History of the Opium Problem
The Assault on the East, ca. 1600-1950

Sinica Leidensia

Edited by

Barend J. ter Haar
Maghiel van Crevel

In co-operation with

P.K. Bol, D.R. Knechtges, E.S. Rawski,
W.L. Idema, H.T. Zurndorfer

VOLUME 105

The titles published in this series are listed at brill.nl/sinl

History of the Opium Problem
The Assault on the East,
ca. 1600-1950

By

Hans Derks

BRILL

LEIDEN · BOSTON

2012

Cover illustration: Honoré Daumier: In China. Western Way of Trade Promotion. (Subtitle:) Inspection of the Opium Smokers, 1859 (The Daumier Website, DR Number 3101).

Library of Congress Cataloging-in-Publication Data

Derks, Hans, 1938-
    History of the opium problem. The assault on the East, ca. 1600-1950 / by Hans Derks.
        p. cm. — (Sinica leidensia ; v. 105)
    Includes bibliographical references and index.
    ISBN 978-90-04-22158-1 (hbk. : alk. paper)
    1. Opium abuse—Asia—History. 2. Opium trade—Asia—History. 3. East and West.
4. Imperialism—Social aspects. I. Title.

    HV5840.A74D47 2012
    363.45095'0903—dc23

                                                                        2012000057

This publication has been typeset in the multilingual "Brill" typeface. With over 5,100 characters covering Latin, IPA, Greek, and Cyrillic, this typeface is especially suitable for use in the humanities. For more information, please see www.brill.nl/brill-typeface.

ISSN 0169-9563
ISBN 978 90 04 22158 1 (hardback)
ISBN 978 90 04 22589 3 (e-book)

This book is printed on acid-free paper.

MIX
Paper from
responsible sources
FSC® C004472
www.fsc.org

PRINTED BY DRUKKERIJ WILCO B.V. - AMERSFOORT, THE NETHERLANDS

CONTENTS

Preface xi
Acknowledgements xix
List of Illustrations, Tables, Figures and Maps xxi

PART ONE. THE OPIUM PROBLEM

1 Introduction 3
2 The Politics of Guilt 11
3 The "Original Sin" 19
4 Conclusions 31

PART TWO. THE BRITISH ASSAULT

5 The Actual Sins 35
   A Private English Asian Trading Company 37
   Opium on a List 40
   A Moral Question 46
6 Tea for Opium Vice Versa 49
   An Analysis from Within 50
   The Bullion Game 53
   The Decision 55
   Opium Shipping 64
   Opium Smuggling 65
   Opium Corruption 68
   Religion as Opium 70
   Opium Banking in a Crown Colony 72
   Exorbitant Opium Revenues 77
   On the Chinese Side 82
7 Indian Profits 87
   Monopoly Opium Production 88
   Monopoly Smuggling 92
   A Western Competitor................................... 95
   Narco-business Revenues 98
8 The Invention of an English Opium Problem 105
   Questions 105
   An English Home Market for Drugs 107

The Creation of the English Opium Problem 113

9 A First Reflection 121

PART THREE. THE DUTCH ASSAULT

10 Portuguese Lessons 135

    Portuguese Elite versus Portuguese Folk 137

    Arab Trade in Peace 141

    On the Malabar Coast 146

    What Did the Dutch learn about Opium from the Portuguese? 154

11 Pepper for Opium Vice Versa 163

12 The Bengal Scene 171

    The Dutch Connection 175

    Mughal Production and Consumption 179

13 The "Violent Opium Company" (VOC) in the East 189

    A "Heart of Darkness" *avant la lettre* 189

    The Dutch Opium Image 191

        Laudanum Paracelsi 191

        The Sailor's Health 195

    The Asiatic Opium Image of the Dutch 196

    Double Dutch Violence 202

    Monopoly Wars 208

    Empire Building 216

    The Banda Case and all that 219

        Other 17th-century Violence 223

        Continuous Dutch Violence 226

    Dutch Opium Trade: General Questions 227

    The Indigenous Producers 231

    Opium Consumption in the East Indies 234

14 The Amphioen Society and the End of the VOC 239

    A Brilliant Economist? 242

    The AS Performance 250

15 The Chinese, the VOC and the Opium 255

    Murder in Batavia 256

    Birth of a Chinese Hate? 259

    Chinese as Victims 264

    Chinese and Early Opium Trade 271

16 From Trade Monopoly into Narco-State Monopoly 277

    A Transformation from Private into Public Interest 278

The Four Van Hogendorps as Opium Dealers 281
The Birth of a Narco-military State 286
17 Tin for Opium, Opium for Tin? 295
The Opium Business of Billiton 302
18 Public Adventures of a Private State within the State 307
A Royal Opium Dealer 309
The State within the (Colonial) State 313
19 The Opium Regime of the Dutch (Colonial State), 1850-1950   319
The Outer Districts 319
The Bali Case 329
The *Opiumregie* 333
The Dutch Cocaine Industry 342
Legal Hypocrisy 348
A Double Dutch End 353
20 Profits 357
The Opium Farmer 358
The Colonial State as Farmer 361
21 Reflections 373

PART FOUR. THE FRENCH ASSAULT

22 Opium in and for *La Douce France* 383
Parisian Fumes 384
The French Pharmaceutical Scene 387
Drugs from abroad 392
23 The French Colonial Scene in Southeast Asia 395
The Beginning of a Disaster 397
The French Opium Performance 400
Revenue Farming 401
The *Opiumregie* 406
The French Concession in Shanghai 411
The End of a Disaster 414
24 The Southeast Asian Context 417
Introduction 417
From "Golden Triangle" to "Bloody Quadrangle" 420
The Tribal Scene 424
The Shan State 427
The Hmong Tribe 431
Consumption Pattern 433

Myanmar (Burma) 438
Thailand (Siam) 443
Malaysia (Melaka, Malacca) and Singapore 447
25 The Role of the Chinese in Southeast Asia 459
About an "Identity" of Chinese Migrants 459
The Chinese Settle(ment) Strategy 464
The (pre-)History of the Chinese Opium Performance 467
Asian Trade 467
'... their industry and economy ...' 469
The 19th-century 471
The Rich "Overseas Chinese" and Opium Criminality 473
The Rich 473
Criminality 477
26 Reflections 485

PART FIVE. THE NEW IMPERIALISTS

27 Japan 493
A Domestic Opium Problem 495
The Annexation of Formosa/Taiwan 498
A Former Formosa 499
A "New Formosa" 502
The Korean Case 509
The Opium attack on China 512
The 'Roaring Twenties' 512
From World Economic Crisis to World War II 516
World War II and after.................................... 519
North China 519
Nanjing China 520
Hong Kong 522
Southeast Asia 525
A Reflection 529
28 United States of America 531
A Domestic Opium Problem from the Early 19th-century? . 531
Rise and Direct Decline of "Free Trade" 537
American–Chinese Opium relations, 1800-ca. 1865 542
The "Mystery" of the Chinese Opium Import 545
The Creation of a Chinese Threat after 1911 551
A first "War on Drugs" and its Limitations 554

The Philippine Case 559
Early 20th-Century Opium and Cocaine Consumption 567
    A Basic Drink 567
    Basic Knowledge 569
    A Mega Consumption 572
    Cocaine Connections 577
Basic Instincts 581
29 A Reflection 587

PART SIX. THE VICTIMS

30 Blaming the Chinese Victims 593
    Introduction 593
    An original image 598
    The Addict "by nature" 601
    Who and How in the Chinese Opium Scene 605
    The Religious Assault 609
    Racism 619
31 The West and its Opium Import in China 627
    A British Inspector 629
    ... and his American Heirs 637
32 Opium Production and Consumption in China 643
    The Healers and the Poppy 644
    The Judge and the Poppy 654
    Chinese Republican Opium Production 657
    Yunnan Opium Production and Trade 666
    Chinese Opium Consumption 671
    About Opium Gangsters 682
    KMT Opium Activities 694
    A Mao Opium Case? 699
33 A Reflection 709

PART SEVEN. THE STORY OF THE SNAKE AND ITS TAIL

The Problem 711
Its History 716
Interpretation History 719
Interpretation Problem 722
What Could Be Done? 729

APPENDICES

Appendix 1   From Rags to Riches to Rags, ca. 1775-1914 735
    Costs of the first treatments 736
    Production of opium in India and its market prices 737
    The work in a British opium factory in India 738
    Public sales 739
    Exports of Indian opium 740
    Destinations 742
    EIC ships from Calcutta to Canton, 1775-1820 748
    Import trade of Canton, 1833 748
    Prices of opium, 1800-1914 749
Appendix 2   The Dutch Opium Import, 1678-1816 753
Appendix 3   The Amphioen Society Swindle 757
Appendix 4   From VOC Opium to Raffles' Heritage 759
Appendix 5   The French and Dutch Opium Factories 765

GLOSSARY 773

BIBLIOGRAPHY 777
    Primary Sources, 1500-1900 777
    Sources 1900-1940 779
    Literature 1940 to the Present 781

INDEX 797

PREFACE

> How came any reasonable being to subject himself to such a yoke of misery, voluntarily to incur a captivity so servile, and knowingly to fetter himself with such a sevenfold chain?
>
> Thomas De Quincey,
> *Confessions of an English Opium Eater* (1821).

> Today some ... call the U.S. invasion of Iraq the greatest strategic military disaster in American history, a massive squandering of lives and resources that will affect the Middle East and reduce the power of the United States ... Yet compared with what is at stake in Afghanistan and Pakistan, Iraq may well turn out to be a mere sideshow ... The U.S. failure to secure this region may well lead to global terrorism, nuclear proliferation, and a drug epidemic on a scale that we have not yet experienced and I can only hope we never will.
>
> Ahmed Rashid, *Descent into Chaos* (2009), p. xlii

De Quincey's idiosyncratic confession was recently (2009) reissued in a series entitled "Great Ideas". Certainly after reading the following text, one can doubt how "great" De Quincey's idea was. That is not our concern, but how should we label the idea of answering the same question by altering 'himself' into 'others' or, more precisely, 'oppressed (and, therefore, *in*voluntary) others' ? That is, indeed, exactly the question dealt with in the following history: why, when and how are foreign people enslaved by making them opium addicts?

The use, trade, chemistry or effects of opium are not a blank page in historiography, anthropology, economics, chemistry or medical sciences, let alone in practical politics and political morality. Books and articles have been written on all these of separate aspects of the phenomenon, mostly by experts and published in not very popular publications. They seldom cover the relationships between all or the most relevant aspects over a sufficiently long stretch of time, so that experts easily lose sight of the larger dimensions of the Opium Question.

However, the most serious failures of the bulk of these publications are the stringent victim approach (poor addicts who must be cured at great cost) and a fundamental distortion of history. Typical sentence:

> In an Egyptian medical treatise of the sixteenth-century B.C., Theban physicians were advised to prescribe opium for crying children just as, three and a half millennia later, Victorian babies were dosed with the opiate Godfrey's Cordial by their nurses to keep them quiet.[1]

Apart from the untenable historical comparison, this leads either to a popular historiography of opium use and the effects of addiction with botanical knowledge about poppy growing, or to one in which the victims (mostly Chinese) are transformed into the perpetrators through a combination of ignorance, prejudice and, eventually, ideological blindness. Unprovable references to remote historical situations are too often used as legitimating the production, distribution and consumption of opium and other drugs. The assessment of these products is also distorted, when isolated from their historical, social or cultural contexts. Finally, one has to acknowledge, that the times of Euro- or Western- centred—historiography are definitely over, which automatically implies that the darker sides of European history shall be stressed more.

Many examples will be given to illustrate all this. A most recent and curious one offered by serious historians—which does not show all of these "misunderstandings"—is the following:

> Chinese consumers and their merchants and middlemen created the market for imported opium, which was thought to be superior to the domestic supply that had earlier provided the major source.[2]

At least four serious mistakes are made in one sentence: (1) as we will prove in all possible detail, the Chinese opium market was created by Western colonizers and imperialists, in particular the Dutch, English and American dealers, smugglers, etc. and their militant governments; (2) Chinese poppy cultivation and/or opium production was started *after* this Western assault was successful and *after* Western coastal colonies in China were established; (3) there was no Chinese domestic supply *before* the Westerners started their Opium Wars, let alone an inferior one; (4) if one writes about 'imported opium', then one may expect that it is not available in China (in sufficient quantities), while import was nearly

---

[1] A. Hayter, *Opium and the Romantic Imagination* (London: Faber, 1971), p. 19.
[2] R. Murphy, K. Stapleton, *East Asia. A New History* (Boston: Longman, 2010), p. 167.

always done by *foreign* (in this case: non-Chinese) importers: who, then, must have created 'the Chinese market for imported opium'?

To avoid all those mistakes and misinterpretations a new approach is introduced, namely to describe and analyze the *History of the Opium Problem*. This is a history of the production, consumption and distribution of opium and its derivatives from the time they form an objective political, social, economic or cultural problem in a specific period and place. The first time that this happened in world history, one of the theses of this study, is on the west coast of India (Malabar or Kerala) after 1660 due to the Dutch assault in the framework of the establishment of their Asian trade empire.

The practical consequences of the Dutch opium policy at the time were far-reaching; even so, in hindsight, it must have had a world—historical significance, because all other opium—imperialists followed the Dutch example to some extent. In addition, we can establish that *before* this "moment" no opium *problem* existed, although there was always some narcotic consumption. This has marked consequences for a historiography covering the substantial moral exploitation of opium use and its problems. Furthermore, a definition of Opium Problems is derived from the practical features "in the field", not based on some theoretical or ideological stand.

The following *History of the Opium Problem* takes a perpetrator's point of view, although it is impossible to forget the victims. Apart from the Asian perspective, attention is also paid to an *autonomous* early internal European opium trade and the household consumption of opium. The intention is to discuss, whether this is problematic as well.

However, the main focus will be on the Opium Question as a creation of Western imperialism and colonialism in Asia. This is not a result of some ideological standpoint, but simply a consequence of proper historical and political-economic research.

It is natural to compare this Western opium assault on the East to slavery between Africa and the Americas. This would not be an exaggeration.[3] The "coolie labor" in the 19th-century was already similar to African slave

---

[3] The most cruel perpetrators, the Calvinist Dutch, did both in the most extreme manner, but even their zealous attempts failed to develop a slave trade in the East as large as that in and between Africa and the Americas (see part 3). They created a *new* form of slavery as K. Ward analyzed and described: empire building through forms of forced migrations, penal transportation, "legalized" slave trade. In this way the Cape of Good Hope colony developed into a penal colony long before the English designed Australia in the same format or long before coolie labor became popular.

labor for contemporaries. The latter was, however, not directly accompanied by the opium trade, which was the case in the coolie trade, often involving the same traders and coolie-holders.

This history still seriously burdens the relationship of the West and the East today, which is too often characterized by wars and serious repressions, of which the two Opium Wars in the 19th-century or the Pacific part of World War II may be the most spectacular. However, from about 1500 onwards, there were hundreds of warlike conflicts started by the West against the East (almost never the reverse: "Pearl Harbor" was the second time in a millennium!), sometimes of a genocidal character.

Ahmed Rashid's quotation above refers to the two wars the Bush and Obama administrations are fighting at present with their English or Dutch allies. The Afghanistan war is definitely a new Opium War from which Rashid hopes that it will not lead to a global 'drug epidemic on a scale that we have not yet experienced'.

Astonishment about this Western behavior is not the only motive to write his bestseller. Rashid:

> Above all, arrogance and ignorance were in abundant supply as the Bush administration invaded two countries in the Muslim world without any attempt to understand the history, culture, society, or traditions of those countries.[4]

Without exaggerating the performance of the Bush family, Rashid's remarks about the present political conduct must be an *Aha experience* for a historian of the *Opium Problem*. Time and again this astonishment was the reaction seen when writing about the opium history from 1500 onwards. It could make readers pessimistic and impatient, but I still hope that this story will help to stamp out this 'arrogance and ignorance' and, more importantly, to avoid the 'drug epidemic' Rashid predicts.

For several reasons explained in the first part of the study, this history of the opium *problem* is not a history of opium use or poppy culture. It starts around 1500 with the Asian activities of the Portuguese in particular. As indicated above, it is the Dutch narco-military machine starting a good century later which plays its lesser-known key role (part 3). Of course, the story is often told of how through the Opium Wars the English imperialists addicted China in the middle of the 19th-century (part 2). They learned this largely from the Dutch and brought it to its logical conclusion by addicting China.

---

[4] A. Rashid, *Descent into chaos* (London: Pelican Books, 2009), p. xlii.

The British and French went further, with the important assistance of American smugglers and their clippers. From their "possessions" in China and Southeast Asia, certain innovations in opium management were introduced. They exported, furthermore, to the other side of the Pacific, the USA, and the opium snake started to bite its own tail. Both are largely responsible for leaving a heritage of present production centers in Southeast Asia and the Middle East of world-economic importance. A new cycle of exploitation and repression of the minds of the people started, which could eventually be followed-up by Rashid's 'drug epidemic'.

This is my outline of the main thesis of the following study. A second thesis shows its limitations.

From the very beginning of the Portuguese and, certainly, the Dutch opium assault on the East, it becomes evident that the decision—makers were well informed about the very nasty effects of opium on the minds of people. They even detested the opium users and prohibited their own people from using it on penalty of serious punishments. Therefore, ignorance can only apply in a limited way to most implementers of the decisions made, but not to most authorities of the time. The moral protests in most Western countries starting during the second half of the 19th-century against opium use, smoking and addiction have, therefore, a soundly hypocritical character.

In addition, they were too late. New drugs like heroin or morphine, derived from opium but with much more devastating effects, were being distributed while people still worried about the comparatively innocent activity of opium smoking. In the 19th-century a new kind of moral agent, representatives of the medical professions (from hospital doctors to apothecaries), counterattacked the anti-opium complaints. As will be demonstrated, they started to defend its usefulness while prescribing its products wholesale. The new chemical and pharmaceutical industries in Europe and the US became the nearly invincible economic interests to support the modern narco-military machines.

Now, the Western gate was opened for the Trojan horse of the narco-military opium industry and their ravaging warriors, the drug-dealers with their supporters in the state and local bureaucracies. The other side of this coin is that the classic Asian opium production (India) and consumption (China, Southeast Asia) lands are largely liberated of the evil. What remains there as regions of production (Afghanistan and Myanmar) is nearly fully dependent on Western consumers.

This is, in short, the second chain of arguments of this study. With both chains, several important details are discussed in their historical or politico-economic contexts: the role of the state (military, violence, wars, prohibitions, etc.); the ideological institutions (religion, churches, missionaries, value systems, etc.); the narco-dealers with their tactics and support; the modern industrialization; the astronomical profits; the effects on foreign policies and other features.

There are also limits to this study since it is not possible to deal with all of the perpetrator or victim countries. The main focus will be on the British, Dutch and French imperialist opium activities in China, India and Southeast Asia, including their function as models for the New Imperialists, Japan and the USA. Since the opium history of the present Indonesian archipelago is not well known outside Dutch archives and some Dutch expert publications, it is treated here in great detail for the first time in English.

This preface ends with some technicalities. The aim of this large global and interdisciplinary study is also to make a new kind of handbook for students of the opium problem. It is the first time that such a book has been written, which implies that it has a certain experimental and introductory character. A study about a historical, social, economic, etc. *problem* like opium, compared rightly by many to slavery, is by definition "controversial". Although slavery is recurring, alas, in several areas at present, it does not have the same social and economic impact as in the 16th-19th-century. The Opium Problem, which originated almost the same time, has in fact increased century after century. It is massively present throughout the whole world. It stands now, of course, also for its derivatives as heroin and morphine, while the cocaine problem is also addressed in passing. In the media and elsewhere it daily leads to highly contradictory arguments and actions.

Certainly with this subject, any author is unable to come up with a value-free description, analysis or judgment. It must be "enough" that no description or analysis is given without a careful argumentation, indication of the sources used, etc.

A handbook presupposes the availability of a broad range of data and that is true in this case as well. This is, furthermore, guaranteed by the method used known as *Gesellschaftsgeschichte* (H.-U. Wehler and others). In many parts new archival material could be used, while the attempt is made in the numerous quotations to reproduce original voices in time and place. These quotations are, therefore, relatively extensive. There are, at the moment, few publications with so much quantitative data over such a long period. Extensive appendices are used and many notes point time and again to alternative interpretations and literature. The result is a specific insight in the socio-economic relations of many countries over a period of several centuries.

The other side of this picture is that many geographical and other names in the quotations and elsewhere are unknown in present spelling and that exotic currencies are often difficult to compare. A glossary is only of limited use to avoid misunderstandings in these fields.

Chronologically, the Dutch assault on Asia occurred about a century earlier than the English one. The latter is chosen, however, as a kind of model for the whole study. Its story is better known, although probably some new vistas are opened on it. In addition, the reader can become more familiar with the—probably unexpected—complexities, which are detailed in the other chapters and parts.

A practical problem of this history is, of course, where to stop. Several logical possibilities were available. Anonymous readers advised stopping immediately after World War II. Many events in a *History of the Opium Problem* indeed came together around that period: the liberation from colonial exploitation of countries like Indonesia, Burma (Myanmar), China, India, etc. These countries played a pivotal role in this history. Finishing an opium history in 2011, inevitably leads to commemorate the important revolution of 1911-1912. A first promising attempt to solve the very extensive Chinese Opium Problem, however, just failed (see ch. 31). This happened not in the least because one had to deal not only with the addiction of a substantial part of the population, but with a most serious political, social and economic problem. One definitely succeeded to solve such an Opium Problem around 1950 for the first time in history, thanks to the victory over the fully opium contaminated Nationalists. For all these reasons "1950" became the end of this history, with the hope that a follow-up to the present can be made someday.

Hans Derks
www.hderks.dds.nl
October 2011

ACKNOWLEDGEMENTS

Many people have helped (in)directly make this book a reality. Indirectly, I owe much to three inspiring spirits who accompanied many of my previous historical and sociological studies personally and in their writings: Bernhard Slicher van Bath, Hans-Ulrich Wehler and Wim Wertheim. The first showed me the intriguing possibilities of quantitative historical research; the second of integrating historical and sociological approaches; the third of the new perception needed for studying the history and society of China, Indonesia and other Asian societies. All of them taught me to paint the historical picture on a large canvas, so that I also discovered what the political philosopher Hannah Arendt demonstrated that, as modern man, the world should be your home.

Directly, this study has been helped not only by the scholarly advices of Frank Bovenkerk but particularly by the highly stimulating comments of Lars Laaman of London University, who critically reviewed the whole manuscript. Furthermore the invaluable help of Alison Fisher should be mentioned, who did a good job in editing my English.

Of course, the initial trust of the staff of publisher Brill, Albert Hoffstädt and Marti Huetink, in this large project was of pivotal importance to realize this *History of the Opium Problem*. Its very professional team of Patricia Radder and Wilma de Weert has seen this large project through the daily process of production. All of them must be thanked wholeheartedly.

The same is appropriate for the editors of the series *Sinica Leidensia*, Barend ter Haar and Maghiel van Crevel, to allow the publication of this history as volume 105.

Furthermore, I would like to thank all those publishers allowing us to use copyright material. In particular, I have to mention *Cambridge University Press* and *Harvard University Press* for granting permission to use maps, figures and illustrations as indicated in the text.

Last but not least, this book could not have been written without the continuing support of my wife and children, to which this book is dedicated.

LIST OF ILLUSTRATIONS, TABLES, FIGURES AND MAPS

ILLUSTRATIONS

1. Papaver Somniferum, Bently & Trimen, 1830 4
2. Frontispiece from *Itinerario,* Jan Huygen van Linschoten, ca. 1595 25
3. The Opium War and China in the cartoons 42
4. Patna, India: four interiors of an opium factory; "mixing", "drying", "stacking", ca. 1850............................... 62
5. Battle at Canton, ca. 1845 84
6. The Pharmacist's Competition, ca. 1866 115
7. The Market of Goa, ca. 1540 142
8. People from the Malabar Coast ca. 1600..................... 156
9. Destruction of three Portuguese galleons at the Malabar coast, September 1639 165
10. Venice and its Treacle....................................... 193
11. List of Medicines in the Ship's Doctor's Chest, ca. 1660 195
12. Several Amputations and the Cauterization of Wounds, 1657 197
13. Cargo List of nine homewardbound Eastindiamen, 1690 209
14. Revolts and Massacres 225
15. Funeral Procession of a VOC Governor-General, 1761........ 249
16. The Dutch Massacre of the Chinese, Batavia, 8 October 1740 . 257
17. Coolie Labor in the Dutch Tin Mines, 1919 300
18. Interior of the Opium factory, Batavia ca. 1935 337
19. Dutch Cocaine Factory, copy of a share 1942 344
20. A Chinese junk amidst Southeast Asian and European vessels, ca. 1820... 468
21. Japanese Overlords and their civilized Savages, Formosa ca. 1920.. 504
22. Dr. Doxey's Elixir 536
23. Happy New Year, 1899! 538
24. A Skeleton in his Closet 546
25. "The Harvest in the Philippines", 1899 560
26. "Those pious Yankees ....", 1902 565
27. Coca Cola: old and new claims.............................. 568
28. How to dope US. babies ca. 1870 574
29. Bayer Pharmaceutical Products, 1898....................... 579

30. Open Air Preaching, 1892 611
31. The Yellow Terror, ca. 1900.............................. 620
32. 'Quan shi jieshi dayan wen' (Essay urging the World to give up opium).. 646
33. The Manufacture of Opium in India, 1900.................. 742

TABLES

1. Trade between England, China and "British" India, 1800-1900   77
2. India's Foreign Trade in select items by Value, 1849-1850 in £   95
3. Balance of Trade of "British" India with selected countries, 1828/9 (x Rs. million) 99
4. Opium Revenues and Expenditures of British Colonial Government in India.. 100
5. Value of Main Export Products from "British" India in selected years, 1813-1930 (Rs. million) 102
6. Exports of Raw Opium from "British" India to Asian Countries, 1922-1935 (in chests)..................................... 103
7. Sources and Quantities of England's Opium Imports, 1827-1900 (in lbs)... 108
8. Import of Opium in Germany, 1910-1925 (x 100 kg) 109
9. Bengal Opium Exported to the Malabar Coast, 1657-1718 (selected years; in Dutch pounds).......................... 170
10. Bengal Opium Exported to the East Indies Archipelago, 1659-1718 (selected years; in Dutch pounds) 178
11. 'Contributions to the Dutch Indies Government by the Billiton District', 1864-1920 (in guilders).......................... 298
12. Profit and *Loss* Account of the Royal Dutch Trade Company, 1824-1834 (selected years; x 1000 Dutch guilders)........... 314
13. Net Output of Opium Leasing in Outer Districts of the East Indies, 1847-1849.. 322
14. Opium consumption (in thails) of License- and Non-License Holders in Java, Madura and Outer Districts (*Buitengewesten*) in the *Opiumregie*, 1930 324
15. Income and Expenditures of the *Opiumregie* and the Colonial State, 1920-1931 (x 1000 Dutch guilders) 339
16. Coca Leaves Export from Java, 1904-1940 (selected years) ... 342
17. Stocks of Coca Leaves, 1933-1938 (x 1 kilogram) 347
18. Prices, Profits and Quantities of Opium of the Opium Farmers in 1887.. 359

19. Dutch Government Net Opium Profits in the East Indies, 1678-1815 362
20. Dutch Government Opium and Colonial Profits in the East Indies, 1816-1915 363
21. Profits from Colonial Products, 1848-1866 364
22. Opium import in Batavia, 1881-1883 in chests and in guilders 368
23. Contribution of the *Opiumregie* to the Government Budget in the East Indies, 1914-1940 (x 1 million current Dutch guilders) 369
24. Dutch trade and Yield in Opium in the East Indies, 1914-1932 371
25. Opium sold to and Income from Revenue Farms in Cochinchina, 1874-1881 405
26. Rentability of the *Opiumregie* compared to the Farm-system in Cochinchina, 1882-1885 (in piaster)..................... 408
27. Costs and Revenue of French *Opiumregie* in Cochinchina, 1882-1898 (x 1000 piaster)............................... 408
28. Southeast Asian Opium Cultivation and Heroin Production, 1992-1996 419
29. Comparison between "legal consumption" of opium in Southeast Asia and the Chinese coast, ca. 1930 434
30. Opium smokers in Indochina in 1906 436
31. Estimated Number of Opium Addicts and Consumption of Illicit Raw opium in Indochina and Singapore–Malaya, 1955 437
32. Value of Estimated Exports of Opium from Burma to Thailand at Various Stages of Transport, 1955 443
33. Singapore Opium Farm Annual Rent, 1820-1882 (selected years; in Spanish $) 450
34. Estimated monthly costs and sales of selected Malayan opium farms, 1903 454
35. Raw Opium Seized in Singapore by Country of Origin and Value opium import, 1954-55 457
36. Opium revenue and Licensed Opium Smokers on Formosa, 1897-1941 (selected years) 505
37. Japanese Cocaine Production, 1934-1939 (x 1kg) 509
38. Opium and Narcotics production in Korea, 1930-1941 511
39. Annual Import of Opium into Tianjin around 1936 516
40. Mengjiang Opium Export, 1939-1942 520
41. Pacific opium import and duties paid in USA and Canada, 1871-1899 (selected years) 549

42. Atlantic Opium Imports and Duties Paid, 1871-1899 (selected years) 550

43. Total Import of Opium and Opium Preparations to the USA, 1850-1924 (selected years) 576

44. U.S. coca imports: medicinal (cocaine) and non-medicinal (cola), 1925-1959 (x kilogram) 578

45. Merck Production and its German Import of Cocaine and Coca, 1880-1915 (x kilogram) 580

46. Percentage Distribution of China's principal Imports, 1870-1910 634

47. Trends in crop acreages between 1904-9 and 1930-3 661

48. Commodity composition of maritime Customs trade in 1908 and 1928 (x million HK taels) 664

49. Opium Smokers in Cantonese Rehabilitation Centers, 1937 and 1941 678

50. A Supply Side of the Opium Problem Around 1970 (in US$) .. 728

51. Expenses and profits of cultivating one *bigha* of Malwa opium ca. 1823 736

52. Production and Prices in Indian districts and Calcutta in piculs and guilders, 1873-1882 738

53. Public Sales of Bengal Opium of the EIC in Calcutta, 1787-1829 739

54. Exports of Opium from India in chests, 1829-1902 740

55. Bengal Opium Export after Sales from India and Financial results of EIC and Government of India, 1787-1900 741

56. Export of *Bengal* Opium from Calcutta to Several Destinations, 1809-1850 in chests (selected years) 744

57. Export of *Malwa* Opium from Bombay to Several Destinations, 1809-1850 in chests (selected years) 745

58. Growth of Opium Trade in Ceylon (Sri Lanka), 1840-1900 in lb 746

59. The Opium Smuggling of Singapore, 1835-1865 in chests (selected destinations) 746

60. "British" Indian Export of Opium to Various Countries, 1911-1920 747

61. "British" Indian Export of Opium to Various Countries, 1911-1917 (in chests) 748

62. Import Trade of Canton, 1833 (in Spanish $) 749

63. Prices of opium per chest, in Spanish $ as given in Canton, Macao or Hong Kong, 1800-1880 750

64. Dutch Opium Import in East Indies by the VOC, 1678-1745 (selected years) 754
65. Dutch Opium Import in the East Indies by the VOC and Dutch Government, 1746-1816 (selected years) 754
66. Dutch Opium Import by the Dutch Government on Java and Madura only, 1817-1850 (selected years) 755
67. Total Dutch Opium Imports in the East Indies, 1678-1850 ... 755
68. Opium performance of the VOC and Amphioen Society (AS), 1721-1768 757
69. Incomes and Expenditures of the VOC in 1795 (x guilders) .. 759
70. Accumulated Profits and Losses of the VOC 1613 to 1693 (x guilders) 761
71. The Budget of Governor-General Daendels ca. 1808 (x 1000 rixdaalder and guilders) 762
72. Comparison between the periods before, during and after Daendels' government (x 1000 ropij and guilders) 763
73. Raw opium import, Preparation and Revenue in French Cochinchina, 1881-1889 766

FIGURES

1. Opium Smuggling into China and Shanghai, 1837-1860 67
2. Decennial Average Opium Revenues in India, 1798-1936 (x 1,000 Rupees) 89
3. Five-year averages of actual and estimated home consumption of opium per 1,000 population in England, 1825-1905 112
4+5. Schematic Diagrams of the Organization of the VOC–General and of the VOC–Asia 203
6. Opium Factory, import raw opium, 1900-1940 (x 10,000 kilogram) 341
7. Revenue from opium tax farms in Java and Madura, 1816-1905 366
8. Percentage Gross and Net Opium Revenue in the French Colonial Budget of Cochinchina, 1864-1895 407
9. Total Opium Consumption in Indochina, 1905-1910 and the Consumption per Head per year, 1906-07 418
10. Opium Consumption in Indochina, 1899-1920 435
11. Average annual opium price in Singapore, 1820-1901 (Spanish dollars per chest) 452
12. Indian EIC Export to China of Bengal and Malwa Opium, 1809-1839 (x 1,000 chests) 743

13. East Indies: Production Cost of Opium Factory and Sales Revenue of Opium Regie, 1900-1935 (x 1 million guilders) ... 769
14. East Indies: Production Cost of Opium Factory and Sales Revenue of Opium Regie, 1900-1920 (thail per guilder) 770
15. East Indies: Opium Factory, Production cost, 1900-1940 (x 200,000 Dutch guilders) 770
16. East Indies: Opium Factory, Production cost, 1900-1940 (per thail x 10 cents) 771

MAPS

1. The global triangle of trade, circa 1820 50
2. Sources of Opium Imported in Britain in the 19th Century ... 106
3. East Asia according to Portuguese mapmakers ca. 1550 148
4. Sketch-map of North Hindostan showing the Opium districts Behar and Benares and the landscapes of the Malwa and Nepal Opium Cultures, ca. 1880 183
5. Octroy area of the VOC during 1602-1795 205
6. Southasian centers of VOC trade during 1602-1795 211
7. VOC trading centers in the East Indies during 1602-1795 218
8. Major Dutch Campaigns in Java, September-December 1678 222
9. The "Dutch" East Indies, superimposed on a map of the United States 320
10. The "Dutch" East Indies and their 'Zones for the Control of Opium Smoking', 1930 326
11. Mainland Southeast Asia, 1880-1930 399
12. Indochinese Zones with different prices of the French Opium-regie, ca. 1930 409
13. Opium Cultivation in Shan State before and after 1963 429
14. Prices of Monopoly Opium in force in various Siamese Districts, ca. 1930 445
15. British Trade routes in the 19th-century and important areas of Chinese Settlements in the Malay world 462
16. Heroin seizures in the United States, 1927-1928 584
17. Estimated Annual Opium Production per Chinese Province, 1908 636
18. Opium Cultivation in China, 1920 659
19. Caravan Routes in the "Golden Quadrangle", ca. 1900 668
20. CIA Map of International Drug "Pipelines", November 2009 .. 732

PART ONE
THE OPIUM PROBLEM

CHAPTER ONE

INTRODUCTION

There are few histories so critical about the relationship between the
West and the East as the history of the opium monopolies, their enormous accumulation of capital in 'the world's most valuable single commodity trade of the nineteenth-century'[1] and the current nearly unsolvable
narcotic problems in the USA and Europe. Their mutual relations in the
heydays of Western imperialism and colonialism could be described as
follows:

> Thus as tea drinking rose in England, opium smoking rose in China ... The
> sale of the Bengal [poppy] crop became so valuable that the East India
> Company ... soon came to depend on its sale for financing the government
> of India.[2]

This might suggest that there was a free relationship between England
(and "its" Bengal) and China. That was not the case: the tea-drinking
English spread death and destruction before they could start consuming
their national drug and before they could dope millions of people in
China.

In the most recent history of the decline and fall of the British Empire,
Brendon recapitulates the many evils of the highly repressive rule of forty
thousand rather stubborn English over forty million Indians. The white
rulers were characterized by their own English boss as 'so vulgar, igno-
rant, rude, familiar, and stupid as to be disgusting and intolerable ...'[3]
These men and women established a 'despotism tempered by paternalism'. Not very innocent, and this easily led to a conclusion like the following, a remark made in passing by its author:

> In economic terms, Company India was engaged in building perhaps the
> world's first "narco-military" empire, an empire in which power and profit
> remained as closely linked as ever they had in the Mercantilist Age of the
> eighteenth-century.[4]

---

[1] F. Wakeman, in J. Fairbank (ed.), 1978, p. 172.
[2] E. Dodge, p. 266.
[3] P. Brendon, p. 48.
[4] D.A. Washbrook, in: A. Porter (ed.), p. 404. Also quoted in P. Brendon, p. 55.

Neither the opium problem nor the West-East relation was confined to the rise or 'decline and fall of the British Empire' alone: as shall be demonstrated below, many similar Western powers preceded and accompanied this most powerful conquering machine, while strongly participating in the attempt to establish a "narco-military (Far) East". Did they succeed in this belligerent aim?

All these West-East attempts were accompanied by poverty, many millions of addicts, substantial extension of wars and genocide, serious corruption on all sides, brutal perpetrators and helpless and even disgraced victims. In the Western colonies of Asia in the 16th to 20th-century one sees how missionaries tried to make the Christian religion in the most literal sense "opium *for*, later, *of* the people" as a well-known writer could have written in 1848 (see, for example, ch. 6 or 13).

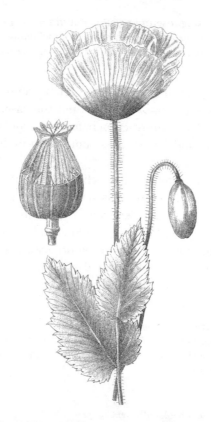

Ill. 1. Papaver Somniferum, Bently & Trimen, 1830
Source: J. Wiselius, 1886, p. 1

It is remarkable that an adequate description of these relationships with the accompanying facts seems still difficult. The main reason is certainly not a lack of sources for the historians. No, this history hits too hard on an open sore in the conscience of the Western colonizers including their "home fronts", and we are, therefore, saddled with largely a legitimizing historiography comparable with the one of a few other items like Western—induced slavery and racism.[5]

In Africa "The West" obtained bodies and brought them to the Americas to work in chains; in Asia they doped the minds in order to create a sedentary, peaceful and quiet workforce.[6] The undeniable guilt of Western governments from the 16th-century onwards is so obvious after even a superficial confrontation with this dossier that one is surprised to find a non-ideological and non-legitimizing historiography only in rather marginal expert literature.

The most clearly demonstrated attitude is silence about the subject or down-grading its importance.[7] In both the UK and the Netherlands, the two most important countries at stake, books from amateurs like Ellen La Motte, Jack Beeching, Maurice Collis or Ewald Vanvugt were the first to

---

[5] See for this relationship in particular J. Nederveen Pieterse, p. 223 ff. or 339 ff. about Christianity as a 'slave religion' under the heading: 'Strange Opium'. Of course, the comparison between slavery and compulsory or induced addiction requires a rather complicated description and explanation, which cannot be given in the following study: I can only point to the phenomenon of the relationship.

[6] Only the British after their long stay and detailed governance in British India started also with an Indian emigration policy in the second half of the 19th-century and exported, for instance, "free workers" to the other colonies in South Africa or the Guyanas (the so-called Hindustani also found in Dutch Guyana). In this way the "political heat" of the proletarians at home could be cooled, while a divide and rule game could be played between the several ethnic groups in the new home.

[7] The most remarkable fact is that in the special volume about the historiography of the British Empire, opium was not discussed besides listing some titles with the word "opium". R. Winks (ed.). Notwithstanding a remark as given in note 3, in this entire five-volume *History of the British Empire*, "opium" is hardly a subject worthy of analysis. In some more specialized literature like T. Rawski and L. Li (ed.) or even the pre-war important publications of C. Remer and F. H. King, opium is not worth discussing. That is strange for other reasons because a high official like H. Morse wrote extensively (and in favour) of opium, as we will see below. For the Dutch Empire, the main historians and main historical works like the old and modern edition of the *Algemene Geschiedenis der Nederlanden*, or special studies of Van Dillen, Boxer until Gaastra and H. van den Doel, opium is, at best, discussed in passing. In France, the situation is not better. The famous F. Braudel, vol. 1, p. 261 treated opium as similar to tobacco and preferred to write about the latter. He also suggested mysteriously that 'humanity had need of compensation' and that opium was one of the "solutions". In the other two volumes opium was awarded only a few words (vol. 2, p. 223; vol. 3, p. 523). In F. Braudel's, E. Labrousse's many volumes of *Histoire Economique*, there is not a single word about opium.

cover up their national opium histories. It is now necessary to make the connections, to provide an adequate context for this fundamental assault on the East, and to ask anew about the characteristics of their own and other colonial empires.

The images the official legitimizing historiography has created, since the two Opium Wars resulted in a Western "victory" were so strong that a full inversion of the roles of perpetrator and victim could occur: for "all men in Western streets" China is still largely identified with isolation ("closed door" policy) from the rest of the world, tea and opium. A general historian provides the most common classical myth as a self-evident truth:

> As European, particularly English, consumption of tea increased, it became the principal cargo and produced enormous profits. But the old difficulty of finding anything to exchange in China, a self-sufficient country, was not easy to solve.[8]

Below I argue that the last thing one should say about "China" is, that it is or was a self-sufficient country: it was always open to international trade and other contacts, even during the late Qing era. In an historical, economical or political sense the first sentence in the quotation has nothing to do with the next. The suggestion, furthermore, that we are confronted here with a constant element in Chinese history, is certainly misleading. In fact, here again the main political economic legitimation is given for attacking China: a country which is 'closed' should be 'opened' by force, etc.

Dodge probably does not know it, but in a theoretical sense we are confronted here with a basic contradiction in nearly all European economic thinking since Aristotle, the antagonistic relationship between the *oikos and the market*. The first concept (literally: house, household) became directly related to an autarkic or self-sufficient state, which too often aggressively strove to become a monopoly in many senses, negating the market forces and interests. Below we shall explain how this is to be understood in the case of China versus the British and other empires. The latter identified itself largely with the global market, but this identification leads to serious difficulties in theory and also in practice.

Carl Trocki opens one of his highly stimulating books with a sentence referring to other fixed opinions about China:

---

[8] E. Dodge, p. 264.

For European observers, one of the most enduring nineteenth-century images of the Chinese ... was that of the opium "wreck". The hollow-eyed, emaciated Oriental stretched out on his pallet, pipe in hand, stood as the stereotype of Asiatic decadence and indulgence. He was the icon of all that was beyond the pale of Christian morality and human decency. Even if we went beyond the picture to learn that it was Westerners, really English and Americans, who were most actively involved in selling the drug in Asia, the association between the "Chinaman" and his pipe was fixed. The victim had come to stand for the crime, and the image has acquired an extraordinary historical durability.[9]

There are other positions to legitimate in opium historiography: the one of the official public perpetrators (here the colonial governments, their bosses in the homelands and the leaderships of the Protestant and Catholic churches) and of their often private official executioners (from producers and traders to military, bureaucrats and settlers supported by their clergy); the one of the homeland supporters (mostly medical staff, politicians) and, ultimately, of the opposition against opium (other politicians, intellectuals and scientists and, in the end, even some individual missionaries). In the victims' countries or circles the legitimated positions are not only of governments or leaders (from emperors to warlords), but also of collaborating producers, smuggling traffickers, etc. and, ultimately, of the addicts and their supporters, who have to rationalize their addiction. Apart from the obvious analysis of the trade, profits and losses, and their contexts, all this is also part of the opium problem as discussed below.

Of course, one can simply deny the ravaging effects of opium and call this 'a misconception'.[10] In the past or at present the most used rationalizations in this kind of literature are found in both the perpetrators' and the victims' media: "Man is by nature cruel and war-like"; "By definition pagans go to hell, unless they are converted to Christianity"; "Man was

---

[9] C. Trocki (1990), p. 1. The image was so strong that also Western and Chinese opponents of opium consumption used it regularly. It is remarkable that Trocki publishes exactly these images and in C.Trocki (1999a). See as well the most recent publication I could consult: J. Lovell, passim.

[10] Even recently by W. Bernstein, p. 289, on highly shaky grounds, 'academic research' (he does not gave a source) should have proved that 'it was largely a social drug that harmed only a tiny percentage of users'. He did not even consider that a 'tiny percentage' in China (let alone in the whole of East Asia) immediately concerns many millions of people. Bernstein writes himself that 'about one Chinese person in a hundred inhaled enough opium to even be at risk of addiction' (Idem). If this kind of reasoning should be relevant, Bernstein does not realize that this concerns at least four million people only in China at the time, apart from their surroundings of related victims.

prepared from time immemorial to eliminate his fellow men", "Man in antiquity was already an addict or consumer of all kinds of drugs"[11], "The Yellow, Black and Red races are clearly inferior to the White race"[12]; "We conquer your country and claim that it is our property" (the classical settler's claim); "It is our world mission to civilize and pacify the earth"; "If you do not want to follow our demands, we have the right/ we are obliged to force you to do so in the name of mankind"; and so on.

A fixed element in all this is the generalizing abstract language, which is immediately neutralized by asking about the concrete details. The European 19th-century, with all its new ideologies, was the richest in inventions of this kind. They still haunt our minds. Its rigidity is camouflaged in legitimating literature at issue by sportsman-like challenge—response dichotomies, etc. Take, for instance, the following text in an important but very imperial English historical atlas. One can read:

> For much of the 19th-century the Chinese failed to understand the challenge presented by Western powers. After a peak of prosperity under the Ch'ing in the 18th-century, they regarded themselves as the centre of world civilization and were slow to realize that Western power, with its superior technology, productivity and wealth, had overtaken them. Such attitudes informed their negative responses to British attempts to develop diplomatic relations from 1793. Matters came to a head when the Chinese tried to end the illicit trade in opium with its damaging economic effects. They were defeated by the British in the First Opium War and in 1842 forced to cede

---

[11] Even C.Trocki (1999a), chapter 2 or P-A. Chouvy in his chapter 1 has the anti-historical attitude to present a prehistory of opium as if this in whatever form can explain or legitimize the spreading of opium under colonial and imperialistic conditions by Western powers. Recently, the same was tried by W. Bernstein, p. 287. The most erudite, detailed and well illustrated example is Merlin's overview of the prehistoric and ancient Egyptian, Greek or Roman experiences with the opium poppy, apart from about 25 other kinds of papaver (in fact 28 genera and some 250 species as J. Scott, p. 1 reveals). The feeling of 'uncertainty' (p. 281) Merlin has about his subject must also arise from the fact that his research on *Papaver somniferum* never came across The Opium Question (or its origins); it was this question which makes his research more interesting than would otherwise be the case.

[12] One of the more clever ideologues of British imperialism, Sir Alfred Lyall, comparing the Roman with the British Empire, ends a study about the many elements of Indian religious sects and the way the British handled this diversity with: 'A modern empire means the maintenance of order by the undisputed predominance of one all-powerful member of a federation ... it is the best machine for collecting public opinion over a wide area among dissociated communities. It is the most efficient instrument of comprehensive reforms in law and government and the most powerful engine whereby one confessedly superior race can control and lead other races left without nationality or a working social organization.' (p. 306). Indeed, it is this powerful race which introduced and managed the production and distribution of opium in a quite mechanical way.

Hong Kong and five treaty ports in which foreigners were permitted to trade free from Chinese jurisdiction.[13]

Did those Western powers really 'overtake' China more than infiltrating some places on the coast? Were 'they' (who?) really regarding themselves seriously as the center of the world and did this really have negative consequences for the West? Were 'they' really so slow to understand the challenge, and which kind of challenge was this? What were, anyway, the attempts of 1793, the Macartney *kotow,* other than a highly arrogant insult of a Chinese emperor by a minor English "diplomat" and a rather fraudulent attempt to make an opium deal with this emperor? Only the word 'illicit' in the quotation could provoke a small murmur and the question of since when was it not allowed to prohibit affairs which were, also at that time, perceived in China *and* England as criminal?

---

[13] *The Times Historical Atlas,* ed. R. Overy, p. 256. See also p. 193 for statistics of relation "export" of Chinese silver and "value of opium" until 1836. See for the narrative of the Opium Wars J. Roberts, chapter 14, E. Dodge, p. 270 ff. and J. Spence, chapter 7, but still the best is F. Wakeman's contribution to the *Cambridge History of China* (1978). It is remarkable that few traits of this appear in the more recent *Oxford History of the British Empire* or the given *Times Historical Atlas.* A better modern treatment is C. Munn, chapter 1 and passim.

CHAPTER TWO

THE POLITICS OF GUILT

We talk of the heathen, the savage, and the cruel, and the wily tribes, that fill the rest of the earth; but how is it that these tribes know *us*? Chiefly by the very features that we attribute exclusively to them ... the European nations, while professing Christianity, have made it odious to the heathen ... On them lies the guilt, the stupendous guilt of having checked the gospel in its career ...

The barbarities and desperate outrages of the so-called Christian race, throughout every region of the world, and upon every people that they have been able to subdue, are not to be paralleled by those of any other race, however fierce, however untaught, and however reckless of mercy and of shame, in any age of the earth.

William Howitt, *Colonization and Christianity.*
A Popular History of the Treatment off the Natives by
the Europeans in all their Colonies (London:
Longman, 1838), p. 7-9[1]

Below, examples are discussed of many warnings about opium at the very beginning of awareness about it in the West. To start with a few 19th-century opinions are given. The question is never explained why even in the English Parliament (April 1840; two years "after Howitt") a Tory politician as famous as Gladstone declared:

I do not know how it can be urged as a crime against the Chinese that they refused provisions to those who refused obedience to their laws whilst residing within their territory ... A war more unjust in its origin, a war more calculated in its progress to cover this country with disgrace, I do not know and I have not read of. The right honorable gentleman opposite spoke of

---

[1] The last part of this quotation is also used by K. Marx, vol. 1, p. 779. The well-known William Howitt (1792-1879) was a Quaker, poet and author of about fifty books. He married Mary Botham, Quaker, poet and author as well. Marx called him 'a specialist in Christianity'.

the British flag waving in glory at Canton. That flag is hoisted to protect an infamous contraband traffic ... we should recoil from its sight with horror.[2]

Gladstone's biographer, Lord Morley, much later summed up his understanding of the case in the following words:

> The Chinese question was of the simplest. British subjects insisted on smuggling opium into China in the teeth of Chinese law. The British agent on the spot began a war against China for protecting herself against these malpractices. There was no pretence that China was in the wrong, for, in part, the British Government had sent out orders that the opium smugglers should not be shielded; but the orders arrived too late, and, war having begun, Great Britain felt compelled to see it through ...[3]

That the British government was willing to accept Chinese complaints seems to be palliative. If true, than the government would not have punished China to pay all costs, to cede many coastal settlements and above all, to accept legal, massive opium imports.

Anyway, Gladstone was preceded by, for instance, the rather paternalistic doctrine of Edmund Burke (around 1795) that colonial government was a trust for the benefit of the subjected people, and that therefore the opium trade should be condemned: this trade is nothing more than a 'smuggling adventure ... the great Disgrace of the British character in India'.[4] It was soo followed by an early representative of the Protestant Church of England, the educator Thomas Arnold of Rugby School, later a historian at Oxford. He mentioned (ca. 1846) that forcing opium on China was 'a national sin of the greatest possible magnitude.' It took much more than fifty years before the first sign of an abolition campaign was heralded and this 'smuggling adventure' of the British could be ended. One reason for this can be found in the Gladstone debate as well.

The right honorable gentleman attacked by Gladstone was the famous historian Thomas Babington Macaulay. He was a Whig member of the cabinet defending the imperialistic attack on China with fierce national-

---

[2] Quoted by F. Wakeman in J. Fairbank (ed.), 1978, p. 195. In J. Roberts, p. 252 and W. Willoughby, vol. II, p. 1090, 1091 there are a quite different readings and quotations of the same part of Gladstone's speech. I combined what all three left aside, hoping they did not err.

[3] Quoted in W. Willoughby, id., p. 1091.

[4] P. Brendon, p. xviii and 103. Burke certainly knew that at the time the EIC officially prohibited the opium trade, but nevertheless stimulated or did not object to smuggling. The EIC and/or its officials traded Bengal opium through Calcutta. Burke, however, was apparently not mislead.

ist rhetoric. Macaulay: those who are forbidden by the Chinese government to trade in opium

> belonged to a country unaccustomed to defeat, to submission or to shame; to a country ... which had not degenerated since the great Protector vowed that he would make the name of Englishman as much respected as ever had been the name of Roman citizen. They knew that, surrounded as they were by enemies, and separated by great oceans and continents from all help, not a hair of their heads would be harmed with impunity.[5]

The government pretended not to attack China in support of opium traffic, but for 'the security of future trade and the safety of English citizens'. Of course, the safety of the English citizens would never have been in danger if the war against China had been stopped. And the profitable and future trade was, in particular, opium, while the successful lobby for the first war came from the largest opium trader, William Jardine and his money!

This way of dealing with the East was only the beginning: a Second Opium War (1856-1860) was also provoked by the British, and it was much more devastating (the destruction of the Summer Palace in Beijing led to an international outcry; etc.).[6] The historical website *The Victorian Web* writes today without any hesitation:

> The Anglo-Chinese Opium Wars were the direct result of China's isolationist and exclusionary trade policy with the West. Confucian China's attempts to exclude pernicious foreign ideas resulted in highly restricted trade.[7]

And in the *Wikipedia* one can still read the opinion, in all respects nonsensical:

> The Macartney Embassy is historically significant because it marked a missed opportunity by the Chinese to move toward greater trade with the Western world, and thus, toward industrialization. This failure to industrialize early would continue to plague the Qing dynasty as it encountered

---

[5] Quoted by F. Wakeman, idem.

[6] P. Brendon, p. 106 etc. His description of the English barbarian behavior and its international reaction is clear, but it is typical for the legitimating (and also here illogical) character of even this book, that he immediately adds a note (p. 108) in which he tries to convince the reader of the miracle that English military could destroy something while it remained intact and that, in fact, the Chinese themselves destroyed the palace!

[7] P. V. Allingham on "The Victorian Web" under 'England and China: The Opium Wars, 1839-60.' The *DTV-Atlas Weltgeschichte* (1997), p. 369 makes history very simple: after "Opiumkrieg" only come the words 'beweist die Überlegenheit europ. Waffen' ('proves the superiority of European arms')!

increasing foreign resistance and internal unrest during the nineteenth-century.[8]

So, even in 2009/10 the reasoning is deemed relevant: it is Chinese's own guilt that the first "regular" relations between the West and the most important country/ government of the East concerned drugs and two narco-wars. This implied: if the Chinese had accepted opium from us, they would not have been killed. Or: if they had accepted being doped, we would not have started a war. In our present public morality this suggests that the underworld has become the upper-world.

It seems as if there is not much difference between blaming the victims in the time of George Macartney ("the man of 1793") or John Adams and today, between an earlier and present attitude to punish the arrogance of those who resist Western repression. Macartney's adventure during his *kotow* (the act of deep respect shown by kneeling and bowing) to the Chinese emperor led a former president of the United States, John Quincy Adams, to tell an audience in 1841 about the first Opium War:

> The cause of war is the *kotow*!—the arrogance and insupportable preten-sions of China, that she will hold commercial intercourse with the rest of mankind, not upon terms of equal reciprocity, but upon the insulting and degrading forms of relation between lord and vassal.[9]

This is one hundred percent demagogy and repeated time and again as the ultimate struggle between the despotic Orient and the "rights" of the democratic West to achieve the Western perception of equality, diplo-macy and commerce![10] It was trumpeted around without any form of res-

---

[8] Wikipedia and New World Encyclopedia under 'Macartney Embassy'. See for this episode part 2-2.

[9] Quoted in J. Roberts, p. 253. Of course here Adams pointed to the *kotow* of George Macartney. See also H. Morse, p. 199, 200 who still defends Adams statement, while using the generalizations "destruction of foreign property" and "the need for better protection" instead of writing about the 1.2 million kilo of opium (!) confiscated by the Chinese author-ities and destroyed, which triggered the war.

[10] See H. Morse, p. 200. Morse (1855-1934) was at the time an important British bureau-crat in China (collaborated with Robert Hart, was Commissioner of Customs and Statisti-cal Secretary, Inspector General of Customs, etc.) and historian, who wrote among others the five-volume *Chronicles of the East India Company, 1635-1834*. Morse quotes here another important person, the Protestant missionary Fr. Hawks Pott (1864-1947), top church bureaucrat of the Episcopal Church in China and twice decorated by the Chinese govern-ment. It is remarkable that Lodwick nowhere mentions this Hawks Pott, although a repre-sentative of his church, Reverend Yen, was 'one of the most prominent of the anti-opium crusaders' (Idem, p. 52 ff.) simply because he was one of the very few Chinese clergymen. Recently (2004), Harry Gelber defended the same position as Adams, which he also repeated in H. Gelber, p. 188.

ervation as Hosea Morse was still doing in 1922 when "evaluating" the first Opium War:

> As has been the rule from the outset, England bore the brunt of the battle in securing the rights of the West, and the privileges secured to her as the result of the war, became the heritage of all the Western Powers coming later into the field.' And the racist element is seldom far away 'where a bold aggressive race comes, especially in matters of trade, in contact with a weaker race ...'[11]

Of course, the British had no rights at all, only better guns. All this does not take into account that the British at that time had, in the propaganda, the same aspirations as the Chinese (to convert the 'rest of the world' into their civilization), with the large difference that the British shot their Christian way through the world with their superior arms technology and the Chinese emperors claimed to impress only Chinese, which largely failed. (Ever seen Confucians trying to convert Western Christians?).

This reasoning and pretext, furthermore, do not belong to the American bourgeois world of John Adams, which had successfully revolted against the colonial British just half a century before, but to a classical *European,* very old-fashioned political thought in which monarchs determine the course of history and all the rest of society and culture does not matter at all. Our way of writing foreign history like the Chinese one is still largely written in this monarchical "Peking Way", as if the duck of the same name is the only food one can swallow in the Chinese kitchen.

And what was the meaning of 'commercial intercourse ... upon terms of equal reciprocity'? This "trade" was only to the benefit of the British state and the merchants, who were looking for state protection of their opium trade. The most famous among the latter was William Jardine, the wealthiest opium dealer in Canton; like all other Westerners he was running a monopoly trade, which was not "free" at all. This kind of armed trade was a classical measure in an oikoidal (colonial) state economic policy which wanted to be compensated for its "loss". Therefore, Adams was not referring to strict (capitalist) commercial trade: Chinese tea, etc. for money; tea which was made a hype by capitalist enterprise, so that they already got huge profits for their small investments. The same was the case with porcelain and silk in the framework of the 19th-century China and chinaware fashion.

---

[11] H. Morse, p. 200. A few years later another authority, the American professor and diplomat Westel Willoughby, provided a strong criticism of the earlier behavior of the British Government.

In addition, the Chinese could *not* use Western products; silver money was enough in exchange for their tea and porcelain. The highest British colonial administrators knew this perfectly well, like the trade commissioner for China, Robert Hart:

> [The] Chinese have the best food in the world, rice; the best drink, tea; and the best clothing, cotton, silk, fur. Possessing these staples and their innumerable native adjuncts, they do not need to buy a penny's worth elsewhere.[12]

No, here the British *state* wanted to be compensated in the trade *balance* which was "negative" vis-à-vis China and the British *state,* including its enterprise in India (British East India Company, EIC), used opium as this compensation by use of arms. What a good definition of "Free Trade"! "Reciprocity" could only concern the way the Chinese defended themselves against this brute intruder. All these were the classical and main elements of an oikoidal political economy, which will be discussed at the end.

However, the main mistake in several quotations above is that at least implicitly—and for the laymen directly—the impression is given that the Chinese were the bad guys: a pagan foreign emperor who pretends to be our ruler and "yellow" Chinese refusing not only "honest trade", but also spreading opium in the world; an assault on the innocent citizens of the West, which had to be punished as severely as possible!

Of course, politicians or their historians did not communicate to the public, that a war on drugs was necessary to increase the profits of Western governments and their traders; instead, it was meant to restore the Christian morality not to be dependent on hallucinating stuff. And indeed, the hypocrisy of the colonial powers was so structured that they forbade opium use for their white citizens but not for the indigenous populations on largely racist grounds: from the Chinese one could accept the tea, but nothing else, that drink was hallucinating enough.[13]

Therefore, the legitimation of these wars had to involve the creation of a so-called foreign enemy, a classical trick. The three most important Western imperialist powers in Asia until ca. 1900 were the Dutch, British and French. They organized the production and trade of opium on the

---

[12] Quoted in W. Bernstein, p. 287. For Robert Hart, see ch. 32.

[13] In 19th-century Canton, the main opium port after the Lintin Island period, opium was always called "tea". H.Morse, p. 360. That is not far from another colonial use, at least during my stay in Kenya in the 1980s where "drinking tea" (tchai) was synonymous with doing corrupt business.

largest possible scale and with tremendous profits with all the consequences not only for the indigenous peoples and societies but for the own
societies as well. Before that date many individual American skipper/
smugglers were heavily involved in the whole region and after that date
the USA started its colonial efforts in Asia. This truth had to be silenced as
much as possible and could be easily given a theological turn in the direction of an original sin.

CHAPTER THREE

THE "ORIGINAL SIN"

> Opium, like alcohol, told an English statesman, is one
> of these few cases in which the imposition of a heavy
> duty enables us to serve God and the Mammon at the
> same time.
>
> J.A. Wiselius (1886), p. 19

To the classical means of political or moral legitimation belongs the history of the "original sin". It is always painted in black and white, but serves important aims. In this case: who or what can be accused of using or producing opium for the first time, must be guilty for ever. The most pleasant option is being able, armed with some blunt historical weapon, to accuse the victims, enemies or competitors: "They did it themselves!"; "Because our competitor challenged us we had to respond!"; "They, the consumers, wanted it themselves!"; "Man is by nature an opium addict!", "From time immemorial people used and liked opium and similar drugs!", etc. Most symptomatic sentences in this legitimating history are quotations like those given above or in the previous chapter. What are the answers to the question of who or what invented and/ or introduced the opium evil? Was it an evil? If not, there is no problem of eternal guilt. If so, people are quick to confess that "the other" made the mistake, notwithstanding the serious problem, that in a Christian theology an "original sin" is inherited. Only Roman Catholics can get rid of it by "baptizing the question", a possibility not available to Calvinist Protestants who are predestined to remain evil. The following answer can be found in a nearly official publication of, chronologically, the first perpetrators and players of the key role in this dossier, the Calvinist Dutch colonial authorities:

> The use of opium seems to be introduced in the East Indies archipelago by
> foreigners, presumably Chinese; upon the arrival of the Dutch its use was
> probably already known in Java, although on a small scale. Soon it was a
> trade product among those of the East Indies Company; opium became

increasingly important until in 1676 the Company got the exclusive import rights in Mataram, in 1678 in Cheribon and a bit later in Bantam.[1]

This looks like a clean chronological story, but the second part of the quote has nothing to do with the first part. That is to say, not in a proper historical sense: it only suggests that some earlier small-scale use and production (if any) increased into a large-scale, booming industry. But this causal relation does not exist as is demonstrated in the third part of this study. Here we have to decide whether one could perceive the specific introduction of opium as an original sin.

A modern Anglo-Saxon historian gave this story of the original sin another turn: of innocent tobacco-smoking Dutch sailors and copying Chinese:

> Opium smoking in China arose from the contact of Chinese traders with the Dutch in Java, who had the habit of mixing a little opium with their tobacco. This practice had an enormous and inexplicable appeal to the local Chinese, who were soon smoking opium straight and who introduced the custom to the mainland in the mid-seventeenth-century.[2]

In a well-documented history of the tea trade and, among others, the practice of exchanging tea for opium (see part 2), Martha Avery blames the Chinese directly:

> The smoking of opium mixed with tobacco had become established in China in the course of the seventeenth-century. Opium was a domestic product, not introduced from outside, as evidenced by the seventeenth-century trade in *shar'* to Bukharan merchants.[3]

She "forgot" that her first mentioning of this *shar'*—here seen as a variety of Chinese tobacco—, included the remark 'it probably contained opium'[4] without any proof substantiating the certainty in the quotation. Let alone, that the information, that the *present* trade route for opium and its

---

[1] *Encyclopaedie,* vol. III, p. 106. One must remember that it looks as if the Chinese were treated in the East Indies and other colonies like the Jews in Europe: they suffered periodically from harsh pogroms. It certainly concerns racist remarks here. Notwithstanding this, one must be careful to extend this comparison too far.

[2] E. Dodge, p. 266. L. Lewin attested this way of smoking tobacco as a typical and original Chinese custom (L.Lewin, p. 62, 63). A peer reviewer, however, informs us, that this habit of *madak* smoking remained confined to the South-Chinese coastline during the entire 18th-century. It was apparently also the reason for the 1729 prohibition of opium by the Chinese emperor.

[3] M. Avery, p. 138.

[4] Idem, p. 117.

derivatives is similar to the old one for Chinese tobacco, can be used as proof![5]

We arrive on slightly more solid ground with an early pharmacological lexicon about drugs, the often translated and republished *Phantastica* of Ludwig Lewin (original from 1924).[6] He, first, comes up with archaeological evidence that Swiss lake-dwellers of 2000 years BCE had a commercial poppy culture.[7] Lewin projects more "certainty" about this through Homer's *Odyssey* because the beautiful Helena mixed wine and some stuff with which one could forget pain and sorrow. Lewin immediately reacts with: without any doubt, this must have been opium, as if he personally made the mix.

In his view ancient Egypt is the oldest location of poppy production, after which this culture spread in the Middle Eastern and Mediterranean regions. And indeed, Lewin can produce several quotations from ancient authors who apparently wrote about poppy including its soporific effects.

There are medical papyri of ancient Egypt which suggest that *Papaver somniferum* is used somehow as a painkiller and means to kill people rather painlessly, as is still done today. This is also the case in most other medical treatises and practices in antiquity up to the Greek and Roman healers like Hippocrates or Galen. The latter two are the main sources for the medical doctors of future centuries. More than proving that opium is

---

[5] The following reasoning is as good/bad as hers. *Wikipedia* informs us as follows: the shar(-pei) is a well-known kind of Chinese dog, already known from pictures of the Han dynasty (200 BCE-220 ACE). After the English invaded China, they introduced their own bulldog, bull-terrier and mastiff as fighting dogs; the English, looking for an inimical Chinese dog, introduced the shar(-pei) as a fighting dog. However, although used as a housedog the *shar* was a very peaceful dog who was a bit 'reserved' towards foreigners and could not fight the English "devils". Therefore, the *shar* had to be saved recently from extinction, and websites (www.worldwidebase.com) can now even report that the *shar* is a typical fighting dog and a cross between a mastiff, a chow-chow and a polar dog!

[6] L. Lewin, p. 53-78.

[7] The same was done recently by T. Dormandy, p. 16 ff. See also *Wikipedia* "Opium". It is mentioned that in Neolithic settlements throughout Switzerland, Germany and Spain, *Papaver somniferum* was found even as far back as 4200 BCE. Since this info is given under the heading "Opium", it is very misleading. All kinds of papaver including opium poppy are used first and foremost for their oily seeds. This kind of use is self-evident since it does not require the rather complicated treatment to produce a medicine or an aphrodisiac. That knowledge is not forgotten, but less well known in particular by those who are looking for solutions to the opium problem in Afghanistan or elsewhere today. See, for instance, the following scientific articles by O.N. Denisenko, G.A. Stepanenko in the journal *Chemistry of Natural Compounds* (1977), p. 477-478; A. Sengupta, U.K. Mazumder in *Journal of the Science of Food and Agriculture* (2006), p. 214-218; M.M. Ozoan, C. Atalay in the journal *Grasas y Aceites* (2006), p. 169-174.

known as a medicine in a very small circle among the elite is not possible, however. For China, Lewin reminds us of a source from about 1000 ACE in which the first mention of opium strictly as a medicine is given.

Most impressive, however, is Mark David Merlin's study of the 'ancient opium poppy'. Every possible trace of *Papaver somniferum L.* is discussed in taxonomy, botany, archeology, and so on.[8] He rightly has been left 'with a feeling of uncertainty' about the controversial result of the current analyses of the 9 sections and 99 members of the genus *Papaver*: only two members of one section (*Mecones*) have been the focus of much biochemical research because they contain morphine.

There is no consensus about the taxonomy, nor about the ancestry of the opium poppy, nor about the use of parts (stem, seeds or leaves) of the plant or the technique of this use. Also the geographical origin of the plant remains in doubt; Anatolia seems to have the best papers. Another important aspect is that Merlin stresses how the opium poppy was used as human food, animal fodder, lubricating and cooking oil, apart from medicine and psychoactive drug for ritualistic and recreational purposes. The archaeological record as such is also strongly modified, but even this author does not or cannot properly link archaeological sites to a typical use of opium.

In European antiquity and medieval times many *herbaria* were made. They form good proofs of the popularity of *Papaver somniferum*. Some include detailed graphic designs, sometimes these designs are transformed into mythical or magical pictures. In the Greek *asclepieia* (places of worship to the god of healers, Asclepios) among the many prescriptions sometimes opium was also distributed, but in the most famous *Capitulare de villis* of Charlemagne (ca. 800 ACE) *Papaver somniferum* is not mentioned at all.[9]

Much later, from about 1000, there was some trade in medicinal products mixed with opium from the Arabian peninsula throughout southern Asia all the way to China. There is some evidence of this in an early Chinese medical encyclopedia, as Lewin already mentioned.

The botanical history must be consulted further. The first printed copies of *herbaria* appear at the end of the 15th-century; the first *systematic* ones seem to have been made at the beginning of the 16th-century in

---

[8] M. D. Merlin, p. 28 ff., 281 ff.
[9] F. Bouman a.o. (ed.), p. 172.

Italy.[10] Bazzi tells how the authors of these collections often refer to authorities in antiquity (Strabo, Galenus, Plinius, etc.), only to make their own views more important, but without a proper support from those authorities.

Bazzi describes one *herbarium* which consists of two parts: the first has 45 pages on which the healing capacities of 74 drugs are given; in the second part 150 plants are given in their 'natural dimension' (?) with their drugs. Only 19 of the latter are given also in the first part. It concerns at least partly a translation of an older work, apparently from the 12th-century or much earlier (Bazzi is not very clear about it), but it is often re-issued. All this is interesting, but I refer to it because one can find there *papavero* listed once in the first part of the codex, while it is never mentioned in the second part.

There is, furthermore, a special kind of literature in the Middle Ages, monographs on specific drugs. The most spectacular are those of the so-called *theriaca*, a wonder drug composed of many ingredients.[11] Below are given more details of its prescription. In this highly detailed study about medieval medicine in West Europe, however, opium is certainly not a common product used in whatever form or for whatever purpose. In addition, it is always used in a mixture with other ingredients; its isolation is a result of modern chemical and/or pharmaceutical experiments.

Recently the study by Leigh Chipman appeared to prove this. It is not a study about opium, but about the highly popular Arabic pharmacology in the 13th-century. In the very long appendix I counted 817 prescriptions for all possible cures.[12] Nearly all of them consists of a combination of herbal products and specifically treated minerals (although in a few "boy's urine" was used) like the following example:

> *ashyāf al-ward* [rose eye-powder with ingredients] ... Maccassar and red sandalwood, rosebuds, gum arabic, gum tragacanth, Socotran aloes, saffron, opium, rosewater, boxthorn, horned poppy' which should be excellent to cure 'external dressing, good for hot inflammations and swellings, analgesic, good for scabies, corrosion of the eyelashes and chemosis.[13]

---

[10] See for the following the article of Franco Bazzi in: G. Baader, G. Keil (ed.), p. 209-227.

[11] See the article by Joachim Telle in: Idem, p. 297. He also reported (p. 318) about the first competition between the "academic doctors" and the popular healers in about the 12th-century. One strategy used was to keep a specific recipe secret to increase its market value. See further ch. 8 and 13.

[12] L. Chipman, p. 185-270.

[13] Idem, p. 237.

In all 817 prescriptions I found opium only 39 times and a reference to different poppy products about 30 times (black, white poppy, horned poppy, poppy seed and poppy syrup). It is a reminder as well that there are many uses of poppy without the possibility of producing opium.

This proves convincingly, that opium and the poppy plants were not at all favorite ingredients among the famous Arab medical doctors and pharmacists. Their most important were camphor, cardomom, frankincense, honey products, mastic, myrrh, pepper, pomegranate, rose and rosebuds or vinegar and violet. This must have had remarkable consequences since these Arab specialists and their knowledge traveled not only in the Mediterranean, but in all countries bordering the Arabian Sea, Indian or Pacific Ocean. They were highly respected in all monarchical or aristocratic courts, which were much later the first targets of the Western merchants and military.

Derived from this tradition was the *Yunani* or *Unani* medical treatment practised by the *hakims* in Islamic India. Around 1200 ACE these doctors could carry out surgical operations for which opium was used as an anaesthetic.[14]

There was an alternative medicine tradition in India derived in some way or other from the vedic. This classical *ayurveda* medical knowledge, developed in the north of India, is quite complicated and applicable to very different aspects of the health problem.[15] Although stories about its ancestry are mostly exaggerated, its sources must have provided a good basis to judge the use of poppy plants or opium. However, the only thing which is mentioned is:

> Also opium was introduced—probably based on Islamic sources—as an efficient medicine to cure diarrhoea.[16]

From all the examples given one may safely conclude, that opium was well known but *not* a very popular substance before—say—the 16th-century in Western Europe and the Mediterranean countries or South Asia, that it was rather expensive, while the date of the *Original Sin* cannot be found in Adam's and Eve's time. Therefore, my decision not to study the history of the use of poppy for its oily content or as medicine or religious

---

[14] The article by Claudia Liebeskind, in: J. van Alphen, A. Aris (ed.), p. 45. She writes in fact: 'The Muslim doctors were among the first to use anesthetics ... Opium, or one of its derivatives was used as a narcotic.' This is highly ambiguous, because these derivatives were the result of modern 19th-century European laboratory isolation experiments.

[15] See the article by Dominik Wujastyk in: J. van Alphen, A. Aris (ed.), p. 19-37.

[16] Idem, p. 21.

ITINERARIO,

Voyage ofte Schipvaert / van Jan Huygen van Linschoten naer Oost ofte portugaels Indien

inhoudende een corte beschryvinghe der selver Landen ende Zee-custen/ met aenwysinge van alle de voornaemde principale Havens/Revieren/hoecken ende plaetsen/ tot noch toe vande Portugesen ontdeckt ende bekent: Waer by ghevoecht zijn / met allen die Conterfeytsels vande habijten/drachten ende wesen/so vande Portugesen aldaer resideerende/ als vande ingeboornen Indianen/ ende huere Tempels/Afgoden/Huysinge/met die voornaemste Boomen/Vruchten/kruyden/ Speecerpen/ende diergelijcke materialen/ als ooc die manieren des selfden Volckes/so in hunnen Gods-diensten / als in Policie en Huys-houdinghe: maer ooc een corte verhalinge van de Coophandelingen hoe en waer die ghedreven en ghebonden worden/ met die ghedenckweerdichste geschiedenissen/ voorghevallen den tijt zijnder residentie aldaer.

Alles beschreven ende by een vergadert, door den selfden, seer nut, oorbaer, ende oock vermakelijcken voor alle curieuse ende Liefhebbers van vreemdigheden.

t'AMSTELREDAM.

By Cornelis Claesz. op't VVater, in't Schrijf-boeck, by de oude Brugghe.
Anno CIↃ. IↃ. XCVI.

Ill. 2. Frontispiece from *Itinerario*, Jan Huygen van Linschoten, ca. 1595
Source: Wikipedia.

medium, but as mass produced and traded luxury, as aphrodisiac, as money, seems reasonable.

Until the 16th-century opium was simply not a historical, social, economic, medical or moral *problem*. Therefore, the questions remain of when and why this occurred and what were the effects. The following study aims to answer these and related questions.

The first mentioning of opium, *relevant to that aim,* is apparently made by the Dutch Protestant scholarly traveler, Jan Huyghen van Linschoten (1563-1611).

Van Linschoten traveled to the East in the service of a Catholic Portuguese bishop of Goa. The English *Wikipedia* (not the Dutch!) writes that he is 'misusing the trust in him, for reasons unknown' by copying top-secret Portuguese nautical maps. None of the present secret services can boast of a similar result: it enabled the British and Dutch East India Companies 'to break the 16th-century monopoly enjoyed by the Portuguese on trade with the East Indies' and to start the conquering of the largest empire ever.[17] However, this was a really world-historical deed in the history of opium also, as is explained below.

The world heard of these secrets in all possible detail after Van Linschoten wrote a bestseller in 1598, which was quickly translated into English and many other languages. It is said to concern the earliest authentic account of the habit of "opium eating". However, 35 years earlier Garcia de (or *da*) Orta (1501-1568), a Portuguese botanist and physician lived in Goa. He mentioned the existence of something like opium with several relevant details quoted by Linschoten. At that time, the famous Italian physician Fallopius (1523-1563) apparently stated that Persians used it to increase sexual pleasure.

However, in my view, it was the Portuguese writer/ trader/ soldier Duarte Barbosa (?-1521) who was really the first of the colonizing Westerners to mention the existence and difficult use of opium.[18] One of

---

[17] See the contribution of Rui Manuel Loureiro in: E. van Veen, L. Blussé (ed.), p. 169 about Linschoten and Cornelis de Houtman who 'had collected enough intelligence to guide his expedition to safe harbour' because he was formerly resident of Lisbon.

[18] D. Barbosa, vol.1, p. 122, 123 described how the king of Cambaya was brought up by eating 'poison' in 'such small doses that it could do him no evil', because his father wished that 'they might not be able to kill him by poison.' Barbosa continued with: 'And he could never give up eating this poison, for if he did so he would die forthwith, as we see by experience of the opium which the most of the Moors and Indians eat; if they left off eating it they would die; and if those ate it who had never before eaten it, they too would die ... This opium is cold in the fourth degree ... The Moors eat it as a means of provoking lust, and the Indian women take it to kill themselves ...' This is nearly literally copied by Linschoten/

the "secrets" Van Linschoten discovered and copied in Goa in his master's library must have been Barbosa's report! In his own text it is easily to see how he copied parts of Barbosa's book, without mentioning the source.[19]

Therefore, the following quotation of the whole of Linschoten's short 78th chapter, titled 'Of Amfion, alias Opium', should be perceived as a compilation of the Western opium knowledge until 1600, but also as the formulation of the original sin. It sounds as follows in old Biblical English:

> Amfion, so called by the Portingales, is by the Arabians, Mores, and Indians called Affion, in latine Opio or opium: [It] commeth out of Cairo in Egypt, [and] out of Aden, upon the coast of Arabia, which is the point of the [land, entring into] the red Sea, sometimes belonging to the Portingales; but most part out of Camaia, & from Decan, that of Cairo is whitish, and is called Mecerii, that of Aden ... is blackish & hard. That which commeth from Cambaia and Decan is softer and reddish. Amfion is made of sleepe balles [or Poppie], and is the gumme which commenth forth [of the same], to ye which end it is cut up and opened. The Indians use much to eat Amfion, specially the Malabares, and thether it is brought by those of Cambaia and other places, in great aboundance. Hee that useth to eate it, must eate it daylie, otherwise he dieth and consumeth himselfe, [when] they begin to eate it, and are used unto it, [they heate at the least] twenty or thirty graines in waight [everie day], sometimes more: but if for foure or five dayes hee chanceth to leave it, he dieth without faile: likewise he that hath never eaten it, and will venture at the first to eate as much as those that dayly use it, it will surely kill him: for I certainly beleeve it is a kinde of poyson. Such as use it goe alwaies [as if they were] halfe a sleepe, they eate much of it because they would not feele any [great] labour or unquietnes [when they are at worke], but they use it most for lecherie: for it maketh a man hold his seede long before he sheddeth it, which the Indian women much desire, that they may shed their nature likewise with the man: although such as eate much thereof, are in time altogether unable to company with a woman, & whollie dried up, for it drieth and wholly cooleth mans nature that useth

---

Paludanus. In a note to this page the editor explains that Barbosa used for opium the word *amfiam* from the Arabic *afyun,* which could be derived from the Greek *opion,* juice. The Dutch used from the beginning the word *amfioen* or *amphioen*. Barbosa indicates on his p. 154 (and vol. 2, p. 214 ff.) that the North Indian Gujarat (Cambaya, Surat, etc.) was the trade connection between the Middle East and the rest of India, but also with Malacca, Sumatra and China. Many products were exchanged, including opium. See also T. Dormandy, p. 19 ff. also mentions the "Greek" *opion,* not knowing that *opium* is a later Latinization of *afyūn,* etc. and, therefore, erroneously suggesting that in ancient Greece and Rome there was a widespread use of opium.

[19] See previous note. In the introduction to the new Dutch edition of Linschoten's *Itinerario* Professor Kern did not mention Barbosa at all, who was certainly Van L.'s source. In the two volumes of the English translation Barbosa is mentioned twice, but only in notes of the editor (vol. 1, p. 46 and 116) and without any relevance to the subject.

it, as the Indians themselves do witnes: wherefore it is not much used by the Nobilitie, but onely for the cause aforesaid.

Back in Holland Van Linschoten worked together with a learned friend called Paludanus.[20] The latter wrote an 'annotatio', a further explanation, for many chapters of the book. In this case, Paludanus clearly differentiates between two kinds of opium. The first is a juice resulting from pressure on the leaves and heads together.[21] The second kind is the juice resulting from cutting the heads, 'which is the right opium'. The former is sweet, the latter is 'heavy, close, fast and bitter'; the smell of it 'provoketh sleepe'. The best opium is 'that which easily melteth in the water [and is] soft, white, and without grossenes or kernels ... and is by the Turkes called Maslac.'[22] According to him, from this stuff Turks eat daily 'a quantity of a pease' whereupon they do not sleep, but which gives them courage when going to war. Paludanus concludes, however, that those who use it daily become stupid and slow, sleepy in their words and work.

Connected to Paludanus and his Dutch context, one can indicate a most important constellation which makes it possible to point to the location of the Original Sin. Paludanus was somehow involved in establishing a *hortus botanicus* as *hortus medicus* in Leiden. These gardens can be considered spatial extensions of *herbaria*. In no other 17th-century European country was the concentration of them as high as in the Dutch Republic. Every university had its garden. In England, for instance, only

---

[20] His proper name was Berend van den Broecke (ca. 1550-1633) and he was born in Enkhuizen (others say Steenwijk), an important seaport at the time. He studied in Padua, was well-known for his collection of curiosities and plants. The University of Leiden asked him to establish a *hortus botanicus* as medicinal garden. The model for this garden had to be the *hortus* of Padua. Recently the lost original design of the garden was found in a catalogue of ceiling designs. See F. Bouman et al. (ed.), p. 27.

[21] Paludanus mentions that the Greeks had a special name for it, *meconium*. This is Latin, however. In Greek, furthermore, *meikoon* has many meanings and uses, as Liddell-Scott, p. 1126 indicates: poppy seed, poppy juice, poppy head or 'the ink-bag of the cuttle-fish' and no connotation to addiction. Even Liddell-Scott is duped as it refers to the Ilias, 8. 306, which does not refer in any way to *Papaver somniferum*. Also, Pausanias does use *meikoon* as *metaphor* for an architectural ornament and not in 5.20.5 but in 5.20.9.

[22] By taking the pains to compare several old dictionaries, one can obtain a good exercise in humility about human knowledge. Their authors too often simply copy their predecessors as Van Linschoten was doing with Barbosa, without correcting the mistakes. Even copying is an art in itself. Take, for instance, *maslac*, the present Turkish word for 'butter' (margarine). The Webster's (1913) writes "maslach" indicating '(med.) An excitant containing opium, much used by the Turks'. A 2002 dictionary (Thomas Nordegren's lexicon about drugs, etc., p. 414) provides four spellings (maslac, maslak, masmach and masmoch) all referring to a Turkish *and* Egyptian 'colloquial term for hashish' or even 'containing hashish', which can be every quantity. A 1818 *Nouveau dictionnaire d'histoire naturelles...* writes (vol. XIX, p. 434) about 'Maslac. Ce nom est celui de l'Opium, en Turquie.'

Oxford had one; in France there were only two; in Belgium the first garden was established at the University of Leuven in 1738, etc.[23] Around 1650, the Dutch Republic was in its Golden Age and leading in these plant collections, but also in the medicines based on these resources or in the publications related to them.

In Amsterdam it was Johannes Snippendaal (1616-1670) who organized the *hortus* for a long period. He wrote an important catalogue of eight hundred plants grown in the garden in which several kinds of poppies are mentioned. About one-third of these plants had some medicinal effect, but nothing is given about some special opium treatments. This was remarkable in the most complicated prescriptions of Nicolaes Tulp (1593-1674), one of the most famous doctors of the Dutch Republic (see Rembrandt's '*Anatomical Lesson from Tulp*').[24]

This Amsterdam *hortus* of one hectare became an experimental garden for the Dutch East and West Indies Companies from 1682 onwards, but again there is no trace of any specific opium treatment.[25] Compared to what "everybody" knew from Van Linschoten's bestseller *Itinerario,* one is tempted to question the specific silence around opium in the most advanced European country and the most abundant trade in the stuff by the same Dutch merchants in Asia. This "mystery" will bring us to the heart of the Opium Problem in our study and the very location of the "Original Sin", in many senses a real Garden of Eden.

In the Middle Eastern culture one can find illuminating parallel histories before the Dutch started their specific trade. Take the region with the ancient custom of *qat* chewing in Yemen, Somalia, etc.[26] Currently, it is a real common people's custom, but that was not always the case. All the details and connotations related to *qat* are similar to those for opium. That concerns not only the present situation where *qat* is the most important cash crop in North Yemen, and indeed 'the most important crop of any kind'.[27]

---

[23] F. Bouman a.o. (ed.), p. 26.

[24] Idem, p. 188 ff.

[25] Idem, p. 209 ff.

[26] It is also known as *chat, jaad,* or *khat* and concerns an evergreen shrub that grows naturally on the mountain sides of specific locations. There is, of course, also a Western medical assessment of *qat* or *khat* as given in an article of S.W. Toennes et al. in the *British Journal of Clinical Pharmacology* (2003), 125-30 or see www.biopsychiatry.com/khat-qat. htm. For history and practice of *qat* see now J. Kennedy, p. 60-79. See also G. Vögler, K. von Welck (ed.), vol. 2, p. 850-872 including the German translation of J. Kennedy's contribution.

[27] According to Kennedy it is, therefore, 'totally unrealistic at this time' to talk about banning *qat* or replacing it with another crop (p. 233).

As a 'recreational drug' it is mentioned for the first time in the 14th-century. Its use is for a long time confined to small numbers of sufis, some wealthy individuals and perhaps some of the farmers who grew it. But around 1565 the elite's knowledge about its negative and positive effects allows detailed comparisons with opium, alcohol and hashish. At that time Al-Haythemi concluded that the use of *qat* must be avoided, but compared to opium it is much milder.

There is also a clear historical and cultural relation with the production and consumption of coffee. Some scholars think that both *qat* and coffee were introduced together by a mystic around 1420; for others this is only one of the legends surrounding the use of *qat*. The Yemeni city Mocha (al-Mukhā), an enormous storehouse and transit harbor for all kinds of products at the turn of the seventeenth-century, also became the logo of the best coffee in the world.[28]

It was drunk, first, by holy men around Mecca both for medicinal purposes and to keep awake during their devotions. The same word for coffee (*qahwa*) was used for *qat*. Coffee drinking spread in the 15th-century from Yemen to other parts of the Middle East; in the next century it was very popular among the "jet set" of Istanbul and Cairo. "Europe" discovered coffee and its trade thanks to the Dutch merchant Pieter van den Broecke, who arrived in Mocha in 1616. Van den Broecke and his followers also purchased opium here.[29]

One hundred years later the Dutch repeated a practice, which we will meet time and again among most colonial powers: to exchange coffee for *qat*[30] or pepper and tea for opium. The earliest decision to make such deals will be discussed in detail below (ch. 11) as the real original sin in opium history.

---

[28] C. Brouwer (2006) provides an excellent and very detailed study of the trade of Al-Mukha (1614-1640) highlighting not only the coffee trade, but also the trade in pepper, cloves, nutmeg, cinnamon, cardamon, textiles, etc. In short, "everything", except *qat,* and only a few remarks about opium. That is symptomatic enough.

[29] Idem, p. 49-51. They were small lots, whereas coffee (*cauwa* in Brouwer's writings) was shipped more systematically and in larger quantities. See also C. Brouwer (1996), p. 228, 274.

[30] *Wikipedia* article "Handelsposten van de VOC in het Midden Oosten".

CHAPTER FOUR

CONCLUSIONS

The search for the original sin brings us, indeed, in or near the Garden of Eden, the Middle East. More importantly, we are confronted with many connotations surrounding the use of Papaver species, including the opium poppy, *Papaver somniferum*. So, up to the beginning of the 16th-century small quantities of Papavers are used among many herbs for personal food and energy (oil of the seeds) and for economic, medical and luxury or recreational reasons. The last two applications in particular could be directly connected to death and poison, to impotence as well as to a sexual palliative or temporary stronger sex activity, to a restricted use among the elite (warriors, etc.). Indeed, in the Middle Eastern medical and court life of the Ottoman empire, many of these elements of Papavers were known. It was surrounded with legends and more or less embedded in an elite culture.

Arab and Muslim traders spread hallucinogenic products, knowledge and customs from the Middle East into the North Indian societies via Hormuz, Surat and similar merchant cities from—say—the 14th-century onwards. At that time it was just a very small item in an extensive trade assortment of these caravan and maritime merchants.

In other words, China has nothing to do with this "original sin". It is also ridiculous to refer to Neolithic circumstances to explain the use of opium as an aphrodisiac; its history can only start where all relevant elements are available concerning ecological, economic, social and cultural preconditions. The most important aspect for our study is: there was *no opium problem* nor an "Opium Question" as a mass phenomenon!

But why then referring to some "original sin"? The answer can be found at the provisional end of our history. A modern highly ambiguous British writer on *The Paradise* also came across Muslim opium producers and traders in Afghanistan. To introduce the second part of his historical analysis, covering the years 1000-1500 (ACE), he talks about such a meeting with an Afghan opium farmer and 'his dangerous but very pretty crops' (!):

> The opium, the farmer said, was not as healthy as it looked ... Did he smoke it? No. People said Iranians liked it, but he personally had never tried the

stuff. How did it make them feel? He shrugged. Like they were in *al-jenna,*
the Garden of Paradise. No, he couldn't sell me a few kilos ...[1]

This British dealer in Paradise reacts like one of the British soldiers in
Helmland, who are accused of only guarding the poppy fields and playing
arch-angel at the gate of Paradise in stead of fighting the Taliban, who
'also got rid of hashish and opium.'[2]

The earliest Western intruders in the Middle Eastern world, those of
the 16th and 17th centuries, started to create these "Afghanistan interest(s)"
and committed the original sin. They pointed to bewildering aspects of
the opium use in a contradictory way as well, because they were confronted for the first time with a regular use of new kinds of herbs and plants in
medicine, the kitchen, religion or elsewhere in the Levant, Middle East or
India. Their curiosity about what could be useful for themselves or in the
militant exchange they organized with these new worlds, also changed in
these centuries in a rather drastic way in the wake of an intensification of
Western imperialism and colonialism: opium became, first and foremost,
an isolated "Asian product" unconnected to any *original* social, ecological
and economic context. This isolation was executed under the most barbarous circumstances: the original sin.

Did an Opium Question originate in the 17th, develop in the 18th-cen-
tury and explode in the 19th-century? Indeed, how this happened and
what are the consequences still felt today form the subject of the following historical analysis, which does not aim at legitimizing any behavior.

Because the English were by far the most exuberant profiteers of the
Opium Problem, their performance will be discussed first. It gives us the
opportunity to sketch the general case, whereupon the analysis of the
Dutch, French or Chinese performances can provide us with the necessary details, definitions of an Opium Question and comparisons. In particular the Dutch assault of the East is interesting not so much due to Jan
Huygen van Linschoten's text as to their "first commitment of the original
sin", the example which was followed by all other Western opium interests.

---

[1] K. Rushby, p. 39.
[2] Idem, p. 43.

PART TWO

THE BRITISH ASSAULT

CHAPTER FIVE

THE ACTUAL SINS

> How did a people who thought themselves free end up
> subjugating so much of the world ... How did an empire
> of the free become an empire of slaves? How, despite
> their "good intentions", did the British sacrifice "com-
> mon humanity" to "the fetish of the market"?
>
> Niall Ferguson.[1]

> As your Ambassador can see for himself, we possess
> all things. I set no value on objects strange or ingenious,
> and have no use for your country's manufactures.
>
> Qianlong Emperor in a letter to King George III (1793).

The opening sentences of the much acclaimed work by David Edward
Owen (1934) about the British opium policy tell us, that it concerns 'the
most curious chapters in the annals of European expansion.'[2] This must
be perceived as an intentional understatement. His astonishment is real:
how is it possible that one-seventh of the revenue of British India was
drawn from the subjects of another state as payment for a habit-forming
drug: this must be 'one of the most unique facts that the history of finance
affords.' Again, a stiff upper-lip exclamation, which continues with the
qualifying phrase, 'still more grotesque', that the opium sent to China was
produced 'under the aegis of a state-administered monopoly which existed principally for supplying that market'. Owen points to only a part of the
problem faced in this study. As so often when subjects are hotly debated,
some authors try to get an "above the parties" position to acclaim authority and objectivity. Owen's book is an excellent example of this genre; a
Chinese contemporary wrote less abstractly about this opium import: '..

---

[1] Quoted by N. Ferguson, p. xiii. It is a pity that Ferguson did not try to answer this
question. Apparently because in the end (p. 365, 366) he was quite satisfied with the
Empire's performance in world history, notwithstanding his demonstration 'how often it
failed to live up to its own ideal.' Happily P. Brendon has done a more relevant job.

[2] D. E. Owen, p. vii. See the relevant remarks of C.Trocki (1999a), p. 174 about Owen
and Morse and their approach.

the import ...it was thought, led to a moral and physical deterioration of the Chinese.'[3]

Eighty years earlier as a direct comment on what happened in China, Karl Marx wrote in the *New York Daily Tribune* (20 September 1858):

> Besides its negative result, the first opium-war succeeded in stimulating the opium trade at the expense of legitimate commerce, and so will this second opium-war do if England be not forced by the general pressure of the civilized world to abandon the compulsory opium cultivation in India and the armed opium propaganda to China. We forbear dwelling on the morality of that trade, described by Montgomery Martin, himself an Englishman, in the following terms: 'Why, the "slave trade" was merciful compared with the "opium trade". We did not destroy the bodies of the Africans, for it was our immediate interest to keep them alive; we did not debase their natures, corrupt their minds, nor destroy their souls. But the opium seller slays the body after he has corrupted, degraded and annihilated the moral being of unhappy sinners, while, every hour is bringing new victims to a Moloch which knows no satiety, and where the English murderer and Chinese suicide vie with each other in offerings at his shrine.

The man quoted by Marx was not simply 'himself an Englishman'. Montgomery Martin (c. 1801-1868) was a British author and civil servant. He was the first *Colonial Treasurer of Hong Kong* from 1844 to 1845. He was a founding member of the *Statistical Society of London* (1834), the *Colonial Society* (1837), and the *East India Association* (1867). In short, a high-placed and esteemed official, supporter of the imperialist adventures of the British Empire. A stronger confession of the British bad conscience is difficult to find.[4]

The "original sin" had several other moral and sometimes theological elements. Take the case of the effects of opium eating or smoking. In the Middle East authorities warned against opium use or prohibited it from the middle of the 16th-century. Despite this ban, the available trade data from the "Arabian" side talk about marginal quantities in the overall trade. Its function was largely: providing medicine and, sometimes, giving pres-

---

[3] S. G. Cheng, p. 149.

[4] A relevant reminiscence to this comparison between slavery and opium addiction can be found in L. Blussé (2008), p. 65 where he states: 'It is indeed ironic that Britain, the nation that prided itself on having first exposed the excrescences of the American slave trade (in which it had been by far the greatest participant) after it had lost the American colonies ... was engaged in the master planning of another kind of enslavement in Asia: opium addiction.' For M. Martin see also C. Munn, p. 47 ff. and a long quote on Idem, p. 21.

ents to smooth the trade; a method soon copied by the Portuguese or British.[5]

This could prove that in the prehistorical phase of our story, the bad effects on individual health and society were already known. In moralistic terms: opium was branded as something rotten, which had to be eradicated. Two centuries later, successive Chinese and other governments prohibited the production and/ or use of opium. They acted accordingly with strong measures but failed for many reasons, as we will see.

At that time they must have reacted mainly to the effects of the Portuguese and Dutch trade results, which will be discussed in part three. From the foreign perpetrator's side, there were not so many criticisms on the use or selling of opium. Protestant religious circles in America and England started a Western anti-movement at the end of the 19th-century (see ch. 29). Apart from the existence of a dubious double morality (one for own people and one for foreigners; let alone for the racially "undervalued" and uncivilized ones), double institutional moralities were asking for trouble. In our case it concerns an immanent contradiction: the normal bourgeois morality perceived opium production, distribution and trading as criminal acts, but the state earning huge profits with them, was accepted for a long period in the West.

A Private English Asian Trading Company

The many East Indies Companies were in fact all ventures of combined state and private interests. Which element dominated varied per country, the strength of the private interests involved and per period. The first English activities in which private interests dominated struggled for survival in Surat on the northwestern Indian coast. This was where the cornerstone of the British Empire in India was build, while everybody thought that the real future of the British in the East was to be found in the spice trade of the Moluccas. In 1920 Rawlinson wrote about the first factors in the beginning of the 17th-century:

> ... there is nothing romantic about the sturdy merchants who founded the factory at Surat. They were not consciously empire-builders. They did not come, like the Portuguese, with drum and trumpet to convert the East to the True Faith. They had no Camoens to sing their praises. They were not even supported, like the Dutch, by the State, from which, indeed, they

---

[5] D. Hall, p. 277.

received scant encouragement. They combined, in Puritan fashion, piety and profit; their objects were the glory of God, and the advancement of the company's (and, incidentally, their own) interests.[6]

It may be that the English did not have a superb poet like the Portuguese Camoens, but Rawlinson's references to Milton ('the greatest of the Puritans') and his *Paradise Lost* was not a bad compensation.[7] Certainly, the Jesuits were eager to convert the pagans and, in particular, to do this together with the rulers of some realm. As a second step, they decided that everybody else in it must be Roman Catholic as well. They were excellent mediators between State and Trade, metropolis and colony.

Maybe the Puritan 'objects were the glory of God', but they had quite different problems: their God and the supporting clergy were theologically in variance with trade and money deals, the very source of all evil in the world. If not or if they had to strike a balance between God and the Mammon, they were fully hypocritical. That was their normal way of life with a bad conscience. But conversion of the naked heathens of India was a clear objective; their moral conduct was distasteful, and if not baptized, they could be killed at will; if baptized, they always remained racially "undervalued". The Dutch were more extreme in this than the English, since the English colonizers had a large proportion of Anglican and more cultivated aristocrats, which largely failed among the Dutch. Both were colonizers like the Portuguese and Spaniards, and both were, in the end, empire builders, while sending a large part of their underworlds to the East.

Whether all this supports the famous Max Weber thesis remains to be seen.[8] Here in India the English company may be 'founded and supported by the Puritan middle class' (as if the Anglicans were absent), but in par-

---

[6] H. Rawlinson, p. 2. The first and second English trips to the East were ca. 1600-1605 and directed to Sumatra and Bantam looking for spices. At nearly the same time, the Dutch traveled to the same destination. The Portuguese and Spaniards preceded them by nearly a century, but that story cannot be told here. During the third English voyage (1608) part of the fleet under Hawkins sailed not to the spice countries, but to India. He arrived at its west coast in Surat, which became the first English basis in India. For Surat and the first Englishmen, see K. de Schweinitz Jr., p. 73-80. See for the differences between EIC and VOC also Idem, p. 75 and M. Roelofsz, p. 70, K. Chaudhuri (1978), p. 6ff. and 19 ff.

[7] H. Rawlinson, p. 19, 20. For the action of the Jesuits, Idem, p. 31 ff. and passim.

[8] Without studying Weber in an appropriate way and very critically, this is simply not done. Even the always interesting Jack Goody forgot his critical mind and did not study the recent literature, while devoting a whole book in order to prove how the 'brilliant' Weber still gave the right answers to Western questioning "The East". See J. Goody. See my writings on Marx and Weber 1978-1, 1978-2, 1999, etc.

ticular in its function of 'inveterate enemies of the Catholic powers'.[9] Still in 1920 Rawlinson treats the first masters of the inexperienced English pupils, the Portuguese who had lived there a century already, in a classically hypocritical way:

> At Goa, and throughout Portuguese India, corruption and venality were widespread, for the Portuguese, too proud to earn money honestly by trade, were driven to make it by less honourable means ... rotten to the core ... justice was bought, public offices were put up for sale, and the martial spirit degenerated into effeminacy, sloth, and indolence, as in the last days of the Roman Empire.[10]

Why hypocritical? Not that the facts mentioned were false, but because he did not refer to the similar situations in the "Puritan" British and Dutch Empires existing long before their last days. By 1630 Rawlinson reports exactly the same stupidities of the English in Surat.[11] Alas, the power of the Puritan God reached far into the East and punished this Sodom by sending a devastating famine in 1631. One did not understand this heavenly message, and hypocrisy continued to rule the deeds of the Westerners in conquering the East and spreading opium.

These Puritan or Anglican Englishmen arriving in Surat (ca. 1607) started practically the largest of these East Indies companies, the British East Indies Company (below: EIC) and the most extensive colonizing practice in India. However, it took these 'sturdy' Puritan merchants nearly 150 years before they definitely ousted their main competitor from India, the Dutch with their company (below: VOC), and later from the position as main profiteer of the opium trade, the most hypocritical trade ever dealt with.[12]

---

[9] H. Rawlinson, p. 19.

[10] Idem, p. 15, 16. He refers to J.H. van Linschoten's story of how the Portuguese women made love to men 'before the very eyes of their husbands, whom they drugged with *datura*' (see also W. Schouten's stories in ch. 10). On p. 19 he continues with: Surat, where the English stayed, 'was not, like Goa, overrun with degenerate half-castes.'

[11] Idem, p. 98. Discipline was poor, prayers neglected: 'Sundays were spent in feasting, drinking and gambling and the beastly sin of whoredom and most polluted filthy talk ... Bribes were freely taken by the authorities ... and all, from the President downwards, indulged in private trade.' See also p. 130, 131. For bribes see also note 42.

[12] For the rigorous competition in the East between the Dutch and English in the early 17th-century, see O. Prakash (2005). This competition had everything to do with the European competition of the two nations in the 17th and 18th centuries. For the different strategies of the Dutch and English and for the dominating mercantile elements among the latter, see also R. Brenner, p. 168 ff. Brenner sketches the internal English transformation of the trade landscape by the "New Merchants". Typical may be an English commentator at the time quoted by Brenner (p. 172): 'The Dutch as they gain ground secure it by vast

While in the EIC the mercantile element may have been much stronger at first than in the VOC, inherent to these companies were continuous conflicts between the headquarters in London or Amsterdam and the companies in the East and their regional headquarters. In England and the Netherlands, the national political changes and ideologies (including moralities) seriously influenced the decisions of the companies. They were more often than not in variance with the trade and military plans in the Far East. And in the Far East serious tensions arose between the bureaucrats of the company headquarters and the commanders or traders in the fields.

In addition, the EIC suffered from competition with other English trading activities of, for instance, the tycoon Courteen, who could even bribe the king with £10,000 to grant a full royal patent.[13] That was not the case with the VOC. After an initial period in which several private companies were set up and voyages to the Indies financed, the VOC received an absolute monopoly in 1602. It became a state within the state, as the EIC did 150 years later.

Opium on a List

At the very start of the EIC adventure, however, all these tensions were far in the future. The first trips to the East did not yield much profit, but every time Londoners were willing to spend capital to build ships and gather enough people to make these dangerous voyages.

The sixth trip of 1609 was a most remarkable one. The King himself was heavily involved and the help of the Puritan and Anglican Gods were invoked since 'blasphemy, swearing, drunkenness, and gambling' were severely punished, and every morning and evening the captains were ordered to join together with prayers to these Almighty Gods for their protection. In all things they were to uphold also 'the honour of our King and the reputation of our traffick'.

From "London" the captains received strict instructions about what had to be their cargo to India and what they had to bring back. One may

---

expenses, raising forts and maintaining soldiers; ours are for raising auctions and retrenching charges; bidding the next age grow rich, as they have done, but not affording them the means.' For the early history of the EIC see Idem, p. 21 ff. It makes no sense to mention the internal English development, not in the least because in Brenner's 734 pages the word "opium" cannot be found.

[13] R. Brenner, p. 171; K. de Schweinitz Jr., p. 40-54.

suspect that this choice was based on the experience of the previous five voyages and of the demands of English consumers:

> Their cargo consisted of cloth, lead, red lead, tin, quicksilver, vermilion, sword-blades, kerseys, and red caps. They were to load up with indigo, calico, cotton yarn, cinnamon, sandal, ginger, opium, gum benjamin, olibanum, aloes and lac ... and above all pepper (400 tons if they could) ..., but too much anxiety for pepper was not to be displayed for fear of putting up the price.[14]

This must be the first time that a Western source asked for Eastern opium. It is in variance with Om Prakash's reasonable opinion concerning the 17th- and 18th-century opium trade:

> Unlike most other tropical agricultural raw materials, Europe did not take any Indian opium whatever. Indeed, the trade in the product had traditionally been confined to Asia.[15]

Rawlinson does not give an explanation for "opium" in this list; it had apparently no specific meaning for him. There is no proof given whether opium was shipped to London. Still: there is no reason to doubt the quotation and, therefore, the question can be posed: who was in need of opium in England at that time?

Certainly, the first decades of the 17th-century were marked by a significant increase in luxury imports as there was, for instance, the sky rocketing consumption of tobacco.[16] Probably this product would have been brought to other Eastern ports in the beginning of the intra-Asian trade, as the Dutch were doing with opium or *qat* later? Was it used as a medicine or as a luxury?

One knew from Van Linschoten's *Itinerario*, the bible for this sixth voyage also, what the qualities of and problems with this product were.[17] Notwithstanding this knowledge, at this juncture one can only conclude that it must have concerned a small amount of opium relative to the very small profit on many products made on this trip and that somebody in London wants to eat from this "forbidden fruit".

---

[14] H. Rawlinson, p. 48. Later (p. 127, 128) he gives a list of goods which were transported to Surat from all directions by caravan and ship. From Persia were imported 'drugs and fine Carmanian wool' and from Calicut came 'garnets, opium and salpetre'. Persia (Egypt, Turkey) was the classical land of opium production used as medicine. For Calicut, see part 3.

[15] O. Prakash (1988), p. 73.

[16] R. Brenner, p. 42 ff.

[17] Probably they had read another Linschoten book, because Rawlinson always talks about the *Itineratio*, p. 31, 34, 153, etc.

Ill. 3. The Opium War and China in the cartoons

Source: published on "Holachina.blog", 29-3-2009, but originally these are French cartoons designed by Honoré Daumier ca. 1860: a British or French admiral forcing opium down the throat of a Chinese person (mandarin?), used time and again on book covers and posters. The other is called 'The Royal Cake or the Western Empires sharing China between them', published in *Le Petit Journal*, 1898.

A second example of hypocritical behavior is related to the historiography of the opium problem. This concerns the period just before the First Opium War, discussed in the next chapter.

Priscilla Napier wants to defend the highly criticized deeds of a famous family member, the unsuccessful Lord Napier (1786-1834), creator of a fiasco called the 'Napier Fizzle'.[18] This 'Chief Superintendent of Trade at Canton' was the first sent by Palmerston to show the Chinese the practice of "free trade with a gun to the head" and to force the "opening of China". In Priscilla's ambiguous defense, however, it is said that this was not Napier's intention but originated 'from the 19th-century American captain' who abruptly ordered 'open up or we fire' in Japan.[19] No, a reappraisal is needed: 'William John', it is true, played his part 'to open up normal

---

[18] J. Beeching, chapter 2; J. Lovell, p. 5-8.
[19] P. Napier, p. ix.

trade with China' but, alas, he was onfronted with 'the disastrous results of Imperial China's refusal to play along with this plan.'

Priscilla Napier went far in her reappraisal and in blaming the victims of the British assault. She dares to stress the

> determination of the British Government ... and of the East India Company's directors in London *not* to sell opium to China ... Dutch merchant seamen, Americans, Parsee entrepreneurs and British get-rich-quick adventurers ... were the bad guys (italics from P.N.).[20]

On the cover of her book Priscilla shows a scene from 9 September 1834: the HMS *Imogene* and *Andromache* bombarding Tiger Island 'in their forcing of the Bocca Tigris passage' up to Canton.[21] The picture does not show what happened thereafter: both ships were rendered totally useless by simple Chinese measures (some cables and twelve sunken barges loaded with stones); they could neither go on nor go back and were completely under Chinese control. Napier failed in a miserable way and died a few days later. However, Priscilla did not mention how Lord Napier was urged to attack by his friends, the most rigorous opium traders and smugglers Matheson and Jardine (see next example).

On the back cover of the book there is a skyline of Hong Kong two years before the handover to China (1997). A text erroneously suggests that Napier established it, although in 1841 the barren, rocky site got its first houses as a result of a new and more successful "free trade's bombarding policy" in order to transform the Chinese into opium addicts.

Long before Priscilla, it was the important American official, Willoughby, who wrote in the 1920s about the hypocrisy of the English in forcing the import of opium and war upon China as follows:

> No mention was made of opium in the Treaty of Nanking, and, therefore, the importation of the drug into China remained illegal under the Chinese law. By a treaty supplementary to that of Nanking, signed a year later, the British Government pledged itself to discourage the smuggling [1843]. This pledge was, however, almost immediately broken, and Hongkong became a base of operations for the contraband trade in opium ... As a further facilitation to this illegal trade, a British ordinance was passed which enabled Chinese boats, many of which were engaged in this trade, to fly the British

---

[20] Idem, p. 65.

[21] It concerns a many times pictured event. See also J. Beeching, plate 3 after p. 192 and the map near the title page. M. Collis, p. 192. The destruction brought by the world's first all-iron steamer, *Nemesis* (1841), is the alternative. See J. Lovell, opposite p. 171.

flag, and out of this permission arose the "Arrow" incident which led to the second war between Great Britain and China[22]

A last example concerns a more complicated case of what could be called "in-built hypocrisy" of the British colonizers from the same pre-Opium War period. The leading figure at the time was Sir Stamford Raffles, one of the main builders of the British Empire in the East. In the British histori-ography he is still pictured as a most humane, enlightened, erudite and competent man; from a Dutch colonial point of view at the time and for later Dutch commentators (like Baud) he was a most controversial man, but that is something like the calling the kettle black. As far as the colo-nized have a voice, they are or should be rather critical about the man.

Anyway, around 1814 he helped his friend Alexander Hare to build a colony on 1400 square miles of land privately acquired in a dubious way from the Sultan of Banjarmasin.[23] Raffles assisted Hare, a man who could have been described in Joseph Conrad's *Heart of Darkness,* who peopled his colony with convicts, slaves and kidnapped women ('of loose morals'). In the middle of it Hare build himself a residence surrounded by dwell-ings of women. His house was 'higher than the tallest tree and [with] 1,650 poles' for which a hundred convicts had to work for twenty months. After Raffles had to leave his job as Governor- General of Java (1816), Hare's col-ony began running at a loss. Hare had to start a new life going from scan-dal to scandal. Like in Australia, this was an example of how colonization was practiced by the British.

It was around 1820 that Raffles himself started the very young settle-ment of Singapore as a model for all colonial ventures to come. Immediately, it was clear who would be the fiercest enemies of this plan: the English bureaucrats and the traders in India. Raffles had to establish Singapore by keeping expenses to a minimum. His representative, Farquhar, however,

> defying Raffles's instructions ... introduced a tax-farming system, auctioning monopoly rights to sell opium and arrack, or Asian spirits, and to run gam-bling dens.[24]

The above mentioned James Matheson, the most vigilant opium trader, cooperated with Farquhar. From Matheson is told and quoted:

---

[22] W. Willoughby, vol. 2, p. 1092.
[23] S. Alatas, p. 36 ff.
[24] C. Turnbull, p. 15.

In May 1819, when Singapore had hardly been taken possession of by Sir
Stamford Raffles, its commercial possibilities were foreseen by the 22 year-
old James Matheson, making his second voyage to China as Supercargo of
the opium ship Marquis of Hastings: "As far as two or three observations
and conversations enable me to speak, I have formed the highest opinion
of Singapore as a place of trade ... the situation of the settlement is truly
delightful, being within 4 miles of the direct tract for China; and the mild
sway of Major Farquhar has attracted settlers from all parts of the village,
which consisted of 200 houses and containing now upwards of 2,000 ... the
Java Government having declined to interfere with our possession.[25]

The cooperation of English and Dutch bureaucrats with this drugs baron
was too much even for Raffles. Upon his return, he intended to eradicate
gambling, opium smoking and the opium trade. But at the very beginning
of the most profitable opium century for the English and Dutch, and
twenty years before the start of the Opium Wars, Singapore had fallen
already prey to Matheson's business:

The well-to-do, who included the Europeans, Jews, Armenians, Eurasians,
Parsees and rich Chinese, suffered mainly from over-indulgence in food and
alcohol ... Among the mass of the population, poverty, malnutrition, over-
crowding and excessive opium smoking took the heaviest toll.' ... 'Much of
this misery stemmed from the deadly habit of opium smoking which was
the centre of controversy. Most Europeans regarded it merely as a bad habit,
soothing and soporific, harmful only if taken to excess. [Those who] cam-
paigned to open the eyes of the government and the community at large to
the medical and social evils of opium smoking ... estimated in 1848 that 20
per cent of the entire population and more than half the Chinese adults
were opium addicts. Rich Chinese, who smoked high-quality opium, were
not seriously harmed, but the poor smoked the refuse. Addicts were reduced
to begging and living on rotten fish and decaying vegetables around the
market, ending up in prison or the pauper hospital, or driven to suicide ...
The well-to-do Chinese found the opium farm lucrative, the less wealthy
Asians made no protest, while European merchants were content to see
taxes levied on opium rather than on commerce, property or salaries ... the
opium farm continued to be the mainstay of the revenue up to the twentieth-century.[26]

---

[25] M. Greenberg, p. 97.
[26] C. Turnbull, p. 62 and 63. In S. Couling's Encyclopaedia (p. 258) Jardine, Matheson
& Co is described without the word 'opium', only that it sent 'the first free ship with free
tea from Whampoa, March 22, 1834'! Also with the text: 'In 1842 business was transferred
to Hongkong. The firm has always been prominent in all efforts for the welfare of the colony.' See also C.Munn, p. 42 ff.

In the next decades Singapore, still a settlement under the direct responsibility of the EIC ("Calcutta") became infamous world-wide for its criminal milieu, many brothels, robbed and beaten sailors and, of course, the
opium business. In the 1880s the world-wide antisemitic movement was
also fostered, thanks to a concentration of Jews in the opium business.
This, however, does not mean the reverse, that opium business was a
Jewish affair, as a Singapore merchant remarked:

> For the opium trade, pure and simple, in itself, I care nothing; it is wholly
> in the hands of Jews and Armenians, and I know little about its ins and outs:
> but there is no doubt that Opium enters largely into, and forms an impor-
> tant part of, the Native trade of this city ... All those prahus and junks which
> we see lying off Tanjong Ru ... are all small parts of one great trade.[27]

The remark again says something about life in Singapore and, furthermore, about the new hypocrisy which was added to the older ones.

A Moral Question

It was at the turn of the century that the anti-opium movement grew
strong enough in the several mother countries to put some pressure on
(colonial) governments. But, for instance in Singapore, this movement
encountered opposition from the tax-farmers, most European and
Chinese merchants and the English language press. A commission
appointed by the Colonial Office advised that opium smoking was a 'fairly
harmless, fashionable vice among the rich' but relatively 'pernicious'
among the poor; only some rickshaw pullers were addicts, etc.

In 1907 this local controversy resulted in what was called a 'compromise': the government took over the manufacture and sale of opium, a
move the Dutch government had already made in Java a century earlier.[28]
In the 1930s Singapore became superficially a more peaceful and safe
place: opium dens were disappearing under the controls and restrictions
on opium smoking and brothels, with mostly imported East European
girls, were declared illegal. Behind secret doors, however, the criminal
societies flourished more than ever and gang fights were common. An
underworld and upperworld divided the Hypocritical Society.

---

[27] Quoted in C.Trocki (1999a), p. 117. Trocki himself adds to the confusing by naming
his chapter 6 'In the hands of Jews and Armenians' without brackets.

[28] Idem, p. 114. Around 1870 the French colonial government of Cochinchina came
with an innovation of this governmental involvement in the opium business, the *Opiumregie*-model (see ch. 19 and 23).

The examples, one of a start and another of a developed constellation, show the characteristics of the perpetrator side in this opium dossier. At least until the beginning of the Second World War this all belongs to rather common scenarios, reactions and developments among the colonial powers and their settler and immigrant populations in the British, French, Dutch and other colonies. There were, however, substantial differences due to the scale of the opium problems in the East Asian region, the accompanying violence, the money interests or the involvement of governments.

These differences are analyzed in detail below. Then it will become apparent that something special exists between "victim country China and Opium". The Chinese inside China are clearly the most affected victims of the European assaults. However, the Singapore example could lead to the question of whether this was also true for the Chinese outside China? This perpetrator-victim relationship requires concrete analysis and differentiation not generalizations (see ch. 15 and 25).

As mentioned earlier, I am not intending to tell a chronological story of the use or trade of opium[29], but rather provide a historical analysis of "The Opium Problem": this concerns the introduction of opium *as a luxury* (not as a medicine which was or is not a problem *before the 19th-century*), as a mass product and as a major element of imperialist policy in the Far East. When can this specific *combination* be signaled in history? And what are the consequences for the course of the opium problem in the main countries affected?

What matters, furthermore, are the enormous profits of the *monopoly* position in production and trade sustained by the power of arms and always extending the scale of consumption. No Chinese in China had or achieved such a monopoly position, only Western colonial governments. Next, it is also a geographical problem: as one of the most important chapters in the history of Western imperialism, this opium history is first and foremost confined to the whole of East Asia before it became a Western problem around the First World War. Therefore, the start of the present drug problem is given here.

But apart from the narrative and its (quantitative) analysis of these subjects, we have to discuss the problem arising from the policy of the British colonial state to become compensated for what it considered the unbalanced trade and monetary relationship with China. That was a

---

[29] A useful chronology is given in E. Vanvugt, p. 416-423.

circumstance which was so fundamental that two wars were fought with the Chinese Empire in order to arrive at a "balanced" situation.

Until the beginning of the 19th-century the British Empire was the most important slave-trading "nation"; thanks to these opium wars it remained a "mind-trading nation" as well for more than a century. The question posed above this chapter has been complicated by the same Niall Ferguson (in the end a remarkable defender of the British Empire[30]), in the following comment on these wars:

> The only real benefit of acquiring Hong Kong as a result of the war of 1841 was that it provided firms like Jardine Matheson with a base for their opium-smuggling operation. It is indeed one of the richer ironies of the Victorian value-system that the same navy that was deployed to abolish the slave trade was also active in expanding the narcotics trade.[31]

This seems to be the best start for the following chapter.

---

[30] N. Ferguson, p. 366.

[31] Idem, p. 166. An interesting illustration of the moral element is, that in the period 1850-1870 of all the cases before the Magistrate (in average about 5,000 a year) less than 1 % was related to opium problems. See C. Munn, p. 133.

CHAPTER SIX

TEA FOR OPIUM VICE VERSA

> Increasing Bengal opium production results in a
> reduction in the profit per unit of opium sold, but it
> will not tend to increase the consumption of the del-
> eterious Drug nor to extend its baneful effects in Soci-
> ety. The sole and exclusive object of it is to secure to
> ourselves the whole supply by preventing Foreigners
> from participating in a trade of which at present they
> enjoy no inconsiderable share—for it is evident that
> the Chinese, as well as the Malays, cannot exist with-
> out the use of Opium, and if we do not supply their
> necessary wants, Foreigners will.

> Governor-General of India to the Directors of the EIC,
> July 1819.[1]

The British opium-assault on China in the 19th-century transformed the
Opium Problem from a one-sided Dutch show of Western imperialism
into its main objective from both a Western and East Asian point of view.
Trocki formulates this differently at the start of the relevant chapter in his
opium history:

> The years between 1780 and 1842 were formative years for the opium trade.
> They were also the formative years of the British Empire. ... Though difficult
> to prove beyond question, it seems likely that without opium, there would
> have been no empire.[2]

The second sentence may be true and the third interesting and provocative. However, the stated years were not the formative years of the trade.
They should be fixed about 120 years earlier as we will see in the next part
of the study. The third sentence, furthermore, is too pessimistic, because
I think that the given thesis can be proved, indeed, *beyond question*.
Although the definite conclusions can be drawn only at the end of the
study, in this part a general support of this aim should be undertaken by
means of a new quantitative and qualitative assessment of the British epi-

---

[1] Quoted in A. McCoy, p. 367.
[2] C.Trocki (1999a), p, 58 and 59.

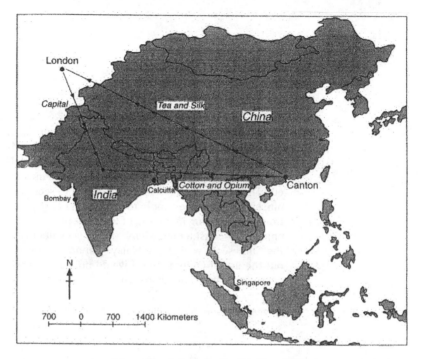

Map 1. The global triangle of trade, ca. 1820
Source: D. Meyer, p. 36

sode in which the Opium Wars occurred. Basic to its understanding is the triangle relationship between China and Britain through India: so, what does it mean "tea for opium vice versa"?

An Analysis from Within

John Crawfurd (1783-1868) was a clever colonial administrators and diplomats in India, Singapore, Java or Burma "running" the British Empire in the East together with people like Robert Hart, Warren Hastings or Stamford Raffles. He was also a prolific author who published, for instance, a three-volume *History of the Indian Archipelago* (1820). Several times in his long career he proved to have a rather intimate knowledge of the opium business. On the eve of the first Opium War, he wrote in 1837:

> Opium is an article calculated to become of vast importance to the agriculture and commerce of India. The growth of the poppy is, at present, confined to a few districts of the lower provinces of Bengal, pretty much in the

same way as the growth of tobacco is confined to a few districts of France, for the purpose of the government monopoly in that country. In the great province of Malwa, however, in the centre of India, it is now freely culti- vated, paying an export duty; and to this we, in fact, owe the vast increase which has taken place in the trade in it, within the last twenty years. In India there is a considerable local consumption of this article, especially in some of the northwestern provinces; but the great marts for its consump- tion are the Malayan islands, the countries lying between India and China, and above all, China itself. We believe we shall not overrate the whole export produce of opium from India, at 24,000 chests a year; nor the export value of every chest, at £120 sterling; making a total value of £2,880,000. The wholesale price of the article to the consumers will certainly amount a sum of not less than three-and-a-half millions sterling. This is probably a larger sum than is paid by foreign nations for all the wines exported from France, Spain, and Italy.[3]

How to assess this "analysis from within the system" in which the main elements of the commercial Opium Question are given? It provides, first, the important sense of proportion. In our present crisis, when everybody talks about billions as if they are packets of butter, we easily forget the tremendous purchasing value of a million English pound sterling, American dollars, French francs or Dutch guilders as -ultimately—the main colonial currencies in the Asian 19th-century.[4]

Crawfurd also gives an estimate of Indian export to the whole of East Asian "clients". A pamphlet at the time (1840) compares the Indian gains of this triangle trade appropriately as follows: it allowed India

> to increase ten-fold its consumption of British Manufactures ... to support the vast fabric of British dominion in the East ... and, by the operations of exchange and remittances in Teas and other Chinese produce, to pour an abundant revenue into the British Exchequer and benefit the British Nation to the extent of six millions annually.[5]

Before the 'white foreign opium devils' poured into China, there existed already a flourishing tea trade with England: in 1668 the first tea (145.5 pounds !) was consumed in England, and it became a booming business from which the English sold twenty per cent to other countries in Europe.

---

[3] Quoted by C.Trocki (1999a), p. 93, 94. See also P. Brendon, p. 102.

[4] It is probably sufficient when Crawfurd compares £2.8 million with "all the wines exported ...". Another measure is that the 30 million pounds of tea consumed every year around 1840 cost only £2 million (P. Brendon, p. 102); it is a tea trade which increased to 85 million pounds around 1870. One can also point to the facts that £1 of—say—the year 1800 is now about £ 32; one Dutch guilder of 1800 would be now twenty guilders, etc.

[5] Quoted by P. Brendon, p. 102.

In the East this trade was divided up between the private company, EIC, and the private individuals known as British Country Traders, 'each stimulating the other' in the 1750s, 1760s and 1770s.[6]

From a Chinese point of view this export was and remained small compared to its own consumption of 1800 million pound around 1850. One concluded, therefore, that it was hardly surprising that the export price only increased by 6 % notwithstanding the enormous increase of the tea export after the First Opium War was "won" and the trade became "free".[7]

Who exactly decided or discovered that tea could be paid not only with silver, through bills of exchange on London, but also by opium from Bengal is difficult to say. Below the EIC decision is reconstructed, but country traders may have discovered the relationship earlier. The export of opium from Bengal is one way to indicate what was going on; the relationship between the company (EIC) and the country traders is another. What Furber says about the latter's prehistory, is a good introduction to what follows:

> In the 1750s the sum raised by the company's supercargoes [in Canton] from the sale of bills of exchange to country traders was negligible; by 1781-82, it reached one million *taels* (c. £333,000), and it was to rise to £500,000 a year by the end of the century. The opium export in country trade from Calcutta rose from 125,000 current rupees in 1774-75 to over a million current rupees in 1786-87 (£12,500 as compared with £100,000). The net annual profits on the English East India Company's China trade were at least £234,000 in the mid-1770s, reaching £418,000 in the 1783-84 season, and rose to £800,000-£900,000 level by the close of the century.[8]

What follows is not only a reconstruction of these trade movements during the end of the 18th-century, but mainly the elementary features and fundamental importance of the opium trade for the British Empire. Remember that this story must be seen as a model for the whole Western opium history, the subject of this book, as still the most neglected part of Western imperialism in the East.

---

[6] H. Furber, p. 176.

[7] P. Brendon, p. 437.

[8] H. Furber, p. 176, see also p. 244 in which he indicates that in the 1790s 'twenty million pounds of tea [went] annually around the Cape of Good Hope to be sold in London for approximately £2,700,000 annually.'

The Bullion Game

This triangle—business became largely an English and American affair before and after the Opium Wars, but it took a long time before this was an undeniable fact. From the beginning of its involvement in the realm the EIC was faced with the necessity of taking out large quantities of bullion and coin to finance its trade. It was a continuous exporter of treasure (mainly silver Spanish dollars/peso) and not many English goods. A symptomatic example: in 1751 five ships left England for China with a cargo of £137,600 worth of silver and only £20,809 in goods.[9]

The Portuguese, Spaniards and Dutch had to do this as well and started much earlier. Over a period of three hundred years the Spanish transported silver and gold at a value of about 400 million "dollars" and the Dutch about 250 million "guilders" in the period 1602-1800.[10] The reason for this is quite simple: the Westerners had next to nothing to offer the Asians and, *therefore*, they had to pay in cash for the goods they purchased.

It is very strange that most later historians and the governments of the traders as main supporters of "free trade" made such a fuss about the most normal exchange procedure. The bullion question is only a bit more complicated, but for our aim the following is appropriate.

England's commerce was an European structured trade and its European goods (woolen goods, broad-cloths, etc. together with some lead and sometimes copper or tin) were offered to the Chinese in such a way that a loss was concealed by a process of bartering for Chinese goods. So, if the selling of these goods (bartered with English goods) was as "profitable" as the costs of the English goods (bought with money in England), the whole transaction was commercially in vain. There was only one

---

[9] H. Morse (1926), vol. 1, p. 307-313 provides a very long list of ships (1635-1753) with their (silver) stocks. The example comes from this list, which is distorted elsewhere. See M. Greenberg, p. 6, and for the following, see his first chapter on 'the old China trade' from which only a few characteristics can be given here. See also J. Beeching, p. 15-40. For a quite different description of the triangle business between Europe, India and China, see J. Richards (1981).

[10] C.Trocki (1999a), p. 42 provides an overly high amount for the Dutch. See for the latter F. Gaastra, p. 139 ff. The strange question always arises of whether profits could be made "under these circumstances". Well, Gaastra only informs us that the goods imported back to Europe with a value (or "Asian cost") of 30 million could be sold for 92 million in the 17th-century. In the 18th-century goods with an "Asian cost" of 90 million could be sold in Europe for 214 million (Idem, p. 147). If a breakdown of "Asian cost" had been given, a much larger profit could have been noted. See Appendix 4 for a relevant discussion around 1810 in the East Indies.

product from China with which very good profits could be made in England and that was tea; with chinaware the profits were not bad, but much less.

In short: in this process the Chinese needs and the private English ones matched; they concerned a normal mechanism of supply and demand. The public (or state) interest in the silver story concerned first and foremost a national relationship between Spain and England, former enemies, and another one between England and China. In addition, the silver was not used that much as normal money but as a means of barter in the form of Spanish silver coins ("dollars" or "pesos"). The big profits with tea were made at home "in English money".[11]

For both trade relations the tea trade was highly profitable until the moment the Spanish coins could not be obtained.[12] That moment came when Spain entered the American War of Independence in 1779 and the silver market was closed until 1785. In addition the competition with Bengal opium started or became apparent for the British. The Malwa and Turkish opium arrived on the Chinese drug market imported, first, by West-Indian, Portuguese and American dealers.[13] It was the start of a fierce competition. After this period the situation went from bad to worse for Westerners. The English and other Europeans wanted to consume more and more tea, while the supply of European silver remained uncertain. A further complicating factor was the specific and not very clear relationship between the English state and a private capitalist enterprise such as the EIC or, practically, their representatives in India.[14]

---

[11] The English state easily could pay its silver owed to Spain thanks to the taxes or licenses it could ask from the tea imports from China. Its next source of revenue was the yearly "profit" of the colony of India.

[12] For the importance of the Spanish-American silver money see the article of Carlos Marichal in: S. Topik et al. (ed.), p. 25-53 in particular p. 41-43.

[13] See below and D. Owen, p. 68 ff.

[14] D. Washbrook in: A. Porter (ed.), p. 409, did not see this whole constellation. He only sees India suffering from a drainage of silver from its monetary system, which lead to the 'effective contraction of the money supply'. Then the question becomes urgent of where the Chinese and the Indian silver went, and there was, in fact, only one address: "London" and not Indian silver for China (p. 403). In addition, Washbrook correctly stresses the importance ofp the opium trade: 'Cotton, silver, and above all opium reached a growing number of consumers in China and South-East Asia' (p. 403). For China he relies only on an unsubstantiated opinion of John Crawfurd. This man proposed in 1837 the opium trade to China 'as a great national advantage' with 400 million consumers for whom 'opium has been more or less an item of consumption ever since we knew them. During the last fifty years it has been constantly on the increase ..' Neither Crawfurd in 1837 nor Washbrook at present mention that this trade to China was prohibited and that one had to wage wars to get it there. Apparently, his 'ever since we knew them' means: since the first time we smug-

So, what could be done in this time of uncertainties? In the Crawfurd quotation above an answer was given, but the following shows its absurdity:

> The solution was finally found in India. It was discovered that while the Chinese had little taste for British goods, they were eager to accept the produce of British India, particularly raw cotton and opium, though China itself produced the one and prohibited the other.[15]

The author does not comment on the remarkable aim to ram something unwanted and even prohibited down the Chinese throat or to plan a trade with products the potential client has in abundance! Still, the very circumstances under which specific persons made the decision to pay for tea with opium remains more or less in the dark. An attempt to reconstruct it runs as follows.[16]

The Decision

One could expect that the decision must have been concocted in India around the year 1781 during the discourse about the Bullion Crisis. The main players here were the Board of Directors of the EIC and the main representative of the English state in India, the first Governor-General, Warren Hastings. But the first initiative "to do something" apparently came from those English people daily involved in poppy planting and opium production in India. They were the civil servants of the Patna factory, who largely worked for their personal benefit. Before 1773 these civil servants of the EIC even claimed a monopoly on the cultivation of poppies.[17]

They constructed the myth that their privileges and immunities were formerly somehow enjoyed by Mughal princes. It was an addictive and poor excuse to legitimize its own wrong actions, but other high spirits among the English like Raffles used the same reasoning.[18] Even Owen

---

gled opium to China and tried to dope its population. For the raw opium from India there were other good clients like the Dutch and French colonizers in Southeast Asia (see below).

[15] M. Greenberg, p. 9; see also G. Cressey, p. 135.

[16] See for the following D. Owen, chapter II.

[17] J. Spencer Hill, p. 1.

[18] S. Alatas, p. 13 wrote in his intriguing Raffles essay that Raffles 'stressed the need to acquire Banka and what he considered to be legitimate British claims by right of conquest. The British, he reasoned, inherited the right on Banka through the Dutch. The Dutch had surrendered its dependency, Palembang.' Banka was (together with Billiton) the main

starts his analysis of this historical decision with reference to the use of opium in Mughal India. It is questionable to refer here to a past practice in subjugated India, apparently to legitimize the further exploitation of the one or subjugation of the other. Owen's remarkable assessment is, that it only concerns 'one of the less savory aspects of westernization of the East.'!

It is, furthermore, 'conceivably, of course' that Mughal rulers 'might have developed' the opium trade and production. This is an untenable proposition since, for instance, the Mughal's power rested on land and never on sea; they never had the intention to conquer something further than their "own" India. Last but not least they prohibited opium use (see ch. 12) and never had the intention themselves to develop even 'an [opium] industry badly organized', apparently 'an essential feature' of Warren Hastings's westernization of India, 'an excellent and convincing rationale'! No, in Owen's words: concerning opium, Mughals were 'incapable of great evil.'[19] An Indian historian, quoting Jan Huygen van Linschoten, gives Owen's words a relevant twist: this 'great evil', opium, consumed by the Mughals in reasonable quantities, was received from the Dutch![20]

---

island with profitable tin mines; it belonged to the Sultan of Palembang but the Dutch had captured it. For this see further ch. 16 with more data about Raffles opium obsession. Raffles behavior in the Palembang Massacre case is described by Alatas (p. 18) as: 'Raffles activity preceding and following the Massacre expressed an amoral political philosophy, but as he was a member of an amoral generation of empire-builders, big and small, he was not alone in holding to this philosophy.' This is a good introduction to the decision process as described below.

[19] D. Owen, p. 18. See also Michael Mann's article in H. Fischer-Tiné, M. Mann (ed.), p. 5. This reader hings on the supposition that some British civilizing mission connected to their colonization of India has some relevance. As is rightly accepted: '... from a colonizer's view, one might conclude that the civilizing mission almost completely failed.' (p. 25). But then follow another 340 pages apparently because 'from the point of view of the colonized, the cultural and civilizational changes and deformations are evident' (Idem). 'Deformations' certainly, but this general statement as such is too ambiguous. In particular, because it is followed by the contradictory statement that the 'effects of the civilizing mission' can be proved 'on individual cases'. A few of these individual cases can be found in the new elite, but that's all: this is too little for billions of colonized people who still suffer from the Western colonization projects. It is, furthermore, an untenable remark that 'with very few exceptions' nobody paid attention to this British "civilizing mission". In a book in which even the name and writings of a Thomas Raffles is negated or Marx is only mentioned once in a distorted way, such an opinion can be expected. See, for instance, the excellent introduction in J. Bastin, p. ix-xx, which should be accompanied by S. Alatas, chapters 1 and 5, in which the practice of the British "civilizing mission" is well illustrated.

[20] S.P. Sangar, p. 204 ff.

The motivation of the greedy English Patna officials, however, was only money. The substantial amounts of this opium money were very welcome and should be increased as quickly as possible since it

> now found a compensation for the scanty allowances made to them by their masters in England.' They were otherwise rigorous people. Notwithstanding a 'dreadful famine' in Bengal 'several of the poorer farmers were compelled to plough up the fields they had sown with grain, in order to plant them with poppies, for the benefit of the engrossers of opium.[21]

Dutch opium interests competed heavily with earlier Indian Patna merchants. When the English returned after one of their defeats, it was no longer in the role of traders, but of foreign occupiers. Indigenous opium merchants were virtually excluded from the opium business. The new English rulers had to cope with the Dutch and French competitors, but succeeded in getting the upper-hand and establishing a monopoly on Patna opium. It is the old policy of all colonial powers to arrive at the sole management of some product and to destroy a "free market". Only a few private persons ('an irresponsible body', Owen) received the profits, and claimed that they exercised a "monopoly" of Mughal origins.

The "Mughal myth" was not unwelcome to Warren Hastings who nurtured it by financially supporting "old Indian" initiatives. In 1772 he was appointed the governor of Bengal and directly confronted with the Patna gang. Fifteen years later he himself was famously accused of corruption (acquitted in 1795). He, as Governor-General, representative of the British state, was also "The Company" (EIC). His position remained very unclear constitutionally. That could not be said of many of his public statements like

> we exercise dominion, founded on the right of conquest' which is no right at all; his patriarchal way of governance 'lessens the weight of the chain by which the natives are held in subjection and it imprints on the hearts of our countrymen the sense of obligation and benevolence...'[22]

---

[21] Quoted by J. Rowntree, p. 16 ff. The author accepted as the truth a historically (and economically) untenable comparison between some 'opium monopoly' of the Mughal emperors and an 'opium monopoly' of the EIC. In fact it concerns a trick of probably Warren Hastings himself to project the English occupation as a continuation of the Mughal empire. As we will discuss later there was no such Mughal monopoly, because a few rich *private* Indian merchants in Patna and Bengal at the time sustained the opium business in conjunction with, among others, the Dutch VOC. What the EIC did was "original" from about 1780 onwards and it was certainly no monopoly in the strict economic sense, but more of a politically hegemonic position expressed in several branches of the economy.

[22] Quoted in *Wikipedia* "Warren Hastings".

This man, notwithstanding his lip-service to free trade, was responsible for the establishment of what is mostly called the EIC opium monopoly. On behalf of this policy he urged that

> opium was not a necessary of life, but a pernicious article of luxury, which ought not to be permitted but for purposes of foreign commerce only, and with the wisdom of the Government should carefully restrain from internal consumption.[23]

The Patna monopoly of some private people became transformed into an opium monopoly of the Bengal government at the suggestion of Warren Hastings (1773). The exclusive privilege of supplying opium was awarded to one Meer Muneer, an Indian who already acted as contractor for the English Patna people.

Muneer, a monopolist in the cultivation the poppies, was obliged to deliver the drug to the factory in Calcutta only, in which it was refined and further distributed by means of public auctions. In this way a regular income developed for the Government as well, which was 'a field for development'. The fundamental principle of this monopoly was that cultivation could be undertaken only with the EIC + government's permission (other cultivation was illicit, heavily fined or destroyed). The poppy peasant (*ryot*) had to sell his product only to the official agency and at the stated price.

The prohibition of opium was never considered. Owen states:

> To blame the company for having refused to embark on such a course would be to impute to the eighteenth-century a standard of social ethics utterly foreign to it. The free traders in the court of directors and elsewhere were moved by no desire to suppress the sale of opium. ... had the Indian administrators sought to forbid poppy cultivation, it is doubtful whether success could have been achieved. There were many more important things to be done, and the company's position in Bengal was too uncertain to have made of prohibition anything but an utopian experiment.[24]

So, according to Owen, false and very opportunistic considerations ruled the crucial decisions based only on strict colonial interests, not influenced by any Indian practice. Owen underestimated, however, many standards of social ethics at the time.

First, Owen's (and Warren Hasting's) considerations negated the many *Chinese* prohibition edicts in the 18th-century as not worth considering.

---

[23] Quoted by J. Rowntree, p. 17 and by D. Owen, p. 23.
[24] D. Owen, p. 25, 26.

The only opposition, the one of the available really free traders in the colonial elite, could not succeed in destroying the monopoly position(s). Their arguments faded away under the heavy load of all the opium money pouring in. Outside England there was strong opposition to the opium business on ethical grounds offered by Thomas Stamford Raffles. Inside England the moral opposition came from Edmund Burke and his allies in the House of Parliament, but even this failed. 'The crux of Hastings's defense is to be found in the profits which his monopoly brought to the company's treasury.'[25]

Another development must have influenced the decision as well. Spencer Hill was one of the few who rightly pointed to it:

> Up to this time, though a very small trade in the drug with China had been carried on, the bulk of the manufacture was disposed of to the Dutch merchants at Batavia. In 1781 however the war with the Dutch ... closed this market, and Mr. Hastings had to find other purchasers for his wares.[26]

The Dutch opium business will be the subject of our story later. It shows that although the English kicked the Dutch out of the poppy fields in Bengal, the opium traders were too dependent on the Dutch money. It must have been this dependence which brought Hastings to look for the Chinese market.

Karl Marx mentioned another important element in this case. There was not only a production monopoly of English officials in Patna, but also a distribution monopoly. This was twofold: for the direction India-London (tea, etc.) and for the India-China route (opium). This

> coastal ship traffic of India and between the islands including the internal Indian trade became a monopoly of the higher officials of the EIC. The monopoly of salt, opium, betel and other goods was a source of inexhaustible wealth. The officials themselves fixed the prices and treated the unlucky Hindi at will. The Governor-General participated in this private trade. His beneficiaries got contracts under circumstances through which they— more clever than the alchemists—made gold from nothing ... The trial of Warren Hastings bristles with these examples. Take this: an opium contract is given to a certain Sullivan at the moment he starts a trip ... to one of the opium districts ... Sullivan sells his contract for £40,000 to a certain Binn; on the same day Binn sells it for £60,000. The last seller and executioner of the contract states, that he later earned a substantial profit. According to a parliamentary list the officials and the Company received six million pound

---

[25] Idem, p. 37. In a decade, 1773-1784 the yield was not more than £534,000, peanuts compared to what was to come.

[26] J. Spencer Hill, p. 2.

sterling in this way from the Indians in the period 1757 to 1766! Between 1769 and 1770 the British policy led to a famine thanks to the buying up of all rice and the refusal to sell it except for unbelievable prices.[27]

Hastings's position is not yet presented in its entirety. He also ordered that the best opium was to be reserved for export and the inferior version sold for home consumption. First, cargoes of opium (3450 chests) were sent by him to Malacca and China on the Company's account (1782). The ships were armed and supplied with soldiers of the Company. The representative of the EIC in Canton was completely surprised when these vessels arrived. He did not know how to handle opium, which was prohibited in China ('it was necessary to take our measures with the utmost caution'). He found two Hong merchants who were willing to buy the stuff, whereupon he gave them a much better price than his superiors in Calcutta had envisaged. The most remarkable message from Canton was that if there was any 'urgency of need' to send a second consignment,

> long credit must be allowed, as the purchaser can have no prospect of selling any considerable part of it here. This is the clear proof that the opium habit was not yet generally prevalent throughout China.[28]

These first steps of the English in the "opium dark" were the result of a far-reaching and rather complicated decision process. It lead to a much discussed follow-up: the first British diplomatic opium mission to China, the abortive Cathcart embassy of 1787.[29] In its instructions it is stated that the prosperity of India

> would be promoted by procuring a secure vent for (its) products and manufactures in the extensive Empire of China, at the same time that the produce of such sales would furnish resources for the Investment (teas, etc.) to Europe.[30]

In fact the Cathcart and Macartney embassies (1793) both failed for different reasons, but the result was important: no deal with the Chinese could be made, while they became warned about the aims of the British and directly renewed the laws prohibiting opium use and trade (1795-96). But the British decision-makers in India and London did not want to

---

[27]   K. Marx, vol. 1, p. 780, 781.
[28]   J. Rowntree, p. 18.
[29]   The British had lobbied for an embassy to go before the Chinese emperor and make requests. The first embassy, the Cathcart Embassy of 1788, was called off with the sudden death of Cathcart before his arrival in China. Another embassy, the much debated Macartney embassy, followed soon thereafter (1792).
[30]   Quoted by M. Greenberg, p. 9.

stop this process anymore and started substantial smuggling campaigns armed to the teeth and on a large geographical scale: now the English narco-military underworld in Asia was a fact.

Remarkably enough,Americans soon joined this world after gaining their independence, making the relationship "tea for opium" applicable worldwide. It is not necessary to recall the event, the Boston Tea Party (16-12-1773), which triggered the American "Revolution".[31] But the Americans had to cope with the same problem as the English in the beginning of the 19th-century:

> If Chinese had not bought opium from the Americans, then United States imports of silk, porcelain and tea would have had to be paid for in silver coin. But there was not enough silver available in the United States ... Opium smuggling had turned out to be good for the dollar.[32]

That was also the case for the pound sterling, because after 1804 little or no silver had to be sent from Europe to China by the EIC. On the contrary: the flow of silver was reversed by 1810. From China millions in silver bullion could be shipped to India to pay for the opium.[33]

In 1827 the Bullion Crisis became a real Chinese one. Fear of this was expressed by the Chinese in an edict of *forty years earlier* (1785) in which it was forbidden to pay for opium with silver. A quick and relevant measure which must have been taken as a reaction to the Bullion Crisis of the British and Warren Hastings's "solution". The Chinese could not know how aggressively the British would jump into opium smuggling and that their greed would motivate even fully fledged Opium Wars.

It was the start of a century of unprecedented profits for the smugglers, EIC, British Indian government, "London" and USA merchants and bank-

---

[31] See H. Derks (ed., 1989), p. 82 ff. It could be a very symbolic story about tea smuggling profitable thanks to an English Tea Tax which led to the Hancock trial, in which this smuggler was defended by John Adams. More important was the theory and practice of the creed: "No taxation without representation!", etc. Two years later the American War of Independence started. It is the same Adams who later defended Ambassador Macartney's *kotow* adventure in China and the British assault on China to carry on the opium trade, etc. See part 1.2.

[32] J. Beeching, p. 36; see also J. Lovell, p. 251.

[33] For the silver reserves of China, see the article of Yeh-Chien Wang in T. Rawski and L. Li (ed.), p. 57 ff. The famous German *Staatswörterbuch* by J. Bluntschli described already in 1857 how European traders paid with silver coins in China in the 18th-century. It continues with: 'Thanks to the opium import of the English, things turned in the other direction: now China had to pay in 1833-34 already 4,976,841 dollars in silver and 375,906 dollars in gold' (vol. 2, p. 436). This is much more than the table indicates. Since no sources are mentioned, I cannot check these figures.

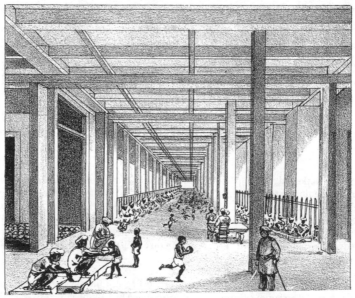

Ill. 4. Patna, India: four interiors of an opium factory; "mixing", "drying", "stacking", ca. 1850

Source: J. Wiselius, 1886, p. 118, 127 and several times reproduced later: see, for instance, D. Duco or (www.plantcultures.org). The preparation of the opium balls is shown in

→

the first picture; the second not only demonstrates children's labor but also the kneading of the balls; these must be dried in a drying department (3) before stored in a 'stacking room' (4).

ers: in the middle of the century opium was—in cash terms—already the largest single commodity traded in the world. Most helpful to this success were the smuggler's infrastructure, the corruption and the "ideological assistance" of religious authorities. A short impression of their importance will suffice.

Opium Shipping

In the first period of the opium trade the drug was smuggled to China in Indian crafts. They used vessels of 500-800 tons built from Malabar teak in the shipyards of Bombay and Hugly. Their rounded lines were unsuitable for beating windward. They ran up the China Sea before the South-West monsoon and returned with the North-East one. They were called *wallahs* by their British owners and commanders. They brought to Canton not only opium but also raw cotton, rice, pepper and tin from the Malay states.

The opium dealers were not satisfied with this 'Country Trade' vessel, whereupon a special type of ship was developed mostly on the banks of Hugly. That became the opium clipper, which was as important as the tea clipper in trade and smuggling.[34] These vessels had

> to beat to windward against the monsoons. They carried the drug from Bombay and Calcutta to the Canton River and Hongkong *via* Singapore ... In the early days the clippers delivered their outward cargoes to the receiving ships lying off Macao or at the Lintin and Cap-sing-moon Anchorages: but after the Opium War Hongkong became their usual discharge port.[35]

---

[34] Basil Lubbock documented in many books the history of the sailing ships, the 'China Clippers', the 'Colonial Clippers', the 'Nitrate Clippers' and, of course, the 'Opium Clippers'. Knowledge of "ship jargon" is a prerequisite. In this last book Lubbock provides a register of the whole opium fleet from 1823-1860 (appendix B), which does not provide all the ships involved in the opium trade, but it is still revealing. From this appendix one can calculate the following figures. In total 99 ships are mentioned with a total tonnage of 20,852. The movement of the trade is as follows: from 1823-1840, 7,822 tons were involved; from 1840-1850 already 10,238 and from 1850-1860 there was a temporary collapse (Opium Wars) to 2,792 tons. The owners were mostly the captains of the clippers, but the largest opium traders had also the most ships: the Scottish-English firm Jardine-Matheson had 14, the USA firm Dent &Co 13 stood far above the others, but the Calcutta-based Cowasjee-Rustomjee family and the USA firm Russell both had 7 ships, etc. Jardine-Matheson became the strongest supporter of the war against China. It is remarkable that the richest opium dealer ever, the Sassoon family, had apparently no ships until 1860 and is not mentioned by Lubbock at all.

[35] B. Lubbock, p. 13.

There was one exception to the general small size of these clippers, which was Jardine Matheson & Co's' famous full-rigged flagship *Falcon* of 351 tons, which carried the drug to ports far outside the treaty areas. Its most important duty was to discover and opening up of new markets.[36] To this aim it was heavily armed with broadside and other guns

> so that pirates and Imperialists, wreckers and marauding fishermen, all hesitated before attacking her, though they thought little of trying to cut off a small schooner.[37]

These clippers were not only able to sail against the monsoon, they could also carry three lots of opium from Calcutta to the depot on the island of Lintin (Canton Bay, twenty miles north-east of Macao) in a single season. The motivation of the opium traders like Jardine, Matheson, Dent, etc. is clearly given as follows:

> Our idea [in building a new clipper] is that the opium trade after the expi-ration of the East India Company's charter is likely to be so much run upon by speculators of every description for the mere sake of remittance without a view to profit that it can hardly be worth our while pursuing on the old plan unless by operating on a large scale, and on the secure footing of always being beforehand with one's neighbours in point of intelligence.[38]

Before the middle of the century another new type, the steamer, was introduced. First and foremost as war-ship (*Nemesis*), so that the gunboat diplomacy could start, and the first commercial steamer was called, of course, the *Jardine*, built in Aberdeen. Now this kind of diplomacy went hand in hand with the opium and tea trade. The profits were too exorbi-tant not to take the investment risks.

Opium Smuggling[39]

Since 1729 it had been strictly forbidden to import non-medicinal opium into China; until the end of the Second Opium War it had to be smuggled in not by the EIC alone, but by many licensed private vessels ("country ships") and American clippers as well. The risks could be minimized by

---

[36] Idem, p. 14.

[37] Idem, p. 14. Lubbock does not give a definition of "Imperialists", but they must be the European competitors of the English, the Dutch or French! For Jardine-Matheson & Co see M. Greenberg, p. 135 ff.

[38] Quoted by M. Greenberg, p. 140.

[39] For the following see B. Lubbock, p. 30 ff., including the quotation. See in H. Morse (1926) under 'running of goods'. Good discussion recently in C. Markovits.

using fast ships, islands off the coast like Lintin, hidden small harbors and bays, Chinese collaborators (*compradors*), corruption, Macao as an old place occupied by foreigners, etc. The English and American smugglers accepted the risks of suffering under draconian anti-opium laws thanks to the very large profits.

The first Chinese edict against opium must have been a reaction to a small import of 200 chests by Portuguese merchants in Macao. The users must have been just a few people in the elite, probably only confined to the court. To control the movements of foreign ships better the emperor ordered that all foreign trade had to be confined to Whampoa, the port of Canton (1745). The next measure imposed ten years later was ambiguous as it demanded import duties, including on opium consignments, which could be interpreted as a kind of approval. If true, it was soon corrected by new government anti-opium directives.

Around the middle of the 18th-century the import was increasing but still limited to 1000 chests a year distributed to several destinations, smuggled by Dutch, Portuguese and some English ships. The EIC considered it, at that time, 'beneath the dignity of the Company to smuggle and would not allow her Indiamen to carry opium.' This honorable motive was soon set aside by company servants and country captains alike. Apparently they "discovered" that opium was the only marketable alternative when specie had become scarce.[40]

Smugglers pocketed the main profits, while "London" could not or did not want to prevent this, as Warren Hastings's decision-making was remarkably ambiguous. The Chinese reacted with new edicts in 1799, in 1800 and in 1809. It took another six years before the first Chinese collaborators of the 'foreign opium devils' were arrested and executed. It was all in vain.

From India the illicit export was pushed so that prices soared (see Appendix 1). Apparently, the English producers and merchants were angered by the new American competition: some Americans smuggled opium from Turkey into China! The American drugs barons Russell and Dent became nearly as important as the English Jardine and Matheson. In the third position came the Jewish Sassoon and Parsee smugglers.

After the First Opium War and the Treaty of Nanking (1842), the ports of Hong Kong and other places were "opened". Still, as Lubbock remarks:

---

[40] H. Furber, p. 292.

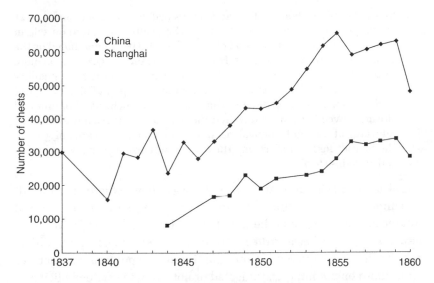

Figure 1. Opium Smuggling into China and Shanghai, 1837-1860

Sources: J. Fairbank, *Trade and diplomacy on the China Coast*, p. 229; Y. Hao, *The commercial revolution in nineteenth-century China*, table 9, p. 130; H. Morse, *The international relations of the Chinese empire*, vol.I, p. 358, 465, table G, p. 556; D. Meyer, p. 62.

'Opium was contraband by Chinese law, but not by British.'[41] He mentions a new legal defense of the Chinese: opium aboard British ships was under British law, but once landed it was liable to Chinese law. Immediately after the treaty in the new colony of Hong Kong, there were 80 clippers engaged in carrying opium to and from this port; 19 of which were registered to Jardine, Matheson and Co. In the interwar period opium imports grew so quickly

> that illegal trade dominated all foreign trade ... and all authorities agree that the drug was the most important item among China's imports until the final decade of the century.[42]

The following figure shows how much opium was smuggled into China, the majority through Hong Kong (1 chest = ca. 65 kilo).

Beeching's description of the situation shortly before the First Opium War is illustrative for the atmosphere of the antagonists, the Chinese Commissioner Lin Tse-hu (Lin Zexu) and the smuggler's with their enormous stocks and backing by the "whole British Empire".

---

41 B. Lubbock, p. 277.
42 E. LeFevour, p. 7, 8.

By 12 May 1839, 1600 Cantonese violators had been arrested, and 42,741 opium pipes had been surrendered ... 28,845 catties of opium on sale in Canton—the equivalent of 2,900 chests—had also been impounded by the authorities in the first onslaught. During the next seven weeks 11,000 more catties of opium were surrendered. But compared with the huge quantity accumulating offshore at Lintin, this was nothing. Captain Elliot, in a letter to the Foreign Office, estimated that nearly 20,000 chests of opium had already arrived in China and waited there unsold. To these must be added "upwards of 20,000 in Bengal, 12,000 in Bombay ... upwards of 50,000 chests ready for the market, and the crop of the current year ... soon [to be] added to this stock.[43]

It took a Second Opium War to erase this legal "flaw": where opium landed simply became an "international concession", so that English and American smuggling could be transformed into legal trade *for the occupied territory*. They became the locations of further smuggling into China. For all Chinese governments (Imperial, Taiping, Republican or whatever opposition) opium imports, smuggled or not, always remained illicit and part of the Western colonization of China. It is difficult to deny this.

What must be seen clearly is that the drugs barons themselves, always in favor of war to "open" China so that legalization could follow, also remained strong supporters of smuggling. In a letter of 2 December 1842 William Jardine wrote to his companion in the opium trade, the knighted Jamsetjee Jejeebhoy in Bombay:

Hong Kong and the smugglers will, to be sure, be powerful engines of counteraction, on our part, bit if slow operations, and not to the extent of preventing much loss and disappointment to speculators, what the future fate of opium Trade is to be is a question of much interest.[44]

Opium Corruption

The second main "help" to the opium success was the corruption and mafia-like practices which spread all over India and all along the Chinese coast from Macao to Manchuria and implicated all of the parties involved. In one quote Greenberg discloses that the opium mafia circuit was well established in 1835 around Canton:

The local Mandarins raised their price for 'protection' to a flat rate of $10 per chest. Dents and Jardines jointly proposed to pay the Chinchew Man-

---

[43] J. Beeching, p. 77; see also J. Lovell, p. 58 ff.
[44] A. Le Pichon (ed.), p. 520.

darins $20,000 per annum and no others to be allowed to trade in the Bay. Jardine wrote Captain Rees, in command of the *Colonel Young*: "If you could manage to make the mandarins attack everyone but your own party it would have a good effect.[!] My principal fear is that *numbers* may bring down the displeasure of the Government authorities on the dealers and boatmen, while competition among sellers will reduce prices very much.[45]

As already mentioned, not only English but also Americans were traders, smugglers, clipper captains, etc. There were, however, a few American merchants who declined on principle to handle opium. J.P. Cushing withdrew from the scene in 1821, Olyphant & Co never touched it.

To this system of corruption belonged not only the receivers of money at some stage or some position but also 'the growing tribe of addicts who needed a steady supply and would gladly break the law to get it.'[46] In 1835 the number of addicts was estimated at two million. Whatever is true (see ch. 31), the corruption knew its conjuncture, anyway: the *Chinese Repository* of April 1839 reported 'Bribes for low-ranking officials and the water forces were set, in the summer of 1838, at the rate of $75 per chest (about 133 lbs).'[47] What would the mandarins raise now, three years later, for their 'protection' if apparently lower officials received seven-fold ?

The opium corruption destabilized the Chinese society much further. The continued influx of British-Indian opium and the subsequent 'oozing out of fine silver' was against Qing law and attested to the complete breakdown not only of the old trade mechanisms, thanks to the continuously increasing smuggling, but also of the government's power of confining the foreigners to Canton-Guangzhou only. It was nearly true that, 'no region of the empire, however remote, was safe from opium's ubiquitous reach, not even the Qing ancestral homeland in Manchuria.'[48]

Prohibition suffered another setback when peasants in coastal areas lured by profits 'ten times that of planting the rice crop' started (or were urged) to cultivate poppies. An incentive was not only the direct payment, but later as the Opium Wars ended, the access to many coastal set-

---

[45] B. Lubbock, p. 141. Italics in original. One cannot say that the captains and owners or the EIC were not warned about the consequences of their illegal trade. This is shown, for instance, in the letter from the 6th of March 1822 signed by the 'Hong Merchants' quoted in B. Lubbock, p. 53 ff. For the consequences see also p. 276 ff. For all opium prohibition acts of the Chinese officials H. Morse (1926).

[46] J. Beeching, p. 36.

[47] L. Kwong, p. 1484 note 55. The *Chinese Repository* was an English-language publication in Canton. See J. Lovell, passim.

[48] Idem, p. 1485.

tlements occupied by 'foreign devils'. These were highly attractive for people looking for work, entertainment and, probably, another belief system. All this corrupted the Confucian or Taoist norms and values concerning the family, self-discipline and self-interest.[49]

Religion as Opium

Everything is extreme in the history of opium and that is also the case with religion at the moment that a European Manifest announces that religion is the opium of/for the people. The third "help" on the opium scene is, namely, formed by the representatives of the Western religious denominations. They became part of the opium scene in many respects.

For many missionaries, it was difficult to communicate in the Chinese language. They all had great trouble expressing their principle thoughts in Chinese, starting with the name and idea of God or the meaning of their basic rituals: the miraculous transformation of bread and wine into Christ's blood and body now had to be made acceptable through the use of rice and tea![50] Only a very few normal Chinese accepted the Western Christian creeds, except for opium addicts: they apparently expected to score their stuff much more easily.

The missionaries had, furthermore, to worry about the conduct of their fellow white devils (nearly all opium smugglers) who sometimes even lived with or—even worse—married an Asian mistress, like a partner of Jardine. Most important, however, it was evidently possible for missionaries and opium smugglers to work hand in hand: a lethal blow to Christian morality and its many supporters?.

The most widely discussed example concerned a colorful German clergyman Carl Gutzlaff (1803-1851) sent by a Dutch Missionary Society to Siam. Later, around 1829, he happened to go to Macao. His influence was based on his ability to speak several Chinese dialects fluently. Soon he was invited by the smuggler William Jardine, who confessed to Gutzlaff as follows:

> ... our principle reliance is on opium ... by many considered an immoral traffic, yet such traffic is so absolutely necessary to give any vessel a reason-

---

[49] See K. McMahon, several chapters; the website *'Asia for Educators'* with selections of Confucius's writings like the *Analects* or Tao (Dao) *Laozi*. The American sinologist Daniel Bell plays a remarkable role as a professor at the Tsinghua University in Beijing and as writer about China's "New Confucianism". See also *Wikipedia* "Religion and Drugs".

[50] J. Beeching, p. 60 ff. also for the following.

able chance of defraying her expenses that we trust you may have no objection to interpret on every occasion when your services may be required ... The more profitable the expedition, the better we shall be able to place at your disposal a sum that may be hereafter employed in furthering your mission ...[51]

Gutzlaff accepted the deal: he 'would be free to spread the gospel ... so long as he did not object to the opium sold from the ships'. He embarked on one of the opium clippers to ensure the success of the opium negotiations with local mandarins and authorities. He was, therefore, directly involved in opium smuggling, but also in deals with other products or in getting detailed information about prices or market conditions.[52]

If necessary, he accompanied the British Navy when it was threatening bombardments of coastal settlements, or acted officially as administrator in Hong Kong.[53] A book in English and a magazine Gutzlaff was printing in Chinese were also paid for by the drugs baron. Happily, that he was on board in a tremendous storm and could call on God to prevent the destruction of the opium clipper *Sylph*.

For Jardine it was more important that his business showed fabulous gains thanks to Gutzlaff's eight years of service. In, for instance, the years 1831-'33 his business increased from 14,225 chests to 23,693 chests of 65 kg. Later Gutzlaff even 'hired an intelligence network of Chinese willing to spy for the British' and was active in opium and military espionage for nine years.[54]

Notwithstanding Gutzlaff's strong support of the use of 'British bayonets', in their service he learned also how to organize door-to-door salesmen, trading by retail in Christian literature. Though not a medical man,

---

[51] Quoted in Idem, p. 61 and in M. Collis, p. 82 ot J. Lovell, p. 27. For another and longer quotation from Jardine's letter to Gutzlaff, see M. Greenberg, p. 139 note 4. I do not know which is the original but, because the gist is the same, I have chosen the better written version. See now also B.Fischer, p. 263. The most illuminating for the role of Gutzlaff is the correspondence between him and Jardine-Matheson given in A. Le Pichon (ed.), starting with p. 144 note 6 (following quote). This correspondence is of the utmost importance for the whole opium affair around the Opium Wars.

[52] A. Le Pichon (ed.), p. 167, without any reason under the fake name 'Humbug' (!), p. 197 or 206, etc.

[53] See, for example, A. Le Pichon (ed.), p. 378, 576. J. Beeching, p. 90 ff., p. 115 ff. Beeching is not convinced of Dr. Gutzlaff's scholarly abilities, but his work (alone and in cooperation with others) on a Chinese translation of the Bible and several books on China (directly translated in Dutch) prove the reverse. See also the *Wikipedia* article 'Karl Gützlaff', called 'the Grandfather of the China Inland Mission'. See also the characterization of Gutzlaff in B. Lubbock, p. 99 ff.

[54] J. Beeching, p. 140 ff., 166 ff., 208.

he 'commended himself to the natives by the practice of medicine among them, having also adopted the native garb and assumed one of their clan names.'[55]

Gutzlaff, a supporter of mass conversions, attracted many Protestant sectarian preachers, and his booklets with controversial translations in Chinese of Biblical texts had a marked influence on the leading spirit of the Taiping, Hong Xiuquan.

The end of his splendid career came when, on a preaching tour in Europe, a competitor of another denomination discovered that these salesmen were often criminals and opium addicts, Chinese devils in stead of white ones. It is remarkable that the most recent Gutzlaff biography is silent about his long opium career, while stressing that the Taiping strongly prohibited opium production and use ('the opium pipe is as a gun directed to yourself.').[56]

The dubious role of missionaries in China is discussed further below (ch. 29). Now we must look at what was the benefit of all this "help" for deliberately expanding an opium market in China, i.e. increasing the number of opium addicts. This profit was first and foremost received in the newest British settlement, Hong Kong.

Opium Banking in a Crown Colony

The rather barren rock on which one of the most important modern money capitals, Hong Kong, would arise was ceded by China to Britain in 1842. It was part of the settlement for the First Opium War. Six warships and 7000 troops were needed to guarantee opium imports by the British. Hong Kong became the center of this naval force (Hong Kong as the 'Gibraltar of the East'[57]) and of the opium trade for a very long time.

The opium was not only destined for China, it was soon exported also to Southeast Asia and the USA. Here and in Shanghai the British policy to transform opium from a luxury good into a bulk commodity was definitely organized and financed. As we will see, this policy followed the example of the Dutch, and with great success. A Hong Kong example: for decades the most important dealer in raw opium, Jardine, Matheson & Co, also traded prepared opium to the USA. In January 1860 'it held

---

[55] K. Chimin Wong, W. Lien-Teh, p. 331.
[56] See the article of Martin Herzog, Gottes zweiter Sohn. in: *Die Zeit*, 2-12-2010, p. 22. See also the article of Jen Yu-Wen about the relationship of Gutzlaff and the Taiping.
[57] G. Endacott, p. 204.

five-eights of all opium stock in the United States. Its agent in San Francisco was Edward & Bailey'[58] (see further ch. 28). And about Shanghai it is written, for example, that in 1904 the foreign (mainly English) tonnage of shipping entered is nearly eight times that of 1864; exports increased nearly seven times in the same period. Silk, raw cotton and rice were the common products in this trade. 'However, opium trade comprised the major balance of general commodity exports.'[59]

Hong Kong was from the beginning the center of the triangular trade described above and in the next chapter. At least officially the India-China opium trade ended after 1911 when the Republican period started in China, and war-lords created a permanent mess until 1949, while exploiting the enormous narcotic market to finance their wars. Mao liberated China from these military profiteers; he also ended foreign domination, opium addiction and trafficking with its related corruption (see further ch. 31). This example was not followed by the British in Hong Kong. On the contrary.

The main players in the opium gangs fled to this city, which had always participated somehow in the illicit business. Now, after World War II it again benefited from the drug trade as in the earlier days and once again Hong Kong became a world distribution center of opium, heroin and other narcotics. Before providing a few data concerning the period until Hong Kong's transformation from British Crown colony into a "normal" Chinese city (1997), some background information on the capital basis of this spectacular opium history is needed.

In the third quarter of the 19th-century the British Empire was at its zenith and Hong Kong celebrated its high position as well. "London" was, therefore, also the world's leading international capital market, providing a string of foreign loans to capital-hungry states, and Hong Kong was its branch in Asia.[60] The City's merchant banks were powerful thanks to the Empire's military-political framework, but they were the most capable ones of providing sterling loans and placing transactions with a broad range of domestic and offshore investors. It is estimated that between 1870 and 1914 total sterling loan issuance amounted to about £4 billion. British merchant banks raised at least 40 per cent of this sum.

Not only a naval, trade and opium center, Hong Kong also became the main banking center. Today it still holds this position in Asia with its sev-

---

[58] E. Sinn, p. 22.
[59] Z. Ji, p. 41.
[60] E. Banks, p. 166 for the following also S. Chapman.

eral hundred large banks. From the beginning the one center was closely connected with the other under the umbrella of the British Crown. It had serious consequences for the behavior of the British in Asia and not only in this Crown Colony. One quote of many:

> And all the British exhibited disdain for the various lesser breeds who shared the colony with them, jumpers on the band-wagon of Empire, the sprinkling of Eurasians and Portuguese, Parsees and Sindhis, Jews and Armenians, Frenchmen and other disreputable Europeans ... Sir Vandeleur Grayburn of the *Hongkong and Shanghai Bank* is said to have commented, "There is only one American in the Bank and that is one too many." But in particular they looked down upon the 98 per cent of the population who happened to be Chinese.[61]

In the most literal sense, the British colonial elite lived in Hong Kong high above the *vulgus*. The most senior British bureaucrats, military men and leading merchants, the *taipans*, lived together on the Peak, the cool heights, overlooking the homes of the Chinese masses. The latter had no rights whatsoever and were ruled in every sense by a British Governor with his supreme power and a direct line to the Colonial Office in London. Even the British expatriates had practically no influence until 1894 and a bit more after some "constitutional reform" in 1916. This dictatorship was "legitimized" with the rationalization: "If We have to give you, Europeans, democratic rights, We have to do this also with the Chinese, which is impossible!"

Hong Kong was a role-model for most of the later foreign coastal settlements of the Western imperialists. The fate of this city can be sketched in a few quotations. The British official Davis reported already in 1844 that

> ... "almost every person possessed of capital who is not connected with government employment, is employed in the opium trade" and later in the year said that opium was in general trade along the whole coast.[62]

Notwithstanding half-hearted missionary lobby work and other pressures, Hong Kong's fate remained closely connected to this specific product and trade, because until long after 1900

---

[61] P. Snow, p. 2, 3. That the British had such an opinion of Americans at the beginning of the 19th-century is more obvious like, for instance, Raffles' American hate as shown in S. Alatas, p. 30 ff.

[62] G. Endacott, p. 73.

the finances of the Hong Kong government have become as dependent on opium as any addict on his drug.' Half of its revenue still derived from the poppy in 1918.[63]

A few backgrounds of the city's banking history seem appropriate since competent analysts also sketch nowadays a broader perspective of Hong Kong's and Shanghai's role in Asia, namely that they

> consciously or unconsciously introduced a complete commercial capitalist system to China. Seeking maximum profits through trade and commercial activities was the main function of commercial capitalism ... The foreign agency houses engaged in opium trade and the cotton business not only through the former East India Company ... but also through Chinese local merchants to build up and expand the distribution networks ... Commercial capitalism was developed before finance capitalism in China.[64]

What about the main actors in this banking history? "London" was, of course, most prominent. The two top merchant bankers of the British Empire, Baring and N. Rothschild, raised a total of nearly £2 billion in sterling loans in the period 1860 to 1904. It was in the 1880s that they received serious competition from the USA from J.P. Morgan.

Chapman provides a table concerning the capital of the leading merchant banks in the whole Empire around 1875. They are divided over three groups of seven banks: the Jewish, the Anglo-American and the Anglo-German groups. The first group has by far the most capital power, with £27 million compared with 7 and 4.2 million respectively.[65] With these transactions they transformed their clients as well, which became now first and foremost institutional investors. They were mostly states like the belligerent Japan[66] and other institutions able to support debts, so that debt issuance gravitated from loans to securities. Individual investors could now easily jump these "debt-wagons" and allowed merchant banks and brokers to place obligations with a broader number of clients.

The top merchant banks, of course, did not enjoy complete control of these foreign loan markets. In particular in the new Asian markets, smaller firms like the colonial *Hong Kong and Shanghai Bank* (HSBC), Jardine Matheson, the *Hong Kong Bank,* etc. or new American bankers like *Goldman Sachs* could make a very good business.

---

[63] P. Brendon, p. 640. See also the excellent article by E. Sinn.
[64] Z. Ji, p. 40.
[65] S. Chapman, p. 44.
[66] E. Banks, 170 ff., 224 note 39.

HSBC, still one of the largest banks in the realm, was established by the opium dealer Dent&Co (1864 -65) and the shipowner Sutherland.[67] It became one of the main financiers of the Chinese government since between 1874 and 1898 HSBC negotiated nine loans totaling £30 million. By the late 19th-century the HSBC was the largest and leading foreign bank in China, because it also issued bank notes in 1, 5, 10, 50 and 100 dollar denominations. For more than half a century until the mid-1930s, the bank effectively set the foreign exchange rate in China's financial markets.

Opium dealers Jardine Matheson were from the beginning of Hong Kong the chief merchant bank and shipowner for a long time. They gradually used their opium fortune to invest in the railway and similar sectors or to provide the Chinese government with loans.

The Hong Kong Bank was strongly involved in loan activities to Japan. Especially before and during Japan's wars against Russia and China, the activities of these merchant banks increased: almost all of Japan's railways, industry, harbors, arms, etc. were bought or erected with the support of the Hong Kong Bank. Later this happened in cooperation with Barings or Rothschild, if the loans were too big as, for instance, a 1923 loan of £60 million. This relationship persisted after World War II as Japan started a new wave of industrialization (see further ch. 27).[68]

The Sassoon family opium and cloth business was also strongly connected to Hong Kong and later Shanghai. The sons extended the business of father David, and it soon became three times larger in the later Edwardian years. Of E.D. Sassoon it was written:

> All the Eastern Banks look upon this firm as quite A1. They are very keen energetic people ... spending very little money ... They possess very considerable property in Hong Kong and other eastern centres and do a very large trade in opium.[69]

Although the older D. Sassoon & Co Ltd was also largely involved in the export of opium from India to China, it was perceived as 'a more or less declining firm'. It was slow to respond to the openings in pure finance and preferred its mercantile past, while leaving much of the initiative in banking and Chinese loans to the Hong Kong & Shanghai Bank, of which it had been a co-founder in 1864. Among the many London-based banks in the

---

[67]   G. Endacott, p. 118, see also p. 258, 259. See table 8.1. in D. Meyer, p. 199. For HSBC see Idem tables 5.3 and 5.4 p. 109 ff. Z. Ji, p. 45-50.
[68]   E. Banks, p. 366 ff.
[69]   Quoted in S. Chapman, p. 131.

period 1885-1915, the main ones specializing in trade to and in India and the Far East were Boustead, Matheson, Dent Palmer & Co, D. Sassoon and E. Sassoon & Co.[70] Nearly all were heavily involved in the opium business (see further ch. 31).

Exorbitant Opium Revenues

It is quite astonishing that older publications like the well-known *British Opium Policy* (1934) could state:

> In the almost perennial friction that marked Anglo-Chinese relations during the nineteenth-century opium must be assigned an important but by no means a preeminent part.[71]

The following table with rather conservative estimates shows how much opium money circulated only at the English national level during an entire century.

Table 1. Trade between England, China and "British" India, 1800-1900[72]

period	annual export from England to China in £	annual export from China to England in £	annual opium-export in given period from "British" India to China in £
[1800-1820]	[500 000]	[2 000 000]	[750 000]
1821-1825	610 637	3 082 109	1 058 252
[1826-1832]	[750 000]	[3 200 000]	[1 500 000]
1833-1835	850 159	3 779 385	1 955 236
1836-1839	911 560	4 273 858	3 209 958

---

70   Idem, p. 58 ff.

71   D. Owen, p. 51.

72   Adjusted computation of J-W. Gerritsen's table, p. 58, derived from successive *Parliamentary Papers* (London). For the details of the first export column J. Rowntree, p. 288, for every year in the period 1859-1903. Adjusted with data mentioned by Crawfurd and Greenberg. See also J.F. Richards (2002-2), 'The opium industry..'. Gerritsen did not indicate that the figures concern the (average) *yearly export in the indicated period* and *not the whole* export in the indicated period as Greenberg's calculations show. He also did not give the figures for all periods which I estimated as given in [...]. During the Second Opium War (1856-1860) there was apparently no interruption of any trade. In addition, Gerritsen has generally lower figures per year than Greenberg, but because the former gives an estimate over the largest part of the 19th-century apparently from one and the same source, I reproduce them here. One can perceive these figures, therefore, as the *lowest estimate*. The third and fourth column concern, of course, "normal" export. His book, one of the latest Dutch books on the opium business, became a thesis from the "Elias School" (J. Goudsblom, A. de Swaan), but he did not consult the main opium literature at all, like M. Greenberg, F. Wakeman, C. Trocki, J. Richards, etc.

Table 1. Continued

period	annual export from England to China in £	annual export from China to England in £	annual opium-export in given period from "British" India to China in £
[1840-1842]	First Opium War	?	?
1842-1846	1 783 888	5 323 388	3 712 920
[1847-1853]	[1 800 000]	[7 000 000]	[5 000 000]
1854-1858	1 961 242	9 157 001	6 365 319
1859-1862 (after Second Opium War)	4 440 402	9 886 403	9 540 211
[1863-1877]	[7 640 000]	[11 000 000]	[10 000 000]
1878-1882	8 054 823	12 662 927	11 909 815
1883-1887	7 956 483	9 951 754	9 770 775
1888-1891	8 585 911	6 717 512	8 207 818
[1892-1900]	[7 600 000]	[6 000 000]	[7 000 000]

These figures need some explanation. Opium export to China initially meant that the British flag followed the British trade. The competition of the Dutch merchant-state in the 17th and a large part of the 18th-century was too strong. English opium trade existed, but remained marginal.[73]

In the 19th-century the Americans and French were the main competitors or enemies (Napoleonic Wars); later also the Russians. At the end of the 19th-century even the Japanese aggressively attacked the British hegemony by joining the club of "Imperialists". However, in the end the British carried off the Chinese prize, but had to leave parts of this cake to all the other as small change or desirable booty.

From the last part of the 18th-century the main export from China to England concerned tea, but porcelain or silk were also beloved articles in England and other European countries. From India they were transported to England for a continuously increasing market.

Apart from the EIC there were numerous private traders-smugglers in India, but until 1834 the EIC was the main mediator between China and England because it now had the monopoly on the opium production in Bengal (Bihar) and in fact also on the export abroad.[74] It had to pay an

---

[73] H. Morse (1926), vol. 1, p. 306 starts his general state of receipts and disbursements to China in 1762 on purpose. Until 1771 there are mostly negative results.

[74] Rajat Kanta Ray in P.J. Marshall (ed.), p. 522. See also an informative article on 'Opium and the British Indian Empire' (2009) on the website of the *Drug Policy Alliance*

annual interest of around £2 million on its debt to the British state. The opium revenues could easily be used to this aim.[75]

After a century of prohibition and under the threat of the British and French governments, China had to legalize opium and the opium trade in 1858 after two wars. It hoped an eight percent tax would help solving its financial woes.[76] But the background of this act is more important while showing in all shocking details what imperialism meant for these Eastern countries.[77]

The British colonial government through the EIC started to import opium into China around 1780. They had to make a sufficiently extensive drug market so that they could compensate for their extensive purchases of tea, silk, porcelain and handicrafts; a nearly *worthless* product received in this way an exorbitant trade value through its upgrading as a mass product.[78]

The table also shows that in the whole century the revenue of the opium export for the state (EIC and/or British Colonial Government) was not less than £526 million for Bengal and Malwa opium together (for Bengal

---

(DPA), www.drugpolicy.org/library/opium india.cfm and, in particular, E. Balfour, vol. 3, p. 28-39.

[75] See table in N. Ferguson, p. 167.

[76] In E. Balfour, vol. 3, p. 37, Sir Robert Hart's statistics are mentioned, among which an import duty, etc. is given of '100 taels of Chinese sycee or silver (£3 = 10 taels)' per chest. This resulted in about £3,000,000 tax annually. See for Hart's calculations also below and in Part 6-3. In W. Willoughby, vol. II, p. 1093 there is a description of how the British negotiator 'permitted' the Chinese government not a duty of 60 taels per chest but only 30, 'a lower duty than England levied on Chinese silks and teas'.

[77] For the following see J. Osterhammel in A. Porter (ed.), p. 147 ff. who did not analyze the dynamics of the British opium trade. In *Wikipedia* under "Opium Wars" the newest novel of the Indian writer Amitav Gosh, *Sea of Poppies* (2008), about the Bengal production is mentioned. It describes more about British trade until 1920. An interesting blog is also *tamala-mind.blogspot.com* with a whole chronology of the opium production, trade and war from 1700 until 2009 in Afghanistan—Helmand were the British troops are, apparently, doing nothing but saving the central production area in the world today. It is good to mention also the earliest British protest against these activities from no one less than a Major-General R. Alexander (who served in Madras) with a book titled: *Rise and Progress of British Opium Smuggling the illegality of the East India company's monopoly of the drug and its injurious effects upon India, China and the commerce of Great Britain* (3e edition; London: Judd & Glass, 1856). Later a *Royal Commission on Opium* (1895) was the start of the prohibition of British involvement in production and trade, although this commission supported opium production and use.

[78] This should be the place to investigate further how the EIC performed this job. This exceeds the aim of this introductory part. One has, for instance, to refer to improved cultivation techniques and also to the pricing policy which was intended to attract the affluent Chinese merchant classes, both around 1800. Much information can be found in A. Le Pichon (ed.). See also below the paragraph 'On the Chinese Side'.

opium alone £337 million; see Appendix 1), which is nowadays comparable to about £ 16,832 million!

Recent calculations (Wakeman, Greenberg) come to substantially higher estimates than Crawfurd's and a bit higher than the estimates in the table. Greenberg, for instance, could provide the *annual* opium shipments from India to Canton alone and expenditures from 1800-1839.

A few rounded off figures from his list of arrivals in Canton are: in 1800 about 4,500 chests valued at $ 2.4 million (= at the time £ 530,000) which increased slowly to a annual export of 5,000 chests (value about £ 600,000) in 1810; in 1820 it is about 5,500 chests (value nearly £ 2 million). In the next decade there is a strong increase until an import of 19,000 chests valued at £ 3 million; in "Crawfurd's 1837" 35,000 chests were imported in Canton valued at probably £ 4 million.[79]

In his magnum opus on criminality in Shanghai Wakeman talks about the other large Chinese center of the opium trade:

> Modern Shanghai was literally built on the opium trade. Before the 1850s Shanghai served as the terminal port for the coastal opium traffic, which was carried on in a semi-public way ... opened to foreign trade on November 11, 1843 and soon afterward Jardine's, the biggest British company operating in China set up a branch and began hiring compradors ... By 1845 ... Shanghai outstripped Chusan ... as a center of opium trade, which rose from 16,500 chests in 1847 to 37,000 chests in 1858, constituting nearly half of the total opium imported to China. By 1860, two years after the opium trade was legalized, Shanghai's share of the trade came to 60 percent of the total.[80]

Wakeman estimates that in 1880 nearly thirteen million pounds of opium was imported from India.[81] The highest estimates, however, come

---

[79] M. Greenberg, p. 220, 221; see also C.Trocki (1999a), p. 95; J. Spence, p. 129; F. Wakeman in J. Fairbank (ed.), 1978, p. 172. All had the same source, namely, Hosea Morse. Li Chien-Nung, p. 26 ff. has substantially larger figures: by 1790 the import was more than 4,000 chests a year; after 1810 this was increased to 10,000 chests; from 1820-1830 the average annual figure was 16,000 chests and in 1836 it totaled more than 20,000 chests.

[80] F. Wakeman (1995), p. 34. Most of this opium was imported by Jardine, Dent, Lindsay and Sassoon. One could also read this quotation to suggest that Chusan rose from 16,500 to 37,000, but that would make the position of Shanghai too fantastic: it is, therefore, supposed that the figures concern Shanghai.

[81] It remains obscure whether Wakeman uses the metric or an English measurement for a pound: in the first case it equals 0.5 kilo and in the other 0.3 kilo: a difference between 3.9 million and 6.5 million kilo, or respectively about 60,000 and 100,000 chests. In my view the two highest figures must be close to what really happened. In a famous German encyclopedia an Indian export is mentioned in 1886/87 of 95,839 chests of 68 kg, which is 6.5 million kg. *Handwörterbuch der Staatswissenschaften* (1900), vol. V, p. 1023. Here, however, the destination of this export is given as only 70% for China, 20% Strait settlements and the rest to Cochinchina.

from two authorities in the late 19th-century opium business. The first is William H. Brereton, a 'well-known pro-opium leader'[82] at the time Protestant missionaries started their ambiguous opposition against opium consumption and the other is Sir Robert Hart, the Inspector General of Customs in China. From his biography one gets the impression that without him there would have been no British Empire in the East. This genius published detailed figures about the consumption, import of foreign opium, production of Chinese opium and their value.[83] Remarkably enough both gentlemen came to the same result: the value in 1881 of the foreign opium import was £16,800,000 and the native opium was worth £8,400,000, so that the Chinese smoked *in one year* the tremendous amount of £25.2 million. In addition, there was also smuggled opium.

If Hart's figures are used, the given total of the opium figures of £526 million must be *doubled* to come close to the "truth" for the foreign opium only and for the Canton import only! Wakeman states that in the early part of the 20th-century, $40 million worth of opium came into the port of Shanghai *every year*.[84] The difference can be explained by the geographical situation.

The figures in the table are derived from data published in London (*Parliamentary Papers*); the figures from Hart are Chinese ones, while India is situated in between. This could mean that the highest and "true" result is gained in China, and in India a substantial part of the booty is "taken apart" before the rest is transmitted to the motherland.[85] That this is still only the trade part of the whole opium picture and its exorbitant profits, and not the production side, will be discussed later.

One thing which remains largely in the dark is the export destination of the Indian opium: usually only about 70 per cent went to China, the rest went to Southeast Asia. After about 1880 this export to China decreases because opium is imported from Persia and Turkey into China, while in this country one started to produce opium as well. The British compensated this "Chinese loss" with an increase of the Southeast Asian export (to its colonies like Strait Settlements, Burma, etc.).

---

[82] K. Lodwick, p. 76, see also p. 84.
[83] The calculations from Hart are given in E. Balfour, vol. 3, p. 37. See further ch. 31.
[84] F. Wakeman (1995), p. 35.
[85] The given possible solution of the problem has an earlier example. Wakeman states (Idem, p. 173) that from 1830 onwards, at least £4 million yearly (of the profits) had to be carried back from India to England.

Furthermore, around 1900 in many Asian countries British, Dutch or American merchants must have taken over large parts of *all* trade (see the Philippine case in ch, 28). Research incorporating all Asian possibilities is not available. If it were, one might not be surprised if the figure of £526 million is *tripled*.

On the Chinese Side

It is much more difficult to find, but the Chinese side also has its quantitative data. In 1800 once again an emperor issued a proclamation forbidding the import and cultivation of opium in Yunnan and elsewhere. Nevertheless, in 1827 the foreign imports had increased to nearly 10,000 chests per year; ten years later to 40,000 chests; in 1856-57 the import was 70,000 and in 1881 it was 90,000 chests of about 65 kilo each. Per chest or pikul a duty had to be paid to the Chinese authorities of £10, which was about 30 *taels*.[86] After about 1885 the imports fell to 50,000 chests annually (1897) until 1905; then it dropped quickly to about 30,000 in 1911, but always 3,000 to 5,000 chests were smuggled in.[87]

Was there much consumption already *before* 1800 along the coasts? Nobody knows, but the affirmative answer cannot involve a Chinese import but a Dutch and Portuguese one or of a British smuggler from India. This smuggling always continued in addition to the British imports and was estimated at 20,000 chests annually in the 1820s.

The *Staatswörterbuch* wrote in the middle of the century about China's import:

> Among the imported goods in particular opium should be mentioned. ... Before 1767 Europeans imported only 200 cases for medical treatment

----

[86] E. Balfour, vol. 3, p. 34. This encyclopedia concluded that in the 18th-century the use of this drug was limited in China to medical purposes only and that its cultivation was limited to the province of Yunnan. Now its suggests that long before the English imported their opium, the Chinese were already addicts. See also D. Meyer, p. 32 ff., 61 ff. or R. Newman (1989), p. 525 who reproduced the propaganda talk of the opium-merchants and/ or the British Government (including its Royal Commission of 1894) that opium was 'an essential part of the lifestyle of millions of Chinese'. Also, Newman does not ask himself why the opium business was laden with so many moral judgments. (Notwithstanding this, he wrote an interesting article: see ch. 31) For similar figures to those of Balfour, see V. Shih, p. 474 who mentions Hosea Morse as his source. J. Fenby, p. 9 writes that by the late 1830s, already 1400 tons (= about 22,000 chests) were landed annually on the Chinese coasts.

[87] See K. Lodwick, p. 12; R. Newman (1989), p. 525 note 1 gives an export figure of 94,835 chests in 1879-80, but this export does not need to be the same as the import in China.

alone. The English import [in China] started in 1780 at a low level. Notwithstanding its prohibition from 1800 onwards it was increased enormously and all attempts of the Chinese emperors to repress the opium consumption, are in vain ... The opium is smuggled in armed ships; the Parsees and other Indian merchants sell it in India; the agents of the large English merchant houses in China advance them 2/3 or 3/4 of the value and the former transport it on [English] cost with quick ships. The profit of the houses Jardine, Matheson and Co must have been 75 million francs in twenty years. The import was in 1849 increased to 36,459 cases and in 1855 to 53,321 cases, but the average price seems to be decreased since 1839 from 966 to 657 rupees. Thanks to this depreciation is the extension of the poppy production in India not favored by the government any more.[88]

That was an ambiguous conclusion. It took some time before the Chinese government reacted in a relevant way to the smuggling and silver drain, but this cannot be a reason for the Western arrogance and brutality: the Chinese government had other things to do dealing with the many peasant revolts everywhere in the country.

Still, fearing the moral downfall of society, it had prohibited the sale of opium already in 1729 and not as thought in 1800 and in 1799 it forbade the import of opium for smoking purposes. There was, furthermore, an ongoing debate among the Chinese mandarins over legalizing the opium trade. Therefore, there must have been much "understanding" (in the sense of 'knowledge') of the impact of the Western opium challenge. The legalizing option was, however, always rejected, and the authorities even issued new prohibition laws involving the death penalty, appointed effective crime-fighters, and tried for decades to avoid by all means the "Western" *illicit* opium trade and smuggling.

This legalizing debate proves, anyway, that the moral question could be superseded. There was, however, also the economic question: the drain of silver to India could cause a depreciation of copper cash against silver; copper money was the normal payment of the land taxes. Discontent increased in some provinces because commodity prices were rising.[89] In addition, the annual export of silver had increased to the alarming level of perhaps ten million dollars in 1839.

At that time the Chinese wanted to ban all British trade to China in order to stop the import of 1,400 tons opium annually by the EIC, whereupon the British *government* initiated its first Opium War incited by the

---

[88] J. Bluntschli (ed.), vol. 2, p. 445. At least this last remark must be wrong as the table shows: very big business had to come, including by and in favor of the British government!

[89] E. LeFevour, p. 6 ff.

opium dealers. The official Chinese crime-fighter, Lin Zexu (or Tse-Hsu), not only ordered the casting of a million kilos of opium into the sea, he even wrote a letter directly to Queen Victoria questioning the moral reasoning of this British government (1839). He asked the Queen:

> Where is your conscience? I have heard that the smoking of opium is very strictly forbidden by your country; this is because the harm caused by opium is clearly understood. Since it is not permitted to do harm to your own country, then even less should you let it be passed on to the harm of other countries—how much less to China.[90]

The letter-writer pointed out that there was a death penalty in China on all dealings with opium. Whether the Queen ever replied is not recorded in the literature; silence reigned also about opium itself in the Treaty of Nanking, the result of the first Opium War. The Chinese refused to legalize the drug, and the British refused to stop its production in India. Matters now aggravated rapidly: the 'social disorder which had probably first stimulated demand increased rapidly after the war' (LeFevour), and already in 1845 the trade probably put China £2,000,000 into debt.

Ill. 5 Battle at Canton, ca. 1845
Source: Holachina.blog, 29-3-2009. See also en-Wikipedia 'British ships in Canton' for another battle (May 1841).

---

[90] Quoted by K. Lodwick, p. 27.

All in vain: the British, assisted by the French, started a Second Opium War, even conquered Peking only to demand the allowance of the opium trade and consumption, whereupon the emperor had to surrender and legalize the opium business (1858). The British poured in a tremendous amount of new opium as the table shows.

The usual corruption of the Chinese bureaucracy could now be enhanced at the same pace as the doping of the Chinese population on a scale that victim "China" became for the whole world the guilty opium country. A royal commission appointed by the British Parliament (1893) 'whitewashed completely' both the opium practices current in India and the opium trade/ production policy of its colonial government in the rest of Asia.[91]

There was, however, another serious effect of the opium assault on China: Chinese (who?) started to produce opium themselves, and this import substitution undermined the British (and French) trade monopoly. In 1879 the British trade had increased to 5,000 tons annually. It is said that at the end of the century the province of Szechwan alone already produced 15,000 tons per year.[92] Half a century later (1908) the emperor and the British government agreed 'to steadily reduce Indian opium exports to China'.[93] But:

> Much of the impetus for ending the trade came from a new, militant form of Chinese nationalism. The self-strengthening movement viewed opium as both symbol and cause of Chinese weakness before the West.[94]

This happened from 1949 onwards due to the new Chinese Maoism. This was not the end of the England-China opium relationship, which was

---

[91] See also the long article on the 'Opium Problem' in *Encyclopaedia of the Social Sciences*, 1949, vol. 11, p. 473. It is revealing how the highest British official in China around 1910, Alexander Hosie, eloquently transformed the Chinese into the "bad guys" (see ch. 30). As usual, this kind of report has a strong alibi character. For this, it is not even necessary to support the current policy directly, but to provide a so-called "balanced" result so that all parties involved can continue with their "business".

[92] J. Osterhammel in: A. Porter (ed.), p. 161. See for this figure ch. 31. Here a serious lacuna in our knowledge arises. First, there is the question of why exactly did the Chinese begin producing opium? Answer could be: after the devastating Taiping and other revolts, the country was so impoverished that planting opium made financial sense and helped save the late Qing economy. On the local or provincial level, some leader must have argued like this. There is the second, no less important question: who started this production? Was it Chinese production or opium production in China, started by a foreign power? Americans could have suggested this plan to undermine the British competition.

[93] R. K. Newman (1989).

[94] DPA article, note 74, p. 7.

formally connected with July 1, 1997 the date of the transfer of Hong Kong to China.

At last, an effect must be mentioned for discussion later (ch. 29), which seems to be the most mysterious aspect: not the English, French and other foreigners who attacked China with devastating effects were made the guilty party in history books and public opinion, instead it was the Chinese, the victims. One example out of many from a serious American scholar at the end of the 1960s:

> The strong identification of opium with China in the public eye can probably be ascribed to the appeal of the romantic, mysterious, and esoteric. The Opium Wars doubtless served to focus attention on the opium habits of the Chinese, but it was the occultation which whetted the interest and invited flamboyant conjecture as to what went on in panoplied opium dens.[95]

This is an "Umwertung Aller Werte", or the victim became the perpetrator.

---

[95] W. Eldridge, p. 3.

CHAPTER SEVEN

INDIAN PROFITS

> In northern India opium was drunk rather than
> smoked, and judging by the frequency with which
> opium shops appear in miniatures of the period,
> opium addiction seems to have been a major problem.
> Since the Company had the monopoly on the growing
> and trade in the substance, which by the 1850s provided
> an astonishing 40 per cent of their exports from India,
> it of course made no attempt to control the problem.
>
> William Dalrymple[1] (2009)

It may be that around 1850 India also had many opium addicts (whatever definition is used by whom), but China was the primary target country of what nowadays would be called a narco-military regime. India was its home base and the country of production of the drug.

It had two major production regions, the northeastern Patna and Benares, oriented to Calcutta, and the central Malwa, oriented to the western Bombay or Goa. Both already had an opium history before the English started colonizing the eastern regions of India from the second part of the 18th-century onwards. This earlier history, which shows India mainly as a victim realm of other Western colonizers, will be discussed in 3.3. As a follow-on from the previous chapter, it is logical to deal now mainly with the 19th-century opium situation in India, the competition between the two production regions and the 20th-century consequences.

Chaudhuri provides a framework for such a task in rather abstract terms:

> The consolidation of the position of opium in the eastern market was
> greatly helped by other circumstances, such as the utilization of the China
> trade as a channel of remittance from India to London, and the increasing
> stake of the Indian government in the revenue from opium.[2]

The meaning of 'utilization of the China trade' is explained in the previous chapter, but what does a 'consolidation of the position of opium'

---

[1] W. Dalrymple, p. 102 note.
[2] B. Chaudhuri, in: D. Kumar, M. Desai (ed.), p. 312.

mean from an Indian perspective? Is this only a matter of more revenue to the Indian government and private interests? We shall have to look into the course of a whole process of production—trade/investments/transport—consumption, including the long-lasting and substantial smuggling practices and some other "details".[3] This again concerns the rather brutal changes of the triangle relationship England—India—China after the Opium Wars. Two of the three parties involved can now be characterized as follows.

The Chinese remained uninterested in English products, had a serious drain on their silver, lost two wars and had to accept a substantial occupation by foreign powers, corruption among many officials, a growing army of Chinese opium addicts and a government which remained strongly opposed to opium. This apart from tremendous revolts started by the Taiping and many other sects to which the fully undermined state was nearly helpless.

The private English merchants including the EIC were, first, overwhelmed by the very quick extension of the highly lucrative tea consumption in the homeland and Europe (much less of other Chinese products). Earlier this had to be paid by the English state with silver bullion, which was difficult to obtain from the Spanish colonies during the war with Spain and Napoleonic wars in general. In establishing a narco-military regime in the Far East as a very profitable and close collaboration between smugglers and the state, its own serious Indian problems could be solved with a very bad conscience. A not unimportant aspect was that the British could upgrade their status of mafia into legitimate merchants and their opium war into a "legitimate conquest". In addition, it could occupy many coastal settlements, strongholds for further imperialist expansion into the interior of China.

The third party in the triangle cannot be characterized briefly, but the following section provides an outline of the Indian opium activities and problems in the given framework and triangle relationship.

Monopoly Opium Production

A quantitative presentation seems to be a good start to discover the "Indian profits" during a long 19th-century.

---

[3] Like E. Balfour, vol. 3, p. 38 and 39.

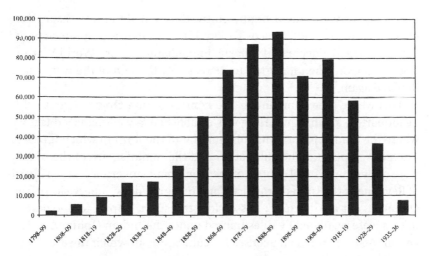

Figure 2. Decennial Average Opium Revenues in India, 1798-1936 (x 1,000 Rupees)
Source: J. Richards, 2002-2, p. 156.

The story of the origin of the EIC+Government monopoly at the end of the 18th, beginning of the 19th-century has already been sketched. How is the situation about a century later?[4]

The EIC had already collapsed (1834), and the British (Colonial) Government had accepted sole responsibility. Its monopoly position was extended now in a typical oikoidal (state-bureaucratic) way. Around 1900 the British Empire in Asia was in its most extensive size. It controlled what now is Pakistan, India, Ceylon (Sri Lanka), Bangladesh, Burma (Myanmar), Malacca and Singapore, North Borneo and Hong Kong and one of the International Settlements in China (including naval station Weihaiwei). In other words: mile after mile the total sea route of the opium trade from India to China was under British military control. Everywhere there were naval stations and army garrisons (both in Hong Kong, for instance).

The production center for all or most of these countries was British India. Around 1915 poppy cultivation was located in 32 districts of the 'United Provinces of Agra and Oudh', south of the Himalaya and Nepal (at present Uttar Pradesh and Uttarakhand). Around 1905 no fewer than

---

[4] E. La Motte (p. 44 ff.) provides very long quotations from descriptions of the Opium Department found in *Statistics of British India, Financial Statistics (1920)*, vol. II, p. 159 ff. These quotations are used in the text. See for a few quantitative data of the production further on and in *Appendix* 1 below.

613,996 acres were under poppy cultivation. For different reasons (increased production in China or Turkey, international anti-opium actions, etc.) this acreage decreased quickly: immediately before World War I it was 144,561, but then it started to increase. At the end of the war, it had doubled again.

This whole area came under the control of one Opium Agent, with headquarters at Ghazipur. Here was established 'a well managed factory where the crude opium is manufactured into the form in which it passes into consumption.'[5] The cultivation and the manufacture of the opium were under the 'general control of the Lieutenant Governor and the Board of Revenue of the United Provinces, and the immediate supervision of the Opium Agent at Ghazipur'. Possession, transport, import and export of opium were regulated by rules framed under the Indian Opium Act. The Opium Agent granted all licenses for cultivation, in which the area to be cultivated is fixed

> and the cultivator is bound to sell the whole of his production to the Opium Department at the rate fixed by Government. ... In March, April and May the opium is made over to the officers of the Department, and weighed and tested, and as soon as possible afterwards each cultivator's accounts are adjusted, and the balance due is paid him. After weighment the opium is forwarded to the Government factory at Ghazipur, where it is manufactured in 3 forms—(a) opium intended for export to foreign countries, departmentally known as "provision opium"—(b) opium intended for consumption in India and Burma, departmentally known as "excise opium" and (c) medical opium for export to London.[6]

This is followed by an instruction about the form and weight of the opium (balls, cakes), its packing in several kinds of the chests (mostly containing forty cakes). The provision opium is sold by public auction in Calcutta; it is the Bengal Government which has to do all the paperwork of the auctions and sales month by month. At these public auctions, apparently sold to private buyers and the China market only, the document states about the situation in 1917:

---

[5] A very detailed description of what happens in India from the poppy fields to the auctions in Calcutta is given in J. Wiselius (1886). I could not discover an English example of this sophistication. Jacob Adolf B. Wiselius (born in 1844) traveled in and wrote extensively about the geography and economy of Southeast Asia, British India or the Philippines. His comparative studies about the colonial systems in British India and the Dutch East-Indies are highly interesting. In 1885 he published a comparison between the prison and compulsory labor systems in both colonies (and added a treatise about the jute production in Bengal). I used his comparison between the two opium regimes (1886) and his earlier analysis of the French in Cochinchina (1878).

[6] E. La Motte, note 4 above.

In addition to this 4,500 chests were sold to the Government of the Strait Settlements, 2,200 to the Government of the Netherlands Indies, and 410 to the Government of Hong Kong. The duty levied by Government on each chest may be taken to be the difference between the average price realized and the average cost.[7]

So apart from sales to private persons there is a not insignificant sale from government to governments. Since the end of the 19th-century, government monopolies had existed in most Asian colonies. In every colony the foreign government regulated the distribution through auctions and government shops. In British India there were nearly 18,000 drug shops at the end of World War I. Apart from opium, other intoxicating drugs like *ganja, charas, bhang,* all forms of *hashish*, were made available. The excise duty only on opium consumed in India was at least £5 million a year from 1907-1912; during the war years this decreased to about £1.6 million a year, but then it increased again to £3 million a year after the war. La Motte concluded in a remarkably American patriotic way:

> A national psychology that can review these figures with complacency, satisfaction and pride is not akin to American psychology. A nation that can subjugate 300,000,000 helpless people, and then turn them into drug addicts—for the sake of revenue—is a nation which commits a cold-blooded atrocity unparalleled by any atrocities committed in the rage and heat of war.[8]

We will see later whether La Motte is sufficiently informed about the American involvement in drugs in those years.

Another, more relevant remark concerns the role of the new imperialist Japan. What is called above the "medical opium for London" was being manufactured into morphine by three British firms (two in Edinburgh and one in London), 'which morphia the Japanese are buying and smuggling into North China.'[9] In the Appendix data are given about the British Indian export of opium to all kinds of destinations, among others, to Japan. In 1911 this export was zero, soon thereafter it is valued at £80,000. From then onwards a tremendous increase can be seen that parallels the definite losses in the export to China after that date. Directly after the war the Indian export of opium increased to £500,000. According to La Motte, the Japanese 'are ardent smugglers', the British monopolist is their source, and the Indians their opium producers.

---

[7] Idem.
[8] E. La Motte, p. 52, 53.
[9] Idem, p. 46 and for the details Idem, p. 11-17.

The consequences and strategic implications will be discussed in the Japan chapter (5.1); in the existing smuggling network the Japanese, indeed, are becoming the new "big players".

Monopoly Smuggling

Let's go back to the beginning of this spectacular development. The in-between nation, India, suffered a sharp decline of its profits from trade in Indian textiles and had to rely strongly on the tea trade, opium production and export.[10] Before the Opium Wars all colonial powers had serious difficulties with the extensive smuggling of opium, which was prohibited by the Chinese government. However, they had to use it and collaborated closely with its representatives the Jardines, Mathesons or Sassoons putting all risks on the shoulders of—in our terminology—mafia bosses. After the Opium Wars the British colonial state was also transformed from a criminal institution into a "legitimate occupier" of foreign territory. Still all depended on the white stuff to keep the money machine, the EIC and the British Empire in the East going.

This triangle relationship was the imperialist setting in which occupied India had to live and act as both victim and perpetrator. All elements mentioned can be found here, but their position within the main opium production country was quite different. Here the British state with its collaborating mafia had to intervene in the production. Let's first take a look into the Indian opium smuggling scene.

One of the most important Indian opium smugglers, Jamsetjee Jejeebhoy (1783-1859; below J. J.), left a detailed business correspondence from which his deeds and results can be derived.[11] He was a Bombay-based merchant from the beginning of the 19th-century belonging to the small but powerful group of Parsees merchants. Their role became important because they acted as brokers to the British.

These Parsees lived here long before the Portuguese physician Garcia de Orta from Goa observed in 1563 that

---

[10] I. Habib, p. 340-347.

[11] For the following, see the article of Asiya Sidddiqi in: Idem (ed.), p. 186-217and the *Wikipedia* article on "Sir Jamsetjee Jeejebhoy, 1ste Baronet". For J. J.'s opium business, see also M. Greenberg, passim and, most importantly, the correspondence of Jardine and Matheson in A. Le Pichon (Ed), passim.

there are merchants [...] in the kingdom of Cambai ... known as Esparcis. We Portuguese call them Jews, but they are not so. They are Gentios.[12]

In fact, Parsees originated from Persia, and they mostly do have a Zoroastrian belief system. Landowners, ship-builders, bankers, money lenders were Parsees. However, it is not very strange that Parsees were confused with Jews, their main competitors. It was David Sassoon (1792-1864) who was the leader of the Sephardic Jewish community in Bombay. Like J. J., he was heavily involved in the opium trade, a middleman between British textile firms and merchants in the Gulf region.[13] Later he became a major player in the triangular trade: Indian yarn and opium were carried to China to buy goods sold to Britain, where he obtained Lancashire cotton products.

Sassoon established an office in Shanghai, and his sons and grandsons were among the largest opium traders to China. It is said that 'one fifth of all opium brought into China was shipped on the Sassoon fleet'. Thanks to opium they became not only the wealthiest family in India, but also the largest real estate dealers in Shanghai. They became, of course, English aristocrats, married into the Rothschild family, and belonged among the richest people in the world. It formed an easy example for the antisemitic propaganda, in this case mainly the British one, of the dubious theory of "Jewish world dominance" (see further ch. 31).

The Parsees built about thirty vessels from Malabar teak for the EIC in the last part of the 18th-century, ranging between 300 and 1000 tons, repaired ships of the Royal Navy and were rewarded by the British with tracts of land. But they were accustomed to other kinds of sea-faring business as well. They served European agency houses, which were the main representatives of the Bombay government at the time. As after 1806 EIC servants were not permitted to trade in order to prevent corruption, the indigenous merchants became part and parcel of a close-knit group.

---

[12] Quoted in *Wikipedia* article 'Parsi'. Garci de Orta played a not unimportant role in the early history of opium. See further ch. 10. For the Parsees see N.Randeraad (ed.), p. 17-41. A. Le Pichon (ed.), p. 83 note 19.

[13] The Sassoon family came to prominence in the second half of the 19th-century based on the earlier work of David Sassoon. See C.Trocki (1999a), passim; the article of Chiara Betta in: I. Baghdiantz McCabe et al (ed.), p. 269-287 (also interesting for the Parsees); the article of Jonathan Goldstein in: D. Cesarani, G. Romain (ed.), p. 271-291 with Zionist apologetic and several *Wikipedia* articles. C. Betta is also published on Internet as PDF, but with the warning "First draft, do not quote" which is rather odd and a good example of abortive communication; besides that, it is rather similar to the article in I. Baghdiantz McCabe et al (ed.).

Monopoly trade was nurtured, and competition among the members of this group was almost non-existent. Nepotism was widespread in this scene of 'friends' and 'neighbors' (as they called each other). It fitted correctly with the monopoly position of the EIC and what was called the Old China Trade, the heart of which was the opium business.

Things became more complicated as industrial Britain expanded, and this community was also shattered by what was called "free trade". Bombay was flooded with new European firms from the rising industrial cities of Liverpool and Glasgow, rather than from London. The old inter-Asian or 'Country trade' almost disappeared. A victory of the "free traders" over the EIC led to a new assault on China of people who were looking to industrialize that country or to find resources for the British industry. They also provided new motives to attack China, which made a mockery of something like "free" trade: it was "free" as long as the British traders profited from it.

The opium career of Jamsetjee Jejeebhoy (J. J.), with his 'best managed business this side of the Cape', started as an agent of various Parsee merchants. In this function he not only made several voyages to China and exported cotton to Europe, he also amassed a fortune during the Napoleonic wars. On one of his trips his ship was captured by a French warship in the Indian Ocean, and on that occasion J. J. made the acquaintance of the young William Jardine. It was the beginning of his opium career: J. J. became the principal collaborator of Jardine-Matheson in Bombay from 1822 onwards. In the 1830s J. J. transacted more than £1 million worth of business annually and remitted to London through China about £150,000 each year.[14] Like all famous opium smugglers J. J. was nominated 'Sir' and 'Baronet'; his son became automatically the 2nd Baronet, etc.

For the Parsee, Jewish, etc. merchants, the 19th-century was a golden period, but the risks taken were substantial as well. When the trade with China was interrupted by the First Opium War, several Parsees of Bombay committed suicide.[15]

---

[14] In the *Wikipedia* article (note 200) opium is mentioned in passing; it is suggested that he earned his money with the trade in bottles. It is also remarkable that a whole paragraph is devoted to his philanthropy, with the remark that Sir J. J. spent in total £230,000 to this aim in his whole life, which is about the amount he remitted in two years to his accounts in London.

[15] A. Guha, p. 1933.

They were later described as typical *compradors*, close supporters and business partners of the foreign occupiers. That was not the most sympathetic position in the eyes of indigenous nationalists. In this very spectacular 19th-century, however, this bond led to other trouble:

> Alongside increasing risks in the opium smuggling business due to a hostile Chinese Government, the Parsi opium traders became increasingly dependent on a single monopolistic European Agency House of China, Jardine Matheson and Co. Together with Remington Crawford and Co and J. J. and Sons as partners, it had ... formed the Malwa Opium Syndicate to control the market.[16]

What J. J. earned is given above, and the Jardines, Mathesons, etc. had a much larger profit, but the smaller traders found themselves cornered, at least during the years of the Syndicate's existence. The following table provides the relative value of the opium trade over other items over two years.

Table 2. India's Foreign Trade in select items by Value, 1849 -1850 in £[17]

	1849	1850
Exports		
Opium	5 772 526	5 973 395
Raw Cotton	1 775 309	2 201 178
Imports		
Cotton Twist and Yarn	909 016	1 131 586
Cotton Cloth	2 222 089	3 371 618

A Western Competitor

The British were not the only Western colonizers left in India after the French were defeated. From the beginning of the 16th-century, the Portuguese and Spaniards were the only representatives of that fabulous Western civilization, who came to plunder and convert the Eastern pagan barbarians. The former are the most important characters in our story.

These Portuguese were first driven out of West India and Ceylon (Sri Lanka) by the Dutch around 1620-1665 and later out of East India by the Dutch, French and English (see ch. 10). In Goa, south of Bombay, they still had a stronghold around 1800 as capital of a colony. It became a

---

[16] Idem.
[17] Idem, p. 1934.

short-lived but spectacular opium region and a real competitor to the English opium trade.[18]

The EIC, in control only of the Bengal opium production in the east (Patna and Benares), attempted by all means to restrict supplies of this opium. After 1810 when trade became a bit more "free", the private traders and smugglers turned to the cheaper but slightly inferior Malwa opium to avoid EIC control. Here one is confronted with the monopoly practice: traders are defined as "smugglers" when they do not obey the rules of the English and their EIC. Chinese governments, who always prohibited opium use and import, were the only ones which could rightly talk about smugglers: the EIC and its supporters. Anyway, three years later the EIC simply prohibited the export of Malwa opium through Bombay.

> The private traders promptly turned to Portuguese ports and the acquisition of Portuguese papers for their ships. Damão in the Gujerat was ideally placed, close to the Malwa production zone, and it became the centre of the Portuguese opium trade, handling about two-thirds of exports in the 1820s.[19]

Diu and Surat could also share in this trade, but Goa was too far south. The British stationed troops in Portuguese India allegedly to "protect" the Portuguese from French attacks; they made several offers to buy Portuguese India; strong diplomatic pressure was brought to bear on Lisbon to prohibit the opium trade. The EIC even bought the whole Malwa crop: all in vain. It only resulted in a massive increase in the production of Malwa opium!

Everybody became increasingly nervous. The Company blocked the overland route between Malwa and Damão, but the opium dealers responded by sending the stuff north across the desert and, in the end, by sea to the Portuguese harbors. Then the EIC forced the Malwa exports through its own ports in West India, Bombay in particular, whereupon the Portuguese reacted by lowering tariffs in Damão. A bitter tariff war between the two cities raged in which the British even blockaded the Portuguese port for a while.

The important studies of Souza reveal that by 1771 the Portuguese imported 800 chests of Indian opium annually.[20] From 1784 to 1799 this

---

[18] For the following I rely mainly on G. Clarence-Smith, p. 22-61, but see also the relevant discussion in C. Markovits.

[19] G. Clarence-Smith, p. 25.

[20] See, for instance, his contribution to E. van Veen, L. Blussé (ed.), p. 357, 358. Souza, p. 358 states that 'at the beginning of the nineteenth-century it is presently estimated at

export to China was increased to an annual average of 1,359 chests, while by 1828 it had again increased to an annual average of 2,196 chests.

The end of the game arrived in 1843 when the British seized the lower Indus valley and cut off the northern route. The Portuguese responded by importing Turkish and Persian opium and even planned to develop a new production zone in its African colony, Mozambique. However, their West Indian opium trade withered away.

The Portuguese had, however, another iron in the opium fire, namely Macao. Around 1800 until the Opium Wars, this city, leased from the Chinese government, became the center not only of the opium trade into China but also of a conspicuous spending of the opium profits. Famous for its fashion, elegance, prostitution, luxury and gambling, Macao had a specific attraction: in 1822 'there were nearly three times as many free non-Chinese women as men'.

After the Opium War the competition with neighboring Hong Kong was too intense, but Macao could still rely on its pirates, who chased profitable opium ships with their well-armed *lorchas*, clashing with the always inimical British. Its new wealth came as the Portuguese renewed their extensive experience as African slave traders and slave holders, and started a Chinese 'coolie' export to all possible destinations including the American Far Western gold fields.

In 1906 representatives of a USA opium commission (including a bishop) stated that much more was wrong with those Portuguese. Blaming the victims was a normal practice, and the 'coolies' sent to the USA 'contaminated' (!) that country. Portugal, however, was a special factor because

> through the possession of her colony of Macao, on the China coast, where considerable quantities of crude opium were annually imported from India, converted into smoking opium, and shipped to United States, Canada, and Mexico.[21]

---

around 4,000 chests annually'. This cannot be true, since Greenberg arrived at 4,500 chests for the Canton import of the English in 1800 alone (see previous chapter). It would have been a bit too strange if the Macao-based Portuguese took up more than half of this opium trade, since Souza also states that 'the Portuguese merchant fleet at Macao as a whole was not a force that could compete with the Companies ...' (p. 358). The importance of Macao is, as indicated in the main text, in providing a much more diversified pattern of its trade, including the important coolie-trade and entertainment services. Sousa's studies make it clear how necessary it is to start new research into the whole pattern of the opium trade in the realm, including a realistic who-is-who in this trade.

[21] Quoted by C. Terry, M. Pellens, p. 632.

Here in Macao an international meeting point of under- and upper-world was, indeed, located, of supply and demand in slaves and drugs.

Narco-business Revenues

All this should be seen as the meaning of 'the consolidation of the position of opium' (Chaudhuri above). The English opium production in India and part of the Eastern trade remained a British government monopoly until 1920. Smuggling was attacked not only to sustain the moral hypocrisy, but first and foremost to uphold the monopoly prices. The following figures demonstrate the value of the production. At its peak around 1890, British government opium was

> one of the most valuable commodities moving in international trade. Each year, export opium leaving Calcutta and Bombay averaged over 90,000 chests containing more than 5,400 metric tons. This staggering amount would meet the annual needs of between 13 and 14 million opium consumers in China and Southeast Asia ... Each year opium revenues poured 93.5 million rupees (9.4 million pounds sterling) into Government of India coffers, approximately 16% of total official revenues.[22]

Let's now illuminate the background interests of this whole constellation in more detail through a short analysis of this Indian middle position in the triangle trade, which is characterized by a duality: both loser and winner in the Western narco-business.

The following balance of trade clearly demonstrates its situation before the first Opium War: the export to the UK is at least 60% tea; the export to China is nearly all opium; the import of the UK dominates fully, while the Chinese import is small; the balance shows how British India depended on China/opium.

As stated, the British opium production was concentrated for a long time mainly in the government opium factories at Patna and Benares and then sent to Calcutta and sold by auction to merchants, who exported it to China until ca. 1850 largely by smuggling. After the Opium Wars, officially, the opium arrived at Canton, where some bureaucrats of the Chinese government and Chinese merchants distributed the stuff along the coast and into the interior of the country.

However, the smuggling along the coast was now officially prohibited by both the Chinese and the English governments. The former because

---

[22] DPA article, p. 2. For a much more detailed estimate see E. Balfour, p. 37 and J. Wiselius (1886), chapter VIII.

Table 3. Balance of Trade of "British" India with selected countries, 1828/9 (x Rs. million)[23]

Country	Merchandise					
	Export	%	Import	%	Balance	%
United Kingdom	53,7	48	34,8	65	18,9	33
China	28,4	26	7,4	14	21	37
France	6,5	6	2,9	5	3,6	6
United States	3,3	3	0,8	1	2,5	4
Total	111,29	100	53,63	100	57,66	100

tax incomes were evaded, the latter because the monopoly prices were negatively affected. Therefore, the Royal Navy also chased Chinese opium junks and India-based opium clippers.

This concerns the so-called "provision opium" (for instance, around 1880 already amounting to 50,000 chests). The British colonial government always kept a changing reserve (for instance in 1878 not fewer than nearly 50,000 chests; three years later 22,000 chests, etc.) with which it could easily influence the prices. There is a third "source", namely the quantity of about 4000 chests of Bengal opium, which are consumed in India itself (called "abkari" or "excise" opium).

The average production cost of a chest of Bengal opium ('including interest on the capital and all indirect charges') is given as 421 rupees; the average price realized on a chest around 1880 was 1280 rupees, and therefore the profit is rs. 859. From outside the British-occupied territory in India, mainly from Malwa, opium is delivered for shipment to China. The British Indian government levied a duty on it of rs. 700 a chest.

During the 19th-century this kind of import became more important. In 1820 its value was only 1% of 53 million rupees; five years later, it had increased to 20% of this total trade valued at 58 million rupees; and ten years later, opium from Malwa is 35% of all import from the interior.[24] Wiselius stresses that opium was the second most important revenue of the British colonial government in 1885 (£9 million) after the land rent (£22 million); in third place came the salt tax (£3.6 million), and this was already the case for 40 years.[25] There was no single product that could compete with this.[26]

---

23 Derived from K. Chaudhuri, in: D. Kumar, M. Desai (ed.), p. 872
24 T. Kessinger in: Idem, p. 253.
25 J. Wiselius (1886), p. 191, 195.
26 It is ridiculous that the maps in the *Times Historical Atlas,* R. Overy (ed.), p. 258-259

About twenty years later it was reported about the triangle relationship that

> it was Britain's heavy adverse balance of trade with China that prevented bullion moving from India to England since the balance of indebtedness between the two latter countries was extremely unfavourable to India.[27]

Based on these figures for the decade with the main profits (1870-1883), the gross and net revenues of the Bengal production for the British were calculated as the following few examples of selected years indicate:

Table 4. Opium Revenues and Expenditures of the British Colonial Government in India[28]

Year	Gross Revenue in £	Expenditure in £	Net Revenue in £
1800	372 502	105 381	267 121
1810	935 996	96 188	839 808
1820	1 436 432	135 726	1 300 706
1830	1 341 988	319 964	1 022 024
1838	----	----	1 586 445
1840	1 430 499	556 222	874 277
1850	3 795 300	1 044 952	2 750 348
1857	----	----	5 918 375
1860	6 676 759	918 467	5 758 292
1871	----	----	7 657 213
1875	8 556 000	2 341 000	6 215 000
1880	10 317 300	2 067 492	8 249 808
1881	10 480 000	2 028 000	8 452 000
1882	9 862 000	2 057 000	7 805 000
1883	9 499 000	2 282 000	7 217 000

One must realize that before the British colonial government (on several levels) started to cash its revenues, many English private entrepreneurs and landowners in India had already made stupendous profits in the Indian poppy production, in the fields and factories or through the land rent (poppy land). In addition, there was a substantial private opium trade. Wiselius tells:

> As said, all opium brought to the Calcutta market is provision-opium, which all is exported to China except a few thousand pikuls. On average, thus, this export is 40-45,000 pikuls. About the same amount of Malwa-opium is imported into China by privates.[29]

---

do not even mention opium among the many products and on p. 190 apparently on the wrong location.

[27] K. Chaudhuri, in: D. Kumar, M. Desai (ed.), p. 872.
[28] Included are data from J. Wiselius (1886), p. 194 and 203 note 1.
[29] Idem, p. 202.

In a proper economic assessment this should be considered as well. One has to realize also that production is sold to the excise department, but the receipts realized by the *provincial* governments on the sale of opium are not included in the table (see also Appendix 1).

The colonial government of the whole of "their" India earned its opium money at the Calcutta auction, from the Malwa pass duty and the cost price money credited by the excise department to the opium department. This last re-sale increased to about £381,000 from, for instance, 1870-1880, but the main deals were made in the other actions. Also the average (=Bengal + Malwa opium) export price per chest increased sharply. In the decades after the Opium war, for instance, the export prices per chest of Bengal + Malwa opium realized at the Calcutta auctions ranged from £127.81 in 1874 to £139.16 in 1882 (see further Appendix 1).[30]

Lord Hartington, a secretary of the colonial state, declared in the House of Commons (16 August 1880) that the revenues of British India are much higher than estimated, thanks to the always increasing consumption of opium and because in British India itself opium is heavily taxed.

The profitability of opium had several consequences. A British colonial commissioner, for instance, thought the land revenue of the peasants 'ridiculously low' relative to the size of the opium consumption in 'his' Assam. Around the 1870s the income from the sale of opium exceeded the land revenue demand by as much as 40%. Therefore, peasants (in his view nothing but 'rack-rent tenants') had to cater for much more land revenue.[31] Cash crops like indigo and opium were typical under the British rule. The British generally did not force opium cultivation (except occasionally), but it was made "attractive" because force was the alternative: opium advances were interest-free; part of the production could be sold to private traders at higher than the fixed government prices, etc.

> However, the vulnerability of the poppy to fluctuations in the weather ... and the rigidity with which the opium advances were recovered by the government ... forced the cultivators into indebtedness, and it was partly because of this that a number of them remained tied to opium cultivation.[32]

The last table demonstrates the value of British India's opium export relative to the two other major export articles, cotton and indigo.

---

[30] According to Idem, table p. 194.
[31] B. Chaudhuri, in: Idem, p. 122.
[32] Idem, p. 146.

Table 5. Value of Main Export Products from "British" India in selected years, 1813-1930 (Rs. Million)[33]

Year	Indigo	Opium	Cotton
1813	15,6	1,2	--
1820	11,3	12,1	5,6
1830	26,7	19,9	15,3
1850	18,4	59,7	22
1860	20,2	90,5	56,4
1870	31,8	116,9	190,8
1880	29,5	143,2	111,5
1890	30,7	92,6	165,3
1900	21,4	94,5	101,3
1910	3,3	127,6	360,5
1920	4,1	25,2	416,7
1930	---	---	464,1

It is only at the end of the 19th-century that the importance of opium export decreases, mainly because the Chinese produced their own much more cheaply, the Indian government agreed to stop opium exports to China,[34] and the smuggling from Southeast Asian production regions was increasing every year. This last story will be told below (part 4). It will be shown as well that the suggestion from this last table (1930 = no opium export) is certainly no indication that the Opium Question was solved. Not in India which remained a production land although, officially, only for medical purposes, and certainly not for the rest of the world.

In all those years British India exported a total number of nearly 80,000 chests or about 5.6 million kilo of raw opium. It was delivered to countries where government opium monopolies existed. On top of this, about the same volume was smuggled to these countries.

The very active *League of Nations Opium Commission* used the following prices.[35] Raw opium was perceived as 70% of the value of the prepared opium; prices are mostly expressed in *tahil* = 38-39 grams metric equivalent. The price per *tahil* of prepared opium ranged from $ 6-8 in Southeast Asian countries, to $ 3-3.3 in Hong Kong or about $1.5 in Macao. This concerns the smuggler's price which is about 15% lower than the official monopoly price.

---

[33] Derived from K. Chaudhuri in: Idem, p. 846. For reading this kind of statistics it is enough to assume that 1000 Rupees = £100.

[34] D. Kumar, in: Idem, p. 919.

[35] Compare Idem, vol. 1, p. 17 ff and the statistics p. 172 ff.

Table 6. Exports of Raw Opium from "British" India to Asian Countries, 1922-1935 (in chests)*[36]

Country	1922	1924	1926	1928	1930	1932	1935
Straits Settlements	1820	3000	2400	2027	1520	1013	253
Hong Kong	150	240	210	196	147	98	24
Ceylon	60	15	35	31	24	16	4
Netherl. Indies	1800	300	1500	964	723	482	121
Siam	1650	1500	1400	1391	1044	695	174
Sarawak	55	12	144	87	65	44	11
British North Borneo	60	84	36	58	43	29	7
Union of Indo China	1700	1355	2420	1762	1321	881	220
Totals	7285	6506	8145	6516	4887	3258	814

* 1 chest = 140 lbs = ca. 65 kg.

Since most of the known 5.6 million kilo raw opium was transported to Southeast Asia, an average value of $5-6 can be taken per *tahil* of prepared opium, which is $ 130-156 per kilo or $ 91-109 for raw opium. It gives a turnover of $509-610 million in thirteen years' time! The smuggler's price is used here, so officially—say—about $ 575-700 million were earned by the government monopolies in the realm.

Two remarks remain. Later on, in particular in the detailed analysis of the most important Dutch opium nation, a much higher turnover and profit for the same years are found. Apparently, only the tip of the iceberg was shown to the members of the *League of Nation Opium Commission*. Furthermore, one has to consider the enormous amounts of money that were extracted from all the people living in these countries, the victims of the opium dealers, most of the time their own governments which were bound to protect them from evil and exploitation. These governments continued until the bitter end with their business, notwithstanding their solemn treaties to stop deliveries and opium production. Indeed, as the last table shows, the Indian deliveries decreased substantially, but no one checked these figures, nor the strongly increased smuggling practices, nor the imports from other countries like Turkey or Iran.

---

[36] Commission, vol. 1, p. 176.

CHAPTER EIGHT

THE INVENTION OF AN ENGLISH OPIUM PROBLEM

> I am told that in your country opium smoking is for-
> bidden under severe penalties ... that is because the
> harm caused by opium is clearly understood ... it would
> be better to forbid the sale of it, or better still, to forbid
> the production of it ...
>
> Letter from Commissioner Lin Zexu (Tse-hsu)
> to Queen Victoria, 1839[1]

Questions

From the earlier chapters it is clear how the British took over every initiative in the East Asian opium business at the end of the 18th-century. In
their "Victorian century" the British not only provoked China as well as
India with huge smuggling operations, wars and stringent exploitation to
swallow and to produce opium, respectively. Trocki's argument can be
supported to a large extent: the British Empire in the East was sustained
mainly by its fabulous opium profits.

This is illustrated well by the cover illustration of Beeching's *The
Chinese Opium Wars*: it is a design of four opium-smoking Chinese (as
puppets, shaven bald and symmetrically seated) under a huge picture of
Queen Victoria (1837-1901). Well, a pioneer study of Berridge and Edwards
demonstrated convincingly that earlier than 1839 a substantial opium
consumption existed in Britain itself among urban workers and peasants,
as well as morphine among medical professionals and the social elite.[2] In
this respect Lin Zexu was not well informed, but he predicted the future
in Victorian England as will be shown.

Now intriguing questions can be tabled. For instance, whether the
same people who were brutal enough to deliberately turn the Chinese

---

[1] Quoted from J. Beeching, p. 75, 76 and others. There are many variations of this letter; it seems as if nobody has read this letter, like me!

[2] See V. Berridge, G. Edwards and I consulted the well illustrated but badly written
website *http://drugs.uta.edu/drugs.html* called 'Victorian's Secret'. E. Kremers, G. Urdang,
p. 92-110.

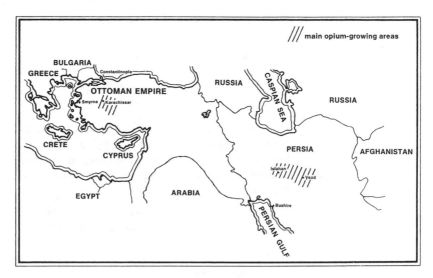

Map 2. Sources of Opium Imported in Britain in the 19th Century
Source: V. Berridge, G. Edwards, p. 5.

society into addicts during the reign of Queen Victoria and were knighted by her for it tried to do the same with "their own kin" in England? More precisely: is it obvious that, while the colonial English (and others) got Chinese tea for their English-Indian opium, the "English-English" got to swallow Chinese tea *plus* Indian opium?

But the use of opium by Europeans in the East was largely forbidden: a white Christian civilized Britain had to be far ahead of indigenous, primitive folk which was—so it was assumed—*by nature* willing to consume opium until addiction followed. Does this imply that there must have been people who brought the stuff to the "homeland", who propagated its use, who made vast sums of money out of it, who tried to keep its excesses silent, who had to struggle against the related criminality or to forgive the sinners if they converted to the decent and prudish Victorian family life?

From the viewpoint of the British practices in the 'homeland', fundamental questions are, of course, how discrepancies between a colony and England could develop and how a use accepted in England could be perceived later as the worst danger for mankind?

Before answering these and related questions, a sketch must be given of the indigenous British opium consumption in and before the 19th-century.

An English Home Market for Drugs

As described in the first part, opium and opiates, in whatever form, were components in many medical recipes used in Europe and the Middle East at least from early modern times. Before there existed a relevant professional medical infrastructure (a network of medical doctors, pharmacies, hospitals, pharmaceutical industry and so on), the population largely had to rely on its own medical knowledge and "home remedies" to cure many kinds of sicknesses, pains and sorrows. In most countries in Europe, this infrastructure did not exist at all before 1900. Even in the most developed part, like England or France, it appeared around 1850.[3] At this time the first restrictive legislation is imposed as well.

In town and country, therefore, one knew the most fantastic recipes handed down over generations. They often were regional, while some families had their own private recipes. Certainly in the 18th-century they were mixed sometimes with "authoritative" prescriptions of famous quacks or university professors from elsewhere in the country or Europe. The confidence in them rose when those quacks had to cure princes, prelates and aristocrats as well.

Among the hundreds of substances the British liked to swallow in times of pain and sorrow was opium. This mostly took the form of laudanum and was generally mixed with something, mainly alcohol. Pure and processed opium was practically unavailable, and had lethal consequences because nobody knew its potential. That was even the case with an uncontrolled intake of laudanum. But what was called 'narcotic deaths' appeared in the statistics only after 1863.[4]

During most of the 19th-century, the corner shop was the center of popular opium use, not the doctor's surgery. Markets often had one stall for vegetables, one for meat and a third for pills. Untrained midwives, "doctors" or herbalists concocted their own mixtures; before 1840 hardly any apothecaries or pharmacists existed. Drug sellers were a motley group with all varieties of qualifications: basket makers, retailers, factory operators and the like. Their number was estimated in the 1850s to be between 16,000 and 26,000. However, there were also people who took an examination set by the Pharmaceutical Society or who worked under the jurisdiction of the Society of Apothecaries.

---

[3] A highly relevant history of the "health-industry" in society is G. Göckenjan.

[4] V. Berridge, G. Edwards, table 3 and 4 p. 275-277. I am not going to comment on this feature of the Opium Problem.

Laudanum was often kept by the shopkeepers in large containers; they measured it in bottles large and small, dirty and clean. This happened not only in urban workers' quarters but also in villages. Twenty or twenty-five drops could be had for a penny; everyone had laudanum at home in some form or another. It was used as a painkiller or a sedative, remedy for coughs, diarrhoea and dysentery.

In short: around 1850 opium was sold openly and quite normally to retailers and customers. These self-medication practices in town and country were based on a *pre-industrial* knowledge.

The opium basic to all kinds of mixtures was only occasionally delivered from India or China. It originated mostly from Turkey and had a quite different trade history: it was a product embedded in old (medieval) trade relations from the Mediterranean directly to countries in Europe. Even at the end of the 19th-century, Turkish opium still made up over 70 per cent of this specific English market as the following table shows.

Table 7. Sources and Quantities of England's Opium Imports, 1827-1900 (in lbs)[5]

Year	Turkey	%	India	China	Persia	Egypt	France	Rest
1827	109 921	97	---	---	---	---	---	3 219
1837	70 099	88	---	---	---	3 768	1 118	5 618
1847	---	--	---	---	---	---	---	---
1857	125 022	92	---	---	---	3 014	---	8 387
1867	258 862	95	---	---	---	---	---	14 660
1870	275 838	74	---	11 002	9 154	50 868	11 559	13 244
1875	381 631	71	25 861	34 182	36 606	---	---	94 617
1880	288 764	72	---	34 699	45 258	---	---	31 653
1885	657 686	93	5 786	3 758	37 040	3 012	---	2 817
1890	360 963	80	9 223	---	30 035	3 543	33 704	13 725
1895	362 572	95	8 240	---	3 890	---	3 180	5 184
1900	619 292	74	96 397	3 317	36 640	---	39 751	37 933

Without elaborating further on the following data, they are given to demonstrate how the Turkish influence persisted also on the continent, in this case Germany.

---

[5] Derived from Idem, p. 272-273. The whole table provides the annual quantities from 1827 up to 1900.

Table 8. Import of Opium in Germany, 1910-1925 (x 100 kg).[6]

Country of Origin	1911	1912	1913	1920	1921	1922	1923	1924	1925
Greece	4	14	15	34	225	230	60	45	182
Swiss	--	--	--	78	--	21	12	74	98
Turkey	638	504	754	500	410	1314	1286	599	904
India	84	19	278	--	14	19	26	77	--
China	103	141	64	8	43	156	18	21	25
USA	--	--	--	5	47	118	--	13	--
total in 100 kg	1040	868	1625	787	790	1906	1409	841	1507
total in lbs	208 000	173 600	325 000	157 400	158 000	381 200	281 800	168 200	301 400

6 L. Lewin, p. 69.

The English data show that the 110,000 lbs from 1827 remained an average until about 1860. In the next decade this import nearly tripled. From 1870 onwards the Turkish import from Smyrna and Constantinople doubled again until 1900. From the other destinations the imports were negligible until the end of the 19th-century.

In previous centuries English opium had come mainly from Turkey, but not many reliable figures are available. There is some evidence that opium was known by a few people in the late sixteenth-century. The quantities must have been very small. An apothecary, Zacharie Linton, had half an ounce of opium among his many drugs in 1593![7] This matched the situation in other European countries, as will be revealed later (ch. 10 or 13).

The opium imports at British ports suggest that it was still not a big business 200 years later: Liverpool imported 120 lb in 1792, Dover 261 lb in 1801. The bulk, however, arrived in London where a small group of "Turkey merchants" dominated the Levant trade from the time of Elizabeth I (1533-1603). This more or less monopoly trade ended in 1825, leaving the import of opium open to free trade.

These merchants used drug brokers in the Mincing and Mark Lane area of London to conduct detailed sale negotiations. On the open market many drugs including opium were sold; auctions of opium took place at Garraway's Coffee House, which was the center for London drug sales. The large players in this business were wholesale houses like Allen & Hanburys and the Apothecaries' Company. In the 1830s there were only three brokers specializing in drugs and spices, but 20 years later there were already about 30.

Opium was just a commodity like tea, and it belonged to a general drugs business closely connected to the apothecaries trade. Later some firms, like Thomas Morson and Sons Limited, became specialized in the pharmaceutical industry. This company did everything: wholesaling, manufacturing and retailing from 1821 onwards. In 1900 it abandoned this last activity. Morson was the first manufacturer of morphine in Britain.

Among its hundreds of drugs, the most prestigious wholesaler, the Apothecaries' Company, manufactured 26 opium preparations in 1868, including two morphine preparations. Others were selling poppy capsules at 1s. 10d for a hundred, opiate plaster, morphine acetate, several varieties of laudanum or syrup of white poppies, raw and powdered

---

[7] V. Berridge, G. Edwards, p. 284 note 8.

opium, etc. Before the *Pharmacy Act* (1868) limited the sale of drugs to the professional pharmacists, the wholesalers' opium stocks were available to any dealer.

Some commentators claimed to differentiate between Turkish and Indian opium; the latter was deemed 'much softer and fouler ..'. Some Indian opium was brought to the motherland and supported by scholars propagating a product of the 'own colony ... rather ... than that we should go to the rascally Turks'.[8] The effort was in vain, as can be seen in the table. The relatively strong increase of the Indian import at the end of the century was most likely due to the dominant position of Sassoon & Co, the largest dealers in Indian opium on the English market as well.[9] At that time many expatriates arrived back in the "metropolis" with their accumulated wealth and conspicuous consumption, including the "real opium" known from the colony.

Among the category "Rest", some opium was from English origin. However, the labor intensiveness of poppy cultivation and of opium collection made English opium uneconomic for large-scale production.

Turkish opium was not grown by large landowners, but by individual peasants chiefly in Kara Chissar and around Magnesia. It arrived at Smyrna by mule, often through the hands of three or four different merchants, which increased the price. In Smyrna the quality was checked, and the opium packed in hermetically sealed zinc-lined wooden cases. In August the shipment to Mediterranean harbors began and from there into other parts of Europe over land and sea. A traveler to this region in 1850 visited the places where this so-called *Opium Smyrnacum* was grown and gave a vivid description of the situation:

> Near a few small dwellings were the poppy fields. In the buildings cauldrons were walled up and vessels and stages constructed to dry the opium cakes. These fields, because of their noxious fumes, were left alone by the old Turkish people during the morning and after sunset. They are perceived as highly dangerous, reason why the peoples hide themselves in the evening in their dwellings ... I myself, experienced in the morning and evening how dizzy, depressive and uneasy one becomes if nearing too close to the poppy fields. This is not the case in daytime. If, after sunset, the humidity of the air increases ... a highly narcotic fume spreads, which gives inexperienced people headaches and unpleasant feelings within a quarter of an hour.[10]

---

[8] Idem, p. 4.
[9] Idem, p. 177.
[10] X. Landerer, p. 293 (my translation. H.D.).

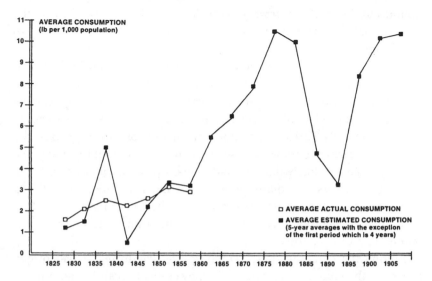

Figure 3. Five-year averages of actual and estimated home consumption of opium
per 1,000 population in England, 1825-1905

Source: V.Berridge, G.Edwards, p. 35.

So, the London 'Turkey merchants' and their clients were warned, and
certainly the pharmacists who had to read this professional publication.
The following table shows how extensive this Turkish trade was in Merry
England in the 19th-century.

The meaning of this becomes clear (?) in the following calculation. In
1827 about 113,000 lbs opium are imported. Next is given an 'actual home
consumption [of opium] in 1,000 lb' of 17,000 lb in 1827.[11] The obvious
question is: what happened to the other 96,000 lb? Exported again? It is

---

[11] Idem, table 2, p. 274 apart from an average consumption per person in this year of
1.31 lb and a not very clear 'estimated home consumption in lb. per 1,000 population' of
nearly 2 lb. There are many difficulties with these data: there is no mention of which population figures were used (from England + Wales + Scotland ?); in table 3 the totals nearly
never correspond with the given breakdown; there is no definition of "actual home consumption" or of "estimated home consumption". It is stated that the latter 'is obtained by
subtracting the amount of opium exported from that imported' which is obvious, but why
estimate when one has 'actual' figures as well? And what do the six *negative* estimations
mean in this definition? That the export is higher than the import minus the home consumption? The total population of England alone in this year is about ten million, so that
an "actual home consumption in lb. per 1,000 population" of 1.31 leads to 13,100 and an
'estimated home consumption in lb. per 1,000 population' of 1.95 leads to 19,500 lb, but
never to 17,000.

important to realize that the import-opium to a large degree was not the same as the export-opium. The latter concerned in all probability end-products, all possible processed goods of the fledgling and quickly expanding British pharmaceutical industry. Eventually, this was comparable to the French import in England. New research should be done to discover the details.

The total population of England in 1827 was about ten million and therefore a supposed consumption of 1.95 per 1000 leads to 20,000 lb in 1827. Samuel Taylor Coleridge (1772-1834), the most famous opium (laudanum) consumer at the time, drank an amount costing two pounds and ten shillings each week. This was a pint (0.5 liter) a day, which must have had some effect on the national statistics.[12]

So, let's conclude that the "opiumization" of the British people in the 19th-century started with these very small amounts of the drugs dissolved into dozens of opium-related products and opiates. In the middle of the century, the opium import had doubled, and the English population had doubled as well. However, the consumption of opium had tripled, and at the end of the century this happened again. To discover the reasons behind this, the following effects and contexts of the "opiumization" of the English must be considered.

The Creation of the English Opium Problem

Let's, first, quote Berridge and Edwards extensively, because they outlined the basic features of the *medical source* of The Opium Problem:

> The medical dimension to the "problem" of opium use was more than a case of professional strategy. There is a danger, in stressing the theme of professionalization in connection with narcotics, that doctors come to be seen as some autonomous body, working out their designs on opium in an isolated way. ... For in reality the medical profession merely reflected and mediated the structure of the society of which it was the product. ... This was at its clearest in the new ideological interpretation of narcotic use which began to be established in the last quarter of the century ... The strict, militant, dogmatic medicalization of society ... (Michel Foucault) found its expression in the nineteenth-century in the establishment of theories of disease affecting a whole spectrum of conditions. Homosexuality, insanity, even poverty and crime were re-classified in a biologically determined way.

---

[12] B. Hodgson, p. 59.

> Concepts of addiction ... of "inebriety" or "morphinism" ... were part of this process. These emphasized a distinction barely applied before between what was seen as "legitimate" medical use and "illegitimate" non-medical use ... the "disease model" of addiction arose through the establishment of the medical profession in society ... The "problem" of opium use found a major part of its origin in ... this form of ideological hegemony ... The moral prejudices of the profession were given the status of value-free norms.[13]

People who are connected somehow to this "medical complex"—apart from politicians and bureaucrats—include Sir Robert Christison (1797-1882), a professor of *Materia Medica* at Edinburgh, who was the investigator of opium eating and advocate of the benefits of coca chewing; Sir Thomas C. Allbutt (1836-1925), Regius professor of physics at Cambridge, who was enthusiastic about hypodermic morphine and an addiction specialist; Dr. Francis E. Anstie (1833-1874), editor of *The Practitioner* and advocate of new and more scientific remedies, including hypodermic morphine; Dr. John C. Browne (1819-1884), the first man to produce chlorodyne; Dr. Norman Kerr (1834-1899), temperance advocate and founder of the *Society for the Study of Inebriety*, who opted for the "disease view" of addiction.[14]

But The Opium Problem did not arise from the minds and outlook of the medical profession alone. This elite, largely with a new, educated, middle-class outlook (upwardly mobile), had to work in a context in which most people had a lack of access to medical care, of whatever quality. Therefore, long after 1850, in the most direct way 'opium itself was the "opiate of the people" [including] in some areas, a positive hostility to professional medical treatment ... in the popular culture of the time.'[15] In some regions, like the poverty-stricken and rheumy Fens, this popular opium consumption was much more extensive than elsewhere and, generally, in proletarian city quarters much more than in the country.[16]

A related development, as indicated in the quotation, concerned the gradual transformation of some shopkeepers into specialized druggists and pharmacists. This process began with the establishment of the *Pharmaceutical Society* (1841) and continued with many activities in the following years to achieve a monopoly of practice for its own members.[17]

---

[13] Idem, p. xxix, xxx.

[14] See Idem, pictures after p. 178.

[15] Idem, p. 37.

[16] See the dramatic description of a Fens district town in B. Hodgson, p. 48 ff.

[17] E. Kremers, G. Urdang, p. 99 ff. Still it took the Pharmacy Act of 1933 before membership of the Pharmaceutical Society was *compulsory*. Therefore: 'Each registered pharma-

THE ORIGINAL
CHLORODYNE,
Invented by RICHARD FREEMAN, Pharmaceutist,

Is allowed to be one of the greatest discoveries of the present century, and is largely employed by the most eminent Medical Men, in hospital and private practice, in all parts of the globe, and is justly considered to be a remedy of intrinsic value and of varied adaptability, possessing most valuable properties, and producing curative effects quite unequalled in the whole *materia medica*.

It is the only remedy of any use in Epidemic Cholera.—*Vide* EARL RUSSELL's *Letters to the Royal College of Physicians of London and to the Inventor*.

It holds the position as the BEST and CHEAPEST preparation.

It has been used in careful comparison with Dr. Collis Browne's Chlorodyne, and preferred to his. Vide *Affidavits of Eminent Physicians and Surgeons*.

It has effects peculiar to itself, and which are essentially different to those produced by the various deceptive and dangerous Compounds bearing the name of Chlorodyne.

See the Reports in 'Manchester Guardian,' December 30th, 1865, and 'Shropshire News,' January 4th, 1866, of the fatal result from the use of an imitation.

_____

Sold by all Wholesale Druggists.

For Retail—½ oz., 1/1½ ; 1½ oz., 2/9 each.

For Dispensing—2 oz., 2/9 ; 4 oz., 4/6; 8 oz., 9/; 10 oz., 11/; and 20 oz., 20/

THE USUAL TRADE ALLOWANCE OFF THE ABOVE PRICES.

_____

Manufactured by the Inventor,

RICHARD FREEMAN, Pharmaceutist,

70, KENNINGTON PARK ROAD, LONDON, S.

_____

CAUTION.—The large sale, great success, and superior quality of FREEMAN's ORIGINAL CHLORODYNE is the cause of the malicious libels so constantly published from interested motives by another maker of Chlorodyne. The Profession and the Trade are particularly urged not to be deceived by such false statements, but exercise their own judgment in the matter, and to buy no substitute for "The Original Chlorodyne."

Ill. 6. The Pharmacist's Competition, ca. 1866

Source: V. Berridge, G. Edwards, p. 128. This praise for Freeman's chlorodyne was advertised at the cost of the dangerous chlorodyne made by Dr. Collis Brown.

In the end the British government became worried and established a *Select Committee on the Sale of Poisons* (1857). Next came the *Pharmacy*

_____

cist conducting an establishment for the dispensing of drugs is authorized to dispense poisons also.' Even: 'Inspectors, who must be registered pharmacists, are appointed by the Society.' (Idem, p. 100). Like other medical professions it became its own judge! One dared to call this new law 'the Magna Charta of British pharmacy' of a 'self-governing community' (Idem.). The American lexicon spiced this by making the comparison with 'the principle employed by England in relation to her colonies ...'

Act (1868), which established a system of registration and examinations basic to this pharmacist monopoly. It also achieved to a large extent a monopoly on prescription and the restriction of the availability of drugs and poisons, including opium and opiates, to specific shops and purses.

However, the government was well aware that overly stringent restrictions on opium sales 'would only create an illicit market'.[18] Now, opium, along with 22 other drugs, was to be kept under lock and key. It could only be sold to adults, in the presence of a witness or on production of an official certificate. This had to be signed by a clergyman or other authority.

The sociologically new aspect was the cooperation for the first time by different factions of the English elite—the political, religious and economic one—in a concerted action against the lower classes.

The given awareness of an "illicit" market and the whole theater of authoritative or religiously legitimated allowances was a reproduction of the shopkeeper's self-interest and the state's or patriarchal elite's willingness to intervene in the lives of the citizens of the lower classes. But, in the same stroke, it created more detailed norms and values every time and, therefore, the sins committed when violating them, including the subsequent punishments.

The third new feature of The Opium Problem was, therefore, the institutionalization and interventionism of the law-and-order state and the invention of a specific criminality. The mood in which this occurred was described by a Dr. Richardson in 1892 who thought that opium smokers were 'very dangerous under those circumstances [smoking. H.D.] ... they might rise up, and be mischievous to anyone who might perform an experiment upon them, however simple it might be.'[19] For Dr. Richardson the alleged 'menace' was not only the supposed criminal act against another individual, but the contamination of the entire English people as well.

Long before Dr. Richardson conjured up again the dangerous character of opium or opium poisoning, it had already become a concern of those involved in the mid-century *public health movement*. For this movement the image was created of opium (in whatever form) as a criminal product (threatening the public health). For example suicide, defined as a criminal act, was at the time very often committed by means of laudanum overdose. This product was also used to kill people of all ages (accidentally or

---

[18] B. Hodgson, p. 117.
[19] Quoted in Idem, p. 199.

otherwise). Berridge-Edwards provides statistics of 'narcotic deaths' from 1863 onwards until 1910 caused by the intake of 'opium', 'laudanum', 'soothing syrups', 'chlorodyne', 'morphine' and 'cocaine'. The last four categories were listed from 1891-1908; they were apparently not available before the 1890s.[20]

The result of this movement, which gained momentum at the end of the century, was the classification of the users of these drugs as criminals, as deviant from the norms of established society, and of opium as a problem drug. Together with the development to define the production and trading of opium (and its derivatives) as 'illicit', the public health movement also created a specific kind of criminal organization, now known as the drugs mafia.

The next feature of The English Opium Problem involves the activities of the strongly religious anti-opium movement.[21] These became important motivators concerning the abolition of 'evils' in China, ranging from opium smoking to foot-binding.

The main organization in this field was the *Society for the Suppression of the Opium Trade* (SSOT) established in 1874, which was dominated by Quakers. The SSOT became a typical pressure group of the Victorian age like the Anti-Slavery Society or the Anti-Corn Law League combining humanitarian and commercial motives. The humanitarian one hinted at the morally unacceptable opium use; the other motive at the failed trade.

Sufferers from the latter motive, mostly representatives of the new industrial world, had an expectation of an enormous trade with the 400 million Chinese population. However, the expected huge profits that did indeed come went to the commercial world (including its bureaucratic support) which accepted and conducted the illicit imports of opium. The "poor Chinese" did not accept British manufactured goods but had to swallow the British "commercial product" opium. A formal pro-opium organization did not exist, but the imperial interests were powerful enough. Important figures in the British-Chinese relations like Sir Robert Hart or W. Brereton (see ch. 31) wrote pro-opium pamphlets.

After 1885 the anti-opium movement and the SSOT weakened considerably. The missionaries among its members tried to form their own anti-opium movement. This was in vain: what could be seen as a major result of the movement, the establishment of the *Royal Commission on Opium*

---

[20] Idem, p. 275-277.
[21] See for the following Idem, p. 173 -194.

(1895), resulted in a polite whitewash of the Anglo-Indian opium government and its business.

The remaining anti-opium societies under the leadership of Joshua Rowntree could not change the unavoidable decline of the movement. Their support within the English population was too small; the government, medical and entrepreneurial pro-opium policy was too strong. The anti-opium stand did remain represented among a section of the medical elite.

Another question to be mentioned here is related to the outbursts of *racism, xenophobia and anti-Chinese (violent) activities* at the end of the 19th-century in London or Liverpool. In the USA the many anti-Chinese actions in those years were much more dangerous for the Chinese victims and had far-reaching consequences (see ch. 28). Still, these English actions are remarkable enough.

In the first place, because there were hardly any Chinese in England! Was this racism largely a reproduction of a bad British conscience? In 1861 in the whole country, an estimated 147 Chinese lived among twenty million people.[22] Twenty years later this was increased to 665. Again ten years later 302 lived here permanently, while 280 had a temporary visa. The settled Chinese serviced Chinese seamen; they lived more or less together in two narrow streets of dilapidated houses.

Indeed, in the 1860s descriptions of opium smoking as a domestic phenomenon started, of "Dark England", of one opium den in the East End visited even by the Prince of Wales. Many famous authors (Dickens, Oscar Wilde, Conan Doyle, etc.) pictured or used opium or cocaine in the 1880s. The anti-opium propaganda advertised the connection to the immoral conduct of the British towards China and created an image of the 'Great Anglo-Asiatic Opium Curse' which 'would somehow come home to roost'. Opium den jokes appeared in *Punch*.

Soon after this decade, the discourse took on a grim tone, like that of a London County Council inspector and ex-policeman who visited an opium den (1904) run by

> cunning and artful Chinamen' and commented later on this 'oriental cunning and cruelty ... was hall-marked on every countenance ... until my visit to the Asiatic Sailors' Home, I had always considered some of the Jewish inhabitants of Whitechapel to be the worst type of humanity I had ever seen ...[23]

---

[22] For the following see Idem, p. 195 ff.
[23] Quoted in Idem, p. 199.

The last feature of The British Opium Problem concerns its *international effects*. It is clear that the main performers, the dealers, were certainly not the main authors of the opium drama, let alone the "willing audience". Who pulled the main strings, let's call them "the imperial interests", could endure the pressure of what could be called "the home interests" for a long time. Around 1900 rather fundamental cleavages are apparent in *both* "groups". At that time *both* had only a limited influence on an increase or decrease of the use of opium, because they never attacked the *colonial* policy or the so-called "free trade" of their governments in any relevant way.

Their controversies were fought far above the heads of the citizens and victims in many international conferences. They were largely attended by Western participants, although the Japanese as new imperialists were also active there to deny their aggressive opium policies in the East (see ch. 27). The 1909 Shanghai conference organized by the US government was one of the most influential. When organizing the follow-up conference (The Hague, 1911), one country, the most powerful one, did not participate and, therefore, did not subscribe to the many recommendations: Great Britain. It did not allow interference in its most profitable business with China. Instead, it sent an interesting series of excuses. The main ones were that it was busy negotiating with China bilaterally about the opium problem on its own terms.

> In addition to this, the British Government was greatly concerned over the morphine and cocaine traffic; for it had been shown beyond a doubt that immense quantities of these drugs were being smuggled into British India to take the place of opium, also that in China they tended to supplant the use of opium which the British Government had agreed that India should soon cease to export, and the production and use of which China on her part had agreed to suppress' ... [On these considerations several other governments were highly interested] ... 'in the manufacture of and traffic in these drugs. They were particularly important to Germany, as one of the largest producers ... the Italian Government has proposed that the production and traffic in the Indian hemp drugs be included as part of the program ....[24]

What had happened, therefore, around 1900 was a serious proliferation of the opium problem into a general drugs problem with quite new aphrodisiacs. Next, the country of British production was infiltrated by these new products. They were produced again by a Western country, by one of

---

[24] Quoted in C. Terry, M. Pellens, p. 635.

the strongest British competitors, the leading nation in chemistry, Germany. The *World War on Drugs* could start.

Whoever still thinks that this "war" only concerns opium and other drugs is mistaken. They have not yet been cpnvinced by the previous analysis of the tea for opium trade or of its above ground and underground elements. All these things concern economic practices with a strong tradition within old British colonies like, for instance, Kenya with its colonial tea production.

From a not very important part of the *Opium Commonwealth*, Kenya, the following message was sent, which also forms an appropriate end of this first historical analysis of the opium problem:

> Kenya will step up lobbying for a review of the import duty charged on tea by Pakistan to help curb smuggling through the neighboring Afghanistan. ... Pakistan currently charges 10 per cent import duty, alongside a 15 per cent sales tax and an additional 10 per cent value-added tax ... Smugglers charge between 15-per cent overall duty on their consignments. Only last month, Kenya raised the red flag over a sudden surge in Afghanistan tea imports with market analyst linking the trend to a syndicate in which suspected billionaire terrorists in the war torn country were seeking to "hide" their dirty money in the wake of a US-led crackdown on opium growing.[25]

The *World War on Drugs* continues. In Kenya an invitation like: 'Let's drink chai (tea)!' is too often the start of a solid case of corruption, a conclusion also drawn by a US *International Narcotics Control Strategy Report*. It assesses Kenya as a 'transshipment point for Southwest Asian heroin and hashish, as well as some Southeast Asian heroin. West African, particularly Nigerian, traffickers are active behind the scenes in Nairobi ...'[26] This stuff arrives for transport to Europe and the US. Indeed, in this year almost 20 mt of hashish was discovered on one of those beautiful beaches near Mombasa, 'one of the largest seizures ever made in Africa'. The traffickers were caught; corrupt police inspectors remained in office, thanks to 'influential politicians and government officials'; a British citizen was arrested for growing 150 opium poppies ... an accident ... [but] ... a previous year 30,000 plants were discovered ...

---

[25] Article from Allan Odhiambo, Kenya seeks reduction in Pakistan tea import duty, in: *Business Daily,* December 30, 2009 (www.businessdailyafrica.com).

[26] US Department of State, 1996. International ..Report, March 1997 in: http://www.state.gov/www/global/narcotics_law/1996_narc_report/index.html.

CHAPTER NINE

A FIRST REFLECTION

As mentioned earlier, this opium history of the British Empire serves as a kind of model for the whole history in this study. The aim is to discover through a short overview the main practical features of The Opium Problem, helping the reader to systematize the whole study of a new and complicated opium history. In part 7 one can read the result of this attempt. The following is only a first reflection on this model.

The most general conclusion is that two contradictory developments were documented in this mainly 19th-century history: the first concerns British imperialism in Asia with its specific consequences for British (and other) perpetrators and Chinese, Indian and other victims. The second development has a largely European impact, in many respects contrary to the Asian one. The former is the subject of this study; the other will be explored in several places below (ch. 10, 13 and 22). Conclusions relevant for the whole study are difficult to make now, but how can we understand this first practical description of a new opium history? Astonishment is an obvious reaction, reflecting that of a contemporary critical *supporter* of the whole opium business, the Dutch traveler Jacob Wiselius (1886). His painstakingly detailed analysis of the British Indian opium culture led to his complaint that the budget of the British colony

> has formed itself to the easily received and conspicuously flowing opium-revenues ... the attentive traveler ... is confronted everywhere and with each step by the extravagant wealth of the governmental services. Thanks to the opium British India could establish itself in grand style and in the develop-ment of this means to wealth it could itself perceive as a state, which not only consumes money, but is able to manage [the colony] so that money is produced as well. It leads, however, to carelessness ... Notwithstanding its fabulous profits and heavy taxing ... it is not enough to compensate the expenses, so that the British-Indian deficit increases per year with three million pound sterling.[1]

---

[1] J. Wiselius (1886), p. 204. To support this opinion, Wiselius reminds not only of the construction of 30 railways at the same time, highly speculative public works, etc., but also the 8-9 month exodus of the entire British administration to a cool mountainous environ-ment or the conspicuous salaries of the highest officials. All made possible by opium.

Wiselius's economic reflection and comparison between the English and Dutch colonial system leads to his conclusion that if the British would lose the opium revenues, 'it should be the financial destruction of the colony'. Reason: opium was a major part of the British budget, while this was not the case in the Dutch East Indies, according to Wiselius. The British knew this: 'But what can we do about it—as has already been asked for years.'[2] The only thing Wiselius wants to criticize about the British opium policy is the hypocrisy of announcing that the continuation with the opium production and trade is 'in the interest of the Indian peasant, to his advantage and happiness'.

Backed by these ambiguous thoughts, the following reflections receive more than a *couleur locale*.

1.

A core problem of the Opium Question seems to be the compensation of the British *state* for a "non-balanced" situation with the Chinese empire or, eventually, the Indian colony. To understand what is at stake here, let's give a not overly simplistic example.

On local shop level it already looks like a quite remarkable problem: if a client wants to buy a Chinese teapot in a shop, he has to pay $ 20 in cash. The normal (and decent) reaction after this transaction is that he or she leaves the shop and goes at home to enjoy the pot. It's a good case of supply and demand. However, the state balance theory and related practice at issue says something very different: After paying for the teapot with the $20, the client tells the shopkeeper: 'Mister, I have a problem: now that I have paid with these dollars, my stock of dollars at home has decreased by twenty, and therefore, I need compensation from you for this loss!' Of course, the shopkeeper is embarrassed ("This is not my problem!"), and after pointing in vain to the fact that the client received a teapot in exchange for $20, the client starts threatening him with hell and the devil. The shopkeeper tries again: 'But I do not ask you for compensation because my stock of teapots has been decreased by one,' but his client insists on getting compensation. The shopkeeper, still polite, after asking which kind of compensation the client proposes: 'You have to buy this white powder from me!' He becomes really upset. Now he can only choose between two serious, bad alternatives: consuming the opium himself and

---

2 Idem, p. 208.

risking becoming an addict or starting to sell this prohibited article and becoming a criminal.[3] While both alternatives lead to a morally and economically based firm denial by the shopkeeper, the next day the client comes back with a gang of thugs and destroys the whole shop. This happens so often that the shopkeeper surrenders and becomes a client of his own client.

This "transaction" was demonstrated by the British colonial state twice in China, and it concerned the triangle relationship between the deliveries of tea, porcelain and silk by the Chinese which were paid through "India" by "London" with the silver coins used at the time, whereupon the English (through India) asked for compensation, and the Chinese had to buy opium from the British Empire ... for silver.

2.

I have demonstrated how closely "a criminal State and illicit Capital" worked together in the colonies under the dictum of 'Free Trade'. It had nothing to do with 'free' or 'trade', but only with a monopoly of violence. Niall Ferguson, as quoted above, should be more critical. Below, the major theme is elucidating this fundamental contradiction between the European capitalist and market-oriented economic development and the oikoidal economic development oriented to state exploitation of Western colonies in Asia.

Indeed, the opium history reveals that in these colonies, Western, strict, narco-military regimes were established, which would have been impossible in the home country. It concerned the cooperation between the English State, its military-imperial arm, imperial bureaucracy and private entrepreneurs in the colonies. The most "spectacular" members were the smugglers, pirates, traders, bankers, gangsters like the Jardines, Mathesons, Dents, Sassoons, etc. with their collaborators in China and India (see further ch. 31). It is a specific cooperation with a history going back to the 16th and 17th-centuries, when pirates did the "dirty work" in European waters for their English, Dutch or French governments.

Now, this cooperation went much further: the pirates are immediately supported and sometimes replaced by the regular army and navy. They

---

[3] A third alternative is also demonstrated in China: throw the stuff away (in the sea), upon which the client is enraged. He cannot get the compensation asked, while the "value" of his product is also denied.

all, including the British government representatives, were dealing violently in only a few products, among which opium often made up the largest share. In addition, they knew perfectly well that they were performing illicit and criminal acts with a product that was undermining the public health and society .

The picture is more complicated: the private entrepreneurs often were or became the English landowners of the poppy fields or their representatives, the English opium factory proprietors or their representatives, the English opium ship builders or the English opium propagandists and church-owners, or the English tax and duty payers and not only the English smugglers.

It is even more complicated: the Jardines or Sassoons became aristocrats; they frequented Queen Victoria's court with all possible pomp and were, therefore, sanctioned by the Queen. She was honored as the Empress of opium-producing colonies. This calls for new investigations in, for instance, the sources of the European monarchical wealth, but also the remarkable fact that the Western narco-military regimes in Asia were of a monarchical nature. Even the republicans at home (Dutch in 17th and 18th centuries, the French at least in the 19th-century) acted as if they were monarchs in the Far East (see for instance ch. 14).

3.

Contradictions between West and East can be found in abundance. Take the Sassoons who became probably the richest family in the world, thanks to their extensive Asian opium empire and including their financial and familial cooperation with the Rothschilds. However, they also gave the growing anti-Semitic movement the "hard" proof that a so-called "World Government of Jews" existed. Nonsensical accusations but the realities behind them had, ultimately, far-reaching and lethal effects for other Jews. They also led to the appropriate renewal of problems like "the guilt of the victims" or much better: ethnic cleansing, taking the relation between the irresponsible behavior of an elite, calling itself Jewish, and the large majority of people who were Jews (or labeled so by others) as a pretext for pogroms.[4]

---

[4] My analysis of the thought of Hannah Arendt (H. Derks, 2004) is, among others, devoted to this problem. For reactions on the opium trade in England see J. Miskel, p. 189-229.

As Dr. Richardson demonstrated in the previous chapter, this "Jewish racism" was immediately connected to the Chinese and Oriental "danger". Apparently, they both triggered a xenophobic and racist movement, but there must have been serious differences between the repression of Jews and that of Chinese. Regarding this relationship between Jews and Chinese, one could suggest that in the East, Jews were among the top opium dealers and Chinese, their main victims.

An influential part of the Chinese elite in Southeast Asia, however, did not act differently from those Jewish dealers (see ch. 25). And in the East Indies, several serious pogroms against the Chinese were organized by both the Dutch colonizers and later the Indonesian authorities. This puzzling constellation did not exist in the West, where too often both Jews and Chinese were the victims. In short: opium played a main role in all these events, and it is worth exploring these relationships in detail in the colonial histories.

4.

Other contradictions between the British opium history in England and its colonies concerned the decision-making political systems.

Under the influence of the French Revolution and Enlightenment in Europe, a separation between the three powers in the state was realized, but—more importantly—a strong separation was achieved between religion and state and between the private economy and public (state) economy, between the civilian-bourgeois and the aristocratic-feudal (aristocracy and church) worlds. What is called the "Industrial Revolution" aggravated all these cleavages in the classical monarchic-aristocratic traditions and countries from 1750, and civilian, bourgeois governments called 'democracies' were established.[5]

But "abroad", through colonialism and imperialism, fully "new" values, norms and customs developed which created the new phenomenon of state-capitalism, which was nothing but a restoration of old practices (aristocratic, absolutist, monarchical, religious) in a new framework. They were important differences, notwithstanding the generally racist attitudes of all colonialists as part of the legitimization of their repression and exploitation: these differences existed between Roman Catholic (Spanish, Portuguese and French) and Protestant (English, Dutch, USA) imperial-

---

[5] See further H. Derks (2008).

ism and colonialism. It should be obvious that these differences became apparent in the opium history as well.

5.

The opium performance of the British lead to exaggerations in the historiography as well. A few examples will suffice. Spence showed how 'profoundly important' opium was between 1830 and 1950

> but they do not prove that without opium there would have been no British Empire, or no state building and anti-Communist victories by the GMD. Both regimes were larger and more enduring than the juice of the poppy that in part sustained them.[6]

Chinese historians and commentators pointed early on to different connections and their consequences. Huang (1935), for instance, wrote:

> Few friends of China ever realized the important role the evil of narcotic drugs played in ruining this great nation .... opium and its allied drugs serving as a check to hold China back from developing into a modern state. In fact, opium has been the source of official corruption, civil strife, famine, banditry, poverty, military tyranny, and other kindred social and economic vices which handicap China's progress ...[7]

Both provocative opinions are worth testing in the following study. To which extent did the British Empire depend on opium? What victory would Chiang Kai-shek have had without opium? And which of the evils listed by Huang were committed by Chinese leaders or regimes? It is certain that Huang's verdict cannot concern China alone. It has to be related to India and Southeast Asia, including the Indonesian archipelago as well.

Until recently, the opium historiography was not more complicated than Spence's or Huang's views. Full attention must be paid to the many contradictions. It is time to incorporate other important elements of the "opium argument", for example, that the West received "a bad cigar from its own Asian box", a tremendous drug problem which is a daily concern of governments in the USA and Europe.

And regarding the earlier periods in this history, one has to consider as well that the current Opium Problem is not simply the historical conse-

---

[6] In the *American Historical Review*, February 2002, p. 171. GMD is an abbreviation for the *Kwomintang* of Chiang Kai-shek.

[7] Quoted from Garfield Huang, Secretary General National Anti-Opium Association of China (21 October 1935) by J. Marshall, p. 19.

quence of Western imperialism in Asia, there is a second source more or less independent of the former. This concerns the lively trade and cultural relations between the Levant and Western European countries from the early modern period onwards.

6.

Arabian and older medical knowledge inspired European pharmacists, apothecaries, doctors, quacks or sorcerers to use opium and opiates in their preparations. Many medical resources, including opium-related products, were traded from the Middle East into Western European ports, from Venice and Marseille to Antwerp, London and Amsterdam. Over several centuries the "doctors" experimented with aristocrats and monarchs, who could not avoid death and pain. Nomadic healers added their experiences about how to cure pains and sorrows to the existing common knowledge among peasants and urban workers. Certainly until the mid-18th-century, the rich enjoyed no longer life expectancy than the poor: '... it was not possible simply to purchase better health'.[8] Then came a European century with regional and temporary differences in this respect.

One assumes that the unhealthy industrialization in England did not improve the health in town and country. Some even talk of a deterioration; some improvements could have been negated by the unhealthy situation. Whatever the case, even at the end of the century, child mortality did not differ in proportion to the family income.

The impact of the *public health movement* must have been limited, although sewer drainage, clean water supplies and a certain professionalization of health officials were not unimportant. This public health 'was supplied "from above " to a public not fully cognizant of its benefits, and even against its will ... the result of paternalistic measures'.[9] Only at the end of the century did improvements appear because this health move-

---

[8] J. de Vries (2008), p. 190. De Vries's fifth chapter, from which the quotation is derived, is full of opinions about the 19th-century English health situation and a search for the 'primary cause' of an improvement at the very end of the century. Whatever the many merits of this book, De Vries has no affinity to the ideological backgrounds of this public health movement or the theory of disease as described by Berridge-Edwards already a quarter of a century earlier. About the consumption of medicines in the household, not a word, let alone one about opium in whatever form. The household-market contradictions (see p. 204 ff.) and their underlying concepts remain too shallow in a book about households. See H. Derks (2008).

[9] J. de Vries (2008), p. 192.

ment 'met with a new positive response "from below" ... a happy conjuncture ..'

Based on the "opium experiences" in the English households, it seems
obvious that after 1860, the learned definitely ousted the experienced, and
a new development started with serious consequences for the Opium
Problem in the West. This concerned something like a permanent struggle between the old "homeopathic" and the new academic medical knowledge.

De Vries still perceives of the household as a production unit. In my
view, this is an anachronism at best, and the opium history demonstrates
it. In the second part of the 19th-century, something new happened in
England. As if they had to colonize a primitive world full of superstition
and magic, the new "medical or health foreigners" in their white uniforms
(apparently inherited from the colonial dress of the masters) acted rigorously: no quarter was given to the home remedies by this new army;
household medicalization had to be replaced by external production
units and professional people in the pharmaceutical, chemical and medical realms.

Their professional knowledge became a monopolized one. Their kind
of knowledge became isolated, specialized and one-sided, without comprehensive relations with other external social or economic relations and
realities. Their products were intended for a market which had first to be
created: the households had to be stripped of any "production-unit" abilities and transformed into "consumption units" first. Next phase: they had
to become consumption units oriented only to specific products and to
swallow more of these new products every time, stimulated by the new
distribution channels from the same professionals.

The consequences were far-reaching. I only point to the fact that the
English consumption of that bad, immoral, sinful, unhealthy product of
opium (in whatever form) doubled and tripled under the new market
conditions in England. Not enough: brand new products like heroin, morphine, chlorodyne, chloral, cocaine, codeine arose ... all successful products from the same sources. All these new products needed consumers;
especially major consumers called "addicts". Household opium products
and recipes had to vanish or were criminalized; only monopoly market
opium was available. Still, the household traditions remained alive in corners of society where they gradually became "utopianized".

This transformation from household medicalization (and its typical
infrastructure and internal European opium trade) to industrialization of

new chemical products (and its new infrastructure) seems to be a major precondition for a worldwide transformation also in the opium trade, business and production.

In the same period, but concerning the other side of the globe, a British *Royal Commission* (1890s) had *not yet* complained that the British 'had fixed a terrible evil upon the Chinese people by the pressure put upon that society to accept the import of Indian opium'.[10] In fact, this commission was one of the most effective supporters of the use of opium ... in the East, which was a last demonstration of an invented Western tradition from the beginning of colonialism. This commission also showed what the medical profession brought to the fore in a most urgent social question. Indeed, at the end of the 19th-century, the new high priests over life and death had occupied the subject and its discourse without much knowledge or experience about it or only with one-sided technical methods..

Around 1900, a new "opium-wave" was organized in the reverse direction within the British Empire: from the East to the West. The traditional dealers in the Far Eastern opium markets were awake and had discovered new opportunities in 'homeland' markets. Their products started to appear as well on the domestic market: the War On Drugs could begin.

It should be a matter of major concern to investigate the role of the pharmaceutical and medical industries and professions in this war. In my view, they occupied a pivotal position in the transformation of an Asian Opium Complex organized by "the West" into a Western Opium Complex organized by "the East".

7.

The tables give an estimate of the opium profits of the British Empire. Is it possible to compare them with the revenues of other products? In this

---

[10] This *Royal Commission on Opium* ultimately produced seven volumes and 2500 closely printed pages, examined 723 witnesses and held 70 days of public hearings in India, because it had to investigate the role of the British colonial government of India in the production and highly lucrative trade. The front of "anti-opiumists" (a majority of Christian Protestant missionaries) was well represented with many witnesses, but in the end the Commission struck a balance and compromised, a fact which meant that the government won the battle. In hindsight, however, it was the beginning of the end of this rather shocking chapter in the imperialist history. In the official Oxford history of the British Empire, it is still a subject which has to be treated in passing. That was not the case in the past as one of the interesting sources for opium proves, George Watt's *Dictionary of economic products of India*, vol. VI-1, p. 17-105 (ca. 1893).

case, there is a difficulty. However spectacular these British profits were, their calculation was for several reasons greatly underestimated. First, the data used concern only the profits received through the exploitation of the British-Indian colony and its trade relations with China. In addition, it is necessary to include the opium profits of some other colonies and their trade relations, like Hong Kong, Burma or Singapore, which gathered immense capital through opium tax farming, etc. Next, one has to consider that these revenues only concern colonial government profits and not the immense profits of private smugglers, bankers or shipping companies.

Still, this does not produce a realistic answer to a highly relevant question like: how much has the West gained by exploiting the East through opium? This British story was copied by Dutch or French, Portuguese or American opium exploitation. In particular, the Dutch opium history is reconstructed below in some detail, so that by the end of this book we can come to a more realistic assessment. Future researchers have to ponder another problem closely connected with this one: should compensation be given to "The East" for their opium exploitation? If the main victims of crimes could be named, they can ask for some form of financial satisfaction. Couldn't they?

8.

Finally, everywhere in Asia and elsewhere in the Third World, "indigenous" voices of protest were heard. One cannot forget the experiences of the victims of Western exploitation. Now that China, India and Brazil are becoming the leading nations economically, they also want to rewrite their histories, and this time not in an Eurocentric or American way. This will unavoidably lead to many very unpleasant histories surfacing about the colonial and imperialistic frameworks, to which also this opium history belongs. A recent study by Madhusree Mukerjee is, for instance, a relevant example from the Indian context.[11]

It discloses how the classic British imperialist, Winston Churchill, while an inspiring war-leader for the British home front, was actually a menace for the whole British Empire. His role in the ridiculous partition plans in Palestine or India served only British interests, while burdening

---

[11] M. Mukerjee, *Churchill's Secret War. The British Empire and the Ravaging of India during World War II* (New York: Basic Books, 2010). which I know only from a book review of D. Rothermund in *H-Soz-u-Kult,* 16-9-2010.

those countries with a very bloody future. Furthermore, he sent two million Indian men into battle to defend their foreign master's interests. Next, Churchill deliberately did not provide any relief or help during the terrible famine in Bengal for mainly racist reasons. In 1943, two to three million people fell victim to this calamity, which could have been avoided.[12]

This history was "forgotten", a fate which could easily happen to the opium history of the Dutch, which will now be described in more detail than the British one. The Dutch role in the opium trade and related businesses is known to some Dutch experts or amateur historians, but not to foreign scholars and a broader public, including a Dutch one. That is a pity, because the Dutch role is historically of much greater importance than the British one, although the latter earned the largest profits from it.

---

[12] In India itself the situation was aggravated by mismanagement of the British colonial government and the speculation of Indian traders, as Amartya Sen already disclosed. Churchill, however, kept his substantial grain reserves for his own use, among others to support the British position in southern Europe at the end of World War II. See also D. Kumar, M. Desai (ed.), vol. 2, p. 530 ff.; I. C. Dear, M. Foot (ed.), p. 438 ff. about the Indian army and p. 891 about the major imperial crisis in India during the war. See Idem, p. 183-188, for a flattering article about 'Churchill as war leader' written by John Gooch.

PART THREE
THE DUTCH ASSAULT

CHAPTER 10

PORTUGUESE LESSONS

From the main competitor of the British colonial state comes the accusa-tion (1906): the opium problem exists

> in particular thanks to the English [who] increased the opium misuse in China tremendously: at the moment this consists of nearly twenty million kilo every year, from which 3/4 is produced in China itself; in all other countries together only one to two million kilo is used as a luxury.[1]

A chutzpah: besides giving the wrong numbers, this competitor was the Dutch colonial government. At that time it was one of the largest distribu-tors of opium and the largest producer of cocaine in the world! In addi-tion, it will be suggested below that the British learned the job of doping a foreign population from the Dutch.

In 1676, for instance, before the EIC, the Dutch East Indies Company (VOC) obtained one of its trade monopolies for raw opium, and appar-ently it was allowed to be the first imperialist to grow poppies.[2] That is only one item in a chain of events and decisions which I want to unravel in this third part. It concerns nothing less than the story of how the Opium Question came into the world as an Original Western Sin and not a Chinese, Indochinese or East Indies one, in short, not as the currently pre-vailing, widespread image.

As the English must have learned much from the Dutch, so the latter were zealous pupils of the Portuguese, eager to copy from them how to live, trade and be cruel in the East as an intruder. The southwestern coasts of India, called Malabar in the 17th-century, now known as Kerala, must have been the area in which their main confrontation took place.[3] At that

---

[1] The Dutch *Encyclopaedie*, vol. III, p. 103.

[2] In their long article in the *Encyclopaedie*, vol.III, p. 102-111 (ca. 1906) and another long article in its 1934 edition, p. 1249-1263 on the Dutch opium performance, the authors were inspired by George Watt's *Dictionary*. They sketch the Dutch history of opium in specific details, comment on the *Royal Commission* report, mention carefully the opinions of sup-porters and attackers (regret the activities of the latter), document extensively the produc-tion, chemical substance, trade, consumption and profits. See for the following also T. Addens; M. de Kort; E. van Luijk/ J. van Ours; J. van Ours; E. Vanvugt.

[3] For the following I largely used the documents and comments gathered in one of the many volumes of the *Rijks Geschiedkundige Publicatiës* (RGP), no. 43 also for the history of

time the Dutch had already established a bridgehead in Ceylon: in 1656 Colombo was captured from the Portuguese after a siege of seven months. Thus, after 150 years in a city they largely built themselves, there came an end to the Portuguese hegemony on the island. Colombo now became the Dutch base for many new operations against the Portuguese empire, the *Estado da Índia*.[4]

In fact, a small part of it was the Malabar coast, attractive not only for its famous pepper but for many other reasons. A description from 1661 details the beauty of its beaches and its cities like Calicut or Cochin. At the same time Wouter Schouten described the surroundings of Quilon as

> the coast with beautiful forests of high fruit-bearing coconut palms. Near the city we saw water on both sides surrounded by handsome green lands. In short, this land of Malabar was beautiful similar to the Earthly Paradise ... And then he saw further on the inimical Malabarians in a village behind a palisade with canons ready to attack us..![5]

Later, in more peaceful times, an 18th-century traveler reminds himself of a Portuguese saying: 'China is a country to earn money, Cochin a place to spend it.'[6]

These interesting qualities of the region could be an additional reason why the lethal competition between the Portuguese and the Dutch lasted for decades before a decision was reached. For the future of the opium trade in East Asia, that "moment" was of the utmost importance.

Notwithstanding their basic unfriendly relationship, there was also some mutual influencing and communication. It is therefore worthwhile to describe the situation along the Malabar coast as a decor for the "clash of civilizations".[7] For both parties the homeland-colony relation was

---

the VOC a main source. Below I call this volume "Kerala". For the meanings of *Malabar* see the interesting lemma 'Malabar' in *Hobson-Jobson*, p. 539-544.

[4] I have to refrain from discussing the important role the Portuguese military, merchants and missionaries played from 1500 onwards in West and East Africa, the Middle East, the Indian Ocean, etc. I only mention here the excellent overview of S. Subrahmanyam (1993) and volumes IV and V of the *General History of Africa*: the contributions of J. Devisse in: D. Niane (ed.), p. 635-673 and of A. Salim in B. Ogot (ed.), p. 750-776. The many volumes on the website of A. van Wickeren are also interesting. More recently, there is the interesting volume by E. van Veen, L. Blussé (ed.) with contributions by Om Prakash (p. 131 -142), George Souza (p. 342-370) and others. Highly informative are the relevant reports of the contemporary travelers (more than the administrative or merchants' reports of the VOC) like the 17th-century bestsellers of J. H. van Linschoten (1595) or of the Dutch medical doctor W. Schouten (1676).

[5] W. Schouten, p. 192.

[6] Kerala, p. xxii.

[7] For general information about this relationship, see the informative website www.colonialvoyage.com organized by A. van Wickeren.

important, not only in a political or military respect but certainly also in cultural terms.

Above I have shown how important the "health complex" was in the English opium situation. Is something similar to be found centuries earlier as a demonstration of this homeland-colony relationship? This will contribute to a better understanding of who were these first Western conquerors and colonizers of India.

Portuguese Elite versus Portuguese Folk[8]

As shown in the English example, the proliferation of opium in society depends on the relationships between the participants in the «health business». Century-long struggles were waged between the medical doctors, apothecaries and pharmacists on the one side, and the folk-healers, who were dominant for a very long time, on the other. The latter could remain active because there was an overwhelming support for them not only among the so-called common folk, but also among the elite: the belief in many kinds of (semi-)magical practices, in particular in matters of life and death, pain and sorrow, was widespread.[9] Portugal was no exception to this rule.

The English example (ch. 8) talks about a revolutionary development in this elite-folk relationship. Around 1850 for many reasons, the "professionals" definitely won the struggle in that country. This was not only a matter of market power leading to a monopoly position with its monopoly prices, but also of the state's definition of power and of intervention.[10] For instance: some definition of disease or health used by the health authorities had serious consequences for which kind of medicine was prescribed and used or not. Consequently, also scholars unaware of the one interest or the other later legitimated the one position or the other.

---

[8] The following is largely based on T. Walker's work about the contradictions between the folk-healers and the academic doctors, which perfectly fits with the Berridge-Edwards study.

[9] Interesting are the articles of Thomas Hauschild, Wolfgang Schneider and Irmgard Müller in the remarkable 1,600 pages work of G. Völger, K. von Weck (ed.), vol. 2, p. 618-650.

[10] To understand this whole complexity, one could read G. Göckenjan's chapter on 'Medical police', p. 94-109 in which police as 'Polizei' had a much broader range of action as a London bobby. His book is a goldmine for the study of the new bourgeois "health-machine" developed mainly in countries like Germany and France in the last part of the 18th and 19th centuries.

Today, this is still reproduced in the regular clashes between the academic professionals in their white uniforms and the homeopathic healers in jeans. The heated debates mostly involve black-white dichotomies. Only wise or tolerant people know, for instance: 'Postulating a sharp division between popular and elite medicines ... fails to capture the medical reality of early modern Europe. Both the lay and the learned worlds shared medical practices and concepts ...'[11]

I think, however, that the negation of those sharp divisions is largely wishful thinking and also a very recent phenomenon in which "chemical doctors" and "plant doctors" have started to cooperate. This happened under the influence of the Chinese health infrastructure in which acupuncture, a wide use of medicinal plants and traditional healing methods go hand-in-hand with modern technology, chemical medicines and the like (see ch. 31).

In early modern Europe all health products, the good and the bad, were still natural products (vegetable, animal and mineral); they were all found in nature. They could not be produced by some technological processing. Those in the profession of medical doctor or healer could not handle those products in any other way than keeping them as they were, crushing or heating them. The usual medicine was a mixture of many of these natural ingredients, probably supposing that if one did not work, the others would. The swallowing of pure, single ingredients must have been an exception. What the Arab handbooks prescribed from the 10th-century onwards was soon common practice mixed up with some local variants of plants, minerals or animals.

In the European Renaissance under the influence of humanism or Venetian trade skills, the first improvements occurred. Still, the differences between academic medical doctors and other healers were not so much related to the medicines prescribed and the related experiential knowledge, but to the class of the patients and of healers/doctors, their positive relationship to the religious and worldly authorities, their work environment (universities) and some specific activities including the related knowledge. One example of the latter: anatomical experiments could never be done by folk healers. Because it concerned an expert activity, these experiments were immediately criticized by other learned people in the harshest terms. Not only the 'disgusting preoccupation of physicians with excrements' and other similar vices were discussed or

---

[11] For this problematic see M. Lindemann, p. 11-17. See also G. Göckenjan, p. 267-305.

their avarice (a common medieval complaint), but the new practices of anatomical experiments as

> a form of public execution in which at one time they used to cut up condemned criminals, still alive and breathing, with savage tortures. Today, on account of reverence for the Christian religion ... the man is first killed.[12]

This was written at the beginning of the sixteenth-century. Learned writers about medicines in this period explained that some medicines worked not just through their combination of elementary qualities 'but through a special occult power inherent in their whole substance or species'.[13] This kind of discourse was essentially common to medicine, natural philosophy, astrology and magic. It concerned the standard discourse among the erudite humanist elite of late Quattrocento Florence.

Cures by non-material means (prayer, incantations) were applied alongside treatments involving internal and external medication. And the stars also had a remarkable influence on human diseases. In addition, the limits of medicine were announced time and again, including the contention that 'the good practitioner can do nothing and the patient dies anyway ...'[14] If detailed prescriptions are given, the symptoms of the patients remain very unclear, so that nobody could check the results.

All this could refer to the specific Portuguese antagonisms at a later stage between the folk-healers and the learned medical doctors. This clash occurred in the first half of the 18th-century. This is, of course, about two centuries after the main clash between the Portuguese and the Dutch along the Malabar coast.

How the Portuguese medical profession dealt with these folk healers was very crude compared to the way the English professionals did much later. The elite perceived those healers as the ones stealing most of their paying patients. However, the Portuguese method to eliminate this competition was of the most rigorous kind. Relations between the Holy Office, the Royal Court and the medical doctors created a constellation in which hundreds of healers were treated like infidels, criminals, sorcerers, heretics; in short as people who could be sentenced or killed under whatever pretext.[15]

---

[12] N. Siraisi, p. 198. See also M. Lindemann, p. 111.
[13] N. Siraisi, p. 227.
[14] Idem, p. 237.
[15] See T. Walker's statistics in the chapters 8 and 9. It is interesting how he could indicate that in a university like Coimbra, the main crime was 'superstition' and in the Inquisition-dominated Evora 'pact with the Devil' (see p. 394).

The subtitle of Walkers' study refers to both 'repression' and 'Enlightenment', for some a *contradictio in terms*. That is not the case, as is demonstrated from around 1715 onwards in Portugal. Indeed, elsewhere in Western Europe the witch hunts were over[16]; these Portuguese trials were very late. But also in Portugal, where folk healers were an accepted phenomenon extending back many centuries, there was a specific constellation needed before the Inquisition trials started.

Here a liberally trained and "foreignized" Inquisitor-General supervised the Holy Office. This institute had the most dangerous definition of power. It was primarily responsible for bringing folk healers to trial after torturing them nearly to death, although before this period it seldom obstructed the healer's work.

This new activity of the Inquisition was directly and indirectly supported from quite different sources: a king, sympathetic to certain enlightenment ideas; expatriate physicians in London, Utrecht and Paris lobbied for it; Portuguese university-trained people, who had infiltrated the ranks of the Inquisition.[17]

In short: it is a similar decision-making elite constellation to the one employed in England 150 years later (see ch. 8). In this perspective Portugal did not lag far behind. The methods used were very crude, but different institutions with different motives cooperated to arrive at the same aim. In Portugal, furthermore, the object of repression was not yet the medicine itself, its production, trade and distribution, but the personal infrastructure of the health industry, including its transformation into a more modern shape.

This Holy Office of the Inquisition, supported by the imperial administration, exercised the policy of sending exiled convicts (*degradados*) to the colonies as a form of forced colonial emigration. Sooner or later, all other Western imperialists did the same. Few of these convicts returned to Portugal due to poor health or the expense of a homeward voyage. A remarkable characteristic of this emigration was the following:

> ... note that no *mágicos* were ever required to leave the Atlantic rim; none were sent east to the *Estado da Índia*. Instead, most were sent to Angola ...[18]

---

[16] In "progressive" Holland, for instance, the last period of the active witch hunts lasted from about 1560-1600. Still thirteen people were weighed to prove whether they were witches in the period 1674-1743 in the town of Oudewater. The suspicion exists that this concerns an ambiguous way of earning money. M. Lindemann, p. 110 writes about the cross-fertilization of religion and Enlightenment in "health" matters.

[17] T. Walker, p. 395.

[18] Idem, p. 303.

Why this is the case is not specified. Generally, the small Portuguese colonies were perpetually in need of "new blood"; soldiers, laborers and European-born women including African slaves. The secular state sent convicts to its conquered lands abroad already from the 15th-century onwards; that the "regular state", the Roman Catholic church, was even more active in this policy was certainly applauded. Magic healers may not have been allowed to go to Asian colonies because much more enlightened people lived in the *Estado da Índia*.[19] Probably one feared that "white magical Portuguese" would undermine the Portuguese idea of superiority in an Arab and Hindu world, much more civilized compared to black Angola: "failed magic" must certainly not be favorable to the authority which is responsible for it!

Anyway, the aggressiveness of the Portuguese elite—enlightened or not—contrasted sharply with the normal, daily behavior of the peoples around the Arabian Sea and Indian Ocean with which they tried to communicate and trade. And, let's not forget, the Arab medical knowledge was miles ahead of the Portuguese, when the latter arrived in the realm around 1500 (see 1.3).

Arab Trade in Peace

Before the Western powers started with their imperialism and colonialism, Middle Eastern powers had lively commercial, cultural and political connections also with the west coastal countries of India with the Arabian Sea in the "middle".[20] Centuries-old trade relations had been developed along the "Arabian coasts" and the many caravan routes. The latter included not only the famous Silk Road, but a whole network from the Middle East (and, therefore, the Mediterranean) into the northern Indian regions and commercial cities like Surat(ta) in the West and along the River Ganges to Bengal in the East. Along these routes opium reached even China, although no quantities are known, and probably only medical professionals or healers were the customers.

In the period 1300-1500 the character of the Asian trade 'was essentially peaceful'. I found a remarkable confirmation of this in the writings of Gijsbert Karel van Hogendorp, the Dutch Minister who played a key role

---

[19] This could be a conclusion from Idem, p. 78.
[20] See for the following the first chapter of A. Das Gupta, p. 1-33; S. Subrahmanyam (1993), p. 74 ff.; M. Roelofsz, p. 1-28; K. Chaudhuri (1978), p. 1-19; T. I. Poonen, p. 1-12.

Ill. 7. The Market of Goa, ca. 1540

Source: J.H. van Linschoten, *Itinerario,* ca. 1595. 'Clear picture of the Goa market with its shops, goods and daily merchants.'

after 1815 in the reconstruction of militant Dutch colonialism and imperialism. His role will be discussed later (ch. 16). In his famous *Contributions to the Political Economy of the State* (Bijdragen) he wrote:

> The trade relations of the Arabs (in India called Moors), whatever their extension through the whole of Asia, appear to be fully peaceful and free of all force of weaponry. The mutual interest and the commercial advantages were the basis of the good relationship between the Arabs and the Princes and People of India ... The Portuguese, however, could get the upper-hand by means of their arms, took possession of the trade notwithstanding the competition of the Arabs.[21]

For two centuries, until the beginning of the fifteenth-century, the Chinese merchants with their large junks had a rather intense relationship with the Malabar coast. The Arab *dhouws* from Egypt or Persia, however, which had always dominated had their basis mostly in Calicut, where they met the Chinese and then departed for the people of Cathay. Merchants from the northwestern trading cities like Surat or Diu participated in these routes to which also the caravan trade was connected.

Apart from classic robberies, trade was peaceful because the different Arabian traders did not compete among each other; to minimize risks they had shares in mutual ventures. Against outsiders they acted as if they exercised some kind of monopoly, although this concept can easily lead to misunderstandings. The Chinese merchants experienced the effects of this as the King of Calicut treated them badly after many decades of peaceful trade, upon which the Chinese took revenge, sacked the city and disappeared from the coast.

Das Gupta explains the Arabian trade morality as follows:

> The inviolability of the trade caravans was generally recognized and plundering of them censured. In the Muslim States that had been the case for a long time before. The unity of the gigantic Caliphate ... had established the freedom of trade and security of the trader so firmly that they continued to exist even after the one large state had been divided into a number of principalities ... As soon as a people participated in international trade it found itself compelled to abide honorably by the unwritten law of the inviolability of the trader because the principle of reciprocity required it and otherwise trade would be broken off. And trade had become a necessity.[22]

This is not quoted here to create some romantic picture of the past; "good old times" almost never existed. It is given because of the tremendous cul-

---

[21] G.K. van Hogendorp, vol. X, p. 3.
[22] A. Das Gupta, p. 7.

ture shock the Western European traders brought. This in all respects: the
Portuguese claim 'to monopolize the spice trade called for a total exclusion of Asian shipping from the Persian Gulf and the Red Sea.'[23] That
meant protracted war against indigenous peoples and powers.

The Portuguese (a century before the Dutch or English and French)
used new kinds of vessels and arms technology. They acted and were soon
treated as invaders only, notwithstanding their different factions (royal
warriors, employees of the *Estado da Índia* with private business, or private traders) with different commercial and shipping interests.

Next, whatever these differences, they all had monopolizing aims,
whereupon trade was automatically transformed from a peaceful into a
military affair. As other Westerners came into the area, they also were
competed against in a lethal way.

In the meantime a permanent religious war was raging in Europe, like
the Eighty Years' War, the Thirty Years' War, and so on. The antagonistic
Christian belief systems were all propagated on the Malabar coast and
elsewhere. But the culture shock was much deeper: Westerners were
highly arrogant, demanding real monopolies with a gun to the head of the
indigenous rulers; they destroyed whole landscapes at will or activated
conflicts between ethnic groups and acted repeatedly in a genocidal way
against indigenous peoples; they did not bring much merchandise from
the West that was useful for the East and became simply new competitors
in the existing inter-Asian trade; they largely perceived indigenous people
as animals or racially "undervalued", obvious prey for fun, hunt and conversion; and so on and so forth.[24]

Many legitimating doctrines were always available in the West. For
this kind of trading practices, there was the code of conduct known as the
Mare Liberum ("From the Liberty of the Sea"; 1609), constructed by the
Dutch lawyer Hugo Grotius. Its rules were acknowledged by all European
powers as a true doctrine. The reason for writing this code was highly
symptomatic: the VOC asked this lawyer to legitimate the capture of a
very large Portuguese ship (the *Santa Catharina*) in the Strait of Malacca
in 1604, which yielded the VOC a profit of 3 million guilders. In fact, the
first draft of Grotius's code was titled *De Iure Praedae*, On the Right of

---

[23] O. Prakash, in: E. van Veen; L. Blussé (ed.), p. 132.
[24] H. van Santen, p. 208, concluded concerning the difference between the VOC and
its Asian competitors: 'The companies seem to have had at their disposal far greater maritime and technological means for enforcing their policies than were available to their
Asian competitors ... Violence was a necessary part of the market strategy of the VOC.'
Below, in ch. 13 we have to elaborate further on the subject "violence".

Piracy![25] A mutual tolerance and cooperation, as the Arabian trading morality prescribed, were not envisaged: the sea is a matter of "free for all" and in practical terms: but for "us" only and "among us", only for the one with the best warriors and guns.

The Portuguese arrived for the first time in India in 1498, more precisely in Calicut, where the ruler was friendly to foreign traders.[26] Just two years later Cabral showed his new military strength by destroying a fleet from several Arabian powers and slaughtered all the people. That was only a testimony of cruelty, not a serious military victory. The Portuguese ships were far better armed and much more manoeuvrable than the Muslim ships, which were mostly small commercial vessels and old galleys.

The petty rulers on the Indian West coast had to accept the new Portuguese repression and occupation. Goa, in the middle of this coastline, became the seat of the Portuguese Viceroy and the headquarters of all operations against the African east coast (Mozambique, Mombasa), the Arabian peninsula and much further to the east up to Macao, the main Portuguese location in China.

The Egyptian Mamaluks and their allies became the fiercest competitors in the Arabian Sea. The Portuguese build a series of fortifications in the Persian Gulf with Hormuz as their main seat. In a time of relative peace, a lively trade developed from this city with the Persians, Turks, and other Arabian peoples and countries. The Portuguese conquered or controlled main centers in this web, after which they tried to get on speaking terms with their former enemies, now backed by their strongholds.

Notwithstanding this, most indigenous peoples and powers remained suspicious and inimical thanks to their periodic, highly cruel behavior.

An important aspect in this trade was that the Portuguese and later the Dutch or English did *not* bring many products needed in the East, but acted mainly as intermediaries between the African, Arabian and Indian countries and buyers of resources for an European market. A network, including its products, was intensified which was already well known to the many African, Arabian, Indian or Chinese merchants. The merchant communities accepted this more or less, because these strong, terrifying Christian intruders could always be bypassed by smuggling and piracy.

---

[25] See a review of the newest edition of *Mare Liberum* (Leiden: Brill, 2009) by F. Jensma in *NRC- Handelsblad* 12-12-2009. Today one relies on this book to legitimate, among others, the catch of whole fish populations in foreign (coastal) waters of weak countries.

[26] For this history see S. Subrahmanyam (1993); the second essay in Idem (2005), p. 17-45 and the excellent website of Arnold van Wickeren www.colonialvoyage.com.

That became the daily practice branded by the European intruders as "illicit", "forbidden" and "asking for serious revenge" and not perceived as legitimate resistance.[27] Notwithstanding this, several famous trade ports could not withstand the new competition and declined.

On the Malabar Coast

This situation existed also on the Malabar coast from the moment Cabral demonstrated the strength of the Portuguese: Calicut or Cannanore declined, while Cochin could adjust to the new situation. In particular, the Zamorin in Calicut—overlord of many Malabar rulers—tried to expel and dislodge the Western enemy. The southern rulers from Cochin, etc. accepted them as a weapon against their own enemy, the Zamorin: the enemy of their enemy became the best friend of the newly arrived traders-warriors.

For nearly a century the Portuguese remained in complete control, which they extended to the Chinese and Japanese coasts as well: in 1514 they arrived off China, while the first English ship came in 1626. The Portuguese onslaught was also responsible for transforming Islamic society in Malabar (Kerala) or, more precisely, for drastically changing the mutual relations of the Islamic and dominant Hindu societies on the coast and further inland regions.[28]

The arrival of the Portuguese was the trigger for the militarization of the Muslim community and a start for its emancipation from Hindu domination as well. From this fighting the Portuguese, and later the Dutch and English, benefited greatly: divide and rule became daily practice, with all the tricks available from extensive European experience. For the Europeans, Hinduism and its variants remained the most foreign religion, as revealed in the many pejorative remarks about Hindu gods, rituals and temples in the European voyage literature. A characterization as

---

[27] A good example of the relation of Portuguese intruder versus "pirates" around the middle of the 16th-century is C. Boxer (1985).

[28] For the following see S. F. Dale, whose frontier concept may be debatable, but who wrote an excellent study about the many effects of the foreign (Portuguese, Dutch and English) assaults on the Malabar societies. See also eyewitness W. Schouten's story (p. 239-249) about the arrival and cruel assault of the Portuguese on the Malabar coast.

Islam, clear cut, individualistic, democratic, simple—Hinduism, abstruse, caring little for the individual, essentially undemocratic and extremely complicated'[29]

is a present-day monotheistic generalization. Islam, represented by the Arab and Muslim merchants, smugglers, pirates and cities like Calicut, was a more direct competitor at sea, however, and an inimical monotheistic religion. Cabral, commander of the second Portuguese fleet, was instructed to remind the Zamorin of Calicut

> that all Christian princes were obliged to fight against Muslims, who should be expelled from Calicut ... [and] that all ships of Meccan Muslims were to be attacked if encountered at sea.[30]

Cabral was, like Vasco Da Gama, highly suspicious and full of misunderstandings about the newly discovered societies and quickly ready to avenge alleged cheating in business. He and his priestly advisers were at first not even aware that there was no Christian society here!

Cabral provoked a round of serious violent exchanges which he ended by seizing five ships from Muslim merchants, murdering or burning their crews alive and then bombarding Calicut. When Da Gama returned in 1502 with a huge fleet armed to the teeth, he burned a pilgrim ship bound for Mecca on the open sea, including all persons who came from Calicut. Then he approached this city to demand that the Zamorin expels the Muslim merchants, the foundation of the Zamorin's wealth and prosperity. The Zamorin refused, whereupon Da Gama seized another ship, decapitated the crew, mutilated the bodies and sent the remains to the Zamorin, while bombarding the city. Message: you had better deal with the Portuguese than with these 'dogs of Mecca'.

---

[29] Quoted in K. de Schweinitz Jr., p. 57.
[30] S. F. Dale, p. 38 ff. also for the following cruel story.

$\rightarrow$

Map 3. East Asia according to Portuguese mapmakers ca. 1550

Source: J. H. van Linschoten, Itinerario, vol. 3 found by J. H. van Linschoten during his stay in Goa and issued anew by him with a Dutch legend: 'Exact design of all the coasts and countries from China, Cochinchina, Cambodia, Siam, Malacca, Arrakan and Pegu including all the neighboring large and small islands. Furthermore are designed all cliffs, reefs, sandbanks, dry places and shallow waters: everything what the old and best maps show which were used by the Portuguese steersmen.'

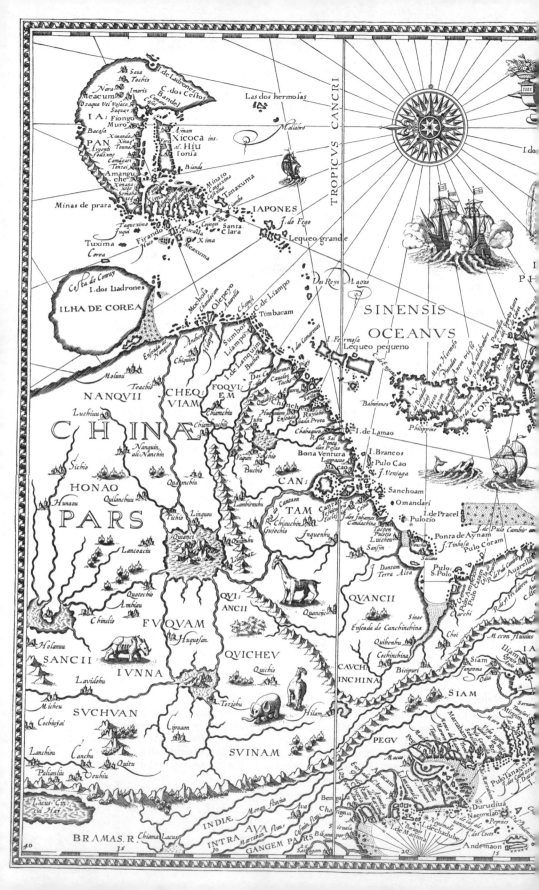

This and other similar events[31] were the start of a systematic attempt to forcibly seize control of the spice trade and initiate the European assault on the East. Before sailing back to Portugal, Da Gama left behind a flotilla guarding their factories and chasing away or attacking "inimical" vessels. It remained there for the rest of the century, which meant a constant state of war.[32] The Muslims countered this blockade by gradually developing a system of naval guerrilla warfare to attack Portuguese ships. The Portuguese retaliation was always carried out in a disproportionate way, so that not only ships were destroyed but also mosques, villages or towns were burned and, if possible, the people killed. The overall militarization of the region resulted in local Islamic societies in which no distinction was made between merchants and "pirates", in fact, resistance fighters against the intruders and Portuguese colonizers. Whatever friendly connections Portugal established against Calicut and trade monopolies, the Zamorin they could not destroy: in 1571 the Portuguese were even kicked off its coasts.

At sea the Portuguese could not stop the Muslim competition from Malabar[33] or from Persia, Egypt or Turkey, while on the land their monopoly did not reach further than the cannons of their many coastal strongholds. Also, several Asian traders of the northwestern coast (from Surat to Hormuz) continued their traditional business with Middle Eastern and East Asian countries. Still, it is clear that the Portuguese had a hegemonic position over nearly the whole west coast of India from 1500 onwards.

---

[31] S. Subrahmanyam (2005), p. 35 ff. mentions another hair-raising event of about 1557 in which the Portuguese destroyed everybody and everything with 8000 victims 'the greater part of them useless [*inútil*] people' for no other reason than the Portuguese lost confidence in some appointment and were tired of waiting. The activities of Simão de Andrade around 1520 in China (e.g. his hunt for young girls of Chinese well-to-do families to sell them as slaves) were shocking. Many times the serious cruelties and devastations on Ceylon are described. See for all these actions C. Boxer (1985), p. 127 ff., 87 ff. (the total devastation and murder of the rich commercial but largely unarmed entrepôt of Broach), the punitive expeditions of Ruy Freyre, etc. See also A. van Wickeren, part 10, ch. 3 and part 12 ch. 3.

[32] S. Subrahmanyam (2005), p. 46 ff.

[33] S. F. Dale, p. 23 ff. about the four communities (two Hindus, two Muslim) who carried out all commercial activities. The Muslim Pardesis, from Persia or Arabia, resided seasonally along the Malabar coast. They were specialized in the very profitable spice trade between Kerala and West Asia, participated in the trade routes from here up to Venice. The second Muslim community, the very influential Mappilas, were also prosperous maritime merchants but bound to the region by intermarriage with the local population. The Portuguese called all these Muslims the 'evil generation [which] continues to increase in Malabar'.

This ended definitively in 1663 at least for the Malabar coast, Ceylon and the Coromandel coast of east India.

The situation became complicated after the arrival of European competitors of the Portuguese. Many times the newcomers were hailed as liberators from the Portuguese plague by people who did not yet realise the menace posed by these northern Europeans.[34] From the beginning of the 17th-century, particularly the Dutch (not yet the English trader-warriors) undermined the Portuguese hegemonic regime bit by bit. Their main base was the Indian archipelago (later Indonesia) from which they expanded their trade relations to China and Japan, but also to the east coast of India (Coromandel, Bengal, etc.) and Ceylon. From the latter island they jumped to the Malabar coast (Kerala), the most southern part of west India.

From the Portuguese the Dutch learned many things. They had had frequent European trade relations with the Portuguese in the 16th-century.[35] In the Asian sphere they first copied the Portuguese organization of the trade by means of combining "passports" (*cartazes*) with monopolies. This concerns exclusive rights of trading with some product or with some country, location or ruler. If someone else wanted to trade at the same location, etc. he needed a *cartaz* of the monopoly holder which could be obtained for a certain compensation.[36] The Dutch added to this procedure the drawing up of a contract in which the trade conditions were fixed. This gave them a "legal" basis for their claims and for reprisals after the inevitable violations of these contracts by "smuggling" practices, etc. Also, the policy of divide and rule using the indigenous potentates was effective after building up a position of strength.

The Dutch next learned that a network of fortifications had to be part and parcel of the monopoly position in the region. And finally, they copied from the Portuguese the habit of combining trade with preaching the Christian belief (Calvinist). A Jesuit missionary explained the situation:

---

[34] That happened also in the Indonesian archipelago as Georg Rumphius, p. 35, 50, 62, 69, etc. could report in 1678. Rumphius *Lant-Beschrijvinge* is a remarkably detailed description of nearly all the settlements in the Moluccas, the spice islands, including their Portuguese history. The most dramatic aspect is the fate of the people of the Banda islands who 'welcomed the Dutch, whom they saw as their saviours from the detested Portuguese': a few years later they were all eliminated by the Dutch driven by their hunger for nutmeg and mace! See J. Villiers, p. 749 and below.

[35] See the contribution of J. Paviot in: E. van Veen; L. Blussé (ed.), p. 24-35.

[36] O. Prakash in: E. Locher-Scholten and P. Rietbergen (ed.), p. 187 ff.

> If there were no merchants searching in the East and West Indies for earthly
> treasures, who could then transport the preachers bringing the celestial
> treasures.[37]

What they did not learn from the Catholic Portuguese was their extensive
cultural accommodation to the local people and cultures: intermarriage
was normal, as was learning each other's languages, customs, clothing,
etc. This always remained a specific characteristic of the paternalistic
Portuguese colonization.[38] The background to this is that their settlers in
Goa, Macao, Mozambique or Brazil tended to separate themselves from
Portugal, whereupon they decided "to go native".

Apart from their excessive greed, the Protestants mostly remained separated from and suspicious-inimical to indigenous neighbors in the colonies; their racial prejudices were quite different from those of the Catholics
(and the Portuguese ones differed from the Spanish). Massacres remained
a more relevant option than racial intermixture.

The Dutch did not copy the Portuguese lessons easily: after excesses
or—at the end of the 19th-century—a so-called "ethical movement" was
propagated to "go native" in order to penetrate the indigenous societies
much better and counteract all forms of nationalism more effectively in
the colonies. Finally, in the 19th and early 20th-century in the Dutch colonies, so-called *Indos* were born as a result of intermarriage between mainly Dutch men and indigenous women. They remained the most staunch
defenders of Dutch interests.

In the 17th-century the Calvinist Wouter Schouten described the differences between the Portuguese and Dutch on the Malabar coast as follows:

> Better than the Dutch they knew how to discipline reluctant people to work
> for them. First thanks to the Portuguese language which could be learned
> rather easily by the Indian people ... Second, there is the Portuguese image-
> worship, which looks so similar to the idolatry of these pagans, as I could
> see with my own eyes. It looks like as if the latter learned many of those
> ridiculous gestures of the Portuguese and vice versa ... Third, the Portuguese
> are able to suppress the Indians quite easily by their flattery and deceitful

---

[37] Kerala, p. xxxvii.

[38] See my article about the Mozambique colonization of the Portuguese in H. Derks
(ed.), p. 63 ff. W. Schouten's description of the Portuguese, p. 247, 248 full of the usual racism. He is, in particular, not a friend of women. Still, there are exceptions: Dutch merchants often married indigenous women in Surat. However, they were of Armenian
descent, foreigners to the inhabitants of Surat, and Christianized. See F. Pelsaert, p. 18 ff.
Highly relevant are M. Meilink-Roelofsz, p. 237 ff. and M. Barend-Van Haeften, chapter 6.

temptations. We have not learned this, so that we have to pay the pearl fishermen much more.[39]

The question is a popular theme in historical research which was, apparently, dominated by a Weberian approach for a long time.[40] This largely concerns a minor problem, however, which is not going to be discussed here.[41] What Schouten describes points to a real difference, but the Dutch lack of ability to deal with foreign societies has been largely sublimated by an enormous cruelty expressed against foreign people in Asia (see ch. 13).

The normal, very Christian-Calvinist-inspired language of people like Schouten already indicates this clearly: indigenous people are not only ridiculed because they worship strange gods ('damned gods'), they are often compared to animals and always treated within the most rigorous friend-enemy framework. Any opposition against a Dutch imperialist assault had to be eliminated (killed) with the help of God, who is a Dutch local War God always urging the elimination of enemies. If one does not succeed directly in this aim—the Dutch can always made mistakes—one has to compromise even with "brown and yellow" people, until one's strength is regained. These thoughts and attitudes would have greatly reduced the Calvinists' willingness and ability to proselytize.

---

[39] W. Schouten, p. 188. Earlier (p. 179, 180) he talks about how at the Coromandel coast (Southeast India) he met Dutch men who were married to Portuguese mestizo women and "even" with Indian women still called 'brown animals', notwithstanding their conversion to Christianity: these "deserters" never intended to go back to "patria". Much later, in the 19th and 20th centuries it was not unusual in the Dutch East Indies for Dutch "whites" to marry indigenous women, from whom the so-called "Indo's" descended.

[40] K. Chaudhuri (1978), p. 145 ff.; S. Subrahmanyam (1993), p. 271 ff.; J. van Leur; J. Goody, passim.

[41] I have devoted many contributions to the Weberian approach. For the latest, see my programmatic article (2008). The much discussed theory of the sociologist J. C. van Leur is uninteresting not because it is very old-fashioned (1955), because it was based on that part of Weber's oeuvre which was already heavily criticized at that time, the Calvinism-Capitalism thesis. It is more important to note that the differences between a Catholic and (Calvinst) Protestant imperialism and colonialism is still relevant if one analyzes them by means of Weber's oikos—market theory. That cannot be done here. For Van Leur see also F. Gaastra, p. 97, 108. For the behavior of Dutch merchants, etc. in Surat (also compared to the non-Calvinist Protestants, the English) see also the Van Linschoten editor H. Terpstra, p. 83 ff. or p. 99 (Baldeus's advices) or the stringent power instructions from the VOC Directors against Surat (p. 100 ff.).

What Did the Dutch Learn about Opium from the Portuguese?

Opium undoubtedly belonged among the many products in the assortment of the Asian and Portuguese merchants long before Dutch or other European ships were seen in the Indian Ocean. Barbosa (1516) states:

> The Chinese are also great navigators ... they go with all their goods to Malacca ... for the return voyage they ship drugs of Cambay, much *afiam*, which we call opium, wormwood, saffron, etc.[42]

The story goes that already during the first phase of the Portuguese assault on the Middle Eastern and West Indian coasts (Aden, Red Sea, Calicut, Diu, etc.), Admiral Albuquerque envisaged a commercial future. In a letter to King Manuel (1-12-1513), he asks him to send a large stock of merchandise. In particular, he proposes to exploit a poppy-growing culture *on the Azores* and to start growing poppies *in Portugal*: thanks to his own devastating attacks on the Middle East, the opium trade to India had come to an end, the price had soared eight-fold, and it was a much beloved article in India. Every year, he wrote, I need a shipload of opium, which is very important.[43]

I doubt whether the Portuguese started to grow poppies at home in order to import opium into the Middle Eastern and Indian realm. To my knowledge the Portuguese trade in opium played only a minor role anyway. Around 1600 it is still so rare that is reported: 'In 1589 and again in 1616, opium occurs in the tariff of duties on imported goods.'[44]

This changed drastically under the influence of the Dutch and English success in the opium trade.[45] Their low profile in the opium business before then is not strange because—notwithstanding Albuquerque's opinion—'the total consumption ... seems to have been quite small until about the middle of the seventeenth-century'.[46] And that was exactly the time the lessons were learned and the Dutch pupils ousted their masters (around 1660; see further next chapter). Until that date the Dutch had traded opium under the same conditions as the Portuguese.

In the Middle East opium was apparently known from the 11th-century. It is, anyway, frequently mentioned in Persian literature and was intro-

---

[42] Quoted by J. Rowntree, p. 7. Barbosa also mentions that the opium coming from Aden commanded a higher price than the Malwa drug from Cambay.

[43] D. Owen, p. 2; A. van Wickeren, part. 6.2. (The Trade with Malabar), p. 2.

[44] J. Rowntree, p. 7.

[45] See among others G. Clarence-Smith, p. 25, 26 and passim.

[46] O. Prakash (1985), p. 145; see also O. Prakash in: E. van Veen; L. Blussé (ed.), p. 136.

duced there from a country west of Iran (Turkey, Egypt?). As in China a century later, in 1621 a Persian ruler, Abbas I, tried to enforce the prohibition of wine drinking and opium consumption. It can be assumed that in the seventeenth-century, it was not consumed only as a medicine.[47] Still, the cultivation, consumption and export remained limited in Persia and elsewhere in the Middle East for the simple reason that the technique of large-scale production became available in Persia from India only in 1850.

Abbas's prohibition of opium consumption came at a time when not only the Dutch and English, but also the Persians challenged the Portuguese might and undermined the *Estado da Índia*. In 1622, for instance, the Persians conquered one Portuguese stronghold after the other with the assistance of six English ships, including the large fortress of (H)Ormuz. But it took another thirty years before the last Portuguese stronghold in the Persian Gulf, Mascate, surrendered to the Persians.

Another opium relationship between the Portuguese and Dutch concerns Jan Huygen van Linschoten, described at length in 1.3. He was a zealous pupil for many years, while serving as the Protestant Archbishop in Goa. He copied "top secret" nautical maps and Duarte Barbosa's treatise about amphioen, amfion, afyūn or related names like *taryāk* (later called *opium*).[48] We may suppose that he also knew the writings of the physician and botanist Garcia de (da) Orta, who lived earlier in Goa, managing a garden with many herbs to study their healing powers. De Orta must have been familiar with the means of treating the many kinds of poppies (including *Papaver somniferum*) as this was common knowledge in the Middle East from about the 11th-century. De Orta (1563) wrote, for instance, that he

---

[47] Regularly, holy men lashed out at those who 'drank '*araq* (an alcoholic spirit), took opium, smoked, played musical instruments, shaved their beards ...' and so on, as was the case, for instance, in Aleppo. See A. Marcus, p. 221. The actual use of alcohol and opium 'remained relatively restricted and almost entirely hidden, due largely to powerful Muslim prohibitions and to limited availability. Smoking tobacco 'mixed with intoxicating drugs ... was widespread and open' (Idem, p. 233).

[48] I thank Dr. Timothy Walker (University of Massachusetts) for his information on the Portuguese performance. In the sixtieth chapter of Linschoten's story, Paludanus refers to a 'Garcius ab Horto' and 'Garciae'. Linschoten lived in Goa about twenty years after the death of Garcia de Orta, but he used De Orta's writings. A large part of Linschoten's chapter thirty on the Portuguese (p. 145-152) is copied by W. Schouten, p. 248 ff. without referring to the source. For the following see also the long and well documented article of S. Shahnavaz. For Garcia de (da) Orta see also J. Villiers, p. 726. See also the contribution of Arie Pos about Van Linschoten's stay in Goa in: E. van Veen; L. Blussé (ed.), p. 89-108. Remarkably enough, Pos posed several interesting questions, but none about the originality of Linschoten, nor about the opium-amphioen problem.

Ill. 8. People from the Malabar Coast, ca. 1600

Source: J.H. Van Linschoten, *Itinerario*: 'The Machometizes of Cananor, the mortal enemies of the Portuguese; Inhabitants of Malabar between Goa and Cochin on the seaside
there where the pepper grows.'

knew a Secretary of Nizamoxa, a native of Coraçon [Khurāsān], who every
day eat three *tollas*, or a weight of 10½ cruzados ... though he was a well-
educated man, and a great scribe and notary, he was always dozing or sleeping; yet if you put him to business, he would speak like a man of letters and
discretion ...[49]

From De Orta also comes the information that opium is mixed by the rich
not only with nutmeg, etc., but even with *ambar*, which is not the well-
known resin *ambre jaune*, but the name for the intestines of the sperm
whale, found floating on the seas in the tropics.[50] Rowntree quotes
Barbosa and some 'Acosta [sic], a Portuguese doctor and naturalist', stating that around 1590 opium was not much heard of outside of medical
recipes. At the same time the reverse is claimed: 'Though condemned by
reason, it is used so extensively that it is the most general and familiar

---

[49] Quoted by the editors in F. S. Manrique, vol. 1, p. 58 note 25.
[50] Idem, p. 59 note 30.

remedy of degraded debauchees.'[51] One may suppose that in those societies the appearance of debauchees was quite exceptional. Until the middle of the 17th-century, indeed, the information is not representative enough and rather contradictory.

Van Linschoten never reports directly about De Orta's studies, but writes extensively about herbs he saw during his *Itinerario* or copied from the Portuguese.[52] For instance, in chapters about the herbs betel and *dutroa* or the *areca* nut, the addictions of Indians and Portuguese are described. It was copied in the seventeenth-century by many writers like the Portuguese priest Fray Sebastien Manrique, who traveled extensively in Bengal, Arakan (more or less East Bangladesh or NW Burma) and China in the 1630s and 1640s. With the approval of the Pope, he published his *Itinerario* about ten years later.

> In Arakan he found 'a plant called Anfion, resembling our hemp ... When it is in flower it is called Posto. From this plant and its fruit a very bitter black extract is obtained, called by them Anfion, which is largely used by Orientals to assist in the gratification of lust and lewdness, by increasing their sexual power ... [then follows the information about the doses and poisonous character well known from Linschoten, De Orta and Barbosa] ... This Anfion mixed with any proportion of oil is a powerful poison ... The rich, moreover, usually mix these drugs [M. points to post, bangue and opium] ... with nutmeg, mace, cloves, Borneo camphor, ambar, and almiscre, all heating substances which act as an incentive towards the attainment of that particular end to which all their barbarous and bestial luxury is addressed ... For, being mere Barbarians and people ignorant of our true and sacred religion, they think only of pleasures of the flesh, believing that the highest pitch of human beatitude lies in them.[53]

During his visits to the Arakan public markets and shops, he is astonished about what is sold there in abundance. Not only all kinds of precious jewelry and stones, but also products from almonds to incense, vermilion to indigo, opium to tobacco, and so on. Among 'drugs' he does not subsume opium, but nutmeg, pepper, cinnamon, mace and cloves.[54] Also on the

---

[51] J. Rowntree, p. 7.

[52] He had many opportunities to plagiarize Portuguese writers. Not only Garcia de Orta, but many Portuguese botanists were active in the same period. Christobal Acosta (1515-1594) studied mimosa, pineapple, tamarind; Filippo Sassati (1540-1588), who was in Goa, came with the acacia; while Barbosa also discovered cardamom on the Malabar coast. They were eager to discover new plants and to merchandize them, like Vasco da Gama himself who discovered the quality and value of the Malabar spices.

[53] F. S. Manrique, vol. 1, p. 58-60. In the extensive notes the editors often refer to Garcia de Orta, Linschoten or some *Hobson -Jobson* article.

[54] Idem, vol. 1, p. 380 ff.

main route to Bengal, he arrived at markets with many kinds of products like 'cotton, cloth, silk, herbs, much opium and poppy-seed, things I have already fully described'.[55] It is noteworthy that he did not report about opium in his reports on China.

Whatever Manrique's opinion about "barbarian lust", his religious enemy, the Calvinist Schouten, gave the following impression of the life and times of the first Portuguese colonizers on the West coasts of India in the same period. Their 'very promiscuous' women are always accompanied in public by their slaves:

> the slaves for bearing their palanquins or parasols, the women slaves for carrying some prayer book [and boxes] with betel, areca nuts and the like. There is no man who may talk to another's husband or daughter without serious trouble, but some women are so tricky ... to play a wonderful theater. They give their husband first the juice of the sleeping herb *dutroa*. When he sleeps sound, she spend a good time with her lover. ... Women ... chew from early in the morning unto late in the evening, at home or in public, betel and *areca* nuts. Many are so addicted to it that they even continue with it in church. They also like very much to take snuff; they always carry with them a small snuff box ... Just like heavy smokers of tobacco they become slaves to their bad customs and dirty lust.[56]

For the effects of *dutroa*, consult the original Linschoten chapter (the 61st) which is written with much more passion and spectacular details: the drug is so effective that her husband can keep his eyes open without seeing how his wife makes love to someone else in his presence, etc. It concerns here a poppy-like herb, which is also deadly if one takes too much of it. Neither Linschoten nor Schouten give comparable details about the use of opium among the Portuguese. This is remarkable with such an attractive environment for it in Goa and other centers.

Recent research apparently shows how the Portuguese bought opium and medicinal plants in Persia from 1550 onwards. Opium was also used 'as a recreational substance or reward for garrison troops'.[57] The main way to disseminate opium and medicinal herbs was through the Portuguese maritime colonial network: officials, commanders and

---

[55] Idem, vol. 2, p. 99, see also p. 118.

[56] W. Schouten, p. 249; in p. 267 he adds that too much of *dutroa* results in 'crying or laughing like mad before death'; is less consumed than 'one is for sixteen hours totally crazy or one sleeps twenty-four hours ...'.

[57] According to a conference report on 'Portugal, the Persian Gulf and Safavid Persia' (September 2007 in Washington) this research is done by Timothy Walker. See www.iran-heritage.org.

missionaries with their organizations were the agents. Indian opium and Indian medicinal remedies were also transferred through these channels.

In the sixteenth-century the Portuguese (like the Asian merchants) brought opium in small quantities from the Middle East as far as NE India, Bengal. It was in the next century that the Dutch arrived in Bengal from Batavia to transport opium further to the Far East, mainly to the East Indian archipelago and also to China. In this way the Far Eastern market was probably opened up initially to Indian opium by Pieter van den Broecke.[58] In July 1614 he was on the Comores writing that Arabs brought textiles here from Gujarat but also 'much anfion'; next month he arrived in Chihiri, two days out of Aden: 'From here comes the best affioen from Arabia Felix, which is exported in large quantities'; in September he reports from Aden that he 'sometimes' bought a lot of 'anfioen'. About Ceylon (1615) he states that the people like 'anfion' as well as many other products like dried fish.[59] About Djibla (1616): 'Here the best anfioen of the whole of Jemen is made ...' as if he is familiar with several qualities of opium. Four years later, he arrives in an Arabian village and reports: 'here the best anfioen of the whole of Arabia is made, which is exported everywhere ...'[60]

During his long stay in Surat, one of the main trading ports in the realm, he must have become very familiar with the Arabic trading business (including opium). One of the very few times he provides concrete figures, he gives the contents of 46 small ships traveling from Goa: no opium is mentioned (1624). The next year 15 vessels from Malabar arrived in Surat with ropes, coconuts, afion 'and other merchandise of little value'.[61]

Therefore, one can safely conclude that opium was not an important product for anybody, although it was regularly sold, a known product, but

---

[58] The most irritating editor of his writings, W. Coolhaas, clearly does not like "Belgians", because he accuses Van den Broecke of excessive careless behavior (in his language as if he had to write as a 20th-century professor or in his bookkeeping in Surat where v.d.B. stayed for eight years, although C. knows nothing about this bookkeeping), of telling stories only in his own advantage, of liking too much wine and women, of vanity, of a lack of authority on the ships he commands, and so on. See introduction to *Broecke,* vol. 1, p. 2 ff.

[59] See respectively *Broecke,* vol. 1. p. 18, 27, 33, 77. Here opium is indicated as *afioen, affioen* or *afion* as a translation of the Arabic *afyūn*; later the Dutch always talked about *amphioen.* Broecke states that the dried fish was named 'bonnitis', which must be the bonito fish, a small kind of tuna fish well-known in the Indian Ocean. After Van den Broecke's rather precise report that this fish was used also as money, Coolhaas thinks it clever to remark that B. is mistaken: it must be kauri-shells (p. 77 note 4).

[60] *Broecke,* respectively p. 99 and 245; see for a similar message, p. 27.

[61] Idem, p. 302 and 304.

not very interesting. This was certainly true for the Dutch. While they already traded along the Malabar coast regularly, the Dutch started to buy opium from Surat in 1640 and earlier.[62] With this step, the VOC also became closely involved in the Arabian and Asiatic trade network. For example, an office in the Persian Gamron (Bandar Abbas) was founded in 1623 where not only silk, wool, spices or cotton fabrics were purchased, but also opium. In Surat, opium arrived from several sources, not just from Malwa.

The VOC—Batavia (Council) placed its first order with

> the Surat factors for a modest amount of 187 pounds of opium. In 1641, the Council received a mere 42½ pounds of Malwa opium from Surat .... It has been estimated that between 1640 and 1652, Batavia received, on an average, only 500 pounds of opium per annum from Surat.[63]

However, Prakash forgot the documents he published earlier about the Dutch relations with Surat.[64] Even in the pre-Van den Broecke period, in 1602, two Dutch factors arrived in Surat, but they were killed by the Portuguese; five years later there were again contacts, which were damaging for the Dutch. Starting a decade later, however, a regular relationship between VOC Batavia and the northwestern coast of India was established.[65] The details are not necessary here.

There were several opium deals between 1620 and the happenings in 1641-1652.[66] The VOC Directors in Amsterdam were informed that opium is also exported from Surat and other places in the region (1620). Two years later (February and March 1622) 1,187 pounds (6 packets) of opium were transported by a Dutch ship, the *Sampson*, from Surat to Batavia (value 1 pound for 1 florin) and 380 pounds by another ship, the *Weesp*. Just a few months later the Governor-General in Batavia himself ordered '200 to 300 catties of good quality opium' of the kind sent by a new ship. Another VOC representative asked in the same month for '300 to 400

---

[62] O. Prakash (1985), Idem. Also for the next chapter this is an impressive and indispensable study. Although he used different archival sources than I did for the next Malabar chapter, his conclusions are not that different from mine. The same can be said from his treatment of the Bengal relation to VOC Batavia (see below chapter 13 and 14).

[63] Idem, note 11.

[64] In O. Prakash (1984) useful documents of the trade in the realm are edited and collected. A new 2007edition could not be consulted. For the early (1620-1650) Dutch profitable trade with Surat and neighboring cities, see H. van Santen. Opium was not yet much traded, but copper, cotton, saltpeter, indigo, etc. were. The Dutch also succeeded in dismantling the large spice trade of Gujarati merchants with the Indonesian archipelago.

[65] Idem, p. 14 ff.

[66] Idem, p. 134, 193, 195, 199, 203

catties of good quality opium' while complaining that the 'lot sent with
the *Sampson* was found to be of very poor quality' (one *catty* weighs 1.25
Dutch pounds).

Again a year later, the VOC Batavia wrote to its representative in
Coromandel (East Indian coast): 'Since a large amount of opium had been
received, no more of it was to be bought until further orders.' Apparently,
opium was also imported in Batavia from the eastern coast, allowing a
comparison of its quality.

Including the information given about the years until 1652, it can be
concluded that the early Dutch opium trade was—like that of the
Portuguese—not impressive at all. Then suddenly a dramatic change
occurred in this trade, which was directly connected to the Dutch take-
over of the Malabar coast. How dramatic this was is discussed in the next
chapter.

When the Dutch started the definite attack on the Portuguese bulwarks in December 1661, our witness is again Wouter Schouten. He
describes at length all the battles in which the Portuguese are assisted by
the so-called *nairos,* a kind of aristocratic warrior, who like the ancient
Spartans do nothing but train in the fighting arts, making armaments and
love to each others wives:

> They do not surrender easily, but remain at their place strong as a post,
> while attacking notwithstanding fire, swords or bullets: by using opium they
> are fully out of their senses. And further on: 'The enemy, frantic by the
> opium, stands like a wall and shoots, hacks and cuts with big knifes every-
> thing and everybody within its reach.[67]

The "opium coast" was conquered, and the consequences of this were so
far-reaching that a detailed analysis of what actually happened is required.
Schouten immediately changes the tone of his information. About the
Zamorin, the overlord of several petty rulers along the Malabar coast, he
reports:

> It seems as if the Zamorin is regularly dazed and his memory lags behind.
> This must be the result of excessive opium use. All the kings of Malabar

---

[67] W. Schouten, p. 194, remarks about opium as one of many merchandises, p. 233, 237
in Surat and Ahmadabad, both cities in Guyarat. Earlier he talked extensively about the
luxury life of the kings and courts of Persia (p. 228 ff.), but without mentioning the use of
opium. For these Hindu warriors, also called "Nayars", see S.F. Dale, p. 16-18 and passim.
They form the basic military force of every Malabar state. Apparently, Barbosa was the first
to report about their existence and function (S. Dale, p. 21 ff., 238, 239 notes 25 and 30, 44).
Dale does not mention opium use.

demonstrate the same behavior, and numerous other people in the whole of the East Indies are addicted.[68]

This is not the East Indies, and we can only conclude that the chiefs and their *nairos* are potential opium users. In addition, Schouten later lists which kind of products are grown in Malabar: between eleven names 'and many more fruits and vegetables', opium is also mentioned without any specific emphasis.[69]

But English merchant-adventurers provided other interesting news from the opium front. Still pupils of the Dutch, they already warned "London" about what was going to happen:

> In their letter dated January 1, 1666, the English factors in Malabar reported to the Court of Directors in London: "the natives of those parts not being able to live without ophium which now they cannot have but from the Dutch ... they have all the pepper which is the growth of those parts in truck for it.[70]

Indeed, there was some specific relation between the Dutch, pepper and opium in Malabar. That was not discovered even by Carl Trocki, who established a pre-English opium trade of the Dutch only in Southeast Asia, where 'the Dutch seem to have been the first to make it a "little" luxury, rather than an exotic medicine' because they changed 'the manner in which opium was consumed.'[71] Alas, such a peaceful attitude was never demonstrated by the Dutch, unless the enemy was too strong, as the following chapters will show.

---

[68] W. Schouten, p. 253, 254.

[69] Idem, p. 267.

[70] Quoted by O. Prakash (1985), p. 170 note 79.

[71] C. Trocki (1999a), p. 34, 35. He made no special study of the case. It is, however, really serious that the most recent Dutch publication, E. Jacobs, missed this whole economic development and thinks that the Dutch started to deal with opium in 1677 on Java only (Idem, p. 128), continuing with statements that the 'VOC shipped the Bengal raw opium only to Batavia' (Idem) and never connected the Malabar (Kerala) coast with the pepper-opium deals. See also Idem, note 249. Further research could reveal whether the Dutch absorbed a few Indian practices, such as blending tobacco with medicinal (and mildly narcotic) herbs.

CHAPTER ELEVEN

PEPPER FOR OPIUM VICE VERSA

From about 1650 until 1663, the Dutch struggled and ultimately succeeded in expelling the Portuguese from the Malabar coast. It was not an easy job. The first Dutch merchants, who had appeared in Surat and on this coast fifty years earlier, were caught by the Portuguese and hanged in Goa. The managers of VOC Malabar did not accept this and initiated the first skirmishes against the Portuguese.[1] It took sixty years before they definitely kicked out their competitor from this region, while the Portugese retained the northern coast with the capital of their empire, Goa.

The Dutch headquarters of the Malabar coast was located in Cochin. The trade carried out by the Dutch was the same as for the Portuguese: export of pepper (64%), rice (10%) and cardamom (6%). Indeed, for all East India Companies, pepper was the product which had the highest priority until the 19th-century, and Malabar pepper was considered the best. It is important to state that from a recent investigation into the Portuguese pepper business in the 16th and 17th centuries, no relationship with opium was discovered.[2]

The Dutch expectations about the profits with this pepper, however, were overly optimistic. Van Goens, the admiral who expelled the Portuguese, wrote to the VOC Directors in Amsterdam, the Seventeen Gentlemen, that four million pounds of pepper were available annually on the Malabar market. He wanted to buy this with goods worth not more than 150,000 Dutch florins. He expected to make at least a 100% profit, and thus a pound of pepper should be purchased for 1½ *stuiver* (five cent piece). Van Goens expected to sell one and a half million pounds of

---

[1] See for the general data about the Malabar period, H. Terpstra, chapter IV symptomatically titled 'The Fighting Corner. The Dutch on the Malabar Coast'; S. Gaastra, p. 52 ff.; S. Subrahmanyam (1993), passim and, of course, the long introduction to Kerala, p. xxii-lxv written by H. K. s'Jacob. It is a pity that the Dutch economic historians, De Vries and Van der Woude, did not understand at all what was going on in these Asian regions. See, for instance, J. de Vries, A. van der Woude, p. 499 ff.

[2] For the Portuguese pepper trade, which was "liberated" in 1570 in the sense that their monopoly was negated and German and Italian business people could join the business, see the article of P. Malekandathil.

pepper in Surat, Ceylon, Persia or Bengal, and the rest could be shipped to Europe. At very least, he needed a pepper monopoly along the Malabar coast.[3] But the situation became much more complicated than testing all these propositions, which was difficult enough.

I could not discover who made the first decision to create a close commercial link between pepper and opium. In hindsight, this decision became the pivotal element in the whole history of opium. In the *Generale Missiven* (GM), the most important VOC documents, I discovered opium (*amphioen*) listed for the first time in the 1641 data. Apparently, it was not worth mentioning earlier, although opium was purchased by the Dutch before that date. In addition, it was also directly connected to pepper in the following way:

> To increase the already attracted capital and to get more pepper we have ordered director Croocq in Surat ... to deliver a quantity of amphioen and similar goods, which are appreciated by the Malabarians ... (12-12-1641)[4]

This, however, seems to be only a way of pleasing political or commercial partners with a present, which we know was the usual method of smoothing deals for the Portuguese. It is very different from what happened ten years later when we read for the first time that

> ships have to bring rice from Bengal to Ceylon, while the yacht *Sperwer* has to bring 480,000 pound powdered sugar to Surat, destined for Persia and 20,000 pound opium to buy pepper in Malabar.[5]

---

[3] Kerala, p. xlvii.

[4] GM, II, p. 145. The meaning of the quotation is not very clear, unless one studies the background extensively, which is not possible or necessary here. For instance: 'the already attracted capital' is my translation of the old-Dutch *aengetogen capitael*, but what opium had to do with this kind of capital is not clear. The attention given in the GM to opium is worth mentioning in all its thirteen voluminous books published so far. The first volume (ed. W. Coolhaas) was published in 1960, the last volume in 2007. I guess that another five volumes will be published. One may hope that one of them covers the many omissions, etc. See *Both*, introduction of P. Rietbergen, p. 12, 13. The first volume covers the years 1610-1638 in which "amphioen (opium)" never appears in the extensive indexes. In the following volumes this is 6 times (1639-1655), 14 (1655-1674), 70 (1675-1685), 77 (1686-1697), 58 times (1698-1713), 63 (1713-1725), 31 (1725-1729), 55 (1729-1737), 56 (1737-1743), 82 (1743-1750), 50 (1750-1755) and in volume thirteen 55 times (1756-1761). This suggests that "amphioen (opium)" is mentioned every time less, but that is not the case, because the volumes cover fewer years every time! In proportion to volume two covering 16 years, the trend should be quite different: 6, 12, 112, 112, 62, 84, 124, 110, 150, 188, 160, and 176 times. This reflects better the attention the product got in these basic VOC writings.

[5] GM, II, p. 447.

Ill. 9. Destruction of three Portuguese galleons at the Malabar coast, September 1639

Source: C. Boxer (1977), p. 23. Portuguese attacked in the Bay of Goa by a Dutch VOC–squadron. Painting by Hendrick van Anthonissen (1653), Rijksmuseum, Amsterdam.

In the same year we hear of another ship which brought 7,000 pound of amphioen from Bengal to Malabar.[6] And more precise, at the time the Dutch controlled the Malabar coast in 1663:

> As elsewhere the VOC tried to pay for this Malabar export as much as possible without money; it was extremely economical with gold and silver money and species. Opium was the main import product and the main means to exchange with pepper.[7]

What did this mean in the daily practice? First, that elsewhere the normal use of opium as a present for the authorities continued or that opium was only one unimportant trade item among many others.[8]

In Malabar, however, the Dutch negotiated with the local rulers (*rajas*) not only an export monopoly (pepper, etc.), but also an import monopoly (*amphioen* = opium). And indeed, most of the *rajas* promised to deliver pepper and prohibited the import of amphioen to all others except the VOC. With Ali Raja, the Muslim merchant ruler of Cannanur, north of Malabar, the VOC had to make special deals. The merchants of Cannanur were the main opium traders with the Middle East, and they mostly imported it via Surat.

---

6 Idem, p. 507.

7 Kerala, p. lvi.

8 See, for instance GM, II, p. 349, 622, 754 or Idem, III, p. 202 (1658), p. 547 (1667), p. 695 (1669), p. 807 (1672) about 'amphioen and other small things', etc.

As early as 1664, the VOC Governor of Ceylon, Hustaert, complained to his commander on the Malabar coast that the costs of the war against the Portuguese were so high that profits from merchandise could not compensate this. In addition, the competition with the "Moors" (the Middle Eastern Muslim traders from Turkey, Egypt, Persia, and north Indian cities like Surat or Cannanur) and the English had not been eliminated. The Malabar rulers were dishonest, notwithstanding the pepper monopoly the Dutch had received in most areas. Now even the import monopoly (opium) was complicated:

> [From the import side] amphioen came by sea and from the land in abundance, so that we did not gain a profit on the main merchandise, but remained ... 30,000 lb unmarketable in the VOC warehouses ... so that we are obliged to think about how all our means can be invested to increase the advantages in the trade.[9]

After making changes in the Dutch management, Hustaert ordered aggressive negotiations with the Muslim merchant-king Adersia now that the VOC had ousted the Portuguese: while it was a new arrangement that he must decrease his imports of amphioen, he should already be aware that any pepper or copper found on his ships would be considered smuggled and confiscated. The Dutch intended to take the same measures against the amphioen delivered by the Zamorin: if he tries to sell it overland to countries like Cochin, etc. 'it shall be declared a good booty'.[10]

The strategic importance of opium is explained through the following section in the instructions of Hustaert (6-3-1664):

> As a good merchant one has to accommodate to different times and circumstances, in which the merchandise becomes cheaper or more costly, like it happened with the amphioen. Two years ago it realized not 100 but 110 lb pepper but now, thanks to the smuggling of a large quantity by sea and over land in several places, it brings not more in than 2½ rixdaalders per lb. This should have been avoided so that such a huge quantity as 30,000 lb not remains unmarketable in the warehouses. Now also 16,000 lb came in from Bengal, we have to sell it against pepper even if the price has to decrease until 60 lb pepper, otherwise the amphioen will wither and be spoiled.[11]

---

[9] Kerala, p. 15. One (Amsterdam) lb is 498 grams.

[10] Idem, p. 19. The Zamorin had refused to give the VOC an opium monopoly, because he asked customs from the Muslim traders of the north (Surat, etc.) who smuggled the opium to/from elsewhere. The VOC now hoped to get an opium monopoly in Surat itself.

[11] Idem, p. 27.

Hustaert's colleague, Godske, wrote a long memorandum to his successor four years later (5-1-1668) in which again the relationship between pepper and opium is stressed. He had quarreled about it with his boss, Admiral Van Goens and had, therefore, to leave his Malabar position for an appointment in Persia. Thanks to this, we can follow a large chapter of the history of the stock of opium in the previous quotation.

Godske complains about the substantial "smuggling" practices over land, but feels they are the result of the price policy of the VOC and, in particular, of Van Goens: They 'have no other origin than the price of amphioen and other merchandise at a fixed and too high level ...'[12] It would take too much space to recount the whole conflict between the gentlemen,[13] but the following substantiation of Godske is illuminating:

> What a serious damage the Company suffered by fixing the price of amphioen at a too high level and by keeping it during four or five years in the warehouse, can be proved as in the previous year in Cochin from a parcel of 10,000 lb 5,000 lb. were cleared with the offices of Calicoijlan and Coijlan: earlier they were willing to pay 90 lb pepper per lb amphioen, while now with pain in Cochin and in both offices only 40 [lb pepper per lb amphioen] could be received. And if this parcel had to remain in stock another year, it was not even worth a stuiver [a five cents piece].[14]

Godske, furthermore, points to another fundamental difficulty of all early imperialist adventures: the Portuguese, Dutch, etc, were quite able to control the coast, sack cities most cruelly to obtain a monopoly position from some ruler, but they could not stop the continuous "smuggling" overland. In addition, the controlling was also a costly affair. In this case, the result was selling even the VOC's 'new perfect Bengal amphioen' for 50 lb of pepper to one lb of opium. Godske proposed:

> no better means is possible [to avoid all the trouble with pepper/amphioen in warehouse and smuggling] to distribute and to make profits both by sea and along the land roads through a proper [and free] marketing ...[15]

He was right, and within a year (November 1669) he got it when it was announced that "smuggling" would be counteracted by lowering the price

---

[12] Idem, p. 52.

[13] Later Van Goens defends himself ambiguously through a letter of two friends to the VOC government (see Idem. p. 78-81) in which they even deny that the opium had to be sold at a fixed price: from the beginning of his appointment, Godske could have lowered the price if necessary (p. 81).

[14] Idem, p. 52.

[15] Idem, p. 53. Literally taken, my translation is probably ambiguous, but Godske's (Old) Dutch is less clear than, for instance, Hustaert's or Van Goens'.

of opium: from 100 lb of pepper per pound of opium, the price decreased to 40 p.p.p.p.o., which is nearly the price of the private "smugglers" (35 p.p.p.p.o.). We assume that the "smuggling" stopped, but free competition was not even considered.[16]

This points to another characteristic of all imperialist and colonialist policies of Western powers: whatever they say about themselves as protagonists of "free trade", they *always* try and succeed to undermine all free marketing of products in a fair competition. They achieve monopolies for areas or whole countries or exclusive rights for dealing in specific products, which means that "free" is used only in the sense of "free for me, but forbidden for you".

Along the Malabar coast (as elsewhere), the antagonism of "free market" versus monopoly with fixed prices popped up time and again. The local Malabar merchants knew how to handle the existence of the monopolies and how to use the passports they received from the VOC. In a very long memorandum with many annotations by other people, a VOC Governor of Ceylon, Van Reede, writes to his officials in Cochin (1681-82) about problems in the city of Kayamkulam, south of Cochin:

> With the amphioen it is nearly the same as with pepper, because they are imported by sea and over land and, thus, difficult to keep to their fixed price. Therefore, one has to follow the market when selling. The merchants of Calicoilan are warned to keep to their contract which was made with them in 1674. However, they insist that they are merchants of the Company and, therefore, have the same rights as those the Company itself received from the rajas: to be allowed to freely trade in all pepper and amphioen, while preventing others from doing the same.[17]

In this way the VOC received a dose of its own medicine. It did not accept this because the consequence was, indeed, a really free market. This was the same as smuggling for the VOC and even worse, the merchants (Baba and Poelicare) had sold amphioen and pepper to the English: 'thanks to this disturbance, the amphioen received a very low market [price]' (Van Reede).

---

[16] GM, III, p. 699.

[17] Kerala, p. 186 -188. Around 1700 there were still many VOC complaints about this city south of Cochin: trade with the English from which it now buys amphioen (Idem, p. 373), while north of Cochin, in Calicut, the seat of the Zamorin, the English have a fixed trading post. Not only they, but all kinds of Muslim merchants from Surat, etc. as well as the French (Idem, p. 366). The Dutch had lost their hegemonic position on the Malabar coast.

Three years later, further information was given about the amphioen stock in Cochin. On the orders of his boss in Ceylon, the main VOC official in town, Huijsman, strongly advised his senior merchant to sell as much amphioen as possible against a lower price. Why? Because

the present contracting parties want to deliver nearly no pepper because they have enough amphioen, which was imported with 20 little Muslim ships from Surat(ta), while also the price of the pepper was increased ... But the main reason and problem was that we, the VOC itself, had about 20,000 lb of bad Bengal amphioen in stock, which shall not improve in quality but grows bad ... [18]

He argues, furthermore, to bring as much bad amphioen on the market so that the price of the smuggled opium collapses.

In 1698 in a memorandum from the VOC official in Cochin, Zwaardecroon, new characteristics of the pepper + amphioen trade are revealed:

The amphioen from Surat(ta) is a product which is rather popular on the Malabar coast, but its quality is not as good as the Bengal one. Still, it can be used as compensation for perishable Bengal amphioen which is to the disadvantage of the VOC. Therefore, it cannot be seen as contraband or confiscated upon orders of the VOC, nor can the Muslim merchants from Surat(ta) be seen as smugglers. However, the Bengal amphioen never received as high prices in our [monopoly] pepper contracts with the [Malabar] rulers as in Batavia and in the east. In addition this, the Bengal amphioen earlier gave rise to fraud and quasi-profits, in particular, when it was used in exchange for pepper, while later this pepper had to bought anyway for cash ... it should be best, therefore, to write off the Bengal amphioen in the future and that the VOC should profit from high market prices [for the Bengal amphioen] elsewhere. ...

It may be known ... that we decided not to sell the last ten chests of [Bengal] amphioen to Cochin.

Apart from all the considerations above, the Malabar coast is flooded by amphioen sold by the pirate William Kidd for next to nothing, while even the English and the Danes ... imported amphioen ... if foreign Europeans do this, we cannot avoid it ... So, it seems the best option to send the ten chests to Batavia ...[19]

Apparently, Zwaardecroon was reacting to complaints by VOC Bengal, which sold opium to VOC Malabar, but did not get its money. The case

---

[18] Idem, p. 206, 207.

[19] Idem, p. 335, 336. Originally the Scottish William "Captain" Kidd (1645-1701) was hired by aristocrats to catch pirates. Thanks to many debts, he became a famous one himself. In the end he was arrested in New York, extradited to London and hanged. Earlier (p. 306) Zwaardecroon reported that Kidd imported more than 100 chests of amphioen.

demonstrates how many difficulties were connected with trade in general and, in particular, with the exchange of pepper against opium. The following table shows how in about half a century of the Malabar pepper trade, the payment consisted of an estimated half a million lbs of opium. It is not only a "proof of the argument", but a good introduction to the following chapter as well.

Table 9. Bengal Opium Exported to the Malabar Coast, 1657-1718 (selected years; in Dutch pounds)[20]

Year	Quantity	Year	Quantity	Year	Quantity
1657	6 238	1669	11 844	1683	8 421
1659	---	1671	N.A.	1688	3 280
1661	6 800	1673	22 713	1690	17 835
1663	16 048	1675	8 555	1692	50 025
1665	N.A.	1677	N.A.	1705	2 900
1667	11 560	1681	22 910	1710	2 610

Total 1657-1666	55 198 + 3 estimates of 4 760 = 69 478
Total 1667-1676	153 753 + 1 estimate of 8 500 = 162 253
Total 1677-1686	57 721 + 7 estimates of 8 400 = 116 521
Total 1687-1696	153 821
Total 1697-1718	6 960 + 1 estimate of 1 450 = 8 410
Total 1657-1718	427 453-510 483

---

[20] Calculated according to O. Prakash (1985), p. 171; see also E. van Veen, L. Blussé (ed.), p. 285 for quite ambiguous data: exports to Malabar are only given in the form of textiles after 1701; p. 288 ff. only exports from Bengal to Europe are given, etc.

CHAPTER TWELVE

THE BENGAL SCENE

> Opium ... The Arab afyūn is sometimes corruptly called
> afîn, of which afîn, "imbecile". is a popular etymology.
> Similarly the Bengalees derive it from afi-heno, "ser-
> pent-home".
>
> Patna ... is the most celebrated place in the world for
> the cultivation of opium. Besides what is carried into
> the inland parts, there are annually 3 or 4000 chests
> exported, each weighing 300 lbs ...
>
> Guillaume Raynal (1777)[1]

The VOC's participation in the Indian trade started with a trading post at
Petapuli (Nizampatnam) in north Coromandel in 1606. K. Chaudhuri
made an interesting general remark about companies like the VOC:

> ... specific examples and the general evidence from the records of the trad-
> ing companies prove conclusively that in the main port towns of India, the
> Red Sea, or China, the organisation of the market in the seventeenth and
> eighteenth centuries followed lines that were to be found in contemporane-
> ous Europe.[2]

An amendment is necessary here: this conclusion does not match the very
violent ingress of the Europeans and the reactions of the indigenous economic and political interests to their repression. That would have been an
exceptional situation in the European trade networks. Until the 17th-cen-
tury the usual reasons for starting a war in Europe were of a religious or
dynastic-political nature. Thereafter, both remain necessary, because
pure trading interests are never favored by war; the *combination* of these
three leads to "monopoly wars", which is nothing but the dynastic motive
to become the sole ruler in a market. The result is still the *elimination* of a
market and, therefore, of the basis of every trade (see further below).

---

[1] Quoted in the *Hobson–Jobson*, p. 641, 642.
[2] K. N. Chaudhuri (1978), p. 145.

This makes Chaudhuri's discussion of Max Weber's thought about types of merchants and the availability of 'capitalistic profit-making enterprises ... [which] ... operate in markets that may be entirely free or subject to substantive regulations'[3] more or less suspect. In their continuous attack the English could be included in the category of these private market-oriented, capitalist merchant-pirates only in the *first phase* of their arrival in the realm. The same is true for the Dutch voyages in the pre-VOC period, the time of the so-called "Voor-Compagnieën" ("Pre-Companies").

The EIC, however, was like a state with an army and monopoly claims. It was first indirectly and later directly supported by the British state (London and the king). This was also the case with the Portuguese, the Spaniards, the French and the VOC, whatever differences there were in the degree of state involvement. "Monopoly" is the catchword in all these state-private ventures, and this remained the main characteristic of Western imperialism and colonialism until far into the 20th-century.

For the historical, economic and other interpretations of the Western collision with "Asia", the following aspect is of overriding importance, about which no misunderstanding should exist: it is much too easy to say that an "open" and "free" Western capitalism conquered the "tradition-bound" or "closed" East.

With the Battle of Plassey in 1757, a new period started in the north and east of India, because it was seen as the start of the British Empire. It was sanctioned more or less by the grant of the *diwani* of Bengal to the EIC, which is the right of rulers and a state to collect taxes. A fundamental British reconstruction of the north and east of India included the opium regime.

The cultivation of poppies remained in the hands of the peasants, but 'the entire crop belonged to the company's government, and private sales were forbidden'.[4] Indian entrepreneurs and merchants who had been active in the opium business did not give it up. They could continue only 'by grace of the enormous bribes they paid to the company servants'.[5] Already in 1786 the English obtained the Benares opium (and saltpeter) monopoly, and the powerful merchant magnates were seriously weakened or eliminated (what happened with the Malwa opium center around Bombay is told in ch. 7).

---

[3] Idem, p. 146.
[4] K. Chatterjee, p. 116.
[5] C. Trocki (1999a), p. 45.

The reverse side of this coin was that English private fortunes were now being made in Bengal, Bihar or Patna. People like George Vansittart, Ewan Law or William Young made handsome profits in the 1770s as the plans for the opium conquest of China were gradually formed. One development went even further. After the Battle of Plassey, the British became the territorial ruler (1772) and now this

> elevation to the status of ruler compelled it to attend to problems that either it had ignored or had fallen outside the scope of its authority prior to 1765. The regulation of taxes and dues, charged upon trade in transit, was one of the first areas to draw the company's attention.[6]

Indeed, this often led to two conflicting interests. The common aim was to exploit the Indians, eventually with the help of Indians (compradors). At the same time, however, the trade interest had to consider the state interest as parasitical: if it could not squeeze enough from the Indians, it had to compensate its costs through the trade interest. This is another definition of the ambiguous position of Warren Hastings (see ch. 6).

The English used their colonial whip to enhance their authority, tease their competitors and increase production. Chatterjee writes about this period:

> The intensified English effort to penetrate the opium business had both a corporate and a private dimension. Through the 1760s, increasingly aggressive British private traders, together with gomastahs employed for the purpose of buying opium for the English company's corporate business, unleashed a regime of tyranny and oppression over the opium growers. Ramchand Pandit's memoir described vividly how the English "gentlemen", as he described them, compelled the opium growers to accept low prices by placing peons over them.[7]

There were, however, also harsh conflicts among the European opium buyers. In the summer of 1767 French *gomastahs* decorated poppy fields around Bihar with flags claiming a right to all the opium produced on those lands. The EIC retaliated by forbidding the peasants to sell opium to the French:

---

[6] K. Chatterjee, p. 129.

[7] Idem, p. 114. Middlemen or agents called *gomastahs* operate between the producers and the great merchants or bankers as the latter's representative; they are mostly engaged at monthly wages. A *peon* is a person with little authority, often assigned to do unskilled or drudgerous tasks; an underling. In this case, it must be someone, who knows how to handle a club or is doing 'police service' (*Hobson-Jobson*).

French *gomastahs* were imprisoned and French *aurungs* were plundered of all opium and other goods stored there. The punitive measures against the French company spilled over into the French textile enterprise and English *gomastahs* destroyed textiles being woven for the French.[8]

Around 1790 after many reorganizations, the revenue administration of the English concerned mainly the land tax, the salt and the opium monopolies, and the customs and excise fees (the *sair*). The opium revenue had been managed ever since 1773 by a contract with Indian merchants, who paid a royalty to the EIC. A few years later the contract was awarded to the highest bidder on a four-years' agreement. The EIC servants had a right of inquiry 'to prevent the oppression of the opium peasants'; the best basis for bribes. The consequences of this rather corrupt constellation for production and trade are sketched in some detail in chapter 6.

There was a specific reason for the harsh regime imposed on poppy growers. No goods other than saltpeter and opium were ever made subject to formal control. Not because both were cultivated exclusively in Bihar, but because both were military strategic goods: the first as a raw material for gunpowder; on the second supported the officials' main governmental and personal profit-making method, while the bullion and tea trade came to depend on opium.[9] For all these reasons the opium history of India in the 19th-century was largely a British government affair.

In the previous chapter, however, it was shown how important the opium trade from Bengal to the Malabar coast was already in the 17th-century when English merchants were not yet very active. In this "Dutch century" the centrality of the Bengal–Bihar (Patna, Benares) scene as the production and trade region is also indicated. We must examine whether and to what extent opium was interesting for other areas than Malabar in this century.

More specifically: is opium also to be seen as one of the major links between Mughal India and the outside world? That world was dominated to a considerable extent by violent Western intruders, with the Dutch becoming much more important than the Portuguese or English and French. The Portuguese appeared on the scene almost at the same time as the Mughals. The dynasty of these important rulers was founded by Babur after entering Delhi in 1526.

---

[8] Idem, p. 115. An *aurung* is 'a place where goods are manufactured, a depôt for such goods.' (Hobson-Jobson).

[9] Idem, p. 155 is not as explicit, but points clearly to this constellation.

The Dutch Connection

The Dutch arrived in Bengal nearly a century later at Hugli on the mouth of the Ganges. They were not yet interested in opium but sought rice, sugar, saltpeter and slaves. In the view of one of the first Governor-Generals, Jan P. Coen, slaves were needed as willing labor in the Dutch colonies in the East Indies. Time and again he urged buying as many slaves as possible. In a letter to Commander Van den Broecke, for instance, he asked (8 May 1622):

> Any number of slaves, particularly young people, could be sent to Batavia. Even if this number was 100,000, the Dutch territories were extensive and productive enough to support them adequately.[10]

In practice, Coen never received such numbers, only about 30-80 slaves from Coromandel or Surat in particular. Soon these requests were not repeated. Indeed, a wide gap existed between what was ordered and what was ultimately delivered, as we will see below for opium also. It proved, however, that the Dutch wanted to be sedentary slave holders in their new East-Indies settlements and not only slave traders.[11] The situation was no different with the establishment of colonies in the West Indies (Surinam, Dutch Antilles).

Regarding the Mughal realm, however, Coen and his successors never intended to establish colonies like the French or English did (except Ceylon[12]), but only to establish trading strongholds in or outside existing settlements. Coen was not very impressed by the profitability of the Bengal region within the framework of his inter-Asian trade network. Later, VOC Batavia judged the cost of the Malabar trade in the period 1663-1702 as too high relative to the profits. This must be taken with a large grain of salt because the Dutch were accustomed to gross profits

---

[10] O. Prakash (1984), p. 203 and passim.

[11] Scholars do not realize the serious differences in theory and practice between the two positions. I discussed them in an analysis of the different positions of the ancient Greeks and Romans: the former were the traders, indifferent to the fate of their "cargo" and the latter the holders, who were establishing their own model society by eradicating an indigenous one by means of a slave labor-force from elsewhere. All Western settlers in history tried to establish societies in the latter way from the Romans to the Portuguese and Spaniards to the Zionists in Palestine. See H. Derks (1986), p. 288 ff.

[12] Its opium history must have been a strange one, because C. Uragoda mentions the Portuguese as masters of Ceylon once, jumps over 150 years of Dutch rule and starts with the English rule from 1815-1915. Before the British introduced opium on the island (see Appendix 1), opium was apparently only used in Ayurvedic medicine.

often exceeding 1,000 percent, at least in their spice trade. But some local VOC officials blamed the building of extensive fortifications and the payment of high salaries instead of attacking the endemic corruption of Dutch officials.[13]

This kind of complaint soon changed in the typical inter-Asian commodity chains. First thanks to the experience that the Indian merchants were at least as clever as the intruders: spices imported by the VOC on the Indian east coast as cheaply as possible in order to create a better trade position for opium were transported overland by the Indian merchants to the west coast. In Surat the strongest competition came from the Indian merchants with their own VOC spices![14] The other side of the trade issue showed that in the 1630s Batavia discovered considerable amounts of inexpensive raw silk in north-east India. It connected this silk trade to Japanese customers, and around 1650 silk was probably the single most important cargo shipped to Japan.

This Japanese trade was highly advantageous for the VOC: Japanese silver was exchanged for Chinese gold in Formosa (Taiwan); this gold could then be invested profitably in textiles on the Coromandel coast. Prakash continues with:

> Due to the importance the Company attached to this trade, its employees were not allowed to engage in it on their individual account. That, however, did not prevent them from doing so on a fairly large scale on a clandestine basis. Indeed, in a high-value, low-bulk item such as opium which was ideal for contraband trade, the volume of the clandestine trade was often as large as that on the Company's own account.[15]

For the first part of the 17th-century, information about the Bengal–VOC relationship is still meager.[16] In that period the level of opium trade of the

---

[13] About this opium corruption see K. Ward, p. 88, 89. Kerala, p. lxxxv gives all the details of the receipts and expenditures over 38 years. If I give the additions (7,211,890 guilders versus 11,502,000), it reveals, indeed, a negative balance of about 4.3 million guilders, which is a very large loss in those times. However, this is only a small part of the story: the huge profits made with pepper in Europe are not considered, and we further know almost nothing of the "value of the costs": in this case opium is bought in north-east India for an unknown price and used as means of exchange. Apart from this, Cochin is largely used as a refreshment station for ships and crews on the long route from Batavia to Amsterdam and that only adds costs!

[14] F. Pelsaert, p. 54, 55.

[15] O. Prakash in: E. Locher-Scholten and P. Rietbergen (ed.), p. 185.

[16] In the Dutch "official" VOC historiography like F. Gaastra (1991) almost nothing is mentioned about this whole constellation. But the more interesting H. Furber, p. 258, 259 mentions several figures on the opium trade between 1613 until the beginning of the 18th-century which are seldom right or presented in a systematic way. Half a sentence refers to

Dutch was also negligible. As shown, this changed in an explosive way after the relative defeat of the Portuguese. But this concerned, first, the quantity in one region.

In the second part of the century, the Dutch exported Bengal opium not only to the Malabar coast, but also to Southeast Asia (Malacca, Manila, Arakan or the East Indies archipelago), Ceylon, Maldive Islands, Gujarat (Surat, Cambay) and the Persian Gulf/Red Sea (Bandar Abbas, Hormuz or Jeddah).[17] Bengal's opium figured in the inter-Asian trade as the VOC's second-best product after raw silk. This leads to a new characteristic of the Dutch opium trade: after 1660 it became not only a mass product for a specific location like the Malabar coast, it was spread over the East in a rather short period. Did it remain a mass product for other areas as well?

The following interesting table shows several aspects, primarily the sharp increase in the quantity of the opium trade for the archipelago. As such, the answer to the question is affirmative.

Next, a certain pattern is found: until 1667 there was a negligible amount of opium traffic apparently everywhere, after which it increased very quickly. In the last ten years 43 times more was officially exported to the archipelago than in the first ten years.

Sinha writes:

> From the beginning the Dutch took the lead in the opium export trade from Hugli, and ... the Dutch succeeded in retaining their lead in this item ... Before Plassey the French and the English together did not export even half the quantity of opium which the Dutch exported.[18]

After the Battle of Plassey, in the period 1765-1775, the English conquered Bihar and Benares, including Patna, the main production area of opium. If we may believe Raynal, as quoted above the chapter, about half a million kilo (ca. 3000 chests x 300 lbs) was exported annually from Bengal around 1770. This is not a bad estimate.

---

some Malabar relationship, etc. Three statements of Furber are certainly true: First, 'there is no evidence for extensive use of opium in the Malay archipelago in the sixteenth-century'. Second: 'Opium was the chief source of corruption in the Dutch company's service in the last half of the seventeenth-century ... private fortunes of hundreds of thousands of guilders were made ... the company had been defrauded of 3,800,000 guilders.' For that time unbelievable amounts of money and at present only comparable with fortunes of billions of guilders. Third: what the Dutch did with opium in Bengal and the East Indies 'laid the foundation for its [EIC's] monopoly of Bihar opium after the conquest of Bengal ... enormous profits for the so-called "opium contractors" among the company servants, who supplied the country traders.'

[17] O. Prakash (1985), p. 28.
[18] Quoted in C.Trocki (1999a), p. 46.

Table 10. Bengal Opium Exported to the East Indies Archipelago, 1659-1718 (selected years; in Dutch pounds)[19]

Year	Quantity Ordered	Quantity Exported
1659	N.A.	1 360
1663	N.A.	–
1667	2 000-3 000	2 346
1671	12 000-15 000	5 600
1675	25 000	26 643
1679	N.A.	28 450
1683	N.A.	33 216
1687	N.A.	43 229
1691	87 000	87 000
1695	58 000	88 305
1699	145 000	69 020
1703	87 000-145 000	120 580
1707	145 000-174 000	39 005
1711	145 000-174 000	116 000
1715	145 000-174 000	159 935
Total 1659-1669: ca. 27 726		
Total 1708-1718: 1 197 845		
TOTAL 1659-1718: 3 614 001		

At that time the Dutch were still the largest opium customer-dealer. They increased this trade in the 18th-century again about 10 times from 1718 onwards. Or: for the whole of the 18th-century, on average 112,000 pounds of raw opium were exported *each year* from Bengal and apparently also imported in Batavia, which comes to the unbelievable amount

---

[19] Quoted from O. Prakash (1985), p. 150-151. The totals are the result of *all* the figures given in the period. D. Duco, p. 41 and 241 note 117, gives different data. J. Richards (1981), p. 61, mentions quite different figures also based on a forthcoming publication (unknown to me) of Prakash: for 'the late 1670s' he mentions an export of '35 Dutch tons' (= 35,000 kilo) a level which is reached twenty years later. For the early years of the 18th-century, 58 tons is given, whereas in 1715 for example about 80 tons are exported. E. Vanvugt (1988), p. 24 ff. has also different and sometimes wrong figures. It is senseless to discuss them here. The trend is everywhere the same, although the most recent (E. Jacobs, p. 128 ff., a Gaastra dissertation) has completely wrong figures. This is unbelievable since she directly referred to the studies of Prakash, Baud and Vanvugt (Idem, p. 400 note 63). In a following note 65, Jacobs refers to an important document, Adriaan van Ommen's memorandum of 1688, suggesting that all authors mentioned above used this highly suspicious document. This remains a wild allegation when it is not mentioned what was wrong with Van Ommen's document.

of 11 million pounds in a century.[20] Compared to this, the English were minor players in the opium trade of this period.

Now, several pressing questions require an answer, if possible.

Mughal Production and Consumption

An obvious question is how opium functioned in the enormous Mughal empire and society? Although there is much support for the thesis of the Dutch "original sin", it would be good to know more about the popularity of opium among the indigenous peoples in the pre-Dutch period. That is not an easy problem, about which I only can make some reasonable guesses.

At the moment scholars do not go beyond the statements of Chatterjee. His excellent study describes how Patna opium drew non-European buyers from all over in the beginning of the 17th-century. He adds: 'The participation of the European companies in this export trade expanded it considerably. But business in ... opium was not a new phenomenon. The additional demand of the European companies merely enlarged its scale.'[21] However, a note is appended to this argument:

> The available sources make it impossible to calculate the extent to which the demand of the European companies enlarged this export trade. But the descriptions of Patna's export market, especially in EFI, volume 1, confirm the view that the presence of the European companies increased the competition among merchants for the purchase of Patna's traditional export commodities.[22]

This is not very helpful. The reference to EFI, William Foster's thirteen-volume document collection, *The English factories in India* (1906-1927), is too British, covers in fact only forty years (ca. 1620-1668) of a period in which the British were still a minor factor in all trade in the realm. There were plans enough to invest in various things, but there is no proof that they did so. Only the Portuguese and Dutch trade is relevant in this framework, and the former were simply not active in the opium trade deserving of this name. The English had no market network at the time in which opium could be sold profitably. And, as shown above, the Dutch really

---

[20] D. Duco, p. 41. Below we have to confront these data with our analysis of the situation in the "Dutch" East Indies.

[21] Idem, p. 27.

[22] Idem, note 70.

started with a relevant opium trade only after 1660. So, we have to walk
on a different path to get to the beginning of an answer about opium production, consumption or trade.

The image of an opium-stricken Mughal India is nurtured in particular
by the much quoted François Bernier (1625-1688). Take, for instance,
David Owen who writes:

> In official circles of Moghul India the poppy and its derivative seem to have
> had their uses. The emperors themselves discovered in the seeds a subtle
> means of dealing with political enemies, "whose heads the monarch is
> deterred by prudential reasons from taking off". An infusion of poppy seeds
> in water, explains Bernier, "is brought to them early in the morning, and
> they are not permitted to eat until it be swallowed. This drink emaciates
> the wretched victims; who lose their strength by slow degrees, become tor-
> pid and at length die.[23]

Fancy stories like this, uncritically publicized by the famous *Report of the
Royal Commission on Opium* (1894-95), functioned largely to portray a
terrible Asian opium past in which honest Westerners played their legal
opium profit game to the benefit of mankind. First, opium *seeds* used in
this way are fully innocent, even if they could be dissolved in water. Owen
did not check the information from the Royal Commission. Bernier did
not wrote about *seeds*, but about the *poust* which

> is nothing but poppy-heads crushed, and allowed to soak for a night in
> water. This is the potion generally given to Princes confined in the fortress
> of Goaleor, whose heads the Monarch is deterred by prudential reasons
> from taking off. A large cup of this beverage is brought to them early in the
> morning ...[etc.]... who lose their strength and intellect by slow degrees,
> become torpid and senseless, and at length die.[24]

Bernier provides this explanation in a story in which a captured prince
was brought before Aurungzeb, who released the handsome man. This
prince proposed to Aurungzeb 'that if it were intended to give him the
poust to drink, he begged he might be immediately put to death'. All this,
however, did not happen this time. The method was apparently known
and feared among the few captured Mughal princes!

Still, it is not very realistic to believe that poppy *heads* do have these
effects.[25] We do not intend to provide a more realistic opium image of
Mughal India here, but the following could form a start.

---

[23] D. Owen, p. 3 ff.
[24] F. Bernier, p. 106, 107.
[25] See, for instance, the long quote in the next chapter of the VOC historian Pieter van

In particular, the Muslim reign of Akbar (1556-1605) was a golden age. A standardized tax system was introduced; there came general prosperity in agriculture and a buoyant trade everywhere. His successors expanded the empire at the cost of the Hindu confederacy of Maratha. It reached its largest extent around 1700 (not the Malabar coast) under the reign of Aurangzeb (1658-1707). European travelers reported about the Mughal court of the latter showed an ostentation without parallel among European courts.[26]

Aurangzeb's orders prohibiting the use and sale of opium may have not been very effective.[27] It proved, however, that there was some opium problem in India. Did it exist only at the extensive Mughal courts? Or did it concern political and economic competitors in trade or production? Is it possible to define this specific Mughal opium problem?

The first aspect is a purely economic one. The Portuguese, Dutch and other foreigners poured in much gold and silver to pay for the local products or as bribes for the many kings. This affected remote inland regions like the Deccan as well as the coast. It is even claimed that the expansion of the Mughal empire depended on this influx of gold and silver. After about 1660 Bengal was a prominent 'silver-consuming region'. Since the Dutch opium trade was pivotal to the foreign presence, it meant that the splendid culture of the Mughals was a product of a narco-military regime. In this case Aurangzeb's opium prohibition was theoretically directed to the very source of his own wealth, which is not very understandable.

But quite a different conclusion could be drawn. Because the opium purchased on a large scale with silver and gold in Bengal was in turn used by the Dutch in a barter exchange for pepper, it is possible that Aurangzeb's prohibition concerned this barter exchange. It also undermined his gold and silver income. This remarkable example of inter-Asian trade, this time between the East (Bengal) and West (Malabar) Indian coast, proved that his power could not be extended to the latter.

Another perspective concerns the internal organization of the Mughal empire. It can be said that the strong centralized administration of the Mughals in the North directed the economy in particular ways. An im-

---

Dam with quite different information about poppy *heads* and that of the VOC physician, Engelbert Kaempfer, about an opium mixture.

[26] See for the luxury of the court, the chapter by Tapan Raychaudhuri in: T. Raychaudhuri, I. Habib (ed.), p. 180 ff.

[27] S. P. Sangar, p. 204. This author discusses opium, post, bhang, dhatūra and tobacco with many quotations from the Mughal period. See also D. Hall, p. 203.

portant factor was that the Mughals had a fairly sophisticated monetary system.[28] Together it formed the backbone of the classical oikoidal society (not the modern), in which the centralized political-military entity is *not yet combined* with economic capitalist monopolies: the powerful Indian opium producers-merchants were private interests, and that is, in fact, even the case with the coin minters.[29]

The modern capitalist concepts and violent practices backed by some Western oikoidal state powers were introduced by the Western invaders. In the 17th-century they could upset but not yet revolutionize the Indian economy and society, as happened from about 1760 onwards. Thus, certainly until this date, people like Aurangzeb were confronted with powerful merchant families in Surat, Agra, Delhi or Benares, Coromandel or Bengal.

Chaudhuri and others gave them a name and described their deeds, including Indians with 'the sinister reputation of Omichund' or Jews, Greeks and Armenians.[30] The latter had already operated for centuries in India and continued troubling the activities of the EIC in the 18th-century. They all had a major stake in the opium trade as did, for instance, the Parsees and Jews in the 19th-century. In short: Aurangzeb's prohibition could have been directed at limiting the economic power of these merchants.

A third view is possible on this remarkable rule which hits at one of the most serious activities of important private interests. Under Aurangzeb's regime the struggle was still raging between the Portuguese and Dutch for supremacy. Since opium was a typically Dutch affair, his prohibition could be a form of taking sides in this struggle. His practices were followed by Muslim scholars active in the Southeast Asian peninsula and archipelago. Hall's description probably illustrates the background of Aurangzeb's prohibition as well:

> The Muslim scholars ... gave impetus to the political expansion of Islam and also strove to promote a sense of unity among the Muslim communities ... in opposing the advance of Portuguese and, later, Dutch power ... it showed

---

[28] K. Chaudhuri (1978), chapter 8 and, in particular, p. 174 ff.

[29] The *oikos* concept is also used by J. van Leur, p. 53-60, but in an ahistorical and uncritical Weberian way. See H. Derks (1986), passim or H. Derks (2008). A more to the point approach can be reached by a "flexibilization" of the classical Marxist positions, starting with Marx's own interpretation of the opium use in India. An interesting article is I. Habib, passim. See for the military side also S. Halperin, p. 136-150.

[30] K. Chaudhuri (1978), p. 146 ff. and the contribution of Sushil Chaudhury about the Armenian merchants in: I. Baghdiantz McCabe et al (ed.), p. 51-73.

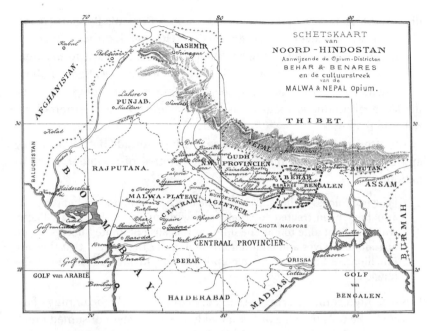

Map 4. Sketch-map of North Hindostan showing the Opium districts Behar and Benares
and the landscapes of the Malwa and Nepal Opium Cultures, ca. 1880

Source: J. Wiselius, 1886, appendix.

itself in punishments for using tobacco and opium similar to those established at the same time by Aurangzeb in Mughal India, in anti-European
propaganda ... in stimulating an interest in Mecca and the pilgrimage, and
in spreading a knowledge of Arabic literary works ...[31]

In this case, however, Aurangzeb gambled wrongly on the losing party.
His own defeat could be seen as a consequence of this choice.

The above considerations concern the production and trade relations
of the opium business in Mughal India.[32] Usually (and erroneously) an
opium problem is only defined as a matter of spreading addiction. What
about this side of the problem?

It is well known that in Mughal India, the consumption of opium
(*afyūn* or *afim*) and many other intoxicants (*bhang, charas, ma'jun, ganja*
or *hashish*) was widespread among the court, as several authors have

---

[31] D. Hall, p. 203.
[32] For a general assessment of the VOC and Mughal India relationship see the article
by O. Prakash in: E. Locher-Scholten and P. Rietbergen (ed.), p. 183-201.

disclosed.[33] A source that uncovers this side is François Pelsaert (1595?-
1630). He was a clever and controversial VOC merchant who lived for
seven years in the center of Mughal India, Agra. In 1627 he wrote an extensive historical treatise and an intelligence report for VOC Batavia about
the previous century of the Mughal society and political developments,
the kinds of products, about coins and measures, or the position of the
rich and poor.[34]

An often repeated remark in these writings sounds both reasonable
and uncritical in the mouth of a representative of a violent Western
nation:

> [The fruitfulness of the land] should be much more abundant but the peas-
> ants have been treated so cruelly and without any mercy. The villages,
> which are not able to pay the full rent (because of limited harvests), are
> abandoned; wives and children are sold under the pretext that they are
> rebellious. ... So lands remain empty and uncultivated, reclaimed by the
> jungle ...[35]

Pelsaert often comments on the subject of opium. At the beginning of his
chronicle, he tells the anecdote that a king 'who always consumed much
opium' fell off the forty steps of a staircase and died in 1556.[36] Another
story reveals how a princely prisoner-addict is personally given his stuff
by the king.[37]

The trade of Agra is described in detail. The exports mentioned are
amphioen (opium), salt or painted cloth.[38] Alas, no quantities are given.
About the present Punjab (Pakistan), he describes how much sugar and
'much amphioen' is grown around the city of Multan, which is transported

---

[33] By a.o. K. Lal; S. Mukherjee; S. Sangar. As I write this, an announcement is circulating of the 21.European Conference on Modern South Asian Studies (26-29.07.2010) in Germany. The abstract of a paper of Nirmal Kumar ('The creation of morals: alcohol and
opium consumption among the Mughal elite') is published as well.

[34] He was controversial because he speculated privately in indigo or in diamonds with
the money of the VOC; sold young female slaves in particular or had a rather dangerous
affair with the wife of an important Mughal official, who died in his house under strange
circumstances, etc. In addition, the adventurer Pelsaert is a clever reporter about the history and society of the Mughals.

[35] F. Pelsaert, p. 295. His description of the sharp antagonism between rich and poor is
also rigorous, p. 308 ff. Although he had to come up with the usual remarks about the non-
Christian pagans (to flatter his own VOC Directors), he is clearly sympathetic to Islam,
while Hinduism remains Greek to him.

[36] Idem, p. 72, 73.

[37] Idem, p. 112.

[38] Idem, p. 254.

to Agra via Lahore[39]; Srinagar is also an opium-consuming city.[40] A general remark about the rich-poor antagonism in Mughal society is that the servants are apparently big opium consumers. After listing their many kinds of labor—a different servant for every task—he writes:

> But they eat constantly much hashish or amphioen, so that they do not feel the continuous labor or fatigue. Therefore, they walk around rather dizzy, so that if somebody asks them something they only answer after being pressed to do so.[41]

It is difficult to understand how somebody can become tired of helping his master onto his horse a few times a day, or ringing a bell if his master has to cross the street, cleaning his master's chair, etc. According to Pelsaert, the reason for the opium consumption is exhaustion: he thinks that a servant walks '25 to 30 coss' every day, where one *coss* equals 5 kilometers! These servants earn 3 to 4 rupees in 40 days. Can they afford opium if they do not have *Papaver somniferum* somehow at their disposal? It is difficult to believe that these servants could be opium addicts. Who then are the opium consumers?

The author writes extensively about the position of the well-to-do women and their wealth 'pressed from the sweat of the poor'. These women must always be prepared to spoil their husbands with all kinds of aphrodisiacs, including opium. Apparently, they themselves constantly drink wine. Pelsaert reports about other representatives of the elite, for instance, that the Rajputs were excellent soldiers 'because the quantity of opium they ate excited them'.[42] This reminds me of the later report of Willem Schouten about the aristocratic *nairos* of the Malabar coast. The Hindu Rajputs or Rajas were also the subject of Bernier's travel report, which has nearly the same information as Schouten. Bernier:

> They might be said to form a species of Gentile nobility ... From an early age they are accustomed to the use of opium, and I have sometimes been astonished to see the large quantity they swallow. On the day of battle they never fail to double the dose, and this drug so animates, or rather inebriates them, that they rush into the thickest of the combat insensible of danger.[43]

---

39 Idem, p. 278.
40 Idem, p. 283, 284.
41 Idem, p. 310.
42 Quoted by S. P. Sangar, p. 203.
43 F. Bernier, p. 39, 40.

Are other soldiers good opium consumers as well, which is not an unimportant question since a Mughal army is quite large? Pelsaert comes up with an extensive calculation of what Akbar left behind as a treasure in gold, silver, books (24,000 'written by great authors'), canons, other weapons (8,575,971) and about two million horses.[44] More recent calculations support this picture more or less. Around 1650 there were 185,000 horsemen, 7,000 cavalrymen and matchlock-bearers, 40,000 artillery men as well as 40,000 infantry. To this should be added about 4.7 million retainers, including 300,000 horsemen in the employ of the *zamīndārs*. Altogether this is close to five million warriors. However, the total of non-military personnel in army service and

> the nobles and the imperial establishment and the families of all the people thus employed ... has been estimated at some 26 million, a remarkably large figure for a population estimated at a mere 100 million ...[45]

The bulk of this 26 million is maintained at a level of bare subsistence, but the five million soldiers mentioned were paid at rates well above that level. If we suppose that the latter are opium clients, is it possible to compare this potential consumption to the production?

It is rather difficult. Bernier goes into extensive detail on the Bengal trade in cotton cloth and silks

> in particular of the Hollanders ... The Dutch have sometimes seven or eight hundred natives employed in their silk factory at Kassem-Bazar ... Bengale is also the principal emporium for salpetre ... Lastly, it is from this fruitful kingdom, that the best lac, opium, wax, civet, long pepper, and various drugs are obtained ...[46]

This must concern information about the early 1660s. It does not suggest that opium is already a booming product in foreign trade (see table above).

---

[44] B. Narain, S. R. Sharma (ed.), p. 33-35. The calculations are not very good: 1,068,248 horses must be 1,962,547; their 7,281 commanders should be 7,312, etc. The same calculations, including the errors, are also in F. Pelsaert, p. 116-121. See for similar calculations Idem, p. 246 ff. about the aristocrats of Agra. In addition, there are numerous wrong numbers in one or the other text. Narain and Sharma reproduce only Pelsaert's chronicle and not the much more interesting *Remonstrantie*, in my view at least, the "intelligence" report for the VOC Directors. But their edition is much more critical than the one of the Dutch editors Kolff and Van Santen.

[45] See the contribution of Tapan Raychaudhuri in: T. Raychaudhuri, I. Habib (ed.), p. 179.

[46] F. Bernier, p. 439, 440.

About twenty years later a more detailed assessment is possible. A VOC account of the year 1688 states that in Bihar the annual output of opium in a normal year is about 8,700 *maunds,* which is about 600,000 Dutch pounds. This account provides the following clue, namely

> that of the total output only about 0.6 percent was consumed within Bihar. Another about 10 to 12 percent was sent to other parts of the Bengal region. The exports to Agra and Allahabad reportedly accounted for yet another 34.5 to 46 percent of the total output. The remaining 41 to 55 percent was exported to other national and international markets. The average amount procured annually by the Dutch Company around this time was approximately 1,000 maunds [68,000 Dutch pounds], accounting for about 11.5 percent of the total output. This, of course, does not take into account the illegal private trade carried on by the Company's servants in this item, which often matched the trade carried on by the Company.[47]

A first conclusion: in this year 1688 the Dutch officially exported to the East Indies 758.82 *maunds* (51,600 pounds) and to Malabar 48.24 *maunds* (3,280 pounds), which is a bit more than 800 *maunds* in total.[48] Therefore, about 200 *maunds* are exported to the other destinations mentioned. Let's suppose that the VOC servants privately traded the same amount, then one can say that the Dutch in this specific year together distributed about 1,600 *maunds,* and about 7,000 *maunds* remained somehow in northern India.

What does this mean? What kind of proportion did this consumption take? A preliminary calculation runs as follows, based on the reasoning that Agra and Allahabad were the most important destinations of the opium export. At that time Agra was a big city of 500,000 inhabitants and Allahabad of ca. 200,000.

Together they consumed, therefore, about 3,500 *maunds* or, on average, 0.01 *maund* per person in a year. This equals about 340 grams or less than 1 gram a day: nobody can become an addict from this! If one should say: opium consumption was only something for the elite at that time (say, about 10% of the population of these cities) a consumption of 3,500 *maunds* results in about 0.05 *maunds* per person per year, or 4.5-5 grams per person per day. There is a good chance of becoming an addict or at least dependent on opium with this daily quantity! Certainly, if it con-

---

[47] O. Prakash (1985), p. 58. On p. 150 for the year 1688-89 Prakash mentions an export of only 51,600 pounds and a quantity ordered of 97,000 pounds. One Bengal *maund* = 68 Dutch pounds = 75 lbs *avoirdupois* = 34.05 kilogram.

[48] O. Prakash (1999), table 6.2 p. 150 and Idem (1985), p. 171

cerns opium of the Patna quality (and not of the Malwa) at the end of the
18th-century, world-famous according to the Frenchman Raynal.

A second calculation focuses on the five million well-paid members of
the Mughal courts and army. If they consumed the 7000 *maunds* of the
remaining Bengal production, the consumption per person per year
should be about 50 gram, an entirely negligible quantity.

There are historians (Sinha) who deny that the cultivation of opium
was encouraged in Mughal India.[49] Probably not by the emperors and the
courts, but certainly by many merchants-producers. The only conclusion
I can draw from the above is that there must have been a reasonable consumption of opium among what could be called the elite. This, however,
did not lead to a substantial addiction problem. In all probability,
Aurangzeb's prohibition must concern not the consumption or even a
moral point of view, but the production and trade relations.

Of course, one knew about the bad effects of excessive opium consumption, resulting in serious personal problems. Several Asian governments warned against opium or prohibited its use, but—for the time
being—we should judge these actions as now analyzed for the Mughal
empire: not from the consumption side.

One thing is clear: in Mughal India there were no negative moral values
associated with aphrodisiacs, including opium. Kumar is right to combine
this moral understanding with the openness about sexuality in the whole
of Mughal society. West Europeans, mainly missionaries, Protestant travelers and British occupiers demonstrated a totally negative Christian perception of sex or lust with, furthermore, not the least understanding of the
common use of numerous herbs. The Portuguese were more flexible in
both respects. Kumar even pointed to the 'criminalization of herbs and
medical preparations' as a consequence of British rule.

Another thing is clear as well: it was the Dutch merchants who pushed
this Bengal opium production, and after the English took over power in
India, they remained the main customer until the British transferred this
trade to the Chinese empire. The target of the Dutch was not India but the
East Indies archipelago. That will be the setting of the next chapters: they
deal with those who brought the real Opium Problem into the world,
which deserve detailed explanations.

---

[49] C.Trocki (1999a), p. 45.

CHAPTER THIRTEEN

THE "VIOLENT OPIUM COMPANY" (VOC) IN THE EAST

> ... a robber-state along the North Sea ... which build
> railways of stolen money and by way of payment dopes
> with opium, gospel and gin those who are robbed..
>
> Multatuli (*Max Havelaar,* 1859)

> It seems as if a royal monopoly is used as a means to
> get an advantage for the state treasury from an abuse,
> which one is unable to resolve.
>
> J.C.Baud (1853).[1]

> 'The Dutch had used the drug in Java and elsewhere
> not simply as an article of commerce—trading it for
> pepper—but as a useful means for breaking the moral
> resistance of Indonesians, who opposed the introduc-
> tion of their semi-servile but immensely profitable
> plantation system.'
>
> Jack Beeching[2]

A "Heart of Darkness" avant la lettre

Joseph Conrad's horror story about Belgian imperialism in Congo (1899; 1902) was published at the same time that Multatuli's famous book found its first readership. Both told the world about what really happened in the colonies: of the Dutch in the East Indies and of their civilized neighbors, the Belgians, in Africa. For the Dutch Guyana ("West Indies") their image as extremely cruel and greedy slave holders was established long ago by the books of the Scottish soldier Stedman (ca. 1790) and others.

The Asian opium history of the Dutch imperialists and colonists start-ed long before these publications were written. Its chain of opium histo-

---

[1] J.C.Baud, p. 194.
[2] J. Beeching, p. 23, 24. In the very British J. Lovell no comparison is made with the Dutch East Indies or whatever other 'opium realm'.

ries documents the "heart of darkness" of world history, the Western assault on a non-Western world. Slaves and opium, the capture of body and mind of non-Westerners in order to establish and expand a Western civilization.

Compared to the magnitude of the Opium Problem in this constellation, the subject is not popular among the general historians of the 20th-century of all political viewpoints. It is largely left to the willing amateur historian, probably to keep the item in the colorful and spectacular world of popular historiography. Notwithstanding their sometimes remarkable achievements, the disadvantage is that it can be neglected and even dismissed by the decision-making elite. Its members expect first and foremost decision legitimating and supporting writings, which are difficult to produce in the opium case. For slavery one can point to the glorious, early 19th-century, British abolition project (Wilberforce), but at the very moment a new wave of fabulous opium profits were pouring out over the Western world. Westerners themselves were still 'strictly against the use of opium by [their] own people'.[3]

In this book the Dutch performance must also constitute the "heart of darkness". It is much less well known than the English one: its history remained in the dark, notwithstanding that it strikes the heart of the Opium Question. The English performance as sketched above can only be perceived as a copy of the Dutch example, which will be discussed below.

General elements, from the bullion game[4] to the accompanying Christian conversion activities, from the colonial organization to the rise of some protests at the end of the 19th-century, will not be repeated or only referred to in passing. Only the basic elements of the opium business will be highlighted: its initiators, aims, scope, profits or corrupting effects on all levels of society and immanent hypocrisy (first importing it, later condemning the indigenous users of the stuff[5]).

---

[3] M. Ricklefs (1993), p. 287 note 3.

[4] For the serious bullion problems the VOC always had, see the documents in GM, II, 754; IV, 442 ff; V, 232, 415, 498; VI 79, 271, 335, 449; VIII, 30, 81; XII, 78; XIII, 54-58, 162 ff. and so on. It is the difficult story of getting gold and silver, exchanging European coins for indigenous ones, re-minting coins, etc. Many millions of Dutch coins were transported from Holland to the East. Many of the ships involved in these transports were lost due to shipwrecks: the sea route must be a cemetery of ships interesting for treasure hunters like Lara Croft, Indiana Jones, etc., but not for us. See K. Glamann, p. 50-73.

[5] Only one example here: Rijklof van Goens, one of the highest and most influential VOC officials around 1660, the admiral who was probably the person most responsible for introducing opium as a mass product along the Malabar coast (see ch. 11), was highly denigrating towards Javanese aristocrats for using opium. See M. Ricklefs (1993), p. 11.

The Dutch Opium Image

An obvious question must be answered at the start: What did the first Dutch conquerors, colonizers and merchants in the East know about the product with which they became notoriously linked in history, opium?

The answer can be found in two sources. Some of these colonizers judged everything as strange, dangerous, good or bad that deviated from their homeland experience. This background knowledge (which can be differentiated at least between elite and common folk information as the Portuguese example shows) had a local or regional European background, it was not necessarily of purely Dutch origin. A large percentage (40-65%) of the largely illiterate, lower-class personnel of the VOC came from abroad, mainly from war-stricken Germany. This rose to 50-80% by the end of the VOC period.[6] The other source of knowledge was based on new experiences as conquerors, traders or colonizers in tropical Asian countries. Let's elaborate for a while, first, on the homeland knowledge about opium, referring to what was already mentioned in ch. 8 and 10.

Laudanum Paracelsi

Before 1800 no relevant health infrastructure existed in England, and there was not much difference between the knowledge of learned doctors and mendicant folk-healers. The majority of families in town and country had to rely on their own inherited knowledge and experience in matters of pain and illness.

However, in relatively developed and rich cities in Western Europe, like the Flemish or Dutch ones, a rather reasonable health infrastructure already existed in the 17th-century, with hospitals, doctors and apothecaries, including an established trade in resources. Local authorities were keen to regulate this still diffuse health market, primarily because they were confronted all too often with serious health hazards. One of the foci of their attention was the medicine distributed or prescribed in town.

One symptomatic example will suffice here. In 1663-64 the Flemish city of Ghent issued the following regulation:

> Article XIV. Because there should be no suspicion of fraud, the [local] apothecaries are not allowed to make [medicines like] the Triakel, Mithridaet ... Laudanum Opiatum ... and the like, unless some of the Doctors College has independently inspected the ingredients needed to compose these

---

[6] F. Gaastra (1991), p. 81.

medicines ... whereupon the Doctor has to give a written testimony to the apothecary in which date of the day and year is given when the ingredient was made and the visitation done ... this on pain of a fine of six guilders for every composite without such a testimony and of confiscation of the composite ...[7]

These three opium products had nearly the same price: per 1 dragma (= 3.9 gram), namely 1 stuyver (= five Dutch cents); the *triakel* was slightly more expensive: seven cents per dragma. The *triakel* (theriaca, treacle, thériaque) was one of the best known.[8] It was imported to Western Europe through Venice, the main mediator between Arab countries and the West. It was apparently invented by one of the internationally famous Arab medical doctors of the 12th and 13th centuries and used as an antidote, wonder-drink and the like, esepcially for kings and popes.

One of these learned men, the Egyptian Aboul Mena ben Abi Nasr ben Haffahd, made the first manual for apothecaries, the fifth chapter of which concerned opiates (ca. 1250). A French translation from 1844 also mentions the *thériaque,* composed of about seventy ingredients, of which honey was the largest one and 'opium choisi' the second.[9] Once the Venetians had distributed the recipe and the product in the second half of the 15th-century, the custom arose of preparing it in public with much pomp, attended by the worldly authorities as well as the "experts". The sales talk about its use in antiquity by Roman emperors made it more expensive and attractive.

As an antidote it was perceived as the ultimate medicine against all diseases, pains and other nasty states. Vanderwiele: ' ... the triakel is a true panacea. It is immediately clear that the healing effects in particular had

---

[7] L. Vandewiele, p. 11, 12.

[8] See P. Boussel, H. Bonnemain, p. 93 ff., 99, 109, 181; M. Lindemann, p. 61, 264; the articles of Wolfgang Schneider and Rudolf Schmitz in G. Völger, K. von Weck (ed.), vol. 2, p. 630-639 and 650-662. Andromachus, a Greek physician to Emperor Nero (AD 54-63) is named as the inventor in Smith's *Classical Dictionary* (not in the *OCD, Lübker* or *Kleine Pauly*). Pharmacists use the Latin, anyway, *theriaca andromachi.* The first publication of his text, a recipe in 174 lines, however, dates from 1607. This makes it rather difficult to expect that authorities in a Flemish city gave detailed instructions concerning some "andromachian" medicine. *Theriaque* is still the name of a US government database about side effects of drugs with 3,300 monographs (see www.ncbi.nlm.nih.gov/pubmed/7855764). Certainly the wonder drink made by Panoramix in a big cauldron, which made Asterix and Obelix invincible, was a good example of a treacle.

[9] See Idem, p. 99. In L. Vandewiele p. 13 all the ingredients are listed as well but without quantities.

Ill. 10. Venice and its Treacle
Source: B. Hodgson, p. 21.

to come from the opium in it.'[10] Even in 1774 there was a public preparation of *theriaca* in Liège.

Of course, nobody knows whether products as spectacular as these resulted in the expected healing. The method of composing something from many components (sometimes the *theriaca* had more than one hundred ingredients) was also a medieval Catholic way of thinking, and pragmatically inspired by the idea that one of them must provide relief. This kind of thinking is still demonstrated in the following illustration and Pozzi's explanation in 1892:

> It was, therefore, not an ill saying, though an old one perhaps, that the government of Venice was rich and consolatory like its treacle, being compounded nicely of all the other forms—a grain of monarchy, a scruple of democracy, a dragma of oligarchy, and an ounce of aristocracy—as the *theriaca* so much esteemed is said to be a composition of the four principal drugs, but never found to be genuine except here, at the original dispensary.[11]

---

[10] L. Vanderwiele, p. 13.
[11] Quoted by B. Hodgson, p. 21 from Hester Piozzi's book, *Glimpses of Italian Society* (1892). For the *theriaca* see also E. Kremers, G. Urdang, p. 56, 438.

Modern times arrived when the components of these composites were 'isolated' and sold as separate products, made by professionals. In a subsequent stage after opium, heroin, morphine or codeine were 'isolated' in the 19th-century.

The next product mentioned in the Ghent regulation, *mithridate* (mithridatum or mithridaticum), was comparable to the first and sometimes even considered *theriaca* itself. It was mostly "defined" as the father of all medicines, the *theriaca* as the mother. Indeed, it was a semi-mythical antidote and poison composed of 64 ingredients. Opium is also an important ingredient, but this time in the form of the thickened juice of poppy heads. Around 1800 in England one could still prescribe this "medicine" and also several other composite preparations.[12]

Laudanum opiatum, finally, is composed of only five ingredients, but here opium is the main one, as the thickened juice of poppy heads. It is normally consumed in pill form; in the 19th and 20th-century it was mostly taken as a tincture. There are many kinds of laudanum. Paracelsus (ca. 1490-1540) is thought to have invented it. The most popular variant is called *Laudanum Sydenhamii* after the English physician Thomas Sydenham (1624-1689), who was a staunch supporter of opium and its treacle form. This was also the case with his well-known contemporary, the Dutch colleague Franciscus Sylvius (1614-1672), and later with the world-famous Herman Boerhaave (1668-1738).[13]

The opium and many other ingredients had to come from the Levant trade with Venice as the intermediary between Turkey or Persia and Western European countries. The position of Venice deteriorated over time, but these trade relations were so strong that in England or Germany certainly the opium for the official health market was imported from Turkey and not from the Far East until about 1930 (see ch. 8).

Another important difference concerned the method of consumption of health products, opium in particular: the majority of the descriptions still considered opium smoking a typical Eastern custom (and, therefore, detestable). Western medicinal consumption of opium involved tinctures, pills and ointments. It concerns one of the many mistakes in the

---

[12] V. Berridge, G. Edwards, p. xxiv.

[13] Idem, p. xxiv for a long quotation of Sydenham. See also B. Hodgson, p. 19, 24. In Germany Johannes Hartmann (1568-1631) experimented with his students in 1615 with numerous opium preparations. In 1674 improvements were reported in one of the first *Opiologia*'s from Georg Wedel. Opium was prescribed for all possible diseases. See Rudolf Schmitz, p. 655. So, what the authorities in the city of Ghent demonstrated was really "modern".

Western perception of the Opium Problem: opium's morphine content, which is the addictive element, is to a specific degree (30%-60%) negated by heat, depending on the smoking method used.

Notwithstanding this, smoking was seen by the representatives of the Western health market as a negative, health-deteriorating activity; only primitive people like sailors smoke, and until recently sailor's tobacco was the strongest kind, whereas civilized city-people smoked with a perfumed and filtered kind of device.

The Sailor's Health

It was the VOC which cared for the health of its sailors much more than the EIC, as they had to go on long voyages to the strange Eastern lands.

Lyſt der Medicamenten tot de Lapdoos.

Empl. Diapalm.
  Defenſiv. Vig. ā̄ ℔ ẞ.
  De Labdano ℔ ẞ.
  Diapomphol.
  Mucagin.
  Diachyl. c. Gum.
  De Ranis c. ☿ io. ā̄ ℥iv
Ung. Alb. Camphor. ℥viij
  Baſilic.
  Digeſt.
  Popul: ā̄ ℥iv
Laud. Opiat. ℨ ẞ
Mel: Roſar. ℔ ẞ
  Commun. ℔j
Syr. Pap. Rhæad. ℥vj
Conſ. Roſar. Rubr. ℥viij
Aq. Cinnamomi p. ẞ
  Roſar. p. j
Sp. Cochlear. ℥vj
  Nitri Dulcis ℥ij
  Vitrioli ℥j
Tinct. Al: & Myrrh. ℥x
Succus Citri ℥x
Balſ. Copayvæ ℥vj
Extr. Cathol. ℥j
Oc. Cancr. ppt: ℥iv
Antim. Diaphor. ℥j
Pulv. Adſtring. ℥iv
Sperm. ceti. ℨẞ
Cantharid. ℨẞ
Tutia ppt: ℨẞ
Sacchar. Alb. ℔j
Succus Liquiritiæ ℔ẞ

Crem. tart. ℥x
Sal. Prunell. ℥iv
  Abſynth. ℥ẞ
Merc. Dulcis.
  Præcipit. Rubr. ā̄ ℥iv
Tart. Emet. ℨẞ
Alum. uſti ℥j
Rad. Altheæ
  Conſolid. Maj. a. ℔ij
  Liqiuritiæ ℔j
  Rhabarb. ℥iv
  Jalapp. pulv. ℥ij
  Liquiritiæ pulv. ℥ij
Therebint. Venet. ℥viij
Reſin Guajac. ℨẞ
Fol. Senn. ℥xij
Croci Orient. ℨ1ẞ
Herb. Philandr. ℔ẞ
Flor. Chamomill.
  Sambuc. ā̄ ℔j
  Papav. err. ℔j
Boviſt. ℥ij
Twee Sponſen.
Twee Blaaſen.
1 ℔ Spaanſe Seep.
2 ℔ Werk.
1 oud Laaken.
Een Brief groote Spelden.
Een ſchaaltjé met een Doosje Gewigt.
Een glaaſe Mortſer en Stamper.
Een Clyſteerpypje.
Een Boek Papier.

Ill. 11. List of Medicines in the Ship's Doctor's Chest, ca. 1660

Source: A.F. Leuftink, p. 31. This list contains a typical European selection of medicines which seems obvious, but is not: one did not resort to indigenous Indian or East Indies cures and methods during those centuries. Laudanum Opiatum is mentioned (left row 12th place from above); in the middle of the other row 'Therebint. Venet.' could refer to the Venetian theriaca, while another Papaver-extract is given as well.

Medical personnel were available on nearly all ships, with their instruments and a specific chest full of pills, tinctures and ointments.

After long deliberations among the decision-makers of the VOC, with advice from medical doctors, a list of 144 ingredients was drawn up for the medicine chests on their ships. They consisted of some single products like specific seeds, oils or minerals. Most of them, however, were preparations like ointments, tinctures or syrups based on complicated recipes: 'For the preparation ... of the often prescribed opium preparation Theriac, one used 60 different ingredients.'[14]

Indeed, the content of the chest in the 17th and 18th centuries was ultimately based on old European knowledge and traditions. Because the overriding idea was that diseases were caused by bad fumes in the environment leading to fermentation or putrefaction inside the body, one needed preparations causing vomiting, laxation, coughing, sweating and so on, and specific treatments like blood-letting. Opium in whatever form (laudanum, belladonna) was used as a painkiller, to stop excessive diarrhoea, and added to many proprietary cures like a stimulant for sweating, against syphilis, typhoid and the like.[15] The market was large for these opium products: in the 1770s about 2,000 sailors per year died of typhoid alone on VOC ships.[16]

Leuftink rightly concluded:

> There seems to be a remarkable contradiction between the large interest ... in the availability of medicines and the evidence of being powerless against the serious diseases on board.[17]

That was not the only contradiction: the West European use of opium as a major means to relieve oneself of pain and sorrow contrasted strongly with the West European perception of Eastern opium.

The Asiatic Opium Image of the Dutch

It is likely that the first knowledge about "Asia" was derived from Jan Huygen van Linschoten's *Itinerario* (1596) and other writings at the time (Barbosa or De Orta), although one cannot exclude the possibility

---

[14] A. Leuftink, p. 30.

[15] Idem, p. 127, 137.

[16] Idem, p. 139. For related USA chests for military use during the American Revolution (ca. 1776), see E. Kremers, G.Urdang, p. 153.

[17] A. Leuftink, p. 30.

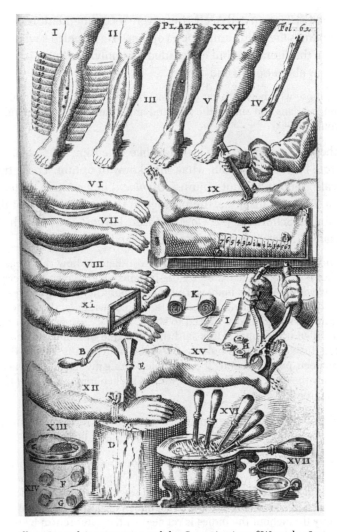

Ill. 12. Several Amputations and the Cauterization of Wounds, 1657

Source: A.F. Leuftink, p. 213, originally published in Johannes Scultetus, *Magazijn ofte wa-penhuis der chirurgijns* [*Arsenal of the physicians*], 1657. As painkiller one used alcohol and also opium (laudanum), if they were available!

that Portuguese or Spanish merchants or prisoners talked about it somewhere.

In the first relevant analysis of the opium problem and trade, Baud's 1853 study, he reviewed the earliest Dutch and English travel literature around 1600, but could not find many references to opium. Concerning the Moluccas, Bantam and Aceh, there were recommendations to trade in many products including amphioen (opium). He revealed several contradictions in this literature, but concluded that only the "Spice Islands" certainly knew about opium and

> that those who began to eat or smoke opium could be found only among foreign Asians and among the rich and important people of the indigenous population.[18]

Later, there were many Dutch travelers like Valentijn, Schouten, Pelsaert who wrote extensively about what they knew of opium. These traveler-writers also reported about opium (*amphioen*) in a context of death and delirium. Take, for instance, the passage in the popular story of the surgeon Wouter Schouten, the *Oost-Indische Voyagie* (1676), which was immediately translated into several European languages:

> In this month of February [1659] I saw in Batavia how the breasts of an Indies man were pinched off by the hangman with glowing pincers. Next, the lower parts of his body were broken upon the wheel. The reason was that the man after using amphioen (a wicked custom of these Indies men) became mad and drunk, started to shout "amuck" ... in which condition he had killed five people ... It is said that this kind of killing was committed often, inside as well as outside Batavia. The reason is mainly the use of amphioen, popular among these people. During my stay in Batavia this was already the third amuck runner who was broken upon the wheel thanks to his murders.[19]

A report from Engelbert Kaempfer (1651-1716), a German physician who had joined the VOC, confirms that opium is smoked in Java:

> [There is] also [another] strange use of opium among the nigritas [Javanese]; for they mix with it tobacco diluted with water so that when kindled the head spins more violently. In Java, I saw flimsy sheds [made of] reeds in which this kind of tobacco was set out [for sale] to passers-by. No commodity throughout the Indies is retailed with greater return by the Batavians than opium, which [its] users cannot do without, nor can they come by it except it be brought by ships of the Batavians from Bengal and Coromandel.[20]

---

[18] J. C. Baud, p. 89. See also J. Meiss, p. 56.

[19] W. Schouten, p. 50. Schouten reports here about a slave from Bali, a certain Polo, who first killed his Chinese master, then himself. His corpse was brought to the gallows as food for the birds; see Idem, p. 109 note 14. That he killed five people must be an exaggeration.

[20] Quoted by C. Trocki (1999a), p. 35.

Again, like the Portuguese, the Dutch ships arrived with opium in very small quantities. In all probability both copied the behavior of earlier merchants like the Arab or Middle Eastern ones which traded in all kinds of drugs and aphrodisiacs. In the East Indies, for instance, Bantam (Bantĕn) on West Java was an important commercial center long before the Portuguese came. For the Dutch, who refrained largely from becoming users themselves, opium remained a means provided for economic—strategic reasons: it smoothed the trade with indigenous rulers as they started to settle here and there in the archipelago.

VOC physician Kaempfer reported about other qualities of opium and confirmed Schouten's remarks:

> People who have an unstoppable aversion in life or in their diseases ... prepare themselves for their death. In their revenge against their fate, they also look to kill other people. To this aim they swallow a piece of opium with the result that they are overcome by a frenzy to such a degree that they go on the street with a dagger to kill all they meet, friend or foe, until they themselves are fatally stabbed ...[21]

In Palembang (Sumatra) in 1642, the VOC obtained a monopoly from the Sultan to import opium and textiles. The population of the entire Sultanate was obliged to maintain a fixed number of pepper plants. Neglect of the gardens 'was severely punished, as were opium smoking and gambling'.[22] This must have been an order of the Sultan, who was interested increasing production as much as possible. If the Dutch could not buy pepper, there were always other Europeans available. For the Dutch this was smuggling and in variance with the monopoly contract in a double sense: neither the pepper nor the opium trade was supported.

Elsewhere, the opium strategy had another face. The notoriously repressive clove cultivation of Ambon or Amboina was fully developed by the Dutch in the 1660s. To regulate the yields, the Company not only carried out *hongi* expeditions (destruction of yields to keep the price as high as possible) but 'even considered importing opium, in the expectation that it would make the Ambo(i)nese lose their work motivation'.[23] Indeed, cloves were for the European markets (and some Asian VOC clients); opium, like slaves, only for the indigenous market. These strategies did not change until opium (amphioen) became a profitable trade product in its own right. This situation developed in the 1660s through the barter trade

---

[21] Quoted by R. Schmitz in G. Völger, K. von Welck, vol. 2, p. 658.
[22] E. Jacobs, p. 66.
[23] Idem, p. 18.

on the Malabar coast as indicated earlier when opium served as "money" and as a mass product. Only from that date onwards is Baud's conclusion valid concerning the period 1620-1740:

> In one and a half centuries [the VOC] succeeded in increasing the use of opium on Java twenty-fold, while continuously complaining that the turn-over was not large enough.[24]

What about the Dutch headquarters of the VOC where the lawyer Pieter van Dam (1639-1701) worked? He was the first officially appointed historian of the VOC. The Board, *The Seventeen Gentlemen*, explicitly ordered him to write its history in detail, including all the failed actions, so that they could learn what to avoid in the future. Normally, the historians of a company exaggerate the glorious deeds of their subject, but here the directors asked for the truth. In 1693 they were deeply concerned about 'the astonishing course of events and near total chaos and corruption in the government of their business in India'.[25]

However, in all seven volumes Van Dam did not answer one of my burning questions: who decided to deal in opium on the Indian coasts in the way described above, and why exactly was this product chosen?[26] Was it so easy or normal to deal in a controversial product as described by Van Dam or Van Linschoten?

Shortly before he died, he published the following about opium, as if the information was not available:

> Amphioen, in Latin opium, comes from Patna and from Gualoor, a landscape in Hindustan; it is the gum from cut up balls, which is rather popular in Asiatic nations, and they like it very much. The young and also the common men use those balls prepared in boiled water instead of amphioen. The Persians say that their aristocrats invented the first use of it, when they could not get to sleep for worrying about important matters. The common man [in Persia] and neighboring countries followed. Only a few people do not use it.
>
> One takes daily a quantity as large as a pea. This doe not so much induce sleep, but strengthens the mind, in particular in war or on long voyages. When runners have to bring messages or letters over land, they are supposed to become strong and to feel no sorrow nor labor. However, most of the time one uses it for sex [literally: for the unchastity]. Those who take it daily become sleepy and stupid or uncontrolled in their words and deeds.

---

[24] J. C. Baud, p. 116.
[25] P. van Dam, GS 63, p. X.
[26] It is the same with the decision to exterminate all who were racially "undervalued" by the Germans. Was this order given in writing? Was it Hitler or not? Etc.

It is a lethal poison, unless one uses it in a modest and prudent way. Therefore, those who like to use it should start with a bit, so that they can become
accustomed to it. But after they stop taking it for four or five days, they can
develop a lethal sickness; those who never used it and swallow 10 to 12
grains will die.[27]

Pieter van Dam wrote this partly based on the reports of captains of VOC
ships or of administrators in the VOC settlements.[28] The author points to
Persia as the country of origin, which is acceptable since the word "amphioen" is derived from the Arabic "afiun".[29] Like Jan Huygen van Linschoten,
whose writings of a century earlier he knew perfectly well, Van Dam differentiates between the use of the juice and the poppy balls. The latter
were consumed by the "lower or uninformed classes" as a kind of arti-
choke; the juice-product was reserved for the aristocrats. And he again
stresses the dangers (poison, etc.) and attractions (war, sex), although
he—as a Calvinist—defined sex as a sin and war as the best means to
punish the unbelievers and primitives.

His contemporary Engelbert Kaempfer arrived in 1689 in Batavia
before continuing on to Deshima, Japan. Here he learned from Japanese
colleagues a specific prescription with *Papaver somniferum*:

.... a secret against impotency, which was communicated to me by an expert
Japanese physician, as somewhat very valuable. Take as much as you please
of crude opium, put it into a piece of linen, and suspend it in the smoke of
boiling hot water; what sweats out of the linen, and sticks to the outside,
affords the best and purest opium. Take this substance, mix it with twice
the quantity of ambergrease, and make it up into small pills. A few of these
pills taken inwardly, at night before you go to bed, are said to be excellent
stimulating medicine in that case.[30]

---

[27] P. van Dam, GS 76, p. 32, 33.

[28] He is partly quoting from J. H. van Linschoten, vol. 2, p. 112, 113 without mentioning
the source.

[29] They say that both "opium" and "afiun" could be derived from the Greek, but this
must be part of the 19th-century legitimation history. According to the OED "opiate" is
used for the first time in 1543 as a purely medical latinization; it is a means inducing sleep.
The OED does not even indicate a year of first use for "opium", which is usually done. It
took another sixty years before one started using the narco-connotations of opiate. In the
19th-century Dutch writers in the East Indies knew perfectly well that the word *opium* had
nothing to do with Latin, but was only a corruption of *afioen* or *apioen*. See N. Struick, p. 3
note.

[30] E. Kaempfer, p. 300 in 1995 edition; same text in the 1727 edition p. 51, 52. Ambergrease is a waxy substance formed in the intestine of sperm whales and used chiefly as a
spice in the East.

It would be interesting to ascertain whether these Japanese physicians had experimented with opium themselves or fell victim to the Dutch (or eventually Portuguese) advertisement of their opium trade. Since 1609 the Dutch had been traveling to Japan for the highly lucrative silver and silk trade, but *en passant* "medical knowledge" was exchanged as well.

The obvious reason for the VOC to circulate opium as a mass product was to save bullion and gain better opportunities in the intra-Asian trade. However, knowing what kind of stuff it was, they must have thought that the end justified the means: everything was allowed when making a profit from "primitive pagans" and, certainly, if you could keep them quiet "in the same stroke".

Double Dutch Violence

Why is the Dutch government also referred to here? In his highly relevant historiography, Van Dam published many documents. One, about the public status and legitimation of the VOC, states

> that the traveling to and trading with the East Indies is not a private venture, but a large, important activity of the State, so that the consequences of its [the VOC's] acts affect the common case ... [elsewhere is indicated] that the investments are made from the State's financial resources, hoping that these in the future will result in large profits benefiting the good inhabitants of our country ... [therefore] ... the military sent out have to swear fidelity to the States General and His Highness, the Prince of Orange ... [The VOC is, therefore, called a] public authority ... to do harm to our common enemy and to promote the right and honorable commerce ...[31]

The decision-making people in the 17th-century could have had their doubts about the honorable character of their trade, but did not mention much about it. So, let us suppose that they had no scruples at all. Both aims ("enemy" and "commerce") are fulfilled in an extravagant way.

The VOC was, indeed, a commercial venture as well as a war-machine. Basic to both are the monopolies and claims its governors (the so-called *Seventeen Gentlemen*), the States General (the Dutch government) and the Prince of Orange (simply an army general, *Stadhouder*, not even admiral of the dominant fleet) announced out of the blue. They were the main means of a threefold strategy: rule by conquest where the VOC claimed direct territorial sovereignty (Banda islands, Batavia, etc.); authority and

---

[31] P. van Dam, GS 63, p. 73, 74.

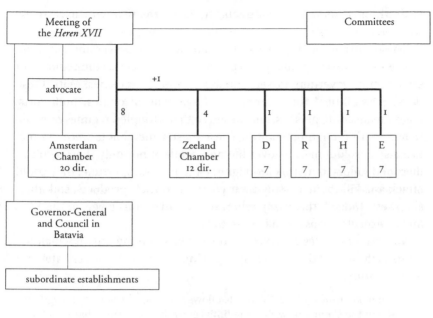

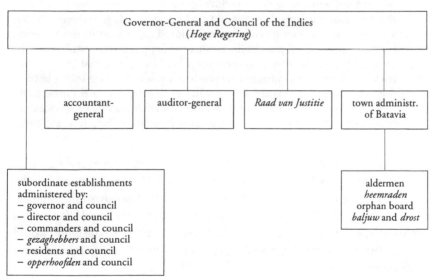

Figures 4 and 5. Schematic Diagrams of the Organization of the VOC—General and of the VOC—Asia

Source: Adapted from F.S. Gaastra, *De geschiedenis van de VOC* (2nd edition, Zutphen, 1991) by A. Meilink-Roelofsz et al., p. 106, 108.

trade through monopoly contracts; trade by treaties with excessively strong Asian rulers.[32]

These aims of the decision-makers provided the power and authority of the executors: captains of ships, admirals of fleets, commanders of strongholds, governors of settlements or whole countries. With these "legal possibilities" they committed large-scale atrocities, built forts, appointed leading persons, encamped soldiers, toppled regimes or made treaties with foreign potentates. These master-merchants were in practice also absolute masters over life and death of not only their own soldiers and sailors, but also of foreigners if that was opportune: they could attack and kill them, destroy their cities, steal their products, sink their ships, etc. Indeed, the *octroy* (charter; authorization) given to the VOC and its executors was also a license to kill.

Van Dam provides the relevant documents like the one in which the limits of the acts of the VOC are given. 'Limits' is here the understatement of the century:

> ... nobody from these countries is allowed to sail, to trade or to negotiate, except the Company, within the limits given in the octroy, that is to say: ... the meridian touching the Cape of Good Hope, which goes directly to the southern and eastern meridian one hundred miles east of the Salomon islands ... [etc.] ... All seas, gulfs, straits, creeks, bays, rivers still to be discovered between those two meridians, will be comprised in this contract. ... here it is forbidden to everybody to trade in the East Indies beyond the Cabo Bona Speï, except the East Indies Company ... it is furthermore forbidden from these countries or royalties ... in someone else's service than of the Company's, to sail or to trade on penalty of loss of life, ships and cargo ...[33]

This and similar *octroys* are declarations of war against everybody who does not act in the interest of the Dutch State—VOC in about half of the world! One can only be astonished about the 'arrogance and ignorance' (see Rashid in the Preface) of these *Seventeen Gentlemen* in declaring this trade war, and assuming that people on the other side of the globe would accept this without counter-violence, revenge, guerrilla warfare and other countermeasures.

---

[32] See K. Ward, chapter two, for a more detailed analysis of these forms of the imperialist power play. J. Somers, p. 57 ff., the newest Dutch political-juridical analysis at issue, does not understand the wrong impact of the *Mare Liberum* doctrine, nor the impact of the monopoly theory and practice.

[33] P. van Dam, idem, p. 76, 77.

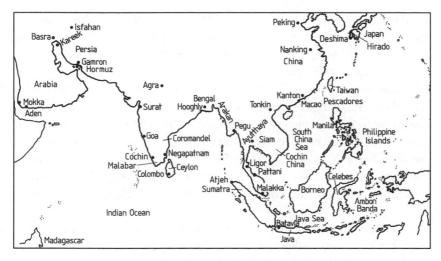

Map 5. Octroy area of the VOC during 1602-1795
Source: M. Meilink-Roelofsz et al. [ed.], p. 101.

It was inevitable that these actions would be taken. They triggered a chain of bloodshed until one of the parties was exhausted, which started again when it recovered. In the Dutch case this endless war stopped around 1950 when they were definitely kicked out of the Indonesian archipelago. The Dutch side (and other Western powers who declared the same wars) assumed it had some 'right to conquer' which was nothing but risking the use of better canons and guns instead of trading in a peaceful way, as it was a *regular daily* practice in Western Europe at the time.

However, it assumed that another does not have such a right or, at least, that he has to accept all consequences resulting from this "right". A new salvo was the only legitimation. The *only* legitimate act, resistance, nearly always led to a greater proliferation of violence from the intruders and not to negotiations with restitution of damages or other acts of repentance. That was, certainly, "forgotten" as a matter of principle when later the unavoidable (and *legitimate*) guerrilla war against the Western repression started. And afterwards, one did not look back in anger.[34]

---

[34] In January 2009 the Dutch Minister of Foreign Affairs, M. Verhagen, visited Indonesia to talk also (along with the usual business) to the relatives of the victims of a Dutch mass-murder incident in the Javanese village of Rawagede (1947). In that year about 450 men were murdered by Dutch soldiers looking for resistance fighters. Verhagen promised much, but did not apologize for this event, nor did he pay compensation as that would have been perceived as a declaration of guilt. Earlier, in December 2008, the Dutch Ambassador had already said "Sorry" about "Rawagede", but refused to apologize for it. In the 350

Who are the enemies of the Dutch State—VOC elite? For this relatively small Calvinist group, the closest enemies in Holland or other provinces were certainly their own inhabitants, bureaucrats, soldiers or sailors. Only a few decades earlier the whole population had been Roman Catholic. The new preachers were fanatic sectarians always ready to fight each other and the fabled "rest of the world". Many of their hairsplitting arguments are to be found in long series of measures fixed in rules and contracts about who is allowed to benefit from captured ships and goods; who will be punished with monetary fines for the slightest mistakes; draconian death penalties for anyone daring to attack the authority of the Calvinist elite or punishments for corrupting everybody outside this elite, and so on.[35]

The legitimation for these continuous internal suspicions and severe punishments is not only the vengeful Calvinist concept of God, but certainly also the relation between an absolute, unassailable position of the elite and the folk who had to do the dirty work for the VOC. This folk belonged largely to the scum of the nation, the mercenaries roaming around in war-stricken Europe.[36] The distance between the rich and the poor in—say—prosperous Amsterdam of the Golden Age is represented in the official annual remunerations: 7000 guilders for the mayor and 200 for a VOC soldier.[37]

In the outside world, the arch-enemies were the former masters, Catholic Spain and Portugal. They had already captured the largest parts of the non-European world. The new Protestant imperialists wanted their share and, if possible, all of it.

In the 17th and the largest part of the 18th-century, England was not a real enemy of the Dutch in the East. They appreciated each other as the enemy of their enemy; as a "well-armed friend", who must sometimes learn a harsh lesson from the strongest in the permanent competition. In addition, the "friend" had the wrong Protestant belief and government,

---

years of the Dutch occupation of the archipelago, it is estimated that several million indigenous peoples were killed by the Dutch. There is not even a list of all the "Rawagedes"; that would be a long list, because at least one conflict was occurring somewhere in the archipelago every year. It took another two years before an official apology and some money was given.

[35] See, for instance, Idem, p. 78-91.

[36] C. Boxer (1965), p. 244.

[37] This 35:1 relation represented no real differences. The mayor could easily get a multiple of that amount through additional sources, while the VOC soldier's payments were reduced by all kinds of fines. For all possible wages, etc. in the 16th–18th-century, see J. de Vries, A. van der Woude, part four.

notwithstanding the fact that a Dutch *Stadhouder* could become king in England (William III). Several English-Dutch Wars were fought at sea in Europe, which were ultimately lost by the Dutch in the West as well as in Asia.

In the East the English only gradually arrived at a hegemonic position thanks to its fleet and the occupation of the largest land mass. This resulted, however, in something of a status-quo at the end of the 18th-century. Roughly: "British" India and the "Dutch" East Indies on opposite sides, "French" Indo-China in between, and China as prey for everybody.

Until about 1750 Holland was still "master of the Asian seas". It was able to make a deal with the English EIC in another *octroy* (1619) which stated that no other body except the two Companies will be allowed to benefit and profit from a mutual treaty.[38] This is a rather exceptional situation. After 1600 the normal daily practice among the main European countries was extensive and cruel religious wars on land and on sea (between "official" fleets of private or state-pirates).[39]

All the people involved in these ventures were accustomed to showing no mercy to anybody, using torture routinely and slaughtering innocent people wholesale. It is very difficult to find elsewhere an example of such a prolonged lethal "friendship" between these West Europeans, who made up their minds to conquer the "rest of the world". Notwithstanding all this, gradually rules of the game developed ("Mare Liberum"; Protestants and Catholics must not fight each other, etc.) and some treaties or bonds which lasted longer than a few months.

Outside the European world, everybody was an enemy by definition. This was due not only to their misunderstood commercial competition but also to cultural self-exaltation or racist and religious connotations in Western belief systems. Here *a general cruelty was envisaged* (to exploit the "other" and to convert them by all means) which was normally *not* done with European enemies.

The main consequences were that Westerners thought they could (for some: had the right to) expropriate and exploit the bodies (slavery) and souls (opium) of those foreign people at will. At least from about the 14th-century, in Western Europe neither slavery nor opium existed as social phenomena, was not allowed or not available on a mass production scale. For the outside world Europeans developed forms of racism to justify

---

[38] Idem, p. 77.
[39] D. Starkey, M. Hahn-Pedersen (ed.), part 1; for the 19th and 20th-century European wars, S. Halperin is indispensable.

slavery and the opium exploitation.[40] The internationally operating
Catholics first invented strategies to incorporate (violently) those who
were deemed "racially impure"; the Protestants were much more rigorous,
always prepared for the sharpest forms of segregation up to genocidal
elimination of specific colored and/or non-Christian groups. This is not
the whole picture but the main context of the stupendous violence and
cruelty of the West European nations towards non-European countries.

Monopoly Wars

From the Portuguese the Dutch learned many things as was described in
ch. 10. One important subject is not mentioned there: *the monopoly game.*
The Dutch learned from the Portuguese attempts to monopolize both the
Euro-Asian and the intra-Asian trade in spices. They soon extended this
to almost all other products. This monopoly game was only successful if it
was based on military power: threatening, destroying or slaughtering peoples and their cities and land for the slightest reasons.

One of the first of the ferocious Dutch civil conquerors, Governor-
General Jan Pietersz Coen, wrote to his VOC Directors in Amsterdam in
1614:

> You gentlemen should well know from experience that in Asia trade must
> be driven and maintained under the protection and favor of your own weap-
> ons, and that the weapons must be wielded from the profits gained by the
> trade; so that trade cannot be maintained without war, nor war without
> trade.[41]

Among the highest Portuguese or Spanish officials, like the Crown lawyer
Joao Pinto Ribeiro, it was commonly held that wars could only be financed
from trading profits. He wrote that the Dutch 'understood this truism
much better than the authorities' in Europe. He should have pointed out
the global constellation in this matter: there was an intimate relationship
between the colonial and the internecine European wars; expansion in
the East provided resources for these European wars and was to a considerable extent generated by them. Or: treaties among European powers

---

    [40] See the article "slavery" in E. Cashmore (ed.), p. 312-316.
    [41] Quoted by C. Boxer, VI-3, also for the following remarks about Joao Pinto Ribeiro. In
F. Gaastra, p. 94 there is a table which gives the figures about the indigenous service personnel and slaves in 20 Dutch settlements ('Indische Comptoiren') in the year 1687-88:
3,605 of the former and 2,384 slaves. The most extensive households were apparently in
Ceylon (nearly 3,000 in total) and Batavia (about 2,000). M. Ricklefs (1981, 1993).

A°. 1690.

GENERALE CARGA,

Ofte Ladinge van Negen Ooſt-Indiſche Retour-Schepen,
midtsgaders een Galliot, met Namen: *Nederlandt*, de *Purmer*, *'t Landt van
Schouwen*, *Sion*, *Capelle*, *Pijlsweert*, *Schielandt*, en *'t Galliot de Snoeper*: Op den
29 December van Batavia; *Pampus* en de *Handtboogh*, op den 11 Maert
van Ceylon vertrocken, te weten:

4219080 ℔ Swarte Peper.	25 ps. Tapyte Cuſſen Stoffen.
2022 ℔ witte Peper.	2307 ps. Chineſe Pangsjes.
351409 ℔ Nooten.	1265 ps Chineſe Gielams.
76 ℔ Mannetges Nooten.	24 ps. Chineſe Caffa.
102333 ℔ Foulie.	20 ps. Schenckagie Stoffen.
40320 ℔ Canneel.	623 ps. Reſtas of Beng. Zyde Stoffen.
1400060 ℔ Salpeter.	643 ps. Nieuwe Modeſſe Bengaelſe
187500 ℔ Japans Staef-koper.	Zyde Stoffen.
657740 ℔ Thin.	30 ps. Japanſe Keiſers Rocken.
32228 ℔ Caleatourshout.	288 ps. Zyde Nacht Rocken.
381285 ℔ Sapanhout.	48 paren Cambajen en Rocken.
15020 ℔ Camphur.	816 ps. Geſchilderde Neusdoecken.
6111 ℔ Radix China en Galiga.	1970 ps. Chitſen van de Cuſt.
923 ℔ Zaatlack.	200 ps. diverſe Allegias.
262 ℔ Draken-bloedt	1760 ps. diverſe Salampouris.
500 ℔ Moernagelen.	400 ps. Allegias Bethilles.
505 ℔ Nooren Oly Koecken.	100 ps. Bethilles Otiſaels.
138 ℔ Vogelnesjes.	1000 ps. Cambajen.
7634 ℔ Benjuyn.	2600 ps. Roemaels.
118 Oncen Amber de Gris.	41 ps. Adathys.
136 ℔ Lange Peper.	250 ps. Pattenaſe Chitſen.
25085 ℔ Indigo Jamboeſer.	650 ps. Effene Gingans.
5598 ℔ Kiermanſe Wolle.	200 ps. Sologesjes.
66302 ℔ Geconfyte Gengber.	200 ps. Terendains.
314 ℔ Marmelade.	1482 ps. Dourias.
16390 ps. Geconfyte Nooten.	1192 ps. Caſſen Bengale.
48543 ℔ diverſe Bengaelſe Zyde.	558 ps. Sanen.
16186 ℔ Florette Garen.	2088 ps. Mallemolens.
2176 ℔ Bengael. Catoene Garen.	160 ps. Percallen.
10695 ℔ Sourats Cattoene Garen.	14400 ps. Corroots.
6490 ps. Armozynen.	320 ps. brede Caetchies.
16876 ps. Toncquinſe Pelangs.	80 ps. Pieremoenemolan Caetchies.
841 ps. Chineſe Pelangs.	3590 ps. divers Guinees Lywaet.
500 ps. Chiourongs.	1040 ps. Tweedradige Zeyl-kleden.

t'Amſterdam, by d'Erfg. van Paulus Matthyſz., Drucker van d'E. E. Heeren Bewinthebberen
der Ooſt-Indiſche Compagnie.

Ill. 13. Cargo List of Nine Homewardbound Eastindiamen, 1690

Source: A. Meilink-Roelofsz et al. [ed.], p. 80. Pepper and saltpetre belonged to the largest
part of the cargo; tin, silk and sapan-wood came next. Whatever other products (dragon-
blood, marmalade or bird's nests) were shipped, no opium was carried back to Europe.

and their changes made it possible/impossible to make commercial agreements in Asian waters between, for instance, the English and Dutch against the Spaniards and Portuguese until the first couple fought in Europe the four English-Dutch Wars.

There are scholars who argue that 'the principal export of pre-industrial Europe to the rest of the world was violence'. In my view this is a rather obvious remark, but Prakash thinks otherwise:

> Violence on sea was a weapon of the last resort, to be used as sparingly as possible, for the simple reason that it was by no means a cheap process. Ordinarily, both sides would first seek to resolve conflict and only in the event of a deadlock would either side resort to actual violence.[42]

Certainly, actions were often costly, and especially for the greedy Dutch, this argument was an important part of the considerations. However, this would mainly concern the actions *on land* which require large bands or armies of Western soldiers and longer (sometimes permanent) occupations, fortifications and so on. Earlier, Prakash made the relevant remark that 'by far the most crucial element in the new situation was the armed superiority of European ships over their Asian counterparts'. To support this, he tells the story of six English ships which in 1612

> congregated off the Arabian coast and hijacked, in succession, fifteen passing ships from India, culminating in the capture of the great 1000-ton vessel Rahimi, which belonged to the mother of the Mughal emperor. The prizes were taken to a nearby anchorage and plundered at will. ... the English could do this with impunity ...[43]

The cost? Nothing, but some ammunition. This is pure piracy in search of a prey. The risks of this were minimal once the ship had arrived in Asian waters, and the gains often enormous. For the underpaid scum of the Western nations, this was not only a welcome, but a necessary "additional income" or status at home. That situation changed as soon as Europeans landed and the Indian potentates knew this perfectly well when they told each other that they could be 'master only of land and not of the sea.'

Of the 4,700 ships which were fitted out by the VOC (transporting about one million people from Europe to Asia), there were only a few which were *not* involved in this kind of piracy somewhere in the realm. Most of them were also involved in bombardments of coastal settlements before they started to plunder these villages or cities and murder all who

---

[42] O. Prakash in: E. Locher-Scholten, P. Rietbergen (ed.), p. 192.
[43] Idem, p. 186, 187.

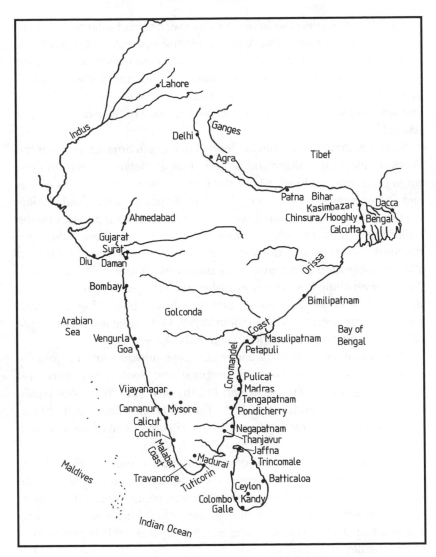

Map 6. South Asian Centers of VOC trade during 1602-1795
Source: M. Meilink-Roeloftsz et al. (ed.), p. 102.

could not take refuge in the jungle or interior. Westerners mostly did not
dare to go there, being afraid of armed enemies (much better guerrilla
fighters) or wild beasts, as well as sicknesses or other "revenge of the countries". For all European conquerors and heavily armed pirate-merchants,
violence was not so much 'a weapon of the last resort' but a necessary
means to arrive at their aims.

All this was not the case, or to a much lesser degree, in the communication and trade between the Asian countries and cultures. Earlier, the example was given of the Chinese merchants who traded peacefully for several centuries with Indian Ocean countries, but once they were treated in a highly treacherous way by Calicut rulers, they violently took revenge and never returned again. That is a good definition of "violence of the last resort"!

Violence, therefore, should be defined in a much broader sense for the Western side, in its culture and setting, than for Asian contexts. In illustrating this, one could start with the quite different perceptions of war and the willingness to use more advanced weapons. Owning and displaying them were always deemed necessary in order to keep pressure on the indigenous people to deliver pepper, tea, opium and other products for the most favorable conditions and prices. In addition, there is a typical Western obsession with war and weapons, which were not available in Asia for a very long time. How astonished the Europeans were to discover in the middle of the 19th-century that the Chinese had had good canons for a long time already, but used them largely for fun and not to kill people and destroy cities or landscapes in genocidal waves.

One cannot forget that when new European powers started to join the imperialist rat-race initiated by Portugal and Spain, they were also involved in genocidal European wars like the the Eighty Years' War (Spain against the Netherlands) and Thirty Years' War (Catholic against Protestant rulers). There was, furthermore, an acceleration in all these wars in all respects.[44]

Next, there were the "rules" of the monopoly game. The Westerners' attempts to obtain a monopoly were nearly always accompanied by a substantial military show to fight off the *European* competitor or to put pressure on an Asian potentate or to help the "other" king, chief or aspiring aristocrats to overrule his/her indigenous competitor.[45] It became a kind of mantra like, for instance:

---

[44] See the overviews in S. Halperin and H. Derks (ed., 1989).

[45] Dutch historians, for a large and dominant part Orangistic and Christian oriented, have always tried to whitewash the *national* history. Hardly any attention is paid to the exorbitant violence of the VOC, let alone its basic elements like the monopoly principle and practice. F. Gaastra, p. 11, even states that the monopoly concept has received a less negative image and stresses only 'the professional and commercial ability' of the VOC authorities. The historians during the Nazi period glorified Jan Pietersz. Coen, one of the most cruel VOC conquistadors among many. Gaastra, now the official VOC historian, still continues with this without any reservation. The alternative E. Vanvugt (1985), p. 48, is

... will the VOC receive permission of the King of Siam that it will trade tin there; [but] Malayan pirates are active there, making the waters insecure; at the moment the Mores export tin, but we must attempt to get a monopoly there ...[46]

Or, when in 1678 the VOC decided again to launch large military operations against some king in Java, one of its leaders

reprimanded the king's officials for having allowed Bantĕn shippers to sell opium and textiles at Jĕpara in violation of the VOC's monopoly ...[47]

And the consequences of obtaining such a monopoly mostly involved establishing a garrison in the capital as a continuous warning symbol, installing the highly provocative Portuguese invention (the *cartaz* or passport system) in which the occupying foreign power "allows" an indigenous private or public power to deal in products of its own country. Time and again the latter tried to "smuggle" or wriggle out of the situation, providing a reason for one punitive expedition after another full of the most cruel murder and genocidal practices.

In short: after the fights end and the *threat of new ones* overshadows all activities, a monopoly (or its variant) is established as a chain of intended violence of an institutional character which basically destroys commercial, social or cultural markets by foreign political-military means; there is no basis of legitimation for establishing such a monopoly, but rather a threat.

The Dutch VOC state was the first in history to establish an opium monopoly in the 17th-century, an example followed by the English EIC at the end of the 18th-century. It was repeated by numerous colonial governments even at the beginning of the 20th-century. Without much exaggeration one can say: since the Dutch established the opium monopoly on the Malabar coast in 1663 through severe military violence, almost all Asiatic wars have had a strong narco-character through to the present, including the Vietnam and Afghanistan wars. In 1677 there followed an opium monopoly for the Mataram (West Java) countries, in 1678 one for

---

wrong as well. He thinks that it is an Eastern custom to secure a monopoly which Dutch merchants learned in Batavia when accustoming themselves to the Eastern way of life. The sources of the monopoly practice and theory must be discovered in Western Europe in late medieval and early modern time (see the scholastic *ius gentium*, etc.), but the "monotheistic way of dealing with economic matters" is not the subject here. See H. Derks (2008).

[46] GM, IV, p. 348.
[47] M. Ricklefs (1993), p. 49.

Cheribon, and so on, although opium *as merchandise* was not very well known at the time.

How the objects of their aggression reacted to this enforced opium trade can be learned from the following examples from 1671, years before a monopoly was obtained and Western opium could be imported. A VOC official communicated in a letter to his superiors (Bantam, 10 November 1671):

> The King with all the aristocrats and wives went today to Pontangh with 50 to 60 vessels, among which 30 to 35 men of war, manned by 1,200 to 1,300 peoples, all amphioen users. When one has arrived on open sea, all these users are inspected for possession of amphioen. If something is found, the person together with his wife and children is sold to Lampon, whereupon the men of war are sent to Landack to start a war ... The King has announced everywhere ... that it is prohibited further to smoke tobacco: if somebody is found who is doing this, he will be punished with the same penalty as the amphioen smokers. Eight days later the same VOC official reports: 'Kei Aria came home from Pontangh and he has summoned us, Englishmen and Frenchmen ..: in the name of the King he ordered us never to smoke amphioen or tobacco mixed with it or to import it or to sell it in the harbor to Javanese of the East or to other foreigners on penalty of confiscation of the ship and all goods. Twenty-five Chinese, amphioen smokers, were sent to the King in Pontangh to work as diggers and field laborers like the other amphioen smokers. This King intends apparently to eliminate all amphioen smokers in his country once and for all.[48]

These messages suggest that if foreigners wanted a monopoly on opium import, the pressure they exerted to get it must have been tremendous.

Here is one example of how this game was played in the daily practice of the VOC's occupation of the "Dutch" East Indies. The English competitor was successfully expelled from the archipelago around 1635. Depending on the periodic English-Dutch wars and treaties *in Europe*, individual ships were allowed to roam around the archipelago or be chased away and destroyed. After the middle of the 18th-century, however, the English came with many more ships, officially as a nation, especially in the northern part of the archipelago, intending to stay, building their fortifications and settlements. That happened also in December 1755 on the Sumatran West coast near Padang. The Dutch Governor-General Mossel reported:

---

[48] Quoted from J. K. de Jonge a.o. (ed.), vol. VI, p. 210 ff. If all 1200 sailors were smokers, their ships still traveled on the open sea. Whatever exaggeration, it is perfectly clear that opium, tobacco and smoking were not the most beloved products and activities.

.... triggered by the new inimical invasion and subsequent stay of the English on the bay of Tappianuly, our ministers extorted ... a contract with one of rulers [*regent*] there in which the two main rulers [*regenten*] of that district not only transferred their lands in full property to the Company, but also their citizens as subjects, if the Company will save them on sea against their enemies. Protests were made against this violation .... but the nation did not bother about it. That is the reason why the ministers asked for law and order to occupy these lands by force to stop its reckless ventures, to sustain our contract and to demonstrate our help. .... [We wait] for this and all other acts for a conclusive answer, but also for an evacuation of the bay and the district of Tappianuly, including reparation of all coastal works in the old condition. And if they attack us by force in order to stop us, then the consequences are for them. ... In addition ... we will construct a small fortification occupied by a militia ..[49]

Hundreds of times the Dutch threatened all corners of the archipelago in the same way from the beginning until the very end and acted accordingly.[50] The indigenous rulers quickly learned what it meant when Dutch officials offered them "help". Indigenous groups, tribes or competitors of the rulers repeatedly revolted to try to liberate themselves from the foreign occupation.

The direct motives of the foreign assaults can differ: sometimes pure power politics against European competitors and their indigenous allies; sometimes direct undermining of foreign or indigenous commercial competitors in a particular product (nutmeg, opium, tin, etc.); sometimes threatening a whole population to stick to the rules of The Contract and continue producing and delivering the right quality and quantity on time. It always concerned the basic violent way of building the Dutch empire.

---

[49] GM, XIII, p. 3. Already at the end of 1757 a war was waged against the King of Johor and Cambodian vassals and the same message reports about the proposal: 'An order has been given to conquer also Battubara, Selangor and Kedah if there is any opportunity to do this, in particular because already for many years competitors deal in opium and tin in Kedah.' GM, XIII, p. 256 ff. The King of Johor is threatened enough to give many lands north of Malacca into the possession of the Company. This produced an administrative problem, because these lands were already the property of the Company thanks to an assault of 1680.

[50] For comparable monopoly contracts concerning land, opium, tin etc. imposed on indigenous people see, for instance, GM, IV, p. 309, 348 (tin), 574 (opium), 592 in Java (opium), 724; GM, V, p. 54 (opium), 188 until GM, XIII, p. 38 etc. For examples of the accompanying passport activities see GM, IV, p. 348 (not allowed to buy opium from others), 418; GM, V, p. 133; GM, XII, p. 256 (opium, tin), etc.

Empire Building

Another such network or chain of violence against people is better known. It concerns the systematic exploitation of bodies and the labor potential of foreign countries, the *holding* of colonial slaves for permanent settlements or the different imperialistic violence of slave *trading*. The VOC was busy with both within an institutionalized violence-labor network. A substantial part of it was recently analyzed by Kerry Ward in an interesting study.[51] It is beyond our scope here to provide the details, but the contours should be sketched, because part of the opium infrastructure was built in the same way.

Ward points to the fundamentals of empire building and in particular the peopling policy of permanent settlements. Her demonstration concerns the relationship between Batavia, the main VOC center in Asia, and the Cape of Good Hope, the main VOC center in Africa.

By the early 1670s the VOC had finally committed itself to a permanent settlement on the Cape. It built extensive fortifications and many other buildings by means of slave labor. A whole chain of events and activities developed gradually and functioned "smoothly" a century later: slave labor networks in the southern part of Africa (Madagascar, Mauritius and Mozambique) were connected with the Red Sea, India (Coromandal coast) and Ceylon. From Southeast Asia came slaves from many island polities across the archipelago, especially from Macassar and the Bugis region of South Sulawesi, the Moluccas and the extensive local slave trade from Bali.

Next, there were forced migrations of Asians, who were defined by the Dutch as exiles, criminals, political prisoners and the like. The ethnic origin of all those transported to the Cape was, therefore, complex. For instance, a group of Chinese was transplanted from the East Indies to the Cape after the 1740 massacre (see ch. 15), including some high-ranking exiles accompanied by their wives and children.

It was the first time that this method of colonization was carried out. It is well known from the English, who were very active in peopling Australia and New Zealand in the 18th and 19th centuries by "cleaning" England of

---

[51] K. Ward. E. Jacobs mentions the use of slaves several times, but in a rather strange context as, for instance: 'The two largest population groups in the city were the slaves ... and the Chinese ... The VOC did not regard slaves as a commodity.' (p. 233). It is not clever to follow this example and never mention slaves in the many product and trade tables at the end of the book and never discuss the topic in a relevant way.

white criminals and the New World of uncivilized, pagan, indigenous groups.

These forced migrations and slavery also presupposed a typical punishment system with the general characteristic that the VOC

> arrested a far higher proportion of their own servants and slaves than any other population group and that these ... were punished more harshly than high-ranking officials who committed crimes.[52]

It went so far that female criminals were transport from the Amsterdam *Spinhuis* (women's prison) to the Batavia *Spinhuis* and later to the Cape.[53] The rather prevalent crime of the high officials was corruption, so much so that upont its demise, the VOC initials were translated as: *Vergaan Onder Corruptie* ('destroyed through corruption'). However, the elite networks mostly saved them from prosecution, while slaves and servants were treated most cruelly. Another example: in 1722, some 26 people of low standing, including 11 European storekeepers, were executed in Batavia for smuggling. These public hangings were not an uncommon phenomenon.[54] They symbolized the colonizing elite's existential fear of riots, thefts in white compounds or slave risings.

Another remarkable aspect is also the general behavior against sick people of low standing. A travel report from Hofhout (1758) mentioned an encounter with 'a horrible group' of sick and half-dead people. According to one comment, they were accompanied by male nurses with big rattans. This was the usual situation in the hospital and outpatient clinic of Batavia where 'the poor patients were robbed and beaten up'.[55] The European patients received luxurious treatment.

These elements of the punishment system were directed at individuals and the behavior in the direct environment (Batavia). More extensive and serious were the punishments meted out when colonial products (coffee, tea, indigo, etc.) were not delivered on time or not under the "right" conditions. De Haan, manager of the colonial archives around 1900, tells in some detail about these cases in which 'a vile cruelty' was shown by or on behalf of the Dutch official (resident). For instance, in the VOC period in

---

[52] Idem, p. 88. For the English way of punishing in the colonial framework, see the excellent C. Munn and his analysis of branding, chain gangs, deportation, flogging, hanging, hard labour and so on.

[53] Idem, chapter 3 which examines the institutions of law and governance in Batavia.

[54] C. Boxer (1965), p. 228.

[55] F. de Haan, vol. 2, p. 543. Officially, sick people received food from the hospital, but that never happened in reality: they had to cater for their own food. Idem, note 4.

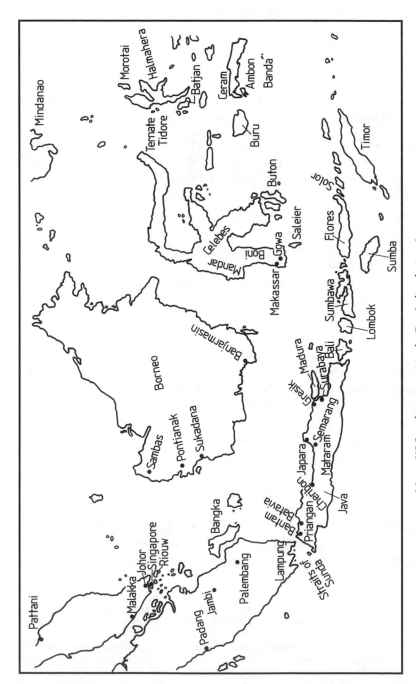

Map 7. VOC trading centers in the East Indies during 1602–1795

Source: M. Meilink-Roelofsz et al. (ed.), p. 103.

the coffee region of Preanger (South-West Java), leaders of the workforce 'who were not industrious enough' got the '*blokstraf*' (pillory) for one or several days, lashings with rattans or chains, etc. Besides the obvious excuse that one has to perceive these punishments from the perspective of a much rougher time, De Haan informs us:

> In our judgment about this we have to consider also the means used by the English in Bencoolen to enforce pepper deliveries from the population against prices as high as the Preanger coffee ... What is the significance of a *blokstraf* or lashings compared to the burning of villages and the destruction of the products in the fields?'[56]

Dutch officials tended to whitewash their own national performance. It also seems that the price of the product was somehow related to the magnitude of the punishment: and the Dutch were much cheaper than the English!

It would be difficult to list all the criminal acts Westerners committed daily for centuries in all the countries now known as the "Third World". Historians in those countries should cooperate in documenting those acts. I described the Portuguese cruelties above, and below I shall confine myself to only a few examples of the Dutch in "their" *Asian* countries.

The Banda Case and all that[57]

One of the first and earliest examples has all the elements of the Dutch way of dealing with the inhabitants of the East Indies. It is, furthermore, a typical example of how Protestant West Europeans conquered "new worlds" with their settlers.

---

[56] Idem, vol. 1, p. 162. De Haan's four volumes contain many documents about the 17th and 18th-century life in Java.

[57] The following is based on J. Villiers who reports mainly about the Portuguese relationship with the nutmeg islands; D. Hall, passim, in particular p. 276-286. Several Dutch VOC websites still write 400 years later in the most abstract terms about the Banda *genocide,* which is the right definition when a whole population is eliminated (see text). One of them writes: 'as a consequence of war acts many thousands of Bandanese died' (Kunst-en-Cultuur. inform. nl), another (VOC Kenniscentrum, KITLV in Leiden) pretends the Bandanese fell in a normal war. It is strange that the present official Dutch historian of the VOC, F.Gaastra, in his book for the general public on p. 45 suddenly refrains from describing what really happened under the pretext that the consequences of Coen's action 'are well known'. Other historians like J. de Vries, A. Van der Woude, p. 453 ff even write that Coen 'strengthened his position by driving out a large part of the population without mercy ...' without even pointing to the strategic importance of demonstrating as much violence as possible in establishing a foreign monopoly or to the strategic importance of opium. And,

It concerns the Banda archipelago about 140 kilometers south of the islands of Ambon and Ceram. This covers about ten small volcanic islands with a land mass of nearly 200 square kilometers. Before the Europeans came, they were the only source of nutmeg and mace for all neighboring countries including Arab, Chinese and Javanese traders. In addition, Banda maintained an important entrepot trade for the regional networks.

The Portuguese were the first Europeans, and they visited several times in the period 1512-1529. The Muslim Bandanese were hostile to Christianity and to the Portuguese. The latter were forced to buy their nutmeg in Malacca, where it was traded by the Bandanese themselves.

In the sixteenth-century nutmeg and mace were highly prized everywhere as important ingredients for cooking and medicine. In the early seventeenth-century an additional value was mentioned in a contemporary Portuguese source (Manrique): rich Bengal opium consumers mixed their dose with nutmeg, mace, cloves, Borneo camphor and other spices to increase the narcotic effect.[58] What we guess about Mughal opium consumption suggests that the direct and indirect Banda–India trade relations were not unimportant.

The Bandanese were very good merchants and large shipbuilders, trading their products not only with Ambon and neighboring islands, but as far as Java and Malacca. A trip like this, for instance, took two or three years, and many of their junks were lost.

The reason why the Portuguese did not succeed in obtaining a nutmeg monopoly is, according to Villiers, 'because they were confronted by a cohesive and united group of *orang kaya*, whose authority derived from popular consent'. Elsewhere, the chiefs were in a constant state of conflict. That was always an advantage for the Europeans, who were experienced in the divide and rule game. These *orang kaya,* a kind of mercantile aristocracy, tried to play this game between the Portuguese, Spanish, English and Dutch merchants. That was, apparently, too complicated a job for them, because they provoked the strongest party, the Dutch.

When the Dutch arrived for the first time (1599), the population totalled about 13-15,000 and included Malay, Javanese, Chinese and Arab traders.

---

of course, without doubting the legitimacy of imperialism and colonialism. For the context see *Both*, vol. 1, p. 91 ff., vol. 2, p. 237 ff. It is a pity, but quite symptomatic, that J. Somers, p. 62, does not elaborate on this Banda case. For the Banda case, see also M. Ricklefs (1981), passim.

[58] J. Villiers, p. 725.

The Dutch were welcomed, were allowed to establish a small factory, and were seen as 'saviours from the detested Portuguese'.[59]

Things soon went wrong: the Dutch occupied the island of Banda and imposed a monopoly for the nutmeg trade on the *orang kaya*. The Bandanese wanted to remain independent, however, they did not need the items offered by the Dutch, and the Dutch seriously mistrusted them. No Bandanese knew what a monopoly contract implied, but they soon learned their first Dutch lesson: the Dutch threatened them with military attacks, if the monopoly agreement was not followed. The Bandanese decided to get rid of these Europeans and killed a Dutch captain with some companions in an ambush in 1609.

Contrary to the Portuguese, the Dutch came back.

In the meantime, they were joined by other Europeans, because the English had arrived, paid higher prices for the nutmeg and built their own fortified factory. Now the Dutch had two enemies; they slaughtered the Bandanese people of one island, but lost 200 soldiers in an English attack (1619).

All this gave the Banda case the highest military priority, and Governor-General Coen himself came two years later with a substantial army and a secret weapon, a company of mercenaries, Japanese samurai. In a terrible massacre the Dutch killed most of the 15,000 inhabitants. Bandanese survivors (ca. 600 people) were caught and transferred to Batavia and elsewhere as slaves. That this was a real genocide according to all possible definitions is proven also by the follow-up.

After Coen prepared this *tabula rasa,* he completed the "victory" by putting his stamp on the empty Banda archipelago: all the available space was divided up into a grid of equal spaces (*perken*) in which nutmeg had to be planted. They were farmed out to Dutch settlers (*perkeniers*) who had to sell their yields only to the VOC for a fixed price; the manual labor was done by slaves imported by the VOC from Batavia. Because the VOC preserved its monopoly on nutmeg for several centuries, the *perkeniers* became tremendously rich.

Of course, this monopoly also had to be sustained by a substantial military deployment. One of the largest fortifications in the East Indies, Nassau Castle, was erected on the main island; smaller fortifications were established on all the others. To eradicate every form of competition and

---

[59] Idem, p. 749.

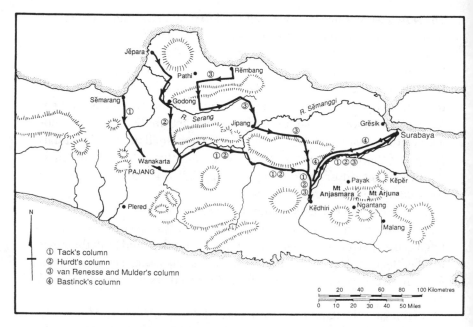

Map 8. Major Dutch Campaigns in Java, September-December 1678

Source: M. Ricklefs, 1993, p. 51.

every suggestion of "free trade", Coen and his successors carried out two rather lethal activities.

First they chased their European competitors, the English, out of the Moluccas, ignoring the 1619 treaty between the VOC and EIC. Revenge for the English role in the Banda case was certainly the main motive. This culminated in the highly debated *Amboyna Massacre* (1623). It concerned a quasi-juridical murder including *waterboarding* practices: the decapitation of ten Englishmen (EIC officials), nine Japanese mercenaries and a Portuguese servant of the VOC. The English public opinion became aroused to such a degree that the massacre was one of the motives for the First, Second and Third English-Dutch Wars. In addition, the fully intimidated English disappeared, and their competition in the Moluccas came to a bloody end.

The second activity was local in nature. Governor-General Coen and his successors repeatedly ordered raids on specific islands. These naval patrols, in fact death squads, were regularly sent around the islands to destroy and burn "unlicensed" nutmeg trees or other valuable plants and, if necessary, their indigenous planters. These so-called *hongi* raids became a standard means of repression for most of the 17th and 18th centuries. The aim was to keep prices as high as possible and to prevent smuggling opportunities.[60] They kept the flame of resistance burning against the VOC and its successor, the Dutch government.

Other 17th-century Violence

All this was the most radical form of repression: the total eradication of an indigenous society and its replacement by a new foreign one. In the East Indies this "signal" was heard and discussed until modern times as the clearest example of the implications of Dutch colonialism. Indeed, in the Banda islands, a typical Dutch Protestant settler society developed. This kind of VOC monopoly game was the ultimate consequence of a model for the Protestant way of colonizing foreign countries, as repeated later in the USA, Australia or South Africa.

This ultimate aim returns in the literature about the first years of the VOC. A highly artificial antagonism is constructed between the "direction Laurens Reaal" (only violence in the last resort) and the "direction Coen" (shoot first, ask questions later). Both were Governor-General of the VOC in the Indies, although the former lasted only a few years (1615/16-1617). The latter was Reaal's successor and stayed nearly unto his death in 1629.

Indeed, Reaal was not a dye-hard Calvinist, military and bookkeeper like Coen, but a moderate, intellectual Protestant (Remonstrant). He was certainly embarrassed by the horrific behavior of the Dutch settlers. He was against the monopoly trade as well and was one of the very few to demonstrate what monopoly trade was all about in his correspondence with the VOC Directors in Amsterdam (1623):

> Do you want to occupy all trade, shipping traffic and all products of the soil of the Indies? From what should the indigenous population live? Do you want to kill them and let them starve? This cannot help anything, because in an empty sea, on empty land and with dead people, you cannot make a profit. In short: with power and violence one intends to do everything in order to provide a monopoly for the VOC, and one is not afraid to use all injustices and even barbaric means to achieve this aim.' And reacting to the Dutch settlers, he asked, who likes to go to the Indies 'to act as hangman or guard of a herd of slaves? ... to be governors and predecessors of free

---

[60] E. Jacobs (p. 18) still thinks that these expeditions were organized 'to temporarily reduce the labor force'.

people who in fact are the scum of our nation; they are able to eat the Company, and they will disclose in the Indies that the Dutch will conquer, mistreat and kill them and that they belong to the most cruel nation of the whole world?'[61]

It is a remarkable expression from one of the highest VOC officials at the very beginning of the VOC's occupation of the East Indies. Alas, he was the first and the last VOC employee who wrote anything like this.

It remained an unusual incident even in his personal history: Reaal plotted against his predecessor Governor-General Both; he stimulated corruption among soldiers and nurtured a dangerous antagonism between soldiers and merchants.[62] Reaal himself suggested the butcher J. P. Coen as his most able successor. Furthermore, he was responsible for all VOC deeds since he remained in the highest VOC position with the most attractive remuneration thanks to 'the herd of slaves' in the Indies. A Reaal–Coen contradiction (if any) had only to do with the question of which is the best (= least costly) strategy to squeeze profit out of a strange, foreign, pagan realm.

The answer was crystal clear. The ink of Reaal's letter was not yet dry before the Banda massacre occurred. Together with Reaal, Coen attacked the English in Jakarta (the later Batavia); the important harbor of Jĕpara (Middle Java) was totally destroyed in 1618 by Block and again in 1619 by Coen himself to avoid English trade or to liberate Dutch people, who misbehaved themselves with indigenous girls; he threatened its Chinese merchants with delivering pepper at fixed monopoly prices; in 1622 Coen attacked Macao; defeated the Chinese a year later in the Pescadores; extensive wars with one indigenous ruler after the other raged for the rest of the century.[63]

Hundreds of thousand of people must have been killed in the East Indies and numerous settlements destroyed before the end of this 17th-century. The sectarian Protestant civilization was notorious for its violence, greediness, corruption and sexual excesses. This tempest over the East Indies had, of course, many consequences for the uprooted indigenous societies, shaken also by the rigorous divide and rule games of the Westerners, their bribery and opium.

---

[61] Quoted in E. Vanvugt (1985), p. 43.

[62] P. Rietbergen in his long introduction to *Both*, vol. 1, p. 102.

[63] M. Ricklefs (1993), p. 75, reports about a similar case fifty years later where VOC solders misbehaved: now they also smoked opium.

Ill. 14. Revolts and Massacres

Source: J. Blussé, 1986, p. 92. Numerous activities like this coincide with the VOC trade expansion in the 17th- and 18th-centuries. This one seems to be of a Chinese revolt in 1740 (see also illustration 16).

Continuous Dutch Violence

Gaastra stated that after 1700, the Dutch were less aggressive than in the previous century.[64] During the 18th-century, however, the rather continuous wars against the indigenous rulers of Bantam (Bantĕn), Mataram, Bali, Java's Eastern Salient (Oosthoek) or Madura can be mentioned.[65] "Banda" massacres also occurred like the so-called *Chinese Massacre of 1740* (see below). The century ended with the lost war against the English (a continuation of the war of 1759 against "British" India) and the occupation of the East Indies by the British. There were as well numerous violent attacks on "enemies" in the rest of the archipelago.

As soon as the Dutch returned to power in 1816, a new period started full of uprisings, revolutionary movements and wars against the Dutch colonial regime. Between 1800 and 1850 there were numerous armed rebellions in Bantĕn, with a peak in 1850. In the period 1825-1830 the Java War was the most devastating attack against these kingdoms under the leadership of one of its aristocrats, the Muslim Dipanagara. This war was also an opium war.[66] Uprisings were endemic until about the 1870, but culminated in the great outburst of 1888 and the thirty years' war against the Sultan of Aceh.[67]

The loss of privilege and collective humiliation that inevitably accompanied colonial rule generated intense resentment and frustration among groups which had lost their traditional position. Protests were often expressed in a religious framework, which was Islam in Bantĕn. Consequently, leaders stressed the Holy War theme. Triggered by so-called modernization projects of the colonial regime, mainly in agricultural practice, the revolutionary movements became peasant revolts, which were also opposed against the urban secularization.[68] The Dutch and the British (during their interregnum in 1811-1816) were simply too bold and arrogant when attempting to revolutionize both the Javanese elite and the peasants. As a result, they joined forces through their common hate of the foreigners, and this antagonism never disappeared.

Once this 19th-century ended, the new and last "Dutch one" began with the serious and devastating wars in Aceh, Bali and Lombok, with a hun-

---

[64] F. S. Gaastra (1991), p. 97. See also M. Ricklefs (1981), p. 91 ff.

[65] See W. Remmelink, J. Talens, C. Boxer (1977), S. Margana, D. Hall, etc.

[66] See C. Holtzappel in: H. Derks (ed., 1989), p. 147 ff.

[67] S. Kartodirdjo.

[68] M. Adas, p. 3 ff. about the situation in Mataram, p. 93-99 about Dipanagara and passim for the Java War.

dred thousand innocent people massacred under the Dutch leadership of the pious Calvinists Van Heutz and Colijn, who had to accept serious losses among their own military. Was it coincidental that these regions were traditional opium "smuggling nests", which undermined the Dutch government's opium profits?[69] The repression continued thanks to the rise of the nationalist movements until the last, unsuccessful, all-out war, euphemistically called the "Police action", in 1946-1949 with the usual massacres of innocent civilians. This time it was also strongly supported by the so-called Socialists of Willem Drees.[70] (A new defeat in a fancy war around "the last colony", New Guinea in 1962, completes this survey.)

It is, indeed, a most tragic period in world history: three hundred years of merciless, violent exploitation of the East by the West in which opium played a major role as a means of repression. Let's now return to this centuries-old Dutch opium trade which was so intimately related to the excessive violence sketched above.

Dutch Opium Trade: General Questions

As described in the 'Pepper for Opium' chapter, the defeat of the Portuguese on the Malabar coast meant the real start of the Western opium trade. The largest portion of the Bengal opium trade was soon directed to the East Indies. One must realize that the archipelago has the surface area of the USA, while the Dutch lived mainly in coastal settlements without forming a true colony. In the 17th and a large part of the 18th-century, their presence was also confined to the middle of Java and only a few locations outside this island. This does not seem very impressive, but the Dutch fleets ruled the waves.

As Appendix 2 indicates, in these years about 40,000-70,000 pounds opium were imported annually from Bengal. It is doubtful that all of it was destined for Java. There must have been other distribution channels. One possibility, which must be seriously considered, is the re-export to Malacca or even China, the land with the most ambiguous opium history

---

[69] E. Vanvugt (1995-2), p. 12 ff. This author also published a so-called "documentary travel novel" *The Bloody War on Bali* (2007). It is the story about two massacres a century earlier in which many thousands of Balinese, including women and children, fully unarmed died from the bullets of the Dutch military. This is astonishingly perceived as examples of *perang puputan*, collective suicide. An effective way to wash away the Dutch guilt.

[70] See H. Derks in: Idem (ed., 1989), p. 296-303.

before its "English 19th-century". Was it easy or possible to sell opium to the Chinese long before the English did? The answer must be negative, and will be discussed here only in a general way.

Malacca in the early 17th-century was a most important location in the Far East, and handled a substantial amount of re-export trade from India to, for instance, China. Large numbers of Chinese junks came to Malacca to trade. Many Arabian, Gujarat, etc. merchants traveled the Persian Gulf, Indian Ocean and came as far as China long before the Western intruders started their violent attacks. The reverse was also true: for centuries Chinese merchants came to the ports in the Middle East and India. In these busy commercial networks, competitors and partners, producers and consumers acted peacefully most of the time and certainly not with imperialistic and or colonialist aims.[71]

Before the Dutch shipped their goods towards China, the Portuguese and Spaniards had done the same. They invented a tradition which became a classic one in the relations with China: in 1679 the Portuguese had conflicts with Chinese officials, because the latter had discovered and discredited Portuguese smuggling. A small quantity of opium was also found on the foreign vessels, which was forbidden on penalty of confiscation of the ship.

The Dutch copied this behavior of the Portuguese even though they didnot have the advantage of a Macao settlement. They intended to start smuggling with small ships but failed as well and complained about the Chinese local authorities, who tried to swindle them.[72] These complaints would not have been heard if they could have made profitable deals with the Chinese.

The violent way the Dutch traded is probably the main reason why matters were blocked in China. Prakash states that success was limited

> to establishing a trading post, by force if necessary, on the coast of China or in its immediate vicinity. The efforts to blockade Chinese trade with Manila were followed by an attack on Macao in 1622 and the subsequent occupation of the Pescadores. But soon after, in 1624, the Dutch were persuaded to move to Taiwan in return for an informal agreement that Chinese merchants would be allowed to go there to trade with them.[73]

---

[71] For the early history see M. Meilink-Roelofsz, chapter 1; K. Glamann, passim. The latter analyzes mainly the East-West trade and not the inter-Asian trade. Therefore, data on opium are not given in his book.

[72] GM, IV, p. 280; see also Idem, p. 11, it was reported that Dutch small ships were smuggling around the Canton islands. See J. Wills, p. 150 ff.

[73] For the following O. Prakash (1985), p. 16 ff.

Still, a small part of the opium the Company auctioned later at Batavia found its way to China, thus opening that market to Indian opium for the first time. The main part of the Bengal production remained, however, in the archipelago.

The Governor-General and Minister of the Dutch East Indies, Jean Chrétien Baron Baud (1789-1859), is probably the first opium historian. He provided the other side of the Chinese story in 1853:

> China, at the moment the country with the most extensive opium consumption, did not produce this remarkable merchandise on a large scale, notwithstanding the availability of poppy and the Chinese knowledge about the characteristics of the moon-juice from their medicine. The import on a large scale for the use of smoking came from the West. This follows from a Memorandum of an important state bureaucrat, Heu-Naetse, to the emperor, who advised allowing the opium import against a tax as was usual in earlier times .... "Originally," Heu-Naetse wrote, "the poppy juice [*heulsap*] was perceived as a medicine; its characteristics are stimulating, stopping excessive defecation, mitigating the effects of bad fumes." In the *materia medica* of Li-Schi-Tschin, from the Ming dynasty, it is called *A-foe-young* ... During the reign of Kien-Lung (1736 until 1796) and also earlier, opium was taxed with the Cantonese tariff of remedies and with an import duty of 3 tael per 100 katti, except an additional duty of 2 tael, 4 mas and 5 condorijn for each package called package money. After this the import was forbidden.[74]

He rightly points to the Portuguese as the one who for the first time "traded" in opium (better: carried opium with them as a present to rulers) and introduced it in the East Indian archipelago through Malacca. Jan Huygen van Linschoten is also used as a source of Baud's knowledge. However, in the earliest travel literature of the Dutch merchant-pirates (Houtman and others), he could not discover any reference to opium in the archipelago. That was already different in Van den Broecke's reports. Baud is clever

---

[74] J. C. Baud, p. 84. Jean Chrétien Baud also refers here to the 'Correspondence relative to China, presented to both houses of Parliament, 1840'. Baud is a highly interesting man. He was sometimes Governor-General in the colony, sometimes Minister of the Navy or Minister of Colonies. In the National Archive (archive no. 2.21.007.58) a substantial archive is available from which can be derived the following. In 1818-1821 he is somehow involved in the organization of the opium lease in the colony, in the prohibition of the opium sale in the Preanger (1824), in the contract with the Bengal opium importer Maclaine Watson & Co (1833). Later he deals with the complaints of the Nederlandsche Handelmaatschappij (see ch. 18) about the difficulties in the opium business (1839) and with the always returning theme of lowering the opium price relative to the extension of smuggling practices (1854). His tract 'Proeve ...' (Essay concerning the Sale and Consumption of Opium in Dutch East Indies) is certainly written by a highly authoritative man and an insider. The first part of E. Vanvugt (1985) is a compilation of Baud's essay.

enough to point to contradictions between the early Dutch and early English adventurers: the latter wrote already in 1605 (erroneously?) that people in Bantam (West Java) liked opium very much, whereas the Dutch had just started to introduce some opium in the Moluccas.

The Dutch pirates did not discover opium on the captured Spanish and Portuguese ships either, 'notwithstanding the fact that several of these ships were Indian coasters from which the cargo may be considered as symptomatic for the dominant needs and customs of the time.'[75] The lack of some opium trade in the archipelago is due, according to Baud, to the war activities of the Dutch during the first forty years of the 17th-century.

Baud, furthermore, wrote quite humorously about the VOC:

> It is quite right that the Company prohibited the opium trade under severe punishments—even the death penalty—but did not include itself in this prohibition. It never detested this trade, but detested the smugglers, who intended to profit from it in the same way. The Company increased the consumption of opium on Java twenty-fold, while complaining constantly that this was not enough.[76]

An important colonial official like Baud was constantly busy with figures and their interpretations.[77] For us, this is a major advantage of his writings. To start with, his following statement is already important:

> From 1640 to 1652 ... the imports averaged 500 pounds. From 1653 to 1665 ... it was on average 1100 pounds annually. From 1666 to 1677 [when the Company was granted the monopoly on the opium trade from the Susuhunan of Mataram, H.D.] the import was on average 10,000 pounds.[78]

---

[75] J. C. Baud, p. 89. That was a similar conclusion to the one I have drawn from Van den Broecke's reports about the Surat traffic.

[76] Idem, p. 116. J. Meiss, p. 56, made of this that the advantages of the opium trade were undermined for a small part by the smugglers, but for the largest part by the fraud (*morshandel*) of the VOC bureaucrats themselves. Generally, the profit increased because the VOC was only interested in this profit and not in prohibiting the use. In Meiss' opinion the opium distribution system is the best, which taxes the use as heavily as possible to the advantage of the treasury (Idem., p. 57).

[77] Baud's major reconstruction of the opium distribution system (1842) involved dividing Java into distribution districts for the opium farmers. They had to sell from the Dutch their largest quantity for a fixed price (210 guilders per *catty*) in a three-year contract. This was called the *tiban*. If there was a demand for more opium, then the farmer could get as much as he liked for the same price. This additional quantity was called *siram*. Later this *tiban–siram* system was changed several times. For example: in 1848 the fixed *tiban* price became 100 guilders per *catty* and the *siram* price 35 guilders. See J. Meiss, p. 56-66; J. Wiselius (1886), p. 13-19.

[78] J. C. Baud, p. 100. This monopoly was reconfirmed in a new treaty around 1705. M. Ricklefs (1993), p. 142.

Baud further provides two long tables listing all the Dutch imports from Bengal into the archipelago. The first is more or less in accordance with Prakash's Bengal *export* data given in the previous chapter (see Appendix 2). From this table and the last quotation, the whole of the 17th-century import in the East Indies from Bengal can be estimated at 2.1 million pounds.

Prakash has given rather precise figures from 1659 onwards. This is the case in Baud's table from 1678 onwards. If we compare the totals from 1659-1718, both have a weight of 3.6 million pounds. There is a difference of 60,000 pounds, but that must be acceptable over such a long period (it's not more than the export or import of an average year).

However, if one compares specific years, serious differences are noted most of the time.[79] If there was always less import in Batavia than export from Bengal, the conclusion is clear: on the long way from Bengal to Batavia, several other customers received opium, which was normally the case. Alas, the picture is not that simple, because sometimes the import was substantially larger than the export from Bengal. In that case other production locations may have been visited, most likely in the Middle East. On the way from Europe to the East Indies, one first passed these opium sources (Surat, etc.).[80]

Based on the Prakash data, I estimated that about 11 million pounds must have been imported from Bengal in the whole of the 18th-century. Appendix 2 shows that around the middle of this century, 6 million pounds are reached, so a total of 11 million pounds is realistic. The growth of the import is exponential, and therefore, it cannot be a surprise that the import for the whole 18th-century was 12.6 million pounds. This was the import quantity from Bengal only.

The Indigenous Producers

The VOC produced nothing, but delivered and sold items. It used to negotiate only if the indigenous producer was too powerful or important for other aims (help in struggle with others, etc.). Take for instance tin from the islands of Bangka and Belitun (Banca and Billiton, south of Malacca)

---

[79] Reasons for this could be the way of bookkeeping, the interval in time between the Bengal and the Dutch notations, the currencies and weights used, the occasional loss of ships, etc. Apparently over a long period all these differences smooth out statistically. Anyway, it is too time-consuming and unnecessary for our aims to go into detail at a year level.

[80] R. Parthesius, p. 45 and 55.

and the surroundings; a highly desired product for the Dutch and English. Their indigenous "partner" was the very rich and powerful Sultan of Palembang. How fierce the competition was between these two main Western powers is demonstrated in a report by a captain of the VOC (1751). He

> had drawn a blank almost everywhere as the tin was being reserved for the English, who had paid in advance with opium and linen ... Only in Kedah, outside the area the Company regarded as constituting its sphere of influence, had he been able to buy a few hundred piculs of tin.[81]

A few years later the VOC sent a special delegation to the region, but it found that not only had the English received a monopoly on tin from a local king in the meantime on the condition that they build a stronghold, but that even in Kedah (in the North of Malacca) they sold 'linen and opium at prices with which the Hon. Company cannot possibly compete'.[82]

This last remark points to a remarkable aspect: the VOC paid the least of all foreign competitors (first and foremost the English, but also all sorts of private traders including Chinese), but on time and closely following the rules of a contract. Private traders were willing to pay between 11 and 15 *reales* for tin; the English were sometimes prepared to pay even 16-17 *reales* per picul.[83] Yet the Sultan of Palembang, the main ruler in the central area of the tin trade and the main receiver of the (silver) *reales*, the most common foreign exchange currency, was not dissatisfied with the VOC behavior.

Later the VOC introduced a passport system to enable cruisers to distinguish "legal" goods from the so-called "smuggled" trade. Every non-Dutch master of a vessel with 'monopoly goods' (spices, pepper, tin, opium and cloth) had to legitimate this by means of a passport received from the VOC. If this was not available, the Dutch decided to confiscate the cargo and/or the ship, but also to destroy everything and sometimes even everybody. In the trade monopoly region, every private trade was forbidden, was smuggling.

This was not only the case for the VOC. The Sultan of Palembang copied this rule. He claimed a monopoly on tin production that was detrimental to the miners and the traders thanks to the practice of an "overweight" system: the miners had to supply the tin for 8 *reales* per picul

---

[81] R. Vos, p. 56.
[82] Idem, p. 58. D. Hall, p. 277.
[83] See Idem. appendices, p. 213-218.

of 150 catties to managers, who sold it for the same price to the Sultan, but using the "light" weight picul of 100 catties. The Sultan in turn received not only the tin for the foreign traders, but also all kinds of necessities for his court. The Sultan sold his tin to the foreigners for 12 *reales* with "some" weight per picul.[84]

The Dutch preferred to pay with hard *reales*. The English, in contrast, purchased *reales* (with goods like weapons, ammunition and saltpeter) and mainly used opium and cloth from India as a means of exchange. The other main difference was that the Dutch preferred to make up contracts with the indigenous suppliers or producers, creating for themselves the "legitimation" to attack and slaughter most cruelly those who breached these contracts. This "Dutch treatment" remained the symbol of its colonial repression until the end.

The aristocratic British imperialists were more flexible since they combined the usual ridiculous "civilizing missions" with a sportsman's acceptance of a lost game. The Calvinist Dutch always had God on their side and handled their business without mercy for the other party as sectarians still behave, certainly when deciding that the entire outer world is their wicked, pagan enemy asking for a trial by ordeal. But local or indigenous people and societies, of course, often act quite differently from a Dutch or Western perspective. The latter is usually characterized by the attitude that the whole area is/was Western property because of its military superiority. How opium activities were organized at the local and regional levels within the rather complicated trade relations before the 19th-century can be demonstrated as follows.

After long and heavy fights the VOC succeeded in 1667 in wresting the trade monopoly from Makassar (Celebes, Sulawesi), mainly for spices, wood and cotton. That one of the largest fortresses in the archipelago, Fort Rotterdam, was needed to consolidate this VOC power is symptomatic of the seriousness of these conflicts. It was a century later that the opium trade also started here with imports and exports of rather small quantities, averaging five *picul* (= about 300 kg) a year. However, twenty years later this suddenly increased about ten times in weight.[85] Apparently, after a long war the elite in Celebes felt the impulse to try the stuff first, leading to some form of addiction and the increase in trade.

---

[84] Idem, p. 26 ff.
[85] G. Knaap, H. Sutherland, table 14, p. 95. For prices see Idem, p. 227, 231.

Opium Consumption in the East Indies

It is very difficult to provide any reliable perspective on the opium consumption question in the archipelago. In the *Generale Missiven*, for
instance, only import or trade figures can be found, but no estimates or
evaluations of consumption. De Haan reproduces from his documents
how 'the chiefs make much of the smoking of madat, but not of inspiring
their subjects to cultivate the fields' (1731).[86] This must be rather difficult
since the author subscribed a few sentences earlier to the classic prejudice of colonialists that 'the common Javanese ... are by nature lazy ...'
A VOC soldier repeated a well-known perception of his opponents in
his report (1672) about 'fights against the opium-stricken Bantam warriors ...'[87] Admiral Van Goens complained hypocritically about the opium
consumption of Javanese aristocrats (ca. 1660), and others repeated this.[88]
So, were Dutch soldiers and Javanese aristocrats the main opium consumers or only the Chinese, who were always blamed for being opium addicts
"by nature"?

To answer this question, Baud is not as good a guide as in the production and distribution matters. He gives very strange and unreliable figures, but his reasoning is still not uncommon today.[89] On several grounds
he estimates that the population of Java and Madura was about four million in 1700 and three million a century earlier. The census from Raffles in
1815 counted 4.6 million people on both islands, with about 2% Chinese.[90]
In Baud's own time the latest census indicated that this population had
increased to 9.5 million. Therefore, there must have been about 5.5 million people on Java around 1745.

Baud assumes next that the opium consumption per head of the population in 1600 was 1/750th of a pound relative to a total annual consumption of 4,000 pounds. A few pages earlier, however, he stated that from
1640 to 1652 the import could not have been more than 500 pounds per
year. In addition, he started his story by mentioning that none of the first
Dutch merchant-adventurers ever reported on opium (amphioen) in the
East Indies. And before 1640 there was a minimal consumption 'only

---

[86] F. de Haan, vol. 2, p. 470. Idem, p. 261 for a similar information (1717) about two
young princes; Idem, p. 544 about 'medak' smoking of Javanese male nurses (1758) in the
Batavian hospital.

[87] Idem, vol. 2, p. 752.

[88] M. Ricklefs (1993), p. 11, 45, 47, etc.

[89] J. C. Baud, p. 114 ff., 160 ff.

[90] Th. Raffles, vol. 1, p. 61 ff.

where those who smoke or eat opium also live', which is among the 'strange Oriental' peoples living in the seaports and among the rich and important people of the indigenous population.[91] He should have remembered this remark.

For the later periods Baud is only a bit more reliable: in 1678 a consumption of 1/54th pound per head per year, in 1707 already 1/39th pound per head, and in 1745 he estimates 1/36th pound per head per year. However, this is rather absurd because this last amount, for instance, is equivalent to 15 grams *a year*: a good business if one can sell this quantity to millions of people, but it is simply nonsense from the point of view of opium consumption. This should certainly concern people who look at smoking opium as an addiction whatever the quantity. The difficulty is here, of course, the too suggestive statistical method of the "per head accounts": in this way not only the product disappears, but also the opium problem, let alone the logistical problem of providing millions of customers with 15 grams of opium a year!

An important source is the reports of Europeans around 1680 who stated

> that opium usage among the Javanese had increased during the war years because of an excess of ready cash' [and also about] 'people starving along the roads of Surabaya and in 1682 identified opium addiction as a cause of poverty rather than a sign of wealth' ... [and] '... The VOC opium sales went well, but in all other products, notably textiles, trade was at a virtual standstill.[92]

We do not know how representative all this is, but a certain conclusion should be drawn to perceive the opium consumption concept in a very different way: it is true that raw opium was imported from Bengal or other places, the official quantities of which are more or less known. It does not necessarily follow from this, however, that these quantities must be consumed in the import country. The largest portion of the trade of the VOC and other similar companies from the 16th-century onwards to their end around the year 1800 consisted of intra-Asian trade. In other words: the products imported in Batavia were not all destined for Java but were re-exported over a huge territory reaching to the Philippines, Formosa and Japan.

---

[91] Idem, p. 89. The concept "vreemde Oosterling/ strange Oriental" is synonymous for Chinese.

[92] M. Ricklefs (1993), p. 70.

Furthermore, the Dutch created opium as a commercial mass product in the Malabar coastal region after 1663. This product was used as equivalent to other trade products, presupposing that opium had an equivalent value. Who else could determine this value than big consumer-traders, connected to a specific and *concentrated* clientele? The common Javanese in the villages could not be reached and, in most cases, had no money; the VOC narco-military could reach only very specific consumers; the smugglers (often Europeans!) were able to reach a much more differentiated network. Thanks to the latter, an opium market could be formed and supported to swallow a mass product.

This leads to another important conclusion for the *Dutch* Indies and a further consequence of Baud's remark about smuggling: there is a strong symbiosis between the VOC traders on the one side and the smugglers or other rather independent indigenous groups on the other. This symbiosis did not exist only relative to the building and further penetration of a specific market, the greediness of dependent customers for easy money, and the lack of every moral restraint to deal in highly controversial products prohibited by several rulers in the East Indies like Amangkurat II (1684).[93]

This relationship between the VOC and the smuggler-distributors is also characterized by its lethal element: the VOC itself is the foreign narco-military force using all means to coerce people into selling their addictive product; the smugglers and the Chinese, those 'strange Orientals', were not only threatened with death penalties but periodically murdered wholesale as well. Much later, in the twentieth-century, even the consumers of this stuff—certainly the addicts among them—became criminalized and prosecuted, but the leadership of the opium *police*, etc. could be accused of stealing and blackmailing on a large scale. This characterizes the whole Opium Complex.

In the 17th and 18th centuries the Dutch gradually created most elements of this complex without any scruples. In the 19th-century the English perfected and extended it and imposed its legality by force. The Dutch in their colony did not need this anymore: they had to continuously wage war to consolidate their power, but they determined what was legally acceptable in the East Indies or not.

Baud, as one of the highest officials, time and again also actively organizing the opium business in the archipelago bureaucratically, had no scruples against this colonial policy nor against opium. On the second

---

[93] Idem, p. 78.

page of his essay, he starts with the criminalization of the consumers at the very moment he was aware of the English, who were waging the Second Opium War against China. He writes:

> There are, indeed, many people who ascribe the most serious consequences to the custom of opium use; others, however, argue that these results are apparent only among the few who degenerate the use into misuse. They can be perceived as similar to our *drunkards*. The majority of users do not experience more harmful consequences, like those among us who swallow a small quantity of liquor daily. Marsden believes that the campaigners against opium [heulsap] are guilty of exaggeration. He acknowledges having seen opium smokers with all the external signs of exhaustion. He, however, adds that these persons were culpable of other excessive behavior ...[94]

and so on (italics added by Baud).

Also for his own period, Baud uses the reasoning involving per head of the population. He arrives, for example, for 1755 at a consumption of 1/34th pound a year (population six million) or for 1816 at 1/133rd pound per head per year (population eight million on Java). In his view, the latter estimate is only a quarter of the consumption in 1755, which is again equal to 15 grams *a year* and in 1816 even 4 grams! Let's go back to the realities of the opium business of those who exploited the East Indies for their own profits. Two groups are always mentioned: the white elite and "The Chinese". Both have the image as the greatest opium profiteers. What is right or wrong? The former are treated in the following chapter, the latter thereafter.

---

[94] Th. Raffles, vol. 1, p. 80.

CHAPTER FOURTEEN

THE AMPHIOEN SOCIETY AND THE END OF THE VOC

Until 1745 the usual organization of the opium business in Dutch East Indies was that the colonial government/VOC imported the raw opium from Bengal (sometimes from Persia or the Levant) and leased or distributed it for further processing and selling to European, Chinese and indigenous 'farmers' through public auctions. The chests became labeled with all kinds of marks and seals to avoid fraudulent actions. The opium could be paid for in cash or on credit. The government's monopoly position concerned, therefore, the import and distribution of opium, a distribution largely confined to Batavia. Sales in Java or elsewhere in the archipelago were done by the opium farmers.

The gross profit for the VOC/government was, of course, the difference between the Bengal purchasing price and the Java auction price. It sustained this monopoly by military force throughout the realm. The costs of this had to be calculated into the net profit. Thanks to this construction, anybody (European or indigenous) trading in opium outside this framework was consequently considered as "smuggling" which "violated" this monopoly. So, every time "smuggler", "smuggling" or "illicit" is used below without these inverted commas, please be aware that it is a VOC judgment. Smugglers and other sappers of the monopoly represent the only available free opium market. It's a view seldom supported by the VOC historians even today.

The VOC morality had another side. From the introduction of opium in the 17th-century onwards, it can be assumed that VOC officials corrupted their own system by becoming involved in some *private* opium selling or other business. This continued, as we shall see, until the last years of the Dutch presence in the East Indies. The general attitude was this is forbidden, but it cannot be avoided; the VOC remunerations are too low, so "they" have to make an "additional, private" income. Therefore, the general practice became: manipulations of the weights, the quantities and quality of the goods, the prices, the bookkeeping, the storage, bribing producers, and so on.[1]

---

[1] See F. Gaastra (1991), p. 94 ff. The OED indicates that since 1608 "Dutch" was 'used in derision and contempt', which must have some ground! There is a substantial difference

The severest punishments for European smugglers and cheaters consisted only of monetary fines and confiscation or a compulsory return home. Sharing the 'silent profits' with the European VOC judges could lead to the avoidance of much of this punishment. Anyway, the barbarous death penalties suffered by non-Europeans were seldom executed on their "own kind". This made the notorious *Amboyna Massacre* (1623) of twenty English convicts, who undermined the VOC monopoly, so exceptional.

From the middle of the 18th-century, something very different happened. On top of all this illicit private business conducted by VOC employees stationed somewhere in the realm, the opium monopoly of the colonial state itself was bartered away, and the actors in this game were the highest officials and some 'free burghers' in both the Dutch and the colonial state. This happened through the invention of the *Amphioen or Opium Society* (AS; 1745-1794). As such, it seems to be the ultimate consequence of the acts of 'the robber-state along the North Sea' (Multatuli).

A contemporary of Multatuli, Governor-General Baud, was certainly not of this opinion, but he must have had a personal, bad experience with the AS phenomenon. He ironically concluded:

> As could be predicted, the Amphioen Society could not fulfill its aim to bridle the smuggling effectively and to provide the Company with the advantages of a regular yearly turn-over of 1200 chests opium ... it was already difficult to arrive at 800 chests ... A remarkable group of citizens, earlier involved in the smuggling themselves, was interested in attacking the illicit import of opium. However, the number of bureaucrats and citizens, who could not become shareholders, remained large enough to be involved in smuggling ...[2]

And what did the inventors of the AS tell the public? In a dispatch (March 1746) to the Directors in Amsterdam, VOC-Batavia described the first experiences of this Opium Society in a frank way never repeated by current Dutch historians. This concerns the perpetual debate about the effects of the price level on opium consumption and smuggling, which persisted in the colony until 1940. The text also provides a shallow legitimation for establishing this Amphioen Society:

---

between the colonization and imperialism of the Dutch and the English or French: in the last two ventures the aristocratic element was much larger than in the Dutch "petty bourgeoisie" one. Only after the Netherlands became a kingdom some Dutch aristocrats (if left) could participate sometimes in the East Indies (see later NHM and Billiton). See for this important aspect J. Nederveen Pieterse, p. 193-223 and passim.

[2] J. C. Baud, p. 124.

A few merchants received in 1745 a ten-year contract [*octroy*] for the trade in opium, because it is impossible to keep the opium price in Batavia as high as during the auctions of the Company in June 1743 and March 1744 and because it is impossible to sell a large quantity of opium without attracting smugglers thanks to the high price. Smugglers risk their life for it, and the indigenous people like to help them if they deliver the opium for a hundred rixdollars per chest cheaper. After the arrival of the [ship the] *Nieuwvliet* from Bengal with only 750 chests of opium, the Society had to sell the opium for 550 rixdollars per chest, meaning: 100 rixdollars per chest lower than the purchasing price from the Company ... If there is a low price, the consumption will increase and smugglers will be discouraged, because they do not want to risk their lives if the profits are too low or have to deliver opium of lower quality than that of the Company, and for a lower price which is not interesting any more. Although it looks as if the Company could get the profit of the Society itself, this is not the case, and the Society gives the Company the most profit. Even if the Society is able to pay 6% every six months, no merchant can compete with it: it is too risky an affair for a profit of 12% in a year. Too much money must be invested which has to be borrowed against a too high interest; therefore, the Society is more advantageous for the Company. The interest of the Company and of the Society is as large a market as possible for the opium, even for a lower price. The price of the shares of the Society is not fixed yet. At the moment there is already an agio of 15 to 20%. Batavia expects that this can increase unto 150%. The Society has all the opium which can be imported through the Strait of Malacca including that which can be captured as contraband of the first degree east of the meridian of the Prince island ...[3]

The relevant Dutch researchers have never reflected enough on Baud's "self-conceit" or the AS initiators' eulogy. That is a pity because what happened there foreshadowed the most important 19th-century development of the Opium Problem, discussed below in some detail.

To explain the backgrounds of this AS, it is necessary to shed some light on the inventor of this innovation. Until now, it was assumed to be the acting Governor-General, Count Van Imhoff, who certainly was highly positive about the new initiative for obvious reasons. In my reconstruction of the case, however, another person should be "credited" for it. Who is this inventor, who built a remarkable VOC career from humble seaman to Governor-General?

---

[3] GM, XI, p. 332.

A Brilliant Economist?

This new key figure in the VOC opium game was Jacob Mossel (1704-1761). He must be considered the first drugs baron, as the first private opium dealer on a large scale.[4] Some current historians see him as a very capable Governor-General together with people like his colleagues Van Hoorn, Van Imhoff and a few others. They all had to do their work among the generally corrupt elite.[5] The most favorable opinion about the man is given by Blussé. According to him, Mossel, the successor of Governor-General Van Imhoff, this 'viceroy', was made a scapegoat since he would have represented all evils of the *ancien régime*.

> He has also been criticized for having made private trade impossible, but here the curious problem poses itself that Batavia underwent a period of prosperity during his reign ... It is striking how historians have parroted each other in this case. A century ago ... Mossel [was described] as the man who only wanted to leave the "trash" ... of the Company's trade to the burghers. Everybody has blindly accepted this verdict without checking it against the sources. Mossel actually was a brilliant "economist", as his contemporaries called him. He indeed forbade private trading between Batavia and the Indian subcontinent, but he was fully in favor of leaving a large share of the trade at Batavia to private entrepreneurs. ... Mossel had a good understanding of the growing commercial interest of the British ... after Mossel's death his successors again drew all trade to the Company as its general condition declined and levied high taxes which totally ruined the citizenry.[6]

---

[4] For the following data see the *Wikipedia* biography, but also www.antenna. nl/~fwillems/nl/nest/mossel.html and Siemen Duys extensive story of the most honorable citizen in the Enkhuizen history at the occasion of a Mossel exhibition: http://toerisme. bruist.nu. The most positive, however, is Leonard Blussé in R.Ross, G. Telkamp, ed., p. 81 ff. The latter used, among others, also an article of W. Coolhaas about Mossel, who apparently is the source of the revision à la Blussé. Same text is published by B. in his (1986), p. 31.

[5] F. Gaastra (1991), p. 97 also referred to Van Lier; in the previous and following pages he gives many examples of this general corruption. This corruption was a standard characteristic of VOC officials from the beginning. See, for instance, *Both*, vol. 1, p. 63.

[6] L. Blussé, in: Idem, p. 81, 82 must have known the earlier C. Boxer (1977), because the author thanks Blussé (p. 112) for sending him a photocopy. Well, Boxer, is one of the fiercest critics of Mossel and Blussé does not discuss the opinion of simply the best scholar at issue. The glorification of Van Imhoff and Mossel, of course, continues in the present official Dutch VOC propaganda, in which prime ministers urge the Dutch public to demonstrate again a VOC spirit (Balkenende, 2007)! In this spirit see also H. Stevens a publication of the Rijksmuseum, Amsterdam: the words "opium" or slavery, for instance, are never heard or used, let alone a reference to the continuous wars and massacres, except the pictures of the beautiful uniforms VOC soldiers apparently wear during their slaughter work. For a quite favorable view on Van Imhoff and Mossel see D. Hall, p. 312 ff.

Mossel must have been a genius if we believe what Blussé writes from his "sources".[7] First, the obvious mistakes in this quotation. That Mossel 'made private trade impossible' is a fundamental misunderstanding of the nature of the Amphioen Society.[8] This argument will be explained further below.

Mossel should be called a clever self-made man with the rather exceptional ability in the VOC of knowing how to write, read and persuade the highest persons in favor of a most stupid plan; he is excessively motivated to make as much money as possible and to give his own person the glamor of a Sun King.

A qualification as 'brilliant economist' can only be invented by people who are not acquainted with the texts of economists, let alone the brilliant ones like those 18th-century contemporaries of Mossel like Colbert, Turgot, Quesnay, Galiani or Adam Smith, David Hume or Adam Ferguson. The immanent problem, aggravated by Mossel's practices, of the contradictions between free trade and the state power was the subject of Pieter de la Court's famous treatise, *The Interest of Holland* (1662; numerous reprints; a new English translation appeared in 1746). It became one of the most influential economic textbooks in the 17th and 18th centuries.[9] There is no proof that Mossel or anyone else in Batavia ever read or discussed this "Dutch" economic treatise.

The very few texts Mossel wrote in his life demonstrate an excessive petty bourgeois bookkeeper's mind like the notorious *Reglement ter Beteugeling van Pracht en Praal* (Ordinance to Bridle Pomp and Splendor, 1754): more than 120 rules related to the proper design of houses, the use and shape of walking sticks, buttonholes and shoe-buckles. It was published by a man who loved excessive splendor during his inauguration as Governor-General, drink-parties and—without doubt—his own lavish funeral.

His next mistake concerned Mossel's alleged understanding of the British commercial interest. This must be a chutzpah: it is Governor-

---

[7] The only source Blussé mentions to support his opinion is an *unsigned* manuscript from September 1794, which is, therefore, written 33 years after Mossel's death. At that time the VOC had already collapsed, and Mossel's many heirs and co-profiteers had, of course, no interest in being blamed for this.

[8] It is a similar opinion to the one made by a well-known judge in 1923, who wrote in a handbook about "East Indies Law of the State": 'The amphioen society and later the anti-opium society agitated against the smuggling and against the lease-system.' J. Slingenberg, p. 91.

[9] C. Boxer (1977) starts his book with a picture and discussion of De La Court's ideas.

General Mossel, who started a war against the English in Bengal and Coromandel in 1759 (after Plassey) without even the faintest knowledge about warfare on sea and land or the ability to organize it. This war was not only a military disaster, it was a serious commercial one as well: *from this moment on, the English definitely took over the position of leading power in Asia.* The Dutch, largely dependent as they were on Bengal textiles, opium and saltpetre, had to pay a dear price as a customer of the British. It took the complete destruction of the VOC and the occupation of Java by the English before the Dutch realized that they had to change their colonial policy drastically (whether they could or did so will be discussed later).

But why do I call Mossel the first private opium dealer on a large scale? Blussé does not write anything about the activity with which Mossel created an innovation in world history, the establishment of the *Amphioen or Opium Society* in 1745. In every biography this is rightly stressed as Mossel's most remarkable activity. Let's first give a few biographical details.

Jacob Mossel was born in Enkhuizen to a humble reformed Protestant family. In the Dutch Golden Age, Enkhuizen was one of the important sea and commercial ports. His poor but rather fanatic father must have taught him how to chase after money; his mother, how to read and write, because she is apparently of impoverished but better standing. It must have been the effect of this education which Mossel demonstrated so exuberantly during the rest of his life: the *nouveau riche* syndrome of humble people becoming rich (he always showed his audience his "family crest", which impressed his colonial entourage, mostly of low descent like himself).

As was usual for poor boys, 15-year-old Jacob went to the East with a VOC ship, as an ordinary seaman for 8 guilders a month (1720). As soon as he arrived at the Cape of Good Hope, the young economist wrote his mother that

> business is bad here, because the Spanish butter and soap are expensive ... Mutton, usually costing two penny (*stuiver*) is here 10 to 12 pennies. I do not buy it, because in Batavia prices will be lower.[10]

It was discovered that young Mossel could write, an exceptional ability in the VOC, which gave him a clear advantage. A year later he had a job on the Coromandel coast well known for its Dutch slave and textile trade where

---

[10] Quoted by S. Duys. When not indicated otherwise, quotations are from this author, who had to write the most favorable text about Mossel for tourists!

he immediately acquainted oneself with the illegal traffic in the VOC's monopoly articles, known as private ... smuggler's trade ... But while high and low smuggled, the big money was only reserved for the elite.[11]

Apparently, the boy decided to become part of this elite: four years later he already occupied the strategically important position of bookkeeper (for 30 guilders a month + bonus of 400-760 guilders a year). Again four years later, he married the 14-year-old daughter of the VOC governor of the Coromandel coast. This gave him a larger monthly income, a better status (main slave trader as 'senior merchant' or head of the administration) and successor to his father-in-law. Boxer informs us how the European servants of the EIC and VOC often worked closely together

> to cheat their respective employers, often also in cooperation with French, Portuguese and Indian accomplices ... a cooperation ... in private trade and smuggling.[12]

Mossel is explicitly mentioned as one of those types. Even for Boxer's sober-minded judgments, he is quite aggressive against those Dutch historians who trumpet the praises of peoples like Mossel, Van der Parra or the VOC performance in general.

When Mossel departed for Batavia, he was already a rich man in VOC terms (with 32,200 guilders saved, which is about one million euros in present value) 'which he could not have gained with his official salary and bonus'. That was not unusual among the elite. A governor of a far-distant VOC post like Mossel officially earned 2,400 guilders a year, but with illicit additional income, one could increase this with some luck and brutality to 100,000 guilders. It was the "official" mentality of the VOC elite to make 'silent profits'.

Still, there were always exceptionally greedy persons like, for instance, Governor-General Van Hoorn, who left Batavia in 1709 with a fortune of 10 million guilders, a "Bill Gates Fortune" in present value. Gaastra called him capable in the meaning of "not corrupt"!

Mossel was also brilliant at accumulating capital. Once back in Batavia (1742) he soon entered the highest ranks in the VOC and could now easily

---

[11] The Dutch have more names for illicit trade, very well known to the VOC people like 'mors-, sluik-, smokkel- or privé-' trade. The last word is, of course, strange, but understandable within the VOC jargon in which everything outside VOC command was illicit, including private trade. Mossel himself wrote that in this VOC trade, people acted 'too extreme and rude beyond any imagination'. As a slave trader he was involved in the most inhuman business of the VOC, as people already knew at that time.

[12] C. Boxer (1977), p. 75, see also p. 80.

see what was the biggest money source in the colony. It was not difficult for him with his bookkeeper's mind and slave trader's experience to make this fixed VOC capital current so that he could fill his own pocket, once he had the key of the treasury.

In November 1745 a ten-year contract (*octroy*) was drawn up between the Dutch colonial state/VOC and a group of private people gathered in a club.[13] For the State/VOC the import part of its opium monopoly remained as it was, but the distribution part was taken over by this AS. The government hoped to stimulate the sale of this already lucrative business and to counteract smuggling by VOC officials, English merchants and others.

It was called a "reorganization of the trade" to produce more profit for the state: nobody was against this. It was also called "privatization": nobody was against that, because the most important people in the colony were invited to participate and accepted becoming profiteers in the game; it was aimed at "avoiding smuggling": nobody was against it, because every participant at this level had the same or similar experiences and wanted to eliminate his competitors. The exclusive object of the trade was opium: everybody knew how easy it was to smuggle this product and how much profit could be gained with it after a century of VOC infiltration.

The invited profiteers of the new activity were only a few rich and influential people, bureaucrats and 'free burghers', who could distribute among each other only 300 very expensive shares of nearly 5000 guilders each (two years of salary for a governor in a VOC region). In their official functions these persons were the leaders of the VOC, and they agreed to offer themselves the most lucrative opium distribution monopoly.

The new club was called the Amphioen Society (AS). Of the 300 shareholders, six did some work as new opium ships arrived from Bengal twice a year. In two meetings the few attendants exchanged part of the VOC monopoly with the AS for a price; largely a movement from one hand to the other. Another two meetings, the auctions, were held between some AS members and the former VOC opium farmers: theoretically, they could have been attended by about 106 AS persons; practically, it may have been a quick meeting between a few representatives of the farmers and a few AS members. Later, two AS members did some administrative work: who had paid cash, who used credit; the transmission of the interests to the

---

[13] For the general data of the AS see R. Manurung, F. Gaastra (2006), E. Vanvugt (1995), p. 106-116.

shareholders. All in all, a few days "hard labor" per year for a fantastic salary.

The AS was, therefore, nothing but an intermediary or "middleman" between the VOC and the opium farmers. It reserved the most promising source of money for itself by emancipating it from the rest of the complicated VOC business. In return, the members promised to buy from the VOC a fixed amount of 1200 chests every year (with some additional conditions). The VOC-colonial state kept the import monopoly and remained responsible for the military security in the whole archipelago: it was, therefore, a construction which gave only advantages to the participants and the costs to the "taxpayer". That is to say: the navy was instructed to chase the "smugglers", the main competitors of the AS participants.

The first director of this purely narco-military AS became Jacob Mossel. He started out by gaving himself a salary of 7,200 guilders a year, which was nearly three times as much as a comparable VOC official could earn in Amsterdam. This brilliant salary, however, was peanuts compared to the forty shares he took for himself. To buy these shares, Mossel must have "earned" about 160,000 guilders in two years (since he arrived in Batavia). Even from a VOC perspective, this is a most astonishing achievement.[14] The only source of it could have been opium through smuggling or administrative corruption. The details are difficult to prove, but the following reconstruction seems to be a reasonable compensation.

Officially, the plan for the AS came from the ailing Governor-General Van Imhoff himself. Of course, a Governor-General in a colony is always

---

[14] The value of the shares was 192, 000 guilders, and he came to Batavia with 32,000 guilders in his pockets two years earlier. F. Gaastra (2006), p. 104 for the first amount. Let us look at the usual incomes at the time. Around 1700 the Netherlands had around 10-20% unemployed, beggars, etc. Next came the soldiers, sailors, unskilled laborers, etc. with an income seldom higher than 200 guilders *a year*. Then there was the petty bourgeoisie (skilled laborers, small shopkeepers, etc.) with a yearly income of between 200 and 400 guilders; a middle class of lower officers, clergymen, small entrepreneurs, etc. had an income of at most 1200 guilders; the upper bourgeoisie (higher officers, large merchants, rentiers, etc.) were well paid with double that amount; finally, there was the 3-4% of the patriarchy (aristocrats, highest government bureaucrats, etc.) with "everything above the last amount". See H. Schipper, p. 110 ff. In the 18th-century the level of the real wages of the petty bourgeoisie was about 10% higher until 1730, but after that year it decreased quickly and substantially to the lowest level in 200 years. See J. de Vries, A. v.d. Woude, p. 722. From the many data mentioned in Idem, p. 647-689, about the 18th-century, one cannot see large differences from those mentioned above: 75% of the Amsterdam shopkeepers had less than 1200; only 2% earned more than 3000 guilders in a year. The largest incomes were earned by the highest government bureaucrats: the mayor and aldermen of Amsterdam with about 7000 guilders per year in 1742. This shows how exceptional the AS opium remunerations were!

the cleverest person, but he was clearly not the boss. A Jacob Cool (the 'Court Jew of Van Imhoff'),who also became a member of the AS board and who was originally the proud possessor of thirty shares, was urged to leave ten of them to his 'favorites'. The result of this shuffle was that Mossel had twice as many shares as anybody else, including Van Imhoff.

As compensation, the latter was nominated "president of the AS" (*opper-directeur*). There must have been specific reasons for this remarkable behavior of Mossel's colleagues: throwing mud and malice at each other was second nature in this rich and corrupt milieu. The most reasonable explanation was that Jacob Mossel was in a position to bribe them all and to buy their silence with the promised profits. A basis for this hypothesis would be a specific relationship with the opium producers in Bengal (doubtless, he had a profound knowledge about the Bengal opium trade) or specific knowledge about smuggling practices, etc.

There is another indirect indication about Mossel's position: after he came from India to Batavia, the opium profits suddenly *trebled* from 512,000 to 1,415,00 guilders. They remained exceptionally high for the next few years, around one million guilders, while the average was not more than half of that (see Appendix 3). It must have been this circumstance which triggered the establishment of the AS, the position of newcomer Mossel as its Director, and Mossel's remarkable sudden wealth. All this made Jacob Mossel the first opium dealer on the largest possible scale at the time. Until his death in 1761, he remained the unchallenged dealer with opium revenues on top of his other lucrative functions.

Although this trade was confined to the inter-Asian realm, Mossel and his AS received fantastic support from the Netherlands as well. Most shareholders lived there. A remarkable participant in this opium game was the royal family, the stadholder William IV himself. This Prince of Orange was invited to became a shareholder with thirty shares in 1748. He was promised that in 1755 he would be 200,000 guilders richer, without having to do anything, when the *octroy* of the Amphioen Society expired. Every time the octroy was renewed, this "stadholder" and his successor, William V, would receive an enormous amount of opium money (e.g. 1,187,280 guilders in 1795).[15] All shareholders together pocketed in total about 13 million guilders; at the time it was a fabulous amount of money comparable to a present value of about a billion guilders.[16]

---

[15] F. Gaastra (2006), p. 105, 106.

[16] The details about these shareholders and most of his text were copied by Gaastra from an unpublished script from I. Mens (1987). Gaastra never altered his favorable opinion about Mossel.

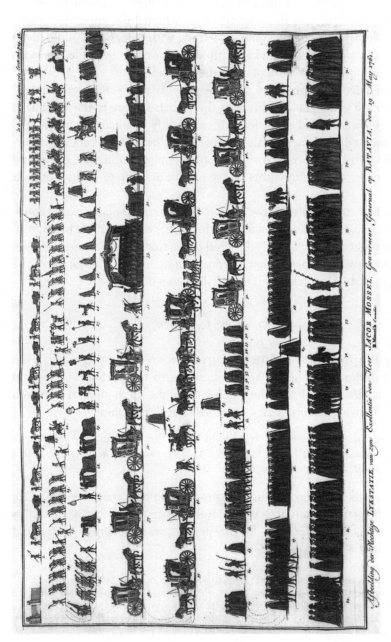

Ill. 15. Funeral Procession of a VOC Governor – General, 1761

Source: Wikipedia 'Lijkstatie van Jacob Mossel, 19 mei 1761'. Governor-General Jacob Mossel, of humble descent, got a funeral in Batavia like Louis XIV earlier in France. This represents well the status of the first large scale opium dealer in history.

Last but not least, Mossel also contributed to the final decline of the VOC by what he did well, in hindsight. In November 1752 he sent a report to the VOC Directors in Amsterdam in which he complained about the marked decline of the company's trade with Asia.[17] The Dutch had a representative in Canton, and enormous profits could be made here with new attention and investments ... in the tea trade.

As detailed in section ch. 6, this was the very product "in cooperation" with opium which, indeed, brought the British Empire to the summit of its power, wealth and extension. Mossel rightly stipulated that the VOC had a marked advantage in this Chinese trade, since it had products available for the Chinese which they liked: tin, pepper, cotton, wax, spices and other goods. Their competitors had to pay for tea with precious metals or opium.

The Directors reacted, however, with a very stupid plan (in hindsight): they decided to bypass Batavia and the VOC, while establishing a completely new organization only directed to the trade with Canton: they created their own competitor and demonstrated, in fact, that for them the VOC (including Jacob Mossel) was as dead as a doornail.

The AS Performance

That is the personal side of the AS story.[18] A more interesting aspect is the opium performance of the AS compared with the normal VOC opium business. What people like the "President" of the AS thought of it is given in the following symptomatic (and nonsensical) reasoning:

> The Society receives the amphioen [from the VOC] for 450 [rixdollars per chest] and sells this for 550 ... It is certain that nobody can sell it cheaper ..[19]; except, of course, the VOC!

In Appendix 2 we have given the comparative data over a period of 24 years. This comparison does not fit in the sense that the "VOC period" is chronologically earlier than the "AS period"; wars or crop failures could

---

[17] For the following see L. Blussé (2008), p. 58 ff.

[18] Appendix 2 to F. Gaastra (2006), p. 113 ff. provides Mens' list of all shareholders in 1801 with incorrect sums (not the indicated 300 but about four less). Only 56 of the shares remained in Batavia and most of the rest in the Netherlands, dispersed over many places and institutions like an orphanage with not fewer than 22 shares and even a pawn-bank with 5.

[19] GM, XI, p. 635.

have taken their toll, which makes historical comparison difficult. But the periods seem to be long enough to make the statistically viable conclusion that the totals of both performances generally did not differ much: the profits per chest were nearly the same (540 and 560 guilders), the profits per pound weight were nearly the same (3.55 and 3.85 guilders), etc.

The next conclusion to be drawn from the table is that the AS on average did not fulfill its promise always to buy 1200 chests from the VOC. All kinds of excuses were given for this (see below), but the table also shows how remarkable regularities occur (see period 1755-1761). It seems obvious that corrupt people like the AS members manipulated the administration; in the VOC table this kind of regularity does not appear.

From other sources comes additional information about those "irregular years" and complaints. Immediately at the end of 1746, the impatience of the greedy is heard in the AS complaints: the profit may be 158%, but in Bengal the purchasing price must be lowered, so that the profit can become 450 rixdollars per chest or 200%.[20] Ten years later 1200 chests were imported from Patna for the price of 1,296,000 guilders (fl. 1080 per chest). That was apparently 200 chests too much for the AS. It requested the government to be exempt from this obligation, 'but the Government had another view about it, whereupon the AS asked to send 100 chests to the West of India, which was agreed with the consent of Bengal'.[21]

Three years later there was a problem with the quantity per chest: in most of the delivery, this was about 70 kilogram too little. The government decided to deliver the shortages to the AS, which was a good subvention.[22] In April 1761 four ships had come from Bengal with the usual 1200 chests of opium. However, the first three carried not more than 293 chests and the last another hundred, while the price per chest was increased by nearly 400 guilders per chest to about 1500. Reason: the indigenous merchant stated that it was impossible to deliver 1200 chests because the constant movement of troops had destroyed a large part of the poppy fields.[23]

Above it was stated that the AS was an intermediary club: profits on two sides, without great risks. The effects of its mere existence were many and serious. Contrary to the long quotation at the beginning of this chap-

---

[20] GM, XI, p. 464; same complaint Idem, p. 634.
[21] GM, XIII, p. 104.
[22] Idem, p. 470.
[23] Idem, p. 621.

ter, the VOC lost the AS's substantial *profits*. Next, this means that the *price* of the product for farmers of the AS was increased by the profits and costs of the AS members and interests of the shareholders. The VOC monopoly price was by definition lower than the AS monopoly price. This led to the opium farmers becoming more motivated to increase the number of their clients; opium being distributed more in society; and more addicts.

However, there was another reaction. The AS was established under the pretext of avoiding "*smuggling*", but the greater the price increase, the sooner the opium farmers would look for alternative suppliers, i.e. "smugglers". Instead of preventing smuggling, the AS must actually have increased the chances for "smuggling". The complaint one reads time and again in the *Generale Missiven* is that the English smugglers from Bencoolen (west coast of Sumatra) were becoming increasingly more active. This "smuggling" represents the workings of a free competitive market (to be counteracted by all means).

Another serious effect of the AS performance was that VOC officials not involved in the AS or who did not belong to the "AS club" felt free to conduct their own opium business. De Haan gives several examples including the fancy prices they made per chest of opium.[24]

These effects of the monopoly opium trade, as emancipated from the rest of the VOC business, contributed to the decline of the VOC. There were more factors involved. One of the means to obtain as much profit as possible was to manipulate the *quality* of the product. A few examples will suffice.

Van Imhoff wrote to Amsterdam (31 December 1746) that private opium dealers are not allowed to trade without a Company pass. And to avoid smuggling, 'one ordered from Bengal 300 chests of amphioen second quality, so that indigenous people can get cheap opium not only from smugglers but also from the Amphioen Society...'[25]

Trouble occurred between the Company and AS as well. At the end of 1751 it was reported to Amsterdam that business had not been good that year due to a lack of pepper and opium. In Hughly 925 chests were pur-

---

[24] F. de Haan, vol. 4, p. 21 ff. the opium business of the "Regentschappen", persons like Nic. Engelhard, etc. with their shameless business morality and exorbitant profits. These persons continued to serve under the new conditions when the AS and the VOC had perished.

[25] GM, XI, p. 396. The AS was even prepared to corrupt its own position to buy opium from smugglers. See Idem, p. 333.

chased, but 263 of them were considered of bad quality in Batavia and as good in India:

> ... the VOC representative [opperhoofd] in Patna, Drabbe, has now to pay a fine of fifteen rixdollars per chest, but the Amphioen Society has already sold them for good quality because of the shortage there was a strong motivation to buy.[26] A year later the VOC obtained again a hundred chests of 'second quality' but sold them to the AS for 432 guilders a chest, but the AS refuses: 'we cannot sell them and want to pay next time not more than 360 ...' which is the Malacca price. This price is so low, because the English are very active in smuggling..[27]

In this way the AS introduced the policy of distributing bad quality as good, which has the same effect as in another political economy: bad money drives out good money. It is a game which was played on a much larger scale a bit later in India by "smugglers in the view of the EIC", centered in Malwa (Bombay). They were struggling against the monopoly of the Bengal-British opium, until the British also captured this part of India, with the effect that from that moment on, the British themselves traded with different qualities. The effect of doing this was to enlarge the opium market because poorer consumers can buy cheaper stuff. This is bad for their health, but dealers were never concerned with that, on the contrary.

For outsiders, the connections between the AS and the VOC were very obvious. The practical status of the AS can be indicated by the following examples.

To exploit its opium resource to the utmost, the AS introduced a lease on smoking prepared opium (*madat*) in districts outside Batavia at the end of 1746. However, this turned out to be a miscalculation: the opium income decreased, and corruption increased. Half a year later, this lease was cancelled: '... the opium leaser has to pay four month lease, half to the Company and half to the Amphioen Society'.[28]

In 1750 the bosses in Amsterdam were thanked for accepting the continuation of the AS for another 25 years, because the opium trade wa 'the most important' for their business: the AS had bought 1300 chests and that gave the VOC an 'income of between eight and nine hundred thousand

---

[26] GM, XII, p. 174.

[27] GM, XII, p. 271, see also Idem, p. 337. The differentiation in several qualities (and prices) of opium is, for instance in 1752/53: of the 1265 chests 998 were 'Behaarse' (617 of which were sold in Patna and the rest in Hughly), while 267 chesst were bad quality from 'Pourannias and Baggelpourian'. See also Idem, p. 504 and GM, XI, p. 407, 408.

[28] GM, XI, p. 598.

guilders'. This was about 40% of all trade in that year.[29] Nine years later (in 1759/60) the delivery of a thousand chests of opium amounted to half of the value of the total delivery of goods (2,125,986 guilders).[30] As shown in Appendix 2 they were exceptionally good years.

The AS status is well circumscribed with a text demonstrating how it fits into the usual monopoly game. It concerns violent quarrels between the VOC and the Sultan of Jambi (east coast of Sumatra) in 1760 and the Dutch blockade of all his ports:

> If the Sultan responds adequately to the just demand of the Company, then the passage of vessels with a pass is freed. Ships which carry spices and opium without the mark of the Company or the Amphioen Society, however, must be confiscated and brought to Batavia without damage, whatever the Sultan may do with our demand. Captains of ships from foreign nations who intend to trade with Djambi must be warned not to do this, emphasizing the exclusive rights of the Company. If necessary, this right will be defended by force in order to avoid disadvantage for the Company's trade ...[31]

In a secret letter accompanying this instruction, the Dutch military are warned not to be cheated by 'those deceitful natives while their own merchants must be saved by threatening the natives with punishments ...' The same page of the *Generale Missiven* reports about the Company's negotiations with a Siamese ruler for the delivery of forty catty of silver. The representative of the VOC is urged by Governor-General Mossel to threaten this ruler as well. Why?

> How reasonable and affable these people may be treated [by us], it appears as crystal clear that this nation abandons itself to unsatiable greed while the possession of only a few goods is more important to them than their honor and decent name, yes, even more than the need and wealth of their countries.[32]

It seems a good formulation to demonstrate how the perpetrators, represented here by the most high-ranked slave and opium trader, are always ready to accuse their victims of their own mistakes to legitimate their repression. This way of silencing their own conscience had the most far-reaching and lethal consequences, as the following story reveals.

---

[29] GM, XII, p. 77.
[30] GM, XIII, p. 609.
[31] GM, XIII, p. 528.
[32] GM, XIII, p. 528.

CHAPTER FIFTEEN

THE CHINESE, THE VOC AND THE OPIUM

Currently, about 40 million Chinese live permanently outside China in 130 countries, most of them in Southeast Asia (*Nanyang*). This phenomenon will be discussed later in more detail (ch. 25). Here some of its early characteristics in the East Indies will be highlighted because it was in hindsight the "role model" for many later developments of the Western Opium Problem in Asia.

The confrontation between the Chinese and the VOC has so much practical and symbolic value for our history that also for the early phase of it, a detailed explanation of its role can be fruitful. The Chinese operated in the East Indies as traders and peasants before the Dutch came. After the arrival of the Dutch, they soon became their main trading partners and later also the important opium farmers. It became a 300-year confrontation between Western and Eastern foreigners, between masters and servants, but also between murderers and victims.

Two hundred years after the first Dutch-Chinese meetings in the East Indies, the British Empire decided to conquer China through bombardment with opium, followed by gunboats and cannonballs. The Opium Problem was transformed into a confrontation between West and East on a world scale. One can, therefore, ask whether this was foreshadowed by the earlier Dutch-Chinese relationship? Let us examine the characteristics of it in this chapter.

Certainly, it is not the first relationship between a Western power and Chinese. The Portuguese were allowed to settle in Macao (Macau) in 1557 with a few people, establishing a few buildings to repair their ships. Slowly some trade developed, which was immediately of a peculiar kind: Chinese were caught and sold to Lisbon as slaves; they were highly desired in Portugal, much more than Arabs or blacks. Although this trade only lasted a few decades before it was forbidden by both the Chinese and Portuguese authorities (1595), it was a peculiar first relationship between a Western country and China. It is also the only occasion of this kind. That was not the case with mass murder in the East Indies.[1]

---

[1] Alas, it became a strange habit to compare the hatred and massacres of Chinese with the Jewish ones by using words such as "diaspora", "pogrom", etc. One has to realize that it

Murder in Batavia

Just before Mossel's arrival in Batavia, terrible things happened there: the Dutch foreigners under the leadership of their highest officials like Van Imhoff and Valckenier massacred the majority of the unarmed Chinese foreigners.[2] This has been ignored, at least in Southeast Asian history. The 'Chinese Massacre of 1740' with about 20,000 mostly Chinese victims is not the only Dutch massacre of this magnitude (see Banda Massacre). It is certainly the first and largest (Dutch) colonial act of Sinophobic violence. Before analyzing this question, we need a few facts.

Around 1740 about 25,000 people (including slaves) lived in Batavia and the surrounding countryside, with the Dutch forming only a small minority (not even 10%) and the Chinese proper (excluding their servants and/or illicit emigrants) 50%. In the countryside corrupt Dutch sheriffs created a "Wild West" lifestyle for the Chinese peasants. As the Chinese domination of the sugar market declined, mass poverty, unemployment and ruin followed. The rural Chinese protested and, in the end, revolted in 1740 under classic banners like "to choose the right day and the right moment" or "follow the righteous of olden times".[3]

---

is a typically Western way of thinking, overloaded as it is by guilt feelings for the murder of Jews. See, for instance, L. Pan, p. 128-153 or J. Blussé (1986) who even uses 'holocaust' (p. 94). Chinese and Jews, however, have nothing to do with each other except some "superficial" characteristics: tragic things like the periodical massacres by "white" torturers and their helpers or their perception as "non-conformists", rich and merchants. The classic mistake is to introduce here ethnic characteristics, but a few moments of reflection on the phenomenon "Chinese Jews/ Jewish Chinese" is enough to cure oneself of it. One can also read H. Derks (2004), chapter 6.

[2] It is strange that in GM, X there are only a very few indications that a Chinese massacre ever happened. The last message from Valckenier dates from 31-3-1740 (p. 461-493) and than nothing until a few lines on 31-10-1740 about 'a substantial rebellion and brutal venture against the Company' (p. 494). The next message of half a page dates from the first of December. It is a request from the VOC chief of Onrust (the island off the coast of Batavia, the VOC's ship-building yard) to his carpenters to return to the island. They apparently assisted the military to combat the Chinese guerrillas. The reason for the silence: the clerks, who wrote the GMs, had to fight as well!

[3] For the following E. M. Jacobs, passim; W. Remmelink, p. 125 ff.; E. Vanvugt (1985), p. 78 ff.; D. Hall, p. 311 ff.; J. Blussé (1986), p. 73-97; N. Randeraad (ed.), p. 23 ff. These rural Chinese cannot be qualified as 'vagabond Chinese' as Vanvugt writes or 'bandits' (Remmelink). Apart from several interesting quotations, the latter mitigates in an untenable way the whole question of the massacre as something which had already happened in Manila six times (Id., p. 96). The relationship Chinese—Spaniards in Manila was much more complicated, with three different Chinese parties (the "pirate-king" Lim Hong who attacked the Spaniards from the seaside as a kind of liberation guerrilla, the Chinese from China who also chased Lim Hong, the Chinese who worked in the city of Manila under bad

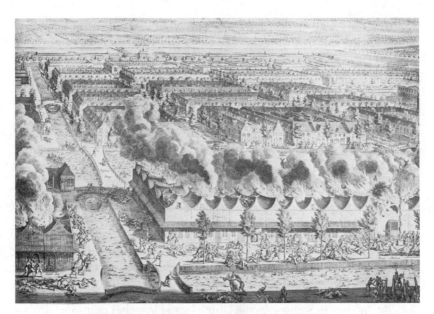

Ill. 16. The Dutch Massacre of the Chinese, October 8th, 1740

Source: C. Boxer (1977) p. 71. Some 12,000 – 20,000 Chinese were killed in Batavia alone; all the houses and shops of Chinese were looted and mostly burned. In the countryside many suffered the same fate 'as a matter of precaution'.

The first phase of the massacre was triggered by this revolt of the desperate, rural Chinese poor. Their urban masters, Chinese captains and officers and Dutch alike, did not want to improve their situation, but killed many and captured others to transport them to Cape of Good Hope or Ceylon. The rumor that they would be thrown overboard during the trip aggravated their anger. They started to attack the city gates, but again many were killed.

The second phase started not only with the easy defeat of these rural poor, but also with the decision of Governor-General Valckenier to attack the urban Chinese. The second highest Dutch official, Van Imhoff, urged the elimination of only the poorly armed urban Chinese. This last plan was carried out, but during this action a few buildings were set on fire by unknown people. This panicked the European population, and assisted by sailors, slaves and servants, they started a hysterical massacre that last-

---

circumstances and revolted three times (1602, 1662, 1686). There was never a massacre of the magnitude of "Batavia", let alone under the same circumstances. See A. McCoy, E. de Jesus (ed.).

ed three days in which Valckenier personally ordered the killing of Chinese prisoners, throwing the sick out of the hospitals, etc. Van Imhoff, the next Governor-General, contributed to this lethal festival by paying a premium to all who could throw a decapitated head of a Chinese person out of the city. It ended by setting the whole Chinese quarter on fire. Definitely 12,000 Chinese were killed; all the houses and shops of Chinese were looted and mostly burned. There are several personal testimonies (1751) of people who plundered and murdered like the German carpenter Georg Schwartz, sent by his boss:

> As I knew that my Chinese neighbor had a fat pig, I intended to take it away ... When my boss ... saw this, he slapped me and told me to kill the Chinese first and then to plunder. I, therefore, took a rice-pounder and with it beat to death my neighbor with whom I so often had drunk and dined'. That was not all; Schwartz discovered a pistol, went outside 'and killed everybody who I met ... I had grown so accustomed to this, that it was the same to me whether I killed a dog or a Chinese.[4]

Outside Batavia, in Semarang, the Dutch leader Visscher considered 'massacring all able-bodied Chinese in the district' as a matter of 'precaution'. In a lethal game of divide and rule, he urged the Susuhunan to fix this job.[5] The Protestant clergyman, Wagardus, declared in the commemorating service after the massacre that God's help was necessary 'to crush this Chinese revolt'. This help was not very effective: what was left over of the rural Chinese initiated a kind of guerrilla war which was so successful that a Javanese ruler of Mataram publicly supported it. The Dutch took several years to suppress this new revolt. In West Java, Bantĕn (Bantam), the Dutch faced a new war, and so on.

   Not every Dutchman was convinced of the need for all this. They lived far away in the Netherlands without much communication. Still, a poet at the time expressed his anger in the following lines[6]:

> Look this Chinese, his wife and kin,
> humbly kneeled,
> a disaster cannot be avoided by him.
> Look how they are all killed,

---

[4] Quoted in J. Blussé (1986), p. 95 who suggests the scum of the VOC is guilty, here a *German* carpenter-servant (Holocaust!). He mentions nothing about the behavior of the VOC leadership. Not so Remmelink, who later rightly stresses 'that the massacre in Batavia had not been a mob action, but an act of policy' (W. Remmelink, p. 128).

[5] W. Remmelink, p. 127, 128.

[6] C. Boxer (1977), p. 96; my translation.

heart and head peeled,
while nobody knows their guilt.

Birth of a Chinese Hate?

Historians counteracted these cruelties by stating in all seriousness that
the VOC people 'after 1700 acted much less aggressively than in the previous period', which was 'not due to their [better] skills..'[7] The longest-term
effect is, anyway, that even after the decolonization, "Chinese hate" was
so thoroughly engrained in this ex-colonial society that even after 1949,
severe anti-Chinese massacres were "successfully" organized several
times in Indonesia. This serious crime directly contributed to a new war
with Mataram (1741, etc.), was an impulse stimulating the great revolt of
Bantĕn against the VOC (1748, etc.), but also the decline of the VOC itself:
the trade with China became too strongly blocked, while it could not be
based on such an aggressive distrust and discrimination.

> Without doubt the junk trade to Batavia was dealt a staggering blow by the
> tragic occurrences of 1740. A large part of the infrastructure and the orga-
> nization of the trade in Batavia simply disappeared because many of the
> Chinese brokers and key figures had been either killed or banished ... the
> junk trade shrank within a few decades to a shadow of its former self.[8]

These are the direct effects of the massacre (see further below), but why
did it happen at that time? I can find three reasons: the existence of a
broadly supported anti-Chinese racism, a typical urban-rural antagonism
in Batavia, and the very limited ability of the VOC leadership to understand and master the situation.

The main sources of sinophobia were mostly hidden in Pandora's Box:
Dutch positive racism ("Chinese are a degenerated race"), Dutch negative
racism (bad conscience about their own murder practice and perpetrator's behavior standardly followed by a "but" ... "they" provoked "us" in
some way or other), Dutch xenophobia ("we" do not like strangers), Dutch
Protestant religious legitimation ("they" are pagans; God is on our side)
and Dutch economic interest ("they" are "our" competitor; "they" are
"rich" and occupy key economic positions).

---

[7] F. Gaastra (1991), p. 97. It is a strange opinion relative to the cruel practices described
here and wars in the 18th-century. The only relevance one could discover behind it is that
the personal violence against their own soldiers and sailors seemed to be less in the 18th
than in the 17th-century. Of course, the regime on the ships was terribly harsh. See, for
instance, Governor-General Both's letter 13 in *Both,* vol. 2, p. 268-271.

[8] J. Blussé (1986), p. 139, 140.

These sources *all* claimed that the Dutch *leadership* thought it necessary from a real-political point of view to teach "them" a lesson "they" will
never forget. It is a message not so much to the alleged "enemy", but to a
substantial proportion of Dutch supporters indoctrinated by the same
doctrines and willing to react. In this case Valckenier and Van Imhoff had
opened Pandora's Box.

The interaction with Europe is obvious. All these sources have a
European background, and memories were still "fresh" after the terrible
religious and economic European wars of the sixteenth and seventeenth
centuries in which sometimes one-third of a population of millions was
eliminated.[9] The application to the Chinese and the *combination* are, of
course, a colonial one and unknown in the West (although the returning
colonialists brought many of these ideas back home). One may suppose
that once the European leadership ventured abroad, these prejudices
were activated much more quickly when arriving in a fully unknown,
strange and tropical world.

Beginning with the soldier-hirelings from these wars, the scum of the
European nations formed the large majority of people engaged in the
colonial ventures.[10] The pious Governor-General J. P. Coen is the Dutch
example par excellence of these terrifying figures or, in this case,
Valckenier or Van Imhoff[11]; the Portuguese, Spaniards or English have
many examples as well. The mediocre leaders of Western colonizers also
showed an unprecedented cruelty against new environments, people as
well as nature.

That cannot be rationalized with an appeal to the primitive peoples,
who are "by nature" barbarous, or something like "the spirit of the time"
(not even: 'the European spirit'). The massacre in question was, of course,
a direct consequence of the Dutch colonial exploitation in which harsh
attacks (bullets against knives) alternate with rigorous divide and rule
games played between the different population groups inside and outside

---

[9] For detailed analyzes of the forms of racism in Western societies, see H. Derks
(2004).

[10] F. Gaastra (1991), p. 81 ff. This was a serious problem from the beginning also relative
to the first European women who were imported in the Moluccas. There were many complaints about their licentiousness, etc. See *Both,* vol. 1, p. 103 ff. Already in 1612 the first
Governor-General, Both, issued the cruelest sentences to counteract their behavior. It
helped only for a short while.

[11] The latter is probably even a "better villain" than Valckenier, because he manipulated the VOC Directors in Amsterdam and the lawsuit so long that one started to believe
that Valckenier was the only one guilty of the murder of innocent Chinese. See C. Boxer
(1977), p. 96.

Batavia and Java. For the Dutch it is a routine case, although the one is much better able to play this game than the other. There is the impression that VOC employees generally belonged to the scum of the European nations and, therefore, relied on violence too quickly, even more than the English did.

This massacre fractured social relations, diminished the workforce and many services formerly provided by Chinese, but it also immediately disrupted the junk trade with China. Merchants from China had lost an important market, and their trading partners for all kinds of commercial ventures elsewhere in Southeast Asia.

When they first arrived (1619), the Dutch were confronted with 400 Chinese merchants, but also with the so-called Mardijkers, ex-slaves of the Portuguese who had a kind of free status. Under the leadership of J. P. Coen, a rigorous population policy was carried out. As given above, he asked for as many slaves as he could get. Generally, people did not live very long in an unhealthy, marshy place like Batavia; "new blood" had to be constantly imported. They also activated the import of new Chinese groups and accepted that rich Chinese would also import Chinese from China. This created the "coolie problem" in mines and plantations and increased the power base of a Chinese elite.

Under Dutch leadership, multicultural coastal settlements developed as islands in indigenous societies which the Chinese dominated, at least in numbers. In Batavia around 1699, they formed 39% of the population (the Dutch 19%) of nearly ten thousand inhabitants, representatives of all sorts of indigenous tribes and parts of Asia. On the eve of the massacre, the Chinese were 58% against the Dutch 18% of a total population of 7,233 (excluding slaves). That figure referred to inside Batavia and not the countryside.

In addition, the Chinese had trade relations with the Dutch in many respects, and the Dutch considered them *unarmed* competitors as well. Because the Chinese were accustomed to the same "maritime business" as the Dutch, they were readily seen as partners in financial and other "maritime business" co-operations. Most indigenous tribes or larger social formations were generally qualified as "lazy" and in a racial sense more "degenerated" than the Chinese.

Even an Englishman of the stature of Raffles copied these dangerous and ridiculous typical Western perceptions when he wrote:

> The Chinese ... are to a high degree more intelligent, more laborious and
> more luxurious. They are the life and soul of the commerce of the country.[12]

And regarding the Malays, for instance,

> that when he has rice, nothing will induce him to work. Accustomed to
> wear arms from his infancy ... he is the most correctly polite of all savages
> ... But with all his forbearance, he is feelingly alive to insult; submits with a
> bad grace to the forms to which, in a civilized life, he finds himself obliged
> to conform; and when these are ... numerous or enforced ... he flies to the
> woods, where ... he feels he is free.[13]

It looks like a positive discrimination of the Chinese. We become suspicious because this man, who had rather intelligent explanations for all
and everything in his history of Java, did not comment much on the Dutch
mass murder of Chinese and the subsequent wars. He only concluded
that the Chinese 'are considered to have much decreased'. The Malays
were degraded thanks to the exploitation of the Dutch, the Chinese or the
Arabs, as well as their own rulers. The British, however, are the Europeans
who were best suited to transform Malays into good Englishmen, if that
suited the British interests.

Raffles writes about other foreigners living in the archipelago in his
History that 'the natives of the Coromandel and Malabar coast ... usually
termed Moors' once were numerous, but their number has considerably
decreased 'since the establishment of the Dutch monopoly and the absolute extinction of the native trade with India, which ... was once very
extensive.'

In his *Memoir*, however, he calls the Arabs 'mere drones, useless and
idle consumers of the produce of the ground', inculcating the most intolerant bigotry. The Islamic religion was nothing but a 'robber-religion'
against which only the propagation of Christianity could be helpful. He
expressed in the same wave of anger his astonishment that among all of
the tribes in the realm ('slaves into the hands of the English') not a single
one could be converted to Christianity; all of them became Muslim, 'and
despise and hate their masters as infidels.'[14]

Indigenous people like the Buginese and other tribes in the East Indies
archipelago, who were at least as clever and skilled at sea as the Dutch,
were seen by the Dutch and English only as pirates, to be eliminated

---

[12] Th. Raffles, vol. 1, p. 75.
[13] Quoted from Raffles' *Memoir of the Life and Public Services of Sir Thomas Stamford Raffles* (London 1830, 1835) by S. Alatas, p. 28.
[14] Idem, p. 30. These are still very popular creeds on both sides of the Atlantic.

wholesale and as soon as possible. When this proved impossible, they could always be recruited for the armed forces for 'good money', as the Dutch used Japanese samurai earlier as killing machines in Banda and elsewhere.

When these people directly acted against Raffles' or British interests, the judgments immediately change into the strongest accusations based on "facts" which he knew could not be true. Thus, without any qualification, he talks about how 'The' Chinese were only 'the agents of the Dutch' from the beginning, acquiring the entire monopoly of opium revenue farms and government contracts.[15] Therefore, the British government was warned against the Chinese:

> Although the Chinese, as being the most diligent and industrious settlers, should be the most useful, they have, on the contrary, become a very dangerous people, and are to be labelled a pest for the country; and there appears to be no radical cure for this evil but their extermination from the interior, a measure which cannot now be effected.[16]

Here, in a statement of an intelligent, learned, leading Western politician—a white elephant anyway—the Chinese hate is expressed by using the verdict of wholesale extermination in an even more stringent way than was the case of the Buginese.

This must be the reason why Raffles failed in his job as historian in the case of the Massacre of 1740. He also paved the way for further acts of lethal violence against "The Chinese", mobilizing enemies of these enemies according to the classical divide-and-rule maxims. Raffles continues his philippic with, among others:

> It is, therefore, of the greatest importance to be on our guard against this pernicious and increasing influence, which preys on the very vitals of the country, draining and exhausting it for the benefit of China. In all the Malay states, the Chinese have made every effort to get the collecting of the port duties into their hands, and this has generally proved the ruin of the trade ... This ascendancy of the Chinese ... should be cautiously guarded against and restrained, and this perhaps cannot be better done than by bringing forward the native population of Malays and Javanese ...[17]

---

[15] M. Adas writes that the Dutch deprived the inland court centers of their trading outlets to the sea and, therefore, of the main sources of revenue. 'The remaining local and inland trade was sizable, but it gradually fell into the hands of the Chinese, who served both the Javanese and Dutch as middlemen, tax farmers, and landlords' (p. 7).

[16] Th. Raffles, Memoir, p. 29.

[17] Idem, p. 30. Raffles should be seen as a true pathological mind; a judgment which seems unavoidable after reading the extensive quotation in S. Alatas (p. 32) about Raffles' description of the cannibalism of the Bataks. It is too obscene to quote here, but after his

Chinese as Victims

Thanks to the occupation and violent repression by the Dutch and English, a hierarchy of norms, values and judgments was established based, of course, on European arms and cultural traditions. Batavia was a copy of a Dutch seventeenth-century city with canals, etc. as was Paramaribo in the "West Indies" and all Dutch colonial settlements in between. From the start, the foreigners violently impressed their Christian culture on the inhabitants of the archipelago, as happened with the Banda islands and others.

One consequence of this whole constellation was that the overseas Chinese seldom or never became enslaved by the Europeans, as was the case with people from India, Java or other East Indies islands, let alone the "blacks of Africa". The Chinese remained "free" but servants, never equals. As such, they were still a "good cargo", notwithstanding the fact that they were pagans and very uncivilized, dirty folk to the barbarians and 'foreign devils' from Europe.

Small wonder, as they were imported as "coolies" under the dirtiest circumstances and in order to do the dirtiest work. The most well-known example is the miners and railway laborers in 19th-century USA, but they were already used in the 17th- and 18th-century Dutch tin mines on Banca and Malacca or on plantations, and they were given opium to consume to keep them working (see ch. 16).

The Chinese already had a Southeast Asian history in which they were not victims in the given sense.[18] They lived in some coastal settlements in the East Indies long before the Europeans arrived (1511). They never had any imperialistic motives, and no traces of discrimination or lethal actions against them are known from that time. Ethnic differences and related cultural differences remained alive. Of course, they were mostly economically integrated, but in a social or cultural sense, there was apparently not much need to become acclimated.

---

extermination verdict of the Chinese, etc., this positive perception of this habit should be called pathological indeed.

[18] See further ch. 25. There are rather irrelevant theories about some resident group of Tang Chinese in Java, but that cannot be our concern here. See C. Menghong, p. 14. See also Th. Raffles, vol. 1, p. 74 ff. It is enough for us to know that as early as the second half of the 12th-century, a Chinese source mentioned the commercial prosperity of Java and 13th-century sources talked about the many and diversified merchandise handled in the old Buddhist kingdom of Çrivijaya (at the site of the later Palembang). They came from the West (Persia, Arabia, etc.), the East (China) and the archipelago itself. There was no opium among the goods. See M. Meilink-Roelofsz, chapter 1; J. Wills, chapter 1.

The Chinese lived in small groups, busy with mining or agriculture, but mainly oriented towards the sea. They were accepted as important mediators to the outside world. In trade and related industrial work they also maintained the communication with China in several ways and supported the junk trade in all respects, from money exchange to ship reparation.[19]

Since their emigration from China, they had established settlements which could later form a network allowing the exchange of labor, work, capital, goods, etc. The Chinese functioned well in a rather vital Asiatic commercial world centered around the Malacca (Melaka) peninsula, including parts of the East Indies like Bantam in the south or the Moluccas in the east. More precisely, in the existing lively trade networks of the Javanese or Moluccans, the Chinese helped to extend these networks in the direction of China and settlements with overseas Chinese and to activate the relations between the regions of the Indian Ocean and the China Seas.

Apart from the usual personal daily conflicts, problems with or against indigenous folk did not occur on any large scale. None of the parties had any intention to overrule the other. Cultural ties in Java remained self-evidently shallow in this situation: intermarriage existed but was not widespread outside the three large settlements of Batavia, Semarang and Surabaya. People descending from a mixture of Chinese and indigenous folk were so numerous that they received a special name, *pernakans*.

This relative mutual "living apart together" was still active when after a certain period the the Chinese undertook agricultural work in the surroundings of their settlements. When the Dutch arrived in Java, this was more or less the situation they found.[20]

This relatively peaceful world was aggressively forced into the power schemes and trade aims of the Western nations. The VOC played a major role. Meilink-Roelofsz was one of the first to acknowledge this:

---

[19] About the junk trade in the VOC era to Batavia, see in particular the excellent article of J. Blussé (1986), p. 97-155. Raffles stresses the annual return trips to China, but such trips from—say—Semarang to Canton and vice versa were difficult or could not be acocmplished within a year at the time.

[20] For many details of the ambiguous Chinese-Dutch relations, see also J. Blussé (1986), chapter 5 or Idem (1989), a well-illustrated book without making serious attempts to destroy the usual prejudices. The early appearance of the Chinese is already mentioned in the remarkable J. Vleming, p. 1 ff. He used as source an article of W.P. Groeneveldt, the man responsible for the reconstruction of the opium business in the archipelago. See below.

> Naturally in the first half of the 17th-century, it is still too early to speak of the Dutch ... politically dominated East Indies, but nevertheless, economically, the Company represented a power factor in the Indonesian Archipelago ... which seriously disturbed or even utterly destroyed various aspects of the native economy.[21]

The Dutch came to rule and exploit everybody else in an economic, social and cultural sense. They had a keen interest to exploit social and cultural differences among the "available populations". The wars they fought against Mataram and Bantĕn also had a negative effect on the daily life of the Chinese who came to live in and around Batavia. Still, for a long time indigenous people liked to deal with the Chinese, but not with VOC employees. The Banjarese people said that the Chinese "paid much more for the pepper and in addition they carry with them always much more interesting merchandise."[22]

Notwithstanding this, the Chinese now became *middlemen* and therefore distrusted by many, Dutch and indigenous alike. They themselves started to demonstrate this behavior as well. For instance, when the sugar fields of the Chinese were destroyed time and again by Javanese warriors, and life became dangerous for them, they fled to the Company. But if the repression of the Dutch was too severe, the Chinese moved to Mataram or Bantĕn (Bantam) for protection and better living conditions.

However, things must be seen in perspective. From a Dutch point of view, their prejudices about the Chinese are closely related to their prejudices about the indigenous people: they were perceived as antagonists, but the inherent value judgments were fully Dutch: both the Chinese and Javanese had to became inimical to fit in the divide and rule game. During Vischer's visit to the Susuhunan (or "Sunan") in Semarang with his bloodthirsty request to eliminate all Chinese, he also informed him that in Batavia they were prepared somehow to come to terms with the 'good' Chinese:

> In his answer the Sunan expressed his great surprise that the Chinese had had the assurance to revolt. For it was widely known by all leeward nations that the Chinese were like women, without any power of their own. They were only good for trading or managing toll-gates. Wherever they lived, they were supported by the Company, which allowed them to trade and become rich. Without the support of the Company they would not be able to maintain themselves because of their cowardice.[23]

---

[21] A. Meilink-Roelofsz, p. 10, see also idem, p. 28 ff, 40, 174.

[22] GM VIII, p. 97 reported 5-12-1726.

[23] W. Remmelink, p. 128.

This Javanese leader apparently was not aware of his prejudice, but he and 'the whole of Java' was convinced that something miraculous had happened, now the Chinese and the Dutch were revolting, 'who were like two sides of the same coin': it was so inconceivable 'that this could only be a sign of God ... many seemed to believe that it spelled the end of the Company'.[24] That was not far off the mark, but this Susuhunan could easily have found out how the Chinese fought together with the Javanese against the foreign intruders time and again.

The image of the two sides of a coin did have a ring of truth for the Chinese-Dutch cohabitation. They became to be more dependent on each other, but at the same time they became also more equal: the Chinese provided many services relative to the trade with the North, but also the daily food for the Dutch came from Chinese agricultural work in the country. It is, furthermore, a typical characteristic of repressive powers that they urge one-person leaderships (captains) of opposing groups. Not only as representative of the whole group, but also as an adequate means to suppress and control the subjects and antagonists.[25]

This kind of representation urged by a perpetrator is never trusted by the oppressed and perceived as a puppet of—in this case—the Dutch colonial government/VOC. That was also the case with the Chinese captain and his officers in Batavia, gathered in a true Chinese Council (*Kong Koan*): it was only accepted as long as the interests of the foreign occupier were served. The Chinese captain, killed in 1740, knew in his last moments the answer to whether such a representative institution of the weak in an aggressive perpetrator's setting could have any other function than to support the perpetrator's aims.

The method is: be an adviser to the perpetrators, but exert authoritarian power over the community in order to avoid new protests and revolts.[26]

---

[24] Idem, p. 129.

[25] One must, again, realize that this is a typically Western legalistic habit. The most well-known "institution" is the *Judenrat* (Jewish Council) installed everywhere by the Nazis in the occupied countries and in Germany itself. But see also the captain institutions in the Dutch West Indies (Dutch Guyana–Surinam). Blussé is too naive in his description of the case. In the Asian colonies the Dutch system of the "Kapitan China" was adopted elsewhere as well. See N. Tarling (ed.), vol. 2-1, p. 79.

[26] C. Menghong provides much information about the work of this Chinese Council (Kong Koan) in the 19th-century, but has not the slightest idea about the meaning of the ambiguous political-moral position between a colonial repressive regime (illicit) and something like a Chinese community in a Western colony. She reproduces largely the Dutch perception and position in her description of the smooth functioning of the Kong Koan: 'As intermediary between the colonial government and the Chinese community ...

The Dutch were interested only in division to sustain their minority rule: between town and country, between Chinese and indigenous, but also between the Chinese elite and the majority of Chinese lower class people. Therefore, they divided up the different groups into their own camps, quarters, housing blocks and so on within the classical grid-iron lay-out of all colonial settlements.[27] We can be skeptical about the strong attempts to conserve traditional values, folklore and so on in such camps or quarters, while asking whether it is genuine Chinese, Javanese, etc. culture or a Pavlovian reaction to Western colonial demands for division and isolation, the results of the rigorous divide and rule game.

It is, therefore, not at all 'paradoxical' (Blussé), but quite logical that the Chinese in the countryside remained unprotected by their own city-officers and were at the mercy of the Dutch sheriffs and commissaries. It was this Dutch behavior in creating mutual distrust which triggered a Chinese revolt and the massacre. It is not 'paradoxical' that the rural Chinese protesters in 1740 wrote to their urban colleagues that they were going to attack Batavia

> in which city so few Dutchmen and so many Chinese live, and where never-theless [the Dutch] dare to treat the Chinese so harshly and oppress them so unjustly, that it can no longer be tolerated. The Chinese nation is forced to unite and with all force declare war upon the Dutch.[28]

No oppressed people are trusted by the perpetrators: one day they will inevitably wreak revenge for their bad life. The Chinese were, of course, never trusted by the Dutch, notwithstanding their slow acceptance of the "Dutch" captains as even an honorable job for the Chinese elite and the substantial mutual advantages. From the quotation below it seems that they were mutually divided as well, longing for common action against a common enemy.

A Dutchmen, called an 'enlightened person', recalled the Roman Empire's administration as he advised his Governor-General in 1705:

> Look at the example of the turbulent Chinese, who have been and remain subdued by the Tartars with a small force ... The Tartars keep only the army to themselves without giving the Chinese a say in these affairs, so that always a tight reign can be held on them during an emergency.[29]

---

on the one side.. direct rule over its [the Kong Koan's] subjects (sic!) and on the other side ... execution of the colonial instruction as careful as possible.'

[27] For an analysis of these colonial city-systems see my (1986), p. 386-413.

[28] Quoted by J. Blussé (1986), p. 94 from J.K.de Jonge a.o. (ed.), vol. 9, p. lvii.

[29] Quoted by J. Blussé (1986), p. 88.

How the Dutch applied quite different norms if Europeans or Chinese violated their laws is demonstrated in the following examples.[30] Three Dutchmen were caught because of their violent behavior against Dutch citizens, but apparently also because of the discovery of 230 chests of smuggled opium, 'the owners of which could not be found ...'. These Dutchmen were punished by sending them back home.[31]

The comment on this report is interesting: it is a pity that Dutch 'false wage-earners' behave as cheaters, but it is shocking that 'wealthy gentlemen' are doing this. Only the latter can afford to buy such an expensive lot of opium, which could be sold for 67,056 rixdollars. The rich Dutch owner of the contraband was not found in the small Dutch community in which everybody knew everybody. From top to bottom of the Dutch community, people were involved in some form of corruption. However, there were at most twenty people who could pay that amount of twenty times the annual salary of a Governor-General![32]

In the same report, however, there is a description of a Chinese who was caught in the act when forging coins:

> ... he is sentenced to death on the gallows after his right hand is amputated, but in the end this sentence is by us augmented, so that he must die through the fire in order to make it a deterrent.[33]

---

[30] This is not only a Dutch custom but also, for example, a Portuguese one, as M. Meilink-Roelofsz, p. 127 shows. One may perceive this, therefore, in a much more general perspective. In the Portuguese-dominated settlements the higher ranks of nobility, civil rulers and priests 'fell outside civil jurisdiction'. The interference of clergymen in secular jurisdiction was detrimental as well. This apart from the "strangeness" of the mutual (licentiousness) behavior of these foreigners, let alone their criminal behavior as 'acts of violence and piracy against native shipping'. This was too often done by or under protection of 'captains of the forts' who could handle all possible cases largely independently of the colonial government or of the government in Portugal. In principle, this was not different among the Dutch, although some regulations were introduced gradually. But regarding Dutch force exerted against Chinese junks from 1620 onwards, see Idem, p. 238 or 253-256, 264-268 and so on.

[31] What was to happen with them in Holland is not known: the usual punishment of the greedy Dutch authorities was to take all the money these people had saved during their stay in the "colony".

[32] In that year, 1728, there were no more than 1300 Dutch people living in Batavia. The very rich, who could afford this kind of smuggling, made up certainly less than 2%. It is, anyway, the elite from which the members of the Amphioen Society were recruited 20 years later.

[33] GM, VIII, p. 170 reported 31-1-1728. A similar case of smuggling opium from Bengal by Dutch people/ships is described Idem, p. 220, reported 8-12-1728. This concerned again 230 chests of opium; it led to 'freedom' for most; in Bengal 'nothing could be proved', and a few were deported. The same report (p. 221) mentions two Chinese who acted in a "criminal way". Now their sin was that they smuggled '6 picol of coffee'. They were rela-

In an earlier situation other contradictory data about the VOC-Chinese relationship can be found. In 1708 the VOC had 1159 Chinese servants.[34] A decade earlier there were serious conflicts with a group of 70-80 Chinese in Semarang, including women and children. The majority of them were poor and newly arrived; there were also four chiefs [*hoofden*] who had lived there for some years as merchants. A Chinese lieutenant from Batavia, who was arrested for having debts, fled to this Semarang group. They all hoped to support the Susuhunan in his struggle with the VOC. This became a tragic failure: the prince delivered them all to the VOC. The Dutch broke them upon the wheel and killed 46 men of the group.[35]

The "in-between" position of the Chinese also had a quite different aspect. Around 1820 the discontent intensified among the Javanese nobility as well as among their peasants. One of the complaints was that the Dutch had taken full control of the many toll stations on central Java, originally a source of revenue for the indigenous regimes.[36] Because they did not have the manpower to staff these stations and they were anxious to collect easy money, the Dutch farmed the tolls out to Chinese collectors. As long as they paid their agreed-upon quotas, the Chinese could do what they pleased. However, the original Chinese lessees in turn parceled out their toll stations to relatives or the highest bidder. They were always Chinese as well. The result was that the number of tolls was multiplied and the rates raised. Apparently after receiving complaints the Dutch "proprietors" of the tolls started to limit the contracts to one year. The Chinese toll farmers now reacted by squeezing all they could from the defenseless population before relinquishing their station to the next bidder. This squeezing often affected the Chinese merchants more than the Javanese. It was, of course, a new source of internal trouble among the Chinese. The Dutch source of all discontent remained, however, hidden behind a Chinese face.

---

tively lucky: their coffee was confiscated and they were severely flogged ('strengelijke laarsing').

[34] GM, VI, p. 570: 952 in Bantam, 69 in Tandjongkait, 97 in Tanara and 41 in Pontang.

[35] GM, V, p. 646 reported 8-12-1693. Of course, one can also point to very exceptional instances of heavy punishment of Dutchmen by the Dutch authorities. For instance, the act of Governor-General Zwaardekroon who in 1721 'had no fewer than 26 Company servants beheaded in one day for theft and smuggling' (D. Hall. p. 308).

[36] For this example see M. Adas, p. 67.

The example is not only chosen to demonstrate the possible effects of the middleman position. It also shows the mechanism of other Dutch farming systems, of which the opium one was the most important.

Chinese and Early Opium Trade

For centuries the Chinese junks traded in many kinds of products. Meilink-Roelofsz spotted in 1630 the following imported and exported "Chinese products": Brazil or dye wood, cloth, copper, foodstuffs, forest products, gold, handicrafts articles, iron pans, money, much pepper, lacquer, porcelain, salt, silk, spices, sugar, etc. However, no opium is mentioned under whatever name. At the end of the 15th-century, a lively trade from Gujarat with China via Malacca was being carried out: main product was Gujarati cloth and 'very small quantities of the luxury products ... rosewater, opium, and incense, all typical products of the Near East ...'[37] This opium apparently came from Aden.[38] This amount could never become a problem worth debating or researching.

There is another early report in 1610 about the opium trade to East Java (Grise near Surabaya). It was embedded in the much larger spice trade. The king of Surabaya had many junks himself, but the Chinese were intermediaries for the trade with West Java (Bantam) in rice, beans, sugar, fish, cattle, salt, cotton. From the West came many products like Indian fabrics, and opium.[39] The Portuguese brought opium into the East Indies archipelago around this time. They bartered it for gold dust, gold coins and bezoar stones; in Pahang they probably could get rice and dye-woods for it.[40] In a Dutch document of October 1620, opium is mentioned for the first time as 'a merchandise reserved for the Company only' while the import by others 'within the Jacarta jurisdiction' is prohibited.[41]

The first conclusion is again that trade in opium to and in the East Indies archipelago is very limited in quantity (if any) until about 1660. It was most likely used to smooth trade by presenting it as presents to indigenous rulers and their courts. Middle Eastern traders must have done this long before the Portuguese followed the trade movements in the 16th-

---

[37] A. Meilink-Roelofsz, p. 64.
[38] Idem, p. 69.
[39] Idem, p. 271.
[40] Idem, p. 165.
[41] F. de Haan, vol. 4, p. 15. De Haan states that opium is mentioned for the first time in a document from 1667, but that this must be a mistake: October 1620 is the relevant year.

century. The Dutch gradually copied this at the beginning of the 17th-century and joined the opium business as well.

De Haan provides the reports of a certain Oluff Christiaansz (1700) about military expeditions into the interior of Java. The food they carried with them is largely destined for the VOC officials in Cheribon. Apart from coins they have:

> ... 12 bottles of sek [a strong sweet Spanish wine. F.d.H.], 4 bottles olive oil and 4 Dutch vinegar ... 10 pound Dutch butter ... and 4 pound amphioen to distribute here and there among the Javanese chiefs ...' De Haan adds that the VOC representative received opium 'to sell it during the trip for a good price in order to pay part of the cost ...' of the trip.[42]

Something must have been changed in the opium trade 22 years later. Then, according to another report 'opium appears to be the most important import article in Cheribon'.[43] Many Dutch foreigners lived there. Did they use the drug despite the warnings of their bosses not to use opium? From whom did they got the amphioen? From the Chinese, who were the main leasers of the VOC opium according to the stories? Were there enough alternative distributors after the AS was established? Let's try to answer these difficult questions.

English and probably other European invaders also continued to compete with the Dutch to get a slice of the spice and other trade in the archipelago. The question is: whoever held the hegemony in the Strait region, around Malacca, could dominate the trade movements by means of passports and naked power. The Dutch won the game around the 1660s, and everybody else had to stick to Dutch rules at least until about 1750. This was certainly the case for the Chinese junks, which were no match for European pirate/traders ships. The former looked for help to save them from the latter: The Chinese once complained about a Portuguese captain who threatened to destroy Chinese junks. The Dutch arrested this man and kept him in custody until a fortnight after the junks had disappeared

---

[42] F. de Haan, vol. 2, p. 195 and note 4. Later (Idem, p. 470) the Dutch complained about the lazy Chiefs who smoked the opium which they had distributed themselves (also called *madap, madat* or *medak* and *affion*) instead of delivering coffee in time. They, furthermore, remarked in 1672 that they had had to fight 'peoples from Bantam mad from opium' (Idem, p. 752). Even a report of 1786 (Rolff) describes how soldiers had an income from amphioen and coffee (Idem, p. 614 note 5). For opium consumption as a result of presents from the Dutch "government" as early as 1636, see F. de Haan, vol. 4, p. 14. The effect is given directly: the ruler of Djambi 'is stunned from eating amphioen' (1641). In 1657 opium is given as a present to the rulers in Mataram, but twenty years later a Governor-General states that "The Javanese" from Mataram cannot do without opium (Idem.).

[43] F. de Haan, vol. 4, p. 14.

from the harbor. Another Chinese trader received an iron canon to defend himself against pirates, etc.[44]

Probably the Chinese bought some opium as medicine in Malacca from Arabs and imported it to China, but I can find no proof of this. Among the Far Western traders, certainly the Portuguese imported opium for the first time into China via Macao in the same period; that is to say, sometimes they bought opium from the Dutch. In any case, it remained a Western product for the Chinese wherever they lived in Asia and whoever delivered the stuff. The maximum that could be achieved by Chinese merchants was copying the smuggling of the Dutch and Portuguese (a bit later also of the English) of goods into China, which was strongly opposed by the Chinese government. The Dutch were extradited to Formosa and had to leave China; the Portuguese could remain in Macao, clearly a matter of better diplomacy. In and around the Formosa settlement of the Dutch, which ended soon with their ignominious defeat, I could not discover any opium trading.

This Dutch-Chinese opium relationship (if any) must have changed in the 1660s. The Dutch formalized their opium business in Bengal and Malabar and made it one of their major products for the first time. This was immediately important for the East Indies. It lead directly to war and an opium monopoly in Mataram (1678).

In his opium story De Haan reminds us that probably the first revenue farming in Batavia was established in January 1661 and concerned the tax on carved tobacco 'which within this city and its jurisdiction is consumed by the Chinese.'[45] This tobacco was imported from China and later mixed with a little opium, which became *madat*. Apparently because also this opium was imported, this madat was prohibited ten years later (the so-called "Batavia jurisdiction"). This had nothing to do with 'a hygienic measure', as De Haan suggests. More relevant is his remark about the low price of *madat* for the slaves, which irritated their masters. But the main reason must have been that the expensive VOC opium was being undermined by so-called "smugglers".

A similar fear was the context for the opium prohibition among fishermen. However, the fishermen disappeared, and the Chinese opium farmers complained that their business was undermined (and could not pay taxes). Result: the measure was revoked (1672). The following cases demonstrate other aspects of a Dutch-Chinese opium relationship.

---

[44] A. Meilink-Roelofsz, p. 150 reported 30-11-1727.
[45] Idem, p. 16.

In 1725 the Dutch sold to Chinese traders 'excluding amphioen and textiles for only 273,209 rixdollars and bought for 278,604 ... tea and non-coined gold ...'[46] Apparently this concerned a fleet of thirteen Chinese junks who came to Batavia, from which four hundred Chinese were allowed to stay. A year later the VOC publicly sold two lots of opium unfit for use with a poor profit of 13% and 8%. The Chinese (it is unclear whether they were from China or Java) offered to buy 250 chests from these lots for 260 rixdollars each. This was refused as too cheap.[47]

One must suppose that, as mediators in Asian traffic, an elite among these "Overseas Chinese" became involved in this large-scale opium business, but only as servants of the Dutch, the opium suppliers. The growth of the ports attracted more Chinese junks trade. This happened even after the Dutch had consolidated their position in the East Indies archipelago: between 1680 and 1740 the arrivals of these junks in Batavia doubled from 10 to 20 per year.

However, De Haan gave a less optimistic view on the Dutch–Chinese opium relation when he described the dominant position of the high VOC official who covered all relationships with the Javanese in the areas south of Batavia, the *Gecommitteerde tot en over de Zaken van den Inlander*. This fully corrupt person

> had the complete import of opium into [interior districts] ... sometimes including the import of salt. If he was willing he added a cattle business to this. He had a monopoly position and 'in avoiding all competition this must have led to an expensive market for the indigenous population ... the coffee [one was obliged to deliver in a near slavery relation] he paid in merchandise instead of cash money ... which was to the disadvantage of the Chinese who themselves liked a profit ...' etc.[48]

Also, the lower-ranking Dutch officials asked for bribes. How ambiguous the situation was is demonstrated in a report by Rolff (1786) about a per-

---

[46] GM, VIII, p. 31 (August 1724).

[47] Idem, p. 97.

[48] F. de Haan, vol. 1, p. 302. See for this also F. Gaastra (2000), p. 14 who, however, did not refer to the opium mentioned by De Haan as the first item. Later (F. de Haan, vol. 4, p. 9) there is again a reference to the opium monopoly position of this 'Gecommitteerde', while apparently the salt-monopoly was exercised by a lower official, a Commander, 'notwithstanding the taking of a bribe from a Chinese'. Later Daendels was allowed to continue with the opium policy of this "Gecommitteerde" (see F. de Haan, idem, p. 22 ff.). After 1900 the colonial government also kept the opium and salt monopolies in one organization, the *Opium- and Zoutregie* (see ch. 19). At that time the same kind of coercion appeared as, for instance, a century earlier, as coffee was paid by the Dutch with salt (F. de Haan, idem.), etc.

son equivalent to an inspector (with the German name *Waltschedel*) and his helper Weijkert. The former received 105 rixdollars (rixdaalders) from Chinese carpenters so that they could stay, but every year they first paid 200 rixdollars to Weijkert, who pocketed 95:

> .. for this he allowed these Chinese to establish a shop (*warong*) to sell opium (*afion*) and all kinds of merchandise; this is very harmful because these Chinese accept from the garden personnel and the slaves stolen gardening tools in exchange for opium.[49]

The English or Portuguese never disappeared from the entire realm ranging from China to the Southeast Asian archipelago. The English even had a rather strong bridgehead, Bengkulu (Bencoolen, Benkulen) in West Sumatra, before they captured Singapore or Northern Borneo. From there they "smuggled" throughout the archipelago if they did not accept the Dutch rules. As the VOC power decreased after 1750, the English influence increased: now, war and opium were not very far apart.

The following description is illustrative for the Eastern part of Java and Bali (Strait), which was not yet wholly under control of the Dutch. Here the English energetically infiltrated:

> One of the significant effects caused by the British presence in the region was the escalation in free trade or, as the Dutch preferred to call it, *smokkelhandel* or smuggling. The indigenous merchants from the surrounding areas were attracted by the opium and cotton which were distributed by the British at quite a low price, and offered the latter salt, rice and other foodstuffs in exchange. In fact, opium and textiles were also distributed by the Dutch, but the local traders preferred to buy them from the British merchants ... Among these merchants were Buginese and Mandarese who were already acquainted with the British merchants ... [in] Bengkulu ... now ..their voyage was shortened considerably, and they could easily pick up the opium with only a minor risk.[50]

Around the Bali Strait representatives of the Javanese elite and Chinese merchants were also involved in the opium trade. Sometimes they were caught by the Dutch, including their opium cargo, which always appeared to be of English origin. This "free trade" did not concern large consignments of opium: sometimes one and a half chests, another 200 pounds including weapons, or twenty catty of British opium. A Dutch investiga-

---

[49] F. de Haan, vol. 2, p. 614.
[50] S. Margana (2007), p. 42 ff.

tion into this matter revealed even that 'the "legal" opium was used as pretext for the "illegal" one.'[51]

Anyway, the Dutch did not hesitate very long before waging a full-fledged opium war in 1768 in Java's *Oosthoek* (Eastern Salient or Blambangan), using quarrels with neighboring Bali as a pretext to conquer the area. Although quickly won, this war triggered new depopulations, massacres, ethnic cleansings, one revolt after another, religious antagonisms until long after Raffles' time in Java. In this turmoil Chinese merchants also got caught in the cross-fire of their former colleagues, the Buginese merchants. Other Chinese who happened to become involved in the political leadership had to pay with their life. This was the chaos in which a fundamental transformation took place, which was characterized by the definitive destruction of the VOC and its monopolistic trade culture.

---

[51] Idem, p. 45.

CHAPTER SIXTEEN

FROM TRADE MONOPOLY INTO NARCO-STATE MONOPOLY

> The Javanese are a stupid race and, coveting the wealth of Europeans, have gradually fallen into their snare; but who could have calculated on the conquerors proceeding to invent the black fumes of opium, to tempt and delude the natives; urging them to consume this drug as a luxury, until they became so weak and emaciated, so dispirited and exhausted, that they could no longer think of regaining their land, nor conceive the idea of revenging their wrongs. The Javanese ... were readily overcome by this poison, and lost all care for themselves; but we Chinese, of the central flowery land, have also been deluded by them; for no sooner do we partake of this substance, than we lose all anxieties about our native land, have no further concern for father or mother, wife or children, and are plunged into unspeakable misery.
>
> Ong-Tae-Hae (1791), p. 18.

Ong-Tae-Hae's criticism and self-criticism form a worthy conclusion to the previous chapter and probably the earliest forecast of what the Chinese could expect from the Western opium imperialism.

Raffles and his investigator, the famous John Crawfurd, were well aware of this fate. In that year, Raffles explicitly planned an opium-free Singapore! However, they could not repair the damage, only make reports for the bureaucrats and the later historians. Crawfurd prepared a rather hysterical report for Raffles about the latest revolt in which a Chinese landlord and opium farmer of several districts played a major role. Arrogant and without reservation about the British role as colonizer, he documented at the beginning of the English-Chinese century how the Chinese had remained again in an "intermediate position", leading to death and destruction from the end of the former Dutch century.

The climate was created in which the victims were lumped together and accused of being agents of the inimical competitors, the Dutch, of possessing all possible wealth, etc. The Chinese—I repeat Raffles' phrase—

became a very dangerous people, and are to be remarked as a pest to the country; and that there appears to be no radical cure for this evil but their extermination from the interior, a measure which cannot now be effected.[1]

This is the irresponsible language of European authorities preparing the crowds for pogroms.

A Transformation from Private into Public Interest

After the internal assault by the *Amphioen Society,* the loss of the profitable Dutch opium position in Bengal or the Pyrrhus victory in Eastern Java, there followed a failed Dutch–English war (1795, loss of Ceylon) and the Napoleonic wars: the VOC broke down, and the Dutch state in Europe lost its independence. There was even a large opium debt owed to its main competitor, the EIC. In short, it was an easy job for the British to conquer Java and, therefore, "inherit" the rest of the East Indian archipelago.

In both the English and the Dutch case, it was not clear whether all this concerned a general public or a private interest. Both were on the brink of being drastically transformed; a most fundamental change took place now in the general opium history as well. Contrary to the Dutch situation, there was a flourishing private country trade apart from the EIC which formed a substantial 'Indo-British power at sea'.[2] Around 1790 at least 70 ships from different countries called at Cochin. They were equivalent to 27,000 tons of shipping manned by 4000 *lascars* (hired Indian seamen) and defended by 564 guns. Their opium trade to China was worth thirty *lakhs* of rupees (3 million rupees) annually around 1800 and the trade in other goods, about twenty *lakhs.*

Certainly, there existed in the 18th-century something like a private Dutch "burgher" trade which was active around India and Ceylon or the Strait of Melaka. The few data are not very impressive and found in obscure literature; this trade does not exist in the official historiography, let alone it offers competition with the British trade.[3] Although we only deal below with the Dutch case (for the English, see ch. 6), both remained closely connected at least until 1816 (for details, see Appendix 4).

---

[1] Quoted from Raffles' *Memoirs* by S. Alatas, p. 29.
[2] H. Furber, p. 181.
[3] In F. Gaastra (1991), for instance, nothing is mentioned.

To avoid a transfer into British hands, the new Dutch government took over all the VOC shares. This was similar to a nationalization of a private business. In the same stroke the Dutch state became the holder of an opium monopoly and started to produce and distribute opium itself. What does this mean and what are the implications?

First, that the Dutch government in Holland bluntly claimed herewith the "ownership" of the VOC "possessions". This was generously perceived as the entirety of the East Indies archipelago, a territory as large as the USA now! The VOC's personnel was, furthermore, transformed automatically into a state bureaucracy. It was like a Trojan Horse to accept this band of fully corrupt foreigners and set them to govern the East Indies from now on.

In hindsight, this was a rather absurd constellation. After creating a mess with the VOC or in East Java, some state in Western Europe, smaller than West Java alone, and after itself being occupied by a foreign power (Napoleonic France), claimed out of the blue the function of feudal overlord over all the kingdoms in this realm and was held responsible for law and order in this vast realm of a thousand islands. This claim was also clearly in variance with new enlightened ideas about colonialism, slavery, industrialization and all that, which were established in this period of the American and French Revolutions. Indeed, this move resembled a Napoleonic Restoration.

It concerned nearly five million people in Java and Madura alone, of which 2% was Chinese. What were called "European capitals" had 60,000 inhabitants (Batavia and suburbs), Semarang and Surabaya (each about 20,000[4]).

In France or Holland at the time, one could have enlightened ideas about, for instance, the abolition of slavery. However, in the East every Dutch man and woman had several slaves at their disposal. In Batavia 19,000 slaves lived, mostly coming from Bali and Celebes; in Semarang, about 4000 and in Surabaya, 3600.[5] From Bali an estimated 1000 slaves (*sapangan*) were exported each year (from 1650 to 1830 some 150,000 of them were taken away from this island alone).[6]

There was not only a close connection between Dutch repression and indigenous slavery, but also between opium and slavery. The imported opium by the Dutch generated a chain of misery. The indigenous nobility

---

[4] Th. Raffles, vol. 1, p. 61 ff.
[5] Idem, p. 76.
[6] H. Schulte Nordholt, p. 41; see also p. 43-44, p. 96.

started wars to get prisoners, put their people in debt for the same reason, while convicts were mostly sold off. But the background of this is revealed in the following statement of a Balinese nobleman (the patih of Karangasem):

> We wage war upon the others when we, lords, lack money; at such times we swoop down on the weakest of our neighbours, and all prisoners and their entire families are sold as slaves so that we ... have money to buy opium.[7]

That is the clearest perversion of life brought by the Dutch exploitation of these islands when they addicted the nobility and enslaved the common folk. Gradually, the use of opium by other people who had money became apparent in the course of the 19th-century as the Dutch pressure to increase opium consumption became stronger and more systematic thanks to the enlightened Europeans and Daendels' opium dens.

In other words: from about 1795-1815 the excessive Western *private* narco-military exploitation of a foreign territory by slavery and opium, *supported by a foreign public institution* (the Dutch state), was transformed into a *foreign public* narco-military exploitation of a foreign territory by "free slavery" and opium, sometimes mainly *exercised through foreign private interests*.

A new phase of Western imperialism started: the European Dutch government began to conquer a foreign territory, which was exploited just in the previous period. When this foreign power finally had to leave the territory forever, through the lost war of 1945-1949, the conquering of this so-called "colony" remained unfinished.[8]

---

[7] Idem, p. 41.

[8] The newest Dutch political-legal analysis of the Dutch exploitation of the East Indies, J. Somers, is still unable to acknowledge the illegal character (in all respects) of the Dutch activities in this part of the world, 60 years after the war of liberation of the Indonesians. This should be the starting position for this kind of analysis. Then one can provide an explanation of why a permanent state of war was necessary from the start until the very end, with one massacre after another at regular intervals: in every part of the archipelago and in every period of these Dutch exploitative activities, people, tribes, and governments of indigenous states revolted against the white intruders. Now, Somers, does not argue against the dubious claims of the VOC Directors in the beginning of his history and ultimately supports the view that the present Indonesia was a creation of Dutch imperialism. For my view on imperialism, Martin Shipway's approach is much more interesting, although it does not go far enough. Disappointing in these respects is also H. Fischer-Tiné, M. Mann (ed.), in particular Mann's confinement to the reproduction only of the "civilized ideas" of Hastings and Cornwallis and to British ideas, without any moderation or investigation into the attitudes of the victims of these ideas.

The Four Van Hogendorps as Opium Dealers

What about the implementation of this transformation? In the Netherlands the fate of the suspect and influential Van Hogendorp family symbolizes this rigorous change in a most perfect way.[9] The father, William, (1735-1784) lost the largest part of his fortune through investments in the EIC. He went to the East Indies to become rich again and obtained lucrative bureaucratic positions. He had his own ship and "officially" smuggled opium worth a substantial fortune. On his return trip to a fantastic retirement in Holland, he drowned near the Cape of Good Hope. People stated: the ship had to sink because W. had too much gold on board. On Java, William was not only busy gathering a fortune in vain, but for some reason he supported smallpox vaccinations for the indigenous people. Furthermore, he was the first Dutchmen who attacked slavery and proposed to change this into a free labor relationship still within a colonial context.

William's eldest son, Dirk, was first and foremost a soldier; first a Prussian officer he ultimately became a Napoleonic general! Before he took this step, he went to the East Indies, where he fought in several of the many revolts against the Dutch repression in Malakka and the Riouw archipelago (1784). In Batavia he tried to re-organize the Dutch army. People laughed at him and, fully disappointed, he became one of the fiercest critics of the corrupt VOC elite.

In 1786 Dirk acted, however, as merchant in Bengal (Patna): at that time people came here for no other reason than to make a fortune with opium. Indeed, Dirk expected to leave the place with at least 100,000 guilders; he was not as greedy as colleagues, who returned home with millions.[10]

Back in Batavia Dirk was appointed commander of the military operations in eastern Java (Oosthoek; 1794). A highly critical report about the VOC Government in Batavia (particularly the main official, Nederburgh) and about the opium business led to his imprisonment. He could flee, however, went to Holland and published his critical report. He formulated a very liberal program for the "colony": the indigenous people were not lazy, they must be allowed private property (something which was unknown anyway), no slavery, no opium, no special emoluments for the

---

[9] For the following see the biographies in E. Du Perron, p. 284-304; E. Vanvugt (1985), chapter 12; F. Gaastra (1991), p. 100 ff.; J. Somers, p. 82 ff.

[10] F. Gaastra (1991), p. 100.

Dutch bureaucrats ... In short, he propagated free labor in order to receive the blessings of an enlightened colonial regime; a progressive program which was never realized.

When the Netherlands were fully occupied by Napoleon, Dirk joined the army even after the Emperor "came back" to be defeated at Waterloo. This rather fanatic collaborator with the French occupier appears in Napoleon's testament! All this made him rightly and officially a traitor to his country.

William's second son, Gijsbert Karel (1762-1834), underwent a military training in Berlin together with Dirk, but choose to become a lawyer and ended up as a gifted organizer of the new Dutch state and colony. Gijsbert Karel and two other aristocrats stood at the founding of this state. After the disappearance of Napoleon, these three staged a coup (1813) to establish a Dutch kingdom for the first time in history, slightly less autocratic than the previous regime. This "out of the blue king", William I, was the son of the last *stadhouder*, William V the Fat, who garnered an opium fortune through the *Amphioen Society*. William I not only inherited this opium money (see ch. 17) but could easily be called the First Opium King, as will be revealed below.

Gijsbert Karel became the prime minister of this autocratic king and main supporter of a newly organized opium trade in the East Indies. This lead to an unprecedented exploitation of the East Indies, new, devastating wars and excessive profits from the opium business. It was the parallel development of what happened with the new opium policy in China exercised by the British Empire. Gijsbert Karel was strongly influenced by the British experiences and by Crawfurd's and Raffles' histories of the Indies archipelago.[11]

In the last volume of his famous *Contributions*, Gijsbert Karel gave a long historical analysis of the Dutch assault on the East Indies.[12] He described how the Portuguese were conquered; how the Dutch skillfully applied the European principle of *balance of power* in the East Indies between the different peoples and competitors (the divide and rule principle); how the most important task—'to capture all the costly goods and manufactures'- was solved. In particular, he stresses the transformation of the private EIC into an activity of the British Crown, which had to stimulate the activities of the private merchants. The trade of the latter could not be stopped by the EIC: now this "private" trade was much larger than that of the EIC.

---

[11] G. K. van Hogendorp, vol. IV, p. 1-14; VII, 339, 370 ff., 381 ff.
[12] Idem, vol. X, p. 1-110.

The fundamental global changes are indicated by the author as follows after concluding that the EIC was left only with an opium monopoly on the Chinese trade:

> ... it is common knowledge that it compensated the losses in all other branches of its trade with the profits of this monopoly. One of the most remarkable effects of the free traffic and trade is ... that the cotton wares are not going anymore from India to England but the reverse ... In a short time the English factories, by means of machines, are able to provide the whole world with cotton goods, while the cheap Indian labor has become obsolete through the technical innovations. ... England even makes the cotton products for the Indian people ... Through the way of life of the English in India ... the English taste in clothing, furniture, ornaments ... is spread among the sixty to one hundred million souls of the British Empire in Asia ... The profits and advantages are so enormous ... and the national interest is so well served, which could never have been the result of whatever balance in one's favor of a commercial company [like the EIC]. At the same time that the British Empire developed in this way, the Dutch society gradually declined ...[13]

According to Van Hogendorp the main reason for this decline was the personal interest of governors and officials which prevailed over the general interest of the Company, the VOC-EIC. A second reason was that the production and running costs of these companies were much too high in comparison to the English and later the American private trade. Also, the Dutch could not stand this private competition. In addition, the monopolies of the Dutch had a negative effect on the 'civilization of the indigenous people, while the new system of free trade, accepted by the English, enhanced the civilization of these people, and derives huge profits and commercial advantages even from this civilization.'[14] The long war with England from 1795-1813 was the death blow for the Dutch 'possessions' in Asia.

After this conclusion, Gijsbert Karel van Hogendorp provides a key confession, because he was personally responsible for staging a coup. The "we" in the quotation has, therefore, a special meaning in what follows about his own time:

> Now everything is quiet in Europe, we got our independence back, and England returned our East Indies possessions ... Now we have done what England intends to do, but not realized fully at present. We have consigned the government of the Dutch Empire in Asia to the care of the Crown, with

---

[13] Idem, p. 8, 9. See also vol. VII, p. 355 ff.
[14] Idem, vol. X, p. 12.

a specific exclusion of all Companies, and we have freed the travel and trade, not only for our own subjects, but also for all foreign people through payment of heavier import and export duties. What is left of the monopoly consists of the spices and nutmeg from the Moluccan islands and of the trade with Japan ...[15]

In fact, he is proud to have reorganized the Dutch-Asian "possessions" into what could be called for the first time a "colony". This was done in close collaboration with the British.[16] As could be expected of a Van Hogendorp, the first thing he mentions is:

Our armed forces, at sea as well as on land, are substantially larger than they were any time in the past. All the costs of the Government and this army and navy are paid from regular taxes in the possessions itself, so that they do not bother the State ... Our own [Dutch] surplus population can find a way out as soldier or sailor... The more these countries flourish, the more they can contribute to this Government and Army.... Our civilized Government is able to bring these people into a state of civilization ... our armed domination is compensated through civilization.[17]

The indigenous population had to pay for its own repression and what that meant was very soon crystal clear. He himself 'has much heard about revolts ... in the Moluccas ... Java ... Cheribon ... Sumatra ... Palembang ... Maningkabo ... West coast Borneo ... Celebes ... at present, we directly govern these countries. This method of conquering is nothing new, not for us and not for the English ...'[18]

Indeed, nothing new under the sun, except that this sun burns in Asia much harder: in the VOC period, the Dutch lived and acted from some bulwarks on the coasts of Java; now a regular conquering of all lands and islands was started. The legitimation (these people live under despotism, we bring civilization) was quite new: in Van Hogendorp's time Hegel was still alive, who invented the theory (not the word) of *Oriental Despotism*.[19]

---

[15] Idem, p. 12, 13.

[16] It was clear that it was "physically impossible" for the English to occupy the East Indies archipelago as well. In addition, they needed the support of the Dutch in Europe to form a buffer-state against France; the new King William I also became king of what was later called "Belgium". Result: there was an exchange of British with Dutch "possessions" in Asia (for instance, Cape of Good Hope or Singapore became British; Bencoolen on Sumatra Dutch, etc.); several treaties between the countries were concluded which, indeed, resulted in peace after two centuries of sometimes severe wars. G. K. van Hogendorp was the author of these treaties as Minister of Foreign Affairs and many other functions.

[17] Idem, p. 40, 41.

[18] Idem, p. 42, 44.

[19] See the really poor treatment of this concept in M. Mann's contribution to H. Fischer-Tiné, M. Mann (ed.), p. 5 ff., 29 ff. See H. Derks, 1978-1+2.

The colony had to pay for itself; the state in Europe wanted to receive only the profits. One problem remained for the Western foreigners. This did not concern the indigenous people, who could be killed, but the English and American merchants. They had already established commercial houses in Batavia and other places. It was not proper to kill colleagues, as happened in an earlier period. There was now "free trade" in which the Dutch merchants seriously lagged behind. During the Raffles period the English had greatly extended their earlier "smuggling" practices, while the Dutch were absent.

> In addition to their manufactures the English also imported here amphioen from Bengal, which is used and demanded there generally among the people like tobacco in Europe ... in particular, the island of Singapore is transformed into a port, roads, market with the best and most spacious buildings ...'[20] These examples are sufficient for Van Hogendorp to realize how the English got their profits 'and that we have to learn how the Dutch could get their profits ... We have everything that the English possess ... and we can speculate on the needs of the indigenous as the English have done. ... Do we need amphioen to add to our manufactures, we can buy it in Bengal, and we can buy it also in the Levant, where it seems to be much stronger.'[21]

The opium history of the Van Hogendorp family did not end with the important interventions of Gijsbert Karel. His son, also a William, asked his father (November 1826) why it was not possible to grow opium in Java itself. He pointed to an earlier Dutch initiative of investigating this possibility in Bengalen through the mission of a Frenchman Maurevert. This man had 'to collect amphioen and other seeds' in Bengalen and to advise about some poppy culture in the Dutch "possessions".[22] Apparently son William planned such an activity on Java. Already half a year later (June 1827) he reported his father how some influential medical doctor had condemned it strongly. Apparently William's initiative fizzled out, but his obvious idea or initiative had a much longer life. Still an opium expert as the later Governor-General and Minister of the Colonies, Jean Chretien

---

[20] G.K. van Hogendorp, vol. X, p. 50.

[21] Idem, p. 52.

[22] Told and quoted by P. van der Kemp, p. 92. This M(e)aurevert was a draughtsman and botanist originally living in Pondicherry (East India). He was attached to the Dutch *Natuurkundige Commissie* (Commission for Natural Sciences) in the 1820s. M(e)aurevert was also known as collector of an orchid discovered on Java. Another Van Hogendorp (1812-1891), son of Dirk, was also active as administrator (resident) in several parts of Java. It is not known whether or how he supported the opium trade or consumption in the regions of his jurisdiction, Amboina, Semarang, Kadoe, Japara, etc. For these districts see chapter 20.

Baud (1789 – 1859), is confronted time and again with the same advise. Another Governor-General, Rochussen, asked, for instance, his colleague and friend Baud whether he liked the memorandum of a former Governor-General Van den Bosch in which the latter proposed to grow poppies on Menado (present North Sulawesi):

> Before I read about the idea of Van den Bosch I myself studied the poppy culture of Bengal. We spend about a million to import the opium and there is, furthermore, the opportunity to export the own opium to China. Against this idea there are two questions: 1. Can all this succeed? 2. Is it clever to inform the population about a product which can be grown so easy and cheap, but which is so expensive for them to buy? ...[23]

Baud answered that his enemy in the colonial bureaucracy, the Director-General of the Ministry of Finance, proposed already in 1827 to grow poppy. There was as well an important advise of the President of the *Royal Dutch Trading Company* (see below), G. Schimmelpenninck: the opium culture is risky and we make much profit at the moment. In addition, it will be difficult to uphold our monopoly position thanks to the scattering of poppy seed. This man even argued that in this case the immorality among the whole population should increase.[24]

The above is enough to learn the mentality, ideology, role model and actions taken of/by the highest Dutch officials. Below, some details will be added to this.

The Birth of a Narco-military State

The Van Hogendorp family symbolized in the most perfect way how the excessive Western *private* narco-military exploitation of a foreign territory through slavery and opium *supported by a state* was transformed into a *public* narco-military exploitation through "free slavery" and opium mainly *exercised by private interests.* For the victims of this last new imperialism, the situation was not new, except that they soon learned about a much harsher opposition of the foreign military against their attempts to liberate oneself of Dutch oppression. Reason: this new state imperialism was accompanied by a much stronger Western military involvement in the foreign territories. Mainly the English and Dutch demonstrated this

---

[23] J. Baud, J. Rochussen, vol. II, p. 24 (a letter from July 1845), p. 235 (a letter from April 1847). Jan Jacob Rochussen (1797-1871) was a Governor General as well.

[24] Idem, vol. III, p. 5 and 9.

policy. In addition, they promised each other in 1816 not to interfere in each other's territories. The French needed at least half a century to recuperate from the Napoleonic disaster and—in my view— they never succeeded (see part 4).

Stronger measures were also imposed to addict the population to amphioen/opium. Already during the "French" period of the East Indies, Governor-General Daendels (1808-1811) rationalized the distribution of opium and tried to stimulate its consumption.[25] He established for the first time many Government opium dens. Furthermore, he ordered every local commander, European or indigenous, to buy a sufficient quantity of opium for a period of six months on credit against a fixed price. The commander was allowed to profit as well from these activities. He also had to report under oath how the consumption in his district and local den(s) was structured. Failure to do so was punished with deportation. Small wonder that the opium income of the state multiplied nearly ten times in 1804 and more than doubled within two years (1809-1810; see appendix 4)!

Daendels' opium system was embedded in a new, typically French, hierarchical organization of the colonial state with the French-Dutch King Louis Napoleon at the summit; there was no place for indigenous princes anymore. They could become a *prefect* in this system of *prefectures* and keep their feudal rights, thus securing their income.

This new system of foreign exploitation was extended into more or less a slave state. The Javanese were obliged under harsh repression to plant coffee trees in every available spot. What Daendels introduced in the opium and coffee business remained more or less intact throughout the 19th-century. He is, therefore, the one who established the main features of a narco-military regime. For the Javanese it was lucky that Daendels stayed only for a short period. Not that their situation improved much afterwards, but some enlightenment could be registered occasionally.

After this French-Dutch period, the East Indies fell prey to Raffles. His very English "liberal reform" was introduced, with its stress on private instead of public initiatives. Contrary to this English practice, however, the Dutch chose later for the combination of harsher military activities, stronger government regulations and privileged private entrepreneurship

---

[25] For Daendels' opium measures, see Appendix 4; E. Vanvugt (1985), p. 134 ff. For his coffee culture and its effects, see J. Bastin, p. 62 and passim. Also, the article by M. Fernando and W. O'Mally in: A. Booth et al (ed.), p. 171-186. During the whole of the 19th-century, nearly 50% of all agricultural households was employed in coffee cultivation. Multatuli's complaints about the Dutch 'robber-state' were based on the practices in this sector.

in every product including opium. This was, in fact, a continuation of the
Daendels system. How the other Van Hogendorps and their autocratic
king fixed this situation will be the subject of the next two chapters. Here
we follow in some detail how the transformation took shape in which opium played such a key role.

The first three Van Hogendorps, each in his way, were aristocratic children of the Enlightenment (like Daendels in fact). They subsequently
demonstrated the phases which led to the autocratic leadership of
Napoleon or the introduction of an autocratic kingdom of the House of
Orange. They all expressed their anger about the highly stubborn, corrupt, selfish Dutchmen in the "colonies". The objects of this criticism were
slavery and opium. Still, these Hogendorps were at the same time very
anxious to amass fortunes in the opium business and/or to propagate opium on the largest possible scale as financial lubricant of the state. This
points to the highest degree of hypocrisy. Since they all held important
and leading positions, this hypocrisy immediately had rather severe,
sometimes lethal consequences, at least for the millions resident in their
Asian "possessions" and new conquests.

This hypocrisy of the Hogendorps was a general phenomenon from the
beginning of the transformation period. There was, for instance, a commission installed to organize a new framework for the opium business
now that the almighty position of the private VOC and its fully corrupt
product, the *Amphioen Society*, had perished. Its president, Nederburgh,
the mightiest colonial bureaucrat to date, was formerly a strong supporter
of extension of the opium business of the private *Amphioen Society*. But
now (1803) he subscribed to the

> 'state maxim ... it is not at all an injustice that the Colonies exist for the
> Motherland and not the reverse', and he also condemned the use of opium
> 'as a slow poison that undermines the mind as well as the body, while it
> makes in the end that men are not able to work and transforms them into
> animals.'[26]

The second part of the statement was an echo of his most sincere enemy,
Dirk van Hogendorp. With this change of opinion, Nederburgh reproduced the position of the new state, which had to cater for several competing interests in the motherland. This lead to his quasi-above-the-parties
position: the combination of the divide and rule and/or the *enemy of your
enemy is your friend* maxims with the stiff-upper lip rule, *what formerly*

---

[26] Quoted in E. Vanvugt (1985), p. 131. See also J. Rush, p. 136.

were the bare facts can now be acknowledged and vice versa. A long-lasting conflict with Van Hogendorp was the result.

A bit later, the confrontation with the Raffles government and ideology had to be mastered. The new Dutch rulers knew Crawfurd's or Raffles' *History of Java* (1817) by heart. Raffles even went to Europe and dined with G. van Hogendorp and King William I in Brussels (1817). He was not impressed:

> [The] King himself, and his leading minister, seem to mean well, [but] they have too great a hankering after profit, and *immediate* profit, for any liberal system to thrive under them ... The King complained of the coffee culture having been neglected, and expressed anxiety that he should soon have consignments; and while he ... assured me that the system introduced under my administration should be continued, maintained that it was essential to confine the trade, and to make such regulations as would secure it and its profits exclusively to the mother-country. (italics of R.)[27]

A matter of greed for money: an English intellectual's judgment about a Dutch intellectual like Gijsbert K. van Hogendorp accentuates quite important differences.

The opium opinions and policies of King William I or the Van Hogendorps are now well-known, but what about Raffles in this respect? In his *History of Java*, there is a special chapter on opium. It starts as usual from the wrong end: it had not been the Dutch and English monopoly and "smuggler" trade that had spread opium in the region, the indigenous people themselves were addicts by nature. He wrote:

> The use of opium, it must be confessed and lamented, has struck deep into the habits, and extended its malignant influence to the morals of the people, and is likely to perpetuate its power in degrading their character and enervating their energies, as long as the European government, overlooking every consideration of policy and humanity, shall allow a paltry addition to their finances to outweigh all regard to the ultimate happiness and prosperity of the country.[28]

Raffles continued his text with a two-page quotation of Dirk van Hogendorp's anti-opium tract in which sentences appear like:

> If a large quantity is taken, it produces a kind of madness, of which the effects are dreadful, especially when the mind is troubled by jealousy, or inflamed with a desire of vengeance or other violent passions. At all times it leaves a slow poison, which undermines the faculty of the soul and the

---

27 Quoted in J. Bastin, p. 66, 67.
28 Th. Raffles, vol. 1, p. 102, 103.

constitution of the body, and renders a person unfit for all kind of labour and an image of the brute creation. ... To satisfy that inclination, he will sacrifice every thing, his own welfare, the subsistence of his wife and children, and neglect his work; so that, at last, he no longer respects either the property of life of his fellow creature ... no law, however severe, could be contrived ... to prevent at least that in the future, no subjects of this Republic, or of the Asiatic possessions of the state, should be disgraced by trading in that abominable poison. ... It is therefore necessary at once, and entirely, to abolish the trade and importation of opium, and to prohibit the same, under the severest penalties that the law permits, since it is poison. The smuggling of it will then become almost impracticable, and the health, and even the lives of thousands will be preserved.[29]

So, the highest officials of England and the Netherlands, the countries most involved in slavery and the opium trade in the world, knew perfectly well the kind of ravaging effects their activities had in their 'Asiatic possessions'. In England, at least, the anti-slavery movement succeeded at this time; the Dutch colonies were the very last in the world to prohibit slavery. The greed of the English (excessive among the Dutch elite) was inflamed to such a degree and the knowledge that opium was the best means to sustain the political peace in the 'possessions' meant that opium was never prohibited.

Dirk Van Hogendorp, Raffles and Gijsbert Karel accepted this as the most promising guideline to get as much profit as possible *for both state and private merchants*:

Opium is one of the most profitable articles of eastern commerce: as such it is considered by our merchants ... it is impossible to oppose trading in the same. In this situation of affairs, therefore, we would rather advise that general leave be given to import opium at Malacca, and to allow the expectation from thence to Borneo and all the eastern parts *not* in the possession of the state' (Italics of Raffles/Van Hogendorp).[30]

The maxim became, therefore, to direct the opium to those Asiatic regions not yet in the "possession" of some Western power: that became, of course, the advice to addict China on the largest possible scale. A variant with the same background is: the English government's opium trade would continue up to the gate to the East Indies, Malacca, where the Dutch would pick it up and distribute it themselves in "their" archipelago. That is what happened in fact. Anyway, it was the guideline which triggered the most

---

[29] Idem, p. 104, 105.
[30] Idem, p. 104.

lucrative opium deals in world history for the Dutch as well as for the English.

The target of the English was China rather than its own colony of India, the production center. The Dutch government had a quite different interest: it directed the poison to its "own subjects" in Asia who were apparently not yet "pacified" enough. After China the East Indies became the largest consumption center thanks to the continuous efforts of the Dutch and their supporters.

The Dutch had nothing to sell in the East Indies except opium. Java and the whole archipelago were to become the sole producer of export crops and mining resources; the indigenous chiefs had to be bound to deliver for the lowest possible prices; from this income they could also buy Dutch opium and later "batiks" fabricated by the Dutch industry in Holland.

This transformation of the VOC + informal governmental support into formal Dutch government opium business is reproduced in Baud's table of the years 1746-1816 (see Appendix 2). However, the "new" knowledge about the poisonous character of opium led to one argument and one conclusion: of course, the colonial state must abandon its involvement with the opium business, but—alas—the English competition was so tough that the compulsory deliveries of the other classical colonial products (coffee, pepper, rice, wood, etc.) should be retained because 'they belong essentially to the Javanese manners and customs'! In short, the opium business had to be continued as usual and extended if possible because it was one of the few profitable ventures.

What is the reality behind these declarations and plans? The British part of this business was characterized in those years by the position of Raffles lying between the interests of the EIC-British government in India and his own interests in Java. "India" expected to transform the new British 'possession' into an easily exploitable producer of agricultural products by indigenous producers. Raffles wanted to go much further: the whole feudal structure with its indigenous nobility had to disappear in favor of a money economy and a direct relationship between the government and peasants in order to make the East Indies also into a market for British manufactured products.

To pay for the occupation of Java, etc. "India" wanted to create a land revenue based upon the principles of free cultivation and free trade, whereas Raffles looked first for commercial and next for territorial revenue.[31] He promised "India" (January 1812) much rice and coffee, Banca tin

---

[31] J. Bastin, p. 17.

and spices. He furthermore expected that his opium monopoly would yield 700,000 Spanish dollars (= ca. 2 million Dutch guilders). Together with revenues from customs and taxes, this could bring the government's income to 5.3 million Spanish dollars (= ca. 15 million Dutch guilders). He only arrived at half this target, and his position versus "Calcutta" was undermined:

> ... the severest of all financial shocks was the abolition of the Java opium monopoly in favor of free importations by Calcutta merchants. The Bengal Government had taken this action in the belief that ultimately the Company would gain more from Calcutta sales by opening markets in the Archipelago than from any local monopoly in Java. ... The loss of the opium revenue and the failure of external commerce led to a big increase in the export of specie from Java by the Bengal merchants ... The result was that the continued adverse balance of trade led to a spectacular flight of specie from the island during the second half of 1812 ...[32]

The Chinese later experienced exactly the same process for the opium-silver exchange with the English smugglers from India (see ch. 6).

The consequence was also that Raffles' anti-opium and anti-slavery policy in Java (whatever its dubious performance) was definitely abandoned. In reality, the old VOC practice, renewed by Daendels, was restored in a pro-slavery and pro-opium fashion. Anyway, a policy was introduced

> thanks to the acceptance of the system ... to make the opium farming as profitable as possible for the colonial treasury' and to expand the lease system also into the Outer Districts.[33]

Before 1800 the tendency was to stimulate opium consumption gradually and to ask low prices in order not to trigger smuggling. Indeed, this approach was definitely abandoned: now, the aim was big money in the shortest possible time and with the most effective methods. At the start, the government targeted three million Dutch opium guilders annually for itself and envisaged a profit of four million for the farmers.

Why? Its new aim of conquering the whole archipelago and colonizing this huge territory on land and at sea had to be paid for by the 'Asiatic pos-

---

[32] Idem, p. 18, 19. The contradictions in Raffles' opium policy are, in fact, more remarkable. During Daendels' regime the opium income came to 16% of the total. Officially (that is to say: according to his own statistics) Raffles diminished this percentage to 12.3 (1812/13), to 13.4 (1813/14) and then even to 5.7. However, not only his land rent income doubled during his regime and the leases increased in a substantial way, but the opium *import* increased in 1812-1816 from 40,500 chests to 73,250 (see appendix 2). This is clearly in variance with his own statistics.

[33] J. C. Baud, p. 161.

session' itself. It was, furthermore, a task which had to be exercised by the Dutch state-in-the-new-colony in close cooperation with *specific* private interests.

How this was done in the 19th-century is recounted here in two stories. A first short story tells about how tin was mined on the island of Billiton, in which the private initiative (the *Billiton Mining Company*) was stressed, and the government tin exploitation on the neighboring island of Banca remained more or less in the background. The second, longer story demonstrates in a rather spectacular way how the public-private cooperation has lead to the activities of a state-within-the-state, the *Royal Dutch Trade Company*. In both stories opium plays an important, but different, role, and in both stories the same is true for the new Dutch royalty.

CHAPTER SEVENTEEN

TIN FOR OPIUM, OPIUM FOR TIN?

The early history of a *Billiton Mining Company* (BM) is of interest here for two questions: what is the relation between tin production and opium, and how does this concern the dependency/independency of the private industry on the Dutch colonial state.[1] That from this early industrial activity it ultimately developed into the largest mining company in the world today, BHP-Billiton, is another rather complicated story. This is, of course, an interesting fact, but irrelevant here.[2]

Until the middle of the 19th-century, these foreign mining activities were only a matter of what was called the "Dutch Government in the East Indies" and the "English Government in Malacca". Tin mining was done at least from around 1700 onwards when the Sultan of Palembang, also ruler of the islands of Banca (Bangka, etc.) and Billiton (Beilitung, etc.), already had serious quarrels about tin with English and Dutch merchants. There were some loose contacts between the VOC and the islands: from 1640 onwards there is some trade between Batavia and Billiton (iron in the form of little axes and knifes exchanged for textiles).

Twenty-five years later, some people asked the VOC to protect them against the Sultan, but the islands were soon abandoned to what was called "pirates".[3] From 1709 the Sultan delivered sufficient tin to Batavia at a fixed price in a regular way, apparently to keep the Dutch out of the region.

At the beginning of the 19th-century, the English reported that potentially 40-50,000 piculs at a cost price of 10 Spanish dollars per picul could be sold in China for 22 to 26 dollars. The EIC could make much more of it, 'if the Company were to monopolize the whole supply, the price might be raised at whim'.[4] At this time the population of Banca was estimated at 10,000, of which 2,000 were Chinese, who worked the tin mines exclusive-

---

[1] The official name in Dutch was: *Naamloze Vennootschap Billiton Maatschappij* (Billiton Company Ltd.). For the following history, I used M. Gruythuysen—R. Kramer, G. A. de Lange, J. Loudon, J. Mollema, F. Stapel, C. Swaving, R. Verbeek.

[2] See an interesting article about the present BHP Billiton in *The Economist*, 21-8-2010.

[3] F. Stapel, p. 14-25.

[4] Idem, p. 29.

ly. They were organized in so-called *kongsehs* or *kongsis*. If, so expected Raffles, the British took over the management of the island, Chinese would 'flock in great numbers to Banca'.

After the English disappeared, the Dutch started their conquering program. The Sultan of Palembang was defeated by General De Kock (1821). The latter bought the support of the "pirates" in the region, nominated an indigenous ruler and occupied Billiton as well by forming a military establishment of 50 soldiers. Chinese from Banca were imported into Billiton to teach the population how to mine tin.

The Dutch began tin-mining in the "governmental" *Banca Tinwinning* (BTW) from the 1820s onwards; Billiton, still seen as a pirate nest, was too wild for them.

The tin was usually auctioned in Amsterdam. Batavia got its fee for this "service" also. Batavia, indeed, earned a great deal of money by doing nothing: just in the years 1852-1881 this amounted to nearly 110 million guilders from the tin source only! In this period the net profit per "gross picul" was not 26 dollars, as envisaged by the English, but already 75 guilders.[5]

The Chinese captain Tan Hang Kwee, one of the leaders of the Chinese tin-miners on Banca, concluded a contract with the Dutch (1827) to start tin mining on Billiton as well.[6] This Chinese leased a concession 'at his own risk and expense', starting with 300 laborers. The Dutch guaranteed their safety, although everything had to be paid for by the Chinese, who had to look for collaboration with the indigenous population. The tin had to be sold exclusively to the Dutch government, which paid over four years a price of 12 Spanish dollars per picul, assuming that the market price was not lower than 20 dollars p.p. The Chinese were obliged to pay for housing and food for the 40-50 soldiers stationed on Billiton. Article 16 says that for the time of the contract, the Dutch shall not introduce 'the amphioen, arak and gambling licenses on Billiton'. Indeed, without the Chinese, neither the colonial state on Banca nor later BM could mine tin; they both had to buy the tin from *kongsis* at fixed prices.

The Chinese first discovered tin ore on Billiton[7]. They did not ask for money in advance, as was usual; everybody was happy, including King William I who signed the contract. A Dutch Minister in the Netherlands,

---

 [5] G. de Lange, p. 30 note. To provide an idea of the change in value is not easy, but this could be helpful: around 1850 $26 is worth £5.33 and 75 guilders around £7.5.

 [6] For this contract see F. Stapel, p. 66-74.

 [7] See J. Loudon, p. 9.

however, acted the spoil-sport. He did not understand the way things worked on these islands. This man warned that now the Chinese could handle the tin-mining business for themselves, 'the old evil, the piracy and smuggling' will return. This ungrounded suspicion led to new measures imposed by the Governor-General in Batavia, to a new Dutch inspector on Billiton and even to the dismissal of Tan Hang Kwee (1829). This muddling through continued on for two decades.[8]

In the meantime the name "Nederlandsch Oost-Indië" ("Dutch East Indies") was invented as a consequence of the wave of conquests in the archipelago.[9] As Minister of Colonies, Baud started procedures to make it possible for European private companies also to start mining activities in the archipelago. As a result, BTW remained on Banca running a Dutch public mine while on the neighboring island, Billiton, Dutch private interests could start with a license from the Dutch colonial government.

The trigger to this activity was His Royal Highness Prince Henry, who wanted to invest much money in tin mining on Biliton together with another aristocrat.[10] The will of a member of the House of Orange could not be negated. The clever John Loudon became his representative, who was the public enemy of the representative of the Dutch in Batavia, the bureaucrat Croockewit. The latter told everybody that there was no tin on Billiton, but Loudon easily and quickly proved him wrong. Apparently, Batavia feared to lose its lucrative tin-business with the Chinese.

That was a well-grounded fear: in 1852 the first 500 picul of tin were mined. Eight years later very rich deposits were found along the east coast

---

[8] Happily for the Chinese, the stupidity on the side of the Dutch was unbelievable since there exists as well an accompanying report from the local Dutch official about the contract with Tan Hong Kwee, which stipulates that the advantage of the contract is wholly on the side of the Dutch and that at least a hundred thousand guilders per year can be gained from the Chinese labor. See Idem, p. 123.

[9] Earlier people used sometimes "Dutch India" (1653), but whether this referred to some "imperial drive" remains to be seen. Therefore, it should have been an official name used by the Directors of the VOC Amsterdam or a Dutch government. This was not the case. See F. Gaastra (2000), p. 8.

[10] The initial investment capital was five million guilders. Prince Henry spent 2/5th of it, Baron Van Tuyll van Serooskerken another 2/5th and John Loudon 1/5th. These people also issued shares of 1000 guilders among 35 mainly aristocratic friends. Prince Henry had 600 of these shares and apparently he expected to get 124,000 guilders interest per year. However, another aristocratic shareholder, Beelaerts van Blokland, earned a profit of 530,000 in 1882 which was increased to 701,000 ten years later. See R. Verbeek, p. 9. This must be his personal profit since the net profit of Batavia in 1882 was 179,130 which is 10% of the net profit of the company. One may suppose that the "costs" of the shareholders had already been deducted from this net profit. For the profit debate, see also G. de Lange, p. 25 ff., and for all the details of the royal contract, Idem, appendix b.

of the island, which gave BM a bright future as a company and Batavia received the crumbs of the cake. Even they were worth a lot of money as the table below shows.

The Dutch "government" license was an expensive one: 10% of the net profit + export duties, import duties, auction costs, many other taxes and ... opium costs. The table gives part of the result for the whole district, which is similar to the island of Billiton, including the BM. Roughly one-third of the total payments had to be paid by the indigenous population, the rest by BM. This costly license is a reproduction of the permanent tensions between the very greedy Batavia bureaucrats (themselves always in conflict with Dutch bureaucrats in Holland) and the private interests, whether the so-called smugglers, foreigners or Dutch private interests.

Table 11. 'Contributions to the Dutch Indies Government by the Billiton District' (in guilders)[11]

Year	Government part of BM profit (a)	Opium income (b)	Taxes and other expenses (c)	Export duty (d)	Total Payments to government (e)
1864	---	14 500	44 910	12 463	44 910
1870	75 161	32 400	154 913	73 575	230 074
1875	90 598	110 000	303 051	123 882	393 649
1880	164 338	123 600	427 501	169 033	591 839
1885	123 873	247 152	599 718	152 865	723 591
1890	155 153	223 100	679 462	183 977	834 615
1895	360 896	204 000	622 244	166 014	983 140
1900	4 333 615	180 000	527 202	175 000	4 860 817
1905	2 278 259	180 012	516 965	154 000	2 795 224

[11] J. Mollema, appendix 4. Only a part of this appendix is reproduced in the text; it, furthermore, describes taxes paid by Chinese and Europeans working in BM, the direct tax paid by the indigenous people, auction costs, etc. In addition, it provides the data per year. Mollema was nearly the Chief Administrator of BM after 1900. Later the Directors of BM complained about the 'weak spots' in Mollema's book. See F. Stapel, p. 7. Probably they were referring to this table with mistakes: in the 1864 row (c) and (e) are the same, which is impossible; all the numbers ending in "000" must be dubious; the comment given on column (a) is not very clear: for several years 3% is paid by BM in natura (in tin, one may suppose), but are the data given equivalent to the 3%, or the 7% cash or the full 10%? Let's suppose it is the last percentage, because then it is easy to determine the full net profit of BM: the substantial amount of 620 million guilders or on average 11 million a year split among the few shareholders. For other amounts see J. Loudon, p. 111 ff.

Table 11. Continued

Year	Government part of BM profit (a)	Opium income (b)	Taxes and other expenses (c)	Export duty (d)	Total Payments to government (e)
1910	1 230 995	275 229	742 673	150 000	1 973 668
1915	881 949	440 000	1 095 954	183 000	1 977 903
1920	2 560 577	634 000	1 209 438	274 000	3 770 015
	---	---	---	---	---
TOTAL	62 793 954	11 709 029	33 515 933	8 570 470	96 309 887

(a) from 1865-1891 BM had to give 10% of the profit, of which it gave 3% *in natura*;
(b) in 1909 the *Opiumregie* (see below) became effective on the island of Billiton; before that date the amounts concern the lease payments;
(c) a total of several taxes (income tax; tax on Chinese workers; patent tax, etc.);
(d) paid partly by BM and partly by the tin-buyers in Batavia;
(e) total of (a), the direct contributions, plus (c) the indirect contributions.

Opium, 11% of the total, was the single most important income for Batavia after the tin license. How and whether these opium costs were divided between BM and the indigenous population remains unknown. The following could give us a clue. Without going into great detail, the important role of the Chinese laborers must be stressed again.

From the beginning of tin production, the Chinese played a prominent role. They were, in fact, their own boss under the leadership of one or more captains. In Banca they did all of the work in a technical, social and commercial sense. Twenty years later, however, they were free laborers under the amateur leadership of white Batavia bureaucrats on Banca and aristocrats imported from Holland on Billiton. The former were apparently too greedy to invest, the latter were only interested in as high a dividend as possible. For the Chinese this did not make much difference.

On Billiton their housing situation was miserable, as the medical doctor Swaving explained.[12] In the months of February and March 1860, some 700 Chinese miners died, mainly from beriberi (a deficiency of thiamine,

---

[12] C. Swaving, p. 1 ff. In full detail he sketched the building (*kongsi* house of 30 x 10 x 5 m) in which 200 Chinese lived, with one entrance and no windows or other ventilation possibilities. Per person they had 7.5 meter at their disposal, 'which is only one-sixth of what they deserve'. Every year beriberi decimated the Chinese population. When more profitable deposits were found, around 1870, this situation was alleviated. For the serious labor conditions in the tin mines of Malaya, see C. Trocki (1990), p. 67 ff.; B. Watson Andaya, L. Y. Andaya, p. 135 ff.

Ill. 17. Coolie Labor in the Dutch Tin Mines, 1919

Source: B. Manders, 2010; *Historisch Nieuwsblad*, September 2010. Chinese "coolies" had to work under "strangle contracts" and severe circumstances in mines, along railways or on plantations. The picture shows a tin mine on the island Banca or Billiton. The East Indies were also "governed" by racism with the notorious rule: 'The more pigment, the less payment.'

vitamin B_1, in the diet). Five years later 60 Chinese died in a week or 63% of the workforce in a month.

Swaving also pointed to the very muddy and wet work of tin miners, the poisonous miasma and starvation.[13] All this together must have debilitated their stamina. In the Billiton administration the column next to the one giving dividend per share indicates the 'Mortality Percentage of the Miners'.[14]

In the initial period of BM, the workers were paid 20 guilders per picul of pure tin as the market price was three or four times as much. This amount must have taken several days of work for one person. Later they were paid much less: around 300 guilders *per year* (from 1900-1918 even on average 280). This is equivalent to less than one guilder per day. BM's notorious administrators had many possibilities to exploit these mostly

---

[13] C. Swaving, p. 4, 5.

[14] J. Mollema, appendix 3. The percentage was 6-23% per year in the 1850s; this decreased to around 10% in the 1870s and further to 2-3% per year. That looks beneficial, but the number of the Chinese miners increased quickly from about 600 in the 1855s to about 2,500 in the 1870s, to 8,000 in the 1880s, 11,000 in the 1890s and 28,990 in 1920. In these last few years the mortality was 1-2%, which is still about 300 Chinese workers every year! At that time, 70 years after the establishment of BM, about 15,000-17,000 Chinese tin miners must have perished on this island of Billiton. The rest was exploited to the maximum.

immigrant workers.[15] The mentality of the new Dutch management is demonstrated as Loudon noted in his diary:

> 27th August. ... According to Dekker the Chinese are found and brought by Tuyll; bad people; Hokloh Chinese; fighting, opium smoking and gambling. He says it is difficult to keep discipline among them. In addition, there is much too much paid for them ... The Chinese do not want to eat the rice bought by Tuyll ... this is investigated and indeed confirmed. [New rice] is procured with a 15% loss; also too expensive.[16]

This greedy Dutch leadership itself started to crimp immigrating Chinese. Another day Loudon brought the following salute to the dying Chinese. He discovered on his inspection tour that Chinese were playing the "poh"-game:

> [I] threatened them with strokes by the stick [*rotting*] if they did it again. A few sick Chinese were dying. At Rembing everything looked sad. The kongsi-house was full of sick and dying Chinese; most of them had large, dirty wounds on their legs; these do not come from the climate ... and certainly not from the heavy work, because they are too lazy to work; anyway, this *doing nothing* will last some days and then it's over and out.[17] (italics by Loudon)

None of this is reported about the situation on Banca for whatever reason.

In the 1880s a big row in the Dutch parliament was organized about the old animosity: BM as a company for the benefit of the colony and eventually the Dutch state (say the Batavia–The Hague bureaucrats) or

---

[15] For these data, see J. Mollema, appendix 3. His explanation of the annual payments (Idem, p. 157 ff.) is far from convincing, but it is not my duty to discuss the case. Anyway, in his BM memorial book, he still proudly remembers that in 1920/21, 974 miners returned to China with savings of 386,388 guilders or about 400 guilders per person after *three* years of hard labor (Idem, p. 156, 157)! A hilarious story describes how once BM had good luck, because the rate of the dollar had declined from 2.55 to 1.35 guilders, and the Chinese workers were paid in dollars. Happily for them: in inland China they were not aware of this, so the miners still got more dollars for their guilders (p. 163). Etc.

[16] J. Loudon, p. 45. Dekker and Baron Van Tuyll are Loudon's Dutch assistant and boss, respectively. Later the bookkeeper of BM was sent to Singapore to recruit Chinese: he came back on a ship with 150 Chinese *sinkehs,* 40 miners from Malacca, etc. (Id., p. 58). Chinese people came in small boats from Malacca to Billiton (p. 62). Loudon repeated here that the Hokloh Chinese 'were the worst kind of people, terribly lazy, opium addicts and thieves who all belong to secret societies ...' (Idem, p. 62).

[17] Idem, p. 67. On the next page L. mentions himself the reason for getting wounds on the legs: 'The most serious sicknesses were wounds on the legs, which usually started with very small unimportant sores, mostly got by felling trees in the woods of the [mining] areas; soon they are transformed in the most hideous wounds; they end up with cold fire and death' (Idem, p. 68, 69). He never thinks about shoes for the workforce or covering their legs: that cost money, and apparently Chinese lives were deemed worthless.

the "private" interests, in this case the House of Orange and related aristo-cratic shareholders. The latter were not exactly the best examples of "pri-vate" interests. This row led to the dismissal of the Minister of Colonies, who defended the Royal purse, but BM did not become nationalized.

Indeed, from the beginning this (semi)private character was jeopar-dized.

Time and again De Lange argued for the support of BM as a state enter-prise: from the first visit of Loudon, he was accompanied by state-mining engineers and warships; the contract envisaged that the BM administra-tors had official police authority, etc.[18] This was particularly important for the virulent opium smuggling: the administrators did not protect the opi-um leaseholder enough, but argued, 'the cheaper the opium, the better for the Chinese miners' ('better' here means: the more they buy, the more I gain).

Because a prince and important aristocrats were involved in BM, supervision by the state was neglected. This happened even in the sense that a quarter of the island was given to BM every time; by 1861 the whole island was BM property; only the rich deposits were mined; much less than 10% of the net profit was no longer paid to the state; the King inter-vened time and again in favour of BM, etc.[19] All this was the subject of the row in the 1890s.

The Opium Business of Billiton

In the BM memorial book in 1922, it states that BM did everything to combat the use of opium among the miners.[20] It was the mantra repeated by all authorities at the time. What is hidden behind it looks much less pious, however.

It is remarkable that no explanation is given for the 12 million guilders paid (see table above) for the opium lease, an amount mentioned in this memorial book. The title of this table is misleading (therefore the quota-tion marks) which tries to suggest that the district was not BM itself from 1861. Who thon on the island of Billiton paid the Dutch government this fabulous amount, and what was the relationship between leaser BM and its "customers"? The memorial author involuntary gives us a small clue to

---

[18] G. de Lange, p. 6, 7.
[19] Idem, p. 9 ff., p. 20 ff
[20] J. Mollema, p. 167.

an appropriate answer. He writes about the alleged Chinese inclination to gambling and opium smoking:

> Well, it is true that even a substantial use of opium is not as morally and physically devastating as the alcohol misuse of the Europeans. However, the very expensive opium as luxury expense is a too large part of the budget of the miner (one hoon, which is one pipe, costs 22 cents). ... The possibility to save money becomes, therefore, for the weak brothers so difficult that the aim of the emigration to a foreign country is missed.[21]

Above I mentioned that the miner is paid on average one guilder a day; one *hoon* is, therefore, more than 1/5th of this wage. There is, however, a rule that in official opium dens (including the one on Banca and why not on Billiton), the minimum quantity for consumption was two *hoons* = 1/50 *tahil.* In this case, the BM consumer already smoked away nearly half of his daily wage.

Next, because he is paid once a year, "somebody" gets into debt and another claims the annual wage. This must be the mystery behind the difference between what the miner receives on paper and in reality, both documented in the memorial book. That must also be the reason that the miner returns to China after three years, having received only 130 guilders a year. Even for those days a bare minimum for bad work, acceptable only for the migrating destitutes in Southeast Asia.

The receiver of the rest must be the official government leaseholder, BM on Billiton. This company apparently earned a lot of money to addict its own miners, a kind of truck system.[22] At the beginning of the 19th-century, it was not uncommon in the industrial cities of Europe. For the Chinese immigrant miner who wanted to go back to his village in China, the reality was given in the popular song "... I can't go; I owe my soul to the company store" ('Sixteen Tons').

From the earlier history of BM, the problem was similar. The BM pioneer Loudon understood perfectly well the classic Banca situation in which the Dutch in Batavia delivered and leased the opium:

> The leases of opium, pawnshops and liquor concerned those of Toboalie on Banca. The major of the Chinese in Muntok, who is the main leasee, leased himself to somebody on Billiton who paid him 1800 guilders per year.[23]

---

[21]　Idem, p. 167.
[22]　See Robert Elson's contribution to N. Tarling (ed.), vol. 2-1, p. 143-144, 148.
[23]　J. Loudon, p. 18.

Loudon does not inform the reader who this 'somebody' is. He himself used laudanum as a medicine on Billiton, which he must have purchased elsewhere.[24] The highly lethal character of the labor and a corrupting influence of the European administrators made opium smoking into a necessity. Loudon's hypocrisy is quite remarkable. That people praise themselves in their autobiography later, certainly vain people like Loudon, is understandable. The way he is doing this is not.

In 1852 he knew how the opium business was organized and exploited by his own administrators; thirty years later he also knew from experience how bad opium was in every respect, and also thanks to several Dutch critics. In retrospect, he had to legitimize his behavior and wrote that in March 1852 he asked Batavia to prohibit the import and distribution of opium on Billiton:

> The aim of this was purely philanthropic. What happened, however? We did not envisage that one needed the means to realize an aim and to vindicate a prohibition. Those means were not available on Billiton, and this open island became poisoned with opium from all sides. Opium became so cheap that nearly all Chinese, who never smoked opium ... became addicts [*opiumschuivers*]. Therefore, I was obliged later to ask the Government to introduce the opium—lease on Billiton ...[25]

Loudon "forgot" not only that the opium lease already existed on Banca (and through this somehow on Billiton); he was probably misled by the new Batavia plan to introduce an *Opiumregie* in the 1880s. In this case he did not realize what he was talking about: the *Opiumregie* was worse than the evil, as is shown below.

Loudon, furthermore, "forgot" that his own administrators had police authority (which was an illegitimate exercise of authority by a private firm, but that is not the problem here); he, Loudon, personally had the means to prohibit it, but he did not. A few sentences further, he even bluntly denied that his administrators had this police power (it existed, according to him, only on Banca), the subject of one of the big controversies in the Dutch Parliament at the time![26]

---

[24] Idem, p. 44.

[25] Idem, p. 57.

[26] This Loudon must have lost his mind in 1883 since he, first, mentions (Idem, p. 58) that his administrators 'were *no* Government officials!' (italics and exclamation mark from Loudon, H.D.). Exactly fourteen sentences later he wrote: that the Government '... decided under certain conditions to provide the administrators of the company with the same police power ... as on Banca ...' In addition, if he was in need of authority, there were many Dutch military on Billiton (as well as on Banca): the army and navy were always mobilized

The French medical doctor, Georges Thibout, illustrated the misery of the opium addict in 1912:

> Many individuals even prefer opium over liberty. The Chinese who work on Billiton to harvest pepper or work in the mines are treated in fact as slaves during the four or five years of their contract. When they give way to the temptation of the small houses along the border of the works where they can find opium, they cannot leave and lose all hope of liberation for the rest of their life.[27]

In short: like dealing in people, like exploiting people for a miserable slavery existence, Loudon and the BM management were also in favor of opium to discipline and silence opposition among the work force, but also to recoup part of the wages through their own opium shop.[28]

---

against opium smugglers. Loudon himself used the available military to chase Malacca Chinese (p. 63).

[27] G. Thibout, p. 91.

[28] In the administration of the *Opiumregie*, this difference between Banca and Billiton is clearly shown through the difference between the licensed and non-licensed opium deliveries on Banca and Billiton. See *Commission d'Enquête sur le Contrôle de l'Opium*, vol. 2, p. 211 ff. for 1928 and below in the section on the Outer Districts–Opiumregie for 1930.

CHAPTER EIGHTEEN

PUBLIC ADVENTURES OF A PRIVATE STATE WITHIN THE STATE

In the beginning of the century, one could not expect that the Dutch opium business would become in absolute terms the most lucrative trade. And despite the terrible wars from the beginning (the Java War against Diponegoro) to the end (the Aceh War fought by the Dutch butcher Van Heutsz). Also, many private (Dutch) opium dealers were very active, and they were "big business"as well. The history of these private dealers must still be written, partly because it remains difficult to get into their archives; partly because their bookkeeping was very dubious, lost or never made.

"Private" is a flexible concept. As demonstrated, the *Billiton Mining Company* was a private venture of the public House of Orange. As such, it also belonged to the second phase of the opium history of the new Dutch royalties. This BM construction was paralleled and followed up by another and more spectacular "adventure".

It concerns the largest and most influential of these "private" Dutch opium dealers, who operated alongside the American and British one, the Royal Dutch Trading Company (*Koninklijke Nederlandsche Handel-Maatschappij, NHM*). Private or not, the NHM's fate was strongly dependent on the government's behavior. That is to say, as the baby of the first Dutch King William I, it was directed largely against the established colonial administration. That was not the case with the American, British or Chinese dealers in the East Indies who, therefore, were so often called 'smugglers'. Their fate was still influenced by, in particular, the new high price setting of Batavia which made these "smugglers" rich in advance.[1]

As stated, this was not predicted around 1816 when the British occupation ended. The government's opium policy switch was triggered, first, by competition between the Bengal raw opium and the Middle Eastern one. Baud tells how the latter was imported by American merchants, and how in the beginning the indigenous Chinese dealers did not like this. The Americans dumped the prices as low as possible so that these customers could not refuse them.

---

[1] For the following see E. Helfferich; W. Mansvelt; E. Vanvugt, chapter XV.

More important was that the Netherlands became an autocratic monarchy for the first time in 1815 thanks to, in fact, a coup by some aristocrats.[2] The first king, William I, was a private merchant as well and ensured that his own pockets were filled with as much money as possible in the colony as well. For the colonial exploitation he personally established a new company, the NHM, which became a state-within-the-state in the colony and had a strong position in Holland as well.

During the highly profitable 19th-century with its new drive in opium farming, the VOC tradition (and stumbling practice) of private enterprise in combination with the military-bureaucratic state involvement developed into an typical form of oikoidal capitalism.

The King's ideology was expressed at the establishment of the NHM:

> ... its aim is to integrate all branches of industrious activities into one whole, of which the NHM is the nucleus; the Chambers of Commerce, the factories and the agricultural committees are the main branches of this whole ...' The NHM also had to be 'the *nucleus* between the general government and the industrious population of the Netherlands, so that the Company becomes the *adviser* of the government and the *champion* of the interests of the civilians in matters of industrious activities' (italics added by the author).[3]

William went so far as to make the NHM responsible for all commercial activities once exercised by the colonial state, expecting a serious reduction in the state expenses, including the import of opium. Even the colonial state bureaucrats had to be transferred to the NHM, which had become the very 'banker, controller and solicitor' of the colonial state, which lagged far behind with its payments to the "motherland":

> Because, the King said, whatever the high position of the government of the East Indies ... relative to the indigenous ('Inlander') and foreign Asian people, above all must reign the great rule that it is subordinated to the motherland ... has to follow-up the commands from here and has to serve the interests of the motherland.[4]

Of course, all this was a nonsensical idea of a dictator, and neither the leadership of the NHM nor the King himself had the ability to realize it even in a rudimentary way. The impression gained is that William painted a grand vista to make money out of it. Mansvelt concluded a century later during the NHM commemoration that it remains obscure whether the NHM or the State benefited from most of these plans.

---

[2] J. L. van Zanden (2000), p. 137 ff.
[3] Quoted by W. Mansvelt, vol. I, p. 87.
[4] Idem, p. 88.

This overriding aim of Dutch imperialism was expressed time and again in Mansvelt's biography of the Royal NHM, e.g.:

> ... one has to realize that the colony in an administrative sense is not considered as an autonomous part of the Empire, but as a State *company* ... as a municipal tram, gas or water works ... (italics by author)[5]

This situation was stressed to the utmost in the discussion of the new Dutch involvement in its colony, called the *Cultuurstelsel* (best translated as *Cultivation System*).[6] The consequences of this royal idea and system for the East Indies people were far-reaching, turning a large majority into badly treated "free slaves". From 1830 onwards, the indigenous cultivators had to reserve 20% of their best land for the cultivation of "Dutch products", which were gathered, managed and sold by the Royal NHM.

Later, the Dutch themselves started to cultivate all kinds of tropical products in plantations (sugar, coffee, indigo, tea, rubber, etc.) which made life for the population in the colony even harder: the indigenous people were simply expelled off their soils and could become poorly paid laborers and were perceived as opium addicts *by nature*. Mansvelt describes this transformation:

> Once fortune is lavished upon them through the famous sugar contracts, the Dutch got the appetite to try it for themselves with the help of free laborers.[7]

The fabulous profits with opium in the 19th-century are closely connected to this *Cultivation System* and its aftermath: "free slavery" and "free addiction" were the main advantages of the Dutch East Indies peoples.

A Royal Opium Dealer

To enter this colonial paradise, the Dutch had to sin grievously many times, and King William did the same, whatever his personal activity in monarchical money-making. He and his advisers organized a remarkable financial construction after collecting the enormous amount of 37 million guilders through NHM shares, while promising the Dutch public a financial heaven on earth.[8] The Dutch taxpayer had to guarantee a net

---

5   Idem, p. 212, p. 213.
6   Idem, p. 211.
7   Idem, p. 211.
8   See table 3.5 in J.L. van Zanden (2000), p. 140.

profit to the NHM of 300,000 guilders annually. Protective import duties were imposed on foreign traders to counteract competition of the NHM.

These substantial amounts of money at the time soon paled into insignificance as the millions poured in and out and remained, anyway, invisible for normal people. The King himself bought 4 million shares, but was—apart from the NHM leadership—the only one who not only got his money back quickly, but earned nearly the same amount again within thirteen years.[9] Later, the Royal involvement was hidden as much as possible. Even the NHM commemoration publication frankly writes about the usual double-Dutch bookkeeping in favor of the King, always called the "Garant", he who guarantees the profits for a happy few:

> This fully different outcome originates in as favorable a method of booking as possible for the Garant and in less than clear concepts of capital and profit ... one did not concern the arrears of the previous fiscal year in favor of the Garant.[10]

Here it is calculated that the King received 1.3 million too much from the NHM in 1830. Indeed, the billions of the private fortune of the present House of Orange originate partly from this source.[11] Another colonial venture, Royal Shell, established at the end of the century, catered for its completion and continuation. (Until 1921 the King got a weekly report from the President of the NHM informing him/her about his/her and the NHM's financial position.[12])

What did this "Garant" do for his money? King William and his advisers told the NHM not to remain in the East Indies alone. Apparently thinking of the old VOC glory, they divided the world into five target regions for the NHM trade.

> He intended to conquer the trade of the East Indies later. The Company had to get control first and foremost of the cotton and opium trade. Therefore, it had to establish its activities in the Levant, Egypt, China, America ...', and so on.[13]

---

[9] See W. Mansvelt, appendix II in vol. II, which unintentionally demonstrated this fabulous game with millions, while denying with a stiff upper lip that he, the King, benefited.

[10] Idem, vol. I, p. 233.

[11] The NHM was until 1936 the most important financial power in the colony, owner or financier of many plantations and other ventures. Gradually, it developed bank facilities in the colony as well as in China or Singapore. After World War II it became one of the largest Dutch banks, the ABN, and through a fusion with the AMRO bank one of the largest banks in the modern world.

[12] Idem, p. p. 235.

[13] Idem, p. 90.

The available capital was also divided over these regions and disappeared: in a few years' time only 24 million were left of the original 37 million. In the meantime money had to be earned directly with the two government monopolies in the East Indies (opium and salt). They provided so much revenue that the disappointment with all other ventures was compensated: royal and colonial mismanagement meant that the NHM nearly collapsed, and thanks to its opium business, this fate was not fulfilled.

The trade with South America, the Mediterranean or the Black Sea had to be abandoned, except for opium trade in the latter two regions.

To save William's dream, the Royal NHM had to become the state opium dealer for a lease of 3 million a year and had to concentrate its activities on the Dutch East Indies specifically and on East Asia in general. Here one was confronted with the same bullion problem as the British (EIC) first and China later: to pay for the Bengal opium, one needed silver which drained Java; Japanese copper could provide a substitute.[14] To solve these opium problems, the NHM became more involved in the intra-Asian market customs and also triggered a kind of currency reform in the East Indies.

The NHM as the main opium farmer of the colonial government ended up in a much better position than the Amphioen Society earlier. Nevertheless, its official announcement stated that opium was

> disastrous for the morality, for the zest for work and for the procreation of the population.[15]

It even used sometimes the very old VOC method to bargain opium for other goods and vice versa (opium for coffee; tin for opium).[16]

How can we comprehend this opium and salt monopoly? Mansvelt starts his explanation quite symptomatically, as the following reminding us of the situation of 25 years earlier:

> The opium trade and distribution were at the time of the VOC already a monopoly given to a special body: the *Amphioen Society*, which must have done good business as it seems. Later this monopoly was leased to whoever offered the most. This lease was the largest which the Indies Government had to offer: it alone concerned an amount of two to three million guilders

---

[14] Idem, p. 198. See also Idem, vol. II, p. 23 and note 2 p. 24, which reported how many silver coins the NHM bought for the government. For instance, in 1834 it was 1.2 million guilders, but five years later this was already 5.7 million.

[15] This had already been published in an *Annual Account* of 1829/30. See Idem, vol. II, p. 22; also quoted by E. Vanvugt, p. 199.

[16] J. Schmidt, p. 22, notes 119, 120.

annually. Since there were no financially strong Dutch people in the colony, the main lease (*hoofdpacht*) was given to English houses. These houses made sub-contracts for small European or Chinese houses in the districts ... The opium contract itself was not made public ..[17]

It is right to see the NHM as a kind of modern Amphioen Society: it now involved not the highest oikoidal officers, but the *primus inter pares*, the King, himself. The suggestion is made by Mansvelt that the NHM did not like the offer of the opium monopoly, because 'it was afraid that the Java War had had too many negative effects on the sales'. In addition, it knew that its predecessor, the English house, Deans&Co (or Dent&Co?), 'had used the last months to push very large quantities onto the market.'

After long negotiations the NHM leased the opium monopoly for 2.6 million guilders annually and for 2/7th of the net profit. However, if it could prove that the Java War had had negative effects, it would receive a compensation. In addition, it could terminate the contract after a year, although it officially lasted for three years. The NHM received 'a not unfavorable profit of half a million per year. Instead of being damaging, the Java War was highly profitable ... because the army was the best customer'![18]

During the negotiations about the renewal of the contract, it was disclosed that the government had a spy in the NHM's opium business, 'who secretly submitted all kinds of information.'[19] That is how friendly the mutual relations were between the established colonial bureaucracy and the new money-making toy of the King.

The relationship with the producers of the raw opium became complicated as well. In the VOC era, nearly all opium was bought in Bengal and further processed by the local, mostly Chinese, leasees. Now it was reported:

> The opium monopoly automatically implied a relationship with Bengal, although one satisfied its needs for 2/3 with Turkish opium, that—imported as raw opium from the Levant—was processed in the Netherlands.[20]

It is the first time in the Dutch opium history that such a relationship with the "motherland" was made.

The NHM leased its opium monopoly out for 3 million to a Chinese sub-farmer, which was the same amount the NHM was obliged to pay

---

17 W. Mansvelt, vol. I, p. 188.
18 Idem, p. 189.
19 Idem, p. 189.
20 Idem, p. 197.

back to the colonial state. This Chinese sub-farmer, however, was also obliged to

> accept a fixed quantity of opium every month (4/5 Levantine and 1/5 Bengal) against prices which greatly exceeded the purchasing prices ... This price increase was the source from which the Company derived its own profit and its annual payments to the government.[21]

So, without doing anything, it already cashed a net profit of 300,000 Dutch guilders, some "import profit" and some "farm-out profit". These amounts do not show up clearly in the NHM balances below. This Royal Construction was a worthy continuation of the double-Dutch practices of VOC and private Dutch adventurers.

The State within the (Colonial) State

Notwithstanding this, the NHM received something of another monopoly. The colonial government needed all kinds of goods from Holland or elsewhere for its own needs. This was in fact a continuation of a tradition already established in the first years of the VOC as its Directors made up a list of items it needed (the so-called *Eis,* Demand) with the status of a delivery contract.[22] The colonial government did the same, and the NHM could buy the goods (even including meat, indigenous wheaten flour, etc. but not weapons![23]) and deliver them for a profit of 16%. It was a very lucrative contract because the profit on this substantial business (see table) must have been much higher. In addition, Mansvelt simply reports, this delivery contract 'escaped the control of the Ministry'.[24]

---

[21] J.C. Baud, p. 164. Indeed, Baud positioned himself as someone who could give orders to the NHM, which was not directly accepted by the NHM. See W. Mansvelt, vol. I, p. 119 ff. It was, furthermore, logical that the colonial elite was not happy with a Royal NHM as watchdog. See also Idem, p. 127, which mentions the inimical attitude, about place-hunters, etc.

[22] J. de Vries, A. van der Woude, p. 457 ff., 511

[23] It must be a slip of the pen, but much later the author reports that weapons were also bought for the government already in the 1830s. W. Mansvelt, vol. II, p. 23.

[24] Idem, vol. I, p. 189; see also p. 190. Gradually, the NHM also created banking facilities, the *Java Bank*, for which Baud designed the articles of association, but it succeeded also to get the monopoly on all payments of pensions, etc. to the Dutch East-Indian clerks of all bureaucracies, including the officers, their widows, etc. I only mention it here to demonstrate how the NHM became not only the spider in the East-Indies web, but a new large bureaucracy fueled by private profits. Idem, p. 209, 211. For all transactions a provision of 2% could be collected. The NHM even succeeded in not paying in cash but in

In the following table the NHM performance in the first years is given, and the items opium, government business and own activity are listed separately.

Table 12. Profit and Loss Account of the Royal Dutch Trade Company (selected years; x 1000 Dutch guilders)[25]

	1824/5	1826	1827	1828	1829	1830	1831	1832	1833	1834
own trade in East Indies	35.2	367.4	31.5	*814.7*	*530.4*	*464.4*	1303	1659.2	615	303.1
on behalf of government	---	582.5	165.9	317.6	423.6	274.9	14.4	218.1	335.2	1006.5
opium lease and trade	---	---	606.7	345.3	621	484.9	374.3	571.2	185.9	98.8
trade with China	---	*908.2*	*310.5*	*734.6*	*43.7*	25.9	243	*55.4*	*85.7*	8.9
Profit or *Loss*	*279.3*	*438.8*	1253	*615.2*	1268	434.8	1404.4	3036.1	1832	2085.6

What about the NHM's opium record for the following years? The answer is given by several authors including Schmidt:

> By the 1850s, the opium income constituted 16.8% of the revenue collected in the Indies. Between 1860 and 1910 this level was more or less maintained at an average of 15%.[26]

This is a necessary but not the most interesting element of the NHM's performance.

Baud could have asked, for instance, how was it possible that within a NHM deal, Levantine opium played such a prominent role? Had NHM officials made a deal with the Americans? Baud knew perfectly well how the colonial Dutch had relied on Bengal opium for centuries. As a Minister of Colonies, he had to negotiate frequently with the NHM.

In a rather unnoticed publication, Jan Schmidt disclosed at least part of the "mystery". He assumed that the Dutch participation in the international opium trade was marginal because it should have been confined to the East Indies only. The British and Americans had a hegemonic posi-

---

goods, the transport of which was again paid by the Dutch taxpayer. And so on and so forth.

[25] W. Mansvelt, vol. I, p. 232 ff or Appendix in vol. II. Quoted in E. Vanvugt (1985; 1995), p.410 ff; see also Idem (1988), p. 35-38.

[26] J. Schmidt, p. 27.

tion outside this realm. Within the archipelago, the latter extended their influence from the moment the first American ship arrived in Java (1789). This lasted, however, only for the period of Raffles government up to 1816.[27] The new Dutch deal with the British Empire was the end of the American penetration and the beginning of a new Dutch start, now more profitable than ever.

Whatever one thinks about the performance of the NHM, it succeeded in overcoming its serious blunders and losses thanks to the substantial and continuous financial support and guarantees from King and Country, while still expanding quickly throughout the whole of Asia.

Its second large financial source was its ability to exploit the colonial state in a rather absurd way, from weapons to pork-meat and pension deals: this parasite could be found everywhere. Only its opium monopoly from this colonial government was perceived as 'nothing but a guaranteed income of three tons of gold, while the government was the suffering party'.[28]

And its third—in my view main—source was its ability not to show to outsiders how the first and second sources became linked to each other *only* in the pockets of the NHM. In other words: its turnover, profits, costs or activities could not ultimately be controlled from either Holland (royal or not) or Batavia. It is even uncertain whether the NHM bookkeepers really could audit what was happening in all the many "departments" in so many countries and with so many products (illicit) and customers. The exploitation of these three pillars and continuously playing the divide and rule game between the first two made the NHM 'a robber state' in the "Multatulian sense", but also towards the two Dutch governments.

According to the above table, the opium business seems to be only one of its activities. Schmidt himself demonstrated in detail how the NHM itself was the buyer of Levantine opium in Turkey (Anatolia) or Egypt, which was also known to Mansvelt. Secondly, he showed how the NHM once bought, for instance, 40 chests of illicit opium offered by an American

---

[27] J. Schmidt, p. 20 ff. He largely based this opinion on the study of Owen's *British Opium Policy* and on studies showing how the economic situation in Europe went from bad to worse. His mistake was that he did not acknowledge the dynamic of the Dutch intra-Asian trade. From time immemorial this was the greatest support of the Dutch colonial empire. Concluding, for instance, that 'the number of ships arriving in and departing from Holland declined every year ... Amsterdam had ceased to function as one of the most important staple ports in Europe' (p. 20, 21), etc., he thought that the same misery was apparent in the East Indies or in East Asia.

[28] Quoted in J. Schmidt, p. 28.

captain in Java; 30 chests were for the government, 8 went to an opium farmer in Padang (north-west coast of Sumatra) and 2 were kept

> at the disposition of one of our most important linen buyers, which he needs for the undertaking of a small, experimental Expedition to the Peppercoast (Sumatra) ...[29]

He also disclosed a constellation in Izmir from before 1800 in which private Dutch and other European opium dealers closely collaborated with Anatolian producers, shipowners of all nationalities, smugglers and the NHM or other private dealers in the East Indies (often Armenians).

The opium (later also morphine and heroin) dealers in Izmir were, therefore, not Turkish but Dutch dealers with names now representative of the Dutch Protestant elite: members of the Van Lennep family, the Wissing family, the Dutilhs, etc. They also interchanged their commercial activities with political jobs as consuls of the Dutch state. The Levantine opium, morphine and heroin were also attractive for other nations. A symptomatic remark for the situation around 1900:

> In the years before the First World War, four major opium dealers were active on the Izmir market: the British firm of Barker Brothers, the Austrian house of F. Fidao & Co and two Dutch firms: that of A.A. Keun & Co and A. Lavino & Co ... Both firms indirectly supplied opium to the Colonial Minsitry. Keun delivered through the agents G. Briegleb, Van Eeghen & Co (both of Amsterdam) and G.W. Koning (Rotterdam) ...[30]

He made a rather spectacular report about a remarkable criminal case in 1897 in which a Dutch private detective alarmed the Ministry of Justice in The Hague that an Armenian opium dealer, Andreas, from Java

> tried to interest the firm of W. Hemsing & Co (Spuistraat 36, Amsterdam) "in making a lot of money in the smuggling trade in opium, particularly by means of bicycles, whose tubes, frame and tube under the saddle-pillar lend themselves excellently to the import of clandestine goods". Once the trade had developed satisfactorily, Holland would also be used as a base. ... A. was going to the Indies to act in the interest of the enterprise, using his experience and acquaintance with officials of high and low rank, all of them ... easy to cheat or bribe. All opium was to be obtained from the Levant ...[31]

---

[29] Idem, p. 25.

[30] J. Schmidt, p. 173.

[31] Idem, p. 31. This case is also "spectacular" for another reason: I lived for a long time near this address in the Spuistraat in Amsterdam, where my bicycles were repaired as well, but I was never asked to smuggle opium; therefore, I remained poor and could not buy a Rolls Royce: the advantage is, I hope, that this book was written!

This kind of double-Dutch opium trade continued, in fact, until 1940-41. Probably the main relationship could be discovered in the table as well. Below the amounts of the opium trade proper (in the end the NHM was the official opium dealer for the colonial government), the data about its China trade are indicated. These are the years of the largest opium-smuggling activities of the English and Americans into China. It would be strange if the greedy Dutch opium traders did not participate in it. Indeed, a Chinese source complains that 'large quantities' of opium came from the 'Dutch East Indies', which was simply similar to the NHM.[32]

This outcome must have serious consequences for the assessment of the opium trade of the NHM (now almost 50% of its activities) and for the Dutch colonial state as well. Is it true that all opium import destined for Java, Madura and the rest of the archipelago arrived here and not in China? If so, the addiction of the East Indies was much less than always suggested, while the smugglers' activity or collaboration of the Dutch colonial bureaucracy or King William I was much larger.

It is impossible to continue this history of the Dutch private opium dealers including the NHM story. It gained a bad image world-wide thanks to Multatuli's famous book, *Max Havelaar, or the coffee auctions of the Nederlandsche Handelmaatschappij* (1859). From this title it becomes clear that Multatuli despised the NHM management of the coffee plantations. However, as the table shows, the opium business was its most profitable activity originally. Even in the beginning of the 20th-century, the NHM belonged to the cartel of importers and producers of coca leaves, the *Association of Coca Producers*.[33] As such it had great influence in the running of the Dutch Cocaine Factory (see below).

Last question: within the Dutch East Indies economy the private NHM was indeed the state within the state. Was it the 'robber state' Multatuli condemned? From the above one can already conclude that most or a very large part of all opium profits went into NHM pockets. Even from Mansvelt's two-volume biography of the NHM (a commission of the NHM), it seems certain that the King (and the House of Orange in general at least until 1921) benefited the most from NHM's opium deals, when William I himself is not the "inventor" of these deals. From other professional Dutch historians one cannot expect more information in this case since they failed to come up with any reasonable *economic* history of their

---

[32] Quoted in A. Hosie, vol. 2, p. 203, 204.
[33] M. de Kort, in: P. Gootenberg (ed.), p. 131.

colonies.[34] From abroad, as so often, must come the "material of the truth"; in this case the study of Helfferich (1914) about the NHM and other 'Kulturbanken' (financiers of the cultivations/ plantations).

In this period the NHM developed into such a dinosaur that its opium (and also including the later cocaine business) not longer had the relative weight and basic importance as in its initial period.

The in-depth study of Helfferich on the situation around 1914 comes, however, to the same conclusion as Mansvelt for the initial period, namely, that the NHM bookkeeping was a mess. For people like Helfferich or any external expert, it is inscrutable; one may add for the largest majority of the internal ones as well. A few quotations must suffice about one of its most profitable, long-lasting and largest activities (sugar plantations and factories) which concern a general judgment about all cultivation projects as well:

> The profits are calculated after internal depreciation and payment of bonuses from which the amount is unknown ... and after [calculating] a fixed interest for the invested capitals, while on top of this from the net profit 500,000 guilders are reserved ... It is a pity that there is a lack of relevant documents ... thanks to the typical NHM accounting methods ... is it impossible to calculate the profitability of the present "participations" ... Furthermore, there are absent in all Year Accounts from the beginning until now the yields and the output of the sugar factories, their production costs and the sales prices, the depreciation of newly bought things or bonuses; in short, all those data are absent in the Year Accounts which belong to the most important economic documents of a firm of the ancestry and importance of the Dutch Trade Company.[35]

And so on! It is a litany of sins not known to Multatuli when he directly attacked the NHM as the most serious partner in the Dutch 'robber state'.

---

[34] A start could have been made by J.L. van Zanden (1996) and better (2000), p. 137-149 and 220-231, but it received no follow-up, apart from the normal situation among Dutch historians that "opium" is not considered at all. Anyway, no progress compared to the first economic history, written by the German E. Baasch, p. 364-384, 569-584, let alone the German E. Helfferich, p. 100-120 and passim. Van Zanden is, like Helfferich, happily already convinced of the manipulations (p. 222) in the official bookkeepers' information about the so-called "Batig Slot", the balance of profits of the colony.

[35] E. Helfferich, p. 116, 117.

CHAPTER NINETEEN

THE OPIUM REGIME OF THE DUTCH (COLONIAL) STATE, 1850-1940

Multatuli's 'robber state' was also a state with a state bureaucracy. It was a colonial state directed at the exploitation of foreign territories without being asked to do so by the indigenous rulers and population, and whether legally or morally allowed, relevant or desirable. At the beginning of the 19th-century, this state and its bureaucracy were rather abstract entities; thunderclouds in a Western tempest with devastating lightning strikes. Of course, the elite had no knowledge of who lived there "far below"and under what conditions and, therefore, what effects this "natural disaster" had. And had forgotten how immense the area was in which this Western Tempest played havoc. For the new Dutch rulers, the island of Java was the only area they ruled for a long time; the enclosed map was not at their disposal.

Therefore, the actual opium distribution in Java had to be done by indigenous people who knew the ways to reach the consumers. The colonial state had to use *opium farmers*, but this changed at the end of the century as the Dutch became more accustomed to the East Indies and the East Indian people to them.

Then the *Opiumregie* was introduced, and its grip on the opium market became unparalleled compared to the VOC or the previous period. This time not only Java and Madura were the center of all activities, but the whole of the archipelago became occupied in a new series of devastating campaigns. Officially, however, the *Opiumregie* was aimed at minimizing or even eradicating opium consumption. There was no place for competition, not even of the NHM: the *Opiumregie* had a monopoly, not only in Java and Madura but also in the rest of the archipelago. Therefore, let us start with a few remarks about this "rest", and later the performance of the *Opiumregie* itself will be scrutinized.

The Outer Districts

As stated above, the better penetration of the Dutch opium business into the Outer Districts was already another feature of Dutch rule in the 19th-

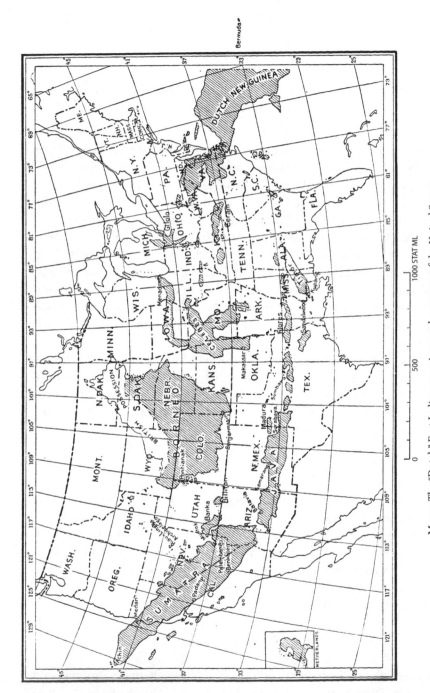

Map 9. The "Dutch" East Indies, superimposed on a map of the United States

Source: A. Vandenbosch, p. 2. Comparative Map no.2, United States Coast and Geodetic Survey.

century and a parallel effect of the protracted conquest of parts of this archipelago; conquests which were followed up at the beginning of the 20th-century a few years before the Dutch were kicked out of the realm. Neither the VOC nor the *Amphioen Society* cared much in this respect for other parts of the archipelago than Java and Madura. They certainly had their customers on specific islands like Bali, but there was no regular, let alone systematic, export from Batavia to elsewhere in the archipelago.

Many of these Outer Districts were situated on the route from Bengal along Sumatra, the Strait of Malacca (Melaka), Singapore, Borneo, etc. Along this route they were visited mostly by non-Dutch traders, who were immediately called "smugglers" by the Dutch. The English country traders and Chinese were the most important ones, but the Buginese traders were also rather active. This non-Dutch network was strengthened after Singapore became more important as the main port in the trade between India–East Indies–China.

Another important reason was that Dutch opium was always cost more than the opium from elsewhere. This situation did not change from the Napoleonic era, through the British occupation of Java or in the 20th-century. On the contrary, British and American opium traders now had the best chance to attack their traditional Dutch competitor. Their only limit was Raffles' strong anti-opium and anti-slavery stand and the military protection the high-priced opium got from the Dutch. To avoid consumption, the British only levied an opium tax in the Outer Districts, but it is doubtful whether anybody cared to collect it.

Yet the rationalization of the opium distribution by means of government opium dens (Daendels, 1809) was continued after the restoration of the Dutch government. Opium dens were also spread over the Outer Districts, leading to a more systematic distribution of opium.[1] In Ambon, Timor, Ban(g)ka–Belitung (Billiton) or Celebes, official opium dens were established. However, the license-holders often had to collect their opium *not* from the Java-based government but from the "smugglers"! At the end of the 19th-century, with the establishment of the *Opiumregie,* this big hole in the government opium network started to close. The closing of it required at least one real Opium War (see below). Until this new organization was functioning, the leasers of the opium dens had to pay for the license and taxes relative to the consumption.

---

[1] J.C. Baud, p. 192 ff.

The reasoning behind it must have been a pragmatic one for an exploiter: what was lost to the smugglers should be shifted towards their "own" consumers. It was a system which allowed many possibilities for corruption on all sides. As long as the government in Batavia could collect its half a million guilders annually from the districts, it was not concerned. The following table gives examples of how that half million was distributed over most districts in the middle of the 19th-century. One must realize that it was Baud, one of the highest officials in the colony, who estimated the so-called "smuggling".

Table 13. Net Output of Opium Leasing in Outer Districts of the East Indies, 1847-1849[2]

DISTRICT	1847 (Guilders)	1848 (Guilders)	1849 (Guilders)	Estimated smuggling (chests)
Moluccas	25 767	32 421	32 187	19
Bali, Timor, etc.	2 150	3 120	3 300	10
Macassar	53 037	81 880	34 240	40
Banjarmasin	12 787	4 480	15 482	9
Pontianak	56 900	71 300	59 466	115
Riau	63 000	67 500	55 200	50
Banca	68 482	60 789	63 010	21
Padano +Aceh	200 022	189 640	192 490	160
Bencoolen	19 125	20 810	21 120	80
Palembang	23 460	25 900	29 760	12
TOTAL	509 049	523 407	531 834	516

This table reveals a few remarkable things. When this distribution occurs, the total opium income of the Dutch colonial state in these years was 6.7, 6.5 and 6 million guilders, respectively.[3] This means that about six million guilders were provided every year by Java and Madura alone. These two islands are the most populous ones and the headquarters of the Dutch occupation and the NHM, but this is untenable. Also, the weights for Java and Madura (Baud: 390-375 chests per year in the period 1845-1849) in relation to the earnings are ridiculous. The first conclusion is, therefore,

---

[2] Idem, p. 193. Padano (Padang) is situated at the middle West Coast of Sumatra above Bencoolen; Banjarmasin is a district in the south of Borneo; Riau is suggested as belonging to a group of islands south of Singapore. The sales in these districts are estimated for the years 1849-1850 by Baud, p. 180 ff.

[3] Idem, p. 220. See also the article of R. Elson in A. Booth et. al (ed.), p. 41 column 2, who does not indicate which factor applies to "guilders": ×100 or ×1000.

that the official Dutch statistics are quite dubious. This problem is in need of further investigation, but that cannot be done here.[4]

Looking for a further explanation, it could be assumed that the data are related to negotiations between the Dutch bureaucracy and the NHM: if the former got its money and the NHM its opium, then everybody must have been "satisfied"; data are only interesting for the motherland. The NHM as the main opium farmer "in Batavia" sells the opium to its own (unknown) customers somewhere in the whole realm. One must remember that the NHM trade operations reached even into China, the largest market for opium!

In this perspective, Baud's estimates of "smuggled" quantities in the archipelago receive a specific meaning, although they cannot be seen in relation to the other columns in the table. Baud's reflection on these smuggling data is:

> ... at the moment only among the leasers one can find the smugglers of substantial quantities ... in the VOC period there existed a right which every collaborator of the Company expected to have on the yield of so-called *silent profits*; at the moment the smuggler is confronted everywhere with the opinion that these profits are not only against the law, but are immoral as well ... if there should exist exceptions to this, one can find them only among the poorly remunerated personnel of low rank. It may be perceived as certain that the Chinese, who were major collaborators of the smugglers in the previous century, are still the same perpetrators ...[5] (italics from Baud)

Therefore, we can also conclude that the NHM, with its extremely close relation to the Chinese traders and opium leasers, belongs among the main smugglers; we can at least expect that smuggling occurs with the *silent approval* of the NHM and that Baud, not a friend of the NHM, is suggesting this assumption.

---

[4] More people do have difficulties with the statistics. Take the example of J. Meiss' doctoral dissertation from 1883. J. Meiss, p. 65, reproduces the same table as given in the text without the smuggling estimates, while adding the totals of 1844-1846 (respectively 838,071; 840,031 and 825,089) and of 1850-51 (respectively 561,248 and 496,220). However, it is a pity that Meiss did not see a printing error in his table (in Bangka, 1847), but that all his totals from 1847-1849 are wrong is a remarkable mistake. The differences are between 250,000 and 300,000 guilders. My only explanation is that Meiss, for whatever strange reason, has taken only the totals from another source like Baud, namely the *Koloniaal Verslag*. In that case, it could be that the large differences between Meiss and Baud originate from a notation of *tiban* plus *siram*, while Baud's data could be based on the *tiban* only. But is this to be expected of Baud, the inventor of the tiban-siram system?

[5] J. C. Baud, p. 182.

Table 14. Opium consumption (in thails) of License and Non-License Holders in Java, Madura and Outer Districts (*Buitengewesten*) in the *Opiumregie*,1930[6]

AREA	HOLDERS OF A LICENSE						NON-LICENSE HOLDERS				Total in thails x 100
	Europeans		Chinese		Indigenous		Chinese		Indigenous		
	no.	thails	no.	thails	no.	thails	no.	thails	no.	thails	
West Java	2	27	1943	36916	626	4258	5093	38731	3036	5570	85
Middle Java	2	59	2702	50241	16184	61947	1874	14514	3193	5384	132
East Java	1	---	3469	80108	33269	113677	1463	24106	1306	5226	223
Djogjakarta	---	---	456	9906	2132	9028	---	–	–	–	18
Soerakarta	---	---	935	14451	16630	52856	---	–	–	–	67
total Java + Madura	5	86	9496	191622	68841	241767	8430	77351	7535	16180	527
OUTER DISTRICTS (selection)											
W.Sumatra	–	–	280	5331	44	233	–	–	–	–	5
Palembang	–	–	217	6176	7	35	1115	22343	20	199	28
E.Sumatra	–	–	148	2857	117	924	36829	339542	3515	14221	357
Banca	–	---	7205	49862	7	54	–	---	–	–	49
Billiton	–	–	–	–	1	4.23	1319	24810	–	–	24
Borneo	–	–	291	6429	18	134	634	12915	107	277	19
Moluccas	–	–	275	8748	274	1431	---	–	–	–	10
Bali, etc.	–	–	541	9546	1292	7629	–	---	–	–	17
total Outer Dist.	---	---	10808	124605	3680	20583	52028	575550	6382	28902	749
Total 1930	5	86	20304	316227	72521	262350	60458	652901	13917	45082	1276
Total 1928	5	100	19552	337012	81491	338628	70266	868348	14805	56879	1601

1 thail = 100 mata = 38.6 gram; 1 ounce = 2.59 thail.

All this points to a more profound context, the struggle between the colonial state representatives (like Baud) and the private entrepreneurship within their realm: the former do have the prerogative to define what is moral or immoral for whatever reason. This resembles the *'Staatsraison'*

---

[6] This table is given in the article of C. Steinmetz in: *Indie en het Opium*, p. 159. From the Outer Districts only a selection is given here. Therefore, the given total is not the total of the given districts, but of all Outer Districts. The totals of 1928 are derived from a table in *Commission d'Enquête sur le Contrôle de l'Opium*, vol. 1 p. 80 ff., vol. 2, p. 211 ff.

of the highest state bureaucrats. In that case, the state knows perfectly well what it involves to distribute a substance like opium in a narco-military framework: it needs the money for its household and servants, and therefore its own activity is defined as of a high moral standing and its competitors as smugglers, enemies who should be eliminated.

Here we can provide another view on the relationship between the Outer Districts and Java plus Madura from several decades later, which results in new questions.

The first thing to deduce from the table is that in the Outer Districts in 1930, about 467 chests are consumed and in Java + Madura, about 328. This is more or less the same proportion as eighty years earlier (516 to 380).[7] In this period, however, the population on Java increased from about ten million (around 1850) to 41 million (1930). In almost all other parts of Southeast Asia, there is a similar spectacular growth.[8] The given data, provided by the Dutch *Opiumregie*, are therefore not very convincing, to say the least.

From this table one can learn many things, more about the *Opiumregie* itself than about—say—the degree of opium addiction in the population. In fact, the table contains data about the inhabitants of the districts and the average opium use per year of the several groups in those districts. As such, it symbolizes an important aspect of the opium monopoly: the ability to combine (and use) all kinds of information about the exploited subjects and the ability to define problems (dubious or not). The registration of five Europeans asking for and obtaining a license to smoke only 86 thails *in a year* is not only a demonstration of European "innocence and civilization" of the opium importers, but also of absurd state interventionism.

It is suggested that there were about 80,000 Chinese licensed and non-licensed opium smokers in 1930 and 90,000 indigenous smokers of the stuff provided by the *Opiumregie*. A holder, however, is not the same as a user; he could be a dealer or shopkeeper, a non-smoking buyer or a family member. Furthermore, in the explanation one always used the Dutch

---

[7] The Outer Districts total of 749,600 thails = about 28,942 kg = about 467 chests; the Java + Madura total of 527,000 thails = about 20,347 kg = about 328 chests. When comparing the several districts in the two tables, one is confronted with serious differences. This supposes, of course, that the reasonable guess of Baud about the smuggling in 1850 should be the whole consumption. This is certainly not the case, but also during the regime of the *Opiumregie*, statistics must have been used to cover government activities, because there was also a substantial amount of smuggling.

[8] N. Tarling (ed.), vol. 2-1, p. 158.

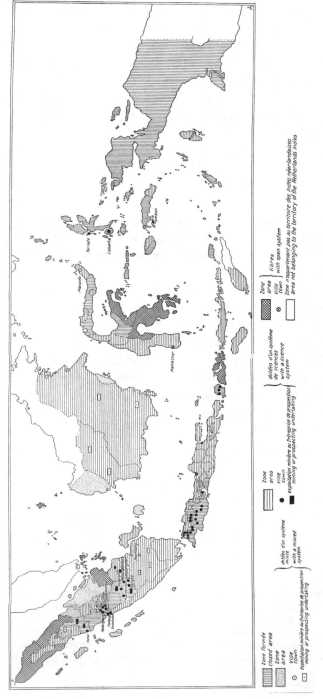

Map 10. The "Dutch" East Indies and their 'Zones for the Control of Opium Smoking', 1930

Source: Commission d'Enquête sur le Contrôle de l'Opium, League of Nations. The Dutch developed rather complicated prohibitive and restrictive measures with respect to the possession, the ownership, the transportation and the use of government opium and its derivatives. The map illustrates this for the whole of the archipelago.

word 'schuiver' for these "smokers", which was for most readers synonymous with addicts (see below). In addition, hardly any reader cared or knew something about the important difference between an opium eater and a smoker (the first consumes oin average much more morphine than the latter, etc.). Most commentators think that at least the same number of smokers were reached through the smuggling circuit.

The table gives the consumers of the *legal opium* (in Dutch: *Wettig Opium*). According to this, on average 1 in every 15 Chinese in the archipelago (7% of all Chinese) and 1 in every 684 indigenous inhabitant (0.2% of all indigenous people) were smokers. In the Outer Districts this ratio was 1 in 10 Chinese and 1 in 1800 indigenous people.

There are specific districts in which the opium consumption is much larger than elsewhere.[9] Officially, there were even districts without any smokers. A spectacular aspect invovles the Ban(g)ka district of the tin mines where 30% of all Chinese consumption can be noted. Some 30% of the Java consumption is concentrated in Eastern Java, etc.

If we try to define an opium *addict* in the 1930s, we can derive from the table that an average of 12 *thail* was consumed per Chinese smoker per *year*, while an indigenous man consumed almost 4 *thail a year* (463.2 g and 154.4 g a year, respectively).[10] In other words, 1.27 gram and 0.42 gram *a day*, respectively. In terms of money, this consumption is calculated as follows:

> Per head of the population in 1930, one spends 38 cents on Java and Madura for Opiumregie opium, in the outer districts 118 and in the whole of the archipelago 67 cents per *year* in a population of about 60 million souls' (italics added, H.D.).[11]

With these figures we can make a few interesting calculations to support our concept. First, the average of 67 cents paid in 1930 amounts to 40.2 million Dutch guilders earned by the *Opiumregie* or the state. The table provided by the Director of the Ministry of Finance, one of the most important figures in the *Opiumregie,* indicates the gross income for 1930 about 5 million *less*.

A second conclusion is that it is physically impossible to become an addict on 1.3 gram a day, let alone from 0.4 gram. To compare this, for

---

[9] See map in J. Rush, p. 5 for a situation at the end of the 19th-century.

[10] Suppose that the numbers in the table represent the consumers, which is suggested but not very convincingly. These *Opiumregie* figures, anyway, represent consumption of *Opiumregie* opium.

[11] C. Steinmetz in: *Indie en het Opium*, p. 157, 158.

instance, with a present packet of cigarettes of 28.3 gram (20 cigarettes) is rather complicated, because one has to compare the morphine with the nicotine content and their addictive effects. However, it is illustrative to say that Steinmetz' opium addicts smoke something similar to about 1/3 to one cigarette a day.

And what does it mean that one spends 38, 67 or 118 cents *a year* on opium? The lowest ranks of the police earned at the time a maximum of 25 Dutch guilders *a month*; the so-called *mantri-politie*, specialized in attacking opium smugglers, earned double that amount.[12] This is thus 300-600 guilders a year. If one earned the minimum and consumed the maximum of 118 cents on opium, this should amount to the negligible sum of 0.4% of the total annual budget (for a "coolie" with his yearly budget of about 180 guilders, it is still less than 1%).[13]

Caring about these "addicts" seems to be only an artificial case aiming at quite different matters than avoiding addiction. Therefore, one can easily conclude: the only explanation for all the fuss about the Opium Problem in the Dutch East Indies then is legitimating and securing a substantial financial contribution to the foundations of the colonial state through a well-known bad and controversial product.

This should have negated a major element of this Opium Problem: for middle- and upper-class well-fed consumers of opium, these quantities are not at all unhealthy for their purse or body. But the above calculations are averages of all classes, while we concentrate on *specific* users, their concentrations in the tin mines or their wanderings.

They are met, for instance, in chapter 8 about the *Billiton Mining Company,* a model for all work sites. Through the whole of the archipelago, hundreds of thousands of men and women were wandering between the many "white" plantations, mines, factories or cities. Between 1913 and 1925 about 327,000 contract "coolies" departed *from Java alone* for plantations and work sites in the outer islands. They were the opium clients and victims described as follows:

---

[12] M. Bloembergen, p. 86. Elsewhere (p. 63) she states that household personnel (or 'the normal coolie') got 14-15 guilder a month plus free lodging; top police officers received 250-400 guilders a month.

[13] The well-known economist J. H. Boeke studied household expenditures in 1886 and 1888. The lowest income was found in a small mountain *desa*, and he gave 3844 cents as the annual income for a family in which the man had to cultivate coffee for the government (78 times) and village services (72 times). In: *Indonesia*, p. 54 ff. The other examples given are interesting as well in this respect.

Their wages were low (for women only half to three-quarters those of men), and what disposable income remained, men often spent on gambling and prostitutes; systematic indebtedness was a useful means for plantation managers to maintain their workforces. With appalling living conditions, disease was rampant, and death never far away ... To ensure a docile or at least compliant workforce, the plantation management could call upon the authority of the state, embodied in such legislation as the Netherlands East Indies Coolie Ordinances of 1880, 1884 and 1893 which imposed fines, imprisonment or extra labour obligations ... physical beatings and financial penalties ...[14]

A million poor people spending a few cents a year on opium will make a few people very rich, the statistics impressive, and allow the state to pay its police force easily to repress rebelling workers.

The Bali Case

It is appropriate to sketch the Opium Problem also from the perspective of a district instead of through the eyes of "Batavia" (*Opiumregie*). One example from the Outer Districts is Banca, on which were located 70% of all Chinese holders of an opium license in 1930, while on Billiton there was not a single one. Only Chinese non-license holders lived there, because it was at the time practically the private property of the *Billiton Mining Company*, which had its own opium policy.

A different situation existed on the island of Bali. There the Balinese nobility and princes dominated the scene rather than a Dutch company. As stated above, they had reacted to the Dutch opium import with the establishment of a true slave export already in the 17th and 18th centuries. In the 19th-century several factors led to important changes.[15]

Balinese slaves were no longer in demand, which was not due to a sudden abolition movement among the Dutch: instead, the Dutch state itself had started to colonize through strong military repression, and this procured cheap local labor. The imported slaves from Bali became too expensive. Raffles' anti-slavery and anti-opium ideas remained largely proposals; they had no relevant impact on the archipelago's economy.

---

[14] See the contribution of Robert Elson in N. Tarling (ed.), vol. 2-1, p. 156, 157.

[15] H. Schulte Nordholt, p. 96 ff. It is not understandable why Clifford Geertz should be 'biased' in his opinion 'that opium was the main driving force of Balinese trade' because he referred to the 'conditions in northern Bali' only (see, Idem, note 35 p. 96). It can be expected that Geertz understood how the importance of opium remained as he indicated for at least half of the 19th-century, and changed afterwards as argued in my main text.

Quite the reverse. He strongly facilitated the private English country traders who risked dealing with opium through Singapore, energetically supported by Chinese and Buginese traders. The Balinese authorities had soon discovered that their opium was much cheaper than the Dutch. In this way they compensated for the relative losses in the slave trade, but this must have given them little comfort.

A second source for cheap labor was also tapped by probably the same English, Portuguese (Macao) and Chinese opium traders: the "coolie" trade. And a third reason to gradually abandon the Balinese slaves-for-opium trade was a natural disaster, the eruption of the Tambora volcano on a neighboring island (1815) which caused crop failures, a plague of mice and famine in the south of Bali.

The longer term effect, however, was that for about two decades fewer people could be spared for the slave trade, while in the subsequent period Bali became the 'chief granary for Singapore'. Rice-for-opium could replace the slave-for-opium trade, and in this transformation manpower in Bali became very important after 1850. In the north of Bali, a coffee-for-opium trade gradually developed.[16]

The relations between Bali and the English Singapore with its many Chinese strengthened and, therefore, the influence of the Dutch weakened. Balinese leaders understood the shifting times and the changing importance of opium. They were

> aware that the royal center should make an effort to increase control over the changing market, as indicated by ... monopolizing of opium imports and the additional taxes introduced with an eye to centralization of organized exports.[17]

The consequence of all this was that the use of opium penetrated more deeply into Balinese society in the second half of the 19th-century. Wiselius documents this as follows.[18] From the Calcutta annual opium exports, 12,000 picul were destined for Singapore. According to the *Annual Reports* of the Dutch Consul-General in Singapore, the export from here to the "Netherlands-Indies" was on average 3,700 picul per year in the years 1878-1883. Of this, 25% went to Batavia, 50% to Bali, and the rest to other ports. Wiselius stresses how strange it is that a Dutch consul knows of these practices and that nobody in Batavia protests against

---

[16] Idem, p. 126 ff.

[17] Idem, p. 102, 108 ff. Rochussen wrote in December 1847 also about opium activities of English merchants on Bali. See J. Baud, J. Rochussen, vol. II, p. 320.

[18] J. Wiselius (1886), p. 21 note 1.

them, and the fact that every year about 3,000 piculs of opium are apparently distributed by "smugglers". That is double what the Dutch colonial government distributed to its opium dealers.

But the Dutch became increasingly angry about the more independent Bali and its wayward princes' orientation towards Singapore. As usual, they started wars. The first one (1846) led to the destruction of a palace, new contracts on Dutch terms, and quarrels between the Dutch and the Balinese decision-makers about what to do next.

The second war (1848) was a true Opium War, but less successful than the first English one of a few years earlier. It started when one prince 'put up defenses and bought large quantities of weapons and opium in Singapore'.[19] This operation was an utter failure: the Dutch were heavily defeated, and strange Dutch stories were made up to explain this loss of prestige away.[20]

In the next war of 1849, the Dutch mobilized for their biggest military expedition with an army of 12,000 men under the command of an experienced general. Small successes were won for this army in the beginning, but it all ended in failure again. The general lost his life, surprise attacks by the Balinese cost many lives, 'unfamiliar conditions' and dysentery did the rest. A peace had to be concluded which the Dutch sold to "Batavia" and the homeland as a victory, but their defeat guaranteed an independent Bali for many decades to come.

The permanent mutual competition among the Balinese nobles was their Achilles heel. Some of them tried to strengthen their own position by asking the Dutch to support them (*the enemy of my enemy is my friend* principle). This led to two small military expeditions of the Dutch (1858 and 1868) against specific nobles, but the Dutch apparently did not dare to attack the whole island anew.

Until the end of the century, Bali even became more and more independent of "Batavia" in an economic sense. Buleleng, the main harbor in north Bali, developed into a prosperous and free port (no import or export taxes); non-indigenous merchants (Chinese, Buginese, Arabs, etc.) became more important and active.

---

[19] H. Schulte Nordholt, p. 165.

[20] The most ridiculous story was that the Dutch commander did not dare to send reinforcements to Bali 'fearing that the revolution which swept over Europe in 1848 might spread to the colony' (Idem, note 24 p. 166). Another story only mentioned that the Balinese nearly lost this war because of 'lack of ammunition and opium' (Idem, p. 166).

> Particularly significant was the opium trade. Raw opium was imported in
> large quantities from Singapore, refined in Buleleng, and for the most part
> smuggled to Java. This lucrative smuggling ... attracted many Chinese immi-
> grants who soon completely controlled the opium processing and trade.
> Part of the opium ... found its way to the Balinese hinterland ... The most
> important Balinese export product was coffee, the cultivation of which,
> concentrated in the central Balinese mountains, expanded rapidly.[21]

The opium trade was really booming. In 1861 opium imports were valued
at 294,321 Dutch guilders; sixteen years later this had increased to the
enormous sum of 4.5 million guilders, ten times more than the second
largest import—textile goods. And so the importance of Buleleng
increased, along the main trade route to Singapore; southern Bali became
dominated by the opium-coffee part in the north.

In the last stage of the Dutch rule in the East Indies, probably the most
devastating one, Bali also had to bear its share of what was officially called
the Dutch 'Ethical Policy'. Along with Bali, the Dutch military machine
tried to eradicate resistance in Aceh, Jambi, Southeast Kalimantan, Flores,
South Sulawesi or Lombok. It did not take long before anti-Dutch revolts
raged everywhere in the archipelago, and the last fully fledged war ended
with the elimination of the colonial regime. Before that happened, hundreds of thousands of dead had to be mourned again.

The massacres in Bali (1901-1906) were part of this endgame. Opium
again played a main role. First in the perception of the Dutch authorities,
which claimed to have a

> civilizing task which implied that "royal arbitrariness", slavery, and opium
> smuggling should be done away with. Governor-General W. Rooseboom
> formulated this vision as follows: "We ... shall, wherever there is injustice ...
> not be able to remain inactive in the protection of the weak and the
> oppressed. This is in complete accord with the ethical direction in colonial
> politics."[22]

In several waves the Dutch army conquered Bali; many thousands of
Balinese lost their lives; princes and nobles lost their influence; direct rule
from "Batavia" became the punishment.

In the last military expedition to establish this lethal *Pax Neerlandica*,
a royal 'resistance to the introduction of the colonial opium directive in
April 1908' was crushed.[23] In other words: this Opium War was waged to

---

[21] Idem, p. 169.
[22] Idem, p. 210.
[23] Idem, p. 215.

establish the *Opiumregie* and its opium dens in Bali and to eliminate the so-called "smugglers"; the competition to the Dutch opium dealers had to be eradicated, not the Dutch opium business. That was the 'civilizing task'.

The table 14 demonstrates the effects of these massacres: Bali became the Outer District with the most indigenous holders of an opium license and nearly 30% of all opium consumption! Apparently, the traditional Balinese resistance against the Dutch disappeared in the opium smoke. This tactic was known among the many enemies of the Dutch *kafirs* like Muslims in Aceh. They told followers there in 1928 that the Dutch tactic to disarm their enemies was executing

> the following scheme: they introduce gambling and opium-smoking, and some set themselves up as toll-collectors as in Java. With great devotion they encourage the people to gamble ... They make the law, the damned *kafirs*, and they rule with new methods.[24]

An important instrument to manage this is the subject of the following paragraph.

The Opiumregie[25]

The man who after much commotion ultimately prepared the decision to transform the opium farming[26] "system" of the Dutch into a centralized state bureaucracy, the *Opiumregie,* was Willem Pieter Groeneveldt (1841-1915). At that time his was a rare intellect with a long and interesting career in East Asia, starting as interpreter for Dutch embassies in Canton and Peking, writer of a scholarly book about the Malay archipelago, and ending as vice-president of the Board of Netherlands Indies, one of the highest functions in the Dutch colony. This man was sent to the French colonies (Cochinchina, Tonkin or Cambodia) to study the French experience with a similar transformation in the opium management. His clear and extensive report with many quantitative data was a long and well

---

24 Document from 1928 reproduced in *Indonesia,* p. 211, 212.
25 For the following, see the 1890 advice of W.P. Groeneveldt, who studied the French *Opiumregie* in Indochina. See also J. Rush, chapter 11 and the "War on Opium" (chapter 10), which allegedly triggered the *Opiumregie.* E. Vanvugt (1985), p. 269-377 gave a very detailed and relevant description of the establishment and activities of the *Opiumregie.* M. de Kort, p. 45 ff.
26 For more details about the opium tax farming in the East Indies and Southeast Asia (except in this section), see below in ch. 23.

argued plea to take the step to a centralized system (see ch. 23). His arguments in favor of the *Opiumregie* can be summarized as follows.[27]

First try out the new system in Java and Madura before introducing it elsewhere in the archipelago, but do not establish a pilot project on, for instance, the island of Banka. Such a project delivers no other experience, as already known in Cochinchina. If one can experiment in a region as large as part of Java, then one is surrounded by leasers whose existence is threatened. Failure cannot be avoided. Like the French dared to do in Cochinchina, the Dutch must act firmly in the East Indies.

An *Opiumregie* depends first and foremost on a strong opium police at sea and struggling against every form of opium smuggling on land. The police cannot handle this task alone, they must be embedded in a network of district police, customs offices and the Ministry of Finance. This proposal led to a modern way of fighting criminality. These measures 'must not have been perceived as favorable to the leasers ... Where the monopoly is in the hands of the Government ... it should be an honor for everybody to cooperate ...'

Nothing changed regarding the purchasing of the raw opium in Benares or elsewhere, except that this could be done much more cheaply, as proved in Cochinchina.

In the technical part of his proposals, Groeneveldt criticized Struick (Haak and Wiselius) for not understanding the way raw opium is treated to obtain *tjandoe* (prepared opium). The main suggestion was to establish a centralized production in an opium factory in Batavia. This happened about ten years later.

Apart from the factory-produced *tjandoe,* there is an indigenous kind, called *tiké* (tikeh). This is raw opium mixed with pulverized *awar-awar* leaves:

> The minor quality of this second kind of tjandoe derives from the preparation in which a substantial quantity of sugar is mixed in and during the remainder of the cooking is treated with lemon juice to extract all the morphine out of it. In this way ... one gets 12 to 17 thails per catty raw opium, whereas with the normal tjandoe one gets only 10 to 11 thails.[28]

---

[27] W.P. Groeneveldt, p. 127-139; the quotations come from these pages. See also J. Rush, p. 208 ff. although Rush uses the wrong title of G.'s publication. Rush much prefers the small pamphlet by N. Struick, published a year before Groeneveldt's large analysis. For the whole discussion for and against the *Opiumregie*, one has to read Rush's chapters 10 and 11.

[28] Idem, p. 129. See for the *tikeh* production Appendix 5.

If the morphine is gone, opium addiction seems impossible (see Appendix 5 for morphine content).

Another theme of Groeneveldt's proposal was the packing policy of the opium: one has to exercise "direct mail" as far as possible, avoiding middlemen who increase the price and reduce the quality. The main argument against middlemen (and, therefore, against the whole farming system) is in fact 'that through the use of middlemen, a large part of the advantages given by the work of the Regie is lost ...'[29]

To sell directly to the users, one has to provide the smallest quantities. In Cochinchina it had been discovered that even deliveries of 20 g (about 1/2 thail) were too large. Furthermore, the opium dens were gradually transformed from locations to consume into places to buy the stuff. Consumption took place largely outside the dens, except when smoking could be combined with prostitution. Anyway, this led to the conclusion that a rather normal consignment of 1200 pikul (= 75,000 kg) raw opium bought in Bengal by the government had to be sold to the consumers as 120 million small boxes of a few grams (mata). Groeneveldt proposed making small tubes of tin or copper for these small quantities. (It became lead and a battery of filling machines entered the opium factory.) These tubes carried specific marks so that the consumer could not be cheated.

The *Opiumregie* became the bureaucratic machine to execute the government's opium monopoly. Historically, it is a variant or an extension of the monopoly established by the government after it took over the heritage of the VOC, which was already based on a specific monopoly management. Now the farming system present until 1894 was modernized and industrialized: a very modern opium factory was opened in 1902, and the opium business became a 100% government task.

In the period that the colonial bureaucracy decided to establish an *Opiumregie*, the Dutch state earned no less than 14 million guilders per year (1896 -1898) which was the largest source of income after the land rent (ca. 17 million).[30] Of course, bureaucrats complained that this was too small and claimed out of the blue that this income had to follow the population increase: in the last few years the population had increased by 4% and the opium income by only 0.6%; it doubled every 42 years. Production, distribution, administration or anti-smuggling measures, all this and more had to be rationalized, automated and so on.

---

[29] Idem, p. 136.
[30] According to a document published in 1901 in *Indonesia,* p. 59 ('rents on opium' and 'opium monopoly').

Many new laws had to be designed which also transformed life in the colony (for the juridical side of the *Opiumregie*, see below). Retailing was forbidden outside the 1100 opium dens managed by the *Opiumregie*. As stated, the *tjandoe* got a specific and obligatory packing in the opium factory. Once opened, these tubes were difficult to close; specific marks were made on them so that fraud could easily be detected (see for details appendix 5).[31]

It took about fifteen years before this *Opiumregie* functioned rather smoothly throughout the archipelago. The leadership always denied that this new institution aimed at increasing opium consumption. But Groeneveldt was clear in his secret report:

> The Regie with exclusion of everybody else aims to satisfy the opium needs. There is no reason to complain about this relative to the sheer extent of this task, because it did not create this need ... if it did not fulfill this task ... important centers of consumption would have to rely on smuggling ... In the system of the Opiumregie, there is no place to reduce the quantities which could be sold; it is necessary to help every buyer.[32]

For the publicity, of course, one cherished the hope that the closest possible management of all elements of the opium problem, like in a police state, would solve this problem in the long run and, therefore, should drastically discourage consumption. How long that "run" should be was not disclosed, but it was clear to all from the beginning, except these bureaucrats' publicity, that this expectation was pitched too high. "On purpose", argued the opposition. Anyway, the first more or less independent investigation into the matter was crystal clear about the *Opiumregie*'s legitimation to act as it did:

> This conclusion [reduction of consumption, H.D.] is not supported by the Colonial Reports, which show that the use of opium in Java has increased from 735,000 *thails* in 1904 to 870,000 *thails* in 1912 in spite the closing-down of a considerable number of shops and dens ...[33]

In January 1934 the *Opiumregie* was extended by the *Saltregie* (Zoutregie). With 'salt' was meant not only kitchen salt, but also 'salts and other derivatives from morphine, diacetylmorphine and cocaine'.[34]

---

[31] A specific ordinance was issued for the packing of the regie opium: see *Opium- en Zoutregie*, p. 57-64 with a very detailed description of an opium tube in articles 3 and 4.

[32] W.P. Groeneveldt, p. 137.

[33] Document from 1914 reproduced in *Indonesia,* p. 88.

[34] *Opium- en Zoutregie*, p. 12. See also Idem, p. 93 ff.

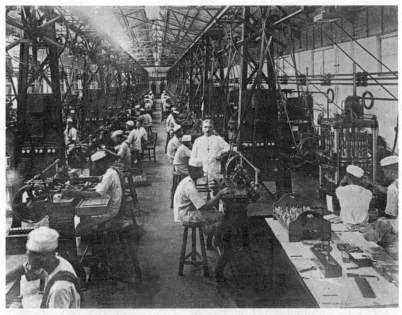

Ill. 18. Interior of the Opium factory, Batavia ca. 1935

Source: Collection Royal Tropical Institute. In the first hall the opium is pressed into small metal capsules of several sizes. The second picture shows the hall in which the opium capsules were packed in wooden boxes (for the details see Appendix 5).

Steinmetz, head of the *Opiumregie* in the 1930s, wrote:

> The existing penal law relative to the import, manufacturing, consumption and distribution of opium, morphine, morphine preparations and derivatives, used for other than medicinal purposes, is being tightened up, and new rules were announced for cocaine, eucaine and other narcotics.[35]

This monopoly combined not only trade, refining and distribution using a factory and about 1100 distribution centers in the whole archipelago. This control system of everything and everybody included a rather substantial police force to attack "smugglers", etc. and covered also the private lives of the consumers. So, the official bookkeeping of 1927 revealed that there were 177,122 opium addicts in the archipelago (92,873 indigenous people; 83,242 Chinese and only 7 Europeans). For cocaine see below.

The *Opiumregie* became, symptomatic enough, a department of the Ministry of Finance. This immediately resulted in the criticism that the profit of the *Opiumregie* landed in the state's coffer with all its consequences for the eradication of the opium addiction: the more addicts, the better for the colonial state finances. As we have seen, that was indeed the standard practice, motivation and rationale behind all measures.

The highest bureaucrats of this Ministry were never tired of explaining that 'the Opium monopoly in Dutch East Indies has in principle [*in wezen*] not a fiscal but a social aim ... the maximum limitation of the use of opium ...' after which another 15 rules follow which contradict this announcement with several "if's".[36]

Even during the International Conference of Shanghai in 1909, the Dutch government had to defend itself with a specific declaration that it 'will never refrain from taking measures ... to minimize gradually the use [of opium] on financial grounds ...' It had envisaged a period of about fifteen years before a definite prohibition could be declared.

However, it then declared that this period cannot *start* because the poppy-producing countries (British India, etc.) were not ready to take this step. The British replied, of course, that countries like the Dutch East Indies were not ready to *start* that famous period. As a result, nothing changed, although to everybody's surprise the Chinese government succeeded in eradicating the opium production in Szechwan or Yunnan to a substantial degree; an embarrassment for the British, Dutch, and French and their opium production facilities.

---

[35] C. Steinmetz, director of the Opiumregie, in: *Indie en het Opium*, p. 149.
[36] C. Van den Bussche, director of the Ministry of Finance, in: Idem, p. 117.

Another main criticism of the Dutch concerned the extremely high price the government asked for its opium; a price which increased in 1926 to the highest level in East Asia (and, therefore, in the world) of 30 Dutch guilders per *thail* (=38.6 g). The following table is given to support the government opium policy. It has to prove that there is no fiscal aim of the opium policy: the opium profits never pay for more than 7.3% of the normal expenditures of the colonial state.

Table 15. Income and Expenditures of the *Opiumregie* and the Colonial State, 1920-1931 (x 1000 Dutch guilders)[37]

Years	Gross income Opiumregie	Income for the ordinary service	Income for the extraordinary service	Normal expenditures of the state	Column 3 in % of column 5
	2	3	4	5	6
1920	53 640	42 671	---	672 982	6.3
1921	53 318	43 471	---	586 740	7.3
1922	44 220	35 098	---	514 054	6.8
1923	37 583	31 061	---	440 801	7
1924	35 317	28 494	---	408 024	6.9
1925	36 640	28 755	---	421 110	6.8
1926	37 727	29 471	---	437 860	6.7
1927	41 617	24 955	6 582	472 726	5.2
1928	42 871	25 727	8 828	510 213	5
1929	40 982	26 200	6 939	514 993	5
1930	34 599	26 921	564	523 995	5.1
1931	26 000*	21 000*	---	532 288*	3.9

* Only a half-year estimate

Government sophistry was extreme: the price increase *could be* a way to avoid smuggling, although the obvious rule was that the higher the official price, the more smuggling was encouraged. Is it not so that

the geographical position of the archipelago makes it less vulnerable to smuggling'[38]; the smokers are accustomed to this price, so we can keep it like this[39]; if all our anti-smuggling measures are not successful, we still can decrease the price; the international situation has been changed in such a way 'that it is not necessary to consider a reduction for the time being'.[40]

---

[37] Data provided by the *Opiumregie* in the article of C. Van den Bussche in: *Indie en het Opium*, p. 118.

[38] Idem, p. 120.

[39] Idem, p. 121.

[40] Idem, p. 121.

All this was an answer to an increased anti-opium sentiment and action in the motherland. That was in fact a reason why the Dutch copied the system of a 100% government monopoly of their main competitor in the realm, the French.

Steinmetz himself mentions price increases on Celebes from 3 guilders in 1926 to 30 guilders in 1931![41] In short: no reduction of the price following the normal fiscal aims, increased smuggling, increased corruption among the top bureaucrats. As a last defense of its policy, these officials attacked their critics and the public opinion with the "argument":

> ... it is also important to realize the correct appreciation [of our opium policy], because the wrong understanding of this policy and the specific suggestive effect of the criticism, we should only follow fiscal aims, ... only supports the wild prohibitionists, ... so that we, in the end, have to abandon our careful and efficient anti-opium policy.[42]

These "prohibitionists" were several kinds of anti-opium lobbies in and outside the Dutch East Indies as, for example, in the USA, including officially the US government. Happily, the many critics of the government policy were not impressed, as will be demonstrated in the next chapater. One example comes from Herbert L. May. He conducted a survey of opium smoking in the Far East (report 1927) and became a member of the *League of Nations Permanent Central Opium Board*; in short, an expert in the right place. This man concluded:

> Existing government prices most everywhere are too high, however, especially in the Netherlands Indies. Not only do they encourage smuggling, but they constitute a high penalty against the man who obeys the law by buying government opium and a high reward for the one who buys smuggled opium at the much lower price. Divans (public smoking establishments) apparently have a social feature which makes smoking more attractive. Therefore, since the object is to reduce or stamp out the vice, divans should not be permitted.[43]

This colonial state with its always growing social and political unrest was constantly in need of large amounts of money, while the motherland was always unwilling to spend more on its colony. To be more specific: the motherland expected the colony to pay for itself and provide in addition

---

[41] C. Steinmetz in: Idem, p. 150.

[42] Idem, p. 122. Other "official" contributions to this interesting reader come from the head of the *Opiumregie* (Steinmetz), a Director of the Opium Factory (Buck), who explains the working of morphine on the mind or from a Chief of the Opium police.

[43] Quoted in A. Vandenbosch, p. 283.

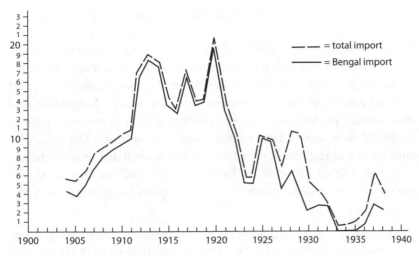

Figure 6. Opium Factory, import raw opium, 1900-1940 (x 10,000 kilogram)

Source: H. Derks based on the *Year Accounts of the Opiumfabriek, the Opiumregie and of the Opium- en Zoutregie* (Batavia, 1913-1938).

raw material for the home industry, a market for its end-products and a place for the recruitment of a rich Dutch bureaucratic and military elite, including a substantial financial contribution to the welfare of the greedy motherland.

This lead to serious competitive pressure among the top bureaucrats for personal gains in the intentionally criminalized opium scene. In 1923 one of the highest police officers in the colony was arrested because he had carried out fraud for the enormous sum of one million guilders; a head of the criminal opium investigation department was accused of opium smuggling; another was dismissed for being a morphine addict; others blackmailed Chinese brothels, etc. for an amount of 2,000 guilders a month, etc.[44]

Fabulous amounts of money in the colony circulated "underground", as was usual in the period of the VOC. One can safely conclude that the whole opium business of the Dutch during the forty years after 1900 yielded *at least* a profit of close to 1-1.5 billion guilders (current value. This level of profit was never reached with the other narco-activity.

---

[44] Idem, p. 227. The official monthly salary was about 500 guilders.

The Dutch Cocaine Industry

The narco-military activities of the Dutch were unprecedented. Apart from opium and its whole infrastructure, including an opium factory, the Dutch government also strongly facilitated the production of coca leaf and co-financed at least two cocaine factories, one in Amsterdam and later another in the colony. These activities started at the same time as genocidal wars were waged against people in the Outer Districts, who once again were fighting for their liberation (Aceh, Bali, Lombok, etc.).

In the *Annual Accounts* of the *Opiumregie*, information about the cocaine factory and its activities in Java is given in passing as if it was unimportant:

> Concerning the cultivation of the coca and the use of coca leaves *by the population*, there exist no other peculiarities than given in the previous report ... The plant is grown only on Java on a scale of about 1600 hectares. Not included are cultivations along roads, in hedges, etc. In 1923 the total production of coca leaves was 922,866 kilogram; the exported quantity was 907,335 kilo. (italics added by me, H.D.)[45]

This *Annual Account* also tells us something about prices and export destinations. The prices of the leaves varied from 60 to 160 Dutch guilders per picul (= here 60.5 kg) according to the cocaine content. Although most of the export was destined for the cocaine factory in Amsterdam, the Japanese were becoming more active buyers. They even bought a whole Java harvest for a fixed price of 75 guilders per picul without any guarantee of the cocaine content (1923).

Table 16. Coca Leaves Export from Java, 1904-1940 (selected years)[46]

Year	Coca leaves in kg	Year	Coca leaves in kg
1904	25 836	1924	1 118 000
1906	122 000	1926	1 043 000
1908	417 000	1928	385 000
1910	430 000	1930	354 000
1912	1 075 000	1932	209 000
1914	1 353 270	1934	105 000

---

[45] *Opiumregie* (*Verslag*, 1923), p. 36.

[46] From the article of Paul Gootenberg in: S. Topik et al. (ed.), p. 334. Here only a selection of his data is given. See also L. Lewin, p. 105-109.

Table 16. Continued.

Year	Coca leaves in kg	Year	Coca leaves in kg
	407 984	1936	125 000
1916			
1918	661 968	1938	50 000
1920	1 676 621	1940	125 000
1922	1 283 503		

The total export of coca leaves from Java in these same years was not less than 21 million kilograms. The *minimum* price of 100 kilo was 50 guilders, so that in these 40 years there was a turnover of some 10 million guilders in coca leaves only. But apart from leaf production, there was also cocaine production. The price of leaves was coupled to the price of cocaine: for one kilo of pure cocaine, one needed 123.56 kilo of leaves.[47] This means that not less that 170,000 kg cocaine could be made from the total Dutch leave export alone.

The value of this cocaine can be estimated as follows. In 1884 the Dutch journal for the medical profession was very positive about cocaine: the only disadvantage was the price of 9,000 Dutch guilders for one kilo.[48] This leads to a turnover of 1.53 *billion* Dutch guilders! Of course this is the theory. It indicates, however, in which level of money market cocaine business has been arrived after 1900. It learns, furthermore, that the available government statistics must be taken with many pinches of salt; they all strongly underestimate – on purpose or not—the relevant levels of production or profit.

The rapid rise of the Dutch on the world cocaine market took the established parties like the Peruvians by surprise. From 26 tons in 1904, production immediately soared at a tremendous pace. The reason behind this spectacular growth was quite simple. First and foremost, the combination of an effective colonial production of raw material for a cocaine industry in the homeland, a willing state bureaucracy and enough private investors, also partly channeled through state-sponsored banks like the large Dutch *Colonial Bank*. When expansion and success were apparent, the Dutch diplomacy in the international negotiations to prohibit the drugs

---

[47] Quite different figures are mentioned, but the most reliable in this respect seems to be the Dutch expert A.W. de Jong, p. 885. After an analysis of the German, British and American leave – cocaine ratio De Jong concluded: 'The quantity of coca leave necessary to produce 3,480 kg cocaine is, therefore, about 430 ton.'

[48] M. de Kort, p. 39.

Ill. 19. Dutch Cocaine Factory, copy of a share, 1942
Source: www.deresearcher.nl

business was very willing to slow down the American anti-drugs policy ("prohibitionists") and the private anti-opium leagues. This game was played together with the British, who had similarly large drug interests.

There was no *Cocaine–Regie* imposed as in the opium case and, therefore, no cocaine monopoly system. The formal reason was that this enterprise was a private one, established by the *Colonial Bank,* property partly of the Dutch royal house. Therefore, it was not a clearly capitalist private business either, let alone a prerogative of some mafia, as was clearly the case a few years later. In the research, raw material and distribution side of this cocaine problem, the Dutch colonial state was dominant or, at least, very helpful with its experienced, bureaucratic drugs infrastructure and opium money.

Cocaine production involves a much more sophisticated chemical process than opium, and had to be managed by a European and American pharmaceutical industry. Famous names such as Boehringer (Germany), Hoffman-La Roche (Switzerland), Merck (Germany, USA), BASF (Germany), Rhône-Poulenc (France), etc. were all heavily involved in cocaine production and distribution. This was because they had in the meantime (from about 1870) gained experience with the production of the opium derivatives, morphine and heroin. In this cocaine scene the Dutch played again a major, sometimes the most important, role.

The cultivation of coca plantations on Java began around 1885 when the relevant botanical experiments spread among several European colonial powers. It was a stroke of luck for the Dutch that their special variety of *Erythroxylon novogranatense* contained twice the cocaine content of the usual Peruvian kind. Dutch botanists had done a "good job" in the well-furnished gardens of Buitenzorg.

Parallel to the Opium Factory, a Cocaine Factory was established, first in Amsterdam (1900).[49] It used patented German technology (*Farbwerke*) to extract cocaine from coca leaves imported from Java. It furthermore enjoyed the advantage of the well-organized plantation systems in the Dutch colony: cheap Asian labor, four annual harvests, economies of scale, intercropping with colonial rubber and tea. The performance of this cocaine industry impressed foreign investors so much that even Merck USA started its own coca plantation on Java with great success in the 1930s.

The *Nederlandsche Cocainefabriek* (NCF) became the largest in the world. It even created a new product, *novocaine*, a fully synthetic sub-

---

[49] The fate of this factory became recently subject of a highly interesting movie by Jeanette Groenendaal, *The Dutch Cocaine Factory* (2007) and of a novel by Conny Braam (2009).

stitute for cocaine. It was a less poisonous drug than cocaine with more or less the same vein-constricting effects; as such, it was considered more suitable for the dental practice. Nowadays, it has been replaced by more effective drugs. This activity in Holland triggered other initiatives there. It is not surprising that one of them, the *Chemische Fabriek Naarden*, soon became involved in obvious mafia practices of smuggling morphine and heroin to China.[50]

Almost as quickly as it arose, the Dutch position in this market vanished. In particular, the decline was very fast after 1925. The reasons for this are partly obvious: the international competition strongly increased, and governments made agreements like the *Geneva Convention* (1925) to restrict the business to trade for 'medical and scientific purposes'. Just before implementing this system, the Dutch sent a million kilograms of leaves out from Amsterdam warehouses.[51]

As can be seen in the table, during First World War and the Great Depression, the demand for cocaine collapsed. That is contrary to the persistent legend that European soldiers were doped with cocaine to fight longer and better: cocaine has always been a peacetime product, a luxury for those who can afford it.[52] There are obvious reasons for this: the deliveries are hindered in wartime, although the demand may increase; the price for an individual portion may be sky-high in Europe, but the price for a total harvest of leaves dropped sharply.

In the following table the Dutch disadvantage (?) is shown from a different angle: the geo-political position from its huge stocks of coca leaves.

Before World War I there were cartel-like arrangements between the largest European cocaine manufacturers which guaranteed the highest prices. But even in Holland there were three cocaine factories competing with each other. After the war each manufacturer had to manage its own business, with the result that the competition strongly increased and prices fell, despite a growing demand.[53]

In one of its last massive reports (before the Second World War), the *Central Opium Board* (League of Nations) assessed the drug traffic,

---

[50] M. de Kort, p. 98-110; M. de Kort in: P. Gootenberg (ed.), p. 140.

[51] Idem in: Idem, p. 131.

[52] Although not so unequivocal as in the Java statistics, the Peruvian exports with a different market show the same trend for the World Economic Crisis of the 1920s and also for the whole World War I period of 1911-1919. Remarkable are also the fluctuations in the US coca imports during World War II. See S. Topik et al. (ed.), p. 338 and 342.

[53] M. de Kort in: P. Gootenberg (ed.), p. 130.

Table 17. Stocks of Coca Leaves, 1933-1938 (x 1 kilogram)[54]

Country	1933	1934	1935	1936	1937	1938
Germany	56 200	50 247	52 250	39 400	45 424	72 862
United KIngdom	17 625	313	9 391	9 909	6 689	11 465
United States	204	191	203	197	197	197
France	32 613	11 781	15 556	31 370	46 446	59 374
Netherlands	577 825	541 120	462 191	391 456	331 357	136 508
Switzerland	21 931	310	10 390	251	2 740	2 619

production and consumption of the new products as follows.[55] The gradual decrease in the manufacture of the three main drugs—morphine, heroin and cocaine—stopped: the first increased by 11.5 per cent, the other two showed a slight increase. However, as concluded above, the consumption in this time of crisis decreased by 10 per cent for the second drug and 4 per cent for the other two.

The increase in *morphine* production occurred mainly in the UK (from 1,292 kilo in 1932 to 1,873 kilo one year later); cocaine also increased (from 238 kilo in 1929 to 427 kilo in 1933). The main producer of morphine was the US with 7,459 kilo in 1933, while Japan manufactured most of the cocaine (920 kilo). In this last country, the consumption of cocaine was also the largest (14 kg per million inhabitants). In Europe, the largest cocaine consumer was France (9 kg per million).

The history of the NCF continued: apart from new products such as novocaine, it also started with already well-known products like codeine, benzedrine (amphetamine) and efedrine. From 1932 onwards it even began processing raw opium into morphine.[56]

There was, however, no future for Dutch cocaine anymore: in the same year the dry coca-leaf production of Peru had already reached the 3,500 tons with an export of 85 tons; in the other South American production country, Bolivia, plantations with a surface of 8,333 hectares produced 1,735 tons and exported 347 tons of dry leaves.[57]

---

[54] A.W. de Jong, p. 885. It is nearly for sure, that at least the USA figures are a bit misleading: such small stocks of leaves do not have any value for the preparation of raw cocaine. It is not sufficient for Merck alone. This besides the fact that the USA has several much more important South American coca leave sources. The value of the table is mainly to show the relative importance of the Dutch position.

[55] I used here the summary in the *Newcastle School of Medicine Centenary*, Oct. 13, 1934, p. 686.

[56] For the following I used information from the National Archive, The Hague, *De Nederlandsche Cocainefabriek* (12-3-2010).

[57] A. W. de Jong, p. 870, 871.

While the relationship with the Dutch state had mostly been an indirect one, this gradually became a direct one. During the occupation in World War II, the NCF was fully incorporated into the German war economy. Poppies had to be planted in Holland to obtain enough raw opium under the direction of a Department of Medicines. The growers were told that the morphine extracted from the poppies was only destined for 'own land and *Volk*', which was untrue. Only those produced in the province of North Holland remained in the Netherlands; the production in all other provinces went to Germany.

The profit construction of the NCF was unbelievable: it received 165 tons of raw material for free, and it could charge its processing costs to the state. The price to be paid was that end product of raw opium became state property. Then the NCF bought the raw opium from the state to produce pure morphine and other derivatives from it. The transaction price of 130 guilders per kilo of raw opium was far below the cost price, so that the NCF realized fabulous profits on its morphine during the war. Soon after the war AKZO Nobel bought the company for an unknown price.

Legal Hypocrisy

One may conclude, relative to the East Indies drug position, that there was no reason to complain about the substantial and profitable opium and cocaine business. But Steinmetz, head of the *Opiumregie* in the 1930s, wrote:

> The existing penal law relative to the import, manufacturing, consumption and distribution of opium, morphine, morphine preparations and derivatives, used for other than medical aims, is tightening up, and new rules are being announced for cocaine, eucaine and other narcotics.[58]

The latter was never realized, and the penal side of the problem never received an adequate treatment.

Still, with the establishment of the *Opiumregie*, opium factory or cocaine factories, the colonial government had to provide some legal framework to regulate the production or distribution of narcotics: the government of the homeland urged the colony to pay for itself. It was, however, also obliged to minimize the consumption of narcotics or eventually to warn and save the citizens from them: the public and religious

---

[58] C. Steinmetz, director of the *Opiumregie*, in: *Indie en het Opium*, p. 149.

opposition against governmental opium distribution in the homeland had to be satisfied. In short, in practical and moral terms, these aims were conflicting and the involved interests clashing.

The result is legal hypocrisy: suggest doing one thing, but try to realize the other. As all colonial governments were far from democratic, they played this hypocritical game only superficially. Even the fear of repercussions in the Dutch homeland was bearable. The representative of the mightiest economic power in the colony, Royal Dutch Shell, was Dr. Hendrik Colijn, the Calvinist and colonial military butcher, who had been a homeland-politician and prime minister until the Second World War.

It is a major reason why the most remarkable clashing interests were all within the colonial government itself: to pay for the costs of the colony (to put it as broadly as possible), opium was a most suitable product from the very first time Dutch merchants and the VOC arrived in the archipelago.

In the twentieth-century the situation was still the same: more consumers, more addicts were needed; the distribution should be better organized, and so on.

As everybody knew at the time, including the members of the many International Opium Conferences, this conflicted with the aim to eradicate the opium habit. The word consumption cannot be found in the relevant legal texts, let alone some ordinance devoted to the subject of how to diminish opium consumption. Only regulations to better organize the production and selling to get as much financial benefit from the investments as possible.

The clash within the Dutch colonial government was well documented by Wim Wertheim. In the 1920s he was a young legal adviser to the Dutch colonial government.[59] For his own boss, the Minister of Justice, he had to design new, severer laws concerning the trade and consumption of opium, while the Ministry of Finance owned and exploited about a thousand opium dens through its *Opiumregie*. He concluded therefore:

> ... this Department of the Opiumregie had to generate in these years of economic crisis a substantial part of the state income through the opium trade. Therefore, in the complaints about the dangers of misusing opium was hidden a good portion of hypocrisy. The state, in fact, aimed only at attacking its own competitors, which also happened in a juridically inappropriate way ...[60] And about the situation around 1900: 'Very shortly after

---

[59] He wrote the preface to E. Vanvugt (1995), p. 7-12.
[60] Idem, p. 8.

a new colonial war was won, the first building which was erected belonged to this Department of the Opiumregie or was an opium den. Even in areas like Lombok or Aceh ... the indigenous rulers stuck to their own severe punishment of opium consumption ...[61]

The first law or ordinance concerning opium was issued in 1872, and many followed.[62] In May 1927 an attempt was made to collate all those separate ordinances into a single one, the *Regie Opium Ordonnantie*. After its first article with the necessary definitions came the following two articles:

> Article 2. It is forbidden to grow poppy and Indian hemp. Article 3. The import, the possession and property, the stock and preservation, the transport, the preparation, manufacturing, processing, sale, use and export of narcotics, poppy and Indian hemp, including the import of coca leaves, are prohibited except as specified below.[63]

After learning what we have about the *Opiumregie*, opium and cocaine factories in those same years, we can only repeat the words of Baud, the 19th-century Governor-General, about the earlier VOC policy:

> It is quite right that the Company prohibited the opium trade under severe punishments—even the death penalty—but it did not include itself in this prohibition. It never detested this trade, but detested the smugglers, who intended to profit from the same advantages. The Company increased the consumption of opium on Java twenty-fold, while complaining constantly that this was not enough.[64]

This remarkable continuation reproduces the immanent contradictions of every foreign colonial occupation.

The first modernization which took place was in 1927. Baud's remark is, in fact, explicitly mentioned in article 28: the prescriptions and decisions of this law 'do not concern the import ... manufacturing ... distribution ... [etc.] ... of the Government'. In addition, we have shown that the opium consumption not only did not decline up to the Great Depression, but that it was facilitated with new products like cocaine and that the government's profits increased tremendously. True, it is now difficult to prove that the consumption of opium on Java increased twenty-fold as Baud mentioned, but its price certainly did!

---

[61] Idem, p. 11, 12.
[62] *Opium- en Zoutregie,* p. 6-9, mentioned all 44 of them until the ordinance of 1927, a separate one for every part of the archipelago.
[63] Idem, p. 12.
[64] Idem, p. 116.

The second modernization concerned the punishments. No longer the death penalty for the slightest infringement but, on the contrary, small fines for serious offences: 100 guilders for the druggist who sticks his narcotics in an unlocked drawer; somebody who plants large fields with poppy or Indian hemp (hashish) can get a maximum fine of 1000 guilders; a 1000 guilder fine can be imposed on a captain if his ship transports narcotics without the necessary papers and licenses (no quantities are mentioned); if this captain declares that he knew nothing about all those strange chests in his hold, he certainly pays less; if he is stupid enough to admit that he deliberately transported all these chests, he can get the maximum fine of 10,000 guilders, but he earns at least twenty times that amount from the cargo.[65]

Another modification was that the *Opiumregie* was established as a monopoly for the sale and manufacturing of *tjandoe*. As stated earlier, this must have been the result of a serious internal clash in the colonial bureaucracy. Even the first law of May 1927 provided the *Opiumregie* and its factory with an important position, but not the leading role. Given the overwhelming attention to medicinal matters, the responsible party must have been the Ministry of Health.[66] This changed already in July 1927, while its power was extended by January 1934 into an *Opium–en Zoutregie* (Opium–and Saltregie) and the leading party was the Ministry of Finance, which did not care about the health of the people, but only about its balance sheet.

The self-conceited perception of *Opiumregie* preceded this legal fixation: a multicolored map of the *whole* archipelago, always enclosed in its *Annual Accounts* from at least 1916 onwards (the first I could consult), is proudly announced as a 'General Map ... of the Area of the Opiumregie' while its 'Explanation' starts with 'The Property, etc. of the Opiumregie are ...' (see map 10 p. 326).

---

[65] Idem, p. 28 ff the long article 25.

[66] The *Opium- en Zoutregie* publication reproduces a chaotic situation from the point of view of law making. First, in this official publication of 1937, texts of—say—1927 are published time and again in the corrections of a later date. In this way it is difficult to reconstruct the bureaucratic struggles underlying these corrections. The first long ordinance (called the 'Narcotics Ordinance') is dated 12 May 1927 (p. 5-34). At the same day the equally long 'Regie-Opium Ordinance' was issued about the same subject (p. 45-55). In between a very short one (p. 35, 36) was published apparently only to fix the decision-making power among the various departments: for the import of raw opium, the head of the *Opiumregie* was responsible; for all opium business (from import to export) concerning medicinal aims, two other top bureaucrats (army and Ministry of Health); for coca leaves, the Ministry of Agriculture, etc. They all have the power to issue specific licenses.

Notwithstanding this attitude of a monopoly, the *Opiumregie*'s jurisdiction had its limits or, better, the consumption of its products (tjandoe,
djitjing, tikee, raw opium) was limited. If you cannot pay with cash, you
cannot buy the stuff. It was Queen Wilhelmina herself who "rightly" gave
this order by Royal Decision (*Koninklijk Besluit*), apparently because a
substantial percentage of it still arrived in her pocket through her share-
holding of the *Royal Dutch Trading Company* (NHM). Furthermore, the
Queen insisted that you had to be at least 21 years of age before starting to
smoke opium.[67]

Other limitations of the *Opiumregie* were more serious. They were
derived from a 'Circle Theory' and, in particular, a Circle practice.[68] The
archipelago was subdivided in 'open circles', 'mixed circles', 'license circles' and 'closed circles'. Within these areas, including the adjacent territorial waters, different rules apply for who was allowed to use the
regie-opium (not its derivatives or even cocaine). A few remarks will suffice here.

Throughout the whole archipelago, it was forbidden for all military and
police to use regie-opium, but this concerned all Europeans, in fact. In the
few 'closed circles', specific areas where local leaders had forbidden narcotics for some reason, nobody was allowed to use government opium
(and had to rely—if necessary—on smuggled narcotics); in 'license circles' nobody could use it without a license, a rule mostly in favor of
Chinese license-holders (about 75%); in 'mixed circles' license-holders
and specific non-license-holders were both allowed to use the stuff; in the
few 'open circles' there were no limitations, which concerned cities like
Batavia or Surabaja and specific regions like one in East Sumatra or the
Riouw archipelago. In the latter cases it was, apparently, too difficult for
the *Opiumregie* inspectors to control matters.

The theory involved must concern some rather complicated knowledge about the ethnic composition of the archipelago's population and
many regions. In the two appendices of this ordinance, all these locations
are mentioned and who is allowed (or not) to accept the blessings of the
bureaucrats of the *Opiumregie*.

---

[67] For this very short text of 29-11-1932 see Idem, p. 55, 56.
[68] In a law of 3 February 1934, this is legally fixed. See Idem, p. 64-89.

A Double Dutch End

At the beginning of the Second World War, it must have been clear for every undergraduate analyst that the position of Dutch colonialism was untenable: the world had turned upside down, and nationalism destroyed the colonial basis internally. This happened everywhere in Asian colonies. Clever people realised this from 1900 onwards as a storm developed into a devastating tempest. First result: 1914-1918. For the second phase the Dutch government (in and outside Indonesia) apparently followed the French example of ignoring this weather forecast. It intended to fight against the hurricane to secure its "own property" and not to follow the English example of hiding since 1920 under an umbrella like the *British Commonwealth*.

The last Dutch colonial war became another disaster, whether the "enemy" was destroyed or not. As before, the Dutch were fighting in a country in which they were foreign exploiters. Neither the Calvinists nor the Catholics nor the Social Democrats showed any relevant understanding of this situation or of the legitimacy of repressing foreign people. The bill they had to pay now was again a huge one.

First, they had to fight three wars in a short period: against the Germans 'at home', the Japanese 'abroad', and now it invaded a sovereign and independent Indonesia. This under loud and continuous complaint of having lost a beautiful tropical milking cow called *Tempo Doeloe,* while blaming it on the victims. Next, the Dutch inevitably lost all "their" property, industrial enterprises, plantations, trade relations for decades, their goodwill with the USA and Asia, and so on. However, there was one advantage: the Dutch also lost the basis of their opium and coca image as—without any doubt—the first and largest drugs dealer in world history. Until now, Dutch historiography has tended to display *blaming the victims* attitudes, while generally unable to describe their past behavior and experiences in Indonesia in a realistic and down-to-earth fashion. Even this farewell to an opium dealership was celebrated by means of a very loud silence.

After its *Declaration of Independence* (17th of August 1945), the new, inexperienced and poor Indonesian Republic had to consider distributing opium in its first years also. Together with salt, forest products and petrol/oil, opium belonged to the products with which it could gain some profit and pay for the costs of the new beginning and, in particular, a new army.[69]

---

[69] B. Bouman, p. 102, 108 ff. It is important to say that the author is an historian, but also a Dutch general, who was a Dutch military and no deserter during the invasion of

This was necessary because the Dutch had announced their intention to invade Indonesia, and they came back, armed to the teeth, to teach 'the rebels' a good lesson. This invasion started on the 20th of July 1947. The Indonesians experienced how fragile their liberty was. Two and a half years after the return of the Dutch, the invaders definitely lost (27th of December 1949).

The Japanese had handed over the opium factory to Indonesia in September 1945, whereupon an Indonesian copy of the *Opium- en Zoutregie* was established as the *Djawatan Tjandoe dan Garan*. The new head was an experienced man, Raden Mukarto Notowidigdo, who had earlier served both the Dutch and Japanese management of the factory. At that time there was a stock of 24 tons of raw opium and one ton of pre-pared opium.[70] Prices were announced in the press and

> ... in the period 1st of October to 31st of March 1946 the *Djawatan Tjandoe* contributed 8.1 million guilders to the revenues of the state ... this was about four times the revenues of the Dutch in 1938, notwithstanding the loss of the markets of Sumatra, Banka and Billiton.[71]

As shown in Appendix 5 this conclusion is far from correct: the Dutch had a net opium profit of about 9 million guilders in 1938![72] In addition, the triumphalism of Bouman is quite symptomatic.

The most serious mistake, however, is that the General simply changed rupiahs into guilders, apparently to support the comparison made with the pre-war Dutch situation and to demonstrate how "good" Dutch people were compared to these rebels. Only a few pages earlier, the first budget was reproduced in *rupiahs*, including the addition: 'All figures are in Japanese occupation currency.'[73] This money is, in fact, worthless inter-

---

Indonesia. For this episode see my article in H. Derks (ed., 1989), p. 296 ff. See also a main source of Bouman, R. Cribb, who wrote a highly ambiguous—to say the least—analysis of the Indonesian use of opium directly after Independence Day.

[70] R. Cribb, p. 703 writes about 22 tons of raw and 3 tons of refined opium, which makes a substantial difference in value also. I have to reproduce simply what is told by Cribb and Bouman, who derived their data largely of suspected Dutch police, military and secret service sources.

[71] B. Bouman, p. 108.

[72] What makes the difference between before and after the war is demonstrated by the Dutch *Central Office of Statistics* (CBS): if the 1900 guilder = 100, the 1940 guilder = 152.9 and the 1950 guilder = 312.4.

[73] This last quotation comes from R. Cribb, p. 705, note 5, in all probability Bouman's source. But this Cribb made similar mistakes in his attempt to morally condemn the Indonesians of trading in opium. Once he wrote about the earliest provision of opium from the Indonesian government to the armed forces; it concerns a 'consignment of ninety kilos of raw opium ... therefore ... some 158,900 tubes of refined opium were provided ...' (Idem,

nationally. In addition, immediately after the war at least four currencies circulated: Japanese, Dutch, "guerrilla-money" and the new rupiah!

The story continues: when the Dutch appeared on the horizon again, the Indonesians planned to transport the opium factory and a factory for medicines into Middle Java.

> Between the end of November and the beginning of December 1945 the largest part of the opium stock—22 tons of raw opium—... was transported to Djokja and Klaten by a group of medical students.[74]

After this, nobody knows where the opium went: some say that 80 drums with raw opium went to East Sumatra from whence they were transported to Singapore. Anyway: the general report states that until May 1947, 'nearly no opium was sold'.

In that month (eight weeks before the Dutch invasion), there was no money left in the Indonesian Ministry of Finance (the manager of the opium during the Dutch regime), and it was decided to sell raw opium gradually in portions of 80 kilos. Again a month later, a Chinese merchant in Singapore paid 282,000 Straits dollars for 1,500 tons of maize and opium, whereupon the cabinet decided to sell all opium abroad. This opened new inroads into the Singapore connection, but we cannot follow that further.[75]

Apart from all the quantitative mistakes, which only prove that they are not very familiar with the subject they describe, it is more important that Bouman and Cribb exploited a perspective on this opium history

---

p. 718). Appendix 5 clearly explains how in the opium factory from about 200,000 kilo of *raw* opium, about 110,000 kilo *prepared* in tubes can be derived (including the weight of the leaden tubes). Thus, the 90 kilos of Cribb can never provide 158,900 tubes refined opium, but at most 99,000 tubes.

[74] R. Bouman, p. 109.

[75] If one follows the chronology mentioned by the General and calculates the quantities of opium involved, then this story becomes quite ambiguous. Take, for instance, the use of 80 drums with raw opium: suppose it concerns the standard oil drums of 55 USgal = 200 liter, then we are confronted here with 16 tons of raw opium. Earlier he writes about 1 ton *prepared* opium in 'two drums of 500 liter': each drum holds 500 liters? two drums hold 250 liters each? Eighty drums of 500 liter gives 40 tons of opium (raw? prepared?), which were not available. In terms of chronology, the problem is not clear either. From October 1945 to the 1st of April 1946, apparently 8.1 million guilders was earned, but on November 1945 the whole stock had already been transported to a safe place, and until May 1947 no opium was actually sold. Or on the price side: is it possible in a rather chaotic Indonesia to sell raw opium within half a year for 8.1 million *guilders* (whatever the definition)? Or: per *thail* (= 0.04 kg) the price of opium is on average 25 to 30 guilders in 1938; 8.1 million guilders would be equivalent to 270,000 to 324,000 *thails* or 11-13 tons of raw opium. This is far from the 22 tons which was left or the original stock of 24 tons. And so on.

which must be perceived as distorted after so many decades: for them the Dutch *rightly* returned to invade a then sovereign country and, anyway, foreign territory; the Dutch also *rightly* chased after the Indonesian opium traders, etc. Both write extensively about the opium (and rubber) 'smuggling' activities of the Indonesians, but they have "forgotten" that the latter were simply *trading in their own country*, which only the Dutch considered smuggling. It is a point of view with far-reaching consequences dating from the VOC time. And if the authors had had a genuine aversion against opium, they would have complained first against the Dutch *Opiumregie* which the Indonesians, compelled by necessity, had to copy for a limited time.

General Bouman dedicates his study 'to my Indonesian friends, former antagonists'. He and Cribb still wrote as enemies, probably overwhelmed by the data mostly provided by Dutch police, Dutch military and bureaucrats, including their secret services. All this cannot lead to an unbiased historiography.[76]

---

[76] And not only this. As recently as 2010 the Dutch government refused any form of ideal or financial compensation for the slaughtering of Indonesian villages (several "My Lai's" must be celebrated) during this last colonial war.

CHAPTER TWENTY

PROFITS

At the end of this long part about the Dutch East Indies, we have to settle the bill. Which bill? In the opium business profits are made on different levels, wages or bribes paid and received, revenues gained. The levels concerned are not only local, provincial or state ones, but also the classes in society and the time when the profits were received (accidental, during contract years or permanently) and the location within the whole production and consumption chain.

It is nearly impossible to demonstrate the opium profits and losses for all possibilities and levels. Nevertheless, in Appendix 1 an attempt is made to provide an example of such a chain. Because there was no poppy production in the East Indies, a chain had to start from the imported government opium. The one given in the appendix concerns the largest possible route, that between Bengal–India and Shanghai–China.

Here we shall assess the profits/revenues in the East Indies on two levels: for the opium farmer, relevant only until the start of the *Opiumregie*, and for the colonial state until its collapse. A feeling for proportion can be gained, when confronted with the large capital sums in the opium business, if one realizes that around 1870 the lowest payments on the plantations were 4-5 cents a day. Often 8 guilders *per year* was paid (indigo cultures) or even 4.5 guilders *per year* (coffee cultures).[1] This apart from the large portions of daily beatings. They did not have any possibility to pay for any addiction for long.[2]

One of the most eloquent Dutch supporters of opium distribution, Jacob Wiselius, bases his case on the following quasi-logical calculations:

> The government provides the farmers with ca. 1600 pikul, and the import of illegal opium should be calculated at about double that, so that the number of users in the archipelago is about 16% of the 25 million ... who use together 4,000 pikuls of opium. Every pikul contains 125,000 gram (= 1,600 thail = 160,000 mata) and, therefore, every smoker uses one and a half thail

---

[1] E. Vanvugt (1985), p. 211 ff.

[2] This is seriously doubted by J. Meiss, p. 63 note 2: '... because I was never confronted with the proper figures proving that a population which pauperize looks for savings by reducing its consumption ... of alcohol or opium.'

per year or 1/2 mata opium per day. Suppose that the average price of one mata, bought from the farmer, is 8 cents, then it follows that on average every smoker's expense per day is 4-5 cents.[3]

He adds in a note that the price depends on the quantity of smuggled opium in circulation. Often a mata costs 10, sometimes even 15 cents. However, if the user buys the opium per thail, Wiselius thinks, it may be cheaper. Of course, wholesale prices were always cheaper, but wage earners could never afford that sum. According to Wiselius the consumption of 'every smoker' was 1½ thail per year, which is worth 15-22 guilders, equivalent to a slave's existence for 3-5 years and saving all the money one has earned, while not paying for food, drink, and housing.

The irrational aspect of this calculation starts with the assumption (which can never be proved) that smuggling amounted to twice what the Dutch imported. In addition, this smuggling is styled as a nightmare of the honest Dutch colonial exploiter: it is a function of the Dutch greed. Later we shall return to this element of the story. Perhaps the opium farmer can provide us with a solution in this typical colonial problem.

The Opium Farmer[4]

A quotation like the following about rich Chinese families appeals to the imagination and prejudices:

> The wealth of the Cabang Atas was conspicuous. Aside from endowing charitable institutions and temples, the great opium farmer–Chinese officers of Semarang built luxurious family compounds nestled in gardens laid out in the Chinese style, with fish ponds and ornamental mountains and caves made of coral. The Be family compound was known as ... the Eastern Garden ... the Western Garden, home of the Tans ... the peranakan elite ... great feasts and parties ... The most striking was the gleaming, palatial villa of an immensely wealthy retired opium farmer ... And so on.[5]

Around 1890 three of these rich Chinese families dominated thirteen of Java's twenty opium farms. The Be-Tan group owned four farms: Batavia,

---

[3] J. Wiselius (1886), p. 6. Indeed in 1881 there were 1667.38 pikul available for the farmers, in 1882 there was one hundred less, while in 1883 only 1390.19 pikul were placed at the disposal of the farmers. Idem, note 1.

[4] For the background of the revenue farming in Southeast Asia and the East Indies in particular, see J. Bucher, H. Dick (ed.) in which an excellent contribution by F.W. Diehl (p. 196-232) deals with the East Indies in the long 19th-century.

[5] J. Rush, p. 95.

Krawang, Bantam and Bagelen. A rival, Ho Yam Lo, from a Semarang-based group, ran 'three lucrative farms in central Java': Semarang, Djokjakarta and Kedu. The third group, headed by Han Liong Ing (the 'Kediri kongsi') managed the farms in Cheribon, Tegal, Pekalongan, Rembang and Japara with familial ties to two others.[6]

It was Struick, an inspector of the Dutch Finances in the East Indies, who investigated the profit and loss structures of the twenty farms around 1890 (a few years before the *Opiumregie* started). His results more or less destroy the relationship 'immense wealth' and 'opium farm'.

Table 18. Prices, Profits and Quantities of Opium of the Opium Farmers in 1887 (prices in guilders) [7]

Location Opium Farms in Java	Purchasing prices of the farmers per catty of raw opium	Average sales price per 1 catty of raw opium**	Average sales price of prepared opium		Quantity received from Dutch provider in catty	Number of official opium dens
			per thail = 1/16 catty	per mata = 1/100 thail		
Bantam*	137.63	177.69	16.69	0.24	7860	40
Batavia	---	---	16.8	0.2	---	---
Krawang	---	---	18	0.27	---	---
Lampong districts	---	---	22.9	0.32	---	---
Cheribon	135.08	143.34	15	0.25	1625	11
Tegal	187.56	244.51	12	0.15	2300	21
Pekalongan	174.48	180.81	12.24	0.16	2500	33
Semarang	168.8	186	16	0.17	13400	61
Japara	125.08	164.3	15	0.18	5683 1/4	47
Rembang	132.05	167.34	14.04	0.17	6350	42
Surabaya	131.54	156.37	14.4	0.14	14300	48
Pasuruan	185.58	178.64	13.15	0.17	3740	20
Probolinggo	122.73	156	12	0.18	2680	14
Bezuki	107.83	130.43	13.6	0.14	1830	21
Banjumas	80.23	156	14	0.25	3600	10
Bagelen	123.05	151.34	13.5	0.18	2400	28
Kedu	156.2	178.9	15.5	0.2	2900	31
Djokjakarta	120.54	155.14	15	0.16	5500	93

---

[6] Idem, p. 95, 96. For the Chinese *kongsis* in the East Indies see J. Vleming, p. 57-71. In this very positive and detailed, juridical analysis about all possible commercial deals with Chinese (1925), one cannot find the word opium or a reference to Chinese opium business.

[7] For the following see N. Struick, p. 24-28. Prices are in guilders.

Table 18. Continued

Location Opium Farms in Java	Purchasing prices of the farmers per catty of raw opium	Average sales price per 1 catty of raw opium**	Average sales price of prepared opium		Quantity received from Dutch provider in catty	Number of official opium dens
			per thail = 1/16 catty	per mata = 1/100 thail		
Surakarta	160.77	183.25	12.33	0.15	7800	146
Madiun	165.37	158	11.7	0.18	8425	57
Kediri	197.82	206.69	14	0.25	13300	100
Madura	112.07	121.48	14.25	0.13	1901 1/2	32

* The first four districts belong to one opium farm with the same prices for *raw* opium as indicated.
** This average sales price is an estimate of N. Struick. The difference with the previous column is, therefore, the profit or loss per catty for the farmer.

It is clear from the table that, for instance in Pasuruan and Madiun, one has to accept a loss directly at the start of the process. A more spectacular example is Surakarta with the largest number of official opium dens (secret dens seem to be more numerous).

Financial inspector Struick comes up with a calculation of the management costs (one person earning 80 guilders a month, 30 guilders for rent and other expenses) of 1320 guilders per den per year. For all dens, therefore, a total of 192,720 guilders per year. As the table reveals, the gross profit per catty is 22.48 (183.25 minus 160.77) which makes for the 7,800 catty requested from the colonial government a total of 174,344 guilders. Conclusion: only the management of the dens in Surakarta costs 18,000 guilders more per year than the gross profit. Similar calculations for Kediri reveal a loss of 14,000 a year, for Cheribon 1,100, Pekalongan 30,000 and Madura 25,000 guilders.

In addition, these amounts must certainly be too low, because only the management cost of the dens are considered, not the expenses of the farm administration, the preparation of the opium, payments for bookkeepers, transport, interest on capital loaned, expenses for food and drinks, and so on. In short, it is difficult to find an opium farmer who earned a big profit from his farm.[8]

---

[8] In the correspondence J. Baud, J. Rochussen, vol. II, p. 174 is mentioned by Rochussen that the chief farmer of Samarang had a loss of 600,000.– guilders in 1842, a fortune. Reason: the too heavy competition among the Chinese. In September 1847 is reported: 'The chief farmers lost fortunes and are more or less ruined ...' (Idem, p. 292). Reason: the

According to Struick it is, in fact, only the opium farmer of Banjumas, an 'industrial entrepreneur' (in fact, the indigenous resident of the district itself), who is happy with his opium farm. Reason: he paid the lowest government rent (*pachtschat*), nearly three times less than the Chinese boss of Pasuruan, half of the Chinese boss of Pekalongan, etc. Moreover, Banjumas seems to be the only farm which requested the maximum quantity of opium available for his location. The rest of the farms asked only 50% or 30% of the opium which they could have gotten.

Why did the Banjumas resident have such an advantage? He paid the lowest rent thanks to the absence of 'free competition' in Banjumas: for many years he was the only one dealing in opium and related products. He, furthermore, can rely 'on an army of obedient bureaucrats', while no Chinese dared to compete with him. Thus, the resident of Banjumas was in the position to deal with the Dutch colonial government in the sense of: I demand this price, otherwise no opium in my district!

The question remains, therefore, why were the Chinese in the first quotation so rich? Not from the opium bought from the Dutch. According to Struick and many others, they were all heavily involved in opium smuggling as well, which was facilitated by their farm and its relation to the Dutch opium monopoly: this relationship meant that the farmer was allowed to possess large quantities of opium; it was his guarantee that he could smuggle!

However, it seems to me an excessively clever reasoning for Dutch colonialists, who were always very jealous of the profits of others. Also, Struick had to acknowledge that there was no proof of Chinese opium farmers' smuggling. It is, therefore, more logical to suppose that the opium farms, through which enormous capital sums circulated, provided the proprietors with *highly lucrative economic power positions throughout the economic infrastructure, the credit market and merchandise trade*. The only position which was economically and politically strong in the colony was the narco-military Dutch one.

The Colonial State as Farmer

The question seems simple: what was the net profit gained by the Dutch since the 16th-century by making the people of the Dutch East Indies into

---

new distribution system. Two years later: most sub-farmers are ruined and the consumption decreases (Idem, p. 379). Reason: the opium leases are too expensive.

opium addicts. It was difficult to answer such a simple question. Let's give here, first, the simplest and certainly an incorrect answer. The table provides the *summary* of the data so abundantly published by a superb Dutch colonial bureaucrat, J. C. Baud.

Table 19. Dutch Government Net Opium Profits in the East Indies (1678-1815)[9]

Periods	Current Dutch Guilders
1678-1700	6 872 555
1701-1723	8 876 947
1724-1746	14 772 415
1747-1769	15 060 792
1770-1792	9 336 758
1793-1800	12 629 414
1801-1815	9 607 822
TOTAL	77 156 703

More revealing is what the VOC Directors in Amsterdam wrote in 1686 to VOC Batavia:

> It is truly not a small profit which is gained with the amphioen according to your last letter: in Patna you bought it for 64 rupees [about 80 guilders] per maund [40 kg] and on the east coast of Java it is sold for 320-340 rix-daalders [about 825 guilders] per pikul [62 kg]. Therefore, it is urgent ... to keep this business for the Company as best as possible.[10]

This resulted in a profit per kilo of opium of 11.3 guilders. The VOC sold about one million kilo of opium in the period 1678-1700 for a profit of nearly 7 million guilders. Still, a fabulous sum for that period.

After the turn of the century, prices in Bengal increased from two to four guilders a kilo (g/k) in 1730. Later, the fraudulent mechanism of deals between VOC officials, Bengal producers and English EIC officials apparently worked very efficiently (see discussion of *Amphioen Society*): around 1760 the Bengal price had soared to six g/k, and in 1764 it increased even to ten g/k. As we have seen in Appendix 3 every figure decreased from 1760 onwards. This, however, does not mean that the personal profits of the dealers involved decreased, but that the VOC received much less opium and got much less total profit.

---

[9] Calculation based on J. C. Baud, p. 216 ff.
[10] Quoted in E. Vanvugt (1985), p. 108, although his source is not well indicated. See this page also for the following figures.

The following table and figure concerning the 19th-century are much more complicated. There is a specific meaning behind tables like these in which a comparison with national accounts is implied. This is discovered in the usual comment accompanying them: if only a low percentage of opium contributes to the national or colonial wealth, then the Opium Problem cannot be as serious or large as the anti-opium propaganda claimed. It is a tricky reasoning.

Only by using the most abstract definitions, like 'the contribution of agriculture' to the national income instead of something like 'the usual contribution of opium is mostly 10%' can the bad conscience be eased. We have to compare specific items like rice or oil to a product like opium to discover its relative value for the "Wealth of the Dutch Nation". In that case, certainly during the 17th until the end of the 19th-century, opium scores among the top three products. Before taking the discussion further, let's look at the figures resulting from all the above calculations and deliberations.

Table 20. Dutch Government Opium and Colonial Profits in the East Indies,1816-1915[11]

Period	Net Opium Income in Million Guilders	Total Colonial Income in Million Guilders	Profit Balance in Million Guilders	Loss Balance in Million Guilders
1816-1822	8.1	129.4	9.2	---
1823-1833	30.3	284.3	---	51
1834-1847	88	887.9	118	---
1848-1865	145.1	1 779.1	503.9	---
1866-1875	103.8	1 290.5	199.6	---
1876-1885	157.6	1 416.4	---	73.9
1886-1895	180.7	1 298.5	---	5.6
1896-1905	153.1	1 426.4	---	100.6
1906-1915	211.9	2 251.6	---	115.2
TOTAL	1 078.6	100 764.1	830.7	346.3

It is not an easy matter to assess this table. It remains problematic which method is used in the national accounts and which aim must be served with a calculation: to convince the homeland state bureaucrats of something or its politicians, the king or the taxpayers. Apart from this, one

---

[11] J.-W. Gerritsen, p. 62. See also E. Vanvugt (1985), p. 414; A. Booth in: A. Booth et al (ed.), p. 210 ff. and other computations (Frits Diehl).

must realize that most colonial profits are not made in the colony but in the homeland.

For example: in the 1848-1865 period the total income from the colony for the Dutch was nearly 2 billion guilders, of which about 45% was earned in the East Indies itself. From this last amount (928 million), about 20% (180 million) resulted from the opium sold by the government.[12]

As shown in the table, the first years after the English occupation were difficult (Java War, introduction of losses of the *Royal Dutch Trading Company*, NHM). This makes the average opium income over the whole century about 10%.

Calculations were made to compare the profit rates for the main colonial products in the middle of the 19th-century. This coincided more or less with the 1848-1865 opium period in the previous table. The result of this comparison is given in the following table, which does not need any comment.

Table 21. Profits from Colonial Products, 1848-1866 (x 1 million guilders)[13]

Product	Cost Price	Selling Price	Profit	Profit %
coffee	215.8	637	421.1	195
sugar	176.6	254.9	78.3	44
indigo	22.3	45.5	23.2	104
tin	25.1	103.8	78.7	313
other	38.1	69.4	31.3	82
Monopolies				
salt	34.5	100.3	65.8	190
opium	21	176.9	155.9	742

There are, of course, several methods for calculating opium profits. Struick gave a good example of it for the year 1887 and the islands Java and Madura alone. It is interesting because it highlights the cost, income and profit sides of the state opium business. Not all details can be mentioned but the following are informative enough.[14]

In this year 150,000 catties of Bengal and Levantine raw opium were bought for 1.4 million guilders. Strange enough, this is not the largest expense. The Dutch colonial state had to pay 2,500 opium sellers in its opium-den network for 3.5 million, while the same amount was spend by

---

[12] See the calculations of Diehl given in E. Vanvugt (1985), p. 413.
[13] Quoted from F. Diehl by E. Vanvugt (1985), p. 393 note 33.
[14] N. Struick, p. 58-62.

the opium police fighting in vain against the "smugglers". There are, furthermore, some small costs for preparing the raw opium, the payment of agents, bookkeepers, inspectors or chemists. Nearly 10 million guilders were spend to meet all these expenses in 1887.[15]

Struick supposed that the prepared opium is sold for 15 guilders per *thail* and 20 cents per *mata*. In total the state could earn 24 million guilders gross which was in his calculation 14 million guilders net, *if all the opium farmers should pay their duties*. Struick suggests that this was not the case; the opium was sold by the state at a small loss. In the mean time an army of Dutch bureaucrats earned a living in this opium business. So, what is a loss?

In the following figure the 19th-century opium ups and downs are well illustrated. It concerns only Java and Madura and not the Outer Districts, but covers the bulk of the profits. The revenue obtained each year was 'determined by the amount of licence fees paid by the opium revenue farmers and by the amount of profit made by the government on its sale of opium, for which it held a monopoly'.[16] It is, however, not true what Diehl states after this: 'Each component was affected by general market fluctuations ...' etc. They had little influence in fact: there was not a proper market in the East Indies, which presupposes rather autonomous participants playing in a peaceful supply and demand constellation.

Here a Dutch narco-military power fixed monopoly prices and squeezed the buyers of the stuff as long as a profit could be got which it deemed sufficient. That is to say: at least ten times the purchase price in India (see below).

One has to realize that when monopoly prices are used, any market is negated (except the fluctuations the monopoly holder accepts for personal motives). This means in narco-military terms: for strategic reasons relative to the degree of repression of the indigenous populations, including those who distribute the opium among the indigenous consumers. One must not forget when examining all these tables and figures that from the beginning to the end of the 19th-century, the Dutch waged one devastating and bloody war after another against the East Indies populations.

It would also not be wise to defend the position of the Dutch, who constantly complained about "smugglers" undermining their profits or intim-

---

[15] Struick did not mention in his cost analysis the transport costs in Bengal and from Bengal to Batavia, the loss of 45% when raw opium is made into prepared one, etc. This last loss is mentioned at the wrong place.

[16] F. Diehl, p. 209.

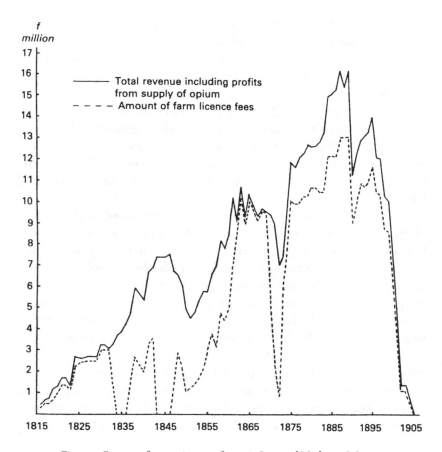

Figure 7. Revenue from opium tax farms in Java and Madura, 1816-1905

Sources: Embrechts, 1848; Baud, 1853; de Waal, 1864; *Koloniaal Verslag* and *Bijlagen*, annually from 1849 to 1915 used by F. W. Diehl, p. 210 .

idating the opium farmers not to buy the Dutch opium. This blurs the fact that the Dutch asked usury prices for their product, which only tremendous rich farmers could afford. In addition, the smugglers were rarely or never caught, except 'the arrest of the usual suspects'. The existence of the "smugglers" (if they were not created to support the highest possible prices) is the only feature which resembles a free market!

This figure concerns, thus, the period of the revenue farm opium. The steep fall at the end does not mean that the profits disappear. On the contrary, the *Opiumregie* takes over the "sqeezing job" with much greater success.

Another perception of profits lists them per century of the VOC and Dutch government. Including the results of our analysis of the *Opiumregie*, the totals over the centuries are:

17th-century:	6,872,555	(is in today's currency	0.518 billion euros)
18th-century:	60,676,326	("	5.185 billion)
19th-century:	799,704,716	("	45.240 billion)
20th-century:	1,064,150,000	("	35.112 billion)
40 years.			

The easiest conclusions from all these figures are: there is no *single item* in the *Eastern* colonial history of the Dutch which *constantly* caters through the centuries for such a substantial income; there is no single product which *increases in revenue* so quickly (ten times every century). Considering that the result for the 20th-century was gained over only forty years and that the government swore by all Christian saints that it would eradicate the narcotics, it seems to be the best proof of the untenability of that promise.

Only a few observations are left to make here. First, we must stress again that these amounts only concern *government revenues*. In the literature, it was accepted that the smuggling practices of opium (defined as non-Dutch trade) were responsible for half of the opium business and profit. Although the Chinese were accused of it, many Europeans were also smugglers; for a long time Americans were certainly in the majority. Also, the substantial narco-profits of companies like the Royal NHM or Cocaine Factory are not included in the above figures.

The qualification of opium as the most profitable product for a very long period should be qualified by three remarks. In the 17th and 18th centuries, pepper or textiles were certainly more profitable, but they lost their lead to coffee or rubber in the 19th and 20th centuries; in turn, oil took over.

The status of this opium, furthermore, was achieved in the *Asian* production and trade, because it was *not* produced for the European market. (From about 1850 onwards Levant opium gradually penetrated the East Asian markets through, for instance, NHM activities). All this drastically changed after World War II.

Finally, the chapter on the introduction of opium as a mass product (pepper for opium; ch. 11) after 1663 demonstrated the real value and profit of opium: it became the Asian means to gain a Western profit for the West.

There are different ways to put these opium profits in figures. In a puzzling way some economists say this about the 19th-century Dutch performance:

> Over the whole of the period 1816-1915 the accumulated colonial surplus was 485 million guilders. But absent the opium revenues ... there would have been a deficit of 600 million guilders.[17]

To make this less abstract, one could quote Ewald Vanvugt. He arrives at the following result for just the thirty years before 1913:

> From 1884 to 1892 one got from the opium farming a profit of 110 million guilders; in the years 1893 to 1899 this was 137 million; and from 1900 to 1906 it amounted to 120 million. After establishing the *Opium Regie* the profits increased in the years 1907 to 1913 to about 135 million. So in these thirty years the profit was about 500 million.[18]

Based on the tables of Appendix 2 of the imports (and Baud's tables) and compared with the above, it can be calculated that the Dutch government alone earned a net profit for the first period of 14.26 guilders; for the second period 48.28 guilders; and for the third period 116.83 guilders for every imported *pound* of opium.

For the last period before the establishment of the *Opiumregie*, the following table is revealing:

Table 22. Opium import in Batavia, 1881-1883 in chests and in guilders[19]

	1881		1882		1883	
	Imported chests	Price per chest in guilders	Imported chests	Price per chest in guilders	Imported chests	Price per chest in guilders
Levant opium	770	1845.39	826	1316.49	615	1332.5
Bengal opium	900	1545.74	800	1460.89	950.5	1380.41

The Dutch bought their opium in Calcutta or in the Levant. The auction in Calcutta gave as a normal auction price 1225 guilders per pikul—chest. On top of this 10% could be added for all sorts of costs (freight, insurance,

---

[17] E. van Luijk, J. van Ours, p. 4 note 7.

[18] E. Vanvugt (1995), p. 394; in Idem (1985), p. 360 there is a quite different text.

[19] J. Wiselius (1886), p. 144. The average price of a chest between 1873 and 1883 was £125 14 sh. This equaled more or less 1225 Dutch guilders (Idem, note 1).

etc.) which makes a price per chest in Batavia of nearly 1350 guilders. In a previous table I indicated the prices the opium farmers had to pay: on average 140 guilders per *catty*. Since one chest—pikul contains 100 catty, the Dutch received on average 14,000 guilders. This is nine to ten times the amount they had paid in Calcutta! There was no other product which gave this kind of profit margin. Wiselius, one of the most astute defenders of the opium trade, is not satisfied even with this result. He proposed depressing the Calcutta price by at least 50 guilders per chest, so that Batavia could cash at least 50,000 guilders more.[20]

For the period 1900 to 1940 we are also able to provide an assessment. This period is characterized by modernization in all respects: industrialization in factories, the full application of chemical-pharmaceutical knowledge, and rigorous distribution methods. To meet the needs of a modernized opium business, the Dutch government took a progressive step by establishing the *Opiumregie*. The following table provides the opium profits in a different way than in a previous chapter.

Table 23. Contribution of the *Opiumregie* to the Government Budget in the East Indies, 1914-1940 (x 1 million current Dutch guilders)[21]

Year	Opium Revenue	Total Revenue	Opium % of Total	Opium Profits	Profit as % of Opium Revenue
1914	35.0	281.7	13.5	26.7	76
1915	32.6	309.7	11.2	25.2	77
1916	35.3	343.1	10.8	28.4	80
1917	38.2	360.1	11.4	30.4	80
1918	38.8	399.7	10.2	30.1	78
1919	42.5	543.1	8.2	33.2	78
1920	53.6	756.4	7.5	41.6	78
1921	53.3	791.8	7.1	42.1	79
1922	44.2	752.6	6.2	34.5	78
1923	37.6	650.4	6.1	30.1	80
1924	35.3	717.9	5.1	28.1	80
1925	36.6	753.8	5.2	28.7	78
1926	37.7	807.9	5.2	29.1	77
1927	40.6	779.1	5.7	31.4	77
1928	42.8	835.9	5.7	34.6	81

[20] Idem, p. 145.
[21] S. Chandra (2010). The figures for 1934-1940 are derived from the combined accounts of the *Opium- and Saltregie*. Chandra indicates that they 'underestimate the profitability of opium'.

Table 23. Continued

Year	Opium Revenue	Total Revenue	Opium % of Total	Opium Profits	Profit as % of Opium Revenue
1929	40.9	848.5	5.3	32.7	80
1930	34.5	755.6	5.3	27.1	79
1931	25.3	652.0	4.6	19.0	75
1932	17.3	501.8	4.5	12.3	71
1933	12.7	460.6	3.7	8.6	68
1934	11.1	455.2	3.2	7.2	65
1935	9.5	466.7	2.6	6.1	64
1936	8.9	537.8	2.2	5.7	64
1937	11.5	575.4	2.5	7.7	67
1938	11.9	597.1	2.6	8	67
1939	11.5	663.4	1.7	8.6	75
1940	11.7	N.A	N.A	8.5	72

In an older encyclopedia the Dutch still accused the British in the 20th-century for all their own opium misery. This was largely motivated by jealousy that they themselves could not trade twenty million kilo of opium a year. This was quite hypocritical because the Dutch government *distributed* at least 150,000 kilo a year at that time, which increased to 200,000 in 1920.[22]

In addition, several reports state the substantial consumption in Java and Madura alone: in 1909 there were already 146,723 native opium buyers, of which about 80,000 were regular ones.[23] With this business the government earned no less than 45 million guilders *gross*. Later it increased the price and lowered the production so that it still earned 35 million guilders *net* in 1929 with only 57,000 kilo. And it could tell the motherland and the anti-opium lobby that it had decreased production. In addition, the Dutch bureaucrats made their usual deals with the opium "smugglers", who managed a substantial "illicit" opium trade without much interference from the authorities.

Other interesting aspects can be derived from the 1816-1915 table above: for instance, that the Java War occurred in the period 1825-1830. This war was also an opium war.[24] During these years the opium profit did not

[22] *Encyclopaedie,* 1934 edition, p. 1255.
[23] T. Addens, p. 84.
[24] See NHM story above; also C. Holtzappel in: H. Derks (ed., 1989), p. 147 ff.

decrease, and directly after its ending, it increased quickly to pay for the devastation and to renew the colonial profitability.

Half a century later the democratic government in the Netherlands introduced the *Opiumregie* in the colony to prevent smuggling. As usual, all possible rationalizations were given to cloak the profit motive, including the medical and religious arguments—"we can help the addicts better now"—that went down well in the motherland. But the "smuggling" also continued, not the least because it became dominated by American and British traders, and the system itself was as fraudulent as possible. This monopoly position allowed the prices to be manipulated as Wertheim already concluded in his autobiographical remarks:

> Was the price decreased, the aim was trying to avoid the use of smuggled opium among ordinary folk. If increased, than the aim was quite the same!'[25]

In addition, the colonial government had to cope with an increased anti-opium sentiment and action in the motherland. That was in fact a reason why the Dutch copied the system of 100% government monopoly from their main competitor in the realm, the French. Now it was easier to announce to the motherland that the production had decreased "again". One of its main effects is given in the following table of data for *selected* years.

Table 24. Dutch trade and Yield in Opium in the East Indies, 1914-1932[26]

Year	Opium sold in kg	Yield in millions of guilders	Yield per kg in guilders
1914	98 810	35	354
1919	91 714	42	458
1924	50 342	35	695
1929	58 806	41	697
1932	24 427	17	696

A conservative estimate about the opium turnover and profits in the years 1914-1940 states that the Dutch government made a *net* opium profit of 625.7 million current guilders in a turnover of 810.9 million; for every guilder of cost, there was nearly three guilders in profit! And these costs included, for instance, the lucrative salaries of many Dutch officials.

---

[25] In his preface to E. Vanvugt (1985; 1995), p. 11.
[26] Adjusted from the table in J.W. Gerritsen, p. 65.

Notwithstanding the strongly increased price per kilo (and, therefore, greatly increased smuggling), the overall yield for the state decreased. This occurred in the years of the Great Depression (1930-1936), but the sales increased again to 1940. Officially, the government sold at least 12,000 kilo in 1935 and 20,000 kilo in 1940.

The last remark about opium profits brings the above data into the right perspective: they concern only the initial analysis of three hundred years of opium revenues of some Dutch *government* agencies (and its predecessors) in the East Indies archipelago (ca. 1650 to 1940). What are not mentioned yet are the profits of *private individuals* as seen, for instance, in the *Amphioen Society,* which concern multi-million amounts. The third kind of opium profits are related to *private companies.* The best example is the *Koninklijke Nederlandsche Handelmaatschappij* (NHM). Here, again, the opium profits can only be estimated at "several hundred million guilders". In NHM-related publications one cannot find a proper analysis nor an assessment of the opium trade between the East Indies and China. It was the Chinese government which in 1906 complained about the substantial opium imports from the 'Dutch East-Indies'![27] One could also refer to private companies like the Dutch cocaine and heroin factories in the years after 1900.

Therefore, in addition to the assessment of the government profits or revenues over ca. 350 years (in total nearly 86 billion in today's euros), one could estimate the opium profits from the two other sources at 0.5-0.75 billion or 20-30 billion guilders, respectively. Certainly until about 1950 this makes the Dutch, without any doubt, the largest opium dealers in world history: not only Shanghai or Hong Kong weare built on opium, Amsterdam and The Hague were as well.

---

[27] A. Hosie, vol. 2, p. 203, 204.

CHAPTER TWENTY-ONE

REFLECTIONS

1.

At the end of this *History of the Dutch Opium Problem*, it is good to realize that there were also Dutch people who criticized the imperial and colonial projects of the Dutch. In the 17th-century one of the very few VOC intellectuals, Reaal, tried to change the dominant drive of his organization. Above, the famous dictum of Multatuli is quoted as one of the harshest judgments of the colonial regime. He was certainly not alone, but the criticism was often rather ambiguous.

Take the following quotation relative to the Dutch "public opinion" in Holland in the 19th and early 20th-century. People who all were highly responsible for the colonial regime and its narco-military policy acted like they were characters from Multatuli:

> The arguments of Dirk van Hogendorp [1761-1822], who called the opium monopoly one of the most hurtful and injurious features that dishonor the administration of the Dutch East Indies; of Minister of the Colonies Rochussen [1832-1912], who put opium on a line with the plague; of Minister of the Colonies Loudon [1824-1900], who classed it with poison; of Minister of the Colonies Sprenger Van Eyck [1842-1907], who spoke of its use as a great evil; of Minister of Colonies Keuchenius [1822-1893], who characterized it as a means to debauch and ruin the population—all these arguments could not prevail, even with those who brought them forward when their colonial politics needed some moral leavening, against the consideration that there is money in opium.[1]

This is an effective demonstration of the immanent hypocrisy of the Dutch colonial elite vis-à-vis opium. Scheltema from Yale University, who wrote this in 1907, concluded from this ambivalent behavior that the Dutch colonial spirit 'is the spirit of trade' and in italics: *'Trade before everything!* ... at present no less than in the time of the East India Company ... a rather flimsy foundation ... not developed into something of broader conception, more in keeping with the great movement of expansion on principles ... a very limited circle of thought ...', and so on.

---

[1] J. Scheltema, p. 248; the life data in the quotation are given by me.

As alternatives and worthy successors, attention turned to the Americans in the Philippines or the Japanese in Formosa. Part 5 is devoted to both "New Imperialists". Here it can be said that if they are the alternative to those old Dutch colonial rulers, we should not be surprised to be confronted with exaggerated arguments, concerning a change from bad to worse.

Scheltema suffered from a symptomatic ideological blindness.[2] He really thought that only the money-making of criminal individuals was the motor behind all the opium traffic and that the government only had to eliminate them to solve the opium problem. Notwithstanding his severe and honest criticism of the Dutch colonial leadership, it is remarkable that he did not conclude from this that colonialism or the colonial government was a main part of The Opium Problem. Therefore, he expected the solution to lie in new-style colonial governments.

It is, furthermore, untenable to accuse trade as such for creating "evil" (at present, similar critics use 'the market'). This resembles the medieval accusations of mainstream theologians. It avoids seeing another serious problem in the undermining of all trade through the widespread *monopolization* of trade (nearly a contradiction in terms). This made free trade impossible and, therefore, trade on an equal and normal basis of supply and demand with indigenous people.

Scheltema's main target was the *Opiumregie*. This was a monopoly institution par excellence. In his daily newspaper, the *Bataviaansch Nieuwsblad* (September 1902), he criticized the government for its 'hypocritical' and 'immoral' behavior.[3] This led to his imprisonment for three months. He took revenge in his AJS article, which had a great impact in the international press at the time. It had repercussions in the Dutch Parliament in Holland as well. The colonial bureaucrats reacted, however, in the obvious way: those members of Parliament had no knowledge of the Indies and knew nothing about opium. A reduction of the opium con-

---

[2] Idem, note p. 250, 251. J. Scheltema was born in 1855 in Macassar (Celebes) where his father was "president" of the local Court of Justice. He served the Dutch government in Singapore and elsewhere; became a journalist in 1883; editor of several papers in Java; in 1903 'imprisoned for the publication of some observations on the opium policy of the Dutch government, too true to be tolerated in a Dutch dependency'. After his release, he settled for a year at Yale University, and succeeded in publishing there a long article in a scholarly journal without any relevant academic background. Anyway, his article was apparently accepted in the AJS, because it aims to provide the American government with advice on how (not) to handle the opium problem in the Philippines.

[3] J. Rush, p. 237.

sumption or production of opium (heroin, morphine) and cocaine were not envisaged.

Not only in Scheltema's writings, but generally, the criticism was not directed at the monopoly position of state institutions: if there had been free trade in opium in the East Indies, the price of opium would have collapsed; the widespread knowledge of the connotation "opium = colonial repression" had seriously undermined this market thanks to the anti-Dutch sentiments.

2.

For a world history of opium, nothing is so important as the Dutch assault on the East. In hindsight, it remains, possibly, the only fact of world historical importance concerning the Dutch colonization of the East, as the Dutch slave trade was for the colonization of the Americas and Africa. Apart from some architectural locations of memory, nothing is left of the realm once proudly called the Dutch Empire.

There never was such a "thing": from the beginning to the end (1600-1949), the leading concept and practice of this venture was, indeed, *exploitation* in horror scenarios. The silences in between two events were only recuperation time.

The VOC was satisfied with a network of coastal settlements that interfered in the affairs of the indigenous powers in order to exploit the available worthwhile agricultural and mining products in exchange for opium and fear. A fleet effectively connected these settlements. The many massacres permanently created the fear on which the exploitation was based. The unexpected *hongi* trips to destroy agricultural products, in order to keep the monopoly price as high as possible and competitors at home, are the most symptomatic methods of the general exploitation; they were guerrillas against the indigenous peasants.

This imperial or hegemonic construction was the VOC's strength and weakness: it had no friends, and its enemies were weak. It perished largely through its own incompetence, internal corruption, antagonism between VOC Holland and VOC East Indies, as well as European wars (Napoleon).

3.

The substantial investments in capital and manpower the Dutch used in the East were only directed to the creation of "monopoly profits": quite symbolic for this was the highest possible price-setting of a worthless product like opium.

Profit-making (whatever its definition) was and is still inherent in every supply and demand situation in product exchange. Profit was also the aim of the VOC, EIC and all other European colonial ventures. However, they mostly had no products which were of interest to the indigenous Asian people: thus, there could be no normal trade, supply and demand. Only demand was left, with an iron fist.

To use this last instrument was "easy" because all of them nurtured the astonishing arrogance and dangerous presumption of having the right and ability to claim large parts of a foreign world as their own property. And all of them used the scum of the European nations to do their dirty work in the tropical environments. And all of them were harassed by serious internal corruption and criminality even from the point of view of current value systems like Protestantism and Catholicism.

There were, however, marked differences between VOC and EIC. First, there was a very short period of free (pirate) trade, symptomatically called "pre"-companies, in the VOC case. This lasted about a century and a half for the EIC, only about a decade of two for the VOC.

In the EIC case the whole project was organized in a dominant way by the British aristocratic elite; in the Dutch case mostly by petty bourgeois bookkeepers. A European so-called "civilizing mission"—whatever its meaning nowadays—was a leading British activity much earlier and longer, and rescued the English language from oblivion. The more "Catholic" Anglicanism was practically more tolerant than the fanatic Dutch Calvinists or die-hard Catholic Portuguese and Spaniards.

There was also the following main difference. Already in 1602 the powerful Calvinist VOC arrived on the imperialist scene. This was from the beginning a military-, state- and God-supported attempt to create lucrative opportunities for monopoly profit-making. It took more than a century before the English state started a relevant strong support of the EIC after which, indeed, colonization could begin.

Contrary to the EIC, the VOC had from the beginning all the traits of a national project with a strong military-royal influence to destroy The Enemy (= the rest of the world). Fanatically, it traded only according the principle "deliver your products, or I shoot" and the principle "I must have the monopoly position". The basic *octroy* (1602) fixed this position, which was confirmed time and again. The VOC, indeed, 'acted the part of the Prince' as a contemporary commentator remarked. In a memorandum of 1741 a future Governor-General of the Dutch East Indies, Imhoff, told his readers that the VOC was

> no mere Merchant, but also represents the Power of the Dutch Nation, and that whereas it journeys and trades in the former capacity, it is in the latter capacity that it is established there; to achieve its true goals the Company must assure its existence in both capacities and on the strength of both capacities, so tightly is the political interwoven with the mercantile, and vice versa.[4]

This resulted in a continuous war against all European competitors and indigenous producers.

4.

The above formed the breeding ground for producing, trading and distributing on a large scale a product which was known to be bad for the health and mind of the users: opium. Before this, opium was either used only in medicine in Europe or medicine plus luxury in a very limited number of Middle Eastern or other Asian scenes (royal). The Portuguese used it as a present in order to smooth their trade. The Dutch continued with this but made something like a cash crop of opium (*amphioen*), with which they created The Opium Problem in world history. Opium was, however, much more than this.

Slavery and opium deliveries were the methods to keep a willing labor force available to do the heavy work in the fields and mines until far into the 20th-century. Opium also had the "function": to keep the indigenous elite dependent. From the 1660s until about 1950 Asian opium was seldom shipped to Europe, but remained the most profitable Asian product and trade. The third function was: opium as a substitute for money and as product for barter (opium for pepper, etc.).

---

[4] Quoted in R. Vos, p. 1.

5.

The Dutch were the first to discover all these advantages of opium, and they were the first to push opium into Asian countries on a massive scale. It was the model for the British Empire in its treatment of China. By doing this, the VOC became the unbeatable and first international narco-military power from about 1660 onwards, as it conquered the Portuguese along the Malabar Coast. This remained the case until 1800 when the English took over this "honorable job" and the Dutch had to accept a very profitable secondary position. They proved that the mutual opium competition of the European imperialists (mainly Dutch, English and French) formed the "engine" by which this could proliferate into the present world Opium Problem.

6.

Not only the external competition is important, but for the VOC so is the internal one. It concerns the internal mutual competition between Holland and the East Indies. The VOC and later the "state" elite in Holland were jealous of the VOC and "state" elite in the East Indies for the enormous capital one could accumulate there *personally*. This antagonism formed a strong internal dynamic for the Dutch leadership in this imperialist and colonialist venture. The latter, however, had a rather autonomous field of operation and profit, the inter-Asian trade. This was difficult to control by VOC Holland, which was concerned only with the voyages outward and home-bound.

The most pernicious project "to make peace" between both groups was the *Amphioen-Opium Society.* This brought both factions of the Dutch leadership and shareholders multi-million profits in the 18th-century, sanctioned by the House of Orange, one of its largest profiteers.

This constellation remained fully intact, was even perfected and more strongly legitimated, after the VOC perished through internal and external circumstances, and a new Dutch Colonial State was invented and established. Narco-military exploitation remained the leading practice and principle. This was immediately apparent in the House of Orange constructions and participation in the *Royal Dutch Trading Society* (in fact a much extended *Amphioen Society*) or (Royal) *Billiton Mining Company* and later in (Royal) *Unilever* and *Shell.*

7.

The post-VOC regime was in fact a construction of the Dutch, French (Napoleonic Holland, Daendels) and English (Raffles' occupation of Java). The result was a continuation of the VOC regime as occupier of the East Indies, but now aimed at a full occupation and colonization of the whole archipelago. The Dutch state itself became responsible and acted more extensively as narco-military occupier of the East Indies. The penetration with opium was now systematized and extended to all corners of this archipelago.

Around 1900 it was again extended by the world's largest coca leaf and cocaine production and trade and a state monopoly on the industrial production and distribution of opium (*Opiumregie*). Without doubt, there was no other product in the Dutch Asian history from 1600-1949 which can compete with this lucrative drug business. The end of this Dutch opium history was also the end of the Dutch influence in the world.

8.

"How the snake could bite in its own tail" is perfectly demonstrated in the Dutch opium history after 1950. This cannot be discussed here, but a provocative view on the future could be the following.

Without its lucrative colonies, the Netherlands could continue its economic life largely as a harbor region of Germany. In the 1960s, a kind of cultural revolution took place in the Netherlands more than elsewhere, in the heavy smoke and smell of marihuana, hashish, opium, cocaine, LSD, mescaline and many other aphrodisiacs. They all were (and are, more or less) publicly available.[5] And since the 1980s the Netherlands has become known in Europe for a new market concept to provide consumers in special shops with nearly everything they need to forget the serious dullness, etc. of Dutch culture.

In the meantime the old rice, rubber and coca plantations in *Tempo Doeloe* were replaced by extensive hashish plantations inside Holland itself, and the original Dutch cocaine production is now replaced by extensive ecstacy (MDMA) and other chemical drug laboratories.

---

[5] See H. Derks (ed., 1989), p. 215-225.

PART FOUR

THE FRENCH ASSAULT*

---

* The name *Indochina* is used as a general name for the large southern "peninsula" between China and Indonesia with the present countries Vietnam, Laos, Kampucheia (Cambodia), Thailand (Siam), Myanmar (Burma), Malaysia and the Republic of Singapore. Because the French assault on this part of Asia dates officially from 1867, this date is also the beginning of the opium history in this part of the study. French Indochina is, of course, much smaller. In 1887 it was formed by Annam, Tonkin and Cochinchina (together the present Vietnam), the kingdom of Cambodia and Laos.

CHAPTER TWENTY-TWO

OPIUM IN AND FOR *LA DOUCE FRANCE*

It is well-known that the Western methods to rule their so-called colonies differed between a direct and an indirect form.[1] The first resulted mostly in the construction making the colony part of the motherland (metropolis), like *La France d'outre-mer* in which all inhabitants became Frenchmen. In practical terms, they were second-class citizens, but formally Frenchmen. The Portuguese went even further and strongly advocated a racial mixture (*luso-tropicalism*).[2] This kind of political and racial integration nearly never happened in the Anglo-Saxon, Dutch or American colonies. In them, a rather large cultural and political gap remained and was cultivated between the rulers-perpetrators, the indigenous rulers and conquered-victims (racial segregation). This is the background to why the Opium Problem also took a different course in the various Western colonies.

Next, there is the not unimportant fact that the French colonized Southeast Asia–the main opium source or location after the 1950s–relatively late. They started after the middle of the 19th-century when the colonial exploitation was already in full swing elsewhere in the realm. The integrative moment is probably the reason why, more than other "whites", the French expatriates popularized East-Asian opium consumption in its own European capital as an oriental luxury. In many illegal ways they extended the colonial markets by making opium smoking socially acceptable in France and Europe.[3] In the USA opium was popularized first as a medicine in local "pills and powders markets", but remained inimical to "The East". In France it became a "tool" in the elite communication, an obvious element of the orientalism and *chinoiserie* hype. There are more

---

[1] C. Trocki (1999b), p. 90 ff. uses a clever study of Furnivall (my edition is from 1948) to demonstrate the differences. Indeed, in daily practice 'there was no sharp line between direct and indirect rule'. This is not the place to discuss or criticize Furnivall's approach. In my view, Furnivall does not understand the legal status with its serious consequences. To this aspect I refer only in the main text.

[2] See my analysis of the Portuguese–Mozambique relations around 1800 in: H. Derks (ed., 1989), p. 63 ff.

[3] See, for instance, ch. 8 the export from France into England during the 19th-century.

differences, how the "bite of the snake" was given and received, but these are the most noteworthy.

To show the main elements of this boomerang effect there is no better way than to describe in this first chapter the French opium landscape from around 1900.

Parisian Fumes

In the 1901 issue of a *Journal of Mental Science* a review under the heading 'Opium-smokers' runs as follows:

> Opium smoking seems to be on the increase in Paris; and, as the smoking is carried on in private apartments, those who reside in them become intoxicated by the fumes. This occurred in the case of a young woman, who prepared her husband's pipes, so that a craving was induced. To obtain sleep she became dependent upon opium-smoking and the atmosphere created by another smoker. Very soon symptoms of intoxication appeared-hysterical convulsions, neurasthenic anxiety, paralysis of will, excessive timidity, etc. Treated by hypnotic suggestion, she gave up opium-smoking and got well. Bérillon observes incidentally that the cat of the house and a servant who lived in the room exhibited signs of craving after the opium-smoking had ceased there.[4]

The inhabitants on the other side of the Channel must be lucky, since being near or handing a bottle to a laudanum drinker did not addict bystanders like the Parisian fumes apparently did. But if at that time a *Parisienne* had to prepare her husband's opium pipes, it can be assumed that this is a custom in a wealthy family. And we can be assured that several oriental paraphernalia were present in the "opium room", creating an addictive, oriental atmosphere.

Of course, laudanum drinkers or opium (heroin) syringe users like De Quincey, Coleridge, Oscar Wilde and Conan Doyle's Sherlock Holmes gave opium its relative status among the cultural elite in the Anglo-Saxon world as well. Their opium must have been largely imported from Turkey and processed in England into laudanum and heroin. Is that why De Quincey or Wilde so often expressed their anti-orientalism? Romantic exaggerations were everywhere, but there must have been a strong relation between these negative feelings and the rather aggressive and popu-

---

[4] Found on http://bjp.rcpsych.org/cgi/pdf.

lar oriental horror and murder thrillers with sinister Chinese mandarins (Fu-Manchu novels of Sax Rohmer).[5]

The Japanese mostly received better treatment among the Dutch, Americans and English (see ch. 27). This continued even after World War II with highlights like James Bond films (1967, *You only live twice*) or the Hollywood one in which the ideal-typical American hero, Robert Mitchum, even offered a finger to a mafia boss in a Japanese ritual as compensation for American guilt (*The Yakuza*, 1975).

In France, however, smokers like Baudelaire (1821-1867), Rimbaud, le *Club des Haschischins* with its famous writers Hugo and Balzac, nearly all authors from Mallarmé through Cocteau (1889-1963), the Surrealists or Walter Benjamin (1892-1940), all made la France 'douce' from the opium fumes. They all nurtured a rather positive, romantic orientalism. More revealing: laudanum drinking was known, but most of them smoked opium or hashish, a custom which came from the Far East, in this case the French Indochina or the French concession in Shanghai. Probably, as in England, the French opium for the daily use of the common folk, laudanum, originated from the Levant, but this is not well documented.

From Paris, the cultural capital of the Western world, the seduction was irresistible for many who wanted to belong to the 'scene'. Early French films like *Dandy-Pacha* (1908) or *Le rêve d'un fumeur d'opium* (1908) were made; numerous novels like *Les Fumeurs d'Opium* or *Lélie, fumeuse d'opium* (1911) mythologized the drug, while composers like Berlioz composed a 'symphonie fantastique' on the psychedelic adventures of French opium users.[6]

Indeed, the orientalism and exoticism surrounding opium were soon mixed up with many kinds of sexual connotations and practices. Opium dens in, for instance, Montmartre were mostly exotically furnished and expensive meeting points for the cultural elite. France in particular was known to harbor a great number of opium users.[7] Reports at the time claimed that in 1901 Paris had up to 1200 opium-smoking establishments.

---

[5] G. Lee, p. 4 ff..

[6] Many relevant French titles are mentioned in B. Hodgson, p. 87 -101; M. de Kort, p. 120. On the highly interesting website http://jclandry.free.fr many documents from the French opium scene are collected. Many examples refer directly to the French Asian colonies. At the moment I am correcting this text the 'symphony fantastique' is performed in a concert hall of drugs capital Amsterdam (October 2011).

[7] For the following, including the quotation, see www.salon.com/archives/welcome/history2.html.

A cosmopolitan atmosphere of the big city, still undisturbed by rumors of revolt, helped increase interest in the new aphrodisiacs.

Most famous was the *Moulin Rouge* in Montmartre, already decorated in glittering lights in the 1890s. Visitors had to pass through scarlet-colored halls and enter into an aromatic garden with a giant-sized, mock elephant. This was the ultimate opium den where visitors could indulge in their opium-smoking habit. Cabarets and salons like the Cabaret Voltaire (Zürich) or the Bohemian Salons existed in most big cities in Europe and the United States. Those for the poorer representatives of the cultural elite were characterized 'by lack of money ... long hair, loud ranting against the bourgeoisie, unruly sexual behavior and copious consumption of wine, absinth, opium, hashish and other *substances d'abus*'.

The scandals followed on soon afterwards, but they only added to the creation of the nimbus. This seduction is still being exported today and not only by fashion moguls such as Yves Saint-Laurent, who launched his OPIUM perfume recently.[8]

"Opium in Europe" was not only an interest of the "seduction industry" (from copywriters, movie-makers to Freudianists). Arts and literature were important as well. It is not my job to consider the pros and cons of addicted poets or fiction writers: It is up to literary critics or psychoanalysts to decide whether Baudelaire, De Quincey, Poe, etc. became good, better or bad writers thanks to opium or another narcotic.[9]

One thing is clear: these famous writers made narcotics interesting for the elite in Europe and the USA as aphrodisiacs or stimulators of creativity. Addicted scientists or non-fiction writers never received a nimbus as in literature or art: Freud, who experimented with cocaine in this period,

---

[8] A new TV-program on art entertainment in the Netherlands is called "Opium"; a new band is called "Opium", etc.; Jean Cocteau is still mentioned in most opium publications, for instance, K. McMahon, X. Paulès, etc. A specific luxury yacht model built in Marseille is named "Opium"; the "best" aphrodisiac drink "Sex Opium"; MP3 albums by "Opium Jukebox" (Amazon. com) and so on. For the effects on consumers one can consult "Somni Forum", subtitled with 'The continuing adventures of the world's most controversial flower, poppies.org.'.

[9] The poet Georg Trakl (1887-1914) is apparently the first well-known modern poet-addict. The "Opiomaniacs" of the 19th-century smoked the soft opium or took *laudanum* (opium mixed with alcohol; mostly freely available), Trakl started with the heavy opium derivatives heroin and morphine, added later cocaine. It may be true that alcoholics do live a much shorter life, but it seems to be exceptional for a heroin addict to make it to the age of 50. Hayter's conclusions from her interesting literary comparisons of eight famous authors is illuminating: "No clear pattern of opium's influence on creative writing ... has emerged from this survey ... They had nothing in common except that they lived in the same century, were imaginative writers, and took opium' (A. Hayter, p. 331).

is only of interest to a small coterie of adepts. That was not the case with the drugs as such: they became an aim in themselves, of interest later to the pharmaceutical industry, psychologists and even secret services.[10]

The question here is how did this Parisian environment at the end of the 19th-century become "addicted" by opium which could not be harvested from the Champs d'Elysées, while referring to the easy life lived by the gods.

The French Pharmaceutical Scene

Around 1900 the rather new pharmaceutical and chemical industry already worked in close collaboration with medical scientists, apothecaries, state bureaucrats, and so on in a "health complex", which had serious consequences for other corners of society. Famous names like Merck or Bayer industries are mentioned not for their discovery of heroin (1874), but for its exploitation.[11] The French competition and jealousy were fierce.

The most important French industrial region became Rhône–Poulenc.[12] It is part of a new, specific, modern and Western scene developed from the middle of the 19th-century in West Europe, later in the USA: its young European and American history explains how medical products search for markets, patients and diseases with all possible consequences.

---

[10] For the 20th-century development after 1945 in this field, see C. van Campen, who started with the analysis of the French writers and poets like Baudelaire (*Les paradis artificiel*, 1860), Gauthier, the *Club de Hachichin* or the remarkable study of Jean Moreau (1845): *Du hachisch et de l'aliénation mentale, études psychologiques*. The climax of this development was the highly controversial LSD experiment with Dutch Holocaust victims and the CIA's MKULTRA project. See http://www.angelfire.com/ar2/Handleidingen/MKULTRA.html.

[11] What the relationship was between Freud and the notorious opium and heroin factory E. Merck (now one of the largest multinationals in the pharmaceutical industry) is apparently given in an article by A. Hirschmuller titled "E.Merck and cocaine. On Sigmund Freud's cocaine studies and their relation to the Darmstadt industry". See: www.cocaine.org/history/merck.html.

[12] The history of the pharmaceutical industry is of the utmost importance to highlight the backgrounds of the drug problem in Europe, the USA and the world. Rhône-Poulenc is a combination of 19th-century initiatives in the field: the Poulenc apothecaries from Paris with similar entrepreneurs from Lyon. In 1928 they merged, the first of a long series of merges. In 1999 Rhône-Poulenc merged with the German Hoechst AG to form Aventis. This in its turn merged in 2004 with Sanofi, making Sanofi-Aventis at the moment the third largest pharmaceutical industry in the world. It must be clear that in this volume this side of the history cannot be dealt with. E. Kremers, G. Urdang, p. 286-294, 322 ff.

To create patients and diseases in response to the need for multinationals to survive and expand was not understood in the 19th-century, and probably not before 1945.[13] As in other countries at the beginning of that century, it was the individual performance and leadership which prevailed. After the Second World War, however, social and economic institutionalization led to increased centralization and monopolization of markets. A few remarks and details about this development in France will suffice.

The French Enlightenment must have had many effects in its country of origin because French chemists, apothecaries or medical scientists discovered one useful drug and pain-killer after another: in 1804 *morphine* (Séguin and others), in 1809 *nicotine* (Posselt a.o.), in 1819 *caffeine*; *codeine* was directly "isolated" from opium and *atropine* from belladonna (ca. 1832). A related compound was *chloroform* (1831), its use doubled from 1855 to 1875; *ether* trebled in the same period; *chloral*, introduced in 1869, was consumed more than chloroform six years later. The consumption of *morphine* increased from 250 grams in 1855 to ten kilo in twenty years' time. Opium was the most popular among the traditional pain-killers. It continued to be employed in quantities of 150 kilo per year.[14]

Remarkable figures, because—as discussed in ch. 8—the French opium export to England was, for instance, already about 11,000 lbs in 1833. This strongly decreased, but in 1870 there was again a French export of that magnitude. After this year this import exploded, with even several years of about 60,000 pounds.[15]

---

[13] Of course, it is not appropriate to discuss here modern developments in the pharmaceutical (and related chemical) industry, but the present scandals involving these industries are rather alarming: through the well-known international channels one is able to create unnecessary mass vaccinations against rather innocent flues, etc.; forbidden tests of new products are carried out in Third World countries; very expensive HIV medicines are distributed in a monopolized relationship, while very cheap medicines are available; and so on. In the UK the activities and many publications of Charles Medawar and the *Social Audit* organization give very detailed information. Not by accident is the Joseph Rowntree Charitable Trust sponsor. The history of this trust is strongly connected to the anti-opium struggle from the end of the 19th-century. See C. Medawar, B. Freese and J. Rowntree.

[14] Th. Zeldin, vol. 2, p. 784 ff.; P. Boussel, H. Bonnemain, p. 206 ff., E. Kremers, G. Urdang, p. 318 ff. Normally only the German inventors are named, like Gaedeke, Sertürner, Niemann, Losen and many others (M. de Kort, p. 33 ff.), but the French were as important as the English or Americans. They all belonged to an initial phase of a new industrialization which expanded globally from the 1880s onwards.

[15] V. Berridge, G. Edwards, p. 272. Zeldin should have mentioned whether everything was re-exported (except 300 lbs). Probably there is a misunderstanding in how "opium" is

Zeldin is more reliable in finding a connection between 'an enormous increase in drug-taking' in the Second Empire and 'a recourse to the asylums'. Indeed, the number of 'madmen' in asylums increased from about 8,000 (1838) to 88,000 (1900). The French professionalization of medical practitioners resulted not so much in better health (environment) for the common people, as in new and more profitable definitions and institutions. As elsewhere, this professionalization of the medical field was not only the result of a fight for a higher status and remuneration, but also of an extension of the "sphere of influence": the expulsion of the lay healers and the gradual monopolization of the health system.[16] This included a monopoly on the prescription of opiates, cocaine and other poisons.

The asylums were one of the bulwarks in this system: state and medical interests merged here. Mostly old people were transported to them, who could not obtain a place in the quickly overcrowded old people's home in their villages and regions, if they were available at all. According to the medical personnel, old people are only in need of tranquilizers, for which hashish was mostly chosen. The doctor-patient relation in the northern villages is brilliantly described in Flaubert's *Madame Bovary*. I do not remember whether any form of drug use was known in her village: Emily took arsenic and not opium to kill herself.

Cannabis (hashish) was chosen by Jean Moreau of a Parisian hospital in his publication *Du haschish et de l'aliénation mentale* (1845).[17] Moreau could rely on a certain tradition, because during the Napoleonic occupation of Egypt, the intoxicating property of cannabis was discovered. Back in France, authorities were quick to impose heavy penalties on selling, using or trafficking in cannabis. For Moreau, these rules did not apply.

The "doctors" in the villages were not familiar with it, however, and their urban colleagues were probably still afraid of the authorities, because in the urban hospitals alcohol is used excessively:

> ... in 1855-1875 the consumption of alcohol in Paris hospitals rose from 1,270 to 37,578 litres and that of red wine from 17,000 to 163,000 litres-though the number of their patients remained the same.[18]

The "doctors" and their helpers became very thirsty with all those "insane" peoples or the patients instead of restoring them to health. This excessive

---

defined here. Is Z. referring to 150 liter of laudanum? And does this require 11,000 lbs "opium"?

[16] M. de Kort, p. 37, 43.

[17] V. Berridge, G. Edwards, p. 212.

[18] Th. Zeldin, idem, p. 785.

alcohol consumption apparently was the result of the warnings of other scholars who stated that cannabis was the *cause* of insanity.

To understand what happens in France one can depart from two important phenomena: the widespread distribution of drugs for recreational purposes, and the emancipation or "isolation" of a health complex as a monopoly.

The first leads nearly automatically to a consumer, addict and patient orientation. In practice, this is followed by the establishment of a whole gamut of assistance and healer institutions, let alone criminal investigators, drug departments of the police and entertainment industry (see above).

As told, opium and hashish gradually became popular for recreational purposes among the elite already at the beginning of the 19th-century. This development quickened after the 1840s. With the introduction of the hypodermic syringe (ca. 1850), morphine became the painkiller of choice for civilian and military doctors, but also the drug of choice for the bourgeoisie. Twenty years later everybody talked about the *morphinomanie,* morphine addiction. The doctors, who were largely responsible for this, had created new patients by curing the morphine addiction with cocaine and heroin.[19] Is this introduction of stronger and more dangerous drugs done on purpose or simply through ignorance? The latter is difficult to believe, and the former an unbelievable assault on humanity. The only innocent effect was the proliferation of a whole lexicon of addictive *manies.*

The second development is much less spectacular but, in my view, more important because it concerns the origins or roots of the Opium Problem. A new phenomenon is hidden behind what has been discussed so far: the legal power of "people in a white coat" to negate the freedom of individuals and to lock up people for short or long periods without any form of lawsuit, trial or even obligatory consultations. Just the judgment of some medical man with a limited knowledge about the victim and his/her "disease" was enough for this far-reaching execution. Many scandals and accusations of trade with "lunatics" for asylums were unavoidable. However, the new drug scene and the *manies* in addition threatened the whole of *La Douce France* with much more spectacular cases.

As in England, this "white coat" power developed into a monopoly for the whole "professional health complex". To strengthen this position, the

---

[19] H. Padwa, p. 341.

same policy was used as all power groups aspiring to a monopoly, like churches, state bureaucrats or the military: to produce fear in order to advertise oneself as the savior of the nation; once this is acknowledged, the bill must be paid:

> By the 1880s doctors were beginning to condemn these drugs as agents of degeneration, capable of wreaking chaos on both the individual and social bodies if allowed to spread. Both a sign and a catalyst of medical and social decay, drug abuse needed to be stopped before it, like a variety of other degenerative behaviors and conditions, spread and facilitated the physical and moral decline of the nation.[20]

The most positive thing one can say about this is that the doctors who opened Pandora's Box did warn us that it was opened. The practical consequence was that the consequent health complex, facilitating both the perpetrators and their victims' helpers, became strongly economically interested in the continuation and expansion of the "scene": morphine, heroin, cocaine 'broke out of the doctor's office' and took hold as a recreational drug in select Paris salons and brasseries by the late 1880s. Once the first reliable statistics about addiction were available, the situation became clear:

> In the 1920s there was a great increase in it: Paris is said to have had 80,000 cocaine addicts in 1924, but they were not otherwise criminals. The consumption of drugs fell drastically after that (80 kilogrammes of heroin was the official estimate in 1939, 12 kg in 1950) without obvious results [on criminality].[21]

Another consequence was that in France the medical profession never abandoned its most prestigious, old-fashioned, absolute power. There was apparently no need for improvements, authority was enough: the opium preparation belladonna was still prescribed as a cure for colds in the 1960s.[22]

---

[20] H. Padwa, p. 342.

[21] Th. Zeldin, Idem, p. 911.

[22] Certainly not for the health of the French population as Zeldin's analysis shows, in which the French remained far below the health levels in other Western countries. See Th. Zeldin, vol. 2, p. 630-636. In nearly every respect France lagged behind: it was in the 1960s 'that medication was drastically revised and put on a more scientific basis' (Idem, p. 636), but not for belladonna.

Drugs from abroad

The dimensions of the French Opium Problem at the time must have made many authorities quite uneasy. One main source of unease was the troubles between the Treasury and the Colonial Offices. They were worried not only about the growing anti-opium movement in Europe, but much more the growing costs of the colonial administrations, which were urged to become self-sufficient, to keep their opium for themselves and to stop making trouble. A few French examples will suffice.

In 1907/08 a scandal arose when a navy ship, *La Nive*, was involved in a serious accident because its officers were opium addicts. At the same time the Ullmo opium scandal reached the world press.[23]

This naval officer smoked 37 pipes a day! According to 'a well-known French admiral':

> Ullmo certainly smoked opium, but no more than his fellow-officers. Only one remedy is possible in the existing state of affairs. The habit is contracted in Indochina by officers, both old and young, who are assigned to that station. The French government has a monopoly on opium there, and draws from it a rich source of revenue. If the government is willing to renounce its profits in this nefarious trade and suppress it altogether, the victims of it will be bound to disappear, not only in Indochina, but also in France. This is the sole means of rescuing the navy from its present grave menace.[24]

Neither the government in France nor that in its Asian colonies listened to the admiral. The only effect the Ullmo affair had was a decree issued in 1908, which instituted strict controls on the commerce and consumption of opium. It did not became an antisemitic row either, because Ullmo confirmed the accusations. The affair led to the first step France took against recreational drugs.

Five years later, a report by a French journalist about opium consumption in the French Navy in southern seaports triggered a larger scandal (1913). In Toulon, the chief naval port, there were no fewer than 163 opium dens which 'menaced ... the effectiveness of the Navy as a national defense'.[25] The author of these words also wrote for an international forum:

---

[23] See also G. Thibout, p. 144-149 including the scandal story of the naval officer Ullmo, who was spying to get money and was sentenced to life imprisonment. The scandal was compared to the Dreyfus affair (because Ullmo was an 'Israelite') and even with the Mata Hari affair (because in his villa he had to care for a costly prostitute, "la belle Lison").

[24] *The New York Times,* March 1, 1908. See also Idem, October 26, 1907

[25] www. druglibrary.org. An article in *The New York Times*, April 27, 1913, cabled to New York by Mr. Dorcieres, a journalist of *Le Matin*. It stated that the police and civic authori-

that this terrible scourge is actually one of the principal State manufactures in France's greatest colony, Indochina, where it is sold under a State guarantee as freely as tobacco is here and contributes more than one-sixth of the entire revenue of the country ... the annual production of opium in that colony is over 260,000 pounds, bringing an average revenue of $2,102,000. Through smuggling, however, the consumption is at least double that shown by the official figures.

They are not very encouraging messages one year before the outbreak of the First World War. They would become worse. In the war, suspicions and accusations around drugs reproduced the war-psychosis clearly. The French deputy, Charles Bernard, declared in 1916:

It seems that the Germans can't beat us with their fire or their asphyxiating gas, so now ... they're using cocaine and morphine to wear us down.[26]

Also after the war there was no evidence for such a Teutonic plot. There was a simple reason for this. The majority of the drugs in French criminal hands came from colonies in North Africa and Indochina. They reached France through neutral Switzerland or England. Still, the anti-German suspicion about the drug assault on France was wide spread with exclamations as:

Given that German pharmaceutical companies like Merck and Bayer were among Europe's leading producers of these substances, why would the Germans not use their pharmacological capacities to wage a more covert form of "chemical warfare"? ... 'Let's not forget that factories on the other side of the Rhine sent us ... their morphine and cocaine' ... 'the extermination of the French race by all means is the ultimate goal of the German plan' ... 'The spread of addiction since the start of hostilities is both disturbing and mysterious ... if we think about it, it's easy to see that Germany is behind this.[27]

The most remarkable thing is that this kind of Germanophobic and nationalistic drug discourses remained intact after the war. As late as 1922 they could be found in French ministerial messages. However, after the war it was revealed that the German chemical firms BASF, Bayer and Hoechst developed poison gas to be used deliberately for the first time. A researcher and fanatic propagandist of this gas was the Jewish chemist Fritz Haber, who came in uniform to test his weapon himself in the

---

ties can do nothing: 'Under the present laws only dealing in opium is a penal offense. To smoke it, to induce others to smoke privately or for money or to possess a large stock of the drug is perfectly legal.'

[26] Quoted in H. Padwa, p. 340.
[27] Idem, p. 347, 348.

trenches and instructed his generals on how to use it profitably. After World War II Haber certainly would have been hanged as a war criminal.[28]

From a French point of view, therefore, such an evil as opium and the many other drugs could only have come from abroad, from "The East", whether Germany or the Far East, easily substituting the French colonists for "racially degenerated Chinese".

---

[28] Illustrative enough his wife (1914) and son (1946) both committed suicide thanks to his behavior. As a reaction British and French chemists started to develop the same chemical weapons. For Nobel prize winner Haber (1868-1934) see D. Kaufmann (ed.), passim. Remarkably enough one can still find rather perverse defenders of Haber (also inventor of Zyklon B but, of course, not responsible for its use in Auschwitz, etc.) even in present-day Israel, which has still several "Fritz Haber" institutions! Institutions named after Haber's colleague, the Nobel prize winner Debye, were renamed after it was recently discovered how he had cooperated with the Nazis to a less serious degree than Haber instructed the military in WW-1.

CHAPTER TWENTY-THREE

THE FRENCH COLONIAL SCENE IN SOUTHEAST ASIA

> Les Français sont incapables de créer des colonies
> prospères.
>
> Quoted from critical Frenchmen
> by J. Wiselius (1878), p. 277

At the end of the 19th-century, the New Imperialists, USA and Japan, requested their share, and in Europe the recently formed German Empire aspired to have a colonial branch as well, while the Russian Empire tried to expand in the Far East. In the end the British Empire had to pay the largest price, the French a lesser one, but it played the game less well. The USA claimed the Philippines and, in fact, the whole of Central and South America as their hunting grounds; Japan claimed large parts of coastal China including Korea and Formosa; the European «scramble for Africa» divided up this continent, but was too expensive, came too late and did not provide a satisfying basis for the usual exploitation. The legitimation for these conquests was absent. The consequences of all this was a permanent threat of war in the world culminating in the First World War, exhausting all the classical European imperialists.[1]

Indeed, world imperialism at the end of the 19th-century also determined the fate of the exploitation of the colonies by means of opium. The new fundamental creed was: private profits had to be transformed into European state bureaucratic monopoly profits. The old opium import monopolies of most colonial governments (except for the English in India) combined with a private farming system were replaced by a "regie-method". This made the state monopoly position complete. The only free trade in opium was called smuggling. This was paralleled by the warring states which now took the lead over private capital; that is to say, only

---

[1] S. Halperin, p. 7, thirteen large wars were fought between and by colonial powers from 1870-1912 just in East Asia, as many as in the previous 70 years. I think that several French and Dutch conflicts in Southeast Asia are not considered. Still, they cannot alter the impression of the incredible aggressiveness of the Western powers also in this part of the world.

private monopoly capital like the NHM in the Dutch East Indies could accommodate to this new situation.

This state had an image formed of European political thoughts, revived from the bourgeois onslaught on 'feudal' (aristocratic, monarchical and religious) aspirations and claims. The playground for these new aspirations became the colonies: the military repression and exploitation increased there tremendously.[2]

However, all this led to a very bloody flight and to a miserable end for the European powers. Within half a century the indigenous contra-powers like China, India or Indonesia were mobilized to such a degree that they could not be destroyed, and the "whites" had to flee. A few years later, around 1945, the game was in fact over.

Some could not believe or accept it, like the French and the Dutch. The total destruction of their colonial empires was necessary to teach them the new realities. In particular, the French were clearly the most stubborn colonizers of all. It took two long and devastating wars and the help of the USA before both definitely lost their position not only in Asia, but in the world at large. From triumphant winners in a long 19th-century, they transformed into "eternal losers" doped by what they first had sown in the colonies: the snake had bitten its own tail hard.

The French drug scene with its connections deep into the French navy reproduces most features of this decline-and-fall process: the Asian countries as resources for the foreign colonial government, which is the "source" of the military users and addicts, who brought "it" back to the homeland; there, the rich expatriates could be found in *Le Moulin Rouge*; the homeland in which the problem was settled through the opium den infrastructure and its deliverers; a new, politically compromised and socially criminal Western drug scene could develop in *La Douce France*; the colony itself stumbled into its last colonial drama performed in the mud of Dien Bien Phu (1954).

Because of its spectacular character and its most serious consequences for the world at large, a rich literature exists on this part of the opium history. First and foremost, there are the "bibles" of modern drug historiography, Alfred McCoy's *The politics of Heroin in Southeast Asia* or Carl Trocki's study about the Singapore scene, *Opium and Empire*.[3] I have to confine

---

[2] For this transformation see H. Derks (2008).
[3] McCoy's study is now fully available on-line: see www.drugtext.org/library/books/McCoy/default.htm.

myself here to adding newer data here and there to try to give a sketch of the "French scene" in Southeast Asia, in Indochina and its wider context.

The Beginning of a Disaster

In 1800 the British and the French had already nearly two centuries of lethal Asian conflicts and mutual wars behind them. They were largely located in and around the Indian subcontinent. After they had recovered from the devastating Napoleonic European wars, they both started to move eastwards, gradually infiltrating Indochina and China. Not only in a military sense, but also in a cultural-religious way by sending missionaries who preached a strange, militant belief and sometimes the use of opium. In part 2 this kind of British (and American) assault on China was given globally.

On their way to the Chinese opium-Walhalla, the EIC's Bengal opium transports, those of the private "country traders" and many other transports of Arabs or Chinese had to pass the Straits. Some bridgeheads in Arakan (the later Burma) and coastal settlements were quickly constructed by the British. They, furthermore, had to deliver opium to their main client in the East Indies.

To ease this venture, Raffles occupied Singapore, which soon became the main naval and merchant base in Southeast Asia. After Napoleon's defeat, he could occupy the Dutch "possessions" in the East Indies as well. It could be used to negotiate with the Dutch, making them more or less loyal allies once the East Indies were returned to the Dutch with their new conquering plans.

For the French, from their point of view, there was not much territory left in Indochina. As losers of the large European wars, they were also much slower to take their share of this Indochina cake, although they started early enough. This was a remarkable and symptomatic beginning, and not only in hindsight.[4]

Here they had already relations with local rulers, while French missionaries spread the Catholic *civilization française* in the usual arrogant and aggressive way. It is one of the rare examples of Western missionaries arriving before the military occupation.

---

[4] For the following see D. Hall, p. 461 ff., 608 ff.; N. Tarling in: Idem (ed.), vol. 2-1, p. 30-48. For the French in Laos I used M. Stuart-Fox.

The military now could come, for example, in Vietnam to "protect" the Paris Foreign Missions Society. The Vietnamese elite saw these Catholic priests, obviously, as a cultural and political threat. King Minh-Mang, who succeeded to the throne in 1820, hated these 'barbarians from the West'. Also, a most influential faction in the dynastic system, the courtesans, detested the priests as well because they preached monogamy.

Even after three French attempts, Minh-Mang remained unwilling to conclude a commercial treaty or even to receive a letter from the French king. He broke off all official relations with France. As a strict Confucian and admirer of the Chinese culture, he even started to persecute Christianity as had happened in an earlier period as well. The First Opium War of the British against China changed his mind, but he died soon thereafter, and his successor revived the policy of persecution with even greater vigour.

This Opium War was also a reason for France to change its Southeast Asian policies. Now it became as brutal as the British and sent a warship to Hué, which was coincidentally called the *Héroine* (1843). Next, they looked for some *modus vivendi* with the English and even battled in the Second Opium War alongside their greatest enemy. In this way, opium brought military peace and a peaceful competition between the Dutch, British and French only. Even with the first Western power in East Asia, Spain, the British made peace because they needed the Spanish silver to buy the Chinese products.[5] Only the Americans had difficulties in participating in this Western concert (see ch. 28).

However, like the Dutch, the French were also left alone in their military adventures in Southeast Asia: they seized Saigon (Cochinchina) in 1862; a year later a protectorate over Cambodia was established, which gave them control of the lower Mekong. The expectation was that this river should bring the French right into the south of China, Yunnan. This was not confirmed by expeditions to the sources of the Mekong, and the interest shifted to the Red River. Hanoi was seized in 1873, Lao territory east of the Mekong followed, and ca. 1885 the whole of Vietnam including Tonkin was in their hands. The rest of Laos west of the Mekong and the western provinces of Cambodia surrendered to the French in the first years of the 20th-century. Their main imperial challenge remained the largest country, Siam (the later Thailand). To achieve its goal, France used

---

[5] For Anglo-Spanish projects at the time see N. Tarling in: Idem (ed.), vol. 2-1, p. 21 ff.

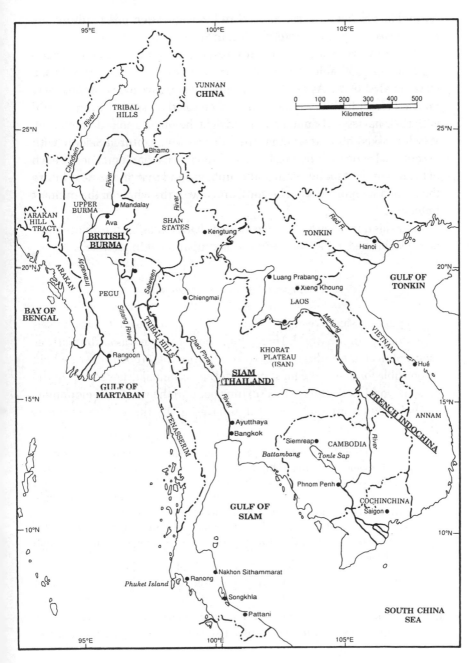

Map 11. Mainland Southeast Asia, 1880-1930

Source: N. Tarling, vol. 2-1, p. 78.

old and flimsy Vietnamese claims to an Indochinese empire to ultimately create a *casus belli* for an intervention in Siam.

These military expeditions did not result in a reasonable basis for making colonies profitable from a Western point of view. Jacob Wiselius, a clever analyst of the Asian Western imperialism, gave a devastating view on the French inability to colonize wherever they landed in the world with their navies and military. In hindsight, he made a sound prediction. Wiselius asked himself whether the admiral who captured Saigon 'with exceptional good luck' in 1862 had the faintest idea that it meant a breach of peace among Annam, Siam and Cambodia and that 'in the near future the French weapons should be confronted with the whole of the militant Indochina'.[6]

After this quick overview we have to go back to basics: the opium business, established to pay for the French occupation of Indochina.

The French Opium Performance

Among the classical Western colonialists the French were the last to settle in this part of the world. Their opium performance was as dramatic as their political and military one. In our history the French must be held responsible for one of the most powerful and criminal drugs scenes in the present world. Let's start with a turning point in the whole development.

Their important and peaceful innovation in the opium scene is described as follows:

> Of major importance were the gradual restriction and then rapid termination of revenue farming, especially the lucrative opium farms ... In Indochina between 1897 and 1904, the French established state monopolies on the sale of opium, alcohol and salt; this confirmed and at the same time centralized earlier and generally unsuccessful local French initiatives to abolish revenue farming, and greatly increased the weight of these consumption taxes so that they formed the major revenue item for the French colonial state.[7]

This transformation from revenue farming to centralized government monopoly in 1882, became the model for all colonial powers. The "French general change" took place around 1900 everywhere in Southeast Asia. The legitimation was similar among all Europeans: we have to reorganize

---

[6] J. Wiselius (1878), p. 285.
[7] The contribution of Robert Elson to N.Tarling in: Idem (ed.), vol. 2-1, p. 153.

(= in this case: centralize) the whole opium production and distribution to minimize opium consumption as a concession to the many criticisms at home against the governments's opium business. And the factual motives everywhere for this transformation were, first and foremost, that the bureaucrats of the colonial state wanted the private profits of the mostly Chinese opium farmers for themselves. This was consequently accompanied by a general racism directed, this time, against the Chinese.

The motherlands ("metropolis"), furthermore, urged the colonies to look after themselves, but it also asked for an increased exploitation in order to pay for its own military expenses, which were incurred in the Far East as well. It this contradictory struggle of interests, the colonial bureaucrats normally won. Whatever was claimed about the dangers of opium, the immorality of this business, and so on, no influential officials with any authority cared much about the opium consumers, nor about the opinions in the motherlands. The best proof of this was the remarkable jump opium consumption made when the *Opiumregies* were installed.

Revenue Farming[8]

In the 19th-century all Western colonies in Asia (as well as the independent kingdom of Siam) regulated their opium, as their single most important source of revenue, through a farm system:

> The entire colonial enterprise in Southeast Asia was financed by revenue farms. Every colony, every state farmed out the bulk of its revenues to Chinese tax farmers. ... We cannot understand the nature of European colonialism in Southeast Asia without acknowledging the role of opium.[9]

States, colonies or state-private institutions like the VOC or EIC used the means of the highly lucrative revenue farming as explained in ch. 19. The alternative was a separate, substantial and expensive tax organization. In the case of the foreign occupiers, an additional disadvantage of this alternative was the provocative measures of the unpopular tax collectors among an indigenous population. Farms did not bear too close an examination. The European authorities, furthermore, could easily blame the Chinese for spreading and extending the opium vice against the many complaints from indigenous and later Western sides.

---

[8] For the following see the contributions of Carl Trocki and Robert Elson in: N. Tarling (ed.), vol. 2-1, p. 85 ff., 147 ff. and in particular several contributions to J. Butcher, H. Dick (ed.). See also C. Trocki (2006), p. 28 ff.

[9] C. Trocki (2006), p. 28.

Revenues were drawn from many products and regulations, but every-where the opium revenues were the most profitable ones for the states or colonies. The method used involved taxing exports of tin or rice, head tax on Chinese. In the Straits Settlements there were farms for alcohol, gambling, betel-nut, pork, pawnbroking and even markets.[10]

A well-known example: the opium and spirit farms for Singapore Island were the largest and most lucrative in British Malaya.[11] They were led by the wealthiest and most powerful Chinese businessmen and regularly constituted between 40 and 60% of the entire state revenue. This was possible because in Singapore much more than elsewhere there was a commitment to free trade and a lack of taxable exports (see below).

The French understood the strategic importance of revenue farms as well. They started on a small scale collecting the money in Cochinchina. This was extended later to Cambodia and Annam-Tonkin but failed. Crawfurd wrote in 1820:

> The smallness of their numbers does not admit of the employment of instruments either sufficiently cheap, or sufficiently expert. They are but unwilling for and unequal to the task of bestowing the necessary attention to the minute details of a laborious business.[12]

They were largely unable to control their subordinates, who kept most of what they collected for themselves.

Crawfurd's opinion is that of the colonial administrator, of the foreign occupier, who ultimately had to rely (to his regret) on foreign help to collect money. The fact that they as European powers had to rely on Chinese help to get the "fruits of their repression" proved how weak their power was. It was the acknowledgment of this fundamental weakness which underlay the so-called indirect rule system of the English or the Dutch in the VOC period.

The institute of revenue farming was also well known in Europe. The reason for using these collectors was because the rulers who installed the people endowed with these "functions" trusted them. In Europe very often Jews were used as tax collectors, which realistically explained their unpopularity and their large capital sums. In this way a Jewish elite formed a tiny minority heavily dependent on the rulers who could also easily dismiss or eliminate them without much protest. Not for anti-

---

[10] A. Foster (2000), p. 255.

[11] C. Trocki (1990), p. 96 ff. offers an overview of the opium farm annual rent from 1820-1882 with astonishing figures.

[12] Quoted by J. Butcher, in: J. Butcher, H. Dick (ed.), p. 22.

semitic, probably xenophobic reasons, but mainly due to jealousy of their accumulated wealth gained from the very unpopular dirty work for the "boss".[13]

In Asia there were in fact not enough Jews available to do this kind of work. They had other things to do like the Sassoons: opium smuggling, banking, shipping between India and China. In Southeast Asia, however, there was a tiny Chinese elite available to do this job.

It is, in my view, not so much that 'European or Southeast Asian [political leaders] relied on revenue farming mainly because they could gain *more* income', as Butcher thinks, but to receive a *regular* income through taxing people instead of the normal colonial robbery by foreigners.[14] Taxing is, furthermore, a prerogative of an accepted government. Like all colonizers, the French acted as if this was the case, but foreign colonial regimes were only feared and hated. The natives only collaborated within a socially or economically artificial framework.

How artificial it was becomes apparent from the fallacies French occupiers used to defend their distribution of the opium everybody knew to be pernicious. Even in this early phase of their Southeast Asian activities, complaints were made several times that they poisoned the indigenous people with their opium. The important official, Dussutour, replied:

> A government which is ahead of the European civilization and which has a true providential mission in these countries cannot be itself the treacherous executioner (*le bourreau empoisonné*) of these peoples ... [it] is able to sell this task to others ... and close their eyes waiting for the period in which one could say: "it is enough" and put this announcement on all the borders of Cochinchina ...[15]

Along with this most cynical form of hypocrisy, there were also childish reactions to the complaints, claiming that distribution could not be stopped abruptly because of the health hazards like withdrawal symptoms. This moment occurred anyway in the next century when the French had to leave after the disaster of 1954. Others pointed to the high price of the opium and concluded that opium was only fit for the rich people of Amman and the Chinese. As elsewhere, the argument was also heard that only an overdose was bad, and the misery which followed was sketched in colorful details: but ... you had to be stupid to take an overdose.

---

[13] H. Derks (2004), p. 160 ff.
[14] J. Butcher in: J. Butcher, H. Dick (ed.), p. 23 (my italics. H.D.).
[15] Quoted by C. Descours-Gatin, p. 39.

The journal *Le Courrier de Saigon* (10th of March 1864), official publication of the French administration, was also quite original when writing about the current annual budget: the morality of the French administration was proved beyond doubt since from the total of 3,012,000 French francs, 10% was spent to propagate the Christian faith and education among those poor opium addicts.

Despite these "arguments", there was almost no French supervision of the revenue farms, which were established around 1862. Therefore, the available data are not reliable, while the Chinese farmers' testimonies in the French part of their bookkeeping are described as outright falsification.[16] Later Groeneveldt wrote how also the French bureaucrats were fraudulent.[17]

For about two decades the French were satisfied with their opium income. This was derived from several sources: from the *tjandoe* which was sold for about $1.8 per thail; next, from the petals of the poppy flowers, called *écorces*. It had nearly no opium residue and was chewed by the poor people as a kind of *sirih*. Still in 1880 and 1881 a quantity of it of 176,683 and 104,346 thails was sold for $50,000 and $30,000, respectively.

One bought, furthermore, the dross from the pipes (*tai amfioen*) which was mixed with the *tjandoe*. The licenses to open an opium den produced another income of about $20,000 a year. Finally, opium was exported to neighboring countries, but Groeneveldt could not discover how much.

In 1862 the revenue of the French colonial state was $61,334, which increased four years later to $210,182 and further to $465,000 in 1873. For the following years Groeneveldt summarized his findings in the next table.

This opium income in this period was always about 20% of the export earnings of rice, the main source of income. In 1874 an opium factory (*bouillerie*) had already been established in Cholon near Saigon.

However, Wiselius reproduces in his analysis of the French budgets in Cochinchina, etc. the 1877 budget of Cochinchina in full detail. The landrent brought in 3.5 million French francs (25% of the budget income) and as second main source was mentioned the 3.1 million francs (22%) from the opium revenue farms.[18] Why his contemporary, Groeneveldt,

---

[16] W. Groeneveldt, p. 26 ff. It is a pity that Descours-Gatin did not know this detailed and reliable source about the opium economy and management in Cochinchina, Tonkin, Cambodia or Amman in the years to 1890.

[17] Idem, p. 30.

[18] J. Wiselius (1878), p. 74. There are as well 1.5 million francs in revenues from other farmings as there are arak, fisheries, birds' nests or the slaughtering of animals.

Table 25. Opium sold to and Income from Revenue Farms in Cochinchina, 1874-1881[19]

Year	Opium sold in thails	Gross income from opium farms	
		in $-piaster	in French francs
1874	429 320	972 438	5 348 409
1875	486 953	949 470	5 222 085
1876	601 975	1 169 772	6 433 746
1877	699 647	1 337 490	7 356 195
1878	851 080	1 717 603	9 446 817
1879	837 906	1 603 531	8 819 421
1880	763 605	1 472 093	8 096 512
1881	710 875	1 332 185	7 327 018

came to a substantially different result only a few years later is not known: some difference between gross and net seems to be much too high; probably, it is a matter of fraudulent bureaucrats, about which he complained.[20]

Wiselius, a strong supporter of Western colonization, was rather critical about several French thoughts and practices experienced during his stay and travels in the colonies.[21] First, he did not agree with the typical French direct rule through which all inhabitants are administratively transformed into 'Asian Frenchmen' with all the advantages of *liberté, égalité et fraternité,* of which they did not understand a syllable.

It would have been better, according to Wiselius, if the indigenous people were 'slowly prepared for freedom'! He displayed the most ideal-typical expression of the oikoidal principle when he proposes that, if a government of a state is formed in accordance with a people's need, one has to look at the organization of its households. In addition, he criticizes the enormous quantity of rules, regulations and standing orders issued: the indigenous people did not understand the need for this and did everything they could to negate them. He continues with:

> It is not so much that we perceive it as a mistake of the state to subordinate the passions of the people to the treasury, but it is utterly wrong if the rules of the state do have a paradoxical character ... gambling is prohibited except on New Year's Day in Annam, and the sale of opium is forbidden as well. A few years ago—or probably still today—in Siam opium smokers had to have a Chinese tail and to pay six dollars a year for it. Whoever did not accept this was killed. The French government in Cochinchina, however, makes it easy for everybody to smoke opium for the annual price of 3.25

---

[19] Idem, p. 27. The $ = piaster = 5.5 French francs.
[20] C. Descours-Gatin, p. 27 ff. does not allow a solution in this matter.
[21] J. Wiselius (1878), p. 108 ff.

million francs, and through the establishment of numerous opium dens, it brings the habit even into the village households ... (the only effect of it is) ... that the savings of the indigenous people are spent on opium ... so that he has to build his hut even more primitively than his Javanese colleagues or his hut becomes more humid and unhealthy ...[22]

Those were the methods to *force* the Chinese to smoke opium.

The Opiumregie

The French invented this tradition, including its ambiguous background. The Dutch soon followed it in the East Indies, as was described in the previous part. Whatever the motives of the colonizers, an important aspect in all motherlands was that the colonies had to pay for themselves, and thus their exploitation had to be stepped up. This had to be realized in addition to the money, which had to be transmitted in standard form to the metropolis.

This also explains why the opium revenues strongly increased instead of diminishing through the *Opiumregie*, the military involvement of most colonial powers increased at the end of the 19th-century again, and an industrialization of the opium production was realized in many new opium factories. It is the period in which the euphemism "pacification" was used everywhere: in fact this word covered one of the most bloody periods in colonial history.[23]

The *International Opium Commission* (Shanghai, 1909) reported the following data in its typical way, as if all countries had fabulous statistical offices:

> In 1906 ... opium provided 16.25% of the revenue in French Indochina, 29.02% in Hong Kong, 53.3% in the Straits Settlements, 10.8% in the Federated Malay States, 14.91% in the Netherlands East Indies, 14.3% in Formosa, 25.7% in Macao ..., and 15.55% in Siam. Burma, as a province of the Indian Empire, did not report separate figures.[24]

Still, they are impressive enough, in particular by suggesting how widespread opium use was in all those countries. The farmers had to pay more money in order to win the franchise, and they were eager to create as many consumers as possible, preferably addicts. The still well-known tricks among drug dealers were also used by them: selling cheaply or

---

[22] Idem, p. 109.

[23] See for the detailed overviews S. Halperin, p. 136 ff, appendices 2 and 3, p. 299-445; H. Derks (ed. 1989), passim.

[24] A. Foster (2000), p. 256.

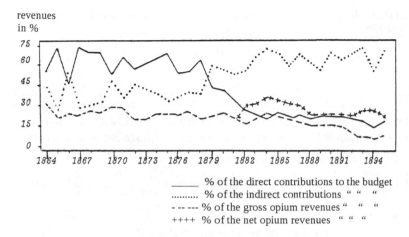

revenues
in %

_____ % of the direct contributions to the budget
.... % of the indirect contributions "   "   "
- -- --- % of the gross opium revenues "   "   "
++++ % of the net opium revenues   "   "   "

Figure 8. Percentage Gross and Net Opium Revenue in the French Colonial Budget of Cochinchina, 1864-1895.

Source: C. Descours-Gatin, p. 100, based on *Budgets et comptes administratifs de Cochinchine, 1864-1895.*

giving away opium to lure people into addiction. Critics in the West were also impressed by the figures quoted, knowing that without these revenues the colonies were difficult to finance, including the projects in the framework of the "mission civilisatrice". Reform of the farm system was, therefore, necessary, but not discontinuation.

There came, however, an end to this farming system, not so much out of compassion for the victims or international criticism, but for greed: it was decided that it would be better to collect the profits the farmers made.[25] The colonial decision-makers had to finance the increasing military, administrative and luxury costs of the foreign settlers and their expatriates, i.e. their personal wealth: from the end of the 19th-century, one costly building after another arose everywhere for Western hotels, banks or government palaces; the whites built themselves large villa quarters with excessive gardens on the best spots.

The French were the first to transform the farm system into a centralized *Opiumregie* in 1882. That was a profitable move as the following table demonstrates.

---

[25] C. Descours-Gatin. p. 90 ff.

Table 26. Rentability of the *Opiumregie* compared to the Farm-system in Cochinchina, 1882-1885 (in piaster)[26]

Year	Gross income Opiumregie	Total cost	Stock	Net income Opiumregie	Advantage compared with farm-system of 790 684 piaster
1882	1 355 657	605 674	+ 12 034	734 949	- 52 705
1883	1 627 736	622 315	+ 28 719	976 701	+ 186 047
1884	2 105 704	780 234	- 16 730	1 342 200	+ 551 546
1885	1 868 222	730 375	+ 19 508	1 118 338	+ 327 684

Table 27. Costs and Revenue of French Opiumregie in Cochinchina, 1882-1898 (x 1000 piaster*)[27]

Year	Gross Income	Costs					Profits	
		Opium buying	Production in %	Personnel in %	Building etc. in %	Total costs		in % of gross income
1882	1 356	328	6	27	13	605	751	55
1884	2 106	537	8	19	4	780	1 326	63
1886	2 015	553	8	22	4	836	1 179	59
1888	1 855	412	10	28	4	704	1 151	62
1890	1 653	344	8	34	2	606	1 046	63
1892	1 815	814	8	19	2	1 157	658	36
1894	2 686	1 524	5	19	3	2 098	588	22
1896	2 981	1 218	4	28	2	1 869	1 112	37
1898	4 092	1 003	6	32	6	1 792	2 300	56
Total 1882-1898	*37 915*	*12 420*	*7*	*26*	*4*	*19 165*	*18 750*	*50*
–	–	---	---	–	---	–	---	–
1919	17 981	---	–	–	–	5 133	12 848	71
1920	13 321	---	–	---	–	2 947	10 374	78
1921	15 099	---	–	–	–	4 717	10 382	69
1922	17 862	---	–	–	---	6 190	11 672	65
1923	18 332	–	–	–	–	6 730	11 602	63
1924	14 912	–	–	–	–	6 429	8 483	57

* The Southeast Asian piaster refers to the Mexican dollar. Therefore, the indication is often with a $ sign. One piaster is in this period valued at 5.55 French francs; until 1913 this is nearly equal to 1 US$.

[26] Idem, p. 110.

[27] C. Descours-Gatin, p. 108; the figures for the years 1919-1924 are from T. Tong Joe, p. 92. The latter only gave gross and net income. For additional data on this period see Appendix 5.

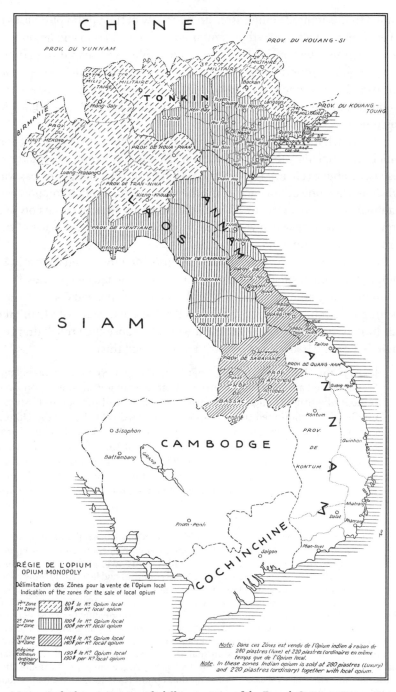

Map 12. Indochinese Zones with different prices of the French Opiumregie, ca. 1930

Source: Commission d'Enquête sur le Contrôle de l'Opium. League of Nations. In the East Indies the differences concern the bureaucratic measures, here they are related to prices.

Added to this limited comparison, an overview of the opium purchases is given. From 1862 to 1882 they remained between 20,000 and 40,000 kg, but from 1882 they immediately doubled, tripled and soared sometimes to 170,000 kg around 1900. Without any doubt: the *Opiumregie* was big business for the French compared with the farming system. Moreover, the quantities of opium started to flood Cochinchina in their search for new customers.

The French introduced the *Opiumregie* in Indochina in the early 1880s, which was copied by the Dutch in "their" East Indies twenty years later as discussed above (ch. 19). The centralization of all parts of the process was finished when one opium factory for the whole of the French colonies was established in Saigon (1900). This modern factory was an extension of a previous plant, one which was operational already in the last years of the farm period (see Appendix 5).

In 1929 the opium revenue in French Indochina increased to nearly $8 million for a much smaller quantity than earlier, i.e. 140,000 pounds.[28]

Immediately after the Second World War, the US pushed France to end its drug trafficking. In 1946 it looked as if the French were willing to take this hint. It took another five years, however, because the French dragged their feet on the issue. What followed is described thus:

> In 1951 the Opium Purchasing Board ceased operations. Two years later France signed a United Nation protocol agreeing to end all state-sponsored trade in the drug. Though France was officially out of the opium business, unofficially it continued to trade in the drug. Two years before the Opium Purchasing Board officially closed its doors, the French Expeditionary Corps began buying opium from hill tribes throughout Indochina ... For a time (between 1949 and 1951) the Expeditionary Corps purchased only a fraction of the opium harvested by the Hmong. But the trade picked up substantially in 1951, when France's intelligence community took over the

---

[28] *Encyclopaedie,* 1934 edition, p. 1258. T.Addens, p. 26 reproduces all sorts of League of Nations figures for the 1930s, but does not mention any production figures for French Indochina and the Dutch East Indies, where the cultivation and production of raw opium were largely confined to respectively Laos, the Meos countries and Java. He acknowledges that his figures for China are 'extremely inaccurate' and 'without doubt erroneous' (p. 28); the largest production of raw opium comes from India, Iran and other countries in 'Asia Minor' (mainly Turkey). T. Addens's doctoral dissertation is probably the most detailed exposé of the ecology, production, consumption and trade of raw and processed opium before 1940 (mainly the 1930s). About the health effects of smoking or eating prepared opium Addens supports Lyall's conclusion 'that a license to smoke opium is in truth a warrant authorizing a man to cut off a third of his life' (p. 83). At the same time he doubts this conclusion and also makes a case of proving that opium leads to less criminality than alcohol. This judgment must be based on a very narrow definition of criminality.

operation and greatly expanded purchases of Hmong opium. The motive was not only to make money, but to deny the opium to the communists.[29]

Indeed, the French High Command financed its war against Ho Chi Minh's *Viet Minh* also through an extensive opium business. Thanks to this, the Hmong tribe, which delivered the stuff, became directly of strategic importance with all the consequences for its own later development (see below).

The French Concession in Shanghai

Thanks to their military cooperation with the English enemy in the Second Opium War, the French received a large part of the International Settlement in Shanghai in return. The growth of this city was fabulous after World War I. Between 1910 and 1930 the population almost tripled to three million.[30] One-third of them lived in the International Settlement (nearly one million Chinese and 36,471 foreigners). In the French Concession (FC) there were 434,885 Chinese and 12,335 foreigners.

In particular, the FC was well-known for its exclusive and elaborate entertainment business which was mixed up with the narcotic scene in many ways. This life exploded after World War I. Overnight Shanghai became a cabaret town, a city of expensive nightclubs, brothels and the like. In 1915 in the International Settlement, there were officially about ten thousand prostitutes of all classes and nationalities with American and Russian ladies "at the top". Five years later the municipal authorities estimated this figure at 70,000 in the foreign concessions only. In the FC alone, there were 40,000 prostitutes.

Nearly all Chinese of any political creed believed that the enormous narcotic, gambling and prostitution industries of Shanghai

> depended upon the protection of the consular system of extraterritoriality set up under the "unequal treaties" of the nineteenth-century ... even the most jaded urbanite had to be dismayed by the underworld's more violent manifestations in the form of kidnapping, robbery, and homicide committed by criminals who based themselves in the French Concession or International Settlement.[31]

---

[29] K. Quincy, p. 85.
[30] For the following see F. Wakeman, p. 9 ff.
[31] Idem, p. 13 also for the following quotations.

Observers stated that if anything socially unsound was discovered in the International Settlement 'it is immediately removed to the French Concession, where it comfortably settle down.' The FC became known as 'the dirtiest spot in the Orient'. Indeed, it had the largest opium dens, the biggest brothels, the fanciest casino's and the most brazen prostitutes and in the FC the police was 'doing nothing to stop this immoral traffic in contrast to other parts of the International Settlement'. The reason for this typical character of the FC is indicated by Chinese contemporaries as the consequence of the French laxity towards all their colonies: '... let the "natives" go to degradation and demoralization; their fate is no concern of the French nation.'

The corruption in the FC was endemic, also among French officials. Du Yuesheng, boss of the Green Gang, not only the main drugs-criminal that time in Shanghai but creator of one of the world's largest illicit cartels, was always intimately connected with "high politics" (see mainly ch. 31):

> [He] ... was holding a series of conferences with the French authorities over gambling and opium ... had come to dominate the gambling and narcotics rackets in the French Concession under the protection of Chief Etienne Fiori and Consul General Koechlin ... the Green Gang boss had gotten the help of certain Cantonese investors and opened four gambling houses in the French Concession. ... Each gambling house quietly paid a daily protection bribe of $2,500, which was discretely passed on to the highest authorities by Du Yuesheng himself.[32]

Du became a real Godfather. He was frequently requested by the rich of the FC to settle disputes arising over the division of inherited property, divorce and other personal problems; this gave him more reasons to enrich himself. More importantly, he was also the mediator in labor conflicts. This provided Du with the strike weapon in several labor unions of the FC.

"Paris" became embarrassed now the entire FC seemed to have been turned over to Chinese gangsters.[33] From the French colonial government in Hanoi came the first complaints; press voices in the FC followed, and the FC police authorities answered first with "rounding up the usual suspects". That was not the end of this story: hostilities with Japan started in January 1932. A straightforward French admiral declared martial law in Shanghai and immediately prohibited gambling and drugs.

---

[32] Idem, p. 201.
[33] Idem, p. 202 ff.

Du Yuesheng mobilized a thousand armed gangsters with tricolored armbands supplied by the French police, while rallying in support of the French Consul General Koechlin. The French navy cleared the streets in the FC of those dubious supporters of the French police: Du Yuesheng, Koechlin and Fiori had to resign.

The revenge of the first did not take long. A month later during a luncheon organized by Du, five high French officials were poisoned, of whom four died, including Koechlin. Fiori survived, though extremely ill, and left the FC to spend the rest of his lucrative opium life in a villa at Cagnes-sur-Mer. Large numbers of corrupt policemen in the FC were dismissed and replaced by disciplined people. The drug-related crimes now soared sky-high: they had increased in 1933 to six thousand, a year later the rate of eleven thousand was reached.

Probably because the poisoning "could not be proved", the new French leadership of the FC tried to negotiate with the Godfather: they were bribed or threatened with murder. Only one possibility to get rid of him remained: to provide him with attractive facilities outside the FC. Thus, negotiations were started with the Chinese municipality about what could be offered to Du.

> There were a number of small factories—often only a single room just large enough to contain a laboratory—scattered around the French Concession where crude morphine manufactured in eastern Sichuan was refined into morphia and heroin by Chinese, Japanese, German and Russian chemists. If the Nationalist authorities, who had been trying once again in 1931 to establish a legal opium monopoly, could be persuaded to come to an agreement with Du Yuesheng, then these refineries might be relocated outside the French Concession in Greater Shanghai.[34]

So, the new French officials also played the game with the Godfather in exchange for Du's ability to prevent a strike of the French Tramway Union. How the Chiang Kai-shek part of the opium story developed will be dealt with in ch. 31. All this showed how deeply the French officials remained involved in criminal practices: sometimes as initiator, sometimes as profiteer, sometimes suffering from their own machinations.

During the Sun Yat-sen government the relationship with the Western occupation was already critical but generally of a polite character. That situation changed with his death in March 1925. Chinese opposition from all corners protested publicly against the foreign occupation in the International Settlement, against the centers of narcotics and Western

---

[34] Idem, p. 205.

decadence, or against the Western or foreign labor exploitation. Strikes in foreign—owned industries became regular and time and again British, French marines or Japanese guards machine-gunned 'thousands of rioting coolies'[35]

After 1930 the influence of France and Britain in China faded away quickly, and the USA and Japan replaced them.

The End of a Disaster

> Between June, 1940, and March 9, 1945, Japan enjoyed full control of Indochina with the compliance and assistance of the French colonial authorities. The colony was the main base for Japan's southward push against the Philippines and Southeast Asia after the attack on Pearl Harbor.[36]

This sentence contains the most serious allegation against the French possible: it is the betrayal of the Indochinese people, of their Western colleagues and their civilization. The latter fought the Japanese in the Pacific, Burma or the East Indies and succumbed to superior numbers. The betrayal of the Indochinese people was more direct: it concerned not only the collaboration with the enemy, but during the Japanese occupation, the French troops fought and suppressed the Indochinese resistance against the Japanese!

It is often shown that resistance movements against unpleasant regimes joined the new powers as liberators, the Germans in Europe or Japanese in Asia, hoping to obtain help in toppling that regime. The Flemish in Belgium; the Ukrainians in Russia; the Croatians in the Balkans; in India as well as in the Dutch West Indies, there was a pro-German movement; etc. They all supported the Germans or Japanese because they helped to expel the French, Soviets, Serbs, British or Dutch, respectively. Examples in Asia include the nationalists of Sukarno in Indonesia, certain Chinese warlords in China, or an Annamite monarchist movement in Indochina. This is rather understandable, although politically not very clever to collaborate with a much stronger warring party, and risking the exchange of one occupation for another.

However, I do not know of another example in which a former occupier collaborated with a new one. Certainly, also in Indochina there were individuals like General Catroux who rallied for De Gaulle and against the

---

[35] J. Taylor, p. 49 ff.
[36] H. Isaacs, p.156.

dominant Vichy Fascists, but they were exceptions without an army or other support.[37]

This all ended in many actions by parties trying to save their skins or to take advantage of the existing chaos. For example: in the permanent power competition throughout Southeast Asia between the British and French, Siam remained largely unoccupied as a kind of buffer between the "European possessions". In 1939 it was renamed Thailand, and after 1945 it recaptured lost territory.

This was about three years before the English had to flee the realm and a decade before the French lost their last battle in Dien Bien Phu (1954). The Americans took over the colonial heritage, learned next to nothing from it, and had to leave Vietnam again two decades later in a chaotic flight with their tail between their legs. The result: a disillusioned American citizenship and dishonored military defeated by a small, self-conscious, poorly armed and rather weak, developing country.

Ho Chi Minh, the gravedigger of French and American imperialism in Asia, also destroyed their opium and heroin activities (see below). He had earlier singled out the French opium and alcohol monopolies as two of the definitive outrages of French colonialism. The *Declaration of Independence* of the First Vietnamese Republic (1945) accused the French of trying to 'enfeeble a Vietnamese race' through opium. The French must have perceived this as communist propaganda. However, Chantal Descours-Gatin confirmed this.[38] Time and again this was repeated about the Dutch and British as well.

The French imperialism and colonialism were probably the most dishonorable and humiliating type from a Western point of view. After collaborating with the Japanese during World War II, France tried to restore its corrupt colonial power in a most provocative way (by breaking one promise after another) and in a highly cruel war against the Vietnamese resistance. This was formed in a struggle against the Japanese (and French) occupation and as the legitimate republican representative of the Vietnamese people. A lost affair practically by definition.

In Indochina the end came as the brilliant General Giap's forces were trained and ready, Mao Zedong had won in China (December 1949), and the American-guided Cold War had been initiated. Pierre Mendès-France told the French parliament that things had gone too far *not* to negotiate

---

[37] R. Paxton, p. 80 ff. and passim. See also the contribution of David Marr in: A.McCoy (ed.,1980), p. 125-159.

[38] C. Descours-Gatin.

with Ho Chi Minh. For, he argued (October 1950) in a most remarkably dubious reasoning (and overdue):

> It is the overall conception of our policy in Indochina which is wrong ... It is a fact that our forces ... are unable to bring about a military resolution, especially since the evolution of the Chinese situation, and it is a fact that our policy of making feeble concessions, and then withdrawing or denying them, has failed, and now, alas, will increasingly fail, to rally the mass of the Vietnamese people to our side.[39]

Their defeat in Vietnam was not the end of their controversial role in world politics as they continued their bloody repression in Africa (Algeria) and interventions in West African affairs or their dubious role in the Rwandan genocide (1990s).

---

[39] Quoted in M. Shipway, p. 108.

CHAPTER TWENTY-FOUR

THE SOUTHEAST ASIAN CONTEXT

Introduction

Southeast Asia is, of course, much larger than Indochina as defined above and incorporates also the Philippines and all the islands in the East Indies archipelago, now known as Indonesia. New Guinea is on the border, notwithstanding the fact that half its territory is now Indonesia. This is not very relevant for our history of the opium problem. Many countries are located in this huge part of the globe (the East Indies archipelago is already as large as the United States).

In 1600 its population was estimated at just over 22 million. Vietnam, the largest country at the time, had nearly five million, Java four million, Burma three, etc.[1] Two hundred years later the entire region had increased by about 50%. Compared with most other large units (Europe, China, India, etc.) it had still a very low density of 5.5 persons per square kilometer (China had about 37). The endless wars and religious conflicts among the many kingdoms were the main reasons for this low population level.

The primary characteristic of Southeast Asia is the dominant islands populated with very different tribal people with many languages, and large stretches of sea separating them. Nearly all people, except a few on the large land masses, were more or less strongly oriented to the sea: ports, trade, pirates, merchants, foreigners, and many other mercantile features including shipbuilding, money-dealers, etc. belong to the standard "outfit" of Southeast Asia from its earliest history onwards.

The permanent labor shortages made "manpower" into a highly esteemed product and the target of the numerous pirate groups. They had the clear function of bringing people from areas with a "supply" to those with a "demand". Consequently, slavery had quite different characteristics under the indigenous peoples than under Western colonial masters. Apparently, warfare among the former had largely the function of "getting

---

[1] C. Trocki (2006), p. 3 ff.

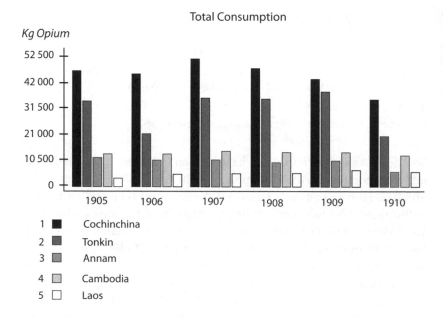

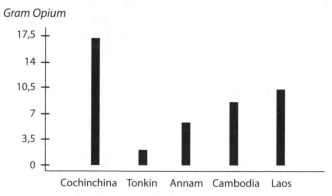

Figure 9. Total Opium Consumption in Indochina, 1905-1910 and the Consumption per Head, 1906-07

Source: C. Descours-Gatin, p. 211 according to *Inspection Meray, rapport no. 61; Memorandum Lauret, 1911*. Also the Laos figures represent the results of the *Opiumregie*. It is too difficult to evaluate the results of the smuggling activities as well. For the consumption per user per year see table 29.

people" more than killing, and never had the genocidal nature of the European assaults. Still, they were men-consuming ventures:

> The larger states mobilized a substantial proportion of their male popula-
> tion into vast, ill-organized armies, without providing adequate supplies

either for the soldiers or for their families left behind. Thousands of captives were marched back home by the victorious armies of Burma and Siam, or shipped home by Aceh and Makassar [pirates], with incalculable losses on the voyage. Perhaps an even more important factor demographically was the need to be constantly ready for flight in troubled times. This probably meant avoiding births at least until the older children were able to run by themselves.[2]

Colonization by Western powers was started first by the Spaniards in the Philippines; the Portuguese formed several settlements together into a rather busy trade network, but conquests of large tracks of land had no priority. The Dutch VOC conquered large parts of Java in order to consolidate its military and economic position, but the new Dutch regime in the East Indies in the 19th-century started with a rather systematic conquest of the whole archipelago.

At the same time the British and the French divided the heartland of Southeast Asia between themselves: the British conquered the Western, the French the Eastern part, and in between remained a large country, Siam, left colonized as a kind of buffer between the two foreign powers.

It cannot be a coincidence that the opium history was confronted here in the British and French colonies with most dramatic developments: the narco-military Western regimes changed into very powerful narco-military Southeast Asian regimes. The latter dominate today's opium and heroin production like the British did in the 19th-century.

The combination of the following table and figure 9 present the whole perspective for the next chapter.

Table 28. Southeast Asian Opium Cultivation and Heroin Production, 1992-1996 [3]

	1992	1993	1994	1995	1996
Net poppy cultivation in hectares					
Myanmar (Burma)	153 700	165 800	146 600	154 070	163 100
Laos	25 610	26 040	18 520	19 650	25 250
Thailand	2 050	2 880	2 110	1 750	2 170
Total	181 360	194 720	167 230	175 470	190 520
Potential opium production in metric tons					
Myanmar (Burma)	2 280	2 575	2 030	2 340	2 560
Laos	230	180	85	180	200
Thailand	24	42	17	25	30
Total	2 534	2 797	2 132	2 545	2 790

---

[2] Quoted from Anthony Reid by C. Trocki, idem, p. 5, 6.
[3] UNODC figures quoted from the *Frontline* website www.pbs.org.

Table 28. Continued.

	1992	1993	1994	1995	1996
Potential opium-heroin in metric tons					
Myanmar (Burma)	190	215	169	195	213
Laos	19	15	7	15	17
Thailand	2	4	1	2	2
Total	211	234	177	212	232

The head of the United Nations Office on Drugs and Crime (UNODC) for East Asia, Gary Lewis, reported in December 2010 that the Burmese output had soared over the past four years to 95% of Southeast Asian production.[4] Of this most is produced in Shan State, the large eastern part of Myanmar (Burma). In this "state" of military and criminals, there is a struggle for mastery over the opium-heroin-amphetamine, etc. resources. The last sentence of his article says:

'Most experts agree that as long as there is conflict in ethnic Burma, drugs production will follow as a means to fund it.' According to the UNODC Myanmar is pouring, probably *the largest opium-heroin production* over the Western world. And *The Economist* reports not only that the cultivation has increased by nearly 50% since 2006, but also that now 'more than one million people in Myanmar are involved in producing opium, up 27% from the year before.'[5]

In this chapter we follow the history of this future until about 1950. We shall try to discover why this area became what it is now, described as 'Poisoned Hills' by the local, highly courageous *Palaung Women's Organization* in Burma. It recently accused the military and militias of many criminal deeds and atrocities against women, children and innocent people; in the end all opium-induced crimes.

From "Golden Triangle" to "Bloody Quadrangle"[6]

Even when describing the creation of the *Golden Triangle,* the ultimate opium logo of this part of Southeast Asia, historians cannot refrain from

---

[4] Dan Withers on the website of *Democratic Voice of Burma*, 20 December 2010.

[5] *The Economist,* 16th of March, 2010: 'Myanmar's opium crop. Steady hand on the till. But who is to blame for the spike in cultivation?'

[6] Apart from the McCoy and Trocki studies, are used UN Special no. 626 (February 2004) written by Evelina Rioukhina (UNECE) on www.unspecial.org/UNS626/UNS_626_T07.html and M. Jelsma, T. Kramer, D&C, no. 16, August 2008. C. Lamour, M. Lamberti, part 2.

pointing to 'ancient Greek fertility cults' as the 'first references to opium use' as if this should be relevant, although it is incorrect.[7] B. Renard knows that the first references to opium use in Southeast Asia date back 'to 1366 (Thailand) and 1519 (Burma)'. The obvious conclusion is not drawn that Arab and Portuguese traders, respectively, must have brought some as a present to native rulers. Nowhere in those years did any form of large-scale opium business in Asia exist, and there was no opium problem whatsoever.

Next, the information that in neighboring Yunnan (China) opium cultivation was introduced in the 18th-century 'from which it spread to northern Burma (Kachin State and Shan State) and Laos' is unreliable as well. In that century no opium was cultivated in China or Yunnan, and certainly there was no one who could expand into such a large area. More precisely:

> In Southeast Asia the use of opium does not play an important role before the 19th-century. ... Generally it is true that opium consumption ... was initiated and stimulated by European merchants ... for profit. In Thailand, at that time still called Siam, the use of opium was introduced by the English, who discovered how they could smuggle opium under the British flag.[8]

The Yunnan invasion referred to above must be the one between 1870 and 1880: Hmong tribal people, who now knew how to grow poppies, were expelled by the Chinese military. They apparently taught other hill tribes how to grow this useful plant for their own consumption.

Early in the 19th-century indigenous rulers in Siam and Burma, like the Chinese emperors, strongly opposed the smuggling activities of the English and other Westerners (including Americans). Outside the tribal areas these rulers could prohibit the import and use of opium or tried to regulate them before they were overruled by the French or English.

> In Siam there '... is a strong anti-opium movement ... resulting in the prohibition of selling and consuming opium of 1811 by King Rama II. Nearly ten years later, in 1829, his son, Rama III, even ordered the death penalty for the opium trade ... Also in Burma, the kings prohibited the use of opium until 1852. When the English conquered parts of the south, the opium commerce started there. This happened in the form of a controlled monopoly by the occupying forces ... This expansion of the British continued, and in 1886 the Shan state of Burma was occupied as well. ... In Vietnam ... Cochinchina ... the government was also against opium use. Opium is prohibited

---

[7] M. Jelsma, T. Kramer, D&C, no. 16, p. 4.
[8] D. Duco, p. 55.

by the court, while breakers of the rules were punished severely ... In the end opium use was accepted from 1857 onwards by the French colonists ...[9]

The opium is largely imported from Benares (India), and it is only in the period after 1880 that a change occurred from Benares import to Yunnan import, and the English started to complain about "Chinese competition".[10]

In short, the opium image still given in the usual touristic information: 'For centuries, these countries have produced the opium that has attracted traders from Europe and elsewhere'[11] must be utter nonsense. It only fits the widespread "blaming the victims" stories (see ch. 29).

There is nothing romantic about this best-known Asian drug (opium, heroin, amphetamine) region. Its name is derived from the location where three countries, three nations and cultures come together: now the border zone of Thailand (Siam), Myanmar (Burma) and Laos with the river Salween in the middle. It forms a really symbolic triangle, each side belonging to another country. The triangle is a geographical mistake with several serious consequences. The fact is that it does not concern a borderland region of three countries, but of four.

Yunnan (China) is of strategic importance for the functioning of this "triangle" as opium center. Long after the British introduced opium as a mass product in China, that country developed the first counterattack through its own Chinese production (from around 1870 onwards). Yunnan became a center of Chinese opium cultivation (see ch. 31). We should therefore speak of the *Golden Quadrangle*. In reality, however, all the border regions together make up the center of the Burmese drugs business as quantified above and, therefore, one of the most criminal regions in the world.

Recently, *The Economist* published a news analysis about this same area, looking around in Meng'a, one of China's main points of entry into Myanmar.[12] In quiet days Chinese from Yunnan arrive here on a day trip 'to escape their country's ban on gambling by visiting Bangkang's casino'. It is not quiet any more, however, because the usual mutual conflicts between the several militia—all very busy with the production and trade

---

[9] Idem, p. 56, 57.

[10] C. Descours-Gatin, p. 209, 210.

[11] E. Rioukhina, p. 3.

[12] *The Economist*, 27th of November 2010, 'Myanmar's border with China. Good Fences.'.

of opium, heroin or amphetamine—have started again, together with those against the junta in Rangoon.[13]

China faces a remarkable and complicated dilemma: it supports the junta because a new pipeline (gas and oil) from the Bay of Bengal had to cross Myanmar's territory. China also supported the militias because of their traditional ties with the Communist Party of Burma (CPB), from which some militias evolved many years ago. The junta also plays different games: it relishes China's backing in the UN, but it also courts China's rival, India. Last but not least, China is doing everything to fight drugs trafficking through its officials in Yunnan, and it has a keen interest in keeping the border areas calm because of its substantial investments in mining, rubber and other industries. If successful, the opium-stricken region would certainly be renamed a "Golden Quadrangle". But not yet: narco-militarism can still be studied here first hand!

It must be clear now that neighboring China is historically and currently of the utmost importance for the fate of this whole *Bloody Quadrangle*.

Still, there are some grounds for optimism. In 1989 the US State Department, not the best source of information about drugs, told the world that the Golden Triangle 'produced a total of 3,050 metric tons of raw opium, equivalent to 73 percent of the world's total illicit supply ... America's leading single source of heroin'.[14] This production has decreased as shown in table 28, but it is practically impossible for it to increase again. However, McCoy points to the reality that 'the globe's great opium reserve in northern Burma had merged with the world's premier heroin market in the United States'. This foreshadows one of my main conclusions.

In his many famous studies, Alfred McCoy made crystal clear how

> all Western attempts at interdiction ... have not only failed to eradicate this resilient global commodity, they have contributed, quite directly, to an expansion of both production and consumption. ... During the 40 years of the Cold War, moreover, government intelligence services, particularly

---

[13] The ethnic militias in the border areas between Myanmar and China are: in the northern so-called Kachin State operates now the *Kachin Independence Army* (KIA); more to the south in the Kokang region and the "Special Region no. 2" (with cities like Meng'a and Bangkang) the largest army of the *United Wa State Army* (UWSA) with 20,000 well-armed soldiers; along the border of China, Laos and Myanmar the *National Democratic Alliance Army* (NDAAD) is active. In addition, in the so-called Shan State, a large potential of junta enemies are concentrated with a highly militant tradition.

[14] A. McCoy in A. McCoy, A. Block (ed.), p. 237.

> the ... CIA ... served as protectors of Southeast Asia's key opium traffickers ... contributing to an initial expansion of production and the failure of later interdiction efforts.[15]

Therefore, what is it about this area? This question should be answered from the perspective of the French colonization and not so much from its "use" after 1950 by the CIA or any other power. McCoy has great merits in uncovering the Cold War's strategic use of opium; its pre-history is highlighted below in which none of the opium parties in Southeast Asia even dreamed of the production figures and position in the world's drug scene today.

The Tribal Scene

Traditionally, opium has been used in the many tribal regions of Southeast Asia for a variety of purposes. We still do not know whether it originated as a custom brought centuries ago by Arab, Portuguese or Dutch merchants or colonizers. Anyway, for the 18th, 19th and a large part of the 20th centuries, tribal people in Southeast Asia (not the urban population) must have perceived opium use as a *genuine indigenous custom.*

It is used medicinally to cure diarrhea, to lessen the effects of malaria, to reduce heart palpitations and as a painkiller and tranquilizer. It was also employed in veterinary medicine. A village custom in parts of Southeast Asia used it to cure animal diseases, but most importantly it could be applied to tame and train elephants for all forms of heavy work and transport. Furthermore, poppy seeds (*graine de pavot*) were used to give flavor to bread or other culinary products and to made oil (*l'huile d'oeillette*). Last but not least, there was a specific recreational use of opium smoked mixed with tobacco or drunk in tea.

This means that the poppy plant was a rather elementary part of the daily life of indigenous people in the villages. A substantial part or all of this consumption could be grown locally. It was perfectly relevant, effective, good, legitimate and so on and was derived (sometimes still is) from old tribal wisdom and knowledge.

A comparison with the European situation from before 1800 is quite revealing.[16] The main difference is that the Southeast Asian tribes could grow poppies for themselves and, therefore, could discover many more

---

[15] Idem, p. 238.

[16] See ch. 8 for England, ch. 10 for Portugal, ch. 13 for the Netherlands and ch. 22 for France.

applications than just medicinal ones over the course of time. In both cas-es the use of opium was for a long time an intimate part of their daily life, without all kinds of legal or criminal obstructions. And in both cases this situation came to an end and was transformed into an external matter of fear and repression.

In the European case a combination of external factors (state repres-sion, differentiation of class interests, religious-moral repression, Enlightenment, development of specific modern health infrastructure) also put an end to the home-oriented use of opium embedded within a mixture of social and cultural customs and related knowledge. Here in Southeast Asia the foreign colonial regime and its rigorous settler's activi-ties insisted on destroying the indigenous belief systems and customs. Also here, the relationship between Enlightenment and modernized imperialism is important to consider (see ch. 28 the Philippines case). What may be left of it today should be good for tourism only.

All this is symbolized in the orders of the French and English colonial states: indigenous opium is forbidden, and only the French and British opium regimes are allowed. This is accompanied by the French and English definition of power for their religious representatives: opium is a social evil that needs to be banned. Modern, imported knowledge (medi-cal, pharmaceutical, chemical and the like) of an "isolated" kind must replace the comprehensive and socially embedded knowledge of the trib-al people.

In the meantime there was a *traditional need* for opium which could only be satisfied by external economic interests: locally grown poppies were forbidden in favor of European-owned or -guided interests based on strong state support. The *criminalized villagers* suddenly became depen-dent on external powers (state bureaucrats, military, missionaries) and their criminal supporters (tax farmers, for instance): the only thing which was left for them was to revolt or resign, to defend their traditions or remain isolated in a new urban society with a foreign character.

Long after this, the drama enrolled as reported:

> Those that relapsed became seen as failures holding the village back from the fruits of modernization that development agencies and government officials are promising to the "model" villages that are relatively successful in removing opium addiction ... This adds to the sense of shame and hope-lessness that many opium smokers feel and only increases their dependence on opium ... Regardless of the fact that the pervasive presence of opium and its practical and symbolic value in specific medical or social contexts makes abstinence a difficult and at times impossible task, addicts are increasingly

marginalized because of their imputed personal responsibility for their addiction and its implications for the village's material development. This kind of punitive atmosphere began creating a sub-population of "degenerate addicts".[17]

This statement concerns village life in Laos. After many interventions by the state, military or "modernizing" expatriate developers, the old bonds were fully destroyed. Too many people became defenseless individuals. After the colonial wars were over and a new power vacuum was filled, opium consumption rates in the rural areas soared to the highest in the region. Many people were unable to stand the alienation and to fulfill the expectations of a strange, modern, urban world; they fell victim to the urban opium criminals. This pushed them into a fully hopeless situation of dependence on heroin. Opium use was decreasing, but opiate dependence increased.

That was the situation in village life in this part of Asia from around 1980 onwards. But let's return to the 1940s and 1950s, and provide more details about this tribal scene in Southeast Asia, because there are many misunderstandings circulating about it.

The third Western colonial government involved in large-scale opium production and trade, the French, had a monopoly for its own Southeast Asian colonies. Not only did its colonial activities have widespread effects in the whole of Southeast Asia, but the same effect was gained as in the British-Chinese relation (see part two and ch. 30): in the propaganda, the victims were transformed into the perpetrators as a whitewashing campaign of the white colonizers. By the end of this "game", some victims indeed acted as perpetrators and acknowledged the prejudice. In Southeast Asia some tribes underwent this fate.

The peculiar characteristic of Southeast Asia is that without a substantial and, in fact, powerful tribal scene, opium production or distribution or trade was very difficult. This is true not only for the period after the end of the long 19th-century. Tribes have been settled in the hills of the Chiang Rai area for centuries (the Akha, Lahu, Lisu, Mien, Hmong, Shan or Thai-yai, Mon and Karen). A certain symbiosis between these areas with their wild nature, colorful tribes, rather militant tribal life and opium production and trade easily leads to exaggeration. One always hears, "Opium has been here already for centuries" which is a quasi-truth never properly substantiated.

---

[17] Quoted by M. Jelsma, T. Kramer, D&C, no. 16, p. 22.

The Akha are very tradition-bound and well-known for their attractive dresses, wearing skilfully embroidered silken jackets in their everyday life. The small group of the Lahu live in villages located above 1,000 meters. They farm poppies, dry rice and corn as cash crops. Many of them have been converted to Christianity. The Lisu form the smallest tribal group in Thailand. They arrived from Burma in 1920, live at a very high altitude, and are well-known for their hard work and competitiveness. They are considered the most successful of all Thailand's tribal people. The small tribe of the Mien are in all respects the most Chinese oriented. They practice rotational agriculture, depending more on rice and corn rather than poppies.

More to the east, in Vietnam the ethnic situation is possibly even more complicated, although most people are not aware of it. They think of Vietnam only in terms of its lowlands and the Kinh (ethnic Vietnamese), which is understandable because the Kinh (literally: 'people of the capital') form the majority (85%). However, Vietnam is three-quarters mountainous and hilly, in which about 20% or 14 million of the inhabitants live.[18] There are seventeen ethnic groups. In Vietnam at the moment, opium does not play a significant role among these ethnic groups. We have to turn, therefore, to the three most important tribes in the Southeast Asian opium story: the Shan, Hmong and Karen (or Red Karena).

They are border tribes connecting Burma, Thailand, Laos and China, countries which share over 1,000 miles of border. Historically, they suffer and benefit from their buffer position between often warring countries. The border tribes constantly have to choose, switch and deal in order to survive. After about 1960 the direction of their choice was clear: most tribes were against the Burmese military regime and pro-Thai. A few remarks about the Shan and Hmong can clarify the previous picture.

The Shan State

For the Shan there are specific reasons for maintaining a peaceful relationship with Thailand and hostility against Burma. The former serves as the transit and refining area for the annual 400-700 tons (1980) of opium from the Shan, while Thailand's main cities (Bangkok, Pang, Mae Hongson, etc.) are centers from which heroin trafficking is financed and controlled. The Burmese military regime, however, is very eager to control the Shan

---

[18] For the following see the article of A.T. Rambo and N. Jamieson, in: H.V. Luong (ed.), p. 139-171.

State itself so that the opium, heroin or morphine revenues can support its despotic regime.

In 1956 the CIA concluded that 'the majority of opium exported from Burma originates in the Shan State' and 'that the annual production of opium in Burma is at least 150 tons'.[19] This is an estimate for the whole of Burma and still very far from the 400-700 tons estimated 30 years later just for the Shan State. Estimates in these cases, however, remain guesses, too often "political guesses".

So, first, who are these Shan? A short "opium answer" must suffice here. Immediately after the end of World War II, Burma became independent of the British colonizers. The British Empire withdrew in disgrace, leaving a social, cultural and economic mess behind, as it did in Palestine, India, and so on. We may consider what was "better" measured by the quantities of blood shed: a direct liberation war against the British or the prolonged massacres which still continue today in Palestine, Kashmir and Burma. As usual, the British took the cheapest option, although they must have known what would happen later.

In Burma, for instance, representatives of the Shan together with the Kachin and Chin tribes (the United Hills Peoples, SCOUHP) met in February 1947 in Panglong to conclude agreements with representatives of the Executive Council of the Governor of Burma. A few days earlier the SCOUHP had already concluded a mutual agreement supporting each other's right to form an independent state and 'to secede after attainment of freedom from Confederation with Burma if and when we choose'.[20]

The representative of "Rangoon", Aung San, accepted an agreement in which, for instance, 'a separate Kachin State' was envisaged, the citizens of the 'Frontier Areas shall enjoy [democratic] rights and privileges' or that they were 'entitled to receive from the revenues of Burma ... similar to those between Burma and the Federated Shan States'. Aung San, however, was killed soon afterwards in a military coup.

The Shan exile, Chao Tzang Yawnghwe (alias Eugene Thaike), is an eloquent supporter of the Shan case. He was chief-of-staff in the Shan State Army (SSA) until 1976 and one of the very few people who can explain the local opium situation well. He is very critical of the frenzied efforts by governments and international agencies to eradicate opium in Burma

---

[19] Central Intelligence Agency, p. 8.
[20] In the appendices of C. Yawnghwe, p. 253 ff. the relevant documents are given. "Rangoon" was also defined as 'Interim Burmese Government'.

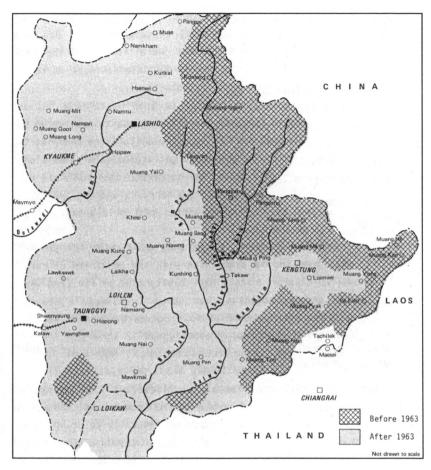

Map 13. Opium Cultivation in Shan State before and after 1963

Source: C. T. Yawnghwe, p. 56. Compiled from "Situation Reports and Intelligence Data', Shan State Army GHQ Office, 1963.

through Thailand, 'which is like trying to pull out a tooth in order to cure a stomach-ache'.[21]

What is the independent opium view of this Shan nationalist, who seems to be a monarchist as well? Yawnghwe:

Why is opium extensively cultivated in Shan State? Is it, as alleged by Rangoon, because the Shan and tribal peasants are forced by Shan rebels and the CPB [Communist Party of Birma] to do so? It is not easy to force peasants to grow anything since there are many ways to get around such com-

[21] Idem, p. 268.

pulsion. For forced cultivation of opium to succeed, it must be run plantation-style with peasants forced into barracks under guard, among other things, which implies that rebel armies must hold secure areas, and this has never been the case.[22]

The next question he tries to answer is whether the peasants grow opium for profit. The obvious affirmative answer is not given; Yawnghwe first points to many other things. A peasant rarely makes substantial profit from what he grows. In addition, he states that a peasant family growing opium under the best weather, soil and social conditions 'will produce at most about 12 kg a year'. He continues with a realistic economic analysis:

> The field price of one kg of opium is as follows: 300 kyat in the mid-1960s; 600 kyat in the early 1970s and 1000 kyat in the early 1980s (kyat and baht are about equal, unofficially). It is indeed rare for a family to be able to produce the maximum amount. However, let us say that a certain peasant family did produce 12 kg of opium in 1980. Its annual income would be 12,000 kyat or baht ... In terms of purchasing power, the family's maximum income would ... be only 4,000 baht (less than $250) a year . The vast majority earned far less. ... Most opium cultivators, moreover, like most peasants of Southeast Asia, are indebted to buying agents or local moneylenders before planting and have to hock the yield, or borrow usually at 30 to 50 per cent interest per season. It is thus amply clear that Shan and other tribal peasants are not growing opium for profit.[23]

Yawnghwe agrees with comments that opium cultivation is widespread in the Shan state, but this would have amounted at most to 60-80 tons in 1958. The government in Rangoon made of this 400-600 tons in 1970; Washington and the United Nations repeated this without any form of investigation. This is unbelievable, 'a revolutionary leap never seen before in agricultural history ...' Rangoon made a mess of its statistics, while it 'does not control the rural areas'.

The true cause of the Shan opium and heroin trafficking is 'a deep economic, social, and political malaise arising from Rangoon's harsh rule, economic foolhardiness, and arrogant defiance of socio-economic and political realities'.[24] In addition, in all their proposals to end the opium problem, the Shan always welcomed foreign observers. Rangoon, however, always told the international community that the opium and heroin problem was 'our internal affair and concerns no one'.

---

[22] Idem, p. 55.
[23] Idem, p. 57.
[24] Idem, p. 58.

Rangoon's solution to the Opium Problem is: "Eliminate Shan rebels!" It immediately received international military aid. This is comparable to the century-old creed in the "Dutch" East Indies or in "British" India when the British stopped their own activities: "The Smuggling" prevents us from eradicating the Opium Problem consistently and gradually. The true reason for this was that the "government" wanted to have the monopoly without any form of opposition or 'free trade' (see *Opiumregie* policy).

In addition, the international military and/or economic aid was given wholeheartedly in the framework of some "domino theory" to encircle Chinese Communism. But Rangoon's problem lies elsewhere: its nationalism is an ethnic nationalism

> trying to impose its concept of nationhood on the other by force ... to subjugate them or destroy their ethnic identity. Rangoon's attempts to gain control over the various homelands is, therefore, linked to the problem of narcotics only because of negative and short-sighted policies. A solution lies ... in ... what is known as "good government", a relevant and rational point which international policy makers, bureaucrats, and scholars gloss over when discussing the problem of drug trafficking in Burma.[25]

Yawnghwe adds to this argument a clear threat: in 1961 the Shan rebels totaled not more than 1,500 men, but twenty years later they are a well-armed army of 7,000 to 9,000 men, which is fighting in its own familiar territory. He suggests that even with Western military assistance, there is no chance of an easy victory, while in the end only the CPB will come out as the winner, 'through its ability to provide arms, be able to take over the various nationalist movements and armies'.[26]

Nationalists fighting nationalists while both have "foreigners" as enemies, the Communists, and both have an ambiguous relationship with Westerners.

The Hmong tribe

The Hmong or Meo became notorious by collaborating with the USA during the Vietnam War. Earlier they also had a remarkable history:

> Between 1898 and 1922 Hmong rebelled against colonial rule; however, relations improved in the 1940s once the French used Hmong opium to supply state-run opium dens throughout Indochina and later, employed

---

[25] Idem, p. 60.
[26] Idem, p. 59.

> Hmong guerillas to resist Viet Minh (Vietnamese communist) efforts to establish a bridgehead in northern Laos.[27]

Thanks to their assistance given to the American forces, many Hmong were allowed to come to the USA.[28]

The Hmong number about 65,000 in Thailand (in 2000). Paul Hillmer, their most recent historian, perfectly demonstrated the ambiguous effects of prejudice. To undermine them, he states that among the Hmong, opium has only a 'limited use as a folk remedy, stimulant, and pain reliever... while opium addiction exists, it was rare and socially stigmatizing ...'[29] However, only a few lines further on, we can read that opium is primarily used

> as a cash crop—both to pay taxes, a practice encouraged by the Lao government and the French colonizers, and to trade in exchange for other necessities. Opium netted a family more wealth per acre than the other crops they grew.

Here the mechanism is indicated thorugh which regular opium production as a cash crop is provoked. In the meantime the Hmong sometimes played an important role in the whole "triangle-quadrangle game" in Southeast Asia, in war and peace. In the highly complex situation of Southeast Asia it is often difficult to discover who was first and who has to follow along as a mere act of survival or out of existential fear for repercussions. Whoever is prepared to take a more independent stand will certainly point to the devastating role of the former colonizers the Meo were familiar with, notwithstanding their bad press as collaborators of the French and Americans.

During World War II the French officials exploited the tribal opium sources in "good collaboration" with the Japanese occupation. The most important opium-growing provinces were Xieng Khouang Province in northeastern Laos and the Thai country of northeastern Tonkin. Both regions had a high concentration of Meo (Hmong) tribesmen. The French rigorously intervened in the tribal relations and conflicts by choosing Touby Lyfoung as their opium broker in Laos and Deo Van Long in the

---

[27] K. Quincy, p. 1.

[28] It is a similar fate to the Ambonese and Moluccan collaborators of the Dutch colonial regime: after the lost Dutch war of 1945-1949, they could stay in the Netherlands as a discriminated minority, which they expressed time and again in a violent way and in the establishment of a "return-to-Indonesia" movement.

[29] P. Hillmer, p. 28.

Thai country. These choices had remarkable consequences for the French colonial future.

Consumption Pattern

In the following table a comparison is made between most regions of Southeast Asia. The data must have been received from the Dutch *Opiumregie*. It is not easy to make such a comparison, let alone to check its figures for the simple reason that, in fact, there are no proper sources (the *International Opium Commission*?). Indochina, here the French colonies only, has the highest sale in kilograms, followed by Siam and the Dutch East Indies. All three had an effective *Opiumregie*. However, the Indochinese figures can be checked thanks to the excellent study of Descours-Gatin.[30]

She used different kinds of figures so that it is also possible to discover some pattern in the opium consumption of Indochina.

For all regions, one of the most important practical changes was the gradual replacement of the Indian import by the Yunnan import after 1880. For example: of a total import in 1904 of 113 536 kg, about 40% came from Benares and 60% from Yunnan. Three years later Yunnan imported already 70% (76 317 kg of 108 005 kg.).[31]

But consumers retained their preference for a special taste. Rich Chinese in Cochinchina preferred the Benares opium with a special soft flavor and a low morphine content (4-5%). In Tonkin, they liked the rougher, stronger taste of the Yunnan opium with its morphine content of 7- 8%.

Cochinchina (the southern part of the present Vietnam with Saigon) has the highest consumption per head. In 1907 about 50,000 kg was consumed by 90,000 smokers. The Chinese here smoke about 1.5 kg per annum, while the Vietnamese use only 300 g on average.

Tonkin is the second largest opium region. In 1907 about 36,000 kg were sold by the *Opiumregie* (nearly all from Benares). This amount is, however, far from realistic: ' ... according to Inspector Meray the quantities available through fraud equal half the total consumption' (1908).[32] Meray thinks that about 40% of adult male Chinese are smokers, whereas this

---

[30] In particular C. Descours-Gatin, p. 209-222.
[31] C. Descour-Gatin, p. 209-210.
[32] Idem, p. 210.

Table 29. Comparison between "legal consumption" of opium in Southeast Asia and the Chinese coast, ca. 1930[33]

Country	Burma	Siam	Indo-china	Straits Settlements	Dutch East Indies	Hong Kong	Macao	Formosa
Sales in kilogr.	23 619	61 000	68 268	43 200	57 100	6 800	12 356	34 970
Price per thail*	14,31	32,25	50,68	36,5	62,19	24,18	3,9	10,3
Opium users	54 282	unknown	unknown	39 503	186 114	unknown	unknown	26 942
Average consumption per year per user in grams	435	unknown	unknown	1 094	295	unknown	unknown	1 151

* in Swiss francs (2 October 1930)

[33] Derived from a table in *Encyclopaedie van Nederlandsch-Indië* (1934 edition), p. 1258.

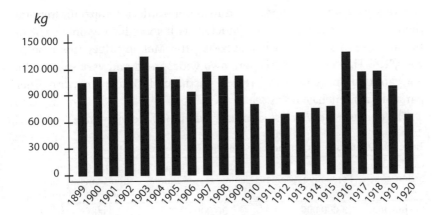

Figure 10. Opium Consumption in Indochina, 1899-1920

Source: C. Descours-Gatin, p. 218. For the years 1899 to 1907 the data are according to the *Inspection Meray, appendix to report 61*; for the years 1908 to 1920 is used *Inspection Merat, appendix II.*

percentage is only 2.5% among the Vietnamese. Others are of the opinion that indigenous people do not smoke at all: only the Chinese are opium consumers. The representatives of the tribes all react differently: among the Chams, Khas and Mois minorities, the "opiomanie" is 'quasi unknown'. Among the mountain tribes, Meos and Mans, in Tonkin, who have a poppy culture, there should be a very limited number of smokers.

Amman and *Cambodia* consumed more or less the same quantity of opium in 1907 according to the *Opiumregie* administration, 10,124 kg and 13,560 kg, respectively. They have, however, different characteristics: the first has nearly double the number of smokers, and in Cambodia 60% of them are Chinese, smoking about 1.4 kg per year, whereas in Annam the Chinese smoke on average 1.7 kg. In Annam, furthermore, they smokes almost only Yunnan opium, while in Cambodia they have just the Benares form; in the latter there are 572 opium dens, but in the former not one. And so on.

Laos is a different case, although this could be the result of contradictory figures. First, the opium comes exclusively from Yunnan. In 1907 the *Opiumregie* sold 4,716 kilo of opium there. They say that this assumes a consumption of 10 gram *per year*, a quantity by which nobody can become an addict, not even a regular smoker. This would give, however, an unreliable smokers population of 471,600 people. And with a factual population of about 630,000 this, in turn, would lead to 6,300 kg consumption or a smokers population of 75%. In addition, according to specific reports there are serious regional discrepancies, with some having only 2-3% of the adult men smoking, whereas along the Mekong river this rose to 30-35%.[34] The "smuggling" is here also widespread and very easy to do. For Laos there were no data given, so I estimated some in line with other parts of the French colonies.

The above is more or less summarized in the following table.

Table 30. Opium smokers in Indochina in 1906[35]

Land or region	Total Population	% Chinese	Total smokers	Total Chinese smokers	Total non-Chinese smokers	% Chinese smokers
Cochinchina	3 000 000	4,7	90 000	20 000	70 000	22
Annam	5 000 000	0,12	23 000	2 500	20 500	11
Tonkin	6 000 000	0,7	132 000	9 000	123 000	7
Cambodia	1 600 000	7,16	12 000	7 200	4 800	60
Laos	630 000	0,08	18 000 *	1 000*	17 000*	6*
Total	16 230 000	1,9	275 000	39 700	235 300	14

* Laotian smokers are "real" estimates and, therefore, the totals as well

A comparison with the Burmese consumption is revealing. The figures used by the CIA in the 1950s must be derived from the estimated annual production of 150 tons, of which 120 tons were exported:

> It is estimated that 60,000 opium addicts, concentrated principally in the producing areas and in the Bhamo and Myitkyna districts, consume 30 tons of opium a year ... This estimate is derived by assuming that the annual consumption of a Burmese addict is similar to that of a Thai addict: 500 grams a year.[36]

The consumption figures of so-called addicts given here are fully in variance with those revealed above with differences ranging between 10 grams, 500 grams and 1.5 kilo a year. These differences result not only from ignorance and inaccurate reporting, but to a large extent from wrong definitions: a smoker is not necessarily an addict, while an addict is always a smoker in these regions; it is, furthermore, utter nonsense to call a 500 gram smoker a year an addict; in an earlier table, in which a comparison is made between several Southeast Asian countries in 1930, some 54,000 'opium users' are mentioned, the most vague definition possible.

---

[34] Idem, p. 213 and note 45.
[35] Idem, p. 214 rounded figures.
[36] Central Intelligence Agency, p. 8.

After World War II and the Japanese occupation the situation in Southeast Asia became quite chaotic with a war of liberation against the French or several military coups and assassinations with an ethnic background. The reports of the CIA are one of the few sources available and they are used with caution.

Table 31. Estimated Number of Opium Addicts and Consumption of Illicit Raw Opium in Indochina and Singapore-Malaya, 1955[37]

Province	Number of Addicts	Illicit consumption in metric tons
South Vietnam	55 000[a]	30
North Vietnam	60 000	45
Laos	10 000	8
Cambodia	20 000	15
Total Indochina	*145 000*	*98*
Singapore + Malaya	115 000	100

[a] 'Approximately 15,000 of these addicts receive legal opium "detoxification" doses from governments stocks rather than illicit opium.'

This table covers the same realm as in the previous one. The largest differences concern "North Vietnam" which is the earlier Annam + Tonkin. This cannot be explained only by the use of different definitions (addicts versus smokers). For South Vietnam (former Cochinchina), a source is accidentally mentioned: 'Mr. Tran Van, a Deputy Director of the South Vietnamese Police and Sûreté'. This man estimated the annual consumption in his province at about 36 to 48 tons, of which about 30 tons arrived through the illicit circuit.

As a rule of thumb it is estimated that about half the opium produced is consumed locally in these provinces (except South Vietnam). In Laos (now estimated at a population of 1.3 million) there is a slightly different regime. Consumption does mean here probably 'the amount retained by the Lao after the official collection'. The largest part of the opium retained after the official collection 'was purchased by private opium dealers and resold in Indochina, Thailand, Burma and Communist China'. The smallest part is estimated 'at about 68 tons'.[38]

In particular, the strategically important Laotian production-consumption is treated in a bewildering way as follows. It is already difficult

---

[37] Idem, p. 13. The data for Singapore are added from Idem p. 15. The report used 'disintoxication' in stead of 'detoxification'.

[38] Idem, p. 14.

to make a connection to the 8 tons in the table and the 68 tons of what is called 'personal consumption by the Lao'. However, the following rather spectacular description can be partly an explanation for the bewildering figures:

> Thus, total consumption in Indochina could amount to approximately 100 tons a year. As approximately 125 tons of opium are produced annually in Laos, approximately 25 tons of Laotian opium are available for hoarding and for export to other countries. Opium is sold quite openly in Laos. [X] recently reported: "Opium can be purchased in village markets in Sam Neua ... Luang Prabang and Xieng Khouang provinces, as well as in the northwest. It can be bought right in the town of Xieng Khouang." With a readily available source of supply at competitive prices, opium smuggling from Laos is a relatively large-scale operation. Airplanes and trucks, both civilian and military, are used extensively for the clandestine movement of opium from the Laos collection centers to the markets.[39]

I can only point to this situation as a demonstration of what can be done with statistics, while I am not in a position to do new research on this matter. And that is necessary, not only for the Burmese case, but for the whole of the Opium Problem. Since the Myanmar narco-military regime belongs today to the largest opium and or heroin producers in the world, it is worthwhile to re-examine this country for the period up to the 1950s.

Myanmar (Burma)

Quite at the beginning of his interesting study, Ronald Renard provides us with a most relevant opening sentence:

> Involved parties ... agree that it was the British who were mainly responsible for introducing opium to Burma proper on a large-scale basis. Although ... the British were not directly involved in developing the cultivation of opium as a major cash crop in the Shan areas of Upper Burma, the role of the East India Company in spreading opium to Burman areas and popularizing it there is undisputed.[40]

---

[39] Idem, p. 14. If 68 tons is the consumption in Laos only and its production 125, than 57 tons remain for export. Apart from this, 100 tons are mentioned as consumption for the whole of Indochina *including* the Laotian 68: this leaves 32 tons for all the other Indochinese countries or provinces. According to the table 145,000 minus 10,000 (=Laos) addicts must be served with 90 tons. From where do the missing 58 tons come? This apart from 25 tons mentioned for hoarding, etc.

[40] R. Renard (1996), p. 2, 3.

Once told this, it is senseless and a-historical to start a new chapter about early drug use with an unproved and unprovable story about 1000 BC or 800 AD in which it *seems* as if cannabis or opiates are used: by whom? how much? how? imported? grown oneself? If one cannot answer questions like these with some kind of certainty, then it is much better not to speculate. That is, besides, an art in itself.[41]

The year 1519 in which the ruler of Martaban made an agreement with the Portuguese to bring opium has parallels elsewhere (China). But it still does not provide any relevant information.

The further historical information is mostly useless. A son of a king at the end of the 16th-century died from opium, whereupon the sentence follows:

> However, there is virtually no mention of opium or alcohol in the Burmese chronicles until the nineteenth-century. By this time, usage was more widespread, although the elite still shunned it. A 19th-century observer noted that "a respectable Burman would hesitate to be seen around a Government-licensed [liquor] shop" and that opium use among the "better classes of Burmese is extremely rare. ... Burmans have no taste for ganja".[42]

The British penetrated China not only from the sea, they tried later to enter it through Tibet. During the British conquest of Burma from 1885 onwards, exploratory expeditions were sent particularly to the border regions with China (Third Anglo-Burmese War). Here one expected trade routes into China, the "Golden Road to Cathay", among others for their opium. It is perfectly possible that the tribal poppy cultures on the other side of the practically non-existent border, in Yunnan or Szechwan, were an off-shoot of this Burmese conquest. The fact is that poppy cultures among the hill tribes started to flourish only after the Opium Wars with China (see ch. 30).

The story goes that an early James Bond, the bagpiper Sir James Scott, discovered many hectares with poppies in the 1890s in the Shan state that resembled rice fields. Other discoverers soon arrived here in Kokang and gave their own, very differing estimates of the availability of opium. They vary from 4,000 to 30,000 hectares ![43]

---

[41] If I see on the kind of sources on which this "ancient old" information is based (a *Police Journal* from the year 1941; an obscure magazine like the Burmese *Mooyit*), I have to question the procedure followed even more.

[42] Idem, p. 16.

[43] Idem, p. 28.

As a good bookkeeper Scott estimated a yield of 2.6 kg per hectare with a market price of 6-7 rupees (= about £1 at the time) per kilo just after the harvest and 10 rupees during the off-season. Whatever the estimates, this price leads to a substantial income for the region. Its popularity was greatly increased during a convention of the League of Nations (1930), when it was declared that Kokang opium was 'the best in the world', thanks to its high morphine content!

By 1900 opium was, anyway, the dominant crop in the Kokang region. From here the cultivation spread to other areas, while cultivators came from several directions. We could expect to find reports of how the practice of opium smoking, trade and smuggling increased rapidly. Scott's assessment of the use in 1900 is expressed as follows:

> It is to be noted that there are no victims of opium in these opium-producing districts, any more than there are in Ssu-ch'uan, where the people are the wealthiest in China and half the crops are poppy. It is only in places where opium is prohibitive in price that there are victims to opium. There to buy his opium, the poor man must starve himself. He dies of want and opium is blamed. Where opium is cheap, the people are healthy and stalwart. East of the Salween, the universal opinion of opium is that of the Turk, who stamps on his opium lozenges *Mash Allah*, the gift of God.[44]

To underline his view, Scott refers to opinions among hill-tribes like the Lahu or Akha who 'smoke opium because [they claim] it is the best thing for their health they know of'. In other tribes, like the Shan, Kachin or Palaung, however, who had already copied the European cant about opium, they started to lie, acted defiantly or responded hypocritically when questioned about opium use. In his time, according to Scott, in Kokang everybody was smoking opium 'and at all hours'. The rulers of Kokang governed an area so remote and earned profits so large that they did not control anything until the 1960s. That was not the case for the rulers of the southern part of Burma, where one had far greater opium problems.

And the British occupiers?

> It was to opium revenue that many British colonial officials became addicted. Not only did this differentiate them from the Burman rulers in the past, who had little if any use for opium or its revenue, this addiction also kept the British from ever taking serious actions to finally eliminate opium.[45]

---

[44] Quoted in Idem, p. 29. Apparently "Ssu-ch'uan" is the same as the Chinese province, Szechwan. The Salween is a river originating in Tibet and ending after nearly 3,000 kilometer in the sea near Rangoon in the south of Burma.

[45] Idem, p. 30.

The latter is a euphemism, since following the British takeover the opium consumption immediately grew rapidly thanks to the promotion campaigns of the EIC and the British colonial government in India. It was the Burmese authorities and the Mon Buddhists who strongly opposed the spread of opium use. Anti-opium tracts soon appeared, and demonstrations were held of hundreds of elders who went down on their bended knees with their head on the ground to implore that 'the opium plague should be removed ...' These elders were even willing to pay to compensate a loss of the Government's opium revenue.

And indeed, King Bodawpaya prohibited opium consumption in 1826, making it a capital offense in the Burmese state. After fierce British pressure a commercial treaty between the king and the viceroy of India was concluded in which, of course, trade in opium was permitted (1862). But sixteen years later there came a real Opium Act for Lower Burma (in 1888 also for Upper Burma) with royal sanctions against opium use. A remarkable aspect was that this act was not restricted as elsewhere to Chinese only or to any registered opium user in Lower Burma. Opium shops were closed down throughout Burma except in Rangoon, and so a whole network of anti-opium rules and laws gradually came into being.[46] Widespread actions against cannabis were launched as well.

Not many figures can be found about later years, but Balfour writes that in Burma the import 'has greatly increased, even more rapidly than the population'.[47] The consumption of 1869 had doubled ten years later; one reason for this was the continuous flow of Chinese immigrants

> and their use of the opium pipe is without any bad results. Amongst the Burmese, however, the demoralization, misery, and ruin produced by opium-smoking presents a painful picture.

But Chinese traders also played a role, as a Norwegian explorer remarked in 1881:

> Occasionally a caravan of Haw or Yunnan traders brings a fresh supply of merchandise into the city, principally wax ... [and] opium, a great quantity of which they smuggle under their wide coats and trousers ..[48]

The Burmese elite, under the influence of all kinds of modernisms brought by the English, started to develop a nationalist creed from the 1920s onwards. A historical theory was adapted in which the Burmese tribe was

---

[46] In a useful appendix (Idem, p. 115-123) Renard has listed all measures from 1782-1991.
[47] E. Balfour, vol. 3, p. 37.
[48] A. Maxwell Hill, p. 8, 9.

perceived as a nation, whose kings had by feats of valor created a Burmese kingdom (Golden Peacock throne) subordinating most tribal lands, dynasties or people like the Shan, Arakan, Karen, Chin and so forth. 'This unity was shattered by Britain, the kingdom dismembered, and separatism encouraged in keeping with the divide and rule strategem of foreign imperialists.'[49]

The British left in 1948. It is the year in which one of the few indigenous politicians who could keep Burma united, Aung San, was assassinated with his whole cabinet by Burmese coup-plotters. This was the beginning of a new wave of bloodshed and wars among "Rangoon" and nearly all tribal states. Furthermore, hundreds of thousands of persons, mainly of Indian descent, emigrated. The Burmese middle class "disappeared", leaving the economy in shock, from which it still has not recovered. The consequence was that the remaining people had to rely on an active black market fostered through a strong exchange of goods between Burma and Thailand.

This situation was highly favorable to the opium business and the rise of Burma as one of the main narco-countries. The CIA assessed this as follows:

> Opium is exported from Burma to overseas markets by sea from Rangoon and, after traveling through Thailand, from Bangkok. It is estimated that 30 tons were exported from Rangoon in 1955. This estimate is based on the following considerations: (a) it is estimated that 12 tons were exported to Singapore and Malaysia in 1955 from Burma [see table 35, p. 467 H.D.], and (b) Rangoon is one of the two principal supply ports for the Hong Kong and Macao markets. The opium traffic from Burma to Thailand is much larger than the shipments from Rangoon and is estimated to amount to approximately 90 tons.[50]

It is interesting how this report continues with a table in which the accelerated increase of opium prices is given relative to the distance the opium had to travel. The transport concerns 90 metric tons and about 1,500 km:

---

[49] C. T. Yawnghwe, p. 51. The author, himself a Shan nationalist, immediately added that this perception 'does not quite fit the facts', pointing to the language policy of the British to make English the national language. This must be a proof that one state was desired over separatism. He forgot that every European colonizer wanted its language to become the dominant one, but that politically the *indigenous* opposition was fought in endless battles and that it was a standard policy to prevent by all means a united front arising against the foreign rulers. Divide and rule by force or by bribes, and therefore, being friendly to one group (like the Shan nationalists!) and angry against another, and so on.

[50] Central Intelligence Agency, p. 8.

Table 32. Value of Estimated Exports of Opium from Burma to Thailand at Various Stages of Transport, 1955[51]

Stage of Transport	Value in wholesale prices x $1000.-
Producers location	1 350
Kentung, Burma	3 970
Thai–Burmese border	5 310
Chieng Mai, Thailand	6 840
Bangkok, Thailand	9 540

In 1988 the World Bank estimated that 40% of Burma's gross national product (US$3,000 million) changed hands on the black market annually.

This has been immensely profitable for the Karens and other rebels since the start of their rebellion in 1948. The Burmese government controlled only a few isolated points on its eastern border, so that the rebels could easily conduct big business to finance their military activities.[52]

Thailand (Siam)

Shallow historical evidence reveals that opium (or something which was designated as such) played some role in early Thai history. There is a law from 1350 pertaining to banditry stipulating that the public was prohibited from smoking, eating or selling opium. This cannot be considered reliable information.[53] The next mention of opium apparently concerns a late 18th-century source from the Bangkok Period. In the 19th-century Kings Rama I to IV decreed that those caught with opium must be punished, apparently an offense of the elite: confiscation of property; the defendant's families and slaves would become property of the realm; the opium was to be destroyed or publicly burned by monks. These performances received a specific name, *kratham chapanakit phao fin*, opium cremations. One of these kings undermined his own anti-opium regime in the 1840s:

---

[51] Idem, p. 9.

[52] R. Renard (1996), p. 47.

[53] T. Chaloemtiarana, p. 125. If this concerned opium, business on a rather large scale must have been carried out for some time. I know at the time no poppy growing, processing or exporting took place in the Far or Middle East with trade relations to this region. See also D. Duco, p. 55 ff.

Rama III's attempts to control trafficking in the drug were unsuccessful, however, because of the great profits to be had from the illegal opium trade. Accordingly, the government of Rama III began importing opium from India and selling it by auction to the highest bidders, who were called *nai akon*, or tax officials.[54]

Whether this happened on his own initiative or a foreign one is not known. Anyway, the next king, Mongkut (1804-1868), returned only partly to the old prohibition policy by restricting the opium use to the Chinese community. Thais were prohibited again and from that time on opium became associated with the rise of Chinese secret societies. It was an attempt to corner the opium market, as if Chinese needed secret societies to get free opium. This approach, in the framework of the so-called 'bamboo policy', was certainly fixed under the pressure of the English-Chinese Opium War and the American threatening of Japan (1854). [55]

Chinese secret societies did not have much to do with this, but they feared being the next target of the Western assaults. Therefore, Mongkut quickly made a deal with the English through the governor of Hong Kong, Sir John Bowring, as official representative of Queen Victoria. Sir John arrived with his personal steamship in Bangkok (1855). The result of this very British demonstration was a costly treaty for both parties: Mongkut had to abandon the traditional system of princely monopolies and farmings, the main income of his household, in favor of a simple import-export system which allowed the British to import, for instance, opium when and how much they liked. The prince was left with 3% import duty.

That the British were also allowed to rent or buy land and houses near Bangkok gave them the opportunity to establish an English settlement to control the implementation of the new treaty and to organize the selling of British opium in Siam.

That was not all: within a few years time Mongkut was forced to conclude similar treaties with France and the United States (1856), Denmark and Portugal (1858), the Netherlands (1860) and several other Western countries which smelled profits. Although they had never read the *Illias*, Mongkut and his successor Rama IV experienced the effects not of one but of many Trojan horses: in 1867 Siam lost its power over Cambodia to the French, and so on. Envy arose among Westerners regarding the fine position Bowring had obtained for the English.[56]

---

[54] T. Chaloemtiarana, p. 125.

[55] See the article of Henk Zoomers in R. Feddema (ed.), p. 42 ff.

[56] Explicitly mentioned by a Dutch negotiator with the Siamese authorities. See *Idem*, p. 57. This negotiator, Loudon, is highly arrogant and discriminating vis-à-vis the Siamese

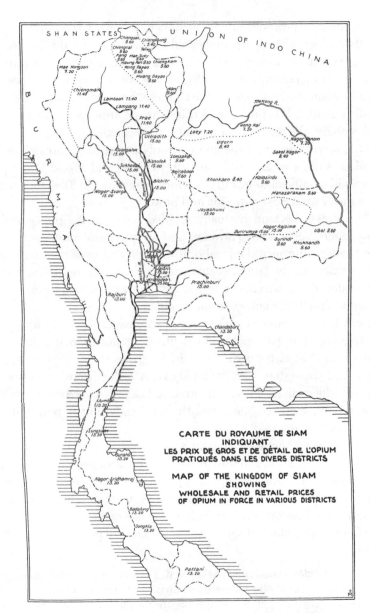

Map 14. Prices of Monopoly Opium in force in various Siamese Districts, ca. 1930
Source: Commission d'Enquête sur le Contrôle de l'Opium. League of Nations.

---

rulers: it is a shame that Bowring had given these childish simple 'Toeans' a prince-like status, who did nothing but established a harem and smoked too much opium (L. writes remarkably enough about 'belladonna'; idem, p. 59).

Although all powerful families in Siam lost thanks to the "Bowring treaty", the influential Bunnag family could compensate for this by strengthening its already strong position in the opium, alcohol and gambling business by increasing the prices.[57] The specific relation it had developed with its main consumer group, the Chinese, must have made the Bunnag family enemies. It is probably in this inimical atmosphere that the idea and probably the practice of Chinese secret societies arose.

Still, secret societies exist and certainly in the fully corrupt scene of Thailand's elite, where until long after the Second World War 'opium remained an official source of government revenue in Thailand, becoming a major source of corruption and power'.

This power became gradually divided between the police and the army, police general Phao Siyanon and army general Sarit, respectively. The former controlled the local opium trade and used it to finance his police machine; the latter became the leader of the country, a despotic paternalist, through a coup in 1958. Sarit's power base was strong military support of the USA's anti-communist policy.

Sarit hated hoodlums, opium, uncleanliness and social impropriety. Therefore, no long hair, rock-and-roll music, modern dancing, tight pants, and so on, but also no dirty roads, littering, stray dogs or beggars. Urbanized youngsters from the villages driving 'pedicabs' and using opium were the main target of Sarit's arrests. In a few years time nearly 8,000 were caught, sentenced for a month and mostly sent to reform institutions to be "re-educated".[58]

One personal hobby was to fight arson and fires, which often occurred in times of depression and sometimes with devastating effects. Sarit used these events to blame unpopular groups, e.g. Chinese or communists. They "confessed"—before they themselves were executed—to setting fires in the framework of a larger plan to create chaos.

After his coup Marshal Sarit announced his 37th proclamation with the words:

> Now, the designated time has arrived. The first minute after midnight on July 1, 1959 marks the ultimate termination of opium consumption in Thailand ... The sale and use of opium are illegal ... Alien offenders will be deported, and Thais will be marked as traitors who refuse to make sacrifices for the nation, which is equivalent to not cooperating with me personally

---

[57] Idem, p. 52.
[58] T. Chaloemtiarana, p.121 ff.

... I can sacrifice even my life. I consider that opium is a national menace, and I will do anything to save the nation.[59]

Opium dens were meant to be closed within six months, treatment centers were established to help addicts, 43,000 opium pipes were publicly and ceremoniously 'cremated', heroin producers in Bangkok arrested. The decision to wage all-out war on opium and heroin brought fame to Sarit and earned him the respect of the public.

This act of moral purity was counteracted, however, by Sarit's substantial cruelty and corruption to enrich himself, his family, eighty mistresses and friends. Upon his death (1968) they all quarrelled over about approximately US$140 million. Not opium but women, gambling (lottery) and excessive drinking appeared to be his weak spots. The Thai opium dossier will have to be explored in another publication.[60]

Malaysia (Melaka, Malacca) and Singapore

From the middle of the 18th-century, the Malays and other inhabitants of Melaka had many reasons to question the VOC's military preparedness.[61] For at least a century the Dutch were the dominant power. However, the serious conflicts between the commercial Bugis of Sulawesi and the Malays from around 1750, in which the latter asked for the protection of the Dutch, showed an unexpected weakness of the VOC.

In exchange for their help, the Malays Sultan Sulaiman promised the Dutch toll-free trade and other privileges. The lethal attack on the Bugis was planned by both. They did not wait, however, but took the initiative and laid siege to Melaka, burned houses in the suburbs and even raided the town itself. It was a shocking experience for the Malays, and in the following decades these events only strengthened the position of the Bugis.

The Dutch were not able to retaliate until 1761, but it was the last active Dutch campaign. Once they discovered that the cost of their presence in the region was becoming prohibitive, all parties realized what a contemporary observer expressed. He compared the VOC 'to a man infected with a creeping disease which, if not cured in time, would prove fatal'. A few years later it was over and out for the VOC.

---

[59] Quoted in Idem, p. 126.
[60] The start of it is described in C. Lamour, M. Lamberti, passim.
[61] For the following see B. Watson-Andaya, L. Andaya, p. 97 ff.

Its main competitor, the EIC, became gradually more important because the English controlled the cloth-producing and poppy growing areas in India after "Plassey".

> Malays had been smoking opium mixed with tobacco since the seven-teenth-century, when the Dutch began importing the drug into the area. A hundred years later their consumption had reached such heights that the Governor of Melaka could tell his superiors that "the people of Rembau, Selangor and Perak, like other natives, cannot live without opium", while Chinese accounts show that east coast Malays were equally addicted. No entrepot could compete in this new economic environment unless it had ready supplies of opium, and in 1786 Francis Light was to recommend the import of large quantities of the drug to Penang specifically to attract mer-chants.[62]

In particular, the English country traders, speaking fluent Malay, were highly successful thanks to their smuggling of weapons and opium, which were forbidden by the VOC. It was around 1800 that the region definitely became an important trading center on the road between India and China.

The main beneficiary on the indigenous side was the Bugis-controlled Riau archipelago, the 'key to the Straits'. Here vessels from all over the region flocked to trade: Riau became the principal point of exchange for smuggled spices, opium and other products like tin or cloth.

Instead of the Dutch, the British took over in the region. Singapore strengthened its position as holder of the "(military) key of Asian trade" and as center of tin mining, rubber plantations or shipbuilding. The whole peninsula and the opposite Sarawak (North Borneo) became a most strategic position. As explained in ch. 2, the relationship Raffles-Farquhar-opium tycoon Matheson resulted a century earlier in the (re)establish-ment of Singapore and surroundings as the internationally well-known pleasure center and "one big opium den" with all possible nasty conse-quences.

Newbold reported about 'that pernicious drug, opium' as the second main article and nearly equal in value with the first, Indian and other piece-goods (the third is tin):

> The total value of this article imported in the year 1835-6 amounted to the enormous sum of upwards of a million of dollars. Two hundred and fifty two thousand of which was the value of the quantity exported to China, most part of the remainder went to the east coast of the peninsula, to Java,

---

[62] Idem, p. 100.

Borneo, Celebes, Cochinchina, and Siam, and a considerable quantity to America. The opium trade with China is contraband. The total value exported annually from Calcutta and Bombay to the East is supposed to amount to about 3,000,000 lbs. The Patna opium is the most prized ... and sells from 710 to 720 Sp. drs [per chest]. Benares sells from 645 to 650 Sp.drs, and Malwa from 580 to 600 Sp. drs. Turkish opium, though disliked at first, has latterly come into greater demand.[63]

Here is demonstrated how Singapore was in the earliest phase already a world distribution center of opium; the "brand new" United States were not free from this 'pernicious drug'.[64]

There was, however, another side to this medal. In the period that the English had to earn their fortunes as owners of mines, plantations or banks, and as narcotic dealers or smugglers, they detested the Malays as too lazy to do the dirty work in the tin mines or on the rubber plantations. The British opium smugglers-investors used their lively trade with China to bring back a substantial Chinese labor force for the tin mines, plantations and, later, as operators of the tax farms.

Around 1835 the best paid Chinese hand-laborer got from 4-6 Spanish dollars a month and a Malay only $2.5-4.5. A skilled Chinese man like a carpenter got about 15 dollars, whereas a skilled Malay carpenter received only 5 dollars per month. Adult Malay women employed in weeding and similar work got 3-8 cents a day.[65]

As a rule of thumb the British believed that this import of Chinese workers was a reliable index of economic progress. They were right. The global framework changed drastically between the beginning of the 19th-century and the end of the Opium Wars. It is well described by Trocki:

> Most important was the expansion of the global market communicated to Singapore through the major trades: opium, capital, and manufactures from India and the West. Pepper, gambier, tin, and the other major commodity flows generated in Southeast Asia originally moved with the Western trade to China. ... In addition to redirecting the commodity flows to the West, the

---

[63] Th. Newbold, vol. 1, p. 363. Also elsewhere (Id., p. 57) he writes about 'that most debasing and pernicious drug, opium' in combination with the Chinese secret societies 'of which spring many of those daring outrages and robberies that disgrace our settlements.' See the article of B. ter Haar about 'secret societies' in D. Leese (ed.), p. 883-885.

[64] See Th. Newbold, Idem, p. 20, which reported that there was a commercial convention between Great Britain and the United States (1815), which restricted the American privilege of trade to Calcutta, Madras, Bombay and Prince of Wales' Island. Singapore was not mentioned because it did not yet exist (1818). An American tried to enter Singapore in 1825, but was "arrested". But 'an inconvenient and clandestine sort of traffic was still maintained' (Id., p. 21), until the matter was solved.

[65] Th. Newbold, vol. 1, p. 14, 15.

shift created a vast demographic eruption. It was as if the current of wealth flowing out of China began to pull with it the Chinese peoples themselves. Singapore came into being as a result of these global forces ...[66]

Opium played in this global shift the most crucial role. Singapore's opium scene in the 19th-century is, therefore, much more important than only in a local or regional context. It can be summarized in a table in which the whole constellation is symbolized. Trocki's central thesis that the British Empire in Asia was built on opium is certainly supported by the fate of Singapore. Together with Hong Kong, Singapore represents the fate of this empire. Officially, nearly half of all revenues of the British was earned here by opium, as the next table shows. This concerns, of course, only the colonial profit for the British. It cannot demonstrate how much private or individual British officials, military men or bankers earned. Indirectly, it also suggests how much a very few super-wealthy people (Chinese) pocketed as their share of the opium rents in this century.

Table 33. Singapore Opium Farm Annual Rent, 1820-1882 (selected years; in Spanish $)[67]

Year	Rent (x 1000)	Total Revenue (x 1000)	Percentage 2 from 3
1820	7	16	46
1825	24	76	32
1830	39	96	41
1835	58	119	48
1840	65	143	46
1845	108	232	47
1850	88	---	---
1855	148	288	51
1860	267	493	54
1865	270	671	40
1870	361	876	41
1875	398	967	41
1880	600	1 277	47
Total all years 1820-'82	11 551	25 669	Average: 45 %

---

[66] C. Trocki (1990), p. 220, 221.
[67] Idem, p. 96-97. Instead of the used indication 1820-21 I prefer 1820 etc. All figures are rounded.

Ellen La Motte added to this table the revenues of the years 1898-1906 as found in a report of the *Straits Settlements Opium Commission* (February 1909).This report gives all possible details about all possible aspects of the Opium Problem in the Straits Settlements. Among its members the opinions were divided about the harmfulness of opium, but

> as a means of raising revenue, the traffic was certainly justifiable. It was proven that about fifty per cent of the revenues of the Straits Settlements and the Federated Malay States came from opium trade and, as was naïvely pointed out, to hazard the prosperity of the Colony by lopping off half its revenues was an unthinkable proceeding.[68]

The table proves probably much better than others how dependent Western colonizers were on the opium business they themselves initiated or—in a positive perception—how successful their invention or colonial exploitation was.

Certainly it is important that Singapore is an axis in the colonial military and trade web of the Western powers. Let us also recall what Crawfurd and Raffles said about "their city" (ch. 2) and how the latter's mission was to make Singapore opium-free! Raffles got a beautiful statue in innocent white marble for it in Singapore.

Little is known about the early opium farms in this port. The British records say almost nothing about their identity or their organization. The British occupiers of the place, like Crawfurd, were only interested in maximizing their profits. They were successful: in the first decade the total revenue increased by a factor of six, while the opium rent in it increased by a factor of 5-6. The second decade presented only a slight increase for both, which was also the case for the period 1840-1850, apparently as a side effect of the Opium War with China.

Spectacular, however, was the growth in the opium business during the following period, the start of the booming years for the British opium dealers, traders, bankers or shippers and, therefore, also for Singapore, although the competition with Hong Kong wais fierce. The end of the Second Opium War was, of course, the definite turning point for the whole opium business. The British had taken control of the commerce of India, China and Southeast Asia in less than fifty years.

---

[68] E. La Motte, p. 24. For 1898 the opium revenue was 46%, in 1901 it had increased to 53% and in 1904 even to 59.1%.

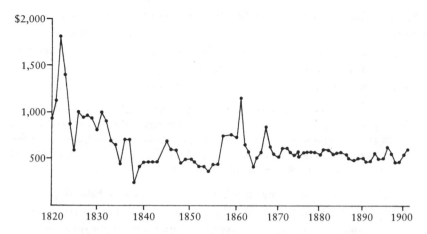

Figure 11. Average annual opium price in Singapore, 1820-1901 (Spanish dollars per chest).
Source: C. Trocki, 1990, p. 59. Compiled from various issues of SFP and ST.

It is difficult to see how the British succeeded in doing this without opium. It was the major form of economic leverage.[69]

The table of Singapore's opium export in Appendix 1 complicates this picture for, at least, the period 1830 to 1870.

We could have expected that when such enormous amounts of money are earned in a very cheap way by relatively few people, they would make a deal in order to divide the profits fairly. Instead, the reverse occurred: the parties involved became greedier and the mutual struggles increased. One thing remained relatively quiet after the Second Opium War: the opium prices. In the preceding period the competition was fierce, the political and economic situations unstable, the fate of the individual dealers uncertain.

For Singapore, Trocki identified and described in detail the fate of four "parties" involved in the 19th-century opium business: the British merchants and officials; Malay chiefs; Chinese merchants and revenue farmers; Chinese *kongsis* or brotherhoods.[70] For the Chinese side of this constellation, see next chapter. They were involved or had an interest in a specific side of the Opium Problem: consumption, trade, speculation, control, taxation, etc. Their local games were played in a new world

---

[69] C. Trocki (1990), p. 221.
[70] Idem, p. 220 ff.

economic constellation, which became much more important thanks to the core opium function of Singapore in it.

Singapore as British "Cape of Good Hope" also meant recuperation for everything (ships, etc.) and everybody (leisure, entertainment and retirement home for white, rich colonialists). Quite different images of the Malays were created along with these different functions. The "leisure" image is reproduced, for instance, by a naive expatriate, Frank Swettenham (1913):

> The real Malay is courageous ... but he is extravagant, fond of borrowing money and slow in repaying it ... He quotes proverbs ... never drinks intoxicants, he is rarely an opium smoker ... he is by nature a sportsman ... proud of his country and his people, venerates his ancient customs and traditions and has a proper respect for constituted authority ... lazy to a degree ... and considers time of no importance.[71]

Ideal people for those who belong to the 'constituted authority' as the dominant minority of those "English at ease". One may ask where this Swettenham resided. If he had walked along the sandy beach of Pasir Panjang, in the southwestern part of Singapore, he could have visited the *House of Tiny Tin Tubes*. This was the state-owned opium factory.

In 1910 in Singapore, the development from opium farming to *Opiumregie,* like elsewhere, was completed by the opening of a modern opium factory. Once the mechanization of opium production and distribution was a fact, mass addiction could be realized. Of course, the usual nursery tales of diminishing opium consumption are told, but the fact is that their factory could produce a million *tahils* of opium a year or some 450,000 two-*hoon* tin tubes of *chandu* daily. A Mr. Walling wrote enthusiastically:

> The machines which do this are beautiful, highly technical and impossible for me as a layman to describe. After sealing, they [the tubes] are weighed by delicate, automatic, weighing machines, and packed in small boxes, two hundred at a time. They rest there like miniature Sainsbury's cooking eggs!'[72]

However, Swettenham was not a simple English expatriate and was not really naive, because he was the governor of the Straits Settlements. He must have known perfectly well what was going on in his area of "opium jurisdiction", because he personally ran the periodic opium auctions. Furthermore, he was the one who organized the basic transformation

---

[71] Quoted in B. Watson-Andaya, L. Andaya, p. 175, 176.
[72] Quoted by C. Trocki (1990), p. 224.

from opium farm system into *Opiumregie*. The following table provides the details, although it suggests that only the Chinese in Malaysia and Singapore used opium. In an ethnically diverse landscape, many groups were available.[73] Swettenham's opinion about Malays quoted above should be seen as a typical Pavlovian reaction of all foreign Western colonizers to divide and rule the available ethnic groups immediately upon arrival.

Table 34. Estimated monthly costs and sales of selected Malayan opium farms, 1903[74]

	Singapore	Pinang	Melaka	Johor	Kedah
Estimated Chinese population	164 000	98 000	19 000	150 000*	39 000
Estimated chandu sales in *tahils*	140 000	74 337	11 000	80 000	28 000
Gross chandu sales in $	433 740	230 432	33 000	140 000	76 000
Estimated costs in $	138 540	66 749	9 150	58 600	30 200
Opium farm rent in $	215 000	172 000	26 000	80 000	43 000**
Spirit farm rent in $	50 000	45 000	5 000	10 000	
Net profit or loss in $	30 200	- 53 317	- 7 150	- 9 000	2 800

* This figure was thought to be 'greatly overestimated'
** This figure is the combined opium and spirit farm rent

The table gives an overly pessimistic picture, because the spirit sales are not included, although its rent is. Even in present terms a pure profit of $30-35,000 per month (360,000 to 420,000 per year) is substantial for people in the street business. A century ago this was an enormous profit in Malaysia or Singapore. Apart from this, the money capitals which circulated every month among tax farmers or consumers in the opium business (half of the bureaucratic machine of the British) were unbelievable for a region in which wages were counted in cents per day.

Ellen La Motte visited Singapore in January 1917 and stayed in the first-class *Hotel de l'Europe*. The first morning at breakfast, she was already confronted with an opium-addicted waiter, 'a handsome young Malay', who was in such a state that it was impossible for him to handle the nor-

---

[73] In 1970 the Malays numbered 47%, Chinese 34%, Indians 9% and among the rest one could find Arabs, Filipinos, Dayaks or Thais. In the Borneo part, the Chinese were between 20-30%.

[74] C. Trocki (1990), p. 201. Johor is the first region on the peninsula past Singapore; Kedah is the most northern region on the border with Thailand about 800 kilometer north of Singapore.

mal breakfast orders.[75] In her tours through the streets, she was confronted time and again with opium dens selling always the same

> little, triangular packets, each containing enough for about six smokes. Each packet bears a label, red letters on a white ground, "Monopoly Opium" ... House after house of feeble, emaciated, ill wrecks, all smoking Monopoly Opium, all contributing, by their shame and degradation, to the revenues of the mighty British Empire.[76]

That evening after dinner she read an article in a copy of the *Straits Times* (a Reuter's Telegram, 17th January 1917). It concerned a row involving the Chinese in Liverpool: the previous night 31 Chinese were arrested during police raids on opium dens; great quantities of opium were seized; the police were attacked in one place by the Chinese, who threw boots and other articles from the roof. La Motte reflected:

> It must be very perplexing to a Chinese sailor, who arrives from Singapore, to find such a variation in customs. To come from a part of the British Empire where opium smoking is freely encouraged, to Great Britain itself where such practices are not tolerated. He must ask himself, why it is that the white race is so sedulously protected from such vices, while the subject races are so eagerly encouraged. It may occur to him that the white race is valuable and must be preserved, and that subject races are not worth protecting ... as if subject races were fair game—if there is money in it ... Is this ... what we mean when we speak of "our responsibility to backward nations" or of "the sacred trust of civilization" or still again when we refer to "the White Man's burden"?'[77]

Still, this Malaya including Singapore was also perceived as a model colony for the whole of Southeast Asia in the *Interbellum*. For the British expatriates this country was most attractive as 'a Tory Eden in which each man is contented with his station', because they were in full control of the local elites through a variety of administrative systems. The three "races" were kept in balance: Malays in the paddy fields, "British Indians" on the immense rubber plantations and the Chinese in the shops and tin mines. Indeed, Malaya was the largest producer of tin and rubber, but thanks to the government monopoly in the manufacture and sale of opium half of the country's income still came from this source. The colonial Governor was already familiar with the rationalizations in 1924:

---

[75] E. La Motte, p. 18-22.

[76] Idem, p. 20, 21.

[77] Idem, p. 22. In 1917 in the official *Blue Book* was published that the total revenue of the 'Colony of the Straits Settlements' is $19,672,104.- and that $9,182,000.- came from opium (47%). (Idem, p. 25).

> Opium smoking in Malaya is not the awful scourge believed in by western sentimentalists ... [it] is not doing as much harm as drink in England. It can never be stopped in Malaya ... Smuggling is impossible to prevent, and the money now coming into revenue would go to the smugglers. Any attempt to earmark our opium revenue ... to humanitarian works ... would play the devil with our finances.[78]

This tells us as much about the position of the immigrant Chinese as about opium and their British "masters". The latter acted also in a spectacular way during the Japanese occupation by suddenly issuing a total prohibition of all opium activities immediately after the war (for the period of the Japanese occupation, see ch. 27). However, after the war nothing happened in this direction.

After the war, London still believed: if India was the jewel in the imperial crown, Malaya was the industrial diamond.[79] Sixteen years later the new Governor estimated (same as his predecessor) that Malaya (Singapore) was 'worth' about £227.5 million to the British Empire; about 50% must derive from opium. Most of this disappeared mainly to the City of London. Its status as most profitable British colony was achieved, of course, not only by its resources (tin, etc.):

> The key to the great public works and civic conceits of the Strait Settlements was opium. Duty on opium accounted for between 40 and 60 per cent of its annual revenue. Its production was monopolized by the government "Chandu factory" on Pepys Road in Singapore which turned out 100 million tubes a year. Much of the revenue burden of Malaya therefore fell upon the Asian, particularly Chinese, labourers who were the greatest consumers of opium. The British crescent in Asia was supported by narco-colonialism on a colossal scale.[80]

This remained at least until the 1960s. A change of opium provider took place: instead of the British Empire opium from India, it came from the Middle East. At the end of the history in this book, Singapore was still considered the primary opium port in the Far East by the CIA. An impression of its importance can be given through the perception of this secret service.

---

[78] Quoted by P. Brendon, p. 338.
[79] See for the following Ch. Bayly, T. Harper, p. 33.
[80] Idem, p. 33.

Table 35. Raw Opium Seized in Singapore by Country of Origin and Value Imports, 1954-55[81]

Country of Origin	Quantity Seized (in pounds)		Percent of Total Seizures		Estimated Value of Imports of Raw Opium in US$ b/
	1954	1955	1954	1955	1955
Iran	1 834	2 333	46,5	50	19 849 750
"Yunnan"[a]	914	965	23	20	5 440 060
India	546	552	14	12	5 513 892
Burma	656	547	16,5	12	3 705 132
Unknown	9	498	---	6	2 140 800
Total	3 959	4 695	100	100	36 649 634

[a] 'This term is used by local traffickers to indicate opium received through Thailand and probably consists of illicit supplies originating in the adjoining areas of the Wa States and Kentung State in Burma, Laos, and North Thailand as well as in Yunnan.'
[b] CIF values (Cost, Insurance, Freight)

The first five columns of this table do not tell us much about the normal imported quantities of opium, but first and foremost about the ability of the Singapore customs organization. And this 'ability' could also refer to: either the stupidity of the Iranian smugglers or the change they left for the custom officials, but also to the corruption of the Singapore custom officials *not* to seize the competing opium from "neighboring" Thailand, Laos and Burma.

The *Singapore Central Narcotics Intelligence Bureau* estimates that the markets in Singapore and Malaya distribute 100 tons of illicit opium annually. The total number of opium addicts in Singapore and Malaya is estimated to be 115,000. Since neither country has any domestic production, the opium must be imported from elsewhere.

It remains remarkable that, notwithstanding the relative proximity of opium, the Iranian form was preferred. We can assume that this preference was based on ease of import and availability. Furthermore, the high morphine content (9-11 per cent, compared with 6-9 for the "Yunnan" type) seems to have been attractive.[82]

It is more interesting to note how soon close opium relations between the two most important opium-producing regions were realized after the Second World War. CIA reports state that

---

[81] Central Intelligence Agency, p. 16. and 19. In tables on page 17 and 19 the same figures are used as in the %-columns of table p. 16, but now they have to refer to 'Amount (Metric Tons)'!
[82] Idem, p. 16 ff.

a small syndicate of Bahreini Arabs trades in opium on a very large scale from Dubai to Aden, East Africa and Singapore. The opium is procured from Iran and shipped to Aden concealed in cargo where it is transferred to oceangoing vessels ... The town of Qasbat, Iran, is the center for smuggling opium into Kuwait ... Opium smugglers have also used commercial aircraft to move opium from Iran to the Malayan area.[83] Regarding the second destination in the table, it was reported that nearly every ship or commercial airplane arriving from Bangkok carried illicit narcotics, usually opium. Smuggling by airplane concerned a small-scale and intermittently used means. Furthermore, there must have been considerable transports over land and by rail from northern Thailand to Haadyai, apparently the smuggling center of South south Thailand, but also directly across the Malaysian border.

The estimated values of the transports into Malaysia and Singapore reveal that opium was the sixth largest import into both countries. The cost of importing into Malaysia was very high. Apparently, an artificial measure:

Bribes alone are reported to account for almost half of the delivered costs. In 1955, opium could be purchased in Bangkok at $105,831 a ton, or approximately 39 percent of the price in Malaysia.[84]

It is a conclusion symptomatic for the general (opium) corruption in the whole of the Southeast Asian realm.

---

[83] Idem, p. 17, 18.
[84] Idem, p. 19.

CHAPTER TWENTY-FIVE

THE ROLE OF THE CHINESE IN SOUTHEAST ASIA

> The emigrating portions of the Chinese people come from a relatively minute area in the provinces of Kuangtung and Fukien, but wherever they go ... their adaptation is so quick and so perfect, their industry and their economy so in excess of those of the natives of these lands, their solidarity and their power of mutual cohesion so phenomenal, that it is necessary for the security of the remainder of the human race that "the Chinese must go!"
>
> Rev. Arthur Smith (1894)[1]

About an "Identity" of Chinese Migrants

Smith's exclamation reverberates in the many present discussions about the identities of foreigners in most Western countries. And remind us of old-fashioned discourses about racism and nationalism, although they are now often clothed in highly abstract and rather meaningless words, not even concepts. To reflect on something like "the identity of the Southeast Asian Chinese" must lead to questions of who defined "The Southeast Asian Chinese " and under which circumstances? Almost certainly, we would arrive at British or French colonial sources of around 1850 qualified by a large degree of ignorance, prejudice and fear of "the other" of the "white" settlers, missionaries, administrators and military. It is not surprising that recently it was still argued 'that the Chinese nationalist movements in colonial Malaya', including those in which prominent Straits Chinese figures participated, were China-oriented and uninterested in developing 'a separate overseas Chinese identity' or in getting involved in local 'indigenous nationalism'.[2]

---

[1] A. Smith (1894), p. 146, 147. See also A. Smith (1907) chapter two for many details on 'A Great Race' and about the opium question p. 73-80.

[2] D. Goh, p. 484. Important is the article of Wang Gungwu about the overseas Chinese (*huaqiao*) in D. Leese (ed.), p. 123-128 .

Of course, Chinese have migrated away from China for centuries, originally did not belong to the indigenous population, and had no other alternative than to do what the American Reverend Smith demonstrates: therefore, they were attractive for the other "white" foreigners; sometimes also for the indigenous population, in which case they were promoted to *peranakans*. These are locally born "indigenous foreigners", who could marry the indigenous daughters. In contrast to the *peranakans*, the Westerners were brutal and war-like from the very beginning, always focused on finding enemies.

At the start of the confrontations between the British and the Chinese, the former had difficulties with xenophobic opinions, which were not yet accompanied by racism and aggressiveness à la Reverend Smith. One of the few available examples of this early perception comes from Newbold, who wrote his extensive books in the time the British opium smuggling was about three decades old and already highly profitable.

The Englishman Thomas Newbold (1806-1850; soldier, administrator, traveler, writer) reproduced the classical English-colonial way of reasoning in his *British Settlements* (1839). Immigrant Chinese from Canton, Fukien or Macao had the following characteristics:

> They are active, industrious, persevering, intelligent, educated sufficiently to read, write, and to use the swampan or reckoning board. They are entirely free from prejudices of caste and superstition, which are grand stumbling blocks to the natives of India. On the other hand, they are selfish, sensual, ardent lovers of money, though not misers; inveterate gamblers, and often addicted to smoking opium. The Chinese will expose himself to all dangers for the sake of gain, though he would not stir a finger to save a drowning comrade. They make bad soldiers, it is said; but the experiment has not ... been yet properly tried under British authority. They are capable of any crime, provided they run no direct personal risk ... ruled by the strong hand of power, they form an excellent class of subjects; but where the reins of government are slack, they are apt to turn refractory and rebellious.[3]

Newbold also created the highly dangerous fear of the 'secret fraternities' with which the Dutch in Java had such a 'bad experiences' and which in China 'are deemed so dangerous to the government, as to be interdicted under penalty of death'. Chinese perjury, bribery and sometimes open violence was also well known in Singapore, according to him.[4] (He could

---

[3] Th. Newbold, vol. 1, p. 13. He gathered the information for his 1000-page book in the years preceding 1835.

[4] Newbold later contributed to the anti-Chinese sentiments. C. Trocki (1990), p. 20.

demonstrate how the giving of bribes was criminal, and not demanding or receiving them).

Remarkably enough, the British Singaporeans reacted to this and other remarks about Chinese immigrants by not selling Newbold's book. They objected strongly and publicly in newspapers against the denunciation of the 'greedy Chinese' since 'they regarded the pursuit of material gain as one of the main virtues of Chinese settlers'.[5] The book was, furthermore, discredited because of other 'unfashionable opinions' (his proposal to tax the remittances exported by the Chinese settlers or to abolish a part of the British bureaucracy in Singapore). Turnbull does not mention Newbold's anti-opium stand in the spirit of Raffles, which must have been the main source of criticism: half of the Malaysian and Singaporean budgets came from opium; the turnover of the annual trade was already at that time a million Sp. dollar.

In present Europe and the USA, migrants are feared by the settled, while there are many reasons for the migrants to fear the settled: the former may work for a trifle, and then be forced to return to where they came from. How one defines an identity is never discovered in these migrants, because only their labor is interesting, not their minds. Some very basic facts are forgotten.

The largest minority, if not a substantial majority, of all people in the world leave their birthplace sooner or later for many other environments; they undoubtedly develop several kinds of quite different allegiances with other men and women than their family; most of them use or have to learn more than one language or dialect. Many kinds of other mobilities are familiar as well.

Once turned around, the problem looks different: the political and religious choices are basically intolerant, they destroy "identities" more than they create them; patriots, seen as identity-supporting, are without doubt waning in increasingly larger political constellations. Small pockets of them radicalize quickly; and so on and so forth.

The influential Reverend Arthur Smith demonstrates aberrations of the identity discourse perfectly, concerning "Chinese who left their birthplace to find a future outside China". Later, the reverend was thankful that the present Chinese did not migrate wholesale, like their ancestors at the time of Djenghis Khan: 'it is hard to see what would become either of us, or of our doctrine that only the fittest survive'!

---

[5] Idem, vol. 1, p. ix in C. Turnbull's introduction.

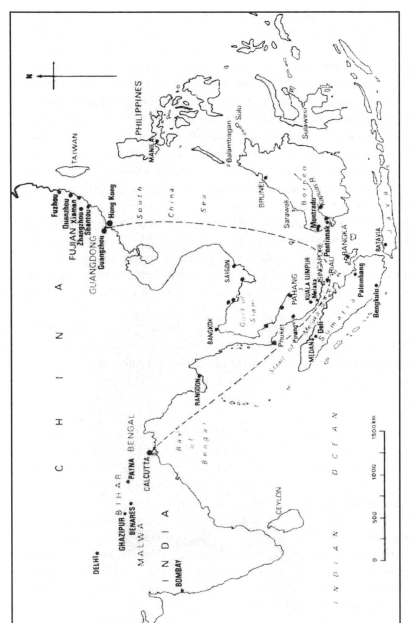

Map 15. British Trade routes in the 19th-century and important areas of Chinese Settlements in the Malay world.

Source: C. Trocki (2004).

It is remarkable that in his social-Darwinist perspective, he forgot the already invented tradition of "Chinese isolation" and the "Chinese aversion against an Open Door". Apparently, the newer racist discourse has replaced it and now supports notions like: Chinese do not want contact with us, hate us, do not acknowledge the benefits of a Western civilization; they, therefore, are primitive and will be strangers whom you must fear and attack if possible. The other side of the old coin?

It should be investigated further whether the extended colonial practices of the West have proven a fundamental and basic inability of the Western elite to communicate with the outer world in other than a war-like manner. This was apparently the case when they felt guilty about their own opium production and distribution in these Asian countries. It seems as if the highly mobile life inside and outside of the *many* Chinese regions (border or coastal) or ethnic groups was never acknowledged, nor were the often dramatic fate and extreme poverty of Chinese in Western countries working in mines, plantations, on railways and so on.

It is disappointing that, even today, most acclaimed studies place the problem with this Chinese emigration in an ambiguous context. Take Philip Kuhn's recent study with its substantial merits.[6] To explain the background of the Chinese emigrations in the past, he starts to look into China's internal agricultural situation and problems like land shortage. That is not unimportant, although one has to make a more complicated "push" story, considering that land shortage can be solved inside the enormous Chinese territory rather than by migrating overseas.

There are, furthermore, very different regions and circumstances leading to emigrations: natural disasters like floods or famines in China, bloody revolts or the collapse of local industry by cheap foreign imports and extreme exploitation. Why peasants migrate from the interior and why fishermen, traders or sailors along the coasts migrate are different stories. It seems reasonable to expect that people acquainted with the seas will and can migrate sooner to foreign countries (the straight distance between Canton and Batavia was 3,000 km and along the coasts about 4,000 km; a trip of one or two years!).

Still, the reasons given apparently do not cover the most relevant issues. Differences between permanent and temporary leaves should be considered as well. For instance, homesickness was very widespread under the coolies and Chinese literati alike. The return movements are considerable, which result in something other than "overseas Chinese".

---

[6] Ph. Kuhn.

No, the real problem with these emigrations is situated in the "host" countries. There is a considerable "pull" movement, trade in Chinese labor for Western colonial enterprises (see ch. 17 about the tin mines). A part of this coolie force remains in the foreign country. Chinese migrants are flexible and rather romantic people; they are prepared to give their labor for low wages, but mainly because they expect to get some "Golden Future" in return. In particular, later emigrations and the reuniting with already "arrived" family. This perspective will not only lead to quite different investigations, but also to other proposals for eventual solutions. The approaches are as varied as "blaming the Chinese" versus "blaming the Western assault on China".

More to the point is, therefore, Daniel Goh's study of the so-called Straits Chinese. The richer strata among them repeatedly show a conservative loyalty to the British Empire, which secured their safety only as long as the British patience lasted, their labor remained cheap, and some Chinese purses were so abundantly filled that the British always could "borrow" them.[7] In a more extreme way this kind of loyalty is shown, for instance, by the Parsis and Jews of Bombay.[8]

It concerns the producers of the opium, the product with which the largest and most long-lasting profits could be gained. For the Opium Problem, it seems inappropriate to study the migrations; only the context in which the "Chinese overseas" had to operate until the 1950s is relevant.

The Chinese Settle(ment) Strategy

The first features Western observers associated with this subject are "secret societies", *triads* or *kongsis*, which were well-known after the 1860s.[9] It became a hype comparable to what we have to swallow every day about a nearly mythical al-Quaeda. After the British stopped their Opium Wars, the European creators of the Opium Problem simply disap-

---

[7] D. Goh mentions relevant examples of this from a British Governor, Swettenham (1901), who knew perfectly well about the real relationship between the British Empire and "their" Chinese (p. 497 ff.) compared to Lim Boon Keng's speech from 1917 (p. 499).

[8] N. Randeraaad (ed.), p. 33 ff. which has all the traits of a fanatic collaborating with the foreign occupier, which inevitably leads to great suspicion and inimical reactions among nationalist Indian groups (Id. p. 39).

[9] In Vietnam there were Chinese organizations called *bangs* based on language and geographic origin (so Cantonese, Hokkien, Hakka, etc. *bangs*). They organized all things relevant to Chinese culture from schools to hospitals. Therefore, they cannot be compared to *kongsis*.

peared behind the widely publicized, alleged criminal activities of these Chinese *kongsis*.

As Trocki recently described them for the first time, the *kongsis* represent an effective strategy to settle in a foreign, often inimical, environment. This refers to both environment (of the mines and plantations) and settlement (town and city). Social, economic and cultural similarities and contradictions between town and country are covered by this. Sociologically, it concerns quite normal group formations for people of more or less the same background and everyday experience who do not yet know the new language, customs, etc. In the economic perspective of the 19th-century world, there is a close relationship between the Chinese *kongsis* and the provision of Asian resources to the European "industrial revolution" as demonstrated in ch. 17. This concerns thus both the resources and the labour necessary to obtain them.

It is similar to the situation in Western Europe, where hundreds of thousands of *Wanderarbeiter* (migrant laborers) came from Germany or East European countries to work in the Belgian, French and Dutch mines and factories. They were housed in very overcrowded conditions, exploited by ruthless proprietors and mostly spoke unintelligible dialects; they drank too much, and in exceptional cases they chose a criminal way of life. If they joined established trade unions, they protested within the normal channels for protesting; if they started their own strikes for obvious reasons, the trade unions were their fiercest enemies, and the mining or factory management could play an easy divide and rule game.

Many returned back to the homeland after a few years with some savings; a substantial number remained in Belgium, etc. and became more or less reasonably acclimated (very recently one of them became even prime minister in Belgium). For the latter their original isolation was a temporary disadvantage, for the former a temporary advantage, making their estrangement of the homeland less severe.

Compared to this Western mobile labor force, the Chinese one in Southeast Asian mines, plantations and other locations had to work under much more severe circumstances: many of them soon perished due to their poor treatment. Those who survived and stayed in Malaysia or the East Indies must have been mostly addicts. They were definitely in need of much support, which could be received from missionaries (if they accepted some Western belief) or Chinese "rescue" organizations.

The Western occupiers remained suspicious of the latter normal (temporary) support: "unknown activities" of 19th-century proletarian groups in Europe or here in Southeast Asia transformed them automatically into dangerous, criminal and secret groups.

In both areas the definitions and laws are made by the British, French or Dutch bosses. They were themselves foreign in Southeast Asia and were now confronted with other foreign "guests". In addition, these Western occupiers were not the most generous people in Europe; they preferred not to invest capital to alleviate the life of the destitute migrant workers.

While Southeast Asians were willing or obliged to offer their labor and inventiveness, they largely had to depend on the Western foreigners. In this triangle game between Westerners, Chinese and indigenous people, the Chinese immigrants were the weakest party for a long time: labor competitors of the indigenous, labor dependents of the Westerners and, therefore, exploited to the utmost.

Indeed, the *kongsis* provided some safety and shelter for its Chinese members or supporters. They made them stronger in the daily fights and made it more difficult for the Westerners to exploit them. They, further-more, became more competitive towards the indigenous interests: irrita-tion about this competition, suspicion, jealousy, ignorance form the best combination to make others dangerous and even criminal, if the social barriers become too high for them to surmount within a reasonable time.

Trocki formulates this as follows for Singapore *kongsis* around the time Reverend Smith wrote his bestseller:

> The failure of British observers to dwell on economic factors when dealing with the Chinese *kongsis* appears linked to the general tendency of the Europeans to criminalize *kongsi* activities. If the *kongsis* were essentially illegal organizations, then the possibility of their playing a necessary eco-nomic function in the British settlements was not at issue. If the cause of strife could be located in China or in some deviant characteristic of Chinese culture, rather than in the immediate economic environment of the colony, the British could easily deny the possibility that they themselves should bear responsibility for being a partial cause of the strife.[10]

The negative perception of these Chinese groups was specifically appar-ent after 1850 when many more Chinese "coolies" appeared in the streets, mines, railways and plantations. At that time many impatient Western adventurers of the types described in chapters 17 and 18 arrived to estab-lish mines, plantations and factories. It is also the era that opium started to influence all relationships in a large part of the world where Chinese

---

[10] C. Trocki (1990), p. 37.

migrants appeared. That cannot be a coincidence, and it is not difficult to decide now which is cause and effect.

Tens of thousands of Chinese migrated to North America, Australia or New Zealand in the 19th-century (see ch. 28). Rice, silk and tea already belonged in a flourishing world market. These immigrants created a new world market for all Chinese products and activities; not only the *chinoiserie* hype at the end of the 19th-century, but also other features ranging from Chinese restaurants to the cheap, colorful playthings and nightclub accessories (see further ch. 22).

Markets are communication systems in which producers and consumers are connected in many ways, of which the exchange in goods and money is the most important one. Chinese emigrants connected their new locations with their Chinese homes by transmitting money back to their families left in China and receiving all kinds of products from China. Opium forms the *leading* commodity in the old and the new markets, with all possible consequences.

The (pre-)History of the Chinese Opium Performance

In the reconstruction of the Dutch opium history, we were confronted several times with the role Chinese immigrants played. It is important to note that the Chinese had a long history in the East Indies. It extends back at least to 1400 when trade developed between Banten and China, and the Chinese started to settle on Java and probably elsewhere in the archipelago. They slowly mixed with the Javanese population and established an original part of the Javanese population.

Asian Trade

Ong-Tae-Hae wrote already in 1791:

> The virtuous influence of our government extending far, all the foreigners have submitted, and thus mercantile intercourse is not prohibited. Those who ply the oar and spread the sail, to go abroad, are principally the inhabitants of the Fokien and Canton provinces, who have been in the habit of emigrating, for the space of 400 years; from then early part of the Bêng dynasty (AD 1400) up to the present day ...[11]

---

[11] Ong-Tae-Hae, p. 2.

Ill. 20. A Chinese junk amidst Southeast Asian and European vessels, ca. 1820
Source: J. Blussé, 1986, p. 152. Note the passenger cabins at the stern of the junk.

Therefore, long before the White Man looked for a new burden and created his Chinese isolation myth, the Chinese had an extensive maritime
and land trade system and migrated over huge distances.[12] Their migrations were not confined to that enormous country of China itself, but
encompassed the whole of Asia from at least the thirteenth-century
onwards. Apart from and together with a lively trade, there were small
groups settling all along the trade routes of the caravans or ships. This not
only concerns the famous Silk Route, which still connects the Far East
with the Middle East and has hundreds of settlements along it. There is
also the old caravan trade route with Southeast Asian countries and, in
particular, the extensive trade by junks deep into the Indonesian archipelago long before Western powers came to dominate the markets in the
East.

---

[12] See even H. Gelber and J. Spence (1998) for many examples of this European and
American myth. A main source of them is, indeed, the Macartney opium mission of 1793
which was accompanied by the most stupid anti-Chinese propaganda, including the myth
about the two cardinal vices of Chinese men: 'their passion for gambling and their appe-
tite for opium' (Spence, p. 102). D. Willmott, one of the few who studied the internal structure of Chinese enterprises, was confronted with Chinese business failures ascribed to the
'speculative nature' of the Chinese (p. 52). Acknowledging that speculation is a characteristic of Chinese business, he concludes anyway: 'But it is doubtful whether Chinese entrepreneurs are any more speculative in business than their counterparts in other ethnic
groups.' (Id.) He should have added: and than Western capitalist entrepreneurs.

The best-known voyager was Zheng He (or Cheng Ho, 1371-1435).[13] He was made an admiral of a fleet of 200-300 large, 6-9 masted junks (these ships were four times larger than the ship Columbus used). During seven trips Zheng He visited Arabia (Aden or Hormuz), East Africa (Mogadishu, Malindi), West India (Calicut, Cochin), Ceylon, Southeast Asia (Malacca, Siam), South Asia (the Indonesian archipelago). Some say that this fleet or ships of it also traveled the Atlantic Ocean.

Trade was the first aim, but some suppose that also imperialistic motives played a role since a substantial army always accompanied the fleet. However, no colonies or even strongholds were established. The aim of these voyages was to gather as much knowledge as possible about all the countries visited, from which detailed maps and chronicles were prepared (Ma Huan, 1416).

The military power must have had a defensive purpose, but Zheng He used it ruthlessly to suppress the many pirates in the Chinese and Southeast Asian waters. Pirates had plagued the lively Chinese or Arabian trade and fishery in these waters for a long time. Furthermore, these substantial fleet movements were used to relocate large numbers of Chinese Muslims to the nascent Malacca and other places. From that time Malacca became one of the most important international trade centers. In addition, in many countries small settlements of Chinese (mostly Muslims) were established along the coasts as trading and industrial centers, or Chinese lived in a quarter of an indigenous settlement.

... their industry and economy ...

At the time the Portuguese or Dutch entered the East Indies, every important town had such a "colony" of Chinese merchants and shopkeepers. From China they imported household pottery and porcelain, cotton goods, silk and paper, while they exported to China pepper, nutmeg and cinnamon. Junks came and went regularly and in large numbers. It did not take long before the Chinese established sugarcane mills; they were involved in wine, candle and peanut oil production. The Chinese elite from Batavia, Banten or Semarang, who had strong relations with the Southeast Asian and Chinese junk trade, also traded in the 18th-century in large quantities of opium imported by the VOC from Bengal. Early in the 17th-century local Indonesian rulers had already established some

---

[13] See J. Roberts, p. 172 ff., H. Gelber, p. 88 ff.; D. Willmott, p. 3 ff. and the relevant *Wikipedia* articles.

system of farming out monopoly tax rights, including import and export duties, the head tax or market fees.

So the wealth accumulated from several sources and the population increased: steadily new immigrants arrived, not the least attracted by the lively junk trade or revolts in China (for instance around 1644 when the Manchus overthrew the Ming), while there was a growing number of Indonesian-born Chinese. In every respect, this was a really free trade and not an "ideological one", including all possibilities for the Chinese to accumulate substantial capitals.

The Dutch, always very busy with war-mongering in the 17th-century, needed these Chinese to consolidate their positions. In turn, these Western newcomers became another source of wealth for the Chinese. This dependence of the mighty Dutch Calvinists created the other side of the coin: this Chinese industrial and economical behavior and activity led to the "Reverend Arthur Smith reaction" among the Dutch. "The Chinese Must Go!" could have been the main drive behind the terrible massacres of the Chinese by the Dutch around 1740.[14]

Rural Chinese groups (not yet defined as but practically organized as *kongsis*) protested against their exploitation by Dutch VOC officials. Notwithstanding contradictions between the urban Chinese elite including their urban support groups and these rural groups, both suffered from the lethal Dutch repression. The consequence was that other Chinese groups tried to join the Javanese indigenous protests against the Dutch occupiers. However, they were betrayed by the indigenous ruler, extradited to the Dutch and massacred. This is a typical example of how the triangle game between Western foreigners, Chinese foreigners and the indigenous elite could be played.

This game remained one-sided as long as the Chinese could only effectively function as middlemen between the Dutch and the indigenous rulers, merchants or common people. It became a "normal" triangle-game when local East Indies rulers and aristocrats started to farm out monopoly taxes and duties, market rights or gambling concessions to wealthy Chinese merchants. Until the end of the Raffles government, the fate of the Chinese on this level was not further affected than in the 1740s. In the fully corrupt VOC culture, clever and rich Chinese could gain large advantages.

---

[14] N. Randeraad (ed.), p. 23-25.

However, poor Chinese could also benefit from a certain trickle-down effect and slowly developed the stratum of Chinese shopkeepers. As usual, the local population did not like to pay taxes and certainly not to repressive rulers, as most of them were. Those Chinese who were rich supporters and instruments of those rulers or of Dutch occupiers became representative of and scapegoats for the overlords, while all resentments could easily be directed against an influential Chinese middle class. This could eventually be compared with the basis of the Western antipathy of the Jews. The framework is the same at least: the combination of state and private capital in privileged positions or even monopolies.[15]

This picture is not complete without the remark that among the always small minority of the Chinese (except in cities as Singapore), there existed at least two and mostly three options in the strategy of collaboration between the Chinese and others: with the dominant Western colonizers, with the indigenous authorities or with nobody. This last option was followed, for instance, for a long time after the massacres and wars of the 1740s. In the 17th and part of the 18th-century, with the extensive junk trade between the East Indies, Southeast Asia and China, this option was in principal always open to every Chinese.

The 19th-century

The grip of Western foreigners on "their colonies" was strongly intensified in the 19th-century, and much changed in a fundamental way on the Chinese side as well. As indicated already, the very different 19th-century migrations from China happened in several large waves. In the USA, Chinese are found from about 1850 onwards participating in the gold rushes and the construction of the railway network in very inhospitable regions. From Yunnan or several coastal provinces, numerous people fled south, establishing permanent Chinese settlements in the cities and regions of Thailand, Burma, Malaysia or the East Indies, now called "Dutch East India". Soon they were involved in all kinds of trades in their new homes, but sustained relations with China itself.

After Raffles and the English occupation disappeared, the Dutch started a general repressive regime in 1820-1850 by introducing a pass-system and travel restrictions for the Chinese; specific Chinese quarters were formed, and Chinese living elsewhere were required to move their

---

[15] See for the well comparable European situation H. Derks (2004), p. 149-187.

residences into these "ghettos".[16] In this well-known, racialist-induced segregation of a military-bureaucratic regime, the mask of colonial paternalism was thrown off in an attempt to regain some "former prestige". The foreign occupiers and their state companies like the NHM took most of the opium profits, not the well-to-do Chinese middlemen and opium farmers, while the Dutch soldiers were among the best opium customers: they had to do the dirty work (Java War, etc.).

But after 1850, Chinese middlemen were soon back in their lucrative and dangerous position. The reason for this was that the Westerners could not communicate effectively with the indigenous majority without the Chinese networks. In addition, they needed a new kind of Chinese laborer to make the "Industrial Revolution" in the homelands complete. The middlemen were the best at labor acquisition among a new Chinese workforce.

We already described the example of the exploitation of the tin resources on Banka by the Dutch colonial administration and on Belitung (Billiton) by Dutch private entrepreneurs. Here and in the Malaysian tin mines, the exploitation of a new kind of Chinese worker, the imported coolies, took on a grim character like never before: slavery went here hand in hand with opium addiction.

As elsewhere in Southeast Asia, the *kongsi* constellation was adopted on several levels and for several purposes, which must be kept clearly separated. First, they were organized for labor solidarity among people suffering the same fate, including induced opium consumption as part of their exploitation. It concerned a new phenomenon, Chinese proletarians, who immigrated massively from China, with Singapore acting as a central distribution point. For these miners/coolies, indeed, as Trocki formulated: opium was both the worst thing and the best thing available to them.

Of the three options mentioned above, the last one was standard among many Chinese coolie immigrants. They remained somehow in permanent contact with the homeland, so that they could return to China without much difficulty.

There was also a very different *kongsi,* however, described by Rush in the 1870s when the Chinese opium farming had its heyday. It concerned the already long established procedure at the opium auctions of the Dutch administration:

---

[16] D. Willmott, p. 6.

For the Chinese [opium farmers], forming partnerships was among the most important aspects of preparing for the auctions. The Dutch required prospective farmers to have two formal guarantors who, along with the farmer, signed the farm contract and bound themselves to its obligations. In most cases these three men ... represented a much larger association of backers—the opium farm kongsi—who actually financed the farms.[17]

Only *kongsi* leaders became wealthy as Chinese opium and tin farmers on Banca. On Billiton the private Dutch firm acted, in fact, as the opium farmer of the Dutch administration in Batavia and sold opium directly to the *kongsi* people and were paid by their labor; a lethal form of labor lasting only a limited number of years and a lethal kind of narcotic compensation.

On the other end of the Chinese spectrum stood the wealthy and super-wealthy. They were the opium kings.

The Rich "Overseas Chinese" and Opium Criminality

If the populations of Hong Kong (before the transformation) and Taiwan are included, the total number of "Overseas Chinese" in East and Southeast Asia (excluding North and South Korea and Japan) amounts to somewhere between 17 and 23 million in the 1990s, although higher estimates exist. Who are the rich *huaqiao* among them? Certainly a very small minority; if we estimate 1% rich people among them (the large majority of "Overseas Chinese" now belongs to the shopkeeper category) than we are talking about 200,000 people. Opium or drug tycoons, so well known today in Colombia or Mexico, were not so prevalent in Asia or Southeast Asia in the period until 1950. In this time the trade was largely conducted by Europeans (including Jews) and some Parsis from India with Chinese support. We now want to deal only with the problem of the latter, who operated in organizations conducting numerous kinds of trade, distributions and so on.

The Rich

For the *present* situation Hodder assesses the economic performance of this small minority in Southeast Asia only in superlatives.[18] They control a larger share of regional trade than do other ethnic groups, generating

---

[17] J. Rush, p. 46. Rush did not write about the Banca or Billiton kongsis.
[18] R. Hodder, p. 3, 4.

the equivalent of a GNP two-thirds the size of China's. The three countries which are populated largely by these Chinese (Hong Kong, Taiwan and Singapore) possess larger foreign reserves than either Japan or the United States. Excluding the first two, the "funds" of the Overseas Chinese in the region are conservatively estimated at $ 400 billion.

In Indonesia the small Chinese minority controls half the country's trade and about three-quarters of private domestic capital. In Thailand the majority of the corporate assets, nine-tenths of investment in commerce and manufacturing, and half the financial resources of Thai banks are owned by Chinese. In the Philippines 40% of the assets of private domestic banks are Chinese property. And so on and so forth.

Many and varied reasons are given to explain this formidable position apart from the broader macro-economic policies or international trading strategies pursued by governments. The usual suggestions are that the Chinese happened to be in the right place at the right time; that they had the skills, drive and commercial experience in urban networks already during the period of European imperialism and colonialism; that they were patient, hard-working, frugal and possessed sharp business acumen. There is much which can serve as a warning against these easy explanations; in particular, the analysis so far.

Hodder's conclusion is certainly right:

> ... in reality there is no group, no "Chineseness": there is only the *idea* of a group, culture or society, and the limited, unidimensional and static *presentation* of changing and multidimensional contexts.[19] (italics from R.H.)

They do not form a homogeneous group; they originate from many parts of China, though mostly from southeastern China; they speak different dialects, posses different beliefs and values; they often do not differ much from indigenous people like the *babas* in Malaysia or *peranakan* in Indonesia; they often adopted indigenous names or foreign religions like Catholicism and Protestantism; most of them are nationals. Since the dubious racial and racist judgments persist, the "racial purity" (whatever that may mean) is very difficult to find since they mixed with indigenous peoples from the beginning. "Ethnicity" is mainly conjured up by outsiders and is in this case nearly meaningless.

In short, sweeping generalizations about "Overseas Chinese" or similar concepts cannot be accepted. There is simply no monolithic bloc called "Overseas Chinese". The economic success of some of them is to be under-

---

[19] Idem, p. 8. See for the alternative view F. Dikötter, B. Sautman (ed.).

stood partly by European colonialism, the Communist revolution of 1949, Japan's economic growth (itself built upon American strategic concerns). Most crucial in Hodder's perception

> is the desire of many Chinese to achieve material progress or, more accu-
> rately, the desire of many Chinese to "turn" institutions towards the exten-
> sion, safeguarding, legitimization and institutionalization of trade and its
> associated wealth values.[20]

In a less abstract way characteristics of the Overseas Chinese super rich can be given as follows. Indeed, one generalization is probably appropriate: one is confronted here with real capitalists operating in a real free market: free for them (and monopolies for others). Two controversial things often form the lucrative, *starting* activities to make the jump to the top: opium and local politics; once on the road to the top, it is necessary to free oneself of both.

"Free" is related to an overriding characteristic of their capitalist activities: free from active involvement in politics, and free from the bureaucrats by bribing them. Besides these "apolitical" elements, crucial economic elements should be added that were derived from their location: *only* these "Chinese Overseas" had a *threefold* advantage by remaining strongly in touch with the motherland, whatever the political regime in China or in their own settlement.

First, the profuse selling of many cheap gadgets, small and bulk products in the immense Chinese open internal market. The conglomerate is, therefore, the most beloved company model. Second, the effective use of the internal Chinese mega-sized industrial capacities, which were established very quickly after 1900. They can potentially outdo every kind of competition in their branches. The third advantage concerns the interaction between the previous two and financial and investment programs. Such a large internal open market for the Chinese, and a large competing open market outside China, is not available anywhere for others.[21]

For those who could profitably exploit these opportunities, there was only a limited need to deal in opium and a limited willingness to take the risks of losing the opportunity to exploit the indicated threefold advantages. In economic terms: the chance that a management of risks in dealing with very large money capitals will lead to a zero-solution is high, and

---

[20] R. Hodder, p. 22.
[21] See for modern data the articles 'Industrial Policy', 'Industrialization' and 'Information Technology' in D. Leese (ed.), p. 486-492.

certainly much higher than those super-rich who remain involved in politics as well. In other words: dealing with many large countries, with many products, with many branches outside the political conflicts carries a very low risk and the strongest possible basis for accumulation of capital.

There are rather interesting biographies of the (super)rich and powerful Chinese in Southeast Asia.[22] One example will suffice here, and it concerns the Semarang-born Oei Tiong Ham (ca. 1866-1924).[23]

Oei was the last of Java's nineteenth-century Chinese "kings" and the first of the 20th-century corporate businessmen and modern community leaders. Of course, he was 'opium monopoly holder for Semarang and three other residencies, had made a profit of 18,000,000 guilders'.[24] His father, Oei Tjie Sien, arrived in Semarang in 1858, having fled China during the Taiping chaos, married into a locally established family, and made a successful and traditional career of *peranakan*: first, a small shop (his 'Kian Gwan kongsi'); next, a bigger one; savings enough to take advantage of an economic crisis and to buy an opium farm for a bargain, which was lost by another; once economically established, he also became socio-politically involved by his nomination as Chinese lieutenant of Semarang. This combination was the basis for a quick accumulation of capital: after the first opium farm, he acquired four others. The basis he laid for the career of his son Oei Tiong Ham was, in all respects, solid.

Although Oei Tiong Ham never learned Dutch, kept Semarang as his hometown and always spoke Amoy-Chinese or Malay, he was one of the first to wear European dress in public, cut off his Manchu queue, which was followed by many other radical changes. Around 1900 the *Kian Gwan kongsi* was extended into a *Kian Gwan Handelsmaatschappij* with still the largest opium monopoly and sugar monopoly in Java.

In the meantime, however, a shipping company was added. Soon his company became one of the largest exporters of all kinds of products, moved to Singapore, abandoned Chinese bookkeeping practices, hired teams of Western-trained accountants, and so on:

---

[22] See part III in J. Butcher, H. Dick (ed.), p. 249 -281 with five biographies.

[23] For the following see Idem, p. 272-281; D. Willmott, p. 24 ff. and J. Rush, p. 248-252.

[24] D. Willmott, p. 24. On Idem, p. 149 we learn that Oei Tiong Ham netted this sum only with opium in the years 1890-1903. Also at that time an extraordinary amount of money. Compare this with the Singapore table 34 p. 454 in which a monthly net profit of $30,000 per month is given; over 13 years this is about $5 million.

Oei's true competitors were not his fellow Chinese merchants, but large European trading firms ... such firms as the Nederlandse Handelsmaatschappij [NHM] and the Internationale en Handelsvereeniging Rotterdam ...[25]

As described in ch. 18 the NHM became not only the largest industrial and commercial Dutch conglomerate, but laid the basis for its Dutch monopoly position through an original and solid opium position. In 1924, therefore, Oei's fortune and commercial "empire" can be measured in values amounting to hundreds of millions.

Criminality

In ch. 31 the item of "Chinese opium criminality" is discussed in detail, but this concerns the situation inside China from about 1900 to the establishment of Communist China. There is less information about *Chinese* opium criminality in Southeast Asia.

The logo of the Southeast Asian opium problem, the *Golden Triangle*, is at the moment directly connected to narco-criminality on a world scale. This phenomenon started not earlier than World War II. It is perfectly possible that the leaders in Burma, Thailand, Laos, Singapore, etc. used local Chinese. It seems to me the most insignificant feature of the drugs criminality in Southeast Asia whether or not local Chinese were available in those functions. Of course, it does not make any difference in the present Opium (and its derivatives) Problem.

Is that true? Not entirely: if that kind of *ethnicity* could be attested, it could be used in Western anti-Chinese propaganda in many kinds of racist discourses and publicity campaigns. Secondly, there is the reasoning: since "Overseas Chinese" became fabulously rich, they stand, "therefore", at the basis of this *Golden Triangle* story. Take Ronald Renard's remarks in his opium history about new banks established in Thailand after 1960:

> These firms were generally dominated by first- or second-generation immigrants from southern China. Their emigration ... had been taking place since the mid-nineteenth-century ... many stayed in Thailand, others returned, out of which emerged a network linking the Overseas Chinese with those in China ... these Chinese controlled the conglomerates ... By the 1960s, most of the country's [Thailand's] major commercial banks and principal trading houses were run by these families. Rags to riches stories abound. To mention just ... a family in the pawnshop business expanded in real

---

[25] J. Rush, p. 250.

estate, establishing the Land and House real estate company capitalized at 62 billion bath in 1995 ...[26] And so on.

This, however, is calling a Chinese connection "fundamental". In this way, decades ago, every flu in Europe was called "Mao flu" (Mao exists, flu exists, but the combination is pure propaganda); today it is "Mexican flu" and that is "also" a major drugs paradise!

As indicated above, even the CIA was aware of the fact that the Chinese were not involved in poppy production around 1950. This concerned, however, only, the Chinese inside China and the CIA of about 1950, which rapidly changed colors. And today these Chinese play at best a small role (if any) in this area, but *historically* and thanks to Yunnan production, we have to talk about a *Golden Quadrangle* until the new Communist regime terminated the connections with the *Golden Triangle* (see further ch. 31).

Daniel Goh's clear analysis of the political factions and ideological stands of "Overseas Chinese" before 1942 and the large contradictions between the several new China-oriented groups (from Nationalists to Communists) is not very helpful. It is certainly too adventurous to move from this to linking an opium banking network between "Overseas Chinese" and Communist Chinese at the time.

Anyway, Renard provides only loose threads in a highly complicated history. These arouse suspicions, but have limited value in a proper research study with proper questions. For instance: How to define or understand a *criminal* relationship between Chinese-*outside*-China and opium in the pre-1950 period? Trocki sketches the problem at stake in the following way:

> Opium, the preparation, distribution, and consumption of which was the other integral part of the Chinese economy of Singapore, was not only part of the system of labor exploitation but actually made the system work to the profit of the shopkeepers, the secret societies, the revenue farmers, and the colonial government. Opium was the grand "common interest" of the Anglo-Chinese elite of Singapore. For the laborers, it was both the worst thing and the best thing available to them ... the worst because it was addictive, and habituated consumers were ready to sacrifice first their profits, then their labor, and finally their lives and futures to obtain it ... the best because, in an environment so deprived, it was virtually the laborers' only source of pleasure. Not only did it substitute for women and banish loneliness, but it may have been more than a luxury when the workday was long and the toil strenuous.[27]

---

[26] R. Renard (2001), p. 23, 24. If I have counted well this is still US$ 1.8 billion at a rate of 100 baht = US$ 3!

[27] C. Trocki (1990), p. 67.

This concerns largely the consumer side of the problem, and since all or most of the involved parties in Singapore had a keen interest in opium, including the addicts, criminality or perpetrators were difficult to identify.

On the production side of the Opium Problem, the connection is also difficult to find: the production was in the hands of non-Chinese tribal groups or concentrated in non-Chinese countries in Indian and European hands. Therefore, one has to look for them in the trade, distribution and financial sectors. New research has to uncover the relevant data. We need, however, to obtain some indication about what was meant by "criminality" in earlier periods.

The historical record provides some examples of this last problem. Around 1800 the Chinese traveler, Ong-Tae-Hae, keenly observed, for instance, the customs under a corrupt VOC regime and how "Overseas Chinese" merchants reacted to it. About these Java-Chinese he wrote:

> Our rich merchants and great traders amass inexhaustible wealth, whereupon they give bribes to the Hollanders and are elevated to the ranks of great Captain, Lieutenant, Commissioner of insolvent and intestate estates ... but all of them take the title of Captain ... When the Chinese quarrel or fight, they present their cause to the Captain ... The rights and wrongs, with the crookeds and straights of the matter, are all immediately settled, either by imprisonment or flogging, without giving the affair a second thought. With respect to flagrant breaches of the law and great crimes ... reference must invariably be made to the Hollanders. Those who journey by water and land must all be provided with passports, to prevent their going and coming in an improper way; from this may be inferred how strict the Hollanders are in the execution of the laws, and how minute in the levying of duties.
>
> The life of man, however, is not required at the hand of his next neighbor.[28] ... when men are killed, they are either thrown out into the streets, or suffered to float downstream, every one being silent without inquiry, and nobody daring to stand forward as a witness. Alas! alas! that the important affair of human life should after all be treated so lightly. With respect to the Dutch, they are very much like the man who stopped his ears while stealing a bell. Measuring them by the rules of reason, they scarcely possess one of the five cardinal virtues ...[29]

---

[28] The 1850 editor adds: 'In China, if a dead body is found, the nearest inhabitants are taken up and required to discover the culprit; the Chinese writer laments that it is not so in Batavia.'

[29] Ong-Tae-Hae, p. 4; see also D. Willmott, p. 148, 149.

As if the above is not enough, there follows a long, harsh and impressive criticism of the Dutch that I had never encountered before or since: the Dutch do not score satisfactorily on any single feature of these five cardinal virtues (benevolence, righteousness, propriety,wisdom and truth): 'it is scarcely worthwhile wasting one's breath upon them'![30] But Dutch gardens south of Batavia are beautiful and in their manners Europeans aim to be polite against the rich and powerful "other".

Again, who was wrong and/or a criminal? The answer is clear: the Dutch had stringent laws with heavy penalties to prevent, for instance, bribery in any form, and that was not the case among "Overseas Chinese", wealthy or not. In addition, the Chinese were apparently not instructed about these Dutch laws, which were for them anyway laws of foreign barbarians with red hair, long noses, grey eyes.

However, this example already provides a main criterion, a legal one: if a law is violated, it is a criminal act, which can and has to be punished.

Indeed, no laws, no crimes? The historian and sociologist will point to other circumstances and, at least practically, to different criteria. Take already an obvious extension to the argument given: no state, no laws, no crimes? This refers to a rather famous discussion about the so-called 'primitive law', which will not be repeated here, at very least because "primitives" do not create an Opium Problem.

However, in that discussion the moral value of a law which is imposed on the "primitives" by a foreign state was *not* a theme, while at the same time it was a law *exclusively* aimed at these "primitives". The highly ambiguous nature of this was also known among "primitives" 200 years ago and relative to opium. Ong-Tae-Hae wrote in 1791:

> In every case it is the same. At the same time Europeans forbid their people the use of this drug, and severely punish those who trespass; how is it then

---

[30] See also Ong-Tae-Hae, p. 14, 15 where he severely criticizes the Javanese from Bantam, because they are so afraid of the 'Hollanders', building them even a fort which has the sole aim to control them, erroneously thinking that the Dutch respect them; etc. The Dutch only 'form plans for entrapping the people ... till they have sufficiently subdued their minds ..'. Ong-Tae-Hae forgets or does not know how the people from Bantam in a decades-long struggle against the Dutch were repressed in a genocidal way from the harsh reign of Governor-General J. P. Coen onwards. So, their fear is well grounded and perhaps became a basic element in their collective memory. There is a Dutch translation of Ong-Tae-Hae's booklet: 'Chineesche aanteekeningen omtrent Nederlandsch-Indie' (The Hague: Martinus Nijhoff, 1858). However, it has only 48 pages of the 80 + xv in the English translation of W. Medhurst. I could not find a copy of it to check whether the fierce criticism of the Dutch had been censored or not.

that we Chinese, together with the Javanese, are so thoughtless as to fall into the snare!'[31]

Without any doubt this is a strong legal argument: the Dutch VOC-State used its excessive violence and the fear of it to impose their Western martial law, which had nothing to do with the laws and customs of indigenous Javanese or "Overseas Chinese". Furthermore, they created a habit of opium smoking among a mass of Javanese based on this basic fear, in order to tame those "primitives". This law was exclusively issued for the sake of a profit for the foreign VOC-State.

Many questions arise now: was this allowed according to the prevailing international law (Grotius, etc.)? Was opposing this law a criminal act? The dominant Calvinist Dutch must have affirmed these questions, because they formed the government imposed upon the pagans thanks to God's will and by virtue of their Christian civilizing mission. Anyway, they sometimes punished violations severely, as mentioned earlier (ch. 13 and 15). But, even today, these Calvinists and their Christian enemies have never succeeded in convincing Asian people of their West European and Christian truth. They yielded fear, but not respect.

Speculating about Ong-Tae-Hae's answer and assuming that he experienced the opium smuggling practices of the British and Americans back in China, he must have known which scenario would follow. The next step could be to protest publicly (which was done by the Chinese government, in vain); to take prohibitive actions (which was done by the Chinese government, in vain) and to start a defensive war (which was done by the Chinese government, but it lost). What next? There was not yet an *International Criminal Court.* In fact, it was Mao Zedong in the 1950s who introduced the first effective systematic anti-opium measures *in history*— whatever one thinks about it.

Back to Ong-Tae-Hae's Java and the bribery example. This shows that what was a criminal act in Holland or in the VOC was not the case in China or among "Overseas Chinese". It must have been around 1725 that a Dutch Governor-General punished bribery in a draconian fashion for the last time; after that date, this never happened again. The social and economic practice apparently undermined the validity of this Dutch law, although it formally did not disappear (nor did bribery: in the 1930s high Dutch police officials in Java demanded bribes from Chinese opium dealers; ch. 19).

---

[31] Idem, p. 19.

During the VOC era officials should be judged in a different way than for the period after 1820 when the Dutch attempted to establish a state in the East Indies. The VOC bosses in Amsterdam wanted to prevent their employees conducting all kinds of business for themselves; in the state period, the state-bureaucratic officials should not be bribed, because they had to stand above all parties and interests to safeguard the common good, or to judge *sine ira et studio*. In the VOC period a practical argument was dominant, and in the state period, an ideological one.

It is certain that Oei Tiong Ham bribed a Dutch official to get his title of lieutenant (later major). In many cases, this *illegal* practice should be a reason to change the law. In addition, there were no official or legal criteria for becoming a captain. The practice in the East Indies was, first and foremost, to promote a person who could be a good "tool of the Dutch", in Singapore a "tool of the British Empire", etc.[32]

After 1865 the criteria for the nomination of Chinese officials in Singapore were stated by the British Governors as 'details of Chinese racial character, such as natural corruptibility, criminality and clannishness ...'[33] Stronger even than the Dutch, the British were willing to change the basis under the law to declare the giver of a bribe as a criminal rather than the British receiver of the bribe.[34] This was not a "normal" criminal, but somebody who had a racial inclination to bribe people, who was a *natural criminal.*

Again, many Chinese being a "natural trading folk" had no law against bribery; they felt that nearly all acts in life were a matter of supply and demand; they were the real "free traders". However, there must have been exceptions, otherwise all moral criteria (and there were many of them, for instance, in Confucian value schemes) would be invalid. Opium was such a subject, which was prohibited time and again not only by Chinese

---

[32] D. Willmott, p. 151.

[33] D. Goh, p. 490. His article is one long discussion about the criteria of Chinese "unofficials" as 'loyal colonial subjects' or not and how these changed in the course of time until 1942.

[34] Now many Western companies are competing heavily to get a Chinese profitable relationship, they bribe Chinese officials on a large scale. The *Los Angeles Times* (August 10, 2007) reports that Zheng Xiaoyu, head of China's food and drug agency, was executed because he accepted a bribe of $850,000 from Western pharmaceutical industries. The title of the article is: 'Chinese bribes: Better to give than to receive' and inside it reads 'Bribe-givers tend to get off relatively easy in China, according to legal experts, government statistics and media accounts.' The same procedure was demonstrated in the recent, well publicized Rio Tinto (Australia) affair in which the four receivers of bribes got draconian sentences. See *The New York Times,* March 29, 2010.

emperors (law), but also in moral codes and public opinions (Confucianism or Taiping ideology).

Gambling was another vice defined by Ong-Tae-Hae as a 'perversion'. With special dances and songs the Chinese in Batavia were enticed by the Chinese gambling farmer (who paid 10% of the stakes annually as tribute to the Dutch).[35] Earlier I quoted extensively about how he castigated the use of opium by "Overseas Chinese" and Javanese as well as the conqueror's invention of 'the black fumes of opium'.

How strong Ong-Tae-Hae condemned the opium "invention" or gambling and the perversion of Chinese farming these activities, he had no "crime definition" for it as Westerners had. The authorities in China at the time used criteria like "bad for the health and the mind", "bad for society" as this "perversion" was the subject of business in the streets, "dependence on uncivilized barbarians", apart from macro-economic complaints about the loss of silver, etc. In China he could have referred to verdicts ("laws") of the Emperor, which was not the case in overseas territories, which at that time had been conquered by the Dutch more often than not.[36]

One may suppose that the rich "Overseas Chinese", who were also opium farmers, had no scruples about earning money in the opium business because their activities were extensions of foreign-induced trade, of the law-makers themselves and, therefore, legal (= without danger). What Hodder stated above seems applicable here as well, that there is 'no "Chineseness", there is only the *idea* of a group, culture or society': as *peranakans* they lived outside China in a fully different world *in between* a dominant small minority of heavily armed Western people and a large majority of non-Chinese: materially on the side of the British, French or Dutch; culturally on the side of the Malayasians, Javanese, etc.

As *in between* people, however, there are again several modes of behavior, which are very different for the rich and for the large majority of the "Overseas Chinese": in the process of accumulating wealth, they lost every trace of an in-between position and became "Western" (see rich Singapore and Hong Kong Chinese) and freed themselves of dependence and of such things as opium.

If "Overseas Chinese" operate as opium (heroin, etc.) criminals, then it must be in a Western environment, Western gangster methods, etc. and

---

[35] Ong–Tae–Hae, p. 61, 62.
[36] Idem in his Section III he describes most islands in the whole archipelago and always mentions whether they are subjected to the Dutch.

in all probability in combination with other Western criminal activities like gambling or prostitution. "Ethnic Chinese" are no longer seen as Chinese, but as other Western citizens who can be cheated, exploited, etc. But even in this milieu one may expect the development that as someone becomes richer, he moves away from the bad activities and looks for a more "honest" field. A remarkable example of this is given by Sinn.

She describes how a notice in a San Francisco *Chinese* newspaper warned consumers against fake opium (14-1-1906).[37] Two firms, claiming they were renowned and registered in Hong Kong and Macau, announced that they sold opium from old raw Patna (India). In support, they also state that their brands are patronized by rich merchants in the USA. Their warning concerned the activities of criminals using their names to sell cheap and low-grade opium under false pretexts. Only one person, Mr. H. G. Playfair, was authorized to import their product.

This is a good example to introduce the following section in which the "New Imperialists", Japan and the USA, write their part in the *History of the Opium Problem* and implement the most extensive criminal laws against opium production and consumption.

---

[37] E. Sinn, p. 16, 17.

CHAPTER TWENTY-SIX

REFLECTIONS

It is important to stress again that this part of the *History of the Opium Problem* refers to the opium history up to the 1950s (1954 Dien Bien Phu). However, this history has the most serious consequences for its future up to the present, much more than the other parts. Therefore, these reflections are devoted to one question: why did such consequences follow from the history as described? It is clear that an answer cannot be given in a systematic way. That must be reserved for another study, but these reflections show that such a study could have several advantages.

1.

The Southeast Asian opium economy was relatively unchanged at the end of the Second World War and ready to play its role in the new era of the Cold War. Before Afghanistan took over the lead, the *Golden Triangle* region of Burma, Thailand and Laos was the largest producer in the world. "They" increased the total production from about 80 tons a year to 1,000-1,200 tons by the end of the Second Vietnam War.[1]

However, that was not yet apparent directly after World War II. Foreign opium supplies (Iran, India, etc.) were imported again legally, and the overland smuggling from Yunnan flourished also. The number of Indochinese addicts had grown as well, which was estimated at 250,000 around 1970.

Singapore and Malaysia formed exceptions as the number of addicts dropped sharply from about 186,000 in 1945 to 40,000 just 25 years later.

2.

Three main features of the Southeast Asian opium constellation should be highlighted: apart from their mutual competition (with Siam-Thailand as a buffer state) there were the continuous attempts of the British and

---

[1] A. McCoy et al. p. 87.

French to use all the northern and northeastern borderlands as potential inroads into China. The conquest of this huge country, using *'the Golden Road to Cathay'*, was the long-term goal. The short-term goal with the highest priority was to establish an opium infrastructure; not for long, because the white Christian civilization at home was against opium addiction and—as a French official wrote—he and his fellow colonists 'cannot be the treacherous executioner (*le bourreau empoisonné*) of these peoples'.

This leads directly to the second main feature. The mutual competition of the French and British facilitated in all possible ways the trade position of the tribal regions in Southeast Asia, and on top of this, the China conquest option had the same effect. Together they made the position of all the regions of the so-called *Golden Triangle* nearly unassailable and extremely desirable. Since the borderland with China was geopolitically the most important one, I propose talking about the *Golden Quadrangle*.

Both features are directly connected with the third one, which is related to the tools to achieve the indicated goals: whoever was in power in the *Golden Quadrangle* always used the tribal narco-military regimes. They were armed by foreign narco-military powers, whether official ones and/or political-criminal ones like uncontrolled secret services with their "licenses to kill".

3.

Indeed, French involvement in highly war-stricken Southeast Asia was strongly intertwined with the British before 1900 and with American opium policies after 1945. The opium production areas in the north or northeastern parts of Burma, Thailand and Laos became the practical centre of interaction between the Western opium policies and their militant ethnic producers; the main cities in the realm (Bangkok, Rangoon and Singapore) became the distribution and money centers, delivering the opium and its derivatives to all corners of the world.

These remote regions could expand and become institutionalized in world-economic and world-political schemes because the Western military and political powers, including their local allies, gathered here to fight nationalism and communism. "Vietnam", the former French Indochina, was the country in which these fights were repeatedly decided in favor of anti-Western policies and could not be connected any longer to opium as under the French and American regimes.

4.

Opium policies became the most beloved tools in the harsh ideological and political struggles of the Cold War. The reverse is also true: opium production, consumption, distribution and criminality took on world dimensions because opium became the main tool in the anti-China policy. That became clear around 1950 for the insiders and during the Second Vietnam War for everybody.

Before that period, the USA's criticism of classical colonialism and imperialism was still strong enough to avoid "classical imperial actions". This was probably the background to the CIA report of 1956, which was certainly not welcome to the Harry Anslinger crusaders in the USA (see ch. 28 below), the Taiwan Nationalists and anti-Communists or Nationalists in Southeast Asia. Still, the Cold War had already left serious impacts on this report, starting with the formulation of the task the CIA had to fulfill: 'to obtain sufficient reliable information to characterize the possible involvement of Communist China in the opium situation in Southeast Asia and in other markets.'[2]

The conclusions of the CIA at this juncture are remarkable, and show a quite different perception to a decade later in the midst of their strong illegal involvement in Laos, Burma and South Vietnam. Therefore, they are worth summarizing in the following section.[3]

5.

A small amount of raw opium produced by minority tribes in Yunnan is exported to Burma, the value of which does not exceed $500,000 annually. Any Communist Chinese involvement could not be more than tolerating 'unruly tribal producers' busy with their 'traditional economic and social pursuit'.

The 'major opium producers in Southeast Asia are Burma and Laos', not China. Coupled with Thai production facilities, they supply a large domestic market and provide a sizable export potential. Bangkok is the main export center from Southeast Asia, supplying significant quantities of opium to Malaysia, Hong Kong, Macao and Indonesia. 'Singapore, Hong Kong and Macao are important intermediate transit points for the supply

---

[2] Central Intelligence Agency, p. 24.
[3] Idem, quotations come from p. 24-26.

of opium to other world markets.' Refinery facilities to service the markets for morphine, heroin, etc. are established mainly in Thailand, Hong Kong and Macao: 'There is no evidence that Communist China exports opium derivatives.'

Southeast Asian producers receive only a very small return for their opium crop. Opium produced for the illicit trade is apparently in surplus supply. 'This surplus may be the result of the virtual disappearance of the former large Chinese market since the generally successful opium-addiction-suppression campaign of the Chinese government on the Chinese mainland.' The middlemen and government officials get the lucrative profits, and do this job purely 'for personal gain'. Members of local Communist parties may be involved in order to finance their activities, 'but there is no available evidence indicating that such involvement is substantial or that it is systematically directed by the Chinese Communists. The trade appears to be dominated by non-Communists ... There does not appear to be any evidence of Chinese Communist influence in this trade [of opium derivatives. H.D.]'. 'One US seizure report indicates that Communist China was the suspected origin of a shipment of contraband heroin which was transshipped from Hong Kong. Hong Kong authorities and US Treasury representatives in Hong Kong state, however, that they have no evidence that opium or derivatives from Communist China enter Hong Kong.' These are the CIA conclusions so far.

6.

Foreign opium was always imported to French and British Southeast Asia from India and the Middle East. After the British left the realm, it seemed as if Southeast Asia was totally cut off from all foreign opium. On top of the British disappearance came the collapse of the French colony. In the battle of Dien Bien Phu (1954) the Vietnamese people demonstrated again that they wanted to be liberated from Western occupation, including its opium regime.

At the same time other major developments had created drastic changes in the international opium trade:

a. In 1953 the major opium-producing countries in Europe, the Middle East and Southeast Asia signed the United Nations protocol: no selling of opium for legalized smoking or eating. One consequence was that the *Golden Quadrangle* became again a *Triangle*:

Although this international accord ended large shipments of Iranian opium to the Thai and French opium monopolies, international smugglers simply took over the Iranian government's role.[4]

b. Much more serious was the victory of Mao over the nationalists of Chiang Kai-shek. The last supporters of the latter (a *Kuomintang* militia) were driven out of Yunnan. Consequence:

> ... the People's Liberation Army began patrolling the border in the early 1950s ... most opium caravans were halted. By the mid-1950s People's Republic agriculturalists and party workers had introduced substitute crops, and any possible opium seepage into Southeast Asia ceased.[5]

c. The changes in the international opium trade thanks to the earlier decisions and developments favored Iran. This country became the major supplier of Southeast Asia. In 1953 it provided nearly half of all opium smuggled through routes via Lebanon, Arab states and Europe. This gave Iran substantial revenues but also a bad reputation in Asia, which was not in the interest of the Shah's foreign policy. Consequence:

> ... in 1950 Iran began to reduce production sharply; exports declined from 246 tons in 1950 to 41 tons in 1954. The final blow came in 1955, when the Iranian government announced the complete abolition of opium growing ... Turkey filled the void in the west, but Southeast Asia was now at a crossroads.[6]

d. There was, however, a strong force counteracting all previous favorable developments. The USA did not wanted to accept the loss of this French colonial bulwark against the "Commies"and jumped into this position.

7.

Before he started speculating in 1972 about "What Can Be Done?" to end 'America's heroin plague' (see part 7), Alfred McCoy described a kind of film scene symbolic of the international entanglement of several nations in one area and in one product, opium and its main derivatives, heroin and morphine.[7]

---

[4] A. McCoy et al, p. 88 referring to the reports of the *Bureau of Narcotics and Dangerous Drugs*, "The World Opium Situation" (Washington, DC, 1970).

[5] Idem, p. 88.

[6] Idem, p. 89.

[7] Idem, p. 352 ff.

A crude opium den in a corner of a Yao village general store is occupied 24 hours a day. It is located not far from the Kuomintang (KMT) headquarters, whose soldiers frequent the den. Near to it lies the rest of a road-building works started by a US combat engineering unit. It concerns a road built under the auspices of USAID's *"Accelerated Rural Development Program"*. The false impression is given that while development aid arrived, it only helped the counterinsurgency: the road is meant to give easy access to rugged mountain areas in times of insurgency. What is certain is that the KMT's involvement in the international narcotics traffic is strongly facilitated by this road.

> Before the KMT caravans leave for Burma, arms, mules, and supplies are shipped up this road. And after they return, opium, morphine base, and no.4 heroin come down the road on their way to the international drug markets. The road has reduced the KMT's transportation costs, increased its profit margin, and improved its competitive position in the international heroin trade.

It is a typical example of the way the American secret services worked (and work), how the US allies against the "Commies" were supported, and how these allies received "additional income" in the narcotics business, in particular by doping the generous USA!

8.

The opium potentials of Southeast Asia were not exhausted with the destruction of the French opium colony. Earlier, the USA-CIA started to develop the former British colony, Burma, into Myanmar and one of the largest narco-military powers in the world. This happened with remarkable success. Although its opium production had decreased since 1996, the UNODC Report 2009 on Southeast Asia states in the preface:

> Worrisome is the situation in Myanmar where cultivation is up for the third year in row—an 11% increase from 28,500 ha in 2008 to 31,700 in 2009. Most of this increase came in the Shan State where 95% of Myanmar's poppy is grown. More than a million people ... are now involved in opium cultivation in Myanmar, an increase of more than a quarter over 2008.[8]

---

[8] UNODC (2009), p. iii. See also UNODC, 33rd Meeting (2009), p. 6.

PART FIVE
THE NEW IMPERIALISTS

CHAPTER TWENTY-SEVEN

JAPAN[1]

Compared to all previous imperialist powers, Japan was formally the last nation which started imperialist adventures by waging war with Russia and China and occupying and exploiting foreign countries (parts of them) like Formosa, Korea and North China from 1897 onwards.

The deliberations of the *International Opium Commission* in Shanghai (February 1909) revealed many tensions between the imperial powers. In the US delegation, missionaries like Tenney and Brent exerted great influence. They could not understand the British reluctance to move rapidly toward comprehensive opium controls. Their intellectual and political level is best characterized by their report to the US Government which states:

> That part of the convention having to do with central governmental control of the drugs is based on the best European and Japanese practice, which on the whole is far in advance of the practice of our Federal Government.[2]

The European practice has been described in detail in the previous chapters and the American one will follow in the next. So, how far in advance was Japan?

Commenting on the results of the next international conference on opium (Geneva, 1924-'25), the British ambassador to Japan, Charles Eliot, could not answer this question. He informed his London base:

> I do not understand very clearly what has happened at the Opium Conference except that Japan is taking sides with America against us. This no doubt means that Japan is glad to show America that in spite of the exclusion clause she has no objection to friendly cooperation on occasion. It is also a hint to us ... Japan also sometimes feels it prudent to defer to this

---

[1] For the general background of this chapter I relied much on W. Walker III. Only quotations from it will be indicated. It is, furthermore, advisable to study B. Wakabayashi to discover specific backgrounds (ethnic differences involved, post-war Japanese political correctness or ideological constraints on historical scholarship) relative to the 'imperial Japanese opium operations ' in China and elsewhere. The following chapter is, in fact, a quick overview of these operations.

[2] Quoted in C. Terry, M. Pellens, p. 637. Bishop Brent and Dr. Tenney were the leading figures of the Philippine Opium Commission (1906), see below, and Brent was again the main voice in this Shanghai commission. For Brent see D. Musto, passim.

same powerful country though in so doing she may to her great regret inconvenience her former ally.[3]

The British, let alone their diplomats, did not understand that the end of the British Empire was a fact after World War I. Japan and the USA had taken over; they supported each other in many fields as "New Imperialists", although they were also competitors. Mutual praise and criticism could be noted.

Probably this British ambassador read in the then famous American *Terry's Guide to the Japanese Empire* the abundant praise for Japan which gave Manchuria (not yet conquered!) 'a promising future' while it is 'being developed and modernized by the capable and progressive Japanese'.[4] Notwithstanding the Chinese initiative to build the link to the Trans-Siberian Railways, the *Guide* continues, it is thanks to the 'present able Japanese management [that] the rapidly spreading system has become one of the great highways of the world, and it is as modern, as safe, and as dependable as the best American railway'. The 'order-loving, thoughtful Japanese are of imperishable interest to the average traveler'. The Japanese victories at Port Arthur (1894 and 1904) 'have made of the region one of the most interesting and instructive battle-fields.' And so on. Other remarkable examples of American "Japanophile" behavior are given below.

However, it is almost certain that this British ambassador did not have the information discovered by a journalist of the *New York Times* five years *earlier.* This journalist reported in a very long and detailed article (February 1919) that the Japanese government 'secretly fosters the mor-phia traffic in China and other countries in the Far East ...' He further informed his readership that 'morphia' can no longer be purchased in Europe, but that the seat of industry

> has been transferred to Japan, and morphia is now manufactured by the Japanese themselves. Literally, tens of millions of yen are transferred annu-ally from China to Japan for the payment of Japanese morphia ..."[5]Before discussing the serious contradictions at issue, first, a brief sketch of the Japanese background is necessary.

---

[3] Quoted by H. Goto-Shibata, p. 97.
[4] *Terry's Guide,* p. 756.
[5] Quoted in E. La Motte, p. 11.

A Domestic Opium Problem

After the Meiji revolution (ca. 1867-1877), a radical oikoidal political economy developed in Japan.[6] From the start of industrialization, a close cooperation was established between the state (including the emperor) and economic family trusts (Mitsui, Yasuda or Sumimoto). As pure *oikoi,* like that of the Western Rothschild, they controlled banks, industries or trade. They urged control of foreign resources (coal, etc.) and markets for their end-products, which became the basic motive for Japanese imperialism and the military build-up. The military state power and its monopoly of coercion also became subject to competition between *oikoi,* the clans of the Choshu (army) and the Satsuma (marine).

Whatever their mutual differences, the main targets of all interests were Formosa (Taiwan), Korea and, in particular, China. What all other imperialist powers did (army to conquer, opium to addict China) was copied by this newcomer in the usual excessively violent way. It arrived at its targets much more quickly, however: apparently, it had no time to lose to become a "honorable member of the imperial (opium) club".

Also in this Japanese variable of the well-known story, the attackers cannot claim that they did not know what opium was all about. In the midst of the Meiji Revolt or "Restoration", the very first statement of the new government, issued in June 1868, with orders to post it throughout the country, was:

> Opium is a product that decreases a person's energy and shortens life. Foreigners are forbidden by treaty from bringing it in[to Japan], but recently [the government] has found out that it is being smuggled in, which will lead to disaster if it spreads among the public. Buying and selling are of course prohibited, as is smoking. Violations of the prohibition policy will be severely punished. This [policy] will be strictly observed in perpetuity.[7]

Selling drugs for profit was punishable by beheading, and the maximum penalty for enticing people into smoking opium was death by strangulation; for consuming it, one could be banished or imprisoned. Knowing how corrupt bureaucrats are, the Japanese anti-opium law did not forget the officials who had to uphold the law: if they failed, they were liable to the same penalties.

---

[6] For the Meiji revolution see my contribution to H. Derks (ed., 1989), p. 164 ff.

[7] Quoted in J. Jennings (1997), p. 8.; also for the following Idem, chapter 1.

Before this Meiji Revolt, the Japanese elite knew enough of the political troubles surrounding the introduction of opium. The humiliating assault on China by the British and French in order to spread opium was fraught with unpleasant possibilities for Japan.

Both the Western aggressiveness and the devastating effects of opium were heightened by the Americans. They wanted to be in the Shogun's good graces after their own assault on Japan (Perry's squadron, 1853) and outdo their British competitors. The first American consul-general in Japan, Townsend Harris, played upon those fears four years later. He described the trouble opium had brought to China: millions of Chinese were addicts; the yearly opium import cost $25 million; etc. Harris painted the potential future of Japan:

> Opium is the one great enemy of China. If it is used, it weakens the body and injures it like the most deadly poison; it makes the rich poor and the wise foolish; it unmans all that use it, and by reason of the misery it brings robbers, and acts of violence increase and ... England will not prohibit it, because the trade is profitable ... China has prohibited the importation of opium, but the English bring it in armed vessels and smuggle it in. ... It appears that the English think the Japanese, too, are fond of opium, and they want to bring it here also ... the English want to introduce it into Japan.[8]

Of course, Harris did not mention that American clippers were found among the main opium smuggling ships and American firms among the main providers, and of course, he told his Japanese diplomatic partners: 'If you make a treaty with the United States and settle the matter of the opium trade, England cannot change this, though she should desire to do so.' This message must have had the envisaged effect, because a year later Japan signed a treaty with the Americans, which was a clear break with the past since Japan only traded with the Dutch and Chinese until that date.

There was, however, a remarkable provision in the commercial treaty between the USA and Japan (1858): American ships could import opium, but not more than three *catties* (four pounds) per ship. This treaty became the model for similar treaties with the Netherlands, Russia, England and France. I do not know how many Western ships arrived each year, but the total import must have been far from full prohibition. The acceptance of opium import by foreigners, and therefore domestic consumption, meant that Japan became "a little bit pregnant" with an opium problem.

---

[8] Quoted in Idem, p. 7.

In the following years they were confronted with British smuggling practices, other attempts of Western powers to force opium trade on them and, in particular, the smoking attitudes of Chinese sailors and residents. Observations like the following about their habits say something about the panic-stricken reactions of Japanese authorities:

> In the Chinese merchant ships ... they smoke something called opium-tobacco. This is a paste stuffed into the bowl of an opium pipe, lighted and smoked. One of the qualities of opium is that one never feels sleepy; consequently, the pilots use it in order not to fall asleep at sea ... However, this opium is smoked in doses, and if the dose is exceeded, it becomes a poison. Moreover, many pilots die after three or four years. Everyone says that the poison of opium brings on other sicknesses.[9]

Later (1868), a Nagasaki newspaper reported about the death of four prostitutes allegedly because they got opium from Chinese residents. Apparently, it concerned an anti-Chinese racist action, but the authorities reacted by publicly posting a proclamation with the warnings:

> Opium smoking scorches the lungs and deranges the mind, and finally it causes addiction and is a threat to life ... Now [the government] ... discovered that the vice is being gradually spread from the Chinese to our own people. Therefore, from now on it is forbidden to land [opium] ...[10]

It was the beginning of a national anti-Chinese campaign after the Japan-China negotiations (1871) remained ambiguous: Japan decided unilaterally to inspect all Chinese ships for opium and all houses of the Chinese community in Japan. This led to serious incidents. The Sino-Japanese War was then not very far off.

These far-reaching anti-opium actions were counteracted by a gradual development into an opium monopoly of the government. First, the government tried to control the local distribution of foreign opium, but accepted more responsibilities and took steps to improve and regulate production for medical use only. That did not remain confined to medical use, but another market was provoked; smuggling and smoking increased; more control and bureaucratization were the answer. In 1876 the next step was taken to a full-fledged opium monopoly of the government. One reasoned:

---

[9] Quoted by J. Jennings (1997), p. 13. About the earlier Chinese-Japanese relations, see J. Murdoch, vol. III, chapter 3 and p. 272 ff.

[10] Idem, p. 13.

that if the government directly imported the drug to make up for shortfalls in domestic production, smuggling and opium smoking could be more easily suppressed.[11]

This monopoly was still confined to medical production and consumption with the necessary import. The morphine content was important for the Japanese physicians. In 1880 the production was not more than 262 kilo raw opium, which increased six years later to 975 kilo annually. The cultivators received '6.3 yen per 375 grams of opium with a morphine content of 6 percent, and a bonus of 0.7 yen per additional percentage point of morphine content'.[12]

These rather contradictory domestic experiences led to a rather consequent approach of "victims of opium" in conquered territories (advertised as "soft") and a quick and more extensive establishment and management of an Opium Monopoly. Japan with its image as the modernizing Asian power *par excellence* was at that time also an example for Chinese students. Returning from Japan they 'agitated for opium control after seeing a government monopoly there and on the island of Formosa apparently reduce the incidence of smoking'.[13]

Were these students victims of effective propaganda? Japanese imperialism can easily be judged as one of the harshest forms of a narco-military regimes. Even this is a "profession" which must be learned, and in Formosa a certain "soft" approach was practised. Wasn't it?

The Annexation of Formosa /Taiwan

When Japan occupied Formosa as the outcome of the Chinese–Japanese war (1895), it received public approval from the American government and public opinion. That was three years before the USA followed this example and occupied the Philippines (see next chapter). The two newcomers on the international scene created for each other the "right" to follow the old colonial and imperialist practices. As the old ones had done so successfully, both newcomers were willing to exploit the immanent weaknesses of the beleaguered Ch'ing dynasty.[14]

---

[11] Idem, p. 9.
[12] Idem, p. 10.
[13] W. Walker III, p. 14.
[14] An interesting reflection (1919) on the new ascendancy of Japan in the Far East is S.G. Chen, p. 278-289.

Most symbolic for this constellation was a long and unbelievably posi-tive article in *The New York Times* (25 September 1904) about the Japanese occupation and colonization of Formosa, in particular about its opium policy. It is titled: *'Savage Island of Formosa Transformed by Japanese. Wonders Worked in a Few Years With a People That Others Had Failed to Subdue—A Lesson for Other Colonizing Nations'.* The message: the Chinese were 'glad' that Japan 'demanded' such a wild, primitive, opium smug-gler's nest to civilize. The Spanish or Dutch colonizers 'gave it up in despair'; the French and English preferred 'not to put their foot' on such a savage island, while for the Chinese government it was an outlet for its own outlaws, pirates, robbers and similar individuals or bands. Before dis-cussing this article, it is good to comment first on the allegedly savage character of Formosa, a main "argument" to capture it "rightly".

A Former Formosa[15]

It was the Portuguese who gave this island off the Chinese coast its best-known name *Ihla Formosa* (Beautiful Island) in 1544. Spanish traders from the Philippines followed, but both refrained from colonizing it for some reason or other. The Dutch, eager to trade with China, decided to occupy the island (1624) and largely used it as a service station for the ships sailing to China and Japan.[16] A story about the 'original sin' is con-nected to this Dutch stay in Formosa: the Dutch brought opium to the East Indies and then to Formosa. Owen, reproducing Engelbert Kaempfer, states:

> Here the malaria-tainted jungle made opium an esteemed addition to the rudimentary *materia medica*. Opium divans soon appeared and with them confirmed addicts, who, in the words of a Chinese writer, unless they "be killed will not cease smoking". Once in Formosa the new vice easily found its way to the mainland.[17]

This is simplified historiography. The Chinese, however, did not accept this occupation and defeated the Dutch through the mediation of a kind of pirate king, Zheng Chenggong ("Koxinga"). He transformed Formosa

---

[15] See for the following www.howardscott.net; www.maritimeheritage.org/ports/tai-wan.html;

[16] One of the best descriptions of the Dutch trade in Japan is still J. Murdoch, vol. III, chapter VIII; about Formosa, p. 276 -281. F. Gaastra has next to nothing of interest and mentions Engelbert Kaempfer as the main source of Murdoch's story only once in passing (p. 106).

[17] D. Owen, p. 15. See also H. Morse (1926), vol. I, p. 5, 44.

into a Chinese trading center for the Portuguese, British, French or Dutch and integrated the island better into the extensive Chinese trade networks. Remarkably enough, this Koxinga was also made a Japanese hero.[18]

Until the Chinese prohibition laws of 1729, opium smoking was confined to Formosa and Fukien (Owen). Indeed, Formosa was always intimately connected in the Western perception with the opposite islands and cities of the mainland, Amoy (now Xiamen) and Ku Lang Hsu (now Gulangyu), about 150 miles from Formosa. Everywhere in the realm lived pirate-fishermen of Japanese and Chinese origin, who regularly raided the Fujian coastal settlements and captured foreign ships, smuggled salt and opium in the 19th-century.

They must have learned about that profitable product from pirate-smugglers of European origin, who settled in this region as well, and undertook opium smuggling as the most lucrative contraband. It seems appropriate to identify the latter with the heavily armed American opium clippers who could sail through the Formosan Channel against the northeast monsoon. They were often the property of the British opium dealers Jardine-Matheson & Co. or the American Dent &Co. Owen talks about the glorious reception of one of these clippers, the *Eamont,* by the Formosan "natives" and "whites":

> On one occasion she was sent to open Formosa as an opium market, and in the course of her visit, had to repel the assault of hundreds of natives as well as to ride out a typhoon. Everything was shipshape aboard the better clippers, the crew well paid and well fed. One of the Eamont's company has testified that "The officers of Her Britannic Majesty's ships on the station were very often delighted to come on board these opium-clippers and spend a pleasant evening, the more so that the table was much better than any of the hotels that were then in existence in the far-off Eastern land". Service on a clipper was regarded as a desirable appointment ...[19]

If a Western opium dealer's representative has to "open" Formosa for the opium market around 1830-40, it must be clear that before that time Formosa was "closed". Apart from this, the quotation shows how the narco-military relationship was celebrated in luxury in its earliest phase.

After the First Opium War the Ch'ing government was obliged to designate Amoy as one of the five Treaty Ports (1842), after which Ku Lang Hsu became the internationally notorious center of excessive gambling, drinking, prostitution and opium trade. Most of the wealth on display on

---

[18] J. Murdock, vol. III, p. 275.
[19] D. Owen, p. 201.

Ku Lang Hsu is to be seen in the still present colonial architecture reproducing the opium profits of the former owners.

In the 1870s the export of sugar brought riches to the Takow traders, but according to the well established colonial system, the British tried to "balance" their sugar trade with opium; if necessary, opium of the lower Persian quality.[20] Soon sugar made up fully 90% of the export and opium 90% of the import.

At that time (ca. 1865) the Dutch physician, Jos Bechtinger, needed twelve days to travel in a Chinese junk and in bad weather from Amoy to Formosa's Tamsui, near the present Taipei.[21] During his stay, Bechtinger met Odd, a British opium dealer from Dent & Co. in Hong Kong who was stationed there. This man had his opium store in a 'customs office' run by an American, John Dodd. Bechtinger experienced the lawless life there, when the British opium dealer cut the queue of a Chinese worker, whom he had caught stealing. A German opium dealer, Mellet, described how he had chased away Chinese employees, who had removed the gunpowder from his canons, and so on. They became Bechtinger's friends.

These opium dealers traveled the islands to sell opium to Chinese and tribal people, who lived a quite separate life. Other Westerners from Poland or Spain visited Formosa at the same time. All were attacked by the Chinese and/or "savages", of which there were many tribes. Bechtinger's story gives the impression that Formosa was divided between Chinese villages or small towns with a Chinese population on the coasts and several tribes in the interior. The latter are painted as savages, sometimes cannibals; the former as inimical to the white foreigners. All inhabitants are described in a rather denigrating way.

Other Western travelers reported in 1888 how the original population mixed with Chinese in East Formosa. About the last of the indigenous, daughter of a king, he said:

> One daughter remained; she married a Chinaman, took to opium and sold the crown to some Chinese virtuoso. By the way, the aboriginal women, who marry Chinese, nearly all become confirmed opium-smokers. Their husbands are chiefly to blame, by enticing them to try just one smoke, as they clean and light the pipes.[22]

---

[20] Idem, p. 287, 288.

[21] J. Bechtinger, p. 3 ff.

[22] Quoted from an interesting series of old articles reproduced on the website http://academic.reed.edu/formosa/intro.html. Parts of Bechtinger's story can be found there as well. The quotation is from G. Taylor's article in *The China Review*, 16 (1888). The next one is from J. Thomson's article in the *Journal of the Royal Geographical Society*, 53 (1873). The

An earlier (1873) report of a British geographer-discoverer tells:

> The imports of Takow consist of opium, cotton and woolen piece-goods, raw cotton, hemp bags, nankeens and prepared tobacco; and the chief exports, of brown and white sugar, sesamum-seeds, rice, sweet potatoes (extensively used as food by the natives) ... The enormous increase in trade and the corresponding revenue is mainly due to the energy of the foreign traders, although partly to the slightly more liberal policy of the Chinese Government and to the rapidly developing resources of the island ...

This optimism soon faded away because the arrival of the steamers made it necessary to improve harbor facilities, but the local Ch'ing leadership failed to do this, and the trade shifted from Takow to Anping. This is probably one reason why the Ch'ing lost confidence in Formosa and were willing to accept the Japanese demands in the Sino-Japanese war.

Another reason, or indication of this, could be the desolate condition of the Chinese soldiers on Formosa, who could not match the vigilant Japanese army. A Presbyterian missionary, George Ede, visited the camps of Chinese soldiers in Eastern Formosa which were 'anything but clean' (1891). He also saw:

> Of the sixty soldiers at this camp only three did not smoke opium. The whole set of them were in a most plighty condition. Many were in rags, and not a few had their bodies covered with most offensive sores. On asking if the soldiers had not regular drill, I was told by a fellow-traveler that the only exercise they went through was with the "big gun", which is a name jocularly given to the opium-pipe ... In place of money, the soldiers receive a large share of their wages in opium. Most of the men say that they began taking this ... "dirt" ... to alleviate the pain of their body ailments, for they have no means of obtaining medical treatment in times of trouble.[23]

When the Japanese army entered Formosa a short time later, they did not fight these poor soldiers alone. *The New York Times* provides the details.

A "New Formosa"

Japan took until 1901 before the 'last revolutionary elements' were killed.[24] The country enjoyed 'only a few years of complete peace'. Indeed, these six years of war must have been a very bloody and costly affair. It was the

---

same kind of information about the opium import-export of Formosa (Takow) was given in 1867 by N.B. Dennys.

[23] The quotation is from George Ede's article in the *Presbyterian Messenger* (1890-1891) given on website in the previous note.

[24] For the resistance of the Formosans see C.-M. Ka, p. 83 note 1.

first assault of the Japanese army on Chinese soil. But the journalist reports simply that already in 1901, 'the natives begin to understand the blessings of Japanese rule and to praise it'! The 'enlightened laws of Japan' were introduced and applied in full measure for the Japanese colonizers, but not for the uncivilized aboriginal inhabitants, who were unable to appreciate civilization without training.

Every new colonizing regime is eager to improve the infrastructure (roads, railway and telecommunication) in order to make the repressive military more mobile. For the homeland the resources of the colony are exploited (here: forests and mining). For their own colonizing settlers, health and medical provisions must be made similar to the standards of the homeland. They become show places for foreign visitors, seldom places where indigenous people were cured in a relevant way. The same is true for the educational facilities. Japan did or intended to do all this in Formosa and later in Korea. The unnamed reporter of *The New York Times* noted everything.

However, he spends the first half of the article blessing the Japanese rule, the new and soft opium policy:

> Even the opium habit has in so far been respected that the natives are not punished for consuming opium, though opium smoking and dealing in opium is a crime for which Japanese citizens in Japan and in Formosa as well are punished with penal servitude of varying degrees.

The Japanese government has adopted a policy of making 'the opium trade a monopoly, which it judiciously uses for at the same time permitting and discouraging opium smoking'. Full control is organized around consumption, addicted persons (clearly defined as 'opium smokers'), distribution by means of opium dens, import, and so on.

Also statistics are included. According to *The New York Times* there were about three million inhabitants on Formosa in 1900, of whom exactly

> 169,064 were opium smokers. By the end of March 1902, only 152,044 were registered and licensed as opium smokers, the decrease of 17,020 having been caused by death or by the discontinuance of the opium habit, and this number will no doubt rapidly be further reduced by the wise policy that is being pursued. The value of the opium imported was fixed in 1900 at an amount of 3,392,602 yen. The obvious result three years later was '1,121,455 yen only'.

It is, of course, doubtful whether one could have statistics, let alone reliable ones, in such a 'savage island', full of warring parties. A journalist

Ill. 21. Japanese Overlords and their civilized Savages. Formosa ca. 1920
Source: www.flickr.com/formosasavage/2758.

should have been very suspicious when hearing that 17,020 people died from opium smoking in a short time. This is impossible. These figures must be seen, therefore, as advertisements of the good, wise, Japanese colonization.[25]

The following table demonstrates this again.

Table 36. Opium revenue and Licensed Opium Smokers on Formosa, 1897-1941 (selected years)[26]

Year	Opium revenue in yen	Opium revenue as % of total revenue	Opium revenue as % of monopoly revenue	Number of licensed opium smokers	Smokers as % of population
1897	1 640 210	30.9	100	50 597	2.1
1899	4 249 577	41.8	124.6	130 962	5
1901	2 804 894	23.9	35.4	157 619	5.7
1905	4 205 830	19.4	33.2	130 476	4.2
1909	4 667 399	15.2	21	109 995	3.5
1915	5 870 408	15.3	50	71 715	2.1
1920	7 847 739	9.5	---	48 012	1.3
1930	4 349 818	4.4	---	23 237	0.5
1935	2 567 588	2.1	---	14 644	0.3
1940	2 278 542	0.9	---	8 594	0.14

The New York Times reports that the *general* revenue in 1896 is 2,711,822 yen; in that case the opium revenue must be about 60 per cent of the total revenue. The effects of an opium monopoly are seen, for instance, in the figures of 1909 and 1915: while the number of licensed smokers decreases by about 40%, the revenue increases by 30%: the prices of the opium for the consumers are strongly increased by "the dealer".[27]

---

[25] In the most positive assessment one can imagine that the Japanese fixed a certain number of smokers in say 1903 or 1905. To show for the outside world how "good and wise" their treatments were, one has to fix a much higher figure earlier in time, etc. Again it must be remembered here that smokers are not identical with addicts.

[26] A combination of the tables 2.1 and 2.2. in J. Jennings (1997), p. 24 and 29. These figures are in variance with those mentioned in T. Tong Joe, p. 70. The latter are based on a Japanese article (1924) and a speech of the Japanese representative, Sugimura, in the first *International Opium Conference*. The fourth column is derived from C-m. Ka table 2.2 and 2.3, p. 55, 56.

[27] T. Tong Joe, p. 69 ff. accepts everything that the Japanese propaganda states: there is no opium smuggling in Formosa, not only because of an effective police force but also thanks to the very low prices asked of the addicts, so that smuggling is not lucrative. The

What cannot be shown is whether there was the usual corruption of the monopoly officials in Formosa. In most other cases (the VOC and EIC corruption with their government backing were notorious), it remains impossible to trust the cat to stay away from the cream. The price manipulations clearly point to an affirmative conclusion.

In Japan the colonization of Formosa was not popular, because it was too costly due to the underestimated resistance and, therefore, long military involvement. It was even proposed to sell Formosa to a Western country.[28] The fourth governor-general, Kodama Gentaro, and his civil affairs bureau chief, Gotō Shimpei, came up with a new approach: in short, Formosa had to pay for itself, but this deserved an initial investment for roads, railroads, harbors and, of course, prisons. Gotō had made a master plan to develop the infrastructure of Formosa (1898). Earlier Japanese investments were only directed at colonial government buildings and military expenditures. The new master plan focussed on economic growth and exploitation of the island; the financing involved, therefore, a government loan of 35 million yen to the Japanese Formosa administration that should be repaid with interest. Land tax reform was one source of revenue.

> As a means of repaying public debts and reducing Japan's fiscal burden in a period of public disapproval of the colonial adventure ... Gotō explored another important source of revenue: government takeover of the monopoly benefits held by foreign traders on opium and camphor [sixty per cent of the import was opium]. An opium bureau was set up in 1897 to monopolize the production and sale of opium. According to Gotō's plan, opium prices would be marked up to obtain an annual income of 1.6 million yen. Combined with the customs on opium imports, this revenue would allow the government to gross at least 2.4 million yen annually, about as much as the tax revenues of the Office of the Governor-General in 1897.[29]

It is like reading a report of a Dutch, British or French colonial Governor-General. Indeed, whatever the differences in the details, once again the twofold function of opium in the exploitation of a conquered foreign land is documented here: to pay the cost of the military conquest and occupation, and to keep the opposition in the population under control; a third

---

price is only a quarter of the Hong Kong price: 117 Yen per kilo for first-class opium and 87.6 Yen per kilo for second-class.

[28] See C-M. Ka, p. 50 ff.

[29] Idem, p. 53, 54.

and fourth function could be developed only on top of these two: to conduct a profitable international business for members of the occupying power elite and to make a sound basis for further conquests.

The main effect of the narco-military monopoly also here in Formosa was that the government had to become the dealer in all respects and chased away all foreign competitors. It also had to look overseas for resources and to become a player in the international opium game, including smuggling practices.

The opium monopoly triggered others: in camphor, tobacco, salt and alcohol. Indirect taxes could be kept as high as 50-60% of the tax revenue at the expense of the consumers.

The Japanese knew perfectly well that

> the measures employed to achieve financial independence were expedients that could cause embarrassment if discovered by foreigners or the newly colonized people and could never be relied on permanently.[30]

Gotō stated this later in a lecture to the Yuki club. A clever remark showing understanding for the fact that you cannot continue to turn on the tax screw, but he did not mention the opportunities given: being so experienced, the same tactic could be repeated after a new conquest. That is what Japan did. and the fear of foreigners could be sublimated as well.

New imperialists are, indeed, modernized. Not only occupation and exploitation of foreign territory are saved, also modern public relations in attracting tourists. This documents the rather rare American *Terry's Guide to the Japanese Empire.*[31] In it, Formosa is 'a bizarre blend of civilization and savagery', and it offers 'the blasé traveler an unusual thrill—that of hobnobbing with savage head-hunters who secretly covet the visitor's head but are prevented by Japanese law and watchfulness from taking it unless the traveler is willing!' The tourist can watch savage dances under the secure protection of 'their Japanese masters'. Their aim was to make of Formosa an exceptionally attractive tourist resort with its mixture of savagery and modern hotels and comfort.

There is praise in this *Guide* of 1930 for the

> advanced educational ideals of the Japanese as colonizers' while rescuing 'a savage race from moral, commercial, and intellectual oblivion' in a 'war

---

[30] Idem, p. 54, 55. See also Idem, p. 61
[31] *Terry's Guide*, p. 761-791.

of regeneration or extermination ... being conducted with characteristic Japanese vigor'. These savages 'die in defense of their wretched huts ... [32] The Japanese guards of the tribes live in bamboo houses along a broad road cut through the cleared jungle 'surrounded by barbed-wire fences, and supplied with firearms, grenades, field-guns, telephones, etc. ... entanglements are electrically charged and sunken mines are laid for the savages.[33]

In short: highly attractive for American tourists who can play the hunting-savages game here and attend the show because 'sometimes whole parties are ambushed and massacred'.

Elsewhere on the island one could enjoy other spectacular things:

> The Monopoly Bureau where the bulk of the world's supply of camphor is refined, and where all the opium smoked on the island is elaborated, is highly interesting. ... The visitor is shown the complicated process of ... treating the crude opium. The hotel manager will plan a visit ...[34]

The tourist information about opium (in Japanese *ahen, afuyō*) is quite precise and allows us to cross-check the official data given in the table. There are also marked differences with the Dutch East Indies practices. After some remarks about the origin of opium and the information that it is forbidden for Japanese to smoke it, the description of their opium factory is as follows:

> The process of crushing it [the imported raw opium from India, China or Turkey. H.D.], then steaming it in huge vats, and adding wine and other relishes to impart a piquant taste, is interesting. The rooms are filled with the disagreeable odor of burning medicine. None of the 300 or more employees smoke. The finished product is packed in 1-lb tins in three grades; the best quality retailing for about ¥21, the 2d at ¥17, and the 3d at ¥13. The Bureau pays out about 5 million *yen* a year for materials and for expenses, and nets about 1 million *yen*—a considerable item of the island revenue. There are upward of 100,000 smokers in Formosa, each of whom uses about 37 grains a day, for which 6 *sen* are paid. The death-rate among them is high.[35]

There are in 1930 apparently four times as many smokers as given in the table. However, if all these 100,000 smokers have to pay 6 *sen* a day for

---

[32] Idem, p. 763 and 769.
[33] Idem, p. 770. The description continues with many kinds of morbid details.
[34] Idem, p. 781.
[35] Idem, p. 782. In 1930 a *yen* equals about half an American dollar; one *sen* equals 1/100 of a yen (Idem, p. xix). The purchasing power of a dollar was large: from Seattle to Japan a first-class cabin on a luxury steamer cost about $200, to Hong Kong $290, etc.; a 'Round the World Tours' (from Seattle via Shanghai, Singapore, Suez to London and back to New York) for $910.

their dose, the total annual income is about ¥ 219 million, which is fifty times more than the income given in the table! If one, furthermore, thinks about opium as a 'considerable item of the island revenue', it concerns a statement 'considerably' beyond the aim of the Japanese colonizers that this opium contribution should be as greatly diminished as possible. With this outcome all other figures become suspicious, and specific questions (like: who has pocketed all this non-registered money?) demand new investigations.

Another rather unknown aspect of the Japanese occupation of Formosa concerns the Japanese cocaine production. De Jong mentions that

> Japan and Formosa use nearly all their leaves to produce cocaine. They use themselves the largest part of it and export the rest. Formosa exports most leaves to Japan.[36]

Their cocaine production is as follows:

Table 37. Japanese Cocaine Production, 1934-1939 (x 1kg)[37]

	1934	1935	1936	1937	1938	1939
Japan	910	900	900	896	900	900
Formosa	40	84	75	90	85	80
Total	950	984	975	986	985	980

The conclusion seems to be that one attempts to hide the reality behind the announcement of the outstanding colonial performance of the Japanese apostles of civilization, and has to tame the brutal and systematic elimination of defenseless indigenous peoples by means of cocaine, opium and its derivatives.

The Korean Case

Opium smoking in Korea was a late 19th-century phenomenon. It arrived in all probability from neighboring Manchuria around 1880 when the British import into China had reached its highest levels. Like all other governments, the Korean one prohibited the use, cultivation and import of opium and even of opium pipes (in vain). In 1910 the Japanese took over control, and they repeated the prohibition according to the strict Japanese law. Everywhere in the spheres of Japanese influence, however, the con-

---

[36] A. W. de Jong, p. 884.
[37] Idem, p. 884.

tradiction between law and practice was dangerously large. That was well known internationally but was not always opportune in the diplomatic discourse.

The New York Times (March 30, 1919) published a long letter presented to the American minister in Peking written by the representatives of the Korean people living in China. It is one long complaint about the Japanese colonizers, their economic, religious, ethnic and cultural exploitation. They also wrote:

> The Japanese Government has established a bureau for the sale of opium and under the pretext that opium was to be used for medicinal purposes has caused Koreans and Formosans to engage in poppy cultivation. The opium is secretly shipped into China. Because of the Japanese encouragement of this traffic, many Koreans have become users of drugs.

This cannot be very far from the truth. First, opium addiction was officially eradicated thanks to severe punishments, but morphine and heroin addiction was introduced and encouraged without any form of effective control and with very low fines. In 1924 'there were four thousand addicts in Keijo (Seoul) alone, creating "enormous havoc". Nor was the problem confined to the cities'.[38] Six years later, there was a thousand more, representing only a fraction of the total.

Furthermore, Japanese Korea emerged as a major exporter of raw opium, because the Japanese pharmaceutical industry used the colony as resource production in North Korea. It established a branch office and morphine factory in Keijo as well. The colonial government apparently created the demand through its soft morphine policy.

It was still not large enough. Along the border with China, illicit production and smuggling developed during World War I. This created a disparity between an official anti-narcotics policy and an attractive extension of a profitable market in Korea and abroad (mainly China).

An opium monopoly was established in 1919, which was ineffective, if one expected to eradicate the opium and its derivatives problem. Under this monopoly, production, distribution and consumption increased dramatically, and the relations with the Japanese-controlled parts of North China, the *Kwantung Leased Territory* and Manchukuo, intensified year after year. The following table provides the details.

---

[38] J. Jennings (1997), p. 31.

Table 38. Opium and Narcotics production in Korea, 1930-1941[39]

Year	Raw opium in kilo	Area in hectares	Government payment in yen	Morphine in kilo	Heroin in kilo	Medicinal use opium in kilo
1930	1 400	736	35 572	195.58	103.1	10.93
1931	5 654	1 054	166 051	272	155	12.49
1932	7 634	1 087	235 153	274.93	135.79	10.35
1933	14 059	2 241	401 149	267.01	156.76	---
1934	11 339	2 178	343 028	310.32	100.81	9.9
1935	18 348	2 481	565 922	84.25	---	5.03
1936	27 305	2 385	796 776	---	---	11.9
1937	28 848	2 557	792 618	---	---	59.71
1938	27 712	5 004	718 914	87.05	---	22.4
1939	27 702	6 597	724 245	141.57	4.1	45.38
1940	32 929	7 295	1 348 821	239.03	2.7	25.01
1941	50 725	8 462	2 592 661	---	---	---

It may be true that the rapid emergence of Japan as a major producer of narcotics was 'a response to the international shortage of medicinal drugs during World War I' (Jennings), but the nationalism in Japan with its strong imperialistic drive and immanent racism *vis-à-vis* the Chinese and Korean "races" created that dangerous combination between military and industrial interests, the narco-military state. In one international conference after the other, Japan erected a smoke-screen to hide vigorous activities on the military and opium fronts.

The Japanese colonies of Korea and Formosa were used as the basis for the opium assault on China. 'At Harbin and Mukden, the drug trade was in the hands of Koreans who seemed to local officials to have no other way of making a living.'[40] The open hostilities in China began in 1937, but their previous history must be elucidated as well.

---

[39] J. Jennings (1997), p. 36 and 37 adjusted by Idem (1995), p. 814, 815; why Jennings added the figures for 1938-1940 in his table 2 and not in the more recent publication is unclear. They are reproduced here as well.

[40] W. Walker III, p. 90. The 'North China Imbroglio' is covered by Idem p. 90-96.

The Opium attack on China

The "Roaring Twenties"

Neither its victory over China in 1894-1895 nor its defeat of Russia in 1904-1905 lead to the acknowledgment of Japan as world power. This acceptance had to come, first, from the almighty British Empire. Several agreements with the British (1902, 1905 and 1911) gave their relationship the status of an alliance. For Japan there were two main aims: protection of its naval-building program and of its opium policy, i.e. its prominent role in the lucrative morphine trade. Japan and the British Empire both had strong interests in blocking the proposed anti-opium reforms as long as possible, and for both, China remained the largest market of their addictive products.

The astonishment of the British ambassador Eliot (1925) quoted in the beginning of this chapter had, indeed, some reasonable grounds. Still, between the last agreement and 1925, a world war had happened and Japan's opium interest in Asia was about to replace the British. The British opium policy was attacked not only by the new imperialists, America and Japan, but also from within, a rather powerful British and European anti-opium lobby.

Japan's Chinese opium interest tried to infiltrate Manchuria steadily. In the Japanese perception, opium and its derivatives were major tools to conquer larger parts of China, exploiting the one revolutionary upheaval in China after the other. The main motives to attack China militarily and with opium addiction programs originated ultimately from Japanese racism: Chinese were "by nature" inveterate opium consumers because they were culturally and racially inferior to the Japanese race and culture.

As a general statement, here is one example of this Japanese opinion:

> Despite its disastrous aftermath, the Chinese believe in the medicinal qualities of the drug, and they blow smoke in the faces of new-born children to make them utter the first cry. Smokers are in misery until they procure opium, and if thwarted will become frantic and commit excesses.[41]

The long Chinese tradition of anti-opium measures could scarcely result in Japan's sympathy. Thanks to the active pro-opium policy of the Chinese warlords, Japan was constantly re-affirmed in its racial thinking and anti-Chinese attitudes and practices.

---

[41] *Terry's Guide*, p. 783.

In the period 1910-1920 Japan became the largest opium buyer in Calcutta.[42] It apparently tried to copy the earlier British Empire policy in China. Members of a *White Cross* association from Seattle, connected to a *China Club*, disclosed a more complicated relationship in 1920:

> that foreign morphine was being shipped across the United States to Japan to be smuggled into China and also that some American narcotic drugs were going to Japan for eventual use in China.[43]

Many people cried shame about this affair. It urged new US legislation after commercial interests from Seattle convinced members of Congress that the US was 'poisoning' its relation with China, a 'customer ... able to take more American goods than any other nation'. In addition, an international conference immediately noted that Japan promised 'the strictest possible investigation into the illicit traffic in morphine', whereupon it advised the Japanese government to clear up the discrepancies between the Japanese import and export statistics.[44] It is the diplomatic language customary in an abstract world which starts bothering about their mutual relations only after crimes against humanity are committed in the real world.

That was also the case now, as the *New York Times* (February 14, 1919) reported in full detail:

> In South China, morphia is sold by Chinese peddlers, each of whom carries a passport certifying that he is a native of Formosa, and therefore entitled to Japanese protection. Japanese drug stores throughout China carry large stocks of morphia. Japanese medicine vendors look to morphia for their largest profits. Wherever Japanese are predominant, there the trade flourishes. Through Dairen, morphia circulates throughout Manchuria and the adjoining province; through Tsingtao, morphia is distributed over Shantung province, Anhui, and Kiangsu, while from Formosa morphia is carried with opium and other contraband by motor-driven fishing boats to some point on the mainland, from which it is distributed throughout the province of Fukien and the north of Kuangtung. Everywhere it is sold by Japanese under extra-territorial protection.[45]

La Motte did not like this article: it is 'more anti-Japanese than anti-opium'. Another commentator, the Englishman and well-known China-

---

[42] See Appendix 1 table 60; L. Lewin, p. 65.
[43] D. Musto, p. 192, 194; see also E. La Motte, p. 46.
[44] C. Terry, M. Pellens, p. 667 seventh recommendation.
[45] Quoted by E. La Motte, p. 11, 12. T. Tong Joe, p. 72 does not make any critical remark in dealing with the Japanese occupation of Kwantung: it is the same optimistic story as told about Japan's opium policy in Formosa.

watcher Putnam Weale, attacked the Japanese assault on China at the same time. All Chinese ports with Japanese commissioners of Maritime Customs were also centers of contraband trade. Opium and its derivatives were smuggled so openly 'that the annual net import of Japanese morphia (although this trade is forbidden by International Convention) is now said to be something like 20 tons a year—sufficient to poison a whole nation'.[46] Again, La Motte did not like this Englishman either, because he was too anti-Japanese and not enough anti-opium.

In her opinion, A.J. Macdonald, a Cambridge scholar or English missionary, presented the facts in a 'more balanced' manner (1916) and, therefore, more anti-opium. Macdonald wrote:

> In the North of China another evil is springing up. The eradication of the opium habit is being followed by the development of the morphia traffic ... by the action of [Japanese] traders ... China is being drenched with morphia ... It is said that in certain areas coolies are to be seen "covered all over with needle punctures". An injection of the drug can be obtained for three or four cents. In Newchang 2,000 victims of the morphia habit died in the winter of 1914-15. Morphia carries off its victims far more rapidly than opium.[47]

At this time morphine was not produced in Asia. The bulk of the manufacturing took place in England (in Edinburgh and London), in Germany and Austria. In total, 5½ tons were produced in 1911, according to Macdonald, which increased to 14 tons in 1914. After the war it increased again to 20 tons in 1919. Japanese agents traded it, but the fact that three British firms supplied 'China with morphia for illicit purposes is a condemnation of English Christianity'.

The *New York Times* article triggered a strong response in the US. The Japanese, growing impatient with all the blamed although they were only the distributors, reacted with remarkable background information. Putnam Weale was attacked directly because he did not accuse the British producers. Large quantities of morphine were shipped from Edinburgh to Japan. The Japanese stated, however:

> ... the shipments to Japan dropped from 600,220 ounces in 1917 to one-fourth that amount in 1918 ... 113,000 ounces of morphia arrived in Kobe

---

[46] Idem, p. 14. B.L. Putnam Weale (pseudonym for Bertram Lenox, 1877-1930) lived in and was a strong supporter of Republican China. From his many China books and articles most can be read on-line today (see, for instance, the fabulous *Project Gutenberg*). For the political Chinese "Roaring Twenties", they are important sources. E. La Motte (p. 13, 14) quotes an article from him in the journal *Asia* (1919).

[47] Quoted by E. La Motte, p. 14, 15.

from the United States in the first five months of 1919 ... this morphia is being transhipped in Kobe harbor to vessels bound for China. Dr. Paul S. Reinsch, who has resigned his post as Minister to China, has stated that he will use every resource in his power to stop the shipment from America of morphia intended for distribution in China, in defiance of the international convention which prohibits the sale of the drug in that country.[48]

The message of this statement is clear, namely, to demonstrate that in opium matters the British producer, the American and Japanese distributors had a common interest and that China was the common target.

It is understandable that Ellen La Motte in her powerful attack on the British Opium Monopoly tried to mobilize all opposition against its manipulations: 'America to the rescue! It must have been a close squeak for poor old China.'[49] She witnessed how the Chinese President Hsu Shih-ch'ang decided to destroy nearly eighty tons (!) of opium in a costly public burning at Shanghai. Specially constructed furnaces burned the stuff from 1200 confiscated chests in eight days (17-25 January 1919). It was a spectacular apotheosis of the large anti-opium campaigns several Chinese governments carried out at the beginning of the 20th-century.[50] Publically, the British, Americans and Japanese applauded this and the activities of the Peking-based International Anti-Opium Association. Meanwhile, a completely new era in narco-militarism had been started based on the chemical manufacturing of the opium derivatives morphine and heroin.

The opium burning was the last all anti-opium act of the Chinese government in its revolt against Western and foreign aggression. It was also the beginning of the opium nightmare of Republican and Japanese China, which ended with the establishment of a unified Chinese government in 1949. The two new imperialists, Japan and the United States, played the key roles.

---

[48] Idem, p. 16, 17. The source of the quotation is *The Japan Society Bulletin* (1919/1920), which quotes other Japanese sources. The reference to the well-known professor of political science Reinsch, a China expert and writer of several books about China (1869-1923), is remarkable. As American Minister to China he had to resign after the American government assigned German rights in the Shantung Peninsula to Japan during the Peace Conference in Versailles, while Reinsch had told the Chinese government that the Americans would support Chinese interests. See an article in *The New York Times*, August 28, 1919. Later Reinsch criticized the Chinese government several times (see *The New York Times* September 6, 1920 and September 13, 1921). The Japanese government could see in him a friend of Japan.

[49] W. Walker III, p. 29.

[50] Idem, p. 28. Reinsch was closely involved in the discussions. See Idem, notes p. 231.

From World Economic Crisis to World War II

The economic world crisis did not stop the opium business, it only slowed it down for a while due to stagnation on the production side. It was quite logical that the "old days" should return once the combination of army-violence plus drugs trade was restored. Indeed, it was soon unavoidable that as the Japanese military activities extended, the Japanese addiction activities in China did, too.

The Nationalists of Chiang Kai-shek started to work against the Japanese activities and published alarming data about the annual import of opium into the Japanese foreign concession in Tianjin, home of the illicit trade in opium and narcotic drugs in North China.

Table 39. Annual Import of Opium into Tianjin around 1936[51]

District of Production	Quantity in Ounces	Number of Importers
Ganzhou	2 600 000	over 20
Liangzhou	9 100 000	50
Ninxia	2 600 000	20
Chahar	100 000	7
Suiyuan	200 000	10
Shaanxi	700 000	6
Jehol	600 000	1

The quality of this opium was low. The Japanese concession contained 42 illicit opium firms and 160 opium dens. Chinese authorities were powerless in dealing with this foreign concession. The only thing they could do was to catch the drug smugglers who went in and out of the concessions. This smuggling was done not only by Chinese subjects, but also by Japanese and Koreans. They often sold heroin and morphine to foreigners in the other concessions, in particular the French one.

Now both England and the USA were prepared to bring pressure to bear against these activities, although this was done half-heartedly: the British still had 'vital commercial interests' in the realm, and Roosevelt was not prepared to abandon his rather hypocritical 'restrictive neutrality'. That was even the case after the genocidal activities of the Japanese army, including the Nanking Massacre (December 1937) with its criminal bombardments of civilian targets, its 300,000 murders and about 25,000 rapes. What was the difference with the German policy of Chamberlain on the other side of the globe, which got all the publicity?

---

[51] Quoted in A. Baumler (ed.), reading 17, p. 158.

Roosevelt's advisers did not fail to inform him quite clearly

> that Tokyo intended to use narcotics as a weapon of war against a defense-
> less people' or 'that the Japanese intended to establish an opium monopoly
> in North China under the North China Army and in Central China under
> the army based in Shanghai.[52]

Also *Time* (December 5, 1938) reported about the narco-military activities of Japan. Earlier, *Time* had provided the information that under the
supervision of the Japanese army, Iranian opium was being imported into
China. Now, six months later, this situation had changed drastically:

> The bustling Japanese now produce most of China's narcotics in Japanese
> factories in Manchukuo, transport the supply down from Dairen to Shang-
> hai and Nanking. ... [A report from Dr. Miner Searle Bates, vice-president of
> the US-supported University of Nanking, declares] ... In Nanking 50,000
> persons, one-eighth of the population, are being slowly poisoned by heroin
> ... sold by Japanese-directed rings. At least 5,000,000 Chinese dollars are
> made every month in the Nanking area by dealers belonging to or allied
> with the Japanese Army. Out of this, Japan's puppet Chinese
> "Reformed"Government gets a sizable cut. Japanese and Korean prostitutes
> "attached" to the Japanese Army brought into Nanking 80 cases of opium
> a fortnight ago. Japanese agents three weeks ago delivered 400 cases of
> Iranian opium to Nanking's Opium Suppression Bureau, which ostensibly
> was set up to curb the traffic but which actually distributes opium through
> its own sales agencies.[53]

The opium business was so lucrative that the Japanese army and navy
were caught in intense wrangling over the control of the profits, while
Japanese in the municipality of Shanghai also demanded their share. The
Japanese authorities acted in the same way as the previous warlords and
the Kuomintang: war, army and the support of puppet governments
should be paid by the opium victims.

However, the income from opium and its derivatives was insufficient
and could not compensate the multi-million flight of labor from China's
cities and the destruction of urban industries.[54]

Every opportunity to gain opium money was seized: in North China
and Manchuria the puppet-government abolished all anti-narcotics
and anti-opium laws (24-2-1938); from each opium den, an impost of one

---

[52] W. Walker III, p. 119.

[53] Find this article at www.time.com/time/magazine/article/0,9171,760383,00.html.

[54] For the dubious and lethal relationship between the Japanese and the gangs in
Shanghai, in particular to Du Yue-sheng, see J. Marshall, p. 39 ff.

percent was imposed on its gross intake; insiders even feared that Tientsin was going to serve as 'the supplying center of heroin for Europe'.

Of course, notwithstanding the available information a British undersecretary of state expressed that there was 'no evidence that the increased drug traffic ... is aimed at the systematic demoralization of the Chinese people'. US officials were less "reluctant", but they had not had a colonial career in India as this undersecretary had.

The US vice consul in Manchukuo informed the British and American governments continuously in 1938 and 1939 of the activities at the opium front and 'the protection of [official] revenue', the curbing of competing, illicit traffic in drugs. Coincidentally, he lived next to a small heroin factory and was confronted once with the corpses of drug addicts 'dumped naked into the slime'. He reacted:

> It was difficult not to conclude that the Kwantung Army was satisfied that the Chinese of Manchuria should be debauched. Dope addicts do not overthrow governments.[55]

The Manchukuo govermment attempted to do something against the opium addiction. The US consul at the time was rather positive about it, but others condemned Manchukuo 'for exacerbating China's opium problems' and 'intentional narcotization'.

The attempts were not very successful in any case. Drug smuggling from Chosen (Korea) increased; authorities found it difficult to give up the lure of opium revenues; the monopolization of the opium business was, as elsewhere, only a means to increase the revenues. Opium peddlers around Nanking sold drugs in relief camps, supplied by Japanese *rōnin* or gangsters. Some believed that this was part of the policy of drugging the Chinese people.

In addition, George Morlock, a well-informed American working for the Division of Far Eastern Affairs of the US government, learned that 428 cases of Iranian opium had reached Tientsin in mid-April 1938; three hundred of them were in Japanese hands at Shanghai. Another 1000 cases were being held in Macao, where the Special Service Agency of the Japanese army was trying to set up a heroin factory.[56]

---

[55] W. Walker III, p. 121. The *Kwantung Army* was the name of the Japanese invasion army.
[56] Idem, p. 125.

Notwithstanding all these activities at the opium front, no 'party' in the game could gain control over the market since there were too many competitors for the profits.

World War II and after

The historiography of the Japanese in World War II remains a superficial affair.[57] It seems as if the dramatic fate of the 'comfort women' got most of the publicity, after the usual period of total silence about the war period by victims as well as perpetrators. The certainly exaggerated victor's historiography glorified the few heroic deeds, which was not pleasant for perpetrator countries like Japan. However, contrary to the Germans, the Japanese have had great difficulty to develop a critical way of writing about their own war crimes and war ideology (racism, biological experiments, concentration camps or emperor adoration), about the pre-war years performance in Asia (Nanking, opium policy), etc.

Last but not least, the data about Japanese policies in the occupied territories, in particular the important opium policy, are even scantier. John Jennings's and Bob Wakabayashi's writings belong among the first to document this. Their research has revealed a more detailed insight into the development of the Japanese war opium policy.

North China

Mengjiang (literally: Mongolian Territories) was a puppet state of Japan more or less corresponding to the southern part of the present Mongolia including border provinces of China (1936-1945). In 1939 it received its final shape, but at the end of the war, it was abolished thanks to the invasion of the Soviet Red Army. Now the area is called Inner Mongolia, the northern part of the People's Republic of China (PRC), populated by a large majority of Han Chinese.

For Japan, this area was important for its mineral resources (iron, coal). Its establishment as a national state may have intended to provide a buffer against China with its own army, a section of the Japanese Kwantung Army. As the table shows, the Japanese used Mengjiang also as a safe production location for opium exported to China.

---

[57] One of the better examples in this genre is the long article of Hatano Sumio in I.C. Dear, M. Foot (ed.), p. 476-501.

Table 40. Mengjiang Opium Export, 1939-1942 (volumes in 1000 taels = 36 kg)[58]

destination	1939	%	1940	%	1941	%	1942	%	totals	%
Internal	141.4	16.3	252.3	6.2	144.1	2.6	166.3	1.8	704.1	3.6
Shanghai	100	11.5	2005	49.2	3848	70.1	5027	53.5	10 980	55.4
Beijing	300	34.6	1205	29.6	1200	21.9	1300	13.8	4 005	20.2
Tianjin	100	11.5	520	12.8	---	–	–	–	620	---
Jinan	100	11.5	---	---	---	–	–	–	100	–
Tangshan	100	11.5	---	---	---	–	–	–	100	---
Manchuria	–	–	---	---	---	–	2000	21.3	2000	–
Guandong	–	–		---	300	5.5	–	–	300	---
Elsewhere	27.31	3.1	90	2.2	–	–	58.4	0.6	175.4	0.5
Japan	–	–	–	–	–	–	841.6	9	841.6	4.2
Totals	868.4	100	4072.3	100	5492.1	100	9393.3	100	19826.1	100

It seems as if the Japanese had a kind of domino theory about opium. As such, this Mengjiang production potential formed the most northern link of a chain, which involved fields and factories for opium, heroin and morphine in Manchukuo, perhaps Japan, Korea, Formosa, Hong Kong and the southern occupied countries. To uncover this whole chain will take considerably more research, but the following is a small compensation.

Nanjing China

There was a most remarkable effect of the Japanese opium activities in the occupied territory: Japanese soldiers themselves had to pay 'extortionate amounts for supplies in the bazaars, especially for the opium on which many of them had become dependent'.[59] This conflicted with the Japanese racist idea that only the Chinese were so degenerate that they needed opium.

The reason this was possible was probably disclosed in 2007 by Reiji Yoshida, staff-writer of *The Japan Times*. He wrote an interesting series of articles on the relationship between World War II and opium from which the following is derived.

A newly found 1942 document showed that opium dealer Hung Chi Shan Tang sold as much as 300 million yuan worth of opium in 1941. At that time, the annual budget of the Nanjing government was 370 million yuan. The dealer belonged to a Shanghai-based company headed by the

---

[59] B. Wakabayashi, p. 19.
[59] H. Sumio, p. 404.

Japanese Hajime Satomi. This was the dominant opium trader in Japanese-controlled central China until early 1944. Satomi had to testify before the *International War Crimes Tribunal* (Tokyo, 1946), but his opium business was apparently ignored.

Jennnings could not have known about this new document. It remains remarkable that he mentioned Satomi only once in passing without realizing that he was the spider in the Japanese opium web in China.[60]

During World War II, from December 1941 to August 1945, the Japanese Army established a military administration in Hong Kong and issued military bills called *gunpyo* as a currency. Hong Kong residents were forced to exchange Hong Kong dollars for *gunpyo*, and the use of Hong Kong dollars was subsequently banned completely. On the back of each *gunpyo* there was a note stating: "This bill may always be exchanged for Japanese yen of equal value". Opium was used to support this military money with which Chinese materials were procured. This means

> that to buy opium, locals would need to buy *gunpyo* first by selling their legal tender ... This would push up the value of *gunpyo*. In short: a rather complicated way of stealing on a large scale. In 1942, for instance, the opium exchanged for *gunpyo* was valued at nearly 100 million yuan.

These dealings were kept secret for a remarkable reason: 'Opium was too dirty, and it has been kept secret until now,' said Yoshida's spokesman.

The new Satomi document reveals how profitable this *gunpyo* was relative to the operating costs, the wholesale prices of the opium, local currencies, Hung Chi Shan Tang's commission (8%) on top of insurance fees and tax; the air transport cost in one year rose up to three million yuan, and so on.

Hung Chi Shan Tang was, in fact, a private opium farmer of the Japanese puppet government in Nanjing. In practice, he was the farmer of Hajime Satomi, who was the middleman between the Japanese occupation force and Japan's wartime ministry in Tokyo. The opium farmer, in his turn, sold six million "liang" or 222 tons of opium to local-level Chinese dealers alone in 1941. The earlier North Chinese governments under Japanese control (Inner Mongolia, Manchuria) systematically grew poppies to raise revenues: in 1942 opium accounted for as much as 28% of their annual budgets. Satomi further declared that opium was the only product with which foreign currency could be earned. In addition to Mongolian opium,

---

[60] J. Jennings (1997), p. 94.

Satomi's company imported the product from Iran as well as from the state monopoly of the Manchukuo regime.

Apart from raw or prepared opium, these Japanese-Chinese dealers sold morphine and heroin as well. The document reveals that Hung Chi Shan Tang had 999 kg of morphine made in Manchukuo and even '277 kg of cocaine processed by the Japanese colonial government in Taiwan as of June 1, 1942'. Morphine and cocaine, Satomi reported, could be sold immediately on the Chinese market at street prices, which were twice the book value.

The narcotics were originally prepared for the wartime Southeast Asian market. Satomi states that Chinese residents were his main clients. However, the relationship with the opium-consuming Japanese soldiers is also clarified with this information.

A remarkable relationship could have been uncovered: the later Prime Minister Kishi, a wartime Prime Minister, General Tojo, and many other politicians were, in fact, on his payroll. This 'Opium King' died in 1965 at the age of 69. Kishi rendered him the last honors.

Hong Kong

This Crown colony was explicitly a target of a Japanese invasion plan in 1936.[61] The Japanese Chief of Staff was reacting to a re-fortification of Hong Kong and Singapore by the British. It took another four years before this plan was realized, because Japan was so frustrated with the colossal and endless China war. But the Hong Kong authorities did not confine themselves to a re-fortification.

The military manpower had to be strengthened, which for the British overlords was always a subtle matter of divide and rule in which racist and cultural prejudices played an important role. First, a Portuguese unit was formed, which was ultimately trusted the most, notwithstanding the fact that they were historically the main competitor in the opium trade of neighboring Macao (were not the mixed Portuguese-Chinese nearly the same as the mixed British-Chinese?).

Next came a police or army unit formed by Indian *sepoy* troops (had not Hong Kong 'flourished for decades as a receiving station for Indian opium'? And could they not be better trusted than the Chinese police forces, who could have inherited something of the Chinese Revolution of 1911?). European expatriates, the most powerful group in Hong Kong after

---

[61] P. Snow, p. 34. Also for the following Snow's very detailed study is mainly used.

the British military, were against an emancipation of the Chinese, including opportunities for Chinese in the police departments. Therefore, Indian sepoy were used to break up strikes of Chinese laborers, when they could not be silenced enough through opium deliveries.

Notwithstanding the English, international or Chinese Nationalist's pressures, the 'Colonial Office had dragged its feet' in reforming the opium business. In 1914 it had replaced the old system of farming out the opium stocks to private companies by a government monopoly. As mentioned above, this monopoly acted only as a 'tidy revenue earner' and never reduced the number of drug users: it provided 50% of the government's total income. Later this decreased, at least officially, to about 10% around the time Japan made its first invasion plan. The result can be assessed as follows.

A few months before the Japanese take-over, there were reportedly 5,577 rationed and non-rationed opium smokers. More revealing are figures like the existence of 2,500 opium divans used by 20 smokers a day, which makes 50,000 users every day. In addition, there were 30,000 heroin pill addicts.[62]

Of course, the Japanese succeeded in toppling the old British colonial hierarchy by setting up the usual New Order for the New Men of all authoritarian regimes. This time a pan-Asiatic ideal defined by Japan and realized by Japan was the guiding principle. A fundamental part of this was to abandon every Western influence:

> On his arrival in February [1942] Governor Isogai proclaimed the replacement of selfish Western materialism by the 'spiritual values' of the Orient ... on "traditional Asian morality" ... the authorities publicized their resolve to wipe out that great evil which had underpinned Hong Kong's founding and rise to prosperity and which the British had been so slow to eradicate— the consumption of opium. In late March Isogai announced the introduction of an Opium Suppression Policy. All secret opium divans were to be "cleaned up" and steps taken to control the opium traffic ... a register was compiled of the colony's opium addicts, with a view to ensuring that these addicts should receive their fix only through designated sales outlets, at a high price and in quantities that were to be reduced year by year.[63]

These are plans already familiar to readers when confronted with the French colonial opium monopoly or the Dutch *Opiumregie*. Also in the follow-up, the parallels are striking.

---

[62] See the article of Harold Traver in: H. Traver, J. Vagg (ed.), p. 44.
[63] P. Snow, p. 99.

The Japanese occupiers had started to squeeze all wealth out of the Hong Kong citizens by introducing worthless 'military yens' (M¥) at a greedy rate of HK$2: M¥1, later even HK$4: M¥1. They, furthermore, imposed a whole series of steep taxes not only on business profits, but on many other things. The announcement regarding the Opium Problem in January 1943 was remarkable: the number of addicts in the colony is so large that an abrupt suppression of opium smoking would be 'difficult to carry out' after all. Instead, the authorities decided to 'suppress opium by taxing it'.

Like the British, they planned to create an official monopoly by establishing an Opium Sale Syndicate. This was meant to manage the traffic, to take charge of retailing the drug, to register smokers at a suitable prohibitive price, and so on. In short: as usual, this government also milked the craving for opium to its own profit. To create a smooth business and, therefore, as much profit as possible, the Japanese were even able to bring

> large consignments of the drug ... into Hong Kong by the Army from regions of north China such as Chahar and Jehol.[64]

In a much more profound way, the Japanese occupier was involved in the Hong Kong opium business. Isogai had promised to eradicate the city's substantial gangsterism (the Triads). That did not occur, but his successor, General Tanaka, incorporated the gangsters Street Guards into his repression machine from late 1943 onwards. The Street Guards in each district elected a Protective Guards Body which cooperated and dined with the chairman of the Police Bureau and the Police Committee, which should have arrested them. Through the black market, which was already a Triads business, the Protective Guards allegedly took over the distribution of food to the populace during the last part of the occupation.

In addition, Tanaka made some deal with a Triad chieftain, a certain Wan Yuk-ming, concerning the 'Western amusements' which were condemned by Isogai:

> During the following months gambling joints multiplied once again. The red light districts boomed, and the colony became dotted with an estimated 8,000 opium dens, many of them large-scale and operating in full public view.[65]

---

[64] Idem, p. 153, 154.
[65] Idem, p. 218, 263. See also note 59 p. 409.

Through investigations conducted directly after the war, Isogai could have been accused of participation in an opium racket. Because that information led the authorities to a Chinese warlord, Xu Chongzhi who cooperated with Isogai, this aspect of his government was silenced. Reason: this Xu was formerly a commanding officer of Chiang Kai-shek.[66]

The last element of the Japanese treatment of the Opium Problem, this time in Hong Kong and during the reign of Governor Isogai, is:

> Disregarding the pious noises put out by the Governor's Office, which warned of "severe treatment" for anyone caught taking heroin pills, the Kempetai also set up their own depot for the sale of heroin—with fairly striking results. A report which leaked out of the colony in June 1942 observed that this new drug "was much cheaper than tobacco and was becoming popular" ...[67]

There follows a list of names and objects of the worst kind of corruption among the Japanese military bureaucrats.

Southeast Asia

The Japanese active opium policy towards Southeast Asia dates from 1902 when the Japanese navy established undisputed mastery of the South China Sea. All sea traffic between Indochina and the West became difficult. This gradually brought an end to the steady supply of opium from Turkey and Iran, a substantial source for the French narcotic business.

Japan practised a treacherous policy in this part of its "eternal empire": profiteering as much as possible from the opium, while at the same time condemning the Western colonialists of having exploited the opium resources to repress the indigenous people. But the French were no less corrupt and collaborated with the Japanese for profit, while claiming Indochina again after the war as if nothing had happened. The French stakes were high:

> At the beginning of World War II Indochina's 2,500 opium dens and retail shops were still maintaining more than 100,000 addicts and providing 15 percent of all tax revenues. The French imported almost sixty tons of opium annually from Iran and Turkey to supply this vast enterprise.[68]

---

[66] Idem, p. 306.
[67] Idem, p. 162.
[68] A. McCoy et al, p. 76.

However, when the war blocked most trade routes Indochina was also cut off from the poppy fields in the Middle East. Most French officials collaborated easily during the Japanese occupation, but those who had to manage their Opium Monopoly were faced with a major fiscal crisis. Smuggling from Yunnan could have filled their pockets again and eventually solved the addicts problem. A better solution was found to inducing the Meo (Hmong) of Laos and northwest Tonkin to expand their opium production. The transformation of the tribal opium economy succeeded in 1939-40 under the fierce surveillance of the French officials.

Indochina's opium production jumped from 7.5 tons in 1940 to 60.6 tons in 1944, an 800 percent increase in just four years! This was enough for the French and the more than 100,000 addicts, and yielded an increase of government revenues from 15 million piasters in 1939 to 24 million in 1943.

The Japanese propaganda exploited the widespread hate and animosity against the British, French and Dutch colonialism, which had an insidious effect: it was too easy to accept half the truth of this propaganda. During and after the war most nationalist movements in Southeast Asia received their anti-imperialist lessons from the Japanese occupiers. If one promised to become part of a Great Japanese Empire "later", requests for independence "later" received a willing Japanese ear.

Both the traditional colonialists and the many Communist liberation movements had to cope with this nationalism, for instance, in the confrontation with Buddhist–Nationalism and new military regimes in many Southeast Asian countries including Indonesia. Many of the complications of the Vietnam Wars, arrogantly waged and dramatically misunderstood by the colonialist and the Americans, had their origin in the Japanese occupation. The same was true for the Dutch colonialism and its lost war after the Japanese occupation.

In their turn, the foreign powers in the realm *accused* the indigenous liberation movements of collaborating with the Japanese, which was one of their main enemies at least during World War II (but not before the war and not after it). So, for instance, Sukarno in Indonesia or Aung San in Burma looked first for help from the Japanese to get rid of the Western powers and they were given this help until both discovered that the Western repression was being exchanged for an Asian one. As such these were obvious moves, demonstrated elsewhere in the world as well (see, for instance, the Flemish resistance movement against the French, which

welcomed the German occupiers; etc.). The Western accusations were
rather hypocritical.

In Singapore, occupied by Japan in February 1942, 'the Japanese took
advantage of the huge stocks of opium left behind by the British as a
source of immediate revenue. They carried on sales in the Government
Retail Shops.'[69] Because the import duties fell rapidly increasing dependence was placed on, among others, the opium revenues. Typical war
measures were taken:

> In November 1943, the British Government announced total prohibition of
> opium (import, export, possession, sale or purchase) would replace its
> policy of gradual suppression of opium in enemy occupied territories in the
> Far East after the War. The Opium and Chandu Proclamation, enacted on
> 1 February 1946 called on those in possession of opium, chandu, pipes,
> lamps or utensils to surrender them. This prohibition could not stop the
> craving of those pre-war registered addicts and those who had acquired the
> habit during the Japanese Occupation. Traffickers quickly saw a golden
> opportunity to make fortunes when the addicts went underground. Com-
> munications were reestablished with sources of supply and the highly prof-
> itable of the smuggling of the drug was resuscitated.[70]

In the Dutch colonies the Opium Factory and the whole *Opiumregie* infrastructure were simply handed over to Japan (see ch. 19).

> The Opium-Regie's distribution network on Java ... appears to have survived
> the war largely intact, and there remained some twenty-two tonnes of raw
> opium and three tonnes of refined opium in the factory at Salemba, as well
> as unspecified quantities of refined opium in Central Java, when the Japa-
> nese surrendered in August 1945.[71]

Cribb concludes from this that, compared to pre-war consumption of
refined opium, it 'declined during the three and a half years of occupation.' A reason for this could be that the Japanese policy of regional economic autarchy, which prohibited trade between occupied regions,
deprived the regime of its most lucrative markets, the islands of Banka
and Belitung (Billiton).

If, however, the Japanese did in their vivid opium (heroin and morphine) business what they did elsewhere, then there were no barriers
erected in the opium trade. Therefore, there is another more relevant reason for a possible decline: until 1940 the opium for the East Indies had to

---

[69] See the Singapore government website www.ica.gov.sg about the ICA history.
[70] Idem.
[71] R. Cribb, p. 703.

come largely from Bengal-India and a small portion from the Middle East. Both regions were closed to Japan for obvious reasons. The Burmese and Thai resources were large enough to fill this gap: the newly opened Indonesian market could be reason why the production and opium trade flourished as never before. Because of this central position of the Indochinese opium sources and the French collaboration with the Japanese, a few more details of the situation will suffice.[72]

After 6000 Japanese invaded the north of Vietnam (September 1940) and, later, many more appeared on bicycle in the streets of Saigon, the French colonial government surrendered. They made a corrupt deal with the new occupiers: they would remain and administer "their" Indochina under the umbrella of the Japanese. The gist of this deal was: full autonomy for the French bureaucracy as long as Japan received favorable terms of trade for Indochinese rice, coffee, rubber and opium. In addition, they had to pay for the cost of the Japanese occupation (200 million piaster per year).

During the Second World War the French *Opiumregie* (Opium Purchasing Board) could continue to manage the opium business. This implied that the contracts with the Hmong opium producers were made more lucrative for the Hmong (schools built in their territory in return). Gestures were made by them as well to accord the Hmong a significant role in the political future of Laos.

Their opium production increased and by 1943 the lion's share of the opium needed, sixty tons, came from North Laos to replace the lost opium imports from elsewhere. The greater part of the large payments in silver piasters for this flowed into the pockets of private opium brokers. They invested this again in the general economy to such an effect that the inflation 'soared into the stratosphere'. For ordinary people the necessary commodities were priced beyond their reach and many could no longer afford to feed themselves, let alone smoke opium.

Only the Hmong were often rich, at least by their own standards (see further ch. 24). Although they had mixed feelings about the Japanese, the Hmong opium business was also business. A Japanese trading company, Shiowa, with offices in Luang Prabang, regularly sent agents to Xieng Khouang Province to purchase Hmong opium.[73] The transactions drove up local prices, 'which greatly pleased Hmong farmers.' Another Japanese

---

[72] See for the following K. Quincy, p. 54 ff.
[73] Idem, p. 62 ff.

firm exploited an old silver mine in the region where hundreds of people were used as forced laborers until a shaft collapsed killing 200 miners.

In December 1944 British commandos[74] were parachuted from India into Laos, but the Japanese responded with a very quick buildup of their presence. This was financed 'with the sale of a truckload of Hmong opium confiscated from Chinese drug merchants.' It did not help Japan: a few months later this war was over.

A Reflection

Wakabayashi estimates that the Japanese opium operations (1933-1944) comprise already the enormous amount of 13,000 tons opium or an average of 1.25 kg per capita year consumption in the occupied territories leading to an average number of 9,059,112 addicts supplied/year.[75] In my view, further research will lead to an increase of, at least, the consumption estimates.

There were three motives leading to these opium operations: the need to finance collaborator states (similar to the old imperialistic aim that colonies had to pay for themselves) and to fund undercover operations that facilitated Japanese aggression. Opium profits, furthermore, went to right-wing societies in Japan (there is even evidence 'to link laundered wartime opium monies with early postwar conservative parties').[76] As shown, there was since the middle of the 19th-century until shortly before World War II and afterwards, a remarkable "community of interests" between Imperial Japan and the USA.

In North American foreign policy research there is the widespread view that Japan should be treated as an 'independent' and 'mysterious entity, to be loved or reviled'. Cumings, one of the main US experts on Asian foreign policy argues rightly, however, that Japan, like Taiwan or South Korea

> have nested for most of this [the 20th] century in a Western hegemonic regime and are nowhere near the self-definition and comprehensive autonomy that local nationalists have long sought' (and feared by many Western hegemonic observers!).[77]

---

[74] A few French accompanied them, which later became the pretext to occupy Indo-china anew by De Gaulle.

[75] B. Wakabayashi, p. 19.

[76] Idem, p. 5.

[77] B. Cumings, p. 23, 225.

It is an outcome of the Second World War and the subsequent Cold War that Japan became a partner of "The Western Bloc". Geopolitically— another way of thinking is not available in the Pentagon or the State Department: Japan, Taiwan and so on adequately "encircled" the Enemy (Soviet Union and China).[78] Altering this position in an independent setting would mean an unacceptable "Gap in the Wall": Japan has to remain a subordinate partner of the US, the self-styled policeman of the "West".

Therefore, after the Soviet Union disappeared as Enemy No. 1, the US even deepened its containment grip: apparently Enemy No. 2 has had to be treated in the same way as No. 1. In addition, the US and Japan clearly feared, partly for different reasons, that Enemy No. 2 would not only replace Enemy 1 in a political-ideological sense, but also override any economic importance of the former Enemy 1.[79]

In this perspective, it seems to be a bold conclusion of Cumings that since the late nineteenth-century Japan 'usually' thrived within such a network of politico-economic subordination: the only *exception* was the period between "Pearl Harbour" (7-12-1941) and "Midway" (June 1942), the decisive battle in the Pacific against Japan. This simply means that Japan was liberated from the US for half a year.

For our opium history this bold conclusion has far-reaching significance and leads to other bold conclusions as well.

As sketched above, from its first assaults against Russia and China, Japan developed an aggressive narco-military policy as a fundamental part of its Eastern conquests. This narco-military policy must, therefore, be part and parcel of Japan's subordinate partnership with the United States! Will China remain deeply suspicious of some "tandem US-Japan" including a re-start of the narco-military assault?

This is not an optimistic suggestion, but one which should be combined with Rashid's prediction given in the *Preface*. It is, anyway, the best transition to the next chapter about the other new imperialist in East Asia.

---

[78] In I.C. Dear, M. Foot (ed.), p. 307 under "Formosa" one can read the remarkable sentence: 'At the Cairo conference in November 1943 ... it was pronounced that the island had been stolen from China and would be returned to it, which it was.' Interesting for the reconstruction of the USA–Japanese post war relations is H. Moulton, L. Marlio (1944), p. 54-93; included is a remarkable assessment of Japan's pre-war colonialism in which any reference to opium is avoided.

[79] Cumings could have added that the Pentagon/ State Department not only deepened its containment policy as indicated, but took the opportunity to aggravate it even by attacking Russia with a missile shield at its West border and urging Japan to start new quarrels about the property of a few rocks opposite the Siberian coast.

CHAPTER TWENTY-EIGHT

UNITED STATES OF AMERICA

In dealing with the opium history of the United States of America until about 1950 under the heading of the "New Imperialism", one has to stress more the "new" than "imperialism". For most present commentators, all of the "real" imperialist adventures of this country (from Chile to Nicaragua and Grenada, from Israel, Iraq to Vietnam and Afghanistan) started later. Indeed, the earlier ones from the end of the 19th-century are nearly forgotten. This period followed soon after a genocidal war on the indigenous population at home and a very bloody war among the white settlers-conquerors themselves.

Below, some details of this *mixture* of early imperialism with domestic opium problems come to the fore in Philippines or Mexican policies. The complexity is obvious, not least because this history precedes the global *War On Drugs,* officially launched twenty years after 1950. The question is whether the earlier "Philippines" and the present "Afghanistan" have something in common, apart from being both "opium wars".

The period with which we have to deal ended in a rather spectacular anti-climax: instead of the USA succeeding, like Japan and Germany or the older imperialists, in "conquering the world", it was itself conquered by the Opium Problem. In a way, the USA became the most tragic victim land in the West and the best example of how the snake has bitten in its own tail. How paradoxical: it happened in exactly the same period that China successfully jumped over its own shadow in its own civil war, the bloody competition between Nationalists and Communists.

Let's start with the end: the domestic opium problems. Then we shall consider in detail the American version of imperialism.

A Domestic Opium Problem from the early 19th-century?

From the Singapore statistics of 1835 we learned that opium was shipped in a 'considerable quantity to America' (p. 448f.). Nothing more is known, so we can easily take this as a mythical opium year and try to discover the American consumers.

It probably only concerned raw opium, since Courtwright states that 'smoking opium began to be imported in significant quantities in the mid-1850s, when the first wave of Chinese immigrants arrived in California'.[1] In the Jacksonian era (1820-1850) cotton was frequently imported from India, which easily could have been accompanied by opium (and opium was probably "needed" given the panics and bankruptcies happening around this cotton import).

So, who are the *potential* white opium consumers? People familiar with American history always point to aggressive religious sectarian settlers. These Calvinist Puritans believed they were predestined from the time of setting foot ashore to win against all "foreign" elements in the "New Jerusalem" they had captured from the original inhabitants. They became the new bosses and had to become very practical: profit must be made under all circumstances. They started a double-entry bookkeeping of their victims, making a good business from killing, using the following market prices:

> Those hard-headed virtuosi of Protestantism, the Puritans of New England, in 1703, by decrees of their assembly set a premium of £40 on every Indian scalp and every captured redskin: in 1720 a premium of £100 on every scalp; in 1744, after Massachusetts Bay had proclaimed a certain tribe as rebels, the following prices: for a male scalp of 12 years and upwards £100 (new currency), for a male prisoner £105, for women and children prisoners £50, for scalps of women and children £50 ... The British Parliament declared bloodhounds and scalping for "God-given and natural means".[2]

---

[1] D. Courtwright, p. 21 and note 45 p. 156. For the announced 'objections' see below.

[2] Karl Marx, *Das Kapital. Kritik der politischen Ökonomie* (Berlin: Dietz, 1971), vol. 1, p. 781. A famous German Lutheran theologian, Helmut Gollwitzer (1908-1993), who was Marxist oriented and prominently involved in the political debates ensuing in the late 1960s and 1970s (e.g. pastor to the RAF-terrorist Ulrike Meinhof), referred to this same period and location. He, however, wanted to prove that 'the church had with the gospel the weapon at hand against class society, which those discovered who wanted to avoid that the slaves and the subjected by colonial powers could receive the Christian message and education'. Gollwitzer added in a note: 'This was forbidden in several North American states until the end of the 18th-century. In 1708 the missionary ... Ziegenbalg was imprisoned for several month by the commander of the Danish East Indian Company ... Also the English in India were as inimical ...'. See H. Gollwitzer, *Die kapitalistische Revolution* (Munich: Kaiser, 1974), p. 117, 118 and 131. It is a pity that this pastor did not read his Karl Marx. To get the whole picture clear, it almost suffices to read a review about present-day Indian problems in the USA and the reasons why the reviewer is disappointed: Christopher Vecsey. "Review of Huston Smith, *A Seat at the Table: Huston Smith in Conversation with Native Americans on Religious Freedom*," H-AmIndian, H-Net Reviews, March, 2007.

This is quoted by Karl Marx in his famous analysis of the Christian character of the so-called 'original accumulation' in which he tells one terrible
story after another about Dutch or English colonization and conversion
practices.

The Dutch Calvinists had already ruthlessly decimated the populations
of East Indian islands in a nearly genocidal way; their American fellow-
believers made a profitable business out of it. The English Anglican
Protestants demonstrated several times how to organize mass-deaths by
causing and/or exploiting severe famines. They forcefully requisitioned
all of the rice several times in order to sell it for fabulous prices, a practice
which cost the lives of a million Hindus in the Indian province Orissa in
1866 alone.[3] A typical example of monopoly trade, which was only possible in Western colonies.

Apparently, they did not regret the nearly total elimination of the
indigenous population of the Caribbean islands and adjacent territories
in the 16th and 17th centuries, forcing them to re-populate the islands
with black people from Africa and colored ones from Asia. Did all these
slaves consume opium to forget their misery like the coolies in the Asian
mines?

What was the United States like around "opium year" 1835? It was a
result of irrational claims of Western conquerors from Spanish, French,
British, Dutch and even Russian origin (the latter claimed Alaska): the
indigenous people were destined, of course, to be eliminated as had
already happened in the Caribbean.

The victorious British could write a most heroic history, certainly after
their settlers did what European settlers always dreamed of: deciding to
govern the colony without interference from the mother country. A few
"states" in the East formed a federation, and from old England came the
farewell greeting of Dr. Johnson to the rebel Americans: 'They are a race of
convicts, and ought to be thankful for any thing we allow them short of

---

[3] See the still prudent formulations in the history of these disasters in David
Northrup, Migration from Africa, Asia and the South Pacific, in: Andrew Porter et al. (ed.),
The Oxford History of the British Empire (Oxford: OUP, 1999), vol. III, p. 93; see also,
p. 406 ff. For another interpretation of Marx's Orissa story see Vincent A. Smith, *The
Oxford History of India* (Oxford: Clarendon Press, 1928), p. 740 ff. and Dharma Kumar (ed.),
The Cambridge Economic History of India (Hyderabad: CUP, 1984), vol. II, p. 528 ff. 'The
Orissa Famine of 1866' and 'Famine in India', in *Wikipedia*. Prabhat Mukherjee, The Orissa
famine of 1866, in: *Orissa Historical Research Journal*, 6:1 (1958 for 1957), p. 69-95; David
Hall-Matthews, Inaccurate Conceptions: Disputed Measures of Nutritional needs and
Famine Deaths in Colonial India, in: *Modern Asian Studies* (2007).

hanging.'[4] Indeed, this became a normal activity for the decades to come as the white settlers performed the drama called "Winning of the Far West" with all the nasty and lethal consequences for millions of the indigenous peoples, their animals and territories. Was their collective bad conscience silenced by the strongest possible antidotes: opium and/or religion ?

Around 1835 in the east of the territory, there lived an imported, English-speaking population of about 13 million ex-Europeans and new Americans, still a rural farm life with a few towns like Boston, New York or Philadelphia. In a large part of the west and south, Spanish imperialism ruled until 1845 -1848. Here, too, there were a few small settlements under the guidance of fanatic friars of San Francisco, thinking of themselves as *Los Angelos*. The population was much smaller (probably half a million including the indigenous one). Outside these settlements indigenous people often dwelt in pueblos, while hacienda or rancho life was reserved for the conquerors. In between, in the remaining third of the territory, a few French-speaking settlements existed along the Mississippi River, including New Orleans. This "French" territory had probably a half million people in total around 1835.

Again: who needed so much opium from Asia, while it is unclear whether it arrived in San Francisco or New York? Courtwright produced a statistical analysis for the earliest possible period he imagined, in 1827.[5] He fixed the average dollar value of opium imports from this year until 1842 at $75,000. This is equivalent to an average consumption of 27,000 pounds per year. In this period there was no duty on opium: 'No duty means no smuggling ...'[6] In short: there was no opium problem at all, and many people could get their daily dose (27,000 or 63,000 pounds). To indicate some proportionality, one can suppose a "normal" consumption of 2 to 3 grams a day. In this case one has to reckon with 12,000 to 19,000 con-

---

[4] Quoted in V. Kiernan, p. 27, a most stimulating book by a typical imperialism historian.

[5] D. Courtwright, chapter 1. A rather curious definition of foreign trade ('imports minus exports without real exports') was used at the time (or by C.?), which is not discussed here. Exactly around 1835 his difficult figure 1 (p. 20) indicates that the "imports" are valued at about $450,000 and the "exports" at $280,000. Well, "imports" minus "exports" of $170,000 must be similar to a consumption of 63,000 pounds (according to C.'s value of $2.77 per pound). However, based on the opium export price in Singapore (C. Trocki) of $480 per chest in 1835, a pound of opium had to cost $3.69. This export price to America is still excluding the transport cost, but probably the Spanish $ is at the time not equal to an American $.

[6] Idem, p. 20.

sumers, respectively, or 29,000 to 43,000.[7] Whether this is a large proportion, relative to the population, is difficult to say.

The first potential users of opium must have been settled pharmacists or traveling salesmen, who could transform the raw opium into their laudanum tinctures and pills. They relied upon English knowledge. In 1820 the first American pharmacopoeia was published, and in 1833 the authoritative *Dispensatory of the United States of America* was written by the learned men, George Wood and Franklin Bache. Philadelphia was the place of publication, and it cannot be a coincidence that later a flourishing pharmaceutical industry was established there. How "wild" the USA remained may be proven by the appendix of the edition consulted (18th from 1899): it had a long list of medicinal herbs used by the indigenous people, the so-called Indians.[8] At that time they were already non-existent for most Americans until revived a decade later through Hollywood.

Whatever the texts in the period of the first editions, the practice of apothecaries was still not very different from the one in colonial times: an *experienced and learned* apothecary had to act as surgeon, provide medical treatment, deliver babies and prepare prescriptions. The largest majority, however, as in England or France, was more of a traditional rural healer or medical handyman; his income extended as far as people could trust him. His practice was often not different from the one of Dr. Samuel Doxey. Apparently, he is a "good" representative of the profession until far into the 19th-century in the largest part of the USA, but not in the cities.

Around 1800 in the USA, alcohol use was already endemic as was tobacco smoking, but a poppy culture existed only in the gardens of nostalgic European settlers. Attempts are always being made to subsume all drugs under one umbrella, which is a bad custom for the historical "treatment", comparable to a standard reference to "ancient Greeks" or "archeology". The drugs differ, in particular because of individual socio-economic preconditions and environment. It does not even make much sense to talk about "drugs", let alone a *War on Drugs* if normal daily life cannot do without medicines, coffee, sugar or tobacco.[9] It also seems obvious not to use

---

[7] Because in all probability the import concerns raw opium only, the lowest estimates are the most realistic, because the transformation into prepared opium cost much of the weight.

[8] See also E. Kremers, G. Urdang, p. 377.

[9] S. Tracy, C. Acker (ed.), p. 2 rightly made a similar remark and pointed to a possible relation between the use of a drug and another. "The 'War on drugs' has given many a sense that the nation has enjoyed a drug-free past ... and that there may be a drug-free future. Such thinking is naive and historically myopic." (Id.) This argument has its limited

Ill. 22. Dr. Doxey's Elixir

Source: Morris, *Lucky Luke* nr. 7, 1955. Dr. Doxey tells his audience: ' ... after 30 years of continuous research, I have the pleasure, the duty and the honor to demonstrate the public
the most stunning discovery the world has ever seen ...' Only one page further this audience was seized with cramp and more serious pains; dogs which licked it up, died immediately ... and Dr. Doxey was glad that none of the bullets this audience sent after him hit
home.

unsubstantiated suggestions like opium as 'an Eastern vice' or exaggerations about the 'unmatched analgesic power' of opium.[10]

Relative to this period: the 1835 Singaporean opium export to America
was certainly not a Chinese export. To my knowledge, Chinese junks never reached any American harbor. The British, American and Indian opium smugglers never had any idea about their opium as the new universal
Chinese painkiller. It is difficult to find something other than "naked prof-

---

value thanks to the *abstract use of general concepts* as "drugs": there was an American past
without settler's alcohol (say: before 1585), without opium (say: before 1800) and without
heroin (say: before 1880) and certainly without an Opium Problem (say: before 1860). And
for a massive number of people, who stopped smoking cigarettes, there is a future without
this "as device". It is very important to be precise and concrete as possible, apart from not
denying the historical certainty that people can change their bad conduct (mostly very
slowly—see religion—sometimes very quickly—see eating habits) or that bad conduct
must first become a social problem before it can be considered bad. In addition, the medicalization of the present American society has reached an unprecedented level compared
to that of probably all European countries, and certainly all other societies in the world.
That is the reason why Tracy and Acker lightly speak of a 'commanding presence of
socially acceptable psychoactive drugs such as alcohol (not, for instance, in Islamic countries) ... antidepressants, estrogen and testosterone in our daily lives' (Idem).

[10] E. Kremers, G. Urdang, p. 120.

it" as a reason for introducing opium in a foreign non-opium country, including the new American states.

In addition, in an early American practice, opium could never compete with alcohol as a painkiller. Around 1800 this was consumed in approximately twice the rate prevalent in 2000 (four to six gallons per capita per year):

> The efficiency and profitability of turning corn into whiskey, heavy frontier drinking, the spread of urban saloons, and the arrival of beer-drinking Germans and whiskey-swilling Irish encouraged the nation's bibulous tendencies.[11]

Later there were better opportunities for opium:

> In the Jacksonian era, many Americans not only brewed, fermented, and distilled their own alcohol, they treated their own ills. On farms and in villages and towns, women used herbs and tonics to maintain their families' health and care for them in times of illness. In this system of healing, medicines were expected to restore the body's balance and to relieve symptoms: to revive, to calm, to brace, in short, to make one feel better.[12]

Whatever the serious problems the settlers had to solve, here is, therefore, the same conclusion as for the English or French situation: until the Civil War, there does not seem to have been an opium problem in the United States. It is, therefore, time to look at whether an American opium performance abroad is as unproblematic.

Rise and Direct Decline of "Free Trade"

By the time the US is able to expand abroad *as a nation*, about seventy years have gone by, and the world is still in the stranglehold of classical imperialism. In the largest part of the 19th-century, expansion abroad was a matter of individual trade activities and many individual trade connections. Both the individual and the national opium business are "defined" by the relation with China, although the opium relation with Europe cannot be neglected as will be demonstrated below. And both are subsumed under the heading "free trade": at first a reality, later only an ideology.

The following anecdotal start of the US in the Western imperialist concert of the 19th and 20th-century seems perfectly suitable as an introduc-

---

[11] S. Tracy, C. Acker (ed.), p. 4.
[12] Idem.

Ill. 23. Happy New Year, 1899 !

Source: A. McCoy, F. Scarano. ed., p. 36. This is a cartoon published in *Judge*, January 7, 1899 (US Library of Congress). It says: 'It ought to be a happy new year: Uncle Sam and his English cousin have the world between them.' Both figures showed no trade but war ships on their breasts, because both had a canal near Suez or Panama to their disposal to wage war as quickly as necessary or as possible.

tion. It concerns the arrival in the Philippines of a US governor-general, Francis Burton Harrison (6 October 1913). It is, formally, one of the first official appearances of a civil US official on the scene. We will deal with the context in which he has to operate later.

Two days after his arrival, Harrison was already confronted with headlines in *The Manila Times* of 'Two Trunks of Opium in Harrison Baggage':

how "clever" the smugglers were because they "took advantage of the foreknowledge that the courtesies of the port would be extended" to Harrison's party to try to smuggle in two trunks containing "440 tins of the highest grade opium" by labeling them as the property of Manuel Earnshaw, resident commissioner from the Philippines to Congress.[13]

Although in the following days "the usual suspects" were rounded up, not only Harrison was mortified (and his friends, accusing him 'for having become the arch opium smuggler of the Far East') and the ineffectiveness of the US opium policy demonstrated, the immanent hypocrisy of colonialism was laid bare as well. In the Philippines, still strongly upset about the harsh USA colonialism which replaced the Spanish (see below), the Harrison affair could only confirm this aversion. And, indeed, it is difficult to deny this.

Twenty years later in his published memoirs, Harrison criticized Britain's opium policy of cynical exploitation, contrasting this with the US respect for indigenous traditions. He dared to continue *rightly* with:

> The White Man's Burden has been materially lightened by the money thus derived, and by the state of physical and moral ruin to which the people have been reduced. If they are thoroughly doped, they are more willing slaves.

This affair, this combination of controversial behavior and high moral judgment, is the attitude continuously demonstrated in the Dutch, French or British propaganda, nurtured by the colonial elite defending their luxury lives and standing against the jealous home-front, which has to satisfy itself with thoughts about some civilizing mission and ineffective moral exclamations about those poor and destitute opium victims far away. The new imperialists in East and West had quickly learned this cheap policy, as was demonstrated by Harrison or the "innocent" behavior of the Japanese in international conferences at the time.

The USA opium policy as presented here is largely devoted to the opium or drugs elements of the Asian "adventures" of the USA. As is well-known, there is also a South and Central American drugs foreign policy of the US ("Colombia", "Mexico", etc.), but its strongest activity occurs outside the scope of this book. Still some elements of this will be discussed later as a consequence of the dominant Dutch cocaine position between 1900 and 1925.

The first necessary remark concerns the obvious need to differentiate between the activities of individual Americans and the "nation USA". This is more appropriate than expressed in recent literature because it actually concerns two different and often antagonistic worlds: the one of the

---

[13] This story is told by A. Foster (2000), p. 253 ff. including the following quote.

Federal government with its State Department and Ministry of Defense/ Attack; the other is of the entrepreneurs, of the scientists or other private actors, who are often strongly hindered by the public tax claims, control measures or imperial aspirations. These differences are certainly developed more strongly on the European continent, with England in between.

As a nation the USA came late on the international scene, but rather rapidly took on an overwhelming role. After the previous chapter it is not difficult to assess the first performance of this nation "in the field". That was not so much the Japan adventure of Commander Perry (1853), which only showed that the USA had aspirations. Their realization followed nearly half a century later around a then rather unimportant archipelago in the Pacific. Here Harrison's diplomatic and military predecessors acted quite differently (see below).

In the opium minefield the American nation acted for the first time through the Philippine Commission, appointed in 1903. Its members also visited Japan. It was one of its 'most illuminating experiences'. After the previous chapter it must be highly "illuminating" to read about

> the one oriental country whose attitude towards the drug habit was indubitable and whose law was enforced with an effectiveness unknown elsewhere in the Far East. From Japanese authorities, who pointed out that "China's curse has been Japan's warning", the committee learned of the horror with which the vice was regarded. The Philippine report ... led not only to the prohibition of opium in the Philippine Islands but also to the first attempt to deal internationally with the problem.[14]

Anyway, the performance of this Philippine Commission, combining the utmost misunderstanding about the Opium Problem with ignorance about, for example, the Japanese opium policy, is indeed a beginning of the *official* USA involvement in the international drug scene.

What about *individual* Americans? For a long time they were already active as captains, sailors, bullion traders, opium dealers or ship builders, starting soon after the British colonies in North America gained independence (1783). The British did everything to counteract the new American competition, as Harrison's anger still showed. In reality, the "New American" clippers cooperated with the British in smuggling and competed with everybody in trading.

Notwithstanding this, the "Old China Trade", the early commerce between China and the US until the First Opium War, was lucrative for both parties and, therefore, not combined with American imperialist

---

[14] D. Owen, p. 327, 328.

motives or activities. It became *real free trade* since the Chinese could sell Americans many kinds of Chinese products for a willing American market: from tea, cotton and silks to lacquer-ware, porcelains and floor-matting, all available even for poorer people. In every American household at the time, some Chinese product could be found. The main thing Chinese bought from the Americans was bullion, silver Mexican dollars ($62 million between 1805 and 1825), followed by the much appreciated ginseng from the Appalachian Mountains and furs.

This American "Old China Trade" was rather unique because the other Westerners were not only representatives of colonial or imperialistic powers but were also strongly involved in the intra-Asian trade including opium trafficking.

The Americans, however, gradually slipped into these older "not free" trade networks. They were attractive because of their use of quick clippers, but the consequences were far-reaching: it brought them into direct competition with the "older" British, French or Dutch traders and in direct involvement in the opium trade. Until then, the Chinese had perceived of them simply as one of those 'foreign devils'. In addition, it brought these American traders their first confrontation with America *as a nation*, with state bureaucracies and foreign policy with increasingly more military and imperialistic overtones and activities.

The foreign competition with these American "older traders" was accomplished through technical superiority (clippers) and the strategically important bullion trade. Both aspects soon lost their importance: the clippers were replaced by steamers, and the Chinese had to swallow opium instead of buying bullion. The Americans lost their exclusive position and became just one of the many who had to stick to the British narco-military activities.

Indeed, thanks to the First Opium War, the 'Old China Trade' definitely came to an end, the first and last example of free trade of a Western nation with Asian countries. Now the Americans had to follow the British Imperial Flag, for the first time *as a nation* (see John Adams in ch. 2). A new period of emancipation from British domination was initiated until the USA became a full-time imperialist nation of its own with representatives like Mr. Harrison.

Because of the importance of this period in hindsight, it seems appropriate to specify the above by assessing the question of whether this "Chinese" was only related to a geographical location, to an "object" for profit, or to a problem with ethnic or cultural connotations.

American–Chinese Opium Relations, 1800-ca. 1865[15]

As indicated, private Americans, shippers and merchants, arrived for the first time in Canton around 1800 to establish a trading center of their own. With their quick and well-armed clippers, they were among the most fanatic opium smugglers. They often cooperated with Chinese *compradores*, a school for a new kind of opium criminal.

The famous American businessman who started a regular opium trade with China was the already very rich John Jacob Astor (1763-1848), born German with a Waldensian or Jewish background.[16] In 1784 the first American trading vessel to China, *The Empress of China,* departed from New York. Later that year fourteen more American ships sailed for the Indian Ocean and beyond. Reason: their favorite area for trade, the West Indies, was closed off by the British, and they had to look for different destinations. They brought back a good profit, which inspired people like Astor to extend his trade with fur, sandalwood and tea.

It came abruptly to an end due to the inactive and unpopular *US Embargo Act* (1807) invented by Jefferson. Nine years later, however, Astor joined the opium smuggling trade camouflaged by his *American Fur Company*. He could not get his cargo in India and purchased ten tons of Turkish opium and shipped this contraband to Canton. To confirm this once again: this was officially smuggling for Britain and illicit for the Chinese government.

Astor was preceded by a smuggler from Boston, Charles Cabot, who attempted to purchase opium from the British and smuggled it into China under the auspices of British smugglers (1805). Another American, John Cushing, employed in his uncles' business, James and Thomas H. Perkins Company of Boston, acquired his wealth from smuggling Turkish opium to Canton (1812). Many other Americans established this illicit trade to China.

After the opium clippers were exchanged for steamers, the American firm Russell and Co (= Delano, great-grandfather of President Roosevelt) was apparently 'the third-largest opium dealer on the China coast'.[17] It is this firm which introduced opium into the Americas and not the Chinese,

---

[15] See for this C. Terry, M. Pellens, p. 630 ff.

[16] See for this Astor A. Madsen and *Wikipedia.* This Astor was the first "richest man of the US" and he is subject of many stories and legends triggering that special hobby of sectarian Americans, knowing the tricks of the conspiracy trade, like the highly controversial L. Larouche, etc. See for normal science L. Blussé (2008), p. 60 ff.

[17] H. Gelber, p. 166.

who did not have the right ships for crossing the Pacific. And Russell went so far as to make people think of it as trade by the Chinese.

The combination of illicit trade, smuggling, camouflaging controversial products behind innocent names, hiding a whole "White Race" behind a "Yellow Race", the ambiguous support of the authorities if provided with enough "licenses", the intentional creation of addicted "clients" etc.; all these acts created the corrupting secrecy and conspiracies long before a so-called 'organized crime' was established.

Soon Americans were also well known along the China coasts for other things: insulting and quarreling with the British sailors as their mutual *War of Independence* had to be continued and fought abroad. There are also remarkable legends claiming that the habit of smoking opium via a pipe-smoking merchantman was spread in the 17th-century 'from America'![18] Apparently, some Sioux or Comanche chief came to smoke the "peace pipe".

Priscilla Napier, who told this story, is not very fond of Americans since Americans competed with the English from the end of the 18th-century by selling 'Indian and Turkish opium along the China coasts'.[19] The English Bengal opium monopoly was definitely undermined (a little).

The later legends about "the bad opium and the good Americans" weare established soon after the First Opium War when gold was found in California and thousands of Chinese emigrated to this "paradise". This *Gold Rush* was soon accompanied by, of course, the 'Gold Mountain opium'. During and after the Second Opium War, it was an American adventurer, Frederic Ward, who helped the Chinese imperial army to struggle successfully against the Taiping. That is probably the reason why Priscilla mixed up many things by stating:

> The Chinese empire had already been badly weakened by the Taiping Rebellion ... led by a communist rebel from the south preaching Marxism before Marx was, laced by draconian notions of equality picked up from American missionaries, and causing more deaths than those suffered by everybody on both sides in the First World War.[20]

Later, at the moment of the highest opium profits of competitor England (around 1880), the to-and-fro traffic between Hong Kong and San Francisco grew exponentially into thick and multilevel networks.

---

[18] P. Napier, p. 91.
[19] Idem.
[20] Idem, p. 239.

At home Americans had already developed a habit of opium eating or smoking in the form of pills, drinks and powders. Probably as an impact of the American Civil War, one report about opium consumption in 1867 stated:

> The habit is gaining fearful ground among our professional men, the operatives in our mills, our weary serving women, our fagged clerks, our former liquor drunkards, our very day laborers, who took gin a generation ago. All our classes from the highest to the lowest are yearly increasing their consumption of the drug.[21]

It is remarkable enough that reports like this could already be made at this junction. But the following is quite wonderful in light of the above quotation: in 1882 some Citizen Kane reports that

> a sporting character by the name of Clendenyn was the first white man to smoke opium in San Francisco in 1868. The second ... induced to try it by the first, smoked in 1871'![22]

Kane continues with the more reliable story of how smoking led to new city ordinances, many arrests of young girls and men of respectable families and heavy punishments: opium *eating* was allowed in pills and powders for everybody with a doctor's prescription and *smoking* also, but then only for the Chinese in US *Chinatowns*.

At this time there was also the division of labor between *prepared* opium and the *raw* form. Preparing opium for export became a monopoly of the Hong Kong (and Macao) British (Portuguese) opium farms. Their revenue made up a quarter of the Hong Kong government's income from 1860 to 1890.[23] After that date Hong Kong was often called the "Drugs Capital of the World" and similar expressions, while still the main direction of this trade was the United States.

As will be shown below: three years after the "first American white smoker" made his discovery, already 30,000 lbs of smokers-opium was being imported! This was certainly not only for the Chinese immigrants working in gold mines and on the railway projects. And it was deemed a bad habit out of racist motives, anyway, whatever the legality of the import. The main sources for the knowledge of this early opium use were the physicians and druggists, who were 'alarmed' that year after year, they had to sell more opium, morphine and laudanum.

---

[21] C. Terry, M.Pellens, p. 5.
[22] Idem, p. 73.
[23] E. Sinn, p. 19.

Against the background of these lively opium relations, the flirtation between American governments and successive Chinese leaderships can only be perceived as ambiguous.[24] It started in 1844 and lasted to about 1949. In 1844 the *Treaty of Wang Hea* forbade American citizens from trading in opium in that country. Violators were dealt with by the Chinese government, which at that time beheaded opium smugglers and traders.

Immediately after the Opium War, the US government changed its opinion drastically and repeated the same language as the English conquerors: in the *Tientsin Treaty* (1858) Americans had "negotiated" to become 'free to engage in the opium traffic'.[25] In the same year, however, a commercial treaty with Japan prohibited opium import by Americans. To apply such a double standard would remain the most solid element in the foreign policy of the Americans, a cynical attitude copied from their old colonial masters.

They were soon dissatisfied with their tiny piece of the opium pie. Along with a fear of losing a reasonable commercial future in China, the Americans again changed colors drastically in a new commercial treaty with China (1880). This again 'forbade American citizens from engaging in the import of opium into any of the open ports of China', while Chinese subjects were also prohibited from importing opium into the USA. This was affirmed in the next *Treaty of Commercial Relations* (1903).

The "Mystery" of the Chinese Opium Import

The first table below, however, shows that after 1880, the opium import mainly from Hong Kong into the ports on the USA Pacific coast *increased* instead of the reverse. Cynical conclusion or a genuine mystery? Cynical in every respect, because this government policy became the "argument" used to repress the Chinese as being the *Yellow Peril* and as opium *Smokers who Poison the Nation*. Serious pogroms were organized against the *Chinatowns* in the US at the same time as pogroms in Russia occurred against another minority, the Jews. This serious repression culminated in the extradition of the Chinese from this hospitable country for immigrants (*Chinese Exclusion Act*, 1882; even extended as the *Geary Act*, 1892 which was extended again in 1924).[26]

---

[24] See also S.G. Chen, p. 278, 290 ff.
[25] For the negotiations around this treaty see J. Beeching, p. 260 ff.
[26] The *Statistical Abstracts of the US* (1880) state that the immigration 'from Asia' (95% Chinese) was in 1871 already 7,236, three years later 20,326 and again three years later

Ill. 24. A Skeleton in his Closet
Source: Puck, magazine 3-1-1912 by L.M. Glackens.

The mix of the usual Christian racism (developed as a strategy against
the American Indians) with "scientific" racist theories[27] and the demoni-

22,943. But under the influence of all anti-Chinese measures and actions, it decreased to
5,879 in 1880. See further *Wikipedia* article 'Chinese American History'. The interrelations
between the immigration of Chinese and import of opium (in whatever form) should be
scrutinized anew: T. Tong Joe, p. 72 ff. states that the Chinese population in the USA doubled in the period 1860-1870 but the opium import only increased by 88%.; from 1870-1890,
however, the Chinese population doubled again, but the import of prepared opium
increased ten times, apart from smuggled and raw opium. Although these figures are difficult to check, his conclusion is right: there is no clear correlation between the existence
of the Chinese in the USA and the consumption of opium. Or: "white consumption"
increased much quicker, which made the anti-Chinese measures even more dubious.

27 In 1849 American scholars like Morton published as result of his craniology (skull
measurement) that English had 96 cubic inches of brains, Americans 90, Negroes 83 and
Chinese 82. Indians lagged behind with 79 cubic inches. T. Gosset, p. 74. Twenty years later
another urged putting all Negroes and Chinese in reservations (Id. p. 262). Especially in
California the Chinese were repressed from 1854 onwards as they were described as 'morally, the most debased people on the face of the earth' and a Supreme Court decided that
Chinese were barred from giving testimony in cases involving whites (Idem, p. 290). In the

zation of opium smoking by the American missionaries must have contributed strongly to these extraordinary actions.[28] It was a bizarre fact that when the import of Chinese cheap labor strongly decreased from around 1880, the opium import increased greatly! The American-Chinese relations were seriously affected by these unprecedented actions: during the Boxer rebellion, revenge on the fanatic American missionaries in particular was carried out. And this gave a legitimation for the previous repression in the USA, in hindsight, and a legitimation to extend the Western extraterritoriality claims in China, and so on.

The increase in the opium import is not a mystery, however. We must realize that after the Opium Wars it was legal trade *from a Western point of view*. It concerns largely *British* trade carried out mostly by *British* or American ships, exported by a *British* colony (Hong Kong) and distributed in America mainly by American wholesalers (later called 'the organized crime' or mafia) and by American pharmacists with their 'Overseas *Chinese*' shopkeepers as middlemen. In addition, many American businessmen were settled in the new foreign concessions of Shanghai or in Canton and Hong Kong under the British umbrella.

For American consumers, taxpayers and uninformed authorities inside the USA, all this was "Chinese business", a highly symbolic transformation of a "white" trade. The same authorities gratefully accepted the substantial import duties. The mix of this added an institutionalized hypocrisy to the already existing secrecy around the real dealers, profiteers, etc.

Furthermore, a new source of opium was found; this time a true American one. The Civil War (1861-1865) and the Opium Wars in China had brought marked initiatives among entrepreneurs. The Civil War led to an army of addicts since the main painkillers were opium and morphine: nearly 10,000,000 opium pills and over 2,841,000 ounces of other

---

1870s and 1880s the Californian trade unions including Jews like Samuel Gompers were the most active in the anti-Chinese activities. In his opinion Chinese were people 'without morals', 'without nerves and without digestion' and he sinisterly predicted that they shall 'overwhelm the world' (Idem, 291 ff.). It is a good example of the classical *antisemitic* discourse by an important Jewish leader, which puts this discourse in a quite different light.

[28] E. Sinn, p. 36 note 9. See further ch. 29. Sinn further writes (Idem, note 17): 'Later on white Americans also smoked opium, but interestingly, when the import of prepared opium was banned in 1909, they were the first to switch to the syringe.' As a thesis should be perceived: the anti-Chinese activities which are completely out of all proportion must have connotations with the guilt of the Americans towards the genocide on "Indians", who—according to a popular theory—descended from "Mongols". See the Philippine adventure.

opium powders and tinctures were issued to Union forces alone.[29] We can guess that the new American pharmaceutical industry based in Philadelphia had done well. New promising market opportunities were seen as well by many people.

In 1865 Mr. Robertson in Virginia started to produce opium, which yielded 4% of morphine along with narcotine. Dr. Black in Tennessee produced an opium with a 10.2% morphine content (1868). In North Carolina as late as 1894, opium production was initiated. The learned pharmacists announce:

> Very fine opium has been produced by Mr. J.H. Flint of California ... 1874 ... also in Minnesota by Mr. E Weschke ... 1886 ...; but in the opinion both of Mr. Flint and of Mr. Weschke the high price of labor forbids the profitable production of opium in the United States ...[30]

This seems not to be the main reason to me. The Civil War was fought among other reasons to keep cheap plantation labor in the country for the northern industry, while very cheap Chinese labour poured in through the ports of the West coast. Probably the main reason was that the stuff imported from Singapore or Hong Kong by the British or American merchants was too cheap. The following two tables make additional remarks possible.

From this table one can learn that in the last quarter of the 19th-century a minimum of 2 million pounds of opium were imported into North America just through the Pacific ports. This gave the state and its bureaucrats an additional advantage of at least $15 million. It can be expected that the distributors in the USA and Canada calculated this amount in the consumer prices of the opium.

There is a mysterious aspect to this "Chinese import". Wood and Bache's *Dispensatory*, the source of the experts *par excellence*, states about this "Chinese opium":

> Chinese opium probably never reaches the European market. It is imported to some extent into the United States through San Francisco, but appears not to find its way into the ordinary channels of trade, and is probably used exclusively by resident Chinese for smoking purposes. The U.S. duty upon opium is one dollar a pound, but the custom-house authorities view the Chinese variety as an extract, and levy six dollars a pound; hence, probably, the ever-recurring attempts at its smuggling. It occurs in flat, oval cakes, wrapped first in white tissue, then in thin brown paper, labeled in Chinese

---

[29] D. Courtwright, p. 55.
[30] G. Wood, F. Bache, p. 981 note also for the following production data.

Table 41. Pacific opium import and duties paid in USA and Canada, 1871 – 1899 (selected years)[31]

Year	Quantity in lbs	USA Duties in $	Canadian Duties in $
1871	37 825	265 259	---
1874	---	---	2 493
1875	62 775	376 648	4 836
1876	53 189	319 137	15 331
1880	77 196	463 176	13 668 [1881]
1882	141 476	848 836	---
1883	220 867	1 325 202	---
1885	54 434	554 340	---
1887	65 397	653 970	53 172
1889	44 674	446 740	101 244
1890	77 578	818 912	137 050
1895	116 354	698 124	36 056
1896	43 692 [4 months]	261 852	---
1897	---	---	51 580
1899	---	---	39 705

characters with the name of the province and the seller ...[32] We must realize, however, that notwithstanding the official declarations of governments, the many critics of the opium trade targeted the *smoking* of opium only. Opium was legally used in many medicines and concoctions under different names (laudanum, etc.), in many households and available through most medical doctors from about 1860 onwards.

There was, indeed, a quite different source for the very lucrative pharmaceutical business which was established mainly in Philadelphia, the basis for the largest modern multinationals in the field like Merck or Glaxo-Smith-Kline: this was a British-Turkish variety imported mainly into New York. As described in section 2.4, the British "household opium" came from Turkey, and it was this traditional link which was extended to the former British colony, the USA.[33]

[31] E. Sinn, p. 34 and 35 quoted from Kane (1882) and Masters (1896). Data from three different sources are combined by me (not by Sinn). For 1871 two different figures are mentioned in two Sinn tables, which I have added. I suppose that both tables concern, in fact, San Francisco Customs statistics. One may suppose, furthermore, that the San Franscisco import arrived mainly from Hong Kong. The Canadian data come from the interesting site *web.uvic.ca/vv/student/chinatown/ opium/p3.html* and they concern the duty on imported opium in British Colombia.

[32] G. Wood, F. Bache, p. 986.

[33] It remains symptomatic that the American Lyndon LaRouche sect published in 1978 a report *"Dope: Britain's Opium War against the US"* constructing a British and Jewish

Table 42. Atlantic Opium Imports and Duties Paid, 1871 – 1899 (selected years)[34]

Year	Quantity in lbs	USA Duties in $ in New York	USA Duties in $ aggregate of all other ports	Total US in $
1871	265 416	1 511 474	415 441	1 926 915
1874	250 604	1 470 099	1 070 129	2 540 223
1875	171 582	1 170 985	866 808	2 037 793
1876	183 243	707 413	1 098 492	1 805 906
1880	326 352	1 427 687	1 358 919	2 786 606
1882	158 127	481 959	1 345 089	1 826 998
1883	99 552	328 894	2 809 245	3 138 159
1885	152 703	426 173	892 098	1 318 271
1887	355 348	764 341	568 424	1 332 765
1889	202 741	369 289	1 084 808	1 454 097
1890	204 268	486 341	966 957	1 453 298
1895	191 447	388 981	1 261 694	1 650 675
1896	...	...	735 134	735 134
1897	542 132	1 108 100	2 209 488	3 317 588
1899	364 915	866 390	1 185 764	2 052 154

It is, therefore, reasonable to assume that the price effects about which Mr. Flint or Weschke (see above) complained were the result of the competition between the European-New York and Asian-San Francisco opium dealers. This antagonism probably formed the basis of the drugs gangs which started to operate after the economic interests involved were forced to go underground by social agitation and new legislation. Around 1900, however, it was still rather quiet on all these "opium fronts".

Whether the white Christian immigrant society of Canada demonstrated the same traits is not very clear. The communication between the two coasts was very limited at the time. The role of San Francisco was played for a long time by Victoria until Vancouver took over all activities around 1900. It is said that trade between Hong Kong and these Canadian ports was 'practicable' since the former was a British colony and the latter a British Confederate. Opium sellers in Canada needed a license. In 1865

---

conspiracy to rape the US innocence. This in fact patriotic pamphlet combines, as usual in this kind of writings, a bit truth with many suspicions. It is still available on the Internet: www.fourwinds10.com.

[34] whc.newyork.chamberofcommerce.opium.import.export.pricedata.xls (read-only) -OpenOffice.orgCalc

this cost $100; a year later it was $250, and about twenty years later one had to pay nearly $500.

Among the Chinese, mostly working for the *Canadian Pacific Railway*, a lethal competition raged between the six opium factories until one of them decreased its price so far that most competitors perished. Still a few years later there were new ones, and thirteen factories with a annual turn-over of 90,000 lbs at $15 a pound, realising a gross income of $10 a pound on these deals. That was not much, and additional sources of income were needed like prostitution and trade in human beings. Smuggling was also common, because the duty in Canada was $5 a pound and in the USA $10. Nothing was done against it by authorities, 'simply because the trade helped to promote opium manufacturing and thus generating revenue for the government.'[35]

The Creation of a Chinese Threat after 1911

Kremers and Urdang still write in 1963:

> Nevertheless, it was in the second half of the 19th-century before the great European trading nations and the United States of America became aware of the threat to themselves of what originally was considered to be pecu-liarly an Eastern vice.[36]

It concerns here, of course, not a 'Chinese vice' but a British product imported into China and elsewhere resulting in the addiction of numer-ous Chinese. Yet they mention in passing that the English government overcame the attempts of the Chinese government to stop the opium import, but that it was 'an irony of history' that the poppy cultivation of the Chinese themselves made opium into a Chinese export article.

In the meantime serious scientific research has gradually formed a common view on China after 1911, the end of the Chinese empire. A period started of widespread renewal of opium cultivation resulting from politi-cal chaos, provincial or "national" warlords and the chance for high profits and army revenues. The criminal activities of these generals (including Chiang Kai-shek) in conjunction with gangster organizations (foreign) and dubious speculators (foreign), periodically antagonized many observ-ers (foreign). To discover something of the reality behind the prejudices and propaganda took much time.

---

[35] web.uvic.ca/vv/student/chinatown/ opium/p3.html.
[36] E. Kremers, G. Urdang, p. 119.

Marshall about 1934 states:

> American officials, concerned that over 90 percent of the world's opium grew in China, were particularly critical of Nationalist policies. Some State Department officials were less concerned that the drugs were entering the United States than that the opium trade was diminishing China's potential to absorb American goods.[37]

Even on the top of this Chinese production, most opium was produced in India, the Middle East and Southeast Asia. In the *League of Nations* reports on opium, certainly those from the 1930s, China is mentioned as the main *consumption* country.[38] Its production diminished strongly during World War I in the framework of an international deal and was later largely confined to Chinese consumption only.[39] In addition, substantial foreign, mainly Western, interests in Chinese opium production and consumption always remained.

American officials reacted ambiguously. One of them objected to Chiang Kai-shek's use of opium 'to further his designs for a "Nazi" style dictatorship'; a colleague emphasized the enormously corrupting influence and charged that Chiang broke the anti-opium laws for personal enrichment. Diametrically opposed to this was the policy of officials close to the Rockefeller Foundation (the "Oil Group"), which supported Chiang's minister T.V. Soong establishment of a national opium monopoly, as was done earlier in French Indochina or the Dutch East Indies. It had become clear in the meantime that this kind of monopoly never stamped out the use of opium, but only worked to provide the state with regular and generous opium revenues. This implied, of course, price as well as consumption increases and further state involvement. The American Ambassador, Nelson Johnson, called the Soong move, therefore, 'pathetically naive and a little ridiculous' (1932).

The still obscure Joseph Stilwell (the later controversial—"Vinegar Joe"—general in World War II) was military attaché in China specialized in the opium business (1935). He had a keen eye on Chiang Kai-shek's maneuvers to monopolize opium as a means to monopolize the political power in China. Stilwell wrote:

> By means of secure domination of the opium traffic [Chiang hoped] to increase the political power of the National Government over provinces whose allegiance is doubtful ... opium is the chief prop of all power in China,

---

[37] J. Marshall, p. 22.
[38] See *Commission d'enquête.*
[39] T. Tong Joe, p. 25 ff., 102 ff. and below part 6-2.

both civil and military. No local government can exist without a share of the opium revenues. If the central government can control the opium supply of a province, that province can never hope to revolt successfully.[40]

Later (ch. 31) will be discussed whether and how Stilwell exaggerated (which he did).

There were also people who acted as fear-mongers warning of an opium assault on the USA *by Chinese or "China"*! An US consul reported (April 1934):

> One of the results of the development of an organized drug traffic in China is the increasing export of opium and its derivatives (morphine and heroin) from China to foreign countries, including the United States. It is reported that important members of the international drug ring now reside in Shanghai to control this traffic.[41]

Anslinger's *US Bureau of Narcotics* reported a few years earlier (1931) that most of the opium smuggled into the US came via Seattle and San Francisco. One wonders why such an office needed to circulate information that was nearly half a century old (see above); an office which dares to report next that the exact sources were still unknown, but that the 'greater bulk' was 'manufactured and packed somewhere in the Far East ...'! Of course, such mysterious people or organizations were 'impossible to stop because ... the smuggling of opium into the United States is conducted on a huge scale by well organized highly financial gangs'.[42]

It was never investigated whether "Chinese export" really was Chinese export or only export from elsewhere or by non-Chinese interests choosing some Chinese address or from a Western nation operating from Hong Kong, Macao or other "international settlement". The most remarkable aspect was that they apparently did not know anything about the lively export to the USA by the Jardine-Matheson company, the largest opium dealer. Their USA export around 1850 from Amoy or Hong Kong to Havana (Cuba) concerned *coolies* for the US mines and railways, who were erroneously deemed all opium addicts.[43] Easy business: you deliver the workforce (nominally illegal!) and the means to keep them quiet in one deal.

---

[40] Quoted by J. Marshall, p. 25.

[41] Idem, p. 27. The consular mentions a name of an old friend of Chiang Kai-shek which sounds very Chinese for some bureaucrats in Washington, but who cannot be found in Chiang's best biography from J. Taylor or other relevant literature.

[42] Idem, p. 27.

[43] D. Meyer, p. 69; G. Endacott, p. 127 ff. The opium-missionary Gutzlaff was even involved in this trade. This coolie-opium combination was certainly still standard after 1900. See D. Meyer, 115 ff.; G. Endacott, p. 275 ff.

The great Harry Anslinger himself repeated in 1934 the message of his "man in China", now adding several times that it was 'confidential police information': it must have been a tradition invented to mask ignorance, amateurism or propaganda behind so-called "security" or "national interest" announcements. He also mentioned that several from the 'notorious international narcotics traffickers' now also had offices in Europe, without mentioning relevant information. Of course, they 'were known to continue to be immune from prosecution ...'

This is not to suggest that this smuggling of heroin and other narcotics did not take place. But it took decades of operating rather publicly before parts of the international "ring" of the aristocratic Jardine's and Sassoons or of the Ezra Brothers (including their many political connections) were "discovered" (see further ch. 31). Indeed, some had their base in Shanghai (in the foreign concession), but operated world-wide after World War I. Mostly *Western* smuggling "rings" with foreign collaborators exported opium, heroin or morphine from many places in the world on *Western* ships.

Anslinger's crusade, developed in these years, continued after World War II and was the proper preparation for the "War on Drugs", which was formally announced by President Nixon (17 June 1971).[44] Anslinger's outright anti-Chinese racism, his ideological and practical mixture of foreign and domestic drug policies, became the most controversial aspect of the US *War on Drugs*. That is not the subject of our *History of the Opium Problem*, but the following preparation of the domestic part of this "war" could easily form part of the controversy.

A first "War on Drugs" and its Limitations

The moral criticism of many 19th-century religious pressure groups in the USA was not bothered about foreign policy and macro-economic trends. The effect of this criticism was to denigrate the image of opium and give it immoral or criminal connotations. It was the necessary prerequisite for action and legislation.

It is estimated that by 1895, around 3% of the population (65 million) was addicted to morphine, which is equivalent to 2 million people. The

---

[44] President Roosevelt publicly supported a uniform drug act (1935). The *New York Times* came with the headline: 'Roosevelt Asks Narcotic War Aid.' It sounds like Anslinger's cowboy-language. See *Wikipedia*'s article 'War On Drugs'.

majority of them was classified as 'high-income women', known as *habi-tués*.[45] This must be a gross exaggeration, despite morphine's popularity after the invention of the hypodermic needle: it would suggest that *all* high-income women in the USA were addicted.[46] Whether serious or not, this situation became the source of one scandal after the other, and all kinds of Christian women's organizations (apparently not addicted) start-ed campaigns which were supported by missionaries, anti-alcohol lobbies and many other agitation groups. The targets were local, state and federal politicians and bureaucrats. The *honorables* of San Francisco (with at that time about 200,000 inhabitants) reacted adequately.

This Pacific coastal city, the main port for the opium trade and busi-ness, had numerous opium dens and very few wholesalers. An article of 1892, an interview with the opium authority Dr. Masters, sketches a remarkable situation in this city, criticizes the anti-democratic behavior of a double-dealing government, and presents a Chinese solution:

> In San Francisco a city ordinance attempts to regulate the selling of smok-ing opium by a high license proportional to the gross business done, and in 1889 another ordinance made it "illegal to sell any extract of opium except on a written order of a practicing physician, and requiring that the amounts sold, with the name, sex, color and residence of the purchaser, and the name of the prescribing physician, be entered in a book. The City Council thus passes an ordinance practically declaring a business illegal which it has already legalized, and from which it is not ashamed to draw a revenue." The right way to deal with the problem, Dr Masters thinks, is to follow the advice of the better class of Chinese, and remove prepared opium from the tariff list, declare it contraband, and confiscate it wherever found.[47]

Police state practices and solutions already surrounded the San Francisco opium problem, at that time a rather liberal city. It is the first time that these consequences of the Opium Problem can be demonstrated in any Western country. The most serious attacks from a Moralistic State were still to come. But could it be worse than reported in the same 1892 arti-cle?

---

45 G. Recio, p. 23.

46 In a population of 65 million there were at the time about 13 million adult women, from which around 5% or 650,000 could belong to the high-income class. See for these women, D. Courtwright, p. 36 ff. The syringe needle was invented in 1857, and Merck had distributed the stuff in 1827 first when he was still a pharmacist shop-owner.

47 This article is published on the site of the excellent *Schaffer Library of Drug Policy* and quoted from *The Review of Reviews* (5 June, 1892), titled 'San Francisco Opium Joints'.

Complaints that the 'opium vice' demoralized not only the Chinese but also white Americans made the latter afraid to go to the joints to purchase their own imported doses. Dr. Masters advised, therefore, as follows:

> If done at all ... it must be very secretly. The movements of white people about Chinatown are so carefully watched, and the different hells under almost half-hourly surveillance, that it would be impossible for them to frequent these places without soon attracting the attention of the police. There is plenty of smoking done by American people, but it is carried on in private houses or in rooms secretly kept by white people.[48]

Not in the Philippines, as McCoy thinks, but here in the United States itself, the police state was invented with all possible practical and theoretical consequences.

On the federal level this example of San Francisco was not followed, despite what the willing and powerful anti- or pro-opium federal institutions or private organizations could generate in terms of repressive measures. The box of Pandora was opened, however, and remained so.

In 1909 the *New York Times* published a long article about the attempts 'to stamp out the use of opium and many other drugs'.[49] It reported, first, about the Shanghai conference of that year in which Great Britain announced a reduction to $35 million *a year*. Elsewhere in the article the real meaning of this promise is given: Britain 'was making $35 million a year from her opium in India'. And it agreed 'to reduce the exports of opium from India 10 per cent a year for ten years, and China agreed to reduce the production of the drug within her boundaries at an equal rate'.

The journal was not suspicious about the British proposals: if Chinese production was dismantled from where the Chinese addicts should get their stuff? There was only one provider left at the time: British India. The journal did not mention that Britain was cheating the international community also by bringing in the *value of a certain quantity*, while the *price* per unit would increase. In this way the envisaged reduction in income was not achieved. It is the same trick the Dutch government employed in the East Indies. If reductions followed, it was not due to positive actions of the imperial powers. That other countries represented in the Shanghai conference did not promise the same, notwithstanding an opium monopoly in its colony or country, should have been a warning for analysts.

---

[48] Idem.
[49] *The New York Times,* July 25, 1909 reprinted on www.druglibrary.org. The quotations come from this article.

The British and the Dutch governments were the largest opium provid-ers or distributors. The only country without such a monopoly was China, the country which always had to pay the bill. There was, however, one spoil-sport in this game: against all expectations only the Chinese govern-ment realistically reduced the Chinese opium production by rigorously suppressing the opium peasants, traders and fields (see ch. 30 and 31).

However, *The New York Times* reported other quite interesting matters. First, that the governments in the Shanghai conference understood that after solving the Opium Problem they, including the United States,

> will take just as resolute steps to abolish in every civilized land the growing traffic in cocaine, hasheesh, absinthe, chloral, and other drugs that fasten themselves upon mankind.

This points to the very new development that opium became the world-wide raw material for specific bulk chemical products like heroin or codeine from the 1885s onwards, as it was already for morphine. Furthermore, the excessive profits of the poppy exploitation stimulated the search for other similar plants suitable for large-scale cash cropping: that became *Erythroxylum coca* from which the coca leaves produced cocaine or *Cannabis sativa,* which provided hashish or marihuana (bhang, ganja, etc.). As shown above, the Dutch government was not only one of the main opium distributors, it also started cultivating coca leaves at the end of the 19th-century and the production of cocaine. In this field it became a world leader (see ch. 19). The quick spread of these new drugs was made possible by the well developed infrastructure for the opium trade, smuggling, and production for mass addiction. *The New York Times* specified:

> The tremendous increase in the use of cocaine that followed the passage of the restrictive laws against opium may be gathered when it is known that in 1904—before the United States took up the cudgel against the Oriental habit—the importation of cocaine was only 58,000 ounces, and of coca leaves ... was 53,000 pounds. In 1905 300,000 pounds of coca leaves were imported ... because rather than pay a duty of 25 per cent, ad valorem, the chemists had started the manufacture of the drug in this country on a large scale. In 1906 the importation of coca leaves was 2,600,000 pounds. ... No drug on the market seems to have anywhere near such a demoralizing effect on the human system.

According to this paper the prohibitory laws against smoking opium in the US had such an effect that only ten days after their announcement, the Portuguese 'opium farm' in Macao closed its business. The crude opium was imported into Macao, prepared for smoking and exported nearly entirely to the US. The paper was in all probability too optimistic.

In the opium business, a serious transformation took place. Not only from "Yellow" customers into "Whites", but also from the importing of smoking and crude opium, so that further manufacturing could take place into heroin and morphine in the US itself. In 1907 a total of 160,397 pounds of *smoking* opium were imported, which decreased to about 40,000 pounds two years later. However, just New York imported 123,427 pounds in 1908, and nearly 300,000 pounds of *crude* opium was imported through all US ports together. And the rise in the price of smoking opium was from $1.50 a pound to $50 a pound in the big cities![50]

All this points to the basic transformation of the "natural" production into the industrial, pharmaceutical, one. This was also the start of the transformation from a more or less legal into a criminal business, from the rise of the drug mafia divided over the tremendously rich, white, Westerner and international dealers-transporters, the local producers (poor peasants) with their rich and criminalized local clients. The first two could be assured of political protection in most cases, the last one never, if only to keep the prices as high as possible and the medical, police and social services going.

In short: in these years, particularly in the USA, one is confronted with the *transformation of the Opium Problem from an assault on the East into an assault on the West.* From the point of view of the big drug dealers and their political and military friends, their finest hours were still to come.

The citizens of the USA, however, could now add a new item to their superlative language: we are the first in history to initiate in response to the self-created Opium Problem a *War on Drugs* on the local level and serious pogroms against an ethnic minority throughout the country, which led to a police state and an assault on the intimate private life of the citizens of San Francisco. Was this the model for a similar project with the same name after 1950: a federal and/or a global police state?

---

[50] The journal also talks about the spreading of the crude opium over the USA. So in 1908 New York imported 123,427 pounds, Philadelphia imported 153,081, St. Louis 6,885 pounds and Detroit only 430. The crude opium together is valued at $1,151,207, while the prices of the rather small amount of smoking opium increased so much that its total value became $1,336,703. This smoking opium, however, had quite a different distribution. In 1908, the last year of a substantial import of about 150,000 pounds, about 90% entered in San Francisco, Hawaii got 1,400 pounds, Puget Sound 156, Willamette (Wash.) 119 'and the district of Montana and Idaho combined, just one pound'.

The Philippine Case[51]

Before the internal American developments are discussed further, we have to continue with the external (colonial) activities which Americans developed under the same circumstances as any other Western colonizer. To have some political weight in the Eastern (opium) power game, one needed an Eastern power base. The Philippines became this stepping stone to reach to the bigger prey, China and Japan, a venture which came too late and failed from the beginning: the actions of Commodore Perry in the Japanese waters, who was trying to copy the successful assault of the British opium assault on China, 'ironically dubbed the Open Door policy'.[52]

Because of this late arrival *as a nation*—and like Japan or Germany—its main antagonist was the dominant imperialist, the British Empire: from about 1870 onwards competition with England became the leading maxim of American foreign policy and its architect, the bureaucracy of the State Department. And for similar reasons—and again like Japan and Germany—it tried to form an empire of its own in the East (Alaska, 1867; Hawaii, 1897; Philippines and Guam, 1898) or in Central America (Puerto Rico and Cuba, 1898; later followed by Panama, Haiti, etc.).

For both policies, it could certainly rely on a not unimportant, traditional anti-Anglicanism among the American population, part of an always remarkable nationalism or patriotism of a settler's society. In the many American cartoons illustrating "Uncle Sam's" entrance in world politics, "his" position was seriously exaggerated, as if it really could compete with the British Empire.

During the 19th-century the American elite expressed two different, but not original, ideas about how to cope with foreign countries. That is to say, those countries that were interesting as markets for American products or as sources of raw materials and other foreign products or as both import and export destinations. The earliest US traders decided to stay for a relevant, rather short period in an existing coastal settlement rather than conquer a substantial territory with its own settlers. The reason for this is not an enlightened idea about the ridiculous claim to grab a foreign country as one's own property. No, it was already very busy conquering 70% of the American territory and colonizing it and, therefore, there was

---

[51] For the following see Idem and A. McCoy, F. Scarano (ed.), in which at least twelve of the ca. 40 articles concern the Philippines. For the colonial history of the Philippines see in particular H. Kamen.

[52] A. McCoy, E. Jesus (ed.), p. 66.

Ill. 25. "The Harvest in the Philippines", 1899

Source: These words were below the cartoon published by *Life*, July 6, 1899 (Wisconsin State Historical Society). See also A. McCoy, F. Scarano, ed., p. 399.

simply no American manpower available to conquer territory at the other end of the world as well. US traders are, furthermore, not very willing to cooperate with US military and a federal government by which their own freedom to trade will be directly limited: traditionally, one has to act on one's own behalf.

Around 1800 the very racist American settler's society was still inventing itself as a "white nation" and faced a very bloody civil war among its own tribe. At the same time it was organizing a genocide of the original population, the "Red Race", and the "liberation" of the imported "Black Race" in order to get cheap labor for the new industries in the North instead of the plantations in the South. In such a rigorous situation, dreaming of a Greater America and nurturing imperialist activities in

Central and South America (Monroe Doctrine) or making America the dominant power in the Pacific Basin demonstrated an unbelievable lack of realism and an excess of naïveté.[53]

This changed a few decades after the Civil War. There was no lack of warnings against an imperialist adventure. A *New England Anti-Imperialist League* reminded the public that 'when we undertake to govern subject peoples separated from us by half the world, let us remember how we despoiled the Indian'.[54] Time and again this comparison was made between local tribal heathens and those far away; the massacres in the Philippines were immediately compared with "Wounded Knee". What happened on those far-away islands in view of the reactions at home is symptomatic for all US foreign "projects".

The Philippine Revolution (1896-1898) resulted in a liberation of the archipelago from the Spanish occupation. There had already been sporadic uprisings against the Spaniards before, so that in 1872 a "national" liberation movement could be established. The Filipinos definitely ousted the Spaniards with the help of the Americans. As such, it was the first of a long chain of similar 20th-century liberation movements in Asia and elsewhere.

However, no politicians or military and spiritual leaders in the West were prepared to perceive this as the beginning of the end of their imperialist fixation. Certainly not the lately arrived New Imperialists, all of whom became involved in genocidal actions against indigenous people: the Americans in the Philippines, the Japanese in China, and the Germans against the Herreros in Southwest Africa. It looks as if the achieved death rates made them "adult imperialists".

Not that the Old Imperialists stopped with similar practices, as the Dutch proved in their very bloody campaigns against largely unarmed indigenous peoples of North Sumatra, Bali or Lombok. These "Old Butchers" heralded that Americans had joined the slaughterers' club, while the Americans taught them the new technique of "water-boarding torture against Muslim people" or concentration camps, immediately copied by the British in their South African struggle against Zulus and the first colonizers, the Calvinist Dutch Boers.[55]

---

[53] A. McCoy, F. Scarano (ed.), p. 66 ff.

[54] Idem, p. 401.

[55] It is symptomatic for the Pavlov reaction to burden The Enemy with all the criminal acts oneself is committing. Notwithstanding the widespread publicity concerning the "waterboarding" practices of American torturers in Guantanamo Bay at present, an intelligent American, the Poet Laureate of the USA, Charles Simic, still writes in the *New York*

The Americans did more. As soon as they landed in the Philippines as liberators, they betrayed the indigenous people and started their first Asian colony with probably the First Genocide of the White Race in the 20th-century. Under the leadership of generals like Pershing, Wood or Smith, they did their dirty job while executing infamous orders such as: *'Kill every one over ten!'*[56]

When the main killings stopped (guerrilla fighting continued until 1913), between 500,000 and 1,000,000 Filipinos had lost their lives from a population of nine million. Concentration camps were established, and *waterboarding* became a routine method of torture. At that time, American generals in the Philippines referred explicitly to their campaigns against the Indians in the Far West.

After the gunpowder smoke had cleared and at least in the main settlements something like a normal life resumed, the new colonial USA government discovered that it had also inherited a serious opium problem from Spain. A few remarks about the preceding opium history will do.

The first Spanish conquerors arrived in the Philippines in 1565. Though few in number they, like their predecessors the Portuguese, were able to capitalize on the possession of firearms and especially of ship's cannon. Gradually, all of the islands were captured but this remained confined practically to coastal areas; the natives simply vanished into the bush. Guerrilla fights and revolts were a regular phenomenon from that time onwards.

But Spain ruled here until 1898: the official language became Spanish; the religion Roman Catholicism of a primitive kind nurtured by the rather dictatorial rules of the friars (Franciscans and Dominicans); a complicated racism supported the social hierarchy (the percentage of Spanish blood influenced one's social or economic possibilities), even the indigenous peoples were caught in a system of racist categories.

In the middle of the 18th-century, this Western colony became part of the mutual wars between the Western competitors: the EIC captured

---

Review of Books (February 11, 2010, p. 9): 'Borrowed from Soviet and Chinese Communists and other repressive regimes ... these "techniques" were fine-tuned with ... the Department of Justice ... CIA officials ...', etc.

[56] Idem, p. 401- 409; see also the *Wikipedia* article 'Philippine Revolution'. It was the same brand of American generals who at the very end of World War 1 wanted to continue with the very bloody fighting, despite the fact that the surrender of the Germans was known and signed. This stubborness cost a few thousand American and German soldiers their lives. General Pershing was a commander in the Philippines as well as in World War I.

Manila (1762), but lost it again a few years later.[57] Still, this year is seen as the beginning of the end of the Asian Spanish colonial rule: the English and Dutch infiltrated further every time, pirates of all sorts had their undisturbed playground, and the Islamic Sulu Sultanate was established in the south and feared for its extensive and long-standing slave raids and trade. It occupied mainly the island of Mindanao and the adjacent islands in the Sulu Sea, located between the Chinese mainland and the islands of Borneo and Celebes.

The opium history of the Spanish Asian colonies started in fact as a modernization project.[58] Based on Enlightenment ideas, a radical critique of Spanish imperialism was made by Spanish administrators, intellectuals pointing to the huge profits the Dutch and English received from their ventures. Everywhere in Spain as well as in its colonies, "Economic Societies of Friends of the Country" (*Sociedad Económica de los Amigos del País*) were established in the 1780s-1810s, which proposed all sorts of modernization projects.

Instead of the strict oikoidal system, they supported a system of "free trade" (especially with America) as the only way in which Spain's hidden potential might be developed. Silver from America remained the fuel of the Spanish empire also, notwithstanding the fact that the Spanish trade was largely in the hands of foreign merchants (British, French and Dutch). They were eager enough to upheld the Spanish imperial illusions. The most lucrative product of the strict oikoidal "Spanish" trade (largely trade with Spanish destinations) remained slaves to North, Central and South America, while a large proportion of goods were transported through extensive smuggling practices, the free trade.

In East Asia there was just as much smuggling, but the slave trade was confined to specific "addresses" like the Sulu Sultanate on Mindanao. Opium was much more profitable, as the Spanish authorities learned mainly from the Dutch, but served the smugglers' free trade. In the Philippines the new governor, Basco y Vargas, not only established a *Society of Friends of the Country*, but encouraged the growth of new crops for export such as indigo, tea, silk, tobacco, abaca (a kind of hemp suitable for ropes, etc.) and opium. Foreign merchants came to dominate this trade (of the thirteen trading houses, seven were British and two American) so that the Philippines could not lose in a competition with,

---

[57] H. Kamen, p. 482 ff.
[58] For the following Idem, p. 458 ff.

for instance, the same British firms trading in Chinese tea and silk or Indian opium.

As elsewhere in the Far East under Spanish rule, an opium monopoly of the government had existed since 1843 and opium tax farming was farmed out to Chinese. Only 70,000 Chinese lived here, most of them in the capital Manila.[59]

After its annexation by the USA, this monopoly was abolished and replaced by an American one. This was, in fact, an *Opiumregie* system, including heavy taxation plus free opium trade. Considerable public revenue was obtained now along with a marked increase in consumption, especially among the Filipinos, so that opium became the main government income. 'This was partly the result of a cholera epidemic in 1902, partly of the looser nature of the American system, which did not forbid the non-medicinal use of opiates by native Filipinos.'[60]

Later, after a shift in its China policy and criticism of American missionaries, the new colonizers started a prohibition campaign. If it should be true that 'the United States was the only power to give up the lucrative opium revenue voluntarily' (A. Foster),[61] it is strange that the US has remained ever since the most lucrative market for drugs in the world. Apart from this, the *New York Times* (August 6, 1904) reported more correctly about the Opium Committee appointed by Governor Taft, including the immanent contradiction:

> The committee recommends that the opium traffic be made a Government monopoly at once so that at the end of three years the importation of opium may be absolutely prohibited, with the exception of medical requirements; that only confirmed habitués of the drug who are over twenty-one years of age be granted smokers' license; ... that the punishment of Chinese found guilty of importing opium be deportation.[62]

As elsewhere in East Asia, the colonial government monopolized trade or distribution in order to get more profit and control; they decreased the

---

[59] T. Tong Joe, p. 73 ff; D. Courtwright, p. 80 ff.

[60] D. Courtwright, p. 80.

[61] Quoted in a review of F. Schumacher in: H-Soz-u-Kult, 26-04-2006 of a reader about the Americans in the Philippines by Julian Go and Anne Foster, which I could not consult. Probably it is the same as Foster's short and naive contribution to A. McCoy, F. Scarano (ed.), p. 95-105. She writes (Id., p. 95) about something most ambiguous as the 'American leadership of the anti-opium movement.' More support could be found for the reverse hypothesis that the US became the most serious victim of the same movement! That, however, is not the aim of my writing.

[62] *The New York Times* archive article 'Federal Opium Monopoly'.

Ill. 26. "Those pious Yankees ...", 1902

Source: Life, May 22, 1902 (Wisconsin State Historical Society) published this cartoon as probably the first warning about the US waterboarding practices. All Old Imperialists – Britain, France, Germany, Spain and Holland – sang a chorus in the background: 'Those pious Yankees can't throw stones at us anymore". See also A.McCoy, F.Scarano, ed., p. 405.

quantities but increased the prices in the colonies, stimulating not only serious bureaucratic corruption but also smuggling. Also here the Chinese always got the blame; the "white" British and American importers or the main smugglers were largely spared.

Main customers at the end of the 19th-century belonged to the Chinese emigrant population, which became directly dependent on the government deliveries. But other consumers were also spotted by, for instance, the *American Pharmaceutical Association* in 1903:

> While it has not been practicable to obtain exact figures, it can be stated that the drug habit is alarmingly increasing among the men of our army and navy. The number of men using opium in the army has greatly increased since the occupation of the Philippines, many "opium smokers" acquiring the habit there from Chinese or natives ... Quite a number of enlisted men have been discharged from both army and navy during the last year because

of their being detected as habitual users of opium or morphine ... Not a single case of drug habit coming from the prescribing of an opiate by a medical officer can be recalled ...[63]

The Anglican bishop Brent was the most influential member of the *Philippine Opium Commission.* In his view the consumption of opium was not merely a matter of personal weakness, but a social vice and a crime. At that moment, for church people, there was no alternative after the foreign missionaries in China had changed colors in order to save their business of converting Chinese. The commission members accepted their opinion that Chinese of all classes used opium,

> the poor inevitably suffered most from the high prices. Missionaries reported that men sold their businesses and families to satisfy their habits. Apparently, the missionaries did not perceive an appropriate solution in making opium available at lower prices ... Missionaries thus perceived opium use as frustrating their own ambition.[64]

In doing so, they contributed strongly to the habit of blaming the victims (see further ch. 29).

As usual in other colonies, the commission recommended a government monopoly to effectively control the use of opium, aiming at the repression and abolition of use and traffic, but in fact leaving the huge profits not only to the large "white" opium dealers like—in this case—the Dent & Co firm.

However, the results from Brent's proposals were conspicuous by their absence. The US government did not accept the proposed opium monopoly and its rather complicated management. In a new law (3 March 1905) it stated that in three years' time, every opium import in the Philippines should be illegal, except for medical purposes. Also, all opium selling and consumption should be prohibited.

It is not very understandable that, according to Tong Joe, much later Bishop Brent acknowledged that this was the only right decision.

---

[63] C. Terry, M. Pellens, p. 23, 24. Why the non-activity of the medical officers is mentioned here so explicitly must have a specific reason: not much later C. Terry discovered from empirical studies that indeed half of the addicts picked up their habit from treatments by physicians and the activities of druggists! That gives a specific background to the last sentences in the quoted report: 'At the present, it is calculated that there are over a million opium smokers in the United States, the importation of opium smoking purposes being double that for medicinal uses, amounting to more than 500,000 pounds last year, valued at $3,500,000!' . See also D. Courtwright, p. 100 ff.

[64] D. Richards, p. 162.

When it is discovered how lucrative a method it is for purposes of revenue, Governments easily dissemble with themselves and postpone reform indefinitely.[65]

The Philippine reality was that 'anyone who wishes to buy prepared opium can buy it at a moderate price.'[66]

A rather official investigation from the New York-based *Opium Research Committee of the Foreign Policy Association* concluded diplomatically in 1927:

> It is not difficult after an unofficial investigation of opium and smuggling in the Philippine Islands to understand why the United States is somewhat under suspicion internationally for failing to produce Philippine opium statistics. Illegal opium is coming into the islands in such quantities as to make smoking opium procurable freely at very low prices, but lack of reliable figures on the number of Chinese in the Islands makes any estimate of the extent of opium smoking difficult.[67]

Smugglers are normally not impressed by the availability or not of figures. They act when the profit is reasonable compared to the risks and costs. In the Philippines smuggling opium remained an intensive activity, and in particular from Amoy, Hong Kong, Macao, Kwang Chow Wan, British North Borneo and Formosa. This opium trade network operated smoothly until World War II when the Philippines arrived near the eye of the storm.

The result of all the Philippine mess is a highly repressed population robbed of its dignity of having fought for its own liberation and addicted to Eastern opium probably more seriously than before, falsified statistics or not.

Early 20th-century Opium / Cocaine Consumption

A Basic Drink

In the USA an original home-bred way of addicting many people was invented. In 1865 the pharmacist John Pemberton was wounded in the Civil War, and like many wounded veterans he became addicted to morphine. Searching for a cure, he began experimenting with coca and coca wines, comparable to a diluted form of laudanum. He called the result

---

65 Quoted by T. Tong Joe, p. 74 note 1.
66 Idem, p. 75 quoting a report of May about the Philippines.
67 Quoted in A. Vandenbosch, p. 283 note 34.

Ill. 27. Coca Cola: old and new claims, ca. 1902

Source: Many marvelous mental medicines circulated around 1900 in the USA including the wonderful Coca Cola. See www.bonkersinstitute.org/medshow/cola.html. This advertisement of 1902 urges people 'when the Brain is running under full pressure' to drink a glass of Coca-Cola: it 'enables the entire system to readily cope with the strain of any excessive demands made upon it.' At that time the drink still contained cocaine. Later it contained only(!) an extract of coca leaves.

Pemberton's French Wine Coca. His medicinal concoction was advertised as being particularly beneficial for

> ladies, and all those whose sedentary employment causes nervous prostration, irregularities of the stomach, bowels and kidneys, who require a nerve tonic and a pure, delightful diffusable stimulant.[68] When drinking a Coca Cola nowadays, only a few people know that it has this medical background.

---

[68] Article 'John Pemberton', in: *Wikipedia*.

The company does not promote the historical knowledge of its product, consumers cannot be stimulated by it to 'have their Coke'! Without any doubt, however, Coca Cola is the top addiction product of American citizens in the 20th-century.

The original formula allegedly called for 8.46 mg of cocaine, while an average dose of the street drug is between 15 and 35 mg. As Pemberton's business partner invented the name Coca Cola (1885), the company claimed that it was a medicine to cure morphine and opium addictions, among a multitude of other health benefits. An advertisement of 1886 stated about this 'intellectual beverage' (!) that it was not only a delicious etc. drink but that it was a cure 'for all nervous affections – sick, headache, neuralgia, hysteria, melancholy', etc.

Neither Pemberton nor anybody else until today has proven whether these claims are true or that it is just a new product in the overstocked US quack's market (see Dr. Doxey's Elixir above).

Notwithstanding all anti-narcotic campaigns after the 1880s, the *claim* in the advertisement campaigns was sufficient to seduce enough Americans to make the drink relatively popular. It wasn't until the Second World War that Coca Cola became the multinational company with bottling plants all over the world, including the Philippines.

Basic Knowledge

In the 1899 copy of the authoritative *Dispensatory of the United States of America* written by learned men like George Wood and Franklin Bache, Coca Cola was not mentioned. It had become the handbook for many generations of American pharmacists and apothecaries (24th edition in 1947, etc.). One of the longest articles in it concerns opium.[69] Its sources are British, French and US pharmacopoeia.

Its opium article starts with details about the *Papaver somniferum Linné* plant, its capsules and juice; its preparation had a content of between 9½% and 10½% morphine ('not more'). Then it continues with a 'Commercial History', containing some loose remarks about the opium imported and its destination: 'For various reasons India opium no longer enters Western commerce to any extent'. Following the European pattern, the USA apparently received opium mainly from Turkey directly or through different European ports. In 1897 a total of 1,072,914 lbs was imported from that source, valued at $2,184,727, which makes $2.03 per lb.

---

[69] G. Wood, F. Bache, p. 980-1005 very dense printed texts. Quotations come from these pages.

In addition, 157,061 lbs of 'prepared opium for smoking' was imported, valued at \$1,132,861, which makes \$7.21 per lb.

The French port of Marseilles was the main transit harbor and the location of extensive frauds:

> The opium taken thither from the Levant is first softened, and then adulterated with various matters which are incorporated in its substance. To use a strong expression of Guibourt, they make the opium over again at Marseilles. Our traders to the Mediterranean would do well to bear this assertion in mind. ... Sand, ashes, the seeds of different plants ... gum arabic ... aloes, even small stones and minute pieces of lead and iron, are mentioned among the substances employed in the sophistication of the drug.[70]

There follows a long list with sometimes extensive comments on the available kinds of opium and researchers who tested them: Turkey with export ports Smyrna and Constantinople (12 kinds); Egypt; India (3); Persia (3) and even Mozambique before the Chinese market.

Regarding China it states that its opium never reaches the European market, but enters the United States through San Francisco. There it is mainly consumed by the resident Chinese for smoking purposes. The San Francisco custom house apparently wanted to make a big business out of this import. As told earlier, it did not asked the normal US\$1 duty a pound, but \$6 by inventing a new definition: this imported opium is 'an extract'! The pharmacists conclude: '... hence, probably, the ever-recurring attempts at its smuggling'.[71]

This list of kinds of opium is followed by a review of all *alkaloids*, which are usually the 'active principles of the plants in which they are found ... and been applied so advantageously to the treatment of disease'; in short, a review of *morphine, codeine, thebaine, laudanine* and more than twenty other alkaloids, all with the ability to transform people into addicts instead of curing diseases, with which "too little money" can be earned.[72]

---

[70] Idem, p. 982. This must be the real background for the movie *The French Connection* (1971) in which a New York policemen arrived in Marseilles and another civilization to fight the French drug mafia in the American cowboy way; a brilliant role of Gene Hackman. See C. Lamour, M. Lamberti, p. 29 ff. for the situation in the 1970s.

[71] There is also mentioned a second "Chinese" opium with the mysterious name *Boston Opium* (elsewhere called "pudding opium"). Without lifting the veil about this name, we can say that it concerns a 'sophisticated article, skilfully adulterated so as to reduce the percentage of morphine to the lowest point compatible with getting through the United States Custom-House and yet to get the physical appearance of a high-grade opium.' Idem, p. 986.

[72] They all have the chemical combination of C, H and NO elements as, for instance, morphine $C_{17} H_{19} NO_3$ or codeine with $C_{18} H_{21} NO_3$, etc.

This *Dispensatory* provides so many rules and recipes about how to treat opium that any layman can make his own opium preparation; the greatest difficulty is the sheer volume of this extremely large book.

This copy from 1899 also details what a consumer can expect of his/her opium. When a healthy person takes a moderate dose, it increases the frequency and force of the pulse, invigorates the muscular system, etc.

> and gives new energy to the intellectual faculties. Its operation ... is directed with peculiar force to the brain, the functions of which it excites sometimes even to intoxication or delirium. However, 'in a short time' this excitation subsides and 'a calmness of the corporal actions, and a delightful placidity of mind, succeed ... forgetting all sources of care and anxiety ... pleasing fantasies ... a quiet and vague enjoyment. At the end of half an hour or an hour ... all consciousness is lost in sleep. ... All the secretions ... are in general either suspended or diminished ... pain and inordinate muscular contraction ... are allayed and general nervous irritation is composed.[73]

Unfortunately, the quantity of a normal dose in the relevant cases was not mentioned.[74] Therefore, the explanations of what happens if the doses are 'insufficient' or 'large' result only in the obvious remarks that the reactions are slower or more intense, respectively, as described. The details of what happens after swallowing 'quantities sufficient to destroy life' conclude with the obvious: 'Death soon follows, unless relief be afforded.' It is, however, not very reassuring to learn that after consuming 'very small quantities', this occasionally gives 'rise to excessive sickness and vomiting and even spasm of the stomach ... restlessness, headache and delirium ...'![75]

It is remarkable that after this more or less technical information, it starts recounting fairy tales about other people: that in 'all parts of the world opium is habitually employed', which is happily not the case, and that Mohammedans and Hindus use opium as 'the most pleasing substitute for alcoholic drinks'. This is logically and factually incorrect.

Where alcohol is unknown, something else cannot be a substitute for it. Throughout most of history and the largest part of the globe, alcohol and opium were absent among the majority of the population before the

---

[73] Idem, p. 1001.

[74] Later (p. 1003) one mentions what the authors prescribe in *catarrh* and *diarrhoea:* not more than one-fourth or one-third of a grain (0.016 or 0.02 gram); in acute peritonitis one jumps even to 'the equivalent of seventy-five grains (5 gram)' ! Is this the dose after which the relatives must be told: 'Death soon follows, unless relief be afforded'? Anyway, this is insufficient for general treatment purposes as relative to the function of this *Dispensatory.*

[75] Idem, p. 1002.

Dutch or English pressed native inhabitants to swallow the stuff. In addition, Mohammedans (see ch. 30), Hindus or Buddhists are in general not opium users, excluding some Mughal elites. In Islam (Qur'an) there is even a formal prohibition against using any alcohol and drugs, when not medically prescribed. In Hinduism some gurus consume only cannabis, and some opium is used in Ayurveda medicine. The same is applicable to Confucianism or Taoism. Only in specific local rituals are substances with opium-like qualities used, like *peyote* by specific shamans. Only Christians and Jews are well-known users of all forbidden products.

The *Dispensatory* states: 'In India, Persia and Turkey it is consumed in immense quantities, and many nations of the East smoke opium as those of the West smoke tobacco', but this is far beyond the credibility of the explanations given above: 'Death soon follows, unless relief be afforded'! In India, Persia and Turkey this relief is not afforded, so there should have been many reports of deaths! Therefore, all this looks like a legitimation of the *American* behavior and the saving of the bestselling product of pharmacists. And, indeed, this behavior demands a strong legitimation; an impression confirmed by the next section, in which the old stories about the ancients (Diagoras, Hippocrates) are told.

Indeed, seven kinds of useful applications of opium to cure something are mentioned; this time without the double-blind proofs of the results, let alone the provision of alternatives.[76] After this short digression, the text continues again with discussing contra-indications.

No single remark is given about the social, political or economic aspects or effects of opium (or morphine, etc.) use. There is, probably, shame about doing so because a few years later it is crystal clear that a serious anti-opium opposition has developed. It still remains incomprehensible that in the 1918 edition of the *Dispensatory*, no article appeared on opium, morphine or heroin.[77] That was when the consumption of these drugs rocketed sky-high in the United States.

A Mega Consumption

The Americans are the ones who have to pay the largest bill for the deeds of their 19th-century ancestors and their Western colleagues. Against

---

[76] Idem, p. 1002, 1003.

[77] This 20th edition with its 1576 pp. can be studied on-line: www.swsbm.com/Dispensatory/USD-1918-complete.pdf. It is edited by Joseph Remington, Horace Wood and others. There was only a short article on "poppy capsules", p. 1143-1145, not even one on 'papaver'.

their enormous profits with the opium trade, the chief medical officer of the City of New York reported already as early as 1921 that

> Americans consume twelve times more opium than any other people in the world. More than 750,000 pound are imported every year in the USA, which equals around 2.5 gram per person. The legally allowed opium consumption is not less than 70,000 pound a year.[78]

It is in particular after 1918 that people caught by the police as opium addicts increased by nearly 800%. These figures must be exaggerated compared to data given below, but the question is whether it is possible to come up with more reliable figures.

It was something like common wisdom that a relatively high level of opium consumption was established in the United States. From all sides—Europe, the Far East, Mexico or Canada—large consignments of opium could be imported (legally and smuggled) and consumed.

A first attempt to uncover opium addiction comes from O. Marshall (1878), who interviewed 200 key figures in about 100 townships and villages all over Michigan. Based on these results, he estimated that of the 1.3 million people in the whole state, 'the total number of opium eaters ... would be 7,763'. There were also many more female 'eaters' than males.[79] These figures do not tell us about addiction, the quantities involved, and so on; they only claim that the druggist could sell substances freely to mainly female customers, people with sleeping problems, pain or whatever.

A government report of 1919 concerning addiction in the country guessed 'that the total number of addicts in this country probably exceeds 1,000,000 at the present time'.[80] A 1924 estimate starts in a more realistic way by stating that it is impossible to make a reliable account of the addicted persons 'because of the social and legal factors tending to make addiction a secret practice'.[81] After scrutinizing all kinds of studies and figures, the highest estimate for the period 1915 to 1922 is likely to be 269,000 for the whole country, with a minimum of 104,300 addicts (Lawrence Kolb).

The first sound evaluation of the opium problem in the USA was carried out by the *Committee on Drug Addictions* in collaboration with the

---

[78] L. Lewin, p. 77.
[79] Idem, p. 11-15. See also D. Courtwright, p. 36 and table 2, p. 13 for addicts per location around 1920 (Kolb).
[80] Idem, p. 32.
[81] Idem, p. 42.

Ill. 28. How to dope US. babies ca. 1870.

Source: D. Duco, p. 107. This soothing syrup for babies was one of the best known laudanum products.

Bureau of Social Hygiene, Inc. The results were published in 1928; with over one thousand pages, it was one of the most extensive reports at the time.[82]

The study starts with an assessment of the extent of the opium problem which resulted in the table below. Nearly half of it is occupied by the very detailed discussion of the medical side of the problem; a quarter of it concerns the control measures to be taken at international, national and municipal levels; about 10% is filled with texts of some international treaties and most US states measures. Only 0.5% is devoted to the opium problem. For a *History of the Opium Problem* they are the most interesting chapters, and include some background.

One of the authors, Charles E. Terry, a dedicated health officer in Florida, initiated a most controversial medical approach.[83] He established a city drug clinic to provide the habitués with free narcotic prescriptions. With this, he became the forerunner of the methadone maintenance clinics which now exist in most large Western cities. The municipal law to do this was passed in Jacksonville (Florida) in 1912.

After a year Terry had registered 646 habitual users, 1% of the Jacksonville population. Among them, the white habitués outnumbered

---

[82] C. Terry, M. Pellens.
[83] For the following see D. Musto, p. 97 ff.

the blacks by almost two to one; women outnumbered men by about three to two, and the latter preferred opiates to cocaine. He, furthermore,

> came to the conclusion that 55 percent of the habits had been acquired through treatment by physicians, 20 percent from advice of acquaintances, and 20 percent through dissipation. Only 2 percent arose from chronic and incurable disease treated with narcotics.[84]

Terry also chastised the druggists, who reaped an extravagant profit from their narcotic sales, and strongly emphasized that addiction problems should be left to health departments and not to the police. Consequently, Terry had confidence only in "public physicians".

In an atmosphere of USA "cocainomania", Terry's results were an assault on the general racist anti-black and anti-foreigner attitudes of government institutions or private and religious associations and on the general adoration of "people in the white coats", the medical professionals. They also did not support the anti-feminist belief in the general sinfulness of women as "based" on the Genesis story. And they contradicted the widespread political belief that 'perfidious foreign nations' were usually responsible for American drug taking.[85]

The widespread xenophobia is, for instance, expressed by the influential *Philippines Opium Commission* of Bishop Brent and others. The three members represented the USA in the international opium conference in Shanghai (1909). Their attitude and probably their strategy were to blame the Chinese and the Chinese government as much as possible, which they expressed, for instance, as follows:

> The original idea was that the opium traffic and habit as it existed in the Far East was to be investigated. But during the passage of the diplomatic correspondence it developed that the opium habit was no longer confined to Far Eastern countries, and that the United States especially had become contaminated through the presence of a large Chinese population.[86]

In this catalogue of participants, together responsible for the opium problem, Terry's characterization of the non-institutionalized institution, the underworld, or of the general opium business, must be added:

> It is not unnatural ... for the head of a penal institution in which cases of chronic opium intoxication are treated to come to the conclusion that the underworld and criminal classes are especially prone to this condition; for

---

[84] Idem, p. 98.
[85] Idem, p. 279 note 3.
[86] Quoted in C. Terry, M. Pellens, p. 632.

the head of a state hospital to conclude that the mentally unstable form a considerable majority of these patients, and for the proprietor of a private institution, where the cost of treatment is within the means of only a favored few, to claim that financiers, individuals highly successful in the business world, and professional groups able to pay the highest prices to a large extent are susceptible to opiumism.[87]

In Terry's study is given also the following table:

Table 43. Total Import of Opium and Opium Preparations to the USA, 1850-1924 (selected years)[88]

Year	General imports		Entered for Consumption		
	Crude opium in lbs	Opium prepared for smoking in lbs	Opium entered for consumption in lbs	Smoking opium entered for consumption in lbs	Morphine and its salts entered for consumption in oz
1	2	3	4	5	6
1850	130 349	---	---	---	---
1855	111 229	---	107 632	---	---
1860	119 525	---	116 686	---	---
1865	110 470	13 703	92 099	31 918	172
1870	254 609	[34 000]	121 185	12 603	3 187
1875	305 136	[53 000]	188 239	62 775	4 252
1880	533 451	[60 000]	243 211	77 196	19 386
1885	351 609	37 475	351 609	37 475	20 710
1890	473 095	34 465	380 621	58 982	19 954
1895	358 455	139 765	357 981	115 709	16 029
1900	544 938	142 479	537 004	129 335	26 208
1905	594 680	159 380	456 563	144 997	21 396
1910	449 239	[100 000]	439 379	[118 500]	13 085
1915	484 027	---	391 938	---	8 676
1920	211 277	---	225 528	---	31 909
1925	96 848	---	96 848	---	[65 000]

This table should be given to students to teach them the pitfalls of making statistics: is the title of column 3 similar to that of column 5 as only the 1885 data suggest? Column 2 + 3 is only in one case, 1865, similar to 4+5: where have all the differences between 'general imports' and 'entered for consumption' gone? Generally, the transformation from crude into pre-

---

87 Idem, p. 513, 514.
88 Idem, p. 50-51 from official sources.

pared opium reduced its weight by 50%: how is this to be seen in the table? Is column 3, therefore, to be added or subtracted from column 2 (and 5 from 4)?

In addition, it is an interesting exercise to compare this table to the two given earlier about the Pacific and the Atlantic opium import. For example, in 1870/71 the addition of these two gives an import of 303,231 lbs, while the entirety for the USA gives about 50,000 lbs *less*! Ten years later the same procedure leads to a weight of 129,905 lbs, which derives from other ports than San Francisco and New York. For 1890 this amount is even 191,249 lbs.

The import quoted earlier from Wood and Bache's *Dispensatory* is a multiple of what is mentioned here as the import for 1895. A new study of these figures is welcome to clarify whether the differences result from imports in other ports, from smuggling, from "secret" imports needed in the pharmaceutical industry, from corruption in the custom offices, and so on.[89] Whatever its value, the table indicates clearly the kind of quantities of opium swallowed by American consumers.

Cocaine Connections

Above is quoted an alarming article from *The New York Times* (1909) which informed the reader that five years earlier only 53,000 pounds of coca leaves were imported, but that this had jumped to 2,600,000 pounds within two years. This last figure is approached only in 1943; it only nurtures my suspicion about official US statistics.

As remarked in ch. 19 for the export of Javanese cocaine, the drug consumption of the soldiers in World Wars I and II and during the world economic crisis strongly decreased instead of the expected increase. The figures in the table also suggest the same development. Smuggling cannot be represented in reliable numbers or in estimates of a non-reliable drugs police. Even if one supposes that the consumption of soldiers is hidden in the medicinal data (and, therefore, that non-medicinal figures are confined to the civilian consumption at home), the given downward trend in times of crisis can be supported. Still how can we explain the remarkable jump of consumption in the non-medicinal realm *after* the world crisis or at the beginning of World War II: are they only "home front data"?

---

[89] It seems as if people busy with narcotic statistics are themselves seriously addicted. The many reports about the number of addicts in the USA are notorious, which often lead to big rows because of the bad image the USA could get abroad if they were too high. See D. Courtwright (p. 121 ff.) about the Harry Anslinger period and his surveys.

Table 44. U.S. coca imports: medicinal (cocaine) and non-medicinal (cola), 1925-1959 (x kilograms)[90]

Year	Coca Leaves		
	Total Imports	Medicinal	Nonmedicinal
1925	72 255	72 255	---
1930	89 699	89 699	---
1931	221 236	122 748	98 487
1933	81 699	81 699	---
1934	85 551	81 070	4 481
1935	110 331	94 469	15 862
1940	352 201	146 189	206 011
1941	420 389	127 484	292 905
1942	360 656	80 849	270 806
1943	447 396	207 409	239 987
1944	202 057	67 555	134 502
1945	316 224	45 359	270 865
1950	112 743	112 743	---
1955	141 290	141 290	---
1956	184 096	184 096	---
1958	112 501	112 501	---
1959	135 223	135 223	---

Furthermore, what does "medicinal" means? Resources for the pharmaceutical industry? Let's take the example of Merck. At least until 1933, this company was a world leader in legal drug production and even a monopolist for cocaine, heroin and morphine. Like Bayer and others, it stuffed its painkillers and many other products with these components. Concerning the consumer side of the Opium Problem, it seriously contributed in this way to the collective addiction or dependence on medicinal products in general instead of good and differentiated food, better collective hygiene or better information about health and related subjects.

Firms like Merck, Boehringer or Bayer exported tons of these drugs annually over the whole world without any form of external control. In 1922, for instance, the production figures were: 1.2 tons of cocaine, 2.5 tons of morphine and 4.2 tons of heroin. The demand by the «international

---

[90] Quoted in the article of P. Gootenberg in: S. Topik et al. (ed.), p. 342. The source is the notorious US Department of Treasury, Federal Bureau of Narcotics (1960). Only selected years are given. Before 1930 coca leaf is not clearly separated; separate reporting (but not imports) ceases after 1947. The figures are rounded.

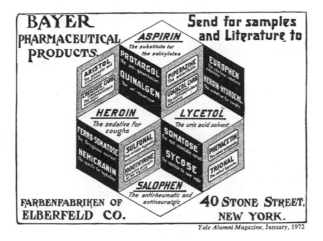

Ill. 29. Bayer Pharmaceutical Products, 1898

Source: A. McCoy et al., 1972, p. 4.

community» to control this kind of production was not in the interest of the German pharmaceutical industry and, therefore, not of the German government.

«Darmstadt», the German base of Merck, became one of the three production centers in the world for cocaine: the *Dutch Cocaine Factory* was the largest, and the American New Jersey Merck the second.[91] Thanks to this concerted competition, the values of Peruvian coca and crude cocaine dropped by some 95% in the 1920s.

As a main offshoot of their prominent position, the pharmaceutical industry pursued patent rights on its products.[92] In most countries it was not possible to patent vital necessities of daily life, as it is a form of monopoly. New definitions are easy to find. In the USA in 1870, the patent law was revised to make even that possible. Anyway, drugs and their method of production can be patented. This had far-reaching consequences:

> The extensive development of large pharmaceutical firms, based on research, could not have occurred in the same way without patent laws. The fact that the industry, the ingenuity and the money invested in the discovery of new drugs and processes have been rewarded by a temporary

---

[91] Apparently, private individuals could get their dose from Merck. 'Freud obtained some cocaine from the pharmaceutical firm of Merck &Co of Darmstadt and started to take doses of 50 milligrams dissolved in water.' Th. Dormandy, p. 369 and that was the beginning of an addiction and supporter so that friends were addicted as well.

[92] For the following see E. Kremers, G. Urdangs, p. 113 ff.

Table 45. Merck Production and its German Import of Cocaine and Coca, 1880-1915 (x kilogram)[93]

| Year | Merck production | Coca imported | | Crude cocaine imported from Java |
		from Peru	from Java	
1880	0.05	25	---	---
1885	70	18 396	---	---
1890	557	---	---	---
1895	791	---	---	---
1900	1 418	---	---	---
1905	2 146	---	58 967	919
1910	5 241	---	186 127	3 183
1915	265	---	203 972	2 966

monopoly has helped to stimulate the startling advances since the last quarter of the 19th-century.[94]

An application of this patent right is the monopoly on trademarks, which even makes it possible to acquire 'unlimited exclusive rights to the brand name' and 'to enjoy a virtual monopoly on a given product'. This led to many excesses, but the patent + trademark "principle" remained intact. For the whole drug scene, it had the practical effect that the industry's trade in cocaine, heroin, morphine or any other "trademark" was invented by the advertisement people, could be defined as "legal"and remained unchecked. Competitors had to pay big fines, prison or worse, if confronted with an Italian mafia or the Mexican police.

The largest cocaine imports into the USA were organized from Mexico. Not without difficulty as experienced, for instance, by the Zionist David Goldbaum around 1916.[95] This man occupied a remarkable position as a

---

[93] From the article of Paul Gootenberg in: S. Topik et al (ed.), p. 326. Only a selection of his data is given.

[94] Idem, p. 114. See also Th. Dormandy, p. 413, 414 for Merck patents. As one of the few, the founder of the present Eli Lilly concern still had, anyway, the right idea to commit 'himself to producing only high-quality prescription drugs, in contrast to the common and often ineffective patent medicines of the day' (*Wikipedia*, 'Eli Lilly). At the moment it produces world-wide products like the controversial *Prosac*. Things can change also in other directions: In January 2009, the largest criminal fine in U.S. history was imposed on Lilly for illegal marketing of its best-selling product, the antipsychotic medication, Zyprexa.

[95] G. Recio, p. 34. This David Goldbaum was a Zionist, suspicious of the plans to settle in Palestine and, therefore, member of the so-called Territorialist Faction (start in 1905) of the Zionist movement. He and other Zionist settlers in Baja California arrived there in the 1880s, and they planned to buy a large part of the peninsula to establish there the "New

representative of Chinese opium dealers! He got a concession for the handling of smoking opium from Esteban Cantú, governor of Baja California. This Cantú, however, charged a fixed fee of $45,000 and monthly instalments of $10,000. It was a deal he had made not only with Goldbaum. The US Treasury Department caught this clever opium trafficker, but most of his colleagues had more luck.

For cocaine Mexico provided the only trade route. In the 1920s Mexico instituted more rigorous laws on trafficking, but the smugglers responded by planting opium in several border states in Mexico and extended and refined the distribution network within the USA. From this labor they are still profiting today.

Basic Instincts

A notorious report from Hamilton Wright (1910) argued that 'the general criminal population' was addicted, at a rate more than 250 times that of the general adult population.[96] In many pressure groups, whose activities led to the *Harrison Narcotic Act* (1914), similar sounds were heard. The question of who belonged to the opium or drug mafia was easy to answer: the mafia were criminals; addicts were criminals, too; therefore, all addicts belonged to the mafia. This false assumption became canonized as the highest form of wisdom about addiction by Congressman Porter or the US surgeon general, Rupert Blue.

In the latter's view, addicts should be divided into two classes: the legal or medical class with a few members with some disease, injury or pain requiring relief and those who habitually used narcotics for other than medical reasons, who are the real addicts similar to 'psychopaths, neurotics and criminals'.[97] The first class should be cared for by medical doctors, pharmacists and the pharmaceutical industry, the three sources of their addiction. The second class consisted of clients of the police, prisons, and, of course, the pharmaceutical industry as well, which had to provide the means to cure the craving. High-ranking police officers (1924) used readymade arguments like, for instance:

World Israel", an autonomous Jewish state. Certainly a better plan than what happened in Palestine. Goldbaum also wrote a booklet to support this plan: 'Towns of Baja California. A 1918 Report. ed. by W. Hendricks (Glendale, Cal.: La Siesta Press, 1971).
[96] D. Courtwright, p. 145.
[97] Quoted by D. Courtwright, p. 142.

> Whether an addict becomes a criminal or a criminal becomes an addict, the fact remains that they spring from the same soil—namely from the group of mental, moral and psychological inferiors.[98]

People acquainted with the basic addiction problems protested against these discriminatory platitudes. They pointed to the effects of legislation (even possession of drugs became a crime in itself) making a user a criminal by definition and not by act. They, furthermore, argued: when a user does commit a crime like theft, it is solely to obtain cash to pay for his drug. The reason why was not discussed: because the law has driven the price of the drug to excessive heights.[99] To the known criticism at the time, Courtwright adds that the use of police records in these addiction-criminality cases is fraught with peril. So, the prohibition policy exercised by the authorities with their typical supporters only increased the revenues of the pharmaceutical industry, its pharmacists, doctors and the underworld and aggravated The Problem.

The question of who belongs to the Opium Mafia leads, therefore, to complicated answers. It would be better to talk about a *Mafia Complex* in order to cover both causes and effects and a large grey zone in which all kinds of ideologues, decision makers, executioners and distributors operate, as do the mafia members. An example: in the *Harrison Act* the bureaucratic rule was set that addicts, as unregistered persons, had to obtain a prescription for their drugs. "Dope doctors" provided them for a fee:

> During a single month one New York City doctor "wrote scrip" for 68,282 grains of heroin, 54,097 grains of morphine, and 30,280 grains of cocaine.[100]

The alternative for the addicts was (and often is) the so-called black market, which is in the hands of the "real" underground. That inroad was, however, forbidden by the authorities through stiff penalties so that the "white market" of the doctors and pharmacists could keep their business; the industry, producer for everybody, could earn from both the underworld and upperworld.

---

[98] Quoted by Idem, p. 145.

[99] D. Courtwright, p. 144 mentions many proponents of this criticism in his note 123. See also W. Eldridge, p. 24 ff. and p. 116 ff.

[100] D. Courtwright, p. 107. If around 1920 the average price per ounce of morphine is $100, of cocaine $50 and heroin $53, then this prescription trade has a value of nearly $8,000. If the 'dope doctor' got a fee per grain, he could have earned 152,000 x $0.5 per month, a multitude of what the President of the United States cashed every month. What inflation means in the drug business can be ascertained from the present price of heroin, which is $59-$88 per gram or $22 for 1/3 gram. If an American ounce = ca. 29 gram, its price today is $1,711-2,552. See www.thegooddrugsguide.com.

For heroin, which came on the white and black markets around 1910-20, Courtwright concludes:

> ... addiction was moving from the upperworld to the underworld, and the principal forces behind that shift were medical and demographic, rather than legal ... the background of the typical addict in 1940 ... would have been a lower-class white male, living in a decaying urban area. He would have had a history of what contemporaries called vice (gambling, excessive drinking, or consorting with prostitutes), and perhaps would have committed more serious criminal acts ... The law did not create the underworld addict, but it did aggravate his behavior.[101]

Heroin was the illicit opiate *par excellence*. For the dealers it had the principal advantage that it could be adulterated easily. Profits could be doubled or quadrupled by cutting heroin with milk sugar or a similar substance. Around 1940 the heroin was one-third pure, very potent for present standards. Heroin was also an ideal substance for smuggling and, in this period, much cheaper than morphine and 'cheaper for the amount of kick in it'.[102]

Once the police seizures of heroin were mapped, the diffusion could be followed easily: radiating outward from New York City by the mid-1920s, it had reached coastal cities north and south of New York. Then it spread westward. This process continued until around 1932 when heroin had supplanted morphine to a considerable degree as the drug of addiction in nearly every part of the United States.

This map indicates the failure of the law which prohibited the production and import of heroin (1925). It, furthermore, shows how the mafia (here a general concept for the underworld) took possession of the United States. Of course, not only drugs (from alcohol to heroin and cocaine) were their source of revenue, although there was always a specific internal division of labor, so that gambling or prostitution were covered as well.

The entry into the underworld, heroin department, was also stimulated by the way one took it. Around 1910 heroin was mostly sniffed, a decade later the hypodermic technique was widely diffused among addicts. Again later, addicts started to appreciate a subcutaneous, intramuscular or intravenous injection. In these acts the social (criminal) environment became lethal thanks to the following circumstances.[103]

---

[101] Idem, p. 146, 147.
[102] Idem, p. 108.
[103] For the following see Idem, p. 110-111.

Map 16. Heroin seizures in the United States, 1927-1928

Source: D. Courtwright, p. 109 from *Extracts from the Report of the Commissioner of Prohibition, 1928.*

In the 1930s there was a steadily declining purity of street heroin. It was the time when an aggressive new generation of Italian gangsters infiltrated the business, replacing the Jews in particular. The Italians increased the prices and lowered the level of adulteration. The Jewish dealers, apparently, got the image of the "good gangster", who traded a 'decent product' making 'a high but not exorbitant profit' by exploiting 'their' addicts. Both had only a different way of looking at this macabre market: you can treat addicts 'decently' to exploit him/her longer (Jewish way) or you can squeeze the money quickly out him/her, because you never knew how long this looser had to live (Italian way).

This American Mafia Complex had, of course, an international element as Trocki indicated when he described that in these years drug transformations occurred in China also:

> In fact, the production levels of opiates now gave China a surplus that made it possible for China to turn the tables on the western powers and begin exporting drugs to the United States and Europe. American gangsters beginning with Arnold Rothstein and going on to Meyer Lansky, Charles "Lucky" Luciano, Louis "Lepke" Buchalter and Jasha Katsenberg, forged links with Chinese drug lords, both in Shanghai and California, to obtain supplies for the growing American narcotics market.[104]

---

[104] C. Trocki (1999), p. 133.

A remarkable number of Jews (or people who were called as such[105]) and people with a Jewish background were busy in this drug scene and not only in America (see ch. 31). They are part and parcel of the Mafia Complex, which deserves to be entangled better than in the Hollywood glamour productions.[106]

---

[105] A Jew is only somebody who accepts the Jewish religion as his/her creed, whatever part or sect of it. If only one or two parents believe(d), than one can only speak of somebody 'with a Jewish background'. See further H. Derks (2004), chapter 7. One is too often confronted with highly exaggerated expressions, which also people with a Jewish background copied from Americans with an inferiority complex. In the mafia history this habit is demonstrated in the most ridiculous fashion in, for instance, Arnold Rothstein's biography in the *Jewish Virtual Library* (American-Israeli Cooperative Enterprise) or on websites in which this gangster, murdered like many others of his kind, is called even 'the spiritual father of American organized crime' (www.carpenoctem.tv/mafia/rothstein.html). Nick Tosches's *King of the Jews. The Arnold Rothstein Story* (2005) supplied a religious hagiography of this very mediocre figure.

[106] A good example is the study of F. Bovenkerk and Y. Yeşilgöz about the Turkish mafia.

CHAPTER TWENTY-NINE

A REFLECTION

1.

During the one and a half centuries from 1800 to 1950, the Opium Problem underwent several transformations within the territory that became later the USA. First, of course, the fact that in 1800 the USA occupied about 30% of its current territory and acquired the rest within fifty years. The Opium Problem existed only outside this territory in East Asia where American clippers aggravated the Chinese opium problems. Internal problems only arose locally and through individual actions ("Dr. Doxey").

This was comparable to the "household situation" in England before about the 1850s. An American Opium Problem was created *around* the period of the Civil War. Opium and its derivatives were abundantly produced and consumed. A combination of factors was necessary for this creation.

First, the rise of an American pharmaceutical industry and further professionalization in the health sector as was seen in Europe as well. Second, the increasing opium import divided over two separate streams: one for the Chinese inhabitants from the East imported through San Francisco and one for the "whites" from the West (Turkey and Europe) imported through New York or Philadelphia. The former was only crude or prepared opium; the second more sophisticated, crude opium as resource for the pharmaceutical industry and morphine, codeine or products like laudanum, opium syrups for babies or adults. Third, a much larger market of clients: the soldiers in the Civil War, the army of its addicts thereafter; Chinese inhabitants; the hype of lady-morphine addicts; and, generally, a huge collection of opium pills and powder swallowers. As a crown on this booming US *narco-consumer complex* came Coca Cola in the 1880s.

From about 1885 onwards a new period started in which all features of the Opium Problem became aggravated in a way that no one knew how to handle. This was already sufficient reason for why the Opium Problem got completely out of hand. First, the widespread sectarian and religious campaigns of moral lobbies created a highly exaggerated moral problem for which they did not give an adequate solution except praying, abstinence and paying on God's own accounts.

Second, from the local to the federal level, laws were invented by authorities which criminalized the use of opium, leaving the producers largely undisturbed. In some cities even a full-fledged police-state was created against the behavior of the normal citizens.

The excessive urbanization and foreign immigration, furthermore, led to a radically new kind of client: urban low-class men became notable consumers instead of higher-class women. The urban and migrant dropouts could easily organize in gangs, and what was criminalized by the "aboveground" was the obvious field of activities for the newly created "underground": first and foremost, all kinds of prohibited stuff and drinks (not Coca Cola).

Fourth. The excessive stress on the consumer side of the Opium Problem (using as disease, as health hazard, as criminal act, and so on) concentrated all theoretical (scientific) and practical attention on the person and personalized the Opium (Drug) Problem. This resulted in numerous "psychoactive" studies and rules, new definitions, new medical procedures, new professionals and new drugs ('to attack drugs with drugs' like opium with cocaine). No relevant comprehensive explanation(s) of the whole Opium Problem were produced.[1]

Next, in the 1890s the American pharmaceutical industry started developing into a multinational industry and consequently its lobby and price-setting potentials grew. Like every other industry, it suffered a certain set-back in the economic slump period, but the World War II period was detrimental for its global extension. After 1950 they often rose into the category: "Too Big to Topple" with all the nasty consequences.

2.

The American foreign policy aspects of the Opium Problem seldom interested people outside academic circles, secret services and the army. The

---

[1] That was not only the case in the period 1880-1950, but it is difficult to find such a study nowadays. Take for example the contribution of one of the most successful American social scientific drug experts, Erich Goode, in the excellent *The Social Science Encyclopedia* (ed. Adam Kuper and Jessica Kuper), 1999, p. 197-200. Despite the advice to follow the Dutch policy of flexible enforcement. The author even deemed it necessary to start with so-called examples to prove that throughout human history people have evidenced drug (ab)use.

many practical conflicts between England and the USA concerning opium from 1800 onwards resulted in a loss of a serious world problem for England, whereas the USA inherited one. This developed far beyond its power, its understanding and—for some analysts—its ability and even willingness to solve it. The beginning of this drama until about 1950 was a main subject of this chapter.

It should certainly contribute to the lively debates about "formal US imperialism" which rage among US academics. The most logical way of dealing with this imperialism is to study not only its actions (attacks on foreign countries, exploitation of them, their religious or cultural conversion, etc.), but also the reactions of the victims. Recently, this approach received the name of 'imperial reciprocities'.[2]

This is defined using the very ambiguous center (metropolis)-periphery model. In the 1970s it was used for the first time (from Galtung to Gunder Frank or Wallerstein) to explain the effects of Western capitalism in the Third World. This largely uni-directional and soon outdated theory is not interesting for us, but some practical results of it as used by Alfred McCoy are.

According to him and his colleagues, the opium activities of American imperialism in, for instance, the Philippines were the start of the world's first "surveillance state".[3] This was imported during and after the First World War into the USA. The prohibition of opium in the Philippines became, therefore, the root of the American drug legislation and even of the modern *War On Drugs*. For him it is a good example of how a colony (= periphery) can function as a kind of testing ground for social and political reforms implemented at home (= center). As shown, however, the first example of a police state as a consequence of the Opium Problem was San Francisco in the 1880s. Therefore, the internal situation of the USA should be researched more carefully when looking for reasons leading to a War on Drugs after 1950.

Another crucial problem in American's foreign policy and its Asian opium policy as indicated by Bruce Cumings. He emphasized in 1999 that with the return of Hong Kong to China and the growing investment and trade ties with Taiwan and people of Chinese descent in Southeast Asia, a

---

[2] D. Owen, p. 10.

[3] Idem, p. 107 ff. He rightly criticized Max Weber for his one-sided definition of a state by its monopoly of legitimate use of physical power in a given territory. Weber did not understand that the modern state uses violence to penetrate into the privacy of its citizens.

development had been started comparable to that of Korea and Taiwan since the 1970s.

His advice was not to look for an aggressive US policy versus a new China like the Korea or Vietnam Wars. He argues that a 'wise policy begins with China's long-term humiliation at the hands of the West, and therefore Western humility'.[4] Herewith an alternative way of looking at new or old US-Chinese relations is given.

It is no luxury to view problems also from this angle, where even today voices and publications are asking for war with China: even by its very performance this country, apparently, threatens the political domination and economic hegemony of a troubled America.[5] Secret services, mostly highly involved in drugs policies, play(ed) a crucial role in Asian politics, but never in stimulating peaceful developments. The close relationship between imperialism and opium is modernized into opium policy as part of aggressive foreign policy. This should be discussed and not denied.

---

[4] B. Cumings, p. 170.

[5] See an article of Charles R. Smith (China and War, August 14, 2001) on archive. newsmax.com or the contribution of Dr.Jeffrey Record (Thinking about China and War, December 6, 2001) on www.airpower.au.af.mil/airchronicles/apj/apjo1/wino1/record.html which is particularly important since his institute at the Johns Hopkins University often did simulation war-games. In March 2009 some of them were leaked. Their conclusion: War-games against China had bad results for the USA!

PART SIX

THE VICTIMS

CHAPTER THIRTY

BLAMING THE CHINESE VICTIMS

> ' ... the use of opium is not a curse, but a comfort and benefit to the hardworking Chinese; that to many scores of thousands it has been productive of healthful sustentation and enjoyment.'

Messrs Jardine, Matheson & Co, opium dealers (1858).[1]

> 'We forced the Chinese Government to enter into a treaty to allow their subjects to take opium.'

Sir Rutherford Alcock (1871)[2]

Introduction

To introduce this last part, it is necessary to explain in a few words why and how victims have played an important role in this *History of the Opium Problem*. The obvious answer almost suffices: because the many-sided historical description of it above highlighted the kinds of institutionalized perpetrators who cannot act normally without making opium victims. They are mutually dependent on each other; they constitute a relationship. Thus, a description of the victims' positions must follow to create a comprehensive story and make a complicated definition of an *Opium Problem* possible (see part 7). Although this history could be called "perpetrator oriented", one may hope that this more or less abstract introduction and the following chapters provide enough compensation to give the alternative a reasonable profile.

As announced, in this book a "productive approach" of the Opium Problem in history was chosen: in short, for describing and analyzing the political economy of the problem mainly in the framework of Western imperialism and colonialism. Therefore, the relations between perpetrators and victims are perceived in this same framework. They differ greatly,

---

[1] J. Beeching, p. 263 combined with the slightly different wording in J. Spencer Hill, p. 31.

[2] Quoted by W. Willoughby, vol. II, p. 1094.

of course, in the development of the Opium Problem in European countries from which these perpetrators came. The relationship changes drastically in both histories but remains intact as indicated, for instance, in
the image: *the snake which bites in its own tail.*

In this "productive approach" victims cannot be perceived *as such*, nor
their suffering, while certainly solutions for their sorrows cannot be given
without referring to the *reasons* for their addiction. Analyses, descriptions
or explanations in a "productive approach" inevitably point to the role of
the state and its bureaucracy, military and police; large economic interests; opium production, trade or marketing; legitimising thoughts and so
on. We only arrive at the victims and their personal and dramatic stories
as derived from these "acts".

The opposite is much better known in narco-literature. It can be called
the "consumptive approach", which starts with the *personal* sufferings of
addicts and proceeds with the success or failures of their cure by religious,
medical, social or bureaucratic (police) workers; the success or failure of
the state to protect society from this drug menace which costs the taxpayer astronomical amounts of money. The bad guys, the mafiosi, are promoted as the most "beloved" targets in films, books or theater. This
approach is, as a rule, much more personal and emotional. In my view, it
is the main reason why a comprehensive picture of the social, economic
or political backgrounds of these dramas is seldom arrived at (or not).

It is logical that in this part Chinese victims, as the most spectacular of
all opium victims of the West, receive special attention within the framework of a "productive approach". Therefore, no pictures of emaciated
Chinese addicts sucking on their pipes in opium dens managed by other
mysterious Chinese, which were spread after 1850 through all Western
dailies and books for ambiguous reasons. Indian, Southeast Asian or
Indonesian addicts do not show up often. What will be discussed is, I
hope, appropriate also for these victim countries: China represents here
an "Oriental model", an image which was (and often still is) not at variance with the existing "Orientalism" in the minds of many or most
Western observers.

To choose the example of China as a victim country (Chinese victims
are derived from it, therefore) was not difficult since no other country
was attacked from all sides and by all Western countries including Japan:
all expected to find there the most abundant sources of wealth. The
attacks involving opium and weapons were as long-lasting and heavy as
the expectations were great and the disappointments severe: there were
many reasons to blame Chinese victims!

Understanding the victims' positions on this level, however, is not easy. How tricky a victim-perpetrator connection can be is demonstrated in the ongoing discussions concerning the most "spectacular" modern example, the ambiguous relation between Israel and Holocaust victims.[3] Through a notorious decision of the United Nations (1947), the pre-war Zionist and Jewish settlers of the British were allowed to establish a new state in Palestine and expelled nearly a million persons of the indigenous population and exploit and repress the remainder of these Palestinians on a massive scale. In the end the only legitimation or pretext was that *some* of its newly imported Europeans with a Jewish or Zionist background were victims of the Nazi regime (never more than 8% of the new Israeli population). One of the most unfortunate effects was that the Holocaust victims' position was immediately degraded through its use as a tool in an internationally criticized foreign and internal policy or, worst, as revengeful new perpetrators.

Many other examples can be given (Balkans, Kashmir, Rwanda, etc.) in which victims later became stupid perpetrators as well, forgetting which kind of injustice was done to themselves. Revenge at this level always means a bloody, long-lasting and difficult to pardon collective affair. In looking for solutions, one can never forget the *reasons* for all this bloodshed before blaming the original victims.

A victims discussion should be concentrated on the case at issue and on the right level. In this book, therefore, this is something like "massive addiction through opium by external (military) powers from the West during one and a half or three centuries". The roles of perpetrators, European and Chinese criminals and authorities alike should be highlighted as well on the same general level. Objections could be raised and criticized.

Under the influence of *present* positions or developments (from *after* 1950, the last year of this *History of the Opium Problem*), some scholars produce rather harsh judgments about a pre-1950 history. It is too easy to transform this into a demagogic trick. A scholarly discussion has to remain as "clean" as possible: we should, at least, differentiate between occasional expressions of someone's emotions and structural elements of a phenomenon; it seems obvious not to blame a whole society for the misdeeds

---

[3] H. Derks (2004), chapter 6 and 7. How ambiguous this relation is follows from the writings of Israeli historians like Tom Segev (*The Seventh Million*) and Idith Zertal (*Catastrophe to Power*) or, more recently, from Hajo Meijer (*The End of Jewishness*).

of one inhabitant or of a specific (criminal) coterie, and it is less obvious, but very understandable, not to blame earlier "good behavior" under the influence of later "bad behavior".

In blaming people, pejorative language is often used, while discrimination is normal. Here are two examples of how not to discuss our case ('blaming Chinese victims'): the first concerns my own writings below and the other is related to the highly interesting scholar Frank Dikötter, who seems to point to "Chinese racism" as a kind of excuse for Western racism. Below we shall discuss the main elements of this Western racism vis-à-vis China and the Chinese to show how untenable this position is.

An enthusiastic peer reviewer of this *History of the Opium Problem* also remarked in passing that I should avoid 'subjective comments' like 'mafia' when referring to the Jardines and Sassoons: 'they were simply doing what they knew how to do best, trade by all means, just like their Chinese counterparts'. Still, I decided in ch. 31 below not to alter this 'mafia' because of the many similarities to the classical and original mafia and to stress the remarkable position of these and similar gentlemen.

For decades both the Jardines and Sassoons were involved in the illegal drugs trade, smuggling, probably piracy. Later, when the former left the opium business, the Sassoons became increasingly involved in pure modern gangsterism (see below). Indeed, this was 'trade by all means' and on purpose, but normal trade is *by definition* peaceful and legal and not involved in illegal products which are seen officially and by Jardine himself as immoral—also in the beginning of the 19th-century. The many Chinese prohibitions, the debates in the English Parliament at the time or the discussion with Gutzlaff (ch. 6) are illuminating in this respect.

The Sassoon family, even more than the Jardines, Mathesons or Dents, was indeed a family (the classical meaning of 'mafia') which cooperated with similar criminal 'families' like The Ezra gang. Last but not least, all of them were knighted and arrived in the position of all later drugs-*barons*. Altogether, there are quite objective reasons to use a label like 'mafia'.

The Dikötter example is more important as an excellent representative of the "consumer approach" as defined above. Here it concerned his use of "racism", a qualification often used when blaming victims. Dikötter tries to prove his case by extensively quoting some journalists and an "Overseas Chinese", Su Xiaokang (1991). This person, living in the USA, sees "Chineseness" primarily as a matter of biological descent, physical appearance and congenital inheritance: one is Chinese 'by virtue of one's blood', whatever his/her social background, birthplace in this immense country, profession, ethnic allegiance, language, etc.[4]

It is already remarkable that Dikötter pays attention to this fully out-dated and controversial opinion, knowing its consequences when used at state levels and in state propaganda. He also quotes two other examples: a very primitive form of racism relative to black people in the writings of Kang Youwei (1858-1927)[5] and a pure reproduction of anti-Chinese racism transformed into a positive exclamation about his China ('The greatest force is common blood', etc.) of Sun Yatsen (1866-1925).

The former is perceived as a monarchist or a reactionary virtuosi but, in my view, he is a perfect example of a national-socialist ideologue. Anyway, in China he is also considered a highly controversial political thinker. It is not necessary to criticize Sun Yatsen, father of the Chinese Republic, for his occasional statement. In a European racist discourse, however, his dictum that 'the Chinese belong to the yellow race' can only be supported by radical racists (see below).

Dikötter's aim with this discussion remains unclear and is based on very shallow grounds. Youwei's and Sun Yatsen's opinions reproduce the modernized Western ideological choice in China around 1910. I cannot discover more than a concern about *present* African students, who are 'periodically' subjected to racial attacks at some Chinese university, or about Tibetans and Uighurs who are officially discriminated also on racial grounds. To relate Sun Yatsen and the other to African students or Muslim Uighurs is a "mission impossible".

No context or proportionality of the case is given. Racism in a country with hundreds of ethnic minorities certainly exists locally, but it must be underdeveloped in all respects and cannot be equated with "Chinese Racism". For instance, tensions between local Han versus other tribal peo-ples are expressed high in the north in Chinese Mongolia but also in the deep south (see Yunnan below): they are fully unrelated and not compa-rable since the local circumstances are very different for all parties involved. Only outsiders can construct some commonalities.

Compared to what the enlightened societies in Europe, the United States or Australia demonstrate at present in this respect ("gypsies" are still killed in several East European countries like the Mexicans along the border with the USA; people with an Islamic belief are seriously discrimi-nated against in nearly all Western Christian countries, and so on); com-

---

[4] F. Dikötter, B. Sautman (ed..), p. 1.
[5] See D. Leese (ed.), p. 118-121 and passim.

pared to all this, "racism of some Chinese" must be seen as insignificant.[6] This, however, can never be an excuse for acting in a racist way or being silent about it.

Concerning the opium use itself is Newman's and his pupil Dikötter's argument of interest

> that nineteenth century opium use was a pleasurable and largely harmless aspect of popular sociability and that relatively few users were addicted.[7]

Newman's remarkable view is discussed below. Here I refer only to the relevant criticism of Harrison who points to the untenable downplaying of the socio-economic effects of drug use. Her research in the Shanxi villages reveals how the effect of drug taking on rural family finances was often devastating. It is also important that she considered the transition from opium to refined narcotics like morphine and heroin as a problem in its own right.

The last thing one should say about the drug-scene in post-1911 China, as described below, is that it concerns 'a pleasurable and largely harmless' constellation! Anyway, in this way the case of the opium victims was blurred by unnecessary "noise". The obvious question is now how and why are the Chinese opium victims blamed for "their" sins?

An original Image[8]

There is the indestructible image of "the Chinese" as both opium producer and addict formed from about 1870 onwards. Pictures of Chinese smoking pipes in an opium den were an absolute hype in all dailies and illustrated journals. In the 1960s every flu was called a Mao-flu. Even in the 1970s in the Netherlands and elsewhere, using heroin—a typical

---

[6] Dikötter should listen to F. Dikötter (1995), p. 6, where this author warns: 'It is dangerous to reduce the cultural categories of a period to the expressions of a dozen authors, and the hagiographic conventions which endlessly parade figures ...' All this cannot have the aim to disqualify Frank Dikötter (and his co-authors). Below, many excellent publications by him are used, and F. Dikötter, L. Laamann, Z. Xun is a highly informative tome concerning the "consumptive approach", the alternative of the "productive approach" adhered to in this *History of the Opium Problem*.

[7] H. Harrison, p. 154. It is a pity that I came across Harrison's long article too late to use it in a proper way below. I am anyway glad that she can support my rather positive conclusion about the role of the Communist Party in eradicating the drug culture in the 1950s (see p. 176).

[8] See for more background the article of Andreas Pigulla in: D. Leese (ed.), p. 110-113.

European chemical product—was called 'chase the dragon' and even 'to chinese'. Heroin itself is also named 'Chinese White', notwithstanding its invention and exploitation by German-American pharmaceutical firms like Merck or Bayer.

An older and well-known characteristic is of the Chinese or China as *Weltfremd*, isolated from the rest of the world. We have already met this time and time again. It was evident in the English offensive which already started at the end of the 18th-century in McCartney's opium mission. Not much later seducers like the opium dealers Jardine, Matheson & Co, Sassoon, Dent and politicians from Palmerston to John Adams attacked the Chinese reluctance to accept opium as dangerous isolationism, xeno-phobia, anti-Western and anti-free trade enmity and so on. Old and new prejudices and half-truisms were mixed up to win a propaganda battle in which the real victims became transformed into the offenders. Present historians continue too often in this mood, as quoted in the *Preface*, or by declaring out of the blue that opium

> was ... an essential part of the lifestyle of millions of Chinese, for whom opium smoking was a social relaxation, a release from pain or a temporary escape from a miserable existence. With such an insistent demand for the drug ... the opium trade was able to continue into the twentieth-century despite official disapproval in China ...[9]

However, from about 1900 onwards, not only Chinese governments but all kinds of Chinese victims from Nationalists and Communists to Republicans started to organize all forms of protest against opium-impe-rialism: it was foreign to Chinese traditions and cultures, as well as being an economic assault destabilizing society. It is the time when industrial-ization and urbanization created a large Chinese audience for these com-plaints.

Foreigners reacted with a virulent racism. This was widespread in the United States, Europe or Australia and not confined to foreigners in China. It made serious victims among the overseas Chinese as well. It is from this time that China definitely took another direction of develop-ment and very quickly became a highly distinctive society. And 'never the twain shall meet', Kipling's famous dictum, was repeated time and again, as if there existed a necessity to do this.[10]

---

[9] R. K. Newman (1989), p. 525, 526.
[10] See an interesting discussion around this subject in M. Jacques.

Something of these images was true for the simple reason that the Chinese territory was as large as Europe, and they never could "handle" more. We do not accuse the ancient Romans of conquering only half of Europe or of knowing nothing of the Chinese. They were contemporaries of the Qin and Han dynasties, the Great Walls of which attract more tourists than the Colosseum in Rome, let alone the Hadrian's Wall in Britain. Like the Romans, the Qin and Han were always busy with border conflicts as a routine matter, so why not perceive the attack of the 'foreign white devils' as just the next border conflict?

This kind of reasoning is largely nonsense; underestimating its propagandistic "value" in the intolerant Christian societies is unwise as well. A remarkable example of its impact can be found early in the quite learned, liberal and Lutheran *Staatswörterbuch* (1857) in which one can read a theory about "the" Chinese: they are not the original people, but invaded the present area thousands of years ago from the Northwest, ousting the original people to the periphery before they themselves arrived at last at the coast:

> Because they were from time immemorial an agricultural people from the interior and surrounded by uncivilized tribes, the Chinese only could develop themselves without any impulse from outside. Thanks to this situation the Chinese people became one-sided, limited, extreme conceited [*dünkelhaft eingebildet*] and remained so after arriving at the coast of the wide ocean: still they communicated insufficiently with other less cultivated peoples like themselves ...[11]

And when "the" Chinese started such a distorted communication, they could not learn anything from the other, 'not in agriculture, industry or trade and not in religion, art or science'. This is, of course, incompatible with modern science from the beginning to the end, but still a substantial part of the discriminating "yellow race theory".

It is only possible to come up with general characteristics of "the" Chinese if one takes the impossible bird's eye view in which all Chinese are treated alike. Even after the long-lasting, unifying influences of the CCP—rather unique in Chinese history—there are currently hundreds of different ethnic groups with rather contradictory characteristics (from language to lifestyle or economic performance) and remarkable differences between hundreds of regions of this immense country.

Let's first take opium as "typically Chinese" to demonstrate the untenability of this generalization.

---

[11] J. Bluntschli (ed.), vol. 2, p. 440.

The Addict "by nature"

Long before the British, French, Dutch and other traders and smugglers did their rather nasty work in the Chinese realm against the will of Chinese governments and laws of the country, opium was used in China *as medicine*. We can safely conclude that until the arrival of the 'foreign devils', a select group of Chinese (in a select part of this vast country) used opium in very small quantities among the hundreds of other vegetable medicines. And probably, who knows, a few became addicts. They could buy it and learned how to handle it from Arab caravan traders or from the many visits of Chinese fleets to the lands in the Indian Ocean or Arabian Sea.

Another use of opium in China was in some religious rituals like those concerning the Tsao Wang or Kitchen God in North China. He is one of the oldest household deities who 'looks after the hearth' and 'has constituted himself the censor of morals of the family'. As such, he is perceived as 'the connecting link between God and Man' who makes an annual report about the family to be laid before the All Highest.[12] To make this report as favorable as possible and to ensure that he will say only kind things or even to silence him altogether, the mouth of his picture or sculpture is smeared with something like opium (in other cases one used wine) to render him drowsy at the time of making his report.

During the Manchu era there existed a sect of girls in some secret guilds like the 'Golden Orchid Society' who vowed never to marry. Breaking their celibacy by enforced marriage regularly led to suicide by using white arsenic or opium.[13]

A rather famous historian of Chinese history, Wolfgang Eberhard, wrote: 'The Chinese were familiar with opium under its Near-Eastern name, *afyûn* (*a-fu-yung*) probably since Sung times.'[14] He, first, cannot provide any proof for this and uses 'the' and 'familiar' as if all Chinese at the time knew about all forms of the drug. For a period of at least four hundred and at most seven hundred years later, Eberhard continues the former quote with the first concrete and very symptomatic information:

> In the Ming era, the emperor received 200 pounds for himself and 100 for the empress from Thailand, but from the eighteenth-century on, opium arrived in China from the coast. At the time of Ch'ien-lung [1711-1799; H.D.], the court received between 200 and 1,000 crates from the Portu-

---

[12] V. R. Burkhardt, vol 1, p. 76, 77.
[13] Idem, p. 108.
[14] W. Eberhard, p. 298 also for the following quotation.

guese. In 1729, the government confiscated 34 pounds in the storeroom of a merchant in Chang-chou (Fukien). Thus, opium is not a drug, recently imported into China, but has a long history in China.

The opium presents for some Ming emperor and his wife were apparently nothing but an accident in a period of three hundred years and did not affect the 200 million Chinese inhabitants at the time. The information tells us also about who gave the opium: indeed, 'foreign devils'. Their big opium present was enough to addict the whole court and, anyway, aimed at provoking an opium market. We do not know whether it was repeated, but it was confined to the court only and had exactly the "wrong" effect: the emperor started a new offensive against opium from 1729 onwards! And that for a ridiculous quantity of 34 pounds in the house of a coastal merchant several thousand miles from the court? Perhaps this was not as ridiculous as it seems, because the next information is about the other classical phenomenon around opium trade: smuggling of the now prohibited substance and illicit distribution from the coast to some interior.

During the Yongzheng reign in four coastal prefectures, sworn brotherhoods started their organized criminal work in the use and distribution of opium around 1755.[15] As usual, their work also led to fierce village conflicts in those prefectures, reason enough for a government to interfere. At this time the only sources of the opium were Bengal and some Middle Eastern locations, while the trade was largely a monopoly of 'foreign devils': Dutch, English or Portuguese traders from Macao. In a mild form (compared to what happened in the next century[16]), all the ingredients of the Opium Problem were available: foreign opium assaults versus government defence and in between, the market battle of smugglers and criminals concerning a very small and illicit market.

Until about 1750 it cannot be true that Chinese other than courtiers and the well-to-do used opium *sometimes* as a luxury or that *some* physicians knew how to use it as a medicine *if it was available to them*. The other ritual uses of opium mentioned are confined to very specific occasions or locations from which it is uncertain whether it was really opium of the many available herbal remedies (raw, prepared?) which was used.

Indeed, from about 1790 when the British and other opium traders arrived for the first time in Canton, everything changed in a fundamental way: the new era of mass-produced and mass-imported illicit opium had

---

[15] J. Lipman, S. Harrell (ed.), p. 43.
[16] See also idem, p. 52.

arrived, the smokers followed. Not only governments but also the Chinese opposition, the most spectacular being the Taiping, were against opium production and consumption:

> Although opium had been smoked in China for many years, it became a serious problem after the beginning of opium importation from India. Taiping leaders had witnessed the smuggling of opium and the resulting Opium War as well as the demoralizing effect the smoking produced among the people. China's defeat in the Opium War must have given them an added cause for wanting to eliminate all opium smoking.[17]

So, telling an uninformed Western audience that the "Chinese knew about opium already for centuries before we arrived" as an obvious defense of their own criminal activities is one of those examples of the political use of generalizing statements and of a bad Western consciousness.

Next, we fix the beginning of the Opium Problem in China during the British and other Westerners' gradual organization of the assault in the First and Second Opium Wars. The details are discussed in part 2. Palmerston's operations, the failed opposition of Gladstone and others, and the hypocritical way treaties were made with China and immediately broken are sketched. The follow-up is also completely under the constant pressure of the English. An example from an insider:

> During the years immediately following the Opium War, the British Government made repeated efforts to induce the Chinese authorities to legitimize the importation of opium into its borders. Lord Palmerston, in 1843, instructed the British representative in China "to endeavor to make some arrangement with the Chinese Government for the admission of opium into China as an article of lawful commerce"; and advised Sir Henry Pottinger that he should "avail himself of every possible opportunity strongly to impress upon the Chinese plenipotentiary ... how much it would be for the interest of that Government to legalize the trade.[18]

Pottinger started his networking through private conversations with the Chinese anti-opium commissioners. The latter asked the Englishman why the foreigners would not act fairly towards them by prohibiting the growth of the poppy in India and thus effectually stopping 'a traffic so pernicious to the human race'. Pottinger's answer is worth recalling:

---

[17] V. Shih, p. 226. Poems were made to express the hatred for opium and opium-smokers (id., p. 228); the Taiping social policy was wholly directed toward the prohibition of opium (id., p. 443); opium smokers were simply threatened with execution (id., p. 70).

[18] W. Willoughby, vol. II, p. 1092; J. Rowntree, p. 68-73 about the "negotiations" of Sir Henri Pottinger.

This, he said, in constituency with our constitutional law, could not be done; and, he added, that even if England chose to exercise so arbitrary power over her tillers of the soil, it would not check the evil, so far as the Chinese were concerned, while the cancer remained uneradicated among themselves, but that it would merely throw the market into other hands. It, in fact, ... rests entirely with yourselves. If your people are virtuous, they will desist from the evil practice; and if your officers are incorruptible and obey your rulers, no opium can enter your country. The discouragement of the growth of the poppy in our territories rests principally with you, for nearly the entire produce cultivated in India travels east to China. If, however, the habit has become a confirmed vice, and you feel that your power is at present inadequate to stay its indulgence, you may rest assured your people will procure the drug in spite of every enactment.[19]

It is an answer worth of a diplomat of "Perfide Albion": blaming the victims for everything at the end of the First Opium War, while negotiating the Treaty of Nanking (1842), the most humiliating treaty the Chinese had to sign. As a reward for his service, Pottinger became the first governor of Hong Kong, from then on the center of the opium trade.

Notwithstanding the financial temptation to follow this diplomatic language of a narco-military order, the Chinese emperor refused to take the step to legalize opium. He even replied:

It is true that I cannot prevent the introduction of the poison; gain-seeking and corrupt men will, for profit and sensuality, defeat my wishes; but nothing will induce me to derive a revenue from a vice and the misery of my people.

A new Opium War and new humiliations further, the Chinese still retained their objections.[20] The possibility to connect practical consequences to

---

[19] Quoted in J. Rowntree, p. 72, 73 from the diary of a Captain Loch, author of *Campaign in China* (ca. 1860). Rowntree adds that he hoped the Chinese had insufficient knowledge of "our constitutional law", so that they were debarred 'from following the extraordinary propositions' of Pottinger.

[20] It remains an incredible coincidence that the English commander responsible for the Second Opium War and the most serious devastation, Lord Elgin (the son of the Elgin who had stolen the Karyathides from the Parthenon in Athens, whereupon they were called the "Elgin Marbles"), later showed strong disapproval of the opium traffic and of the two wars which were unjustifiable upon the part of the British Empire (quoted in Idem, vol. 2, p. 1094). He wrote in his memories: 'I have hardly alluded in my ultimatum to that wretched question of the *Arrow* which is a scandal to us, and is so considered, I have reason to know, by all except the few who are personally compromised.' And elsewhere: 'I thought bitterly of those who for the most selfish objects are trampling under foot this ancient civilization.' Etc. See J. Beeching, p. 318 about the destructive plundering of Peking by the English and French. The disgust of Lord Elgin is worthless since he was responsible for the conduct of his soldiers.

this moral appeal, however, was bombed out of their hands. Forty years later as the agitation in England against the constant opium imports from India reached considerable proportions, the absurd attempt was made to blame the Chinese themselves: 'to show that the legalization of the importation of opium had been freely assented to by China'.[21]

Half a century after the last war China could repeat its criticism with some initial success. It definitely succeeded in solving its Opium Problem after 1949. It is, therefore, worth considering the following question.

Who and How in the Chinese Opium Scene

After the opium wars, the important territorial losses, the huge payments and so on, the anti-opium campaigner Joshua Rowntree (1906) concluded nearly correctly:

> Great Britain had at last accomplished its desire, so long worked for, so little avowed. The Government of India was no longer to be the chief accomplice, the unsleeping partner of Chinese smugglers. The great drug trade was regularized by law. China had yielded to steady, continuous pressure, which it had not the strength to resist.[22]

This is nearly correct since these "Chinese smugglers" were the small fish in the English and American business of Messrs. Jardine, Matheson & Co, of the Sassoons or the Russells.

It is also obvious that once the foreigners imported opium into the coastal ports, there was a need for some Chinese merchants to bring it into the interior, if they were convinced that it was profitable to do this. Here the foreigners practically created a new opium market and found willing customers. The means to do this involved corrupting key-persons in bureaucracy or trade (direct contempt of law), smuggling and keeping every phase of the process in their foreign hands, (in)directly threatening foreign revenge.

Take the example of the coastal port of Tianjin in the north directly on the road to Beijing which received (in)directly foreign import in the 19th-century:

---

[21] W. Willoughby, vol. II, p. 1094. A most important contribution to this problem is G. Lee, who started from the pioneering Berridge-Edwards study used above at the end of part 2.

[22] J. Rowntree, p. 93.

... foreign goods and foreign opium. Merchants from the interior sold their products in Tianjin and bought opium with the proceeds; just before the Opium War, Tianjin was the central point for drug shipments into North China.[23] 'In the first years of the treaty port ... opium and cotton cloth dominated the import trade. From the end of the Sino-Japanese War (1895) to World War I, the scope of foreign activity in China greatly expanded. In Tianjin the net volume of foreign trade increased, in spite of reduced activity during the Boxer Rebellion and the last few years of the Qing dynasty. Cotton yarn, cloth, sugar, kerosene, dyes, and opium were the major imports. During and after World War I, many foreign firms began to import military hardware for warlord customers.[24]

This shows the differences between the beginning of the 19th-century and the end. But it is too easy to think that the Chinese merchants simply bought the stuff at the quay or embankment and departed for the interior as missionaries suggested (see below):

From 1860 until 1949, foreigners controlled every stage of the passage of goods into and out of the port of Tianjin.[25]

Here "every" must be stressed because their control covered the customs service, foreign loans and money, ships (mostly owned by the British and later by the Japanese), shipyards, the business of unloading ships, transferring the cargoes to barges destined for the interior, and so on.

Actual trading was carried on by the foreign-owned yanghang, which usually hired a Chinese comprador to act as agent with native merchants.[26]

An insider, an important civil servant of the British Empire, Maurice Collis (1889-1973), reminds us about the early 19th-century start of this business in his history of the opium trade and opium wars:

The Company [the EIC] controlled the cultivation of opium in India, having in fact almost a world monopoly of the drug. The eleven million dollars sold by the country firms in China was procured at Company auctions held annually at Calcutta. Thus, the Company was the source of the opium traffic.[27]

Again foreigners controlled the proliferation of the drug from the earliest stage, not only the foreign merchants and their factory helpers in Canton, but also missionaries were 'attractive potential allies for merchants while

---

[23] G. Hershatter, p. 12.
[24] Idem, p. 26.
[25] Idem, p. 27.
[26] Idem, p. 27.
[27] M. Collis, p. 71.

also giving accounts of their mission a literary appeal' and by influencing 'the crafting of foreign policy for the Opium War as the political situation in China intensified due to opium trafficking'.[28]

A century passed between this start and the situation in Tianjin. Yet present historians still blame the Chinese. For example, the simple comment made by amateur historian Priscilla Napier. She excuses, first, the EIC's opium monopoly as 'a necessity' thanks to the Napoleonic wars, and she continues with:

> At the other side of the world, thousands of South Chinese seemed unwilling to endure the continuous toil, poverty and hardship of their lives without opium's instant but fatal alleviation.[29]

The following reasoning of a professional historian about the situation at the end of the 19th-century is already more sophisticated:

> Western liberals and missionaries argued with growing passion that the West was guilty of corrupting China. The Chinese said Western opium was deeply responsible for China's weakness and decline. None of it was true. What was keeping Chinese from Christianity was Christianity, which was deeply subversive of China's social order, while the people preaching it were of course foreign agents. The truth was that no one, Chinese or foreigners, knew how to persuade Chinese not to grow or use opium. Still less could anyone prevent foreign merchants from shipping it into a very willing market. In any case, the great majority of China's opium supply was by the 1860s and '70s being grown at home. One guesstimate is that by 1900 there were about 40 million consumers of opium in China, about 13.5-15 million of them addicts.[30]

Let's say it again: from early on, opium was imported into China; it was not home grown. That was the case in the 16th and 17th-centuries when opium was imported from the Middle East as medicine. This is fully irrelevant for Gelber's reasoning, however. Opium as a result of "legal" *Chinese* poppy growing started *after* the two Opium Wars.

Before those events Chinese who tried to produce opium or to grow poppies risked being killed because it was not only forbidden by Chinese law, but there was also an active prosecution and repression from, at least,

---

28 B.L. Fischer, abstract.

29 P. Napier, p. 65. Elsewhere (p. 91) she gave another classical "argument" in the framework of "blaming the victims": 'Although the Chinese had been growing and eating opium on a minor scale since the 700s, the habit of smoking it on a considerable scale did not begin till the 17th-century.' No source is mentioned for this wisdom.

30 H. Gelber, p. 223, 224. For alternative consumption figures see Idem, p. 451, 452 note 8.

around 1800 onwards. Foreign merchants were prevented officially from importing opium, whereupon the 'foreign devils' (mainly English, English-backed Indians and Americans) organized extensive smuggling activities.

As this illicit trade became effectively blocked by the Chinese authorities, the English (supported by the French) opened up the opium market by the use of substantial *military violence*. That is the truth which is not only neglected by Gelber and others, but actively denied since he also claimed that the Chinese 'emperor decided to make war on the laws of supply and demand'[31] or that the Chinese 'did want to buy more ... opium from India'[32] instead of pointing to the cutthroat consumption to which they were destined by the English in the 19th-century.

Whether, furthermore, Chinese opium was home-grown during most of this century cannot be concluded from the previous analyses. In the next chapter the Chinese consumption pattern will be discussed in all possible detail with *nearly* the same result. Still, a major question remains unanswered: who owned, initiated or financed this poppy cultivation in China? This would be a good research project for Chinese scholars.

Thus, many "foreign devils" knew perfectly well how to make some Chinese into opium addicts: by military violence, by importing mass-produced opium and by organizing the supply far into the interior by various means (see the Tianjin example). Of course, it is self-evident that after 1860 producers started to grow poppies in Chinese regions where this was possible like Yunnan.

However, it is easily forgotten that prolonged military violence was needed in one way or another: not only the Opium Wars or the rather continuous fights against smugglers of all sorts, but the very rebellious period also caused warlords to stimulate or organize opium production and trade to pay for their weapons and keep their soldiers satisfied. That started during the Taiping and other revolts and continued after 1900 to 1945 (see ch. 31).[33]

---

[31] Idem, p. 186 which contains also a nearly explicit defense of the British assault: the smuggling of opium (by the British, etc.) is 'China's problem, no one else's', etc.

[32] Idem, p. 173.

[33] Regarding the warlord practice, Gelber reports only one case (p. 275), the alleged Mao's opium trade, without mentioning any source. He not only neglects the overwhelming practice of trade in opium and other narcotics of Chiang Kai-shek and other warlords, he also neglects the professional literature of—say—a profound drugs and Chinese historian like W.O. Walker III, chapter 4 and 5. If Mao dealt in opium, Walker should have mentioned this immediately (with sources!). See also C.Trocki (1999a), p. 134 who mentions for this one source, but of a suspect kind, a young American author, E. Devido, without further experience except in Taiwanese and Buddhist relations.

In short, it is purely blaming the victims to suggest that "the Chinese" formed a 'very willing market' or that 'nobody knew' how to stop this mass addiction. It was nearly stopped between 1908 and 1918,[34] and it certainly *was stopped* after 1945 by the Maoist regime: by ending foreign opium import; by harsh measures against the Chinese producers and traders; by mild but firm procedures for the addicts. In a few years time the opium problem belonged to the past in China! In the century before this remarkable date, it seemed as if the whole world was attacking and addicting China from all sides and with all possible weapons, as will be demonstrated below.

The Religious Assault

Blaming the Chinese opium victims was also a result of Western religious activities.[35] It was remarkable that clergymen like the Reverend Charles Gutzlaff were highly active in spreading opium by means of the Holy Cross. This is documented also in Maurice Collis's report about the relationship between Gutzlaff and the opium tycoon Jardine.[36] The aim of the priest was so high,

> to convert to Protestantism at last the teeming millions of a country, which for millenniums had been plunged in darkness, and bring to it not only light and truth but the uncounted blessings of free commercial intercourse with those chosen nations to which God had revealed Himself. As Mr. Jardine had so truly said, the exchange of commodities more respectable than

---

[34] As is apparently proved by J. Madancy, but see R.K. Newman (1989) and next chapter.

[35] That is not new information: an unexpected announcement comes from the German race theoretician W. Schallmayer, p. 283 ff. who provides numerous examples of the low intellectual level of missionaries, their irritating behavior always under the umbrella of foreign arms, the many unfounded prejudices and disdain for the Chinese culture. His main target is the famous American missionary and author A.H. Smith, and his main support is apparently the one-liner of Prince Kung (ca. 1870): 'Do away with missionaries and opium, and our mutual troubles are gone as well!' In addition, Schallmayer criticizes the very superficial knowledge about China among the German population.

[36] M. Collis, p. 82 ff. For Gutzlaff see also C. Carr, p. 47 ff. and Th. Klein, R. Zöllner (ed.). This last reader shows that it is easy for Gutzlaff to substitute the qualifications "stubborn colonial bureaucrat", "fundamentalist missionary", "non-scrupulous merchant in East Asia" or "marketing genius". Indeed, these qualifications concentrated in one person, named Gutzlaff, deliver the appropriate range of attitudes demonstrated by the foreign missionaries in China or other parts of East Asia. It is far from a 'natural inclination' of missionaries to condemn opium consumption as R. Newman, p. 768 thinks. See recently B.L Fischer, chapter IV, p. 245-355 about Gutzlaff, in particular 'Gutzlaff, Opium Merchant', p. 261 ff., 322 ff.

opium was impossible unless funds were provided by sale of the latter. And there must be commerce if there was to be evangelization; the two were indissolubly bound together.[37]

Collis stresses that we must not forget that the 'rubbish' this reverend and his tycoon communicated was the opinion of the largest majority of the English and far beyond: the EIC, the Parliament, all Europeans held the conversion of the Chinese to Christianity 'to be highly desirable'. Notwithstanding our knowledge about this religious adventurer with his extensive opium network, it is still a remarkable surprise for present-day Christian historians when one discovers:

> Westerners and opium were associated in the minds of the Chinese, who blamed the foreigners for bringing opium to China and addicting the Chinese to it in an effort to weaken them so that Westerners could gain more privileges from the Chinese government.[38]

Immediately after this correct conclusion Lodwick, who aims at describing the heroic fight of American Protestant missionaries in China against opium, neutralizes this statement in the classical Christian way by insisting that

> smuggling opium into China in the early years of the nineteenth-century could never have taken place if Chinese themselves had not been the foreigners' accomplices who transported the drug into the interior for sale to other Chinese.

This almost incorrect conclusion (see previous section) leads directly to the old game of blaming the victims, who must anyway be converted to a foreign belief system: they are sinners, and if they could be converted to this Christianity (a project that was too difficult and unsuccessful, as was generally the case throughout Asia), they remained an inferior kind of Christian because the so-called "yellow race" was "racially impure" for too many Europeans and Americans.

This ends also in the classical mistake of substituting the behavior of some individual Chinese for that of the whole nation, culture, etc. and the reverse. Basic to these mistakes are the attempts (often deliberate) to

---

[37] M. Collis, p. 84.

[38] K. Lodwick, p. 2. In fact, the same opinion as Gelber as quoted above. The very American Protestant B. Fischer, who has many interesting things to say about Gutzlaff's opium gospel + bible books business, also demonstrates why historical understanding must fail here: he remains preaching against the sinner Gutzlaff. The latter did not understand that 'the good news that Christ's atoning sacrifice was available to save all people' (p. 267) independent of material objects like a Bible ('part of Western intellectual property') and opium from the West.

Ill. 30. Open Air Preaching. China Inland Mission, 1892
Source: en.Wikipedia.org: 'Open Air Preaching' by a China Inland Mission, London.

avoid discussing the context or proportions of the behavior, thought or action: how many people in a given time or place can be "blamed"? And why is this relevant? Are they public or private persons? And so on.

An defender of the missionary position at the time, Spencer Hill, tried to be as concrete as possible in his research and concluded, therefore:

> ... the alleged insincerity of the Chinese proved on investigation to be due, partly to administrative impotence, partly and chiefly to violent action on our part and our practical encouragement of the unlawful trade.[39]

---

[39] J. Spencer Hill, p. 92.

Lodwick also points to a specific kind of hypocrisy within the Christian circles. For the missionaries

> opium addicts were untrustworthy and hence banned from church membership. With so many Chinese automatically excluded from the possibility of conversion, missionaries began to campaign against the drug.[40]

Although these missionaries acknowledged the disadvantage of the foreigner-opium association and although they must have had knowledge about the recent opium propaganda of colleagues and countrymen, they paradoxically identified the opium evils of Chinese social and political life with its non-Christian religion and morality. It was a consequence of their dominant position, spatially as well as culturally, as described clearly by Paul Cohen:

> The missionaries lived and worked in the highly organized structure of the mission compound, which resulted in their effective segregation ... The missionaries really did not want to enter the Chinese world any more than they had to. Their whole purpose was to get the Chinese to enter theirs.[41]

In addition, Lodwick does not make obvious remarks about the era, the 19th-century, in which one revolutionary movement after the other developed and criminals—always in need of money—were found "all over the place".[42] No obvious remarks were made either about the many underpaid corrupt bureaucrats, who were very helpful in spreading opium. Let us not forget either that the enormous extent of China does not allow for abstract generalizations.

Of course, Lodwick also "forgets" that in a rebellious and hunger-stricken China, it was very difficult for the provincial or imperial authorities (who nearly all forbade opium consumption as a luxury, not as a drug in medical treatment) to control the thousands of kilometers of coastlines or the criminal helpers of the foreign smugglers.[43] Aside from the possibility that the Royal Navy was aiding these British and American smugglers. The existence of these categories and circumstances cannot be an excuse for foreigners to deliberately dope parts of a population.[44] Ultimately, the

---

[40] K. Lodwick, p. 181.

[41] Quoted in Albert Feuerwerker's contribution to J. Fairbank (ed.), p. 172. Here also useful data about the many kinds of missionaries (Idem, p. 165-177).

[42] D. Richards, p. 162.

[43] A contemporary like J. Spencer Hill, p. 93, mentioned the difficulties that the central Chinese government was unable to control the provinces (Taiping, etc.) and that the English should help the central government. This was not done, and one gets the strong impression that the English did the reverse.

[44] See C.Trocki (1999a), p. 124, about the exaggerations of the missionary Edkins.

largest mistake of the foreign missionaries and their present historians was that only a very few individuals among them were brave enough to blame the foreign assault *as such* and blame the introduction of opium as a *foreign* assault on the minds of the Chinese.

What stopped them from doing this was their racist attitude. A few examples suffice here before I elaborate on this theme in the following section. In the swelling choir of moral anti-opium critics in the 1880s, Spencer Hill can be viewed as an honest man with a profound knowledge of the history and even economics of the opium traffic. But even he accepts highly dubious opinions as if 'the sentiments of morality and the powers of self-control are the weakest and most uncertain' among the Chinese:

> In them the animal and sensuous elements of their nature are most fully developed, while their relish of momentary and immediate pleasures is particularly keen and regardless of the consequences, a combination of characteristics which renders them specially liable to, and unable to resist, any temptation that may be presented to them.[45]

This, however, was the reason for him to accuse the British ('a nation great and powerful', etc.) 'to take advantage of the weakness or the vice' of the Chinese instead of caring, protecting and helping these poor creatures to overcome their mental backwardness. (And to act like this, one is, of course, in need of an army of missionaries as, later, development workers in Western aid programs.)

Everywhere in the world opium or its derivatives have been prescribed for many ailments: in Western wars it is popular among soldiers as painkiller, etc. As a luxury, Westerners drank or injected the stuff; in India it was eaten:

> The Chinese alone chose to consume the drug by smoking, and apparently this difference made the Westerners view the Chinese addicts with disgust. ... opium was smoked in public dens. This visible use conflicted with Western standards of propriety and added to the foreigners' contempt for the Chinese.[46]

J. Spencer Hill, chapter 2 is probably the exception to the rule. He rightly bases his analysis of the "morality of the opium traffic" on: 'The history of the trade in Opium ... was carried on mainly by British subjects with the support and protection of their government, in open defiance of the rulers of China and in direct contravention of the laws of that empire' (Idem, p. 29).

[45] J. Spencer Hill, p. 56.

[46] K. Lodwick, p. 4. This smoking story is a very strange one, because from the production side (the whole rather complicated treatment of poppy into consumable opium),

Lodwick provides other astonishing examples of missionary tactics like the one of an archdeacon who told the *Society for the Suppression of the Opium Trade*: when preaching to the Chinese, 'when someone shouts out, "Who sells Opium?", my answer is, "Who smokes the Opium?" I have thus silenced them hundreds of times'.[47] A classical demagogic trick by equating producers with consumers.

This had apparently insufficient effect because in the 1890s there was 'the almost universal Chinese idea' that the missionaries themselves were strongly involved in the opium business, so much so that the term 'Jesus opium' was in use everywhere. Small wonder that many missionaries found the opium question so embarrassing that they were reluctant to admit they were citizens of the British Empire or the USA and transformed themselves into Chinese, including a queue. Remember there was a treaty between the USA and China (1881), which prohibited Americans from engaging in the opium trade. The immediate response to the treaty was the racist *Chinese Exclusion Act* of 1882, a significant move in identifying a group seen as non-assimilable and threatening.[48] No single American missionary organization protested against this law.

The position of the missionaries was not only determined by their perception of China and the Chinese or their intolerant behavior. According to many analysts one has to see their position within the imperialist exploitation system. America's *ad hoc*

> colonial administration was often held together not by a strong civil service but by the army and the navy ... aided in considerable measure by a strong voluntarist ethic in the nongovernmental sector in which services were contracted out to missionaries, the YMCA, and other nongovernmental organizations. [49]

The American empire had 900 missionaries in China in 1890, while 30 years later there were 14,000 which largely argued that the 'American

---

smoking is not the most obvious method, to say the least. Smoking in a pipe must have quite a different history in the Western world where the Portuguese and, in particular, the Dutch colonizers, who were the first to deal with opium as a luxury, were classical tobacco and pipe-smokers. Hashish as a luxury was smoked long before the East Asians knew of the stuff around the Mediterranean and in the Middle East. Both backgrounds should be combined in explaining why *not only* in China, but also in the whole of Southeast Asia the opium pipe was preferred and not eating it as in India. See D. Duco, passim.

[47] Idem, p. 33, which is still a main "argument" of people like Harry Gelber (see previous chapter).

[48] E. Cashmore (ed.), in the informative article 'Law: Immigration USA', p. 189.

[49] A. McCoy, F. Scarano (ed.), p. 30 also for the following two quotations.

empire should be moralized and turned into a moral state'. The meaning of this was crystal clear once an alternative opium policy was adopted, namely 'to assert American hegemony in East Asia to undermine the moral authority of the British and to aid the process of modernization in China'. As shown above, the Spaniards and Portuguese in the 16th and 17th centuries had already introduced fanatic conversion policies, and the Dutch and English Protestant colonizers did the same after they had conquered their Catholic predecessors. The New Imperialists USA, Germany and Japan again introduced a religious assault along with the military and opium one.

There remained differences between the nations in this respect. The British and American missionaries largely remained in the "opium-stricken" Chinese cities. The many strongly anti-foreigner resistance movements, including the Boxer Rising, encouraged them to do this. The Japanese tried to conquer whole provinces, as was shown above, and also produced propaganda for their national religion. The Germans, more heroic, tried to convert the peasants in the countryside.[50] After 1933 their motivation to do this was clear and should be read in German:

> Dem Deutschen liegt es im Blut, nicht auf die Verfeinerung des Volkes den größten Wert zu legen, sondern auf die Volkskraft. Er hat ein klares Auge dafür, daß in den Städten die Volkskraft verdorben und verbraucht wird, daß das Land die Städte überhaupt nur am Leben erhält. ('It runs in the Germans' blood not to insist so much on the cultivation of the people but on strengthening its immanent power. The Germans perceive it quite clearly that this Power of the people is spoiled and wasted in the cities, while the countryside is the force which nourishes the cities.) [51]

This application of the *Blood & Soil* doctrine for Chinese aims suggests that in the countryside the peasant customs are still prevalent and the people control each other much more; somebody who aspires to become a Chinese Christian has a much higher "value" in the countryside than in the cities. There were complaints about how difficult it was to convert these peasants: apart from the obvious problems of poverty and lack of education, there were specifically the Communist attacks, who turned the mission into a hazardous venture.

Thanks to the studies of Wolfgang Eckart, realistic backgrounds are now known for these German missions. His detailed description of the

---

[50] J. Müller's contribution to J. Richter (ed.), p. 94 ff.
[51] Idem, p. 95. The Japanese "soul" was perceived as similar to the German 'Blut und Boden' (p. 101).

Deutsches Schutzgebiet Kiautschou around the city of Tsingtao (Quingdao) on the coast of the Yellow Sea shows the sharp distinctions and mutual aversions between the poor Chinese and rich German military, bureaucrats and missionaries.[52] This part of coastal China was "freely occupied" by and under the command of the German navy.[53] The Europeans and Chinese lived quite isolated from each other. The former planned a kind of garden city with all possible luxury; it was even announced as a seaside resort. For the Chinese, the *European* contractors planned and built something very different. 'The development of the Chinatown Tapautau, however, ... was [around 1900] characterized by a government-inspired ghetto, an always increasing influx of indigenous laborers in far too few houses ... a continuous danger for the health of the inhabitants ... houses for more than 500 Chinese laborers ... new suburbs ...' which formed with the older buildings a hierarchy of poverty, dirt and misery.[54] In the Germans own words, it was a 'Drecknest' with health conditions of an 'epidemic character', while in garden city Tsingtao, sicknesses decreased annually. Eckart continues with:

> That the Chinese population was accused of being guilty itself for this may sound today as cynical, but was understandable in the colonial mentality of the European Herren of Kiautschou.[55]

This still sounds very cynical today, since the Chinese had to suffer health hazards, etc. thanks to the European actions, which were done on purpose. This went to further extremes: for example, the German marines nearly all had venereal diseases, but continued to infect Chinese women in remote villages. Willingly and knowingly, the German occupiers also organized an opium regime for the Chinese population:

> Contrary to the directions of the International Opium Commission ... the opium consumption was not prohibited and even taxed. Also after 1909 every inhabitant of Kiautschou could get an *Opiumschein* [opium permit] for 1 dollar ... other revenues were gained by opening, controlling and taxing of opium dens. Between 1904 and 1907 the opium consumption in

---

[52] W. Eckart, p. 458-505. In particular, he describes the health infrastructure in the "Europäerstadt Tsingtau" in contrast to the planning of the "Chinesenstadt Tapautau". This part of the coast was occupied by the German navy as revenge for the murder of two German missionaries (November 1897).

[53] See S.G. Chen, p. 280 ff., 291 ff. about the remarkable move of the German to give their *Schutzgebiet* to Japan with far-reaching consequences also for the opium policy of this country (see chapter 27).

[54] Idem, p. 462.

[55] Idem, p. 464.

Kiautschou increased from 6,575.47 kg to 8,697.97 kg. In 1908 there were 3,150 addicted opium smokers registered. The Opium Law of 1912 did not alter this situation, but stabilized it.[56]

The large concentration of missionaries in Kiautschou stabilized this situation as well.

From Chinese sources there are only a few testimonies of the missionaries' personal activities. Sun Shuyun discovered the fate of a few of these German missionaries in the 1930s and described them as sellers of 'the other opium', religion, 'the poison of the mind'.[57] In the first thirty years of their stay in China, missionaries apparently converted fewer than 100 Chinese:

> The Chinese were frightened of them, thinking the missionaries were dev-
> ils, and their grey and blue eyes were due to their lack of nourishment,
> which they made up by eating the eyes of Chinese children. They stoned
> the missionaries, set fire to their houses, and petitioned local officials to
> throw them out.[58] German missionaries achieved some success with the
> Miao tribe in Yunnan and Guizhou in the early 1910s. This mountain peo-
> ple was active in opium smoking and trade (see next chapter). The dis-
> crimination of the Miaos in Yunnan brought them together with the German
> 'foreign devils'. When the Red Army on its Long March arrived in a small
> country town, Shiqian, the settlement was thrown into panic. Soldiers
> found three German priests and some nuns. Two of them escaped, and the
> third died of hunger in captivity.

Another German priest, Rudolf Bosshardt, of the London-based China Inland Mission, was caught by a part of the 2nd Red Army and helped it to join with another part. He was released in 1935 after a long imprisonment and payment of $20,000 silver dollars. Bosshardt's day-by-day account of his captivity is one of the most complete reports of the *Long March*, displaying the cruel reality of the Red Army's methods of supplying itself.

After about 1935 there were almost no Western missionaries left in this "mutually inimical" China in which they had become "foreign mud" for nearly all Chinese, Nationalists as well as Communists. They never returned. It has not been forgotten, however, how all these representatives of the Christian West perceived the Chinese as a detestable *Yellow Race*. The Reverend Arthur Smith provides the best introduction to the next paragraph with his elaborations on the Chinese 'physical vitality'.

---

[56] Idem, p. 464 note 34.
[57] S. Shuyun, p. 103.
[58] Idem, p. 104.

This vitality is for him excellent: A Chinese person recuperates very quickly from all the serious disasters in his time, which costs millions of people their life. However:

> The only permanent and effective check upon the rapid increase of the Chinese population appears to be the confirmed use of opium, a foe to the Chinese race as deadly as war, famine, or pestilence.[59]

Herewith a new argument of doping Chinese is given, and the reverend's advice as panacea to 'the terrible *vis inertia* of Oriental apathy and fatalism—that dumb stupidity' is the action of 'some force from without'. As such, this influential religious official does not point to diplomacy. No, what is

> needed by China ... is unrestricted intercourse, free trade, and the brotherhood of man. The gospel of commerce is the panacea for China's needs; more ports, more imports, a lower tariff and no transit taxes.[60]

Smith's bestseller *The Uplift of China* provides the outlines of an 'American Moral Empire' with the aim to 'lay deep the foundations of an Oriental Christian civilization'.[61] This "empire" seems to be equivalent to America exploiting opium-stricken, pagan Chinese. At the end of the 19th-century, new imperialists still advertised the same ideas and practices as at the start, including the "free" and massive import of opium in exchange for silk, porcelain and tea, supported by a royal and republican navy (no diplomacy, but military power). The *Chinese Exclusion Act* (1882) covers both aspects: they are so inferior thanks to their opium smoking that they all must be returned to their own opium country. The victims are not only blamed, but also punished.

---

[59] A. Smith (1894), p. 145.

[60] Idem, p. 325, 326.

[61] A. Smith (1907), p. X. I could not consult Ian Tyrrell's book with the effective title: *Reforming the World. The Creation of America's Moral Empire* (2010) but only a highly favorable review of Barbara Reeves-Ellington (*H-Soz-u-Kult* 03.06.2011). It is an up-to-date analysis of all possible American religious reform movements and organizations of the second half of the 19th-century. Their interconnectedness created the networks of empire that for Tyrell lie at the heart of American imperialism, even if reformers did not always meet their goals. Some are liberal (in the US sense), most fundamentalist sectarian. They all intersected with the state to promote the gospel of some American Dream which, *therefore*, always has to remain a dream. In Tyrrell's words it concerns 'the exercise of power under a shared moral and political order in which that power is the subject of multilateral contestation among nations and classes'.

Racism

A major source of blaming victims was and, indeed, still is racism as developed in the wake of colonialism and imperialism of mainly the 19th-century.[62] It is too popular a means to disqualify "The Enemy". No serious people today use "race" as a concept providing any knowledge about large groups of people, let alone individuals. Also with the new DNA knowledge and hype, most biologists—the traditional 19th-century and early 20th-century sources of erroneous and dangerous race theories—rightly accept their own layman's knowledge of social, economic or cultural developments in societies. Nevertheless, it is, alas, appropriate to elucidate the pitfalls of racism as a function of nationalist enmity. This was the racism endemic from the middle of the European and American 19th-century. In hindsight, it was not surprising that it was exactly in new imperialist nations like the USA and Germany, who arrived too late for a profitable piece of the Eastern pie, that this imperialist racism had so much support.[63]

At the beginning of the 19th-century, the Chinese were seen as people who stupidly resisted "free trade", the mutual exchange of tea for opium or their conversion to Christianity. At the end of the century once their exploitation by the West had reached its peak, they were seen as the most terrible enemies of mankind, who contaminated the human race with *their* opium, who were ready to conquer and enslave the rest of the world and had already sent thousands of emigrants to the USA, other Western countries and their colonies in order to steal "well" paid jobs, forming at the same time a secret army preparing to conquer the West, and so on.

This perception was accompanied everywhere in the West and their colonies (Australia, New Zealand, etc.) by the slogans of the *Yellow Danger, La Race Jaune,* the *Yellow Specter, het Gele Gevaar,* the *Gelbe Gefahr,* or the *Yellow Terror* and the *Yellow Race.* They were conjured up in the same way as antisemitism was spread, namely, by means of terrifying anti-Chinese cartoons, writings, pogroms or movies. Most of the pictures were of addicts sucking on their pipes in opium dens. In particular, union leaders

---

[62] See E. Cashmore (ed.), p. 264-279 as a reasonable but outdated analysis of race and racism. Racism was also a main motive in 16th-century colonialism and missionary activities (the Roman Catholic Spain and Portugal), but it was not yet combined with nationalism and state-capitalist monopolies as in the 19th-century dominated by Protestant/Calvinist countries like the English, Dutch and Americans.

[63] For the following see U. Mehnert, the detailed *Wikipedia* article "Yellow Peril" with many present-day examples.

Ill. 31. The Yellow Terror ca. 1900
Source: en.Wikipedia.org 'Yellow Terror in All his Glory'

feared that the Chinese would undermine American or British labor (the Chinese population reached a peak of 2,419 in 1931 in the whole of Britain!). The Chinese were also accused of introducing iniquitous practices such as gambling and opium smoking. Sex was added in the classical manner to these fear elements by pointing to miscegenation. This was considered immoral, unnatural and endangering The Empire.[64]

---

[64] For this kind of racist problems in Britain, see the interesting Sascha Auerbach. See also the review of this book by David Lloyd Smith (who does not know that Sascha is a well-known Jewish female name) in: H-Net Reviews (Jan. 2010). He made the remark that a highly influential racist book of Sax Rohmer, *Dope: A Story of Chinatown and the Drug Traffic* (1919) 'is a repellent novel-racist, anti-Semitic, and xenophobic, and mired in reactionary politics', but not a sinophobic work. Jews are described by Rohmer 'as the primary threat to the hegemony of the Anglo-Saxon race'. To substantiate this, he quotes from another Rohmer book describing a positive element of the 'Chinese heart', i.e. a deep distrust of the police. This is not convincing, when no further qualification is given. In addition, one can ask which police is distrusted: if it is Chinese police, it is difficult to suppose sinophobia. If it is the white police of the International Settlements (which must be the case here), then the quotation points to remarkable practices of sinophobia: considering

Germany and the USA were the main sources of this racism, and it is highly symbolic that the German Emperor Wilhelm II could write to the President of the USA at the time, Theodore Roosevelt (September 1905):

> I foresee in the future a fight for life & death between the "White" and the "Yellow" for their sheer existence. The sooner therefore the Nations belonging to the "White Race" understand this & join in common defense against the coming danger, the better.[65] Roosevelt was, indeed, the right address. Reflecting on what might cause 'new nations of an old stock to spring up in new countries' like Australia and the United States, he expressed the opinion:
> 'the peopling of the great island-continent with men of the English stock is a thousand-fold more important than the holding of Hindoostan for a few centuries.' [It was the] 'ethnic conquest' of a territory ... The presence of the 'Chinaman' [whether in Australia or the United States would be] 'ruinous to the white race' [but these democracies] 'with the clear instinct of race selfishness, saw the race foe, and kept out the dangerous alien.'[66]

A large part of Australia has a tropical climate, and at the time it was difficult to get a "white" labor force for the plantations and similar work. These entrepreneurs hired Chinese and other Asians. As soon as these newcomers were noticed, they became competitors of the whites, and like in the US, the Australian trade unions initiated strong racist actions: for them the Chinese were of a 'depraved and dissolute' race; or 'The risks to white male health were alcohol, opium and Asian prostitutes', and so on.[67] The liberal (Australian definition) president, Samuel Griffith, immediately changed laws so that Asians could be extradited (1892).

Particularly in the USA, these images and opinions were combined with the slave-like situation of most Chinese immigrants working in the mines or on the railway projects. Since that time, opium addiction has been described in the United States as 'un-American' and 'non-Western'.[68]

Chinese as pariahs 'who may therefore be robbed, beaten and even murdered by his white neighbours with impunity.'

[65] Quoted by U. Mehnert, p. 9.

[66] Quoted by W. Anderson, p. 254.

[67] Idem, p. 88. See also p. 90: A Watson told: 'The yellow, the brown, and the copper-coloured are to be forbidden to land anywhere.'; the chief objection to Chinese immigration was 'entirely racial' (Senator Pearce); the Chinese 'cannot mix with us. We know from the teachings of science that they cannot' (Senator Smith), etc.

[68] D. Musto, p. 2; U. Mehnert, p. 49 ff. points to the fact that Chinese in the USA of the 1870s concern about 4% of the total, mainly European immigrants of 2.8 million people. The always highly racist trade unions in the USA (led by Jews like Samuel Gomperz) were the source of the anti-Chinese (later anti-Japanese) actions. Japanese were attacked from the 1890s onwards, but their immigration was much lower than the Chinese: 0.001% of the

It led to a heavy repression of Chinese in this country and even their extradition around 1910. In the end an "explanation" for all this was found in the doctrine of the "Yellow Race", a non-doctrine reproduced in all sorts of pejorative slogans, rationalizations and chimeras.

In 1868 the racist Henri George (later famous for his *Progress and Poverty,* 1879) published his reasons why 'pagan, untrustworthy, voluptuous, cowardly and cruel' Chinese should be excluded in order to save 'the racial homogeneity' of the Americans.[69] Another provocative book was *The Chinese Invasion* (H. West, 1873) in which the Chinese were compared to the 'great plagues [which] overran Egypt'; pogroms against the Chinese were regular events like the one in Tacoma, Washington (1877) in which a whole Chinese quarter was burned to the ground, etc. A few years later the *Chinese Exclusion Act* appeared. Around 1895 the anti-Chinese and anti-Japanese propaganda everywhere reached its high point.

After the turn of the century, the phrase *"Yellow Peril"* was daily food for the readers of the Hearst newspapers in the USA. An influential US evangelist, G. Rupert, preached about the same peril and warned in 1911 of the assault on the West by China (" ... only Jesus Christ can stop these attacks"). In 1914 the famous author Jack London wrote about the coming world hegemony of China, as did the novelist Nowlan with his novel *Armageddon* (1928) at the moment China was close to a total collapse!

In Europe the situation was not very different. Thanks to their continuous resistance against British, French, etc. assaults, the Chinese were characterized in the 19th-century publicity as unreliable, cruel and sly; their nation as reactionary and despotic. And nearly always these qualifications were followed by references to their gambling and opium addiction.[70] The German Emperor Wilhelm II promised his nation that he would eradicate this *gelbe Gefahr* (*Die Hunnenrede,* July 1900)[71]; in

---

whole US population. From then on the Chinese stereotypes became similar to the Japanese ones. They also became 'inferior, unreliable and tricky' (Idem, p. 55). Japan, however, received many more comments because a political-military development of becoming a world power accompanied the racist discourse.

[69] U. Mehnert, p. 52.

[70] A well-known German commentator on world politics, Paul Dehn, used these qualifications (1905) referring to western 'experts of the Far East'. U. Mehnert, note 7 p. 22.

[71] In this notorious speech to a German expedition army to the Far East, aimed at crushing the Boxer Rebellion, the German Kaiser compared this 'Prussian Christian army' with the revenging Huns of Atilla. He ordered them not to take prisoners and behave as ruthlessly as possible, 'so that the name of Germany in China is feared in a way that never again a Chinese tries to squint at a German'. A classical example of how racist remarks were transformed in disqualifications of The Enemy is that "Huns" became since this speech the name for barbarous Germans during World War I.

England, M. Shiel published the bestseller *The Yellow Danger* (1897) about the murder of two missionaries by Chinese.

There are remarkable parallels with present publicity because, for instance, Rupert preached what he called 'British Israelism', while now Zionist writers like Margalit or Morris and Samuel Huntington and other *Occidentalism* writers warn about global attacks by Islam and China on the West; new US evangelists preach war against the modern China. Mehnert also points to the strong parallels between the Yellow Race slogans and the present concepts like "the Asian Challenge" or "Japanese Challenge" which ask for "Our" response or directly for a new war against Islam or whatever enemy is needed to assuage the "Western" bad conscience.[72]

The excuse that the 'Yellow Race' was specifically attracted or suited to opium possibly cancelled Western guilt. It was soon mixed up with all kinds of *Orientalisms*. Here are two examples. An interesting detailed article in a famous (pre-war) encyclopedia states

> that behind the opium problem there is a fundamental divergence of attitude between East and West. The custom of eating and smoking opium has by this time become deeply ingrained in the social fabric of the eastern countries—so deeply ingrained in fact that it cannot readily be eradicated without the full cooperation of the western powers.[73]

The misleading reference to the "age-old use of opium" in China accompanies the accusation that 'colonial interests' exploited these 'eastern habits'!

A variant on what the opium dealers like the Jardines, Mathesons or Sassoons told the world as quoted at the start of this chapter provides the next example:

> It is true that opium is not likely to become popular among an active and industrious race like the Anglo-Saxon, whose preference must always be for the more potent, though less permanent stimulus, of ardent spirits, the "gross and mortal enjoyments" of which are far more suitable to the character of that race than the "divine luxuries" of opium ... Orientals ... will choose the stimulant which multiplies and gives a livelier coloring to ...

---

[72] The present Samuel Huntington crusade is an old one. Already, Hugh Lusk published in the *North American Review* (1907) an article titled 'The Real Yellow Peril' in which he states that the thread of the Asian people is not so much a military or economic thread: 'The real peril is to be found ... in the collision and competition of civilizations'. Quoted in U. Mehnert, p. 53.

[73] *Encyclopaedia of the Social Sciences*, vol. XI, p. 472 (1949) clearly written around 1935 by H.H. Moorhead and H. Tobin.

ideas, rather than that which ... excites to muscular exertion and boisterous mirth.[74]

Of course this is phraseology and has nothing to do with the practice physicians experienced in their therapeutic observations and written down 20 years earlier, let alone what numerous observers have reported since the 16th-century:

> The greatest sufferings ... are those which attend the state of depression, always existing when its direct influence is no longer felt. There are excessive restlessness, a universal and indescribable uneasiness, feelings of intolerable distress, especially in the epigastrium and lower extremities, an irksome sense ... of incapacity both for intellectual exertion and for mental or emotional enjoyments ...[75] and so on.

Indeed, the "Anglo-Saxon Race" was vulnerable to 'more potent' drugs which became the derivatives of opium like heroin and morphine.

The intellectual level of discourses about race and drugs in the United States, which had such far-reaching effects, displayed strange mixtures of negative and positive elements. For example, certain drugs were dreaded because they seemed to undermine specific restrictions keeping groups and races under control:

> cocaine was supposed to enable blacks to withstand bullets which would kill normal persons and to stimulate sexual assault. Fear that smoking opium facilitated sexual contact between Chinese and white Americans was also a factor in its total prohibition.[76]

Every racial group received so its "prescription" largely adjusted to the political demands of the day.

After about 1890 it was clear enough that Japan, contrary to China, was achieving a prominent role in world politics and becoming an imperialistic competitor of the Western powers, including Russia. In the *Yellow Race* doctrine, however, the Chinese and Japanese were lumped together. That situation had to change, however, as soon as new friend-enemy relations developed. The most prominent among them was the Berlin-Tokyo axis of Nazi Germany against its strongest enemy at that time, England and its British Empire.

German racial theorists, earlier in the forefront of the *Yellow Danger* (*Gelbe Gefahr*) publications, had to rewrite their textbooks into a remark-

---

[74] Quoted in C. Terry, M. Pellens, p. 95.
[75] Quoted from dr. G. B. Wood (1856) in Idem, p. 138.
[76] D. Musto, p. 244, 245.

able mixture of the classical position and a "Yellow Lovestory". Still, the 'Northern Germanic Race' must remain in the leading position, which led to a highly ambiguous treatment of the East.

So, in his historical 'applied racial theory', Heinrich Wolf fully agrees with the policies of Australia and New Zealand, 'where the indigenous people are fully destroyed by the whites', and that they strongly oppose the immigration of Chinese coolies and Japanese peasants: it is, indeed a struggle between 'Germanisation or Orientalisation'.[77] Wolf's proto-Nazi racial stand was soon followed by one of its prominent ideologues.

In his *Mythus* (1930, etc.) Alfred Rosenberg was not only enthusiastic about the impact of Confucianism and Taoism on the racial characteristics of the Chinese and their society. He also gave a long overview of the British opium attacks, which was introduced by some general remarks on the economic imperialism of the West that

> cotton and opium, waste-products of Europe, could infiltrate into China to destroy first the equilibrium of Chinese life in coastal cities and later every time farther into the interior ... even learned Chinese started to beautify their homes ... with Western kitsch ... but protests came from Chinese and Japanese intellectuals ... to start a movement of racial renewal and liberation of the East ... Today China has lost its typical mythical ideal ... One may hope that missionaries, opium dealers and dark adventurers have to leave China soon ... Like the large movement of renewal in Germany, China struggles for its myth, for its race and its ideals against the commercial race which dominates today all stock-markets and the deeds of nearly all governments.[78]

The *Yellow Race* doctrine is flexible enough to be used in the game "the enemy of my enemy is my best friend". What is to be done, though, when both friends and enemies disappear like opium smoke? After the Japanese were conquered in 1945, happily for the heirs of the old empires, the rise of Mao and its "communism" in 1949 could keep the doctrine fresh and alive.

---

[77] H. Wolf, p. 325. Wolf has headed a paragraph 'Die gelbe Gefahr' referring to Houston Chamberlain's *'Grundlagen des 19.Jahrhunderts'* and, in particular, Wilhelm Schallmeyer's influential *'Vererbung und Auslese'* which accuses the British and French of occupying China 'in a barbaric way', whereupon it was subjected to 'das schädliche Opiumlaster' (p. 327; 'the noxious sin of opium').

[78] A. Rosenberg, p. 652-654.

CHAPTER THIRTY-ONE

THE WEST AND ITS OPIUM IMPORT IN CHINA

The image of the Chinese was not very favorable in the Western perception to use an understatement. What was China's own contribution to the world's Opium Problem apart from providing the largest number of opium consumers at the end of the 19th-century? To qualify this last question immediately, we can reveal that Chinese already around 1830

> routinely depicted [opium smokers] as physically and mentally decrepit, with a skeletal frame, a grey complexion, weak stamina, stained teeth, diminishing willpower and a lack of incentive to work.[1]

Many missionaries used similar words at the end of the century in their propaganda directed at the homeland to coax funds for the poor missions in such miserable countries like China.

Around 1830, these opium victims were hated because they exposed the weakness of the Qing state, and they permanently demonstrated the Chinese defeat, the serious humiliation by the 'foreign devils': Opium was the poison of the West. Whoever supported these criminal Western foreigners was himself a criminal. Consumption of the poison was no less a crime than helping these foreigners to distribute the opium or assisting them in other ways (from money changing to translations). It is difficult to condemn Chinese governments or local officials for these reactions.

There is, furthermore, the classic reaction of all shopkeepers and some historians: "The Chinese wanted to buy the stuff itself, so we delivered!" This is an insufficient as well as a demagogic answer: "The Chinese" do not want anything, only specific Chinese people do. It presupposes preliminary knowledge available only to the sellers, and products available only to the importers. Aside from the fact that both sellers and importers knew perfectly well how poisonous the stuff was.

Still, it is clear enough that too many Chinese were eager to buy opium so that "China" became synonymous with Opium. This reached such a degree that some Chinese started cultivating poppies, which contributed to the perception in the West known as the *Yellow Menace.* In all cases,

---

[1] L. Kwong, p. 1485; for the same kind of depiction from 1895 see R. K. Newman (1995), p. 766 with many other examples in Idem, note 3.

however, opium 'was intricately involved with the unfathomable interaction between China, India, Britain, the United States, France, and other European nations ...'[2]

Under the impact of the present Chinese economic domination, the West has started to look more thoroughly into this Chinese opium history. Some consensus about the Chinese victim position is being hesitatingly accepted among serious Western scholars.[3] How the Chinese handled this problem themselves mostly remains unclear. It is, therefore, the time to look at details of the Opium Problem from the victims' viewpoints. How active were Chinese producers, traders and mafia, and how were they treated and dealt with by the Chinese governments mainly in the period 1900-1950?

The Chinese producers and distributors knew perfectly well how unlawful and morally objectionable their work was in official Chinese eyes and discourses. They helped the foreigners to spread the Opium Problem across the country after the Opium Wars were lost. The large international context in which they operated must be stressed, and this made a fundamental distinction necessary between the Chinese in China and those living elsewhere in Asia (see ch. 25). Sometimes they interacted, which gave the Chinese side of the Opium Problem a nearly universal Asian profile. Below, remarks about this context will precede the main subject of this part, which is the Chinese opium production and consumption. Who can better describe this mutual relationship than the man, who—as representative of the British occupier—had to play a remarkable intermediary role?

---

[2] K. McMahon, p. ix.

[3] One has to stress the word 'serious'. A Dutch historical journal published recently an article from its 'correspondent' in China, B. de Groot (*Historisch Nieuwsblad*, September 2010, p. 27). In China it was until 2009 normal to come up with a massive number of 'colonial clichés' . But 'now there is an economic crisis and China needs Europe desperately', China even forgets the anniversary of the Second Opium War. However, the schoolbooks still tell these 'colonial clichés'. An example of this is the following sentence, according to this expert: 'In October 1860 the bandits from the West imposed a dishonest treaty on the corrupt Qing-government ... To enrich Europe the Chinese people had to become addicted.' Long before 1860 in the British Parliament, judgements about the Opium War were couched in similar language, while Multatuli wrote about a 'Dutch robber state'. Even the robbers themselves, like Warren Hastings, thought of the opium trade as a kind of criminal act (see above). For De Groot all those stories are only told 'to blacken Europe'. What is in crisis here?

A British Inspector ...

Who could better judge the opium situation in China than the top representatives of those who produced and imported the opium? A most energetic example was the British diplomat, traveler, writer and inspector, Sir Alexander Hosie (1853-1925). He made several long trips through many provinces of China, visited the same locations several times, and reported in many books about the differences and similarities, mostly in a dry accountants' language. Hosie was also a member of a delegation to the *Shanghai International Opium Commission* (1909). He occupied a responsible position. Largely based on Hosie's positive advice and unconfirmed investigations, the British government was practically obliged to officially stop the lucrative opium imports from India (1917). However, the "Perfidious Albion" cynically built in loopholes in its treaties with China.

The report which is important for our endeavors is Hosie's two-volume *On the Trail of the Opium Poppy* (1914). They sketch journeys through six provinces, partly still unexplored, which were the chief centers of Chinese opium production. The results of this were published earlier in *Parliamentary Papers* around 1912. Two long appendices in this work explain the inception, organization and methods of the anti-opium crusade; the second is a very useful summary of all the data he had gathered in the six most important opium provinces, Shansi, Shensi, Kansu, Szechuan, Yunnan and Kueichou.

The introduction to the first appendix is interesting, because it tells how it "all" started: during a British invasion into Tibet in 1903/04. The British exerted lethal force with their new Maxim machineguns against poorly armed Tibetans. A treaty was imposed on Tibet by the British occupier, but the British were not satisfied by this: 'the seal of the Amban, the representative of China—the suzerain of Tibet' was absent. This led to new negotiations between the British Empire and China.[4]

A special Chinese Envoy was send to Calcutta (September 1904) to negotiate with the Government of India. During this visit the Chinese Envoy, T'ang Shao-yi, 'derived the impression that India was prepared to dispense with her opium revenue'. Hosie continues with the remarkable and symptomatic sentence that this Envoy

---

[4] See A.Porter (ed.), the contribution of R. Moore, p. 434 ff. and the contribution of J. Osterhammel in Idem, p. 160 ff.. See also the *Wikipedia* article "Expedition to Tibet".

on his return to Peking ... informed his Government that it was the Chinese craving for the drug, and not England's desire to force it upon China, which was responsible for the continuance of the traffic in Indian opium. Thus was initiated the campaign against the cultivation of the poppy and the consumption of opium in China ...[5]

From every point of view, this is breathtaking information! A very British man like Hosie, and one of the few opium experts, writes this baldly without any remark. Whether Tang Shao-yi made a bold diplomatic manoeuvre or not by spiriting away the pivotal role of the British in addicting the Chinese, the fact is that—in hindsight—this became an opening move to solve one of the most complicated, large-scale and fundamental questions of a society. It is unbelievable that a Chinese Envoy would inform his own government of such a lie. One can only imagine that the British told the envoy to inform his government that no agreement would be possible if any accusations whatsoever were launched against the British (they could easily lead to very costly compensations in this Opium Case). In short, it would be worthwhile for someone to look in the archives again for the background of the negotiations about Tibet between China and the British.

In my view, the British Balfour government's arrogance and ignorance merged Curzon's geopolitical speculations about Russia's aims in China, and the interests of Calcutta's cotton and opium merchants to make a Tibetan deal with China. In the long term, the British could have aimed at a Western land route into China (a rather utopian aim militarily), while intimidating Russia from doing the same. Both perceived China as a colossus on feet of clay.[6] The Chinese interest must have involved negating its dependence on Britain (and foreigners in general), which largely hinged on the British-Indian opium business.

In any case, the Chinese were very quick to exploit the situation. An *Imperial Decree* (September 1906) was issued, expressing the worries of the Emperor about the ruinous effects of the opium in his country and commanding 'that within a period of ten years the evils arising from foreign and native opium be equally and completely eradicated'.[7]

---

[5] A. Hosie, vol. 2, p. 191, 192. The quotations below are from the following pages.

[6] Both calculated their political future also in regard to Japan, which had already won a Chinese-Japanese War. The Russians wanted to secure their presence in the Far East (Vladivostok, Port Arthur); the Japanese were certainly the most aggressive as described in ch. 27.

[7] Quoted in Idem, p. 192. See also K. Chimin Wong, W. Lien-Teh, p. 566, 603.

Two months later a series of detailed proposals were submitted that practically aimed at a strong central government grip on the poppy fields, production, consumers and trade. Contrary to similar attempts in the Dutch or French colonies, the Chinese central government really wanted to eradicate the entire poppy culture. The proposals did not intend to establish a state opium monopoly, as is often claimed.[8] Some officials probably put forward such a plan, but that was not only contrary to several 1906 proposals, the existence of the international settlements or Hong Kong made such a scheme impossible. Peking needed to destroy the *poppy culture as part of the foreign occupation.* That is what happened as testified by Hosie and others.

The main difficulty was, of course, how to deal with the huge British-Indian opium interest of the main occupier. In article 10 an arrangement with the British was proposed

> with a view to effecting an annual decrease within the next few years of the import of foreign opium, *pari passu* with the decrease of native opium, so that both may be absolutely prohibited by the expiry of the time-limit of ten years. Besides India opium, the drug is also imported from Persia, Annam and the Dutch Indies in no small quantities. In the case of Treaty Powers negotiations should similarly be entered into with their representatives in Peking to effect the prohibition of such import ... [9]

In stronger wording, the article continues to talk about 'morphia ... the effects of which are even more injurious than those of opium itself..' and about the need to ban also the 'instruments for its injection'.

A new series of concrete proposals were submitted (January 1907) to serve as a basis for negotiations concerning the import and taxation of Indian opium (raw and prepared), the consumption in the foreign settlements in China, and the import of morphia: reduction of Indian import by 10% every year starting from 1907; duties on native and Indian opium must be raised (but since the Indian opium is twice as strong as the native one, the tax increased twice as much); the large Hong Kong prepared opium stock must be taxed with a very high duty, if its import into China cannot be prevented; prohibition of selling opium in brothels, tea-shops, hotels, opium dens, restaurants or other public resorts in the foreign settlements; prohibition of export of morphia to China including the syringes or injection needles.

---

[8] For instance, recently by B. de Groot (previous note 3).
[9] Quoted in A. Hosie, vol. 2, p. 203, 204.

Of course, they were followed by counter-proposals from the British-Indian government: instead of reducing the import into China, they would be willing to reduce by one-tenth the annual export to China for three years (from 1901-5 this was 67,000 chests, of which China took 51,000). And they promised also that if China diminished its own production and consumption, they would 'undertake to continue in the same proportion this annual diminution of the export after the three years in question'.[10]

His Majesty's Government wanted to receive additional information from Peking on several other minor issues. Only the gist of this first counter-reaction is important here: we, the British, will accept many things if you, the Chinese, do what you promised to do. This seems logical, probably reasonable, but this was not the case: it was only reasonable to assume that the Chinese could *not* entirely abolish opium, so the British-Indian import could continue anyway. It would have been logical if the British opium perpetrator had proposed a scheme for stopping its exports, since it had earned at least a billion pounds in this opium trade (see ch. 6 and 7), after the international outcry about its opium performance, and since the abolition of slavery had been realized a century earlier.

Several other proposals were exchanged. A new aspect was that the government of the United States interfered with a proposal to establish a joint International Commission to investigate the opium trade (May 1908). This had the effect that the Chinese-British negotiations could no longer remain secret, but had to proceed in the light of the media and public and that for the first time statistical data were gathered about the Opium Problem in many countries.

They formed the preparations for the rather famous *Shanghai Conference* (1st to 26th February 1909), the start of a long series of international conferences which still continues today, in fact. The good news for the Chinese was that a period of ten years was accepted after which the British import of opium was fully stopped; the bad news was that in a new agreement with China (May 1911), England put so many conditions and demands on the table that it gives the impression the British wanted to blow up the whole affair.[11]

In the ten long articles plus annex of this latter agreement, the British demanded that the diminishing of the Chinese opium production should

---

[10] Idem, p. 208. The Persian-Turkish opium import was fixed at only 1,125 piculs annually (Idem, p. 212, 213), negligible compared to the British.

[11] The literary text of this agreement is given in Idem, p. 220–227.

go 'in the same proportion as the annual export from India' for seven years; this export will only cease 'if clear proof is given of the complete absence of production of native opium in China'; it did not permit closure of the Canton and Shanghai ports for Indian opium until the very end of the whole process; India will stop its export only when China 'has effectively suppressed the cultivation and import of native opium' into any Chinese province; on confirmation of the agreement, China will immediately withdraw 'all restrictions ... on the wholesale trade in Indian opium ... and ... all taxation on the wholesale trade ...'; British officials must be allowed to continuously investigate the Chinese diminution of cultivation and 'their decision as to the extent of cultivation shall be accepted by both parties to this agreement'; and so on.

The important British official carrying out this controversial work was the inspector, Sir Alexander Hosie. With a stiff upper lip, he produced an agreement like this without any comment. Even worse, at the end he put his "signature" below the following repetition of the lie the Chinese Envoy, T'ang Shao-yi, tried to sell to his government in 1904 (according to Hosie):

> Thus was taken the first step towards the eradication of an evil for which the Chinese themselves have alone been responsible all along, and which a policy of drift has permitted to be widespread. The evil had its origin in China itself, and I feel bound to say that but for the help of Great Britain ... the progress that we see to-day ... would not have been realized. ... The Government of China ... has recognized that assistance, and repeatedly expressed its gratitude to the British Government.[12]

Indeed, officially, there came an end to the Indian-China opium relationship. This was a rather abstract result, because many concurrent events of magnitude happened, including the abdication of the Empress and the start of something like a republic, which made this end different than the result of all previous negotiations.

The fate of Hosie is probably symptomatic of this. How often he complained about the false estimations made by other experts! In the second long appendix in which he described his voyages through six Chinese opium provinces, his own investigations were as superficial as all previous ones. Without any doubt, he made interesting and sometimes useful observations, but mostly he simply reproduced the opinions of missionaries. Generally, he provided a poorly amateurish performance.

---

[12] Idem, p. 231.

For example, Hosie visited Szechuan in January 1910, the province with the largest opium production, claimed to be not less than 238,000 piculs in 1906, which was reduced to 159,000 two years later. Hosie informs us further that the opium arrivals in 1910 in Ichang, the Yangtsze port, still amounted 28,370 piculs. In fact, during his trip a few days later 'I ascertained that poppy cultivation had entirely ceased after the season of 1908-1909.'[13]

Newman was not surprised about this mystery as he read from Hosie that in Szechuan now 'hardly a stalk of poppy could be found'.[14] The patriarchal Sir Alexander could not avoid adding the very British comment that China now was raised 'with all her faults in the estimation of the civilized world': a new attempt was being made to transform victims into perpetrators. Indeed, in these crucial years a serious change took place, which can best be shown in the next table concerning the opium and other imports.

Table 46. Percentage Distribution of China's principal Imports, 1870–1910[15]

Years	total value (HK taels x 1,000)	Opium %	Cotton piece goods %	Cotton yarn %	Kerosene %	Machinery %
1870	63 693	43	28	3	---	---
1880	79 293	39	25	5	---	---
1890	127 093	20	20	15	3	0,3
1900	211 070	15	22	14	7	0,7
1910	462 965	12	15	14	5	2

It was about 70 years earlier when this "civilized" world smuggled opium to addict China on a large scale in favor of a few British soldiers, bureau-

---

[13] Idem, p. 270. The interpretation or use of Hosie's judgments is still ambiguous, even by a fine historian like McCoy; see his contribution to A. McCoy, A. Block (ed.), p. 245. Although he is clearly and rightly analyzing his case from the perspective of European colonialism as the creator of mass addiction, poppy cultivation and mass promotion of opium, the consequences of this are not followed with the same rigor. For instance, he (like all historians) presumed that the opium business was largely legal (Idem, p. 238). This was, however, only in the perception of the colonialists: from the start until the end, many if not most indigenous leaders protested against this opium trade. It is, furthermore, ahistorical and rather irrelevant to trace the use of opium back to several millennium B.C. (Idem, p. 239 ff.).

[14] R. K. Newman (1989), p. 548.

[15] A. Feuerwerker, p. 49. I have rounded the figures. The table is larger, but that is not very relevant here. One must realize, however, that in absolute terms the 1870 import concerns 27, 388,000 taels and in 1910 it is twice as much, 55,556,000 taels. The cotton piece goods come from Lancashire; yarn and opium from India.

crats in India and England, and opium criminals like the Sassoons, Jardines, etc. The majority of the 19th-century opium was the single most important Chinese import. Only in the 1890s was it surpassed by cotton piece goods. Whatever Hosie and others stated about the competing Chinese opium production, in these years apparently not a gram of Chinese opium was exported. Tea and silk remained the largest export goods.[16]

The actual Chinese defense against the opium assault was a direct follow-up of the earlier defense under the spectacular leadership of Commissioner Lin Zexu.

Now, at the end of the Indian-British-Chinese opium relationship (February 1918), a British gunboat manoeuvred in a remarkable way along the coast, and opium was again burned by Chinese officials. They also suggested that the opium stocks of the foreign merchants or governments should be repatriated to India from which they were sent. Apart from government actions, there were substantial anti-opium protests—largely identical with anti-British and anti-foreigner opposition—which brought people into the streets. The highest British diplomat in China, Jordan, eager to get opium off the British diplomatic agenda as quickly as possible, now supported this Chinese suggestion because the

> spontaneous withdrawal of the stocks would produce an excellent impression and be a just and generous act which would form a fitting end to a trade which has become a moral anachronism.[17]

Indeed, the time for a luxury existence of foreigners in China was running out. The Chinese had to put up with their provocative behavior until the end of World War II. The Chinese opium drama remained spectacular until the end. The gradual British retreat, which coincided with the abdication of the Empress and the start of the Republican period, had many consequences.

As in the beginning of the opium game, the largest opium profiteers, the Sassoons, made fabulous gains again: prices rose from about 3000

---

[16] The value of the tea export in 1870 is 27,647,500 taels, and in 1910 it is 38,083,000 taels; for silk these figures are 21,565,050 taels and 95,208,250 taels, respectively. Generally, in nearly all those years, China had a negative import-export balance with mainly the UK (British Empire). Also in this respect, the exploitation was going on until long after 1900. See Idem, table 16 p. 46 ff.

[17] R. K. Newman (1989), p. 557. For Jordan see also W. Willoughby, vol. II, p. 1096.

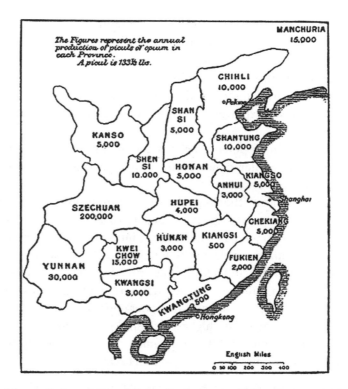

Map 17. Estimated Annual Opium Production per Chinese Province, 1908

Source: en.wikipedia.org (China and Opium). The sources used by the mapmaker(s) are unknown; this map probably belongs to the propaganda efforts of the British government. See also map. 18 below. The map is reproduced from the *British Government White Paper, China, No. 1, 1908*. Piculs are nearly equivalent to chests. The figures represent the annual production of piculs in each province. Added to this map is the comment of Lord Justice Fat: 'We English, by the policy we have pursued, are morally responsible for every acre of land in China which is withdrawn from the cultivation of grain and devoted to that of the poppy; so that the fact of the growth of the drug in China ought only to increase our sense of responsibility.'

taels to 16,000 *taels* per chest.[18] And again: 'Moral anachronism' or not, under the umbrella of some British governmental institution as compensation for their "losses", the Sassoons got nearly 'a virtual monopoly in the other Far Eastern markets on which India itself was now having to rely'.[19]

---

[18] During the financial year 1912-13 the Government of India received Rs. 43 million from opium taxes, etc. and the opium "merchants" (again the Sassoon family leading) Rs 35 million in the same year. Idem, p. 555. That was a profit on the purchasing in India only, not yet on the selling in China.

[19] Idem, p. 557. During the last phase of this Indian-British-Chinese opium relation-

In addition, the Shanghai Municipal Council, the governing body of the International Settlement in this city, failed to cooperate: 'from 1907 to 1913 the number of licensed opium shops in the Settlement increased from 87 to 560 and the revenue from licenses from 4,290 taels to 86,386 taels'.[20]

In the power vacuum the British left behind, the USA and Japan entered. In particular, the new imperialist Japan started a raging opium war, more cruel than the former and extending over a large part of East Asia. Japan had a particular opium relation with the Middle East (Persia, Turkey) and could circumvent India and the British. It used other methods as well and copied the old imperialist game of importing opium to addict Chinese, it also renewed or refined this game by starting production of heroin and morphine on Chinese soil in the newly conquered parts of North China, Manchuria and Jehol, eventually with the assistance of some Chinese warlords.

... and his American heirs

To counteract the British dominance, the other new imperialist, the USA, was transformed from the main opium transporter and smuggler into the main provider of American missionaries agitating in an anti-opium mood. It also gave a demonstration of dollar diplomacy by granting Peking a large loan. However, the aim to replace the British as the most favorable commercial partner of the Chinese came too late: the Japanese were earlier, closer and more aggressive. The opium import in the USA became an increasing concern, and it gradually developed an anti-Japanese strategy.[21] Its official anti-opium stand, however, was characterized by puzzling about whether the narcotics now imported on a large scale came from India, China or Japan.

In China, its main concern became another British heritage: the big problem of extraterritoriality, the autonomous political and legal power of the occupying Western powers in the International Settlement. Here the British and the French still dominated. During the extensive negotiations on the problems in the International Settlement in one conference

---

ship, it was the controversial Sir Edward Grey, the English Minister of Foreign Affairs (responsible for the outbreak of the First World War), who came to the conclusion 'that the right thing to do was to give in to David Sassoon ...' (Idem, p. 555).

[20] W. Willoughby, vol. II, p. 1098 note 12.
[21] W. Walker III, p. 44 ff.

after another, the American Willoughby proved to be the best expert on opium in the scene. He quotes a Japanese writer, Kawakami (1924), to explain his case:

> Not only is China surrounded by opium-using countries, but she has within her own territories several centers of the opium trade. Foremost of these centers is Shanghai, followed by Hongkong, Canton, Macao, Harbin and Dairen. The International Settlement in Shanghai is said to have at least 500 opium stores, and the French Settlement 140. In the Foreign Settlements the import and sale of opium is not forbidden, and it is but natural that they should become favorite rendezvous of opium addicts and the vantage-ground from which crafty smugglers, both foreign and native, make inroads into the interior of China.[22]

Indeed, Willoughby's long discussion of all the international conferences shows the distressing reality that first and foremost the British and French governments obstructed the anti-opium measures with all possible tricks and lies in nurturing their extraterritoriality in China, while pretending at the same time that they were officially suppressing the opium business once and for all. Their interests coincided with those of the large opium dealers.

That did not concern the Americans. Their government mostly suggested that they were the best supporters of the Chinese case, while their private economic interests (American smuggling, banking, transportation through Hong Kong) continued as usual and without relevant government intervention.

Therefore, the story of the imported opium did not stop, but entered a quite new phase after 1911 as will be detailed in the next sections. The main *practical* elements of the story, how the Chinese involvement in the opium production and consumption rose and declined, will be described later.

We are left here to interpret the story of "China and its Imported Opium Problem". It seems as if there is still a cultural Opium Problem, which represents the most basic notions of the Western relations with China. One aspect of this is that we can find something of the truth only through the enemies of Britain. From the German side, for instance, the influential sociologist Max Weber wrote around 1905 the following statement which is difficult to find in present-day British or American literature:

---

[22] W. Willoughby, vol. II, p. 1141 note 29.

Opium, the narcotic perceived as of a specific Chinese nature, was still imported in modern times; it must be well-known that its acceptance in the country followed only after the fiercest opposition of the dominant elite was broken by a war from outside.[23]

This import was, therefore, not the result of a civilizing mission or something similar (if Germans had been involved), but only of naked conquest by a 'perfidious Albion' and its brutal, mainly American smugglers.

There are, however, quite different remarks found in the Anglo-Saxon historiography, probably thanks to Hosie's "positive approach" or British propaganda. The opportunity to demonstrate this is given by probably the most influential Western China watcher. Indeed, if we want to know how and why a new situation in the international relations emerged, we would receive 'only one recommendation: read John King Fairbank!'[24] A wise advice because in assessing the impact of the Western opium assault on China, Fairbank (1907-1991) went, in fact, one step further than Sir Alexander Hosie.

After a study lasting many decades, he made the following remarkable

final proposition, that the most natural way to meet the West on equal terms was to follow a Chinese minority tradition which had more in common with Western ways of commerce and violent competition than with Chinese ideals of bureaucracy and harmonious compromise. For example, one peculiarly menacing aspect of the "Western Ocean" (Hsi-yang) people in the early contact at Canton was that their uncouth and greedy ways appealed to tendencies deeply latent among the Cantonese populace. The outright commercialism of the Western "barbarians" met a quick response among the shopkeepers in Hog Land behind the opulent ghetto of the Thirteen Factories. Once Indian opium was brought by the private merchants in the Country (local) trade from India, commercial greed fostered the growth of the opium trade on both sides. It became the great bilateral Sino-foreign joint enterprise of the nineteenth-century, and it succeeded far beyond anyone's fears or foresight. It requires only a modicum of imagination to see the Cantonese opium entrepreneur, who did his bit to usher China into modern international commerce, as the inheritor of the Chinese tradition that had much in common with the Western trading world. Some of the seemingly "foreign influences" of the Republican Revolution may turn

---

[23] M. Weber, vol. 1, p. 519. Other remarks about opium can be found in Idem, p. 250, 296 notes, 506 and in Idem, vol. 2, p. 292. Weber and his colleagues were critical opponents of the British "market behavior". See for this H. Derks (2004), p. 102 ff. Max Weber never protested against the genocide German colonizers were committing in Southwest Africa against the Herrero at the time that he made this remark. This assault was loudly announced as part of a civilizing mission of the Germans in Africa.

[24] L. Blussé (2008), p. 100.

out at second glance to have coincided with or grown from older Chinese
trends that shared certain traits with the foreigners.[25]

One wonders what prevails in the mind of a brilliant historian who knows
all the facts as described in detail in his many voluminous books. Anyway,
there is no trace of a perception of the victim side of the Chinese or China.
On the contrary, he equates at the start of a new episode in Chinese history (1911) 'a Chinese minority tradition' with a Western 'uncouth and
greedy' commercialism. Now the victims truly become perpetrators.

Fairbank proposes that a mix between these two (and not the old 'harmonious', bureaucratic dominant tradition) was the basis of a Republican
revolution. This mix became the new spirit for a new age which ultimately brought China 'on equal terms' with the West. In the end, Fairbank's
final proposition implies that the catalyst for all this was, indeed, opium.

It is senseless to counteract Fairbank's moralistic 'final proposition'
with another moral appeal.[26] Hard political-economic facts are more
than enough. First, the reliance here on the private merchant's opium
business alone negates that two devastating opium wars and "peaceful"
pressure exerted with a gun were needed to establish a so-called "free
trade". This trade was, therefore, not free at all. In addition, it was no
trade: the Chinese could not participate in it unless they stuck to the
Western rules relative to the product (opium) and the handling of the
profits and the organization of the trade (through foreign mediators,
banks or shipowners), to avoid undermining the British-Indian import
position.

It should have been realized, therefore, that this had nothing to do
with "commercialism", which is by definition a peaceful mutual relationship between two parties on equal terms. Not only was it largely a military
affair, the West (or, generally, all imperialists) had simply nothing on
offer: throughout the 19th-century they had no products demanded in
China; they came to conquer, to convert and to silence its victims by
means of mass consumption of worthless opium, which had to be bought
for high prices.

---

[25] J. Fairbank (ed.), p. 8, 9.

[26] Interestingly, Fairbank belonged to the so-called 'China Hands' with Theodore
White, Owen Lattimore, Edgar Snow and others. They were foreign service officers, jour-
nalists, American scholars and advisers to the USA government during World War II and
afterwards. They were soon accused by the McCarthy administration of being too soft on
Communism, that they had helped to defeat Chiang Kai-shek and a lot more nonsense.
See *Wikipedia* "China Hands".

It should also have been obvious that all this had nothing to do with a 'great bilateral Sino-foreign joint enterprise' but instead a one-sided harsh assault. The prey of the assault was too big, however, for the British and other old imperialists. During a 50-year-long assault by the New Imperialists, they soon understood that fixing such a job was only possible by "Vietnamization" of the struggle: to keep Chinese fighting against Chinese and seek what could come out of it in order to renew its original grip (USA by supporting Chiang Kai-shek *and* Mao Zedong; Japan by setting up Chinese puppet regimes, cooperation with warlords, etc.).

And what about the 'quick response' to the Western assault of those 'Cantonese opium entrepreneurs' or some 'Chinese minority tradition', whatever that may be? It was largely through a Western-organised management that the West's program of creating a mass market for opium in China was executed. It cannot be denied that 'it succeeded far beyond anyone's fears or foresight' (although one can debate the degree to which this happened; see below consumption—production analysis). However, we cannot deny either that Chinese governments always remained highly motivated to suppress this *opium habit as a Western import* product (whether they were successful or not is another story). Mao Zedong and his CCP were no exception at the end of the Republican period and, indeed, continued a two centuries old tradition![27]

The last comment on Fairbank's 'final proposition' concerns the product opium as handled in the British Crown colony Hong Kong until 1997. Fairbank could have checked what was left of his 'great bilateral Sino-foreign joint enterprise' in this British colony in China. Seven years after his text was written, a well-informed commentator wrote:

> In the 1990s, Britain faces one of the most frightening and dangerous influxes of crime that it has ever encountered. Before Communist China takes over Hong Kong in 1997, the world's most ruthless criminal cartel will be stepping up its bid to take control of the underworld of Western society, and to spread within our culture like a criminal cancer. This cartel is the Chinese Triads—the yellow peril of the East, and now the West.[28]

---

[27] On 22-12-2009 it was reported in my newspaper that "China" wanted to execute a British man (with the typical British name: Akmal Shaikh) because he imported four kilos of heroin. Gordon Brown has personally intervened, while the Foreign Office accused the Chinese authorities of not caring about the shaky mind of the smuggler: he must have been 'psychotic', 'unbalanced', 'misled by others' and so on. An old tradition in all respects!

[28] Quoted in Y-K Chu, p. 1.

That he is playing with the classical Western racism concerning the Yellow Danger must be clear after the previous chapter and that it is exaggerated will be discussed later. He rightly points, however, to the nasty effects of the *British stay* in China. Under its colonial responsibility, it offered a haven to a serious international criminal network based on opium and its derivatives, and now it is involved in the usual activities of local gangsters: gambling, prostitution, etc.[29] Certainly in this extent, it would not have been possible under Chinese rule.

---

[29] See also W. Walker III, p. 170–171 for how the American officials were misled by the British and Hong Kong government (including the nearby Portuguese colony of Macao). See for the British Hong-Kong opium history around 1900, the article of E. Sinn.

CHAPTER THIRTY-TWO

OPIUM PRODUCTION AND CONSUMPTION IN CHINA

The imported opium led to a whole gamut of reactions in the Chinese societies: war, criminality, addiction, large profits to new experiments in law and healing practices. First, this word 'societies' is written on purpose in the plural, because in an immense country like China with its large ethnic, cultural, and political diversity, a fully unknown product like opium must have had very different effects. Hosie already reports that 'Mahommedans, Thibetans and Mongols are not addicted to the habit, and not more than 1 per cent of the former are thought to be opium smokers'.[1] They are also inhabitants of China and, therefore, Chinese. Aren't they? The anthropology of the Chinese opium consumer would be a very interesting chapter in our history, but apart from the few data below, there is nearly nothing known at the moment about this subject.

Some compensation for this is given in the first two sections below, before the real production and consumption data are analyzed. In previous parts the health and medical aspects of opium use have been discussed. Some brief remarks about the traditional Chinese medicine and Western medicine in China are made for reasons of comparison to stimulate more relevant research: Chinese medicine has become world famous through the acupuncture hype and the herbal basis of its prescriptions. But around 1900, what was its relation to Western thinking about health and its practice? More specifically: was there some relation with opium, let alone heroin and other chemical derivatives from *Papaver somniferum*?

A very different aspect of the Chinese reactions to the foreign imported opium is the moral-legal one. How did judges cope with these new habits which quickly captivated a million addicts with all possible consequences?

So, before discussing any misunderstandings about the production and consumption patterns in the first half of the twentieth-century, let us look at the following notes on grassroots reactions to the Opium Problem from Chinese medical officers and judges.

---

[1] A. Hosie, vol. 2, p. 253, 256.

The Healers and the Poppy

What was concluded about the European struggles between folk-healers and Enlightenment medical science can be repeated in some sense also in the case of China and India (see ch. 8, 10, 13, 22 and 28). The English or French intruders and aggressive opium dealers were also representatives of this Enlightenment science, and it was, therefore, no surprise that the opium import got unequivocal support from the Royal Commission (1893) thanks to its European medical members. In the most rude way, these medical doctors legitimated not only this socio-economic and political assault, but violated as well the spirit and practice of the traditional Chinese and India health care system.

The latter is well-known at present as Ayurvedic medicine, which uses opium in its prescriptions. It is, however, reported that the 'earliest reference to its medicinal properties is in the *Yogaratnakara*, an Ayurvedic book written in Sinhala verse in the sixteenth-century.'[2] At that time the Portuguese were in the realm, and they had the custom of bringing opium to kings and important people as a gift, not making a commercial profit from it. It could be, therefore, that the Ayurvedic scholars received the stuff (how much? for which kind of prescriptions?) from the Portuguese as one of the earliest proofs of West-East opium communication. I do not know whether something similar happened in Chinese medicine.

All this was similar to an assault on a health monopoly, which arose from the Enlightenment criticism of the folk-healing or lay medicalization in Europe: this had to be eliminated to the advantage of the monopoly profit and status of the "people in the white uniform". That foreigners introduced diseases like syphilis or opium and foreign doctors had no adequate treatment for them was one side of this inflated coin. That the latter did not bother about or understand any aspect of the indigenous healer theories and practices demonstrated their one-sided arrogance. As always, there were exceptions, but they did not influence the general attitudes.

Still, like the missionaries the imported foreign medical personnel also in the end discovered that this Chinese snake was a bit too huge to swallow; one had better get on speaking terms with it before trying to create a performing dragon. There is no better method to do this than making friends through the provision of health services. They must, however,

---

[2] C. Uragoda, p. 69 also for the following information.

be understood as an improvement compared to the existing Chinese system. Was that the case?

The Western doctors had just gained authority thanks to their new monopoly positions, and here in China they were backed in the end by the Western might: until the Boxer Rising they had nothing to fear. However, in Ch'ing China there was a generally unfavorable attitude towards the medical profession, especially by the educated class.[3]

The practice of medicine has been considered 'as an avocation, a side occupation, or else purely a business'. The patient's relatives and friends largely decide whether a prescribed medicine is 'cooling' or 'heating', suitable or unsuitable to the patient. The richer the family, the more doctors who are engaged to write a prescription and explain the supposed cause of the illness. Chimin Wong and Lien-Teh were critical of this tradition, but they could not change the fact that the Western alternative had the handicap of being based on doctors and foreigners.

They even quote at length a long poem from around 1750, entitled 'Lament of Medical Practice', as if it was still relevant in 1936 with sentences like:

> Having nothing to do they take to healing. What do such people know about the value of human life? Or that saving people is not a business proposition? ... Before starting practice they just inquire what medicine the popular quacks are using and then try it on their patients. If some good results happen, they are themselves surprised ... How many innocent boys and girls, young husbands and wives, aged fathers and mothers have you killed? ... etc.[4]

There were even writers who propagated the abolition of medicine. They did not have much influence, but it was symptomatic for a general anti-

---

[3] For the following, K. Chimin Wong, W. Lien-Teh, p. 178–193. The 1000 pages of this history contain a fabulous compilation of medical data of all sorts, in particular about the 19th and early 20th-centuries. It documents in all possible detail 'the struggle between the old and new forces' (p. 159 ff.) in medical practices triggered by the arrival of Western foreigners. Certainly, the second part is an extremely detailed who-is-who of foreign missionaries working in medical services after the 1850s and of physicians working after 1911. They died so quickly or stayed for such a short time that the book is overloaded with names! Apart from the establishment of many small hospitals, a few large ones and other medical institutions like many small opium refuges around 1900 in many places, the overall performance of the missionaries and their doctors is not spectacular. Still, this book is rather unique for its data collection. Nearly all Medical Colleges (national, provincial and private) were established after 1911 (p. 795 ff.); in 1934 there were 426 hospitals with 2,086 physicians, 4,212 nurses and 27,553 beds. Of course, about one-third of all items were located in Kiangsu, with cities like Shanghai and Nanking (p. 814).

[4] Idem, p. 178, 179.

Ill. 32 'Quan shi jieshi dayan wen' (Essay urging the World to give up opium)

Source: This spectacular anti-opium poster was published ca. 1895 by the Shansi Mission (American Board of Commissioners for Foreign Missions Archive).

Western attitude (in this case) combined with an anti-medical doctor one. This is not different from the general attitude about medical doctors in Europe before the Enlightenment. Daumier in mid-19th-century France made the doctors into one of the main targets of his sharpest cartoons thanks to their critical performance. They were the doctors who appeared in the European colonies!

The emancipation of some Chinese doctors occurred through the adoption of Western knowledge and through the relative respect or fear which existed for those "white devils". Their knowledge was spread in China for the first time by an English medical doctor, B. Hobson, who translated some English medical textbooks already in 1851. Very slowly, some Chinese took over much of the new knowledge so that with the establishment of the Republic (1911), radical changes occurred immediately in every walk of life: the super-powerful '*Imperial College of Physicians* was abolished and modern (= Western) trained doctors were for the first time in history appointed as medical officers in the President's office'.[5]

Here, the study of Dikötter on the impact of the modern medical sciences is highly relevant.[6] He documents in detail how a sexual revolution took place in a short time and mainly in all major cities. Here, indeed, the media were the message: many sex periodicals competed with each other for massive profits; sophisticated marketing strategies were successfully developed with the effect that for a few cents new ideas could penetrate

---

[5] Idem, p. 159.
[6] F. Dikötter (1995).

also in the lower classes of society about sex education, the repressive position of women, marriage customs and so on. That in the same flood of publications the typical Western quasi-medical traits of contemporary racial and racist studies (from eugenics to biometrics and race purification) could also be distributed as the ultimate modern idea is the other side of this coin.

Unavoidably, contradictory forces (cultural) clashed when all modernizing groups and movements were all more or less radical anti-Western as in the nationalist movement.[7] This dialectics of modernization resulted, therefore, also in the saving of much traditional Chinese medical knowledge. This support was not only based in the countryside. It resulted also in an enormous drive to self-mobilization conflicting with all attempts to strengthen the uniforming power of the state.

The victory of the CP China, Red Army and Mao did not alter this situation: that attractive, typically Chinese mixture of "old and new" resulted from this constellation, so that acupuncture, ginseng, massage and specific gymnastic exercises became immensely popular around the world in the 1960s.

Therefore, the difference between a Chinese and a Western approach in health matters continues to haunt world politics and economics as the following example demonstrates. On the 10 October 2010 Zhou Xiaochuan, Governor of the Chinese Central Bank, met colleagues from the Western Central Banks in Washington. He was invited to give the speech of the day. He is called 'friend' and 'partner' by his German colleague, and now Zhou aims to explain what is, in fact, a partner today. According to the German weekly *Die Zeit,* he told the meeting:

> The Western method is to prescribe pills, which would be able to solve a problem overnight. However—Zhou paused a while and smiled—he sticks to the Chinese healing methods in which one mixes ten herbs and waits for its long(er)-term effect.[8]

It is also based on this "mixture" that Chimin Wong and Lien-Teh judge the opium problem as 'one of the knottiest problems for China in the Modern Period'.

---

[7] Example: After 1930 the curriculum for medical colleges starts in the first year with 36 lectures 'Principle of Kuomintang'. K. Chimin Wong, W. Lien-Teh, p. 792.

[8] Marc Brost, Mark Schieritz in: *Die Zeit*, 11-11-2010, p. 26. It is a pity that the authors refrain to provide this answer to 'What Zhou means by this, becomes clear two weeks later' (at the G-20 conference).

They start their history with the usual speculation about the introduction of opium in Chinese history: it is mentioned once as an ingredient in a prescription in the first half of the eighth-century, a second time in a treatise in the tenth-century, next time in a popular work of 52 volumes with nearly 12,000 recipes (*Pen-Ts'ao Kang-Mu* or *Great Herbal*; 1596).[9] All this has, of course, nothing to do with their 'knottiest problem'. Ultimately, the first mention of opium smoking comes from foreigners on Java and 'as the Dutch controlled Formosan trade from 1624 to 1662'. In a Chinese publication of 1724, opium *smoking*, confined to a tiny part of the elite on the coast, is mentioned and explained for the first time:

> The confirmed opium smoker is described as black-faced, weak-voiced, watery-eyed, with prolapse of the bowels, and prospects of an early death.[10]

This characterization appears at the same time as the first known government prohibition of opium (1729).

A quite different story concerns the use of the poppy as *capsules* and then as an extract. This custom came from Arab merchants, partly by sea to Canton or overland from Burma and India. It was never widespread, because the poppy was grown only piecemeal.

The most worrying for the authors is the present use of morphia injections and heroin pills ('red pills') which led to a suicide epidemic. A report by the *Shantung Road Hospital* (Shanghai) concerning the years 1921-1926 mentions a total of 4,802 cases of suicide. Of these, more than half were patients using opium. 'No wonder people call opium the great curse of China.'

The first treatments of opium addiction resulted in a remarkable cooperation between Chinese and Western peoples. One of the latter, an American medical doctor and missionary, Macgowan, was inspired to this treatment as follows (ca. 1845):

---

[9] K. Chimin Wong, W. Lien-Teh, p. 105. The title is also written as *Bencao Gangmu* and published at nearly the same time that Paracelsus worked in Europe, but much more relevant than this "inventor" of European homeopathy. Several similar encyclopedic projects were published before, but this one of Li Shi-chen (1518–1593) was not only a critical revision of them but added thousands of lesser-known recipes. About 2,000 substances (clearly divided into mineral, animal and plant) were discussed, including the famous *ginseng*, 'the most celebrated plant in the Orient, on account of its root ... the cure-all ...' (Idem, p. 110). The status of opium in the European pre-Enlightenment medicine and folk-healing (teriaque) was more or less comparable with that of ginseng, which is also used as aphrodisiac. Even more comparable was ephedrine, which was well-known as a stimulant in Li Shi-chen's 900 books.

[10] Idem, p. 182.

A philanthropic Chinese issued handbills where he recommended a simple mixture as a cure for the evil, insisting at the same time upon immediate and total abstinence from the drug. Because the remedy advocated was cheap, few trusted it. However, seeing that some success was obtained, Macgowan adopted this idea and began to administer"empirical remedies, addressed chiefly to the imagination ... to a number of applicants"—not without some good results.[11]

Twenty years later another American medical doctor-missionary, Barchet, opened a 'Homeopathic Dispensary and Opium Refuge' at Ningpo, and the funds for it came eventually from a government official who had earned much money as inspector of the opium manufacture in India. He felt so much guilt that he sponsored the *Church Missionary Society* by giving £3,000 'for curing opium-smokers and combating the evil in other ways'.[12] The treatment was done with 'anti-opium pills' (it is a pity that no ingredients are mentioned) which were also sold to opium smokers. There was such a demand for them that it 'threatened to lose its charitable character'; a remark too pious for pious people?

As in the European and Arab traditions, the Chinese folk-healing was based on a natural foundation of plants, animals and minerals. Therefore, it could not avoid being highly suspicious of the imported chemical and pharmaceutical pills and recipes. The large difference with the European situation was, of course, that in China opium as a non-medical mass product was introduced from outside in a military setting. From the same external address this autonomous product (isolated from its natural environment or robbed of its function as one ingredient among many others) is used as a basis for "chemicalization": heroin, morphine, etc. And later, this heroin or morphine are used in their turn as the source for other new products that produce new and stronger (better marketable) means to addict.

This procedure was also followed with another herbal product, coca leaves. Once it was functional within a specific ethnic, medicinal constellation of Peruvian mountain tribes. When European chemists started to

---

[11] Idem, p. 347, 348.

[12] Idem, p. 379, 433. The 'results had not been very satisfactory' because the missionaries had not enough personnel nor buildings. The *Homeopathic Dispensary* was, in fact, opened in 1878 (Idem, p. 420). In 1868 addicts had to pay $1 'as security' (Idem, p. 407), and ten years later this was $3 (Idem, 420). In Peking an *Opium Refuge* was established in 1878 through cooperation of a Chinese Anti-opium Society and the foreign missions in the city. In 1878 there were 78 smokers admitted with an average stay of 28 days; the next year there were 68 persons sheltered (average six weeks), while 385 were treated outside (Idem, p. 425).

extract cocaine from it and sold this product on the world market, every link to this previous constellation was gone. And, too often, the chemists and pharmacists started making jokes about this previous "primitive" constellation, denying the medicinal or other workings of the plant (animal or mineral) basis.

The best one could expect of this East-West confrontation was demonstrated by the Dutch-American physician Snapper, who spent a few years in Beijing during the Second World War (partly as a prisoner of the Japanese). He must have been one of the last Western physicians serving in China. His main object of inquiry was the differences between diseases called "Western" (in fact: New York) and "Chinese" (in fact: Beijing).[13] The obvious discovery was that the food, the daily diet, was the main reason for these differences, although the Japanese occupation resulted in serious malnutrition among the majority of the population. This is not an ideal situation to inquire into the food comparison.

Therefore, Snapper comes to the wrong conclusion that the Chinese are vegetarians: that is always true if there are no animals left to eat and one is ill-informed about Chinese diets which vary from region to region anyway.[14]

Snapper is more skilled at telling about his actual experience with opium and heroin addicts in his hospital, the *Peiping Union Medical College*.[15] First, he rightly emphasizes that addicted opium smokers should not be identified 'with the opium and morphine addicts of the Western part of the world'. In China, the opium smokers generally do not show the progressive degeneration of the personality which is seen in the West: opium-addicted people suffer here and in the West from different diseases. The former can be treated safely in the common wards, which is fully impossible with the latter. For the Chinese he prescribes:

> In these cases usually the administration of a few cc. of opium tincture or of a mixture containing scopolamine, pilocarpine and dionine is sufficient to still their craving for the opium pipe and to make them reasonably comfortable. Very often these patients beg to be cured of their opium habit, and a gradual decrease of the quantities of opium tincture given for relief of the craving usually suffices to eradicate the addiction.[16]

---

[13] I. Snapper, chapter 1. See also an interview with him in *Time*, 22 December 1941: 'Medicine:Torments of China'.

[14] About the Chinese diets in several parts of the country, see H. Derks (1999), p. 7–12.

[15] For the following see I. Snapper, p. 339–342.

[16] Idem, p. 339. Scopolamine is a drug isolated by a German scientist Ladenburg in 1880; it is derived from a plant of the nightshade family and is one of the active compo-

This prescription and treatment are completely impossible with Western opium addicts: a morphine addict cannot be treated in a common ward, not even in a private room of an ordinary hospital. The patient becomes clinically depressed and is always in danger of committing suicide. There is, furthermore, the dangers of vasomotor collapse and cardiac failure, which is only seen in exceptional cases during the treatment of Chinese opium smokers. Evidently, smoking opium is much less dangerous than consumption by mouth or injection, while opium smoking seldom lead to 'degeneration of the personality'. However, the patients in his hospital told Snapper that this degeneration could have been first and opium smoking secondary.

Also in China heroin addiction poses a fully different and much more dangerous problem. This kind of poisoning is, according to Snapper,

> remarkably frequent here. Per year the emergency clinic ... handles about 100 cases of acute opium poisoning. The fear of death in China is much less developed than in the West, and a relatively slight emotional upset is often sufficient, especially in girls and women, to result in suicide. In Peiping, the taking of opium is the favorite method of accomplishing this purpose.[17]

Between July 1938 and July 1940 there were 198 cases of opium poisoning: 41 died within 24 hours; 16 others later; only 16 recovered. What happened to the rest is not clear; they still needed treatment after July 1940.

It is clear that all the (anti-)drug treatments lagged behind laboratory practice or microbiological and pharmaceutical research by about thirty years. After 1900 this backward position began to be reversed, but the turmoil in the country was not very supportive. In hindsight, there was, however, a remarkable advantage to this backwardness.

In China a very long tradition of folk-healing exists with now famous products like ginseng (imported from the USA in the early 19th-century). This was accompanied by several rather sophisticated kinds of medical

---

nents of products like belladonna. Pilocarpine is an antidote for scopolamine or atropine poisoning. Dionine is better known as ethylmorphine and, therefore, one of the many derivatives of opium. It was invented by Merck in 1884. See for the details the relevant *Wikipedia* articles. At the moment dionine is a product of the Ghazipur opium factory, which also produces codeine, morphine, narcotine or thebaine. The Ghazipur factory is called by *BBC News* 'the world's largest opium factory' (2008/07/21).

[17] Idem, p. 340. Snapper writes that, although he cannot affirm the curative influence of the drug *coramin* on the poisoning, this drug 'seems to have a beneficial influence in this intoxication ...' (Idem, p. 342). I can imagine why: this drug is produced from the cattle and pig cardiac muscle, which must be beneficial to Chinese vegetarians!

techniques and methods. Massages, gymnastic exercises and acupuncture became well-known thanks to the many international, alternative, social and religious movements beginning in the 1960s.[18]

As TCM ("Traditional Chinese Medicine"), it has nowadays emancipated into a 'recognized medical system in the western world'. However, the Western branch of it does not much resemble what Chinese apothecaries and pharmacists present on the corners of normal Chinese streets. The strong herbal basis of this folk-healing and its relative present popularity also among Western people have led to prescriptions aimed at healing opium or heroin addiction as well.[19]

It is remarkable that in the new *Peoples Republic*, debates among Chinese medical and pharmaceutical scholars started immediately along the classical divide between traditional and modern. But already by the mid-1950s, the government 'made a full-scale commitment to the wholesale acceptance and study of traditional Chinese medicine' with 'some fascinating discoveries, and has made Chinese medical practice today rather unique in the world'.[20] A new embedding of healing methods in social and cultural settings was developed.

Cooperation between the several hundred thousand traditional Chinese herbalists and acupuncturists became absolute necessity, even without the positive incentives: otherwise, too many people had no medical care at all. Another improvement concerns the health infrastructure. The barefoot doctor program and the policy of 'the mass line' became

---

[18] Two examples from many: in 2009 one in ten Australians received acupuncture treatment by some experts. Health insurance funds offer rebates; statutory regulations have been implemented; acupuncture begins to integrate into mainstream health care; and so on. See article of C. Changli Xue et al, in: *Chinese Medicine*, 4 (2009). The Australian background of it can be traced back to the 1850s when the first Chinese immigrants arrived and worked in the gold fields. Acupuncture remained unregulated until 1970, when professionalization started. See for the following also www.nursegroups.com/article/traditional-chinese-medicine.html. In 2006 a new journal *Chinese Medicine* (University of Macau) was published because since the 1990s 'there has been a phenomenal growth of interest in traditional medicine knowledge and practices, which is evident in the increasing World Health Organization (WHO) activities and publications, such as Global Strategy for Traditional Medicine (2002-2005).' Editorial no. 1.

[19] For instance the OHAH product (Opioid + Heroin Antagonist Herbs) of www.natureproducts.net. Another example: in the *American Journal of Chinese Medicine*, 4 (1976), p. 403-407, an article about the acupuncture treatment of drug addiction in Pakistan (Shuaib BM) describes how Professor Wen's technique of electro-acupuncture was used successfully for treatment of withdrawal symptoms in 19 drug abusers. Especially for opium addicts this kind of treatment was effective: much shorter than with codeine substitution therapy, effective, simple and more economical. See www.ncbi.nlm.nih.gov.

[20] The article of Kenneth Levin in: G.B.Risse (ed.), p. 107.

spectacular and well-known. Both grew out of China's woefully inadequate medical facilities and poorly trained personnel.

The barefoot doctor program has been since 1965 a highly effective tool to improve the health of the majority of the peasants all over this immense country. It is oriented to the specific diseases and illnesses common in the area; traditional Chinese herbal medicine and acupuncture are standard in this program; the medical personnel are recruited from a specific region and return after the training to their area. For Third World nations and for war situations (Vietnam), it was much more advantageous than the Western programs, which were characterized by expensive and often inefficient practices, which almost never reached peasant populations since they were bound to cities.[21]

The policy of 'the mass line' concerns the mobilization of the whole population to help the medical workers.[22] The first projects were campaigns to clean up the cities and eliminate the so-called "four pests": rats, flies, bedbugs and mosquitoes, but in some areas also lice and grain-eating sparrows (only the latter received special attention in Western newsreels, largely making fun of the people doing this action). Other 'mass line' projects concerned community hygiene, widespread vaccination programs, and they led to the virtually complete elimination of venereal disease. These kinds of projects were probably even more important to create a common solidarity, in which destitute, poor or degenerate people also found acceptance and a social task.

For the drug addicts there were special treatment and rehabilitation courses in special centers from 1950 onwards. But, in my view, it was this general improvement of health, the health infrastructure combined with the traditional medicinal techniques and mass actions which eradicated the large-scale opium and narcotic problems. It was the first country which succeeded in this task; folk-healing became healing of the folk.[23]

---

[21] See the article of Paul G. Pickowicz in: G.B.Risse (ed.), p. 124–147.

[22] K. Levin in: G.B.Risse (ed.), p. 109 ff. The success of the "mass line" projects was also favored by the new Marriage Law of 1950 in which the status of women was completely reversed with the passage of equal rights legislation. They constituted half of the population which became rather satisfied.

[23] The present situation falls far outside the scope of this book. Now there is strong urbanization, individualization and increased wealth, reports are published regularly about a new drug addiction problem in China: it is estimated that in Yunnan province there are annually 50–60,000 heroin addicts thanks to Burmese heroin import. More than 50 methadone treatment clinics have been opened in Yunnan. See article of Francis Wade, 16-11-2010 in www.dvb.no "Burma fueling China's heroin crisis". Another report says: 'With drug abuse on the rise in China, there could be estimated 2.3 million drug addicts in the country, according to a health official', etc. in: www.thaindian.com 26 June 2008. The same

The Judge and the Poppy

The heritage of the British, French and other foreigners in the coastal ports or the International Settlement had serious criminal aspects (see ch. 6 and 23). As the Western foreign occupiers slowly retreated and the Chinese had to take their fate into their own hands, they had to cope with brand new problems in many respects. Solutions had to be found by trial and error and often under the threat of competing warlords. An important, but not properly researched aspect was the way judges had to cope with the new problems. The following acquaintance with their struggle for justice is another introduction to the analysis of the whole internal Chinese opium situation at the beginning of the 20th-century.

The starting point is the fact that nearly all previous Chinese governments (national and provincial, notwithstanding their mutual tensions) regularly prohibited (and prosecuted) opium criminals, fought in wars against foreign opium nations, opium traders, opium users or opium production.[24] Indeed, some paid only lip-service to the general norm: Suppress Opium! and started or continued the illicit opium business. Except in the stories told by grandfathers and fathers, after 1911 every Chinese knew that this was an illegal and criminal trade. How were these opinions formed?

First and foremost by a huge anti-opium campaign of the national government before 1911. At all other Chinese levels, this triggered smaller initiatives. The judges only had to cope with the consequences. One of the main means through which this was done was a rather new criminal law practice. A Supreme Court (SC) was established by an imperial edict as a striking innovation (December 1906).[25] After the revolution of 1911, the

---

source reports a year later that 'Number of young women drug addicts escalating in Beijing' (26 June 2009). The difficulties with these reports is that their sources are not mentioned or are so ambiguous that they can also concern the usual secret service spam.

[24] In the four volumes of H. Morse (1926), the prohibition of opium is documented time and again from vol. I, p. 215 onwards. For literal texts of these 'Special Edicts' and letters from the Hoppo or the Hong merchants in 1820 only, see H. Morse (1926), vol. III, p. 385–388. Their last words were often 'Feel a cold Shiver at this'. Apparently, it made no impression on the EIC because the number of its ships increased year after year as Morse's statistics after these Edicts indicate (Idem, p. 389–398): in 1805 there were 17 EIC ships, in 1816 already 29 and in 1820 still 23. All 311 ships had opium in the cargo apart from other 'Western Goods' not beloved by the Chinese. By no means were they the only foreign ships; many American, French, Dutch, private English or Indian vessels were involved in the opium smuggling.

[25] For the following including the quotations, see M. van der Valk (ed.), p. 59, 60, 63, 64, 67, 73, 74. This is a collection of 559 rules of the SC in 1915 and 1916 in Chinese and Eng-

new constitution of Nanking guaranteed the law-courts' independence. They functioned remarkably well until the warlords created so much chaos and civil war that this innovation also perished. Therefore, the rulings of the SC in these two years concerning opium and its use represent a serious attempt to come to terms with this phenomenon.

We must conclude that—quantitatively—opium cases belong here to the less important subjects. Apparently, the large anti-opium campaigns of both the imperial and early republican government must have had their effects. The overwhelming majority of cases concern family problems (marriage, abortion, adoption, divorce, inheritance and so on). I count only 18 "opium cases". Here are a few examples:

'A substance not actually opium' is sold for the purpose of blending it. How shall we deal with it? The SC told a procurator of a High Court that the meaning of this is too unclear: if the substance is like opium, but blended with other matter and falsely designated as opium, it shall be punished according to article X; if the substance has nothing to do with opium, the offense shall be punished according to article Y.

In the same month (January 1915) the question was posed of whether swallowing opium as a form of medicine is included under smoking. SC answer: smoking is not the same as taking medicine. However, if opium medicine is taken as a substitute for smoking, it is certainly an offense. The making and using of morphia (in pills) is sometimes done for the purpose of withstanding 'the craving for morphia'. What to do? asks the Fukien High Court, whereupon the SC answers: in all cases mention 'the making of pills shall be punishable in virtue of ... article ...'

The Ministry of Justice reported to the SC about a proposal to punish dealing in poppy seeds or keeping poppy seeds in order to deal in them. The difficulty was that the text of the proposal did not cover the case well enough. This could imply that keeping a stock, without the intent to deal, is always punished which is 'in disharmony with the principle of proportion between offense and punishment'. Do you, SC, agree with this interpretation? This question was affirmed but, in my opinion at least, the

---

lish translation. They were mostly answers to requests of provincial or local law courts about whether their rulings were right or wrong. They represent as such a phase in the development of the modernization of the whole judicial system. 'The SC has drawn into the discussion a large number of factors, which formerly were quite unknown in China; praiseworthy, indeed, but from the point of view of the simple district-magistrate highly confusing. Still ... they aim at either maintaining, or supplementing, sometimes even at altering the written law in force ...' (p. 26). It is impossible to discuss the highly interesting and complicated background of this development.

judgement was itself unclear since the necessary distinction was not made between possession in order to deal or to use it oneself.

The SC also created a serious problem when the Shanghai district court asked: '... Shall the smoking of opium to which a tax stamp of the Ministry of Finance has been attached be punishable? ...'[26] This time the answer was crystal clear: '... the smoking of opium is always punishable, irrelevant whether tax has been paid or not ...' We do not find the obvious conclusion that the Ministry of Finance was receiving money from criminal acts or, by necessity, becoming involved in criminal networks.

Another case mentioned here concerns a Kansu peasant accused of illicit planting of poppy. He was contracted by A for a certain sum of money. In turn, A contracted B for all the young poppy plants. At the time of the harvest, however, it was discovered that the peasant had absconded. Question: should A and B still be punished? The SC replied in the affirmative.[27]

This casuistic continues with: if somebody keeps opium in his possession, never uses it but provides another with it, without having any profit, who is punishable? The SC rules that the original possessor is punishable.[28] And so on.

Because of their low number, these cases suggest that, contrary to what happened later in China, the opium problem is under control at this time. They also show that nearly every *internal Chinese* element of this problem is somehow covered by legal activities and judgments.

This demonstration of an orderly, managed society is given in a period in which, according to all imperialists and their historians, China was on the brink of collapse, the old empire disappeared in favor of a Republic, and warlords started to carry out their nasty business.[29]

Dikötter made an extensive study of crime and its punishment in a later period. The opium problem was not addressed in particular, but a few data can be illustrative for the development of this problem in the Republican period.

---

[26] Idem, p. 107; p. 129 the same question is asked by the Kwangtung High Court.

[27] Idem, p. 311.

[28] Idem, p. 328.

[29] Recently, J. Madancy published a book about this anti-opium action. I could not use it. See also W. Willoughby, vol. II, p. 1095–1098, C. Trocki (1999a), p. 128 ff., while R.K. Newman (1989) covers the same period and attempts to eradicate the opium production and traffic in an interesting way. I hope Madancy analyzed in much more detail the performance of all parties in the opium game, because Newman here largely confined his story to the British top bureaucrats in London, India and China.

In 1920 'the largest category of sentenced criminals among a registered national total of 41,911 cases were thieves (4,369) and opium smokers (2,939) sentenced to terms of several months ...'[30] This is only 7% for the latter. A few years earlier, in a Fengtian province prison, about 10% of the inmates were convicted for opium-related crimes.[31] In 1920, however, in another prison 'a vast majority' was sentenced for morphine addiction; in 1928 elsewhere a quarter of the inmates were sentenced for morphine possession, but in both situations only a handful for opium consumption.

Throughout republican China the majority of criminals were poor people coming from the countryside sentenced to relatively short terms; the reverse was also appropriate: the higher the status of a social group, the lower its representation in prison populations.[32] This is no exception from the daily practice in modern Western society. This is also true for the conclusion that prisons became sites of drug consumption and dealings.[33]

An important element in all these Chinese republican prison and crime data seems to be a clear shift from opium to heroin and morphine use. Also, there was a clear shift from theft as the main reason for imprisonment until about 1920 to drugs-related crimes later: around 1930 a third was convicted for a drugs-related offense and a quarter for theft, while already a year later the former was perceived as 'the most common crime'. Indeed, now the Opium Problem has been aggravated into a heroin and morphine problem. Still, one wonders how relatively few people were "treated" by the judges and their prisons, in view of the supposedly huge consumption of drugs and local production.

Chinese Republican Opium Production

Fairbank knew perfectly well that at the end of the 18th-century, opium was not yet a mass product in China spread by 'uncouth and greedy' Western merchants but only one of the many luxuries available to a few representatives of the elite. Obviously, it was already something illegal

---

[30] F. Dikötter (2002), p. 77. One of these must have been a morphine addict, Li Youling, a recidivist who had stolen iron bars because he was short of cash and desperate for a new dose. In 1917 he was given a two-month sentence after which he was sent back to the local court for supervision (Idem, p. 84).

[31] Idem, p. 97. In identifying the ca. 1,000 prison inmates in Fengtian province (1914), it appears that 256 inmates were convicted for theft, 143 for murder or wounding, 116 for gambling and 107 or 10% for opium-related crimes.

[32] Idem, p. 99.

[33] Idem, p. 126.

and illicit. And he also knew that a Chinese opium production on some scale started *after* the Opium Wars. Who took the initiative to start a *Chinese* production which could bear this name is still an unanswered question, but it apparently happened despite the many exaggerations. It even became an import substitution that worried the British-Indian producers and importers. It was long after the end of the Second Opium War, around 1875, however, when the following production level was reached.

For the pre-1911 situation the only production estimates from a reliable source that I could find were: in the provinces of Fukien, Kiangsi and Kwantung the production was less than 2,000 *piculs* per year (= 100 metric tons); even closer to the coast in the provinces of Chekiang, Kiangsu, Shantung and Chihli it was 3,000-10,000 *piculs* per year (= 150-500 metric tons); and in some provinces along the Yangtze river (Hunan, Hupei and Anhwei) it was the same. A substantial production of more than 10,000 *piculs* could be found in Manchuria, Shensi, Kweichow and Yunnan. The absolute exception was the province of Szechuan with a production of 250,000 *piculs* a year (12,500 tons).[34] In about ten provinces there was no opium production at all.

It was the dying empire which was able to launch an opium suppression program that was so successful that even in the province of Szechuan 'hardly a stalk of poppy could be found' (British inspector Hosie). If Fairbank's 'great bilateral Sino-foreign joint enterprise of the nineteenth-century' had existed, it was now eradicated. This is so far the larger context of the Chinese's own performance. What happened later?

It is in fact Lossing Buck's famous investigation of 17,000 Chinese farms all over the country which provides the first sound statistical results from before 1945.[35] They concern, however, the utilization of the land. An economic assessment of poppy growing has to rely on more and other data. Still, Lossing Buck's study is a necessary prerequisite to arrive at such an assessment.

He cooperated with many experts, including the well-known geologist and geographer Cressey. Their work was very difficult in a land flooded by foreign enemies, civil agitators and bandits of all sorts. Cressey tells, for

---

[34] W. Walker III, p. 8, 15.

[35] J. Lossing Buck (1964), which concerns a reprint of the 1937 edition. Unfortunately, J. Lossing Buck et al. (1966) contains a most unreadable contribution in a Taiwanese propaganda publication. It is only interesting that in this last book, no word about opium can be found. His pre-war investigations are fully indispensable contrary to the information received from amateur travelers or missionaries. See for this K.McMahon, p. 98 ff., which has a typical victims' approach.

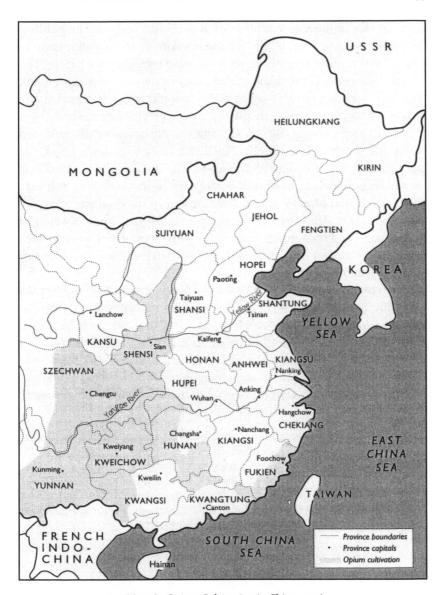

Map 18. Opium Cultivation in China, 1920'

Source: W. Walker III, p. 33. Compared to map 17 much less provinces are affected;
it should have been the reverse taking into account the efforts of the war lords.

instance, that at the moment his book was about to appear, the publishing plant was destroyed by the Japanese invasion of Shanghai early in 1932: all maps, photographs, etc. were lost, and he had to start again. The map reproduced here provides a global image of the poppy-growing areas. It must be seen as a possible regional division and not as an actual one.[36]

Lossing Buck's study already provides more precise information about the location of a poppy culture. His study is divided over the northern wheat and southern rice regions. The former is broken down into three and the latter into five agricultural areas. The opium type of farming is located in only two areas of this rice region: in the Szechuan rice area about 11% is occupied by opium farming and in the Southwestern rice area, about 19%. The latter covers the provinces of Yunnan, Kweichow and Kwangsi and the former, most of the provinces of Szechuan, Hupeh and Hunan. Another indication is that of the 156 localities studied, 29 or 19% sold opium somehow.[37]

The table indicates in fact a dramatic development. The attempts of the Chinese government to diminish the poppy culture reported above in the "Hosie paragraph" was successful. In North China farmers increased their planting of beans or other products as a substitute cash crop. But thanks to the subsequent anarchistic warlord period, this success was reversed.[38] What more can be said about opium production in China?

One of Lossing Buck's larger comments on the Opium Problem is quite symptomatic:

> The growing of the opium poppy is affected by political policy but is confined largely to the frontier provinces, since its value per unit of weight is high, and is, therefore, easily transported. Tsinghai is an exception, as the provincial authorities do not allow its culture in that province. As one crosses the border of Kansu and Tsinghai, between Lanchow and Sining, one finds a sharp demarcation between the areas growing the opium poppy and those where it has been completely suppressed.[39]

---

[36] Nowhere could an analysis or even a reasonable guess be found of the square miles of *cultivated* land per agricultural product per province (and period), so that also for opium a relevant analysis could be made.

[37] Idem, table 1 p. 34 and table 22 p. 234. The types of farming altogether do not cover the full 100%, so I added 'about'.

[38] Idem, p. 9.

[39] J. Lossing Buck (1964), p. 206. Below it is impossible to cover all remarks about opium, which are many more than indicated in the index: see, for instance, also p. 34, 78, 80, 87–91, 230–232, 304, 309, 313, etc.

Table 47. Trends in crop acreages between 1904-9 and 1930-3[40]

	Number of localities reporting	Estimated percentage of total crop area in the reporting localities			
		1904–9	1914–19	1924–9	1930–3
Crops whose acreage increased or was unchanged (selection)					
Corn	22	11	14	16	17
Cotton	29	11	14	18	20
Opium	13	14	3	11	20
Rice	17	40	41	37	40
Soy-beans	7	8	9	10	8
Sweet potatoes	18	10	11	12	13
wheat	29	26	27	27	27
Crops whose acreage decreased (selection)					
barley	10	24	23	20	19
millet	15	22	18	17	17

That the growing of the poppy is a matter of politics is an understatement in a country in which many political and military leaders (warlords) after about 1920 had connections to the opium underworld to get their activities financed. Cressey tells:

> In many provinces farmers have been forced by the military authorities to raise opium for taxation purposes, and in this way considerable areas of the best land have been removed from food production.[41]

The warlords' constant money demands led to a farmer's dilemma: because this demand is so severe the peasants have to grow poppies, as it is the only product with which could pay such high "taxes", while it is very risky to refuse. In addition: what happens after the harvest? Is the result paid in barter as "tax" to the military or first marketed before paying "tax" in cash? And are these "taxes" nothing but compulsory deliveries? All this remains in the dark or should be read between the lines. However, even at the time of Lossing Buck's investigations, 1929-1933, there were still Chinese governments which prohibited opium growing: a remarkable example of "civil courage" in this chaotic period, when corruption is the country's greatest plague.

---

[40] Quoted in A. Feuerwerker, p. 8 from J. Lossing Buck.
[41] G. Cressey, p. 144. See for the warlord's opium revenue also James Sheridan's contribution to J. Fairbank (ed.), p. 291 ff.

Not all of the provinces mentioned border foreign countries. However, the location of many poppy fields points to an important characteristic of the opium production: it concerns a cash crop and apparently largely an export product for Southeast Asia from Canton, for further sea export or other locations in China. At least, we have to conclude with Lossing Buck that opium together with tobacco belong to the crops of which 75% is sold (opium seeds nearly 80%). Only 15% of rice is sold and, therefore, 85% is used on the farm for consumption or payments. Poppy products are also used for food and energy on the farm (about 20%) and for paying rent (1%).[42]

While the above concerns some orientation to a market, another element of opium production is related to the state-bureaucracy:

> Taxation often influences land utilization, and in China this is most noticeable in certain frontier provinces with the high opium tax which compels the farmer to plant opium in order to meet his tax bill.[43]

Also in this case, a farmer's dilemma exists and a bureaucrat's burden: to pay these state taxes, opium has to be grown, and when opium is planted, one has to pay a special high opium tax. The investigators counted 188 different taxes for different grades of farmland. From 1908 to 1933 the tax burden was doubled. Generally, on high-grade land in China as a whole, the opium tax was 5% of all taxes, the road tax 10% and the military tax 23%. There are, however, large differences in tax burdens.

In the wheat region the average on low-grade land was $4.05 per acre; in the rice region it was $7.05. By far the highest tax was paid in three localities in Szechuan: $27.85 per acre. Once broken down, the two largest components of this amount were $5.48 as opium tax and $10.94 for roads; the rest is for many other local purposes. On the highest-grade land in the wheat region, one had to pay on average $7.63 compared to $9.42 in the rice region. For the three expensive localities in Szechuan, the average was $33.56, of which $6.10 was the opium tax, $11.14 for roads, etc.[44] From

---

[42] J. Lossing Buck (1964), p. 233, table 22 p. 234, figure 5 p. 235 and table 23 p. 237. Opium stalks are all used on the farm mainly for fuel (86%) and the rest for 'industrial' purposes such as thatching and other building purposes, sandals or rope (see table 24, p. 238 and p. 239).

[43] Idem, p. 323. See also G. Cressey, p. 316 for opium as 'the most attractive crop for taxation' in Szechuan. In p. 144 one can read: 'In many provinces farmers have been forced by the military authorities to raise opium for taxation purposes, and in this way considerable areas of the best land have been removed from food production.'

[44] Idem, p. 325.

these taxes roughly 55% went to the *hsien* (county) government and the rest to national or local authorities.

There is also a most dramatic picture of what the populations had to suffer from 1904 to 1929 in terms of calamities, famines, starvation and even cannibalism (which was confined to some parts of the wheat region). The opium areas experienced a crop destruction of 20-80% during all these calamities. Whatever we know about the fabulous profits of the opium trade, the peasants who have to do the dirty work earned the lowest wages of all![45] In particular in the Southwestern rice area, peasants must belong to the poorest of China: their savings and the value of their farm buildings are far below the Chinese average, while it houses the densest farm population.[46] That's also opium life in China.

The last general question which remains concerns the danger of a Chinese world pollution with narcotics as, for instance, Black envisaged after 1997. Did this fear already exist in the Republican period?

It must be a matter of gangster and smuggler activities for which, of course, no statistics exist. Neither Lossing Buck nor Cressey provide official data about opium as a Chinese export.[47] Only from the first decade of the twentieth-century could the following table be composed about the value of opium trade compared to other products. It concerns all overseas trade, which is not necessarily confined to foreign destinations. Chinese coastal traffic is intensive and far-reaching. It cannot be all Chinese trade either, as a substantial part concerns trade done by foreign companies. So, 'domestic trade' is here exclusive of the overland and river trade that does not reach the customs authorities.

This illustrates the proportion of the opium export or domestic trade, which is 0.3% and 7% of the total, respectively. It involves sums of $351,000 and $4,563,000, respectively, which are not at all impressive even in the currency of the time. The first is less than the Yunnanese opium smugglers made in one trip in 1917 (see below). It is a pity that there are no data for 1928, although the opium business flourished much better.

If we should increase the 1908 opium figures 1.5 times proportionately to the increase of the export-domestic trade, the result is around 1930: $1.890.000 and $29,110,000 respectively. If one takes a given price per

---

[45] Idem, table 1, p. 37 the heading 'Wages of farm year labor, including value of food and other perquisites (in yuan)" is accompanied in Szechuan with nearly the lowest intake of calories 'per adult-male unit per day'!

[46] Idem, table 1, p. 38. An explanation for this is probably the high taxation in the area (Id., p. 81).

[47] See G. Cressey, p. 137–142.

Table 48. Commodity composition of maritime Customs trade in 1908 and 1928 (x million HK taels)[48]

	Exports Abroad 1908	Domestic Trade 1908	Exports Abroad 1928	Domestic Trade 1928
Silk	83	14,1	187,6	7,7
Tea	32,8	4,1	37,1	19,7
Cotton and cotton textiles	12,9	5,4	73	258,4
Grain and flour	---	23,9	37,4	88,7
Beans and bean-cake	23,4	15,2	201,3	40,8
Oils and seeds	15,1	11,1	58,4	28,7
Tobacco and cigarettes	2,7	6,5	25,3	70,5
Sugar	1,4	5,2	0,3	2,6
Opium	0,9	11,7	--- [3.83]	--- [74.65]
Other	104,5	64,9	371	171,5
TOTAL	276,7	162,1	991,4	688,6

ounce of $2.7, these export-domestic trade amounts represent weights of respectively 700,000 ounce (about 21,000 kilo) and 10,781,481 ounce (about 323,500 kilo).

Why do I introduce these details? Because of a political statement in 1930 made by a State Department official, Stuart J. Fuller, an expert on narcotics; a statement similar to the one of Black in 1997. For some years Fuller was a consular official in Tientsin, but his main "qualification" was that he closely collaborated with the activist Harry Anslinger, the most influential designer of the American foreign policy on drugs before and long after 1945. In a London meeting (May 1936) Fuller sketched a Chinese opium problem of immense proportions:

> Total opium poppy production in China amounted to 12,000-18,000 metric tons, only 1,325 tons of which were grown in Manchuria and Jehol. Yunnan, where suppression officials ordered farmers to grow poppies, produced more than 4,600 tons; Szechuan totaled nearly as much. Shensi and Kansu also showed signs of unusually large increases in opium growth from earlier years. ... a narcotic menace to the rest of the world. In 1934 alone ... some 24,000 kilograms of acid acetic anhydride were imported into Shanghai,

---

[48] D. Perkins et al, p. 121, 361. Perkins thinks that 'the only aspects of Chinese trade' with 'a clear negative impact was the import of opium'. Alas, he refrains from studying it because 'it is customary for economists to eschew moral judgments' (p. 133). Albert Feuerwerker in J. Fairbank (ed.), p. 122 ff. provided the available official trade data without a differentiation of export and domestic trade and, most remarkably, without mentioning opium, notwithstanding his knowledge (Idem, p. 125) that 'opium was the most important import into China' until the 1890s. Apparently, it suddenly disappeared.

enough to produce 4.4 million average doses of heroin. China ... had the capacity to produce thirty to sixty times the world's legitimate annual heroin requirements ...[49]

Fuller also condemned the illicit traffic to Canada and the United States from North China, accusing directly the Japanese Ministry of the Interior for its permission to produce the drugs. A year later the crusade against Japan's and China's production was stepped up; he called special attention to the clandestine manufacturing of narcotics in areas of China under Japan's control (Peiping, Tientsin and Hopei). It is clear that Fuller greatly exaggerated. That is not to say that the Chinese Opium Problem in the Republican Period was a minor one. At that time the ambiguous "War On Drugs" was invented. In particular, the remarkable role of Japan should have been stressed.

The *South China Morning Post* wrote about it as one of the strongest indictments of Japan's opium policy and concluded with:

> Humanity has come to rely heavily upon American aid in the war on drugs.[50] Indirect accusations were made that Tokyo 'not so much intended to poison the Chinese people' but ...

Fuller oversimplified contradictory information, and he accepted also the allegation that 90% of all illegal narcotics marketed internationally was of Japanese origin, including the 500 kg of heroin that reached the USA weekly. This alarmed American officials, but did not lead to any relevant actions towards opium suppression. The alarm and fear incited was enough, as usual with bureaucrats, but the relevant measures must be initiated by exterior sources or circumstances.

The *Shanghai Evening Post and Mercury* wrote that around 1937, about 700,000 people worked in the opium business, China's only billion-dollar retail trade. More than three-quarters of them lived in Kweichow, Szechuan and Yunnan. It even warned critics of the government in Nanking to be cautious because of its alliance with the former opium racketeers 'now perfumed into respectability' without changing 'its essential nature of gangsterdom'.

But Chiang Kai-shek's alliance with opium was no reason for the British or the Americans to reconsider their own interests: it could have meant not only an anti-Chiang and anti-Japan policy, but also a coalition between them and the many Chinese anti-opium organizations, including the

---

[49] Quoted in W. Walker III, p. 99.
[50] Idem, p. 102.

Communist Party of Mao Zedong. The early successes of the Japanese army against Chinese cities, however, put the opium question in the background and the association with China at war as more urgent.

Fuller mentions Yunnan as producing (or trading?) 4,600 tons of opium (per year?). Yunnan was, indeed, an "opium sucked province". Is it possible to get a straight picture of the situation here without using Fuller's figures?

Yunnan Opium Production and Trade

Yunnan (about 110,000 square miles) is a province with many hills and rough mountains with peaks above 5,000 meters and oval valleys (*Ba Tze*).[51] About 80% of these valleys are planted with rice in the summer and broad beans, wheat and opium in the winter. The degree of terracing is high compared to other areas. The size of parcels, of not quite two-thirds of an acre, is below the average for the region, and the size of the fields (0.12 acres) is the smallest in China. Cultivation must be intensive since the yields are high compared to all other areas. The cultivated acreage of Yunnan in the Republican period was about 25 million *mou* or about 1.7 million hectares (about 17% of the total surface).[52]

To give an impression of how labor-intensive opium production is, it is illuminating to know that to make one raw opium ball implies 230 *hours* of labor; one hectare results normally in about 13 kilo of opium, for which one has to work 816 labor*days*.[53] In winter, the cultivated acreage must be divided over three products. How much is used for the poppy culture is not known to me, but in the previous table we can see how important beans are for food and export. So let's suppose that 10% is reserved for opium or about 170,000 hectares, then this would result in a production of about 2.2 million kilo of raw opium. Under military or bureaucratic pres-

---

[51]   See for the following Idem, p. 87–91, p. 97 ff. G. Cressey, chapter 20 and D. Perkins et al, passim who made a reassessment of Lossing Buck's figures of all crop yields and output data in Yunnan and the other provinces from 1914–1957. See the article of M. Swain in D. Leese (ed.), p. 1066 ff. Also interesting is D. Duco, passim.

[52]   Calculated from Perkins table B. 14, p. 236 an average of the 1913 and 1933 figures. It is not possible to calculate further the winter acreages of beans, wheat and opium, which is important data to assess the opium output. It is only logical that opium takes the minor position of the three: beans are after silk the largest export article of China in this period, and wheat is a most important food in winter time. This argumentation, however, is not necessarily the one of the Yunnanese peasants!

[53]   D. Duco, p. 238 note 62.

sure this percentage can, of course, increase. In that case, the production of 4,600 metric tons remains very high, but becomes a possibility.[54]

The production of opium here is a copy of the Indian method and started after 1860. Many Yuannanese migrated to the southern parts of the province bordering what in the 20th-century became the *Golden Triangle* (Quadrangle).

In China the end product is not provided in opium balls but in slabs which are typically called *Yunnans*. In other aspects of the opium production, like the making of opium pipes or boxes, special tables or drawers, etc. "opium provinces" like Yunnan or Szechuan excel. Yunnan produces the cheapest pipes of *pakton(g)*, Chinese silver, but also the most beautiful ones for the landlords.[55]

Not unimportant for the production circumstances are the many tensions between the Han Chinese (only 20%) in the valleys and the Hakkas or the descendants of many older aboriginal tribes in the mountains. The Han are mostly the landlords and the Hakkas the tenants, while the mountain people carry on their old tribal mode of life. They are, however, the landlords who insist that farmers sow poppy fields, while threatening to harm anyone who attempts to stop the farmers.[56]

Rice is, of course, the dominant product, but Cressey mentions that in 1923 poppy occupied two-thirds of the cultivated land during the *winter* season, as was the case in Kweichow. This is not well founded by Lossing Buck's study. About Yunnan the latter states:

> The area is suitable for production of the opium poppy because of the difficulty of transporting more bulky and less valuable products, and the revenues of this trade have had an important influence on the political situation of the provinces within the area. Moreover, income from an acre of opium poppy is much larger than from any other winter crop which might be planted.[57]

---

[54] It is, therefore, a physical impossibility to produce 100 million taels of opium, which is about 67 million kilo, as J. Marshall, p. 25 states (the Cantonese *tael* = 1.33 lb.). Under very strong (military) pressure, one can squeeze about 5 million kilo raw opium out of Yunnan. Also, the other figures about Yunnan are exaggerated.

[55] In Duco the most excellent collection of pipes, etc. is given. Small wonder, because he is the Director of the Amsterdam Pipes Museum, with one of the most outstanding collections in the world. Www.pijpenkabinet.nl.

[56] W. Walker III, p. 23. Elsewhere (Szechuan) the republican provincial authority ordered this, and in Kansu it was the officials who did the same.

[57] J. Lossing Buck (1964), p. 89.

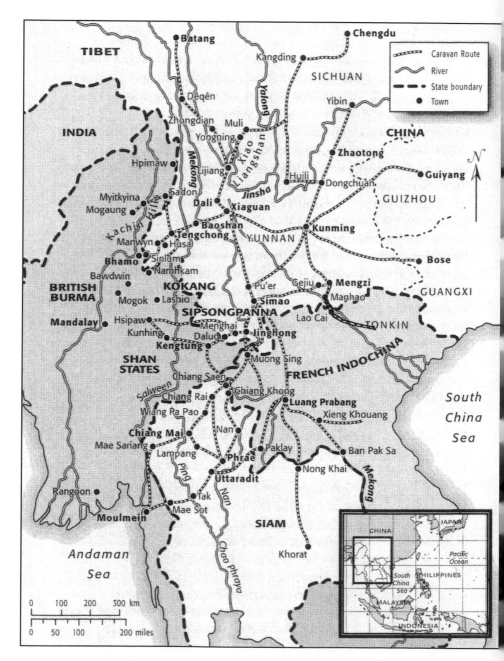

Map 19. Caravan Routes in the "Golden Quadrangle", ca. 1900

Source: A. Maxwell Hill, p.39

The area was quite inaccessible except for the French railway from Indo-China into the capital Yunnanfu, and a limited mileage of paved roads. Lossing Buck's recommendation for the area is, therefore, the improvement of transportation to other parts of China. This is followed by:

> With such a development the growing of the opium poppy could be more easily suppressed and the mountainsides could be devoted more readily to uses such as forests and special tree products.[58]

At that time it was a very optimistic recommendation. Cressey's information about the capital Yunnanfu (about 140,000 inhabitants) states that

> it is said that 90 per cent of the men and 60 per cent of the women are addicted to the habit of opium smoking. Many hsien produce from one to two million ounces and the removal of so much first-class agricultural land from useful production has induced a serious food shortage.[59]

This is not confirmed by Lossing Buck's later study because the relationship opium farming-food shortage is not made. Famines occurred many times and for many reasons (floods, droughts, insects, war or frost), mostly in the wheat region, double as many as in the rice region in which the opium areas are situated.[60]

Cressey, furthermore, makes the classic mistake of perceiving smoking as addiction. His remark could concern here a smoking habit largely comparable to cigarette smoking, he has no data about real addiction and smoking habits. When he complains about the statistics for Yunnan and Kweichow, we have to consider 'it is said' as the whispering of some missionary.[61] Still, with his remark Cressey pointed to a specific market for Yunnan opium, which brings us to the trade aspects of the Yunnan case.

Because Yunnan is one of the few production areas, its export must be important. Modern studies reveal that this was increasingly the case after the quantities imported from British India had begun to decline thanks to this Yunnan (and Szechuan) import substitution:

> The opium trade in the later years of the empire and throughout the Republican era (1912-49) was one of the most lucrative, but dangerous, enterprises for Yunnanese traders. Periodic government prohibitions, heavy

---

[58] Idem, p. 91.
[59] G. Cressey, p. 375.
[60] J. Lossing Buck (1964), p. 124–128.
[61] His study was paid for by the American Baptist Foreign Mission Society (p. viii).

taxation of the cultivation and transport of opium, and banditry were largely responsible for the high-risk/high-gain nature of the trade.[62]

This remark concerns, of course, the institutionalized smuggling practices. From 1906 to 1911 the opium suppression was rather effective in Yunnan as elsewhere. In the mid-1930s there was also a short period of prohibition. However, in every year there was always some opium grown and not only in remote areas.

Part of this production remained in Yunnan (the "Yunnanfu market"), a part went in a northern direction into China. A substantial part, however, was exported by caravan to the Southeast Asian countries, but traders also *imported* opium of a different quality from the southern Shan states. Chinese sources rightly maintain that opium was not an important export from the Yunnan production area

> until the 1920s, when the poppy was so widely cultivated that mountain people were no longer self-sufficient in food grains ... opium became ... a kind of currency in Yi areas, where goods from Chinese caravans were measured in terms of their worth in opium.[63]

The southern part of Yunnan bordering Kokang became of strategic importance for opium smuggling and not only for this product. There was a regular trade between, for instance, Burma and Yunnan in tea, raw cotton, cotton yarn and 'probably opium'.[64] In these districts local and foreign people were accustomed to intermingling with each other in some kind of business. Here, every winter and spring, caravans of 5,000 to 6,000 mules were organized, carrying commodities into and from Yunnan. It was only part of the extensive trade networks from northern Yunnan to the southern Shan states in British Burma and ultimately Rangoon, Siam, Laos or Vietnam as the map shows.

Trade between Yunnan and Southeast Asian countries must have had a long history, but the given routes were certainly also used for the opium trade from about 1860 onwards and after the 1920s when this trade became more and more illicit.[65] It was favored by the increasing domination of specialized traders and transporters from Yunnan who, among others, still delivered 'opium for the Siamese Government from the Shan States'.

---

[62] A. Maxwell Hill, p. 41.
[63] Idem, p. 43.
[64] Idem, p. 25 ff.
[65] For the following see Idem, p. 34-45.

Opium from the Shan States into Yunnan (and further into the Chinese interior), however, had to be smuggled during periods of effective government suppression of the drug and poppy growing.

The Chinese entrepreneurs involved made huge fortunes by managing heavily armed transports, but they also had substantial costs as the following report (1917) demonstrates:

> The whole expedition carried with it $400,000, which in Burma would be enough to purchase about 150,000 ounces of opium. There were about 200 members and 160 horses when they started, but ... the band increased to 300 people and 200 horses, with 170 rifles and pistols. It took 172 days to make the round trip. The group stayed in Rangoon for 42 days and camped 47 times on the way.[66]

From 1900 onwards the main intermediary region of the opium trade and production was the Shan State Kokang or Guogan. It was in fact a "great entrepôt" for opium. The Yunnanese opium also went by caravan to Tonkin (via Mengzi, Lao Cai, etc.) or to Siam via the so-called Golden Road: Kengtung to Chiang Saen and Chiang Mai. Import and export of opium through this region were under the control of the Siamese government. It maintained an opium monopoly from 1906 until 1957 (for the other developments in Southeast Asia, see the relevant chapter below).

Around 1930, during the Nationalist regime, there was no pretense about the suppression of opium in Yunnan (or other provinces/regions), and opium shipments often received military protection.[67] The illicit business became so intense that an anti-opium association complained that in Yunnan, 'the black (opium) calamity is much worse than the red (communist) calamity'.[68]

Chinese Opium Consumption

Here I have to limit myself to some remarks about the local Chinese consumption during the heydays of the foreign opium power. That is easy because no reliable data about earlier periods are available. Accidental

---

[66] Quoted in Idem, p. 42. The price of an ounce (0.03 kilo) of opium is, therefore, about $2.7 or 10 *yuan* (1933 dollar) or 6.7 *taels*. See Perkins's equivalents, p. xvii. Of course, this is only calculated to get a reasonable grip on figures, weights or prices at the time. There were only a few caravans a year, but still, 150,000 ounces or 45,000 kilo are large transports. It is a pity that no information is given about whether it concerns raw or prepared opium.

[67] W. Walker III, p. 48.

[68] Idem, p. 69.

remarks like the following can be found in a letter from a mandarin to his emperor (1838):

> There are opium dens in every prefecture of the country, and they are kept as a rule by magistrates constables and soldiers from the army, who gather together dissolute youngsters from rich local families to indulge in the pipe where they can't be seen. As most of the clerks in the magistrates share the same taste, they are sure to be protected. I beg your majesty to set a date a year from now after which all smokers who persist in their addiction will be put to death.[69]

Happily for the smokers the emperor decided not to attack the demand but the supply side, the English and the smugglers who had already been operating for four decades along the Chinese coasts. Carr, in turn, mentions in a classical exaggerating way the unbelievable story that as the EIC lost its monopoly on the opium trade in 1834, 'private smugglers entered the game; within a year more than 2 million Chinese were addicts' as if somebody was interested in counting them and could diagnose opium addiction.[70]

From the quotation we note the memorable information that before the Opium Wars, opium use was confined to the well-to-do and involved Chinese bureaucratic corruption and assistance from the army. This is apparently confirmed from Taiping sources after the Opium Wars.[71] "Western" figures must be used, however, which are unreliable as well, but they do exist.

Now, the following reasoning is *possible*: one of the Chinese reactions to the Second Opium War was to produce opium locally, which is a good example of import substitution. Once this China-India competition developed on the Chinese market, the British-Bengal producers made apparently so much product that prices decreased, and more Chinese people could afford to smoke opium. A booming consumption was the result, and the number of addicts increased into the many millions. Source: the amount of Western export divided by opium consumption per grain. Will this reasoning lead to a relevant explanation of the situation?

Several estimates exist about the consumption of opium in China. Balfour mentions one by Brereton for the year 1881:

> ... from the 400 million inhabitants three million were opium smokers. From these, the smokers of foreign opium are estimated at 1,000,000. The

---

[69] Quoted in C. Carr, p. 45.
[70] Idem, p. 45.
[71] See V. Shih, p. 474 note 6.

total estimated value of the opium smoked is £ 25,000,000 sterling, viz. Indian, £16,800,000; Chinese, £ 8,400,000. At these estimates, the smokers of foreign opium spend 11d. per man daily, and the smokers of the Chinese opium 2¾ d. daily.[72]

Here the judgment of Gelber is already complicated: it may be true that around 1870 a 'great majority' of the consumers smoked Chinese-grown opium, but in value the situation was exactly the reverse: the Indian opium yielded double the turnover of the Chinese. Furthermore, Brereton did not differentiate between consumers and addicts. If we use the Gelber estimate that a third of the consumers in 1900 was addicted, then twenty years earlier there were one million addicts. In the last part of the century there must have been a tremendous increase in addicts.

The most sophisticated calculations come from Sir Robert Hart, inspector General of Customs with arguments like 'every time a smoker needs 30 to 40 pipes, which is x maces which makes 1,120,000,000 maces and, therefore, ...'. Still they allow us to answer roughly a question like who could pay for this stuff in China—say—from 1870 to 1920.

Spence has the simplest answer: 'for a few coppers people could get a pipeful of opium ... in reach of urban dwellers and the poor'.[73] What is a "pipeful"? A statistician like Hart went so far as to determine the value of one mace of prepared opium at

about 3½d (English). Divided by the number of days in the year, the quantity of prepared opium smoked daily ... 3,068,413 mace, and the value ... £ 46,027 ...[74]

which must be an immense fortune at the time in 1870 as well as in 1920. It was available only to the very happy few and not to millions of ordinary

---

[72] E. Balfour, vol. 3, p. 37. About the many ambiguous methods of calculating the Chinese opium consumption, see the introduction of X. Paulès, p. 141–145, even without the examples given in my text.

[73] J. Spence (1990), p. 130. To substantiate this, Spence provides only examples of very well-to-do people like eunuchs, Manchu court officials from the palace bureaucracy, 'women in wealthy households', 'secretaries in the harried magistrates' offices', 'merchants preparing for business', 'soldiers on their way into combat' (Idem, p. 131). That is not an answer to his own suggestive question: 'Why did the Chinese of the mid- and late Qing begin to smoke so much opium?' Like most other Western historians of foreign peoples and countries, Spence is also ridiculing his subjects because of an in-built and unfounded superiority: as the Qing government allows opium as medicine, but severely prohibits pushing the drug to users, Spence thinks of it as an 'uneasy compromise' (p. 131), while that was for decades the normal Western way of dealing with opium by family doctors and the authorities after the Chinese introduced this innovation two centuries ago!

[74] E. Balfour, vol. 3, p. 38.

Chinese smokers. Hart supposes that the average smoker consumes three mace of prepared foreign opium. This suffices for 30 to 40 pipes, so that Spence's 'a pipeful of opium' must be a ridiculous remark, which cannot lead to any form of addiction.[75]

In detail, Hart's reasoning runs as follows relative to the situation of about 1880:

> ... the results arrived at are that 200,000 chests, or almost 13,000 tons (1680 catties = 1 ton), of unprepared opium are consumed annually by 2,000,000 opium-smokers; that these smokers expend £25,000,000 on opium; that this is an expenditure of, say, from 5d. to 11d. daily by individual smokers ... from the statistical point of view it is safe to say that opium-smokers in China constitute simply two-thirds of one per cent of the population. On the supposition even that the quantity of native opium produced is ten times that of the foreign opium imported, the total will not yet suffice for the consumption of even four per cent of the population. Four percent is a small percentage, but in China it means 12 millions of people. It is hardly credible, however, that native opium is produced in such quantity ..[76]

This last warning is needed because Balfour quotes missionaries and travelers, who gave the impression that from deep in the south of China unto the highest cold north, one is confronted only with 'a sea of poppies ... superseding the growth of cereals', so that normal food was not grown any more and hunger spread quickly.[77] That was far from the reality.[78]

---

[75] The expert D. Duco, p. 103, provides the details: the smoking of opium is not immediately addictive; the first time one smokes opium, one cannot feel anything. It fails because one smokes too little or too much, which is followed by sickness and vomiting. After one is accustomed, after one or two months, then one is really an addict. Spence's 'one pipe' must be less addictive than one cigarette. K. McMahon, p. 92 ff. provides details as well and several contradictory opinions: a beginner smokes one or two pipes (1841) or 3 to 6 grains at a time (1853); sixty grains was a mace which would fill twelve pipes, and this should be the dose of a 'temperate smoker' (1895); two maces daily must be the dose of a serious addict, and few can bear this for any length of time (1895). Another thinks of it as a common dose (1908), while rich people can smoke even three to five maces, according to the same source (he probably means that a rich man can pay for this quantity). Still, novelists created persons who could swallow ten to twenty maces a day. A *mace* = about 4 gram; a *grain* = 0.06 gram; a *pipe* must be something of 0.18 gram.

[76] E. Balfour, Idem.

[77] Idem, p. 29.

[78] F. Wakeman in J. Fairbank (ed.), p. 178 suggests that Hart's calculation resulted in too low numbers of addicts; Jonathan Spence (1990) takes even 10% of the population as smokers (which is about 40 million or "better" about 30% of all adult men) with 3-5 % or 15 million as heavy smokers. This is H. Gelber's source. For about 1920 G. Cressey, p. 144 states that 'in many provinces farmers have been forced by the military authorities to raise opium for taxation purposes, and in this way considerable areas of the best land have been removed from food production'. If he has to write more concretely, it is only in the provinces of Kansu (p. 192, 193), Szechuan (p. 315 ff.) and Yunnan (p. 375) that poppy fields

The difficulty, however, with Hart's calculation concerns the relationship income-opium consumption. The latter averaged 8 d daily according to Hart, elsewhere he supposes that it is 10¾ d (which makes £17 *a year*). Around 1930 the highest wages in modern urban factories were ca. 23 yuan per month and the lowest, ca. 12 yuan.[79] Therefore, the highest wage was equivalent to £2.3 a month, whereas Hart's smokers spent on average about one whole pound, which is close to half of their income in this category. For the lowest wage, equivalent to £1.2, it is nearly the entire monthly wage.

For most workers around 1910, local factory wages paid no more than home handicrafts. They did not differ much from the above wages, although there were also privileged jobs like supervisors with 32 yuan per month.[80] It seems safe to conclude that foreign opium smoking cannot be an activity for the low echelons in society, so they eventually had to cope with the native opium of poorer quality or simply no smoking. This alternative—let's remember—was exercised by the large majority of the Chinese.

The dictionary tells us that the foreign drug was about three times as expensive as the native product, mainly produced and consumed in 'Szechuen': one estimate is that 25,000 chests are produced annually, another estimates this at 265,000 chests, but the dictionary itself accepts two "facts":

> .. the one is that, so far as we know to-day, the native opium produced does not exceed the foreign import in quantity; and the other, that native opium was known, produced, and used long before any Europeans began the sale of the foreign drug along the coast.[81]

No details are given for the second statement. It refers possibly to a very small native production somewhere in the vastness of China for medical purposes only. Lodwick even exaggerated this further by stating that the

---

replace normally cultivated land. In particular, Yunnan must be a center of opium production.

[79] G. Hershatter, p. 148. The Chinese money system is very complicated and highly variable per province and period; the data to compare the different currencies in a particular period are very difficult to find, while the real Western experts (like H. Morse) do have a complicated way of explaining the comparable and foreign exchange values. I will spare the reader the method I found that around the year 1900 in Canton one *yuan* must be one-tenth of a pound (1£= 240 d), of course, before the pound sterling was subdivided into 100 pence in 1971.

[80] See Susan Mann in: Th. Rawski and L. Li (ed.), p. 264 ff.

[81] Idem, p. 37, 38.

Chinese cultivation of opium began in the late 18th-century 'and gradually spread to all parts of the empire. By the late 1880s it was a major crop in some parts of China ...'[82] Again, no supporting details follow.

What should we think about this consumption story? It is repeated in general terms in most histories of the period without any proof and largely based on the propaganda of missionaries or the guesses of anti-opium authorities, and disbelieved by far too few people: they are all more or less dubious estimates about millions of Chinese addicts. In the beginning of this section, I provided a model of how to think about this consumption, but I have the feeling that this way of thinking must be falsified. The problem is how, but about the "why" we can consider the following.

There exists a formidable *export* of opium to the USA and Europe. Macao in China is mentioned several times[83] and, indeed, it is well located to organize this export. Canton, Hong Kong and Macao are not only situated very close to each other, all three were centers of a lively opium trade in all directions.

It remains remarkable that around 1900-1915 the Chinese government nearly succeeded in controlling the opium problem in a rather short time and that about thirty years later, Mao's regime succeeded in eradicating the opium problem fully in a few years' time. With so many millions of addicts and the complicated intermediary systems needed between producer and consumer, this must have been a difficult task. Unless the sources of the propaganda can be disclosed, there were probably many fewer addicts than cited, fewer production areas, lower production levels or, simply, false statistics in which, for instance, smokers are included with addicts, export figures in one country were combined with import data elsewhere, and so on.

The following four examples give us much to think about because they are the only ones I found which are more or less based on Chinese practice and probably not on estimates, models or propaganda. The first concerns the 1934-36 suppression campaign the government organized

---

[82] K. Lodwick, p. 12. See also p. 13 for ahistorical remarks mixing up situations from after the two Opium Wars with long before. She mentions herself the result of Robert Hart's investigation that still in 1864 'native opium was known in all ports, but few acknowledged it being grown in their areas' (Idem, p. 13, 14). Indeed, this contradictory information not only negates Lodwick's suggestions in the framework of her "blaming the victim" attitudes, but points in my view only to the smuggling practices and forced imports of the English, French, Dutch, etc., which had been occurring already for more than a half century.

[83] See C. Terry, M. Pellens, p.639; W. Walker III, passim.

nationwide in order to show foreign nations the KMT's serious intention to get rid of the opium problem.[84] It became a bloody affair: 2000 narcotics offenders or addicts were simply executed by firing squads; exactly ten times as many were prosecuted, and 43,020 opium *addicts* registered. In the whole of China, four million *smokers* were registered.

Between May and September 1936 a new campaign was held, this time in Shanghai only, in which 24,144 addicts were registered (included in the previous example?). Of these, about 5,600 (or 17,600 in another source) were sent to detoxification clinics. One must realize that Shanghai (about three million inhabitants) was 'built on opium' and that here the heydays of the opium business were celebrated by many money interests. The supposed result of both examples: from a national population of about 500 million, less than 1% were *smokers* and less than 0.01% were *addicts*; in Shanghai itself, less than 1% of the population was defined as *addicts*.

The third example is from two years later. In 1938 the government of Manchukuo tried to take control of the opium business.[85] This part of China was estimated to have between 500,000 and one million opium smokers. Not a bad estimate: in August 1938 more than 585,000 smokers had registered themselves in response to propaganda from the Central Commission for Opium Suppression.

At the same time about 20,000 addicts were treated in some fifty national and local infirmaries. Smokers are not necessarily addicts, but a total of 20,000 addicts in a population of about 35-40 million is not much. The USA had the same population around 1870 and 77,000 opium addicts.[86]

In 1938-1939 Manchukuo suffered from war and a most rigorous foreign occupation during which 16 million people fled the region. This was not the case in the USA when recovering from its terrible civil war. Of course, the example does not permit us to extend the result over the whole of China, and it is possible to modify the comparison between the USA and Manchukuo (is a similar definition of an opium addict used?[87]).

---

[84] F. Wakeman (1995), p. 271–272 and several notes on p. 414-415 for the first two examples.
[85] W. Walker III, p. 122.
[86] C. Terry, M. Pellens, table IV, p. 44.
[87] The table I used here belongs to a discussion about numbers of addicts in the USA which must be confusing even for insiders with sentences like 'It is, therefore, believed that at no time have there been more than 246,000 opium addicts in the United States' (1924). If that should be the case, the number of addicts in Manchukuo is peanuts in an absolute sense!

The last example is probably the most realistic one and concerns Xavier Paulès's analysis of the procedures in two Cantonese rehabilitation centers for drug addicts in the years 1937 and 1941. The following table summarizes his findings. It provides a view on some social and demographic features of the opium problem in a big city, which is probably a model for other similar cities in this period.

Table 49. Opium Smokers in Cantonese Rehabilitation Centers, 1937 and 1941[88]

Professions in male population Canton 1928 in %	Professions patients 1937 in %	Age group	Male population Canton 1928 %	Male patients 1937 in %	Male patients 1941 in %
workers	43	48	0–5 year	7	---	---
jobless	19	12	5–10 year	7	---	---
merchants	17	18	11–15 y	8	---	---
coolies	7	16	16–20 y	11	1	---
soldiers	4	1	21–25 y	10,5	7	2
policemen	2	---	26–30 y	10,5	22	17
peasants	1	4	31–35 y	10	25,5	18
others	7	1	36–40 y	10	17	30
			41–45 y	7	11,5	14
			46–50 y	6	6	7
			51–55 y	6	5	7
			56–60 y	3	3	4
			+ 60 year	4	2	1
100	100		100	100	100

A large proportion of these Cantonese smokers had a daily consumption of opium of less than one *qian* (= 3.8 gram) which corresponds to six or seven pipes smoked in about half an hour. This is drastically different from Hart's estimates, which has serious consequences for his much acclaimed calculations. It concerns here some individuals who smoke on social occasions. Therefore, about 10% of the male patients (in total about 1000) refused to call themselves a patient. Probably, their health was not deteriorating, or they did not think of themselves as addicts. The real addicts are clearly a subgroup. Also, this differentiation of Paulès is an improvement over previous interpretations.

[88] Derived from the four figures given in X. Paulès, p. 174, 175.

In the Cantonese press, however, every smoker is an addict. This must be the result of the fierce anti-opium propaganda stressing the health problems of the individual and financial problems of his family. It described every user as an enemy of the Chinese nation, as supporting the humiliation of China and the imperialist repression, and many other right or wrong accusations. The users received specific names like 'opium-smoking devils' (*yangui*), 'the spirits of the poppy' (*furong xianzi*), 'the damned' (*heiji zhongren*) or 'the immortals' (*xian*). This supports the point of view in which opium smokers, whatever their degree of addiction, are isolated from non-smokers and could be brought to the rehabilitation clinics, if some authority would do so.

Even the Cantonese experts do not know how many smokers or addicts lived in the city: the estimates change from 21,721 in a rather precise investigation to 80,000, but the the most realistic conclusion is 40,000. The population of Canton was 1.2 million around 1930, making about 3% a user. Paulès thinks that about half of them were addicts.

The table indicates that these smokers and addicts are concentrated in specific strata of the population: especially male manual workers in the 25-48 age bracket. Certainly the rickshaw pullers are strongly represented. This demonstrates the importance of opium as an energizer to compensate for physical exhaustion, but also the kind of relationship between the pullers and their patrons, providers of their rickshaws and housing. The coolie profession scores high on everybody's perception of opium consumption.

This table suggests, furthermore, that there is a fundamental difference between the consumption during the work to earn a living and the consumption outside this in leisure time. The town-country distinctions feature in this table as well. Indeed, relatively many peasants lived in major Chinese cities before World War II, including their small businesses, compounds and swines.[89]

It is remarkable that no representatives of the "higher classes" were found, which must be the result of a selective police policy. Big city life in the last phase of the Republican Era was a severe and daily struggle against great miseries for a large majority of the population. That there were only 3% of smokers in Canton does not seem alarming. If this percentage applied in all large cities (together at the time about 50-60 million inhabitants), then there were about 1.5-1.8 million smokers and half as many

---

[89] H. Derks (1999), p. 17 ff.; Idem (2004), p. 59 ff.

addicts. Still, there are too many "Republican addicts" for all participants in the Opium Problem.

Enough suspicion is raised, however, by these examples. We need to inquire further: all this can lead to the conclusion that some of the Indian export to China as given above *never reached the Chinese internal market.* Within the Canton-Hong Kong-Macao region, this import could have been divided over *two other directions*: to the South (starting in Korea to Singapore and further to the Dutch East Indies) and to the USA. They are the most logical routes, certainly after about 1930 when morphine and heroin laboratories were erected by the Chinese mafia and the Japanese.[90]

In addition: there is not only export by sea. As the Yunnan case proves, the overland export was also sizeable. Both exports can be *subtracted from a Chinese inland consumption* potential and incentives.

The least one can say is: this argument and its consequences for the consumption and image of the Chinese should be the subject of very thorough new research.

My conclusion so far is that among the Chinese at the time, there were no more smokers and addicts than elsewhere in Asia. New research into this matter should, however, *not* take the direction Newman suggests and not just because of his following provocative conclusion:

> It is clear, therefore, that the wilder accounts of Chinese opium consumption cannot be correct. The stereotypical addict of the missionary literature was only one small part of a varied cast of opium users. Most opium smoking in imperial China was a harmless and controllable recreation.[91]

It is certainly true, as Sinn also argues, that in studying the opium problem, one has to suspend conventional prejudices; the personal use is often harmless (assuming a healthy lifestyle) and far from a crime.[92] It is, furthermore, good to repeat time and again that opium smokers are not necessarily addicts.

Still, one must be cautious with calling the use of opium harmless: it is too intimately connected with illicit production, smuggling, mafia, corruption and so on, let alone the *direct* relationship between opium and pogroms against the Chinese in the USA and elsewhere or the often serious political-economic effects on societies, including wars.

---

[90] C. Trocki (1999a), p. 133. For the earlier history of the Hong Kong-USA relations, see the excellent E. Sinn.

[91] R. K. Newman (1995), p. 789.

[92] E. Sinn, p. 18.

In addition, there are real health hazards among the poor users, because they have to rely too often on poor quality stuff or vile adulterations. One cannot isolate one from the other: together they form the Opium Problem, with different gradations for each country. In my view, it is much better to differentiate all this by means of the perpetrator-victim dichotomy and its practice, while considering the following.

Because Newman reduces opium use to a medical case, he opposes in an untenable way the idea that opium is a 'curse visited by imperialists on a weaker nation'. The poppy's presence in China should be seen as 'part of the geographical diffusion of a useful crop, and possibly as an element in the diffusion of central Asian cultures'.[93] All this means: opium is a negligible item in its physical effects and in its cultural and social impact on Chinese society and history.

Newman reduces opium, furthermore, to a purely Chinese phenomenon (blaming the victims!) and denies the use of opium as an imperialist means to destabilize successive Chinese and Asian societies in favor of the private profits of some drug criminals or the imperialist doctrine of the so-called "free trade". It is, however, not very clever to avoid sound historical analyzes of the Opium Problem and its origins or the many critical comments of contemporaries.

Newman provides interesting data but does not follow the right methodology sufficiently: systematic research of the relationship between consumption-production-distribution of opium and its history. He is also remarkably uncritical about the backgrounds of the *Royal Commission on Opium* (1893-94)[94]: its conclusion concerning the harmlessness of opium is the opinion of dealers like Jardine or Sassoon and of the British and Dutch governments. As demonstrated at length, these governments were never prepared to lose their substantial opium profits, the trade and banking mechanisms to finance and sustain their empires, and a work drug for the *coolies*.[95] Whatever texts of treaties promised a solution for the Opium Problem, it immediately organized an underground way of con-

---

[93] R. K. Newman, p. 790, 791.

[94] Idem, p. 768.

[95] C. Trocki (1999a), p.144. Whether there is a direct relationship between the result of the Royal Commission and the rapid expansion of the opium consumption in China (Idem, p. 130 ff.) should be studied further. There is, furthermore, a serious gap in our *detailed* knowledge about the question of why between 1860 and 1880 in China there was such an explosion in opium consumption. Who advertised this? Who organized this apart from, of course, the Sassoons, Jardines or Dents who were the best to exploit the possibility created by the British conquest?

tinuing the trade through its colonies like Hong Kong or Burma, where the Jardines, etc. were allowed to do what they always did.

In addition, a new party with opium interests, the medical professionals with relations to the pharmaceutical industry, presented their untenable case for the first time: the "people in the white jackets" think of themselves as the ultimate fount of opium knowledge and decision-making.

> The medical doctors are, furthermore, eager 'to increase people's dependence on doctors to prescribe medicine, sought to curtail their right to use opium as a form of self-medication.[96]

It is strange that Newman does not discuss the repeated attempts of Asian governments to prohibit the opium production and consumption from the beginning of the 17th-century until the Chinese successes in Szechuan around 1910, and he does not discuss (only ridicules) the political economic constellation created by the Western imperialism, the "pepper and tea for opium" mechanism, which made the Chinese economy largely dependent on the many foreign intruders. He does not discuss the moral conflict explicitly arising among the colonial leaders in Asia (Warren Hastings, Raffles, Crawfurd, Coen, Mossel or Hogendorp and many others) between their detailed knowledge of how *socially bad* opium was and their decision to use and exploit it anyway in their political and economic decisions.

Last but not least, the British and other Western colonial powers did not introduce "modernization", "democracy", "capitalism" and whatever other values they preached at home. The violent narco-military assault hit Asian societies which were revolutionizing like the Chinese in the most unexpected and most unwelcome manner: this assault only aggravated and exploited existing misery and created new miseries to such a degree that China was unable to counter new external enemies like the Japanese. Before leaving the country in disgrace, the West had performed only a criminal act by creating unprecedented criminality. All the above belongs to the Opium Question.

About Opium Gangsters

To illustrate the above criticism, a short history of the origin of all present opium gangsterism is appropriate. Almost by definition that origin must

---

[96] E. Sinn, p. 18.

be found in the framework of Western imperialism, Asian department. Herein the first commercial exploitation of the poppy was established in the middle of the 17th-century by the Dutch VOC (see ch. 11). Further preconditions for creating a narco-military organization of a mixed private-state nature were developed then. The Dutch *Amphioen Society* (see ch. 14) could be seen as the first autonomous, purely private opium-dealers organization backed by a state on a purely private profit basis, which was deliberately dealing in a "morally wrong product" in a corrupt way. That they earned fabulous amounts of money with this activity is, in fact, also perceived as a basic element of a criminal opium organization: only successful ventures get publicity!

Still something is "missing" in all this if one wants to become a full-fledged criminal organization: the breach of law. But that was available, even among the Dutch. In the 17th-century there were many crimes which were punished severely by the VOC. They did not concern dealing in or producing opium as such, although everyone knew how dangerous (and attractive) this drug was. The private business of VOC employees was officially prohibited and perceived as a criminal act, but mostly connived at. Occasionally, this corruption was attacked with draconian measures. That was the Dutch custom.

At least from the beginning of the 17th-century, several Asian governments can be found which prohibited opium smoking and trade, threatening them with serious punishments; in the 18th-century it was already difficult to find one which did *not* prohibit it. This was the case with governments in the Middle East, Mughal India, China or the East Indies. It was also perceived as a typical "foreign crime", introduced by the Western merchants-pirates-conquerors. This made the crime worse.

Finally, there were not only geographical differences between laws, but many others which do not need elaborating here (see ch. 25).[97] Anyway, the so-called "law of conquest" does not apply to them, but only to conquests. There is, furthermore, the remarkable fact that conquerors

---

[97] See the discussion about the study of law in the colonial context from Simon Roberts in T. Ingold (ed.), p. 973–976. What was "customary law" and what was its relationship with the "colonial project"? From this "project" (what a misleading name!) is derived colonial legislation as an application of colonial rule including its usual ridiculing of *adat*-rules and similar indigenous legislations Still, even this excellent handbook does not hide the extensive reliance of anthropology as a scientific discipline on the "colonial project": the question of whether this "project" was a criminal one is not discussed and that is, according to me, the basic question which we can easily affirm.

themselves, time and again, from Jan Huygen van Linschoten onwards, thought of opium distribution as something morally wrong.

The comparison with slavery points automatically to the remarkable discrepancy: at the same time that the British successfully fought the abolition struggle, they embarked on the largest opium "injection" of foreign people ever (which was seen by many in England as a genuine criminal act) and on the *coolie* trade between China and the USA, a trade in "free slaves".[98]

The conclusion from the above seems unavoidable: the opium introduction in China by the English was a criminal act, a matter of gangsterism as the ultimate consequence of the Western assault on China. Let's see whether empirical data can support this complicated thesis, by showing how Chinese society was destabilized and who did it. This, furthermore, has to highlight that it happened through opium as a source for profit and political gain and not through the opium addicts, as some still believe.[99]

One thing must be understood: opium *gangsterism in China* is something very different than *Chinese gangsterism*. The former dates from ca. 1800 and is conducted by Western smugglers, traders, bankers and the like (including their Chinese collaborators), who together made the opium business.

Chinese gangsterism received its main influence (and got the most publicity) in China through Shanghai in the 1930s but existed from ca. 1900. This was the time when gangster wars in Chicago were reported daily.

The main characteristic was, of course, that in the 19th-century, *Chinese* laws were constantly being violated, fundamental differences between legal and illegal, trade and smuggling, Western and Chinese views, narcomilitary actions and peaceful commercial negotiations were deliberately and constantly blurred or provoked by foreign intruders under the cloak of their extraterritoriality.

---

[98] G. Endacott, p. 127 ff.; D. Meyer, p. 115 ff. and ch. 17 the use of *coolies* in the Dutch East Indies in the tin mines on Billiton. The Dutch were, anyway, more consistent: they were the last in the world to abolish their extensive use of slaves (1868), embarked immediately on an extensive coolie trade and use, and its government always continued to exploit opium until kicked out of Indonesia.

[99] Of course, the following is based on and only a shadow of the highly intriguing work of Brian Martin, Jonathan Marshall and Frederic Wakeman. In ch. 6 and ch. 7 mention is made about the background of the Sassoons, etc. Here mainly their activities in China are highlighted. See also S. Chapman, p. 131 ff.

Around 1900 it was clear that a transformation had developed in all this: instead of an *external* assault from foreign pirates, smugglers, "legal" and illegal opium dealers, there were established *internal* interests ruling a Chinese underground. That transformation and its consequences are discussed here.

Shanghai was opened to the opium trade at the moment the biggest British opium dealer, Jardine, arrived in town (November 1843). He immediately hired Chinese collaborators for the distribution, who must have been viewed as terrible traitors. It took only a few years before half of the total opium imported to China was concentrated in Shanghai; the other half was imported in the Hong Kong-Canton-Macao region. Profit from opium had given the Jardine firm a commanding lead in both export from India and import into China. Thanks to its large shipping fleet, this firm could sustain a coastal distribution system. It 'ensured that this lead would be held whether opium imports were legalized or not'.[100]

Jardine, Matheson and Co's negative assessment about the possibilities for manufactured goods in China (and about the heavy tax on tea in England) encouraged, continued and accelerated investments in opium. This meant not only closer links to Indian opium production or transport, but also that 'a more elaborate and expensive distribution and sales system in China' had to be developed. A large network of Chinese employees, merchants or officials was gradually established 'who provided the market information and the smuggling facilities which made the trade possible'.

This trade was so effective and profitable that in the House of Commons and in the manufacturing branch, opium was blamed for absorbing the purchasing power of the Chinese to the detriment of all other imports. The complaints were directed first and foremost to Jardine personally, who defended himself by arguing that profit from opium was the catalyst of China's foreign trade.

Along two lines his company practically defended the opium trade as such. First, 'to secure the opium trade from the possible interference of the British government through the British navy'.[101] Second, to avoid the competition of 'men of small capital' and to *oppose* a legalization of the trade, because

---

[100] E. LeFevour, p. 8 also for the following quotations.
[101] Idem, p. 12.

abolition of the smuggling system would lower delivery costs and thus would certainly increase competition and encourage the "men of small capital" arriving in China with high hopes for trade under the treaty. Legalization might also have confined opium sales to Hong Kong where the quasi-monopoly advantages of the coastal system would have been impossible.[102]

From this one can learn how an underground system works in an imperialistic setting: of course, outside legality, but also as monopoly (fighting against competitors) and through its own distribution network based on bribes; if something went wrong, this foreign company must be confident that it could rely on the navy.

The Opium Wars gave Jardine, Matheson & Co. a great advantage: their share in the Indian export rose to two-thirds of the total with monopoly (and therefore high) prices. Its ships became better armed so that they could fight the Chinese underground competitors, pirates looking for profitable opium ships. These gangster fights became regular practice, the total number of *illicit* participants in the opium business increased exponentially.

From the 1840s Jardine easily mastered these new challenges and created a new substantial extension to this whole opium network by moving from the Canton-Macao- Hong Kong region to Shanghai. He extended his firm as well by its cooperation with Dent, forming a 'duopoly' and mixing legal (tea, silk, cloth) with illegal trade. In fact, this negated the border between what today would be called the upperground and underground, spreading corruption on a larger scale in society. The money details of the deals and trade are mentioned elsewhere (part 2 and appendix 1).

The Chinese helpers of Jardine and other foreign dealers were concentrated in Canton before the First Opium War. They acted as compradors, interpreters, shroffs (to detect bad coins) and clerks. Each Jardine ship had a standard equipage of a comprador, a shroff and an interpreter. Gradually, some of them established their own firms to deal with the foreigners. At the headquarters in Hong Kong or Shanghai, there was a large Chinese staff for repairing ships, warehousing and accounting. But these works always depended 'upon the willingness of Chinese dealers to face the risk and expense of a nominally illegal trade'.[103]

How the internal Chinese opium market really functioned is not very clear from the Jardine-Matheson papers, probably because the huge

---

[102] Idem, p. 13.
[103] Idem, p. 22.

imports were enough to know that it functioned anyway. But during the Taiping Revolts it was reported 'that Chinese dealers could not supply areas where the imperial administration no longer existed since official approval, or Taiping hostility, apparently determined conditions of distribution and sale'.[104] Apart from the necessity of assistance from state bureaucrats who depended in difficult times often on revenue from opium sales, this information is not very helpful.

In coastal regions, however, sometimes specific Chinese guilds were established which controlled the distribution and became specialized in the illegal opium trade like at Swatow (now Shantou), north of Canton. The Opium Guild here frequently bought supplies from Hong Kong. It is said that the Chinese opium criminals stimulated the cultivation of locally grown poppies and that they mixed this with the foreign one after the 1850s. If available, this Chinese production must have been very small for decades and certainly did not influence the continuously increasing foreign imports at least until the 1890s.

In addition, the mutual cooperation of Chinese and foreign merchants, bankers, pawnshops, etc. in the treaty ports led to relatively few investment opportunities. New business was put forward just when the profits of the Indian opium trade began to decline and Chinese firms of Jardine's size were established.[105]

For the time being, the main activities in the opium business can be seen, therefore, on the "foreign opium front". After 1860 it was concentrated in the "autonomous" international settlements. In these decades, therefore, a criminal infrastructure must have been developed which covered an immensely large coastal area from Macao to Shanghai and their direct hinterlands with many "bridgeheads" in between. When "Peking" at last accepted legalization of the opium trade under intense pressure from the British and French governments, the European and American infrastructure became "legalized" as well, but *not* the Chinese part of it. This Chinese part could now hide behind the Westerners, though, and it grew in quantity and quality.

The moment the Chinese government was allowed (or could not be hindered) to return to its traditional anti-opium stand (in the 1890s), this infrastructure had to disappear underground again. Its opportunities were now much better: a few million opium customers had to be "served"

---

[104] Idem, p. 23.
[105] Idem, p. 25.

now; coastal smugglers with their inland branches had to cope now with developed and mutually competing urban gangsters.

On the "foreign opium front", matters changed more profoundly. There was the competition between the Bengal and Malwa opium in India, practically a competition between the Jardine, Matheson, Dent group and the Sassoon group of Bombay and Hong Kong (see ch. 6).

In Hong Kong David Sassoon had already opened a branch in the 1830s which concentrated on the illegal opium business. His firm was also established in Calcutta and Singapore. In the 1850s, like Jardine and his colleagues (mostly in cooperation with the Americans Lindsay and Russell), the Jewish Sassoons (later in cooperation with the Jewish Ezra people and some Parsis) could therefore connect every link in the India-China opium chain by the extension of their *Peninsular and Oriental Steamship Company*'s services.

The Sassoons (& Co) had made a fortune with raw cotton exports from India to China. In India they were originally only involved in the opium business through banking activities (loans to poppy producers). In China, therefore, they could make quite different trade connections (legally also in Chinese eyes). These eased their entry into China at the moment they started their opium business.

Opium was used as payment for up-country purchases of tea and silk. They soon imported not only raw cotton, but staggering quantities of opium for staggering numbers of consumers and addicts (see Appendix 1 for the precise data).

It is difficult to say which of the two groups, the British-American or the Jewish, was the most successful. Until the First Opium War Jardine's certainly was. The competition became harsher during and after the Second Opium War when Sassoon sales on the coast were linked with increasing speculation at the Bombay sales and Calcutta auctions. They, furthermore, obtained a stake in the poppy production. This yielded considerable benefits from the 1870s onwards, while Jardine went on the defensive.[106] Jardine's withdrawal from the trade was not far away:

> Early in 1871, the Sassoon group was acknowledged to be the major holder of opium stocks in India and in China; they were owners and controllers of 70 per cent of the total of all kinds. ... Strict control of costs in India had allowed the group to undersell all others in China for five years and against

---

[106] Idem, p. 27. See also Idem, p. 165 note 82 where Jardine wrote in a memo 'how long this ruinous business' of the Sassoons could last.

this organization Jardine's was defenseless; its withdrawal from the trade became inevitable ...[107]

This underselling involved not only taking smaller margins, but also by selling its "own" Malwa instead of the more expensive Bengal opium. The moment the Sassoons achieved a monopoly position, the prices of Malwa also increased. Another effect, however, was much more important: the cheap opium greatly increased the number of consumers and, because this opium was of an inferior quality, the health hazards increased as well. This certainly happened in the lower classes, who lived in the cities without a decent standard of living.

Until the 1870s Jardine, Matheson & Co. had made a profit on their own opium investments of about 15% and 4% on agency business. That is what LeFevour found in their archive, but a proper cost-benefit analysis as attempted in Appendix 1 suggests much higher profits. Anyway, with these profits the company could easily overcome its withdrawal from opium and started investments in other branches (railways and banking, for instance).[108] Not only had their success turned upon the pivot of opium,

> trade in drug also had the effect of channeling a major part of the commercial enterprise of several large Western and Indian firms in China into the sale and servicing of one commodity for several decades. There was no alternative before the 1870s.[109]

The substantial Chinese opium consumer market at the end of the 19th-century was, therefore, created by concerted actions from several directions: first and foremost by the decades of activities of the two large Western opium tycoons (the Jardines and the Sassoons), both backed by the Royal Navy; the activities of numerous Western "men of small capital"; the competition between expensive and cheap opium; the Chinese assistants of the Westerners, who gradually started their own business; the

---

[107] Idem, p. 29.

[108] For Jardine's banking activities see E. Banks, p. 167, p. 206 ff. (relations with Rothschild or Samuel-Marcus bankers), p. 441 (Jardine, Matheson, Fleming 'had emerged as the dominant corporate finance house in Asia'); p. 507 (Fleming purchased in 1998 the remaining 50% of Jardine Fleming from Jardine Matheson for $300 million), etc. See also S. Chapmann, p. 113 ff for the Hong Kong & Shanghai Banking Corporation (HSBC) which was supported by 'the leading Far Eastern merchant houses like Sassoons and Dents from the first [1865], but the most eminent British firm in China, Jardine Matheson & Co, held aloof for a dozen years, until 1877.' Idem, p. 142 ff. in which is shown how Jardine Matheson & Co. developed into a kind of NHM in the Dutch East Indies as discussed in ch. 18 including their original reliance on opium in order to establish a multi-functional enterprise.

[109] E. LeFevour, p. 30.

continuously increasing populations of the International Settlements and their many opportunities for criminality of all sorts.

Around 1900 the imports from India and elsewhere declined because opium production was established in China itself by someone (Sassoons?). At the end of World War I, $40 million worth of opium still arrived annually only in Shanghai. The city had over eighty shops for selling the crude opium and 1,500 opium houses. Many of them were visited by *coolies* who smoked a mixture of opium and the residue (*dross*) of more fortunate smokers. The owners of these dens bought their supplies from three major opium businesses in the International Settlement: the Zhengxia ji, Guoyu ji and Liwei ji.

> All three were owned by Swatow (Chaozhou) merchants who constituted their own guild which in turn, around 1906, bought the Persian and Indian opium from four foreign merchant houses: David Sassoon & Co, E.D. Sassoon, S.J. David and Edward Ezra.[110]

Four foreigners who worked so closely together that they practically acted as one firm. Swatow people connected Cantonese gangs with Shanghai ones known as the Red Gang. The four foreign merchants were originally Jews from India. They reacted to the relative decline of the opium imports with a triple strategy: 1. they linked their businesses into the *Shanghai Opium Merchants Combine* (1913) and signed an agreement with the Swatow gangsters to buy their Indian (Bengal and Malwa) and Persian opium exclusively; 2. they made an agreement with the Municipal Council so that in the International Settlement the *Combine*'s opium had the monopoly; they, furthermore, asked from the Council to close down the small retail shops dealing in "smuggled" opium; 3. they reached a profitable opium duty agreement with the Yuan Shikai's government (1915) in return for specific payments.

After these foreign and local gangsters had created a monopoly, they increased the prices, claiming that the Indian opium was of much better quality than the Chinese one. It helped: from 1912 to 1916 the price of their Bengal opium increased sixfold and of Malwa fivefold. These were usurious prices, because the world prices were much lower.[111] They even managed to forge an agreement with the warlord Feng Guozhang to sell their remaining stocks for $14 million payable in government bonds at 40% of

---

[110] F. Wakeman, p. 35.
[111] Idem, p. 327 note 73.

face value. The warlord's pleasure lasted only briefly, because in January 1919 most of these stocks were destroyed.

But again Jewish opium dealers were accused of being behind all this. The medical doctors K. Chimin Wong/W. Lien-Teh reported in their *History* concerning the successful prohibition campaign of the central government:

> The combine of Jewish merchants, who had been the principal promoters of the trade, began to rush opium into the country and accumulated a huge stock at Shanghai. Eventually, a bargain was struck with some unscrupulous officials, and about 1,500 chests of opium were purchased on behalf of the Central Government at the price of Tls. 6,200 per chest. When the news leaked out, the people all over the country raised an outcry, especially as the excuse for buying the opium was that it was destined for the manufacture of medicine![112]

Once the legal trade ended the Swatow gang organized a new and illegal monopoly. But part of the opium money was available for speculation in real estate. In particular, the new quarters of the foreign rich were the objects of speculators, rapidly raising land values by 973% between 1906 and 1936.[113] One of the Ezra brothers even sold his property to the US Government.[114]

In the meantime all opium relations were established underground: the import, distribution and Chinese production. Nearly all warlords asked for their share in exchange for military protection of the opium in transit. Competition among gangs with gang fights occurred, and the four foreign providers had to go underground. The whole circuit was now a criminal one for all parties and for all legalistic considerations.

Its international connections can be sketched by means of a most notorious example known as the Ezra opium case, involving a deal of the Ezra brothers. Their opium business was hidden behind the *Dahloong Tea Company*.[115] The tea-for-opium mechanism remained intact long after its initiation. Their *Combine* once bought (1923-24) a multimillion-dollar cargo of high-grade Turkish opium. This was shipped by a Japanese vessel from Constantinople to Vladivostok, where it was transshipped for the destination China. However, the captain of the ship made his own deal with rival opium smugglers: when he arrived at the coast near Shanghai,

---

[112] K. Chimin Wong, W. Lien-Teh, p. 603.
[113] Idem, p. 66.
[114] J. Marshall, p. 28.
[115] F. Wakeman, p. 37 ff. and p. 328 notes 83–85.

he unloaded fifty chests of opium into a waiting junk and pocketed the profits. The smugglers brought the stuff to Shanghai where it was stored in one of the many underground warehouses in the French Concession and elsewhere in the International Settlement.

One of the Ezra brothers, Alexander, became aware of this. He went to his friends among the police who started an investigation. Indeed, they discovered an elaborate storage depot for opium, complete with false walls, secret doors, and a warren of tunnels. Alas, for the Ezra brothers and their colleagues, the revelations about their opium syndicate were publicised which

> shocked the world and led to a recommendation by the League of Nations that all ships heading for the Far East be searched at the Suez Canal. Japan refused to support this measure, and the scheme was never adopted.[116]

The downfall of the Ezra brothers followed a routine narcotics arrest (April 1933): Judah Ezra, just arrived at San Francisco, was arrested with his brother. Agents discovered an entire warehouse full of drugs worth $50 million. The Ezras were sentenced to twelve years in prison. Both were released in 1940, whereupon Judah returned to Japanese-occupied China. In 1947 their names circulated again in the press after workmen discovered a huge stash of narcotics hidden in the ceiling while renovating a former Ezra house. Anslinger's *Bureau of Narcotics* accused Judah seven years later of supplying a large narcotics ring out of Hong Kong.[117]

The details of the history of Jewish opium gangs in China or the USA still remain to be uncovered, as does the investment history of the opium profits. The pious Ezra established several synagogues in Shanghai. The Sassoons speculated in all kinds of International Settlement real estate,

---

[116] Ezra himself never recovered the opium, because he was in serious difficulty concerning his nationality: if he had had the "right" nationality, he could have enjoyed extraterritoriality and recovered the opium. Alas, it was discovered that he had the Turkish nationality and not the Spanish one as he claimed. Turkey, as a member of the central European powers which had fought against China, had forfeited its treaty privileges. Documents seized in the Ezra raid revealed, among others, that the Jewish opium syndicate had a deal with the Chinese navy, army and police to protect their narcotics. Publicity about it was now not beneficial for the Ezra brothers.

[117] J. Marshall, p. 28, 29. Here one can find also all the details about the Ezra brother's chief Shanghai Chinese collaborator, Ye Ching Ho, a most notorious and clever gangster with many political connections. He was very close to the Japanese occupiers as well as to Chiang Kai-shek. His story is comparable to the famous leader of the Green Gang, Du Yuesheng (see below). For the Western part of the opium business, Marshall also points to other American Jewish gangster bosses, which—like it or not—suggests a specific explanation.

but also in land on the outskirts of the city. This happened on such a scale that the Chinese authorities were afraid that the foreigners wanted to extend the Settlement, including its extraterritoriality privileges.[118]

One conclusion from this short history of the opium criminality introduced by foreigners in China is that there was a fundamental transformation from an illegal external assault by private Western smugglers inducing a learning process for Chinese smugglers and dealers violating Chinese laws, to the internal involvement of the same private foreigners in strong cooperation with full-fledged Chinese gangs.

Another conclusion is that initially, these British and Indian-Jewish smugglers were backed (in)directly by the British Navy, EIC and British government: without this support, ready to wage war for the benefit of an opium market of/for British entrepreneurs, it would have been impossible for the Jardines or Sassoons and their Chinese criminal supporters to obtain their huge profits. For the period after the transformation, it was again the combination of foreign and Chinese criminals which could not succeed without the backing of military and state officials. This will be explained further in the next section about the relationship of the Kuomintang (KMT) movement with the opium business.

The last conclusion is a technical one: the "Jardine approach" was characterized by a straightforward conquering of a market with a new product, opium, involving all kinds of unorthodox methods (from the Gutzlaff Bible assistance to bribing everybody on the way ahead), and illegality was preferred since legality was too time-consuming. Cooperation with many helpers on a few aspects after the product was bought at auction: money, transportation, distribution to a place where it could be handed over to other parties; in short, act as mediators.

---

[118] *The Economist* (May 29th 2010, p. 57) reports about the reopening of one of these synagogues, the Ohel Rachel, built in the 1920s. Judaism is too limited in China and not one of the five officially recognized religions. Everything can change, they must have thought by opening this building without mentioning its history: '… the heritage signs posted on them typically give little detail about their previous significance'. The rabbi who organized the opening believes that Shanghai's economic revival has made officials more confident in treating its complex history, and able 'to use the past to benefit the future—even if the past was not so much to their liking'. It is a pity that Jewish propaganda was not far away, because talking about a Jewish ghetto in old Shanghai is far beyond reality. The article ends with the words: 'Some history is still too hard to face.' Let's hope for the rabbi that the Jewish opium history will not be faced again. It will be difficult to negate C. Trocki's (1999) sixth chapter which is headed 'In the hands of Jews and Armenians' (p. 109 -137).

The "Sassoon approach" was characterized by management from the production in the poppy field all the way to the consumer-addict, which allowed a "squeezing out" of every phase in the process in order to end up with the largest profits for the lowest cost. The work done through this last approach had to remain underground from the first smuggling to the final cooperation with their own Shanghai acquaintance and largely executed by one's own kin[119]; in short, it is the self-sufficient form of a classical gang concentrated in one branch.

The last remark concerns the drive for public respectability, knowing the highly dubious character of their work. This applies to the Jardines and to some Sassoons, some of whom managed to became British aristocrats: "respect" remained the dangerous concept of honor in the mafia scene.[120]

KMT Opium Activities

The estimation at the time was that just the Shanghai drug traffic brought in $6 million a month 'to whomever controlled the city'. This contraband trade was, therefore, an irresistible lure for warlords. The most famous among them, the Kuomintang (KMT), was no exception. More than other warlords, the KMT leadership was intimately connected with the fabulous and very quick transformation of an immense country like China from an imperial and/or feudal-patrimonial state with religious-moralistic overtones and a strong agricultural base into an industrial, heavily urbanized, republican nation.

From 1911 (abdication of emperor) to 1949 (victory of the Communist Party, CCP) this nation was politically dominated by many warlords and a few civil ones like Sun Yat Sen and Mao Zedong. They fought with each other in various coalitions about what to choose as the main model of state and society: a nationalist or a socialist one.

After 1927 the KMT of Chiang Kai-shek became the leading organization in the military-nationalist arena and the CCP of Mao Zedong led in

---

[119] A quite typical Jewish glorifying picture of the Sassoon family and their stay in Shanghai is given by David Kranzler on the *Sugihara* website www.pbs.org. For the Ezra brothers see *Wikipedia* 'Edward Isaac Ezra' and for the whole Jewish scene in Shanghai, see the article of Robert Cairns, Colorful Jewish community contributed much to Shanghai, in: www.dangoor.com/issue76/articles/76096.htm, etc.

[120] Without any doubt the largest opium criminal of all from 1912-1951, Du Yuesheng, was still invited even after the war by the British Embassy as an honored guest, along with distinguished diplomats. J. Marshall, p. 43.

the civil-socialist one. Both had to rely at some stage wholly or partly on the support of one or more imperialist powers. The simple reason was that these foreigners could not be removed from the Chinese coasts without a military power which the Chinese did not have. In addition, they were a major source of money income for the feuding Chinese parties. In the Republican period the foreigners no longer contemplated conquering China, except Japan which perished like all the others. The foreigners were confined to playing the divide and rule game: the USA supported both Chiang Kai-shek and Mao at some stage; the Chiang's *White Terror* against the Communists was not only assisted by gangsters, but also by police squads and the leadership of the French Concession (indirectly by other foreign powers in the International Settlement).[121] Warlords and also Chiang Kai-shek during the *White Terror* played the power game by blackmailing representatives of foreign powers to pay huge sums in exchange for "protection".

It made Chinese life in this period pretty complicated and bloody: opium addicts and Communists were murdered wholesale. Gangsters, police and military killed at least four thousand Communists or people who are defined as such. This is the main context of China's exterior position, to which an equally important interior choice must be added.

A paradoxical development can be seen. While notoriously anti-urban, the military-nationalists were practically confined to the new urban world, while the typically urban CP had to rely on the agricultural countryside, so that both had in fact the wrong ideological base to fulfill the tasks they wanted to perform. The warlords, including the Kuomintang (KMT), intended to conquer large parts or the whole of China with or without Japan, perceiving their military rule as a replacement for the imperial or old provincial rule, and to construct a society according to the top-down military hierarchy with all its consequences. It was the classical land-based state model overruling town and country.

The socialists wanted a bottom-up civil society anyway, but ultimately had to replace the urban proletariat by peasants and much later by countryside communes and urban neighborhood organizations.

The combination of these different interior and exterior positions determined to a large extent not only the outcome of the struggle between the military versus the civilians, the KMT versus the CCP, the mutual civil wars from 1911-1949, the fate of the many imperialist intruders, but also

---

[121] F. Wakeman, p. 122 ff. and passim.

the development of the opium business, consumption and production. Only this latter development will be illustrated here with the following examples.

For the outsider it was, anyway, highly confusing: around 1935 the whole country seemed to be one great opium den if one could believe the papers and the mostly very exaggerated (dis)information from all sides. According to the American observer Woodhead (December 1934):

> It is rather curious to read in the newspapers on the same morning a report from one Chinese news agency stating that altogether 204 opium traffickers have been executed in China during the current year; from another that at present there are about 30,000,000 opium and drug addicts in the country; and from a correspondent in Poseh (Kwangsi) a description of the arrival in that city of a caravan carrying 1,800,000 ounces of opium, which was stored in the offices of the Opium Suppression Bureau ...[122]

It is important to consider the intimate relationship between the warlords' armies, including the KMT, and opium. Apart from the land taxes, opium was one of the main means to finance their wars and state or provincial bureaucracies.[123] After the last energetic anti-opium campaigns of the central government, opium became the concern of two powers: the upperground operating warlords and bureaucratic leaders from Peking or the provinces and the underground of several Chinese gangster organizations. Both were looking constantly to cooperate suspiciously with each other without losing their grip on their own fate. The rather complicated story of the warlords, their cliques and networks cannot be described here.[124] Some opium relations of the first and a short profile of the Chinese mafia must suffice.

Besides the KMT, there was the notorious warlord Wu P'ei-fu, main antagonist of Chiang Kai-shek and head of the so-called Chihli (or Zhili) Clique. Against all previous successful suppression measures, by mid-1920, officials of this clique stimulated opium cultivation on a large scale in Fukien, Honan and Shensi. The related Canton government organized opium production in other parts of Fukien, Kweichow, Szechuan and Yunnan. In Manchuria poppy cultivation was started on a lower level, but

---

[122] Quoted in J. Marshall, p. 22.

[123] About the many kinds of land taxes invented in this time to squeeze the peasants, see J. Sheridan, p. 24 ff.

[124] For the following J. Fairbank (ed.), passim, mainly p. 294 ff.; W. Walker III, p. 31 and entry 'Wu P'ei-fu' in: *Encyclopedia of World Biography* (Thomson Gale, 2004).

in most of China all remained "silent" on the opium front. Often one used the slogan: *'Salvation from Poverty through Opium growth!"*

Another one is the 'Christian General', Feng Yü-hsiang, active in the period 1912-1925 in Hunan and the northwest of China.[125] He was one of the very few warlords who actively struggled against the opium business. When he settled in Ch'angte (Hunan), he embarked on a program to stamp out three vices: narcotics, gambling and prostitution. He estimated that 5% of the population here was addicted. He prohibited the sale and smoking of opium and had opium traders arrested. Feng's men confiscated all possible drugs and just before he left Ch'angte in the spring of 1920, he publicly burned the stocks. The fire lasted three days and nights.

Feng also looked to treating the victims. A sanitarium, stocked with medicine and food, was set up in order to cure the addicts. They were encouraged to come voluntarily for treatment, but those who were unwilling were brought by force. If the treatment was successful, they were offered a job. All this was a rather clever program, although it had its limits: Feng was lax toward the upper class; no landowner, official, merchant or other prosperous person was urged to go to the sanitarium.

By 1925 Feng Yü-hsiang had a reputation as a reformer. He was now operating in the northwest and had an 'excessive preoccupation with the question of funds', and notwithstanding his reputation, he started to profit from opium sales. Opium was sold openly and illegally in Kalgan, so that a tax could be imposed. The only thing that can be said about it was that it came too late to save Feng's position and generated too little money. A year later he invaded the distant Kansu along the Mongolian border, apparently motivated by the lucrative Kansu opium tax.[126]

This example demonstrates that even the "white elephant" of a military-warlord-reformer had to rely on opium due to the high cost of his military enterprise and the lack of other resources. That was never the case with the most spectacular example of the Shanghai Green Gang under the leadership of Du Yuesheng (or Yue-sheng) described earlier.[127] His relation to the main warlord must be highlighted below.

---

[125] For the following see J. Sheridan, p. 91 ff., 157 ff. and passim.

[126] Idem, p. 193, 196, 246.

[127] For practical reasons, for the following I had to rely on, first, B. Martin (1995), although F. Wakeman (1995) and B. Martin (1996) are much more extensive. Martin and Wakeman collaborated. See also C. Trocki (1999a), p. 133 who relies on Jonathan Marshall's study on opium business of the government. See also P. Brendon, p. 346 ff about the Shanghai opium situation: 'at least half' of the police officers was 'involved in the opium traffic', etc. "Green Gangs" had a countryside and an urban base. The Shanghai GG had a

From 1927 (takeover of Shanghai by the KMT) there was a rather unstable relationship with this Green Gang, but after 1932 it was fully integrated into the nationalist's power structure. Its functions: opium financing, anti-communist struggle and "special (intelligence) operations".

Initially, Du Yuesheng tried a divide and rule policy:

> According to the minutes of the ... CCP Shanghai ... Du Yuesheng ... offered to keep in check the activities of all Green Gang groups throughout Shanghai in return for the CCP's not moving against the opium traffic ... There is reason to believe that just such a deal lay at the heart of the Green Gang's cooperation with the ... [KMT] ... in the anti-Communist coup of April 12, 1927 ...[128]

The gangsters knew everything about "protection", and since they accepted the KMT's protection, they had to pay a substantial price. Also, the KMT-Nanjing government, in order to "regulate" its taxes, always contemplated the possibility of an official opium monopoly. The entrenched interests of the Green Gang were seriously challenged, and before 1933 it paid $40 million in opium revenue, which later jumped to $30 million *monthly*. By that time Du Yuesheng's company ('Da Kongsi, The Big Company'), like the Japanese in Tianjin, had set up heroin and morphine laboratories. It was so successful that "China" could start a very profitable export of these substances to the USA.

The consequences were serious and had a global impact:

> American gangsters beginning with Arnold Rothstein and going on to Meyer Lansky, Charles "Lucky" Luciano, Louis "Lepke" Buchalter and Jasha Katsenberg forged links with Chinese drug lords, both in Shanghai and California, to obtain supplies for the growing American narcotics market.[129]

---

country base as well; its traditions provided organizational and legitimizing structure for the criminal activities in this multi-million city. They constituted 'one hundred thousand or so gangsters' in Shanghai spread over distinct and competing groups busy with opium, prostitution, gambling, kidnapping, protection and labor contracting. Du Yuesheng is also prepared to organize on a substantial scale boycotts of or resistance to the Japanese or relief for refugees. He never forgets his financial opium interests when cooperating with the Shanghai bourgeoisie. His original power base was situated in the French concession, cooperating with representatives of the French government. From 1932 he succeeded in establishing a Chinese power base in this concession after some difficulties: as the gangster boss of bosses, he also played an important role in the politics of Shanghai. And this is only part of the Du Yuesheng story: his close relations with the Kwomintang, the Japanese but also the American secret services is astonishing reading. See J. Marshall, p. 38–42.

[128] B. Martin, p. 65, 66.

[129] C. Trocki (1999a), p. 133. They are nearly all gangsters with a Jewish background. It seems at least logical that they also had relations with the Sassoon opium and Shanghai real estate empire with all its connections to an upperworld.

Du and other right-wing leaders in the KMT were also involved in establishing "fascist cells" of black-shirted bully-boys to raid left-wing presses, bookstores, schools and universities. He also became the 'sworn brother' of Dai Li, "Chiang's Monster"; the Mayor of Shanghai was on his payroll for Ch$500,000 a month! As the spider at the centre of the web of an official opium monopoly, it enabled him 'to promote his opium interests quite openly', and so on. After 1933 the KMT and gangsters developed many ties so that what Marshall concluded became true: Chiang Kai-shek

> pragmatically forged alliances with provincial bosses and urban gangsters who demanded protection for their stake in the opium traffic. Chiang himself soon learned the political potential of the traffic and used it to finance his wars against the Japanese, Communists, and rival warlords. By moving to centralize the traffic under his personal control under the guise of "suppression", he sought to extend his regime's control. As a result, corruption and gangsterism, part of Chiang's unhappier inheritance, thrived as never before.[130]

This policy continued in fact until the victory of the Red Army and the CCP could definitely end the opium menace in China. However, *outside* China the system Warlords + Opium remained intact in Southeast Asia and elsewhere as we have seen, while the Chinese remained involved in the opium traffic. For Americans, far away in some Washington office, it was difficult to discover the difference between one Chinese and the other.

A Mao Opium Case?

It is well-known that after Mao came to power, one of the first programs implemented was against the use, trade, production and cultivation of opium. In February 1950 Premier Zhou Enlai issued an extensive order against opium. The first action of its kind had been started about forty years earlier (1906), but after a spectacular beginning, it stopped through the subsequent *warlordism* and the massive spread of opium and its derivatives by nearly all warring parties (propaganda also claimed the same of Mao and his compatriots, but it was never proved). The 1950 program, however, must be qualified in all probability as the first concerted action on this scale which was successful. Therefore, some details must be mentioned. The key parts of this opium liberation program as executed at

---

[130] Quoted by C. Trocki (1999a), p. 133.

the county level (in this case in Yanhe, a county of Guizhou) are the following:

> 1. Deep and broad propaganda about the dangers of opium, encouraging the masses to participate in opium suppression. 2. Prohibiting poppy growing. The local cadres, anti-bandit troops, and leaders of mass organizations were to carry out inspections and encourage peasants who raised poppy to uproot it themselves. Those who refused were to be dealt with by the Public Security Bureau. 3. To prohibit opium shipment, manufacture and sales. Those things are entirely evil, and those who dared to challenge the law would be punished. Those who produced opium had to give up their equipment to be destroyed by the masses ... 4. Prohibiting opium smoking. As opium had been poisoning the county for a long time there were many opium addicts, with the greatest numbers among the workers and the peasants, and it was important to educate them so that they could cure themselves. Those who were deeply addicted ... could be registered and receive anti-opium pills ... Those who, in the end, could not be cured, besides undergoing forced labor, would not be eligible to receive the fruits of the struggle with feudalism ...[131]

Chao Zhongli tells how in Yanhe county in December 1950, 1663.3 ounces of opium were found. In addition, 274 pipes were confiscated, 15 opium addicts were 'purified', and only 6 *mu* (= ca. 1 acre) of poppy were discovered. The latter achievement was due to the fact that poppy sprouts were difficult to see in this season among other sprouts. In January of the next year, 10 *mu* was found somewhere in the mountains, while 'the evil landlord Xiao Xiaofeng' had hidden 10 *jin* (= ca. 13 pound) of opium.

At the end of 1951, the yield of the police was not bad: 6,171 *mu* (= ca 1,000 acres) of poppies were uprooted, 148,000 ounces of opium collected, 272 pipes burned, and 36 opium criminals sentenced from four months to two and a half years. During the third and fifth campaigns, some opium was found, but the report says that after two years, opium 'vanished like a puff of smoke'.

The only thing we can say about these figures is that notwithstanding its location in or near a classical opium region, the given quantities are not very impressive. Elsewhere, the period necessary to make this change

---

[131] From Document 19 in A. Baumler (ed.), p. 181–186. It concerns a translation from the Chinese of Chao Zhongli' s memoirs published in: *Guizhou wenshi ziliao* 2(1990), p. 87–93. In 2007 this district was situated in the prefecture of Tongren with about four million inhabitants; on average the districts have about 400,000 inhabitants. In 1950 this must have been substantially lower. A reasonable guess seems to be 80,000 to 100,000 people. See also an article in a *China Now* magazine (1977), reproduced on the SACU (Society for Anglo-Chinese Understanding) website: www.sacu.org/opium.html.

would be much longer. Working at top speed, it could take between two and four years in rural areas, and five to ten years in urban centers, depending on demographic features and the patience of the investigators. This must have been achieved because, indeed, the Opium Problem in China 'vanished like a puff of smoke' after 150 years of Chinese struggle against the foreign import. The subject, however, did not disappear as a propaganda item.

During the years 1940 to 1949, Mao Zedong and his compatriots still had many remarkable friends in the USA in the highest echelons of society, including the US Army ("China Hands"). There existed a substantial distrust of Chiang Kai-shek and his nationalists.[132] This friendly relationship could easily change with new persons in the State Department or secret services. In these circles a strange mixture of opportunism and hypocrisy with sectarian belief-systems was (and is) the rule: cooperation with Chinese opium criminals like Du Yuesheng or with Chinese pirates could be perceived as highly attractive regardless of the official anti-opium policy. As a "Cold War" raged, everything became possible, as the following story demonstrates.[133]

In Alfred McCoy's unsurpassed *The Politics of Heroin*, there is an appendix with a clear title: *'Isn't It True That Communist China Is the Center of the International Narcotics Traffic? No'*.[134] McCoy's argument runs as follows, which is symptomatic of his highly sound complaint about the devastating agitation of secret services in the present world.

Once Mao and the CCP founded the People's Republic of China (PRC), official and unofficial spokesmen in the US and Taiwan charged that 'the Chinese Communists were exporting vast quantities of heroin to earn much-needed foreign exchange'. In particular, the American director of

---

[132] J. Taylor, passim; see, for instance, the rows between the conservative general Sitwell and Chiang Kai-shek, whereas the former was heavily influenced by Mao-friendly authors like Edgar Snow, Harold Isaacs, etc. Sitwell explained that 'it was not in the nature of Chinese to be Communists', etc. (see idem, p. 191 ff.), in his mouth a form of "philosemitism".

[133] See J. Marshall, p. 42 ff.

[134] A. McCoy, p. 145–148. Quotations are from these pages. They concern the radical right-wing Harry Anslinger (1892–1975), a hard-boiled intelligence addict, 'the Father of the War on Drugs' or 'America's first drug czar'. In the 1930s, as Director of the Federal Bureau of Narcotics (within the Treasury Department!) he became well-known for his crusade against marihuana with messages like: 'There are 100,000 total marijuana smokers in the US, and most are Negroes, Hispanics, Filipinos and entertainers. Their Satanic music, jazz and swing, result from marijuana usage. This marijuana causes white women to seek sexual relations with Negroes, entertainers and any others.' Quoted at present on all websites on "Anslinger". See D. Musto, passim in particular chapter 9.

the Federal Bureau of Narcotics (FBN), Harry Anslinger, was busy spreading this accusation together with Taiwanese officials. As late as 1961 he reports:

> One primary outlet for the Red Chinese traffic has been Hong Kong. Heroin made in Chinese factories out of poppies grown in China is smuggled into Hong Kong and onto freighters and planes to Malaya, Macao, the Philippines, the Hawaiian Islands, the United States, or, going the other direction, India, Egypt, Africa and Europe.

According to Anslinger, Los Angeles alone received 40% of the smuggled contraband from China's heroin and morphine plants. After his retirement, Taiwanese officials continued with the propaganda like 'Red China exported some US $800 million worth of narcotics last year ...', etc.

It was quite easy to check these messages since Hong Kong and Burma were always named as transit points. The English customs and police officials in these locations regarded the charges as ridiculous. One of them declared (1971):

> We've never had a single seizure from China since 1949, and I've been here since 1947. We have customs posts out on the boundary, and the search is quite strict. There is only one road and one rail connection so it is quite easy to control.

In the Burma-China borderlands, several leaders of Shan rebel groups (usually conservative, Christian and monarchist) asserted in 1971 that there 'are absolutely no opium caravans' crossing the Chinese border. This was a confirmation of the findings of a BBC television crew six years earlier, but also of CIA agents who were very active in the region. Their intelligence teams learned during the 1960s that the Chinese had transformed the patterns of the hill tribe agriculture in Yunnan so that opium would not be a major crop.

On top of this came the written declarations of former collaborators of Anslinger. The bureau now concluded that there had been a major postwar upheaval in the international opium trade: 'the rapid suppression of China's illicit production' in the mid-1950s. There were, furthermore, several complaints (1971) about the abuse of the name of the FBN by Anslinger like:

> Every time Anslinger spoke anywhere he always said the same thing—"The Chicoms are flooding the world with dope to corrupt the youth of America" ... It was kind of like the "Marijuana rots your brains" stuff the old FBN put out. It really destroyed our credibility, and now nobody believes us. There was no evidence for Anslinger's accusations, but that never stopped him.

Notwithstanding this, Taiwanese officials continued with their damning of the People's Republic, but now the chief of the FBN, John Warner, offered the following explanation (October 1971):

> The Taiwanese floated a series of nonattributable articles in the right-wing press, quoting ... British police officers in Hong Kong saying "we have seized five tons of opiates in Hong Kong this year". And the article would then state that this came from Red China. Actually, it comes from Bangkok. The real object of this sudden mushrooming of this kind of propaganda is to bar China from the U.N.

Twenty years later the expert William Walker declared:

> Available evidence does not support this conclusion [the Anslinger-Taiwan allegations. H.D.]. It therefore ought to be relegated to the array of misperceptions of the PRC held by U.S. policymakers that served to prolong a hostile relationship.[135]

So many proofs of policy lies are seldom available; normally, they are published and go unpunished. In that case it should be a premium on the substantial morphine, etc. import from England and the USA. They were cynical enough to organize this through their enemy Japan. At the time they tried to reverse this policy, 'Japanese, Koreans and others were ready to fill the gap ...'[136]

In addition to McCoy's and Walker's information, it is possible to point to the following. From a much earlier publication, the Anslinger people could have realized the ambiguous content of their propaganda. There was already a CIA report from 1956 which explicitly examined charges of Chinese Communist involvement in the opium trade.[137] The first sentence of the summary is crystal clear, although written in the Cold War terminology of the day:

> There is no reliable evidence to indicate that the government of Communist China either officially permits or actively engages in the illicit export of opium or its derivatives to the Free World. There is also no reliable evidence of Chinese Communist control over the lucrative opium trade of Southeast Asia and adjacent markets. There is evidence, however, that small quantities of raw opium produced by minority tribes in Yunnan Province, Communist China, move over the Burmese border. The annual earnings of the

---

[135] W. Walker III, p. 219.

[136] Idem, p. 218.

[137] See Central Intelligence Agency (1956). This secret report was approved for release in November 2003, and it is now available on the Internet under its report title. Even so, several large parts of even this 54-year-old report are blotted out, and the 'source references' (appendix C) are left off.

Chinese Communist tribes from such sales probably would not exceed US $500,000 per year.[138]

Time and again this CIA report indicated that one has to look at Burma instead of China or that there 'are a considerable number of unreliable reports alleging that Communist China is involved ...' etc.[139] The indications the CIA had for its judgment referred to the 'intensive campaign against opium production, trade and addiction' of the CPC, the 'complete lack of reliable reports on extensive production of opium' and to reports 'that other Bloc countries of the Soviet Bloc have been buying opium from the Free World'!.[140]

Blaming the Chinese victims has varied aspects, and many foreign institutions had an interest in doing so, which does not alter the relationship between the original opium perpetrators and their victims. It is a pity that even recently, professional historians still proceed on the same road, which can be demonstrated with another example.

In Taiwan there was a research fellow working at the Institute of Modern History called Yung-fa Ch'en. He recently 'discovered that profits from opium production and sales by the CCP made a substantial contribution to the economic development of the Shaan-Gan-Ning base area and the financing of its government'.[141] This happened in the period 1941-1943 when the Communist Party suffered from a serious financial crisis with the Japanese and Nationalist enemies before the gate. Later, Mark Selden, one of the famous American pro-CCP scholars, stated that the 'Yan'an Way' of economic development was demonstrated for the first time in that area, which became the model for the Cultural Revolution and for the Third World as well. This was the so-called "Dazhai experience", which was soon afterwards dropped by the CCP as irrelevant.[142]

Ch'en says, therefore, that this Yan'an (Yenan) Way would have been 'simply impossible' without the opium trade and that Selden made a big mistake. The CCP acknowledged this last "fact" later as well for *different*

---

[138] Idem, p. 1.

[139] Idem, p. 28, but see also p. 3, 5, 7.

[140] Idem, p. 5.

[141] C. Yung-fa, p. 263, 264.

[142] The importance of the Yan'an (Yena) episode is comparable with the whole 'Long March' story. If one is seriously able to corrupt a story like this, one has indeed arrived at an important result (propaganda). However, even the American political scientist David Apter's contribution to T. Saich, H. van de Ven (ed.), p. 193–235 does not support the following Chen Yung-fa's paper, although it analyzes Mao's role in Yan'an as a contribution to collective action. See, in particular, p. 232 note 31.

reasons. A bit more interesting is the historical question of whether the CCP crisis of the 1940s and some use of opium by the CCP could be attributed to a Nationalist economic blockade and Japanese offensives?

It seems to me quite understandable that Mao under such miserable circumstances tried to solve at least his financial problems with the means both the well-armed Nationalists and Japanese had used since the very beginning of their threatening regimes. He needed money or, probably, the opium itself, because incentives had to be given to enhance the cotton production in the area (his soldiers depended on this cotton for their clothes) while threatened by the Nationalists and the Japanese. Still, all this must be proved![143] Whatever one thinks about Mao's policies, it is a fact that only a few years later Mao definitely solved the Opium Problem for China like no one had before.

Through Ch'en, the Taiwanese propaganda makes of this: as self-styled 'most fervent champion of Chinese national interests', the CCP 'loudly condemned the Western powers for their opium trade' and now it contributed itself to 'this infamous trade'. This Nationalist Taiwanese accusation is clear, and the profit one supposedly gained from it must be obvious in circles of people uninformed about the Nationalist's backgrounds. We may be happy, anyway, that now also this side acknowledges that it concerns 'an infamous trade'.

Accusations published in scientific publications have to be measured against scientific and not political criteria. Is that possible in this case? I am very glad that Yung-fa Ch'en confesses immediately after his accusation:

> ... I should emphasize that the statistical evidence used is far from precise. That evidence is drawn primarily from a documentary study ... published in the political atmosphere of post-Mao liberalization. I have no way of checking the accuracy of these materials. But from my own experience in handling original party documents collected by the Nationalist intelligence

---

[143] Also in an earlier CCP and Mao period (1930s), the rather easy exploitable opium was a logical source in case of financial difficulties, and the Communists had only a few small sources of money except the opium *business*. See F. Wakeman (1995), p. 139, 140. S. Shuyun, on numerous places, describes how during the *Long March* the Red Army or parts of it had to rely on opium (eventually dissolved in water) as medicine for the soldiers or looted stocks of opium in the settlements they arrived at. Shuyun, therefore, could write that opium 'was one thing that the Red Army was never short of' (p. 103). Still, this is something very different from a regular involvement in growing poppy, producing opium or its derivatives heroin and morphine, or trading-smuggling these products with the help of gangsters like the Nationalists and all other warlords were doing.

apparatus, I have no reason to doubt the authenticity of these Communist-compiled documents ... held in libraries on Taiwan.[144]

In addition to this, the author apologizes for 'carelessness by transcribers', 'numerical contradictions', etc. and still all this 'casts no serious doubts on my sketch ...[and] ... my conclusions with respect to the importance of the opium trade'! Later on he, for instance, mentions 'obvious errors that I cannot explain' or refers to 'only the fragmentary materials noted above', etc.[145]

Last but not least, this article copies and is therefore based on only one intelligence report produced 40 years later than the events they describe. It is quite paradoxical that Ch'en's statistical adventure is based on an intelligence report of the Taiwanese secret service led by Dai Li (1897-1946). His office was called the *Bureau of Investigation and Statistics* while Dai Li himself was for some 'China's Himmler' and for Jonathan Spence, anyway, 'Chiang's Monster'.[146] This is hardly worthy of a scholar.

And it is clearly not the judgment of China watchers like Tony Saich when he accepted Yung-fa Ch'en's intelligence report as a scholarly contribution to his reader. It is also serious that recent publications not only copied Ch'en's results but uncritically used and even exaggerated them in the framework of anti-Mao or anti-Chinese publications like Fenby's history or Chang-Halliday's and Taylor's biographies.[147]

Let's take a look in, for instance, the Mao biography by Chang and Halliday. They wrote a chapter entitled 'Revolutionary Opium War (1937-45)'. It starts with remarks about a grain tax Mao imposed on the Yenan peasants and the salt potentials of the area which were neglected. No sources are given for either item. The chapter continues with:

> The German invasion of Russia in June 1941 made Mao look round for an alternative source of funding in case Moscow was unable to continue its

---

[144] C. Yung-fa, p. 264.

[145] Idem, p. 290 and 294 note 2.

[146] J. Spence (2004), p. 29 ff.

[147] J. Fenby, p. 308 ff. used Chen Yung-fa's product and called it a 'groundbreaking study' without mentioning the Taiwanese secret service source, let alone McCoy's devastating criticism of that secret service or the provisos Yung-fa made himself. J. Taylor, p. 242 also simple adopted the KMT report, symptomatic of his one-sided portrait of Chiang Kai-shek. Even an excellent study like C. Trocki (1999a), p. 134 produces strange information about opium production and export in Shandong (Shantung) from 1927-1952 under CCP leadership. This northeastern coastal province was a classical area of "famous" warlords (Zhang Zongchang, Han Fuju) from 1924 until 1937 when Japan took over full power until its surrender in 1945, after which the KMT-Red Army fought severely until 1949. No, there was no peaceful year to grow poppies in this region for the arch-enemy of the occupiers!

subsidy. The answer was opium. Within a matter of weeks, Yenan bought in large quantities of opium seeds. In 1942, extensive opium-growing and trading began. To a small circle, Mao dubbed his operation 'the Revolutionary Opium War.[148]

The information came from 'Mao's old assistant, Shi Zhe' who also said about growing opium: 'It did happen ... If this thing gets known, it's going to be very bad for us Communists.'

That is the propaganda message, which presupposes that Chang and Halliday also think of opium as 'an infamous trade'. That is, again, the only positive remark. If the authors had written what Sun Shuyun quoted in extension from an official source (*Second Army History Committee,* 1991) about the role of opium in some parts of the Red Army during the famous *Long March,* nothing could have been 'going very bad for Communists'.[149] The authors also refer to a 'carefully researched study' from 'that year' which put the opium growing area at 30,000 acres, the credentials of which are given above. Yung-fa Ch'en states that Mao made his alleged opium decision under the influence of the Nationalist and Japanese attacks; the 'German invasion of Russia' had, therefore, nothing to do with it, but "sounds better". It is, furthermore, very difficult to find some information about the informant Shi Zhe. I agree that this 'old assistant' is much more sympathetic than information of the 'Assistant of Dai Li, Chiang's Monster'.[150]

---

[148] J. Chang, J. Halliday, p. 337. "Yenan" is another name for Yan'an in the central north province of Shaanxi.

[149] S. Shuyun, p. 103 and note 9 chapter 5, p. 290.

[150] Whether now the Opium Problem was solved in China must be taken with some grains of salt. What was left was apparently a heroin problem and a related HIV/AIDS problem. Of course, it must have been a small problem compared with the many millions of opium addicts from before 1950. During a stay in September 2002 at a conference organized by the World Health Organization/Beijing Institute of Mental Health, David Smith heard about 'an escalating heroin problem in China ... and because of frequent needle sharing there is a dramatic escalation of HIV/AIDS'. See www.drdave.org/Articles/csamwin04.htm.

CHAPTER THIRTY-THREE

A REFLECTION

This part of the study is aimed at the only historical investigation into the opium victim problem. It seems logical that it leads to the following reflection.

From the very beginning of this *History of The Opium Problem*, we have been confronted with its *basic* complexity, which it never lost. This complexity could never be reduced to a personal problem of one person or victim. This has many, rather important consequences.

This means directly, for instance, that scholarly disciplines like medical or psychological sciences are not very helpful for understanding, let alone solving the Opium Problem. I do not imply that medical "facts" can be left out of consideration, as is not done in this *History* either: see 2.4; 3.1; 3.4 and so on. They are a substantial *part of The Problem itself*, certainly for the 19th-century Western opium history.

At least for analytical purposes, therefore, we should always perceive this Opium Problem as an *externally induced* problem: it originates from outside and then develops into something.

If personalized, this perception is important for the following reasons: neither a victim's problem nor an addict's problem can be solved from "inside" the victim or addict (probably only the "side-effects"). In the treatment of addicts and victims, we encounter the same "internal myth", when opium addiction is expected to be treated by other addictive drugs like cocaine or medicines, or that LSD can help to prevent a concentration camp "syndrome" as if the victim had invented concentration camps in his own mind.

Basically, therefore, medicalization, psycho-treatments, meditation, etc. are useless, largely sources of income for therapists, while in exceptional cases interesting for curing side-effects. The victim's problems should be explained, understood and treated or related to, first and foremost, "actions" in social-cultural or political environments appropriate to the victim or addict, from which some individual treatment should be "derived".

How substantial a part of the Opium Problem this is can be seen in the relation between this medical knowledge and profession and the sociobiological approaches invented and implemented in the European and American 19th- and early 20th-century. The often claimed natural or racial disposition for opium or gambling and other vices of the Asian or the Chinese (laziness of the Javanese!) does not exculpate the Western introduction of opium. The most extreme consequence of this perception is that opium (or cocaine for that matter) is imported and distributed among the people in order to make them work harder and longer (for the boss) or deliver more money for the industry/financiers of for drugsdealers and that victims of this "treatment" are seen as criminals to be locked up or, worst, eliminated as worthless bodies.

In other words: in the treatment of all those externally induced vices on victims or victim-countries, the environment or *outside world and its history* should be considered of overriding importance rather than of limited value. The success of the collective treatment of the Opium Problem in the largest victim-country, China, after 1950 is that in a *political, economic and social* way, this treatment was induced. In fact, it was *methodologically* along the same path as its introduction by the Western states and their criminal smugglers and other dubious supporters.

PART SEVEN

THE STORY OF THE SNAKE AND ITS TAIL

The Problem

This complicated *History of the Opium Problem* from about 1600 to 1950 has brought us to all the corners of the world. It is inappropriate in this last chapter to come up with something like conclusions or "lessons to be learned for the future". This future, the history of this problem from 1950 to the present (and later!) must first be told and analyzed. The dark predictions of Ahmed Rashid in the Preface do not sound very optimistic, but we cannot avoid describing the paths to that future, analyzing the problems or testing propositions. The aim of this last part is to do this concisely and not very systematically.

If this history needed to be abridged to a few one-liners, we could use: "The West produced the Opium Problem for and from the East" or "In the period 1900-1950 the West stumbled into the reverse movement" or "The West has now become the China from after the Opium Wars" or "The Snake (for many in the proportion of a Dragon) has bitten in its own tail which can lead to a lethal injury" (Rashid's prediction).

Interested readers cannot be satisfied with this. For them, the following reflections are made, which supplement those given after every part of the study. First, they *describe* more or less basic elements of *the Opium Problem*, starting with a kind of problem definition. Next, the specific *history* of this problem will be annotated through some main features, followed by *interpretations* of both the problem and the history at issue. In short: the *History of the Opium Problem* is too complicated to be captured in one-liners or in conclusions.

1.

The following six main elements of the original Opium Problem show its complexity from the very beginning of its existence.

There is, first, *a producer/production Opium Question*. It is formed by a Dutch overproduction of opium in Bengal and an underconsumption of VOC opium in Malabar and the inability of the VOC to pay for the Malabar pepper in cash. This is, in my view, the origin of the Opium Problem in world history.

Using opium (for the East) in order to buy a bulk good like pepper (for the West) leads to the creation of opium *as a mass product* with some invented market price. This was not a simple question of supply and demand, but more a matter of "challenge and response" in the framework sketched. From the end of the 18th-century onwards, the English had to cope by exchanging opium for Chinese tea; this also increased the activities of all competitors in both the tea and the opium trade and production.

If the Dutch had not waged so many wars against their competitors, they would have had cash enough to pay for the pepper: instead, they decided to use opium as money. From a commercial point of view, certainly a clever idea at the time, and in the long term it provided the Dutch, English and French with unheard profits unmatched by any other trade product until oil.

The effects after 1663 were that all competitors of the Dutch (first and foremost the English, but also the Portuguese or French) started to increase the production of opium and used it in exchange for pepper or as money to buy other products. This attracted merchants from everywhere, including pirates, "smuggling" or selling the stuff and eager to make a profit as the Dutch were doing. The consequence was that, particularly with opium, the harsh competition led to large quantities of cheaper opium on a market: even the Dutch with their import and export monopolies had to exchange one pound of opium for 110, 100, 60 and even 50 or 40 pounds of pepper.

Second, there is a *quality Opium Question*: the VOC Bengal quality was soon given a higher commercial and user's value than the indigenous one from the Middle East or from Malwa. The English experienced the same opium competition between Bengal and Malwa about 150 years later and solved it by military and bureaucratic force. After this internal Indian Opium War (ca. 1800) the English had to deal again about 75 years later with the same kind of difference between the Bengal opium and the indigenous Chinese one.

This leads, next, to *a consumer Opium Question*. The quality differences already determined to a large extent not only the price, but also the kind of consumers. In the former period the relatively small quantities were consumed by the elite as medicine, for pleasure and, eventually, for killing competitors. Now a tension arose between the rich and the poor or less rich people. This developed in such a way that by the end of the 19th-century, the "less rich" were transformed into the poor thanks to the introduction of a new management construction called the *Opiumregie*. The poor often had to consume poor quality stuff mixed with all kinds of undefinable fillers; more often than not, this was an additional assault on their health.

Another crucial element of the consumer side is that the intruders actively searched for consumers, if needed by force, in order to continuously enlarge the opium market. The most "healthy" supply and demand was formed by as many addicts as possible. The continuous state of war introduced in the realm by the assaults of the Portuguese and Dutch created this market through the fighting customs of the many thousands of *nayros,* indigenous warriors.

Whether a *social-cultural Opium Question* arose on the Malabar coast should be studied anew. Anyway, travelers' reports mention several times how these *nayros* were stupefied by the drug and killed en masse by the Western weapons. Furthermore, the frenetic attempts to spread Christianity lead to remarkably xenophobic, intolerant or racist remarks and probably segregation measures. In addition, opium was reserved for the pagan primitives and not for the Europeans.

This immediately created the *moral Opium Question*: the Dutch decision-makers knew *beforehand* how bad this product was from the literature (Van Linschoten, ca. 1595) and from the Portuguese with their rather extensive health infrastructure in Goa. The medical doctor Willem Schouten and other contemporary travelers also warned of opium's bad effects, but this was used as a reason to blame the victims, not to accuse the producers and traders as, for instance, a Persian ruler did as early as 1621. Because this indigenous ruler prohibited opium use in a production area, a *legal Opium Question* developed as well.

This original six-fold Opium Problem developed in history in the sense that new elements were added, but nothing of the original complexity was lost. In particular after the second half of the 19th-century, the medical and pharmaceutical elements were added in both Europe and Asia. Furthermore, the criminalization of the Opium Problem after about 1890 led to the establishment of an extensive underground and gangsterism.

2.

The Opium Problem did *not* exist in the Asian world before the 1660s. There was no opium *problem* in European societies and the Americas before the middle of the 19th-century. No opium problem in all non-Asian societies before that date. There was also no such problem in

Spanish and Portuguese Asian colonies before the competition with the Dutch got out of hand. This is remarkable since they knew about opium and its qualities. The knowledge of "Asian opium" (*afyūn*) was spread in Europe by the Portuguese. They had done much research, on which the other Europeans relied. Apart from a few Portuguese sources, the Dutch and English learned something about Asian opium for the first time in Van Linschoten's writings about *amphioen* (ca. 1595).

3.

The competition among Western "colonizers" and traders in Asia must have been an astonishing and ridiculous spectacle for the indigenous people. Until the 17th-century the usual reasons for waging war inside Europe were of a religious and dynastic-political nature. For centuries trade *as such* was peaceful, including in the much more developed Arabian or Chinese trade networks; "warring trade" was identical with piracy.

However, from that period onwards and mainly outside Europe, the *combination* of religion, dynasty (state) and trade led to Western "monopoly wars". This is nothing but the dynastic motive to become sole ruler in a market. It was the normal European way of communication with the people in the East and of the mutual European competition in the East. The result was always: the *elimination* of a specific market and, therefore, of the very basis of trade; trade in an imperialistic framework can never be "free" and was, therefore, directed by war, repression, intolerance and exclusion.

New research must be done on this topic, but also on the question of why the West started communicating in such a belligerent way with territories outside Europe from the beginning. The former answer "the Western need for slaves" is no longer sufficient. The world's latest experiences in the Afghan opium war demand a new explanation, in which the course of the opium history should be a main feature.

4.

Before 1950 there were three different *opium circuits* with their own resources and histories:

a. the internal European one in which Levant (mainly Turkish) opium is distributed through Mediterranean ports like Venice and Marseille. The opium from this source is used, processed, consumed from about the

15th-century, in fact, only for medical purposes at least until 1900. The parties involved were, in particular, West European merchants, distributors (folk-healers, apothecaries, pharmacists, medical doctors) and all sorts of consumers in town and country. Until about 1860 this trade and consumption were fully legal.

Opium was one of many hundreds of ingredients used in all kinds of healing practices; it was normally mixed with other substances and never used pure. This purification, characteristic of modern science, happened in the middle of the 19th-century in the framework of a new division of labor: apothecaries, pharmacists and medical doctors, backed by a new pharmaceutical industry, distanced themselves from a "lay public" and marketed new opium products like laudanum, heroin, morphine, codeine, etc. They were used in West Europe and the USA to cure many pains and sorrows as separate medicines for all ages.

These drugs were now only available on prescription. The new professionals were superimposed on "everybody and everything else" as masters in a health infrastructure strongly intertwined with state institutions and the pharmaceutical industry. They were mainly responsible for the "side-effects": addictions, criminal circuits, extensive policing, new authoritarian laws and so on. From this background developed the internal-Western Opium Problem at the end of the 19th-century.

b. the internal Middle Eastern-Indian one in which mainly Persian and Indian opium is distributed through ports along the coasts of the Arabian Sea like Hormuz, Surat or Cochin. The opium from these sources is produced, processed and distributed mostly for medical aims (mixed with other substances), but also for recreational purposes at the many courts. In addition, it is said that it was used by warriors going into battle and as a poison to kill competitors in princely milieus. This concerns the period from the 13th-century to the middle of the 17th-century.

c. the external European circuit prepared by the Portuguese but really opened up by the Dutch VOC as it distributed opium as a bulk product for the first time, and poppy as a cash crop. This happened after 1663 when the Dutch chased the Portuguese away and defeated them on the Malabar Coast (southwestern India), while importing opium as payment for Malabar pepper. This Opium Box of Pandora was opened exclusively in Asian countries in the framework of Western imperialism and colonialism.

5.

The most spectacular example of how the "Western Snake" (this time in the shape of the American CIA) bit its own tail is the transformation of the British colony Burma into one of the largest narco-military powers in the world (see ch. 24), which is probably the main opium, heroin, etc. producer for American and European consumers.

Even today, Myanmar is handled with kid gloves as a consequence of the outworn American containment policy of the Cold War. Japan, as the USA's first Asian partner, gave Myanmar $1.2 million to eradicate opium cultivation: in the Shan area opium farmers should be encouraged to shift to alternative crops (2003). It did not help the opium farmers, as the following quotation reveals, but benefited their military rulers.

Therefore, McCoy's highly relevant statement at the time of the Vietnam War still sheds light on the present situation in which Myanmar and Afghanistan play the leading roles in opium business:

> After pouring billions of dollars into Southeast Asia for over twenty years, the United States has acquired enormous power in the region. And it has used this power to create new nations where none existed, handpick prime ministers, topple governments, and crush revolutions. But U.S. officials in Southeast Asia have always tended to consider the opium traffic a quaint local custom and have generally turned a blind eye to official involvement ... [which] has gone far beyond coincidental complicity; embassies have covered up involvement by client governments, CIA contract airlines have carried opium, and individual CIA agents have winked at the opium traffic. As an indirect consequence of American involvement in the Golden Triangle region, opium has steadily increased [until about 1996. HD.], no. 4 heroin production is flourishing, and the area's poppy fields have become linked to markets in Europe and the United States. Southeast Asia's Golden Triangle already grows 70 percent of the world's illicit opium and is capable of supplying the United States with unlimited quantities of heroin for generations to come.[1]

Its History

1.

It is inappropriate to start this *History of the Opium Problem* in prehistory or antiquity, in old Indian or Chinese history before the attempts to eliminate them by aggressive representatives of the "white race" with their

---

[1] A. McCoy et al., p. 353.

Christian civilizing mission. In all these periods, there was no opium problem whatsoever. *If* the poppy was used among many other herbs, it was for its oil or taste of its seeds, for the energy generated by burning its stems and bulbs. Only in a few cases was its juice used as an ingredient in a specific medicine for a few people. This was true for both the European history of medicines and pharmacy and for the Indian or Eastern one; for the European *teriaca* as well as for the Eastern Ayurveda prescriptions.

It, therefore, makes no sense to refer to these old histories to legitimize drug use or production today or to start popular histories of opium and other drugs to suggest that "people" are addicts *by nature*. This is certainly not the case for opium or cocaine and, of course, for their derivatives: the Opium Problem came into existence after the middle of 17th-century in the framework of Western imperialism.

2.

A geographical limitation of this *History of the Opium Problem* is the following. Although European imperialism also affected Africa and the Americas, it is only in Asia that opium became a spectacular means of European economic and political repression and the largest and most long-lasting source of extracted wealth. In the Americas opium was introduced not earlier than the 19th-century. Coca leaves, an indigenous South American product, were also used locally by the Spanish intruders like opium (17th-century), but as cocaine its use dates from the end of the 19th-century. Opium in Africa is a recent phenomenon now that Nigeria has been transformed into an important drug traffic center between the East and the consumer markets of Europe and the USA.

3.

From about 1450 small quantities of opium were not exceptional within the normal (and legal) European and later American cash "medical trade networks" on shop levels. Four hundred years later, this was still the case.

In the East, however, a very different situation existed. The quantities traded after 1650 were very much larger (bulk trade) and mostly not for medical aims, while the trade networks were narco-military ones. During a large part of this period, there was a fundamental weakness: "the West" had *nothing on offer* for "the East", while they could get pepper, spices and many other interesting products and resources only by cash payments. Therefore, this trade was largely transformed into barter until far in the 19th-century: opium for pepper (Dutch), opium for tea (British).

4.

It was the *Dutch East Indies Company* (VOC) which introduced the Opium Question into world history in the period 1663 to about 1700 along the Malabar coast by starting the exchange of opium for pepper on a large scale. It is worthwhile recapitulating this historical introduction.

Until the 1660s the Dutch bought opium through the "normal" market route: in the available markets, for current prices, cash money for quite "normal" customers (the VOC itself or for its royal clients). Over the *whole* period of about 1620-1663 the maximum amount purchased and sold in this way was in total 6,000-7,000 pounds or about 160 pounds per year on average.[2] Indeed, this half a pound a day is a very small quantity and was used in all probability largely as medicine or as gifts to authorities. It was, therefore, a product which yielded no profit relative to its cost, certainly not for a company accustomed to 200% profits or more on its deals.

From 1663 onwards, once the Dutch were the military masters of the coast, a new policy was adopted: opium in exchange for pepper, which resulted over the next 35 years in an exchange of about 500,000 pounds, which is about 12,500 pounds per year on average or 35 pounds a day. This equals the regular consumption of many people. Only as an indication of how many, a simple calculation is sufficient: with a daily use of 2 grams per person, about 9,000 persons could be supplied. But the story is not just that 500,000 pounds of opium were exchanged for 40 million pounds of pepper only on the Malabar coast over 35 years (average of 80 lb pepper for one pound *amphioen,* the current Dutch word for opium).

It is the first time in history that quantities of opium like this were in circulation; it is the first time that they were needed to buy the top-priority product of all European colonial trade (until the beginning of the 19th-century), pepper. And it is the first time that opium replaced large payments with cash money.

5.

A major element in the opium history is, thus, the close connection between Western imperialism and colonialism in the East and opium importation. This happened, first, with the explicit aim to earn as much money as possible and to create the possibility to transport pepper, tea, etc. to Europe. From the end of the 19th-century, the European powers

---

[2] See, for example, O. Prakash (1984), p. 193-195 and passim.

changed their *raison d'etre* in the East from trade profits into exploitation through colonization. Now, opium was given an additional purpose: to make the workforce more willing, and weaken human protests.

Interpretation History

1.

The valuation of trade products varied greatly in the many landscapes and territories encountered: Japanese silver could be exchanged for gold in China; saltpetre was worthless or not needed in northern India, but in Europe the possession of it decided whether one could win a war or not; etc. The consequences were that Europeans always had to choose between piracy, war, robbery, conquest, paying with silver and gold bullion or bartering Asian products with Asian products. The last aspect led to an energetic intra-Asian trade by Europeans. Thanks to this, they became strong competitors of the traditional Arab, Indian and Chinese maritime traders.

The overland-trade was too difficult for Europeans and remained, therefore, in the hands of the indigenous merchants and other interests. For the new European merchant-conquerors, this overland-trade became "smuggling", which should be eliminated (stimulus for many guerrillas). Apart from the lethal competition among the European competitors, there were endless reasons on sea and land for small or large conflicts with indigenous interests. The West and the East were caught in a permanent war after the arrival of the European Christians. A Kipling question, "whether the twain shall meet", was most likely inspired an utopian naiveté.

2.

It would be a serious mistake to perceive the *History of the Opium Problem* separately from the history of imperialism and colonialism of the East. This started with the Portuguese and Spaniards, then the Dutch, a bit later the English and the French; the Danes, Swedish, Russians, etc. somewhere in between. I am not referring to a chronological sequence.

After a short period in which the Portuguese were "alone", representatives of nearly all these Western countries were "on the scene". In different periods, different intruders held the hegemonic position somewhere in Asia. The Dutch and the English were the most spectacular ones and covered the largest territories. All this seems obvious, but it is not.

For the opium history, complementarity is important. In some way or another, all foreign intruders played a more or less important roles, because after the Dutch brought large quantities of opium into the markets of several coastal areas in Asia, in due time all the others took over this lucrative initiative and spread the use of opium among a much larger population. The most successful were the English and their assault on China.

This led to reactions among indigenous merchants (both inside and outside "their" countries) which again deepened the penetration of opium with all its devastating social and economic consequences.

All these interests competed with each other in reaching the customers, needing as many addicts as possible, lowering prices to enter the markets, and increasing prices once a monopoly position was achieved.

3.

Recently, the centenary of the *Shanghai International Opium Commission* of 1909 was commemorated in Shanghai with much pomp. The *United Nations Office on Drugs and Crime* (UNODC) belonged, of course, to the organizing institutions. In many publications and websites this important event in 1909 nowadays leads to often contradictory comments.

It will be difficult to discover the differences between 1909 and today in one of the first sentences of a report:

> Although the original plan was to limit the conference to the situation in Asia, it was argued that the issue could only be addressed if all the major producing, manufacturing and consuming nations attended. A compromise that ensured that delegates only acted in an advisory capacity to their governments allowed most of the colonial powers of the time to attend.[3]

China was in 1909 the only nation which could report progress in the prohibition of opium. It was at the time the country with perhaps the largest production and, certainly, the largest consumption. However, the whole world knew that the British Empire was the most responsible party and which Western nations it supported in their drive to fabulous drug profits.

In 1909 it was the British who objected against a realistic reporting of the drug relationships. The "poor addicts" stand was chosen to polish the

---

[3] On the UNODC website www.unodc.ord/unodc/en/frontpage/this-day-in-history-the-shanghai-opium-commission-1909.htm.

image of the British imperial producers, let alone the involved financiers, bankers, traders or American shippers.

Of course, the other main producers-distributors like the Dutch or Japanese supported the British. Also in all following international conferences, nothing was said nor researched about the backgrounds of these producers or financiers of the Opium Problem. It took 90 years before a program against money laundering could be started by UNODC in 1997, and only because the USA had launched the so-called *War on Terrorism*.

The British objections in 1909 aimed at a bilateral agreement with China without interference by third parties. Officially, they promised to gradually eliminate their opium sales to China, while apparently expecting that China would not eliminate its own poppy cultivation. As the British inspector Hosie could see and report: the Chinese government largely kept its word, to everyone's surprise. Alas, in the period of the Chinese warlords until their defeat by the People's Republic Army and the CCP, this promising result was largely negated.

The centenary of the 1909 Shanghai conference also led to the publication of a history of this period. The preface by Antonio Maria Costa, Executive Director of the UNODC, starts with the following paragraph:

> For those who doubt the effectiveness of drug control, consider this. In 1906, 25 million people were using opium in the world (1.5% of the world population) compared with 16.5 million opiate users today (0.25% of the world population). In 1906/07, the world produced around 41,000 tons of opium—five times the global level of illicit opium production in 2008. ... the illegal production of opium is now concentrated in Afghanistan (92%). Same for coca. ...Today coca leaf production is concentrated in three Andean countries: Colombia, Peru and Bolivia. International drug control can take some of the credit.

At the moment Costa has the best information about the drugs markets at his disposal. However, one may seriously doubt whether this is also the case for the historical data. Was, for instance, the world production in 1906 'around 41,000 tons'?

In 1922 the *Opium Commission of the League of Nations* estimated the annual world production at 3,515 tons. At the same time the *Committee of Experts* of the League estimated it as 8,600 tons, of which 5,000 concerned the Chinese production.[4] This last figure is also the bottleneck in the reasoning: for 1906 one expert gave 584,000 *pikul* as the total Chinese production and another 76,063 *chests,* which decreased to 40,000 *chests* in

---

[4] Quoted by T. Tong Joe, p. 12, 13.

1909-10.[5] If one accepts that a *pikul* and a *chest* are both about 62 kg, one arrives at estimates for China alone between 36,208 tons and 4,716 tons, respectively (2,480 in 1909-10). An impossible result relative to Costa's 41,000 tons for the whole world; this apart from the temptation to show the *absolute* number of 1.5% and 0.25% of the world population in respectively 1906 and 2008!

4.

At the *end* of the 19th-century, both Asian and West European developments were interrelated in some way thanks to the following developments:

a. the Western chemical industry and science had replaced the herbal basis of drugs;
b. the Western pharmaceutical industry and science had replaced the traditional herbal knowledge and experience;
c. the Western missionaries replaced the usual opium-is-good-for the-Orientals into an opium-is-bad-for-the-Western moral (and, therefore, less good for the Orientals);
d. the Western national states, based on moral and racist concepts, started to replace the liberal non-intervention of the state by increasing intervention into the private lives of its own citizens.

Interpretation Problem

1.

The "mechanism" for why the situation grew from bad to worse in French Southeast Asia can be summarized as follows. The French colonists, like all other colonial regimes, were urged by the mother country-state (which was attacked from all sides, including by the anti-opium lobby) to curb opium consumption and, therefore, the related criminality. At the same time, however, these regimes wanted (and were urged by the mother country) to increase the colony's profitability. The moral wishes could be met and the greed of the colonial bureaucrats satisfied by increasing the prices on all levels and, therefore, negatively affecting the "public" consumption.

---

[5] Idem, p. 25; the last two figures are from Holmes in note 4, which was published in the *Encyclopedia Britannica*.

But if these bureaucrats were not personally involved in the smuggling, they had detailed knowledge about the smuggling they stimulated. The bureaucrats' high monopoly prices stimulated the smuggler's lower prices, while increasing consumption and criminality. The strict oikoidal wish 'to remove the private profit motive that had encouraged consumption and addiction'[6] had, therefore, the reverse effect: opium smuggling in Indochina became more widespread after 1900 with the 100% state monopolies and was so strongly stimulated that it evolved into a real scourge.

This criminality led to new state measures, (secret) military and police organizations, more widespread corruption or a stronger competition between the various colonial governments. Through this spiral the (colonial) state and its (expatriate) bureaucrats proved their necessity: for a long period they had built up substantial experience with the smuggling phenomenon, especially with opium from the beginning of the 17th-century.[7] That this occurred only after the foreign powers themselves defined what was "smuggling" and criminality was silenced loudly.

The problem is, of course, that the Western state and its self-styled monopoly is representative of the foreign conquering state only. Basic to this state is, first, the policy from the mother country that the main tasks of the colonial state are to organize the *exploitation of the colony in favor of private interests in the mother country* by means of securing the safety (military) and create the preconditions for continued undisturbed exploitation (infrastructure works; legal facilities; police). The second policy guideline of the mother country immediately limits the first: the *colony has to pay for itself.* The third maxim adds to the effects of the second one: the colony has to *contribute to the wealth of the mother country-state.* This last maxim led to an acceleration of the exploitation, which would have been unnecessary if the mother country had paid for its bureaucrats.

Thus, the colonial bureaucrats (military, police, officials) had to remain very involved in the narco-military organization of the opium, cocaine,

---

6 E. van Luijk, J. van Ours, p. 1.

7 E. van Luijk, J. van Ours demonstrate how scholars can became ideologues of a specific state policy. They had no realistic view on the effects of state monopolies in this period but concluded (p. 16) 'that the change in policy *per se* did indeed induce a substantial reduction in opium use. Apparently, by taking over the opium market the government removed the profit motive to stimulate consumption' (italics by authors. HD). Simply astonishing is the 'lesson' they derive from their analysis, 'that the consumption of even addictive drugs is price-responsive, and a policy of socializing the hard-drug trade need not be as immoral as it sounds' (p. 16, 17). What the state is doing cannot be immoral ...

heroin, etc. trade because their own income depended on the drugs profits, their own status in the bureaucratic hierarchy depended on the result of their work in the exploitation of the colony; their own possibility to make a fortune as an expatriate in the colony depended on their freedom to exploit an underground. It is only through fear and terror that this underground spread and gave these bureaucrats the freedom to fill their pockets undisturbed.

The French colonialism was quite different in its ideological setting from the Dutch or English. This concerned not only the superior position of the bureaucracy and its direct rule. In the East Asian setting it concerned the way the model French *gouvernement* opium monopoly became organized in a highly centralized and repressive way. But the most astonishing development was still to come.[8]

2.

"Opium management" by the American state was handled by McCoy et al. as the introduction of the "surveillance state" at home, imported from the colony (Philippines), where the practice of it was tested in rather rigorous form. Based, however, on this new history of the opium problem, the mechanism could receive a more universal character.

In the first place the Portuguese started in the 16th-century with a system of passports for all traders, so that their traffic and the content of the cargo could be controlled. This was done to limit the Dutch or Arabian competition and "smuggling" (their definition). The control was executed by Portuguese warships mainly in the Arabian Sea and along the Indian West coast.

The Dutch not only copied this system in the VOC period in the East Indies, but extended it much further in several ways. The Chinese traveler Ong-Tae-Hae reported that already before 1780, Chinese groups needed passports to travel around and to check whether they lived in "ghettos". Apparently, this surveillance was introduced after the Dutch massacred about 20,000 Chinese in Batavia (1740), their main competitors in the opium trade (instead of "pious consumers") who were always accused of "smuggling", etc.

The French introduced the *Opiumregie* system after about 1870 in Indochina. This was also copied by the Dutch and extended into a detailed

---

[8] A. W. McCoy et al. See also for an update on www.a1b2c3.com/drugs/opi011.htm based on the 2003 edition.

control system of the private lives of the addicts and users, who needed specific licenses. They established a special Opium police as well with an extensive and expensive surveillance apparatus with its own navy to control the many government opium dens and "smuggling".

All these measures were a consequence of the opium monopoly position of the states, which they spontaneously claimed for themselves to ensure regular revenues to sustain their officials, the state bureaucracy, the army and navy. They were in fact only directed against *specific foreigners* and added, therefore, to the general racism in the colonies and at home (the Dutch, English or French did not consider themselves as foreigners: the colonies were their property, weren't they?).

The main effect of all these practices was that foreign criminals were automatically created.

This was also the consequence of quite different surveillance practices, which were described for the city government of San Francisco already around 1880, and foreshadowed the countrywide repression of non-conformist behavior of their *own* citizens by the Anslinger administration later. This is the first narco-policing of the *own* Western citizens.

While the opium surveillance activities in the Philippines colony were directed to the *specific foreigners*, in the San Francisco case their own citizens became foreigners for the bureaucracy and its leadership.

3.

At the end of Part 2 we showed how around 1900 the "British-Induced Opium Problem" had proliferated into a world drug problem, still with opium as its nucleus, but now with derivatives like heroin and morphine and alternatives like cocaine. The latter three products added brand-new techniques from a rather new technology (chemistry) to the opium production and trafficking. Before they left the German laboratories and factories (Bayer, Merck, etc.) or US gadget shops and created an immense drug problem, we had entered the first decade of the twentieth-century.[9]

---

[9] As was the case for opium, it is useless and ahistorical to refer to some old practice from Peruvian Indians for cocaine comparable to the qat chewing in Yemen, Somalia, etc. Certainly, the Spanish colonists did deal a bit with coca leaves like the Portuguese or Dutch with *Papaver somniferum*, but they never created a problem comparable to the Opium Problem, nor made coca into a business product outside the Potosi mines in Bolivia. Coca was used there to stimulate the miners to work harder and longer. The Spaniards were much less commercially oriented than the Portuguese; they were the settler colonists who used drugs to extract more energy from the slaves on their plantations, mines, etc. No, cocaine was re-invented by German chemists as a new drug in the second

The problems related to these new chemical products became first and foremost confined to the Western world, in particular the USA. In addition, the whole infrastructure created by the opium production and trade through the official and illicit channels has made it much easier for these new Western products to find a world market. In reverse, the opium which was largely confined to the East Asian countries could now come much more easily into the Western hemisphere, not in the least because heroin and morphine are derivatives from the same *Papaver somniferum.* Therefore: without opium, no heroin and morphine. Indirectly, the enormous financial profits created by the opium production and trade must have been the stimulus to give cocaine its very quick expansion.

To show how the West received "a cigar from the own box" and created many present world problems with its new chemical products, it is not necessary to go into detail about the chemical background and characteristics of the products involved. The experience with opium and the Opium Problem was definitely the basis on which the new products could be launched successfully. That happened in particular in the period 1900-1940. What happened during and after World War II was an exponential growth of the same problem.

4.

The chapter devoted to a *History of the USA Opium Problem* became a consumer-oriented story for two main reasons: after the Civil War the USA discovered a serious Opium Problem at home. The very fine Christians with their bright Bible knowledge who now occupied this ex-British colony discovered nearly always the mote in their brother's eye and never the beam in their own. Certainly, in particular the USA was increasingly the victim of massive opium imports from all corners of the globe.

In addition, its own new pharmaceutical industry, mainly busy with opiates and cocaine-related medicines, contributed seriously to the medicalization of Americans. Secondly, the "side effects" of this victimization were counterattacked in several ways:

a. the prevailing view of the opiate addiction as a vice;
b. the guilt was largely placed on the back of the Chinese. At the end of the 1960s, a serious researcher of the narcotic problem wrote that

---

half of the 19th-century and became a commercial product creating a Cocaine Problem in the beginning of the 20th-century.

there is a mystic scene of oriental opulence where languid mandarins gently puff ivory-inlaid pipes, filling the air with a sinister blue haze.[10]

c. the pharmaceutical industry not only created part of the problem, but also came with the "solution": medicines to cure and the experts to prescribe these medicines (further medicalization);
d. the spiritual or moral experts had the same double-sided "face": they created the "vice" and the "crime", after which could come the solution: the religious prescriptions (of competing sectarians) and the establishment of a rigorous legal and prison system;
e. the bureaucrats on the different (competing) political levels created the "vice" by adding a big increase on top of the normal market prices through taxes and duties, which made the products so expensive that smuggling had to be organized which later was called the "underground", the "mafia" and "organized crime".

It is not surprising that David Courtwright concluded his in-depth study on the addiction problem before 1940 with a devastating criticism:

> Another fundamental feature of American narcotic laws is that they were passed, interpreted, and defended on the basis of misleading, even fraudulent, information. In attempting to assess the extent of addiction at different points in time, I have necessarily considered a variety of official estimates. These figures consistently were shaded either upward or downward, depending on whether government officials were attempting to obtain more stringent regulations or defending the stringent regulations already in place. The ethic that intelligent narcotic policy should be predicated on accurate data was almost totally lacking prior to 1940 ...[11]

5.

The following table is appropriate here without much comment. It documents an important supply side of the Opium Problem and how the "bite of the snake" functions. It, furthermore, shows the development of that "cosy" Turkish opium scene for medical aims only of the 19th-century into a post-World War II global production center (see ch. 8). This scene has now definitely lost its innocence. The expenses are related to bribes, travel and conversion; X in the first row is related to seed and labor. It is evident that there were more drug supply routes, but they did not differ much in principle.

---

[10] W. Eldridge, p. 1.
[11] D. Courtwright, p. 7.

Table 50. A Supply Side of the Opium Problem Around 1970 (in US$)[12]

	Weight	Buying Price	Selling Price	Expenses	Profit
Opium					
Turkish producer to first middleman	10 kg	---	180	X	180 minus X
First middleman to agent	---	180	250	---	70
Agent to Istanbul exporter	---	250	280	---	30
Crossing of Syrian border	---	280	650	90	280
Cost of conversion of opium into base morphine	---	650	850	60	140
Morphine					
Crossing of Lebanese border	1 kg	850	1000	50	100
Refining of morphine in Lebanon	1 kg.	1000	1200	50	150
Transport to Beirut (couriers and accomplices)	---	1200	1500	75	225
Beirut–Marseilles (couriers)	---	1500	2000	100	400
Commission to local agent in Marseilles	---	2000	3000	200	800
Conversion to heroin in Marseilles	---	3000	4000	150	850
Heroin					
Marseilles–New York (couriers)	---	4000	7000	500	2500
Entry into US	---	7000	12500	1000	4500
American wholesalers	---	12500	22500	---	10000

These are moderate wholesale prices; exaggerated figures circulate widely like, for instance, 28,500 dollars a kilo in New York or 36,000 dollars a kilo in Chicago; the UN even calculated a street selling price of heroin of 430,000 dollars a kilo in 1971 ! In the American streets at the time, pure heroin was sold in bags of 5 milligram for US$5. However, too often the addict had to pay this price for heroin "cut" with 50% lactose. Whatever the substance, 1259 people died as a result of a heroin overdose in 1971 in New York alone.

---

[12] C. Lamour, M. Lamberti, p. 67, 68.

What Could Be Done?

This question was posed by Alfred McCoy at the end of a most thrilling and influential scientific analysis of the modern opium problem.[13] The painstaking way in which he uncovered the role of secret services like the CIA in the narcotic business as the main tool in a dubious and unsuccessful foreign policy has undoubtedly produced shock-waves among largely embedded journalists, politicians and bureaucratic decision-makers. The cure of the "Commies Problem" in Asia, mainly directed against China, has become the Western nightmare no. 1. That it was proved once again how naively the new imperialists entered the international scene with conquering plans, fully overestimating their own capabilities, is one side of McCoy's study; an important aspect, but still a side-show, in this history of the Opium Problem.

Concerning this Problem, he demonstrated how from before World War II until the 1970s, Western governments and their bureaucratic institutions, in particular their police and army, were unable and too often unwilling to stop neo-colonial policies in which the narcotic business (always accompanied by illicit weapons deals) is a most important element.

His study also had a moral incentive: 'to end America's heroin plague'. It is not McCoy's fault that his nearly heroic attempt did not have the result he hoped for. 'Obviously, something must be done,' he wrote, proposing to use one of the following three strategies:

> (1) cure the individual addicts; (2) smash international and domestic narcotics syndicates; or (3) eliminate illicit opium production. Since it is extremely difficult to cure individual addicts without solving the larger social problems and almost impossible to crush the criminal syndicates, the only realistic solution is to eradicate illicit opium production.[14]

One point can be made immediately: the first strategy does not concern my study, and there are many means available and experimentally proved for the individual curing of addicts. For the Asian countries the social treatment Chinese addicts got after 1950 seems to be the most successful one. In addition, however dramatic personal problems may be, they are minor compared to the problems related to the other two strategies. Therefore, we shall concentrate on them here.

---

[13] A.C. McCoy et al., p. 354-362.
[14] Idem, p. 355.

Many scholars followed McCoy's example and documented the direct (and most often indirect) assault of British and American policymakers on East Asia, more specifically on China. Carl Trocki's conclusion, twenty years after McCoy, is still correct, alas, ten years after his own well-known study:

> Ironically, it was the combination of opium and warlords which on the one hand destroyed the Qing, but on the other sowed the seeds for the next opium plague, one which would sweep out of Asia and wreak a kind of poetic justice on the former colonial powers.[15]

Indeed, the boomerang effect of this kind of Western assault on Asia has received new a much broader empirical basis, a more complicated historical explanation and meaning in this study.

This opium history demonstrates that one thing never can be left out of consideration: to question the role of the state which hides itself in the West behind dubious Christian morality and policing or suggesting it would save its citizens from the bad world outside; it is a state which acts, *once out of sight of its citizens*, in (neo)colonies, as the worst violator of everything it stands for at home.

The Chinese history teaches us how difficult it was to resist these attacks by the West, but it succeeded by *partly* copying the quasi-invincible strongest weapons of the West, its technology and dubious imports of opium. It demonstrated an effective case of import substitution, in economic terms, while half a century later a regime came to power which effectively eradicated opium production, consumption and trade. An example to be followed by "the West"?

Other proposals to solve this opium problem are given time and again. They are mostly far from realistic. One has to consider the different market constellations also in the prohibition of private opium consumption in Western and Eastern countries, because in the former it was/is confined largely to the well-to-do circles and in the East to the poorer ones. Addens' reasonable four-point program to solve the opium problem was directed only at combating Eastern opium consumption: 1. an improvement in labor conditions; 2. better medical provision for the population; 3. control of the production of raw opium, including the prevention of illicit traffic and 4. 'above all, the filling up of the spare time of the populations by recreation and sport for instance'.[16] An interesting approach with

---

[15] C. Trocki (1999a), p. 171.
[16] T. Addens, p. 86.

reminiscences of the successful 1950 anti-opium programs in the new China.

It is now 60 years later. The latest information about Chinese criminality refer 'to the golden years of social order in the 1950s when ... it was not necessary to lock one's door at night'.[17] Whether this was a myth or not is not important here: *if true*, the present situation sketched seems alarming. The author writes:

> About 40 per cent of the heroin from the Golden Crescent of Afghanistan and Pakistan ... is now trafficked into China and beyond. The same percentage of the heroin originating in the Golden Triangle of Laos and Burma also flows into China ... The drug consuming market in China has exploded in recent years.

The central thesis of this new study seems to be: "the market created the crime", and this is utter nonsense. In modern China supply-demand relations for all products, services or information do not exist. That is the case, often for different reasons, in most countries in the world! She apparently does not demonstrate the relativity and proportionality of her Chinese crime and execution figures, for instance, by comparison with the "market" society par excellence, the USA: her story feeds sensationalism.

But apart from all this, the author could know that her central thesis cannot be proved or supported: the reasons she mentions herself are revealing enough. Many crimes are committed 'by itinerant rural workers fleeing the countryside, where there are too many people chasing too little work'; there is 'no criminal code' only a 'culture of punitiveness'; the corruption among police, party and government officials is widespread; large government anti-crime campaigns in the 1980s 'were encouraging crime'; serious political struggles ...

All this has nothing to do with the Market (whatever definition one uses), but with a serious malfunctioning of the state, provincial or local bureaucracies, fundamental urban-rural contradictions and discrepancies in the basic care of the people (see further Addens's proposals above). Specifically, drug criminals—social-economic criminals par excellence— can easily find out how to exploit all these bottlenecks. And, as in the case of the USA-CIA, a specific Chinese foreign policy of supporting Burma,

---

[17] This quotation and the following data are from a review in the *Times Literary Supplement* (28-1-2011, p. 10). This is the last information I could consult for this history of the Opium Problem. It concerns a study of Susan Trevaskes (*Policing Serious Crime in China*). Of course, this book falls outside the scope of my history.

Afghanistan, and Pakistan makes China vulnerable to accepting their main export articles: drugs.

Anyway, this is not covered by this *History of the Opium Problem*. A sequel should study the reasons why the Opium Problem in the "New China" became aggravated again. In this case, one can be pessimistic about the future to which Ahmed Rashid referred in the preface; an opium future in the 1950s was for China still a 'golden' one.

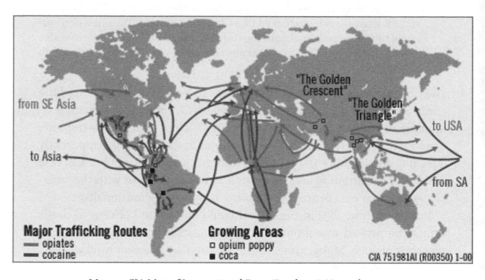

Map 20. CIA Map of International Drug "Pipelines", November 2009
Source: en.wikipedia.org (Drugroutemap.gif)

APPENDICES

FROM RAGS TO RICHES TO RAGS, CA. 1775-1914

There were several theoretical approaches in the past (from world systems approach to dependence and neo-liberal theories) to try to understand the very imprecise concept of "globalization". They were all too abstract, could not withstand empirical criticism and produced extravagant nonsense (Wallerstein, Gunder Frank). The *practical* idea of the *commodity chain* (Topik, Gootenberg, etc.) is much more revealing. It provides the opportunity to look in a proper way into the connections between production (labor), consumption and distribution (trade), including the interventions of state bureaucracies and similar institutions or price fluctuations.

It is surprising that no one has looked into the spectacular tea/pepper-opium-silver, etc. chains, thanks to which we can add another important variable, the relationship between the different "uppergrounds and undergrounds".

In theory, a commodity chain is certainly not enough by itself: in the links of the chain, it is important to look around and see how and why the existing networks there operate. That is much more complicated than just a flow of commodities and money. The important features in the chain and network "inspire" each other in making a realistic history possible. I hope that this book contributes to the making of a chain-network of the opium history.

A small compensation for this aim is the following answer to the question: Is it possible to make a numerical reconstruction of the whole process from planting the poppy in 19th-century India to consumption of opium in China? It could result in a chain of production, distribution and consumption starting with the poor peasant and ending with the poor consumer, while showing the main features of the existing networks. Somewhere in between we can find the field in which enormous profits were made by the foreign bankers, traders and so on. Indeed, a chain from rags to riches to rags. In fact, this is overstretching the possibilities of the sources at the moment. However, much more and detailed data can be found in other sources.

The following must be perceived, therefore, as an effort to pave the road to that result, in the hope that somebody takes up the challenge. For the time being the data given show a sequence of
* planting of the poppy by the peasant;
* production and circulation of opium in India;
* work in a Patna or Benares opium factory;
* sales of the end-product (raw or prepared opium) in public auctions in Calcutta (or Bombay);
* export from India to several destinations, but mainly to China;
* import in Canton;
* distribution (prices) in China;
* consumption and addiction in China.

The comments are confined to some explanation of the given tables. The excellent *Digital South Asia Library* (DSAL) contains the historical statistics of British India from 1840-1920 (*Statistical abstract relating to British India*). They are used as the main source and correction of other sources. However, additional information is badly needed.

Different authors often provide different data while consulting the same sources. Sometimes contradictory conlusions are drawn. If they do not differ too much, I leave it as it is. Otherwise I devote a short discussion to it.

Costs of the first treatments

In Bengal the British planted about 550,000 acres of poppy every year (= 2,225 million square meters or 750,000 bighas).[1] About 3/4 of this was irrigated. The average production is 4½ seer per bigha or 15 English pounds per acre, which makes about 60,000 chests in total.

'There is, in fact, no crop known to the agriculturist, unless sugar-cane, that requires so much care and labour as the poppy' (E. Balfour, p. 30). After which follows a detailed description of all the work and how it has to be done in the Malwa region. 'One acre of well-cultivated ground will yield from 70 to 100 pounds of chick. The price of chick varies from three to six rupees a pound, so that an acre will yield from 200 to 600 rupees worth of opium at one crop' (Idem).

Next, this harvest underwent several treatments (separation of the oil, etc.) and ended with making balls of eight to ten ounces each. They are finally packed in chests of 150 cakes; 'the total cost of the drug at the place of production being about fourteen rupees per chest including all expenses' (Idem, p. 31).

Table 51. Expenses and profits of cultivating one *bigha* of Malwa opium ca. 1823

Expenses (rupees)		Receipts (rupees)	
5 seers of seed	0.9	5 seers (pukka)	40
manure	2	sale of seed (3 M.)	4
watching expense	4	total income	44
weeding, plowing, etc.	6		
cutting and gathering	4	*minus* expenses	29.9
watering	6	*minus* village dues	1.8
linseed oil	1		
rent to Government	6		
Total	29.9	Net Income	12.15

Source: John Malcolm, *A Memoir of Central India Including Malwa and Adjoining Provinces ...* (London: Kingsbury, Parbury & Allen, 1823), quoted in C.Trocki (1999a), p. 183, see also p. 68.

---

[1] See the very detailed data in J. Wiselius, (1886), p. 196 ff.

A *bigha* corresponds to about 2/3 acre or about 2700 sq. meters. One *seer* is about 1 kg. One Rupee is 2 shillings; it was devalued in 1899 to 1s 1d.

In the table are given the data for a "good season". For a tolerable season the expenses were estimated at 31.10 rupees and the receipts at 32.11 so that a net income is left of 1.01 rupee. In a bad season a loss per bigha is estimated of 9 rupees. Because in a bad season the prices of opium were probably higher, the loss may turn out to be a little less.

The peasant could hope for a production of 4-5 seers (kg) per bigha and an income of Rs. 200 for about 14 bighas. Wiselius informs us that the Behar (Bengal) poppy planters received 25 shilling gross per year, reminding us that much is deducted 'before the planter receives this money'. Per bigha the peasant is paid 33-38 shilling gross. In Benares the peasants got more from their bigha, 38-42 shilling gross.

In the 1870s the peasants gradually stopped working for the British government and in particular the poppy production, since they preferred the better paid sugar, potatoes, etc. for the local Indian market: the British were forced to respond with an increase in the "poppy wages". In addition, it is more expensive to buy Malwa opium in the independent states than Bengal opium on government contracts. The former is nearly twice as expensive. There is also the trend, however, that the yields in Bengal decrease whereupon Malwa opium must be bought in order to sustain or expand the export.

Production of opium in India and its market prices

In Bengal (NW Provinces and Oudh) in 1797, the total area of poppy cultivation amounted to 9,460 bighas, but nearly a century later it has increased to 928,241 bighas (E. Balfour, p. 31).

In 1878-79 the total output in British India was 91,200 chests with an export value of £12,993,985, and the net profit to the British Indian Government was £7,7000,671 (Id., p. 30); about half Bengal and half Malwa opium. Of this about £1,000,000 was exported to Burma and the Malay settlements, the remainder to China.

From the year 1784 to 1801 the market price of crude opium from the cultivator ran from 16 to 21 salimshahi rupees per durri, a measure of 5 pucka seers, each seer being 90 sal. rupees. 'This was the price of the drug by the grower in the first stage and a better criterion than that of the manufacturer in its prepared state' (Id., p. 30). In 1801 this price rose to 25 rupees, in 1804 to 27, quickly increasing to 42—its maximum—in 1809. Later it gradually fell to 29 in 1814, then rose again to 33 in 1818; it reached 38-39 in 1820.

For later years the following table documents the situation:

Table 52. Production and Prices in Indian districts and Calcutta,1873-1882 (in piculs and guilders)

		Chests-piculs provision and abkari opium produced in the agencies	Cost price for government per picul in guilders	Chests sent to Calcutta	Chests sold in Calcutta	Sale price per chest in Calcutta in guilders
1873	Behar	30,771	389	26,770	25,500	1,305
	Benares	19,512	390	19,000	16,500	1,229
1874	Behar	33,936	391	30,856	26,244	1,242
	Benares	25,068	384	23,860	18,756	1,200
1875	Behar	32,702	396	29,340	25,800	1,269
	Benares	23,146	386	22,414	19,200	1,215
1876	Behar	38,108	396	34,957	26,800	1,309
	Benares	34,109	388	33,094	20,200	1,243
1877	Behar	35,575	389	32,166	25,000	1,298
	Benares	36,027	380	35,001	23,000	1,229
1878	Behar	19,003	361	18,140	30,000	1,280
	Benares	26,153	323	25,000	24,000	1,199
1879	Behar	33,108	252	29,786	30,000	1,189
	Benares	22,483	356	20,175	30,000	1,112
1880	Behar	34,453	309	31,118	28,200	1,361
	Benares	22,028	350	21,851	28,200	1,292
1881	Behar	27,407	393	24,200	28,200	1,358
	Benares	26,884	348	25,532	28,200	1,345
1882	Behar	28,379	381	26,022	27,900	1,261
	Benares	28,548	392	28,017	28,200	1,221

Source: J. Wiselius (1886), p. 201.

The work in a British opium factory in India

There exists a painstakingly detailed description of the work in an opium factory, the Ghazipur Factory, forty miles below Benares. The writer is Rudyard Kipling, who visited the factory in January 1888.[2] His friend was the Opium Agent at Ghazipur, Harry Rivett-Carnac. This man earned 3,000 rupees a *month,* equivalent to £2,700 per *annum.* In that case, in 1888 £1 = Rupees 13.3; 1,000 Rupees is about £76.0. Other exchange rates are also available. At the time Kipling, who was addicted to both alcohol and opium, earned one-fifth of the wage of this Opium Agent.

---

[2] R. Kipling. See for detailed information on Kipling's trip www.kipling.org.uk/rg_opium1.htm. Colonel Harry Rivett-Carnac held a 'second-rate appointment—the opium commissionership at Ghazipore ...' The Indian bestselling author of *Sea of Poppies,* Amitav Ghosh (2008), provides the present image of the opium factory (still running): 'The Ghazipur and Patna Opium Factories together produced the Wealth of Britain.' Interview: www.outlookindia.com.

Public sales

Table 53. Public Sales of Bengal opium of the EIC in Calcutta, 1787–1829

Year	Chests sold	Average price per chests In rupees	Results of sales In rupees
1787	3693	470	1 735 710
1792	2982	525 (535)	1 884 624
1797	4172	426 (286)	1 777 272
1802	2840	1378 (1383)	3 913 520
1807	4208	1276	5 369 408
1812	4769	1955	9 323 395
1817	3552	1876 (2178)	6 663 552
1822	3360	2062 (3089)	6 928 320
1827	7461	1328	9 908 208

Source: J. Rowntree, p. 284, 285 statistical tables supplied by Maurice Gregory. The data are derived from the *Report of the Royal Commission on Opium* (1895), vol. 7, p. 61 and 62. For the second column see also J. Richards (2002-2), p.159 (except for the year 1827). One *chest* is about 140 lbs which differs from 60–72 kg; one *seer* = about 1 kg.

In the original tables the year is indicated as "1829-30", which is here given as "1829". The selected data indicate the sales or export or revenue in the given year. For all years see J. Rowntree, p. 284 ff. and J. Richards (2002-2), p. 159 ff.

Table 53 differs sometimes considerably from the one given in C.Trocki (1999a), p. 65 of the same period. His figures are given as well in brackets in the third column. Part of the explanation is that Trocki only provides Patna data, but this is not true for data after 1798. Further reasons for the differences are not known. The table from H. Morse (1926), vol. iv, p. 383 titled 'Opium, 1818-27' gives no information about which phase of the process is covered and is, therefore, useless.

From 1860 to 1880 the annual average production of 'provision' opium was 50,154 chests, and in that period the price of crude opium varied from Rs. 4.8 to Rs. 5 a seer. The actual cost of a chest of Bengal opium 'including interest on the capital and all indirect charges, is as follows:

'68 seers 2 chittak at 75° consistence, equals 73 seers at 70° consistence at Rs. 5 per seer .... Rs. 365 (Behar.) .... Rs. 341 (Benares)

Cost of manufacture and packing, interest on capital, charges for pensions, and leave allowance of officers   71   66

Total .... Rs. 436   .... Rs. 407

Being an average of Rs. 421' (E. Balfour, p. 38).

Exports of Indian opium

This important subject is documented by many sources, and it could be expected that then the question would become crystal clear. Alas, the reality is different. There is even the suspicion that many people have an interest to create a chaos to hide interesting backgrounds. To entangle the real constellation here would be too time consuming.

Table 54. Exports of Indian opium in chests (1829-1902)

Year	Exports of opium in chests	Net revenue to indian government in rupees
1829	9 678 (9 678) [16 257]	---
1832	16 083 (9 385) [21 985]	---
1837	29 679 (19 307) [34 373]	15 864 450
1842	35 887 (16 518)	15 765 810
1847	23 877 (23 877)	16 633 848
1852	61 157	37 179 320
1857	74 966	59 183 750
1862	82 217	61 991 980
1867	86 930	70 480 650
1872	82 934	68 704 230
1877	92 820	65 216 520
1882	91 800	72 167 780
1887	90 096	60 908 870
1892	75 384	63 906 840
1897	56 069	27 906 550
1902	65 603	48 649 985

Source: J. Rowntree, p. 286, 287 statistical tables supplied by Maurice Gregory. He derived these data from *Financial and Commercial Statistics of British India,* 10th Issue (Calcutta, 1903); see also E. Balfour, p. 38, 39 for these revenues in £ for the years 1871-1881 and for 1800-1860.

The figures in parentheses in the second column are mentioned by J.C. Baud (1853), p. 214. The given differences are quite mysterious since two times similar data are given and three times much lower ones. This table also differs considerably from M. Greenberg/C.Trocki (1999a), p. 95. Their data are given in brackets. In this case the matter could be solved as follows: there must be a large difference between data from the *arrivals* of opium from several sources in Canton and the export from India (see next paragraph "Destinations"). At last, this table differs by 50% from J. Richards (2002-2), p. 160-162.

Table 54 is, anyway, not clearly defined: is it the total export or only of Bengal opium? An answer is suggested by B. Lubbock (p. 286), who gave details about the sales during 1845. They were attended by contenders of five nationalities: English, Scottish, American, Parsee and Hindi. The Bengal sales (Patna + Benares) of opium were 21,526 chests and Malwa opium sales 18,321 chests 'making an export for the year of 39,847 chests'. In the missing details of table 54, an amount of 36,942 chests is indicated for '1844-45' and an amount of 20,553 chests for the year '1845-46'. It is not logical to choose '1844-45' to compare with Lubbock's data of 1845, as then a gap of nearly 20,000 chests must be explained. My suggestion is that in table 54 only the data about *Bengal opium* are given. The remaining difference of nearly 1000 chests can be explained as follows: it must be the quantity left for consumption in India, or it is simply a typing error.

To get a better grip on these figures, ten-year totals are calculated from the same sources as Rowntree reproduced. Although there is a question of definition between the two, they are combined in the following table:

Table 55. Bengal Opium Export after Sales from India and Financial results of EIC and Government of India, 1787-1900**

Years	Chests	Results in rupees
1787–1800	51 427	25 764 000
1800–1810	39 474	55 302 000
1810–1820	41 788	84 687 000
1820–1830	48 464	90 990 000
1830–1840	228 507	159 123 000*
1840–1850	363 370	214 041 000
1850–1860	670 421	405 565 000
1860 1870	777 232	586 361 000
1870–1880	919 028	681 049 000
1880–1890	898 721	681 576 000
1890–1900	702 039	478 308 000
Totals 1787-1900	4 740 471	3 371 068 000

* During this decade in the first five years there was no indication of the net revenue to the Indian Government. For the other five years, the revenue was 67,425,000 rupees.
** The third column gives round sums.

Let's suppose that the 1870 rule of 1000 rupees = 100 pounds was appropriate for the whole period. Then the EIC and the British Indian government received from the sales of *Bengal* opium alone £337,106,800 largely as net revenue. During this period nearly five million chests of *Bengal* opium were exported, which is 325 million kilo. Together with the Malwa opium there must have been an export of about 600 million kilo of opium, if one supposes that the 1829 division (see below) is appropriate for the whole period. Can this estimate be substantiated further through data about the destination of the Indian opium?

Ill. 33. The Manufacture of Opium in India, 1900

Source: The picture is probably made in Ghazipur north of Calcutta by Bourne & Shepherd; www.plantcultures.org.

Destinations

The opium export from India was not only destined for Canton or other Chinese ports (Macao, Hong Kong, Shanghai, etc.). In this section many export data and destinations are given which should be made the subject of further research. In addition, we must remeber that Turkish opium also arrived in Canton, albeit much smaller quantities than Bengal or Malwa (C. Trocki, 1999, p. 95). In the given period it cannot be more than 10%, so one can expect that 600 million kilo also arrived in China during the 19th century plus one decade.

That century started with an Indian export of opium to China of 1500 chests (E. Balfour, p. 34). Baud provides data until the middle of the century, but alternative information about the pre- and post-Opium War period is necessary as well as about specific years.

The following figure 12 concerns the pre-Opium War period and the EIC performance only.

It is worthwhile scrutinizing specific years. Take, for example, the shipping expert Lubbock's stories for 1829 or 1841. In short, he reveals the following.

1829
Lubbock mentions that in this year 7,006 chests of *Bengal* opium were received at Lintin, 137 chests in Macao. Furthermore, 6,542 chests of *Malwa* opium arrived as well. Of this kind of opium, 315 chests were brought to Macao. In a shipwreck 233 chests were lost. In addition, 700 chests of *Turkish* opium were brought to Lintin by American bottoms.[3] The above list of Rowntree gives for

---

[3] B. Lubbock, p. 70.

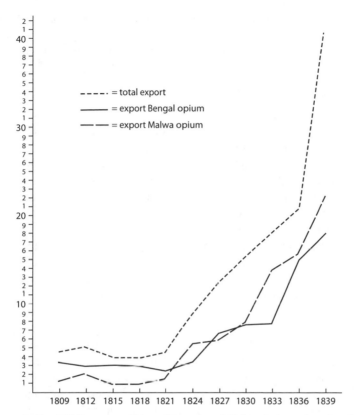

Figure 12. Indian EIC Export to China of Bengal and Malwa Opium, 1809-1839 (x 1,000 chests)

Source: H. Derks based on data from A. Le Pichon, 2007, p. 19; selected years.

1828-29 an amount of 8,578 chests of *Bengal* opium. This means that about 1500 chests or 15% were sold during the voyage from Calcutta to Canton, so that 85% went to China in this year. For the same kind of bookkeeping of the stocks and deliveries in 1833, see H. Morse (1926), vol. iv, p. 372.

1841

On the outward run to China, many clippers arrived first in Singapore. In January and February five clippers landed in total nearly a thousand chests (924).[1] This is about 4% of the total export, so 96% went to China.

---

[1] Idem, p. 241.

Table 56. Export of *Bengal* Opium from Calcutta to Several Destinations, 1809–1850 in chests (selected years)

Years	China	Manilla	Java	Sumatra coast	Strait settle-ments	To else-where	Totals
1809	3 200	---	---	---	---	---	3 200
1811	3 600	---	---	---	---	---	3 600
1813	3 300	---	---	---	---	---	3 300
1816	3 376 (2,700)	74	213	62	583	42	4 350
1818	3 575 (2,900)	12	44	119	549	7	4 306
1820	3 591 (1,700)	57	797	45	657	5	5 152
1822	3 207 (3,300)	9	439	50	395	5	4 100
1824	5 365 (3,400)	65	294	73	1 258	31	7 086
1826	5 861 (3,800)	30	172	64	435	36	6 568
1828	4 903 (6,700)	18	62	23	1 582	7	6 554
1830	5 590 (7,400)	12	162	8	1 344	12	7 116
1832	7 530 (6,800)	12	162	5	1 842	13	9 385
1834	9 480 (7,800)	12	30	6	1 512	20	11 050
1836	10 493 (14,900)	12	132	19	2 107	2	12 734
1838	14 499 (19,600)	12	189	19	3 483	50	18 221
1840	5 817	728	46	19	11 424	123	17 410
1842	11 867	728	75	19	4 505	71	16 518
1844	14 709	728	222	19	3 822	39	18 792
1846	20 668	728	85	19	4 277	45	24 990
1848	27 870	728	50	19	4 352	15	32 287
1850	30 996	728	75	19	3 997	25	35 093

Source: J. C. Baud, p. 214. Instead of Strait Settlements he had «Pulau Pinang and further Eastwards». The 1809–1813 figures and those in brackets are given by A. Le Pichon, p. 19

From this table we can learn not only the large differences between several sources, but also that 75-80% of the Bengal opium on average was destined for China, 10-15% to the Strait Settlements and 5-10% to Java. In all the years together about 434,000 chests with Bengal opium were exported to the given destinations. During the First Opium War with China, the export to China decreased in 1839/40 to 3,755, and the next year it was 5,817. Afterwards, it increased very quickly.

About the Malwa opium Baud provides much less data, as the following table shows. At that time it was still located outside British India. Under the heading 'To Elsewhere' is meant export to Malabar, Goa or Mauritius.

So with the exception of one year, all Malwa opium (about 95%) went to China. This was a total of 227,091 chests.

Table 57. Export of *Malwa* Opium from Bombay to Several Destinations, 1809-1850 in chests (selected years)

Years	China	Manilla	Java	Sumatra coast	Strait settlements	To elsewhere	Totals
1809	1 000	---	---	---	---	---	1 000
1811	1 400	---	---	---	---	---	1 400
1813	1 600	---	---	---	---	---	1 600
1815	700	---	---	---	---	---	700
1817	1 200	---	---	---	---	---	1 200
1819	1 000	---	---	---	---	---	1 000
1821	1 700	---	---	---	---	---	1 700
1823	3 900	---	---	---	---	---	3 900
1825	6 700	---	---	---	---	---	6 700
1827	5 600	---	---	---	---	---	5 600
1829	7 700	---	---	---	---	---	7 700
1831	12 900	---	---	---	---	---	12 900
1833	14 000	---	---	---	---		14 000
1835	11 700	---	---	---	---	---	11 700
1836	20 882 (15,400)	---	---	---	191	---	21 073
1838	17 353 (14,800)	---	---	---	153	9	17 515
1840	12 022	25	---	---	3 700	6	15 762
1842	18 521	---	---	---	376	2	18 899
1844	14 883	---	---		229	59	15 171
1846	17 389	---	---	---	26	158	17 573
1848	21 392	---	---	---	376	48	21 811
1850	16 513	---	---	---	70	14	16 597

Source: A. Le Pichon, p. 19 for the years 1809–1835 and for the figures in parentheses; the rest J.C.Baud, p. 215. The indication --- means: not available and/or not known.

Destination Ceylon (*Sri Lanka*)

Until 1815 Ceylon was a Dutch colony, but the central part of it was formally ruled by the Kandyan kingdom. In that year the English also annexed this kingdom and started to govern the whole island. The first opium arrived as a luxury with them, because opium consumption among the Malay troops in the British army was high, and these soldiers were held in high esteem by the British authorities 'but the use of opium rendered them unfit for service at an early age' (C. Uragoda, p. 71). Apparently, a large part of the imported opium must have come from Malwa, because the British started to levy an exceptionally high import duty of 20 rixdollars per pound. Later this was reduced to 5 rixdollars, by 1840 it became one shilling per pound, and in 1885 even one rupee per pound.

Table 58. Growth of Opium Trade in Ceylon (Sri Lanka), 1840/1900 in lb

Year	Pounds of opium imported
1840	1 562
1850	852
1860	8 379
1870	12 449
1880	10 117
1890	12 807
1900	23 755

Source: C. Uragoda, p. 70.

This enormous growth in the consumption can be indicated also as follows. Around the middle of the century, opium dens were introduced on Ceylon by the English government: the first appeared in 1850, a second came ten years later, but then apparently the sky was the limit: in 1890 there were 31, seven years later 56 and in 1907 already 65. Of course, the revenues for the government increased in the same way: from Rs. 4,100 to Rs. 122,189 in 1907 (Idem, p. 72). The anti-opium lobby made a lot of trouble about it later 'against forcing opium on uninterested countries' (Idem, p. 75).

Key position Singapore

Table 59. The Opium Smuggling of Singapore, 1835/1865 in chests (selected destinations)

Country	1835	1841	1843	1845	1848	1852	1857	1863	1865
China	422	5 437	2 559	1 730	2 746	1 854	1 933	1 887	931
Indochina	4	429	281	329	518	464	209	160	153
Java	164	223	42	14	170	271	804	1 032	676
Penang and Malacca	61	131	57	163	139	257	263	449	400
---	---	---	---	---	---	---	---	---	---
Total	1 285	7 550	3 974	3 196	4 547	4 069	4 188	4 558	3 081

Source: M. van Os, p.66 who copied the data from Wong, *A Study of the Trade of Singapore*.

After the Second Opium War was won by the British, the opium position of Singapore became less important. Hong Kong and Shanghai took over control, and from a British point of view there came an end to the smuggling practices. Furthermore, the use of steam ships made a stop in Singapore less necessary, with all the consequences for the entertainment industry. Still, there was a reasonable compensation for this in the increased opium trade with the East Indies.

The table gives no information about an "internal transformation": the Bengal opium lost much of its dominant position to Malwa and in particular Middle Eastern opium. For this last sort, Singapore retained its key position for the whole of Southeast Asia. The quick rise of the demand from Penang/Malacca (and the ignored Sumatra) is due to the growing influx of Chinese tin-laborers.

Period 1910 to 1918
The British indicated (A. Hosie, vol. 2, p. 208) that from 1901-5 annually 67,000 *chests* were exported, of which 51,000 went to China. It is unclear whether this is Bengal plus Malwa opium. In any case the period of serious reductions of the export to China started around 1907. The next table shows that 75% went to China (1911); at the beginning of World War I (1914) this decreased to 45%. A year later the entire opium export of India to China collapsed to about 10%. Japan and French Indochina remain strong clients during this war. For the Treaty ports the figures for 1904 are also given as about £1.5 million, which doubled ten years later, but fully collapsed at the start of the war.

Table 60. "British" Indian Export of Opium to Various Countries, 1911/1920 (in £; selected years)

Destinations	1911	1912	1913	1914	1915	1918	1920
French Indo-China	207 722	325 500	99 018	129 502	291 425	627 243	386 041
Java	386 825	362 120	383 408	472 199	282 252	?	?
Siam	10 217	190 657	263 177	164 030	204 328	300 097	350 000
Hong Kong	3 963 264	3 019 858	2 400 084	1 084 093	110 712	77 772	130 234
Straits Settlements	1 692 053	1 099 801	704 870	226 500	80 572	83 023	112 880
United Kingdom	927	2 907	1 180	18 433	58 148	---	---
Treaty ports, China	2 203 670	3 614 887	3 242 902	27 833	---	---	---
Macao	---	---	236 420	18 295	---	---	---
Japan	---	76 817	129 545	119 913	100 659	195 957	406 390
Other	45 565	36 420	15 659	19 223	47 543	21 064	74 717
Total	8 510 243	8 728 967	7 539 236	2 280 031	1 175 639	1 605 156	1 9060 262

Source: E. La Motte, p. 9 and 10 quoted from *Statistical Abstract relating to British India. Exports of Opium* and DSAL, 1910-1920 no. 164.

The next table gives the data about the same period but in quantities, in chests.

Table 61. "British" Indian Export of Opium to Various Countries, 1911-1917 (in chests)

Destination	1912	1913	1914	1915	1916
Cochinchina*	805	875	2 690	2 035	3 440
Java	3 010	3 265	2 650	1 835	1 965
Straits Settlements	5 098	1 537	755	605	239
China**	19 575	4 061	1 000	734	500
United Kingdom	11	115	498	199	0
Ceylon	50	105	80	65	80
Mauritius	10	19	23	65	120
Other	2 815	1 929	3 160	3 248	2 366
Total	31 374	11 906	10 858	8 786	8 710

Source: E. La Motte, p. 48 quoted from *Statistical Abstract relating to British India*. Data on Japan are omitted for some reason.
* "Cochinchina" is about South Vietnam and, therefore, only a part of French Indochina.
** "China" must be Hong Kong, Macao and Treaty Ports together.

EIC ships from Calcutta to Canton, 1775-1820

H. Morse (1926), vol. II, p. 436-452 and vol. III, p. 389-398 gives long lists of EIC ships which arrived in Canton. They are certainly not all of the ships that came in China nor all of the English ships. In the 1775 to 1804 period, 499 EIC ships arrived (30 years). From 1805-1820 there were 311 EIC ships (16 years). Most of them brought chests with opium in the cargo, apart from the smugglers and ships of other nationalities.

Import Trade of Canton, 1833

Of course, this table concerns the import of only one year shortly before the outbreak of the First Opium War. Indeed, nearly half of the British import concerns opium. The Americans imported nearly as many "Western goods" as the British, but lagged far behind them in the opium import. A remarkable aspect is the American silver import. As discussed in ch. 6, the "Bullion Game" resulted in a big switch with the turning point in 1827: before then, the British had to pay for their tea by means of silver; later, the Chinese had to pay the forced opium import with silver. The following Chinese silver drain provided a good business for the Americans as this table shows. The table also demonstrates that 75% of the total import came from "Eastern products". "The West" had not much to offer Chinese consumers. In other years this disparity is even more obvious when all the other "Eastern goods" receive their notation.

Morse also gives the data of the export trade of Canton in the same year (1833). The total British export is 21 million dollars; 43% concerns tea, and now they

Table 62. Import Trade of Canton, 1833 (in Spanish $)

Goods	British			American	Total
	Company	Private	Total		
Woollens	2 127 386	389 958	2 517 344	---	---
Cotton goods	275 217	351 957	627 174	---	---
Metals	112 643	48 915	161 558	---	---
Furs	---	17 306	17 306	---	---
Other Western products	---	118 584	118 584	---	---
Total Western products	*2 515 246*	*926 720*	*3 441 966*	*2 907 936*	*6 349 902*
Cotton	1 842 332	4 884 407	6 726 739	---	---
Opium	---	11 618 716	11 618 716	500 000	---
Sandalwood	75	41 400	41 475	---	---
Tin, Banka	---	92 192	92 192	---	---
Pepper	---	190 757	190 757	---	---
Other Eastern goods	---	1 344 448	1 344 448	---	---
Total Eastern products	*1 842 407*	*18 171 920*	*20 014 327*	*500 000*	*20 514 327*
Total Goods	4 357 653	19 098 640	23 456 293	3 407 936	26 864 229
Silver	---	20 500	20 500	682 519*	703 019
Total Imports	4 357 653	19 119 140	23 476 793	4 090 455	27 567 248

Source: H. Morse (1926) vol. iv, p. 369; D. Meyer, p. 42 for the year 1828.
* In addition, there are bills on London for a total of 4,772,516 dollars.

export also silver and gold (valued at nearly 7 million dollars in 1833), the payments for the opium import (33% of the export)!

It is interesting to compare this table with the same one for the year 1820 in H. Morse (1926), vol. III, p. 383. Here the Company imported silver worth 2.7 million dollars, and Americans imported about the same amount. The value of the opium import (only 'private') in 1820 was 6.5 million dollars or about 45% of all goods (double that of all 'Western Products').

Prices of opium, 1800-1914

The fluctuation of prices was in the beginning clearly related to the smuggling activities until the First Opium War. In 1832, the year of the foundation of Jardine, Matheson & Co, the overall value of the opium export to China was estimated at $11.6 million (£7.7 million). The market price of Bengal per chest in this year fluctuated between $940 and $625, Malwa opium between $720 and $490 (A. Le Pichon, p. 19). After the Opium War the prices were "legal" for the Western

Table 63. Prices of opium per chest, in Spanish $ as given in Canton, Macau or Hong Kong, 1800-1880

Month–year	Patna	Benares	Malwa
07 1800	557	525	---
04 1805	1430	1430	---
03 1810	1090	---	---
(?) 1815	---	---	---
12 1820	1550	---	1450
04 1825	780	---	580
03 1830	800	---	745
07 1835	675	630	575
(?) 1840	---	---	---
03 1845	640	580	---
04 1850	510	515	595
04 1855	320	335	420
04 1860	782	770	600
03 1865	415	397	635
09 1870	580	540	570
04 1875	595	570	570
10 1880	610	---	720

Source: C. Trocki (1999a), p. 81, 82. One Spanish $ = 4s 2d = about 2 Rupees; £1 = 4 dollars until 1814, later one used the rate £100 = $ 416.67. The *tael* of currency at Canton was treated as equivalent to 6s.8d or £1 = taels 3 (H. Morse, 1926, vol. 1, p. xxii).

merchants and tended to be leveled down in the mutual competition. Malwa opium, which was always perceived to be a lesser quality than Patna could reach the same quantities and sometimes even more. This does not relate, of course, to Malwa versus Bengal (= Patna + Benares) opium.

'The average price realized on a chest of Bengal opium for the ten years ending 1880-81 may be taken at Rs. 1280; the average profit ... may be taken at Rs. 1280-421 = Rs. 859' (E. Balfour, p. 38).

Another calculation comes from M. Greenberg, p.129: in 1821 the Chinese paid $8,314,600 for 4,628 chests of opium (Malwa and Bengal combined); this is an average price of $1,796 per chest. Two years later this price was dropped to $1,204 per chest. The table above shows that much later the chest price mostly was about $400.

Shanghai, 1913

Ellen La Motte visited Shanghai in 1915/16 and gathered many data on the opium business in the "native city" as well as in the International Settlements. The Chinese authorities were not allowed to enter, this, not in the least because of their nefarious reputation as "big opium dens". In October 1907 there were

87 licensed opium shops in the International Settlement.[2] Less than seven years later there were 663! In 1907 the average monthly revenue from opium licenses, dens and shops altogether was 5,450 *taels*. Seven years later the shops alone produced a revenue of 20,960 *taels*; in total in 1913, a license revenue was received of 86, 386 *taels*. Opium could be officially sold in taverns, foreign liquor sellers, Chinese wine shops, tea shops, a Chinese theater and a club, all apart from special opium shops. Retail-prices are not given.

Production and Prices in China from about 1870-1914

E. Balfour, p. 29 gave the following figures:

Manchuria	400,000	pikuls
Western China total	97,000	„
Western Hou-pe district	2,000	„
Eastern Sze-chuen	45,000	„
Yunnan	40,000	„
Kwi-choo	10,000	„

Most poppy production was not, as bold, in Sze-chuen (Szechuan) and Yunnan. In the former the ordinary price was 820 rupees for 133 1/3 lbs. avoirdupois. At Hankow it had risen to 930 rupees.

The estimates of the Chinese production vary widely, because the authorities almost never visited the poppy fields. What Alexander Hosie did is very exclusive, and it gave his actions and estimates a wide audience. For the situation around 1885, Wiselius (1886, p. 200) refers to an expert, Dr. J. Dudgeon, who stated that the Chinese production was 400,000 pikuls. A consul of Ichang estimated only 200,000 pikuls.

The price of North China opium per Chinese ounce was 2.8 to 3.2 taels; Malwa opium at New-chang 5.8 taels; Patna opium 5.4; Chinese 2.8.

Sze-chuen opium exported to the coast, to Hankow, in 1880 was 927 pikuls; at Hankow a *ad valorem* duty of 7 1/2 percent was added.

In 1776 'the drug which cost in Calcutta Rs 500 the chest, was sold in China for 500 dollars' (E. Balfour, p. 33, 34).

After World War I the mafia (including the Sassoon family and the Ezra Brothers) could not hide behind the *English* legality of the opium import in China. From 1912 to 1916 a chest of Bengal opium increased sixfold in price, Malwa fivefold, because in a combined effort these families had achieved a monopoly position on the Chinese market. These usurious prices were far above the world prices at the time:

> 'In 1914 a chest of Indian opium sold for 6,800 taels wholesale; 10,000 taels retail in Shanghai and 50,000 taels retail in remoter places. Shipped to a non-China market, the same chest was worth the equivalent of only 500 taels' (F. Wakeman, p. 36 and p. 327 note 73).

---

[2] E. La Motte, p. 39–43 quoting Shanghai Municipal Council sources, pamphlets and papers.

THE DUTCH OPIUM IMPORT 1678-1816

J.C. Baud, one of the highest officials in the 19th-century Dutch East Indies, also acted as the first opium historian who luckily enjoyed gathering the necessary figures. He is the source of the following data of the 17th, 18th and beginning 19th-century opium import, mainly from Bengal. They can be compared with modern studies (Om Prakash). I have concluded that the totals are reliable; in the details many differences can be seen.[1]

However, new investigations should be carried out. For instance, Governor-General Speelman (from 1681-1684) estimated the sale of opium around 1677 in Mataram at 600 picul a year, which is about 78,000 pounds.[2] The importer of this opium is not given, so we probably must conclude that Baud's figures, which are lower and certainly not confined to Mataram, represent Dutch imports only. N. Struick wrote that in 1640 the import weighed not more than 187 pounds and ten years later 648 pounds; again 27 years later the opium import was in full swing with 10,025 pounds. For the next year Struick mentions Baud's figure as given in the following table.[3]

For the whole of the 17th-century, the *Dutch* opium import by the VOC weighed about 2.5 million pounds in the East Indies alone; in the 18th-century this increased to nearly 13 million (12,634,145) pounds; until the middle of the 19th-century it was 2.5 million (2,516,875).

---

[1] It is a pity that E. Jacobs' many tables (p. 305–373) differ in a way which cannot be discussed seriously. Although she knows Baud's study, she apparently had other sources but did not indicate why she did not follow Baud. Her figures differ strangely from Baud's. I think that the problem is centered in her methodology. She announces (p. ix) that her study 'does not concentrate on a few years or decades, but ... [on] .. a "long" eighteenth-century'. Her basic material, however, is exactly concentrated on a 'few years or decades': (1) Sep. 1711-Aug. 1713; (2) Sep. 1730–Aug. 1732; (3) Sep. 1751-Aug. 1753; (4) Sep. 1771–Aug. 1773 which is even followed by a period of one year (5) Sep. 1789–Aug. 1790. There are also mis-calculations: previous tables in which sometimes opium is mentioned cannot be summarized in the totalizing table 47 on p. 373. It remains, furthermore, in the dark what was done with all these figures. See also the soft but relevant criticism of G. Souza (2009-1), p. 115.

[2] F. de Haan, vol. 4, p. 14.

[3] N. Struick, p. 8.

Table 64. Dutch Opium Import in East Indies by the VOC, 1678-1745 (selected years)[4]

Years	Dutch pounds	Years	Dutch pounds
1678	67 444	1712	23 345
1680	35 847	1714	159 355
1682	52 181	1716	97 440
1684	74 810	1718	46 690
1686	17 302	1720	110 925
1688	55 533	1722	112 955
1690	63 525	1724	95 700
1692	92 699	1726	46 667
1694	117 067	1728	161 148
1696	105 733	1730	177 915
1698	186 306	1732	124 700
1700	69 020	1734	172 550
1702	60 538	1736	138 096
1704	145 870	1738	127 042
1706	95 864	1740	229 398
1708	---	1742	108 508
1710	104 690	1744	153 090

At the end of the 18th-century, the VOC was suffering from serious corruption and the many wars. In 1798 there came an end to its history, after almost two centuries. The Dutch Government took over all its debts and tasks and continued with the opium "business as usual".

Table 65. Dutch Opium Import in East Indies by the VOC and Dutch or English Government, 1746-1816 (selected years)[5]

Years	Dutch pounds	Years	Dutch pounds
1746	136 143	1782	76 250
1748	217 500	1784	59 550
1750	188 500	1786	184 650
1752	171 514	1788	153 000
1754	180 425	1790	126 750
1756	174 000	1792	34 500
1758	174 000	1794	248 196
1760	174 000	1796	130 000
1762	80 550	1798	153 495

---

[4] J.C. Baud, p. 101, 102. D. Duco, note 117 p. 241 refers to Baud, p. 115 in which, however, the given figures are not provided; in addition, the figures as such cannot be correct. For a copy of Baud's complete list, see E. Vanvugt (1985), p. 405–409.

[5] J.C. Baud, p. 158, 159.

Table 65. Continued.

Years	Dutch pounds	Years	Dutch pounds
1764	62 700	1800	67 500
1766	119 850	1802	67 500
1768	119 850	1804	68 000
1770	108 000	1806	54 000
1772	108 000	1808	54 000
1774	108 000	1810	54 000
1776	81 300	1812	40 500
1778	91 760	1814	73 250
1780	122 870	1816	73 250

Table 66. Dutch Opium Import by the Dutch Government on Java and Madura only, 1817-1850 (selected years)[6]

Years	Dutch pounds	Years	Dutch pounds
1817	68 750	1835	58 125
1819	68 750	1837	52 250
1821	99 625	1839	52 250
1823	60 125	1841	53 250
1825	35 875	1843	54 525
1827	64 000	1845	54 625
1829	72 125	1847	50 625
1831	60 250	1849	52 500
1833	52 875		

Table 67. Total Dutch Opium Imports in the East Indies, 1678-1850

All years 1678-1700: 1 853 578 Dutch pounds weight
All years 1700-1722: 2 196 657 " "
All years 1722-1745: 3 402 073 " "
All years 1746-1769: 3 506 954 " "
All years 1770-1795: 3 092 416 " "
All years 1796-1816: 1 573 460 " "
All years 1817-1839: 1 452 000 " "
All years 1840-1850: 586 125 " "

Totals 1678-1745: 7 452 308 Dutch pounds weight
Totals 1746-1816: 8 172 830
Totals 1817-1850: 2 038 125
Totals 1678-1850: 17 663 263 " " "

---

[6] Idem, p. 172.

THE AMPHIOEN SOCIETY SWINDLE

The VOC opium business in the 18th-century was organized as follows: the VOC bought the raw opium in Bengal (see appendix 2) and sold it in Batavia to its clients, the opium dealers, in an auction. The latter distributed it further among the opium consumers in the archipelago, mainly Java.

The Amphioen Society (AS) opium business was organized as follows: the VOC bought the raw opium in Bengal and sold its distribution monopoly to the AS who sold it in Batavia to its clients, the opium dealers, in an auction. The latter distributed it further among their clients. The AS was, therefore, a brand new player in the opium market and acted as intermediate trader or middleman. This made the chain more complicated and raised the price for the consumer. That is, if the number of the consumers remained the same. After 1745 the opium dealer not only had to pay the usual purchasing price of the VOC + the VOC costs + VOC profits, but also the AS purchasing price + AS costs + AS profits. More than ever, the opium dealers were, therefore, highly motivated to increase the number of consumers.

Table 68. Opium performance of the VOC and Amphioen Society (AS), 1721-1768

VOC opium trade					AS opium trade					
Year	Chests	Pounds x 1000	Profit x 1000 guilder	Profit per chest in guilder	Profit per pound in guilder	Year	Chests	Pounds x 1000	Profit x 1000 guilder	Profit per chest in guilder	Profit per pound In guilder
1721	927	175	790	850	4.51	1745	975	136	633	650	4.65
1722	356	52	152	430	2.92	1746	1200	174	800	670	4.6
1723	941	136	197	210	1.45	1747	1500	218	1000	670	4.59
1724	1113	163	315	280	1.93	1748	1428	207	911	640	4.4
1725	597	87	49	80	0.56	1749	1300	189	817	630	4.32
1726	822	119	324	390	2.72	1750	925	134	569	620	4.25
1727	434	63	171	390	2.71	1751	1199	172	609	510	3.54
1728	1251	181	552	440	3.05	1752	1090	160*	585*	540*	3.66*
1729	985	143	391	400	2.73	1753	1243	180	618	500	3.43
1730	1039	151	380	370	2.52	1754	1295	188	667	520	3.55
1731	1005	146	375	370	2.57	1755	1200	174	634	530	3.64
1732	1405	204	691	490	3.39	1756	1200	174	679	570	3.9
1733	370	54	150	410	2.78	1757	1200	174	733	610	4.21
1734	1354	196	482	360	2.46	1758	1200	174	756	630	4.34
1735	974	141	337	350	2.39	1759	1200	174	974	810	5.6

Table 68. Continued

VOC opium trade					AS opium trade					
Year	Chests	Pounds x 1000	Profit x 1000 guilder	Profit per chest in guilder	Profit per pound in guilder	Year	Chests	Pounds x 1000	Profit x 1000 guilder	Profit per chest in guilder	Profit per pound In guilder
1736	1227	178	601	490	3.38	1760	1200	174	714	600	4.1
1737	788	114	614	780	5.39	1761	537	81	232	430	2.86
1738	668	98	386	580	3.94	1762	210	32	108	510	3.38
1739	997	145	640	640	4.41	1763	418	63	209	500	3.32
1740	1090	158	331	300	2.09	1764	508	76	208	410	2.74
1741	1062	154	512	480	3.32	1765	799	120	352	440	2.93
1742	1532	225	1415	920	6.29	1766	937	141	312	330	2.21
1743	1011	147	1064	1050	7.24	1767	799	120	297	370	2.48
1744	1000	145	1064	1060	7.34	1768	511	77	347	680	4.51
Total	22131	3374	11981	540	3.55	Total	24074	3505	13499	560	3.85

Source: J. de Jonge, vol. 11 (1883), p. 106-116; numbers with * are estimates.

From 1722 onwards, Baud's figures (previous appendix) are in variance with those used by J. de Jonge from less than thirty years later. I do not know why this happened. The differences are, for instance, of a magnitude in 1722 of 112,955 (Baud) and 51,620 (De Jong). A possible explanation could be that in the usual VOC notation of "1722/23" one takes the first and another the second year. For a longer period this difficulty could be negated. Take, for example the period 1728-1737. It leads in Baud to 1,423,436 pound weight against in De Jong to 1,507,778, which is still a difference of 5-6%.

Another explanation is that Baud used a Batavian administration and De Jonge one in Amsterdam. In that case a new source of swindle could be indicated.

The AS existed until 1794. During this half century it kept to its obligation to buy at least 1200 chests from the VOC for only seven years.

FROM VOC OPIUM TO RAFFLES' HERITAGE

In the Dutch language there is a translation of an abridged version of Raffles' famous *History of Java* by J.E. de Sturler, *De Geschiedenis van Java* (1836). Sturler served the Dutch government in the East Indies for about twenty years. In the end he was 'resident of a substantial part of Java' (p. vii). All figures below are derived from this edition, because in the English original of 1817 these data are not given (not, at least, in the edition I had to study).

In the introduction to de Stuler's translation (p. xvii-liv), several "budgets" are given, which are reproduced here. They concern the years 1795-1815 and provide a specific perspective on what happened in the Dutch East Indies in those years. They clearly show how important opium was in the economic life of the colony. In the discussion about these "budgets", Raffles also referred to previous centuries in order to show how advantageous the British government of Java was.

In 1791 a commission was sent to the East Indies by a Dutch "Parliament" (Staten van Holland) to investigate how profitable (or not) the VOC was. According to Raffles, this commission was installed to introduce 'free trade' on Java. Ultimately, it proposed to 'free for private trade' only Bengal and the Coromandel coast (at the time fully controlled by the British), whereas Java was perceived as more closed for private trade to counteract the British competition.

This points again to one of the largest misunderstandings in the current historiography, as if colonialism and imperialism were merely side-effects of capitalist free trade.

The mission also published the following result.

It is called a budget, but it was a list of actual incomes and expenditures discovered by the commission. It announced that the figures 'exclude the direct trade with China', but nowhere is the extent of this trade given.

Table 69. Incomes and Expenditures of the VOC in 1795 (x guilders)

Incomes		Expenditures	
General rights and taxes	2 350 000	*For the "overhead" of the expenses:*	
Freight VOC ships	50 000	on Cape of Good Hope	150 000
Additional incomes	460 000	in Bengal	33 120
1. Profits on the trade in India*:		in Surat	40 000
opium	1 250 000	Army East Indies	2 571 314
tin	228 000	Wages for civilians	1 000 000
mace	43 000	Ammunition, etc.	100 000
nutmeg	90 000	Repair of buildings, etc.	400 000

Table 69. Continued

Incomes		Expenditures	
clove	420 000	Rent praus, etc.	200 000
Japanese copper	292 000	Hospitals	100 000
Profits on the trade in Surat:		Confiscations	18 000
sugar	190 000	Presents to local princes	32 000
camphor	10 000	Interest on Indian loans	100 000
tin	18 000	Transport of VOC goods	200 000
Profits in Japan:	76 000	Unforeseen expenses	100 000
Profits in Coromandel:	33 000	Indigenous products	4 519 400
2. *Profits on the return cargo:*		Insurance on shipments to Indie	212 700
coffee	6 813 281	Freight return cargos	3 300 000
pepper	1 958 273	Sea insurance in Indie	200 000
tin	196 365	Shipments in Indie	699 030
cotton yarn	99 750	Transport 2320 soldiers and civilians	219 240
indigo	110 580	Return trip 450 people	28 350
sugar	1 767 000	Earnest-money for 2020 military	303 000
salpetre	385 605	Gratification for 300 civilians	60 000
sapan wood	61 560	Recognition to Admiralty	360 000
cowries	40 584	Contribution to Admiralty	500 000
camphor	65 025	Total cost of VOC in Europe	1 000 000
cardamom	18 810	Annual interest	4 758 000
tamarind	43 700	Dividend of 12½% to participants	831 000
arack	46 000	---	---
cinnamon	2 000 000	---	---
clove	812 500	---	---
mace	937 500	---	---
nutmeg	561 000	---	---
Bengal piece goods	970 000	---	---
Surat piece goods	550 000	---	---
Freight and recognition duties on private trade	200 000	---	---
Total incomes	23 087 533	Total expenditures	22 035 154

Source: T. Raffles, *Geschiedenis van Java,* p. xxxiv
* In the logic of the table, I suppose, it concerns here India (in practice Bengal), although a term like "Indie" is ambiguous (tin in India?); the later-mentioned "Indische retourladin-gen/ return cargo" must refer to the "Dutch" East Indies.

The advantage ("Batig Slot") is here, therefore, not more than fl. 1 052 379. It is obvious that if proper bookkeeping had been exercised, a substantial negative outcome would have been the result. (Example: if only the depreciation on ships, fortifications, etc. or losses in quality and quantity of products or plantation manpower were considered, the expenditures should have been in excess of 30 million). It is remarkable that nearly a quarter of all given expenditures refers to interest on loans and dividends for the members of the Opium Society (see previous appendix), while another quarter is spent on the repression machine of the army and navy. Thus, the main elements of the narco-military constellation are present.

It is unclear which status such a table had. One may expect that it is an overly optimistic estimation to support the decision to go on with the VOC. It is important that "parliamentary research" in 1795 led to it. Based on these figures, the conclusion was drawn that the VOC show must go on, the trade has to be extended and the costs reduced.

The table documents differences between the inter-Asian trade (everything mentioned under 1; my addition) and the trade directed to Europe. Opium is still the *largest* source of income in this *inter-Asian trade* (nearly 50%). Of course, this is not the case if the total picture is considered. However, before the profit of e.g. coffee could have been figured in, it would have been sold in Europe. Therefore, the reasoning is not appropriate (or much less so): opium was not important for the Dutch in the exploitation of the archipelago. On the contrary: as demonstrated below, the opium business was extended in a remarkable way, notwithstanding the complaints of decision-makers like Van Hogendorp, Daendels or Raffles.

Raffles used the following table to demonstrate how the profits of the VOC diminished decade after decade and fully disappeared in the end. It is an appropriate answer to the previous table and its authoritative authors.

Table 70. Accumulated Profits and Losses of the VOC 1613-1693 (x guilders)

	1613–1653	1613–1663	1613–1673	1613–1683	1613–1693
Total profits	101 704 417	142 663 776	206 072 335	259 250 069	322 735 812
Total expenses	76 177 735	117 616 961	161 271 745	212 282 020	274 416 305
Pure profit	25 526 682	25 046 815	44 800 590	46 968 949	48 319 507

Source: T. Raffles, *Geschiedenis van Java*, p. xxv

In this way it was also estimated that the pure profit

from 1613 to 1697 was only				38 696 527
to 1703	"	"		31 674 645
to 1713	"	"		16 805 598
to 1723	"	"		4 838 925
to 1724	"	"		1 037 777
to 1730	"	"	−	7 737 610
to 1779	"	"	−	84 985 425.

Again ten years later the loss of the VOC was 74 million guilders, which again increased to 85 million, of which 68 million was loaned by 'the Dutch nation' (see the interest to be paid by the colony to the metropolis in the previous table).

A new era was starting after the French Revolution and the subsequent occupation of the Netherlands by Napoleon. One of the most important Dutch collaborators of the French, Daendels, became the new Governor-General in the East Indies.

Table 71. The Budget of Governor-General Daendels ca. 1808 (x 1000 rixdaalder and guilders)

Receipts			Costs		
	rixd.	fl		rixd.	fl
Landrent	2 000	5 000	Wages civilians	1 000	2 500
Opium	1 120	2 800	Army	1 227	3 068
Coffee	4 500	11 250	Ammunition making	180	450
Pepper	160	400	Navy	250	625
Tin	400	1 000	Fortifications, etc.	200	500
Japanese copper	250	625	New works	400	1 000
Spices	1 000	2 500	Law and police	150	375
Wood	250	625	Carrying trade	300	750
Rice	250	625	Transport military, etc.	300	750
Others	500	1 250	Indigenous products	300	750
			Packing, etc.	100	250
			Interest	400	1 000
			Unforeseen	903	2 258
Total receipts	10 790	26 975	Total costs	5 790	14 475

Source: T. Raffles, Geschiedenis van Java, p. liv

This time the 'pure profit' is, therefore, estimated at 5,000,000 rixdaalder or 12,500,000 guilder. Whether this corresponds to reality is doubtful after the serious losses in the previous period and the figures in the following table. It is safe to say that here the intentions of the new Governor-General are shown.

Again opium is among the highest sources of income: 12% of the total income. Daendels needed more than twice as much as the 1795 commission; the military involvement was twice as great as well (50% of all costs concern repression). The narco-military elements were potentially more expressed.

At the end of De Geschiedenis van Java, an interesting comparison is added between the period before Daendels, Daendels' government and Raffles' government. For the opium history it is not necessary to reproduce the entire table. Therefore, the given totals/losses are not the additions of the given subjects; the results are added by me.

One difficulty is that under Raffles the 'Javasche Roupij' (Java rupee) was introduced to replace the Dutch rijks(rix)daalder (nearly 2.5 guilder) and guilder currency. To make a comparison possible, I have converted rupees to guilders in rounded figures.

What is the conversion rate? The answer could be very complicated according to J. Bucknill, p. 195 ff. and passim; the *Wikipedia* article 'Netherlands Indies gulden' is also helpful (see also J. Bastin, p. 19 ff.). Around 1765 the silver *rupee* was worth 30 *stuivers* (= 30 x 0.05 guilder) while a *rixdaalder* was 48 *stuivers* (stiver) and the *guilder* 20. Thirty years later this was more or less the same.

The value the new silver *roupij - rupee* received from Raffles' government seemed to be 30 stuivers (stivers) or 120 duits (doits). Raffles experimented also with copper, tin and paper money. I have chosen to use this last given value, but also to provide the *Java roupij* figures, in case a different conversion rate becomes necessary.

Table 72. Comparison between the periods before, during and after Daendels' government (x 1000 roupij and guilders)

	Before Daendels came					
	1802-1803		1803-1804		1804-1805	
Subjects	Roupij	Guilders	Roupij	Guilders	Roupij	Guilders
Landrent	---	---	---	---	---	---
Leases	594.3	891.5	595.3	892.9	762.4	1 143.6
Opium	54.5	81.8	54.4	81.7	61.3	91.9
Taxes and duties	532.7	799.1	520.7	781.1	616.4	924.6
---	---	---	---	---	---	---
Totals	2 226.4	3 339.6	1 979.2	2 968.8	2 458.8	3 688.2
Costs	1 631.9	2 447.9	2 240.9	3 361.4	1 819.4	2 729.1
Results	594.5	891.7	-261.7	-392.6	639.4	959.1

	During Daendels' government					
	1808-1809		1809-1810		1810-1811	
Subjects	Roupij	Guilders	Roupij	Guilders	Roupij	Guilders
Landrent	34.7	52.1	34.7	52.1	23.8	35.7
Leases	288.5	432.8	720.2	1 080.3	558.2	837.3
Opium	1.5	2.3	215.8	323.7	549.1	823.7
Taxes and duties	290.2	435.3	182.5	273.8	515.7	773.6
---	---	---	---	---	---	---
Totals	2 056.3	3 084.5	2 632.9	3 949.4	3 440.4	5 160.6
Costs	86.1	129.2	2 290.1	3 435.2	3 547.2	5 320.8
Results	1 970.2	2 955.3	342.8	514.2	-106.8	-160.2

	During Raffles' government					
	1812-1813		1813-1814		1814-1815	
Subjects	Roupij	Guilders	Roupij	Guilders	Roupij	Guilders
Landrent	--	--	1 253.5	1 880.3	2 473.2	3 709.8

Table 72.　Continued.

| Subjects | During Raffles' government | | | | | |
| | 1812-1813 | | 1813-1814 | | 1814-1815 | |
	Roupij	Guilders	Roupij	Guilders	Roupij	Guilders
Leases	1 518.3	2 277.5	1 025.1	1 537.7	1 090.9	1 636.4
Opium	614.1	921.2	583.3	874.9	375.3	562.9
Taxes and duties	953.2	1 429.8	672.3	1 008.5	442.6	663.9
Totals	4 995.9	7 493.9	5 418.7	8 128.1	6 549.6	9 824.4
Costs	3 707.9	5 561.9	2 171.7	3 257.6	1 571.4	2 357.1
Results	1 288	1 932	3 247	4 870.5	4 978.2	7 467.3

Source: T. Raffles, *Geschiedenis van Java*, appendix

A few conclusions relevant for the opium history are the following:

1. Before Daendels, the opium income nearly doubled in two/three years' time.
2. During Daendels' government the opium income became nearly ten times larger than in 1804 and more than doubled within the two years 1809-1810! The figures of 1808/09 are not reliable; the differences in all respects with the subsequent periods are too large.
3. During Raffles' government the opium income increased once, but then decreased substantially, while still remaining six times higher than "before Daendels".
4. Compared to the previous period Raffles' government is generally much more profitable, notwithstanding the decrease of the opium income. This trend is not continued. On the contrary: the opium incomes of the new Dutch colonial state increased sky high, along with the general budget problems.

THE FRENCH AND DUTCH OPIUM FACTORIES

Probably the oldest modern opium factory is the Bengal one in Gaziphur (1820), which is still in operation: in 2008 it produced for the USA and Japan together not less than 200-250 metric tonnes of opium (*Wikipedia*)! This is twice the total sold in the whole of Ceylon and Southeast Asia in the best year of 1926. Impressions of this early factory (Patna, 1850) are given on p. 62.

However, the French opened the last factory in the craftsmen era and the Dutch, the first in the machine age. In addition, they both functioned within the new *Opiumregie* system. This was developed in the French Southeast Asian colony of Cochinchina.

From both factories specific numerical data are given below, to show how they operated in detail. First, the French opium factory (*bouillerie*), which operated from the revenue farm period and came under the *Opiumregie* in 1881. It was established ca. 1874 in Cholon near Saigon.

The production process was carried out largely with manual labor. It followed, in short, the steps described in detail in W. Groeneveldt's report (p. 46-49).

The raw opium arrived in the harbor of Saigon from Bengal and was immediately brought to the storehouse of the tjandoe factory. It was packed in chests of 40 balls. The quantity of the balls needed is carried to the first section of the factory (*bouillerie d'opium*), in which four large stoves (*fourneaux pour grandes bassines*) are situated, each provided with two large kettles of 300 liters for opium water. The water is used for boiling the opium and later the peelings of the balls for making the *écorces* (opium bark), a product which was in high demand among poorer people. In this part of the building there were also other stoves, each with 34 fireplaces (altogether thus 136).

The laborers started by cutting the balls in two and taking the opium out of them with wet hands; the peelings were put aside for later boiling, while the inner parts were first boiled in the large kettles. The opium content of 2½ balls was put in a copper pan (52 x 12 cm) together with four liters of opium water and boiled on a charcoal fire until sufficiently concentrated. After it was removed from the heat, stirring continued to prevent the substances from sticking to the wooden spoon. From this a ball was prepared, and two of them had to fill a pan.

This stage took two hours, and then a new procedure was started. The pan was put upside down on a soft charcoal fire, whereupon the substance fell apart in small slices which were removed immediately. These black-brown "pancakes" (*crêpes*) were so crispy within a few minutes that they fall apart if touched. The pieces were gathered in other copper pans (69 x 18 cm), each containing the equivalent of five balls. Twelve liters of opium water were added, and after soaking for about 18 hours, the "pancakes" had disappeared.

This result was filtered twice after the substance was boiled on a hot charcoal fire. After 2½ hours it was beaten until it was cold. The final product was weighed and transported to the factory storage.

In the store it was saved for four months in large, closed, copper barrels (300 liter), filled halfway so some fermentation could take place. After this period the *tjandoe* with a 9.15% morphine content was ready to be packed. This was done in flat square boxes, and the cover was fastened by a drop of solder.

Table 73. Raw opium import, Preparation and Revenue in French Cochinchina, 1881-1889[1]

Years	Imported chests	Average price per imported chest in Saigon in $*	Number of worked up balls (40 per chest)	Quantity in thails		Opium revenue x 1000 $*	
				Tjandoe	Écorces	Tjandoe	Écorces
1881	350	616	---	---	---	---	---
1882	560	601	24 159	716 604	31 406	1 252	43
1883	725	544	29 000	886 589	42 630	1 532	37
1884	956	578	37 758	1 156 003	51 082	1 697	35
1885	850	568	33 038	1 040 068	43 419	1 763	54
1886	1050	543	40 904	1 276 711	61 061	1 891	44
1887	1070	511	38 080	1 192 372	50 638	1 840	53
1888	850	498	31 385	958 459	66 250	1 724	58
1889	800	512	30 609	957 213	71 402	1 407	58

* This $ is not an American dollar, but the indication of piasters. One piaster in this period is valued at 5.55 French francs; until 1913 this is nearly equal to 1 US$.

The Dutch Opium Factory in Batavia was established in 1898 following a secret proposal of W. Groeneveldt (1890). Many discussions for and against exist (J. Rush, chapter 10 and 11). About the technicalities of such a factory, the opinions of Groeneveldt, Struick, Haak or Winselius varied widely. The first had studied the case the best.

A most important aspect of this debate concerned the morphine content of the raw opium and of the *tjandoe* made from it. Today a normal, unadulterated opium of any type, in the air-dry condition, usually has between 8% and 19% of morphine. The principal commercial opiums generally have approximately the following morphine contents: Yugoslavia 15%; Turkey 13%; Iran 11%; India 11% (www.poppies.org).

In the Groeneveldt debate Haak wrote

'that from one catty (16 thails) raw opium 8 thails *tjandoe* are derived, so that the good quality tjandoe (from Bengal opium) has to contain at least 16% morphine, *if during the process no morphine is lost*. According to the same calculation the Levant opium must give a tjandoe of 26% and more morphine content. However, Haak found in the tjandoe of the lease contracts [in East Indies. H.D.] ... not more than

---

[1] The table is a combination of the tables from W. Groeneveldt, p. 44, 49 and 63.

8.85 % morphine, because—according to him—this was mixed with other ingredients to increase the weight. Now, if the Opiumregie should make tjandoe without such a mixture, the users would get tjandoe with 20-30% morphine, which is to a large extent ruinous for them.'[2]

Therefore, Groeneveldt wisely proposed that the factory produce tjandoe of about 10% morphine content. During his visit of the opium factory in Saigon, he found that the tjandoe there had a 9.15% morphine content.

Haak missed the mark because he supposed that raw opium consists only of concentrated poppy juice (*heulsap* in Old Dutch). To a certain degree, however, raw opium also contains poppy leaves. The weight of this element is at least 5 thails in every ball of Bengal opium of 2.5 catty. Therefore, per catty there remains only 14 thails of raw opium.

The above knowledge is incorporated in the following account of the factory process. I have chosen the example of the year 1913, which is in principle not different from the other years. All figures are in *kg* and rounded. The production process is in the sequence 1, 2 ... etc. to 8.

In the factory accounts and elsewhere, the designations A, B, C ... to G, or H and K boxes are used for different contents, cost price and weight: A has 200 small tubes, B 100, etc. to K with two larger tubes. A thousand tubes of the smallest kind weighed about half a kilo; the tubes in box K weighed 24.5 kilo. The smallest measure was 193 mg (1/2 *mata*).

As the pictures show, the Dutch Opium Factory was not small, and it was well equipped with modern machinery. A staff of a dozen Europeans managed it with about a thousand indigenous workers. The Europeans received monthly salaries; the workers' wages were paid per day and calculated per *thail*. In 1912 they were paid 9.4 cents per *thail*, in 1913 it was 8.6 cents per *thail*. That made between 10 and 15 guilders a month; the Europeans got about 50 times more, excluding a specific "bonus" and/or privileges like trips to the Netherlands or Dutch pensions.

In 1913 the factory had already reached its maximum production capacity. However, by expanding the storage buildings, the mixed *tjandoe* could be stored for three months before being used to fill the tubes. This improved the quality of the product and was an argument to increase prices.

Apart from the preparation of the raw opium, mainly imported from Bengal, the factory made specific products like *tikee*. Furthermore, there were opium pills (in tubes I) which were sold only among the tin miners on the islands of Bangka (Banka) and Belitung (Billiton). A special kind of raw opium was also prepared for some elite customers in Java.

---

[2] Idem, p. 130.

1. STOREHOUSE RAW MATERIALS
added to stock:
Bengal raw opium 182,875
Levant raw opium 4,209
djitjing 2,216
total stock 234,554 100%
from this:
a. to mechanical opium prep. 189,684 80%
b. to *tikee* department 894 1%
c. to storeroom 43,976 19%

2. MECHANICAL OPIUM PREPARATION
from 1: 189,684
added:
a. leaking tubes 145
b. from smuggling 332
total 190,161 100%
from this:
a. to mixing 2,903 2%
b. to storeroom prep. 122,573 64%
c. lost in preparation 64,655 34%

3. STOREROOM OPIUM PREPARATION
added:
a. from Mech. O. Prep. 122,573
b. from stock 17,656
total 140,229 100%

from this:
to mixing room 111,284 79%

4. MIXING ROOM
added:
a. from storeroom op. prep. 111,284
b. sugar 2,540
c. increase 906
total 100% 114,730
from this:
to storeroommixed opium 114,730

5. STOREROOM MIXED OPIUM
added:
a. from mixing room 114,730
b. in stock 10,716
total 125,446 100%
from this:
a. to filling room 113,950 91%
b. to *tikee* storeroom 654 0.5%
c. to stock mixed opium 10,842 8.5%

6. FILLING ROOM
added:
a. storeroom mixed opium 113,950
b. stock filling room 1,853
total 100% 115,803
from this:
a. filling of tubes 98% 113,561
b. filling losses 2% 4,973

7. PREPARATION TIKEE, RAW OPIUM, PILLS
from several stocks:
a. *tikee* 647
b. raw opium Bengal 153
c. raw opium Levantine 657
d. opium pills 5,137
total 6,594 100%

8. STOREROOM PACKED TJANDOE
added:
a. from filling room 113,561
b. from preparation *tikee*, etc. 6,594
total 100% 120,155

from this:

to storeroom packed *tjandoe* 6,594

from this:

a. tubes A to G 92% 110,674
b. *tikee* 662
c. raw Bengal opium 191
d. raw Lev. opium 660
e. opium pills 218
f. stock storeroom *tjandoe* 7,750

These last items from 8 are the end products (weighing 120,155 kg) packed in wooden boxes with tubes. They are send to *Opiumregie*, which had to take care of the selling and distribution. So, very roughly, 200,000 kilo of raw opium were needed to make 110,000 kilo of prepared opium in tubes (excluding the weight of the lead tubes).

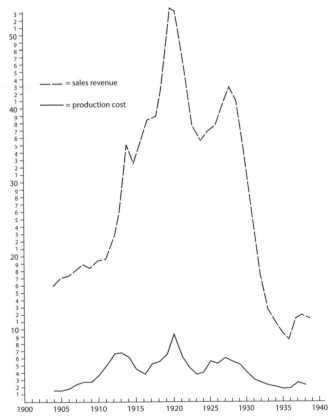

Figure 13. East Indies: Production Cost of Opium Factory and Sales Revenue of Opium Regie, 1900-1935 (x 1 million guilders)

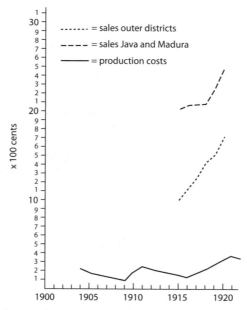

Figure 14. East Indies: Production Cost of Opium Factory and Sales Revenue of Opium Regie, 1900-1920 (thail per guilder)

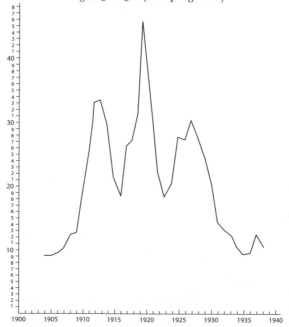

Figure 15. East Indies: Opium Factory, Production cost, 1900-1940 (x 200,000 Dutch guilders)

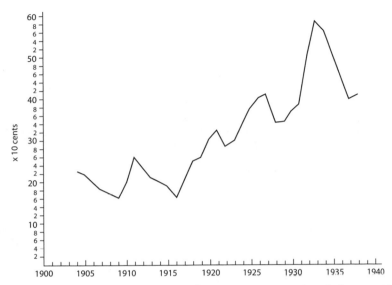

Figure 16. East Indies: Opium Factory, Production cost, 1900-1940 (per thail x 10 cents)

Source: The data for the figures 13-16 are all derived by H. Derks from the *Year Accounts* of the *Opium Factory and Opiumregie,* (Batavia; 1913-1940).

GLOSSARY

Amphioen, affion, afion, afyūn	(Arabia, East Indies) names for products derived from the *Papaver Somniforum*, now called opium.
Awar-awar	(East Indies) leaves from a plant (*Ficus septica*) used for mixing with *tikee* or other opium for smoking in the Opium Factory (Batavia) or elsewhere.
Ball	of raw opium (India) weighed about 3 pounds; measure used at the EIC factories in Patna and Ghazipur.
Bhang	is a cannabis (hashish) preparation originally sold to Indian laborers under the farming system in 19th-century Malaya and India.
Bhar	common weight: in Goa 463 pounds, in Bantam 369 pounds, in Batavia 408 pounds, etc.
Bigha	(India) = 2/3 acre or about 2,700 m^2; in opium districts 1 acre = 1.33 bigha.
Boule	(Indochina) the same as *ball,* but 1.6-1.8 kg.
C(h)andu	(India) opium prepared for smoking (same as *tjandoe*) by dissolving raw opium in water and boiling it several times into a paste.
Candy or Khandi	contains 20 *maunds*; common weight: in Bengal 1493-1642 pounds, but in Bombay 560 pounds and in Surat 746 pounds, etc.
Catty (Chinese) or Kati	1.33 lb or about 605-618 grams or 16 *taels* (or *tahils*); in India 1.25 Dutch pounds; one catty = 16 tail.
Chee	(Southeast Asia) a weight equivalent to one-tenth of a *tahil*.
Chest	(India), Caisse (Indochina) unit of raw Bengal opium = 140 lbs or about 60-72 kg also, indeed, a chest made of mangowood containing 40 *balls* of raw opium.
Ch'ien	(Chinese) = copper coin (with hole); 1000 *ch'ien* is 1 *tael.*
Chis	(Southeast Asia) = weight of 1/4 *tahil*; the maximum quantity for consumption in government dens was two *chis* = 1/5 *tahil.*
Djitjing	(East Indies) is the name of the *dross*, the residue left in opium pipes (also written *jicing*).
Djitjingko	(East Indies) is the smoking product made of *djitjing.*

Dollar	name for the Spanish or Mexican silver dollar which was used for a long time as the standard commercial currency of Southeast Asia and Chinese coastal foreign settlements; worth about 4 shillings.
Dross	see *djitjing*.
Duit, doit	(Dutch) = copper coin; 8 duit is 1 stuiver [around 1817, 4 duit were equal to 1 stuiver (stiver)].
Dutch guilder	(florin) is almost two English shillings.
English pound	20 shillings.
French livre	is about one English shilling.
Geleng	(East Indies) are opium "cigarettes" or "pills" made from a *tikee* mix weighing about 100 mg; 1 thail = 300 gelengs; a geleng is the smallest purchasable quantity of opium.
Grain	(English): 1 lb (avoirdupois) contains 7,000 grains = 454 grams metric which makes the weight of a grain = 0.06 gram.
Guilder	(Dutch currency) = 20 stuiver = 10 dubbeltjes.
Heren XVII	are the *Seventeen Gentlemen*, the Board of the VOC in Amsterdam.
Hoon	(Southeast Asia) = weight of 1/25 *tahil;* the minimum quantity for consumption in government dens in Dutch East Indies was two *hoons* = 1/50 *tahil* = 19.3 *gram*; others define a *hoon* as 'equivalent to one-tenth of a chee' which results in a one-hundred of a *tahil*, which is not an East Indies *hoon.*
Jin	(China) is the same as a catty = 1.33 pounds.
Kati	see *Catty.*
Kongsi	is a partnership, company or even a secret society to run an enterprise or opium farm.
Koyan	1 last = minimum 3,000 Amsterdam lbs = 1,482 kg (this weight varied widely).
Lakh	(India) = 100,000 rupees and £10,000; in Malayan countries it is used for 10,000 rupees (Hobson-Jobson).
Mace	about 3.8 gram or 63 *grains* or about 1/10 of a *tael* (= 4.2 gram).
Madat, medak, madap	(East Indies) general names for smoking opium often mixed with some local (tobacco) leaves.
Mata	(East Indies) about 380 mg; 100 mata = 1 tahil.
Mata-mata	(East Indies) spies or agents of the opium farm.

Maund or Man	(India) whatever the weight always contained 40 seers; common weight: in Bengal 75-82 pounds, in Surat 30 pounds, in Bombay about 76-80 pounds or about 40 kg; 30 maund = 1122 kg
Mu	(China) is 0.16 acre.
Nanyang	(China) name for Southeast Asia.
Pagoda	(India) golden coin worth 6-8 English shillings.
Parekan	(East Indies) dependent servant of a lord.
Peranakan	(East Indies) name for locally born Chinese or "Chinese mestizo".
Piaster	(Indochina) valued at 1:5.55 French franc around 1900; sometimes written as $.
Pikul	(Chinese) = 100 catty or 133.33 pounds or 60.5-61.8 kg (in Dutch-East Indies 62.5 kg); the Malay *picul* or Chinese *tan* was 136 pounds; mostly the same as *chest*; one picul opium = 125,000 gram = 1,600 thail = 160,000 mata.
Pound	(as weight): Amsterdam lb = 494 gram =1.09 lbs avoirdupois (av.); 125 Amsterdam lbs = 1 *pikul* = 100 *kati* = 61.75 kg = 136.14 lbs av.
Puputan	(Bali) literally 'ending'; ritualized, dynasty-ending defeat by military sacrifice or collective suicide.
Rixdollar	(Dutch) = rixdaalder, rijksdaalder = 2.5 *guilders*, sometimes 3 guilders = 60 light stuivers = 48 heavy *stuivers*; equals also 0.888 *Spanish real* (dollar).
Rupee	(silver; India) = 0.1 £ sterling end of 18th-century; 2 shillings (until 1872-3), devalued to 1s 1d in 1899; 1000 rupees is again £100 in 1870, but £50 in 1878; worth approximately one-half of a Spanish silver *dollar*. The silver Java rupee was, for instance, 120 duits-doits in 1817 (see Appendix 4).
Seer	= 1.9-2 lb or about 1 kg or 1 ¼ catty.
Spanish dollar	(rial/real of eight) about five English shillings = 1.125 *Rixdollar* (Dutch).
Straits Settlements	a British colonial construction made up of Singapore, Penang and Melaka.
Stuiver	(Dutch) = 0.05 *guilder* = 16 penning (60 light-stuivers = 1 Rixdollar; 40 heavy stuivers = 1 Rixdollar.
Tahil	= 38 grams or 100 *mata*.

Tael	(silver) = both a weight and a currency. As a currency it is 4s 6d; around 1830 £1 = 3 taels; as a weight, one Canton tael = 1/16th *catty* or about 42 grams or 700 grains; in Indochina 37.6 gram.
Thail	0.04 kg and for some 0.05kg = 100 *mata*.
Tikee	(East Indies) is made for special customers. It is prepared opium mixed with carved *awar-awar*. The cheapest kind of *tikee* has the form of a pill or cigarette consisting of tobacco soaked in opium.
Tjandoe	(East Indies) is the opium product resulting from a series of manipulations of raw opium (like dissolution, roasting, fermentation) so that it can be use for smoking.
Tolas	(Burma) = weight of 0.31 *tahil*; the maximum quantity of opium one is allowed to sell to individuals is 3 *tolas* or 0.927 *tahil* and also the quantity which allows the police to put the proprietor in jail.
Triad	the union of heaven-earth-man; the concept used for Chinese secret societies or brotherhoods.

BIBLIOGRAPHY

Primary Sources (1500-1900)

Balfour, Edward (ed.), *The Cyclopaedia of India and of Eastern and Southern Asia. Commercial, Industrial and Scientific* (London: B. Quaritch, 1885), 3 vol.

Barbosa, Duarte, *The Book of... An account of the countries bordering on the Indian Ocean and their inhabitants* (London: Hakluyt Society, 1918, original 1518), 2 vol.

Baud, Jean C. and Rochussen, Jan J., *De semi-officiële en particuliere briefwisseling tussen ..., 1845 – 1851*. Introduced and edited by Baud, W.A. (Assen: Van Gorkum, 1983), 3 vol.

Baud, Jean C., Proeve van eene geschiedenis van den handel en het verbruik van opium, in: *Bijdragen tot het Koloniaal Instituut* 1 (1853), p. 79-220 (sometimes indicated as: *Tijdschrift voor Indische Taal-, Land- en Volkenkunde*).

Bechtinger, Jos, *Het eiland in de Chineesche zee* (Batavia: Bruining & Wyt, 1871).

Bernier, François, *Travels in the Mogul Empire AD 1656-1668*. A revised and improved edition .. by Archibald Constable (Westminster: Archibald Constable & Co, 1891); on-line edition Columbia University Libraries Digital Collections.

Bluntschli, J. C. and Brater, K. (ed.), *Deutsches Staatswörterbuch* (Stuttgart- Leipzig: Expedition des Staats-Wörterbuchs, 1857).

Both, Pieter. *De Eerste Landvoogd .. 1568-1615. Gouverneur-generaal van Nederlands-Indië (1609-1614)* (Zutphen: Walburg Pers, 1987), ed. Rietbergen, P.; 2 vol.

Broecke, Pieter van den .. in Azië, ed. Coolhaas, W. P. (Den Haag: Nijhoff, 1962); Werken Linschoten Vereniging, LXIII; 2 vol.

Broek, J. A. van den, *Oud Oost-Indië. De lotgevallen van Nederlandsch Oost-Indië* (Haarlem: Bohn, 1893).

Bronnnen tot de Geschiedenis der Oostindische Compagnie in Perzie, ed. Dunlop, H. in: *Rijksgeschiedkundige Publicaties*, RGP, GS 72 (The Hague: Nijhoff, 1930).

Dam, Pieter van, Beschrijvinge van de Oostindische Compagnie 1639-1701, in: *Rijksgeschiedkundige Publicaties*, RGP, GS 63, 68, 74, 76, 83, 87, 96 (The Hague: Nijhoff, 1927 ff.).

Dutch Factories in India, 1617-1623. *A collection of Dutch East India Company documents pertaining to India*, ed. Prakash, O. (New Delhi: Manoharlal Publishers, 1984).

Generale Missiven van Gouverneurs-Generaal en Raden aan Heren XVII der Verenigde Oostindische Compagnie, ed. Coolhaas. W.P. et al. in: *Rijksgeschiedkundige Publicaties*, RGP (The Hague: Nijhoff, 1964 ff.), 13 vol. quoted as GM, I etc.

Gouverneur Van Imhoff op dienstreis in 1739 naar Cochin, Travancore en Tuticorin, en terug over Jaffna en Mannar naar Colombo (Zutphen: Walburg Pers, 2007), ed. Anke Galjaard et al.

Groeneveldt, Willem P., *(Geheim) Rapport over het opium-monopolie in Fransch Indo-China in verband met de vraag in hoever beheer in régie van dat middel voor Nederlandsch-Indië wenschelijk is; uitgebracht in voldoening aan artikel 1 van het Gouvernements-besluit van 21 Januari 1890 no. 1* (Batavia: Landsdrukkerij, 1890).

Hill, J. Spencer, *The Indo-Chinese Opium Trade considered in relation to its History, Morality and Expediency and its influence on Christian Missions* (London: Henry Frowde, 1884).

Hobson-Jobson, *A glossary of colloquial Anglo-Indian words ...* ed. Yule, Henry and Burnell, A.C. (1886); reprint (Sittingbourne, Kent: Linguasia, 1994).

Hogendorp, Gijsbert Karel van, *Bijdragen tot de Huishouding van Staat in het Koningrijk der Nederlanden verzameld ten dienste van de Staten-Generaal* ('s Gravenhage: Weduwe Johannes Allart, 1818-1825), 10 vol.

Indonesia. Selected Documents on Colonialism and Nationalism, 1830-1942 (St. Lucia: University of Queensland Press, 1977), ed. and translated by Penders, Chr. L.

Jonge, J. K. de, a.o. (ed.), *De Opkomst van het Nederlandsch Gezag in Oost-Indië* (The Hague: Nijhoff, 1862-1909), 17 vols.

Kaempfer, Engelbert, *The History of Japan; together with a Description of the Kingdom of Siam* (London: Routledge, 1995; original edition London, 1727).

Kerala, De Nederlanders in .. 1663-1701. De Memories en Instructies betreffende het Commandement Malabar van de VOC, ed. S'Jacob, H.K. in: *Rijksgeschiedkundige Publicaties*, RGP, KS 43 (The Hague: Nijhoff, 1976).

Kipling, Rudyard, *In an Opium Factory* (original, 1888); web edition published by *eBooks@ Adelaide,* 2009.

Landerer, Xavier, Ueber Opiumbereitung in der Nähe von Magnesia in Kleinasien, in: *Archiv der Pharmazie,* 113 (1850), p. 293-297.

Lange, G. A. de, *Mijnontginning van Staatswege op Billiton* ('s Gravenhaghe: Gebr. Belinfante, 1891).

Linschoten, Jan Huyghen van, *Voyage to the East Indies* (London: Hakluyt Society, 1885; orig. 1595), 2 vol., ed. by Coke Burnell, A. and Tiele, P.

———, *Itinerario, voyage ofte schipvaert naer Oost ofte Portugaels Indien, 1579-1592* (The Hague: Nijhoff, 1955-57; orig. 1596), 3 vol.; ed. by Kern, H. and Terpstra, H.

Loudon, John F., De Eerste Jaren der Billiton-Onderneming, in: *De Indische Gids* (Amsterdam: J. de Bussy, 1883), p. 1-115.

Lyall, Alfred, *Asiatic Studies. Religious and Social* (London: John Murray, 1884).

Manrique, Fray Sebastien, Travels of ... 1629-1643 (Oxford: Hakluyt Society, 1927), 2 Vol.; ed. by Eckford Luard, C. and Hosten, .H.

Marx, Karl, *Das Kapital. Kritik der politischen Ökonomie* (orig. 1867; Berlin: Dietz, 1971); 3 vol.

Meiss, Johan H., *Eenige bijdragen tot de kennis van den Inwendigen Toestand van Nederl.-Indië onder het bestuur van Gouv.-Gen. J.J. Rochussen, 1845-1851* (Leiden: Brill, 1883).

Memories van overgave van gouverneurs van Ambon in de zeventiende en achttiende eeuw, ed. Knaap, Gerrit in: *Rijksgeschiedkundige Publicaties,* RGP, KS, 62 (The Hague: Nijhoff, 1987).

Metzger, Emil, Das Opium in Indonesien, in: *Revue Coloniale Internationale,* II (1887), p. 175-202.

Midden-Molukken, Bronnen betreffende de ... 1900-1942 (The Hague: Instituut voor Nederlandse Geschiedenis, 1997), ed. Jobse, P.; 4 vol.

Narain, Brij and Sharma, Sri Ram (ed.), *A Contemporary Dutch Chronicle of Mughal India* (Calcutta: Susis Gupta, 1957).

Newbold, Thomas John, *Political and statistical account of the British Settlements in the Straits of Malacca, viz. Pinang, Malacca, and Singapore; with a history of The Malayan States on the Peninsula of Malacca* (London: John Murray, 1839), 2 vol. (reprint London: Oxford University Press. 1971).

Ong-Tae-Hae, *The Chinaman Abroad; An Account of the Malayan Archipelago particularly of Java* (London: John Snow, 1850); translated by Medhurst, W. H.; the original is from 1791.

Pelsaert, Francisco *De Geschriften van .. over Mughal Indië, 1627,* ed. by Kolff, D. and Santen H. van (The Hague: Nijhoff, 1979), Werken Linschoten Vereniging, LXXXI.

Raffles, Thomas Stamford, *The History of Java* (London: Black, Parbury etc., 1817). Reprint Oxford University Press, 1965; 2 vol.

———, *Geschiedenis van Java .. wat betreft de onderwerpen, welke voor Nederland en Indië wetenswaardig zijn met aantekeningen to verbetering, beoordeeling en vervolg;* vertaald door Sturler, Jacques Eduard de ('s Gravenhaghe-Amsterdam: Van Cleef, 1836).

Remington, Joseph P., *The Practice of Pharmacy. A Treatise* ... (Philadelphia: Lippincott, 1886).

Ro, (A) de, Das Opium in Indonesien. Eine Berichtigung, in: *Revue Coloniale Internationale,* II (1887), p. 553-555.

Rumphius, Georgius E., *De Generale Lant-Beschrijvinge van het Ambonse Gouvernement* ... ed. by Buijze, W. (The Hague: Houtschild, 2001), original 1678.

Schouten, Wouter, *De Oost-Indische Voyagie*; reprint by Breet, Michael(Zutphen: Walburg Pers, 2003, original 1676).

Smith, Arthur H., *Chinese Characteristics* (New York: Revell Company, 1894).

———, *The Uplift of China* (London: British Young People's Missionary Movement, 1907).

Struick, N. J., *Opiumpacht of Opiumregie?* ('s-Gravenhage: Cremer, 1889).

Swaving, Christiaan, Een woord over een kongsiehuis en de sterfte onder de mijnwerkers op Billiton, in: *Tijdschrift Maatschappij ter bevordering der Geneeskunde*, no. 5462 (Batavia: 1869), p. 1-16.

Verbeek, Reinier D., Het Billiton-Debat in de Tweede Kamer. Eenige Beschouwingen naar aanleiding daarvan, in: *De Indische Gids* (Leiden: Brill, 1892), p. 1-64.

Wiselius, Jakob A. B., *De Franschen in Indo-China: geografisch, administratief en economisch overzicht van Fransch Cochin China, Annam en Kambodja* (Zaltbommel: Noman, 1878).

———, *De opium in Nederlandsch-en Britsch-Indie: oeconomisch, critisch, historisch* (The Hague: Nijhoff, 1886).

Wood, George B. and Bache, Franklin, *The Dispensatory of the United States of America* (Philadelphia: Lippincott, 1899); 18th edition revised by Wood, H., Remington, J., Sadtler, S. (1st ed. 1833).

Sources 1900-1940

Addens, Tjako J., *The distribution of opium cultivation and the trade in opium* (Haarlem: Enschede, 1939).

Baasch, Ernst, *Holländische Wirtschaftsgeschichte* (Jena: Gustav Fischer, 1927).

Bucknill, John, *The Coins of the Dutch East Indies. An Introduction to the Study of the Series* (London: Spink, 1931).

Burkhardt, V. R., *Chinese Creeds & Customs* (Hong Kong: South China Morning Post, 1957; original ca. 1925).

Cheng, Sih-Gung, *Modern China. A Political Study* (Oxford: Oxford Clarendon, 1919).

Chimin Wong, K. and Lien-Teh, Wu, *History of Chinese Medicine. Being a Chronicle of Medical Happenings in China from Ancient Times to the Present Period* (Shanghai: National Quarantine Service, 1936).

Commission d'enquête sur le contrôle de l'opium à fumer en Extrême-Orient (Genève: Société des Nations, 1930), 3 vol.

Cressey, George B., *China's Geographic Foundations. A Survey of the Land and Its People* (New York: McGraw-Hill, 1934).

Encyclopaedie van Nederlandsch-Indië (Ed. by Lith, P. van der and Snelleman, J.) (The Hague: Nijhoff/Brill, s.d..), ca. 1900-1905.

Haan, F. De, *Priangan. De Preanger-Regentschappen onder het Nederlandsch Bestuur to 1811* (Batavia: Genootschap van Kunsten en Wetenschappen, 1910-1912), 4 vol.

Helfferich, Emil, *Die Niederländsch-Indischen Kulturbanken* (Jena: Gustav Fischer, 1914).

Hosie, Alexander, *On the Trial of the Opium Poppy. A narrative of travel in the chief opium-producing provinces of China* (London: George Philip & Son, 1914), 2 vol.

Indië en het Opium. Een verzameling opstellen betreffende het opiumgebruik (Batavia: Kolff, 1931), ed. Nederlandsch-Indische Grootloge van de Internationale Orde van Goede Tempelieren.

Kemp, Pieter H. van der, *Oost-Indië's Geldmiddelen. Japansche en Chineesche Handel van 1817 op 1818: in- en uitvoerrechten , opium, zout, tolpoorten, kleinzegel, boschwezen, Decima, Canton* (The Hague: Nijhoff, 1919).

King, Frank H., *Farmers of Forty Centuries or Permanent Agriculture in China, Korea and Japan* (London: Cape, 1927; 4th impression 1949).

Kol, H. van, *Uit Onze Koloniën. Uitvoerig reisverhaal* (Leiden: Sijthoff, 1903).

La Motte, Ellen N., *The Opium Monopoly* (New York: Macmillan, 1920).

Leur, Jacob C. van, *Eenige Beschouwingen betreffende den ouden Aziatischen handel* (Middelburg: Den Boer, 1934).

Lewin, Ludwig, *Phantastica. Die betäubenden und erregenden Genußmittel* (Berlin: Georg Stilke, 1927; second printing).

Lossing Buck, John, *Land Utilization in China. A study of 16,786 farms in 168 localities ... 1929-1933* (New York: Paragon Book Reprint, 1964; original Nanking, 1937).

Mansvelt, W. M., *Geschiedenis van de Nederlandsche Handel-Maatschappij* (Haarlem: NHM, 1924-1926), 2 vol. (at the occasion of the 100-year celebration of the NHM).

Mollema, Johan C., *De Ontwikkeling van het Eiland Billiton en van de Billiton-Maatschappij* ('s Gravenhage: Nijhoff, 1922).

Morse, Hosea B., *The Trade and Administration of China* (London, New York: Longmans, Green & Co, 1921).

———, *The Chronicles of the East India Company trading to China, 1635-1834* (Oxford: Clarendon Press, 1926), 4 vol.

Murdoch, James, *A History of Japan. From the Origins ... to 1868* (London: Kegan Paul, 1925-1926); 3 vol.

Opiumfabriek, Verslag over het jaar ... 1913, 1914, 1916, 1918, 1920 (Batavia: Departement van Gouvernementsbedrijven in Nederlandsch-Indie).

Opiumfabriek, Verslag over het jaar .... 1922, 1924, 1926, 1929, 1932, 1935, 1938 (Batavia: Departement van Financiën in Nederlandsch-Indië).

Opiumregie, Verslag betreffende den Dienst der, over het jaar ... 1916, 1918, 1919, 1920, 1923 (Batavia: Drukkerij Ruygrok – Landsdrukkerij).

Opium- en Zoutregie, Wettelijke bepalingen betreffende opium en andere verdoovende middelen (Batavia: Landsdrukkerij, 1938).

Owen, David E., *British Opium Policy in China and India* (New Haven: Yale University Press, 1934).

Pernitzsch, M., Shanghai, in: *Mitteilungen der Ausland-Hochschule an der Universität Berlin, Abteilung I, Ostasiatischen Studien,* XL (1937).

Rawlinson, H. G., *British Beginnings in Western India, 1579-1657* (Oxford: Clarendon Press, 1920).

Remer, C.F., (ed.), *Readings in Economics for China. Selected Readings with explanatory introduction* (Shanghai: Commercial Press, 1933; reprint New York: Garland, 1980).

Richter, Julius, (ed.), *Das Buch der deutschen Weltmission* (Gotha: Klotz Verlag, 1935).

Rosenberg, Alfred, *Der Mythus des 20.Jahrhunderts. Eine Wertung der seelisch-geistigen Gestaltenkämpfe unserer Zeit* (München: Hoheneichen Verlag, 1937; orig. 1930).

Rowntree, Joshua, *The Imperial Drug Trade. A Re-Statement of the Opium Question ...* (London: Methuen, 1906).

Schallmayer, Wilhelm, *Vererbung und Auslese. Grundriss der Gesellschaftsbiologie und der Lehre vom Rassedienst* (Jena: Fischer, 1920; 4th edition).

Scheltema, J. F., The Opium Trade in the Dutch East Indies, in: *The American Journal of Sociology,* 13 (1907), p. 79-112, 224-251.

Slingenberg, Johan, *De Staatsinrichting van Nederl.-Indië* (Haarlem: Tjeenk Willink, 1924).

Stapel, F. W., *Aanvullende gegevens omtrent de geschiedenis van het eiland Billiton en het voorkomen van tin aldaar* ('s Gravenhage: Mijnbouwmaatschappij Billiton, 1938).

Terry, Charles E. and Pellens, Mildred, *The Opium Problem* (New York: Bureau of Social Hygiene, 1928).

Terry's Guide to the Japanese Empire including Korea and Formosa with chapters on Manchuria ... (Boston: Houghton Mifflin Co., 1930).

Thibout, Georges, *La Question de l'opium à l'époque contemporaine* (Paris: Steinheil, 1912).

Tan Tong Joe, *Het Internationale Opiumprobleem* (The Hague: L. Gerretsen, 1929; dissertation).

Valk, Marinus H. van der, (ed.), Interpretations of the Supreme Court at Peking; years 1915 and 1916 , in: *Sinica Indonesiana*, 1 (1949), p. 1-383.

Vessem, Cornelis J. Van, *Economische Beschouwingen over de Indische Middelen in het bijzonder de Fiscale Monopolies* (Wageningen: Veenman, 1932).

Vleming, J. L., *Het Chineesche Zakenleven in Nederlandsch-Indië* (Batavia: Uitgave Volkslectuur, 1925).

Willoughby, Westel W., *Foreign Rights and Interests in China* (Baltimore: The Johns Hopkins Press, 1927), 2 vol.

Wolf, Heinrich, *Angewandte Rassenkunde. Weltgeschichte auf biologischer Grundlage* (Leipzig: Weicher, 1927).

Literature 1940-present

Adas, Michael, *Prophets of Rebellion. Millenarian Protest Movements against the European Colonial Order* (Cambridge: Cambridge University Press, 1987).

Alatas, Syed Hussein, *Thomas Stamford Raffles, 1781-1826. Schemer or Reformer?* (London: Angus-Robertson, 1971).

Alphen, Jan van, and Aris, Anthony (ed.), *Oriental Medicine: An Illustrated Guide to the Asian Arts of Healing* (London: Serindia Publications, 1995; Dutch translation Rotterdam: Lemniscaat, 1995).

Anderson, Warwick, *The Cultivation of Whiteness. Science, Health and Racial Destiny in Australia* (New York: Basic Books, 2003).

Andors, Stephen, *China's Industrial Revolution. Politics, Planning and Management, 1949 to the present* (London: Robertson, 1977).

Anh Tuân, Hoang, The VOC's import of monetary metals into Tonkin and its impact on seventeenth-century Vietnamese society, in: Worden, N. (ed.), p. 149-172.

Arasaratnam, Sinnappah, *Maritime India in the Seventeenth Century* (New Delhi: Oxford University Press, 2004).

Auerbach, Sascha, *Race, Law and "The Chinese Puzzle" in Imperial Britain* (New York: Palgrave Macmillan, 2009).

Avery, Martha, *The Tea Road. China and Russia meet across the steppe* (Beijing: China Intercontinental Press, 2003).

Baader, Gerhard and Keil, Gundolf (ed.), *Medizin im mittelalterlichen Abendland* (Darmstadt: Wissenschaftliche Buchgesellschaft, 1982).

Baghdiantz, Ina, a.o., (ed.), *Diaspora Entrepreneurial Networks. Four Centuries of History* (Oxford/New York: Berg, 2005).

Banks, Erik, *The Rise and Fall of the Merchant Banks* (London: Kogan Page Ltd., 1999).

Barend-Van Haeften, Marijke, *Oost-Indië gespiegeld. Nicolaas de Graaff, een schrijvend chirurgijn van de VOC* (Zutphen: Walburg Pers, 1992).

Bastin, John, *The Native Policies of Sir Stamford Raffles in Java and Sumatra* (Oxford: Clarendon Press, 1957).

Baumler, Alan (ed.), *Modern China and Opium. A Reader* (Ann Arbor: The University of Michigan Press, 2001).

Bayly, Christopher and Harper, Tim, *Forgotten Armies. The Fall of British Asia, 1941-1945* (London: Allen Lane, 2004).

Beattie, Alan, *False Economy. A Surprising Economic History of the World* (New York: Riverhead Books/ Penguin, 2009).

782 BIBLIOGRAPHY

Beeching, Jack, *The Chinese Opium Wars* (New York: Harcourt, 1975).
Bernstein, William, *A Splendid Exchange. How Trade Shaped the World* (London: Atlantic Books, 2009).
Berridge, Virginia and Edwards, Griffith, *Opium and the People. Opiate Use in Nineteenth-Century England* (London: Allen Lane, 1981).
Betta, Chiara, *The Trade Diaspora of Baghdadi Jews: From Ottoman Baghdad to China's Treaty Ports, 1843-1931*, in: cbetta@ath.forthnet.gr.
Bingling, Yuan, *Chinese Democracies. A Study of the Kongsis of West Borneo, 1776-1884* (Leiden: Leiden University, CNWS Publications, 2000).
Bloembergen, Marieke, *De Geschiedenis van de Politie in Nederlands-Indie. Uit Zorg en Angst* (Leiden: KITLV uitgeverij, 2009).
Blussé,Leonard, An Insane Administration and an Unsanitary Town: the Dutch East India Company and Batavia (1619-1799), in: Ross, R. and Telkamp, G. (ed.), p. 65-87.
———, *Strange Company. Chinese Settlers, Mestizo Women and the Dutch in VOC Batavia* (Leiden: RU Leiden, 1986).
———, *Tribuut aan China. Vier eeuwen Nederlands-Chinese betrekkingen* (Amsterdam: Cramwinckel, 1989).
———, *Visible Cities. Canton, Nagasaki and Batavia and the coming of the Americans* (Cambridge, Mass.: Harvard University Press, 2008).
Boekhout van Solinge, Tim, *Dealing with Drugs in Europe. An Investigation of European Drug Control Experiences: France, the Netherlands and Sweden* (The Hague: Willem Pompe Institute-BJu Legal Publishers, 2004).
Boomgaard, Peter, Droefenis en duurzaamheid. Beheer en exploitatie van de bossen op Java onder Daendels (1808-1810), in: *Jaarboek voor Ecologische Geschiedenis 2009*, p. 53-77.
Booth, Anne a.o., (ed.), *Indonesian Economic History in the Dutch Colonial Era* (New Haven: Yale University, Southeast Asia Studies, 1990).
Bouman, B., *Ieder voor zich en de Republiek voor ons allen. De logistiek achter de Indonesische Revolutie, 1945-1950* (Amsterdam: Boom, 2006).
Bouman, Ferry a.o., *Kruidenier aan de Amstel. De Amsterdamse Hortus volgens Johannes Snippendaal, 1646* (Amsterdam: Amsterdam University Press, 2007).
Boussel, Patrice and Bonnemain, Henri, *Histoire de la Pharmacie ou 7000 Ans pour Soigner L'Homme* (Paris: Editions de la Porte Verte, 1977).
Bovenkerk, Frank and Yeşilgöz, Yücel, *De Maffia van Turkije* (Amsterdam: Meulenhoff-Kritak, 1998).
Boxer, C. R., *The Dutch Seaborne Empire, 1600-1800* (London: Penguin Books, 1965).
———, *Jan Compagnie in Oorlog en vrede. Beknopte geschiedenis van de VOC* (Bussum: Unieboek, 1977).
———, *Portuguese Conquest and Commerce in Southern Asia, 1500-1750* (London: Variorum Reprints, 1985)
Brendon, Piers, *The Decline and Fall of the British Empire, 1781-1997* (London: Vintage, 2008).
Brenner, Robert, *Merchants and Revolution. Commercial change, political conflict and London's Overseas Traders, 1550-1653* (London: Verso, 2003).
Braudel, Fernand, *Civilization and Capitalism, 15th-18th century* (London: Collins, 1983).
Brouwer, C., *Dutch-Yemeni Encounters. Activities of the United East India Company (VOC) in South Arabaian Waters since 1614* (Amsterdam: D'Fluyte Rarob, 1999).
———, *Al-Mukha. The Transoceanic Trade of a Yemeni Staple Town as Mapped by Merchants of the VOC, 1614-1640* (Amsterdam: D'Fluyte Rarob, 2006).
Brown, Ian, The End of the Opium Farm in Siam, 1905-7, in: Butcher, J. and Dick, H. (ed.), p. 233-249.
Buchanan, Keith, *The Transformation of the Chinese Earth. Perspectives of Modern China* (London: Bell, 1973).

Burger, D. H., *Sociologisch-economische geschiedenis van Indonesia* (The Hague: Nijhoff, 1975), 2 vol.

Butcher, John and Dick, Howard (ed.), *The Rise and Fall of Revenue Farming. Business Elites and the Emergence of the Modern State in Southeast Asia* (New York: St. Martin's Press, 1993).

Campen, Cretien van, Gedrogeerde deuren van de waarneming, in: *Psychologie & Maatschappij*, 20 (1996), p. 374-387.

Carr, Caleb, *The Devil Soldier. The Story of Frederic Townsend Ward* (New York: Random House, 1992).

Cashmore, Ellis (ed.), *Dictionary of Race and Ethnic Relations* (London: Routledge, 1994).

Central Intelligence Agency (CIA), *An Examination of the Charges of Chinese Communist Involvement in the Illicit Opium Trade* (Secret Intelligence Memorandum, CIA/RR IM-438, 9 November, 1956).

Cesarani, David and Romain, Gemma (ed.), *Jews and Port Cities, 1590-1990. Commerce, Community and Cosmopolitanism* (London: Valentine Mitchell, 2006).

Chaloemtiarana, Thak, *Thailand. The Politics of Despotic Paternalism* (Suthep, Th.: Silkworm Books-Cornell Southeast Asia Program, 2007).

Chandra, Siddharth, What the Numbers Really tell us about the Decline of the Opiumregie, in: *Indonesia*, 70 (2000), p. 101-123.

——, The Role of Government Policy in Increasing Drug Use: Java, 1875-1914, in: *The Journal of Economic History*, 62 (2002), p. 1116-1121.

——, Economic Histories of the Opium Trade, in: *http://eh.net/encyclopedia/article/chandra/.opium ; 02-05-2010.*

Chang, Jung and Halliday, Jon, *Mao. The Unknown Story* (London: Vintage Books, 2007).

Chan, Kwok Bun, *Smoke and Fire. The Chinese in Montreal* (Hong Kong: Chinese University Press, 1991).

Chapman, Stanley, *The Rise of Merchant Banking* (Aldershot: Gregg Revivals, 1992).

Chatterjee,Kumkum, *Merchants, Politics and Society in Early Modern India. Bihar: 1733-1820* (Leiden: Brill, 1996).

Chaudhuri, K. N., *The Trading World of Asia and the English East India Company, 1660-1760* (Cambridge: Cambridge University Press, 1978).

——, India's Foreign Trade and the Cessation of the East India Company's Trading Activities, 1828-40, in: Siddiqi, A. (ed.), p. 290-321.

——, *Asia before Europe. Economy and civilization of the Indian Ocean from the rise of Islam to 1750* (Cambridge: Cambridge University Press, 1990; eighth printing, 2005, under a slightly different title).

Chesneaux, Jean, *Secret societies in China in the nineteenth and twentieth centuries* (London: Heinemann, 1971).

Chien-Nung, Li *The Political History of China, 1840-1928* (Princeton: Van Nostrand, 1956).

Chipman, Leigh, *The World of Pharmacy and Pharmacists in Mamlūk Cairo* (Leiden: Brill, 2010).

Chouvy, Pierre-Arnaud, *Opium. Uncovering the Politics of the Poppy* (London: Tauris, 2009).

Chu, Yiu-Kong, International Triad Movements. The Threat of Chinese Organised Crime, in: *Conflict Studies*, 291 (1996), p. 1-25.

Clarence-Smith, Gervase, *The third Portuguese empire, 1825-1975. A study in economic imperialism* (Manchester: Manchester University Press, 1985).

Clarke, Robert C., *Hashish !* (Los Angeles: Red Eye Press, 1998).

Collis, Maurice, *Foreign Mud, being an account of the Opium Imbroglio at Canton in the 1830s and the Anglo-Chinese war that followed* (New York: New Directions, 2002; originally 1946).

Courtwright, David T., *Dark Paradise. Opiate Addiction in America before 1940* (Cambridge, Mass.: Harvard University Press, 1982).

Creutzberg, P., *Changing Economy in Indonesia: A Selection of Statistical Source Material from the Nineteenth Century up to 1940. Volume 2: Public Finance 1816-1939* (The Hague: Nijhoff, 1976).

Cribb, Robert, Opium and the Industrial Revolution, in: *Modern Asian Studies,* 22 (1988), p. 701-722.

Cumings, Bruce, *Parallax Visions: Making Sense of American-East Asian Relations at the End of the Century* (Durham, NC.: Duke University Press, 1999).

Dale, Stephen F., *Islamic Society on the South Asian Frontier. The Mappilas of Malabar, 1498-1922* (London: Clarendon Press, 1980).

Dalrymple, William, *The Last Mughal. The Fall of a Dynasty, Delhi, 1857* (London: Bloomsbury, 2009).

Das Gupta, Ashin, *Malabar in Asian Trade, 1740-1800* (Cambridge: Cambridge University Press, 1967).

Datta, Kalikinkar, *The Dutch in Bengal and Bihar, 1740-1825 A.D.* (Delhi: Indological Publishers, 1968).

Davids, C. A. a. o. (ed.), *Kapitaal, Ondernemerschap en Beleid* (Amsterdam: NEHA, 1996).

Davis, Lance E. and Huttenback, Robert, *Mammon and the Pursuit of Empire. The Economics of British Imperialism* (Cambridge: Cambridge University Press, 1988).

Dear, I. C. and Foot, M.(ed.), *The Oxford Companion to World War II* (Oxford: Oxford University Press, 2001).

Departement van Koloniën, *Het Beheer in Nederland van de Geldmiddelen der Overzeesche Gebiedsdeelen in de Jaren 1940-'43* (Zutphen: Thieme & Cie, 1945).

Derks, Hans, *Karl Marx en Lawrence Krader over de "Aziatische Produktiewijze": van 'externe theorie' tot intern probleem* (Amsterdam: University of Amsterdam, 1978-1; Ph.D-thesis).

———, *Stad-Land tegenstellingen en de "Aziatische Produktiewijze"* (Amsterdam: University of Amsterdam, 1978-2).

———, *Stad en Land, Markt en Oikos* (Amsterdam: University of Amsterdam, 1986; Doctor diss.).

——— (ed.), *Kroniek van 3 eeuwen revoluties* (Groningen: Wolters-Noordhoff, 1989).

———, A Note on *homogalaktes* in Aristotle's Politics, in: *Dialogue d'histoire ancienne* (CNRS), 21.2 (1995), p. 27-40.

———, *Autarkeia* in Greek theory and practice, in: *The European Legacy,* 6 (1996), p. 1915-1933.

———, Nomads in Chinese and Central Asian History. The Max Weber Case, in: *Oriens Extremus,* 41 (1999), p. 7-34.

__, *Jew, Nomad or Pariah. Studies on Hannah Arendt's Choice* (Amsterdam: Aksant Acad. Publisher, 2004).

__, Religion, capitalism and the rise of double-entry bookkeeping, in: *Accounting, Business & Financial History,* 18 (2008), p. 187-213.

Descours-Gatin, Chantal, *Quand L'Opium Finançait la Colonisation en Indochine. L'élaboration de la régie générale de l'opium (1860 à 1914)* (Paris: l'Harmattan, 1992).

Diehl, F. W., Revenue Farming and Colonial Finances in the Netherlands East Indies, 1816-1925, in: Butcher, J. and Dick, H.(ed.), p. 196-233.

Dikötter, Frank, *Sex, Culture and Modernity in China. Medical Science and the Construction of Sexual Identities in the Early Republican Period* (London: Hurst & Co., 1995)

———, *Crime, Punishment and the Prison in Modern China* (New York: Columbia University Press, 2002).

———, and Sautman, Barry (ed.), *The Construction of Racial Identities in China and Japan. Historical and Contemporary Perspectives* (London: Hurst & Co., 1997).

———, Laamann, Laaman and Xun, Zhou, Narcotic Culture. A Social History of Drug Consumption in China, in: *British Journal of Criminology,* 42 (2002), p. 317-336.

Dillo, Ingrid, *De nadagen van de Verenigde Oostindische Compagnie, 1783-1795* (Amsterdam: Bataafsche Leeuw, 1992).

Dodge, Ernest, *Islands and Empires. Western Impact on the Pacific and East India* (Minneapolis: University of Minnesota Press, 1976).

Dormandy, Thomas *The Worst of Evils. The Fight against Pain* (New Haven: Yale University Press, 2006).

Duco, Don H., *Opium & Opiumschuiven; een bronnenboek* (Amsterdam: Stichting Pijpenkabinet, 2006).

Durrenberger, Paul (ed.), *State Power and Culture in Thailand* (New Haven, Con.: Yale University Press, 1996).

Ebben, Maurits and Wagenaar, Pieter (ed.), *De Cirkel doorbroken. Met nieuwe ideeën terug naar de bronnen. Opstellen over de Republiek* (Leiden: Instituut voor Geschiedenis, 2006).

Eberhard, Wolfram, *A History of China* (London: Routledge & Kegan Paul, 1977).

Eckart, Wolfgang U., *Medizin und Kolonialimperialismus Deutschland, 1884-1945* (Paderborn, etc.: Schöningh, 1997).

Eldridge, William B., *Narcotics and the Law. A Critique of the American Experiment in Narcotic Drug Control* (Chicago: University of Chicago Press, 1967).

Elvin, Mark, *The Pattern of the Chinese Past* (Stanford, Cal.: Stanford University Press, 1973).

Endacott, G. B., *A History of Hong Kong* (Hong Kong: Oxford University Press, 1977).

Erfurt, Jürgen, *Frankophonie* (Tübingen: UTB, 2005).

Evans, Grant, *A Short History of Laos. The Land in Between* (Crows Nest, Australia: Allen&Unwin, 2002).

Fairbank, John K. (ed.), *The Cambridge History of China* (Cambridge: Cambridge University Press, 1983), vol. 12. Republican China 1912-1949.

Feddema, Raymond (ed.), *Wat beweegt de Bamboe? Geschiedenissen in Zuidoost Azie* (Amsterdam: Spinhuis, 1992).

Fenby, Jonathan, *The Penguin History of Modern China. The Fall and Rise of a Great Power, 1850-2009* (London: Penguin Group, 2009).

Ferguson, Niall, *Empire. How Britain Made the Modern World* (London: Penguin, 2007).

Feuerwerker, Albert, Economic trends in the late Ch'ing empire, 1870-1911, in: Twitchett, D. and Fairbank, J., p. 1-69.

Fischer, Benjamin Louis, *"Opium Pushing and Bible Smuggling": Religion and the Cultural Politics of British Imperialist ambition in China* (Notre Dame, Indiana: University of Notre Dame, 2008), dissertation; etd.nd.edu/ETD-db/theses/available/etd...172638/.../ FischerBL042008.pdf

Fischer-Tiné, Harald and Mann, Michael (ed.), *Colonialism as civilizing mission. Cultural ideology in British India* (London: Anthem Press, 2004).

Foster, Anne L., Prohibition as Superiority: Policing Opium in South-East Asia, 1898-1925, in: *The International History Review*, 22 (2000), p. 253-273.

———, Prohibiting Opium in the Philippines and the United States: The Creation of an Interventionist State, in: McCoy, A. W. and Scarano, F. (ed.), p. 95-106.

Furber, Holden, *Rival Empires of Trade in the Orient, 1600-1800* (New Delhi: Oxford University Press, 2004).

Furnivall, J. S., *Colonial Policy and Practice. A Comparative Study of Burma and Netherlands India* (Cambridge: Cambridge University Press, 1948).

Gaastra, Femme S., *De geschiedenis van de VOC* (Zutphen: Walburg, 1991).

———, De VOC als voorloper van de koloniale staat, in: *Leidschrift*, 15 (2000), p. 7- 21.

———, De Amfioen Sociëteit. Een geprivilegieerde handelsmaatschappij onder de vleugels van de VOC, 1745-1794, in: Ebben, M. and Wagenaar, P. (ed.), p. 101-115.

Geddes, William R., *Peasant Life in Communist China* (Ithaca, NY: Cornell University Press, 1963).

Geertz, Clifford, *Negara. The Theatre State in Nineteenth-Century Bali* (Princeton, NJ: Princeton University Press, 1980).

Gelber, Harry G., *The Dragon and the Foreign Devils. China and the World, 1100 BC to the present* (London: Bloomsbury, 2007).

———, China as "Victim"? The Opium War That Wasn't, in: *Harvard Center for European Studies, Working Paper Series #136* (2007).

Gerritsen, W., *De Chinese Opium-entrepreneurs in Java. James Robert Rush' histoire integrale* .... (Nijmegen: KU Nijmegen, 1982; doctoraal scriptie).

Gerritsen, Jan-Willem, *De Politieke Economie van de Roes. De ontwikkeling van regulering-sregimes voor alcohol en opiaten* (Amsterdam: Amsterdan University Press, 1993).

Glamann, Kristof, *Dutch-Asiatic Trade, 1620-1740* (Copenhagen: Danish Science Press, 1958).

Göckenjan, Gerd, *Kurieren und Staat machen. Gesundheit und Medizin in der bürgerlichen Welt* (Frankfurt a.M.: Suhrkamp, 1985).

Goh, Daniel P.S., Unofficial contentions: The postcoloniality of Straits Chinese political discourse in the Straits Settlements Legislative Council, in: *Journal of Southeast Asian Studies,* 41 (2010), p. 483-507.

Goody, Jack, *The East in the West* (Cambridge: Cambridge University Press, 1998).

Goor, Jan van (ed.), *Trading Companies in Asia, 1600-1830* (Utrecht: HES, 1986).

Gootenberg, Paul (ed.), *Cocaine. Global Histories* (London: Routledge, 1999).

Gossett, Thomas F., *Race. The History of an Idea in America* (New York: Schocken Books, 1963).

Goto-Shibata, Harumi, The International Opium Conference of 1924-25 and Japan, in: *Modern Asian Studies,* 36 (2002), 969-991.

Gray, John, *Rebellions and Revolutions. China from the 1800s to the 1980s.* (Oxford: Oxford University Press, 1990).

Greenberg, Michael, *British Trade and the Opening of China, 1800-1842* (Cambridge: Cambridge University Press, 1951/1969).

Gruythuysen, M. and Kramer, R., *Inventaris van het Direktie-archief van de n.v. Billiton-Maatschappij, 1852-1970* (Den Haag: Algemeen Rijksarchief, 1990).

Guha, Amalendu, The Comprador Role of Parsi Seths, 1750-1850, in: *Economic and Political Weekly* (1972), p. 1933-1936 (www.cscsarchive.org).

Habib, Irfan, *Essays in Indian History. Towards a Marxist Perception* (New Delhi: Tulika, 1997).

Haccou, J. F., *De Indische Exportproducten. Hun beteekenis voor Indië en Nederland* (Leiden: Stenfert Kroese, 1947).

Hall, D. G., *A History of South-East Asia* (London: Macmillan, 1966).

Hall, C. J. van and Koppel, C. van de (ed.), *De Landbouw in den Indischen Archipel* (The Hague: Van Hoeve, 1946-1950); vol. 1, IIa, IIb, III.

Halperin, Sandra, *War and Social Change in Modern Europe. The* Great Transformation *Revisited* (Cambridge: Cambridge University Press, 2004).

Hamilton – Merritt, Jane, *Tragic Mountains. The Hmong, the Americans, and the secret wars for Laos, 1942-1992* (Bloomington: Indiana University Press, 1993).

Harrison, Henrietta, Narcotics, Nationalism and Class in China: the transition from opium to morphine and heroin in early twentieth-century Shanxi, in: *East Asian History,* 32/33 (2007), p. 151-176.

Hayter, Alethea, *Opium and the Romantic Imagination* (London: Faber and Faber, 1971).

Headrick, Daniel, *Power over Peoples. Technology, Environments, and Western Imperialism, 1400 to the present* (Princeton: Princeton University Press, 2010).

Hershatter, Gail, *The Workers of Tianjin, 1900-1949* (Stanford: Stanford University Press, 1986).

Hillmer, Paul, *A People's History of the Hmong* (St. Paul, MN.: Minnesota Hist. Soc. Press, 2010).

Hodder, Rupert, *Merchant Princes of the East. Cultural Delusions, Economic Success and the Overseas Chinese in Southeast Asia* (Chicester: John Wiley & Sons, 1996).

Hodgson, Barbara, *In the Arms of Morpheus. The Tragic History of Laudanum, Morphine, and Patent Medicines* (Buffalo, New York: Firefly Books, 2001).

Hull, Isabel V., *Absolute Destruction. Military culture and the Practices of War in Imperial Germany* (Ithaca: Cornell University Press, 2005).

Inglis, Brian, *The Forbidden Game. A Social History of Drugs* (New York: Scribner's Sons, 1975).

Ingold, Tim (ed.), *Companion Encyclopedia of Anthropology. Humanity, Culture and Social Life* (London: Routledge, 1997).

Isaacs, Harold, *New Cycle in Asia. Selected Documents on Major International Developments in the Far East, 1943-1947* (New York: Macmillan, 1947).

Jacobs, Els M., *Merchant in Asia. The Trade of the Dutch East India Company during the Eighteenth Century* (Leiden: CNWS Publications, 2006).

s'Jacob, Hugo K., Het Hof van Cochin 1670-1710. VOC dienaren als informanten, in: Locher-Scholten, Elsbeth and Rietbergen, Peter (ed.), p. 201-227.

Jacques, Martin, *When China rules the World. The Rise of the Middle Kingdom and the End of the Western World* (London: Allen Lane, 2009).

Jelsma, Martin and Kramer,Tom, The Opium Decline: Figures, Facts & Fiction, in: *Drugs & Conflict [D&C]*, August 2008 (Transnational Institute, Amsterdam).

Jennings, John M., The Forgotten Plague: Opium and Narcotics in Korea under Japanese Rule, 1910-1945, in: *Modern Asian Studies*, 29 (1995), p. 795-815.

———, *The Opium Empire. Japanese Imperialism and Drug Trafficking in Asia, 1895-1945* (Westport: Praeger, 1997).

Ji, Zhaojin, *A History of Modern Shanghai Banking. The Rise and Decline of China's Finance Capitalism* (London: Sharpe, 2003).

Jong, Anton W. K. de, Coca, in: Hall, J. van and Koppel, C. van de (ed.), vol. IIa, p. 866-888.

Ka, Chih-ming, *Japanese Colonialism in Taiwan. Land Tenure, Development, and Dependency, 1895-1945* (Oxford: Westview Press, 1995).

Kamen, Henry, *Empire. How Spain became a World Power, 1492-1763* (New York: HarperCollins, 2003).

Karch, S.B., *A Brief History of Cocaine. From Inca Monarchs to Cali Cartels: 500 Years of Cocaine Dealings* (Boca Raton, Fl.: Taylor & Francis, 2006).

Kaufmann, Doris (ed.), *Geschichte der Kaiser-Wilhelm-Gesellschaft im Nationalsozialismus. Bestandsaufnahme und Perspektiven der Forschung* (Göttingen: Wallstein Verlag, 2001), 2 vol.

Kennedy, John G., *The Flower of Paradise. The Institutionalized Use of the Drug Qat in North Yemen* (Dordrecht: Reidel, 1987).

Kiernan,Victor, *The Lords of Human Kind. European Attitudes to Other Cultures in the Imperial Age* (London: Serif, 1995; original 1969).

Kirby, R.J., *Urbanisation in China: Town and Country in a developing economy, 1949-2000 AD* (London: Croom Helm, 1985).

Klein, Axel, *Drugs and the World* (London: Reaktion Books, 2008).

Klein, Thoralf and Zöllner, Reinhard (ed.), *Karl Gützlaff (1803-1851) und das Christentum in Ostasien. Ein Missionar zwischen den Kulturen* (Nettetal: Steyler, 2005).

Klimburg, Alexander, Some research notes on Carl A. Trocki's publication *Opium, empire and the global political economy*, in: *Bulletin of the School of Oriental and African Studies*, 64 (2001), p. 260-267.

Knaap, Gerrit and Teitler, Ger (ed.), *De Verenigde Oost-Indische Compagnie tussen oorlog en diplomatie* (Leiden: KITLV Press, 2002).

———, and Sutherland, Heather, *Monsoon Traders. Ships, skippers and commodities in eighteenth-century Makassar* (Leiden: KITLV Press, 2004).

Kolko,Gabriel, *Century of War. Politics, conflicts and society since 1914* (New York: The New Press, 1994).

Korf, Dirk and Riper, Heleen (ed.), Illicit Drug Use in Europe. Proceedings of the 7th annual conf. on Drug Use and Drug Policy (Amsterdam: SISWO, 1997).

Kort, Marcel de, *Tussen patient en delinquent. Geschiedenis van het Nederlandse drugsbeleid* (Hilversum: Verloren, 1995).

Kremers, Edward and Urdang, George, *History of Pharmacy* (Philadelphia: Lippincott, 1963). Revised by Sonnedecker, Glenn.

Kuhn, Philip, *Chinese Among Others. Emigration in Modern Times* (Lanham, MD: Rowman & Littlefield, 2008).

Kumar, Dharma and Desai, Meghnad (ed.), *The Cambridge Economic History of India* (Hyderabad: Orient Longman Limited, 1984), vol. 2. c. 1757-c. 1970.

Kwong, Luke S. K., The Chinese Myth of Universal Kingship and Commissioner Lin Zexu's Anti-Opium Campaign of 1839, in: *English Historical Review*, cxxiii (2008), p. 1470-1503.

Lamour, Catherine and Lamberti, Michel, *The International Connection. Opium from Growers to Pushers* (New York: Pantheon Books, 1974).

Lee, Gregory, *The British Imperial Addiction: Ideology and Economics and the Chinese Consumption of Opium*, in: G. Lee, www.gregorylee.net/ (2010; original French 1998 ?).

Leese, Daniel (ed.), *Brill's Encyclopedia of China* (Leiden: Brill, 2009).

LeFevour, Edward, *Western Enterprise in Late Ch'ing China. A Selective Survey of Jardine, Matheson & Company's Operations, 1842-1895* (Cambridge, Mass.: Harvard University Press, 1968).

Le Pichon, Alain (ed.), *China Trade and Empire. Jardine, Matheson & Co. and the Origins of British Rule in Hong Kong 1827-1843* (Oxford: Oxford University Press, 2007).

Leuftink, A. E., *Harde Leermeesters. Zeelieden en hun dokters in de 18de eeuw* (Zutphen: Walburg Pers, 2008).

Leur, Jacob C. van, *Indonesian Trade and Society. Essays in Asian Social and Economic History* (The Hague: W. van Hoeve , 1955).

Lindemann, Mary, *Medicine and Society in Early Modern Europe* (Cambridge: Cambridge University Press, 2010).

Lipman, Jonathan N. and Harrell, Stevan (ed.), *Violence in China. Essays in Culture and Counterculture* (New York: SUNY Press, 1990).

Locher-Scholten, Elsbeth and Rietbergen, Peter (ed.), *Hof en Handel. Aziatische vorsten en de VOC, 1620-1720* (Leiden: KITLV Uitgeverij, 2004).

Lodwick, Kathleen L., *Crusaders against Opium. Protestant Missionaries in China, 1874-1917* (Lexington: University of Kentucky Press, 1996).

Lossing Buck, John; Dawson, Owen and Wu, Yuan-li, *Food and Agriculture in Communist China* (New York: Praeger, 1966).

Lovell, Julia, *The Opium War. Drugs, Dreams and the Making of China* (London: Picador, 2011).

Lubbock, Basil,*The Opium Clippers* (Glasgow: Brown & Son, 1953).

Luong, Hy V. (ed.), *Postwar Vietnam. Dynamics of a Transforming Society* (Singapore: Institute of Southeast Asian Studies, 2003).

Luijk, Eric van and Ours, Jan van, The effect of government policy on drug use: Java, 1875-1904, in: *The Journal of Economic History*, 61 (1995), p. 1-17.

Madancy, Joyce A., *The Troublesome Legacy of Commissioner Lin. The Opium Trade and Opium Suppression in Fujian Province, 1820s to 1920s* (Cambridge, Mass.: Harvard University Press, 2004).

Madsen, Axel, *John Jacob Astor: America's First Multimillionaire* (Chicester: John Wiley & Co, 2001).

Malekandathil, Pius, The Mercantile Networks and the International Trade of Cochin, 1500-1663, in: Veen, E. Van and Blussé, L. (ed.), p. 142-165.

Manders, Bert, *De ontdekking van Tin op het eiland Billiton* (Amsterdam: KIT Publishers, 2010).

Manurung, Risma, *Amphioen Sociëteit en Amphioen Directie. Inventaris van het archief van de Amphioensociëteit en Amphioendirectie te Batavia, 1745-1880* (ANRI: Jakarta, 2007).

Marcus, Abraham, *The Middle East on the Eve of Modernity* (New York: Columbia University Press, 1989).

Margana, Sri, The formation of a new frontier: the conquest of Java's Oosthoek by the VOC in 1768, in: Worden, N. (ed.), p. 184-207.

――, *Java's Last Frontier: The Struggle for Hegemony of Blambangan, c. 1763-1814* (Leiden: University Leiden, 2007).

Markovits, Claude, The Political Economy of Opium Smuggling in Early Nineteenth Century India: Leakage or Resistance, in: *Modern Asian Studies*, 43 (2009), p. 89-111.

Marshall, Jonathan, Opium and the Politics of Gangsterism in Nationalist China, 1927-1945, in: *Bulletin of Concerned Asian Scholars*, 8 (1976), p. 19-45.

Marshall, Peter J. (ed.), *The Oxford History of the British Empire* (Oxford: Oxford University Press, 1998), Vol. II, The Eighteenth Century.

Martin, Brian G., The Green Gang and the Guomindang State: Du Yuesheng and the Politics of Shanghai, 1927-37, in: *Journal of Asian Studies*, 54 (1995), p. 64-91.

――, *The Shanghai Green Gang. Politics and Organized Crime, 1919-1937* (Berkeley: University of California Press, 1996).

Matheson – Hooker, Virginia, *A Short History of Malaysia. Linking East and West* (Crows Nest, Australia: Allen&Unwin, 2003).

Maxwell Hill, Ann, *Merchants and Migrants. Ethnicity and Trade among Yunnanese Chinese in Southeast Asia* (New Haven, Con.: Yale University Southeast Asia Studies, 1998).

McCoy, Alfred W.; Read, Cathleen B. and Adams, Leonard P., *The politics of heroin in Southeast Asia* (New York: Harper&Row, 1972).

McCoy, Alfred W. (ed.), *Southeast Asia under Japanese Occupation* (New Haven: Yale University Southeast Asia Studies, 1980).

――, and Jesus, C. de (ed.), *Philippine Social History: Global Trade and Local Transformations* (Quezon City: Metro Manila, 1982).

――, and Block, Alan A. (ed.), *War on Drugs. Studies in the Failure of U.S. Narcotics Policy* (Boulder-Oxford: Westview Press, 1992).

――, Heroin as a Global Commodity: A History of Southeast Asia's Opium Trade, in: __, and Block, A. (ed.), p. 237- 279.

――, and Scarano, Francisco (ed.), *The Colonial Crucible. Empire in the Making of the Modern American State* (Madison: University of Wisconsin Press, 2009).

McMahon, Keith, *The Fall of the God of Money. Opium Smoking in Nineteenth-Century China* (Lanham, Maryland: Rowman, 2002).

McPherson, Kenneth, *The Indian Ocean. A History of People and the Sea* (New Delhi: Oxford University Press, 2004).

Medawar, Charles and Freese, Barbara, *Drug Diplomacy. Decoding the conduct of a multinational pharmaceutical company ...* (London: Social Audit, 1982).

Mehnert, Ute, *Deutschland, Amerika und die "gelbe Gefahr": zur Karriere eines Schlagworts in der grossen Politik, 1905-1917* (Stuttgart: Franz Steiner Verlag, 1995).

Meilink-Roelofsz, M.A., *Asian Trade and European Influence in the Indonesian Archipelago between 1500 and about 1630* (Den Haag: Nijhoff, 1962).

――, et al (Ed), *The Archives of the Dutch East India Company, 1602-1795* (The Hague: SDU, 1992).

Menghong, Chen, *De Chinese gemeenschap van Batavia, 1843-1865. Een onderzoek naar het Kong Koan Archief* (Leiden: University of Leiden, 2009; diss.).

Merlin, Mark David, *On the Trail of the Ancient Opium Poppy* (London: Associated University Press, 1984).

Meyer, David R., *Hong Kong as a Global Metropolis* (Cambridge: Cambridge University Press, 2000).

Michael, F. and Chang, Chung-li, *The Taiping Rebellion. History and documents* (Seattle: University of Washington Press, 1966-1971).

Miskel, James F., *British Reaction to the Opium Trade, 1839-1860* (Ann Arbor: University Microfilms International, 1979; original 1977).

Mori,Yoshizo, Evolution of Japan opium: empire and its successive invasions to China, Korea and the Southeastern Asias, in: *Bulletin of the Yamagata University. Social Science* (2005), p. 17-57 (in Japanese).

Moulton, Harold and Marlio, Louis, *The Control of Germany and Japan* (Washington: The Brookings Institution, 1944).

Mousnier, Roland, *Peasant Uprisings in Seventeenth-century France, Russia and China* (New York: Harper, 1972).

Munn, Christopher, *Anglo-China. Chinese People and British Rule in Hong Kong, 1841-1880* (Richmond: Curzon, 2001).

Murakami, Ei, The Collapse of the Trade Control System of the Qing Government. The opium trade before the Opium War. *Workshop on Chinese Economic History* (Yokohama National University: May 2009).

Murphy, Rhoads and Stapleton, Kirstin, *East Asia. A New History* (Boston: Longman, 2010).

Musto, David F., *The American Disease. Origins of Narcotic Control* (New York: Oxford University Press, 1987).

———, The History of Legislative Control over Opium, Cocaine, and their Derivatives, in: *www.druglibrary.org/schaffer/history/ophs.htm* (Jan 2010).

Nadri, Ghulam, The VOC's engagement with piracy in Western India in the 18th century: perceptions and the construction of social identities, in: Worden, N. (ed.), p.172-184.

Nankoe, Hakiem; Gerlus, Jean-Claude and Murray, Martin, The Origins of the Opium Trade and the Opium Regie in Colonial Indochina, in: Butcher, J. and Dick, H. (ed.), p. 182-196.

Napier, Priscilla, *Barbarian Eye. Lord Napier in China, 1834. The prelude to Hong Kong* (London: Brassy's, 1995).

Naquin, Susan and Rawski, Evelyn S., *Chinese Society in the Eighteenth Century* (New Haven: Yale University Press, 1987).

Narain, Brij and Sharma, Sri Ram (ed.), *A Contemporary Dutch Chronicle of Mughal India* (Calcutta: Susis Gupta, 1957).

Nederveen Pieterse, Jan, *Empire and Emancipation. Power and Liberation on a World Scale* (London: Pluto Press, 1989).

Newman, R.K., India and the Anglo-Chinese Opium Agreements, 1907-14, in: *Modern Asian Studies*, 23 (1989), p. 525-560.

———, Opium Smoking in Late Imperial China: A Reconsideration, in: *Modern Asian Studies*, 29 (1995), p. 765-794.

Niane, D. (ed.), *General History of Africa. Africa from the twelfth to the sixteenth century* (London: Heinemann, 1984), vol. 4.

Ogot, B. (ed.), *General History of Africa. Africa from the sixteenth to the eighteenth century* (London: Heinemann, 1992), vol. 5.

Os, Maurits van, *Batavia versus Singapore. De handelsrelatie tussen Nederlands-Indie en de Straits Settlements, 1820-1870* (ESG-PhD thesis, University of Amsterdam, 2002).

Ours, Jan van, The price elasticity of hard drugs; the case of opium in the Dutch East Indies (1923-1938), in: *Journal of Political Economy*, 103 (1995), p. 261-279.

Overy, Richard (ed.), *The Times Complete Historical Atlas of the World* (London: Times Books, 2007).

Padwa, Howard, National Security and Narcotics Control in France, 1907-1920, in: *Proceedings of the Western Society for French History*, 33 (2005), p. 340-351.

Pan, Lynn, *Sons of the Yellow Emperor. A history of the Chinese Diaspora* (Tokyo: Kodansha, 1994).

Paoli, Letizia; Greenfield, Victoria and Reuter, Peter, *The World Heroin Market. Can Supply Be Cut?* (Oxford: Oxford University Press, 2009).

Parmentier, Jan (ed.), *Noord-Zuid in Oost-Indisch perspectief* (Zutphen: Walburg pers, 2005).

Parthesius, Robert, *Dutch Ships in Tropical Waters. The Development of the Dutch East India Company (VOC) Shipping Network in Asia, 1595-1660* (Amsterdam: Amsterdam University Press, 2010).

Paulès. Xavier, Les fumeurs d'opium à Canton dans les années 1930, in: *Études chinoises*, xxiii (2004), p. 141- 180.

Paxton, Robert O., *Vichy France. Old Guard and the New Order, 1940-1944* (New York: Colombia University Press, 1982).

Peffer, Nathaniel, Far Eastern Problem, in: *Encyclopaedia of the Social Sciences* (New York: Macmillan, 1949), vol. 6, p. 92-100.

Perkins, Dwight H.; Wang, Yeh-Chien; Wang Hsiao, Kuo-Ying and Su,Yung-Ming, *Agricultural Development in China, 1368-1968* (Chicago: Aldine, 1969).

Phongpaichit, Pasuk and Piriyarangsan, Sungsidh, *Corruption and Democracy in Thailand* (Bangkok: Chulalongkorn University Press, 1994).

Poonen, T.I., *A Survey of the Rise of the Dutch Power in Malabar, 1603-1678* (Trichinopoly: Industrial Scholl Press, 1943).

Porter, Andrew (ed.), *The Oxford History of the British Empire* (Oxford: Oxford University Press, 1999), vol. 3, The Nineteenth Century.

Prakash, Om, *The Dutch East India Company and the economy of Bengal, 1630-1720* (Princeton, NJ: Princeton University Press, 1985).

————, European trade and the economy of Bengal in the seventeenth and early eighteenth century, in: Goor, J. van (ed.), p. 19-33.

————, Opium Monopoly in India and Indonesia in the Eighteenth Century, in: *Itinerario*, XII (1988), p. 73 -90.

————, The Mughal Empire and the Dutch East Indies Company in the seventeenth century, in: Locher-Scholten, Elsbeth and Rietbergen, Peter (ed.), p. 183-201.

————, Alternative Trading Strategies: The Dutch and the English East India Companies in Asia, 1600-1650, in: Parmentier, J. (ed.), p. 167-177.

————, Asian Merchants and the Portuguese Trade in Asia, in: Veen, E. van and Blussé, L.(ed.), p. 131-141.

Quincy, Keith, *Harvesting Pa Chay's Wheat. The Hmong & America's Secret War in Laos* (Washington: Eastern Washington University Press, 2000).

Randeraad, Nico (ed.), *Mediators between State and Society* (Hilversum: Verloren, 1998).

Rapin,Ami-Jacques, Notes sur la technique de la fumerie de l'opium, in: *www.sinoptic.ch/ceria/textes/Notes.fumerie_Rapin.pdf.*

Rashid, Ahmed, *Descent into Chaos. The world's most unstable region and the threat to global security* (London: Penguin Books, 2009).

Raychaudhuri, Tapan and Habib, Irfan (ed.), *The Cambridge Economic History of India* ((Hyderabad: Orient Longman Limited, 1984), vol. 1, c. 1200-c. 1750.

Recio, Gabriela, Drugs and Alcohol: US Prohibition and the Origins of the Drug Trade in Mexico, 1910-1930, in: *Journal Latin American Studies*, 34 (2002), p. 21-42.

Reid, Anthony, The Origins of Revenue Farming in Southeast Asia, in: Butcher, J. and Dick, H. (ed.), p. 69-80.

Reid, Daniel P., *Chinese Herbal Medicine* (Boston: Shambhala [Random House], 1987).

Remer, C.F. (ed.), *Readings in Economics for China. Selected Readings with explanatory introduction* (Shanghai: Commercial Press, 1933; reprint New York: Garland, 1980).

Remmelink, Willem, *Emperor Pakubuwana II, Priyayi & Company and the Chinese War* (Leiden: University of Leiden, 1990; diss.).

Renard, Ronald D., *Kariang. History of Karen-T'ai relations from the beginnings to 1923* (University of Hawaii: Ph.D dissertation, 1979).
———, *The Burmese Connection. Illegal Drugs & the Making of the Golden Triangle* (Boulder, Col.: Lynne Rienner, 1996).
———, *Opium Reduction in Thailand, 1970-2000. A thirty-years journey* (Bangkok: Silkworm Books, 2001).
Richards, David, *Sex, drugs, death and the law: an essay on human rights and over criminalization* (Lanham: Rowman & Littlefield, 1986).
Richards, John F., The Indian Empire and Peasant Production of Opium in the Nineteenth Century, in: *Modern Asian Studies*, 15 (1981), p. 59-82.
———, Changing Land Use in Bihar, Punjab and Haryana, 1850-1970, in: *Idem*, 19 (1985), p. 699-732.
———, Opium and the British Indian Empire: the Royal Commission of 1895, in: *Idem* 36 (2002-1), p. 375-420.
———, The Opium industry in British India, in: *The Indian Economic and Social History Review*, 39 (2002-2), p. 149-180.
Ricklefs, M. C., *A History of Modern Indonesia c. 1300 to the present* (London: Macmillan, 1981).
———, *War, Culture and Economy in Java, 1677-1726. Asian and European Imperialism in the Early Kartasura Period* (Sydney: Allen & Unwin, 1993).
Risse, Guenter B. (ed.), *Modern China and Traditional Chinese Medicine. A Symposium held at the University of Wisconsin* (Springfield, Ill.: Thomas, 1973).
Roberts, J.A.G., *The Complete History of China* (Chalford: Sutton, 2007).
Roelofsz, M. Antoinette, *De Vestiging der Nederlanders ter kuste Malabar* (Den Haag: Nijhoff, 1943).
Ross, Robert and Telkamp, Gerard (ed.), *Colonial Cities* (Dordrecht: Nijhoff, 1985).
Rush, James R., *Opium to Java. Revenue Farming and Chinese Enterprise in Colonial Indonesia, 1860-1910* (Ithaca: Cornell University Press, 1990).
Rushby, Kevin, *Paradise. A History of the Idea that rules the world* (London: Robinson, 2007).
Rutten, Alphons, *Dutch transatlantic medicine trade in the eighteenth century* (Rotterdam: Erasmus Publishing, 2000).
Saich, Tony and Ven, Hans van de (ed.), *New Perspectives on the Chinese Communist Revolution* (New York: Sharpe-Armonk, 1995).
Sangar, S. P., Intoxicants in Mughal India, in: *Indian Journal of History of Science* 16 (1981), p. 202-214.
Santen, Hans W. van, *De Verenigde Oostindische Compagnie in Gujarat en Hindustan, 1620-1660* (Meppel: Krips, 1982).
Schipper, Hans, *Macht in de Zeventiende Eeuw. Engeland en Nederland kwantitatief vergeleken* (Zutphen: Walburg pers, 2001).
Schmidt, Jan, *From Anatolia to Indonesia. Opium Trade and the Dutch community of Izmir, 1820-1940* (Istanbul: Ned. Hist.-Archaeol. Institute, 1998).
Schramm, Stuart R. (ed.), *Mao's road to power. Revolutionary Writings, 1912-1949* (New York: Sharpe-Armonk, 1992-2005), 7 vol.
Schulte Nordholt, H., *The Spell of Power. A History of Balinese Politics, 1650-1940* (Leiden: KITLV Press, 1996).
Schweinitz Jr., Karl de, *The Rise and Fall of British India. Imperialism as Inequality* (London: Methuen, 1983).
Scott, J. M., *The White Poppy. A History of Opium* (London: Heinemann, 1969).
Shahnavaz, S., Afyūn, in: *Encyclopaedia Iranica* (www.iranica.com).
Sheridan, James E., *Chinese Warlord. The Career of Feng Yü-hsiang* (Stanford, Cal.: Stanford University Press, 1966).
Shih, Vincent Y., *The Taiping Ideology. Its sources, interpretations and influences* (Seattle/London: University of Washington Press, 1972).

Shipway, Martin, *Decolonization and its Impact. A Comparative Approach to the End of the Colonial Empire* (Oxford: Blackwell, 2008).

Shiraishi, Takashi, *An Age in Motion. Popular Radicalism in Java, 1912-1926* (Ithaca: Cornell University Press, 1990).

Shuyun, Sun, *The Long March* (London: Harper Perennial, 2007).

Siddiqi, Asiya (ed.), *Trade and Finance in Colonial India, 1750-1860* (Delhi: Oxford University Press, 1995).

———, The Business World of Jamsetjee Jejeebhoy, in: Idem (ed.), p. 186-218.

Sinn, Elizabeth, Preparing Opium for America: Hong Kong and Cultural Consumption in the Chinese Diaspora, in: *Journal of Chinese Overseas*, 1 (2005), p. 16-42.

Siraisi, Nancy G., *Medicine and the Italian Universities, 1250-1600* (Leiden: Brill, 2001).

Snapper, I., *Chinese Lessons to Western Medicine. A Contribution to Geographical Medicine from the Clinics of Peiping Union Medical College* (New York: Interscience Publishers, 1941).

Snow, Philip, *The Fall of Hong Kong. Britain, China and the Japanese Occupation* (New Haven: Yale University Press, 2003).

Somers, Jan A., *Nederlandsch-Indië. Staatkundige ontwikkelingen binnen een koloniale relatie* (Zutphen: Walburg Pers, 2005).

Souza, George B., The Portuguese Merchant Fleet at Macao in the Seventeenth and Eighteenth Centuries, in: E. van Veen, L. Blussé (ed.), p. 342-369.

———, Opium and the Company: Maritime Trade and Imperial Finances on Java, 1684-1796, in: *Modern Asian Studies*, 43 (2009- 1), p. 113-133.

———, An Anatomy of Commerce and Consumption: Opium and Merchants at Batavia over the Long Eighteenth Century, in: *Chinese Southern Diaspora Studies*, 3 (2009-2), p. 61-87.

Spence, Jonathan D., *The Search for Modern China* (New York: Norton, 1990).

———, *The Chan's Great Continent. China in Western Minds* (London: Allen Lane, 1998).

———, Chiang's Monster, in: *New York Review of Books*, 25-03-2004, p. 29- 31.

Starkey, David J. and Hahn-Pedersen, Morten (ed.), *Bridging Troubled Waters. Conflict and Co-operation in the North Sea Region since 1550* (Esbjerg: Fiskeri-og Søfartsmuseets Forlag, 2005).

Stevens, Harm, *Dutch Enterprise and the VOC, 1602-1799* (Amsterdam: Rijksmuseum, 1998).

Stuart-Fox, Martin, *Buddhist Kingdom, Marxist State. The Making of Modern Laos* (Bangkok: White Lotus Co, 1996).

Subrahmanyam, Sanjay, State Formation and Transformation in Early Modern India and Southeast Asia, in: *Itinerario*, XII (1988), p. 91-109.

———, *The Portuguese Empire in Asia, 1500-1700: A Political and Economic History* (London: Longman, 1993).

———, *Explorations in Connected History. From the Tagus to the Ganges* (Oxford: Oxford University Press, 2005).

Talens, Johan, *Een feodale samenleving in koloniaal vaarwater. Staatsvorming, koloniale expansie en ecconomische onderontwikkeling in Banten, West-Java 1600-1750* (Hilversum: Verloren, 1999).

Tarling, Nicholas (ed.), *The Cambridge History of Southeast Asia* (Cambridge: Cambridge University Press, 1999), Vol. 2-1 (1800-1930s), Vol. 2-2 (1940s-present).

Taylor, Jay, *The Generalissimo. Chiang Kai-Shek and the Struggle for Modern China* (Cambridge, Mass.: Harvard University Press, 2009).

Terpstra, H., *De Nederlanders in Voor-Indie* (Amsterdam: Van Kampen, 1947).

Topik, Steven; Marichal, Carlos and Frank, Zephyr (ed.), *From Silver to Cocaine. Latin American Commodity and the Building of the World Economy, 1500-2000* (Durham: Duke University Press, 2006).

Touwen, Jeroen, *Extremes in the archipelago. Trade and economic development in the Outer Islands of Indonesia, 1900-1942* (Leiden: University thesis, 1997).

Tracy, Sarah W. and Acker, Caroline J. (ed.), *Altering American Consciousness. The History of Alcohol and Drug Use in the United States, 1800-2000* (Amherst/ Boston: University of Massachusetts Press, 2004).

Transnational Institute, *Drugs & Conflict, TNI-Briefing Series* (Amsterdam: TNI, 2001-present).

Tripathi, Amales, Indo-British Trade between 1833 and 1847 and the Commercial Crisis of 1847-8, in: Siddiqi, A. (ed.), p. 265-289.

Trocki, Carl A., *Opium and Empire. Chinese Society in Colonial Singapore, 1800-1910* (Ithaca: Cornell University Press, 1990).

———, The Collapse of Singapore's Great Syndicate, in: Butcher, J. and Dick, H. (ed.), p. 166-182 (1993).

———, (ed.), *Gangsters, Democracy, and the State in Southeast Asia* (Ithaca, New York: Cornell University, SEAP, 1998).

———, *Opium, Empire and the Global Economy. A Study of the Asian opium trade, 1750-1950* (London: Routledge, 1999a).

———, Political Structures in the Nineteenth and Early Twentieth Centuries, in: Tarling, N. (ed.), vol. 2-1, p. 75-127 (1999b).

———, *Chinese Capitalism and the British Empire.* Paper presented to the International Association of Historians of Asia; Taipei, December 2004.

———, Chinese Revenue Farms and Borders in Southeast Asia, in: http://eprints.qut.edu.au/10605/ from 2006.

Truong, Buu Lam, *Colonialism Experienced. Vietnamese Writings on Colonialism, 1900-1931* (Ann Arbor: The University of Michigan Press, 2000).

Tsiu-Sen, Lin, *China und Japan im Spiegel der Geschichte. Eine Betrachtung anhand des Werdeganges Chinas und Japans* (Erlenbach-Zürich: Rentsch Verlag, 1944-1946).

Turnbull, C. M., *A History of Singapore, 1819-1988* (Singapore: Oxford University Press, 1996).

Twitchett, Denis and Fairbank, John (ed.), *The Cambridge History of China* (Cambridge University Press: Cambridge, 1980), vol. 11.

UNODC (United Nations Office on Drugs and Crime), *Opium Poppy Cultivation in South-East Asia. Lao PDR, Myanmar* (December 2009).

———, *Thirty-third Meeting of Heads of National Drug Law Enforcement Agencies, Asia and the Pacific* (Denpasar, Indonesia, 6-9 October 2009).

Uragoda,C., History of Opium in Sri Lanka, in: *Medical History, 27* (1983), p. 69-76.

Vandenbosch, Amry, *The Dutch East Indies. Its Government, Problems and Politics* (Berkeley: University of California Press, 1941).

Vandewiele, Lode, Over het Artikel XIV van de "Ordonnantien ende Statuten der Stadt Ghendt ...", in: *Bulletin Cercle Benelux d'Histoire de la Pharmacie,* no. 3, 1952, p. 11-19.

Vanvugt, Ewald, *Wettig Opium. 350 Jaar Nederlandse Opiumhandel in de Indische Archipel* (Amsterdam: Onze Tijd, 1985; 1995 second edition without appendices) with a preface by Wim F. Wertheim.

———, *Het dubbele gezicht van de koloniaal* (Haarlem: Knipscheer, 1988).

———, *De schatten van Lombok. Honderd jaar Nederlandse oorlogsbuit uit Indonesië* (Amsterdam: Mets, 1995-2).

Veen, Ernst van and Blussé, Leonard (ed.), *Rivalry and Conflict. European Traders and Asian Trading Networks in the 16th and 17th Centuries* (Leiden: CNWS Publications, 2005).

Vickers,Adrian, *Bali-a paradise created* (Penguin, 1989; Dutch transl. Nieuwegein: Signature, 1997).

Villiers,John, Trade and Society in the Banda Islands in the Sixteenth Century, in: *Modern Asian Studies,* 15 (1981), p. 723-750.

Völger, Gisela and Welck, Karin von (ed.), *Rausch und Realität. Drogen im Kulturvergleich* (Reinbek b.H.: Rowohlt, 1982), 3 vol.

Vos, Reinout, *Gentle Janus, Merchant Prince. The VOC and the tightrope of diplomacy in the Malay world, 1740-1800* (Leiden: KITLV Press, 1993).

Vries, Jan de and Woude, Ad van der, *Nederland 1500-1815. De eerste ronde van moderne economische groei* (Amsterdam: Balans, 1995).

Vries, Jan de, *The Industrious Revolution. Consumer behavior and the household economy, 1650 to the present* (Cambridge: Cambridge University Press, 2008).

Wakabayashi, Bob T., "Imperial Japanese" Drug Trafficking in China: Historiographic Perspectives, in: *Sino-Japanese Studies*, 13 (2000), p. 3 – 20.

Wakeman Jr., Frederic, *Policing Shanghai 1927-1937* (Berkeley: University of California Press, 1995).

Walker, Timothy D., *Doctors, Folk Medicine and the Inquisition. The Repression of Magical Healing in Portugal during the Enlightenment* (Leiden: Brill, 2005).

Walker III, William O., *Opium and Foreign Policy. The Anglo-American Search for Order in Asia, 1912-1954* (Chapel Hill: The University of North Carolina Press, 1991).

Ward, Kerry, *Networks of Empire. Forced Migration in the Dutch East India Company* (Cambridge: Cambridge University Press, 2009).

Watson – Andaya, Barbara and Andaya, Leonard, *A History of Malaysia* (London: Macmillan, 1982).

Weber, Max, *Gesammelte Aufsätze zur Religionssoziologie* (Tübingen: Mohr, 1920), 3 vol.

Wertheim, Wim, *Evolutie en Revolutie. De golfslag der emancipatie* (Amsterdam: Van Gennep, 1972).

———, De integratie van stad en platteland in China, in: Bruijne, G.A. De (ed.), p. 104-112.

Westermeyer, Joseph, Opium Smoking in Laos: A Survey of 40 Addicts, in: *American Journal of Psychiatry*, 131 (1974), p. 165-170.

Westwood, J. N., *Endurance and Endeavour. Russian History, 1812-1980* (Oxford: Oxford University Press, 1981).

Wickeren, Arnold van, *Geschiedenis van Portugal en van de Portugezen overzee*, in: www.colonialvoyage. com.

Willmott, Donald E., *The Chinese of Semarang: A Changing Minority Community in Indonesia* (Ithaca: Cornell University Press, 1960).

Wills, jr., John E., *Pepper, Guns and Parleys. The Dutch East India Company and China, 1622-1681* (Cambridge, Mss.: Harvard University Press, 1974).

Winks, Robin W. and Low, Alaine (ed.), *The Oxford History of the British Empire* (Oxford: Oxford University Press, 1999), vol. 5. Historiography.

Woodcock, George, *The British in the Far East* (London: Weidenfeld & Nicolson, 1969).

Worden, Nigel (ed.), *Contingent lives. Social identity and material culture in the VOC world* (Cape Town: University of Cape Town, 2007).

Yawnghwe, Chao T., *The Shan of Burma. Memoirs of a Shan Exile* (Singapore: Institute of Southeast Asian Studies, 1987).

Yoshida, Reiji (1) Japan profited as opium dealer in wartime China; (2) Opium King's ties believed went to the top; (3) Japan followed West by drug-peddling in China; (4) Narcotics trade boosted army scrip, in: *The Japan Times*, 30 August 2007 (http://search.japantimes.co.).

Yung-Fa, Chen, The Blooming Poppy under the Red Sun: The Yan'an Way and the Opium Trade, in: Saich, T. and Ven, H.van de (ed.), p. 263-299.

Yu-Wen, Jen, A Further Note on Feng Yun-Shan and Gutzlaff, in: *Journal of the Royal Asiatic Society Hong Kong Branch*, 17 (1977), p. 228-231.

Zanden, Jan L. van, Over de rationaliteit van het ondernemingsgedrag van de VOC: enkele empirische bevindingen, in: Davids, C. A. a.o. (ed.), p. 409-423.

——— and Riel, Arthur van, *Nederland 1780-1914. Staat, instituties en economische ontwikkeling* (Amsterdam: Balans, 2000).

Zeldin, Theodore, *France 1848-1945* (Oxford: Oxford University Press, 1977), 2 vol.

INDEX

Aceh (*see* Indonesia)

acupuncture (see Chinese medicine)

Adams, John Q. (*see* USA)

Addiction xii, xv, xvii, 5n5, 7n10, 28n21, 36n4, 73, 87, 106, 114, 157, 183, 188, 233, 235, 309, 317, 325, 328, 335, 338, 357, 390, 391, 393, 407, 425, 426, 432, 440, 453, 472, 486, 497, 510, 512, 516, 518, 551,557, 569, 573, 575, 578, 579n, 581, 582, 583, 594, 595, 598, 609, 621, 634, 643, 648, 650, 651, 652, 653n23, 657, 669, 672, 674, 704, 709, 715, 723, 726, 727, 735

Aden (*see* Middle East)

Afghanistan (*see* Middle East)

African continent 5, 36, 97, 120, 136n4, 141, 145, 189, 216, 223, 264, 375, 393, 395, 416, 458, 469, 533, 561, 597, 639n23, 702, 717 (*see also* East Africa, South Africa)

afyūn (*see* Opium)

Agra (*see* India)

Akbar (*see* India)

Alatas, Syed H. 44n23, 55n18, 56n19, 74n61, 262n13, 263n17, 278n1

Albuquerque, Alfonso de (*see* Portuguese Empire)

alcohol 19, 30, 155n47, 184n33, 197, 303, 357, 386n9, 389, 390, 400, 402, 410n28, 415, 439, 446, 507, 535, 536n9, 537, 555, 571, 572, 583, 621, 738

alkaloids 570

Allahabad (*see* India)

Amangkurat II (*see* Indonesia)

Ambon (*see* Indonesia)

Amboyna Massacre 222, 240

America, North xi, xiii, 5, 78, 130, 310, 311, 315, 343n47, 375, 383, 387, 467, 534n5, 563, 622, 717 (*see also* Chinese – American relations, *see also* United States of America, USA)

  American Revolution 54, 61, 279, 533

  Boston 61, 534, 542

  Boston Tea Party 61

  Canada 97, 548-551, 573, 665

amfio(e)n (*see* Opium; *see also* Dutch Empire)

amphioen (*see* Opium; *see also* Dutch Empire)

Amphioen Society (*see* Opium, dealers; *see also* Dutch Empire)

Amsterdam (*see* Europe)

anaesthetic 24

Anatolia (see Middle East)

Anglo-Saxon (see British Empire)

Annam (*see* Southeast Asia)

Anslinger, Harry (*see* USA)

annexation 498, 564

anthropology xi, 643, 683n97

anti-British actions, etc. 559, 635

anti-Chinese actions, etc. 118, 259, 460n4, 468n12, 477, 487, 497, 512, 545n26, 546n27, 547n28, 554, 597, 619, 621n68, 622, 706

anti-Communist actions, etc. 126, 446, 487, 698, 706

anti-Dutch actions etc. 332, 375

anti-foreigners actions, etc. 575, 615, 635

anti-German actions etc. 393

anti-Japanese actions, etc. 513, 514, 621n68, 622, 637, 665

anti-opium

  lobby xv, 14n10, 37, 90, 117, 129n10, 340, 370, 392, 421, 441, 461, 514, 564n61, 569, 572, 605, 613, 629, 635, 637, 665, 679, 722, 746

  medicine 344, 535n9, 580n94, 649, 651, 700

  Philippine Opium Commission 493, 540, 566, 575

  policy 66, 90, 289, 292, 321, 329, 340, 363, 441, 443, 481, 495, 497, 512, 515, 517, 552, 603, 638, 646, 654-656n29, 676, 687, 696, 731 (*see also* law)

  societies 46, 118, 126n7, 344, 388n13, 515, 649n12, 671

  Society for the Suppression of the Opium Trade (SSOT) (*see* Europe, England)

anti-urban actions, etc. 695

anti-Western actions, etc. 183, 486, 599, 646, 647

antiquity xii, 8, 13, 21-23, 192, 716

antisemitism 46, 93, 124, 392, 402, 471, 546n27, 619, 620n64

anti-slavery policy 117, 290, 292, 321, 329

Antwerp (*see* Europe, Belgium)

aphrodisiac 21n7, 26, 31, 188, 199, 379, 386, 386n8, 648n9

apothecary 110, 192, 535

Arabian Sea (*see* Middle East)

Arab medical knowledge (*see* medical doctors)

Arabs (*see* Middle East)

Arakan (*see* Southeast Asia)

archipelago (see Indonesia)

areca nuts 158

aristocracy 125, 193, 220

Aristotle 6

Armenia (*see* Middle East)

Asian continent xvii, 4, 5, 16, 45, 47, 51, 53, 61, 70n49, 73, 74, 89, 121, 124, 130, 153, 208, 212, 283, 284n16, 291, 401, 403, 414, 421, 450, 456, 468, 512, 519, 533n3, 561, 628, 682, 714, 717, 730 (s*ee also* East Asia; Southeast Asia)

assault xii, xiii, xv, xvii, 6, 16, 32, 43, 47, 49, 61n31, 85, 94, 146n28, 153, 154, 190, 215, 215n49, 278, 282, 375, 381, 390, 393, 397, 418, 444, 464, 496, 500, 503, 511, 514, 530, 553, 558, 559, 575, 599, 602, 603, 608n31, 609, 613, 615, 622, 624, 635, 639, 639n23, 641, 644, 682, 684, 685, 693, 713, 720, 730 (*see also* foreign policy)

Association of Coca Producers 317

Astor, John J. (*see* Opium, dealers)

asylum 389, 390

atropine 388, 650n16

Aung San, president (*see* Southeast Asia)

Aurangzeb, emperor (*see* India)

Australia (*see* British Empire)

Avery, Martha 20

Ayurveda (*see* India)

Bache, Franklin 535, 548, 549n32, 569, 577

backwardness 613, 651

balance of power 282, 455

balance of trade 16, 47, 48, 73, 85n91, 98, 99, 100, 122, 292, 501, 635n16

Balfour, Arthur J. (see British Empire)

Balfour, Edward 79n76, 81n83, 82n86, 88n, 98n, 441, 672, 674, 736, 737, 739, 742, 751

Bali (see Indonesia)

Banda (see Indonesia)

Bangka (Banca) (see Indonesia)

banditry 126, 443, 670

banking 72, 73, 75, 313n24, 403, 478, 638, 688, 689, 689n108

Bantam (see Indonesia)

Barbosa, Duarte (*see* Portuguese Empire)

Barings bank (*see* British Empire)

Bastin, John 56n19, 287n25, 289n27, 291n, 763

Batavia (see Dutch Empire)

Baud, Jean Chr. (see Dutch Empire)

Baudelaire, Charles 385, 386, 387n10

Bayer industry 387, 393, 578, 579, 599, 725

Bechtinger, Jos 501

Beeching, Jack 5, 42n, 43n21, 53n9, 67, 68n43, 70n50, 71n53, 105, 189, 545n25, 593n1, 604n20

Behar (*see* India)

Beijing (*see* China)

Belgium (*see* Europe)

Benares (*see* India)

Bencoolen (see Dutch Empire)

Bengal merchants (*see* India)

Bengal opium (*see* Opium, production)

beriberi 299, 299n12

Bernier, François 180, 186

Berridge, Virginia 105-107n4, 112, 113, 115, 117, 127n8, 137n8, 194n12, 388n15, 389n17, 605n21

Be-Tan group (*see* Indonesia; Opium, dealers)

betel nut 59, 157, 158

Billiton (*see* Dutch Empire)

Billiton Mining Company (*see* Dutch Empire)

Bishop Brent 493, 493n2, 566, 575

blaming the victims 14, 43, 353, 422, 464, 566, 593, 595, 596, 604, 607n29, 609, 610, 619, 676n82, 681, 704

Blussé, Leonhard 36n4, 242n4, 242n6-243n7, 244, 250n17, 255n1, 256n3, 258n4, 259n8, 265n19-268, 542n16, 639n24

Bodawpaya, king (see Indonesia)

bohemian salons 386

Bombay (*see* India)

Borneo (*see* Indonesia)

Bosshardt, Rudolf 617

Boston; *Boston Tea Party* (*see* America, North)

botany 22

Boxer, C.R. 5, 146n27, 150n31, 208n41, 217n54, 242n6, 243n9, 245, 258n6, 260n11

Boxer Rising (*see* China)

Braudel, Fernand 5n7

Brazil 130, 152, 271

Brendon, Piers 3n4, 12n4,13n6, 35n1, 51n4, 75n63, 456n78, 697n127

Brereton, William (*see* British Empire)

bribes 39n111, 69, 172, 174, 181, 274, 357, 442n49, 458, 461, 479, 481, 482, 482n34, 686, 727

British Empire 4, 5n7, 8n12, 36, 37, 44, 48, 49, 52, 67, 73, 81, 89, 92, 105, 121, 123, 126, 129, 130, 172, 250, 255, 282, 283, 315, 378, 395, 428, 455, 456, 464, 464n7, 482, 494, 512, 533n3, 559, 604n20, 624, 629, 720, 721 (*see also* Asian continent, assault; Europe, England)

Anglo-Saxon 20, 383, 384, 639

Anglo-Saxon race 620n64, 623, 624

Australia xiiin, 44, 216, 223, 467, 482n34, 597, 599, 619, 621, 625, 652n18

Balfour, Arthur J. 630

Barings bank 76

Brereton, William 81, 117, 672, 673

British East India Company (EIC) 12n4, 16, 38-40, 46, 49, 52-55, 57, 57n21, 58-61, 65, 66, 69n45, 78, 79, 79n78, 83, 88, 89, 92-94, 96, 172-174, 176n16, 195, 207, 213, 222, 245, 253, 278, 281-283, 291, 295, 311, 362, 376, 397, 441, 448, 506, 606, 607, 610, 654n24, 672, 693, 739, 741, 743, 748

British India 5n6, 35, 55, 90n5, 91, 98, 99, 101, 102, 119, 121, 556, 669, 737, 741 (*see also* India)

British Navy 71, 93, 99, 685, 693

British Opium Policy 35, 122

Churchill, Winston 130, 131, 131n12

'Closed Door' policy 6, 54, 59, 172, 410, 500, 528, 542, 759

Crawfurd, John 50, 51, 51n4, 54n14, 55, 77, 80, 277, 282, 289, 402, 451, 682

East India Company (*see* British East India Company)

embassy of 1793 8, 9, 13, 14, 60n29

embassy of 1787 60, 60n29

Farquhar, major (*see* Opium, dealers)

Kenya 16n13, 120

Kipling, Rudyard 599, 719, 738, 738n2

Lyall, Alfred 8n12, 410n28

Macartney (*see* embassy)

Macaulay, Thomas B. 12, 13

Morgan, J.P. bank 75

Napier, Lord (and Priscilla) 42, 43, 543, 607

Newbold, Thomas John 448, 449n63, 449n64, 460, 460n4, 461

Old China Trade 53n9, 540, 541

'Open Door' policy 463, 559

Palmerston (Temple, H. J) 42, 599, 603

Plassey, battle of 172, 173, 177, 244, 448

Pottinger, Henry 603, 604, 604n19

Raffles, Thomas S. 44, 45, 50, 55, 55n18, 56n19, 59, 74n61, 234, 261-263n17, 264n18, 265n19, 276, 277, 278n1, 282, 285, 287, 289-291, 292, 292n32, 296, 315, 321, 329, 379, 397, 448, 451, 461, 470, 471, 682, 759, 761, 763, 764

Rothschild bank 75, 76, 93, 124, 495

Sarawak 103, 448

Scott, James 439, 440

Swettenham, Frank 453, 454, 464n7

Victoria(n), (queen) xii, 13, 48, 84, 105, 105n2, 106, 117, 124, 444

'White Man's Burden' xiv, 455, 468, 539, 561n55

Broecke, Pieter van den (*see* Opium, dealers; *see also* Dutch Empire)

brothel 46, 341, 411, 412, 631 (*see also* prostitution)

Buchalter, Louis L. (*see* Opium, dealers; *see also* Jewish gang)

Buddhism (*see* India)

Bugis (*see* Indonesia)

Buleleng (*see* Indonesia)

bullion 53, 55, 61, 88, 100, 174, 190, 202, 311, 540, 541, 719, 748

Burke, Edmund 12, 12n4, 59

Burma (*see* Southeast Asia)

bureaucracy 85, 123, 279, 289, 312, 313n24, 317, 319, 323, 333, 335, 343, 351, 461, 528, 559, 594, 605, 639, 662, 673n73, 724, 725

bureaucrats 7, 40, 44, 45, 74, 98, 114, 206, 230n76, 240, 246, 247n14, 277, 282, 298, 299, 301, 308, 325, 335, 336, 338, 340, 341, 351n66, 352, 361, 363, 365, 370, 374, 387, 391, 401, 404, 405, 425, 431, 495, 525, 553n41, 555, 612, 656n29, 665, 687, 722-724, 727

Bureau of Social Hygiene, Inc. 574

Cabral, Pedro Alvarez (*see* Portuguese Empire)
Cairo (*see* Middle East)
calamities 663
Calcutta (*see* India)
Calicut (*see* India)
Calvinism xiiin, 19, 151-153, 153n41, 158, 201, 206, 223, 227, 233, 349, 353, 376, 470, 481, 532, 533, 561, 619n62
Cambodia (*see* Southeast Asia)
Canada (*see* America, North)
cannabis 389, 390, 439, 441, 557, 572
Cannanur (*see* India)
cannibalism 263n17, 663
Canton (Guangzhou) (*see* China)
Cantú, Esteban 581
Cape of Good Hope xiiin, xiv, 52n8, 204, 216, 244, 257, 284n16, 453, 759
capitalism 75, 125, 172, 308, 589, 682
capsules 337, 569, 572n77, 648
caravan routes 31, 441, 468, 489, 490, 601, 668, 670, 671, 671n66, 696, 702
cartazes (*see* Portuguese Empire)
cash (money) 29, 53, 64, 83, 122, 169, 235, 239, 246, 274, 298, 313n24, 352, 582, 657, 661, 711, 712, 717, 718
cash crop 29, 101, 377, 427, 432, 438, 557, 660, 662, 715
casino 412, 422
Cathay (*see* China)
Cathcart embassy (*see* British Empire, embassy)
Catholicism 7, 19, 26, 38, 39, 125, 141, 152, 153n41, 193, 206-208, 212, 353, 376, 397, 398, 474, 562, 615, 619
Celebes (*see* Indonesia)
Central Intelligence Agency (CIA) 387n10, 424, 428, 436, 437, 442, 456, 457, 478, 487, 488, 490, 702-704, 716, 729, 731, 732
Ceylon (Sri Lanka) 89, 95, 103, 136, 150n31, 151, 159, 164, 166, 168, 169, 175, 175n12, 177, 208n41, 216, 257, 278, 469, 745, 746, 748, 765
Chandra, Siddharth 369n21
Chapman, Stanley 73n60, 75, 76n69, 684n99
chastity 200
Chatterjee, Kumkum 172n4, 173, 179
Chaudhuri, B. 87, 98, 101n31
Chaudhuri, K.N. 38n6, 99n23, 100n27, 102n33, 141n20, 153n40, 171, 172, 182, 182n30

chemists 59, 365, 388, 394n28, 413, 557, 649, 650, 725n9
chemistry xi, xv, 21n7, 120, 725
Cheribon (*see* Indonesia)
Chiang Kai-shek (*see* China)
Chihli (*see* China)
Chimin Wong, K. 72n55, 630n7, 645, 645n3, 647, 647n7, 648, 691
China 6, 7n10, 22, 31, 72, 75, 77-79, 82, 83, 85-87, 98, 105, 109, 119, 123, 126, 207, 229, 273, 303, 414, 417, 422, 423, 434, 439, 449, 463, 467, 478, 487, 496, 513, 530, 537, 542, 545, 590, 599, 603, 607, 610, 618, 627, 629, 633, 634, 639, 641, 643, 653n23, 672, 679, 682, 695, 711, 721, 731 (*see also* Asian continent, assault)
  Beijing 13, 70n49, 520, 605, 650, 653n23, 707n150 (*see also* Peking)
  Boxer Rising 547, 606, 615, 622n71, 645
  Canton (Guangzhou) 12, 15, 69, 265n19, 333, 412, 460, 463, 464, 467, 542, 547, 602, 606, 633, 638, 639, 641, 648, 662, 667, 675, 676, 678-680, 685-687, 690, 696, 735, 740, 742, 743, 748, 750
  Cathay 143, 439, 486
  Chiang Kai-shek 126, 413, 489, 516, 525, 551, 552, 553n41, 608n33, 640n26, 641, 665, 692n117, 694-696, 699, 701, 701n132
  Chihli 658, 696
  China, banks in 73, 75, 76, 80, 123, 403, 647, 684, 688, 689n108 (*see also* Dent, Jardine, Matheson, Sassoon)
  China, North 91, 511n40, 514, 516, 517, 519, 524, 637, 660, 665, 751
  chinatown 544, 545, 549n31, 556
  Chinese – American relations 397, 481, 482n34, 515, 518, 537, 540, 541, 545, 552, 553, 566, 570, 584, 590n5, 614, 623, 637, 638, 640n26, 649, 665, 676, 684, 692, 701, 702
  Chinese – Dutch relations 228, 229, 255, 261, 265n20, 286, 291, 301n15, 314, 317, 346, 499, 628n3
  Chinese Exclusion Act (*1882*) 545
  Chinese – French relations 436, 437 (*see also* French concesssion)
  Chinese – German relations 615-617, 625

Chinese hate 20n1, 117, 118, 256, 259, 263, 545, 546n27, 556, 596, 597, 620-622, 622n71, 625

Chinese – Indian relations 87, 88, 93, 94, 99, 103, 228, 278, 321, 357, 448, 672, 673, 680, 688, 735, 742-745, 746, 748

Chinese – Indonesian relations 265, 372, 449, 460, 467, 469, 471, 472, 474, 476, 483

Chinese – Japanese relations 493, 494, 496, 497, 510, 511-513, 516, 517, 520, 522, 561, 638, 692, 719

Chinese junks 228, 261, 274, 468, 469, 470

Chinese law 11, 12, 43, 60, 66, 67, 481-483, 628, 654-656 (*see also* law)

Chinese Massacre (1740) 216, 221, 226, 256

Chinese medicine (*see* herbs, medical doctors)

Chinese migrants 332, 459, 460, 463, 474, 475, 477, 545n26 (*see also* Chinese, coolie; Chinese, 'Overseas'; immigrant, immigration)

Chinese nationalism 85, 459

Chinese opium (*see* Opium, Chinese)

Chinese, "Overseas" (*see* Southeast Asia, "Overseas")

Chinese poppy (see poppy, Chinese)

Chinese – Portuguese relations 96, 97, 136, 145, 146, 150n31, 159, 273

Chinese Republic 73, 414, 514n46, 551, 657, 694, 697 (*see also* Kuomintang, warlords)

Chongzhi, Xu 525 (*see also* warlords)

Communist China 437, 475, 477, 478, 487, 488, 641, 646, 701, 703, 704

Communist Party 126, 415, 423, 429, 446, 526, 543, 598, 615, 647, 666, 698, 699, 705

Confucianism, 13, 15, 70, 70n49, 398, 482, 483, 572, 625

coolie xiv, 96n20, 97, 261, 264, 300, 328, 328n12-330, 414, 463, 464, 466, 472, 514, 533, 553n43, 625, 678, 679, 681, 684n98, 690 (*see also* Chinese migrants)

Dai Li 699, 706, 707

Du Yuesheng (*see* Opium, dealers)

Formosa 176, 235, 273, 374, 395, 434, 493, 495, 498-500, 501, 501n22-502n24, 503, 505, 505n27-507, 509, 513, 513n45, 520,

530n78, 567, 648 (*see also* Japanese Empire, Taiwan)

Fu(o)kien 459, 460, 500, 513, 602, 655, 658, 696

Hong Kong (*see* China) 9, 36, 43, 48, 66-68, 71-74, 75, 89, 91, 97, 102, 103, 372, 406, 434, 442, 450, 473, 484, 487, 488, 501, 521-524, 543-545, 547, 549n31, 567, 589, 631, 638, 641, 676, 680, 680n90, 682, 685-688, 692, 702, 703, 746, 747 (*see also* Japanese Empire)

Imperial Decree (government) 43, 68, 117, 119, 123, 131n12, 140, 186, 297n19, 375, 493, 529, 543, 630, 654, 680, 687, 694, 695

International Settlement 89, 411-413, 553, 620n64, 631, 637, 638, 654, 687, 690, 692, 695, 750, 751

Kansu 629, 656, 660, 664, 667, 674n78, 697

Kitchen God 601

kongsi 296, 299n12, 301, 359, 359n6, 452, 464, 464n9, 465, 466, 478, 698

kotow 9, 14

Koxinga 490, 500 (*see also* Formosa)

Kuomintang (KMT) 489, 490, 517, 647n7, 693-695

Kwantung Leased Territory 510

Kweichow 658, 660, 665, 667, 669, 696

Long March 617, 705n143, 707

Manchukuo 510, 517, 518, 520, 522, 677, 677n87

Manchuria 68, 69, 494, 509, 512, 513, 517, 518, 520, 521, 637, 658, 664, 696, 751

Mao Zedong 85, 415, 481, 641, 666, 694, 701

Mengjiang 519, 520

Ming dynasty 229

Mukden 511

Nanking (Massacre) 66, 516-518, 645, 655, 665

'Overseas' Chinese (*see* Southeast Asia)

Peking 15, 85, 333, 510, 515, 604n20, 630-632, 637, 649n12, 687, 696 (*see also* Beijing)

Peoples Republic of China 702, 703

Port Arthur 494, 630n6

Qianlong, emperor 35

Quing rule 6, 13

Red Army 617, 647, 699, 705n143, 706n147, 707

Red Gang (*see* Opium, dealers)
Revolution of 1911-12 xvii, 73, 82, 91, 551, 632, 638, 645n3, 654, 694
Shanghai 67, 72, 73, 75, 76, 80, 81, 93, 357, 372, 385, 411, 413, 517, 518, 520, 554, 556, 557, 575, 584, 629, 632, 633, 637, 638, 645n3, 648, 656, 660, 664, 665, 677, 684-686, 690, 693n118, 694, 694n119, 697, 697n127-699, 746, 750 (*see also* French Concession, International Settlements)
Shanghai Opium Merchants Combine 690-692
Shansi 629, 646
Shantung 513, 515n48, 658, 706n147
Shantung Road Hospital 648
shar 20, 21n5
Shensi 629, 658, 664, 696
Sino-Japanese War 497, 502, 606
Summer Palace Beijing 13
Sun Yatsen 597
Swatow gang (*see* Opium, dealers)
Szechwan 85, 338, 439, 440n44
Taiping 68, 72, 72n56, 85n92, 88, 476, 483, 543, 603, 603n17, 608, 612n43, 672, 687
Taiwan 176, 228, 473, 474, 487, 495, 498, 522, 529, 530, 589, 590, 608n33, 658n35, 701-704, 705, 706, 706n147 (*see also* Formosa)
Taoism 572, 625
Tianjin 516, 520, 605-607, 608, 698
Tibet 440n44, 597, 629, 629n4, 630
Tientsin Treaty (1858) 545
Treaty of Commercial Relations (1903) 545
Treaty of Nanking (1842) 604
Treaty of Wang Hea (1844) 545
Treaty ports 9, 500, 687, 747, 748
triad 464, 524, 641 (*see also* gang)
warlords 7, 414, 512, 517, 551, 608, 608n33, 637, 641, 654-656, 661, 691, 694-696, 697, 699, 705n143, 706n147, 721, 730
White Terror 695
Yellow Danger (-Menace, -Peril) 8, 16, 153, 543, 545, 558, 597, 600, 610, 616, 617, 619 – 621, 621n67, 622 – 623n72, 624, 625, 627, 641, 642
Yü-hsiang, Feng 697
Yunnan 82, 82n86, 338, 398, 421-423, 433, 435, 439, 441, 457, 471, 478, 485,

487, 489, 526, 597, 608, 617, 629, 653, 653n23, 658, 660, 663, 664, 666-667n54, 669-671, 680, 702, 703, 751
Zheng He 469
chloral 128, 388, 557
chlorodyne 114, 115, 117, 128
chloroform 388
Christianity 4, 5n5, 7, 11, 19, 153n39, 220, 262, 398, 427, 514, 607, 610, 619, 713 (*see also* assault)
Churchill, Winston (*see* British Empire)
CIA (*see* Central Intelligence Agency)
cigarettes 328, 535n9, 664
city 30, 46, 73, 74, 114, 136, 143, 145, 147, 168, 184, 185, 187, 194n13, 195, 216n51, 257, 264, 268, 268n27, 273, 386, 411, 441, 451, 456, 465, 524, 544, 555, 574, 582, 616, 637, 649n12, 678, 679, 690, 693, 694, 696, 697n127, 725, 750 (*see also* urbanization)
civilization 8, 15, 56n19, 95, 136, 190, 224, 283, 284, 325, 397, 403, 414, 455, 486, 503, 507, 509, 570n70, 604n20, 618, 623n72
class 38, 79n78, 114, 116, 191, 201, 247n14, 268, 328, 357, 383, 411, 425, 439, 442, 471, 532n2, 544, 555, 555n46, 566, 575, 581, 583, 588, 618n61, 645, 647, 679, 689, 697
clergy 7, 14n10, 38, 116, 247n14, 258, 269n30, 609
clipper xv, 64, 64n34, 65, 67, 69, 71, 99, 496, 500, 540-542, 587, 743
'Closed Door' policy (*see* British Empire)
Coca Cola 568, 569, 578, 587, 588
cocaine xvi, 117-119, 128, 135, 317, 318, 336, 338, 342, 343, 343n47, 345-347, 347n54, 348, 350, 352, 367, 372, 375, 379, 386, 387n11, 389-391, 393, 509, 522, 539, 557, 567-569, 575, 577-579, 579n91, 580-582, 582n100, 583, 588, 624, 650, 709, 710, 717, 723, 725, 725n9, 726 (*see also* coca leaves)
cocaine factory 317, 342, 344, 345, 345n49, 367, 579
cocainomania 575
coca leaves 317, 342, 343, 345-347, 350, 557, 568, 577, 578, 717, 725
Cochin (*see* India)
Cochinchina (see Southeast Asia)
Cocteau, Jean 385, 386n8

codeine 128, 194, 347, 388, 557, 570, 570n72, 587, 650n16, 652n19, 715

Coen, Jan Pietersz. (*see* Dutch Empire)

Cold War 415, 423, 424, 485, 487, 530, 701, 703, 716

Coleridge, Samuel T. 113, 384

Colijn, Hendrik (*see* Dutch Empire)

Collis, Maurice 5, 43n21, 71n51, 606, 609, 609n36, 610

Colombia 473, 539, 549n31, 721

Colombo 136

colonialism xiii, 3, 11, 32, 143, 153n41, 172, 219n57, 223, 279, 353, 374, 415, 456, 474, 475, 487, 526, 530n78, 539, 593, 619, 619n62, 634n13, 718, 719, 724, 759

colonial repression xv, 14, 125, 140, 145, 171, 223, 227, 233, 254, 264, 266, 279, 281, 284, 287, 329, 365, 375, 396, 402, 416, 425, 470, 425, 526, 545, 547, 566, 607, 622, 679, 714, 717, 725, 761, 762 (*see also* assault)

colonial state (*see* state, colonial)

colonizer xii, 5, 38, 44, 55, 56, 87, 95, 125, 137, 150, 158, 191, 260, 277, 396, 403, 406, 424, 426, 428, 432, 442, 451, 471, 499, 503, 507, 509, 510, 559, 561, 564, 614, 615, 639, 714

Committee on Drug Addictions 573

commodity (chain) 64, 72, 73, 83, 110, 449, 467, 664, 689, 735

Communist Party, Chinese (*see* China)

competition 23n11, 39n12, 40, 54, 69, 75, 78, 94, 97, 136, 143, 146, 150, 166, 176, 221, 222, 232, 274, 278, 291, 307, 310, 331, 333, 346, 360, 378, 387, 398, 415, 451, 452, 475, 485, 495, 531, 541, 551, 559, 563, 623, 639, 672, 685, 686, 688, 689, 691, 712, 714, 719, 724

comprador 66, 80, 95, 173, 606, 686

concentration camp 519, 561, 562, 709

Conference of Shanghai (1909) 119, 338, 556, 557, 575, 632, 720, 721

conqueror 191, 208, 211, 277, 533, 534, 562, 683, 719

Conrad, Joseph 44, 189

Constantinople (see Middle East)

consumption (*see* Opium, consumption)

contraband traffic (*see* illicit trade)

conversion, religious 38, 72, 190, 533, 610, 612, 615, 619

coolie (*see* China)

Coromandel (*see* India)

corruption 4, 39, 57, 64, 66, 68, 69, 73, 85, 88, 93, 120, 126, 176, 176n13, 176n16, 200, 201n29, 217, 224, 242n5, 247, 253, 269, 340, 375, 376, 412, 446, 447, 457, 458, 506, 525, 565, 577, 661, 672, 683, 686, 699, 723, 731, 754

costs (*see* Opium, related costs)

cough 108, 196

Country Trade 52, 64, 94, 176n16, 278, 321, 397, 448

court, monarchical 24, 31, 181, 181n26, 183, 188, 233, 248, 263n15, 271, 422, 601, 602, 673n73, 715 (*see also* oikos)

Court, Pieter de la 243, 243n9

Courtwright, David T. 532, 534, 534n5, 555n46, 573, 577n89, 582, 582n99-584, 727

Crawfurd, John (*see* British Empire)

Cressey, George B. 658, 661, 662n43, 663, 667, 669, 674n78

criminalization 128, 188, 236, 237, 341, 425, 466, 554, 588, 713

criminality 7, 37, 11, 80, 106, 116, 124, 219, 269n30, 269n33, 316, 334, 376, 391, 396, 410n28, 413, 422, 465, 473, 477, 479, 482, 487, 558, 582, 583, 603, 628n3, 643, 682, 684, 687, 690, 691, 693, 697n127, 715, 722, 723, 731

Criminal Law 390, 461, 480-482, 484, 580n94, 657

criminal organization, 46, 92, 123, 117, 393, 400, 425, 466, 478, 484, 486, 575, 596, 602, 627, 641, 642, 656, 729 (*see also* gang, kongsi, triad)

criminals 9, 72, 116, 117, 120, 123, 139, 216, 217, 374, 411, 412, 420, 426, 466, 481, 483, 542, 581, 595, 612, 635, 654, 681, 683, 683n97, 687, 693, 694, 700, 701, 710, 725, 731 (*see also* gangsters; Opium, dealers; piracy, smugglers)

crop destruction 199, 663

cultivation, cocaine 342, 345

cultivation, opium (*see* Opium, cultivation)

Cultivation System (*see* Dutch Empire)

currency xvii, 232, 311, 354, 367, 521, 532, 670, 750, 763

Daendels, Herman Willem (*see* Dutch Empire)

Dai Li (*see* China)

Dam, Pieter van (*see* Dutch Empire)

Daumier, Honoré iv, 42, 646
death 3, 31, 107, 117, 127, 129, 137, 158n56, 180, 198, 199, 204, 206, 222, 258, 277, 301n17, 329, 497, 503, 508, 533, 543, 561, 571, 572, 621, 648, 651, 672
death penalty 83, 84, 230, 236, 240, 269, 350, 351, 421, 460, 495
decadence 7, 414
delirium 571
demand and supply xiii, 35, 41, 49, 54, 54n14, 58, 69, 84, 98, 101, 122, 179, 230n77, 232, 254, 295, 313, 329, 346, 361, 365, 374, 376, 417, 423, 431, 438, 441, 442, 449, 461, 482, 487, 488, 508, 510, 517, 518, 525, 527, 568, 578, 599, 607, 608, 617, 640, 649, 661, 672, 687, 692, 712, 713, 716, 727, 728, 731, 747, 765
Dent & Co (see Opium, dealers)
derivatives xiii, 21, 24n14, 348, 352, 386n9, 486, 488, 510, 512, 515, 517, 553, 587, 613, 624, 643, 650n16, 699, 703, 705n143, 725, 726 (see also heroin, morphine)
Derks, Hans 61n31, 127n8, 175n11, 182n29, 255n1, 341, 396n2, 403n13, 406n23, 471n15, 495n6, 585n105, 595n3, 639n23, 650n14, 743, 771
Descours-Gatin, Chantal 403n15, 404n16, 405n20, 407, 415, 418, 433, 435
despotism 3, 14, 284
diarrhoea 24, 108, 571n74
Dikötter, Frank 474n19, 596, 597, 597n4-598n6, 646, 656, 657n30
Dipanagara, prince (see Indonesia)
diplomacy 65, 273, 343, 618, 637
Dispensatory of the USA 535, 548, 569, 571, 572, 577
distribution (see Opium, distribution)
Diu (see India)
divide and rule 5n5, 146, 151, 220, 224, 258, 260, 263, 266, 268, 282, 288, 315, 442, 442n49, 454, 465, 522, 695, 698
dysentery 108, 331
Duco, Don H. 62, 178n19, 179n20, 421n8, 443n53, 574, 613n46, 666n51, 667n55, 674n75, 754n4
Dutch Cocaine Factory (see Dutch Empire)
Dutch Empire 19, 20n1, 26, 122, 153n39, 162, 175, 187, 189, 195, 199, 201n29, 202, 204, 207, 214, 216, 218, 221, 224, 227, 231, 234, 236, 239, 239n, 255, 262, 264, 271,
273, 281, 282, 287, 291, 300, 307-309, 311, 317, 322, 326, 328, 332, 338, 348, 357, 362, 364, 365, 369, 373, 375, 378, 379, 397, 406, 431, 467, 469, 482, 508, 556, 689n108, 753, 754, 758, 759, 769, 770 (see also archipelago, Asian continent, assault; Euope, the Netherlands; Indonesia)
amfio(e)n (see Opium)
amphioen (see Opium)
Amphioen Society (see Opium, dealers)
Batavia 59, 159, 160-162n71, 169, 175, 176n13, 178, 184, 198, 201, 208n40, 212n45, 216, 217, 221, 224, 229, 231, 234n86, 235, 239-245, 247n14, 248, 250n18, 253, 256-258n4, 259, 261, 264-268, 269n32, 273, 274, 279, 281, 285, 295, 296-298, 299, 301, 303, 304, 307, 315, 321-323, 329-331, 332, 334, 352, 358, 359, 362, 365n15, 368, 369, 463, 469, 473, 479n28, 480, 483, 724, 757, 766
Baud, Jean C. 44, 178n19, 189, 197, 198n18, 200, 229, 229n74-230n75-78, 231, 234-236, 237, 240, 241, 286, 291, 297, 307, 313n21, 313n23, 314, 321n-323, 323n4-325, 330n17, 350, 360n, 362, 368, 740, 742, 744, 745, 753, 754, 758
Bencoolen 219, 252, 275, 284n16, 322, 322n2
Billiton 295, 296-298, 299-301n16, 302-304, 304n26, 329, 473
Billiton Mining Company 293, 295, 307, 328, 378
Broecke, Pieter van den (see Opium, dealers)
Coen, Jan Pietersz. 175, 208, 212n45, 219n57, 221-224, 260, 261, 480n30, 682
Colijn, Hendrik 227, 349
Cultivation System 309
Daendels, Herman Willem 274n48, 280, 287, 288, 292, 292n32, 321, 379, 761, 762, 763
Dam, Pieter van 180n25, 200, 201
Dutch Cocaine Factory 317, 344, 345, 345n49, 367, 579
Dutch – English wars (see Europe, England)
Dutch Ethical Policy 152, 332
Dutch Opium Factory (see Opium, factory)

Dutch violence xvi, 202, 204, 205, 208, 210-212, 212n45, 213, 216, 219n57, 223, 226, 227, 256, 259n7, 261, 263, 269, 481 (*see also* assault)

East Indies Company (*see* Dutch Empire, Vereenigde)

Heutz, Johan van 227

Imhoff, Gustaaf W. van (*see* Dutch Empire) 241, 242, 242n6, 247, 248, 252, 256-258, 260, 377

Java 19, 470, 476, 479-481, 483, 527, 577, 580, 648, 710, 744-748, 755, 757, 759, 760, 762, 770

Java War 226n68, 307, 312, 364, 370, 472

Kaempfer, Engelbert 180n25, 198, 199, 201, 201n30, 499, 499n16

King (House) of Orange 288, 297, 302, 307, 310, 317, 378

law of conquest 55n18, 683

Lombok 226, 332, 342, 350, 561

Loudon, John 295n1, 297, 297n10, 301, 301n16-304, 304n26, 305

Mataram 20, 213, 226, 226n68, 230, 258, 259, 266, 272n42, 273, 753

Moluccas 37, 151n34, 198, 216, 222, 230, 260n10, 265, 284, 322, 324

Multatuli 189, 240, 287n25, 315, 317, 319, 373, 628n2

Nederlandsche Handelsmaatschappij (NHM) 239n1, 307-310, 311n11-313n24, 314, 317, 318, 323, 352, 364, 372, 396, 472, 477, 689

octroy 204, 205, 207, 241, 246, 248, 377

Ong-Tae-Hae 277, 467, 479-480n30, 481, 483, 724

Opium-Zoutregie (*see* Opium, regie)

Outer Districts 292, 305n28, 319, 321, 322, 324, 325, 327, 329, 342, 365, 770

Paludanus 27n18, 28, 28n21

passports, Dutch 151, 168, 479, 724

Pax Neerlandica 332

Pelsaert, Francisco 152n38, 176n14, 184, 184n34-186, 186n44

perkeniers 221

Prince of Orange 202, 248, 297

Reede, Hendrik van 168

Rochussen, Jan J. 286, 286n23, 330n17, 360n8

Scheltema, Johan 373-374n2, 375

Schouten, Wouter 39n10, 136, 136n4, 146n28, 152, 152n38-153n39, 155n48,

158, 158n56, 161, 161n67, 162, 185, 198, 199, 713

Semarang 258, 259, 265, 265n19, 279, 285n22, 358, 359, 469, 476

Seventeen Gentlemen 200, 202, 204

Struick, Nicolas 334, 334n27, 359, 360, 361, 364, 365, 753

Valckenier, Adriaan 256, 256n2, 257, 260, 260n11

Vereenigde Oostindische Compagnie (VOC) 38n6, 39, 40, 57n21, 135, 144, 144n24, 160, 161, 163-165, 166-168, 169, 176, 187, 190n5, 200, 202-205, 208, 213, 216, 222-224, 236, 239, 252, 267, 278, 279, 281, 308, 362, 367, 375, 376, 378, 683, 711, 712, 754, 757

Wiselius, Jakob 19, 62, 90n5, 99, 100, 121, 121n1, 122, 183, 330, 357, 369, 395, 400, 405, 737, 738, 751

Zwaardecroon, Hendrick 169, 169n19

duties 66, 154, 263, 284, 298, 310, 365, 470, 479, 527, 547, 549, 550, 631, 727, 760, 763, 764

Du Yuesheng (*see* Opium, dealers; *see also* China)

East Asia 47, 147, 311, 339, 563, 615 (*see also* Asian continent)

East India Company (*see* British Empire)

East Indies (*see* Dutch Empire)

East-West relations 14, 126, 128, 192, 228n71, 385, 386, 477, 523, 650, 652, 652n18, 673n73, 711 (*see also* chinatowns, orientalism, West – East relations)

Eberhard, Wolfram 601

economics xi, 613, 647

Egypt (*see* Middle East)

EIC (*see* British East India Company)

Eliot, Charles 493, 512

elite 22, 30, 31, 56n19, 59, 66, 74, 105, 114, 116, 118, 124, 125, 137-141, 184n33, 185, 187, 188, 190, 191, 206, 217, 226, 233, 237, 242, 245, 261, 268, 269n32, 274, 275, 281, 290, 313n21, 316, 319, 341, 358, 373, 376-378, 383-386, 390, 398, 402, 403, 439, 441, 443, 446, 455, 463, 469, 470, 478, 496, 507, 539, 559, 572, 639, 648, 657, 712, 767

embassy of 1787 and 1793 (see British Empire)

empire building xiii, 216

enemy 13, 16, 19, 39, 44, 78, 145, 146, 153, 161, 162, 180, 202, 206, 207, 211, 215, 221,

226, 233, 260, 263, 268, 286, 288, 297,
325, 331, 333, 353, 376, 398, 411, 414,
496, 527, 530, 561n55, 619, 622n71-625,
679, 703, 706n147
England (*see* Europe)
English – Dutch wars (*see* Europe, England)
English Parliament (*see* Europe)
Enlightenment 125, 140, 140n16, 288, 388,
425, 563, 644, 646, 648n9
Estado da Índia 136, 140, 141, 144, 155
Europe 138, 140, 144, 164, 171, 176n13, 179, 181,
191, 192, 205, 208, 210, 214, 215, 231, 260,
285, 303, 345, 347, 377, 383, 386, 392,
403, 424, 461, 478, 494, 518, 540, 554,
587, 599, 622, 628n3, 644, 648n9, 713,
714, 717, 719 (*see also* assault)
    Belgium 29, 127, 284n16, 414, 465
        Antwerp 127
        Ghent 191, 192
    England (UK) 3, 5, 9, 12, 13n7, 15, 28, 36,
        40, 41, 51, 53, 54, 57, 59, 77-79n76, 85,
        88, 100, 106, 108, 112, 112n11, 113, 118,
        124n4, 125, 127, 140, 191, 194, 206, 207,
        216, 283, 290, 347, 383n3, 384, 388,
        390, 456, 496, 514, 516, 532, 533, 535,
        540, 543, 559, 587, 589, 604, 605, 623,
        624, 630, 632, 635, 684, 703, 747 (*see
        also* British Empire)
        English – Dutch wars 207, 210, 214,
            221, 222, 224, 244, 278, 284n16
        English Parliament 59, 81, 85, 532,
            596, 610, 628n3, 629
        Great Britain 12, 44, 79n77, 119,
            449n64, 455, 556, 605, 633 (*see
            also* England)
        Liverpool 94, 110, 118, 455
        London 36, 40, 41, 43, 52, 52n8,
            54n14, 59-61, 66, 73-76, 87, 90, 91,
            94, 94n14, 110, 112, 118, 123, 137n10,
            140, 162, 169n19, 172, 456, 493,
            508n35, 514, 617, 664
        Pharmacy Act (1868) 111, 114n17
        Royal Commission on Opium 79n77,
            82n86, 85, 117, 129, 129n10, 135, 180,
            644, 681, 681n95, 739
        *Society for the Suppression of the
            Opium Trade* (SSOT) 117, 614
        Treasury 59, 189, 230, 246, 292, 392,
            405, 488, 578n90, 581, 701n134
    Europeans 144, 146, 151, 169, 188, 199,
        207, 210, 212, 219-221, 236, 257, 264,

277, 280, 303, 324, 325, 367, 473, 522,
533, 616, 675
France, French, (the) xv, xvi, 42, 51, 57,
74, 96, 173, 282, 287, 333, 334, 338, 340,
353, 371, 378, 379, 381, 383, 385, 385n6,
387, 388, 388n14, 389, 391n22, 394,
395, 397, 398, 400, 404, 406, 407, 409,
410n28, 415, 419, 421, 425, 432, 486,
489, 525, 526, 528, 570, 570n70, 724,
725, 747, 765 (*see also* French Empire)
    French Revolution 125, 279, 762
    Marseille 127, 386n8, 570, 570n70,
        714, 728
    Paris 140, 384, 385, 387, 389, 391, 398,
        412
    Rhône-Poulenc 345, 387n12
Germany 21n7, 108, 109, 119, 120, 137n10,
191, 194, 194n13, 267n25, 345, 347, 465,
514, 531, 559, 565, 615, 619, 621, 622n71,
624, 625
    German 61, 70, 75, 80n81, 163n2, 198,
        258, 501, 515n48, 516, 527, 532, 542,
        579, 580, 599, 609, 615, 615n51, 616,
        617, 621, 622n70, 624, 625, 638,
        647, 706, 707, 725, 725n9
    Germanisation 625
    Germans 200n26, 519, 561, 562n56,
        615, 639
    Rosenberg, Alfred 625
Italy 23, 51
    Florence 139
    Venice 127, 192-194, 714
Netherlands – Holland 5, 28, 40, 140n16,
186, 190n4, 206, 207, 212, 239n1, 243,
247n14, 248, 250n18, 258, 269n31, 279,
281, 282, 290, 291, 296, 298, 299, 308,
312, 313, 315, 315n27, 316, 346-348, 371,
373-375, 378, 379, 386n8, 432n28, 444,
479, 481, 496, 565, 598, 759, 762, 763,
767 (*see also* Dutch Empire)
    Amsterdam 29, 40, 127, 160, 163,
        166n9, 206, 208, 217, 223, 242n6,
        247, 247n14, 253, 296, 315n27, 316,
        342, 345, 346, 372, 385n6, 667n55,
        758
    Spain 21n7, 51, 54, 54n11, 88, 206, 212,
        398, 501, 562, 563, 565, 619 (*see
        also* Spanish Empire)
    William I, king 282, 284n16, 289, 296,
        307-311, 317
    William III, king – stadhouder 207
    William IV, stadhouder 248
    William V, stadhouder 248, 282

United Kingdom (UK) (*see* Europe, England)

expenditures 80, 100, 176n13, 328n13, 339, 506, 759, 760, 761

export (*see* Opium, export)

extraterritoriality 411, 547, 637, 638, 684, 693

Ezra Brothers (*see* Opium, dealers)

Fairbank, John K. 67, 80n79, 612n41, 639-641, 657, 658, 664, 696

famine 39, 57, 60, 126, 131, 330, 463, 533, 533n3, 618, 663, 669

farmers 30, 57, 239, 270, 660, 661, 662n43, 664, 667, 674n78 (*see also* peasant)

farmers, opium (*see* Opium, farmers)

Farquhar, major (see British Empire; Opium, dealers)

Ferguson, Niall 35, 35n1, 48, 79n75, 123

Feuerwerker, Albert 612n41, 634n15, 661

film 384, 385

Florence (*see* Europe, Italy)

(folk)-healer 21-23n11, 127, 137, 137n8, 138-141, 191, 389, 390, 535, 644, 715

foreign crime 146n28, 269n30, 279, 683, 693, 725

foreign devils 431, 480, 501, 541, 600-602, 608, 617, 627, 693

foreigners xi, 145, 152, 181, 198, 204, 207, 214, 215, 226, 232, 233, 255, 256, 262, 272, 284, 285, 298, 403, 411, 417, 459, 460, 466, 467, 470, 496, 554, 575, 588, 599, 603, 605, 606, 610, 612, 627, 628, 630, 635, 640, 644, 645, 648, 654, 690, 695, 725

foreign policy xvi, 153, 169, 204, 205n34, 213, 216, 223, 236, 254, 264, 267, 279, 280, 284n16, 286, 287, 350, 353, 376, 396, 398, 401, 402, 411, 413, 414, 419, 425, 430, 442, 454, 471, 472, 480, 486, 489, 506, 515, 516, 526, 529, 539, 541, 545, 554, 559, 561, 567, 588, 589, 590, 595, 606, 607, 609, 631, 636n39, 639, 640n26, 641, 658, 664, 677, 704, 723, 729, 731 (*see also* assault)

Formosa (*see* China)

Foster, Anne L. 402n10, 406n24, 539n13, 564n61

Foster, William 179

Foucault, Michel 113

France (*see* Europe)

French Empire 5n7, 29, 51, 99, 107, 108, 137n10, 279, 284n16, 345, 347, 383, 383n3, 385, 388-391, 391n22, 392, 393, 396, 398, 410, 414, 415, 444, 496, 535, 565, 625n77, 628 (*see also* Asian continent, assault, Southeast Asia; Europe, France)

French Concession 411-413, 516, 638, 692, 695, 697n127

French Navy 42, 94, 392, 393, 396, 411-414

Indochina 333, 381, 385, 392, 393, 397, 400, 406, 410, 410n28, 414-416, 418, 431, 433, 435-438, 438n39, 486, 525, 526, 528, 552, 723, 724, 746, 747, 748

Mendès-France, Pierre 415

Moulin Rouge 386, 396

Napoleon 78, 88, 94, 278, 279, 281, 282, 287, 288, 321, 375, 379, 389, 397, 607, 762

Tonkin 333, 381, 398, 402, 404n16, 418, 432, 433, 435-437, 526, 671

Toulon 392

Vichy Fascists 415

Viet Minh 411, 432

First Vietnam War 396, 415, 485, 488

fraud 9, 169, 177, 191, 230, 239, 336, 341, 362, 371, 404, 405, 433, 570, 727

free trade 16, 42, 43, 53, 58, 59, 94, 110, 119, 123, 168, 222, 243, 275, 283, 285, 291, 374, 375, 402, 431, 447, 470, 482, 537, 541, 563, 599, 618, 619, 681, 759

French Concession (*see* French Empire)

French Navy (*see* French Empire)

French Revolution (*see* Europe, France)

Freud, Sigmund 386, 387n11, 579n91

friars 534, 562

Fuller, Stuart J. 664-666

Fu-Manchu novels 385

Fu(o)kien (*see* China)

Furber, Holden 52n6, 66n, 176n16, 278n2

Gaastra, Femme 5n7, 53n10, 153n41, 176n16, 178n19, 191n6, 203, 208n41, 212n45, 219n57, 226, 239n1, 242n5, 245, 247n14, 248n16, 250n18, 259n7, 260n10, 274n48, 278n3, 297n9, 499n16

gang 46, 57, 73, 123, 412, 517n54, 588, 690, 691, 692, 692n117, 693, 694, 697, 697n127, 698 (*see also* criminal organization)

gangsters 123, 412, 413, 483, 518, 524, 551, 584, 585n105, 596, 642, 663, 665, 682,

684, 686, 688, 690, 692n117, 695-699, 705n143, 713 (*see also* Opium, dealers)

gambling 39n11, 40, 45, 97, 199, 296, 301, 303, 329, 333, 405, 411, 412, 422, 446, 447, 468n12, 470, 483, 484, 500, 524, 583, 620, 622, 642, 657n31, 697, 697n127, 710

ganja 91, 183, 439, 557

Geary Act (*1892*) 545

Gelber, Harry G. 14n10, 607-608n33, 610n38, 614n47, 673, 674n78

Generale Missiven 164, 234, 252, 254

Geneva Convention (*1925*) 346, 493

genocide 4, 221, 416, 547n28, 560, 562, 639n23

German (see Europe, Germany)

Germanisation (see Europe, Germany)

Germans (see Europe, Germany)

Germany (see Europe, Germany)

Gesellschaftsgeschichte xvi

Ghazipur (*see* India)

Gladstone, William E. 11, 12, 12n2, 603

Glaxo-Smith-Kline 549

Goa (*see* India)

God(s) 19, 22, 38, 39, 40, 70, 71, 146, 153, 206, 233, 258, 259, 267, 376, 387, 440, 481, 532, 588, 601, 609

Godfather 412, 413

Godske, commander 167, 167n13

Goens, Rijcklof van 167, 167n13, 190n4, 234

Goh, Daniel P. 459n2, 464, 464n7, 478, 482n33

gold 53, 59, 61n33, 97, 165, 176, 181, 186, 190n4, 271, 274, 281, 315, 543, 719, 749

Goldbaum, David 580, 580n95, 581

golden age 29, 94, 181, 206, 244, 731

Golden Crescent 731

Golden Orchid Society 601

'Golden Road to Cathay' 439, 486, 671

Golden Triangle (Quadrangle) (*see* Southeast Asia)

Goldman Sachs bank 75

gold rush 97, 471, 543, 544, 652n18

Gootenberg, Paul 317n33, 342n46, 346n50, 578n90, 580, 735

Gotō, Shimpei 506

Greenberg, Michael 45n25, 53n9, 60n30, 65n37, 68, 71n51, 77n72, 80, 92n11, 96n20, 740, 750

Great Depression 350, 372

Groeneveldt, Willem 265n20, 333-336, 404, 765-767

Grotius, Hugo 144, 481

guilt(y) 5, 11, 14, 19, 85, 86, 124, 205n34, 227n69, 237, 255n1, 258n4-260n11, 385, 463, 547n28, 564, 607, 616, 623, 649, 726

Gujarat (*see* India)

Gutzlaff, Carl 70, 71, 71n51, 71n53, 72, 72n56, 553n43, 596, 609, 609n36, 610n38, 693

Haan, Frederik de 217, 217n55, 219, 234, 252, 252n24, 271n41, 272, 272n42, 273, 274n48

Hakka 464n9, 667

Han Chinese 21n5, 519, 667

Hanoi 398, 412

Harbin 511, 638

Harrison, Francis B. 538-541

Harrison Narcotic Act (*1914*) 581, 582

Hart, Robert 14n10, 16, 50, 79n76, 81, 673, 674, 674n78, 675, 678

hashish 28n22, 30, 32, 91, 120, 183, 185, 379, 385, 386, 390, 557, 613n46

Hastings, Warren 45, 50, 55, 57, 57n21, 59, 61, 66, 173, 280n8, 628n3

Hayter, Alethea xiin, 386n9

healers (*see* folk-healers)

health(y) 24, 31, 37, 116, 117, 124, 127, 127n8, 128, 137, 194, 195, 253, 290, 351, 389-391, 391n22, 410, 440, 483, 569, 571, 574, 575, 578, 587, 593, 616, 652n18, 653n23, 678-680

health hazards 403, 588, 616, 621, 643, 644, 647, 652, 681, 689

health infrastructure/ organization 107n3, 128, 138, 140, 191, 425, 616n52, 652, 653, 707n150, 713, 715

Hegel, Georg W. 284

Helfferich, Emil 307n, 318, 318n34

herbarium 22, 23, 28

herbs 23, 31, 32, 107, 155, 157, 158, 162n71, 188, 535, 537, 602, 643, 647-649, 652, 652n19, 653, 717, 722 (*see also* Chinese medicine, medical doctors)

heroin (factory) xvi, 73, 120, 128, 194, 316, 345, 346, 372, 375, 384, 386n9, 387, 387n11, 390, 391, 396, 413, 415, 419, 420, 422, 423, 426-428, 430, 438, 447, 483, 488-490, 510, 511, 515-518, 520, 522, 523, 525, 527, 536, 553, 554, 557, 558,

572, 578, 580, 582, 582n100, 583, 584, 599, 624, 637, 641n27, 643, 648-653n23, 657, 665, 680, 698, 701, 702, 707n150, 715, 716, 725, 726, 728
Heutz, Johan van (see Dutch Empire)
High Court 655, 656n26
Hindu(ism) (see India)
Hippocrates 21, 572
histori(ans)ography xi-xiv, 3, 5-8n11, 9n13, 12, 14n10-16, 19, 20, 24, 30, 42, 44, 47, 53, 56, 57n21, 75, 126, 129n10-131, 153, 163, 172, 176n16, 180n25, 190, 202, 212n45, 219n57, 242, 259, 278, 282, 317, 318n34, 353, 356, 396, 441, 485, 493n1, 499, 519, 533n3, 569, 593, 594, 595n3, 599, 601, 606, 607, 610, 610n38, 613, 625, 627, 628n3, 634n13, 639, 640, 645n3, 656, 673n73, 676, 676n82, 680n90, 691, 692, 704, 707, 709, 711, 714, 716-721, 725n9, 731n17, 735, 736, 753, 759, 762, 764
Hmong (see Southeast Asia)
Ho Chi Minh (see Southeast Asia)
Hodder, Rupert 473-475, 483
Hodgson, Barbara 113n12, 114n16, 193, 194n13, 385n6
Hogendorp, Dirk van 281, 282, 288, 290, 373
Hogendorp, Gijsbert K. van 141, 143n21, 282n11-285, 288-290, 682, 761
Hogendorp, Willem van 281, 285n22
Holmes, Sherlock 384
homeopathy 648n9
Hong Kong Bank 75, 76
Hong Kong and Shanghai Bank (HSBC) 75, 76, 76n67, 689n108
Hormuz 31, 145, 150, 177, 469, 715
hortus botanicus 28, 29
Hosie, Alexander 85n91, 317, 372n27, 629-631, 633, 634, 634n13, 635, 639, 643, 658, 660, 721, 747, 751
household xiii, 127n8, 128, 208n41, 287n25, 325, 328n12, 328n13, 405, 406, 444, 469, 541, 549, 587, 601, 673 (see also oikos)
House of Orange 202, 248, 288, 297, 302, 307, 310, 317, 378
Ho Yam Lo 359
Howitt, William 11, 11n1
Hugly (see India)
Hustaert, Jacob 166, 167, 167n15
hygiene 574, 578, 653

hypocrisy 16, 39, 43, 44, 46, 122, 190, 288, 304, 348, 349, 373, 403, 539, 547, 612, 701
hypodermic syringe 390

ideology xii, xiii, xvi, 5, 8, 8n12, 40, 64, 113, 114, 127, 286, 289, 308, 374, 470, 478, 482, 483, 487, 493n1, 519, 530, 537, 554, 582, 597, 625, 695, 723n7, 724
illicit production 123, 124, 256, 315, 412, 437, 457, 458, 514, 542, 583, 656, 680, 686, 702, 716, 721, 729
illicit trade 8, 66, 68, 73, 83, 116, 117, 240, 245n11, 316, 357, 423, 457, 488, 510, 513, 516, 518, 542, 543, 602, 608, 654, 665, 703, 726, 730 (see also smuggling, smugglers; Opium, trade)
immigrant 47, 301, 303, 441, 456, 460, 461, 466, 467, 470, 472, 532, 534, 544, 550, 621, 621n68, 652n18 (see also China, Chinese migrants)
immigration 545n26, 588, 614n48, 621n68, 625 (see also China, Chinese migrants)
imperialism xiii, 3, 8n12, 32, 47, 49, 52, 79, 121, 125, 127, 141, 153n41, 172, 189, 219n57, 239n1, 277, 280, 280n8, 286, 309, 395, 400, 415, 425, 474, 487, 531, 534, 537, 540, 563, 589, 590, 593, 618, 619, 625, 682, 683, 715, 717, 718, 719, 759
Imperial College of Physicians 646
Imperial Decree (see China, Imperial)
imperial reciprocities 589, 612
import (coca leaves, cocaine) 345, 346n52, 350, 557, 578, 580, 710
import (non-opium, non-coca), xii-xvii, 20, 35, 36, 41, 43, 54, 61, 95, 99, 168, 169, 176, 199, 221, 260, 261, 264, 271, 273, 285, 316, 329, 333, 425, 449, 469, 472, 502, 547, 634, 644, 749
import monopoly (opium) (see Opium, import)
import, opium (see Opium, import)
import substitution 85, 658, 669, 730
in-between people 270, 483
income 77, 239, 245, 247n14, 272n42, 287, 291, 292, 292n32, 298, 314, 315, 327, 328n13, 335, 339, 349, 363, 364, 367, 403-405, 408, 430, 444, 490, 506, 509, 544, 555, 667, 736, 759, 764

India xiii, xv, xvi, xvii, 3, 8n12, 24, 26n18, 27,
    36, 39, 50, 55, 77, 79n77, 87, 89, 91, 95,
    96, 99, 100, 102, 103, 121, 130, 145, 163,
    178, 183, 211, 228, 253, 291, 321, 397,
    403, 406, 410, 422, 441, 448, 456, 457,
    522, 532n2, 572, 629, 631, 719, 735-738,
    740 (see also Asian continent, assault,
    British Empire)
  Agra 89, 182, 184-186n44, 187
  Akbar 181, 186
  Allahabad 187
  Aurangzeb, emperor 181-183, 188
  Ayurveda 24, 175n12, 572, 644, 717
  Behar 183, 737-739
  Benares 87, 96, 98, 172, 174, 177, 182, 183,
    334, 422, 433, 435, 449, 735, 737-740,
    750
  Bengal merchants 292, 362, 365n15, 397,
    672, 690, 712, 740, 747, 749
  Bengal opium (see Opium, production)
  Bombay 64, 68, 87, 92-96, 98, 172, 253,
    449, 464, 688, 735, 745
  Buddhism 264n18, 441, 526, 572, 608n33
  Calcutta 12n4, 46, 52, 58, 60, 64, 64n34,
    65, 87, 90, 90n5, 98, 100, 101, 292, 330,
    368, 369, 449, 629, 688, 738, 739, 742,
    743, 744, 748, 751
  Calicut 41n14, 136, 143, 146, 147, 150, 212
  Cannanur 165, 166
  Cochin 136, 146, 156, 163, 166-168n17, 169,
    176n13, 278, 469, 715
  Coromandel 151, 153n39, 161, 171, 175, 176,
    182, 244, 245, 262, 759, 760
  Diu 96, 143, 154
  Ghazipur 90, 650n16, 738, 742
  Goa 26, 27, 39, 39n10, 87, 92, 95, 96, 142,
    145, 147, 152, 155-159, 163, 165, 713, 744
  Gujarat 26n18, 159, 160n64, 177, 228, 271
  Hindu(ism) 141, 146, 147, 150, 161n67, 181,
    184n35, 185, 533, 571, 572
  Hugly 64
  Kerala (see Malabar)
  Malabar xiii, 27, 64, 93, 135, 136, 139, 143,
    144, 146, 150, 150n33, 152, 156, 157n52,
    159, 161n67, 162-164, 166, 168-170, 175,
    177, 185, 190n5, 213, 273, 711, 713, 718,
    744
  Malwa opium (see Opium, production)
  Mughal India 55-57, 57n21, 174, 175, 179-
    181, 183, 185, 188, 572
  nairo 161, 162, 185
  Parsis 464, 473, 688
  Patna 55, 57, 57n21, 59, 62, 87, 98, 171,
    177, 179, 200, 251, 253, 281, 362, 449,
    484, 735, 738-740, 750, 751, 765
  Srinagar 58, 185
  Surat 26n18, 31, 37, 38n6, 39, 39n10,
    41n14, 96, 141, 150, 152n38, 159, 160,
    163, 164, 166n10, 169, 175, 176, 182,
    230n75, 231, 715, 759, 760
  Zamorin 146, 147, 150, 161, 166, 166n10
indigenous consumers 106, 324, 325, 327,
    365, 425, 435, 509
indigenous market 93, 199, 212, 215, 222,
    239, 251, 275, 287, 307, 331, 333, 374,
    448, 466, 712, 719, 720
indigenous medicine 195, 644 (see also Chi-
    nese medicine, folk-healers)
indigenous nationalism 95, 396, 401, 442,
    442n49, 459, 470, 472, 526, 634n13
indigenous people-societies 16, 17, 106, 152,
    152n38, 153, 153n39, 179, 190, 198, 208,
    212, 215, 215n50, 217, 223, 224, 235, 236,
    241, 252, 261, 262, 265, 266, 274, 279,
    281, 284, 289, 296, 298, 308, 319, 327,
    376, 401, 403, 405, 406, 417, 424, 460,
    466, 469, 474, 481, 503, 525, 531, 533-
    535, 561, 595, 625
indigenous producers 57, 231, 233, 291, 309,
    313, 334, 375, 377, 466, 616, 717, 760,
    762, 767
indigenous rulers 144, 151, 171, 199, 215, 224,
    226, 232, 270, 280, 287, 291, 296, 319,
    350, 361, 375, 377, 383, 421, 470, 471,
    501, 683, 713
Indochina (see French Empire)
Indonesia (see also Asian continent; Dutch
    Empire, VOC)
  Aceh 198, 226, 307, 322, 332, 333, 342,
    350, 419
  Amangkurat II 236
  Ambon 199, 220, 321, 432n28
  archipelago xvi, 19, 50, 126, 151, 151n34,
    159, 160n64, 177, 178, 182, 188, 199,
    205n34, 214-216, 220, 221, 226, 227,
    229-231, 234, 236, 239, 247, 262,
    264n18, 265n20, 271, 274, 279, 280n8,
    284n16, 290-292, 297, 315, 317, 319, 321,
    327, 329, 332, 334, 336, 338, 339,
    350n62-352, 357, 372, 379, 417, 469,
    483n36, 757, 761
  Bali 198n19, 216, 226, 227n69, 275, 276,
    279, 280, 321, 322, 324, 329-332, 342,
    561

Banda 151n34, 202, 219, 219n57, 220-224, 226, 256, 263, 264

Bangka (Banca) 231, 264, 291, 293, 295-297, 299-301, 303-305n28, 322, 324, 329, 473 (*see also* Billiton)

Bantam 20, 38, 198, 199, 214, 226, 230, 234, 258, 265, 266, 270n34, 271, 272, 359, 480n30

Be-Tan group 358

Bodawpaya, king 441

Borneo 89, 103, 157, 220, 275, 284, 290, 321, 322n2, 324, 448, 449, 454n73, 563, 567

Bugis 216, 447, 448

Buleleng 331, 332

Celebes 233, 279, 284, 321, 340, 374n2, 449, 563

Cheribon 20, 214, 272, 284, 359, 360

Dipanagara, prince 226, 226n68

Java (*see* Dutch Empire)

Kong Koan 267n26

Lombok (*see* Dutch Empire)

Madura 226, 234, 279, 317, 319, 322, 324, 325n7, 334, 360, 364, 366, 755, 770

Mataram (*see* Dutch Empire)

Moluccas (*see* Dutch Empire)

Oei Tiong Ham 476, 482

Outer Districts (*see* Dutch Empire)

Palembang 55n18, 199, 232, 264n18, 266, 270, 284, 295, 296, 322, 324

peranakans 460

Semarang (*see* Dutch Empire)

Sukarno, president 414, 526

Sulawesi 216, 233, 286, 332, 447

Sumatra 26n18, 38n6, 199, 214, 252, 254, 275, 284, 316, 321, 324, 352, 354, 561, 744, 745, 747 (*see also* Dutch Empire, Aceh, Palembang)

Industrial Revolution xvi, 125, 472

infrastructure 64, 102, 107, 128, 129, 138, 140, 191, 216, 259, 342, 345, 361, 396, 425, 486, 503, 506, 557, 616, 652, 653, 687, 713, 715, 723, 726

injection needle 514, 583, 631, 651, 684

investigation 79n78, 114, 124, 129, 163, 276, 277, 280n8, 285, 301, 323, 336, 341, 359, 390, 430, 463, 464, 509, 513, 525, 553, 567, 611, 629, 632, 633, 658, 658n35, 661, 662, 676n82, 692, 701, 706, 709, 753, 759

invest(or)ment 15, 60, 65, 73, 75, 76, 88, 166, 176, 179, 202, 241, 250, 281, 297, 297n10,

299, 318, 345, 349, 376, 412, 423, 449, 466, 474, 475, 506, 528, 579, 589, 685, 687, 689, 692

Inquisition 140

International Criminal Court 481, 642

International Opium Commission 119, 120, 349, 406, 433, 493, 505n26, 575, 616, 629, 632, 638, 720, 721

International Settlement 89, 411-413, 553, 620n64, 631, 637, 654, 687, 690, 692, 695, 750 (*see also* China)

international trade 6, 67, 73, 98, 143, 187, 346, 469, 474, 488-490, 507, 511, 552-554, 558, 639, 665, 701, 702

International War Crimes Tribunal 521

Iran (*see* Middle East)

Islam 24, 146, 147, 150, 182, 184n35, 226, 262, 535n9, 563, 572, 597, 623

isolation, economical 13, 32, 390

isolation, political-social 6, 13, 268, 463, 468, 599 (*see also* China, Chinese hate)

isolation, scientific 23, 24n14

Istanbul (*see* Middle East)

Itinerario 25, 27n19, 29, 41, 142, 147n, 156, 157, 196

Japan(ese) Empire xvi, 42, 75, 76, 78, 91, 119, 146, 151, 176, 201, 221, 222, 235, 263, 284, 311, 342, 347, 354, 385, 395, 412-414, 432, 437, 444, 456, 473-475, 493, 494, 496, 503, 517, 529, 530
  colonization 506, 507, 509, 511
  Formosa 498-501, 501n22, 502, 502n24, 503, 505-507, 509
  Hong Kong 522-524
  Southeast Asia 525-528
  Korea 509-511, 517
  Kwantung (Army) 510, 513n45, 519
  Meiji Revolution 495, 496
  Nanjing China 520, 521
  narcotics production-trade 505, 505n25, 505n27, 508, 509, 511, 513, 514, 516, 520
  North China 512-516, 517n54, 518, 519
  Sino-Japanese War 497, 497n9, 502

Jardine, William (*see* Opium, dealers; *see also* British Empire)

Java (*see* Dutch Empire, *see also* Indonesia)

Java War (*see* Dutch Empire)

Jejeebhoy, Jamsetjee (*see* Opium, dealers; *see also* British Empire)

Jewish opium gangs 584, 585, 585n105, 688, 691, 692, 692n116, 692n117, 693, 694n119, 698n129 (see also Opium, dealers)

Jews 20n1, 45, 46, 46n27, 66, 74, 75, 93, 94, 118, 124, 125, 157, 182, 248, 255n, 267n25, 393, 402, 403, 464, 471, 473, 542, 545, 546n27, 549n33, 572, 580n95, 585n105, 595, 620n64, 621n68, 690, 693n118

Kaempfer, Engelbert (see Dutch Empire)
Kansu (see China)
Karen (see Southeast Asia)
Katsenberg, Jasha (see Opium, dealers)
Kedah (see Southeast Asia)
Kenya (see British Empire)
Kerala (see India)
King of Orange (see Dutch Empire)
Kinh (see Southeast Asia)
Kipling, Rudyard (see British Empire)
Kitchen God (see China)
KMT (see China, Kuomintang)
Kong Koan (see Indonesia)
kongsi (see China)
Korea (see Japanese Empire)
kotow (see China)
Koxinga (see China)
Kremers, Edward 114n17, 196n16, 387n12, 388n14, 551, 579n92
Kwantung Army (see Japan)
Kwantung Leased Territory (see China)
Kweichow (see China)
Kwong, Luke S.K. 70n47, 627n1

labor (exploitation) xiii, xiiin3, 63, 90n5, 111, 141, 175, 175n11, 185, 200, 214, 216, 221, 223n60, 247, 247n14, 262, 264, 265, 281-283, 296, 297n8, 299, 299n12-301n15, 304, 309, 329, 330, 345, 377, 402, 412, 414, 417, 449, 461, 464-466, 472, 473, 478, 517, 523, 529, 544, 547, 548, 560, 583, 616, 620, 621, 663n45, 666, 698, 700, 727, 730, 735, 747, 765

La Motte, Ellen 5, 89n4, 90, 91, 451, 451n68, 454, 455, 494n5, 513, 514, 514n46, 515, 747, 748, 750, 751n2
Lansky, Meyer (see Opium, dealers)
landlords, 263n15, 667
land utilization 87, 658, 662
Laos (see Southeast Asia)

laudanum (see Opium)
law 8n12, 11, 12, 43, 60, 66-69, 83, 115, 116, 143, 144, 215, 217, 269, 279, 290, 323, 333, 336, 338, 340, 348-352n68, 392n25, 412, 441, 443, 466, 479, 480-484, 495, 500, 501, 503, 507, 509, 517, 540, 552, 557, 566, 574, 579, 581-583, 588, 601, 604, 605, 608, 612n44, 614, 617, 621, 628, 654, 654n25, 683, 683n97, 684, 693, 700, 715, 727, 762

law of conquest (see Dutch Empire, see also assault)
legalization 68, 605, 685, 687
legal opium (see Opium)
League of Nations 102, 326, 340, 346, 409, 440, 445, 552, 692, 721
legitimation 5, 6, 16, 19, 201n29, 202, 205, 206, 213, 233, 259, 284, 336, 395, 400, 547, 572, 595
Le Pichon, Alain 68, 71n51, 71n52, 91n111, 743-745, 749
Lewin, Ludwig 20n2, 21, 22, 109n, 513, 573
license 54n11, 65, 90, 204, 222, 296-299, 305n28, 321, 324, 325, 329, 333, 351, 351n66, 352, 404, 410, 439, 486, 503, 505, 543, 550, 555, 564, 637, 725, 751
Lindemann, Mary 138n11, 140n16, 192n8
Linschoten, Jan Huygen van 25-29, 32, 39n10, 41, 41n17, 56, 136n4, 142, 147, 155-158, 196, 200, 201, 201n28, 229, 684, 713, 714
Li-Schi-Tschin 229
Lin Zexu (Tse hsu) 67, 84, 105, 635
Liverpool (see Europe, England)
Lodwick, Kathleen 14n10, 81n82, 82n87, 84n90, 610, 610n38, 612, 613n46, 614, 675, 676n82
Lombok (see Dutch Empire, see also Indonesia)
London (see Europe, England)
Long March (see China)
Los Angeles (see USA)
Lossing Buck, John 658, 658n35, 660-663, 666n51, 667, 669
Loudon, John F. (see Dutch Empire)
LSD 379, 387n10, 709
Luang Prabang (see Southeast Asia)
Lubbock, Basil 64n34, 65n37, 65n39, 67, 69, 69n45, 71n53, 740-742
Luciano, Charles 'Lucky' (see Opium, dealers)

luxury 26, 31, 41, 47, 58, 72, 97, 135, 157, 161n67, 162, 181, 271, 277, 303, 346, 377, 383, 386n8, 407, 478, 500, 602, 612, 613, 613n46, 616, 635, 745
Lyall, Alfred (see British Empire)

Macao (Macau) (see Portuguese Empire, see also China)
Macartney Embassy (see British Empire, embassy)
Macaulay, Thomas B. (see British Empire)
madat (madak) (see Opium)
Madura (see Indonesia)
Mafia Complex 129, 582, 584, 585
magic 22, 128, 137, 139, 141
Malabar (see India)
Malacca (see Southeast Asia)
Malaysia (see Southeast Asia)
Malwa opium (see Opium, production)
management xv, 57, 131n12, 166, 296, 301, 305, 311, 317, 329, 333, 336, 354, 360, 404n16, 465, 475, 494, 498, 566, 694, 713, 724
Manchukuo (see China)
Manchuria (see China)
Manila 177, 228, 256, 538, 563, 564
Manrique, Fray Sebastien (see Portuguese Empire)
Mansvelt, Willem 308-315, 317, 318
mantri-politie 328
Mao Zedong (see China)
maps 26, 351, 469, 583, 636, 660
mare liberum 144, 145n25, 204n32, 207
marihuana 379, 557, 701n134
market (see demand)
Marseille (see Europe, France)
Marshall, Jonathan 126n7, 517n54, 552, 553, 667, 684, 691n114, 692n117, 694n120, 696n122, 697n127, 699
Martin, Brian G. 684n99, 697n127, 698n128
Martin, Montgomery 36
Marx, Karl 11n, 36, 38n8, 56n19, 59, 60n27, 182n29, 532n2, 533, 533n3, 543
maslac (see Opium)
massacres 55n18, 152, 205n34, 216, 221, 222, 224-227, 227n69, 240, 242n6, 255n1, 256-263, 268, 276, 280n8, 332, 333, 428, 470, 471, 508, 533, 516, 561, 713, 724
mass line projects 652, 653, 653n22
mass products xvi, 12, 26, 31, 47, 79, 96, 177, 190n5, 200, 202, 207, 236, 367, 378,
422, 602, 608, 618, 634n13, 640, 641, 649, 657, 699, 712, 726
Mataram (see Indonesia)
materia medica 114, 499
Matheson, James (see Opium, dealers)
McCoy, Alfred W. 257n, 396, 396n3, 415n37, 420n6, 423, 424, 485n, 489, 525, 538, 556, 559n, 561n53, 564n61, 589, 614n49, 634n13, 701, 701n134, 703, 706n147, 716, 724, 729, 730
McMahon, Keith 70n40, 628n2, 658, 674n75
Mecca (see Middle East)
mecones (see Opium)
Medawar, Charles 388n13
medicalization 113, 128, 391n22, 709, 727
medical doctors, medicines, sciences (see also apothecaries, homeopathy, pharmacists)
  ancient xii, 21
  Arab, Muslim 24, 24n14, 29n26, 30-32, 36, 41n14, 127, 141, 158, 192, 220, 377, 572, 715
  Chinese 22, 65, 82n86, 229, 273, 512, 602, 643, 645-647, 651n14, 652, 652n18, 653, 655, 673n73, 675, 691, 697 (see also herbs)
  early European 23, 26, 28, 28n20, 29, 45, 47, 108, 128, 137, 137n10, 138-140, 156, 158, 168, 191, 192, 192n8, 194-196, 201, 202, 377, 714, 715 (see also folk-healers)
  Hindu, Indian 159, 162n71, 572 (see also India, Ayurveda)
  modern (Western) xv, 7, 72, 82, 90, 105, 107, 113, 114, 114n17, 118, 127n8, 129, 188, 338, 343, 346, 348, 351, 351n66, 371, 383, 387, 388, 388n13, 389, 391, 497, 499, 510, 511, 549, 566, 568, 573, 574, 575, 577, 578, 580n94, 581, 583, 588, 645, 646, 650, 681, 682, 709, 713, 715, 717 (see also Enlightenment, medicalization)
  tribal 424, 425, 502, 535, 564, 649, 650
Meiji Revolution (see Japan)
Meilink-Roelofsz, M. 152n38, 203, 209, 228n71, 264n18, 265, 266n21, 269n30, 271, 273n
Mendès-France, Pierre (see French Empire)
Mengjiang (see China)
Mekong (see Southeast Asia)

Meo (*see* Southeast Asia)

merchant xii, 15, 20, 29-31, 37, 39, 39n12, 43,
    45, 46, 57, 57n21, 61, 69, 73-75, 79n78,
    88, 98, 143, 163, 172, 182, 204, 211, 220,
    228, 241, 331, 377, 421, 452, 470, 479,
    542, 563, 602, 605, 606, 608, 630, 639,
    640, 648, 657, 678, 683, 689n108, 690,
    691, 712, 719

Merck pharmaceutics 345, 347n54, 387,
    387n11, 393, 549, 555n46, 578, 579,
    579n91, 580, 580n94, 599,   650n16,
    725

Merlin, David 8n11, 22

Mexico 97, 473, 539, 573, 580, 581

Middle East xi, xv, 21, 26n18, 29, 30-32, 36,
    107, 127, 141, 150, 154, 155, 159, 165, 199,
    228, 271, 307, 377, 443n53, 456, 468,
    488, 526, 528, 552, 607, 637, 683, 712,
    715
    Aden 27, 154, 154n42, 159, 271, 458, 469
    Afghanistan xiii-xv, 21n7, 31, 32, 79n77,
        120, 213, 485, 531, 716, 721, 731, 732
    Anatolia 22, 315, 316
    Arabian Sea 24, 141, 145, 601, 724
    Arab medical knowledge (*see* medical
        doctors)
    Arabs 143, 159, 255, 262, 273, 331, 397,
        454n73, 458
    Armenia 45, 46, 74, 152n38, 182, 182n30,
        316, 693n118
    Cairo 30
    Constantinople 110, 570, 691
    Egypt xii, 8n11, 21, 27, 28n22, 41n14, 108,
        143, 145, 150, 155, 166, 192, 310, 315, 389,
        570, 622, 702
    Iran 31, 103, 155, 158n57, 410n28, 457, 458,
        485, 489, 517, 518, 522, 525, 766 (*see
        also* Persia)
    Istanbul 30, 728
    Mecca 30, 147, 183
    Mocha 30
    Persia 26, 41n14, 81, 93, 97, 108, 143, 145,
        150, 150n33, 154, 155, 158, 158n57, 160,
        161n67, 164, 166, 167, 194, 200, 201, 239,
        264n18, 501, 570, 572, 631, 690, 715 (*see
        also* Iran)
    Persian Gulf 93, 144, 145, 155, 158n57, 177,
        228
    Smyrna 110, 111, 570
    Turkey 28, 28n22, 41n14, 54, 66, 81, 90,
        97, 103, 108-110, 112, 150, 155, 166, 194,
        312, 315, 316, 384, 410n28, 440, 449,
            489, 508, 525, 542, 543, 549, 569, 570,
            572, 585n106, 587, 632n10, 637, 691,
            692n116, 714, 727, 728, 742, 766
        Yemen 29, 30

military 123, 124, 126, 136n4, 144, 145, 174, 181,
    182, 196n16, 202, 208,   212, 213, 221,
    227, 227n69, 239, 244, 254, 281, 286,
    296, 304n26, 308, 321, 329, 331, 341,
    349, 376, 396, 397, 406, 419, 427, 431,
    446, 469, 495, 516, 552, 560, 608, 640,
    649, 661, 674n78, 695, 723, 760

Ming dynasty (*see* China)

Minh-Mang, king (*see* Southeast Asia)

Ministry of Finance (*see* Dutch Empire)

Ministry of Justice (*see* Dutch Empire)

missionary 14n10, 70, 74, 151, 502, 532n2,
    553, 609n35, 611, 612, 614, 619n62, 648,
    649, 680

Mocha (*see* Middle East)

modernization 226, 350, 351, 369, 425, 563,
    615, 647, 654n25, 682

Moluccas (*see* Indonesia)

money 16, 26, 229, 236, 241, 243, 244, 245,
    247, 248, 253, 263, 265, 269n31, 280,
    289, 291, 296, 298, 308, 310, 327, 340,
    341, 355, 373, 377, 406, 430, 452, 454,
    475, 502, 517, 539, 579, 584, 594, 656,
    661, 675n79, 712, 718, 721, 735, 759, 763

Mongkut, king (*see* Southeast Asia)

monopoly 6, 15, 26, 35, 40, 44, 47, 55, 57,
    57n21, 58, 59, 79n77, 87-89, 92, 99, 102,
    116, 123, 128, 137, 143, 151, 164, 166, 171,
    189, 199, 208, 213, 221, 223, 232, 239,
    274n48, 283, 292, 311, 312, 325, 334,
    335, 338, 352, 365, 389, 390, 400, 413,
    431, 445, 455, 470, 476, 497, 498, 505,
    515, 523, 533, 543, 552, 557, 564, 580,
    589n3, 636, 644, 686, 689, 698, 720,
    725, 751, 757

monsoon 64, 65, 500

morality xi, 7, 14, 16, 36, 37, 70, 143, 145, 239,
    252n24, 286, 311, 401, 404, 523, 612,
    612n44, 613, 730

Morgan, J.P. bank (*see* British Empire)

morphine xv, xvi, 22, 91, 105, 110, 114, 117, 119,
    194, 195, 316, 327, 328, 335, 336, 338,
    340n42, 341, 345-348, 375, 388, 390,
    393, 413, 428, 433, 440, 457, 488-490,
    498, 510-514, 522, 548, 554, 569, 570,
    576, 582, 582n100, 587, 624, 649, 657,
    680, 703, 728

morphinomanie 390

Morse, Hosea B. 5n7, 14n9, 14n10, 15
Mossel, Jacob (see Opium, dealers; see also
    Dutch Empire)
Moulin Rouge (see Europe, France)
Mozambique 97, 145, 152, 152n38, 216, 570
Mughal emperor (see India)
Mughal India (see India)
Mukden (see China)
Multatuli (see Dutch Empire)
Musto, David 493n2, 513, 574n83, 621n68,
    701n134
Myanmar (see Southeast Asia)

Nagasaki (see Japan)
nairo (see India)
Nanjing (see China)
Nanking Massacre (see China)
Napier, Lord (see British Empire)
Napoleon, emperor (see French Empire)
narco-business xvi, 73, 98, 341, 352, 367,
    442, 449, 490, 513, 522, 525, 554, 575,
    584, 665, 684, 692, 698, 701, 729
narco-consumer complex xiii, 113, 120, 126,
    201n29, 213, 351, 386, 411-413, 457, 477,
    489, 518, 548, 553, 554n44, 574, 575,
    581, 587, 653, 663, 692n116, 697, 725,
    727
narco-military state xiv, 3, 4, 14, 61, 87, 88,
    123, 124, 181, 236, 247, 280, 286, 287,
    325, 342, 361, 365, 373, 378, 379, 419,
    423, 438, 456, 486, 490, 498, 507, 511,
    515, 530, 604, 682, 683, 702, 716, 717,
    723, 761, 762
narcotic death 107, 117, 473, 677
narcotics 73, 113, 338, 348, 350, 351, 367, 386,
    431, 458, 510, 511, 516, 517, 522, 581, 598,
    608n33, 637, 664
nationalism 152, 353, 431, 459, 486, 511, 526,
    559 (see also Chinese nationalism)
nationality 8n12, 692n116
Nederlandsche Handelsmaatschappij
    (NHM) (see Dutch Empire)
Nederveen Pieterse, Jan 5n5, 239n1
nepotism 94
Netherlands (see Europe, Netherlands)
Newbold, Thomas John (see British Em-
    pire)
Newman, R. K. 82n86, 82n87, 85n93, 598,
    599n9, 609n34, 609n36, 627n1, 634,
    634n14, 635n17, 656n29, 680, 681, 682
New York (see USA)
New York Times (see USA)
Nigeria 120, 717

North China (see China)
Notowidigdo, Mukarto (see Indonesia)
nouveau riche 244
novocaine 345, 347

occidentalism 623
occupation, military 57, 145, 205n34, 207,
    214, 215, 224, 228, 244, 264, 291, 321,
    322, 348, 350, 354, 364, 379, 397, 400,
    413, 414, 415, 432, 437, 456, 471, 488,
    499, 507, 509, 513, 521, 524, 526, 561,
    565, 631, 650, 677
octroy (see Dutch Empire)
Oei Tiong Ham (see Indonesia)
oikos, oikoidal 6, 15, 16, 35, 89, 123, 125,
    153n41, 182, 182n29, 302, 308, 309, 312,
    401, 405, 495, 563, 619n62, 723 (see
    also court, household)
Old China Trade (see British Empire)
Ong-Tae-Hae (see Dutch Empire)
'Open Door' policy (see British Empire)
opiates 107, 113, 127, 116, 192, 389, 439, 564,
    575, 584, 703, 726
opiomanie 435
Opium (see also poppy)
    afyūn 27n18, 155, 159n59, 171, 183, 601, 714
    amfio(e)n 26n18, 27, 155, 404 (see also
        amphioen)
    amphioen 155, 155n48, 159n59, 164,
        164n4-169, 184, 185, 198-200, 214, 234,
        250, 252, 272, 272n42, 274, 285, 287,
        296, 362, 377, 714, 718 (see also Dutch
        empire)
    Chinese opium 20, 73, 85, 102, 119, 271,
        421, 440, 601, 602, 607, 633, 636, 667,
        684, 751
    Commonwealth, Opium 120
    consumption (use) xiii, 16, 19, 111-114,
        127, 128, 135n2, 154, 155, 179, 183-188,
        194, 229n74, 230, 234, 235, 237, 240,
        241, 272n42, 280, 285n22, 287, 291,
        292, 303, 319, 321, 324, 325n17, 327,
        327n10, 333, 335, 336, 338, 347-350,
        352, 357, 358, 370, 383, 383, 388, 389,
        392, 393, 401, 418, 421, 423, 424, 426,
        433-438, 438n39, 441, 446, 448, 452,
        453, 472, 478, 496, 503, 510, 523, 527,
        529, 534n5, 544, 545n26, 552, 564,
        566, 567, 572, 573, 576, 577, 603,
        607n30, 608, 609n36, 612, 616, 627,
        630, 631, 640, 643, 651, 657, 671-676,

678, 680, 681n95, 711, 715, 718, 722, 723, 723n7, 735, 741, 745, 746

cultivation xii, 36, 55, 58, 82, 82n86, 89, 90, 101, 111, 155, 171, 172, 188, 318, 410, 419, 420, 422, 429, 430, 438, 440, 490, 509, 510, 551, 606, 608, 630, 633, 634, 634n13, 636, 659, 666, 670, 676, 687, 696, 699, 716, 721, 737

dealers
   American xii, xv, 17, 54, 66, 68, 307, 314, 315, 317, 321, 367, 421, 481, 500, 501, 513, 536, 542, 584, 605, 608, 612, 638, 639, 697, 698, 728
   Amphioen Society 239, 240, 243, 243n8, 244, 246, 248, 252-254, 269n32, 278, 282, 288, 311, 312, 321, 362, 372, 378, 383, 757 (*see also* Dutch Empire)
   Astor, John J. 542
   Be-Tan group (*see* Indonesia)
   Broecke, Pieter van den 28n20, 30, 159, 159n58, 159n59, 160, 175, 229, 230n75 (*see also* Dutch Empire)
   Buchalter, Louis L. 584
   Dent & Co 64n34, 66, 77, 500, 501, 566, 599, 688
   Du Yuesheng 412, 413, 694n120, 697, 697n127, 698, 701
   Ezra Brothers 554, 691, 692, 692n116, 751
   Farquhar, major 45, 448
   Hung Chi Shan Tang 520-522
   Jardine, William 13, 15, 43, 123, 124, 553, 554, 593, 596, 599, 605, 609, 623, 681, 682, 685-689, 689n108, 693, 694 (*see also* Matheson)
   Jejeebhoy, Jamsetjee 68, 92, 94
   Katsenberg, Jasha 584, 698
   Lansky, Meyer 584, 698
   Luciano, Charles 'Lucky' 584, 698
   Matheson, James 44, 45, 45n26, 48, 64n34, 65-67, 71, 72, 75-77, 83, 92, 94, 95 (*see also* Jardine)
   Mossel, Jacob 214, 242-245, 245n11, 247, 248, 250, 682
   Red Gang 690
   Rothstein, Arnold 584, 585n105, 698
   Russell, Samuel 605
   Sassoon, family 64n34, 66, 76, 77, 80n80, 92, 93, 93n13, 111, 123, 124, 403, 554, 596, 599, 605, 623, 635, 636, 636n18, 681, 681n95, 684n99,

688-690,   692-694,   694n119, 698n129, 751
   Swatow gang 687, 690, 691

den, opium 44, 46, 86, 118, 280, 287, 303, 321, 333, 335, 336, 349, 350, 360, 386, 396, 404, 406, 412, 431, 435, 447, 448, 455, 490, 503, 516, 517, 524, 525, 555, 594, 598, 616, 619, 631, 872, 690, 696, 725, 746, 750, 751

distribution xii, 8n12, 37, 59, 73, 75, 91, 128, 140, 227, 230n76, 230n77, 234, 239, 246, 287, 304, 311, 319, 321, 322, 335, 338, 345, 348-350, 357, 361n, 369, 379, 390, 401, 403, 426, 449, 463, 472, 478, 486, 487, 497, 515, 527, 558n50, 564, 581, 602, 681, 684-687, 691, 693, 735, 757, 769

eating 26, 26n18, 36, 114, 272n42, 410n28, 443, 488, 544, 607n29, 613n46, 623

export xv, 5n6, 9n13, 51, 52, 60, 66, 72, 73, 77, 77n72, 80n81, 82n87, 87, 91, 95, 98, 99, 102, 103, 163, 165, 170, 177, 178, 231, 298, 330, 342, 438, 442, 487, 520, 534n5, 553, 632, 664, 670, 676, 680, 735, 740, 743, 747 (*see also* Opium, import)

factory 62, 90, 124, 334, 335, 337, 338, 340n42-342, 348, 351, 354n73, 355, 404, 410, 453, 456, 510, 518, 527, 606, 650n16, 735, 738, 738n2, 765, 766, 769, 770

farmer 31, 77, 230, 239, 246, 247, 252, 255, 292, 319, 357-361n, 365, 366, 369, 401, 404, 406, 407, 452, 472, 473, 478, 483, 528, 716

for tea 3, 6, 15, 20, 30, 52, 64, 65, 92, 98, 106, 110, 120, 123, 174, 212, 250, 424, 564, 619, 631, 635n16, 691, 712, 717, 735

for pepper 30, 30n28, 41, 136, 156, 162, 162n71, 163-165, 167, 167n13, 168, 170, 176n13, 181, 186, 199, 209, 212, 232, 252, 367, 377, 712, 715

Golden Triangle (*see* Southeast Asia)

import monopoly 166, 214, 230, 246, 247, 274, 292, 317, 330, 395, 712

import, opium 12, 61n33, 65-68, 72, 79, 80, 80n79, 80n80-83, 90, 96-98, 100, 106, 108-110, 112n11, 117, 154, 165, 166, 169, 178, 192, 199, 227, 229, 231, 239, 273, 286, 292n32, 308, 332, 341, 351n66, 368, 388, 422, 433, 444, 457, 496, 502, 516, 525, 532, 534n5, 545,

547, 549, 550, 558, 558n50, 566, 576, 602, 605, 608, 627, 629, 631, 634, 637, 639, 641, 670, 680, 685, 690, 726, 746, 749, 754, 755, 766

laudanum 107, 191, 304, 384, 572

(il)legal opium 327, 357, 413, 437, 444, 567, 685, 687, 688, 713 (*see also* Wettig Opium)

madat (*madak*) 20n2, 234, 272n42, 273

maslac 28, 28n22

mecones 22, 28n21

money, opium (*see* money)

monopoly, opium (*see* monopoly)

Opium War, First xii, xiv, 6, 398, 444, 500, 540, 541, 543, 604, 686, 742, 744, 748, 749

Opium War, Second 13, 398, 411, 439, 449, 451, 452, 464, 543, 545, 547, 549n33, 603, 604n20, 605, 607, 628n3, 658, 672, 676n82, 686, 746

peasants 69, 101, 105, 111, 127, 172-174, 226, 255, 256, 270, 291, 375, 429, 430, 463, 557, 615, 625, 653, 661, 663, 666n52, 678, 679, 695, 696n123, 700, 706, 737

pipes 7, 68, 72, 303, 384, 392, 404, 441, 447, 497, 501, 502, 509, 527, 543, 594, 598, 613n46, 619, 650, 667, 667n55, 672-674, 674n75, 678, 700, 727

policy 35, 47, 58, 72, 77, 78n74, 85, 118, 122, 236, 244, 253, 274n48, 282, 289, 292, 292n32, 307, 315, 329, 332, 335, 339, 340, 344, 350, 373, 374n2, 398, 416, 431, 444, 446, 495, 502, 503, 510, 512, 513, 513n45, 518, 519, 523, 525, 527, 530, 539, 540, 545, 552, 567, 582, 588, 589, 607, 615, 616n53, 636, 660, 664, 665, 699, 701, 703, 716, 718, 723n7, 727, 729, 730, 731

production 231, 520, 526, 528, 548, 552, 556, 578, 580, 594, 608, 632, 635, 636, 643, 657, 658, 661, 662n43, 664, 666, 667, 675, 702, 704, 711, 716, 721, 728, 735, 736, 738

Bengal opium 3, 220, 227, 229, 229n74, 231, 235, 239, 241, 244, 246, 248, 251, 252, 269n33, 273, 278, 281, 307, 311, 314, 335, 341, 364, 543, 602, 688, 689, 690, 711, 712, 736, 737, 739, 741-744, 750, 751, 757, 765 – 769

Malwa opium 688, 689, 690, 712, 736, 737, 741, 742-745, 747, 749, 750

prohibition, opium 9, 20n2, 83, 155, 188, 214, 229, 236, 304, 340, 350, 406, 407, 408, 410, 421, 441, 500, 545, 557, 564, 583, 700

regie, Opium 299, 304, 305n28, 319, 321, 324, 325, 325n7, 327, 329, 333, 333n25, 334-336, 336n31, 338, 339, 350, 368, 341, 342, 348, 350-352, 366, 368, 409, 418, 433, 435, 523, 527, 528, 564, 713, 724, 765, 767, 769, 771

Question 711, 712, 713

related costs 12, 53, 166, 173, 176n13, 239, 247, 252, 283, 284, 297n10, 298, 299, 303, 315, 318, 348, 349, 353, 358, 360, 365, 365n15, 368, 371, 392, 407, 408, 454, 458, 490, 521, 567, 594, 671, 686, 688, 736, 757, 761, 762, 763, 770

revenues 77, 79, 89, 98, 100, 122, 129, 248, 292, 354, 367, 372, 402, 406, 428, 450, 455, 518, 526, 527, 552, 553, 616, 740, 746 (*see also* profits)

shipping 73, 130, 144, 223, 278, 403, 476, 607, 685 (*see also* clipper, Chinese junks)

smoking xv, 3, 20, 31, 83, 84, 97, 105, 117, 118, 155, 194, 195, 199, 214n48, 229, 234, 253, 340, 384, 436, 443, 448, 456, 495, 524, 535, 543, 557, 570, 576, 613, 623, 648, 656, 674n75 (*see also* madat)

trade xi, xiii, 12, 350, 369, 370, 372, 421, 444, 446, 449, 451, 488, 489, 496, 497, 500, 521, 527, 528, 541, 549, 552, 555, 564, 567, 573, 599, 602, 608n33, 614, 634n13, 638, 664, 669, 671, 685, 687, 746, 757 (*see also* illicit trade, smugglers)

victims xii, xiii, 4, 7, 7n10, 19, 36, 86, 103, 118, 119, 124, 125, 130, 150n31, 189, 205, 254, 517, 539 , 594, 598, 609, 627 (*see also* blaming, death, death penalty, narcotic death)

war, opium 370, 531, 606, 706, 707, 712, 714

Wettig Opium (*see* Dutch Empire)

orientalism 7, 383, 385, 623

Orta, Garcia de (*see* Portuguese Empire)

Ottoman empire (*see* Middle East)

'Overseas Chinese' (*see* Southeast Asia)

Outer Districts (*see* Indonesia)

Owen, David E. 35, 35n2, 54n13-56, 58, 180, 315n27, 499, 500, 540, 589n2

Padang (*see* Indonesia)

pain 21, 107, 127, 137, 191, 192, 196, 571, 573,
    581, 599, 715
pain killer 21, 108, 196, 197, 388, 390, 424,
    432, 502, 536, 537, 547, 578, 613
Palaung Women (*see* Southeast Asia)
Palembang (*see* Indonesia)
Palmerston-H.J.Temple (*see*   British
    Empire)
Paludanus (*see* Dutch Empire)
papaver somniferum (*see* poppy)
Paris (*see* Europe, France)
Parsis (*see* India)
passports (*see* Dutch Empire, Portuguese
    Empire)
Patna (*see* India)
Pax Neerlandica (*see* Dutch Empire)
Pearl Harbor (*see* American Empire)
peasants (*see* Opium, peasants)
Peking (*see* China)
Pelsaert, Francisco (*see* Dutch Empire)
penal law 338, 348
Peoples Republic of China (*see* China)
pepper (*see* opium, for pepper)
peranakans (*see* Indonesia)
perkeniers (*see* Dutch Empire)
Persia (*see* Middle East)
Persian Gulf (*see* Middle East)
Peru 343, 345, 346n52, 347, 579, 580, 649,
    721, 725n9
pharmacist 111, 112, 114, 137, 192n8, 535, 547,
    548, 555n46, 567, 570, 650, 652, 715,
    717 (*see also* apothecary)
pharmaceutical industry xv, 110, 113, 129,
    345, 387, 387n11, 387n12, 393, 482n34,
    510, 535, 548, 558, 577-579, 581, 682,
    715, 722, 726, 727 (*see also* American
    pharmaceutical association, indus-
    try)
pharmaceutical products 549, 649, 579, 649
Pharmaceutical Society (British, 1841) 107,
    114n17
pharmacology 21, 29n26, 369, 393, 425, 535,
    569, 651, 652
    Arab 23, 29n26, 107, 127, (*see also* medi-
        cal doctors, Arab)
Pharmacy Act (British, 1868) 111, 114n17, 115
    (*see also* Europe, England)
Philadelphia (see USA)
Philippine Commission (*see* anti-opium)
Philippine Revolution (*see* American
    Empire, Spanish Empire)

Philippines (*see* American Empire, Span-
    ish Empire)
pipes, opium (*see* Opium, pipes)
piracy 145, 210, 269n30, 297, 596, 714, 719
Plassey, battle of (*see* British Empire)
pogrom 20n1, 124, 125, 255n1, 278, 545, 558,
    619, 622, 680
poison 26n18, 27, 31, 115, 116, 157, 194, 201,
    277, 288-290, 291, 304, 346, 373, 389,
    403, 420, 486, 496, 497, 514, 517, 545,
    604, 617, 627, 650n16, 651, 651n17, 665,
    700, 715
poppy xiv, 8n11, 21, 21n7, 22, 24, 31, 75, 90n5,
    180, 229, 286, 338, 350, 357, 424, 478,
    490, 535, 557, 603, 604, 607, 613, 629,
    631, 636, 644, 654, 664, 666, 669, 679,
    681, 683, 705n143, 717
    Chinese poppy xii, 604, 608, 629, 631,
        634, 644, 648, 659, 662, 664, 666, 681
    papaver somniferum 4, 8n11, 21, 22,
        28n21, 31, 155, 185, 201, 569, 725n9, 726
    poppy cultivation xii, 3, 32, 50, 55, 58,
        59, 83, 89, 90, 100, 101, 111, 124, 154, 173,
        174, 251, 285, 286, 419, 439, 440,
        443n53, 448, 510, 526, 551, 608, 630,
        631, 634, 634n13, 656, 658, 660-662,
        667, 670, 671, 674n78, 688, 694, 696,
        700, 715, 716, 721, 735, 736, 737, 751 (*see
        also* yields)
    poppy balls 201
    poppy heads 180, 180n25, 194, 572, 648
    poppy flowers 404, 767
    poppy seed 24, 28n21, 110, 158, 180, 286,
        424, 655, 717
    poppy syrup 24, 28n21, 126, 201, 229, 767
Port Arthur (*see* China)
Portugal (*see* Europe)
Portuguese Empire xiv, 26, (*see also* Asian
    continent, assault, Middle East)
    Albuquerque, Alfonso de 154
    Barbosa, Duarte 26n18, 27
    Cabral, Pedro Alvarez 145-147
    cartazes 151 (*see also* passports)
    Macao (Macau) 64-66, 70, 96n20, 97,
        98, 102, 152, 224, 228, 273, 406, 434,
        442, 460, 488, 518, 522, 544, 557, 558,
        602, 638, 676, 680, 702, 742, 747, 748
    Manrique, Fray Sebastien 156n49, 157,
        157n53, 158, 220
    Orta, Garcia de 26, 92, 155, 155n48, 157,
        157n52, 157n53

Vasco da Gama 147, 157n52
Pottinger, Henry (*see* British Empire)
poverty 4, 45, 113, 114, 126, 235, 256, 463, 607, 615, 616, 697
Prakash, Om 39n12, 41, 136n4, 154n46, 160, 160n62, 160n64, 170n20, 175n, 176, 177n17, 178n19, 183n32, 187n47, 210, 228, 231, 718n
preaching 72, 151, 543, 607, 610n38, 611, 614
prehistory of opium 8n11, 716
prescription 23, 24, 29, 107, 116, 139, 201, 389, 535, 544, 580, 582, 582n100, 624, 643-645, 648, 651, 652, 715, 717, 727
prices 167, 167n13, 168, 169, 176n13, 199, 219, 229, 230, 233, 239-241, 244, 251-253, 272, 273, 295, 296, 300, 307, 313, 335, 339, 340, 342, 343, 346, 355n75, 358, 359, 362, 365, 368-372, 375, 405, 430, 434, 452, 505n27, 534, 550, 558, 582n100, 671n66, 691, 728, 737, 738, 749
Prince of Orange (*see* Dutch Empire)
private interest 37, 88, 182, 278, 286, 298, 723
profits xvi, 87, 100, 357, 359, 363, 366, 371, 698 (*see also* opium, revenue)
prohibition (*see* Opium, prohibition; *see also* law)
property 8, 14n9, 45, 76, 215, 215n49, 233, 281, 290, 302, 329, 345, 348, 350, 351, 353, 376, 412, 443, 474, 500, 530, 559, 691, 725 (*see also* real estate)
prostitutes 329, 389, 411, 412, 497, 517, 583, 621
prostitution 97, 335, 411, 484, 500, 551, 583, 642, 697, 697n127 (*see also* brothel)
protection (state) 15, 40, 68, 69, 208, 266, 321, 332, 411, 412, 447, 507, 513, 518, 558, 612n44, 671, 691, 695, 697n127, 698, 699
Protestantism 7, 376, 474, 532, 609
public health (movement) 116, 117, 124, 127 (*see also* health)
Puritan 38, 39, 40, 532 (*see also* Calvinism)

qat (*see* opium)
Qianlong, emperor (*see* China)
Quadrangle (*see* Southeast Asia)
Quincey, Thomas de xi
Quing rule (*see* China)

race (human) 8, 8n12, 15, 259, 277, 393, 415, 455, 459, 459n1, 507, 511, 512, 533, 543, 560, 562, 597, 600, 603, 609, 609n35, 610, 617-619, 619n62, 620n64, 621, 623, 625, 647, 716 (*see also* China, Yellow Danger; racism)
racial purity 474
racism 5, 118, 207, 259, 260n9, 300, 401, 459, 460, 511, 546, 554, 562, 596, 597, 599, 619, 621, 642, 725
Raffles, Thomas S. (*see* British Empire)
Rama, kings (*see* Southeast Asia)
Rangoon (*see* Southeast Asia)
Rashid, Ahmed xi, xiv, xv, 204, 530, 711, 732
Raynal, Guillaume 171, 177, 188
real estate 93, 478, 691, 692, 698n129 (*see also* property)
rebellion 226, 256n2, 443, 543, 547, 606, 622n71
reciprocity 14, 15, 16, 143 (*see also* imperial reciprocities)
Red Army (*see* China)
Red Gang (*see* Opium, dealers)
Reede, Hendrik van (*see* Dutch Empire)
rehabilitation 653, 678
religion 4, 32, 70, 70n49, 139, 140, 146, 147, 157, 262, 474, 534, 585n105, 600, 612, 615, 617, 693, 714 (*see also* Calvinism, Catholicism, Christianity, Islam, Protestantism)
Renard, Ronald 421, 438, 441n46, 443n52, 477, 478, 478n26
repression (*see* colonial repression)
revenue (*see* Opium, revenues)
revenue farm 358n4, 366, 400-405, 765
Revolution of 1911-12 (*see* China)
Rhône-Poulenc (*see* Europe, France)
Richards, John F. 53n9, 77n72, 89, 178n19, 739, 740
Ricklefs, M.C. 190n4, 208n41, 222, 224n63, 230n78
risks 65, 66, 92, 94, 95, 143, 210, 251, 475, 567, 621
Rochussen, Jan J. (*see* Dutch Empire)
Rockefeller Foundation (*see* USA)
Roosevelt, Franklin D. (*see* USA)
Rosenberg, Alfred (*see* Germany)
Rothschild bank (*see* British Empire)
Rothstein, Arnold (*see* Opium, dealers)
Rowntree, Josua 57n21, 58n, 60n, 77n72, 118, 154n42, 156, 157n, 388n13, 603n18, 604n19, 605, 739, 740-742

Royal Commission on Opium (*see* Europe, England)

Royal Navy (*see* British Empire, British Navy)

Rush, James R. 288n, 327n9, 333n25, 334n27, 358n5, 472, 473, 476n23, 477n, 766

Russell, Samuel (*see* Opium, dealers; *see also* British Empire,)

Saigon (see Southeast Asia)

Salween (see Southeast Asia)

salt 59, 99, 174, 175, 184, 271, 274, 274n48, 275, 311, 336, 343, 351, 353, 364, 369n31, 400, 500, 507, 576, 706, 707n150

saltpetre 160, 172, 174, 175, 209, 244, 719

Saltregie (*see* salt)

San Francisco (*see* USA)

Sarawak (*see* British Empire)

Sarit Thanarat (*see* Southeast Asia)

Sassoon, family (*see* Opium, dealers; *see also* British Empire,)

savages 262, 501, 504, 508

Sax Rohmer 385, 620n64

scandals 386, 388n13, 390

Scheltema, Johan (*see* Dutch Empire)

Schouten, Wouter (*see* Dutch Empire)

Scott, James (*see* British Empire)

scum 206, 210, 224, 258, 260, 261, 376

secret service 26, 354n70, 356, 387, 486, 490, 588, 590, 654, 698, 701, 706, 706n147, 729 (*see also* Central Intelligence Agency)

Semarang (*see* Indonesia)

settlers 7, 45, 47, 152, 175n11, 219, 221, 223, 263, 407, 425, 459, 461, 503, 531, 533-535, 535n9, 536, 537, 559, 560, 580n95, 595, 725n9

Seventeen Gentlemen (*see* Dutch Empire)

sex 26, 31, 113, 157, 188, 200, 201, 224, 385, 386, 555, 620, 624, 646, 647, 701n134

Shan (*see* Southeast Asia)

Shanghai (*see* China)

Shanghai Opium Merchants Combine (*see* China)

Shansi (*see* China)

Shan State Army (SSA) (*see* Southeast Asia)

Shantung (*see* China)

Shantung Road Hospital (*see* China)

shar 20 (*see* China)

Shensi (*see* China)

Shuyun, Sun 617, 705n143, 707

Siam (*see* Southeast Asia)

silent (profits) 72, 106, 240, 245, 323, 479, 598, 697

silver (drain) 9n13, 16, 41, 52, 53, 53n9, 54, 54n14, 61, 61n33, 69, 79n76, 83, 88, 123, 165, 181, 186, 190n4, 202, 232, 254, 292, 311, 311n14, 398, 483, 528, 529, 541, 563, 617, 667, 719, 735, 748, 749, 763

Singapore (*see* Southeast Asia)

Sinn, Elizabeth 73n, 75n63, 484, 544n23, 547n28, 549n31, 642n29, 680, 680n90, 682n

Sino-Japanese War (*see* China, Japan)

slavery xi, xii, xiiin, xvi, 5, 5n5, 35, 36, 36n4, 44, 48, 97, 98, 141, 150n31, 158, 175, 175n11, 184, 189, 190, 198, 199, 207, 208, 208n41, 216, 216n, 217, 221, 223, 224, 242n6, 244, 245, 245n11, 254, 256, 257, 261, 273, 279, 280, 286, 288, 290, 309, 329, 330, 375, 377, 417, 443, 472, 532n2, 533, 539, 563, 619, 621, 632, 684, 684n98, 714, 725n9 (*see also* anti-slavery policy)

sleep 27, 28, 156, 158, 158n56, 200, 201n29, 384, 497, 571, 573

Slicher van Bath, Bernhard xviii

Smith, Adam 243

Smith, Arthur H. 459, 459n1, 460, 461, 466, 470, 609n35, 617, 618, 618n61

smugglers xii, xv, 12, 17, 43, 61, 66, 68, 70, 78, 88, 91, 92, 94, 96, 120, 147, 168, 236, 239-241, 252, 298, 316, 321, 323, 333, 350, 366, 370, 449, 489, 500, 536, 538, 542, 565, 602, 605, 612, 638, 663, 672, 684, 688, 693, 710, 748 (*see also* gangs; Opium, trade)

smuggling (*see* illicit trade)

Smyrna (*see* Middle East)

Society for the Suppression of the Opium Trade (SSOT) (*see* anti-opium; Europe, England)

soldiers 32, 39n12, 60, 141, 185, 186, 204, 205n34, 210, 221, 224, 234, 242n6, 247n14, 272n42, 296, 346, 419, 423n13, 460, 472, 490, 502, 522, 562n56, 577, 587, 604n20, 608, 613, 634, 672, 673n73, 678, 705, 705n143, 745, 760

Somalia 29 (*see* Middle East)

Soviet Union 530

Southeast Asia (*Nanyang*) xv, 54n14, 72, 98, 177, 216, 255, 358n4, 395n1, 396, 401, 414, 415, 417, 421, 424-426, 432, 434,

437, 449, 451, 455, 466, 471, 473, 477, 486-490, 525, 613n46, 662, 716, 722, 765 (*see also* Asian continent, assault, French Empire, Japanese Empire)

Annam 381, 400, 402, 405, 414, 418, 435-437, 631

Arakan 157, 177, 397, 442

Aung San, president 428, 442, 526

Burma xvii, 50, 81, 89, 90, 130, 157, 381, 397, 406, 414, 417, 419-421, 423, 427, 428, 431, 434, 437 – 439, 441, 443, 457, 471, 477, 485, 487, 490, 526, 648, 653n23, 670, 671, 682, 702, 704, 716, 731, 737 (*see also* Myanmar)

Cambodia 147n, 215n49, 333, 381, 398, 400, 402, 404n16, 418, 435-437, 444

Cochinchina 46n28, 80n81, 90n5, 333-335, 381, 398, 402-405, 407, 408, 410, 418, 433, 436, 437, 449, 748, 765, 766

Golden Triangle (Quadrangle) 420, 422, 423, 477, 478, 485, 486, 667, 668, 716, 731

Hmong 410, 411, 421, 426, 427, 431, 432, 526, 528, 529

Ho Chi Minh 415, 416

Karen 426, 427, 442, 443

Kedah 215n49, 232, 454

Kinh 427

Laos 381n, 397n, 398, 410n, 418-423n13, 426, 427, 432, 435-438, 438n39, 457, 477, 485, 526, 528, 670, 731

Luang Prabang 438, 528

Malacca (Strait of) 26n18, 60, 89, 144, 147n, 154, 177, 215n49, 220, 227-229, 231, 241, 253, 264, 265, 271-273, 290, 295, 301n16, 321, 447, 469, 746, 747

Malaysia 381n, 442, 447, 454, 458, 461, 465, 471, 472, 474, 485, 487

Mekong 398, 436

Meo (*see* Hmong)

Minh-Mang, king 398

Mongkut, king 444

Myanmar (*see* Burma)

'Overseas Chinese' 265, 274, 459, 459n2, 463, 473, 474, 477, 478, 480, 483, 599

Palaung Women 420

Rama, kings 421, 443, 444

Rangoon 423, 428, 428n20, 430, 431, 440n44-442, 486, 670, 671

Saigon 398, 400, 404, 410, 433, 528, 765, 766, 767

Salween 422, 440, 440n44

Shan (state) 420, 421, 423n13, 426-431, 438-440, 442, 442n49, 490, 670, 671, 702, 716

Sarit Thanarat 446, 447

Siam 70, 103, 147n, 213, 254, 381n, 398, 400, 449, 469, 485, 670, 671, 747 (*see also* Thailand)

Singapore 44, 45, 46, 64, 89, 130, 275, 277, 284n16, 285, 301n16, 310n11, 321, 330, 331, 332, 355, 402, 437, 437n37, 442, 447-452, 454, 456, 457, 461, 472, 474, 478, 479, 482, 485, 522, 527, 531, 534n5, 548, 680, 688, 746

Straits Settlements (see Malaysia, Singapore)

Thailand 381n, 398, 415, 419, 420, 421, 427, 429, 432, 442, 443, 446, 457, 458, 474, 477, 488, 601 (*see also* Siam)

Souza, George B. 96, 96n20, 136n4, 753n1

Spain (*see* Europe, Spain)

Spanish Empire (*see also* Asian continent, assault)

Philippines 235, 395, 417, 419, 425, 474, 498, 499, 539

speculation, economic 131, 452, 468, 688, 691

Spence, Jonathan D. 9n13, 55n17, 80n79, 126, 468n12, 593, 673, 673n73, 674, 674n75, 674n78, 706

spices 38n6, 110, 157n52, 160, 176, 208, 220, 232, 233, 250, 254, 271, 284, 292, 448, 717, 762

Sri Lanka (*see* Ceylon)

Srinagar (*see* India)

Staatswörterbuch 61n33, 83n88, 600

starving 235

state (general) xvi, 15, 16, 37, 38, 40, 54, 73, 75, 116, 122, 125, 126, 137, 141, 172, 243, 284, 287, 319, 335, 375, 395, 396, 402, 418, 442, 471, 480, 482, 495, 511, 589, 589n3, 594, 595, 710 (*see also* oikos, surveillance)

American 15, 423, 474, 496, 530, 530n79, 533, 540, 541, 546, 548, 551, 552, 555, 556, 558, 574, 588, 615, 618n61, 621, 664 (*see also* CIA, State Department)

Asian 64, 88, 143, 161n67, 220, 229, 263, 280n8, 406, 420, 421, 423n13, 427, 441, 451, 485, 489, 490, 529, 597, 627, 647, 670

British 16, 54, 54n11, 57, 79, 88, 92, 122,
     172, 290, 376, 425, 442n49, 496, 518
colonial 47, 55, 79, 88, 89, 92, 99, 101, 121,
     123, 135, 172, 189, 207, 213, 240, 243n8,
     246, 247, 277, 279, 285-288, 291, 293,
     295, 296, 301, 308, 313, 315, 317, 319,
     322-324, 327-329, 333, 338, 339, 345,
     349, 357, 361, 364, 365, 378, 379, 393,
     400-402, 404, 425, 426, 482, 560, 565,
     723
Dutch 37, 78, 172, 189, 202, 204, 206, 278-
     280, 282, 284, 285, 288, 302, 309, 316,
     329, 335, 343, 348, 363, 378, 379, 481,
     482, 628n3
French 172, 387, 389, 391, 393, 400, 405,
     410, 425, 631
State Department (see USA)
state protection (see protection)
Stilwell, Joseph (see USA)
Straits Settlements (see Southeast Asia)
Struick, Nicolas (see Dutch Empire)
Subrahmanyam, Sanjay 141n20, 145n26,
     150n31, 163n1
sugar 164, 175, 184, 256, 266, 271, 309, 318,
     334, 364, 469, 476, 501, 502, 535, 583,
     606, 664, 736, 760, 768
suicide 45, 94, 116, 227, 394n28, 601, 648, 651
Sukarno, president (see Indonesia)
Sulawesi (see Indonesia)
Sumatra (see Indonesia)
Summer Palace Beijing (see China)
Sun Yatsen (see China)
supply (see demand)
Surat (see India)
Surrealist 385
surveillance (state) 526, 556, 589, 724, 725
Swatow gang (see China; Opium, dealers)
Swettenham, Frank (see British Empire)
Szechwan (see China)

taipans (see China)
Taiping (see China)
Taiwan (see China, Formosa)
Taoism (see China)
tax farm(er)s 46, 263n15, 270, 401, 404, 425,
     452, 454
taxing 121, 402, 403, 524
tea (see Opium, for tea)
Terry, Charles E. 97n21, 119, 493n2, 513,
     542n, 544n, 566n63, 574-576, 624n,
     676n83, 677n86
Terry's Guide 494, 507, 512

Tianjin (see China)
Tibet (see China)
Tientsin Treaty (1858) 545
Thailand (see Southeast Asia)
tobacco 5n7, 20, 20n2, 21, 41, 51, 155, 157, 158,
     162n71, 181n27, 183, 195, 198, 214,
     214n48, 273, 285, 393, 424, 448, 497,
     502, 507, 525, 535, 563, 572, 613n46,
     662, 664
Tong Joe, Tan 408n27, 505n27, 513n45,
     545n26, 552n39, 564n59, 566, 567,
     721n
Tonkin (see French Empire)
Toulon (see French Empire)
trade (see Opium, trade)
trade monopoly 232, 233, 277
trade routes 150n33, 462, 468, 526
traditional medicine (see medical doctors)
Tracy, Sarah W. 535, 536, 537n11
tranquilizer 389, 424
treacle (theriaca, triakel, teriaca) 23, 191,
     192, 192n8, 193, 193n11, 194, 195, 717
Treasury (see Europe, England)
Treaty of Commercial Relations (1903) (see
     China)
Treaty of Nanking (1842) (see China)
Treaty of Wang Hea (1844) (see China)
Treaty ports (see China)
triad (see China)
Trocki, Carl A. 6, 7n9, 8n11, 35n2, 46n27, 49,
     51n3, 53n10, 80n79, 93n13, 105, 162,
     162n71, 177n18, 198n20, 299n12, 383n1,
     396, 401n8, 402n11, 419n2, 449, 450,
     452, 454n74, 460n4, 465, 466, 472,
     478, 534n5, 584, 608n33, 612, 656n29,
     680n90, 681n95, 693n118, 697n127,
     698n129, 706n147, 730, 742, 750
Turkey (see Middle East)

underground 120, 341, 527, 550, 582, 588,
     681, 685-687, 691, 692, 694, 696, 713,
     724, 735 (see also uppperground)
United Kingdom (UK) (see Europe, Eng-
     land)
United Nations 430, 488, 595
United Nations Office on Drugs and Crime
     (UNODC) 420, 721
United States of America (USA) (see also
     America, North)
  Adams, John Q. 14, 15, 61n31, 541, 599
  American Civil War 537, 544, 547
  American Empire
    Cuba 553, 559

Pearl Harbor xiv, 414
Philippine Revolution 561, 562n56
Philippines 235, 374, 374n2, 395, 417,
      419, 425, 474, 498, 499, 531, 538,
      539, 556, 559, 562-564n61, 565-
      567, 569, 589, 724, 725 (see also
      Spanish Empire)
American government 43, 374n2, 398,
      415, 475, 493, 496, 498, 510, 515n48,
      518, 545, 552, 560-562, 588, 589, 638,
      665, 699, 716, 724, 727
American heroin plague 489, 730
American merchants 69, 82, 314, 371,
      449n64, 496, 541, 542, 547, 548
American Moral Empire 344, 385, 415,
      460, 532, 536n29, 547, 564, 609n35,
      610, 614, 615, 618, 618n61, 637
American dealers (see Opium, dealers)
American Pharmaceutical Associa-
      tion 535, 565
American pharmaceutical industry 345,
      547, 548, 569, 579, 588, 599
American state (see state, American)
Anslinger, Harry 487, 553, 554, 577n89,
      664, 692, 701n134-703, 725
Boston 61, 534, 542
Los Angeles 482n34, 534, 702
New York 36, 169n19, 508n35, 534, 542,
      550, 558, 558n50, 567, 573, 577, 582,
      583, 587, 650, 728
New York Times 392n24, 392n25,
      482n34, 494, 499, 502, 503, 505, 510,
      513-515n48, 554n44, 556, 556n49, 557,
      561n55, 564, 564n62, 570n70
Philadelphia 534, 535, 548, 549, 558n50,
      587
Rockefeller Foundation 552
Roosevelt, Franklin D. 517, 542, 554n44
Roosevelt, Theodore 621
San Francisco 484, 534, 544, 548, 549,
      550, 555, 555n47, 556, 558, 558n50,
      570, 577, 587, 589, 692, 725
State Department 530n79, 540, 559,
      664, 701
Stilwell, Joseph 552, 553
US Bureau of Narcotics 553
Vietnam War, Second 431, 485, 487, 526,
      590, 716
'War On Drugs' 16, 120, 129, 531, 535,
      535n9, 554, 554n44, 558, 589, 665,
      701n134

'War on Terrorism' 721
   water-boarding 561, 565
upperground 686, 696, 735 (see also under-
      ground)
urbanization 588, 599, 653n23 (see also
      city)
Urdang, George (see Kremers, Edward)

Valckenier, Adriaan (see Dutch Empire)
Van Long, Deo 432
Vanvugt, Ewald 5, 47n29, 178n19, 212n45,
      224n61, 227n69, 229n74, 246n, 256n3,
      281n9, 287n, 311n15, 333n25, 349n59,
      362n10, 363n, 364n, 368, 368n18,
      754n4
Vasco da Gama (see Portuguese Empire)
Venice (see Europe)
Vereenigde Oostindische Compagnie
      (VOC) (see Dutch Empire)
Vichy Fascists (see French Empire)
victims (see Opium, victims)
Victoria, queen (see British Empire)
Viet Minh (see French Empire)
Vietnam (see French Empire)
Vietnam War, First (see French Empire)
Vietnam War, Second (see USA)
village 45, 108, 136, 150, 159, 184, 205, 210, 219,
      236, 303, 328, 356, 389, 406, 424-426,
      602, 616, 736
violence xvi, 47, 123, 144n24, 202, 204, 205,
      208, 210, 212, 212n45, 213, 216, 219n57,
      223, 256, 259n7, 261, 263, 269n30, 460,
      481, 496, 516, 589n3, 608
VOC (see Vereenigde)

wages 173, 206n37, 247n14, 502, 663,
      663n45, 675, 737, 759, 762, 767
Wakabayashi, Bob T. 493n1, 519, 520n59,
      529
Wakeman, Frederic 3n1, 9n13, 12n2, 674n78,
      677n84, 684n99, 690n110, 697n127,
      705n143, 751
Walker, Timothy D. 137n8, 139n15, 140,
      155n48, 158n57
Walker, William O. III 493n1, 498n, 511n40,
      515n49, 517n52, 518n55, 608n33,
      637n21, 642, 658n34, 659, 665,
      667n56, 671n, 677n85, 703
war (see Opium, war)
warlords (see China)
'War On Drugs' (see USA)
'War on Terrorism' (see USA)

Ward, Kerry xiiin3, 176n13, 204n32, 216, 216n51
water-boarding (see USA)
Weber, Max 38, 38n8, 153, 153n41, 172, 182n29, 589n3, 638, 639n23
Wehler, Hans-Ulrich xvi, xix
Wertheim, Wim xix, 349, 371
West-East relations xiv, 4-7n9, 8, 9, 11, 13-16, 24, 32, 37, 38n8, 39, 41, 42, 49, 52, 56, 70, 83, 119, 124, 125, 130, 135, 140, 144, 145, 168, 172, 174, 175n11, 180, 182, 190, 196, 207, 208, 210, 212, 224, 233, 255, 261, 264, 268n25, 280, 319, 383, 395n, 407, 414, 423, 456, 466, 481, 529, 547, 594, 610, 623, 638, 639, 640, 641, 645, 711 (see also assault, civilization, colonialism, East – West relations, imperialism, missionaries, racism)
'Wettig Opium' (see Opium, legal; see also Dutch Empire)
'White Man's Burden' (see British Empire)
White Terror (see China)
William I, king (see Europe, Netherlands)
William III, king – stadhouder (see Europe, Netherlands)
William IV, stadhouder (see Europe, Netherlands)
William V, stadhouder (see Europe, Netherlands)
Willoughby, Westel W. 12n2, 15n, 43, 44, 79n76, 593n2, 603n18, 605n21, 635n17, 637n20, 638, 656n29
Wiselius, Jakob (see Dutch Empire)
World Bank 443

World Economic Crisis 346n52, 516
World War I 47, 91, 316, 346, 346n52, 393, 395, 411, 494, 510-512, 543, 552, 554, 562n56, 577, 589, 606, 622n71, 637, 690, 747, 751
World War II xiv, xvii, 47, 73, 76, 90, 130n11, 131n12, 310, 346, 348, 349, 353, 367, 385, 388, 394, 410, 415, 428, 432, 437, 446, 457, 477, 485, 516, 519, 520, 521, 525, 526, 528, 530, 552, 567, 569, 577, 588, 635, 640n26, 650, 679, 726, 727

xenophobia 118, 259, 575

Yawnghwe, Chao T. 428, 428n20, 429-431, 442n49
Yellow Danger (see China)
Yellow Peril (see China)
Yemen (see Middle East)
Yenan Way (see China)
yields 199, 221, 318, 666, 666n51, 737 (see also poppy cultivation)
Yoshida, Reiji 520, 521
Yü-hsiang, Feng (see China)
Yunnan (see China)
Yunnnanfu (see China)
Yu-Wen, Jen (see China)

Zamorin (see India)
Zeldin, Theodor 388n15, 389, 391n22
Zheng He (see China)
Zwaardecroon, Hendrick (see Dutch Empire)